# Literature
## and the Language Arts
### The American Tradition

THE EMC MASTERPIECE SERIES

**EMC**Paradigm Publishing    Saint Paul, Minnesot

## Staff Credits

### Editorial

**Laurie Skiba**
*Editor*

**Brenda Owens**
*Associate Editor*

**Lori Ann Coleman**
*Associate Editor*

**Diana Moen**
*Associate Editor*

**Jennifer Anderson**
*Assistant Editor*

**Gia Marie Garbinsky**
*Assistant Editor*

**Paul Spencer**
*Art and Photo Researcher*

**Janice Johnson**
*Curriculum Specialist*

**Chris Bohen**
*Editorial Assistant*

**Chris Nelson**
*Editorial Assistant*

### Design

**Shelley Clubb**
*Production Manager*

**Karen Michels**
*Design Manager*

**C. Vern Johnson**
*Senior Designer*

**Jennifer Wreisner**
*Senior Designer*

**Michelle Lewis**
*Senior Design Specialist*

**Julie Hansen**
*Design Specialist*

**Parkwood Composition**
*Compositor*

### Cover Credits

**Cover Designer:** C. Vern Johnson

*Watson and the Shark* [Detail], 1778. John Singleton Copley. Museum of Fine Arts, Boston.

*In the Morning*, Winslow Homer.

*Aspects of Negro Life: From Slavery through Reconstruction* [Detail], 1934. Aaron Douglas. Schomberg Center for Research in Black Culture, New York.

*Something on the Eight Ball* [Detail], 1953. Stuart Davis. Philadelphia Museum of Art.

ISBN 0-8219-2164-9
©2003, 2001 by EMC Corporation

All rights reserved. No part of this publication may be adapted, reproduced, stored in a retrieval system, or transmitted in any form or by any means, electronic, mechanical, photocopying, recording, or otherwise without permission from the publisher.

Published by EMC/Paradigm Publishing
875 Montreal Way
St. Paul, Minnesota 55102
800-328-1452
www.emcp.com
E-mail: educate@emcp.com

Printed in the United States of America.
10 9 8 7 6 5 4 3     XXX 06 05 04 03 02

# Literature
## and the Language Arts

**REDWOOD LEVEL**
DISCOVERING LITERATURE

**WILLOW LEVEL**
UNDERSTANDING LITERATURE

**CEDAR LEVEL**
EXPLORING LITERATURE

**PINE LEVEL**
THE AMERICAN TRADITION

**OAK LEVEL**
RESPONDING TO LITERATURE

**MAPLE LEVEL**
THE BRITISH TRADITION

**BIRCH LEVEL**
EXPERIENCING LITERATURE

**CYPRESS LEVEL**
WORLD LITERATURE

## *Consultants and Writers*

**Senior Consultant**
**Dr. Edmund J. Farrell**
Emeritus Professor of English Education
University of Texas at Austin
Austin, Texas

**Amy Bergstrom**
Instructor
English Education Department
University of Minnesota
Duluth, Minnesota

**Diana Blythe**
Senior Content Manager
Humanities Software,
    a division of Advantage
    Learning Systems, Inc.
Hood River, Oregon

**Cherie Boen**
National Board Certified
    Teacher
Educational Consultant
Minneapolis, Minnesota

**Gloria Canson**
English Instructor
Roosevelt High School
Portland, Oregon

**Linda Christopherson**
Educational Writer
Charlotte, North Carolina

**Mary Curfman**
Language Arts Supervisor
Department of Curriculum
    and Professional Development
Clark County Schools
Las Vegas, Nevada

**Deanna and Roger Hebbert**
Educational Writers
Longmont, Colorado

**Sara Hyry**
Freelance Education Writer
Easthampton, Massachusetts

**Christina Kolb**
Educational Writer
Newton, Massachusetts

**Sharon Kremer**
English Department Chair
A. O. Calhoun Middle School
Denton, Texas

**Corrine Leiferman**
English Instructor
Chamberlain High School
Chamberlain, South Dakota

**Jon Madian**
Senior Instructional Designer
Humanities Software,
    a division of Advantage
    Learning Systems, Inc.
Hood River, Oregon

**Beverly Martin**
Managing Editor
Humanities Software,
    a division of Advantage
    Learning Systems, Inc.
Hood River, Oregon

**Laura Mezner Nelson**
Educational Writer
Minnetonka, Minnesota

**Margaret Palmer**
English Department Chair
Samuel Clemens High School
Shertz, Texas

**David Rathbun**
English Instructor
South High School
Minneapolis, Minnesota

**Eric Schneider**
English Instructor
Patrick Henry High School
Minneapolis, Minnesota

**Elnora Shields**
Educational Consultant
Durham, North Carolina

**Dr. Jane S. Shoaf**
Educational Consultant
Edenton, North Carolina

**Kendra Sisserson**
Research Associate
University of Chicago
Chicago, Illinois

**James W. Swanson**
Educational Consultant
Minneapolis, Minnesota

**Anita Usmiani**
Language Arts Supervisor
Hamilton Township School
    District
Hamilton, New Jersey

**Hope Vasholz**
Teacher of English
Hammond High School
Columbia, Maryland

**Dr. Gary Wiener**
Language Arts Chair
Brighton High School
Rochester, New York

*Blanket*, 1875. Navajo artist.

*Winter Sunday in Norway, Maine,* c.1860. American artist.

*Boy Sitting in the Grass*, c.1882. George Seurat.

*entire reading selec[...]* (handwritten annotation)

*Huckleberry Finn and Jim*, c.1936. Thomas Hart Benton.

*Stone City*, c.1930. Grant Wood.

*White Light*, 1954. Jackson Pollock.

# To the Student

## Features of Your Textbook

### A Guide for Reading

When you open your *EMC Masterpiece Series* textbook, you will find great literature, both classic and contemporary, by a wide variety of authors. You will also find useful step-by-step study strategies for each selection, helpful background information, and activities that allow you to relate the literature to your own experiences and share your point of view.

The **Guided Reading** program in this *EMC Masterpiece Series* book gives you tips before, during, and after you read each selection. Read on for a description of the features you will find in your textbook.

- **About the Author** and **About the Selection** give you background information you'll find helpful in reading the literature selection.
- **Literary Tools** points out and explains literary concepts and techniques that are used in the selection.
- **Guided Reading Questions** within the selection help you check your understanding of the reading.
- **Words for Everyday Use** includes the definition and pronunciation for new vocabulary. A sample sentence demonstrates the use of the word in context.
- **Footnotes** explain unfamiliar terms or unusual words.
- **Art Notes** provide information about the history, culture, or artistic technique of the fine art throughout the textbook and foster critical viewing of the art.
- **Respond to the Selection** allows you to relate the literature to your own experiences.
- **Investigate, Inquire, and Imagine** contains

questions you need to perfect your understanding of the reading, from basic recalling and interpreting questions to ones that ask you to analyze, synthesize, evaluate, and extend your ideas. Some questions also ask you to look at a specific point of view, or examine a different perspective.

- **Understanding Literature** follows up on the literary techniques introduced in Literary Tools and asks you questions to further your understanding.
- **Writer's Journal** gives you three quick-writing options to help you build writing skills.
- **Integrating the Language Arts** contains creative activities that tie literature to other language arts areas such as grammar, vocabulary development, public speaking, study and research, collaborative learning, media literacy, and applied English.

### A Guide for Writing

At the end of each unit of your textbook you will find a **Guided Writing** activity that takes you through the steps of the writing process. The lesson includes models from professional writers and students. Also included are graphic organizers, questions to get you thinking, and an integrated **Language, Grammar, and Style** lesson to help you brush up on grammar points.

### A Guide for Language Arts Skills

The **Language Arts Survey** in the back of your textbook is your resource for information about how to use the English language effectively. It includes tips on what you need to know to write, speak, and read effectively. There are six sections in the Language Arts Survey: the **Reading Resource**, the **Writing Resource**, the **Language, Grammar, and Style Resource**, the **Speaking and Listening Resource**, the **Study and Research Resource**, and the **Applied English Resource**. Do you need to correct a passive sentence? include an Internet site in a research paper? interview someone in the community? write a résumé? It's all here for you.

# Part One
## UNDERSTANDING LITERATURE

*In the Morning.* Winslow Homer.

'T is the good reader that

makes the good book.

—Ralph Waldo Emerson
"Success"

# The Oral Tradition

Are there favorite stories that people in your family like to tell? When you were a child, did people tell you bedtime stories? Did you learn rhymes and jingles and songs from your friends? Have you ever sat around a campfire and told ghost stories? Have you ever heard a minister, priest, rabbi, or teacher tell a story to make a point? If so, then you have experienced the oral tradition.

One pretty good definition of human beings is that we are storytelling creatures. Long before people invented writing, they were telling stories about their gods and heroes and experiences. The best of these stories were passed by word of mouth from generation to generation to form the basis of the literature that we know today. Some early stories were told in the form of poems. Some were in the form of songs. Others were in the form of what we would now call prose tales.

The passing of stories, poems, and songs by word of mouth from person to person is called oral transmission. The body of work created in this way in a particular culture is considered the oral tradition of that culture.

The United States is blessed with enormous diversity in its people. No other country in the world has citizens from so many different races and ethnic backgrounds. The United States cannot, therefore, be said to have a single oral tradition. Rather, it has hundreds of oral traditions with origins in Native American cultures and in Europe, Africa, Asia, and other parts of the globe. From the trickster tales of the Plains Indians to Yiddish tales told by European Jewish immigrants, from work songs and spirituals with roots in Africa to Scots-Irish ballads and western tall tales—America offers a feast for professional folklorists, for students of literature, and for ordinary readers of the many collections of American folk literature.

The following are some common types of oral literature found in the United States:

## ArtNote

*Sky Woman*, 1936. Ernest Smith.

A member of the Seneca tribe, Ernest Smith (1907–1975) illustrated a creation story that has been retold for thousands of years. In this first scene of the long and complex story, Sky Woman falls toward the primeval waters where the world will be created on the back of a turtle. What type of oral literature do you think Smith is illustrating?

**Myths** are stories that explain objects or events in the natural world as resulting from the action of some supernatural force or entity, most often a god. Every early culture around the globe has produced its own myths.

**Tall tales** are stories, often lighthearted or humorous, that contain highly exaggerated, unrealistic elements. Mark Twain's "The Notorious Jumping Frog of Calaveras County" (Unit 6) is a literary version of a tall tale. Other tall tales include stories about Pecos Bill, Paul Bunyan, and Annie Oakley.

**Legends** are stories coming down from the past, often based on real events or characters from older times. Unlike myths, legends are popularly regarded as historical; however, they may contain elements that are fantastic or unverifiable. An example of a legend is the story of George Washington chopping down the cherry tree.

**Spirituals** are religious songs from the African-American folk tradition. Examples of spirituals include "Follow the Drinking Gourd" (Unit 1) and "Swing Low, Sweet Chariot" (Unit 5).

Other works commonly found in the oral tradition include **parables, fables, fairy tales, epics,** and **proverbs.** For definitions of these, see the Handbook of Literary Terms.

*Sky Woman*, 1936. Ernest Smith.
Rochester Museum and Science Center, Rochester, NY.

# Literary TOOLS

**SPIRITUAL.** A **spiritual** is a folk song of deep religious and emotional character. Spirituals were developed among African Americans in the southern United States during slavery. The words are most often related to biblical passages and frequently reflect patient, profound melancholy, even though the songs seldom refer to slavery itself. Spirituals have influenced blues, jazz, and gospel songs. As you read the selection, determine how "Follow the Drinking Gourd" qualifies as a spiritual.

**REPETITION AND REFRAIN. Repetition** is a writer's conscious reuse of a sound, word, phrase, sentence, or other element. A **refrain**, or **chorus**, is a line or group of lines repeated in a poem or song. Look for the use of repetition and refrain in this song.

**THEME.** A **theme** is a central idea in a literary work. As you read, decide what you think is the theme of "Follow the Drinking Gourd."

**ORAL TRADITION.** An **oral tradition** is a work, an idea, or a custom that is passed by word of mouth from generation to generation. "Follow the Drinking Gourd" is part of the African-American oral tradition.

# "Follow the Drinking Gourd"

AFRICAN-AMERICAN FOLK SONG

## About the SELECTION

**"Follow the Drinking Gourd"** is an African-American folk song that was part of the Underground Railroad and used to help fugitive slaves escape to safety. Many people traveled the routes or lines of the Underground Railroad. Although it was not an actual railroad, it used railroad terminology such as *station* for a stopping place and *conductor* for a person who helped the escaping slaves. Many members of the free African-American community, including escaped slave Harriet Tubman, worked diligently for the Underground Railroad. Harriet Tubman, in fact, was called "the Moses of her people" for the huge numbers of slaves she helped to reach the Promised Land, or freedom in the North.

The Underground Railroad extended throughout fourteen northern states from Maine to Nebraska with its heaviest activities concentrated in Pennsylvania, Ohio, Indiana, New York, and the New England states. It extended into Canada as well, where slaves were safe from fugitive slave hunters. Estimates of the number of fugitive slaves aided by the Underground Railroad range from forty thousand to one hundred thousand.

## Reader's Journal

How far would you go to gain freedom?

*The Slave Hunt,* c.1870. Thomas Moran. Private Collection.

# Follow the Drinking Gourd[1]

ANONYMOUS AFRICAN-AMERICAN SONG
OF THE UNDERGROUND RAILROAD

**ORAL TRADITION**
*For African-American slaves in the 1850s, songs and stories were passed from one person to the next by word of mouth rather than in written form.*

When the sun comes back and the first quail calls,
    Follow the drinking gourd,
For the old man is a-waiting for to carry you to freedom
    If you follow the drinking gourd.

---

1. **Drinking Gourd.** Dried, hollowed-out shell of a gourd (a hard-rinded inedible fruit similar to a pumpkin) used for dipping water to drink. In this selection, the speaker is using *drinking gourd* as code words for the Big Dipper, a constellation that served as a guide for escaping slaves.

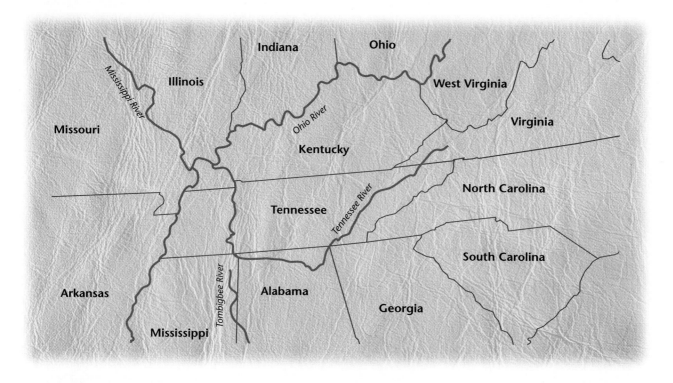

➤ ➤ ➤

**REPETITION AND REFRAIN**
*Note that the refrain, or chorus, recurs after each verse, reiterating the main idea of the song.*

### Chorus

5  Follow the drinking gourd,
   Follow the drinking gourd,
For the old man is a-waiting for to carry you to freedom
   If you follow the drinking gourd.

The river bank will make a very good road,
10     The dead trees show you the way,
Left foot, peg foot[2] traveling on
   Follow the drinking gourd.

### Repeat **Chorus**

The river ends between two hills,
   Follow the drinking gourd.
15  There's another river on the other side,
   Follow the drinking gourd.

### Repeat **Chorus**

Where the little river meets the great big river,
   Follow the drinking gourd.
The old man is a-waiting for to carry you to freedom
20     If you follow the drinking gourd.  ■

---

2. **peg foot.** Wooden foot (replacement for a person's foot)

When the sun comes back and the first quail calls,— fol -low—— the drink - ing gourd, For the old man is a - wait -ing for to car - ry you to free -dom if you fol -low the drink - ing gourd.

Fol - low— the drink - ing gourd, Fol - low— the drink - ing gourd. For the old man is a -wait - ing for to car - ry you to free - dom if you fol -low the drink – ing gourd.

**Respond** to the
# SELECTION

What do you think it would be like to run for your freedom and your life?

# Inquire Imagine

**Recall:** GATHERING FACTS

1a. Who is singing this song? Where are the people going, and why? When are they supposed to travel?

2a. Who waits for the travelers?

3a. How can the travelers use natural elements to help them find the way? What element recurs to guide them? Where do the rivers lead them?

→ **Interpret:** FINDING MEANING

1b. What overriding image is used to guide the travelers toward their destination? Why is this signpost not openly identified? What time of year might be suggested by these natural events?

2b. How will the person who waits help the travelers? Who might he be?

3b. What forces influence the journey of the travelers? Why must they keep "traveling on"? What might "the other side" and "great big river" refer to?

**Analyze:** TAKING THINGS APART

4a. What can you infer about the challenges facing escaping slaves from your reading of "Follow the Drinking Gourd"?

→ **Synthesize:** BRINGING THINGS TOGETHER

4b. How does the map on page 8 help you visualize the path of the travelers? In what ways do you think seeing the "drinking gourd" in the sky helped them visualize their path to freedom?

**Evaluate:** MAKING JUDGMENTS

5a. If you were a slave, how encouraging do you think this song would be in helping you decide whether to escape? Explain.

→ **Extend:** CONNECTING IDEAS

5b. What song, speech, or other inspirational work have you used to encourage yourself to do something difficult? How did it help you?

# Understanding Literature

**SPIRITUAL.** Review the definition for **spiritual** in Literary Tools. In what ways does "Follow the Drinking Gourd" qualify as a spiritual?

**REPETITION AND REFRAIN.** Review the definitions for **repetition** and **refrain** in Literary Tools. What phrase is repeated throughout this spiritual? What is its refrain? In what two ways is it used throughout the song?

**THEME.** Review the definition for **theme** in the Handbook of Literary Terms. What do you think is the theme of "Follow the Drinking Gourd"?

**ORAL TRADITION.** Review the definition for **oral tradition** in the Handbook of Literary Terms. Why do you think a song such as "Follow the Drinking Gourd" was part of the oral, rather than written, literary tradition?

# WRITER'S JOURNAL

1. Write an **ad slogan** that might motivate a young person to achieve a personal goal, such as earning better grades.
2. Illustrate and label a **map** with alternative place names to help a traveler navigate in unknown territory. You might label place names "Spaghetti Junction" (for an intersection that includes multiple freeways) or "The Rollercoaster" (for a series of steep hills that are nearly impossible to bike).
3. Write **song lyrics** to encourage a friend to overcome a difficult situation.

# Integrating *the* LANGUAGE ARTS

## Language, Grammar, and Style

**FINDING THE COMPLETE SUBJECT AND COMPLETE PREDICATE.** All simple English sentences can be divided into two parts, the subject and the predicate. In the most common English sentence, the first part of the sentence tells us what it is talking about. This is the **complete subject**. Then it gives us information about the subject; this second part of the sentence is called the **complete predicate**. In the following sentences, underline the complete subject once and underline the complete predicate twice. For more information, see the Language Arts Survey 3.19, "Finding the Complete Subject and Complete Predicate in a Sentence."

EXAMPLE  You should follow the drinking gourd.

1. The old man is waiting to carry you to freedom.
2. The river bank will make a very good road.
3. The dead trees show you the way.
4. Left foot, peg foot travel on.
5. Escaping slaves listened carefully to the hidden code in this song.

## Speaking and Listening

**ORAL LITERATURE FESTIVAL.** People across the country are experiencing renewed interest in storytelling and folk songs. Form small groups to research and present spirituals, folk songs, and stories from different cultures that reside in the United States. You may want to find professional performances of these works and incorporate them into a multimedia presentation or perform them yourself. Work together to write and present an introduction to each work that explains its history. Include visuals of such things as the lyrics, the musical notation, or images of people from whose culture the selection is taken. To get started, check your local library.

## Applied English

**REQUESTING INFORMATION.** For projects such as the Oral Literature Festival on this page, good source material can be found in many other places besides libraries. The American Folklife Center at the Library of Congress (http://lcweb.loc.gov/folklife/) lists several resources that provide more information about the oral tradition. Compose a business letter requesting information for a class project on the American folk tradition. See the Language Arts Survey 6.5, "Writing a Business Letter."

# Poetry

The word **poem** comes from the Greek root *poíema*, which means "work," and is derived from *poieín*, "to make." Finding a good definition for poetry is difficult, especially because poems can take so many forms. Poetry does not have to be written down; it can be chanted or sung, spontaneous or memorized. Some poems rhyme and have regular, rhythmical patterns, but others do not. Many poems depend on special devices of sound such as onomatopoeia and alliteration, and many use special techniques of meaning such as metaphor and symbolism. Some are simply designs or word pictures, like this concrete poem:

```
             O     O
    B A L L         N
```

Poetry differs from prose in that it compresses meaning into fewer words and often uses meter, rhyme, and techniques such as metaphor and simile. Poetry is often arranged in lines and stanzas as opposed to sentences and paragraphs, and it can be more free in the ordering of words and the use of punctuation. One thing that all poems have in common is that they use imaginative language carefully chosen and arranged to communicate experiences, thoughts, or emotions. Here are some interesting definitions of poetry put forward by important literary figures from the past:

---

**Poetry is . . .**

"the spontaneous overflow of powerful feelings."
—William Wordsworth

"the best words in the best order."
—Samuel Taylor Coleridge

"the record of the best and happiest moments of the happiest and best minds."
—Percy Bysshe Shelley

"[language that] strike[s] the reader as a wording of his own highest thoughts, and appear[s] almost a remembrance."
—John Keats

"musical thought."
—Thomas Carlyle

"conceived and composed in the soul."
—Matthew Arnold

"a mixture of common sense, which not all have, with an uncommon sense, which very few have."
—John Masefield

"the supreme fiction."
—Wallace Stevens

"what gets lost in translation."
—Robert Frost

"not an assertion of truth, but the making of that truth more fully real to us."
—T. S. Eliot

---

The United States has produced many fine poets, including Phillis Wheatley, Henry Wadsworth Longfellow, Ralph Waldo Emerson, Walt Whitman, Edgar Lee Masters, Edwin Arlington Robinson, Robert Frost, Wallace Stevens, William Carlos Williams, Amy Lowell, Ezra Pound, Marianne Moore, Edna St. Vincent Millay, T. S. Eliot, E. E. Cummings, Langston Hughes, Gwendolyn Brooks, Elizabeth Bishop, Judith Ortiz Cofer, Diana Chang, Alberto Ríos, Garrett Kaoru Hongo, Li-Young Lee, and many others. Here is how one of the greatest American poets defined her craft:

"If I read a book and it makes my whole body so cold no fire can ever warm me, I know that it is poetry. If I feel physically as if the top of my head were taken off, I know that it is poetry. Is there any other way?"

—Emily Dickinson

*Something on the Eight Ball,* 1953. Stuart Davis. Philadelphia Museum of Art.

## ArtNote

*Something on the Eight Ball,* 1953. Stuart Davis.

Stuart Davis (1894–1964) brought elements into his abstract paintings that suggest modern music, dance, and poetry. The repeated geometric forms and color combinations suggest the rhythm and improvisation of jazz. The disjointed words and script-like squiggles suggest free-form poetry. What terms for the elements of poetry might also be used to describe the elements of painting?

# Elements of Poetry

**Narrative Poetry.** A **narrative poem** is a verse that tells a story. Examples of narrative poems include Edgar Allan Poe's "The Raven" (Unit 4) and Edwin Arlington Robinson's "Richard Cory" (Unit 7).

**Dramatic Poetry.** A **dramatic poem** is a verse that relies heavily on dramatic elements such as **monologue** (speech by a single character) or **dialogue** (conversation involving two or more characters). Robert Frost's "Home Burial" (Unit 7) is made up of dialogue. Often dramatic poems are narratives as well. In other words, they often tell stories. A **dramatic monologue** is a poem that presents the speech of a single character in a dramatic situation. See Edgar Lee Masters's "Lucinda Matlock" (Unit 7).

**Lyric Poetry.** A **lyric poem** is a highly musical verse that expresses the emotions of a speaker. There are many types of lyric poems. Among the most common types are the following:

**Sonnet.** A **sonnet** is a fourteen-line poem that follows one of a number of different rhyme schemes. Many sonnets deal with the subject of love. See Edna St. Vincent Millay's "Sonnet XXX" (Unit 1).

**Ode.** An **ode** is a lofty lyric poem on a serious theme. It may employ alternating stanza patterns, developed from the choral ode of Greek dramatic poetry. These stanza patterns are called the *strophe*, the *antistrophe*, and the *epode*. However, not all odes follow this pattern. William Cullen Bryant's "Thanatopsis" (Unit 4) is an ode.

**Free Verse.** **Free verse** is poetry that avoids use of regular rhyme, meter, or division into stanzas. The first great writer of free verse in the United States was Walt Whitman. See his "Song of Myself" (Unit 5). See also Li-Young Lee's "A Story" (Unit 1), T. S. Eliot's "The Love Song of J. Alfred Prufrock" (Unit 7), and Langston Hughes's "The Negro Speaks of Rivers" (Unit 8).

**Elegaic Lyric.** An **elegaic lyric** expresses a speaker's feelings of loss, often because of the death of a loved one or friend. See Walt Whitman's "When Lilacs Last in the Dooryard Bloom'd" (Unit 5) and Theodore Roethke's "Elegy for Jane" (Unit 10).

**Imagist Poem.** An **imagist poem** is a lyric that presents a single vivid picture in words. See Ezra Pound's "In a Station of the Metro" (Unit 7), William Carlos Williams's "The Red Wheelbarrow" (Unit 7), and Amy Lowell's "A Lover" (Unit 7).

## TECHNIQUES OF POETRY: METER AND STANZA FORM

**Metrical verse** follows a set rhythmical pattern. **Free verse** does not. Instead, it follows the rhythms of ordinary speech.

**Meter.** The **meter** of a poem is its rhythmical pattern. English verse usually is described as being made up of rhythmical units called **feet**. A **foot** consists of some combination of **weakly stressed** ($\smile$) and **strongly stressed** ($/$) syllables, as follows:

| TYPE OF FOOT | PATTERN | EXAMPLE |
|---|---|---|
| **iamb,** or **iambic foot** | ˘ / | ˘ /<br>afraid |
| **trochee,** or **trochaic foot** | / ˘ | / ˘<br>freedom |
| **anapest,** or **anapestic foot** | ˘ ˘ / | ˘ ˘ /<br>in a flash |
| **dactyl,** or **dactylic foot** | / ˘ ˘ | / ˘ ˘<br>feverish |
| **spondee,** or **spondaic foot** | / / | / /<br>baseball |

Some writers on meter also use the term **pyrrhee,** or **pyrrhic foot,** to describe a foot with two weak stresses, as follows:

```
     anapest        pyrrhee
  ˘     ˘     /   |   ˘     ˘
  un    re    li  |   a    ble
```

The following terms are used to describe the number of feet in a line of poetry:

| TERM | NUMBER OF FEET | EXAMPLE |
|---|---|---|
| **monometer** | one foot | ˘ /<br>Today<br>˘ /<br>We play |
| **dimeter** | two feet | / ˘ ˘  / ˘<br>Following \| closely<br>/ ˘  / ˘<br>Through the \| forest |
| **trimeter** | three feet | ˘  /  ˘  /  ˘  /<br>God shed \| His light \| on thee |
| **tetrameter** | four feet | / ˘  / ˘  / ˘  / ˘<br>In the \| greenest \| of our \| valleys |
| **pentameter** | five feet | ˘  /  ˘  /  ˘  /  ˘  /<br>A vast \| re pub \| lic famed\| through ev \|<br>˘  /<br>ry clime |
| **hexameter or Alexandrine** | six feet | ˘  /  ˘  /  ˘  /  ˘  /<br>In o \| thers' eyes \| we see \| ourselves \|<br>˘  /  ˘  /<br>the truth \| to tell |

A complete description of the meter of a line includes both the term for the type of foot that predominates in the line and the term for the number of feet in the line. The most common meters in English are **iambic tetrameter** and **iambic pentameter**.

**Stanza Form.** A **stanza** is a group of lines in a poem. The following are some common types of stanza:

**COUPLET**
*(two lines)*

We dance round in a ring and suppose,
But the Secret sits in the middle and knows.

—Robert Frost, "The Secret Sits"

**TRIPLET OR**
**TERCET**
*(three lines)*

Children picking up our bones
Will never know that these were once
As quick as foxes on the hill;

—Wallace Stevens, "A Postcard from the Volcano"

**QUATRAIN**
*(four lines)*

By the rude bridge that arched the flood,
   Their flag to April's breeze unfurl'd,
Here once the embattled farmers stood,
   And fired the shot heard round the world.

—Ralph Waldo Emerson, "Hymn Sung
at the Completion of the Concord
Monument, April 19, 1836"

**QUINTAIN**
*(five lines)*

Gaunt the shadow on your green,
   Shenandoah!
The cut is on the crown
   (Lo, John Brown),
And the stabs shall heal no more.

—Herman Melville, "The Portent"

**SESTET**
*(six lines)*

Once upon a midnight dreary, while I pondered, weak and weary,
Over many a quaint and curious volume of forgotten lore,
While I nodded, nearly napping, suddenly there came a tapping,
As of someone gently rapping, rapping at my chamber door.
"'Tis some visitor," I muttered, "tapping at my chamber door—
       Only this, and nothing more."

—Edgar Allan Poe, "The Raven"

**HEPTASTICH**
*(seven lines)*

In Heaven a spirit doth dwell
   "Whose heart-strings are a lute;"
None sing so wildly well
As the angel Israfel,
And the giddy stars (so legends tell)
Ceasing their hymns, attend the spell
   Of his voice, all mute.

—Edgar Allan Poe, "Israfel"

**OCTAVE**
*(eight lines)*

The God who made New Hampshire
Taunted the lofty land
With little men;—
Small bat and wren
House in the oak:—
If earth-fire cleave
The upheaved land, and bury the folk,
The southern crocodile would grieve.

—Ralph Waldo Emerson, "Ode, Inscribed to
W. H. Channing"

## TECHNIQUES OF POETRY: SOUND*

**Rhythm.** The **rhythm** is the pattern of beats or stresses in a line of verse or prose. A regular rhythmic pattern is called a **meter.**

**Rhyme. Rhyme** is the repetition of sounds at the ends of words. The following are some types of rhyme:

> **End Rhyme. End rhyme** is rhyme that occurs at the ends of lines.

> **Internal Rhyme. Internal rhyme** is the use of rhyming words within lines.

> **Slant Rhyme.** A **slant rhyme,** half rhyme, near rhyme, or off rhyme is the substitution of assonance or consonance for true rhyme. The pairs *world/boiled* and *bear/bore* are examples.

**Alliteration. Alliteration** is the repetition of initial consonant sounds. Some writers also use the term to describe repeated initial vowel sounds. Edgar Allan Poe's "The Raven" contains the following example of alliteration: "And the silken sad uncertain rustling of each purple curtain."

**Assonance. Assonance** is the repetition of vowel sounds in stressed syllables that end with different consonant sounds, as in "weak and weary," also in "The Raven."

**Consonance. Consonance** is a kind of slant rhyme in which the ending consonant sounds of two words match, but the preceding vowel sound does not, as in the words *wind* and *sound.*

**Onomatopoeia. Onomatopoeia** is the use of words or phrases that sound like the things to which they refer. Examples of onomatopoeia include words such as *pow, caw, clink,* and *murmur.*

## TECHNIQUES OF POETRY: MEANING*

**Image.** An **image** is a word or phrase that names something that can be seen, heard, touched, tasted, or smelled. A group of images that together create a given emotion in a reader or listener is called, in a phrase coined by T. S. Eliot, an **objective correlative.**

*Note: These techniques are commonly used in poetry, but also appear in other types of literature.

**Figurative Language. Figurative language** is writing or speech meant to be understood imaginatively instead of literally. Many writers, especially poets, use figurative language to help readers to see things in new ways. Following are examples of figurative language:

**Hyperbole.** A **hyperbole** is an exaggeration made for rhetorical effect.

**Metaphor.** A **metaphor** is a figure of speech in which one thing is spoken or written about as if it were another. This figure of speech invites the reader to make a comparison between the two things. The two "things" involved are the writer's actual subject, the **tenor** of the metaphor, and another thing to which the subject is likened, the **vehicle** of the metaphor. In Emily Dickinson's metaphor "'Hope' is the thing with feathers— / That perches in the soul" the tenor is hope. The vehicle is a bird. **Personification** and **simile** are types of metaphor.

**Metonymy.** **Metonymy** is the naming of an object associated with a thing in place of the name of the thing itself. Speaking of *the White House* when one means *the president of the United States* is an example.

**Personification.** **Personification** is a figure of speech in which an idea, animal, or thing is described as if it were a person. *Night embraces us* is an example.

**Simile.** A **simile** is a comparison using *like* or *as*. A simile is a type of metaphor and, like any other metaphor, can be divided into two parts, the tenor and the vehicle. T. S. Eliot's description of evening "spread out against the sky / Like a patient etherised upon a table" is an example. In this simile the evening is the tenor and the patient the vehicle.

**Synaesthesia.** **Synaesthesia** is a figure of speech that combines in a single expression images related to two or more different senses. Archibald MacLeish's line "Dumb / As old medallions to the thumb," which combines the senses of sound and touch, is an example of synaesthesia.

**Synecdoche.** A **synecdoche** is a figure of speech in which the name of part of something is used in place of the name of the whole, or vice versa. The use of *hired hands* for *laborers* is an example.

**Understatement.** An **understatement** is an ironic expression in which something of importance is emphasized by being spoken of as though it were not important.

**Rhetorical Techniques.** A **rhetorical technique** is an extraordinary but literal use of language to achieve a particular effect. The following rhetorical techniques are commonly used in poetry:

**Antithesis.** **Antithesis** is a rhetorical technique in which words, phrases, or ideas are strongly contrasted, often by means of repetition of grammatical structures. An example is Ralph Waldo Emerson's description of the taunting of "<u>lofty land</u> / With <u>little men</u>."

**Chiasmus.** A **chiasmus** is a rhetorical technique in which the order of occurrence of words or phrases is reversed, as in the traditional line "We can weather changes, but we can't change the weather."

**Parallelism.** **Parallelism** is a rhetorical technique in which a writer emphasizes the equal value or weight of two or more ideas by expressing them in the same grammatical form, as in Abraham Lincoln's phrase "of the people, by the people, for the people."

**Repetition.** **Repetition** is the writer's conscious reuse of a sound, word, phrase, sentence, or other element. Walt Whitman used repetition in the line "I celebrate myself, and sing myself, / And what I assume, you shall assume."

**Rhetorical Question.** A **rhetorical question** is one asked for effect but not meant to be answered because the answer is clear from the context, as in Walt Whitman's "Has any one supposed it lucky to be born?"

# "Sonnet XXX"

### BY EDNA ST. VINCENT MILLAY

## About the AUTHOR

**Edna St. Vincent Millay**
(1892–1950) was born in Rockland, Maine, and began to write poetry at an early age. In 1912, her poem "Renascence" was published in a collection called *The Lyric Year.* After attending Barnard and Vassar, she published a book of verse, *Renascence and Other Poems,* and moved to Greenwich Village in New York City. There she refined her poetic talents and worked as both an actor and playwright for the Provincetown Players, which produced her plays *The Princess Marries the Page, Aria da Capo,* and *Two Slatterns and a King.* Millay became a master of the sonnet, one of the most difficult of English poetic forms, and her poetry reached a large and enthusiastic audience. In 1923, she received a Pulitzer Prize for *The Ballad of the Harp-Weaver.* In that same year she married and bought a farm in upstate New York, where she continued her writing, including a sonnet cycle, or group of related sonnets, called *Fatal Interview.* Many of her later works dealt with social and political issues. Works by Millay include *Collected Sonnets* (1941), *Collected Lyrics* (1943), and *Collected Poems* (1953).

## About the SELECTION

Love has been a favorite subject for sonnet writers. Some of the most famous lines in poetry come from love sonnets: "How do I love thee? Let me count the ways" is from Elizabeth Barrett Browning's "Sonnet XLIII," and "Shall I compare thee to a summer's day?" is the first line of Shakespeare's "Sonnet 18." The sonnet sequences of the greatest poets celebrate love. Petrarch's *Canzoniere* is a collection of poems about his love for a woman named Laura. Sir Philip Sidney's *Astrophel and Stella* was inspired by the poet's passion for Penelope Deveraux, who would later marry another. Edmund Spenser's *Amoretti* commemorated his courtship of Elizabeth Boyle. Edna St. Vincent Millay's **"Sonnet XXX,"** which tells of Millay's own great love, continues the long tradition.

## Literary TOOLS

**SONNET.** A **sonnet** is a fourteen-line rhyming poem, often on the subject of love. The *meter,* or rhythm, used in most sonnets is called *iambic pentameter.* Iambic pentameter consists of ten beats per line. As you read, count the number of syllables, or beats, in each line of this sonnet.

**RHYME SCHEME.** A **rhyme scheme** is a pattern of end rhymes, or rhymes at the ends of lines of verse. The rhyme scheme of a poem is designated by matching letters, with matching letters signifying matching sounds. As you read, note which lines in this poem rhyme.

**REPETITION.** **Repetition** is a writer's conscious reuse of a sound, word, phrase, sentence, or other element. Note the use of repetition in this sonnet.

**ALLITERATION.** **Alliteration** is the repetition of initial consonant sounds. Some writers also use the term to describe repeated initial vowel sounds. Look for the use of alliteration in "Sonnet XXX."

## Reader's Journal

What has love meant to you the last year? What has it meant to you over your lifetime?

# Sonnet XXX

### EDNA ST. VINCENT MILLAY

**END RHYME**

*The words* drink *and* sink *are examples of end rhymes, rhymes that appear at the ends of lines.*

**REPETITION**

*The repetition of the phrase "rise and sink" emphasizes a drowning person's continual struggles and, possibly, the rise and fall of any- one's fortunes in life.*

**ALLITERATION**

*The repetition of p and r sounds at the begin- nings of words are examples of alliteration.*

Love is not all: it is not meat nor drink
Nor slumber nor a roof against the rain;
Nor yet a floating spar[1] to men that sink
And rise and sink and rise and sink again;
5    Love can not fill the thickened lung with breath,
Nor clean the blood, nor set the fractured bone;
Yet many a man is making friends with death
Even as I speak, for lack of love alone.
It well may be that in a difficult hour,
10   Pinned down by pain and moaning for release,
Or nagged by want[2] past <u>resolution's</u> power,
I might be driven to sell your love for peace,
Or trade the memory of this night for food.
It well may be. I do not think I would.   ■

---

1. **spar.** Any pole supporting or extending the sail of a ship;
here, the parts of a ship that can be used to keep sailors afloat after
the ship has wrecked
2. **want.** Physical need

---

**WORDS FOR EVERYDAY USE**

**res • o • lu • tion** (rez′ə lü′shən) *n.,* determined state of mind; faithfulness to some person or idea. *Mary's <u>resolution</u> to continue despite her pain was an indication of her courage.*

---

## Respond *to the* SELECTION

Explain whether or not you believe that love is as important as food for a hungry person or release from pain for a suffering person.

# INVESTIGATE Inquire, Imagine

## Recall: GATHERING FACTS

1a. In lines 1–4, what does the speaker say that love is not? According to lines 5 and 6, what can love not do?

2a. According to lines 7 and 8, what might drive a person to make friends with death?

3a. According to lines 9–13, what might move the speaker to sell his or her love for peace? to trade the memory of that love for food?

## Interpret: FINDING MEANING

1b. According to lines 1 and 2, what other things does a person need besides love? In what ways do people, in the course of their lives, "sink / And rise and sink and rise and sink again"? What do the circumstances mentioned in lines 5 and 6 have in common? What needs do people sometimes have that cannot be met by love?

2b. How important is love to such a person?

3b. What question does the speaker consider in lines 9–14 of the poem? How does he or she answer that question?

## Analyze: TAKING THINGS APART

4a. Does the speaker believe that love is a fundamental need? Support your answer with evidence from the poem.

## Synthesize: BRINGING THINGS TOGETHER

4b. What do you think are people's most basic needs? Make a list of these. Is your list the same as the speaker's? How does it differ?

## Evaluate: MAKING JUDGMENTS

5a. Do you agree with the speaker's conclusions? Does the speaker seem convinced that he or she would not trade love for food or release from pain? Explain.

## Extend: CONNECTING IDEAS

5b. Think of the kinds of love you have had in your life: love from parents and family, from friends, or from a significant other. What can love do for a person? What would happen to you if you had never experienced love?

# Understanding Literature

**SONNET.** Review the definition of **sonnet** in the Handbook of Literary Terms. The **English, Elizabethan,** or **Shakespearean sonnet** can be divided into four parts: three quatrains, or four-line sections, and a final couplet, or two-line section. What is the subject of the first quatrain of "Sonnet XXX"? of the second quatrain? of the third quatrain? of the concluding couplet? Paraphrase each of these sections of the poem by stating its main idea in your own words.

**RHYME SCHEME.** Review the definition of **rhyme scheme** in the Handbook of Literary Terms. To determine the rhyme scheme of a poem, assign letters of the alphabet to each of the sounds that appear at the ends of lines. The end rhymes of the first four lines of "Sonnet XXX" have the rhyme scheme *abab,* as follows:

  drink *a*     rain *b*     sink *a*     again *b*

What is the rhyme scheme of the rest of the poem?

**REPETITION.** Review the definition of **repetition** in the Handbook of Literary Terms. What effect does the author's repetition of the words *rise* and *sink* have?

**ALLITERATION.** Review the definition of **alliteration** in the Handbook of Literary Terms. What examples of alliteration can you find in Millay's poem, other than the ones highlighted on page 20? In your opinion, what does alliteration add to the poem?

## Literary TOOLS

**FREE VERSE. Free verse** is poetry that avoids use of regular rhyme, meter, or division into stanzas. As you read, note evidence that "A Story" is a free verse poem.

**NARRATIVE POEM.** A **narrative poem** is a verse that tells a story. As you read, decide whether this selection is a narrative poem.

## Reader's *Journal*

Write about a time someone read to you when you were a child.

*"A Story"*

BY LI-YOUNG LEE

## About *the* AUTHOR

**Li-Young Lee** (1957– ) was born in Jakarta, Indonesia. Because his parents had been forced to flee China, Lee wandered through Hong Kong, Macau, and Japan with his family before finally settling in the United States. Of this experience, Lee has said, "I feel as if [my family's] experience may be no more than an outward manifestation of a homelessness that people in general feel."

Lee earned his B.A. at the University of Pittsburgh and has taught at various schools. Marked by celebration, intimacy, passion, and sadness, Lee's poetry often draws on stories, many about his father, who was a professor before becoming a Presbyterian minister. Lee now has young children of his own and says, "I tell them stories constantly, and they love to hear stories."

Lee's writing includes his poetry collections *Rose* (1986) and *The City in Which I Love You* (1990), as well as his memoir *The Winged Seed: A Remembrance* (1995), which chronicles his family's journeys. His work has been honored with numerous prizes and awards, including a Guggenheim Fellowship and the Lamont Poetry Selection of the Academy of American Poets.

## About *the* SELECTION

**"A Story"** is about a father who is afraid of disappointing his son because he cannot think of a new story to tell him. It has long been known that children whose parents read to them become better readers and writers as they grow older, and usually develop a lifelong love for books. However, children can also be taught important lessons and learn about a parent's values and dreams during storytime. The father may be hoping that the lessons he communicates to his child will be enough to sustain him over a lifetime.

# A Story

## Li-Young Lee

**FREE VERSE**
*Notice that this poem, like many free verse poems, has no regular rhyme scheme or meter.*

Sad is the man who is asked for a story
and can't come up with one.

His five-year-old son waits in his lap.
*Not the same story, Baba. A new one.*
5   The man rubs his chin, scratches his ear.

In a room full of books in a world
of stories, he can recall
not one, and soon, he thinks, the boy
will give up on his father.

NARRATIVE POEM
Just as dialogue is often
included in a story, it
can also be included in
a narrative poem. How
are the lines of dialogue
marked in this story?

10  Already the man lives far ahead, he sees
the day this boy will go. *Don't go!*
*Hear the alligator story! The angel story once more!*
*You love the spider story. You laugh at the spider.*
*Let me tell it!*

15  But the boy is packing his shirts,
he is looking for his keys. *Are you a god,*
the man screams, *that I sit <u>mute</u> before you?*
*Am I a god that I should never disappoint?*

But the boy is here. *Please, Baba, a story?*
20  It is an emotional rather than <u>logical</u> equation,
an earthly rather than heavenly one,
which posits[1] that a boy's <u>supplications</u>
and a father's love add up to silence.          ∎

---

1. **posit.** Assume or claim as true

**WORDS FOR EVERYDAY USE**

**mute** (myüt) *adj.,* silent; unable to speak. *The boy was <u>mute</u> and used sign language to communicate.*

**log • i • cal** (lä´ji kəl) *adj.,* governed by the scientific principles of reasoning. *The character of Spock on* Star Trek *was very <u>logical</u> when solving problems.*

**sup • pli • ca • tion** (sə pli kā´shən) *n.,* humble request or plea. *I responded to the homeless person's <u>supplication</u> by giving what money I had to spare.*

**Respond** *to the* **SELECTION**

If you were the father, what would you do if you could not think of a story?

# INVESTIGATE, Inquire, *Imagine*

**Recall:** GATHERING FACTS

1a. What does the son want? What does the father think the son will do soon?

2a. What does the father imagine he will offer his son to keep him from leaving? How does he imagine his son will react?

3a. What words does the father use to describe the "equation" of his relationship with his son? What does he say the equation is not?

→ **Interpret:** FINDING MEANING

1b. Why might the man feel sad at not being able to think of a story?

2b. Why is the father silent? What could the father do to keep his son from leaving home one day? Would it be possible, or even healthy, for him to make his son stay?

3b. Through this description, what is the father saying about the nature of relationships?

**Analyze:** TAKING THINGS APART

4a. Analyze the father's imagined screams at the end of stanza 5. Based on these lines, what do you think the father realizes about himself, his son, and their relationship? For example, is the father capable of being a "god"? What frustrates him?

→ **Synthesize:** BRINGING THINGS TOGETHER

4b. Why do you think ". . . a boy's supplications / and a father's love add up to silence"? What is the father's worry? Do his worries have to do with telling stories, or do they extend to other areas? Explain.

**Evaluate:** MAKING JUDGMENTS

5a. What kind of father do you think the man will be as his son grows up? Explain your answer.

→ **Extend:** CONNECTING IDEAS

5b. Describe a time when you enjoyed a story that someone told you. What did you learn by hearing that story? Did it make you feel closer to the storyteller? Why, or why not?

# Understanding *Literature*

**FREE VERSE.** Review the definition for **free verse** in Elements of Poetry on page 14. Into how many stanzas is this poem divided? Are the stanzas regular in length? What do the first and last stanzas have in common?

**NARRATIVE POEM.** Review the definition for **narrative poem** in Elements of Poetry on page 14. What is the story told in this poem?

# Writer's Journal

1. Write a **thank-you letter** to one of your parents or to another person who loved and supported you while you were growing up.
2. Compose a **quatrain,** or four-line stanza, about love. Use the rhyme scheme *abab.*
3. Write a **free verse, narrative poem** telling a story appropriate for a child. You could, for example, write a poem about an alligator or a spider.

# Integrating *the* LANGUAGE ARTS

## Language, Grammar, and Style

**FUNCTIONS OF SENTENCES.** English speakers use four kinds of sentences to express four different kinds of complete thoughts:

- A **declarative sentence** gives information. First, it tells whom or what a speaker is writing or speaking about, and second, information about that person or thing.
- An **interrogative sentence** asks a question.
- An **imperative sentence** gives orders or makes requests.
- An **exclamatory sentence** expresses strong feeling.

Write on your own paper whether each sentence below is declarative, interrogative, imperative, or exclamatory. For more information, see the Language Arts Survey 3.17, "Functions of Sentences."

1. Edna St. Vincent Millay was born and raised in Maine.
2. I love her poetry!
3. Have you read the interview that Bill Moyers conducted with Li-Young Lee?
4. It is published in Moyers's book *The Language of Life.*
5. Get Li-Young Lee's memoir, *The Winged Seed,* from the library.

## Speaking and Listening & Collaborative Learning

**ORAL INTERPRETATION OF POETRY.** Select a poem you particularly relate to, possibly one of the poems you found while researching poets for the Study and Research activity. If the poem is long, choose a section of it that can be read alone. Then prepare to read the poem to three or four classmates. First, read the Language Arts Survey 4.19, "Oral Interpretation of Poetry," for tips. As you listen to the oral presentations by others in your small group, record whether each poem is narrative, dramatic, or lyric. When all the presentations are complete, each speaker should reveal what type of poem he or she read, and the other group members should correct their answers.

## Study and Research

**RESEARCHING POETS.** With a partner, research an American poet who interests you. Find out the type of poetry written by this poet and write a paragraph summarizing his or her accomplishments and listing his or her published works. Then make a list of your four favorite poems by the poet. Identify the form of each poem and the techniques of meter and stanza form, sound, or meaning used in each.

# Fiction

The term *fiction* comes from the Latin *fictio,* meaning "something invented." Thus fiction is any prose writing that tells an invented or imaginary story. Some fiction, the historical novel, for example, is based on fact, while other forms, such as the fantasy tale, are highly unrealistic. Fictional works also vary in structure and length, from the newly recognized **short short** (a very brief short story) to the book-length **novel**. Other forms include the traditional **short story** and the **novella**, a fictional work of intermediate length.

## The Development of Fiction

The oldest fictions are the prose stories told in the oral tradition, which include myths, legends, and fables. Early written prose fictions include Petronius's *Satyricon* and Apuleius's *The Golden Ass,* written by Romans in the first and second centuries. The first novel, *The Tale of Genji,* was written by a Japanese woman, Lady Murasaki Shikibu, in the eleventh century. Early fictions from Europe include Boccaccio's *Decameron,* a collection of short prose tales written in the mid-fourteenth century, and Cervantes's *Don Quixote,* a satire of medieval romance tales written in the early seventeenth century.

## The Novel

The novel developed from various kinds of nonfiction writing, including autobiographies, biographies, travel sketches, journals, and letters. Arguably the first full-fledged novel in English was Aphra Behn's *Oroonoko,* published in 1688. Other early novels in English include Daniel Defoe's *Robinson Crusoe* (1719) and *Moll Flanders* (1722), and Samuel Richardson's *Pamela* (1740) and *Clarissa* (1747–1748). By the mid-1800s, the novel had become a popular form in the United States. Important American novelists include Nathaniel Hawthorne (1804–1864), Herman Melville (1819–1891), Mark Twain (1835–1910), Henry James (1843–1916), Kate Chopin (1850–1904), Edith Wharton (1862–1937), Stephen Crane (1871–1945), Theodore Dreiser (1871–1945), Willa Cather (1873–1947), Zora Neale Hurston (1891–1960), F. Scott Fitzgerald (1896–1940), William Faulkner (1897–1962), Ernest Hemingway (1899–1961), Richard Wright (1908–1960), John Steinbeck (1902–1968), Eudora Welty (1909–2001), Saul Bellow (1915–   ), James Baldwin (1924–1987), Toni Morrison (1931–   ), John Updike (1932–   ), Philip Roth (1933–   ), and Alice Walker (1944–   ).

## The Short Story

The short story genre, or type, originated in the United States. Important American figures in the development of the short story include Washington Irving (1783–1859), Nathaniel Hawthorne, and Edgar Allan Poe (1809–1849). Poe was instrumental in defining the genre, which he described as a short work that creates a single dominant impression or effect on the reader. According to Poe, every detail in a short story should contribute to creating that overall impression or effect.

Poe's "The Pit and the Pendulum" and Hawthorne's "Rappaccini's Daughter" appear in Unit 4. Other noteworthy short stories in this book include "The Story of an Hour" by Kate Chopin (Unit 6), "The Life You Save May Be Your Own" by Flannery O'Connor (Unit 10), "The Slump" by John Updike (Unit 11), and "Reassurance" by Allan Gurganus (Unit 12).

*Parisian Books,* 1887. Vincent van Gogh. Private Collection.

# Elements of Fiction

## CHARACTER

A **character** is a person (or sometimes an animal) who figures in the action of a story. The following are some useful terms for describing characters:

A **protagonist**, or **main character**, is the central figure in a story.

An **antagonist** is a character who is pitted against a protagonist.

A **major character** is one with a significant role in the action of a story. A **minor character** is one who plays a lesser role. Because of limitations of length and focus, most short stories have, at most, one or two major characters.

A **one-dimensional character**, **flat character**, or **caricature** is one who exhibits a single dominant quality, or **character trait.**

A **three-dimensional, full,** or **rounded character** is one who exhibits the complexity of traits associated with actual human beings.

A **static character** is one who does not change during the course of the story.

A **dynamic character** is one who does change during the course of the story.

A **stock character** is one found again and again in different literary works. Examples of stock characters include the mad scientist and the absent-minded professor.

**Motivation** is a force that moves a character to think, feel, or behave in a certain way. For example, a character may be **motivated** by greed, love, or friendship. The particular reasons or causes behind a character's actions are his or her **motives**.

## CHARACTERIZATION

**Characterization** is the use of literary techniques to create a character. Writers use three major techniques to create characters: direct description, portrayal of characters' behavior, and representations of characters' internal states. When using direct description, the writer, through a speaker, a narrator, or another character, simply comments on the character, telling the reader about such matters as the character's appearance, habits, dress, background, personality, motivations, and so on. Skillful writers are able to create characterizations through a few well-chosen, significant details. In portrayal of a character's behavior, the writer presents the actions and speech of the character, allowing the reader to draw his or her own conclusions from what the character says or does. When using representations of internal states, the writer reveals directly the character's private thoughts and emotions, often by means of what is known as the *internal monologue*.

## SETTING AND MOOD

The **setting** is the time and place in which a story occurs, together with all the details used to create a sense of a particular time and place. The **mood** is the emotion created in the reader by part or all of a literary work. A writer creates mood through judicious use of concrete details. These details might include descriptions of the setting, of characters, and of events. In fiction, setting is most often revealed by means of description of such elements as landscape, scenery, buildings, furniture, clothing, weather, and the season. It also can be revealed by how characters talk and behave. In its widest sense, setting includes the general social, political, moral, and psychological conditions in which characters find themselves. Many American novels and short stories deal with particular regions of the country (New York City, the western frontier, small towns in the South or Midwest, and so on). Writing in which particular settings play an important role is called **regional fiction.** The details used to create a particular regional setting are called **local color.**

## CONFLICT

A **conflict** is a struggle between two forces in a literary work. A plot involves the introduction, development, and eventual resolution of a conflict. One side of the central conflict in a work of fiction usually is taken by the main character. That character may struggle against another character, against the forces of nature, against society or social norms, against fate, or against some element within himself or herself. A struggle that takes place between a character and some outside force is called an **external conflict.** A struggle that takes place within a character is called an **internal conflict.**

## PLOT

A **plot** is a series of events related to a central **conflict**, or struggle. Often the events of a plot are causally connected. The English novelist E. M. Forster explained, famously, that if the king dies and then the queen dies, that is a story, but if the king dies and then the queen dies of grief, that is a plot. A typical plot involves the following elements:

The **exposition,** or **introduction,** sets the tone and mood, introduces the characters and the setting, and provides necessary background information.

The **inciting incident** is the event that introduces the central conflict.

The **rising action,** or **complication,** develops the conflict to a high point of intensity.

The **climax** is the high point of interest or suspense.

The **crisis,** or **turning point,** often the same event as the climax, is the point in the plot where something decisive happens to determine the future course of events and the eventual working out of the conflict.

The **falling action** is all the events that follow the climax.

The **resolution** is the point at which the central conflict is ended, or resolved.

The **dénouement** is any material that follows the resolution and that ties up loose ends.

Plots are often illustrated using the diagram shown below, known as a plot pyramid. However, many plots do not include all of these elements, and in short stories, the climax often occurs very late in the plot.

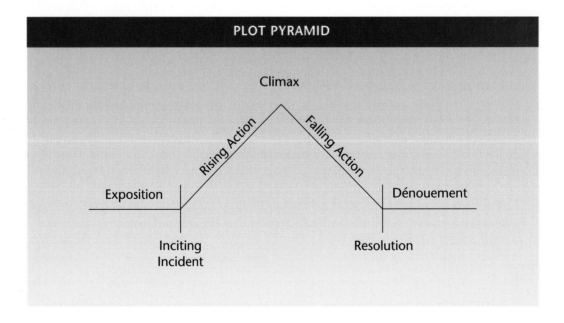

## THEME

A **theme** is a central idea in a literary work. A long work such as a novel may deal with several interrelated themes.

# "American History"

BY JUDITH ORTIZ COFER

## About the AUTHOR

Born in Puerto Rico, **Judith Ortiz Cofer** (1952– ) emigrated to the United States with her family as a child. Her family spoke Spanish, so it was "a challenge, not only to learn English, but to master it enough to teach it and—the ultimate goal—to write poetry in it." Ortiz Cofer says that her family is one of the main topics of her poetry: "The place of birth itself becomes a metaphor for the things we all must leave behind; the assimilation of a new culture is the coming into maturity by accepting the terms necessary for survival. My poetry is a study of this process of change, assimilation, and transformation."

Besides poetry, Ortiz Cofer explored her Puerto Rican heritage in a novel, *The Line of the Sun* (1989). The protagonist, Marisol, learns to balance the American and Puerto Rican aspects of her identity. Living in Paterson, New Jersey, she learns about her Puerto Rican heritage mainly through the stories told by her family. Ortiz Cofer admits that the obsession called "the island" has always been with her. She recreates the scenes of her youth and transforms them with her imagination in her fiction. *An Island Like You: Stories of the Barrio* (1996) includes twelve stories about Puerto Rican teenagers living in a New Jersey neighborhood. *The Latin Deli* (1993) and *The Year of Our Revolution* (1998) contain both short stories and poems. Her story "Nada" won an O. Henry Short Story Prize. Currently Ortiz Cofer teaches literature and writing at the University of Georgia in Athens.

## About the SELECTION

This story takes place on November 22, 1963, the day President John F. Kennedy was assassinated. The narrator, a Puerto Rican girl, struggles "to feel the right thing" for the dead president, even while the national tragedy is overshadowed by a painful experience in her own life.

## Literary TOOLS

The following literary techniques are explored in this story:

EXPOSITION AND SETTING

NARRATOR AND MAJOR CHARACTER

INCITING INCIDENT

MINOR CHARACTER

CONFLICT

RISING ACTION

CLIMAX

RESOLUTION

## Reader's Journal

When have you felt excluded?

**Bare Tree Below Buildings, Manhattan,**
**1944. Brett Weston.**

EXPOSITION
AND SETTING

*In a plot, the*
***exposition*** *is that*
*part of a narrative*
*that provides*
*background infor-*
*mation, often*
*about the charac-*
*ters, setting, or*
*conflict. The* ***set-***
***ting*** *of a literary*
*work is the time*
*and place in*
*which it occurs,*
*together with all*
*the details used to*
*create a sense of a*
*particular time*
*and place.*
*Information about*
*the setting of*
*"American*
*History" is*
*included at right.*

# American HISTORY

## JUDITH ORTIZ COFER

*I* once read in a "Ripley's Believe It or Not" column that Paterson, New Jersey, is the place where the Straight and Narrow (streets) intersect. The Puerto Rican tenement known as *El Building* was one block up from Straight. It was, in fact, the corner of Straight and Market; not "at" the corner, but *the* corner. At almost any hour of the day, El Building was like a monstrous jukebox, blasting out *salsas*[1] from open windows as the residents, mostly new immigrants just up from the island, tried to drown out whatever they were currently enduring with loud music. But the day President Kennedy was shot there was a profound silence in El Building; even the abusive tongues of viragoes,[2] the cursing of the unemployed, and the screeching of small children had been somehow muted. President Kennedy was a saint to these people. In fact, soon his photograph would be hung alongside the Sacred Heart and over the spiritist altars that many women kept in their apartments. He would become part of the <u>hierarchy</u> of <u>martyrs</u> they prayed to for favors that only one who had died for a cause could understand.

---

1. *salsas.* Popular Latin American music
2. **viragoes.** Loud, overbearing women

WORDS
FOR
EVERYDAY
USE

**hi • er • ar • chy** (hī´ ər är´kē) *n.*, group classified by grade or rank. *Phil joined the <u>hierarchy</u> of elite athletes when he won an Olympic gold medal.*

**mar • tyr** (märt´ər) *n.*, person who sacrifices his or her life for the sake of a principle or cause. *Martin Luther King, Jr. was a <u>martyr</u> of the civil rights movement.*

On the day that President Kennedy was shot, my ninth grade class had been out in the fenced playground of Public School Number 13. We had been given "free" exercise time and had been ordered by our P.E. teacher, Mr. DePalma, to "keep moving." That meant that the girls should jump rope and the boys toss basketballs through a hoop at the far end of the yard. He in the meantime would "keep an eye" on us from just inside the building.

It was a cold gray day in Paterson. The kind that warns of early snow. I was miserable, since I had forgotten my gloves, and my knuckles were turning red and raw from the jump rope. I was also taking a lot of abuse from the black girls for not turning the rope hard and fast enough for them.

"Hey, Skinny Bones, pump it, girl. Ain't you got no energy today?" Gail, the biggest of the black girls had the other end of the rope, yelled, "Didn't you eat your rice and beans and pork chops for breakfast today?"

The other girls picked up the "pork chop" and made it into a refrain: "pork chop, pork chop, did you eat your pork chop?" They entered the double ropes in pairs and exited without tripping or missing a beat. I felt a burning on my cheeks and then my glasses fogged up so that I could not manage to coordinate the jump rope with Gail. The chill was doing to me what it always did; entering my bones, making me cry, humiliating me. I hated the city, especially in winter. I hated Public School Number 13. I hated my skinny flatchested body, and I envied the black girls who could jump rope so fast that their legs became a blur. They always seemed to be warm while I froze.

There was only one source of beauty and light for me that school year. The only thing I had anticipated at the start of the semester. That was seeing Eugene. In August, Eugene and his family had moved into the only house on the block that had a yard and trees. I could see his place from my window in El Building. In fact, if I sat on the fire escape I was literally suspended above Eugene's backyard. It was my favorite spot to read my library books in the summer. Until that August the house had been occupied by an old Jewish couple. Over the years I had become part of their family, without their knowing it, of course. I had a view of their kitchen and their backyard, and though I could not hear what they said, I knew when they were arguing, when one of them was sick, and many other things. I knew all this by watching them at mealtimes. I could see their kitchen table, the sink, and the stove. During good times, he sat at the table and read his newspapers while she fixed the meals. If they argued, he would leave and the old woman would sit and stare at nothing for a long time. When one of them was sick, the other would come and get things from the kitchen and carry them out on a tray. The old man had died in June. The last week of school I had not seen him at the table at all. Then one day I saw that there was a crowd in the kitchen. The old woman had finally emerged from the house on the arm of a stocky middle-aged woman, whom I had seen there a few times before, maybe her daughter. Then a man had carried out suitcases. The house had stood empty for weeks. I had had to resist the temptation to climb down into the yard and water the flowers the old lady had taken such good care of.

By the time Eugene's family moved in, the yard was a tangled mass of weeds. The father had spent several days mowing, and when he finished, from where I sat, I didn't see the red, yellow, and purple

NARRATOR AND MAJOR CHARACTER

◄ A *narrator* is one who tells a story. A *major character* is one who plays a significant role in a work. Note who the narrator of this story is and what information is revealed about him or her.

clusters that meant flowers to me. I didn't see this family sit down at the kitchen table together. It was just the mother, a red-headed tall woman who wore a white uniform—a nurse's, I guessed it was; the father was gone before I got up in the morning and was never there at dinnertime. I only saw him on weekends when they sometimes sat on lawn chairs under the oak tree, each hidden behind a section of the newspaper; and there was Eugene. He was tall and blond, and he wore glasses. I liked him right away because he sat at the kitchen table and read books for hours. That summer, before we had even spoken one word to each other, I kept him company on my fire escape.

Once school started I looked for him in all my classes, but P.S. 13 was a huge, overpopulated place and it took me days and many <u>discreet</u> questions to discover that Eugene was in honors classes for all his subjects, classes that were not open to me because English was not my first language, though I was a straight A student. After much <u>maneuvering</u> I managed to "run into him" in the hallway where his locker was—on the other side of the building from mine—and in study hall at the library, where he first seemed to notice me, but did not speak; and finally, on the way home after school one day when I decided to approach him directly, though my stomach was doing somersaults.

I was ready for rejection, snobbery, the worst. But when I came up to him, practically panting in my nervousness, and blurted out: "You're Eugene. Right?" He smiled, pushed his glasses up on his nose, and nodded. I saw then that he was blushing deeply. Eugene liked me, but he was shy. I did most of the talking that day. He nodded and smiled a lot. In the weeks that followed, we walked home together. He would linger at the corner of El Building for a few minutes then walk down to his two-story house. It was not until Eugene moved into that house that I noticed that El Building blocked most of the sun, and that the only spot that got a little sunlight during the day was the tiny square of earth the old woman had planted with flowers.

I did not tell Eugene that I could see inside his kitchen from my bedroom. I felt dishonest, but I liked my secret sharing of his evenings, especially now that I knew what he was reading since we chose our books together at the school library.

One day my mother came into my room as I was sitting on the windowsill staring out. In her abrupt way she said, "Elena, you are acting moony." *Enamorada* was what she really said, that is—like a girl stupidly infatuated. Since I had turned fourteen and started menstruating my mother had been more vigilant then ever. She acted as if I was going to go crazy or explode or something if she didn't watch me and nag me all the time about being a *señorita*[3] now. She kept talking about virtue, morality, and other subjects that did not interest me in the least. My mother was unhappy in Paterson, but my father had a good job at the bluejeans factory in Passaic and soon, he kept assuring us, we would be moving to our own house there. Every Sunday we drove out

---

3. *señorita.* Young lady

INCITING
INCIDENT

The **inciting incident** is the event that introduces the central conflict. One inciting incident is introduced here in the story.

**WORDS FOR EVERYDAY USE**

**dis • creet** (dis krēt´) *adj.*, showing careful reserve in speech or action. *Alicia gave a <u>discreet</u> signal to Keiley to enter the room with the birthday cake.*

**ma • neu • ver • ing** (mə nü´və riŋ) *n.*, strategic movement. *Getting the ambulance through the crowded street required careful <u>maneuvering</u>.*

to the suburbs of Paterson, Clifton, and Passaic, out to where people mowed grass on Sundays in the summer, and where children made snowmen in the winter from pure white snow, not like the gray slush of Paterson, which seemed to fall from the sky in that hue. I had learned to listen to my parents' dreams, which were spoken in Spanish, as fairy tales, like the stories about life in the island paradise of Puerto Rico before I was born. I had been to the island once as a little girl, to grandmother's funeral, and all I remembered was wailing women in black, my mother becoming <u>hysterical</u> and being given a pill that made her sleep two days, and me feeling lost in a crowd of strangers all claiming to be my aunts, uncles, and cousins. I had actually been glad to return to the city. We had not been back there since then, though my parents talked constantly about buying a house on the beach someday, retiring on the island—that was a common topic among the residents of El Building. As for me, I was going to go to college and become a teacher.

But after meeting Eugene I began to think of the present more than of the future. What I wanted now was to enter that house I had watched for so many years. I wanted to see the other rooms where the old people had lived, and where the boy spent his time. Most of all, I wanted to sit at the kitchen table with Eugene like two adults, like the old man and his wife had done, maybe drink some coffee and talk about books. I had started reading *Gone With the Wind*.[4] I was <u>enthralled</u> by it, with the daring and passion of the beautiful girl living in a man-

sion, and with her devoted parents and the slaves who did everything for them. I didn't believe such a world had ever really existed, and I wanted to ask Eugene some questions since he and his parents, he had told me, had come up from Georgia, the same place where the novel was set. His father worked for a company that had transferred him to Paterson. His mother was very unhappy, Eugene said, in his beautiful voice that rose and fell over words in a strange, <u>lilting</u> way. The kids at school called him "the hick" and made fun of the way he talked. I knew I was his only friend so far, and I liked that, though I felt sad for him sometimes. "Skinny Bones" and the "Hick" was what they called us at school when we were seen together.

The day Mr. DePalma came out into the cold and asked us to line up in front of him was the day that President Kennedy was shot. Mr. DePalma, a short, muscular man with slicked-down black hair, was the science teacher, P.E. coach, and disciplinarian at P.S. 13. He was the teacher to whose homeroom you got assigned if you were a troublemaker, and the man called out to break up playground

---

4. ***Gone With the Wind.*** Famous novel by Margaret Mitchell set during the Civil War

**MINOR CHARACTER**

◄ A ***minor character*** is one who plays a lesser role than a major character. How is the minor character Mr. DePalma described?

**WORDS FOR EVERYDAY USE**

**hys • ter • i • cal** (his ter´i kəl) *adj.*, displaying excessive emotion, often through uncontrollable laughter or tears. *Mr. Walker tried to calm Jamal, who became <u>hysterical</u> when he was told he would not be going on to regionals in track.*

**en • thralled** (in´thrôld´) *adj.*, held spellbound. *Sabrina was <u>enthralled</u> by the rap group.*

**lilt • ing** (lil´tiŋ) *adj.*, characterized by a cheerful, rhythmical swing. *The Irishman's <u>lilting</u> voice had an almost musical quality.*

The funeral of President Kennedy, 1963.

"Gross," someone said, and there was a lot of laughter.

"The President is dead, you idiots. I should have known that wouldn't mean anything to a bunch of losers like you kids. Go home." He was shrieking now. No one moved for a minute or two, but then a big girl let out a "Yeah!" and ran to get her books piled up with the others against the brick wall of the school building. The others followed in a mad scramble to get to their things before somebody caught on. It was still an hour to the dismissal bell.

A little scared, I headed for El Building. There was an <u>eerie</u> feeling on the streets. I looked into Mario's drugstore, a favorite hangout for the high school crowd, but there were only a couple of old Jewish men at the soda-bar talking with the short order cook in tones that sounded almost angry, but they were keeping their voices low. Even the traffic on one of the busiest intersections in Paterson—Straight Street and Park Avenue—seemed to be moving slower. There were no horns blasting that day. At El Building, the usual little group of unemployed men were not hanging out on the front stoop making it difficult for women to enter the front door. No music spilled out from open doors in the hallway. When I walked into our apartment, I found my mother sitting in front of the grainy picture of the television set.

She looked up at me with a tear-streaked face and just said, "*Dios mío,*" [5] turning back to the set as if it were pulling at her eyes. I went into my room.

fights, and to escort violently angry teenagers to the office. And Mr. DePalma was the man who called your parents in for a "conference."

That day, he stood in front of two rows of mostly black and Puerto Rican kids, brittle from their efforts to "keep moving" on a November day that was turning bitter cold. Mr. DePalma, to our complete shock, was crying. Not just silent adult tears, but really sobbing. There were a few titters from the back of the line where I stood shivering.

"Listen." Mr. DePalma raised his arms over his head as if he were about to conduct an orchestra. His voice broke, and he covered his face with his hands. His barrel chest was heaving. Someone giggled behind me.

"Listen," he repeated, "something awful has happened." A strange gurgling came from his throat, and he turned around and spat on the cement behind him.

---

5. *Dios mío.* My God

**WORDS FOR EVERYDAY USE**

ee • rie (ir´rē) *adj.,* frightening because of strangeness or mysteriousness. *Right before the storm hit, the sky turned an <u>eerie</u> shade of green.*

**36** UNIT ONE / *GENRES AND TECHNIQUES OF LITERATURE*

Though I wanted to feel the right thing about President Kennedy's death, I could not fight the feeling of <u>elation</u> that stirred in my chest. Today was the day I was to visit Eugene in his house. **He had asked me to come over after school to study for an American History test with him. We had also planned to walk to the public library together. I looked down into his yard. The oak tree was bare of leaves and the ground looked gray with ice. The light through the large kitchen window of his house told me that El Building blocked the sun to such an extent that they had to turn lights on in the middle of the day. I felt ashamed about it. But the white kitchen table with the lamp hanging just above it looked cozy and inviting. I would soon sit there, across from Eugene, and I would tell him about my perch just above his house. Maybe I should.**

In the next thirty minutes I changed clothes, put on a little pink lipstick, and got my books together. Then I went in to tell my mother that I was going to a friend's house to study. I did not expect her reaction.

"You are going out *today?*" The way she said "today" sounded as if a storm warning had been issued. It was said in utter disbelief. Before I could answer, she came toward me and held my elbows as I clutched my books.

"*Hija*,[6] the President has been killed. We must show respect. He was a great man. Come to church with me tonight."

She tried to embrace me, but my books were in the way. My first impulse was to comfort her, she seemed so <u>distraught</u>, but I had to meet Eugene in fifteen minutes. "I have a test to study for, Mama. I will be home by eight."

"You are forgetting who you are, *niña*.[7] I have seen you staring down at that boy's house. You are heading for humiliation and pain." My mother said this in Spanish and in a <u>resigned</u> tone that surprised me, as if she had no intention of stopping me from "heading for humiliation and pain." I started for the door. She sat in front of the TV holding a white handkerchief to her face.

I walked out to the street and around the chain-link fence, that separated El Building from Eugene's house. The yard was neatly edged around the little walk that led to the door. It always amazed me how Paterson, the inner core of the city, had no apparent logic to its architecture. Small, neat, single residences like this one could be found right next to huge, <u>dilapidated</u> apartment buildings like El Building. My guess was that the little houses had been there first, then the immigrants had come in droves, and the monstrosities had been raised for them— the Italians, the Irish, the Jews, and now us, the Puerto Ricans and the blacks. The door was painted a deep green: *verde*, the color of hope. I had heard my mother say it: *Verde—Esperanza.*

I knocked softly. A few suspenseful moments later, the door opened just a

---

6. *Hija.* Daughter
7. *niña.* Girl

**WORDS FOR EVERYDAY USE**

**ela • tion** (i lā´shən) *n.*, state of great joy and pride. *Darla was filled with <u>elation</u> when her story won first prize in the contest.*

**dis • traught** (dis trôt´) *adj.*, upset by doubt or mental conflict. *Mrs. Baccholl was <u>distraught</u> when she couldn't find her five-year-old son anywhere in the grocery store.*

**re • signed** (ri zīnd´) *adj.*, showing acceptance of the inevitable. *Tuck's arguments became weaker, and he finally muttered in a <u>resigned</u> tone, "I guess you're right."*

**di • lap • i • dat • ed** (də lap´ə dāt id) *adj.*, decayed; fallen into partial ruin through neglect. *The neighborhood raised money to restore the <u>dilapidated</u> building into a new youth center.*

**CONFLICT**

◄ A **conflict** is a struggle between two forces in a literary work. A character may struggle against another character, against the forces of nature, or against some element within himself or herself. Note one conflict the narrator experiences as described in the highlighted text at far left.

**RISING ACTION**

◄ The **rising action** develops the conflict to a point of high intensity. The rising action begins in the passage at left.

crack. The red, swollen face of a woman appeared. She had a halo of red hair floating over a delicate ivory face—the face of a doll—with freckles on the nose. Her smudged eye make-up made her look unreal to me, like a mannequin seen through a warped store window.

**CLIMAX**

The **climax** is the high point of interest or suspense in the plot. The climax of "American History" occurs toward the end of the story, as you can see here.

"What do you want?" Her voice was tiny and sweet sounding, like a little girl's, but her tone was not friendly.

"I'm Eugene's friend. He asked me over. To study." I thrust out my books, a silly gesture that embarrassed me almost immediately.

"You live there?" She pointed up to El Building, which looked particularly ugly, like a gray prison with its many dirty windows and rusty fire escapes. The woman had stepped half-way out and I could see that she wore a white nurse's uniform with St. Joseph's Hospital on the name tag.

"Yes. I do."

She looked intently at me for a couple of heartbeats, then said as if to herself, "I don't know how you people do it." Then directly to me: "Listen. Honey. Eugene doesn't want to study with you. He is a smart boy. Doesn't need help. You understand me. I am truly sorry if he told you you could come over. He cannot study with you. It's nothing personal. You understand? We won't be in this place much longer, no need for him to get close to people—it'll just make it harder for him later. Run back home now."

I couldn't move. I just stood there in shock at hearing these things said to me in such a honey-drenched voice. I had never heard an accent like hers, except for

**RESOLUTION**

The **resolution** is the point at which the central conflict is ended, or resolved. Note how the conflict of this story is resolved in the passage at right.

Eugene's softer version. It was as if she were singing me a little song.

"What's wrong? Didn't you hear what I said?" She seemed very angry, and I finally snapped out of my trance. I turned away from the green door, and heard her close it gently.

Our apartment was empty when I got home. My mother was in someone else's kitchen, seeking the <u>solace</u> she needed. Father would come in from his late shift at midnight. I would hear them talking softly in the kitchen for hours that night. They would not discuss their dreams for the future, or life in Puerto Rico, as they often did; that night they would talk sadly about the young widow and her two children, as if they were family. For the next few days, we would observe *luto*[8] in our apartment; that is, we would practice restraint and silence—no loud music or laughter. Some of the women of El Building would wear black for weeks.

That night, I lay in my bed trying to feel the right thing for our dead president. But the tears that came up from a deep source inside me were strictly for me. When my mother came to the door, I pretended to be sleeping. Sometime during the night, I saw from my bed the streetlight come on. It had a pink halo around it. I went to my window and pressed my face to the cool glass. Looking up at the light, I could see the white snow falling like a lace veil over its face. I did not look down to see it turning gray as it touched the ground below. ∎

---

8. *luto.* Mourning

---

**WORDS FOR EVERYDAY USE**

so • lace (säl´əs) *n.,* relief or consolation. *In her grief, Ilse sought <u>solace</u> in the company of her friends.*

Think of a time when adults were deeply moved by some event that you didn't understand.

# INVESTIGATE, Inquire, *Imagine*

## Recall: GATHERING FACTS

1a. What changes occur in El Building the day President Kennedy is shot? What effect does the assassination have on the narrator's mother? How was the president going to be remembered in El Building?

2a. Whom does the narrator watch from her window?

3a. What does Eugene's mother tell the narrator when she comes to visit Eugene?

## Interpret: FINDING MEANING

1b. Why doesn't the narrator grieve for the dead president?

2b. Do Eugene and the narrator make a suitable couple? Why, or why not?

3b. What does Eugene's mother think of the narrator? On what does she base her opinion?

## Analyze: TAKING THINGS APART

4a. Compare and contrast El Building with Eugene's house.

## Synthesize: BRINGING THINGS TOGETHER

4b. Why does the narrator want to enter Eugene's house? Explain whether you think getting her wish would have had the effect she expected.

## Evaluate: MAKING JUDGMENTS

5a. Assess how ethnic prejudice affects the narrator.

## Extend: CONNECTING IDEAS

5b. If this story took place today, do you think the narrator would be treated the same way? Explain.

# Understanding *Literature*

EXPOSITION AND SETTING. Review the definitions for **exposition** and **setting** in Elements of Fiction on pages 29–30. What is the setting of "American History"?

NARRATOR AND MAJOR CHARACTER. Review the definitions for **narrator** and **major character** on page 33. Who is the narrator of "American History"? Who is the major character in the story?

INCITING INCIDENT, RISING ACTION, CLIMAX, AND RESOLUTION. The **inciting incident**, **rising action**, **climax**, and **resolution** are elements of **plot**. Review these terms in Elements of Fiction on page 30. What are the inciting incidents of the story? What happens in the rising action? When does the climax of the story occur? How does the author resolve the conflict?

MINOR CHARACTER. Review the definition for **minor character** in Elements of Fiction on page 28. Why is the minor character Mr. DePalma important to the story? Why is it surprising that he cries the day the president is shot?

CONFLICT. Review the definition for **conflict** in Elements of Fiction on page 29. What types of conflict does the narrator experience?

# WRITER'S JOURNAL

1. Imagine that you are the narrator. Write a **letter** to your cousin in Puerto Rico describing where you were when you heard about President Kennedy's death and people's reactions, including your own.

2. Imagine that you are the narrator. Write a **note** to Eugene explaining what his mother did to you and describing how it made you feel.

3. The narrator says that her parents' dreams are told "as fairy tales." Imagine that you are the narrator. Write a **journal entry** describing your fairy tale about Eugene.

# Integrating
## *the* LANGUAGE ARTS

## Vocabulary

CONNOTATION. Read the Language Arts Survey 1.24, "Connotation and Denotation." Then imagine that you are responsible for finding tenants for the apartments in El Building. Write a radio announcement using words with positive connotations to advertise the apartments and their location.

## Critical Thinking & Collaborative Learning

DISCUSSION GROUPS. The narrator struggles "to feel the right thing" for the slain president. Form small groups and discuss the following questions: What is the "right thing" to feel in such a circumstance? Is it understandable that the narrator can only feel her own pain after being rejected? What is the significance of her refusal to look down at the gray snow at the end of the story? How have you reacted when you have learned of a death of an important figure?

## Study and Research

THE KENNEDY ASSASSINATION. Research the theories about who killed John F. Kennedy. Then write a composition that presents the theory that is the most logical to you.

# Drama

**D**rama is literature enacted in front of an audience by people who play the parts of the characters. No one knows for certain how drama originated, but we do know that ritual performances have been held by people around the globe since long before the beginning of recorded history.

The first literary dramas were created long ago in ancient Greece and may have developed from reenactments of ritual sacrifices. In fact, the ancient Greek word *tragōidia,* from which our word *tragedy* derives, meant "song of the goats." According to one theory, people in ancient Greece would come together to sacrifice an animal to win a god's favor. Eventually, that sacrifice developed into an elaborate show involving an actor, a priest, and a chorus with whom the priest interacted. In the fifth century BC, the Greek playwright Aeschylus added a second actor, and drama as we know it was born.

## Types of Stages

In classical times, dramas were performed in open-air amphitheaters, or **arena stages.** In the Middle Ages, plays were often produced on the backs of wagons in the courtyards of inns. From these developed the **thrust stage** used in Elizabethan England, a platform that jutted into an area open to the sky. In the nineteenth and twentieth centuries, the **proscenium stage,** or **picture stage,** became common. Such a stage is a box-like area with three walls (or curtains) and a removed "fourth wall" through which the audience views the action.

## Types of Drama

Most dramas can be classified as either comedies or tragedies. A **comedy**, in its original sense, was any work with a happy ending. The term is widely used today to refer to any humorous work, especially one prepared for the stage or the screen. A **tragedy** initially was a drama that told the story of the fall of a person of high status, though in recent years the word has been used to describe any play about the downfall of a central character, or protagonist, who wins the audience's sympathies in some way.

## Drama in the United States

The United States has produced many of the world's finest dramatists. Important figures in the history of American drama include Eugene O'Neill (1888–1953), Elmer Rice (1892–1967), Thornton Wilder (1897–1975), Lillian Hellman (1905–1984), Clifford Odets (1906–1963), Tennessee Williams (1911–1983), Arthur Miller (1915– ), Edward Albee (1928– ), Lanford Wilson (1937– ), August Wilson (1945– ), David Mamet (1947– ), and Beth Henley (1952– ).

The earliest American theatrical productions were vaudeville shows and **melodramas**, plays with exaggerated characters, scenes, and situations. From the 1920s through the 1950s, American **Realist theater** blossomed in the work of O'Neill, Odets, Hellman, and Miller. Williams and Albee introduced to American theater many experimental elements, extending and enriching the Realist tradition. For more information about modern drama, see the Introduction to Unit 9, "Modern Drama."

Set for *The Magic Flute,* c.1980. David Hockney. Tamayo Museum, Mexico City.

# Elements of Drama

## THE PLAYWRIGHT AND THE SCRIPT

**Playwright.** The author of a play is the **playwright.** The relationship between a playwright and the play is less direct than that of an ordinary author to his or her text. A novelist or poet has enormous control over the form in which his or her work will be presented to its audience, the reader. A playwright, in contrast, must depend upon the interpretations given his or her work by producers, directors, set designers, actors, and other persons involved in producing the work for the stage. The playwright's art is collaborative.

**Script.** A **script** is the written work from which a drama is produced. It contains stage directions and dialogue and may be divided into acts and scenes.

> **Stage Directions. Stage directions** are notes provided by the playwright to describe how something should be presented or performed on the stage. Stage directions often describe elements of the **spectacle,** such as lighting, music, sound effects, costumes, properties, and set design. They also may describe entrances and exits, the movements of characters, facial expressions, gestures, body language, tone of voice, or other elements related to the acting of the play. Sometimes, especially in reading versions of plays, stage directions provide historical or background information. Stage directions usually are printed in italics and enclosed in brackets or parentheses. In stage directions, the parts of the stage are often described using the terms *up, down, right, left,* and *center,* which describe stage areas from the point of view of the actors.

**Stage Areas**

| Up Right | Up Center | Up Left |
|---|---|---|
| Right Center | Center | Left Center |
| Down Right | Down Center | Down Left |

**Dialogue. Dialogue** is the term used to describe the speech of actors in a play. The dialogue usually consists of the characters' names and the words and other utterances to be spoken by the actors. The dialogue of a play may contain many **monologues,** or long speeches given by actors. A speech given by a lone character on stage is called a **soliloquy.** A statement intended to be heard by the audience or by a single other character but not by other characters on the stage is called an **aside.**

**Acts and Scenes.** An **act** is a major division of a drama. The plays of ancient Rome and of Elizabethan England were typically divided into **five acts.** In contemporary plays, **three-act** and **one-act plays** are quite common. The acts may be divided into scenes. Typically, a **scene** begins with the entrance of one or more characters and ends with the exit of one or more characters. The time and place of acts or scenes may change from one to the next.

## THE SPECTACLE

**Spectacle.** The **spectacle** is all the elements of the drama presented to the senses of the audience—the lights, sets, curtains, costumes, makeup, music, sound effects, properties, and movements of the actors, including any special movement such as pantomime or dance. Spectacle is one major feature that differentiates dramatic from nondramatic works. The following are common elements of the spectacle:

**Stage.** This is the area in which the action is performed. An **arena stage,** or **theater in the round,** is one in which the audience stands or sits around a circular or semicircular open space. A **thrust stage** is one that extends into the audience, which is situated on three sides of the playing area. A **proscenium,** or **picture stage,** is one that has an arch around an opening that acts as a removed "fourth wall."

**Set.** The **set** is everything placed upon the stage to give the impression of a particular setting, or time and place. Sets often include walls, furnishings, and painted backdrops.

**Properties. Properties,** or props, are items that can be carried on and off the stage by actors or manipulated by actors during scenes. Examples of properties include books, fans, gavels, and walking sticks.

**Sound Effects.** These are sounds introduced to create mood or to indicate the presence of something. Common sound effects include thunder, ringing telephones, and police sirens.

**Blocking.** This is the act of determining how actors will move on a stage. Blocking is almost always done by the director of the play.

## Literary
### T O O L S

The following elements of drama are demonstrated in this selection:

STAGE DIRECTIONS

CHARACTER

DIALOGUE

SET AND PROPERTIES

BLOCKING

THEME

## Reader's
### *Journal*

When have you felt social pressure to do something you knew was wrong?

# FROM The Crucible

#### BY ARTHUR MILLER

## About *the*
# A U T H O R

**Arthur Miller** (1915– ) was born in New York City. During his youth, his father's business failed as part of the general economic downturn known as the Great Depression. This failure had a permanent impact on Miller, who went on to write great plays on themes related to social and political justice. After graduating from high school, Miller worked and raised money to attend the University of Michigan. There he began writing plays. His most famous work, *Death of a Salesman* (1949), tells the story of the tragic downfall of its title character, partially as a result of his willingness to do anything for the "almighty dollar." The play is a classic exposé of the consequences of hypocrisy and greed. Miller's other plays include *The Crucible* (1953) and *A View from the Bridge* (1955). In addition to his plays for the stage, Miller has written screenplays, including the script for *The Misfits,* a film that starred his second wife, Marilyn Monroe, and the script for *The Crucible,* a film that starred Daniel Day Lewis.

## About *the*
# S E L E C T I O N

In 1692, a series of trials was held in Salem, Massachusetts, of persons accused of witchcraft. A number of people in the community and in surrounding areas had developed a disease resembling epilepsy, and suspicions arose that the afflictions might be the work of witches. The governor of the colony of Massachusetts, Sir William Phips, began court proceedings. The proceedings were inflamed by accusations made by the daughters of a Salem minister named Parris. These daughters, along with Parris's niece Abigail Parris, pretended to be possessed by spirits and made spectacles in the courtroom during examinations of the accused witches. In all, nineteen persons were hanged as a result of the trials, and one person was pressed to death. Many others were imprisoned and tortured.

Arthur Miller became interested in the Salem witch trials during the McCarthy Era of the 1950s, a time when a similar "witch hunt" occurred in the United States, this one for suspected Communists and other radicals in public office and the entertainment industry. Miller's play explores the psychology of mob hysteria and guilt by association.

# ARTHUR MILLER

*In this scene from the play, John Proctor, whose wife, Elizabeth, has been arrested as a witch, has brought to the court Mary Warren, who has evidence that Abigail and the other afflicted girls have been pretending. As the scene opens, Abigail interrupts an interrogation of John Proctor by the prosecutor, Danforth.*

## Cast of Characters in this Scene

**Abigail Williams.** 18-year-old niece of Reverend Parris. In love with John Proctor, she pretends to be possessed in an attempt to have Proctor's wife condemned as a witch.
**John Proctor.** Farmer in his mid-thirties seeking to free his wife from false charges.
**Mary Warren.** 17-year-old servant of John Proctor.
**Mercy Lewis and Susanna Walcott.** Mercy is an 18-year-old servant girl; Susanna is a little

younger. Along with Abigail, they claim to have been possessed by witches.
**Reverend Samuel Parris.** Zealous minister who begins the witch hunt in Salem.
**Deputy Governor Danforth.** The deputy governor of Salem, prosecutor in this case.
**Reverend John Hale.** A minister who is called to Salem by Reverend Parris to help determine whether witchcraft is afoot.

**STAGE DIRECTIONS**

*Stage directions are notes that describe characters' movements and ways of speaking, the setting, or such elements of the spectacle as lighting, costumes, properties, and sound effects.*

*Abigail, with a weird, wild, chilling cry, screams up to the ceiling.*

**ABIGAIL.**    You will not! Begone! Begone, I say!

**DANFORTH.**    What is it, child? (*But Abigail, pointing with fear, is now raising up her frightened eyes, her awed face, toward the ceiling—the girls are doing the same—and now Hawthorne, Haler, Putnam, Cheever, Herrick, and Danforth do the same.*) What's there? (*He lowers his eyes from the ceiling, and now he is frightened; there is real tension in his voice.*) Child! (*She is transfixed—with all the girls, she is whimpering open-mouthed, agape at the ceiling.*) Girls! Why do you—?

**MERCY LEWIS.** (*pointing*)    It's on the beam! Behind the rafter!

**DANFORTH.** (*looking up*)    Where!

**ABIGAIL.**    Why—? (*She gulps.*) Why do you come, yellow bird?

**PROCTOR.**    Where's a bird? I see no bird!

**ABIGAIL.** (*to the ceiling*)    My face? My face?

**PROCTOR.**    Mr. Hale—

**DANFORTH.**    Be quiet!

**PROCTOR.** (*to Hale*)    Do you see a bird?

**DANFORTH.**    Be quiet!!

**ABIGAIL.** (*to the ceiling, in a genuine conversation with the "bird," as though trying to talk it out of attacking her*)    But God made my face; you cannot want to tear my face. Envy is a deadly sin, Mary.

**MARY WARREN.** (*on her feet with a spring, and horrified, pleading*)    Abby!

**ABIGAIL.** (*unperturbed, continuing to the "bird"*)    Oh, Mary, this is a black art[1] to change your shape. No, I cannot, I cannot stop my mouth; it's God's work I do.

**MARY WARREN.**    Abbey, I'm *here!*

**PROCTOR.** (*frantically*)    They're pretending, Mr. Danforth!

**CHARACTERS**

*The people in a play are its characters. Names of characters are given before the words that they speak.*

**DIALOGUE**

*In a play, the dialogue is the speech of the characters. In a play, dialogue is not placed in quotation marks.*

**ABIGAIL.** (*Now she takes a backward step, as though in fear the bird will swoop down momentarily.*)    Oh, please, Mary! Don't come down.

**SUSANNA WALCOTT.**    Her claws, she's stretching her claws!

**PROCTOR.**    Lies, lies.

**ABIGAIL.** (*backing further, eyes still fixed above*)    Mary, please don't hurt me!

**MARY WARREN.** (*to Danforth*)    I'm not hurting her!

**DANFORTH.** (*to Mary Warren*)    Why does she see this vision?

**MARY WARREN.**    She sees nothin'!

**ABIGAIL.** (*now staring full front as though hypnotized, and mimicking the exact tone of Mary Warren's cry*)    She sees nothin'!

**MARY WARREN.** (*pleading*)    Abby, you mustn't!

**ABIGAIL AND ALL THE GIRLS.** (*all transfixed*)    Abby, you mustn't!

**MARY WARREN.** (*to all the girls*)    I'm here, I'm here!

**GIRLS.**    I'm here, I'm here!

**DANFORTH.** (*horrified*)    Mary Warren! Draw back your spirit out of them!

**MARY WARREN.**    Mr. Danforth!

**GIRLS.** (*cutting her off*)    Mr. Danforth!

**DANFORTH.**    Have you compacted with the devil? Have you?

**MARY WARREN.**    Never, never!

**GIRLS.**    Never, never!

**DANFORTH.** (*growing hysterical*)    Why can they only repeat you?

**PROCTOR.**    Give me a whip—I'll stop it!

**MARY WARREN.**    They're sporting, They—!

**GIRLS.**    They're sporting!

---

1. **black art.** Evil magic

**MARY WARREN.** (*turning on them all hysterically and stamping her feet*)  Abby, stop it!

**GIRLS.** (*stamping their feet*)  Abby, stop it!

**MARY WARREN.**  Stop it!

**GIRLS.**  Stop it!

**MARY WARREN.** (*screaming it out at the top of her lungs, and raising her fists*)  Stop it!!

**GIRLS.** (*raising their fists*)  Stop it!!

*Mary Warren, utterly* <u>confounded</u>, *and becoming overwhelmed by Abigail's—and the girls'—utter conviction, starts to whimper, hands half raised, powerless, and all the girls begin whimpering exactly as she does.*

**DANFORTH.**  A little while ago you were afflicted. Now it seems you afflict others; where did you find this power?

**MARY WARREN.** (*staring at Abigail*)  I—have no power.

**GIRLS.**  I have no power.

**PROCTOR.**  They're gulling[2] you, Mister!

**DANFORTH.**  Why did you turn about this past two weeks? You have seen the Devil, have you not?

**HALE.** (*indicating Abigail and the girls*) You cannot believe them!

**MARY WARREN.**  I—

**PROCTOR.** (*sensing her weakening*)  Mary, God damns all liars!

**DANFORTH.** (*pounding it into her*)  You have seen the Devil, you have made compact with Lucifer,[3] have you not?

*Mary utters something unintelligible, staring at Abigail, who keeps watching the "bird" above.*

**PROCTOR.**  God damns liars, Mary!

**DANFORTH.**  I cannot hear you. What do you say? (*Mary utters again unintelligibly.*) You will confess yourself or you will hang! (*He turns her roughly to face him.*) Do you know who I am? I say you will hang if you do not open with me!

**PROCTOR.**  Mary, remember the angel Raphael—do that which is good and—

**ABIGAIL.** (*pointing upward*)  The wings! Her wings are spreading! Mary, please, don't, don't—!

**HALE.**  I see nothing, Your Honor!

**DANFORTH.**  Do you confess this power! (*He is an inch from her face.*) Speak!

**ABIGAIL.**  She's going to come down! She's walking the beam!

**DANFORTH.**  Will you speak!

**MARY WARREN.** (*staring in horror*)  I cannot!

**GIRLS.**  I cannot!

**PARRIS.**  Cast the Devil out! Look him in the face! Trample him! We'll save you, Mary, only stand fast against him and—

**ABIGAIL.** (*looking up*)  Look out! She's coming down!

*She and all the girls run to one wall, shielding their eyes. And now, as though cornered, they let out a gigantic scream, and Mary, as though infected, opens her mouth and screams with them. Gradually Abigail and the girls leave off, until only Mary is left there, staring up at the "bird," screaming madly. All watch her, horrified by this evident fit. Proctor strides to her.*

**PROCTOR.**  Mary, tell the Governor what they— (*He has hardly got a word out,*

---

2. **gull.** To trick; dupe
3. **Lucifer.** Name for the devil

**WORDS FOR EVERYDAY USE**

con • found (kən found´) vt., confuse; bewilder. *The results of the experiment* <u>confounded</u> *the physicists at first because they appeared to contradict the laws of physics.*

*when seeing him coming for her, she rushes out of his reach, screaming in horror.*)

**MARY WARREN.** Don't touch me—don't touch me! (*At which the girls halt at the door.*)

**PROCTOR.** (*astonished*) Mary!

**MARY WARREN.** (*pointing at Proctor*) You're the Devil's man!

*He is stopped in his tracks.*

**PARRIS.** Praise God!

**GIRLS.** Praise God!

**PROCTOR.** (*numbed*) Mary, how—?

**MARY WARREN.** I'll not hang with you! I love God, I love God.

**DANFORTH.** (*to Mary*) He bid you do the Devil's work?

**MARY WARREN.** (*hysterically, indicating Proctor*) He come at me by night and every day to sign, to sign, to—

**DANFORTH.** Sign what?

**PARRIS.** The Devil's book? He come with a book?

**MARY WARREN.** (*hysterically, pointing at Proctor, fearful of him*) My name, he want my name. "I'll murder you," he says, "if my wife hangs! We must go and overthrow the court," he says!

*Danforth's head jerks toward Proctor, shock and horror in his face.*

**PROCTOR.** (*turning, appealing to Hale*) Mr. Hale!

**MARY WARREN.** (*her sobs beginning*) He wake me every night, his eyes were like coals and his fingers claw my neck, and I sign, I sign . . .

**HALE.** Excellency, this child's gone wild!

**PROCTOR.** (*as Danforth's wide eyes pour on him*) Mary, Mary!

**MARY WARREN.** (*screaming at him*) No, I love God; I go your way no more. I love God, I bless God. (*Sobbing, she rushes to Abigail.*) Abby, Abby, I'll never hurt you more! (*They all watch, as Abigail, out of her infinite charity, reaches out and draws the sobbing Mary to her, and then looks up to Danforth.*) ∎

**Respond** *to the*
# SELECTION

Why does Mary Warren turn on Proctor and make an accusation against him? Explain.

# INVESTIGATE, Inquire Imagine

## Recall: GATHERING FACTS

1a. What does Abigail claim to see on the beam? What does Abigail say is "a deadly sin"?

2a. What question does Danforth ask Mary after she says, "I'm not hurting her"? What does Mary mean when she says that the girls are "sporting"?

3a. Of what does Mary accuse Proctor? To whom does Mary rush at the end of the selection?

## Interpret: FINDING MEANING

1b. According to Abigail, who is making the image appear?

2b. What pressure does Danforth's question put on Mary? What might happen to Mary if the court believes Abigail and the girls? Does Mary see the bird? What explanation for the bird does she offer at first?

3b. Why does Mary change her mind and accuse Proctor?

## Analyze: TAKING THINGS APART

4a. In Puritan New England, debate raged over the admissibility in court of "spectral evidence," the evidence of spirits seen by some people but not by others. What example of such "spectral evidence" appears in this selection? What other "evidence" does Danforth have for believing that Proctor is "the Devil's man"? How would you describe the method of questioning that Danforth uses with Mary? Explain, giving examples from the selection.

## Synthesize: BRINGING THINGS TOGETHER

4b. Would such a method of questioning be acceptable in a court of law today? What is the weakness of this strategy? Explain.

## Evaluate: MAKING JUDGMENTS

5a. What pressures are put on Mary to denounce Proctor? Is what Mary does understandable? excusable? moral? Why, or why not?

## Extend: CONNECTING IDEAS

5b. What would you do in Mary's position? What do you think will happen next?

# Understanding Literature

STAGE DIRECTIONS. Review the definition for **stage directions** in Elements of Drama on page 42. Find examples in this scene of stage directions that indicate parts of the setting and stage directions that indicate how characters are to speak or move.

**CHARACTER.** Review the definition for **character** in the Handbook of Literary Terms. Who are the major characters in this scene from *The Crucible*? Who are the minor characters? Briefly describe the personalities of the major characters, based on their words and actions in this scene. Which characters do you admire? Which do you not admire? Why?

**DIALOGUE.** Review the definition for **dialogue** in Elements of Drama on page 43. Find examples in this scene of dialogue that would probably not be spoken by characters in a modern setting, but that are appropriate to Miller's setting of the play in colonial New England.

**SET AND PROPERTIES.** Review the definitions for **set** and **properties** in Elements of Drama on page 43. If you were designing a set for this scene from *The Crucible,* what elements would you have to include? What properties might you have the actors use?

**BLOCKING.** Review the definition for **blocking** in Elements of Drama on page 43. What movements described in the stage directions for this scene would have to be taken into account by the person, such as the director, who was planning the blocking of the scene?

**THEME.** Review the definition for **theme** in the Handbook of Literary Terms. What do you think is the theme of this scene from the play? What does the scene reveal about the forces that cause people to give in to mob hysteria? Why do some people foresake their convictions in situations like the one described in this scene?

# WRITER'S JOURNAL

1. Imagine that you are John Proctor. Write a **speech,** or **address to the jury,** defending yourself and refuting the "evidence" that has been collected against you.
2. Write a **summary,** or **abstract,** explaining what happens in this scene from *The Crucible.*
3. Imagine that you are Reverend Parris. Write a **sermon** you might deliver to your congregation about how to recognize whether a witness is telling the truth about an accused "witch."

# Integrating *the* LANGUAGE ARTS

## Language, Grammar, and Style

**THE PARTS OF SPEECH.** Review the Language Arts Survey 3.7, "Parts of Speech Overview." Then identify the part of speech of each italicized word in the paragraph below.

[1] *Joseph Raymond McCarthy* entered the United States Senate in 1946. [2] *After* two undistinguished years in the Senate, [3] *he* gained national recognition in 1950 by charging that over two hundred Communists [4] *had infiltrated* the State Department, that part of the government that oversees

foreign relations. At the time, the United States was at war with the Communist government in North Korea, and many citizens of the country were [5] *deeply* fearful about Communist advances in Europe and China. McCarthy's charges struck a chord with the people, and for several years thereafter, [6] *innocent* people were hounded from their jobs in government and in the entertainment industry because of "suspected" Communist activities and "associations" with Communists. Targets [7] *of* McCarthyism included such well-known literary figures as Ring Lardner, Jr., and Lillian Hellman. McCarthy went too far, however, when he made accusations against such popular figures as President Dwight D. Eisenhower. In 1954, the Senate formally voted to condemn McCarthy for his [8] *conduct,* and the McCarthy Era came to an end. Did anything positive come out of the McCarthy Era? [9] *Yes,* this period in American history gave people a new understanding of the dangers of character assassination, guilt by association, [10] *and* mass hysteria. It also gave us Arthur Miller's fine play, <u>The Crucible</u>.

## Study and Research & Collaborative Learning

**RESEARCHING THE SALEM WITCH TRIALS AND THE MCCARTHY HEARINGS.** Your class should form two groups. One group of students research the Salem witch trials of 1692, while the other group researches the McCarthy hearings of the early 1950s. Consider the following questions while researching: What were the origins of your assigned event? How many people initiated it? What motivated the instigators as well as those who subsequently supported the trials or the hearings? Did anyone speak out against these crusaders? What happened to them? Why? Each group should present its findings in class. Then hold a class discussion about the similarities and differences between these two historical moments.

## Critical Thinking

**EXAMINING THE CRIMINAL JUSTICE SYSTEM.** The United States judicial system is based on the principle that a suspect is "innocent until proven guilty." This principle in theory protects people from being wrongly accused of crimes. However, there are cases today in which suspects are wrongly accused of crimes. Using the Internet or the library as a resource, locate a news or magazine article that tells the story of someone wrongly accused of a crime. According to the article, what evidence was used in the case against this person? Was a false confession coerced, or forced, from the suspect? Based on what you learned about the case, was the person truly "guilty beyond a reasonable doubt"? Why, or why not? As a class, discuss the following questions: Why is it important that a person be considered "innocent until proven guilty"? What kinds of evidence are capable of "proving" a person's guilt, and which kinds are merely "circumstantial evidence"?

# Nonfiction

**N**onfiction writing, unlike the other types of literature considered so far, explores actual people, places, things, events, and ideas. Types of nonfiction writing include the following:

**Histories** provide accounts of past events. Histories in this text include excerpts from N. Scott Momaday's "The Way to Rainy Mountain" (Unit 1), from Bartolomé de las Casas's *The Very Brief Relation of the Devastation of the Indies* (Unit 2), from John Smith's *The General History of Virginia, New England, and the Summer Isles* (Unit 2), and from W. E. B. Du Bois's *The Souls of Black Folk* (Unit 8).

Of importance to historians in preparing their works are many types of public records, also nonfiction. These include **speeches, sermons, contracts, deeds, constitutions, laws,** and **political tracts.** Examples in this text include the selection from the Iroquois Constitution (Unit 2), Jonathan Edwards's "Sinners in the Hands of an Angry God" (Unit 2), Patrick Henry's Speech in the Virginia Convention (Unit 3), the selection from Thomas Paine's *Crisis, No. 1* (Unit 3), the Declaration of Independence (Unit 3), Abraham Lincoln's "A House Divided" (Unit 5) and Gettysburg Address (Unit 5), Sojourner Truth's "Ain't I a Woman?" (Unit 5), Robert E. Lee's Farewell to His Army (Unit 5), Chief Joseph's "I Will Fight No More Forever" (Unit 6), William Faulkner's Nobel Prize Acceptance Speech (Unit 7), and John F. Kennedy's Inaugural Address (Unit 11).

Other types of nonfiction, closely related to histories, are **biographies, autobiographies,** and **memoirs,** which can be thought of as histories of individual people. A biography is the story of a person's life. An autobiography is the story of a person's life, written by that person. A memoir is a nonfiction narration that tells a story. It can be autobiographical or biographical and is based on a person's experiences and reactions to historical events. John Smith's *The General History of Virginia, New England, and the Summer Isles* (Unit 2) is an interesting example of an autobiography because, although it is the history of his own life, Smith chose to write from the third-person point of view, typical of biography. Other examples of autobiographies in this text include the selections from *The Autobiography of Benjamin Franklin* (Unit 3), from *Narrative of the Life of Frederick Douglass, an American Slave, Written by Himself* (Unit 5), and from Booker T. Washington's *Up from Slavery* (Unit 5). These autobiographies could also be called memoirs since they tell of historical events.

**Letters, diaries,** and **journals,** which are often used by biographers as source material, are also considered nonfiction. Examples of letters in this text are Abigail Adams's Letter to John Adams, May 7, 1776 (Unit 3), and Abraham Lincoln's Letter to Mrs. Bixby (Unit 5). Henry David Thoreau's *Walden* (Unit 4) and Ralph Waldo Emerson's *Self-Reliance* (Unit 4) were developed from the journals or diaries their authors kept.

An **essay** is a brief work of prose nonfiction. The original meaning of essay was "a trial or attempt," and the word retains some of this original force. An essay need not be a complete or exhaustive treatment of a subject, but rather a tentative exploration of it. A good essay develops a single idea and is characterized by unity and coherence. Examples of essays in this textbook include selections from Emerson's *Self-Reliance* (Unit 4) and Thoreau's *Walden* (Unit 4), Joan Didion's "On the Mall" (Unit 11), the selection from Kathleen Norris's *Dakota* (Unit 12), and Daniel J. Boorstin's "Why I Am Optimistic about America" (Unit 12).

*Room in New York,* 1932. Edward Hopper. Sheldon Memorial Art Gallery, Lincoln, Nebraska.

# ArtNote

*Room in New York,* 1932.
Edward Hopper.

Edward Hopper (1882–1967) recorded city life in a simple, direct way. Rather than a staged portrait, this painting has the feeling of an intimate scene of ordinary life. What can you tell about these people? about their lifestyle? about the historical period?

# Purpose and Organization in Nonfiction

## THE PURPOSES OF WRITING

**Purpose.** A writer's **purpose**, or **aim**, is what he or she wants to accomplish. All writing, including nonfiction, is generally produced with some overall purpose in mind. The following chart classifies modes, or categories, of prose writing by purpose.

| MODE OF WRITING | PURPOSE | EXAMPLE |
| --- | --- | --- |
| expository / informative | to inform | news article, research report |
| imaginative | to entertain, enrich, enlighten, and/or use an artistic medium such as fiction, poetry, or creative nonfiction, to share a perspective | poem, short story, humorous essay |
| narrative | to share a story about an event, often to make a point | biography, family history |
| personal / expressive | to reflect | diary entry, personal letter |
| persuasive / argumentative | to persuade readers or listeners to respond in some way, such as to agree with a position, change a view on an issue, reach an agreement, or perform an action | editorial, petition |

Note that a written work can have more than one purpose. For example, a nonfiction work may start with a brief story, or narrative, to introduce the topic or to make a point. It may then incorporate imaginative writing, provide information, express a personal reaction to that information, and strive to persuade the reader to adopt the writer's view. The emerging form known as "creative nonfiction" in fact combines purposes and aims in new ways.

For more information, consult the Language Arts Survey 2.3, "Identifying Your Purpose."

A writer may structure, or organize, a piece of writing in different ways in order to communicate more clearly. The following chart describes types of writing commonly used in nonfiction, and how these types are typically structured.

| TYPE OF WRITING | DESCRIPTION AND ORGANIZATION |
| --- | --- |
| **Narration** | As with the narrative mode, this method tells a story or describes events using time, or **chronological order**, as a way of organization. |
| **Dialogue** | Writing using this method presents words as they were actually spoken by people. Quotation marks are usually used to set off direct speech. |
| **Description** | Writing with this method portrays a character, an object, or a scene. Descriptions make use of sensory details—words and phrases that describe how things look, sound, smell, taste, or feel. Descriptive writing frequently uses **spatial order** as a way of organization. |
| **Exposition** | Writing using this method presents facts or opinions in an organized manner. There are many ways to organize exposition. Among the most common are the following: <br><br> **Analysis** breaks something into its parts and shows how the parts are related. <br><br> **Classification order** involves placing subjects into categories, or classes, according to their properties or characteristics. These groups are then presented, one-by-one, in some reasonable order. <br><br> **Comparison and contrast order** is a method of organization in which details about the similarities and differences between two subjects are presented in one of two ways. In the first method, characteristics of one subject are presented, followed by the characteristics of a second subject. In the second method, both subjects are compared and contrasted with regard to one characteristic, then with regard to a second characteristic, and so on. <br><br> **Process / How-to** writing presents the steps in a process or gives the reader directions on how to do something. |

## Literary TOOLS

The following literary terms and concepts are described in this selection:

**DESCRIPTION**

**NARRATION**

**CHRONOLOGICAL ORDER**

**ORAL TRADITION AND MYTH**

**TONE**

**CLASSIFICATION ORDER**

**COMPARISON AND CONTRAST ORDER**

## Reader's Journal

Think about a place that has special meaning or prompts strong memories for your family. Why is this place special?

## ArtNote

*Kiowa Funeral,* 1930. James Auchiah.

James Auchiah (1905–1975) was a member of the Kiowa Five, a group of twentieth-century artists who drew on the Kiowa pictoral tradition and combined it with European painting methods. Ironically, museums that collected Native American artifacts rejected these contemporary paintings for not being authentic, refusing to see the changing nature of Native American cultures. What do you think was the artist's purpose in making this painting?

# "The Way to Rainy MOUNTAIN"

### BY N. SCOTT MOMADAY

## About the AUTHOR

**N. Scott Momaday** (1934– ), poet, novelist, playwright, and nonfiction writer, has spent his life teaching and writing about Native American folklore, history, and mythology. Proud of his Native American heritage, the author grew up on Kiowa, Navajo, Apache, and Pueblo Indian reservations. After graduating from the University of New Mexico, Momaday earned a doctorate in English literature at Stanford University. He currently teaches English at the University of Arizona.

In 1969, Momaday won the Pulitzer Prize for his novel *House Made of Dawn*, which tells the story of a young Native American torn between his ancestral roots and twentieth-century mainstream society. In his best-known work, *The Way to Rainy Mountain* (1969), the author combines history, personal anecdotes, and myths imagistically. His 1971 essay "The American Land Ethic" drew attention to the tradition of respect for nature practiced by Native Americans. This essay was followed by two volumes of poetry, *Angle of Geese and Other Poems* (1974) and *The Gourd Dancer* (1976). His more recent books include *The Ancient Child* (1989), *In the Presence of the Sun* (1991), and *The Native American: Indian Country* (1993). Also an artist, Momaday has illustrated some of his books.

## About the SELECTION

**"The Way to Rainy Mountain"** is a nonfiction narrative taken from the memoir of the same name. The excerpt tells the story not only of the journey of Momaday's Kiowa ancestors from the mountains of Yellowstone to the plains of Oklahoma, but also of his grandmother's life from childhood to old age. Momaday also describes his own journey to trace the steps of his Kiowa ancestors. Using poetic prose to describe the land the Kiowas have inhabited, the author evokes ancestral memories. The selection's method of organization varies, from *chronological order* to *classification order* to *comparison and contrast order*.

*Kiowa Funeral,* 1930. James Auchiah. California Academy of Sciences.

# The Way to Rainy Mountain

## N. Scott Momaday

A single knoll rises out of the plain in Oklahoma, north and west of the Wichita Range.[1] For my people, the Kiowas, it is an old landmark, and they gave it the name Rainy Mountain. The hardest weather in the world is there. Winter brings blizzards, hot tornadic winds arise in the spring, and in summer the prairie is an anvil's edge. The grass turns brittle and brown, and it cracks beneath your feet. There are green belts along the rivers and creeks, linear groves of hickory and pecan, willow and witch hazel. At a distance in July or August the steaming

---

1. **Wichita Range.** Mountains in southwest Oklahoma

foliage seems almost to <u>writhe</u> in fire. Great green and yellow grasshoppers are everywhere in the tall grass, popping up like corn to sting the flesh, and tortoises crawl about on the red earth, going nowhere in the plenty of time. Loneliness is an aspect of the land. All things in the plain are isolate; there is no confusion of objects in the eye, but *one* hill or *one* tree or *one* man. To look upon that landscape in the early morning, with the sun at your back, is to lose the sense of proportion. Your imagination comes to life, and this, you think, is where Creation was begun.

> YOUR IMAGINATION COMES TO LIFE, AND THIS, YOU THINK, IS WHERE CREATION WAS BEGUN.

I returned to Rainy Mountain in July. My grandmother had died in the spring, and I wanted to be at her grave. She had lived to be very old and at last <u>infirm</u>. Her only living daughter was with her when she died, and I was told that in death her face was that of a child.

I like to think of her as a child. When she was born, the Kiowas were living the last great moment of their history. For more than a hundred years they had controlled the open range from the Smoky Hill River to the Red, from the headwaters of the Canadian to the fork of the Arkansas and Cimarron.[2] In alliance with the Comanches,[3] they had ruled the whole of the southern Plains. War was their sacred business, and they were among the finest horsemen the world has ever known. But warfare for the Kiowas was <u>preeminently</u> a matter of <u>disposition</u> rather than of survival, and they never understood the grim, <u>unrelenting</u> advance of the U.S. Cavalry. When at last, divided and ill-provisioned, they were driven onto the Staked Plains[4] in the cold rains of autumn, they fell into panic. In Palo Duro Canyon they abandoned their crucial stores to <u>pillage</u> and had nothing then but their lives. In order to save themselves, they surrendered to the soldiers at Fort Sill and were imprisoned in the old stone corral that now stands as a military museum. My grandmother was spared the humiliation of those high gray walls by eight or ten years, but she must have known from birth the affliction of defeat, the dark brooding of old warriors.

---

2. **Arkansas and Cimarron.** Two rivers that join in northeast Oklahoma
3. **Comanches.** Native American people of the plains
4. **Staked Plains.** Plateau region in southeast New Mexico and northeast Texas

**WORDS FOR EVERYDAY USE**

**writhe** (rīth) *vi.,* twist as if in pain or struggling. *During her nightmare, Noreen <u>writhed</u> under the blankets until they became tangled.*

**in • firm** (in fərm´) *adj.,* of weakened vitality, especially feeble from age. *Yolanda helped her <u>infirm</u> grandmother move into a nursing home.*

**pre • em • i • nent • ly** (prē em´i nent lē) *adv.,* first and foremost; most importantly. *For Kelsey, who does not drive, riding a bicycle is <u>preeminently</u> a means of transportation, not a sport.*

**dis • po • si • tion** (dis´pə zi ´shən) *n.,* general nature. *Commando was unfit to be a guard dog because of his friendly <u>disposition</u>.*

**un • re • lent • ing** (un rē len´tiŋ) *adj.,* not softening or yielding in determination. *Mrs. Cunningham found it hard to keep up with the <u>unrelenting</u> pace at the office.*

**pil • lage** (pi´ləj) *n.,* act of looting or plundering, especially in war. *The international community was distressed to hear of the <u>pillage</u> of the ethnic Albanians' homes in Kosovo.*

Her name was Aho, and she belonged to the last culture to evolve in North America. Her forebears came down from the high country in western Montana nearly three centuries ago. They were a mountain people, a mysterious tribe of hunters whose language has never been positively classified in any major group. In the late seventeenth century they began a long migration to the south and east. It was a journey toward the dawn, and it led to a golden age. Along the way the Kiowas were befriended by the Crows,[5] who gave them the culture and religion of the Plains. They acquired horses, and their ancient nomadic spirit was suddenly free of the ground. They acquired Tai-me, the sacred Sun Dance doll, from that moment the object and symbol of their worship, and so shared in the divinity of the sun. Not least, they acquired the sense of destiny, therefore courage and pride. When they entered upon the southern Plains they had been transformed. No longer were they slaves to the simple necessity of survival; they were a lordly and dangerous society of fighters and thieves, hunters and priests of the sun. According to their origin myth, they entered the world through a hollow log. From one point of view, their migration was the fruit of an old prophecy, for indeed they emerged from a sunless world.

Although my grandmother lived out her long life in the shadow of Rainy Mountain, the immense landscape of the continental interior lay like memory in her blood. She could tell of the Crows, whom she had never seen, and of the Black Hills,[6] where she had never been. I wanted to see in reality what she had seen more perfectly in the mind's eye, and traveled fifteen hundred miles to begin my pilgrimage.

Yellowstone,[7] it seemed to me, was the top of the world, a region of deep lakes and dark timber, canyons and waterfalls. But, beautiful as it is, one might have the sense of confinement there. The skyline in all directions is close at hand, the high wall of the woods and deep cleavages of shade. There is a perfect freedom in the mountains, but it belongs to the eagle and the elk, the badger and the bear. The Kiowas reckoned their stature by the distance they could see, and they were bent and blind in the wilderness.

Descending eastward, the highland meadows are a stairway to the plain. In July the inland slope of the Rockies is luxuriant with flax and buckwheat, stonecrop and larkspur. The earth unfolds and the limit of the land recedes. Clusters of trees, and animals grazing far in the distance, cause the vision to reach away and wonder to build upon the mind. The sun follows a longer course in the day, and the sky is immense beyond all comparison. The great billowing clouds that sail upon it are the shadows that move upon the grain like water, dividing light. Farther down, in the land of the Crows and Blackfeet,[8] the plain is yellow. Sweet clover takes hold of the hills and bends upon itself to cover and seal the soil. There the Kiowas paused on their way; they had come to the place where they must change their lives. The sun is at home on the plains. Precisely there does it have the certain character of a god. When the Kiowas came to the land of the Crows, they could see the dark lees[9] of the hills at dawn across the Bighorn

NARRATION AND CHRONOLOGICAL ORDER

*Narration* is a type of writing that tells a story or describes events, most often using time, or *chronological order,* as a way of organization. Whose history does Momaday recount in the highlighted passage at left?

---

5. **Crows.** Native American people who lived between the Platte and Yellowstone rivers
6. **Black Hills.** Mountains in South Dakota and Wyoming
7. **Yellowstone.** National park in Wyoming
8. **Blackfeet.** Native American confederacy of the Montana, Alberta, and Saskatchewan peoples
9. **lees.** Sheltered sides

River,[10] the profusion of light on the grain shelves, the oldest deity ranging after the solstices.[11] Not yet would they veer southward to the caldron of the land that lay below; they must wean their blood from the northern winter and hold the mountains a while longer in their view. They bore Tai-me in procession to the east.

A dark mist lay over the Black Hills, and the land was like iron. At the top of a ridge I caught sight of Devil's Tower upthrust against the gray sky as if in the birth of time the core of the earth had broken through its crust and the motion of the world was begun. There are things in nature that engender an awful quiet in the heart of man; Devil's Tower is one of them. Two centuries ago, because they could not do otherwise, the Kiowas made a legend at the base of the rock. My grandmother said:

> *Eight children were there at play, seven sisters and their brother. Suddenly the boy was struck dumb; he trembled and began to run upon his hands and feet. His fingers became claws, and his body was covered with fur. Directly there was a bear where the boy had been. The sisters were terrified; they ran, and the bear after them. They came to the stump of a great tree, and the tree spoke to them. It bade them climb upon it, and as they did so it began to rise into the air. The bear came to kill them, but they were just beyond its reach. It reared against the tree and scored the bark all around with its claws. The seven sisters were borne into the sky, and they became the stars of the Big Dipper.[12]*

From that moment, and so long as the legend lives, the Kiowas have kinsmen in the night sky. Whatever they were in the mountains, they could be no more. However tenuous their well-being, however much they had suffered and would suffer again, they had found a way out of the wilderness.

My grandmother had a reverence for the sun, a holy regard that now is all but gone out of mankind. There was a wariness in her, and an ancient awe. She was a Christian in her later years, but she had come a long way about, and she never forgot her birthright. As a child she had been to the Sun Dances; she had taken part in those annual rites, and by them she had learned the restoration of her people in the presence of Tai-me. She was about seven when the last Kiowa Sun Dance was held in 1887 on the Washita River above Rainy Mountain Creek. The buffalo were gone. In order to consummate the ancient sacrifice—to impale the head of a buffalo bull upon the medicine tree—a delegation of old men journeyed into Texas, there to beg and barter for an animal from the Goodnight herd. She was ten when the

10. **Bighorn River.** River in northern Wyoming and southeastern Montana that flows north into the Yellowstone River
11. **solstices.** Events based on the position of the sun which in summer causes the longest day and in winter the shortest day
12. **Big Dipper.** The seven main stars of the constellation *Ursa Major,* the "big bear," which form a shape like a dipper

**ORAL TRADITION AND MYTH**

*An **oral tradition** is a work, an idea, or a custom that is passed by word of mouth from generation to generation. A **myth** is a story that explains objects or events in the natural world as resulting from the action of some supernatural force or entity, most often a god. What objects or events are explained in the passage at right?*

**WORDS FOR EVERYDAY USE**

**pro • fu • sion** (prō fyü´zhun) *n.*, great quantity. *As the days grew warmer, the hills were covered with a profusion of purple and orange blossoms.*

**wean** (wēn) *vt.*, free from dependence or custom. *Many people make New Year's resolutions to wean themselves of bad habits.*

**en • gen • der** (en gen´dər) *vt.*, cause to develop; produce. *The flag is a symbol designed to engender feelings of patriotism.*

**ten • u • ous** (ten´ü us) *adj.*, flimsy; weak. *Dobie asked for extra help because his grasp on the material that would be on the test was at best tenuous.*

**rev • er • ence** (re´ver ənts) *n.*, honor or respect felt or shown. *Isa watched the master violinist with great reverence, hoping to learn from the esteemed musician.*

**wa • ri • ness** (wār´ē nes) *n.*, prudence; careful cautiousness. *Jamal tested the ice because the recent warm day had left him with a wariness about the safety of skating.*

**con • sum • mate** (kän´sə māt) *vt.*, complete. *In order to consummate the deal, the two parties signed on the dotted line.*

Kiowas came together for the last time as a living Sun Dance culture. They could find no buffalo; they had to hang an old hide from the sacred tree. Before the dance could begin, a company of soldiers rode out from Fort Sill under orders to disperse the tribe. Forbidden without cause the essential act of their faith, having seen the wild herds slaughtered and left to rot upon the ground, the Kiowas backed away forever from the medicine tree. That was July 20, 1890, at the great bend of the Washita. My grandmother was there. Without bitterness, and for as long as she lived, she bore a vision of deicide.[13]

Now that I can have her only in memory, I see my grandmother in the several postures that were peculiar to her: standing at the wood stove on a winter morning and turning meat in a great iron skillet; sitting at the south window, bent above her beadwork, and afterwards, when her vision failed, looking down for a long time into the fold of her hands; going out upon a cane, very slowly as she did when the weight of age came upon her; praying. I remember her most often at prayer. She made long, rambling prayers out of suffering and hope, having seen many things. I was never sure that I had the right to hear, so exclusive were they of all mere custom and company. The last time I saw her she prayed standing by the side of her bed at night, naked to the waist, the light of a kerosene lamp moving upon her dark skin.

Her long, black hair, always drawn and braided in the day, lay upon her shoulders and against her breasts like a shawl. I do not speak Kiowa, and I never understood her prayers, but there was something inherently sad in the sound, some merest hesitation upon the syllables of sorrow. She began in a high and descending pitch, exhausting her breath to silence; then again and again—and always the same intensity of effort, of something that is, and is not, like urgency in the human voice. Transported so in the dancing light among the shadows of her room, she seemed beyond the reach of time. But that was illusion; I think I knew then that I should not see her again.

Houses are like sentinels in the plain, old keepers of the weather watch. There, in a very little while, wood takes on the appearance of great age. All colors wear soon away in the wind and rain, and then the wood is burned gray and the grain appears and the nails turn red with rust. The windowpanes are black and <u>opaque</u>; you imagine there is nothing within, and indeed there are many ghosts, bones given up to the land. They stand here and there against the sky, and you approach them for a longer time than you expect. They belong in the distance; it is their domain.

Once there was a lot of sound in my grandmother's house, a lot of coming and

**houses are like sentinels in the plain, old keepers of the weather watch.**

---

13. **deicide.** Act of killing a divine being or god

**TONE**

*Tone* is the emotional attitude toward the reader or toward the subject implied by a literary work. Note the distinct tone Momaday uses when describing his grandmother.

**CLASSIFICATION ORDER**

*Classification order* is a method of organization in which subjects are divided into groups, or classes. These groups are then presented, one-by-one, in some reasonable order. Classification order is used in the passage at left.

**WORDS FOR EVERYDAY USE**

o • paque (ō pāk´) *adj.,* not admitting of light. *The <u>opaque</u> shades allowed Keva to sleep during the day.*

**COMPARISON AND CONTRAST ORDER**

*Comparison and contrast order is a method of organization in which details about the similarities and differences between two subjects are presented. Comparison and contrast order is used in the highlighted passages at right.*

going, feasting and talk. The summers there were full of excitement and reunion. The Kiowas are a summer people; they abide the cold and keep to themselves, but when the season turns and the land becomes warm and vital they cannot hold still; an old love of going returns upon them. The aged visitors who came to my grandmother's house when I was a child were made of lean and leather, and they bore themselves upright. They wore great black hats and bright ample shirts that shook in the wind. They rubbed fat upon their hair and wound their braids with strips of colored cloth. Some of them painted their faces and carried the scars of old and cherished <u>enmities</u>. They were an old council of warlords, come to remind and be reminded of who they were. Their wives and daughters served them well. The women might indulge themselves; gossip was at once the mark and compensation of their <u>servitude</u>. They made loud and elaborate talk among themselves, full of jest and gesture, fright and false alarm. They went abroad in fringed and flowered shawls, bright beadwork and German silver. They were at home in the kitchen, and they prepared meals that were banquets.

There were frequent prayer meetings, and great <u>nocturnal</u> feasts. When I was a child I played with my cousins outside, where the lamplight fell upon the ground and the singing of the old people rose up around us and carried away into the darkness. There were a lot of good things to eat, a lot of laughter and surprise. And afterwards, when the quiet returned, I lay down with my grandmother and could hear the frogs away by the river and feel the motion of the air.

Now there is a funeral silence in the rooms, the endless wake of some final word. The walls have closed in upon my grandmother's house. When I returned to it in mourning, I saw for the first time in my life how small it was. It was late at night, and there was a white moon, nearly full. I sat for a long time on the stone steps by the kitchen door. From there I could see out across the land; I could see the long row of trees by the creek, the low light upon the rolling plains, and the stars of the Big Dipper. Once I looked at the moon and caught sight of a strange thing. A cricket had perched upon the handrail, only a few inches away from me. My line of vision was such that the creature filled the moon like a fossil. It had gone there, I thought, to live and die, for there, of all places, was its small definition made whole and eternal. A warm wind rose up and purled like the longing within me.

The next morning I awoke at dawn and went out on the dirt road to Rainy Mountain. It was already hot, and the grasshoppers began to fill the air. Still, it was early in the morning, and the birds sang out of the shadows. The long yellow grass on the mountain shone in the bright light, and a scissortail hied above the land. There, where it ought to be, at the end of a long and legendary way, was my grandmother's grave. Here and there on the dark stones were ancestral names. Looking back once, I saw the mountain and came away. ∎

---

**WORDS FOR EVERYDAY USE**

**en • mi • ty** (en´mi tē´) *n.*, active and typically mutual hatred or ill will. *The <u>enmity</u> between the Browns and the Cliffs surfaced during a legal dispute over property.*

**ser • vi • tude** (ser´vi tüd) *n.*, condition in which one lacks liberty, especially to determine one's course of life. *After seven years of <u>servitude</u>, Jed was no longer an indentured servant.*

**noc • tur • nal** (näk tər´nəl) *adj.*, of, relating to, or occurring in the night. *Star gazing is a <u>nocturnal</u> activity.*

If you were to visit the places described by the narrator, what kind of response do you think you would have? Explain why it would be similar to or different from the experience of the narrator.

# INVESTIGATE Inquire *Imagine*

**Recall:** GATHERING FACTS

1a. What event in the experience of her people did the narrator's grandmother miss by eight or ten years? What does the narrator think she must have experienced despite missing this event?

2a. What ceremony did the narrator's grandmother participate in as a child? Why did the ceremony stop? What does the narrator remember his grandmother doing most?

3a. Where is the narrator's grandmother's grave?

→ **Interpret:** FINDING MEANING

1b. Explain the significance to the narrator of the Fort Sill incarceration.

2b. How did the prayers make the narrator feel despite the fact that he could not understand them? Why might the narrator be impressed with the reverence of his grandmother's prayers?

3b. Why is the location of the grave appropriate?

**Analyze:** TAKING THINGS APART

4a. Identify key events in the journey of the Kiowa as presented by Momaday.

→ **Synthesize:** BRINGING THINGS TOGETHER

4b. Summarize the effect of all of these events on the Kiowa people.

**Evaluate:** MAKING JUDGMENTS

5a. Evaluate the impact on the grandmother's life of changes that occurred in the Kiowa culture.

→ **Extend:** CONNECTING IDEAS

5b. Compare the experiences of the Kiowa and those of the African Americans expressed in "Follow the Drinking Gourd."

# Understanding *Literature*

**DESCRIPTION.** Review the definition for **description** in the Handbook of Literary Terms. How does Momaday use description at the beginning of the narrative? What sensory details does the author include?

**NARRATION.** Review the definition for **narration** in the Handbook of Literary Terms. Whose stories does Momaday recount?

**CHRONOLOGICAL ORDER.** Review the definition for **chronological order** in the Handbook of Literary Terms. What sections of the selection are told using chronological order? What transitions are used in telling the story of Momaday's journey that retraces the Kiowas' migration?

**ORAL TRADITION AND MYTH.** Review the definitions for **oral tradition** and **myth** in the Handbook of Literary Terms. According to the Kiowa, how did they enter the world? How was the Big Dipper formed? How did Momaday's grandmother keep the oral tradition of the Kiowas alive?

TONE. Review the definition for **tone** in the Handbook of Literary Terms. What tone does Momaday use when describing his grandmother in her familiar postures on page 61?

CLASSIFICATION ORDER. Review the definition for **classification order** in the Handbook of Literary Terms. Which section of "The Way to Rainy Mountain" uses classification?

COMPARISON AND CONTRAST ORDER. Review the definition for **comparison and contrast order** in the Handbook of Literary Terms. Which method of comparison and contrast order is used in the description of the grandmother's house as it was in the past and as it is after her death?

# WRITER'S JOURNAL

1. In this selection, Momaday describes a place that is special to him. Write a **description** of a place that is close to *your* heart.
2. Create a paragraph-long original **myth** that explains an object or event in the natural world.
3. An **elegy** is a poem that laments the dead. Write an elegy for Momaday's grandmother or for the Kiowa culture.

# Integrating *the* LANGUAGE ARTS

## Language, Grammar, and Style

FINDING THE SIMPLE SUBJECT AND VERB. The basic units of meaning are found in the **simple subject** and the **simple predicate**, more frequently called the **verb**. For each of the sentences below, use your own paper to identify the simple predicate and verb. For more information see the Language Arts Survey 3.20, "Finding the Simple Subject and Simple Predicate in a Sentence."

1. Winter brings harsh weather.
2. Her forebears came down from the country.
3. Yellowstone, it seemed to me, was a region of beautiful scenery.
4. The sky in all directions is close at hand.
5. The land, descending eastward, is a stairway to the plain.

## Study and Research

RESEARCHING THE KIOWAS. Momaday chronicles several key events in the history of the Kiowas as they relate to his grandmother's life. Do additional research on the Kiowas to learn more about their culture. You might choose from among these topics: history, customs, ceremonies, population, and religion. Use visual aids, such as maps, pictures, and charts, to share the information you find with your classmates.

## Speaking and Listening

NATIVE AMERICAN MYTHS. Choose a Native American myth that you like and tell it to a small group of classmates. Write an introduction telling some facts about the Native American group that created the myth. Before you begin, refer to the Language Arts Survey 4.20, "Telling a Story." After presenting the myth, ask your group what object or event in the natural world the myth explains.

# Guided Writing

## WRITING ABOUT LITERATURE

Before movie critics write a review, they analyze the plot, characters, setting, theme, and mood of the film. Their goal is not to write a summary of the movie, but to evaluate and judge how well the movie accomplishes its purpose. They pay particular attention to any dramatic techniques that are specific to a movie's genre. To analyze a mystery, for example, critics look closely to see if a mood of suspense has been sustained throughout the film. When they write the review, they support their analysis and interpretation by giving examples from the movie. Their goal is to explain why the movie does or does not accomplish its purpose. In this unit, you have read several literature selections from different genres and learned about the literary elements that are specific to the genres.

**WRITING ASSIGNMENT.** Just as a movie critic analyzes, interprets, and writes about a film, for this assignment you will analyze, interpret, and write about a piece of literature. You can focus on the mood or the theme of the piece or on how a literary technique used in the piece fits the particular genre. You will support your interpretation by giving specific examples from the literature selection. Your writing will take the form of an informative essay.

## Student Model

In this excerpt, Keri, an eleventh grade student, analyzes the essay from N. Scott Momaday's book *The Way to Rainy Mountain*. As you read, note how she introduces and supports the **thesis** with specific examples.

> Can you imagine being ten years old and watching your culture fall apart right before your eyes? This is what happened to Aho, an American Indian girl belonging to the Kiowa tribe. The fall of the Kiowa is described in the book *The Way to Rainy Mountain* by N. Scott Momaday, Aho's grandson. Rainy Mountain was the name the Kiowas gave an old landmark—a small, rounded hill northwest of the Wichita Range in Oklahoma. This area is where the

"An essay is a thing of the imagination. . . . it is the movement of a free mind at play. Though it is written in prose, it is closer in kind to poetry than to any other form. Like a poem, a genuine essay is made of language and character and mood and temperament and pluck and chance."

—Cynthia Ozick

A **thesis** is a main idea that is supported in an essay. A well-constructed essay presents a clear thesis supported by ample evidence.

**Theme** is the central idea in a literary work. **Mood,** or *atmosphere*, is the emotion created in the reader by part or all of a literary work. A writer creates a mood through judicious use of concrete details.

- relate an **anecdote** that leads into your topic—everyone likes to hear a story

  *When I was fourteen, my family moved from North Carolina to Arizona. I had to leave everything I knew behind. My world was dev-astated. I thought that no one had suffered so great a loss. Then I learned about Aho. . . .*

- make a surprising state-ment—the unexpected inspires curiosity

  *From sixty million to almost zero—a vast fortune lost! American currency? No, the American buffalo.*

- quote a famous person—people are interested in what celebrities say and do

  *"It makes little difference, however, where one opens the record of the history of the Indians; every page and every year has its dark stain." Helen Hunt Jackson, a nineteenth century activist for Native American Indians, speaking for the Kiowas and other tribes. . .*

Kiowas' defeat took place. As you can imagine, the mood of *The Way to Rainy Mountain* is dark.

Within the first few paragraphs of the essay, you are drawn in with a description of Rainy Mountain's unpleasant weather, and soon find out the narrator's grandmother has died. You also discover her relation to the Kiowas' defeat. Already the essay has taken on a dark mood. Momaday goes on to tell about the Kiowas' evolution through the years and how they had prospered, but you are always reminded that, despite their prosperity, the Kiowas had fallen under the U.S. Cavalry. Momaday describes the landscape in detail, but in the same dark atmosphere. As he says about Yellowstone, "But, beautiful as it was, one might have the sense of confinement there . . . . There is perfect freedom in the mountains, but it belongs to the eagle and the elk, the badger and the bear." He also describes Devil's Tower, a landmark in northeast Wyoming, with an almost horrific manner: "There are things in nature that engender an awful quiet in the heart of man; Devil's Tower is one of them." Momaday's detailed descriptions of the land, the rise of the Kiowas and the journey of the Kiowas remind us of the impending defeat.

**EXAMINING THE MODEL.** In the introductory paragraph, the writer secures the reader's interest by asking a question. The writer provides information about the essay's topic and then presents the thesis statement: "As you can imagine, the mood of *The Way to Rainy Mountain* is dark." The statement also works as a transition that leads the reader to the body paragraphs. The entire essay is included later in this lesson. As you read the essay, note how the writer supports the thesis statement. In the conclusion, the writer summarizes the ideas presented in the essay and gives the reader a satisfying sense of resolution.

## Prewriting

**IDENTIFYING YOUR AUDIENCE.** Before beginning your essay, determine your audience. For this essay, you might consider sharing the insights you have gained from a literature selection with a tenth grade student who, as a junior, would also need to analyze and interpret literature as you are doing here.

**FINDING YOUR VOICE.** Voice is the way a writer uses language to reflect his or her unique personality and attitude toward topic, form, and audience. Consider your attitude toward the topic you have selected. Since your audience is reading an analysis, they will expect to be reliably informed. How can you use your voice to present an interesting, informed, and reliable analysis? Look at the example below. Which sentence reflects an interesting, informed, and reliable voice?

Scott Momaday said the weather was terrible and that Aho's grandmother died.

Within the first few paragraph of the essay, you are drawn in with a description of Rainy Mountain's unpleasant weather, and soon find out the narrator's grandmother has died.

**WRITING WITH A PLAN.** Choose one of the literature selections from the unit that you enjoyed reading. Then copy the graphic organizer onto your own paper and fill in a question that you have about that selection. For example, you might ask yourself: "What is the theme of this piece?" or "Why is the mood the author uses in this selection appropriate to the genre?" Next, freewrite answers to your question for several minutes. Now consider your freewriting. Which part provides the most interesting information? Which part uncovers an idea important enough to write about in your essay? Use the most important part of your freewriting to write a sentence that states the thesis of your essay. The thesis statement is an assertion about your topic, something you claim to be true.

Continue to fill in the graphic organizer with the facts and ideas that you plan to use to support your thesis statement. Lastly, consider your audience and why it will consider the question you are answering to be important.

## Student Model—Graphic Organizer
Keri completed her graphic organizer as follows.

**Literature Selection:** excerpt from *The Way to Rainy Mountain*

**What question(s) do you want to answer in your essay?**
What is the mood? How does the author create it? How well does the author create it?

**Freewrite answers to your question:**
The mood is dark. Everything in the essay is dark—the weather, the grandmother dying, how he sets up the idea that the Kiowas were prosperous, but you know it's not going to end that way, the confinement that he describes. Having to use the hide

"In looking at an essay—or, to a degree, at a story and a poem—it is sensible to check three questions. It helps you to avoid mistakes in reading. First, consider the purpose, moment, or occasion of the writing. Is this a reminiscence or an editorial? A recipe or a denunciation? You must ask: What is it for? Second you must ask: Who is it talking to? Is it addressed to friends or strangers, to initiates or adversaries, to Kiwanis or the Hell's Angels? Third, What is its tone, or assumed vantage point? Is it the humble investigator or the omniscient intelligence? Is it sharing a discovery, piece by piece, or is it handing out the results of a discovery already consummated?"

—Donald Hall, *Writing Well*

"To become truly immortal, a work of art must escape all human limits: logic and common sense will only interfere. But once these barriers are broken, it will enter the realms of childhood visions and dreams."

—Giorgio de Chirico

instead of a buffalo for the sacrifice is probably the darkest moment. Momaday did a good job. I felt terrible about what happened to the Kiowas. The whole time I was reading the essay, I kept thinking about how depressing the whole situation was.

**Write a thesis statement:**
The mood of *The Way to Rainy Mountain* is dark.

**List at least three references from the selection that support your thesis statement:**
the unpleasant weather
the grandmother died
the once prosperous Kiowas were defeated
"the sense of confinement there . . . . There is perfect freedom in the mountains, but it belongs to the eagle and the elk, the badger and the bear."
the Kiowas had to beg and barter for a buffalo
how the grandmother prayed—"[She] never understood her prayers, but there was something inherently sad in the sound . . ."the houses showed age and suffering

**Do you feel the author is on target or could have improved the selection in some way?**
I think the author was on target, especially because he kind of built up the darkness going from one thing that was dark to another that was darker and darker and darker. It doesn't get overwhelming though because the author gives you a break sometimes.

**What else do you want to say about this topic? Explain why your topic is important for your audience—in this case, tenth graders—to consider:**
It's good for everybody to know about what happened to the Kiowas and it's good to know a way to create that feeling so we can really get a sense of what it was like.

**ORGANIZATION.** Your essay should contain an introductory paragraph, several body paragraphs, and a concluding paragraph. The introduction should present the thesis statement, secure the reader's interest, and lead into the body of the paper. The last sentence of the introductory paragraph should contain a transitional "hook" that moves the reader to the first paragraph of the body.

Each paragraph in the body of the essay should contain one idea of support for your thesis statement. The body paragraphs can be organized in different ways. To make the most convincing case for this essay, you may want to present your ideas in the order of their value. In other words, the first paragraph of the body should contain the strongest argument, most significant example, cleverest illustration, or an obvious beginning point; the second paragraph, the next most compelling; and the final paragraph, the weakest or least obvious. Go back to your graphic organizer and number the ideas in the order you plan to use them.

The conclusion should reiterate your thesis and summarize your main points of support. It should also leave your reader thinking about what you have said.

## Drafting

Use the information from your graphic organizer to guide you as you write the rough draft of your essay. Do not focus at this point on the details of spelling, grammar, usage, and mechanics. Instead simply concentrate on getting your ideas down on paper.

Look at the thesis statement you wrote on your graphic organizer. Use it in your introductory paragraph. Remember to secure the interest of your reader and then move on to the body of the essay with a transitional sentence. Support your thesis statement in the body paragraphs by using the three most important ideas from your graphic organizer. Finally, conclude your essay.

## Self- and Peer Evaluation

After you finish your first draft, complete a self-evaluation of your writing. If time allows, you may want to get one or two peer evaluations. For more information, see the Language Arts Survey 2.37, "Self- and Peer Evaluation."

As you evaluate the essay, answer the following questions. You may want to jot down notes that you can use later to revise your essay.

### Introduction
* What is the thesis sentence?
* How clearly does the thesis sentence state the topic of the essay? What improvements might be needed?
* What technique is used in the introduction to secure the reader's interest? How effective is it?

### Body
* How does each body paragraph support the thesis sentence? What additional support might be needed?
* Identify the topic sentence in each body paragraph. Explain how the sentences in each paragraph provide supporting details for the topic sentences.
* What effective transitions does the author use within paragraphs and between paragraphs? Where could the use of transitions be improved?

### Conclusion
* What conclusion is developed? How effectively does it reiterate and summarize the thesis statement and support?

## Language, Grammar, and Style

### Sentence Variety

**IDENTIFYING DIFFERENT TYPES OF SENTENCES.** To avoid monotony in your writing, try varying the length and structure of the sentences you write.

A **simple sentence** is made up of one independent clause. An independent clause has a subject and a predicate (verb phrase). Look at the example below:

The weather is cold today.

You can combine two or more independent clauses to make a **compound sentence**. The clauses are usually combined with a **coordinating conjunction**. A coordinating conjunction is a connecting word such as *and, but, for, nor, or,* or *yet.* A comma is usually placed before the connecting word in a compound sentence. Read the example below.

The weather is cold today, and I want to stay in bed.

The first independent clause is *The weather is cold.* The second independent clause is *I want to stay in bed.* They are joined with the coordinating conjunction *and.*

*continued on page 70*

Look at the two independent clauses in the example below. Combine them into a compound sentence using one of the following conjunctions: *and, but, for, nor, or,* or *yet.*

> I didn't want to walk in the rain. I had to go to school.

Next, identify a compound sentence from the student model that uses coordination.

Instead of using a coordinating conjunction to combine independent clauses, you can use a semicolon between the clauses. Look at the example below.

> Some people don't mind the rain; I'm not one of them.

Combine the two independent clauses below using a semicolon.

> Her shoes were soaked. She felt she might be getting a cold.

You can combine an independent clause with a dependent clause to form a **complex sentence.** A complex sentence is made up of at least one dependent clause and one independent clause. Look at the example below.

> When the weather is cold, I would rather stay in bed.

The dependent clause is *When the weather is cold.* The independent clause is *I would rather stay in bed.*

- How does the conclusion motivate the reader to think about or act on the information in the essay?

## Revising and Proofreading

As you consider your essay and your self-evaluation and peer reviews, think about the changes that are suggested. Which changes will you need to make for your audience to understand your essay? Which changes will you need to make to keep the interest of your audience? Make revisions according to your decisions.

Next, proofread the copy for errors in spelling, grammar, usage, punctuation, capitalization, and paragraph form. See the Language Arts Survey 2.45, "A Proofreading Checklist."

The final copy of the student model is shown below.

## Student Model—Revised

Can you imagine being ten years old and watching your culture fall apart right before your eyes? This is what happened to Aho, an American Indian girl belonging to the Kiowa tribe. The fall of the Kiowa is described in the selection from *The Way to Rainy Mountain* by N. Scott Momaday, Aho's grandson. Rainy Mountain was the name the Kiowas gave an old landmark—a small, rounded hill northwest of the Wichita Range in Oklahoma. This area is where the Kiowas' defeat took place. As you can imagine, the mood of "The Way to Rainy Mountain" is dark.

Within the first few paragraphs of the essay, you are drawn in with a description of Rainy Mountain's unpleasant weather, and soon find out the narrator's grandmother has died. You also discover her relation to the Kiowas' defeat. Already the essay has taken on a dark mood. Momaday goes on to tell about the Kiowas' evolution through the years and how they had prospered, but you are always reminded that, despite their prosperity, the Kiowas had fallen under the U.S. Cavalry. Momaday describes the landscape in detail, but by conveying the same dark atmosphere. As he says about Yellowstone, "But, beautiful as it was, one might have the sense of confinement there . . . . There is perfect freedom in the mountains, but it belongs to the eagle and the elk, the badger and the bear." He also describes Devil's Tower, a landmark in northeast Wyoming, with an almost horrific manner: "There are things in nature that engender an awful quiet in the heart of man; Devil's Tower is one of them." Momaday's detailed descriptions of the land, the rise of the Kiowas, and the journey of the Kiowas remind us of the impending defeat.

The fall of the Kiowas took place on the Washita River above Rainy Mountain Creek. They were going to perform their Sun Dance, a religious dance to their sun god, Taime. The last dance held was in 1887, in which Aho had participated. She was about seven years old at the time. In the dance, there was an ancient sacrifice of piercing the head of a buffalo bull upon the sacred medicine tree. There were no buffalo left in Oklahoma by the time of the next Sun Dance, so a group of men went into Texas to beg and barter for an animal. Momaday uses the words to describe this in such a manner you almost feel the Kiowas' hopelessness. They could find no buffalo, and the Kiowas had to hang an old hide from the tree. Before the

Words that are used to begin dependent clauses are called **subordinating conjunctions:** *after, although, as, as if, because, before, even if, even though, if, if only, rather than, since, that, though, unless, until, when, where, where as, wherever, whether, which, while.*

Combine each independent clause with the dependent clause in the examples below.

> When my shoes are soaked. It's hard to study.

> I should put an extra pair of shoes in my locker. Because rain is predicted all week.

Next, identify a complex sentence from the student model that uses subordination.

The dependent clause may either begin or end a complex sentence, but when it begins the sentence, a comma must follow it.

**FIXING MISUSED COMPOUND AND COMPLEX SENTENCES.** Identify and correct the error in each sentence below.

> Although it was cold and rainy. She went to the bus stop and she rode the bus to school.

> When she met her friend and started talking about the day she forgot about the stormy weather.

> She went outside at noon and the ground looked as if it hadn't rained at all.

*continued on page 72*

Because it was warmer she decided not to ride the bus but to walk home instead.

Select one paragraph in the student essay. What type of sentences does the author use? simple? compound? complex? Fix any errors you see in sentence structure. How could you change sentences in this paragraph to make it more interesting?

**USING A VARIETY OF SENTENCES.** Look at your essay and examine the kinds of sentences that you have used. If you have several short, choppy sentences, try combining them into compound sentences or complex sentences. Check to see if the rhythm or pattern of your sentences lacks variety. You can check the rhythm and flow of your writing by reading your essay out loud and listening for variety. One way to increase sentence variety is to move part of a sentence to a different location. For example, you can put dependent clauses at the beginning of some sentences and at the end of other sentences. You can also change the sentence pattern by adding transitional words at the beginning of some sentences. Finally, alternate short and long sentences to vary the rhythm.

dance had even begun, soldiers from nearby Fort Sill dispersed the tribe. On July 20, 1890, the ten-year-old Aho watched her world fall apart. Momaday describes how his grandmother had prayed—"[She] never understood her prayers, but there was something inherently sad in the sound . . . "— and how the houses of the plains near Rainy Mountain showed the age and suffering. His grandmother, like ancestors before, was buried on Rainy Mountain.

Occasionally, there's a lightness to the essay. The house where Momaday's grandmother lived, for instance, was first presented as a place of gatherings and reunions. Momaday recites elaborate details of prayer meetings, feasts, talk, and faces. You feel the heat of the people filling the house, a warm comfort of people gathering and having a good time. Another example is of Momaday's description of the plains. There is an open, vast freedom about the plains and there the Kiowas feel at home. But again Momaday comes back to the dark mood. After describing the plains, Momaday tells of Devil's Tower and finally of the defeat of the Kiowas. He then returns to the "funeral silence" of his grandmother's home.

The Kiowas had a great and tragic history, an easy setting for an essay with a dark mood. You are constantly reminded throughout the piece that the Kiowas' reign ends with a defeat under the U.S. Cavalry. You feel the helplessness of the defeat as you learn of the dwindling Sun Dances and the soldiers coming from Fort Sill. Though there are a few paragraphs with light moods, the author always threads back to a dark atmosphere. Aho's death seems to be almost a finality for the Kiowas—another member of their tribe is gone. Darkness lingers in the house, and good memories remind the Kiowas of the bad times. Yet Momaday shows that he carries at least some of the culture within him—as though the last Sun Dance will be remembered for generations to come through his essay. Through the dark, hope still filters in between like little rays of sun.

> "What moves men of genius, or rather what inspires their work, is not new ideas, but their obsession with the idea that what has already been said is still not enough."
>
> —Eugène Delacroix

## Publishing and Presenting

Write or print a final copy of your essay. Pair up with a partner in your class. Read and comment on the analysis presented in the introduction, body paragraphs, and conclusion in each other's essays. Then pair up with a tenth grade student and read your essay aloud. Ask the student to comment on the introduction, body paragraphs, and conclusion in your essay. How do the tenth grade student's comments about your essay differ from the comments your classmate made?

## Reflecting

Learning to analyze information is beneficial in many aspects of student and adult life. How did this process benefit you? How do you regard your ability to analyze a piece of literature or an entirely different concept? What were some of the insights you gained through your analysis and the analyses of other students? Were you able to convey your ideas effectively to a sophomore student? How do you predict your ability to analyze and write about literature will change during the year?

# UNIT REVIEW
## *Genres and Techniques of Literature*

## Words for Everyday Use

Check your knowledge of the following vocabulary words from the selections in this unit. Write short sentences using these words in context to make the meaning clear. To review the definition or usage of a word, refer to the page number listed or the Glossary of Words for Everyday Use.

confound, 47
consummate, 60
dilapidated, 37
discreet, 34
disposition, 58
distraught, 37
eerie, 36
elation, 37
engender, 60
enmity, 62
enthralled, 35
hierarchy, 32

hysterical, 35
infirm, 58
lilting, 35
logical, 24
maneuvering, 34
martyr, 32
mute, 24
nocturnal, 62
opaque, 61
pillage, 58
preeminently, 58
profusion, 60

resigned, 37
resolution, 20
reverence, 60
servitude, 62
solace, 38
supplication, 24
tenuous, 60
unrelenting, 58
wariness, 60
wean, 60
writhe, 58

## Literary Tools

Define the following terms, giving concrete examples of how they are used in the selections in this unit. To review a term, refer to the page number indicated or to the Handbook of Literary Terms.

alliteration, 19
blocking, 44
character, 44
chronological order, 56
classification order, 56
climax, 31
comparison and contrast order, 56
conflict, 31
description, 56
dialogue, 44
exposition, 31

free verse, 22
inciting incident, 31
major character, 31
minor character, 31
myth, 56
narration, 56
narrative poem, 22
narrator, 31
oral tradition, 6, 56
properties, 44
refrain, 6
repetition, 6, 19

resolution, 31
rhyme scheme, 19
rising action, 31
set, 44
setting, 31
sonnet, 19
spiritual, 6
stage directions, 44
theme, 6, 44
tone, 56

# Reflecting
## ............... *on* YOUR READING

## The Oral Tradition

1. **SPIRITUALS AND THE ORAL TRADITION.** Why were spirituals transmitted orally instead of being written down? What special historical circumstances made oral transmission of spirituals such as "Follow the Drinking Gourd" necessary? What messages did spirituals convey?

## Poetry

2. **LYRIC POETRY.** How do lyric poems differ from narrative and dramatic poems? What special poetic devices, including devices of sound and rhetorical techniques, are used in "Sonnet XXX"? What characteristics make this poem a sonnet?

3. **NARRATIVE POETRY.** Explain why "A Story" by Li-Young Lee can be considered a narrative poem. What characteristics make this a free verse poem? How is a free verse poem different from a sonnet?

## Fiction

4. **SHORT STORY STRUCTURE.** Into what parts is a typical plot divided? What events in "American History" correspond to these parts?

## Drama

5. **THE SPECTACLE IN DRAMA.** Imagine that you will be directing a production of the scene from *The Crucible* included in this unit. Make a complete list, with descriptions, of the following elements of the spectacle in your production: the stage set, the lighting, the properties, and the costumes.

## Nonfiction

6. **PURPOSE AND METHODS OF ORGANIZATION IN NONFICTION.** What is the main purpose of the nonfiction piece "The Way to Rainy Mountain"? What method or methods of organization does Momaday use?

# *Part Two*
## THE AMERICAN TRADITION

*Penn's Treaty with the Indians* [Detail], c.1840. Edward Hicks. National Gallery of Art, Washington, DC.

Here individuals of all

nations are melted into a new race

... whose labors and posterity

will one day cause great changes

in the world.

—J. Hector St. Jean de Crèvecœur
"What Is an American?"

*Penn's Treaty with the*
*Indians*, [Detail]. c.1840. Edward Hicks,
pages 78–79.

Mindful of the brutal and dishonest
ways in which Native Americans were
removed from the land, the Quakers
were proud of the 1682 treaty that
William Penn made with the Delaware
tribe. One hundred and sixty years later,
Edward Hicks saw in it the Quaker ideals
of peace and equality. Hicks made his
living as a sign painter. His style comes
from rural folk traditions rather than formal art training.

# ORIGINS OF THE AMERICAN TRADITION (TO 1750)

## THE FIRST AMERICANS

Long before the first Europeans set foot on American soil, peoples
from Asia came to the Americas, crossing a land bridge now sub-
merged beneath the Bering Strait. The date of the arrival of the
first humans in America is unknown, with estimates ranging from
twenty thousand to fifty thousand years ago. Other people may
have arrived in South America via sea routes from the South
Pacific, though that theory remains controversial.

## THE PRE-COLUMBIAN CULTURES OF NORTH AMERICA

Descendants of the first Americans populated North, Central, and
South America, creating an extraordinary variety of cultures. When
Europeans arrived in the late fifteenth century, there were perhaps
240 distinct Native American cultures in North America alone and
a population variously estimated at between one million and two million people.
Historians, archaeologists, and anthropologists divide these cultures into eight major
groups, those of the Northwest Coast, California, the Northern Plateau, the Great Basin,
the Southwest, the Plains, the Eastern Woodlands, and the Southeast. Although these
cultures varied widely in their social customs, modes of government, economic systems,
dress, religions, architecture, and languages, they shared a common reverence for and
connection with the natural world. Europeans, in contrast, tended to see the natural
world as something to be subdued, owned, and turned to human ends.

## THE ARRIVAL OF THE EUROPEANS

Historians today believe that the first Europeans to arrive in North America were Norse
sailors. In 1001, **Leif Ericsson** established a very brief settlement in Labrador, which he
called **Vinland**, or "Land of Wine." However, the Norse soon withdrew from the

## LITERARY EVENTS

➤ = American Events

1517. Martin Luther posts his 95 Theses,
beginning the Protestant Reformation

1515. Sir Thomas More's *Utopia* published

1513. Niccolo Machiavelli writes *The Prince*

1510. *Everyman*, English morality play, performed

| **1475** | **1500** | **1525** |
|---|---|---|

➤1492. Christopher Columbus crosses the
Atlantic and lands in the Bahamas

➤1502. Amerigo Vespucci returns from the New World; his account of the
voyage led to his name being given to the New World

➤1521. Aztec capital of Tenochtitlán
falls to Hernando Cortés of Spain

## HISTORICAL EVENTS

Americas, and it was almost five hundred years before Europeans returned. They did so as the result of a misguided attempt by the Italian sailor **Christopher Columbus** to find a route from Europe via the Atlantic to Japan and China. Funded by the king and queen of Spain, Columbus's expedition set sail on August 3, 1492. After months of fear and unrest among the crew, the sailors arrived on October 12 at an island in the present-day Bahamas that Columbus named San Salvador. Thinking that he had reached India, Columbus called the natives whom he met "Indians." Although he made two subsequent voyages across the Atlantic Ocean, Columbus died without realizing that he had "discovered" two continents. These continents were called by Europeans "**the Americas**" because of a mistake made by a German mapmaker who believed, erroneously, that the continents had been discovered by the Portuguese explorer Amerigo Vespucci.

Reconstructions of Columbus's ships, the *Nina, Pinta,* and *Santa Maria.*

After Columbus's initial voyage, European powers competed with one another to seize the opportunity that they imagined the "New World" offered them. Throughout the next two hundred years, many European explorers set sail for the Americas, including Juan Ponce de León, Vasco Nuñez de Balboa, Ferdinand Magellan, Hernán Cortés, Francisco Pizarro, Hernando de Soto, Cabeza de Vaca, Giovanni da Verrazano, Jacques Cartier, Samuel de Champlain, Father Jacques Marquette, Louis Joliet, Robert de La Salle, John Cabot, Francis Drake, Humphrey Gilbert, Walter Raleigh, Martin Frobisher, and Henry Hudson. The Spanish, Dutch, French, and English all established colonies in North America.

For the native population of the Americas, the arrival of Europeans spelled disaster. Millions of Native Americans in North, Central, and South America died as a result of European diseases, to which they had no natural immunities. Millions more were enslaved or driven from their ancestral lands. An account of the devastation of the first Native Americans to come in contact with Europeans is given in the selection from **Bartolomé de las Casas** in this unit.

1591. William Shakespeare's *The Comedy of Errors* produced

1578. Holinshed's *Chronicles of English History to 1575* published

| 1550 | 1575 | 1600 |

1534. Henry VIII breaks with the Church of Rome, founds the Church of England

➤1541. Hernando de Soto discovers the Mississippi River

1558. Queen Elizabeth crowned

➤1565. Spanish found first permanent North American settlement in St. Augustine, Florida

➤1584. Sir Walter Raleigh founds the colony at Roanoke

1588. England defeats the Spanish Armada

Belle Grove Plantation, Virginia.

## JAMESTOWN AND THE ORIGINS OF THE PLANTATION SYSTEM

In 1587, a group of 117 English settlers led by **Sir Walter Raleigh** and **John White** founded a colony on **Roanoke Island,** off the coast of what is now North Carolina. After going back to England for supplies, John White returned to Roanoke in 1590 to find no trace of the colony that he left behind. The fate of the Roanoke colonists remains a mystery.

Settled in 1607, **Jamestown, Virginia,** was the first English colony to survive. The colonists hoped to establish a self-sustaining community, but because they knew little of the new land, they were not successful at first. They endured uncertainty and almost unimaginable hardship, facing fierce weather with little food and, for the most part, hastily fashioned holes in the ground for shelter. The numbers tell the grim story: of the 104 Jamestown colonists who survived the ocean voyage, only 38 lived through the first winter. In the face of such conditions, and with a community made up mostly of upper-class men unaccustomed to manual labor, **John Smith,** a natural leader among the colonists, was forced to proclaim that "he who does not work shall not eat," and to institute a rigorous, organized schedule of planting and working. In his *General History of Virginia, New England, and the Summer Isles,* an excerpt from which appears in this unit, Smith tells the story of being captured by Native Americans and rescued by the young daughter of **Powhatan,** their chief. The story of Smith's rescue by this girl, whose nickname was **Pocahontas,** may or may not be true, but it has captured the imaginations of Americans and contains, at least, a symbolic truth: only with the assistance of native peoples were the colonists able to survive. Native Americans taught the colonists how to build adequate shelters and how to cultivate crops such as corn and tobacco for food and export.

Jamestown did not develop into a community of small family farms, like those soon to be established in New England. Instead, it turned tobacco into a profitable export crop, creating large plantations and importing slaves to do the work. Thus developed the plantation system and the slave trade that would have a dramatic effect on the subsequent course of North American history.

## NEW ENGLAND COLONIZATION AND THE PURITAN ERA

Two other settlements begun in the early colonial years played a decisive role in North American history and literature. The **Plymouth Colony,** founded in 1620, and **The Massachusetts Bay Colony,** founded in 1630, were Puritan settlements. The New England colonists, like the Jamestown settlers, endured great difficulties and depended for their survival on the assistance of Native Americans. The core group of the Plymouth colonists, often referred to as the **Pilgrims,** were **Separatist Puritans,** so called because they had separated from the Church of England after giving up hope of "purifying" that church of what they considered to be Popish, or Catholic, tendencies. After moving from England to Holland to escape religious persecution, the Pilgrims set sail for North America on the *Mayflower* in 1620. They landed on Cape Cod and established their colony by means of the **Mayflower Compact** in what is now the town of Plymouth, Massachusetts. After a difficult winter, the colonists learned from native peoples, particularly **Squanto,** a member of the **Wampanoag** group, how to plant native crops. Under the direction of governor **William Bradford,** the colony flourished.

In 1691, Plymouth incorporated with a much larger settlement of Puritans, the Massachusetts Bay Colony. This group was made up of Congregationalist Puritans who did not separate entirely from the Church of England, believing it could be reformed from within. They found inspiration for their early struggles in America in the belief that their actions were divinely guided. Their governor, **John Winthrop,** would write in his *A Model of Christian Charity* that they were about the business of building, as described in the New Testament, a "city upon a hill" in the new land.

## PURITAN BELIEFS

The first Puritans in these settlements shared several basic religious and social beliefs. First, they had a remarkably strong belief in the importance of the community as a whole. Their belief that they were on a grand historical and religious mission formed a common purpose and sense of support, and they imagined the destiny of the

➤1704. America's first newspaper, the *News-Letter,* appears in Boston

➤1702. Cotton Mather's *Magnalia Christi Americana* published

➤1693. Cotton Mather's *The Wonders of the Invisible World* published

➤1688. Aphra Behn writes *Oroonoko,* the first novel in English

➤1683. William Penn's *A General Description of Pennsylvania* published

1678. John Bunyan's *Pilgrim's Progress* published

➤1741. Jonathan Edwards delivers "Sinners in the Hands of an Angry God"

➤1731. Benjamin Franklin founds first public library company in Philadelphia

➤1729. Benjamin Franklin purchases *The Pennsylvania Gazette*

| 1700 | 1725 | 1750 |

➤1682. William Penn founds Philadelphia; Louisiana territory and the Mississippi Valley claimed by the Sieur de La Salle for the French

1685. James II succeeds Charles II

1688. William and Mary of Orange assume throne

➤1692. Salem Witch Trials begin

1702. Anne succeeds William

1714. George I succeeds Anne

1715. Louis XIV dies in France after a seventy-two year reign

1727. George I succeeded by George II

➤1737. First city-paid police force founded by Benjamin Franklin in Philadelphia

➤1739. French explorers Pierre and Paul Mallet become first Europeans to view the Rocky Mountains

➤1744. King George's War with France breaks out in North America and the Caribbean

*Embarkation of the Pilgrims,* 1857. Robert W. Weir.
Brooklyn Museum of Art.

community as everyone's responsibility. Various consent agreements or compacts, such as the Mayflower Compact, reflected and formalized this communal orientation. John Winthrop envisioned the Puritans bound together in a selfless, harmonious community directed by God. Second, the Puritans believed in **original sin,** the idea that because of the transgression of Adam and Eve, all people were born sinful and could be saved only by divine grace. Third, although they thought they were a chosen people, they did not believe that all souls among them were chosen. They adopted the French theologian **John Calvin's** theory of **predestination,** holding that God has chosen in advance which souls are to be saved and which are not. They understood this to mean they could not change their individual fates directly, by force of will. Since none could be sure of having been saved, however, they maintained a steady and humble watch over their lives for proof that they were among the **elect,** those chosen for salvation by God at the beginning of time. Finally, the Puritans shared a belief in hard work, thinking that material and social successes were signs of God's providence and that such work, though it could not win salvation, was nonetheless a sign of salvation. This complex belief in strict moral propriety, community service, and hard work is today referred to as the **Puritan Ethic.**

## POLITICS, SOCIETY, AND THE PROBLEM OF ORTHODOXY

Despite these shared beliefs, a notable though subdued tension existed in Puritan society and politics between its official, orthodox beliefs and the beliefs of some colonists. Puritan communities functioned as **theocracies,** societies guided by religious law, and early Puritan leaders were largely intolerant of any opposition, religious or political. When **Roger Williams** voiced his objections in 1635 about what he saw as the Puritans' arrogant intolerance of diversity and about the taking of lands from the Native Americans, he was banished from Massachusetts. He went on to found the colony of Rhode Island and to espouse principles of religious freedom. In 1637, when **Anne Hutchinson** bypassed the official church and began teaching her own theories in home Bible classes with other women and their husbands, she was accused of threatening the religion and of being more a "husband than a wife." She was banished from Massachusetts as well. Although advanced among colonies of the time in supporting education for women, Massachusetts was not necessarily interested in being educated by women on matters of church doctrine. Its leaders retained an Old Testament model of patriarchal authority.

Even though pressures from progressive elements led in 1662 to the **Half-Way Covenant,** which relaxed old rules and allowed more people direct membership in the church, tensions remained. Some saw the relaxing of orthodoxy as a sign of weakness, and their concerns surfaced dramatically in the belief that Satan had infiltrated the town of Salem and nearby communities. The **Salem Witch Trials,** begun in 1692, resulted in the execution of twenty people and the imprisonment and torture of many more. Followed by embarrassment and recanting, the trials further diminished the Puritan hold on New England. In 1692, a new Massachusetts charter changed the colony's government from a theocratic one to a secular one in which voting was no longer restricted by religious requirements.

## RELIGION AND ALLEGORY IN EARLY PURITAN WRITING

Religion was a dominant influence and presence in the works of early Puritan writers. In sermons, colonial histories, personal diaries, and devotional poetry, Puritan writers often explored the story of spiritual struggles in personal and public life, interpreting or portraying events as emblems, or **allegories**, of the progress of souls or of God's design. In diaries, writers would record their thoughts from day to day and chart their individual spiritual development, often reading seemingly trivial everyday events or conflicts as signs of God's will working itself out in the world. Puritan writers of history sought to find biblical precedents in current events and in the various travails of their communities as a whole.

Puritan literature was not entirely an expression of official views and beliefs, however, and in it we can find examples of the struggle with orthodoxy and conformity mentioned earlier. For example, in her "Prologue," the poet **Anne Bradstreet** asserted that her male critics' judgment was distorted by their views of women: "For such despite they cast on female wits: / If what I do prove well, it won't advance, / They'll say it's stol'n, or else it was by chance."

Although not all Puritans in seventeenth-century New England were educated, they nonetheless valued and promoted education and reading. They founded **Harvard College** in 1636 and began the first colonial printing press two years later. Writers of this era were influenced by their European counterparts, and some of their works, including the poems of Bradstreet, reveal a familiarity with the styles, themes, and figures of the newly available literature of classical Greece and Rome.

## THE EUROPEAN ENLIGHTENMENT AND THE GREAT AWAKENING

The emergence in mid-seventeenth-century England of scientific and empirical thinking, legitimated and encouraged by the formation in 1660 of a science academy called **The Royal Society,** was to have a significant effect on later Puritan intellectuals such as **Cotton Mather** and **Jonathan Edwards.** English Enlightenment thinkers such as **John Locke** and **Isaac Newton** believed that **empirical inquiry**, the study of human experience and the natural world, was the proper approach for achieving true knowledge. In opposition to medieval theories of innate knowledge derived from God, Locke held that people begin life as blank slates and must slowly build up their knowledge from sense impressions. Similarly for Newton, the proper focus of study was nature, the analysis of which, he believed, supported religious belief by revealing the orderly plan of God's design.

In the preachings and writings of Jonathan Edwards, this Enlightenment emphasis on empirical evidence and human experience gave rise to the claim that one needed to feel or experience God, not just intuit his existence from one's belief or from the Bible. Such experiences, or **awakenings,** as they came to be called, formed the basis for a religious revival, called the **Great Awakening,** which from its beginnings in 1734 in Edwards's Northampton congregation quickly spread to Boston and then throughout the colonies. Edwards's eventual call for a return to stricter church membership requirements and his demand for proof of an awakening and conversion were ultimately unpopular, however, and he was removed from his pulpit in 1750.

# ECHOES

## ORIGINS OF THE AMERICAN TRADITION

Where today are the Pequot? Where are the Narragansett, the Mohican, the Pokanoket, and many other once powerful tribes of our people? They have vanished . . . as snow before a summer sun.

> —Tecumseh, Shawnee chief, on the destruction of Native American peoples and ways of life

The earth receives my body . . . Each in its own turn so that the circle of life is never broken.

> —Anonymous Taos Pueblo saying on the interconnectedness of people and nature

He shall make us a praise and glory that men shall say of succeeding plantations, 'the lord make it like that of New England.' For we must consider that we shall be as a city upon a hill. The eyes of all people are upon us, so that if we shall deal falsely with our God in this work we have undertaken, and so cause Him to withdraw His present help from us, we shall be made a story and a by-word through the world.

> —John Winthrop on the creation of the Massachusetts Bay Colony

I will fear GOD, and honor the KING.
I will honor my Father & Mother.
I will Obey my Superiors.
I will Submit to my Elders.
I will Love my Friends.
I will hate no Man.
I will forgive my Enemies, and pray to God for them.
I will as much as in me lies keep all God's Holy Commandments.

> —"The Dutiful Child's Promises," from *The New England Primer*

Unclean, unclean: my Lord, undone, all vile,
  Yea, all defiled: what shall Thy servant do?
  Unfit for Thee: not fit for holy soil,
    Nor for communion of saints below.
    A bag of botches, lump of loathsomeness:
    Defiled by touch, by issue: Leproused flesh.

> —Edward Taylor, Puritan minister, on the unredeemed state of humankind

I am obnoxious to each carping tongue
Who says my hand a needle better fits,
A poet's pen all scorn I should thus wrong,
For such despite they cast on female wits:
If what I do prove well, it won't advance,
They'll say it's stol'n, or else it was by chance.

> —Anne Bradstreet on men's responses to women writers in the Puritan era

I write the wonders of the Christian religion, flying from the depravations of Europe, to the American strand: and, assisted by the Holy Author of that religion, I do, with all conscience of truth, required therein by Him, who is the Truth itself, report the wonderful displays of His infinite power, wisdom, goodness, and faithfulness, wherewith his Divine Providence hath irradiated an Indian wilderness.

> —Cotton Mather, from *Magnalia Christi Americana,* introduction

Wherever Law ends, Tyranny begins.

> —John Locke, from *Second Treatise of Government,* 1690

*Penn's Treaty with the Indians* [Detail], c.1840. Edward Hicks. National Gallery of Art, Washington, DC.

FROM

# THE Iroquois CONSTITUTION

## About the SELECTION

The **Iroquois Constitution**, dating from the fifteenth or sixteenth century, joined together several peoples who lived on the shores of the Great Lakes into the Iroquois League, or Iroquois Confederacy. Initially, the Iroquois League included the Mohawk, Oneida, Onondaga, Cayuga, and Seneca. In the 1700s, however, the Tuscarora joined the Confederacy, making it the League of Six Nations. Tradition holds that the league was begun by Dekanawidah, a Huron whose words open the constitution, and by Hiawatha, an Onondaga who lived among the Mohawks. Each brought to the league his own special talents. Dekanawidah was a diplomat who envisioned the many branches of the Iroquois people united under his Tree of Great Peace. Hiawatha brought this message of unity—the Great Law of Peace—to the Iroquois people as he traveled the country.

The Iroquois lived by hunting, trading, and raising crops such as corn, beans, and squash. For shelter, they built magnificent long houses, covered with elm bark, that housed several families. Kinship groups, or clans, many named after totem, or symbolic, animals such as the beaver or hawk, were united into half tribes. These were united into tribes, and the tribes into the league. Decisions of the league were made in great council meetings. Each league member had one vote, and all member nations had to agree before any action was taken. The league was ruled by fifty male peace chiefs, who were chosen by the Iroquois women. The political system of the Iroquois was well known to the Founding Fathers of the United States, including Benjamin Franklin, who saw in the Iroquois Constitution a model for representative government.

After the coming of Europeans, many Native American populations were decimated by epidemics of diseases such as smallpox. During the Colonial Period, the total Iroquois population numbered only about twelve thousand, and the total number of Iroquois warriors at any time numbered only a little over two thousand. Despite these small numbers, the Iroquois waged successful war against neighboring groups and held both British and French invaders at bay. During the American Revolution, two Iroquois groups sided with the colonists. The rest sided with the British, leading George Washington to send troops to destroy Iroquois settlements, fields, and stores of food. Later treaties set aside reservation lands for the Onondaga, Seneca, and Tuscarora in New York. The Mohawks and Cayuga settled in Canada, and the Oneida in Wisconsin.

## Literary TOOLS

**SYMBOL.** A **symbol** is a thing that stands for or represents both itself and something else. In the selection you are about to read, several elements of nature are used as symbols. As you read pay attention to these symbols and think about their meaning.

## Reader's Journal

If you were going to design a constitution for a new country, what elements would you include and why would you include them?

## Art Note

*No Nee Yeath Tan No Ton, King of the Generath,* 1710. Johannes Verelst.

The painting on page 88 of an Iroquois chief was made during his visit to Europe. Depictions of Native Americans varied a great deal as Europeans tried to fit them into their worldview. This Dutch artist depicted the chief as a king, while others depicted Native Americans as inferior to Europeans.

**No Nee Yeath Tan No Ton, King of the Generath,**
1710. Johannes Verelst. Private Collection.

# FROM

# THE Iroquois CONSTITUTION

name of these roots is the Great White Roots and their nature is peace and strength.

If any man or any nation outside the Five Nations shall obey the laws of the Great Peace and make known their <u>disposition</u> to the lords of the confederacy, they may trace the roots to the tree and if their minds are clean and they are obedient and promise to obey the wishes of the confederate council, they shall be welcomed[3] to take shelter beneath the Tree of the Long Leaves.

> On what terms would someone outside the Five Nations gain acceptance?

We place at the top of the Tree of the Long Leaves an eagle who is able to see afar.

If he sees in the distance any evil approaching or any danger threatening he will at once warn the people of the confederacy.

The smoke of the confederate council fire shall ever ascend and pierce the sky so that other nations who may be allies may see the council fire of the Great Peace. . . .

Whenever the confederate lords shall assemble for the purpose of holding a council, the Onondaga lords shall open it by expressing their gratitude to their cousin lords and greeting

I am Dekanawidah and with the Five Nations[1] confederate lords I plant the Tree of the Great Peace. I name the tree the Tree of the Great Long Leaves. Under the shade of this Tree of the Great Peace we spread the soft white feathery down of the globe thistle as seats for you, Adodarhoh,[2] and your cousin lords.

We place you upon those seats, spread soft with the feathery down of the globe thistle, there beneath the shade of the spreading branches of the Tree of Peace. There shall you sit and watch the council fire of the <u>confederacy</u> of the Five Nations, and all the affairs of the Five Nations shall be transacted at this place before you.

Roots have spread out from the Tree of the Great Peace, one to the north, one to the east, one to the south, and one to the west. The

---

1. **Five Nations.** The Mohawk, Oneida, Onondaga, Cayuga, and Seneca tribes. These tribes formed the Iroquois Confederacy.
2. **Adodarhoh.** Chief confederate lord of the Onondaga, on whose land the council fire was lit
3. **they shall be welcomed.** The Tuscarora tribe joined the Confederacy in 1722.

---

**WORDS FOR EVERYDAY USE**

**con • fed • er • a • cy** (kən fedʹər ə sē) *n.*, people or groups united for a common purpose. *The three tribes stopped feuding and formed a <u>confederacy</u> to save their homeland.*

**dis • po • si • tion** (disʹpə zishʹən) *n.*, state of mind; general nature. *Angelica's sunny <u>disposition</u> makes her a pleasant person to be around.*

them, and they shall make an address and offer thanks to the earth where men dwell, to the streams of water, the pools, the springs and the lakes, to the maize and the fruits, to the medicinal herbs and trees, to the forest trees for their usefulness, to the animals that serve as food and give their pelts for clothing, to the great winds and the lesser winds, to the thunderers, to the sun, the mighty warrior, to the moon, to the messengers of the Creator who reveal his wishes and to the Great Creator who dwells in the heavens above, who gives all the things useful to men, and who is the source and the ruler of health and life.

*What acknowledgments were made at the opening of a council meeting?*

Then shall the Onondaga lords declare the council open. . . .

All lords of the Five Nations' Confederacy must be honest in all things. . . . It shall be a serious wrong for anyone to lead a lord into trivial affairs, for the people must ever hold their lords high in <u>estimation</u> out of respect to their honorable positions.

When a candidate lord is to be installed he shall <u>furnish</u> four strings of shells (or wampum)[4] one span in length bound together at one end. Such will constitute the evidence of his pledge to the confederate lords that he will live according to the constitution of the Great Peace and exercise justice in all affairs.

When the pledge is furnished the speaker of the council must hold the shell strings in his hand and address the opposite side of the council fire and he shall commence his address saying: "Now behold him. He has now become a confederate lord. See how splendid he looks."

An address may then follow. At the end of it he shall send the bunch of shell strings to the opposite side and they shall be received as evidence of the pledge. Then shall the opposite side say:

"We now do crown you with the sacred emblem of the deer's antlers, the emblem of your lordship. You shall now become a mentor of the people of the Five Nations. The thickness of your skin shall be seven spans—which is to say that you shall be proof against anger, offensive actions and criticism. Your heart shall be filled with peace and good will and your mind filled with a yearning for the welfare of the people of the confederacy. With endless patience you shall carry out your duty and your firmness shall be tempered with tenderness for your people. Neither anger nor fury shall find lodgement in your mind and all your words and actions shall be marked with calm deliberation. In all of your deliberations in the confederate council, in your efforts at law making, in all your official acts, self-interest shall be cast into oblivion. Cast not over your shoulder behind you the warnings of the nephews and nieces should they chide you for any error or wrong you may do, but return to the way of the Great Law which is just and right. Look and listen for the welfare of the whole people and have always in view not only the present but also the coming generations, even those whose faces are yet beneath the surface of the ground—the unborn of the future nation."

*What view should a lord take?*

■

---

4. **wampum.** Small beads made of shell, usually white or dark purple in color

WORDS
FOR
EVERYDAY
USE

es • ti • ma • tion (es´ tə mā´shən) *n.*, respect; value. *At the banquet, the students honored Ms. Shaw, a teacher they held in high <u>estimation</u>.*
fur • nish (fur´nish) *vt.*, supply or provide. *Information <u>furnished</u> by a witness helped Larry solve the crime.*

Do you think people today are as connected to the natural environment as were the Native Americans of the Five Nations? Support your answer. How do people today show their respect for the environment?

# INVESTIGATE, Inquire, *Imagine*

### Recall: GATHERING FACTS

1a. Who plants and names the Tree of the Great Peace with Dekanawidah?

2a. To whom is Dekanawidah speaking? Who is Adodarhoh?

3a. How does a candidate lord show his pledge to the council? What does his offering symbolize?

### Interpret: FINDING MEANING

1b. What is the purpose of the meeting at which Dekanawidah speaks? Why do you think oratory skills were prized by the Iroquois?

2b. Why do you think Dekanawidah refers to the assembled lords as "cousins"? Are they literally related to one another?

3b. According to the constitution, what qualities should a leader have? What qualities should a leader put aside?

### Analyze: TAKING THINGS APART

4a. In what ways does this excerpt from the Iroquois Constitution incorporate nature in the rituals it describes?

### Synthesize: BRINGING THINGS TOGETHER

4b. What does this selection reveal about the relationship the Native Americans of the Five Nations had with nature?

### Evaluate: MAKING JUDGMENTS

5a. In your opinion, are the values and moral code described in the Iroquois Constitution appropriate for the members and leaders of a government? Explain, using examples from the text.

### Extend: CONNECTING IDEAS

5b. Imagine that you and other students have been shipwrecked on an island and have to organize a government of your own. Work with other students to form a constitution establishing the basic laws and political structure of your new country. Which elements of this selection from the Iroquois Constitution would you incorporate into your government? Which types of behavior not included in this excerpt would you regulate by law?

# Understanding *Literature*

SYMBOL. A **symbol** is a thing that stands for or represents both itself and something else. The following chart lists some common symbols used in literary works. In the Iroquois Constitution, what does the tree symbolize? its roots? What does it mean to take shelter under the leaves of this tree? What does the eagle perched at the top of the tree symbolize?

| SYMBOL | CONVENTIONAL INTERPRETATION |
|---|---|
| wind | change, inspiration |
| rainbow | hope |
| rose | beauty, love |
| moon | fickleness, inconstancy |
| roads, paths | the journey through life |
| spring | youth |
| fall, winter | age |
| woods, darkness | spiritual or moral confusion |
| storm | trouble, confusion, anger |
| thorns | trouble, pain, suffering |
| stars | unchangeableness, constancy |
| mirror | vanity, introspection |
| snake | evil, duplicity |
| owl | wisdom |
| fox | craftiness |

# WRITER'S JOURNAL

1. Imagine that you are the leader of a tribe that has been invited to participate in the council of the Five Nations. Write a **thank-you letter** to Dekanawidah expressing your gratitude to him for including your people in the council. Explain why you think it is important for your tribe to join in the confederacy.

2. The writer of the Iroquois Constitution used the metaphor of a tree to describe the confederacy of the Five Nations. Write your own **metaphor** to describe our current government. You might compare our government to another form of nature, or you might choose a metaphor from your own surroundings.

3. Imagine that you are asked to write the **formal procedure** of a meeting of the Great Council. Referring to the Language Arts Survey 6.4, "Writing a Step-by-Step Procedure," make step-by-step directions for the council to follow at its meetings.

# Integrating *the* LANGUAGE ARTS

## Study and Research & Collaborative Learning

RESEARCHING THE IROQUOIS CONSTITUTION. Locate and read a copy of the complete Iroquois Constitution, from the Internet or library. Then, form groups of four and prepare a brief presentation on one of the elements of the Constitution, such as the role of women in the Iroquois government and society; the procedure for deposing a lord who has committed a crime or has not fulfilled his duty; symbolism in Iroquois society; or funeral proceedings for a lord of the council. All members of the group should research the topic, making notes from the Constitution and copying down quotes to include. Another should write the text of the presentation, and another student should edit the text for language, grammar, and style. Finally, one student should create any illustrations or visual aids you would like to include in the presentation. Two students should present each half of the materials so that all have a chance to contribute to the final presentation.

## Literary
### T O O L S

**MYTH.** A **myth** is a story that explains objects or events in the natural world as resulting from the action of some supernatural force or entity. "Song of the Sky Loom" contains elements of Tewa myth.

**METAPHOR.** A **metaphor** is a figure of speech in which one thing is spoken or written about as if it were another, thus encouraging a comparison between features of the two things. The writer's, or speaker's, actual subject is called the *tenor* of the metaphor, while the thing to which it is likened is called the *vehicle*. Songs such as the one you are about to read often employ metaphor in order to create pictures in the mind of the reader or listener.

As you read, make a chart like the one below showing the tenor and vehicle of the metaphors in the poem. An example has been done for you.

|  | Tenor | Vehicle |
|---|---|---|
| Metaphors in "Song of the Sky Loom" | white light of morning | warp |
|  |  |  |

# "Song of the SKY LOOM"

TEWA TRIBAL SONG

## About *the* SELECTION

The language of **"Song of the Sky Loom"** is taken directly from weaving. The Tewa, a Pueblo people of the Southwest, are accomplished weavers. They, in turn, passed the art on to the Navajo, now renowned weavers of blankets and rugs. In addition to weaving, the Tewa make intricately decorated pottery and elaborate baskets. They live in multi-level, multi-unit adobe structures often built into the hard mesas of the Southwest. Like other Pueblo peoples, the Tewa have a vital interdependence with the natural world, performing various rituals and ceremonies related to nature, especially to bringing much-needed rain.

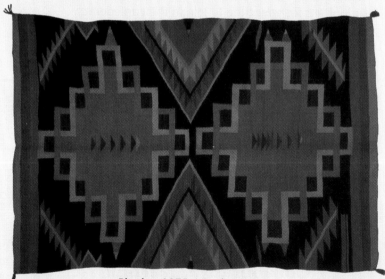

*Blanket,* 1875. Navaho Artist.

## Reader's *Journal*

If you could describe yourself only in terms of an art form, such as a painting, a sculpture, or a musical work, which would you choose, and why?

**Song of the SKY LOOM**

*Tewa Tribal Song*

*Navaho Woman Weaving,* 1988. David Ryan.

O our Mother the Earth, O our Father the Sky,
Your children are we, and with tired backs
We bring you the gifts you love.
Then weave for us a garment of brightness;
5   May the warp[1] be the white light of morning,
May the weft[2] be the red light of evening,
May the fringes be the falling rain,
May the border be the standing rainbow.
Thus weave for us a garment of brightness,
10  That we may walk fittingly where birds sing,
That we may walk fittingly where grass is green,
O our Mother the Earth, O our Father the Sky. ∎

*Who is addressed in this song?*

*Of what will the garment be woven?*

---

1. **warp.** Threads in a loom that run lengthwise
2. **weft.** Horizontal threads in a loom. The weft crosses the warp to make a woven fabric.

## Respond *to the* SELECTION

What images does "Song of the Sky Loom" create in your mind?

# INVESTIGATE, Inquire, *Imagine*

**Recall:** GATHERING FACTS

1a. To whom is "Song of the Sky Loom" addressed? How do the speakers name themselves?

2a. What elements of nature are described in the poem?

➤ **Interpret:** FINDING MEANING

1b. What is the speakers' message? What do "we" offer, and what do "we" ask in return?

2b. What role does each element of nature play in the tapestry woven by Mother Earth and Father Sky? How are the elements linked to one another?

**Analyze:** TAKING THINGS APART

3a. What relationship does the song suggest exists between humans and the divine?

➤ **Synthesize:** BRINGING THINGS TOGETHER

3b. What is the central comparison in "Song of the Sky Loom"?

**Perspective:** LOOKING AT OTHER VIEWS

4a. Based on this song, what attitude do you think the Tewa people had toward their gods?

➤ **Empathy:** SEEING FROM INSIDE

4b. How do you think the Tewa people expected their gods to respond to this prayer song?

# Understanding *Literature*

**MYTH.** Read the complete definition of **myth** in the Handbook of Literary Terms. Every early culture around the globe has produced its own myths, or supernatural explanations of natural phenomena. What mythical elements appear in "Song of the Sky Loom"? What can you infer about Tewa religious beliefs and practices based on this poem?

**METAPHOR.** Review the definition of **metaphor** in Literary Tools on page 92. What are the tenor and vehicle of the central metaphor in the "Song of the Sky Loom"? What is the "garment of brightness"?

# WRITER'S JOURNAL

1. Imagine that you are helping a friend to understand "Song of the Sky Loom." Rewrite a **prose retelling** of the song using informal language.

2. Write this prayer song in the form of a **personal letter** addressed to Mother Earth and Father Sky.

3. A **hymn** is a song of praise or thanksgiving. Imagine that you have been invited to speak at an Earth Day celebration in your community. Write a brief hymn praising or offering thanks for some aspect of the natural world. Model your hymn on "Song of the Sky Loom," using parallelism and unrhymed lines to express your thoughts and feelings. To gather ideas, try creating a cluster chart or sensory detail chart. Refer to the Language Arts Survey 2.13, "Clustering," and 2.18, "Sensory Detail Charts."

# Integrating *the* LANGUAGE ARTS

## Language, Grammar, and Style

**GRAMMAR OVERVIEW.** Answer the following questions, referring to "Song of the Sky Loom" and to the Language Arts Survey 3.7, "Parts of Speech Overview."

1. What interjections are used in the first and last lines of this poem? What nouns of direct address do you find in the same lines?
2. Identify the nouns in lines 5–8.
3. Identify the verbs throughout the poem. Which verbs express state of being? Which verbs express action? (For more information, see the Language Arts Survey 3.60, "Action Verbs and State of Being Verbs.")
4. Identify the modifiers throughout the poem. What words do these modifiers modify? Are the modifiers adjectives or adverbs?
5. Which prepositions serve as linkers? Where do they occur in the poem?

## Study and Research

**EARLY NATIVE AMERICAN ART AND ARCHITECTURE.** The hundreds of different Native American cultures that existed before the coming of the Europeans created a wide variety of exquisite types of art and architecture. Working in a small group, research the early Native American art and architecture of one of the following cultural groups of North, Central, or South America:

- the Penobscot, Algonquin, Iroquois, Ojibway, or Delaware (eastern North America)
- the Cherokee, Creek, Chickasaw, Alabama, Choctaw, Apalachee, Timucua, or Catawba (southeastern United States)
- the Blackfoot, Crow, Sioux, Cheyenne, Pawnee, Arapaho, Kiowa, or Comanche (western plains of North America)
- the Anasazi, Hopi, Navaho, Apache, Zuni, or Pima (southwestern North America)
- the Coast Salish or Wenatchee (northwestern coast of North America)
- the Olmec, Aztec, or Maya (Mexico and Central America)
- the Inca, Chimú, or Nazca (South America)

Refer to the Language Arts Survey 5.18–5.29 for information on conducting research. Present the results of your research in an oral report to your classmates. Use visual aids such as maps and pictures from books to make your report vivid and interesting.

# Literary
## T O O L S

**MOOD.** **Mood,** or **atmosphere,** is the emotion created in the reader by part or all of a literary work. As you read this piece, think about the mood it creates.

**POINT OF VIEW. Point of view** is the vantage point from which a story, whether fiction or nonfiction, is told. A story may be told from the *first-person point of view* by one of the participants, who uses *I* to refer to herself or himself, or from the *third-person point of view* by an outsider who avoids the use of *I*. Pay attention to the point of view used by the author of this selection.

# Reader's
## Journal

What makes one person stand up against injustice when others are afraid to voice their opinions?

FROM

# The *Very Brief Relation* of the
# DEVASTATION OF THE INDIES

BY BARTOLOMÉ DE LAS CASAS

## About *the* AUTHOR

**Bartolomé de las Casas** (1474–1566) first voyaged to the Caribbean in 1502 with his father. He soon found himself taking part in Spanish attacks on the Taino people in response to a rebellion. Such attacks were common and exceedingly brutal. De las Casas was rewarded with a group of Native American slaves for his work in the attacks. He continued to receive such benefits even after becoming a priest in 1512 or 1513.

In 1515 de las Casas realized the cruelty and inhumanity that surrounded him and in which he participated. De las Casas became a spokesperson for rights of the native peoples of the New World. He gave up all of his slaves and urged other slaveholders to do the same. Returning to Spain to plead his case, he was appointed protector of the indigenous peoples. He used oral arguments, writings including *The Very Brief Relation of the Devastation of the Indies,* and his own example to argue his case for the end of enslavement.

## About *the* SELECTION

*The Very Brief Relation of the Devastation of the Indies,* or the *Relation,* as it is sometimes called, exposed the grievous behavior of Spanish explorers in the New World. The excerpt included here focuses on Spanish actions at Hispaniola. Hispaniola, an island in the Caribbean Sea, is thought to be one of Christopher Columbus's first landing sites. Certainly, it is where he began his first colonies. The island, which is now divided between the countries of Haiti and the Dominican Republic, was occupied by the Arawak. While the first exchanges between Columbus and the Arawak were relatively friendly, this situation soon changed. Columbus's later voyages, and the voyages of the explorers who followed him over the years, produced savage treatment of the native people. In combination with European diseases against which the native people had no resistance, Spanish cruelty killed most of the native people of the Caribbean Islands. There are no pure Arawaks living in the Caribbean today.

*Cortez Entering Vera Cruz*, 1500s. Unknown Mayan Artist.
Tozzer Library, Harvard University.

# FROM
# The *Very Brief Relation* of the
# DEVASTATION OF THE INDIES

## BARTOLOMÉ DE LAS CASAS

### From *Hispaniola*

This was the first land in the New World to be destroyed and <u>depopulated</u> by the Christians, and here they began their <u>subjection</u> of the women and children, taking them away from the Indians to use them and ill use them, eating the food they provided with their sweat and toil. The Spaniards did not content themselves with what the Indians gave them of their own free will, according to their ability, which was always too little to satisfy enormous appetites, for a Christian eats and consumes in one day an amount of food that would <u>suffice</u> to feed three houses inhabited by ten Indians for one month. And they committed other acts of force and violence and <u>oppression</u> which made the Indians realize that these men had not come from Heaven.[1] And some of the Indians concealed their foods while others concealed their wives and children and still others fled to the mountains to avoid the terrible transactions of the Christians.

> According to de las Casas, how much did Christians eat?

---

1. **realize . . . Heaven.** Columbus and other early European voyagers reported that the natives took them to be gods who had come from the heavens.

---

**WORDS FOR EVERYDAY USE**

**de • pop • u • late** (dē päp´yə lāt´) *vt.*, reduce the population of, especially by violence or disease. *Plagues and famines depopulated medieval Europe.*

**sub • jec • tion** (sub jek´shən) *n.*, bringing under control or dominion. *The subjection of the American colonies by the British sparked the American Revolution.*

**suf • fice** (sə fīs´) *vi.*, be enough. *One small salad per day will not suffice to nourish a growing adolescent.*

**op • pres • sion** (ə presh´ən) *n.*, keeping down by cruel or unjust use of authority. *The people protested the oppression of the controlling government.*

And the Christians attacked them with <u>buffets</u> and beatings, until finally they laid hands on the nobles of the villages. . . . From that time onward the Indians began to seek ways to throw the Christians out of their lands. They took up arms, but their weapons were very weak and of little service in offense and still less in defense. (Because of this, the wars of the Indians against each other are little more than games played by children.) And the Christians, with their horses and swords and pikes began to carry out massacres and strange cruelties against them. . . .

What did the native people begin to seek?

And because all the people who could do so fled to the mountains to escape these <u>inhuman</u>, ruthless, and ferocious acts, the Spanish captains, enemies of the human race, pursued them with the fierce dogs they kept which attacked the Indians, tearing them to pieces and devouring them. And because on few and far between occasions, the Indians justifiably killed some Christians, the Spaniards made a rule among themselves that for every Christian slain by the Indians, they would slay a hundred Indians.

In what way did the Spaniards say they would retaliate for each Christian slain?

### From *The Coast of Pearls, Paria, and the Island of Trinidad*

[The Spaniards] have brought to the island of Hispaniola and the island of San Juan[2] more than two million souls taken captive, and have sent them to do hard labor in the mines, labors that caused many of them to die. And it is a great sorrow and heartbreak to see this coastal land which was so <u>flourishing</u>, now a depopulated desert.

This is truth that can be verified, for no more do they bring ships loaded with Indians that have been thus attacked and captured as I have related. No more do they cast overboard into the sea the third part of the numerous Indians they stow on their vessels, these dead being added to those they have killed in their native lands, the captives crowded into the holds of their ships, without food or water, or with very little, so as not to deprive the Spanish tyrants who call themselves ship owners and who carry enough food for themselves on their voyages of attack. And for the pitiful Indians who died of hunger and thirst, there is no remedy but to cast them into the sea. And verily, as a Spaniard told me, their ships in these regions could voyage without compass or chart, merely by following for the distance between the Lucayos Islands[3] and Hispaniola, which is sixty or seventy leagues,[4] the trace of those Indian corpses floating in the sea, corpses that had been cast overboard by earlier ships.

Afterward, when they disembark on the island of Hispaniola, it is heartbreaking to see those naked Indians, heartbreaking for anyone with a <u>vestige</u> of piety, the famished state they are in, fainting and falling down, weak from hunger, men, women, old people, and children.

What condition were the native people in when they arrived at Hispaniola?

Then, like sheep, they are sorted out into flocks of ten or twenty persons, separating fathers from sons, wives from husbands, and the Spaniards draw lots, the ship owners carrying off their share, the best flock, to compensate them for the moneys they have invested in their fleet of two or three ships, the <u>ruffian</u> tyrants getting their share of captives who will be

---

2. **San Juan.** Puerto Rico
3. **Lucayos Islands.** The Bahamas
4. **leagues.** Linear unit of measure that varies in different periods of time; usually equal to about three miles

---

**WORDS FOR EVERYDAY USE**

buf • fet (buf´it) *n.*, blow with the hand or fist. *Unable to avoid the <u>buffets</u> of his opponent, the boxer was knocked out.*
in • hu • man (in hyü´mən) *adj.*, unfeeling; cruel; barbarous. *The brutal actions of the Spanish conquistadors were <u>inhuman</u>.*
flour • ish (flʉr´ish) *vi.*, grow vigorously; thrive; prosper. *Because of the rainfall, the vegetable garden <u>flourished</u>.*
ves • tige (ves´tij) *n.*, trace; bit. *The Roanoke colony disappeared and not a <u>vestige</u> remained of its settlers.*
ruf • fi • an (ruf´ē an) *adj.*, brutal; violent; lawless. *The principal warned the bully to cease his <u>ruffian</u> ways.*

house slaves, and when in this *"repartimiento"*[5] a tyrant gets an old person or an invalid, he says, "Why do you give me this one? To bury him? And this sick one, do you give him to me to make him well?" See by such remarks in what esteem the Spaniards hold the Indians and judge if they are accomplishing the divine concepts of love for our fellow man, as laid down by the prophets.

The tyranny exercised by the Spaniards against the Indians in the work of pearl fishing is one of the most cruel that can be imagined. There is no life as infernal and desperate in this century that can be compared with it, although the mining of gold is a dangerous and burdensome way of life. The pearl fishers dive into the sea at a depth of five fathoms, and do this from sunrise to sunset, and remain for many minutes without breathing, tearing the oysters out of their rocky beds where the pearls are formed. They come to the surface with a netted bag of these oysters where a Spanish torturer is waiting in a canoe or skiff, and if the pearl diver shows signs of

> What happened if a pearl diver wanted to rest?

wanting to rest, he is showered with blows, his hair is pulled, and he is thrown back into the water, obliged to continue the hard work of tearing out the oysters and bringing them again to the surface.

The food given the pearl divers is codfish, not very nourishing, and the bread made of maize, the bread of the Indies. At night the pearl divers are chained so they cannot escape.

Often a pearl diver does not return to the surface, for these waters are <u>infested</u> with maneating sharks of two kinds, both vicious marine animals that can kill, eat, and swallow a whole man.

In this harvesting of pearls let us again consider whether the Spaniards preserve the divine concepts of love for their fellow men, when they place the bodies of the Indians in such mortal danger, and their souls, too, for these pearl divers perish without the holy sacraments.[6] And it is solely because of the Spaniards' greed for gold that they force the Indians to lead such a life, often a brief life, for it is impossible to continue for long diving into the cold water and holding the breath for minutes at a time, repeating this hour after hour, day after day; the continual cold penetrates them, constricts the chest, and they die spitting blood, or weakened by diarrhea.

The hair of these pearl divers, naturally black, is as if <u>burnished</u> by the saltpeter in the water, and hangs down their backs making them look like sea dogs or monsters of another species. And in this extraordinary labor, or, better put, in this infernal labor, the Lucayan Indians are finally consumed, as are captive Indians from other provinces. And all of them were publicly sold for one hundred and fifty castellanos,[7] these Indians who had lived happily on their islands until the Spaniards came, although such a thing was against the law. But the unjust judges did nothing to stop it. For all the Indians of these islands are known to be great swimmers.[8]

> Why didn't the judges stop the enslavement and mistreatment of the native population?

■

---

5. *repartimiento.* Distribution (Spanish). A royal decree in 1503 ordered masters of native persons to try to convert them to Christianity and hold their property. In reality it was a system of slavery.

6. **sacraments.** Certain rites believed to be means of grace: baptism, confirmation, the Eucharist, penance, holy orders, matrimony, and Anointing of the Sick in Roman and Eastern Orthodox churches; baptism and the Lord's Supper in Protestant churches

7. **castellanos.** Spanish gold coin bearing the arms of Castile

8. **But the unjust . . . great swimmers.** Spanish judges ignored the mistreatment of the native peoples because their abilities at pearl diving were impressive.

---

**WORDS FOR EVERYDAY USE**

in • fest (in fest´) vt., overrun or inhabit in large numbers. *The old house was <u>infested</u> with termites that gnawed upon the wood.*

bur • nish (bʉr´nish) vt., make shiny by rubbing. *I <u>burnished</u> the candlesticks to make them gleam.*

How do you think Bartolomé de las Casas felt when he witnessed his own people behaving so abominably? How would you feel if you saw a friend behave cruelly? What might you do or say in response?

# INVESTIGATE Inquire, *Imagine*

### Recall: GATHERING FACTS

1a. What did the Spaniards make native women and children do?

2a. How did the Spanish react to native efforts at self-defense?

3a. How were pearl divers treated by the Spaniards? What word does de las Casas use to describe their labor?

### Interpret: FINDING MEANING

1b. Why, according to de las Casas, did the Spaniards want so much food?

2b. Why did they punish the natives so severely?

3b. What was the inevitable fate of the pearl divers?

### Analyze: TAKING THINGS APART

4a. In what various actions do the Spaniards disregard the divine concepts of love for their fellow men? How do the Spaniards seem to regard the Indians?

### Synthesize: BRINGING THINGS TOGETHER

4b. What motivated the Spaniards in all their relations with the natives? What do you think motivated de las Casas in his relations with the natives, after his conversion in 1515?

### Perspective: LOOKING AT OTHER VIEWS

5a. Why do you think Bartolomé de las Casas risked everything, even incurring a charge of treason against Spain, to write the *Relation?*

### Empathy: SEEING FROM INSIDE

5b. What would you do if you were a native of Hispaniola and suffered such mistreatment at the hands of the Spaniards? Would you resist, hiding in the mountains and killing Christians, or would you submit and try to survive the grueling labor? Explain your answer.

# Understanding *Literature*

**MOOD.** Review the definition for **mood** in the Handbook of Literary Terms. Whether sadness, suspense, or humor, mood provides writers with an important tool to engage the reader's attention. Describe the mood of the *Relation*. Find four examples of concrete details that you feel support that mood.

**POINT OF VIEW.** Refer to the definition for **point of view** in the Handbook of Literary Terms. In stories told from a *first-person point of view*, the narrator may be a participant or witness of the action. In stories told from a *third-person point of view*, the narrator generally stands outside the action. From what point of view is the *Relation* told? How can you tell? Why does de las Casas use this point of view?

# WRITER'S JOURNAL

1. Imagine that you are a Lucayan Indian pearl diver working under the Spanish colonists. Write a **journal entry** describing a typical day on the job. Use descriptive detail to explain your thoughts and feelings as you repeatedly dive into the sea.

2. Imagine that you are a reporter from Spain who has witnessed the actions depicted in the *Relation*. Write a **newspaper article** about these events. Since this is a factual article, try to remain objective and do not express any opinion or judgment about the events you are reporting.

3. Suppose you are a Spanish judge or conqueror who has read the *Relation* and wishes to defend herself or himself against the charges of de las Casas. Write a brief **speech** explaining why your actions against the indigenous people are justified. Try to imagine what some of the attitudes of such a tyrant must have been.

# Integrating *the* LANGUAGE ARTS

## Collaborative Learning & Speaking and Listening

**CLUSTER CHART.** Working in groups of three or four, create a cluster chart like the one below showing the injustices done to the Indians by the Spanish conquerors and settlers. In each circle that branches out from the center, write one of the unjust acts cited by de las Casas in his essay. One example has been done for you.

In your group, review and discuss the accusations on your chart as a courtroom jury would in the case of the Lucayan pearl divers against the Spanish colonists who enslaved them. Determine if there is enough evidence to condemn the Spanish for their actions and vote to reach a verdict of guilty or not guilty. Select one student from the group as spokesperson to present your cluster chart to the class, and to declare the jury's verdict, explaining why your group arrived at that conclusion.

## Study and Research

**RESEARCH THE SPANISH INQUISITION.** Research other writing from the 1500s about the Spanish conquest and colonization of the New World. You may want to read from the writing of Hernán Cortes, a Spanish conquistador who conquered the Aztec people of Mexico, the work of Friar Diego de Landa in the book *Yucatan Before and After the Conquest*, or the work of any other early explorer of the Americas. Write a report comparing the attitudes of these authors to those of de las Casas. How are they different or similar? What justification might these authors have for the harsh treatment of the natives described in de las Casas's essay?

Alternatively, you might do research on the life of Bartolomé de las Casas. What was his mission in the New World? What personal failings and personal triumphs did he experience?

Took women and children from their families — Injustices by Spanish colonizers —

## Literary
# T O O L S

**CHRONOLOGICAL ORDER. Chronological order** is the arrangement of details in order of their occurrence. It is the primary method of organization used in narrative writing. It is also common in historical nonfiction writing that describes events, such as this selection.

**POINT OF VIEW. Point of view** is the vantage point from which a story, whether fiction or nonfiction, is told. A story may be told by one of the participants, who uses *I* to refer to himself or herself, or by an outsider who avoids the use of *I*. As you read, notice how the point of view changes as the selection is told.

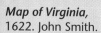

## Reader's
*Journal*

What place would you like to visit where the customs are different from your own? Why?

# ArtNote

*Map of Virginia,*
1622. John Smith.

The map on page 103, drawn by John Smith, depicts the Virginia Colony where his story takes place. "James-towne," the Chicahominy River, and Werowocomoco village are located in the center of the western half of the map. The upper left corner shows Chief Powhatan in his longhouse. On the right side is Smith's depiction of a Native American. He writes in the caption that the natives are "a giant-like people and thus attired."

FROM

# The General History of Virginia...

BY JOHN SMITH

## About *the*
# A U T H O R

**John Smith** (1580–1631) was born in Willoughby, England. As a youth, he worked on his father's farm and was apprenticed to a shopkeeper. At the age of twenty, he went to Hungary to fight against the Turks, was taken captive, escaped to Russia, and then returned to England. In 1606, he joined a group of about one hundred people and set sail for the New World. There, on the Chesapeake Bay, he helped to found the first permanent English colony in America, Jamestown.

Smith explored Virginia, making maps of the land and its waterways. In 1607, he was captured by Powhatan, chief of one of the native peoples of Chesapeake Bay. In later writings, he claimed to have been saved from execution by the chief's young daughter, known to history by her nickname, Pocahontas. Smith served as governor of the Jamestown Colony from 1608 to 1609, at which time he returned to England.

Smith returned to America in 1614, this time to a part of the continent that he called New England. There he made maps of the coastline. In 1615, Smith was captured by pirates but managed to escape. Smith published several maps and accounts of his explorations, including *Map of Virginia* (1612), *A Description of New England* (1616), and *The True Travels, Adventures, and Observations of Captain John Smith in Europe, Asia, Africa, and America* (1630).

## About *the*
# S E L E C T I O N

In *The General History of Virginia, New England, and the Summer Isles,* John Smith presents a detailed and often exciting account of the events in the early years of the Virginia Colony from 1607, the year of its founding at Jamestown, to 1609, the year when Smith departed Virginia, never to return. *The General History of Virginia . . .* was completed in 1624, fifteen years after Smith's return to England. In this part of the account, Smith describes how he was saved from death by Pocahontas, the sixteen-year-old daughter of Chief Powhatan.

*Map of Virginia*, 1622. John Smith. British Library, London.

FROM

# The General History of Virginia...

## JOHN SMITH

### What Happened Till the First Supply

Being thus left to our fortunes, it fortuned[1] that within ten days, scarce ten amongst us could either go[2] or well stand, such extreme weakness and sickness oppressed us. And thereat none need marvel if they consider the cause and reason, which was this: While the ships stayed, our allowance was somewhat bettered by a daily proportion of biscuit which the sailors would <u>pilfer</u> to sell, give, or exchange with us for money, sassafras,[3] or furs. But when they departed, there remained neither tavern, beer house, nor place of relief but the common

---

1. **fortuned.** Happened
2. **go.** Go about; walk
3. **sassafras.** Tree with aromatic bark, the root bark of which was valued for its supposed medicinal qualities

**WORDS FOR EVERYDAY USE**

**pil • fer** (pil´fər) *vt.*, steal. *In the drawer we found Adam's jackknife and many other items John had <u>pilfered</u>.*

kettle.[4] Had we been as free from all sins as gluttony and drunkenness we might have been canonized for saints, but our President[5] would never have been admitted for engrossing to his private,[6] oatmeal, sack,[7] oil, aqua vitae,[8] beef, eggs, or what not but the kettle: that indeed he allowed equally to be distributed, and that was half a pint of wheat and as much barley boiled with water for a man a day, and this, having fried some twenty-six weeks in the ship's hold, contained as many worms as grains so that we might truly call it rather so much bran than corn; our drink was water, our lodgings castles in the air.

> Why might the colonists have been canonized as saints? Why wouldn't the president have been included as a saint?

With this lodging and diet, our extreme toil in bearing and planting palisades[9] so strained and bruised us and our continual labor in the extremity of the heat had so weakened us, as were cause sufficient to have made us as miserable in our native country or any other place in the world.

> What did the speaker feel about the difficulties the colonists had undergone?

From May to September, those that escaped lived upon sturgeon[10] and sea crabs. Fifty in this time we buried: the rest seeing the President's projects to escape these miseries in our pinnace[11] by flight (who all this time had neither felt want nor sickness) so moved our dead spirits as we deposed him and established Ratcliffe in his place . . .

But now was all our provision spent, the sturgeon gone, all helps abandoned, each hour

expecting the fury of the savages; when God, the patron of all good endeavors, in that desperate extremity so changed the hearts of the savages that they brought such plenty of their fruits and provision as no man wanted.

And now where some affirmed it was ill done of the Council[12] to send forth men so badly provided, this incontradictable reason will show them plainly they are too ill advised to nourish such ill conceits: First, the fault of our going was our own: what could be thought fitting or necessary we had, but what we should find, or want, or where we should be, we were all ignorant and supposing to make our passage in two months, with victual to live and the advantage of the spring to work; we were at sea five months where we both spent our victual and lost the opportunity of the time and season to plant, by the unskillful presumption of our ignorant transporters that understood not at all what they undertook.

Such actions have ever since the world's beginning been subject to such accidents, and everything of worth is found full of difficulties, but nothing so difficult as to establish a commonwealth so far remote from men and means

---

4. **common kettle.** Public or general cooking pot
5. **President.** Edward Maria Wingfield (circa 1560–1613), first president of Virginia colony
6. **private.** Private or personal stock
7. **sack.** Dry, Spanish white wine, popular in England during the sixteenth and seventeenth centuries
8. **aqua vitae.** Brandy
9. **palisades.** Pointed stakes set in the ground to form a fence for fortification or defense
10. **sturgeon.** Large, edible, bony fish
11. **pinnace.** Small sailing ship
12. **Council.** Group in charge of the Virginia experiment

---

**WORDS FOR EVERYDAY USE**

**glut • ton • y** (glut´'n ē) *n.*, habit or act of eating too much. *Gladys was sickened by the gluttony she witnessed at the pie-eating contest.*

**can • on • ize** (kan´ən īz´) *vt.*, declare a deceased person a saint in formal church procedure. *Saint Joan of Arc was canonized by the church in 1920.*

**ex • trem • i • ty** (ek strem´ə tē) *n.*, state of extreme necessity or danger. *As they faced the oncoming blizzard, the extremity of their situation instilled fear into the hearts of the skiers.*

**con • ceit** (kən sēt´) *n.*, idea, thought; personal opinion. *Hakim never shares his thoughts, so it is impossible to know what conceits arise in his mind.*

**pre • sump • tion** (prē zump´shən) *n.*, overstepping of proper bounds or the taking of something for granted. *I was shocked when my new roommate had the presumption to throw out my old couch.*

and where men's minds are so untoward[13] as neither do well themselves nor suffer others. But to proceed.

The new President and Martin, being little beloved, of weak judgment in dangers, and less industry in peace, committed the managing of all things abroad[14] to Captain Smith, who, by his own example, good words, and fair promises set some to mow, others to bind thatch, some to build houses, others to thatch them, himself always bearing the greatest task for his own share, so that in short time he provided most of them lodgings, neglecting any for himself . . .

*What type of person was Captain Smith?*

Leading an expedition on the Chickahominy River, Captain Smith and his men are attacked by Indians, and Smith is taken prisoner.

When this news came to Jamestown, much was their sorrow for his loss, few expecting what <u>ensued</u>.

Six or seven weeks those barbarians kept him prisoner, many strange triumphs and <u>conjurations</u> they made of him, yet he so demeaned himself amongst them, as he not only diverted them from surprising the fort, but procured his own liberty, and got himself and his company such estimation amongst them, that those savages admired him.

The manner how they used and delivered him is as followeth:

The savages having drawn from George Cassen whither Captain Smith was gone, prosecuting[15] that opportunity they followed him with three hundred bowmen, conducted by the King of Pamunkee, who in divisions searching the turnings of the river found Robinson and Emry by the fireside; those they shot full of arrows and slew. Then finding the Captain, as is said, that used the savage that was his guide as his shield (three of them being slain and divers[16] others so galled),[17] all the rest would not come near him. Thinking thus to have returned to his boat, regarding them, as he marched, more than his way, slipped up to the middle in an oozy creek and his savage with him; yet dared they not come to him till being near dead with cold he threw away his arms. Then according to their composition[18] they drew him forth and led him to the fire where his men were slain. Diligently they chafed his benumbed limbs.

He demanding for their captain, they showed him Opechancanough, King of Pamunkee, to whom he gave a round ivory double compass dial. Much they marveled at the playing of the fly and needle,[19] which they could see so plainly and yet not touch it because of the glass that covered them. But when he demonstrated by that globe-like jewel the roundness of the earth and skies, the sphere of the sun, moon, and stars, and how the sun did chase the night round about the world continually, the greatness of the land and sea, the <u>diversity</u> of nations, variety of complexions, and how we were to them antipodes[20] and many other such like matters, they all stood as amazed with admiration.

*What did Smith give to Opechancanough?*

*What does Smith say he demonstrated with the compass?*

---

13. **untoward.** Stubborn
14. **abroad.** Outside of the enclosed camp
15. **prosecuting.** Following up or pursuing
16. **divers.** Several
17. **galled.** Wounded
18. **composition.** Habits; customary manners
19. **fly and needle.** Parts of a compass
20. **antipodes.** On opposite sides of the earth

**WORDS FOR EVERYDAY USE**

**en • sue** (en sü´) *vi.*, come afterward; follow immediately. *After Rodney's antagonistic speech, a scuffle <u>ensued</u>.*

**con • jur • a • tion** (kän´jü rā´shən) *n.*, magic; sorcery. *Through a strange <u>conjuration</u>, the cow appeared to vanish into thin air.*

**di • ver • si • ty** (də vʉr´sə tē) *n.*, variety. *The <u>diversity</u> of the museum's collection made it fascinating to people with far-reaching interests.*

Notwithstanding, within an hour after, they tied him to a tree, and as many as could stand about him prepared to shoot him, but the King holding up the compass in his hand, they all laid down their bows and arrows and in a triumphant manner led him to Orapaks where he was after their manner kindly feasted and well used. . . .

What happened to Smith despite his demonstration? Who saved him? How did this person save him?

At last they brought him to Werowocomoco, where was Powhatan, their Emperor. Here more than two hundred of those grim courtiers stood wondering at him, as he had been a monster, till Powhatan and his train had put themselves in their greatest braveries. Before a fire upon a seat like a bedstead, he sat covered with a great robe made of raccoon skins and all the tails hanging by. On either hand did sit a young wench of sixteen or eighteen years and along on each side the house, two rows of men and behind them as many women, with all their heads and shoulders painted red, many of their heads bedecked with the white down of birds, but every one with something, and a great chain of white beads about their necks.

At his entrance before the King, all the people gave a great shout. The Queen of Appomattoc was appointed to bring him water to wash his hands, and another brought him a bunch of feathers, instead of a towel, to dry

***Pocahontas***, c.1616. Unknown Artist, after Simon van de Passe. The National Portrait Gallery, Washington, DC.

them; having feasted him after their best barbarous manner they could, a long consultation was held, but the conclusion was, two great stones were brought before Powhatan; then as many as could, laid hands on him, dragged him to them, and thereon laid his head and being ready with their clubs to beat out his brains, Pocahontas, the King's dearest daughter, when no <u>entreaty</u> could prevail, got his head in her arms and laid her own upon his to save him from death; whereat the Emperor was contented he should live to make him hatchets, and her bells, beads, and copper, for they thought him as well of all occupations as themselves.[21] For the King himself will make his own robes, shoes, bows, arrows, pots; plant, hunt, or do anything so well as the rest.

Two days after, Powhatan, having disguised himself in the most fearfulest manner he could, caused Captain Smith to be brought forth to a great house in the woods and there upon a mat by the fire to be left alone. Not long after, from behind a mat that divided the house, was made the most <u>dolefulest</u> noise he ever heard; then Powhatan more like a devil than a man, with some two hundred more as black as himself, came unto him and told him now they were friends, and presently he should go to Jamestown to send him two great guns

---

21. **him as well . . . as themselves.** He had as much capability as they did.

---

**WORDS FOR EVERYDAY USE**

**en • treat • y** (en trēt ´ē) *n.*, earnest request. *Once Doug has made up his mind, no <u>entreaty</u> will make him change it.*

**dole • ful** (dōl´fəl) *adj.*, full of or causing sorrow or sadness. *Cleo's joyful cry was halted by the <u>doleful</u> look on the messenger's face.*

and a grindstone for which he would give him the country of Capahowasic and forever esteem him as his son Nantaquond.

So to Jamestown with twelve guides Powhatan sent him. That night they quartered in the woods, he still expecting (as he had done all this long time of his imprisonment) every hour to be put to one death or other, for all their feasting. But almighty God (by His divine providence) had <u>mollified</u> the hearts of those stern barbarians with compassion. The next morning betimes[22] they came to the fort, where Smith having used the savages with what kindness he could, he showed Rawhunt, Powhatan's trusty servant, two demiculverins[23] and a millstone to carry Powhatan: they found them somewhat too heavy, but when they did see him discharge them, being loaded with stones, among the boughs of a great tree loaded with icicles, the ice and branches came so tumbling down that the poor savages ran away half dead with fear. But at last we regained some conference with them and gave them such toys and sent to Powhatan, his women, and children such presents as gave them in general full content.

Now in Jamestown they were all in combustion, the strongest preparing once more to run away with the pinnace; which, with the hazard of his life, with saker falcon[24] and musket shot, Smith forced now the third time to stay or sink.

Some, no better than they should be, had plotted with the President the next day to have him put to death by the Levitical law,[25] for the lives of Robinson and Emry; pretending the fault was his that had led them to their ends; but he quickly took such order with such lawyers that he laid them by their heels till he sent some of them prisoners for England.

What did some of the colonists wish to do with Smith? Why did they wish to do this?

Now every once in four or five days, Pocahontas with her attendants brought him so much provision that saved many of their lives, that else for all this had starved with hunger.

Who saved the colonists?

His relation of the plenty he had seen, especially at Werowocomoco, and of the state and bounty of Powhatan (which till that time was unknown), so revived their dead spirits (especially the love of Pocahontas) as all men's fear was abandoned.

Thus you may see what difficulties still crossed any good endeavor; and the good success of the business being thus oft brought to the very period of destruction: yet you see by what strange means God hath still delivered it. ■

---

22. **betimes.** Early
23. **demiculverins.** Large cannons
24. **saker falcon.** Small cannon
25. **Levitical law.** Biblical law from the Old Testament that states "He that killeth man shall surely be put to death" (Leviticus 24:17)

**WORDS FOR EVERYDAY USE**

mol • li • fy (mäl´ə fī´) vt., soothe the temper of. *As Antonio ranted about the fiasco, Carmen tried to <u>mollify</u> him with calming words.*

## Respond *to the* SELECTION

If you had been in Smith's place in Powhatan's village, what emotions might you have been feeling?

# INVESTIGATE, Inquire, Imagine

## Recall: GATHERING FACTS

1a. Describe the people present at Werowocomoco when John Smith is brought there. Who are they, and what do they look like?

2a. Who orders John Smith's execution? Who saves Smith from death? How does she save him?

3a. What does Pocahontas bring to Smith and his fellow colonists regularly after the rescue? How do her gifts help the colonists?

## Interpret: FINDING MEANING

1b. Why do you think Powhatan dresses himself in his "greatest braveries" to speak with John Smith? Why does Smith feel that the courtiers treat him "as if he had been a monster"? Explain why this is a natural reaction to Smith's presence in the village.

2b. Smith's account explains very little about Pocahontas, leaving the reader free to build a story around the bare facts he presents. Why do you think Pocahontas saves Smith's life?

3b. Why is the meeting with Powhatan crucial to the survival of the colony of Jamestown?

## Analyze: TAKING THINGS APART

4a. What qualities did it take to be an early colonist in Virginia? What qualities of character did Powhatan and Pocahontas show in their first meeting with a European?

## Synthesize: BRINGING THINGS TOGETHER

4b. How would you describe the relationship between the colonists and Powhatan's people? How do you think the two groups regard each other, both before and after Smith's encounter with Powhatan? Explain, using details from the selection to support your answer.

## Evaluate: MAKING JUDGMENTS

5a. It is possible that Smith was never in danger from Powhatan at all, that he misunderstood a custom of Powhatan's people and mistakenly assumed he was in mortal danger. He also may have exaggerated the story. Why do you think Smith told this story over and over again and included it in his history fifteen years later? Do you think Smith believed his interpretation of the events fifteen years later, or might he have had other reasons for telling the story?

## Extend: CONNECTING IDEAS

5b. Describe a time in which you exaggerated a story. Why did you do so?

# Understanding Literature

**CHRONOLOGICAL ORDER.** Review the definition of **chronological order** in Literary Tools. Do you think chronological order was an effective choice of order for this selection? Why, or why not? What other method of organization might be used for telling Smith's story, or part of the story? Refer to the Language Arts Survey 2.24, "Organizing Ideas."

Next, create a time line like the one below that plots the sequence of events in John Smith's account. Refer to the Language Arts Survey 2.19, "Time Lines."

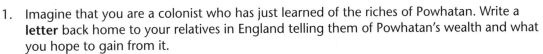

| May 1606 | | September 1606 | 1607 |

Ships return for England   Colonists become ill

**POINT OF VIEW.** Read the complete definition of **point of view** in the Handbook of Literary Terms. In this selection the point of view changes from first to third person. Why do you think Smith chose to use third person point of view? Compare the point of view used by John Smith to the point of view used by de las Casas in the previous selection. Why do both authors use this point of view?

# WRITER'S JOURNAL

1. Imagine that you are a colonist who has just learned of the riches of Powhatan. Write a **letter** back home to your relatives in England telling them of Powhatan's wealth and what you hope to gain from it.

2. In your journal, compose a **speech** that Pocahontas might have given in defense of John Smith, persuading her people to spare his life. Give reasons why Smith should be saved.

3. Imagine that you are one of Powhatan's people and you are present at the capture of John Smith and his meeting with Powhatan. Write a **journal entry** describing your feelings toward John Smith, including your observations about his character and appearance. Use your imagination when describing him, or consult pictures of American colonists from the 1600s for reference on the clothing of the day. Do you view Smith as a monster, a successful pioneer, or in what other way do you see him?

# Integrating *the* LANGUAGE ARTS

## Study and Research & Collaborative Learning

**HISTORICAL RESEARCH.** With a partner, research an element of John Smith's story. For example, you may choose to research the life of John Smith, the culture of one of the native peoples of New England, life in the early colonies of the Americas, or the life of Pocahontas. Present your findings to the class as an oral report.

## Media Literacy

**CRITICAL ANALYSIS OF INTERPRETATIONS.** Compare Smith's factual account of his dealings with Pocahontas with fictional or dramatic interpretations of the Pocahontas story, such as the Disney movie *Pocahontas*. What fictional elements were added to these interpretations?

## Literary TOOLS

**AIM.** A writer's **aim** is his or her purpose, or goal. The aim of the *Primer* was education. As you read this selection, think about what it was trying to teach.

**COUPLET.** A **couplet** is a pair of rhyming lines that express a complete thought. This selection is composed mostly of couplets, with one exception. As you read, try to identify the rhyme that is not a couplet.

Make a chart like the one below to classify each rhyme by the subject area it deals with. (For example, the rhyme for C could go under the classification "Animals.") Identify each class, and list the letters whose verses share the characteristics of that class. Some verses may fit under more than one class.

| Classifications | Animals and Nature | |
|---|---|---|
| Alphabet Rhymes from *The New England Primer* | C | |

## Reader's *Journal*

What do you remember learning from illustrated alphabet books with rhymes or pictures when you were younger?

FROM

# THE NEW ENGLAND Primer

ANONYMOUS

## About *the* SELECTION

*The New England Primer* was the first textbook produced in America to teach reading. Evidence places publication of the first edition between 1687 and 1690. Since the New England colonies were founded for religious reasons, it was only natural that religion formed the basis of all education and therefore dominated the book. Its contents included the Lord's Prayer, the Apostles' Creed, a series of moral and instructive sentences from the Bible, and an illustrated alphabet. The *Primer* was popular throughout the English colonies and was sold in the United States until the nineteenth century. The excerpt here is the alphabet from the 1727 edition of the *Primer*.

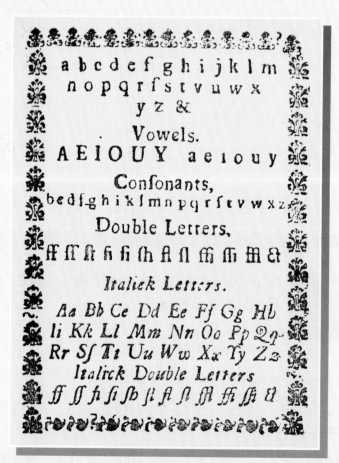

FROM THE NEW ENGLAND **Primer**  ANONYMOUS

**A**
In *Adam's* Fall
We finned[1] all.

**B**
Thy Life to mend
This *Book* attend.

**C**
The *Cat* doth play
And after flay.

**D**
A *Dog* will bite
A Thief at Night.

**E**
An *Eagles* Flight
Is out of Sight.

**F**
An idle *Fool*
Is whipt at School.

**G**
As runs the *Glafs*
Man's life doth pafs.

**H**
My *Book* and *Heart*
Shall never part.

**J**
*Job* feels the Rod
Yet bleffes GOD.

**K**
Our *K I N G* the good
No man of blood.

**L**
The *Lion* bold
The *Lamb* doth hold.

**M**
The *Moon* gives light
In time of night.

**N**
*Nightingales* fing
In Time of Spring.

**O**
The *Royal Oak*
it was the Tree
That fav'd His
Royal Majeftie.

**P**
*Peter* denies
His Lord and cries

**Q**
Queen *Efther* comes
in Royal State
To Save the Jews
from difmal Fate

**R**
*Rachol* doth mourn
For her firft born.

**S**
*Samuel* anoints
Whom God appoints:

**T**
*Time* cuts down all
Both great and fmall.

**U**
*Uriah's* beauteous Wife
Made *David* feek his
Life.

**W**
*Whales* in the Sea
God's Voice obey.

**X**
*Xerxes* the great did
die,
And fo muft you & I.

**Y**
*Youth* forward flips
Death fooneft nips.

**Z**
*Zacheus* he
Did climb the Tree
His Lord to Fee.  ■

*Why should a student pay close attention to this book, according to the instruction for the letter B?*

*What might the description "No man of blood" mean in the description for the letter K?*

*What attitude toward death is expressed in the entries for X and Y?*

1. **finned.** Sinned. The letter *s* often appears as an *f* in the early print style of the *Primer.*

**Respond** *to the* **SELECTION**

If you were a young colonial child reading the *Primer,* what would you learn about religion and attitudes toward life?

# INVESTIGATE, Inquire, Imagine

**Recall:** GATHERING FACTS

1a. What animals appear in the rhyme for the letter *L*?

2a. Which letters have rhymes that might refer to a book?

3a. To what kind of glass does the rhyme for the letter *G* refer?

**Interpret:** FINDING MEANING

1b. What two qualities might the animals referred to in the rhyme for the letter *L* represent?

2b. Explain the couplets for the letters *B* and *H*. To what book might these couplets refer?

3b. What does the rhyme for the letter *F* tell about the treatment of school children during the time the *Primer* was in use?

**Analyze:** TAKING THINGS APART

4a. During an era of political chaos and revolution in seventeenth-century England, the king saved himself from enemies by hiding in a tree. Which letter has a rhyme referring to this incident? Which other rhyme refers to the political leadership of the day? Which rhymes refer to moral teachings?

**Synthesize:** BRINGING THINGS TOGETHER

4b. Based on this selection, how did the Puritans feel about their leadership? What can you tell about the differences between education and culture in the 1600s and 1700s and education and culture today?

**Evaluate:** MAKING JUDGMENTS

5a. At least three rhymes warn of age and death. Identify the letters with these rhymes. Do you think that these are appropriate rhymes for children? Why, or why not?

**Extend:** CONNECTING IDEAS

5b. Make up new rhymes to replace the ones that you think are not appropriate for children of today. Try to incorporate topics that are emphasized in school today, such as cooperation, environmental awareness, tolerance and diversity, drug awareness, and global consumerism. Explain why you wrote each new couplet the way that you did.

# Understanding Literature

**AIM.** A writer's **aim** is the primary purpose that his or her work is meant to achieve. The aim of the *Primer* was education, but education in what areas? What descriptions within the alphabet support your answer?

**COUPLET.** A **couplet** is a pair of rhyming lines that express a complete thought. Which letter is given a verse that is not a couplet? How would you describe that particular verse? Several of the couplets are written in more than two lines of type simply because the width of the page limits the number of characters on a line. Identify one of those couplets, writing it in couplet form.

# WRITER'S JOURNAL

1. In your journal, write three **couplets** about lessons you learned as a child, and then share them with your classmates.

2. A **curriculum** consists of the courses provided by a school. What courses would you need to understand all the references in the *Primer* alphabet? Write a curriculum for your studies, with a short description for each course.

3. Write a **lesson story** for an audience of young children, with the aim not merely of entertaining your audience, but also of educating the children about good behavior. Choose a behavior you wish to promote. Then write a short story that demonstrates why this behavior is desired. You may wish to demonstrate rewards for following the behavior and punishments for deviating from such behavior. Refer to the Language Arts Survey 3.3, "Register, Tone, and Voice."

# Integrating *the* LANGUAGE ARTS

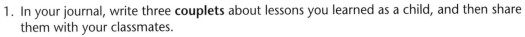

## Language, Grammar, and Style

LINKING VERBS. Read the Language Arts Survey 3.10, "Linking Verbs." On a separate sheet of paper, write each verb from the following sentences. Underline each linking verb.

1. Some modern people feel ignorant when they read Puritan writings.

2. Although the language looks familiar, its meaning is sometimes obscure because of historical and religious references with which modern-day people are often unfamiliar.

3. Footnotes are one means of providing information about obscure references in literary works and other written materials.

4. Religion was the central force within the Puritan community, and all aspects of life felt its influence.

5. That is why Puritan writings were full of religious references.

## Study and Research

ANNOTATIONS. An **annotation** for a literary work is an explanatory note for some part of that work. For example, annotations often appear as footnotes that explain difficult vocabulary and obscure references. If you are unfamiliar with the references in the *Primer*, do some research to familiarize yourself with them. Write two annotations for the section of the alphabet from *O* through *S*.

## Collaborative Learning & Media Literacy

POP CULTURE ALPHABET BOOK. With a small group, create an original alphabet book in which you associate the letters with elements of pop culture or the popular media (example: *R* is for *rap*). Begin with a brainstorming session during which all suggestions are listed. Next, vote on the best word for each letter and decide which form to use—phrases, couplets, or another form. Divide the alphabet among the group members and write the entries. Illustrate them as your group chooses. Finally, assemble the pages, and add a title page and cover.

## Literary
### TOOLS

**HYPERBOLE.** A **hyperbole** is an exaggeration made for rhetorical effect. Notice how Bradstreet uses hyperbole in this selection in order to express her love for her husband.

**PARADOX.** A **paradox** is a seemingly contradictory statement, idea, or event. As you read, look for a paradox in this poem.

## Reader's
*Journal*

When you choose greeting cards for birthdays or special events, what sorts of messages do you prefer? For whom might you buy a poem and for what occasion?

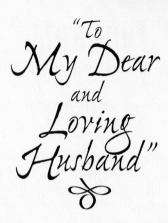

*"To My Dear and Loving Husband"*

BY ANNE BRADSTREET

## About *the* AUTHOR

**Anne Bradstreet** (*circa* 1612–1672) had the advantage of an education unusual for women of her time and began writing poetry as a child. She married Simon Bradstreet, a graduate of Cambridge University and an associate of her father, when she was only sixteen. A year after marriage to Anne, Simon was appointed to assist in the preparations of the Massachusetts Bay Company, and the Bradstreets sailed to the New World. Life in the new world was hard, especially for Anne, who had been weakened by a childhood illness. When her husband became governor of the Bay Colony, Anne's duties increased as well. Despite her many obligations, Bradstreet found time to continue writing poetry, as she had when she was a young girl. Unknown to Anne, her brother-in-law had a collection of her poetry printed in London in 1650—the first published volume of poems by a New World resident.

## About *the* SELECTION

The date of composition of **"To My Dear and Loving Husband,"** like most of Anne Bradstreet's work, is unknown. Originally, she distributed her writings only among family and friends, but after publication of some poems, she then decided to put out a second, authorized edition. That second edition did not appear until after her death, being published in Boston in 1678. "To My Dear and Loving Husband" appeared in the second edition. The poem remains a noble expression of the sustaining and transforming power of love.

# To My Dear and Loving Husband

**ANNE BRADSTREET**

*Elizabeth Freake and Baby Mary.* c.1671–1674.
American Artist, Worcester Art Museum, Worcester, MA.

If ever two were one, then surely we.
If ever man were loved by wife, then thee;
If ever wife was happy in a man,
Compare with me, ye women, if you can.
5   I prize thy love more than whole mines of gold
Or all the riches that the East doth hold.
My love is such that rivers cannot quench,
Nor ought but love from thee, give <u>recompense</u>.
Thy love is such I can no way repay,
10   The heavens reward thee <u>manifold</u>, I pray.
Then while we live, in love let's so <u>persevere</u>
That when we live no more, we may live ever. ■

*How much does the speaker prize her husband's love?*

*If the couple persevere in their love, what will be the consequences?*

**WORDS FOR EVERYDAY USE**

**rec • om • pense** (rek´əm pens´) *n.,* reward; compensation, payment. *The only <u>recompense</u> the volunteers received was the thanks of the people they helped.*

**man • i • fold** (man´ə fōld´) *adv.,* in many forms or ways. *Their parents hoped that the marriage would increase the <u>newlywed's</u> blessings manifold.*

**per • se • vere** (pur´sə vir´) *vi.,* continue in spite of difficulty; persist. *After the battle, the general shouted, "We must <u>persevere</u>! Onward, troops!"*

What is special about the relationship that Anne Bradstreet describes? What enables people to develop this sort of relationship?

# INVESTIGATE, Inquire, *Imagine*

**Recall:** GATHERING FACTS

1a. Both lines 1 and 2 consist of elliptical sentences—that is, not all the words are provided; some are understood. Write out the complete sentences, supplying the understood words. (If you like, use *you* instead of *thee.*)

2a. What is the sense, or meaning, of *prize* in line 5?

3a. *Recompense* means "payment." What is the one thing that can be recompense for the speaker's love?

→ **Interpret:** FINDING MEANING

1b. Why did Bradstreet use elliptical sentences? What effect do they have on the poem?

2b. Complete the comparison suggested in line 7 by the use of the word *quenched:* My love is like _____.

3b. Restate line 10 in your own words.

**Analyze:** TAKING THINGS APART

4a. Is there any objective proof that Anne Bradstreet's love for her husband is reciprocated, or are all her statements subjective? Support your answer.

→ **Synthesize:** BRINGING THINGS TOGETHER

4b. What does the speaker believe about the afterlife and about the consequences of being, in this life, someone who perseveres in love despite its difficulties?

**Evaluate:** MAKING JUDGMENTS

5a. In your own words, how would you describe the relationship between the speaker and her husband? Do you think the poem is an accurate or an idealized picture of the relationship they have? Why, or why not?

→ **Extend:** CONNECTING IDEAS

5b. What sorts of difficulties might these people or any married people face? Why is it important to any relationship to be willing to persevere in spite of difficulties? Do you know anyone who has as loving a relationship as that which is depicted in the poem? Describe their relationship.

# Understanding *Literature*

**HYPERBOLE.** Review the definition for **hyperbole** in the Handbook of Literary Terms. Find an instance of hyperbole in this poem.

**PARADOX.** Review the definition for **paradox** in the Handbook of Literary Terms. What paradoxical statement appears in the final lines of this poem? Why do you suppose the poet chose to use this technique? What is its effect?

# Writer's Journal

1. Write three **hyperbole**, each one about any person, thing, or quality you choose. For example, you might write a hyperbole to exaggerate the sharpness of your wit or the coldness of the weather.

2. Write the text of a **greeting card** you wish to send to a friend or relative to tell them how much you care. You may choose the form of a poem, or you may simply write in prose. Try to use creative language to make your message unique.

3. Sight rhyme is a pair of words, generally at the ends of lines of verse, that are spelled similarly but pronounced differently. Find an example of sight rhyme in the poem "To My Dear and Loving Husband." Then write a short **poem** (4–6 lines minimum) using a sight rhyme couplet at least once. The poem can be about someone you love, or something you love, such as a certain place, a certain activity, or your favorite food.

# Integrating *the* LANGUAGE ARTS

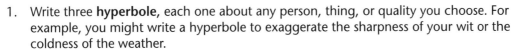

## Language, Grammar, and Style

**INVERTING SENTENCES FOR EMPHASIS.** Read the Language Arts Survey 3.26, "Working with Inverted Sentences." Then rewrite these lines in usual word order, that is, *subject-verb-object.*

1. My love I have not confessed.
2. Not to keep secrets, it's best.
3. Thy love I cannot repay.
4. The heavens reward thee, I pray.
5. My future in your hands I rest.

## Study and Research

**FORMAL NOTE-TAKING.** Read the Language Arts Survey 5.39, "Informal and Formal Note-Taking." Then look up Anne Bradstreet in two library reference books. Take notes from each reference book, using the note form recommended in the Language Arts Survey.

## Collaborative Learning & Media Literacy

**ROLE-PLAY.** With another classmate, role-play an interview with Anne Bradstreet in which one of you plays the role of a modern-day marriage counselor and the other plays Anne Bradstreet. If you play the role of the counselor, ask questions about Bradstreet's relationship with her husband and what makes it successful. Avoid yes-no questions and think of creative questions that will allow your interviewee to give thoughtful, detailed answers. If you play the role of Anne Bradstreet, tell about your shared interests with your husband and explain what makes your relationship a good one. Write out the finished "interview," including both the questions and the answers. Refer to the Language Arts Survey 4.14, "Conducting an Interview," for help.

## Literary TOOLS

**EMPHASIS. Emphasis** is importance placed on an element in a literary work. Repetition and elaboration are two of the techniques used to produce emphasis. This dramatic sermon employs both techniques.

**ANALOGY.** An **analogy** is a comparison of two things that are alike in some respects. Often an analogy explains or describes something unfamiliar by comparing it to something more familiar. A *simile* is an expressed analogy; a *metaphor* is an implied analogy. In this sermon, Edwards uses analogy in order to give his listeners a clear, concrete picture of the abstract ideas he presents.

Create a chart like the one below to list analogies you find in Edwards's piece. In one column write the thing being described, and in the other, write the thing it is likened to. You may restate the analogies in your own words or quote the passage directly if you wish.

| Thing being described | What it is likened to |
| --- | --- |
| Physical means of keeping you alive cannot prevent you from dying and going to hell if God withdraws support. | Thin air cannot hold up a person suspended in it. |

## Reader's Journal

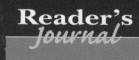

What does the word *grace* mean to you? In what ways can people extend grace to those around them?

FROM

# "Sinners in the Hands of an Angry God"

BY JONATHAN EDWARDS

## About the AUTHOR

**Jonathan Edwards** (1703–1758) was born in East Windsor, Connecticut. He was a dedicated scholar even as a child and was admitted to Yale College when he was only thirteen. Edwards flourished in the rigorous academic setting and devoted himself to the study of theology. Edwards came from a line of noteworthy ministers and was determined to carry on his family's tradition. Edwards moved to Northampton, Massachusetts, where he succeeded his grandfather as minister of the local church, married, and raised a family.

Edwards's goal as a minister was not only to heighten his followers' commitment to religion but to enrich their religious experience. Known for his vivid and fiery sermons, Edwards sought to make religion so moving and real that it was almost a physical experience. Edwards's religious views gained great popularity and began the Great Awakening, a religious revival that swept across the colonies in the 1730s. When he decided, however, to actually name prestigious members of the clergy who were not expressing the proper devotion and reinstate the rite of communion, he was dismissed from his church. Edwards then served as a missionary to the Housatonic Indians and was elected president of the College of New Jersey (now Princeton).

## About the SELECTION

The following excerpt is from "**Sinners in the Hands of an Angry God,**" a sermon Edwards delivered in Enfield, Connecticut, on Sunday, July 8, 1741. Another minister who was present reported that Edwards spoke with calm dignity, yet the effect was highly emotional, with "such a breathing of distress, and weeping, that the preacher was obliged to speak to the people and desire silence, that he might be heard." The text of the sermon was published over eighty years later, in 1829–1830, in a multi-volume edition of Edwards's works.

*The Sermon,* 1886. Gari Melchers. National Museum of American Art, Washington, DC.

FROM

# Sinners *in the* Hands *of an* Angry God

## JONATHAN EDWARDS

You probably are not sensible[1] of this; you find you are kept out of hell, but do not see the hand of God in it; but look at other things, as the good state of your bodily <u>constitution</u>, your care of your own life, and the means you use for your own preservation. But indeed these things are nothing; if God should withdraw His

1. **sensible.** Aware

WORDS
FOR
EVERYDAY
USE

**con • sti • tu • tion** (kän´stə tü ´shən) *n.,* physical makeup of a person. *Fran's <u>constitution</u> suffered from sitting at a desk for hours with no time to exercise.*

hand, they would <u>avail</u> no more to keep you from falling, than the thin air to hold up a person that is suspended in it.

Your wickedness makes you as it were heavy as lead, and to tend downwards with great weight and pressure towards hell; and if God should let you go, you would immediately sink and swiftly descend and plunge into the bottomless <u>gulf</u>, and your healthy constitution, and your own care and prudence, and best <u>contrivance</u>, and all your righteousness, would have no more influence to uphold you and keep you out of hell, than a spider's web would have to stop a fallen rock. Were it not for the <u>sovereign</u> pleasure of God, the earth would not bear you one moment; for you are a burden to it; the creation groans with you; the creature is made subject to the bondage of your corruption, not willingly; the sun does not willingly shine upon you to give you light to serve sin and Satan; the earth does not willingly yield her increase[2] to satisfy your lusts; nor is it willingly a stage for your wickedness to be acted upon; the air does not willingly serve you for breath to maintain the flame of life in your vitals,[3] while you spend your life in the service of God's enemies. God's creatures are good, and were made for men to serve God with, and do not willingly <u>subserve</u> to any other purpose, and groan when they are abused to purposes so directly contrary to their nature and end. And the world would spew[4] you out, were it not for the sovereign hand of Him who hath subjected it in hope. There are

> According to Edwards, what would happen to people if God withdrew his hand? What would fail to save them?

> To what are people a burden, according to Edwards?

black clouds of God's wrath now hanging directly over your heads, full of the dreadful storm, and big with thunder; and were it not for the restraining hand of God, it would immediately burst forth upon you. The sovereign pleasure of God, for the present, stays His rough wind; otherwise it would come with fury, and your destruction would come like a whirlwind, and you would be like the chaff of the summer threshing floor. . . .[5]

> What is hanging directly over the heads of people?

The bow of God's wrath is bent, and the arrow made ready on the string, and justice bends the arrow at your heart, and strains the bow, and it is nothing but the mere pleasure of God, and that of an angry God, without any promise or obligation at all, that keeps the arrow one moment from being made drunk with your blood. Thus all you that never passed under a great change of heart, by the mighty power of the Spirit of God upon your souls, all you that were never born again, and made new creatures, and raised from being dead in sin, to a state of new, and before altogether unexperienced light and life, are in the hands of an angry God. However you may have reformed your life in many things, and may have had religious affections,[6] and may keep up a form of religion in your families and closets,[7]

> Which people are in the hands of an angry God?

---

2. **increase.** Harvest
3. **vitals.** Necessary organs
4. **spew.** Throw up; eject
5. **chaff . . . threshing floor.** *Chaff*—husks of wheat that are left behind; *threshing floor*—place where grain is separated from its husks
6. **affections.** Feelings
7. **closets.** Studies; meditations

---

**WORDS FOR EVERYDAY USE**

**a • vail** (ə vāl´) *vi.,* be of use or advantage. *Maurice's attempts to get concert tickets <u>availed</u> nothing, for they were sold out.*

**gulf** (gulf) *n.,* wide, deep gap or separation. *People cross <u>gulfs</u> upon fallen trees in the movies, but I dared not cross the cavernous drop myself.*

**con • triv • ance** (kən trī´vəns) *n.,* invention; ingenious plan. *I feared we'd be trapped in the pit for days, but Mara's clever <u>contrivance</u> freed us in no time.*

**sov • er • eign** (sä´və rən) *adj.,* above or superior to all others. *With <u>sovereign</u> power, the superintendent decided the truant student's fate.*

**sub • serve** (səb sʉrv´) *vt.,* be useful or helpful; serve. *The pious nun <u>subserved</u> her God.*

and in the house of God, it is nothing but His mere pleasure that keeps you from being this moment swallowed up in everlasting destruction. However unconvinced you may now be of the truth of what you hear, by and by you will be fully convinced of it. Those that are gone from being in the like circumstances with you see that it was so with them; for destruction came suddenly upon most of them; when they expected nothing of it and while they were saying, peace and safety: now they see that those things on which they depended for peace and safety, were nothing but thin air and empty shadows.

How does Edwards address those who may doubt his words?

The God that holds you over the pit of hell, much as one holds a spider or some <u>loathsome</u> insect over the fire, <u>abhors</u> you, and is dreadfully <u>provoked</u>: His wrath towards you burns like fire; He looks upon you as worthy of nothing else but to be cast into the fire; He is of purer eyes than to bear to have you in His sight; you are ten thousand times more abominable in His eyes than the most hateful venomous serpent is in ours. You have offended Him infinitely more than ever a stubborn rebel did his prince; and yet it is nothing but His hand that holds you from falling into the fire every moment. It is to be <u>ascribed</u> to nothing else, that you did not go to hell the last night; that you was suffered to awake again in this world, after you closed your eyes to sleep. And there is no other reason to be given, why you have not dropped into hell since you arose in the morning, but that God's hand has held you up. There is no other reason to be given why you have not gone to hell, since you have sat here in the house of God, provoking His pure eyes by your sinful wicked manner of attending His solemn worship. Yea, there is nothing else that is to be given as a reason why you do not this very moment drop down into hell.

O sinner! Consider the fearful danger you are in: it is a great furnace of wrath, a wide and bottomless pit, full of the fire of wrath, that you are held over in the hand of that God, whose wrath is provoked and <u>incensed</u> as much against you, as against many of the damned in hell. You hang by a slender thread, with the flames of divine wrath flashing about it, and ready every moment to singe it, and burn it asunder; and you have no interest in any Mediator, and nothing to lay hold of to save yourself, nothing to keep off the flames of wrath, nothing of your own, nothing that you have done, nothing that you can do, to <u>induce</u> God to spare you one moment. ∎

According to Edwards, how much control do people who are sinful in the eyes of God have over their destinies?

| WORDS FOR EVERYDAY USE | |
|---|---|
| **loath • some** (lōth´səm) *adj.,* disgusting. *The <u>loathsome</u> beast left a trail of slime in the wake of its destruction.* | |
| **ab • hor** (ab hôr´) *vt.,* shrink from in disgust. *"I <u>abhor</u> snakes," said my aunt, looking at my reptilian pet with disgust.* | |
| **pro • voke** (prō vōk´) *vt.,* anger, irritate, annoy. *"Don't poke the dog with that stick. You'll only <u>provoke</u> him," Derek said.* | |
| **as • cribe** (ə skrīb´) *vt.,* assign; attribute. *Glenda <u>ascribed</u> her success at basketball to her mother's coaching.* | |
| **in • cense** (in sens´) *vt.,* make very angry. *Muriel was <u>incensed</u> when she found Myron had stolen her idea.* | |
| **in • duce** (in düs´) *vt.,* persuade; prevail on. *Despite the rising flood waters, no one could <u>induce</u> Otto to leave his home.* | |

## Respond *to the* SELECTION

Can you sympathize with the members of Edwards's congregation who reacted to this sermon with weeping? Why, or why not? To what emotion does this sermon appeal most?

## Recall: GATHERING FACTS

1a. According to Edwards, what does the average person think keeps him or her alive? To what does Edwards give complete credit?

2a. What are some of the elements of creation that Edwards lists as "not willingly" serving the sinner?

3a. What does Edwards claim is required to take a person out of the sinner classification?

## Interpret: FINDING MEANING

1b. In paragraph 2, Edwards compares the sinner first with a fallen rock and later with chaff on a threshing floor. What does he mean by each of these similes?

2b. Which elements of nature does Edwards use in paragraph 2 to represent God's anger? What qualities do these elements have in common with anger?

3b. What abstract ideal is personified—described as a person—in paragraph 3? In what action is this personified ideal occupied? Why is this comparison frightening?

## Analyze: TAKING THINGS APART

4a. In paragraph 4, what progression does Edwards trace in speaking of the threat to the sinner's existence?

## Synthesize: BRINGING THINGS TOGETHER

4b. Why might this progression be particularly effective in arousing fear?

## Evaluate: MAKING JUDGMENTS

5a. Do you think that this sermon could be influential, on a short-term basis, in inspiring listeners to throw themselves on the mercy of an angry God? What would you expect to be its long-term impact? Why?

## Extend: CONNECTING IDEAS

5b. Read the following speech from William Shakespeare's play *The Merchant of Venice*. Write a brief essay comparing and contrasting the view of God presented in this speech with that presented in Edwards's sermon.

> PORTIA: The quality of mercy is not strain'd,
> It droppeth as the gentle rain from heaven
> Upon the place beneath. It is twice blessed:
> It blesseth him that gives and him that takes.
> 'Tis mightiest in the mightiest, it becomes
> The throned monarch better than his crown.
> His scepter shows the force of temporal power,
> The attribute to awe and majesty,
> Wherein doth sit the dread and fear of kings;
> But mercy is above this sceptered sway,
> It is enthroned in the hearts of kings,
> It is an attribute to God himself;
> And earthly power doth then show likest God's
> When mercy seasons justice.
>
> —act 4, scene 1, *The Merchant of Venice,* William Shakespeare

# Understanding *Literature*

**EMPHASIS.** Review the definition for **emphasis** in the Handbook of Literary Terms. Identify a paragraph in which Edwards uses both repetition and elaboration to emphasize an important concept. State the concept being emphasized. Then identify the repeated words or phrases, and list some additions or changes that elaborate on the original statement.

**ANALOGY.** Review the definition for **analogy** in the Handbook of Literary Terms. Refer to the graphic organizer you completed as you read the selection. Then answer the following questions: Do you think the analogies Edwards uses are effective? Why, or why not?

## WRITER'S JOURNAL

1. Write a **journal entry** about things you would like to do to make yourself a better person. Write about your idea of a "sinner" and your idea of a holy or "pure" person. You do not have to share this journal entry with anyone.

2. Write two **metaphors** and two **similes** about what you imagine the church was like the day Edwards delivered this sermon. Avoid clichéd, or overused, phrases such as "the preacher's voice roared like thunder" or "the woman in the front row was shaking like a leaf." Try to think of creative ways to describe the scene.

3. Imagine that you are explaining the main points of this sermon to a friend. In your own words and in simple, informal language, write a **summary** of the sermon's main ideas. For example, what is the view of God that Edwards presents? Of what does Edwards warn his parishioners?

# Integrating *the* LANGUAGE ARTS

## Language, Grammar, and Style

**CONCRETE AND ABSTRACT NOUNS.** Read the Language Arts Survey 3.52, "Concrete Nouns and Abstract Nouns." On a separate sheet of paper, write each of the nouns in these sentences. Underline the concrete nouns once. Underline the abstract nouns twice.

1. Jonathan Edwards was the last great spokesperson for Puritanism.
2. The bow of God's wrath is bent and the arrow made ready on the string.
3. He wrote and spoke with such power that congregations reacted with barely controllable emotion.
4. For years, his words inspired an era of belief called "The Great Awakening."
5. Eventually, however, his inability to compromise ended in his downfall.

## Speaking and Listening

**VERBAL AND NONVERBAL COMMUNICATION.** Read the Language Arts Survey 4.1, "Verbal and Nonverbal Communication." What are some of the nonverbal signs that a speaker such as Edwards might employ in delivering a sermon? Working in small groups, describe these signs without using verbal communication. Then take turns performing Edwards's sermon, reading from the selection while using the nonverbal gestures you demonstrated earlier.

## from *Of Plymouth Plantation*
## by William Bradford

*Book I, Chapter IX. Of Their Voyage and How They Passed the Sea; and of Their Safe Arrival at Cape Cod*

**September 6.** These troubles[1] being blown over, and now all being compact together in one ship, they put to sea again with a prosperous wind, which continued divers days together, which was some encouragement unto them; yet, according to the usual manner, many were afflicted with seasickness. And I may not omit here a special work of God's providence. There was a proud and very profane young man, one of the seamen, of a lusty,[2] able body, which made him the more haughty; he would always be condemning the poor people in their sickness and cursing them daily with grievous execrations;[3] and did not let[4] to tell them that he hoped to help to cast half of them overboard before they came to their journey's end, and to make merry with what they had; and if he were by any gently reproved, he would curse and swear most bitterly. But it pleased God before they came half seas over, to smite this young man with a grievous disease, of which he died in a desperate manner, and so was himself the first that was thrown overboard. Thus his curses light on his own head, and it was an astonishment to all his fellows for they noted it to be the just hand of God upon him.

After they had enjoyed fair winds and weather for a season, they were encountered many times with cross winds and met with many fierce storms with which the ship was shroudly[5] shaken, and her upper works made very leaky; and one of the main beams in the midships was bowed and cracked, which put them in some fear that the ship could not be able to perform the voyage. So some of the chief of the company, perceiving the mariners to fear the sufficiency of the ship as appeared by their mutterings, they entered into serious consultation with the master and other officers of the ship, to consider in time of the danger, and rather to return than to cast themselves into a desperate and inevitable peril. And truly there was great distraction and difference of opinion amongst the mariners themselves; fain[6] would they do what could be done for their wages' sake (being now near half the seas over) and on the other hand they were loath to hazard their lives too desperately. But in examining of all opinions, the master and others affirmed they knew the ship to be strong and firm under water; and for the buckling of the main beam, there was a great iron screw the passengers brought out of Holland, which would raise the beam into his place; the which being done, the carpenter and master affirmed that with a post put under it, set firm in the lower deck and otherways bound, he would make it sufficient. And as for the decks and upper works, they would caulk them as well as they could, and though with the working of the ship they would not long keep staunch,[7] yet there would otherwise be no great danger, if

they did not overpress her with sails. So they committed themselves to the will of God and resolved to proceed. In sundry of these storms the winds were so fierce and the seas so high, as they could not bear a knot of sail, but were forced to hull[8] for divers days together. And in one of them, as they thus lay at hull in a mighty storm, a lusty young man called John Howland, coming upon some occasion above the gratings was, with a seele[9] of the ship, thrown into sea; but it pleased God that he caught hold of the topsail halyards[10] which hung overboard and ran out at length. Yet he held his hold (though he was sundry fathoms under water) till he was hauled up by the same rope to the brim of the water, and then with a boat hook and other means got into the ship again and his life saved. And though he was something ill with it, yet he lived many years after and became a profitable member both in church and commonwealth. In all this voyage there died but one of the passengers, which was William Butten, a youth, servant to Samuel Fuller, when they drew near the coast.

But to omit other things (that I may be brief) after long beating at sea they fell with that land which is called Cape Cod; the which being made and certainly known to be it, they were not a little joyful. After some deliberation had amongst themselves and with the master of the ship, they tacked[11] about and resolved to stand for the southward (the wind and weather being fair) to find some place about Hudson's River for their habitation. But after they had sailed that course about half the day, they fell amongst dangerous shoals and roaring breakers, and they were so far entangled therewith as they conceived themselves in great danger; and the wind shrinking upon them withal, they resolved to bear up again for the Cape and thought themselves happy to get out of those dangers before night overtook them, as by God's good providence they did. And the next day they got into Cape Harbor[12] where they rid in safety.

---

1. **troubles.** Another vessel, the *Speedwell*, had proved unseaworthy and everything was transferred to the *Mayflower*.
2. **lusty.** Strong; energetic
3. **execrations.** Curses
4. **let.** Hesitate
5. **shroudly.** Shrewdly, meaning wickedly
6. **fain.** Gladly
7. **staunch.** Watertight
8. **hull.** Drift with the wind with short sails
9. **seele.** Roll
10. **halyards.** Rope for raising and lowering a sail
11. **tacked.** Change course against the wind
12. **Cape Harbor.** The ship arrived in Cape Harbor, now known as Provincetown Harbor, on November 11, 1620, sixty-five days after leaving England.

## THE MAYFLOWER COMPACT

I shall a little return back, and begin with a combination[1] made by them before they came ashore; being the first foundation of their government in this place. Occasioned partly by the discontented and mutinous speeches that some of the strangers[2] amongst them had let fall from them in the ship: That when they came ashore they would use their own liberty, for none had power to command them, the patent[3] they had being for Virginia and not for New England, which belonged to another government, with which the Virginia Company had nothing to do. And partly that such an act by them done, this their condition considered, might be as firm as any patent, and in some respects more sure.

The form was as followeth:
IN THE NAME OF GOD, AMEN.

We whose names are underwritten, the loyal subjects of our dread Sovereign Lord King James, by the Grace of God of Great Britain, France, and Ireland King, Defender of the Faith, etc.

Having undertaken, for the Glory of God and advancement of the Christian Faith and Honor of our King and Country, a Voyage to plant the First Colony in the Northern Parts of Virginia, do by these presents solemnly and mutually in the presence of God and one of another, Covenant and Combine ourselves together into a Civil Body Politic, for our better ordering and preservation and furtherance of the ends aforesaid; and by virtue hereof to enact, constitute and frame such just and equal Laws, Ordinances, Acts, Constitutions and Offices, from time to time, as shall be thought most meet[4] and convenient for the general good of the Colony, unto which we promise all due submission and obedience. In witness whereof we have hereunder subscribed our names at Cape Cod, the 11th of November, in the year of the reign of our Sovereign Lord King James, of England, France and Ireland the eighteenth, and of Scotland the fifty-fourth. Anno Domini 1620.

## THE STARVING TIME

But that which was most sad and lamentable was, that in two or three months' time half of their company died, especially in January and February, being the depth of winter, and wanting houses and other comforts; being infected with the scurvy[5] and other diseases which this long voyage and their inaccommodate[6] condition had brought upon them. So as there died some times two or three of a day in the foresaid time, that of 100 and odd persons, scarce fifty remained. And of these, in the time of most distress, there was but six or seven persons who to their great commendations, be it spoken, spared no pains night nor day, but with abundance of toil and hazard of their own health, fetched them wood, made them fires, dressed them meat, made their beds, washed their loathsome clothes, clothed and unclothed them. In a word, did all the homely[7] and necessary offices for them which dainty and queasy stomachs cannot endure to hear named; and all this willingly and cheerfully, without any grudging in the least, showing herein their true love unto their friends and brethren; a rare example and worthy to be remembered. Two of these seven were Mr. William Brewster, their reverend Elder, and Myles Standish, their Captain and military commander, unto whom myself and many others were much beholden in our low and sick condition. And yet the Lord so upheld these persons as in this general calamity they were not at all infected either with sickness or lameness. And what I have said of these I may say of many others who died in this general visitation, and others yet living; that whilst they had health, yea, or any strength continuing, they were not wanting[8] to any they had need of them. And I doubt not but their recompense is with the Lord.

From *Book II, Chapter XII. Anno 1621*

## FIRST THANKSGIVING

They began now to gather in the small harvest they had, and to fit up their houses and dwellings against winter, being all well recovered in health and strength and had all things in good plenty. For as some were thus employed in affairs abroad, others were exercised in fishing, about cod and bass and other fish, of which they took good store, of which every family had their portion. All the summer there was no want; and now began to come in store of fowl,[9] as winter approached, of which this place did abound when they came first (but afterward decreased by degrees). And besides waterfowl there was great store of wild turkeys, of which they took many, besides venison, etc. Besides they had about a peck a meal a week to a person, or now since harvest, Indian corn to that proportion. Which made many afterwards write so largely of their plenty here to their friends in England, which were not feigned but true reports.

---

1. **combination.** Union
2. **strangers.** Those outside the Puritan church
3. **patent.** Document granting a right or privilege
4. **meet.** Suitable, fit
5. **scurvy.** Disease characterized by weakness and bleeding gums
6. **inaccommodate.** Lacking adequate housing
7. **homely.** Intimate
8. **wanting.** Lacking in attention
9. **fowl.** Birds

## "Upon the Burning of Our House"
## by Anne Bradstreet

In silent night when rest I took
For sorrow near I did not look
I wakened was with thund'ring noise
And piteous shrieks of dreadful voice.
5 That fearful sound of "Fire!" and "Fire!"
Let no man know is my desire.
I, starting up, the light did spy,
And to my God my heart did cry
To strengthen me in my distress
10 And not to leave me succorless.[1]
Then, coming out, beheld a space
The flame consume my dwelling place.
And when I could no longer look,
I blest His name that gave and took,
15 That laid my goods now in the dust.
Yea, so it was, and so 'twas just.
It was His own, it was not mine,
Far be it that I should repine;[2]
He might of all justly bereft
20 But yet sufficient for us left.
When by the ruins oft I past
My sorrowing eyes aside did cast,
And here and there the places spy
Where oft I sat and long did lie:
25 Here stood that trunk, and there that chest,
There lay that store I counted best.
My pleasant things in ashes lie,
And them behold no more shall I.
Under thy roof no guest shall sit,
30 Nor at thy table eat a bit.
No pleasant tale shall e'er be told,
Nor things recounted done of old.
No candle e'er shall shine in thee,
Nor bridegroom's voice e'er heard shall be.
35 In silence ever shall thou lie,
Adieu,[3] Adieu, all's vanity.
Then straight I 'gin my heart to chide,[4]
And did thy wealth on earth abide?[5]
Didst fix thy hope on mold'ring dust?

40 The arm of flesh didst make thy trust?
Raise up thy thoughts above the sky
That dunghill mists away may fly.
Thou hast an house on high erect,
Framed by that mighty Architect,
45 With glory richly furnished,
Stands permanent though this be fled.
It's purchased and paid for too
By Him who hath enough to do.
A price so vast as is unknown
50 Yet by His gift is made thine own;
There's wealth enough, I need no more,
Farewell, my pelf,[6] farewell my store.
The world no longer let me love,
My hope and treasure lies above.

## "Huswifery"[7]
## by Edward Taylor

Make me, O Lord, Thy Spinning Wheel complete.
    Thy Holy Word my Distaff[8] make for me.
Make mine Affections Thy Swift Flyers[9] neat
    And make my Soul thy holy Spool[10] to be.
5    My conversation make to be Thy Reel[11]
    And reel the yarn thereon spun of Thy Wheel.

Make me Thy Loom then, knit therein this Twine:
    And make Thy Holy Spirit, Lord, wind quills:
Then weave the Web Thyself. The yarn is fine.
10    Thine Ordinances make my Fulling Mills.[12]
    Then dye the same in Heavenly Colors Choice,
    All pinked[13] with Varnished Flowers of Paradise.

Then clothe therewith mine Understanding, Will,
    Affections, Judgment, Conscience, Memory,
15    My Words, and Actions, that their shine may fill
    My ways with glory and Thee glorify.
    Then mine apparel shall display before Ye
    That I am Clothed in Holy robes for glory.

1. **succorless.** Helpless
2. **repine.** Complain; worry
3. **adieu.** Farewell (French)
4. **chide.** Scold
5. **abide.** Stay; remain

6. **pelf.** Money or wealth regarded with contempt
7. **Huswifery.** Housekeeping, here specifically weaving
8. **Distaff.** Tool that holds the raw wool
9. **Flyers.** Parts that regulate the spinning
10. **Spool.** Part on which yarn is wound
11. **Reel.** Part that takes up the finished thread
12. **Fulling Mills.** Where cloth is beaten and cleansed
13. **pinked.** Adorned

# WRITING A REFLECTIVE ESSAY

Have you noticed that events and time move quickly in your life? One moment, you are a freshman entering high school. Before long, you have your driver's license. Junior prom arrives. Senior graduation looms just ahead. Often, events happen in such quick succession that the full impact or meaning is never realized—unless you make a conscious effort to stop and reflect.

Taking time to reflect gives you the opportunity to contemplate your life now before moving further ahead. Consider these questions: How have you come to be the person that you are today? How have your personal origins contributed to your understanding of the world around you? What role have your family's origins played in your life? Where might the answers to these questions lead you in the future?

**Writing Assignment.** Write a reflective essay to capture and preserve a picture of who you are today. A reflective essay can also be a way for you to share your thoughts and insights with others.

> "The events in our lives happen in a sequence in time, but in their significance to ourselves, they find their own order ... the continuous thread of revelation."
>
> —Eudora Welty

## Professional Model

Rita Dove, the U.S. Poet Laureate from 1993–1995, reflects on her origins as a writer.

> from an American Academy of Achievement interview in 1994
>
> When I first realized what I wanted to do, it was a gradual thing. It really wasn't until I was in college. When I was in college, I took creative writing courses and I began to write more and more, and I realized I was scheduling my entire life around my writing courses, and I said, "Well maybe you need to figure out if this is what you want to do." That was the point.
>
> I loved to write when I was a child. I wrote, but I always thought it was something that you did as a child, then you put away childish things. I thought it was something I would do for fun. I didn't know writers could be real live people, because I never knew any writers.

**Examining the Model.** Rita Dove describes an experience that helped her decide to become a writer. As you read her personal account, identify the experience that Dove is describing.

After you read her reflection, answer these questions. How did Dove benefit from seeing John Ciardi? How might that experience have contributed to the person that she is today—a successful author herself? What understanding and insight might she have gained from reflecting on her experience?

*continued on page 128*

Consider the sentence, "It is possible." Based on Dove's accomplishments, how do you think she feels about that statement now?

The first inkling that maybe it was a possible thing happened in my last year of high school. I had a high school teacher who took me to a book-signing by an author, John Ciardi, and that's when I saw my first live author. Here was a living, breathing, walking, joking person, who also wrote books.

For me, it was that I loved to read, but I always thought that the dream was too far away. The person who had written the book was a god: it wasn't a person. To have someone actually in the same room with you, talking, and you realize he gets up and walks his dog the same as everybody else, was a way of saying, "It is possible. You can really walk through that door too." That was the important thing. That's why I know it's so important to show kids that there are real live people doing these things.

"An effective piece of writing creates the illusion of a writer speaking to a reader. The language, although written, sounds as if it were spoken. Speech is the glue that holds the piece together. The writing voice provides the intensity that captures the reader; the voice provides the music and grace and surprise that keep the reader interested; the voice communicates the emotion and the mood that make the reader involved. Each writer, of course, has an individual voice. But the writer learns how to extend that voice so it is appropriate for the particular piece of writing."

—Donald M. Murray

## Prewriting

**FINDING YOUR VOICE.** Voice reflects the writer's personality and attitude through tone, word choice, and sentence structure. How would you characterize the voice reflected in Dove's comment below?

. . . I always thought that the dream was too far away. The person who had written the book was a god: it wasn't a person. To have someone actually in the same room with you, talking, and you realize he gets up and walks his dog the same as everybody else, was a way of saying, "It is possible. You can really walk through that door too."

Can you hear the hope and exhilaration in these lines?

Dove's reflection on past and present experiences led her to the optimism she expresses. Your reflection on past and present experiences will lead you to express your voice as well. One way to help you develop your voice is to contemplate the emotional and thought-provoking results of your experiences. Have they led you to determination, happiness, regret, pain, or independence?

**IDENTIFYING YOUR AUDIENCE.** Before writing about your experiences, consider your audience. Think of your audience as an understanding friend with whom you are having a conversation while you are writing. Present your experiences using vivid details that will engage your reader. This will make your reader want to discover more about your experiences. However, make sure your details are relevant to your experiences. Such details should make recounting your event more dramatic.

Will your audience include close family members and others likely to be familiar with the event and its context? If so, are there certain assumptions you can make about your readers' familiarity with your material? How much detail is too much and how much is not enough?

**WRITING WITH A PLAN.** One way to approach writing your reflective essay is to focus on a single event or experience that you can use to reflect on your origins and those of your family.

Ben thought about the demands of his after-school life, which centers around his responsibilities at the family's restaurant. Then he thought about how everyone in the family helped out in the restaurant, which his grandparents started when they first came to this country. Brenda, whose parents, grandparents, and great-grandparents have lived in the same farming town for generations, at first thought her family origins were too uneventful to reflect on. But as she thought more about her life, she realized that her origins had given her a real sense of security and confidence. Trevor, who doesn't know much about his family origins, realized that he could rely on his own inner personal strength to accomplish his goals.

The first step in writing this reflective essay is to think about events and experiences in your life. On your own paper, list several. Consider how your origins have contributed to the events and experiences you have listed. Select the event or experience that you feel best illustrates some result in your life from these origins.

As you record information about your event or experience, focus on using your writing as exploration and discovery, as a way of thinking on paper. The goal of reflection is not to find "the answer" or to exhaust the subject. Rather, the goal is to explore the ideas that occur to you. Think of the reflection as an opportunity to try your ideas out. Ask yourself "why" questions and link your ideas.

**Diagramming** is an effective way to organize your thoughts and identify ideas with potential for shaping into an essay. The purpose of a diagram is to put your ideas about the topic on paper in a roughly organized format.

Ben created a diagram that helped him focus on the main ideas he would use in his reflective essay. Copy the diagram on your own paper and complete it using your own ideas. After you have finished, you will have the basic structure for your reflective essay.

"What lies behind us and what lies before us are tiny matters, compared to what lies within us."

—Ralph Waldo Emerson

"...ask your readers to tell you about the tones of voice, habits of mind, and ways of relating to readers that they hear in your words."

— Peter Elbow

## Student Model—Graphic Organizer

> "...the real possibility of the personal essay, which is to catch oneself in the act of being human...means a willingness to surrender for a time our pose of unshakable rectitude, and to admit that we are, despite our best intentions, subject to all manner of doubt and weakness and foolish wanting."
>
> — Tobias Wolff

**Event**
working in my family's restaurant

**Background information about the event**

grandparents came to this country
poor
barely spoke English
determined to do well
grandmother is a good cook
my father, brothers, and sisters worked

**Thoughts and feelings about the event**

hate it sometimes
takes up the time I want to
  spend with friends
sometimes fun, play jokes
grandma and father are cool
keeps us close
how much my family cares —
  college fund

**Details about the event**

hard work
prep, sauces, precooking
dishes, pots, pans, floors,
  cutting boards, walk-in
  refrigerator
vacuuming, tables
4 to 9 every night to 11 on
  Saturday
no life

**Where the event might lead me**

going to college
knowing about hard work
business skills that might help me later

## Drafting

There are several ways of organizing a reflective essay. You can interweave your reflections with supporting details from your event or experience. Or you can begin your reflective essay by presenting your reflections first and then presenting the details about them later. Another strategy is to do just the opposite: present the specific details about your event or experience first and then state your reflections about them.

Remember that you alone have access to all of the memories, images, and emotions that paint the context of your story. To write an effective reflective essay, you'll need to share that context via details. By using details, you can convey a sense of people, places, and events in such a way that your readers feel as if your experience is their own.

At this point, don't focus on spelling, grammar, usage, and mechanics. Instead, concentrate on two things: 1) creating a picture of the situation with words, and 2) exploring and expressing your reflections.

## Student Model—Draft

Every day when the bell rings, students [*What bell?* *for the last class*] head off in a lot of different places. [*overused*] Some go to practise, some go home, some go to part time jobs, some go hang out [*run on sentence?*] at the mall. ~~Do you want to know where I go~~? [*What if they don't want to know?*] I go to my family's restaurant where every day after school and on the week ends I work for the rest of the night. [*how you feel about this comes through!*]
My family's restaurant is a great place. ~~They~~ started it when they first [*my grandparents*] moved to this country. When they got here they barely spoke English they [*and*] didn't have ~~hardly any~~ money, they [*much*] didn't have educations but they were [*run on sentence?*] determined to make something out of their lives. My grandma is a great cook. ~~You should try her chicken satay~~. [*leave this out*] ~~anyway,~~ since she's such a good cook, they decided to start a restaurant. My dad and all of his brothers and sisters

## Self- and Peer Evaluation

After you finish your first draft, complete a self-evaluation of your writing. If time allows, you may want to get one or two peer evaluations. See the Language Arts Survey 2.37 for more details about self- and peer evaluation. As you evaluate your reflective essay or that of a classmate, answer the following questions:

- Does the essay focus on an event or experience? Does the essay stay on track with this event or experience, or does it get sidetracked?
- Does the writing include specific, vivid details to help the experience become real, alive, and important for the reader?
- How does the author feel about the event or experience? What has he or she learned from it? How has it changed or affected his or her life?
- Does the voice invite you along to share the experience and the author's reflections about it? Does it seem that the author is talking to you personally?
- What word choices could be improved? What words could be added or changed to make the details more concrete, specific, and descriptive?
- Does the writer employ metaphor, simile, or comparisons to create more specific images that

*continued on page 132*

convey the uniqueness of the subject to the audience?

For example, notice the difference in the following sentences:

I always thought that the dream was too far away.

I thought I couldn't be a writer.

Which sentence reflects the voice of a person who loves language and aspires to be a writer?

## Language, Grammar, and Style

### Pronouns and Antecedents

IDENTIFYING PRONOUNS AND ANTECEDENTS. A **pronoun** is a word that takes the place of a noun or stands in for an unknown noun. The noun that the pronoun replaces is called its **antecedent**. A pronoun must agree with or match its antecedent because it is a substitute for the noun.

Look at the example below from the first quote:

The events in our lives happen in a sequence in time, but in <u>their</u> significance to ourselves, <u>they</u> find <u>their</u> own order…

Three pronouns refer to one antecedent, *events. They* is a personal pronoun. It replaces the word *events. Their* is a possessive pronoun. It is used to replace the word *events* and to show that the events possess significance and order.

worked in the restaurant most of their lives. ~~And~~ now that ~~they~~ [my parents] have kids, [we] all ~~of us~~ work there too.

It's ~~a lot of~~ [what is?] work too. I have a lot [overused] of different jobs. I do the prep, [what's this?] make the sauces, and do a lot of the [overused] precooking. I also do a lot of clean up [overused] like doing the dishes and the pots and pans. ~~then there's~~ [Besides all that, I] sweeping and mopping [overused] the floors, [sanitizing] the cutting boards, [cleaning the big] walk-in refrigerator, vacuming, [sp] and [setting up the] tables. All of this takes a lot of time. I work from about 4 [spell out] to 9 almost every week night and from 4 to 11 on Saturday. [squeeze] [in to my homework in at the restaurant.] Sometimes I get off because of school work or event, but basicaly [sp] other than school and work I have no life. [When do you do homework?] [what?]

I have to admit I hate ~~it~~ [what?] sometimes. [working in the restaurant] It takes up all of my the time—the time [the] I want just to do what other kids do after school, [like] hang out, go to [the] mall, sleep, [and] watch <u>tv</u>. Sometimes it's fun, like being with my family. We like to [do you have an example?] laugh and play jokes on each other. ~~And~~ [vague] <u>my</u> grandma and grandfather are cool people. So the restaurant keeps us close as a family, and ~~lets~~ me know ~~how much~~ my *all of this work*

(family really cares about me) because *run on sentence?*

some of the money from the restaurant

goes into my college fund, ~~so I can go to~~

~~college when I finish high school~~

So, I may be stuck working in my

family's restaurant now while I'm in

high school, but when I get done, I know

I'm going to college. ~~And~~ when I get

there, I'll ~~probly~~ do ~~good because~~ I
*sp* *well*

will know what hard work is like and I

will know that I can do it. And I've

learned a lot already about getting
*— overused*

along with people and handling money

and a business. *better ending?*

## Revising and Proofreading

If possible, wait a day before you revise your personal essay. Review you self- and peer evaluations. Revise your writing according to decisions you make about these comments. Remember that you do not need to make every change suggested by your peers, but only those changes that you find truly important to your essay. Consider the focus, content, and reflection upon the incident, as well as the agreement of all your pronouns and their antecedents. Concentrate on the realism of the central event and how clearly it comes across.

## Student Model—Revised

Every day when the dismissal bell for the last class rings, students head off in different directions. Some go to practice. Some go home. Some go to part-time jobs. Some go hang out at the mall. I go to my family's restaurant

Read the example below from the student model:

> My family's restaurant is a great place. My grandparents started it when they first moved to this country.

Identify the pronouns and their antecedents.

Go to the professional model and identify the pronouns. What are their antecedents? To what do they refer? Explain.

**FIXING PRONOUN-ANTECEDENT ERRORS.** Look at Ben's essay. Try to identify several errors in pronoun-antecedent agreement. Copy the sentences with errors onto your own paper and correct the errors. Then briefly explain your editing.

For more help on fixing pronoun-antecedent agreement errors, see the Language Arts Survey 3.45, "Getting Pronouns and Antecedents to Agree." For help on identifying a subject and a verb, see the Language Arts Survey 3.20, "Finding the Simple Subject and Simple Predicate in a Sentence."

**USING CLEAR AND ACCURATE PRONOUNS AND ANTECEDENTS.** Circle the pronoun and underline the antecedent in each sentence of your personal essay. Check the pronoun-antecedent agreement for clarity and number agreement. Singular antecedents need singular pronouns. Plural antecedents need plural

*continued on page 134*

pronouns. The relationship between antecedents and pronouns must be obvious, explicit, and clear.

If a number of words separate the pronoun from the antecedent, check to see that the pronoun agrees with the antecedent. Temporarily removing the words in between the antecedent and pronoun can help you isolate the antecedent and pronoun and determine whether they agree.

## Publishing and Presenting

Finally, write or print a final copy of your essay as a letter, memoir, or album with pictures, drawings, and special paper. You might give it to a relative or friend to read, especially someone for whom the incident will also have personal significance. You and your classmates may also want to share your descriptions. You might want to use the topic and details of your essay as a basis for a different type of writing. For instance, how would your incident translate into a journal entry, into a letter of thanks to someone who helped you in your story, or into a song or poem commemorating the event?

where every day after school and on the weekends I work for the rest of the night.

My family's restaurant is a great place. My grandparents started it when they first moved to this country. When they got here, they barely spoke English. They didn't have much money, and they didn't have an education, but they were determined to make something out of their lives. Since my grandmother was such a good cook, she and my grandfather decided to start a restaurant. My dad and all of his brothers and sisters have worked in the restaurant most of their lives. Now that my parents have kids, we all work there too. My grandma still does a lot of cooking and has won awards for her chicken satay.

Working in the restaurant is hard work. I have many different jobs including preparing the vegetables and meats for cooking, making the sauces, and precooking many of the foods. I also do a lot of cleanup like doing the dishes and the pots and pans. Besides all that, I sweep and mop the floors, sanitize the cutting boards, clean the big walk-in refrigerator, vacuum, and set up the tables. I work from about four to nine almost every week night and until eleven on Saturday. I squeeze my homework in at the restaurant. Sometimes I get off because of schoolwork or a special event, but basically other than school and work I have no life.

I have to admit I hate working in the restaurant sometimes. It takes up all of my time—the time I just want to do what other kids do after school like hang out, go to the mall, sleep, and watch TV. Sometimes the restaurant is fun, like being with my family. We like to laugh and play jokes on each other. One time when the weather was really hot, my brother fixed the sprayer for rinsing dishes so that it sprayed cold water on whoever was using it. I got sprayed first. I was a little mad, but then we got laughing and decided to make sure everybody else in the family got sprayed too. We all ended up wet, laughing, and cooled off. My grandma and grandfather are fun people. They help us learn by letting us try to do new things. So the restaurant keeps us close as a family. The restaurant is also helping me with my future, because some of the money from the restaurant goes into my college fund.

So, I may be stuck working in my family's restaurant now while I'm in high school, but when I get done, I know I'm going to college. When I get there I'll probably do well. I will know what hard work is like, and I will know that I can do it. I will know how to take care of a business and how to get along with people. Even though working all the time is tough, I know that working with my family now will lead me to a better life.

## Reflecting

Consider the value of taking the time to reflect on events and experiences in your life and to write down these reflections. What have you gained from this experience? How might you continue to gain from this experience if you reread your reflective essay when you are twenty? when you are fifty?

What was the reaction of the person or persons who read your essay? Compare your reflective essay with one or more of the literature selections from this unit or with Rita Dove's reflections on her decision to become a writer. Are there any similarities between the themes, incidents, thoughts, or feelings? Are the same topics still valid or do they seem outdated? Why, or why not? What has changed and what hasn't?

# UNIT REVIEW
## *Origins of the American Tradition*

### Words for Everyday Use

Check your knowledge of the following vocabulary words from the selections in this unit. Write short sentences using these words in context to make the meaning clear. To review the definition or usage of a word, refer to the page number listed or the Glossary of Words for Everyday Use.

abhor, 121
ascribe, 121
avail, 120
buffet, 98
burnish, 99
canonize, 104
conceit, 104
confederacy, 88
conjuration, 105
constitution, 119
contrivance, 120
depopulate, 97
disposition, 88
diversity, 105

doleful, 106
ensue, 105
entreaty, 106
estimation, 89
extremity, 104
flourish, 98
furnish, 89
gluttony, 104
gulf, 120
incense, 121
induce, 121
infest, 99
inhuman, 98
loathsome, 121

manifold, 115
mollify, 107
oppression, 97
persevere, 115
pilfer, 103
presumption, 104
provoke, 121
recompense, 115
ruffian, 98
sovereign, 120
subjection, 97
subserve, 120
suffice, 97
vestige, 98

### Literary Tools

Define the following terms, giving concrete examples of how they are used in the selections in this unit. To review a term, refer to the page number indicated or to the Handbook of Literary Terms.

aim, 110
analogy, 118
chronological order, 102
couplet, 110

emphasis, 118
hyperbole, 114
metaphor, 92
mood, 96

myth, 92
paradox, 114
point of view, 96, 102
symbol, 87

# Reflecting
## *on* YOUR READING

### Genre Studies

1. **POETRY.** Bradstreet's poem "To My Dear and Loving Husband" is built on couplets. A couplet is a pair of rhyming lines expressing a complete thought. Each couplet expands her notion of love. Examine each couplet and give its central thought.

# Thematic Studies

2. **ORDER, HARMONY, AND JUDGMENT.** Edwards, the Tewa, and the framers of the Iroquois Constitution use extended metaphors to express their themes. What theme does each selection convey? How does the metaphor in each fit the theme? Refer to the definition of *extended metaphor* in the Handbook of Literary Terms.

# Historical/Biographical Studies

3. **POLITICAL THOUGHT AND EDUCATION.** *The New England Primer* was a vehicle for evolving political thought. What view of the English king is evident in the selection printed in this text? Research subsequent editions of the *Primer* and see how this view changed as the colonists headed toward revolution.

4. **SETTLERS' GOALS.** Describe the goals of the colonial settlers. Refer to the introduction to this unit and to the writings of Smith and Edwards.

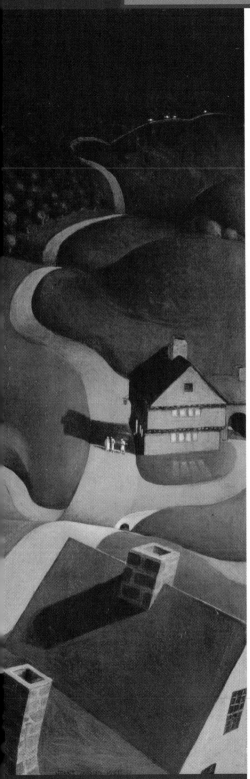

**Midnight Ride of Paul Revere,**
1931. Grant Wood.
The Metropolitan Museum of Art, New York.

T o secure these rights,

governments are instituted among

men, deriving their just powers

from the consent of the governed.

—Thomas Jefferson
Declaration of Independence

*Quaker Meeting.* American artist.
Museum of Fine Arts, Boston.

# THE AMERICAN REVOLUTION (1750–1800)

## THE EMERGENCE OF AMERICAN DIVERSITY

During the Colonial Period, New England remained relatively homogeneous, populated primarily by Puritans of British descent. However, the Mid-Atlantic and the South saw rapid growth and an influx of different peoples, religions, and ways of life. Indeed, by the time of the **American Revolution**, the colonies had achieved a great deal of the social diversity that we now think of as distinctively American.

In the colony of Pennsylvania, **Quakers** of English and Welsh descent established a community based on equality for all citizens and tolerance of religious diversity, for the Quakers believed people to have within them a divine spark that could be demonstrated through love for "all in God's world." In the 1680s, the Quakers became the first group in America to advocate the abolition of slavery, and, unlike the Puritans, they allowed women a voice in religious affairs. As a result of tolerant Quaker attitudes, Pennsylvania by the 1750s had attracted people from a wide variety of ethnic and religious groups, including Native Americans and free persons of African descent. It had also become a center for progressive thinking. **Benjamin Franklin** himself, though he had earlier mocked Quaker meetings in his writings, adopted the Quaker rhetoric of equality and went on to play important roles in the American Revolution, which included helping to establish the terms of the **Treaty of Paris** that ended the war.

## LITERARY EVENTS

➤ = American Events

➤1760. Laurence Sterne's *The Life and Opinions of Tristram Shandy* published

1759. Voltaire's *Candide* published

➤ 1755. Samuel Johnson's *A Dictionary of the English Language* published

➤ 1755. Benjamin Franklin's "Observations Concerning the Increase of Mankind" published

➤1752. George Berkeley's *On the Prospect of Planting Arts and Learning in America* published

1751. Denis Diderot's *Encyclopédie* published

**1750**          **1755**          **1760**

1750. British pass the Iron Act, prohibiting colonies from producing iron products

➤1751. Benjamin Franklin experiments with electricity

➤1752. Philadelphia's Liberty Bell is cast

➤1754. The French and Indian War begins

1759. British win decisive victory over French outside Quebec City

1760. George III succeeds George II

## HISTORICAL EVENTS

In other parts of the Mid-Atlantic, such as New York, New Jersey, and Delaware, which saw new arrivals of Jewish, German, and Irish immigrants, the communal social and economic relations practiced by the Puritans and the Quakers were supplanted by an emerging **Capitalist** ethic of individual profit-making. One result was that in these places land came to be viewed more as a commodity than as part of a homestead or as a source of a community's sustenance. Many middle-sized farms emerged on which owners used wage-laborers, indentured servants, and slaves.

By the mid-eighteenth century the economies of the Southern colonies were centered primarily on commercial agriculture, particularly on the cultivation of cotton and tobacco. The heavy reliance of commercial **plantations** on slave labor had a number of social consequences of concern during and after the revolutionary period, not the least of which was that in many areas (and in some entire states such as South Carolina), the majority of the population consisted of enslaved African Americans.

The overall sense of dynamism and opportunity that the colonies, rural and urban, were coming to represent can perhaps be seen best in the growth of the population itself. In 1650, the total population of the colonies was almost 60,000; by the 1790s, it was 3,500,000. Infant mortality rates were down, fertility rates were up, and many more children were surviving into adulthood. The young country had a young populace; in 1776, the year of independence from Britain, roughly half of the people were twenty-one or younger. Benjamin Franklin and others extolled abroad the virtues of America's healthy environment, as well as the many opportunities that the colonies offered for economic advancement through hard work. Europeans, increasingly non-English ones, heeded the call, often fleeing economic hardship and overcrowding at home.

## REBELLION AGAINST GREAT BRITAIN

The diverse and growing population of the colonies, bound to provide supplies and soldiers for English wars and to help pay for those wars afterward, found subservience to distant England increasingly irksome. In 1763, after the **French and Indian War**, England imposed, through the Stamp Act, the first in a series of heavy taxes that would prove unpopular in the colonies and serve as a focal point of colonial resentment. The colonists began boycotting British goods, leading the British to repeal the

➤1774. Benjamin Franklin's "On the Rise of Progress of the Differences between Great Britain and the American Colonies" published

1774. Johann von Goethe's *The Sorrows of Young Werther* published

➤1773. Phillis Wheatley publishes volume of poetry

➤1772. Philip Morin Freneau and Hugh Henry Breckinridge publish *The Rising Glory of America*

➤1770. *The Massachusetts Spy,* anti-British Whig newspaper begins publication

➤1767. John Dickinson's *Letters from a Farmer in Pennsylvania* published

1762. Jean-Jacques Rousseau publishes *The Social Contract* and *Émile*

| 1765 | 1770 | 1775 |
| --- | --- | --- |

1763. Treaty of Paris cedes Canada to Great Britain

➤1765. British pass Quartering Act and Stamp Act

➤1765. Sons of Liberty clubs formed to resist Stamp Act

➤1766. Stamp Act repealed; Declatory Acts passed

➤1767. British pass Townshend Revere Acts

➤1770. Boston Massacre; British kill colonists

➤1773. Daniel Boone leads settlers into Kentucky against George's edict; Tea Act; Boston Tea Party

➤1774. First Continental Congress

➤1775. American Revolution begins; Battles of Lexington and Concord; George Washington appointed commander in chief of the Continental Army

Boston Massacre.

Stamp Act. Then, in March 1770, British soldiers and colonial citizens skirmished in Boston, resulting in the deaths of five colonists. Among the colonists killed in this so-called **Boston Massacre** was **Crispus Attucks,** the first African American to die in the Revolutionary cause. In 1773, when England imposed a new tax on tea, colonial patriots held what is known as the **Boston Tea Party,** dumping tea from British ships into Boston Harbor. The British Parliament responded with severe restrictions on the self-government of Massachusetts, known as the **Intolerable Acts.** In counterresponse, representatives from the colonies met in Philadelphia in 1774 for the **First Continental Congress.** There they vented their outrage in letters of protest to King George, asked citizens to boycott British goods, and called for the organization of militia, or armed citizens, to defend against British aggression throughout the colonies.

In April 1775, British General Thomas Gage moved troops toward Concord, Massachusetts, with the aim of capturing rebel arms and leaders, but the rebels had been forewarned, thanks to **Paul Revere, William Dawes,** and **Samuel Prescott.** On Concord Bridge, on the morning of April 19, thirty-five militiamen blocked the path of seven hundred British troops. After a brief standoff, a shot was fired, and the American Revolution had begun. That day, fighting between British troops and colonial militiamen in Concord and Lexington left almost three hundred British soldiers and one hundred colonials dead or wounded.

The **Second Continental Congress,** meeting in Philadelphia in May 1775, organized an army under **General George Washington.** In June, after the **Battle of Bunker Hill,** near Boston, King George officially declared the colonies in rebellion against the crown. Early in 1776, Thomas Paine, recently arrived in America from Great Britain, published his pamphlet *Common Sense,* the first work to call for the colonies' independence. In June of that year, acting on resolutions introduced by

**LITERARY EVENTS**

➤ = American Events

➤ 1787. James Madison and Alexander Hamilton publish *The Federalist Papers*

➤ 1783. Noah Webster's *Spelling Book* published

1782. J. Hector St. Jean de Crèvecœur's *Letters from an American Farmer* published

1781. L. Immanuel Kant's *Critique of Pure Reason* published

1778. Fanny Burney's *Evelina* introduces the novel of manners

➤ 1776. Declaration of Independence; Thomas Paine publishes *Common Sense* and *Crisis*

| 1780 | 1785 | 1790 |
|---|---|---|

➤ 1778. France recognizes America's independence

1779. Spain declares war on Britain

➤ 1781. General Cornwallis of Britain surrenders at Yorktown

➤ 1783. Treaty of Paris recognizes independence of the thirteen colonies

1789. French Revolution

➤ 1789. George Washington becomes the first president

➤ 1787. Constitutional Convention

➤ 1788. United States Constitution ratified

**HISTORICAL EVENTS**

**142**   *UNIT THREE / THE AMERICAN REVOLUTION*

Richard Henry Lee, a delegate from Virginia, the Continental Congress voted in favor of independence and appointed a committee, which included **Thomas Jefferson,** Benjamin Franklin, and **John Adams,** to draft a **Declaration of Independence.** Jefferson wrote a draft of that declaration which, with some changes, was adopted on July 4, thereafter known in the United States as **Independence Day.**

## THE PHILOSOPHICAL BACKGROUND OF THE REVOLUTION

The Declaration of Independence was a bold document, for it declared that "all men are created equal," that people have certain "inalienable rights" that cannot be taken from them, that governments derive their right to rule from the consent of the governed, and that when a government fails to protect the natural rights of its citizens, those citizens have not only a right but a duty to rebel. The theories that informed the Declaration of Independence had their origins in the European **Enlightenment,** or **Age of Reason,** and in European **Romanticism.** Thinkers of the Enlightenment, encouraged by discoveries in the natural sciences such as those made by **Sir Isaac Newton,** believed that through reason people could discover principles that would guarantee social and political harmony. Neoclassicists, such as **Joseph Addison,** also valued reason and sought to discover the natural laws by which an individual or a nation could achieve peace and tranquility. The English philosopher **Thomas Hobbes,** though a monarchist, argued that certain natural rights existed that no individual could turn over to a sovereign. Another English philosopher, **John Locke,** reasoned that to ensure the preservation of their natural rights, a people should balance the power of the sovereign against the power of Parliament and retain the right to rebel against oppression. The French philosopher **Jean-Jacques Rousseau** argued that governments are instituted as a **social contract** made by the people for their mutual benefit. Rousseau was one of the foremost thinkers of the **Romantic Movement,** which began in the eighteenth century and continued into the nineteenth century. Among other goals, this movement championed democratic ideals and the rights of

*Paul Revere,* c.1768.
John Singleton Copley.
Museum of Fine Arts, Boston.

1798. Samuel Taylor Coleridge and William Wordsworth publish *Lyrical Ballads;* Thomas Robert Malthus publishes "Essay on the Principles of Population"

➤ 1798. Charles Brockden Brown's *Alcuin: A Dialogue on the Rights of Women* and *Weiland,* or *The Transformation*

➤ 1793. Joel Barlow's *Advice to the Privileged Orders* published

1792. Mary Wollstonecraft's *Vindication of the Rights of Woman* published

**1790**          **1795**          **1800**

➤ 1791. The Bill of Rights becomes United States law

1793. Reign of Terror begins; Louis XVI and Marie Antoinette guillotined

➤ 1793. Fugitive Slave Act passed

1795. Napoleon Bonaparte named commander of the Armée d'Intérieur

➤ 1796. John Adams becomes president, Thomas Jefferson vice president

1799. Napoleon Bonaparte becomes first consul of France; Rosetta Stone discovered

the individual, rights that were to be enshrined in the **Bill of Rights**—the first ten amendments to the United States Constitution.

## THE NEW NATION

In 1777, Congress adopted the **Articles of Confederation,** which created a weak central government and left most power to the former colonies, now sovereign states. In 1781, the British, under General George Cornwallis, suffered a decisive defeat at Yorktown, Virginia. This effectively ended the war, despite sporadic fighting over the next one and a half years. In 1783, the American Revolution officially ended with the signing of the Treaty of Paris, in which Great Britain gave up its claims on the colonies. In 1787, delegates in Philadelphia adopted a new Constitution, beginning with these stirring words:

*George Washington,*
c.1810. Gilbert Stuart.
National Gallery of Art, Washington, DC.

> We, the people of the United States, in order to form a more perfect Union, establish justice, insure domestic tranquility, provide for the common defense, promote the general welfare, and secure the blessings of liberty to ourselves and our posterity do ordain and establish this Constitution for the United States of America.

The task of establishing "a more perfect union" from the diverse peoples of the United States would prove challenging in years to come, but the very diversity that would create tensions in the young country would also be its greatest strength. By the time of the Revolution, America had already produced the first of its great African-American poets in the person of **Phillis Wheatley.** In the years since, its diversity has made American literature one of the finest the world has ever seen.

## A NATION OF READERS

As the population of the young country grew and standards of living climbed, literacy increased dramatically. By the end of the eighteenth century, most of the white population could read, and literacy was blossoming among free African Americans in the North. This burst of literacy created a demand for more and more literature of various kinds, a demand met by technological developments in printing that brought into full flower the "reading revolution." One critical factor underlying the increased demand for printed works was the heightened value that "print culture" (as opposed to spoken or oral culture) was coming to play in shaping the ideals of the emerging nation. Print came to be seen not merely as a means of transmitting information but as a new way of conducting public discourse on important issues. People were beginning to associate print with public debate held without regard to distinctions of status or person. Through the printed word, one might present arguments, as Thomas Paine did in *Common Sense,* and have those arguments stand or fall solely on their merit. Print became, therefore, a vehicle for the new nation's democratic identity and principles.

# ECHOES

## THE AMERICAN REVOLUTION

In reality there is perhaps no one of our natural Passions so hard to subdue as *Pride*. . . . For even if I could conceive that I had completely overcome it, I should probably be proud of my Humility.

—Benjamin Franklin, on pride

Here [in America] individuals of all nations are melted into a new race of men, whose labors and posterity will one day cause great changes in the world.

—J. Hector St. Jean de Crèvecœur, on American diversity

Strange order of things! Oh, Nature, where are thou?—Are not these blacks thy children as well as we?

—J. Hector St. Jean de Crèvecœur, on slavery

These are the times that try men's souls. The summer soldier and the sunshine patriot will, in this crisis, shrink from the service of their country; but he that stands it now, deserves the love and thanks of man and woman.

—Thomas Paine, in *Crisis, No. 1,* on the American Revolution

A little rebellion now and then is a good thing.

—Thomas Jefferson, writing about Shay's Rebellion in a letter to James Madison

The tree of liberty must be refreshed from time to time with the blood of patriots and tyrants.

—Thomas Jefferson, in a letter to W. S. Smith

In framing a government which is to be administered by men over men, the great difficulty lies in this: you must first enable the government to control the governed; and in the next place oblige it to control itself.

—James Madison, the *Federalist Papers, No. 51,* on control of government

To the memory of the glorious Ninety-two members of the Honorable House of Representatives of the Massachusetts Bay, who undaunted by the insolent menaces of villains in power, from strict regard to conscience and the liberties of their constituents on the 30th of June 1868 voted NOT TO RESCIND.

—Paul Revere, inscription on his silver "Liberty" bowl, 1768

Yesterday, the greatest question was decided which ever was debated in America, and a greater perhaps never was nor will be decided among men. A resolution was passed without one dissenting colony, "that these United Colonies are, and of right ought to be, free and independent States."

—John Adams, Letter to Abigail Adams, April 28, 1776

The basis of our political system is the right of the people to make and to alter their constitutions of government.

—George Washington, Farewell Address, September 17, 1796

No More, *America,* in mournful strain
Of wrongs, and grievance unredress'd complain,
No longer shalt thou dread the iron chain,
Which wanton *Tyranny* with lawless hand
Had made, and with it meant t' enslave the land.

—Phillis Wheatley, from "To the Right Honorable William, Earl of Dartmouth"

*Quaker Meeting* [Detail], American artist.

FROM

# THE AUTOBIOGRAPHY OF
## Benjamin Franklin

BY BENJAMIN FRANKLIN

## About *the* AUTHOR

**Benjamin Franklin** (1706–1790) was a writer, scientist, inventor, diplomat, and statesman. Born the tenth son of a man who made soap and candles, Franklin entered the printing trade as his brother's apprentice at the age of twelve. In 1722, at the age of sixteen, he wrote a series of fourteen essays published in his brother's paper under the name "Silence Dogood." That same year, Franklin undertook the responsibility of running his brother's paper while his brother was imprisoned for an article he printed.

At seventeen, Franklin moved to Philadelphia, where he started a printing shop that produced paper currency for the Pennsylvania colony as well as a newspaper, the *Pennsylvania Gazette*. His *Poor Richard's Almanac* was enormously successful and was published annually for twenty-five years; many of the sayings he scattered through each issue preach the virtues of hard work, frugality, and thrift. These enterprises helped to make Franklin quite wealthy. A man of many talents and interests with a keen intelligence and a passion for science, Franklin experimented with electricity and invented a cookstove, bifocal glasses, and the lightning rod. He also founded the first American subscription library and was instrumental in founding the University of Pennsylvania.

Respected for his insight and wisdom, Franklin spent eighteen years in England as an unofficial ambassador, seeking to protect the rights of the American Colonies while keeping them within the British empire. After the Revolutionary War began, Franklin helped draft the Declaration of Independence and secured military and financial support from the French. As minister to France from 1776 to 1785, Franklin helped draft and signed the treaty that ended the Revolutionary War. His last public service was acting as a delegate to the Constitutional Convention at the age of eighty-one. "He seized the lightning from Heaven and the scepter from tyrants," said one French admirer of Franklin's contributions.

# About the SELECTION

Benjamin Franklin wrote *The Autobiography of Benjamin Franklin* over a period of twenty years. It covers his life only until 1758, before his career as a diplomat. He began writing in 1771 and wrote the last two sections between 1788 and 1790, when illness forced him to put the work aside. Although the first part of the book was published in 1791, the entire work was not published until 1868.

Franklin's writing style was developed, he noted, by imitation of great models, primarily of such Neoclassical masters as Joseph Addison. The Neoclassicists of the eighteenth century valued reason and sought to discover orderly principles, or natural laws, by which the life of an individual or of a nation could be conducted in order to achieve relative harmony and tranquility. For more information on Neoclassicism, see the introduction to this unit and the entry on **Neoclassicism** in the Handbook of Literary Terms.

---

An **aphorism**, or **proverb**, is a short saying or pointed statement. The following is a list of aphorisms from the writings of Benjamin Franklin. Many come from Franklin's *Poor Richard's Almanac*, which he edited under the pseudonym of Richard Saunders.

"A learned blockhead is a greater blockhead than an ignorant one."

"A penny saved is a penny earned."

"A word to the wise is enough and many words won't fill a bushel."

"At the workingman's house hunger looks in, but dares not enter."

"Beware of little expenses; a small leak will sink a great ship."

"Creditors have better memories than debtors."

"Early to bed, and early to rise, makes a man healthy, wealthy, and wise."

"God heals, and the doctor takes the fee."

"God helps them that help themselves."

"He that falls in love with himself, will have no rivals."

"He that goes a-borrowing goes a-sorrowing."

"If you will not hear reason, she'll surely rap your knuckles."

"If you would like to know the value of money, go and try to borrow some."

"If you would not be forgotten as soon as you are dead, either write things worth reading or do things worth writing."

"In this world nothing can be said to be certain except death and taxes."

"snug/as a bug/in a rug"

"The early bird catches the worm."

"There never was a good war, or a bad peace."

"Time is money."

"We must indeed all hang together, or, most assuredly, we shall all hang separately."

---

# Literary TOOLS

**STYLE.** **Style** is the manner in which something is said or written. Any recurring feature, such as the selection of words and grammatical structures, that distinguishes one writer's work from another can be said to be part of that writer's style. An interesting stylistic characteristic in Franklin's *Autobiography* is its egotism (or, more sympathetically, enlightened self-interest tempered by a willingness to question his own actions). As you read, look for this characteristic.

**AUTOBIOGRAPHY.** An **autobiography** is the story of a person's life, written by that person. In this selection from *The Autobiography of Benjamin Franklin*, the author describes the time in his youth when he established himself as a writer and printer. Create a chart, listing, on the left, facts about Franklin's life while he was an apprentice for his brother, James. On the right, explain what you learned about Franklin's character from these facts.

| Facts about Franklin's Life | What I learned about Franklin's character |
|---|---|
| He anonymously submitted pieces to his brother's newspaper. | He knew how to surmount obstacles to get what he wanted. |

# Reader's Journal

What have you done to reach a personal goal?

# THE AUTOBIOGRAPHY OF *Benjamin Franklin*

### BENJAMIN FRANKLIN

My Brother had in 1720 or '21, begun to print a Newspaper. It was the second that appeared in America and was called the *New England Courant.*[1] The only one before it was *The Boston News Letter.* I remember his being dissuaded by some of his Friends from the Undertaking, as not likely to succeed, one Newspaper being in their Judgment enough for America. At this time (1771) there are not less than five-and-twenty. He went on, however, with the Undertaking, and after having worked in composing the Types and printing off the Sheets, I was employed to carry the Papers through the Streets to the Customers. He had

---

1. **It was . . . *New England Courant.*** James Franklin's paper was actually the fifth American paper.

*Benjamin Franklin as an Apprentice Printer,* c.1840. American artist.

some <u>ingenious</u> Men among his Friends who amused themselves by writing little Pieces for this Paper, which gained it Credit and made it more in Demand, and these Gentlemen often visited us. Hearing their Conversations and their Accounts of the Approbation[2] their Papers were received with, I was excited to try my Hand among them. But being still a Boy, and suspecting that my Brother would object to printing any Thing of mine in his Paper if he knew it to be mine, I contrived to disguise my Hand, and writing an anonymous Paper, I put it in at Night under the Door of the Printing-House.

> *What was Benjamin Franklin excited to try? Why was he excited? What was his one worry?*

It was found in the Morning and communicated to his Writing Friends when they called in as Usual. They read it, commented on it in my Hearing, and I had the exquisite Pleasure of finding it met with their Approbation, and that, in their different Guesses at the Author, none were named but Men of some Character among us for Learning and Ingenuity. I suppose now that I was rather lucky in my Judges, and that perhaps they were not really so very good ones as I then esteemed them. Encouraged however by this, I wrote and conveyed in the same Way to the Press several more Papers, which were equally approved, and I kept my Secret till my small Fund of Sense for such Performances was pretty well exhausted, and then I discovered[3] it, when I began to be considered a little more by my Brother's Acquaintance, and in a manner that did not quite please him, as he thought, probably with reason, that it tended to make me too vain. And perhaps this might be one Occasion of the Differences that we began to have about this

> *What was one cause of the differences between Franklin and his brother?*

Time. Though a Brother, he considered himself as my Master, and me as his Apprentice,[4] and accordingly expected the same Services from me as he would from another; while I thought he demeaned me too much in some he required of me, who from a Brother expected more <u>Indulgence</u>. Our Disputes were often brought before our Father, and I fancy I was either generally in the right or else a better Pleader, because the Judgment was generally in my favor. But my Brother was passionate and had often beaten me, which I took extremely amiss; and, thinking my Apprenticeship very tedious, I was continually wishing for some Opportunity of shortening it, which at length offered in a manner unexpected.

One of the Pieces in our Newspaper, on some political Point which I have now forgotten, gave Offense to the Assembly. He was taken up, censured, and imprisoned[5] for a Month by the Speaker's Warrant. I suppose because he would not discover his Author. I too was taken up and examined before the Council; but though I did not give them any Satisfaction, they contented themselves with <u>admonishing</u> me, and dismissed me, considering me perhaps as an Apprentice who was bound to keep his Master's Secrets. During my Brother's Confinement, which I resented a good deal, notwithstanding our private Differences, I had the Management of the Paper, and I made bold to give our Rulers some Rubs[6] in it,

> *Why was James Franklin imprisoned?*

---

2. **Approbation.** Approval or commendation
3. **discovered.** Revealed
4. **Apprentice.** Person under legal agreement to work a specified length of time for a master craftsman in return for instruction and, formerly, support
5. **imprisoned.** James Franklin was charged with libel in 1722 because his paper linked local officials to pirates who were raiding outside Boston Harbor.
6. **Rubs.** Insults

<table>
<tr><td>WORDS<br>FOR<br>EVERYDAY<br>USE</td><td>in • gen • ious (in jēn´yəs) *adj.*, having great mental ability. *An <u>ingenious</u> inventor, Henry Ford was the first to use the assembly line.*<br>in • dul • gence (in dul´jəns) *n.*, favor or privilege. *Whenever Mom bought me a candy bar when I was little, I was grateful for the <u>indulgence</u>.*<br>ad • mon • ish (ad män´ish) *vt.*, caution against specific faults. *The teacher <u>admonished</u> Keoung when he wrote on his desk.*</td></tr>
</table>

which my Brother took very kindly, while others began to consider me in an unfavorable Light, as a young Genius that had a Turn for Libeling and Satire.[7] My Brother's Discharge was accompanied with an Order of the House (a very odd one) "that James Franklin should no longer print the paper called the *New England Courant*." There was a <u>Consultation</u> held in our Printing-House among his Friends what he should do in this Case. Some proposed to <u>evade</u> the Order by changing the Name of the Paper; but my Brother seeing Inconveniences in that, it was finally concluded on as a better Way to let it be printed for the future under the Name of Benjamin Franklin. And to avoid the Censure of the Assembly that might fall on him as still printing it by his Apprentice, the Contrivance was that my old Indenture[8] should be returned to me with a full Discharge on the Back[9] of it, to be shown on Occasion; but to secure to him the Benefit of my Service, I was to sign new Indentures for the Remainder of the Term, which were to be kept private. A very flimsy

> How did the newspaper come to be published under Franklin's name?

Scheme it was; but however, it was immediately executed, and the Paper went on accordingly under my Name for several Months.[10] At length a fresh Difference arising beween my Brother and me, I took upon me to assert my Freedom, presuming that he would not <u>venture</u> to produce the new Indentures. It was not fair in me to take this Advantage, and this I therefore reckon one of the first Errata[11] of my Life; but the Unfairness of it weighed little with me, when under the Impressions of Resentment, for the Blows his Passion too often urged him to bestow upon me. Though he was otherwise not an ill-natured Man: perhaps I was too saucy and provoking. ∎

> In what way did Franklin take advantage of his brother? Why might the "Unfairness of it" weigh little with him?

---

7. **Libeling and Satire.** *Libeling*—making false public accusation; *satire*—humorous but critical portrayal
8. **Indenture.** Contract binding a person to work for another for a given length of time
9. **Discharge on the Back.** Release of the remainder
10. **Paper . . . several Months.** Actually, the paper remained in Franklin's name until 1726, nearly three years after he left Boston.
11. **Errata.** Printer's term for errors

---

**WORDS FOR EVERYDAY USE**

**con • sul • ta • tion** (kän´səl tā´shən) *n.*, meeting to discuss, decide, or plan something. *After a <u>consultation</u> with her counselor, Beth dropped her French class.*

**e • vade** (ē vād´) *vt.*, avoid or escape from by deceit or cleverness. *Brian tried to <u>evade</u> his coach's wrath by skipping practice.*

**ven • ture** (ven´chər) *vt.*, undertake the risk of. *Shayna raised her hand, <u>venturing</u> a guess at the calculus problem.*

## Respond to the SELECTION

If you were the young Benjamin Franklin, having just ended your apprenticeship, what qualities and qualifications would you tell a new employer that you possess?

# INVESTIGATE Inquire *Imagine*

**Recall:** GATHERING FACTS

1a. What tasks did Benjamin Franklin perform for his brother as his apprentice?

2a. How did Franklin trick his brother into publishing his writing?

3a. What finally led to Franklin's leaving the newspaper and his job as apprentice?

**Interpret:** FINDING MEANING

1b. How did Franklin feel about the tasks his brother made him do? Why?

2b. Why did Franklin resort to trickery in order to get his pieces printed? Why did he finally reveal that he was the author?

3b. How did Franklin feel about abandoning his apprenticeship at the time he left? How had his attitude concerning the incident and his actions changed by the time he wrote his autobiography? Why had it changed?

**Analyze:** TAKING THINGS APART

4a. What personal qualities did Franklin possess by the end of his apprenticeship that demonstrated he would be able to make it on his own?

**Synthesize:** BRINGING THINGS TOGETHER

4b. Were there more advantages or disadvantages for Franklin in serving as an apprentice to his brother? Cite examples to support your position. How do you think Franklin's view of the advantages and disadvantages might have changed as he matured?

**Evaluate:** MAKING JUDGMENTS

5a. Was Franklin justified in leaving his apprenticeship? Why, or why not?

**Extend:** CONNECTING IDEAS

5b. Have you ever broken an agreement because you thought you were treated unfairly? What happened? Did you regret your decision later?

# Understanding *Literature*

STYLE. Review the definition for **style** in the Handbook of Literary Terms. Then cite an example of the egotism that marks Franklin's style.

AUTOBIOGRAPHY. Review the definition for **autobiography** given in Literary Tools on page 147 and the related graphic organizer you made as you read the selection. What did you learn about Benjamin Franklin in this autobiographical selection that you might not have known if you had read a biography of him instead?

# WRITER'S JOURNAL

1. Imagine that you are James Franklin. Write a **want ad** for the position of apprentice at the *New England Courant,* detailing the duties of the position.

2. Write a **letter** to Franklin's brother, James, telling him what he should do to keep Benjamin as an apprentice at his newspaper.

3. Read the list of aphorisms by Franklin on page 147. Write several of your own modern-day **aphorisms**.

# Integrating *the* LANGUAGE ARTS

## Language, Grammar, and Style

**VERBALS: GERUNDS.** Read the Language Arts Survey 3.80, "Verbals: Participles, Gerunds, and Infinitives." Then identify each gerund and each participle in the sentences below.

1. To young Franklin, publishing was a challenging and rewarding career.

2. Even though annoying disagreements with his brother drove him into running away to Philadelphia, the printing skills he acquired gave him valuable experience.

3. Joining his abilities in writing and publishing with keen business sense, Franklin gained success quickly.

4. Then he enjoyed experimenting with electricity and inventing useful tools, such as the bifocals used by many people today.

5. Retired from business at age forty-two, Franklin spent most of the rest of his life as a diplomat, serving his country as ambassador to France.

## Study and Research & Applied English

**APPRENTICESHIP.** Use your research skills to write a paragraph about an aspect of apprenticeship. For example, you might choose to write about which ancient civilizations used apprenticeship to provide job training, describe the role of guilds in arranging and supervising apprenticeships in medieval Europe, or find out which other famous Americans of the 1700s served as apprentices to learn their trade. You could also write about skilled trades today that require a period of apprenticeship.

## Applied English

**ADVICE COLUMN.** Imagine that you write an advice column for a newspaper. Select an interesting letter from an advice column in your local paper or have a classmate write a letter about a real or imaginary problem. Then write a response to the letter, giving practical advice and insight. Use an aphorism from *Poor Richard's Almanac* or from another writing by Franklin (see page 147) in writing your response. If you prefer, you may write your own aphorism.

## Media Literacy & Speaking and Listening

**TALK-SHOW INTERVIEW.** With a partner, hold a talk-show interview. One person plays the role of Benjamin Franklin as an older statesman. The other plays the role of the talk-show host. If you play the role of the talk-show host, prepare a list of questions to ask Franklin. These may include the tasks he performed, his relationship with his brother, and the influence his apprenticeship had on his life after leaving the *New England Courant*. If you play the role of Franklin, reread the selection from *The Autobiography* in order to give detailed responses to the questions you are asked; in addition, you may find it helpful to do some extra reading about Franklin's life after his apprenticeship to find out more about how that experience influenced his life later.

# Speech in the Virginia Convention

BY PATRICK HENRY

## About the AUTHOR

**Patrick Henry** (1736–1799) was a distinguished statesman and orator during the American Revolution. Born in Hanover County, Virginia, Henry's public schooling was brief, for his education was taken over by his father, a well-educated gentleman. Henry first tried being a storekeeper but proved to be a poor businessman. He then turned to law and received his license in 1760.

Gaining fame as an orator, Henry was elected to the Virginia House of Burgesses, where he became a leader. Taking on varying degrees of political responsibility, Henry served as governor of Virginia, became a conservative member of the Federalist party, but declined membership in the Constitutional Convention and the U.S. Senate. He refused George Washington's offers of appointment as secretary of state and chief justice of the Supreme Court. He was chiefly responsible for the drafting of the Bill of Rights. In 1796, Henry was elected governor of Virginia for the sixth time but refused to take office. His last campaign was for the office of representative in the Virginia state legislature. He won the election but died before taking office.

## About the SELECTION

The **Speech in the Virginia Convention**, probably Patrick Henry's best-known oration, was not written down until years after its delivery on March 23, 1775. It had so captured the attention of its listeners that they were able to recall it for Henry's biographer, William Wirt.

This speech against the Stamp Act in 1765 is considered one of his finest, in which he uttered the famous words: "I know not what course others may take, but as for me, give me liberty or give me death!" The speech was delivered to the Virginia Convention during a time of growing political unrest. Less than a month after Henry's speech, his prediction of open battle in the North was fulfilled in the opening skirmishes of the American Revolution at Lexington and Concord on April 19, 1775.

## Literary TOOLS

**RHETORICAL QUESTION.** A **rhetorical question** is one asked for effect but not meant to be answered because the answer is clear from the context. Speakers use rhetorical questions as a means for reinforcing a point that they have already made or that should, from the speaker's point of view, be obvious to the audience. Paragraph 2 contains this example: "Are we disposed to be of the number of those who having eyes see not, and having ears hear not, the things which so nearly concern their temporal salvation?" As you read, look for additional examples of rhetorical questions in the speech.

**ENLIGHTENMENT.** The **Enlightenment** was an eighteenth-century philosophical movement characterized by belief in reason, the scientific method, and the perfectibility of people and society. It was believed that people could, through application of reason, discover truth relating to the conduct of life or of society. Look for references in this speech that Patrick Henry participated in this movement.

## Reader's Journal

When have a friend's or a relative's words motivated you to take action?

# Speech in the Virginia Convention

## PATRICK HENRY

*Patrick Henry Speaking Against the Stamp Act,* 1800s. American artist. The Granger Collection.

Mr. President:[1] No man thinks more highly than I do of the patriotism, as well as abilities, of the very worthy gentlemen who have just addressed the house. But different men often see the same subject in different lights: and, therefore, I hope it will not be thought disrespectful to those gentlemen, if, entertaining, as I do, opinions of a character very opposite to theirs, I shall speak forth my sentiments freely and without reserve. This is no time for ceremony. The question before the house is one of awful moment to this country. For my own part, I consider it as nothing less than a question of freedom or slavery. And in proportion to the magnitude of the subject ought to be the freedom of the debate. It is only in this way that we can hope to arrive at truth, and fulfill the great responsibility which we hold to God and our country. Should I keep back my opinions at such a time, through fear of giving offense, I should consider myself as guilty of treason toward my country, and of an act of disloyalty toward the Majesty of Heaven, which I revere above all earthly kings.

Mr. President, it is natural to man to indulge in the illusions of hope. We are apt to shut our eyes against a painful truth, and listen to the song of that siren till she transforms us into beasts. Is this the part of wise men, engaged in a great and arduous struggle for liberty? Are we disposed to be of the number of those who having eyes see not, and having ears hear not, the things which so nearly concern their <u>temporal</u> salvation? For my part, whatever anguish of spirit it may cost, I am willing to know the whole truth; to know the worst and to provide for it.

1. **Mr. President.** President of the Virginia Convention

WORDS FOR EVERYDAY USE

tem • po • ral (tem′pə rəl) *adj.,* lasting only for a time; temporary. *Marty's anger was <u>temporal</u>, and soon his good-natured grin returned.*

I have but one lamp by which my feet are guided, and that is the lamp of experience. I know of no way of judging of the future but by the past. And judging by the past, I wish to know what there has been in the conduct of the British ministry for the last ten years to justify those hopes with which gentlemen have been pleased to solace themselves and the house? Is it that insidious smile with which our petition[2] has been lately received? Trust it not, sir: it will prove a snare to your feet. Suffer not yourselves to be betrayed with a kiss. Ask yourselves how this gracious reception of our petition comports with those warlike preparations which cover our waters and darken our land. Are fleets and armies necessary to a work of love and reconciliation? Have we shown ourselves so unwilling to be reconciled that force must be called in to win back our love? Let us not deceive ourselves, sir. These are the implements of war and subjugation—the last arguments to which kings resort.

I ask gentlemen, sir, what means this martial array,[3] if its purpose be not to force us to submission? Can gentlemen assign any other possible motive for it? Has Great Britain any enemy in this quarter of the world, to call for all this accumulation of navies and armies? No, sir, she has none. They are meant for us: they can be meant for no other. They are sent over to bind and rivet upon us those chains which the British ministry have been so long forging.

What guides the speaker?

> But as for me, give me liberty or give me death!

And what have we to oppose to them? Shall we try argument? Sir, we have been trying that for the last ten years. Have we anything new to offer upon the subject? Nothing. We have held the subject up in every light of which it is capable; but it has been all in vain. Shall we resort to entreaty and humble supplication? What terms shall we find which have not been already exhausted? Let us not, I beseech[4] you, sir, deceive ourselves longer.

How have the colonists responded to British threats?

Sir, we have done everything that could be done to avert the storm which is now coming on. We have petitioned; we have remonstrated; we have supplicated; we have prostrated ourselves before the throne, and have implored its interposition[5] to arrest the tyrannical hands of the ministry and Parliament. Our petitions have been slighted; our remonstrances have produced additional violence and insult; our supplications have been disregarded; and we have been spurned with contempt from the foot of the throne! In vain, after these things, may we indulge the fond[6] hope of peace and reconciliation. There is no longer any room for hope. If we wish to be free, if we mean to preserve

---

2. **petition.** "Olive Branch Petition," in which the king was asked to intercede between Parliament and the colonies
3. **array.** Display; assembly
4. **beseech.** Beg; plead
5. **interposition.** Intervention
6. **fond.** Foolish

---

**WORDS FOR EVERYDAY USE**

**so • lace** (säl´əs) *vt.*, comfort, relieve. *The father solaced his young child with a hug.*

**in • sid • i • ous** (in sid´ē əs) *adj.*, sly; crafty. *The dishwasher refused to go along with the cook's insidious plan to steal from the restaurant manager.*

**com • port** (kəm pôrt´) *vi.*, agree; go along. *The politician's actions do not comport with his stated ideals.*

**sub • ju • ga • tion** (sub´jə gā´shen) *n.*, takeover; enslavement. *The subjugation of Earth by fifty-foot ants was the subject of the movie.*

**mar • tial** (mär´shəl) *adj.*, warlike; of the military. *"The Battle Hymn of the Republic" is a martial song.*

**sub • mis • sion** (sub mish´ən) *n.*, act of yielding; surrendering. *The dog showed his submission by dropping the stick and lying down.*

**a • vert** (ə vurt´) *vt.*, prevent. *Snow and ice did not avert the delivery of the mail.*

**re • mon • strate** (ri män´strāt) *vt.*, demonstrate. *Dianne remonstrated her objection with a lengthy argument.*

**pros • trate** (präs´trāt) *vt.*, bow down. *The courtiers prostrated themselves before the king.*

inviolate those inestimable privileges for which we have been so long contending, if we mean not basely to abandon the noble struggle in which we have been so long engaged, and which we have pledged ourselves never to abandon until the glorious object of our contest shall be obtained—we must fight! I repeat it, sir, we must fight! An appeal to arms and to the God of Hosts is all that is left us!

They tell us, sir, that we are weak—unable to cope with so formidable an adversary. But when shall we be stronger? Will it be the next week, or the next year? Will it be when we are totally disarmed, and when a British guard shall be stationed in every house? Shall we gather strength by irresolution and inaction? Shall we acquire the means of effectual resistance by lying supinely on our backs and hugging the delusive phantom of hope until our enemies shall have bound us hand and foot? Sir, we are not weak, if we make a proper use of those means which the God of nature hath placed in our power. Three millions of people, armed in the holy cause of liberty, and in such a country as that which we possess, are invincible by any force which our enemy can send against us. Besides, sir, we shall not fight our battles alone. There is a just God

*What does Henry value more than hope?*

who presides over the destinies of nations and who will raise up friends to fight our battles for us. The battle, sir, is not to the strong alone; it is to the vigilant, the active, the brave. Besides, sir, we have no election.[7] If we were base enough to desire it, it is now too late to retire from the contest. There is no retreat but in submission and slavery! Our chains are forged! Their clanging may be heard on the plains of Boston! The war is inevitable—and let it come! I repeat it, sir, let it come![8]

*Who is favored in battle?*

It is in vain, sir, to extenuate the matter. Gentlemen may cry, "Peace, peace"—but there is no peace. The war is actually begun! The next gale that sweeps from the north will bring to our ears the clash of resounding arms! Our brethren are already in the field! Why stand we here idle? What is it that gentlemen wish? What would they have? Is life so dear, or peace so sweet, as to be purchased at the price of chains and slavery? Forbid it, Almighty God! I know not what course others may take; but as for me, give me liberty or give me death! ∎

---

7. **election.** Choice
8. **The war . . . come!** Boston had recently been occupied by British troops under the leadership of General Howe.

---

**WORDS FOR EVERYDAY USE**

in • vi • o • late (in vī´ə lit) *adj.*, sacred. *Chris's Sunday morning with the comics and a doughnut is inviolate.*
in • es • ti • ma • ble (in es´tə mə bəl) *adj.*, too great to be measured. *You have my inestimable gratitude for solving the problem.*
for • mi • da • ble (fôr´mə de bəl) *adj.*, overwhelming. *Cleaning my room was a formidable task.*
ef • fec • tu • al (e fek´chü əl) *adj.*, effective. *A simple "Quiet" was effectual in silencing the class.*
su • pine • ly (sü´pīn´lə) *adv.*, passively. *I refuse to sit supinely by while you shirk your responsibilities.*

## Respond *to the* SELECTION

If you had heard Henry's speech in 1775, what stand would you have decided to take about the British? Would you have been in favor of war or of a peaceful resolution of the conflict?

# INVESTIGATE, Inquire, Imagine

**Recall**: GATHERING FACTS

1a. According to Henry, what is the only way to arrive at truth?

2a. What evidence suggests strongly to Henry that Britain means to wage war "to force us to submission"?

3a. What is Henry's response to the possibility that war may break out soon?

**Interpret**: FINDING MEANING

1b. Why does Henry feel he must speak out in opposition to the previous speakers who urged moderation and the maintenance of a peaceful attitude toward Britain?

2b. Why does Henry distrust the "insidious smile with which our petition has been lately received"?

3b. What does Henry see as the unthinkable alternative to war?

**Analyze**: TAKING THINGS APART

4a. Compare the colonists' and the British authorities' attempts to resolve the conflict in the colonies.

**Synthesize**: BRINGING THINGS TOGETHER

4b. What British actions would probably have appeased Henry so that he would not have called for war?

**Evaluate**: MAKING JUDGMENTS

5a. Compare the Six Nations' speaker's speech as reported by Benjamin Franklin in "Remarks Concerning the Natives of North America" on page 178 with Patrick Henry's Speech in the Virginia Convention. Which is more diplomatic? Why? What is the purpose of each speech, to persuade or to inform? How can you tell?

**Extend**: CONNECTING IDEAS

5b. What groups of people in the world news today seem to agree with Henry's declaration that death is preferable to a life where no liberty exists?

# Understanding Literature

RHETORICAL QUESTION. Review the definition for a **rhetorical question** in the Handbook of Literary Terms. Then make a chart, listing four rhetorical questions from Henry's speech on the left and the answers that he assumes on the right. One example has been done for you.

| Rhetorical Questions | Assumed Answers |
|---|---|
| "Is this the part of wise men, engaged in a great and arduous struggle for liberty?" | Wise men seeking freedom open their eyes and see the truth. |

ENLIGHTENMENT. Review the definition for the **Enlightenment** in the Handbook of Literary Terms. Look for indications in this speech that Patrick Henry participated in this movement and that he was familiar with classical rhetoric. (a) Where does he support the importance of using reason as a guide to action? (b) The scientific method calls for hypothesizing and predicting, experimenting to test the hypothesis, and basing further action on the results of the experiments. What hypothesis have the previous speakers presented with regard to the political situation in the colonies? What "experimental results" does Henry report? What prediction does he make based on observable phenomena?

# WRITER'S JOURNAL

1. Make a **list** of the steps in Henry's argument.

2. Imagine that you are a loyalist who wants Great Britain to retain control of the colonies. Write your own **speech** to loyalist sympathizers, detailing Henry's treasonous remarks in his Speech in the Virginia Convention.

3. Imagine that, as a newspaper reporter, you attended the Virginia Convention the day that Patrick Henry gave his speech. Write a **newspaper article** summarizing Henry's speech and describing the reaction of the representatives.

# Integrating *the* LANGUAGE ARTS

## Language, Grammar, and Style

**FUNCTIONS OF SENTENCES.** Read the Language Arts Survey 3.17, "Functions of Sentences." Then identify the functions of each of the following sentences from Patrick Henry's speech.

1. Let us not deceive ourselves, sir.

2. This is no time for ceremony.

3. And what have we to oppose to them?

4. There is no retreat but in submission and slavery!

5. Sir, we are not weak, if we make a proper use of those means which the God of nature hath placed in our power.

## Speaking and Listening

**PUBLIC SPEAKING.** Read the Language Arts Survey 4.17, "Steps in Preparing an Extemporaneous Speech." Then think of a cause that you believe in and write notes for an extemporaneous speech on that topic. Try to persuade your listeners to support the cause that you believe in. Use at least one rhetorical question in your speech. Then join with three or four classmates and take turns giving your speeches.

## Applied English

**TAKING MINUTES.** Imagine that you are the secretary for the Virginia Convention. Write the minutes for Patrick Henry's speech. (In the minutes of a meeting, the secretary of an organization summarizes the discussion on each item of business and records formal movements and decisions.)

## Collaborative Learning

**PETITION.** Patrick Henry referred to the petitions that his countrymen had sent to the king of England, seeking what they perceived as their rights as English citizens. Decide something that you would like to petition as a daughter/son, student, employee, or citizen. With a partner, play the roles of a petitioner and an authority figure. If you play the role of the petitioner, identify the rights that you seek and explain why you deserve them. If you play the role of the authority figure, explain why you will or will not grant those rights to the petitioner. After you have completed your role-play, switch roles so you both have the opportunity to be a petitioner and an authority figure.

## Media Literacy

**TELEVISION COMMERCIAL.** With two classmates, write a television commercial to arouse support from the colonists for King George III. For example, you could explain the need for taxation and why the colonists should show allegiance to the king. Draw a storyboard to show the text and visuals to be used in your commercial.

# "To *S. M.,* a Young African Painter, on Seeing His Works"

BY PHILLIS WHEATLEY

## About the AUTHOR

**Phillis Wheatley** (c.1753–1784) was born in West Africa, captured as a child, and brought on a slave ship to Boston in 1761. There John Wheatley, a Boston tailor, purchased the girl to work for his wife, Susannah, who provided an education for Wheatley. A child prodigy, Wheatley rapidly learned to read both English and Latin. By the age of fourteen, she was writing poetry. She achieved fame early for a poem that she wrote about an evangelical preacher named George Whitefield.

In 1773, she went to London with the Wheatleys' son, Nathaniel, partly to seek support for her first book, *Poems on Various Subjects, Religions and Morals.* She returned to Boston before the publication of her work, having received news that Susannah Wheatley was dying. Before Susannah's death in 1774, the family released Wheatley from slavery. In 1776, the year in which America declared its independence from Britain, Wheatley met General George Washington after she had written a poem dedicated to him. In 1778, Wheatley married John Peters, a freedman.

Her later life was one of grief as she endured poverty and the loss of two children. Her third child, ill when Phillis Wheatley died, passed away shortly afterward and was buried with her in an unmarked grave. Rediscovered in the 1830s, Wheatley's poetry shows her to have been an eloquent spokesperson for her faith, for American independence, and for the abolition of slavery.

## About the SELECTION

Phillis Wheatley wrote **"To S. M., a Young African Painter, on Seeing His Works"** in praise of the work of Scipio Moorhead, a servant to the Reverend John Moorhead of Boston. It was published in her volume of 1773.

## Literary TOOLS

**HEROIC COUPLET.** A **heroic couplet** is a pair of rhyming iambic pentameter lines. An iambic foot contains one weakly stressed syllable followed by a strongly stressed syllable:

Cease, gentle muse! the solemn gloom of night

Now seals the fair creation from my sight.

As you read, identify other heroic couplets in Wheatley's poem.

**ALLUSION.** An **allusion** is a rhetorical technique in which reference is made to a person, event, object, or work from history or literature. As you read, look for the way Wheatley uses allusions from Greek mythology in her poem.

## Art Note

*Phillis Wheatley,* c.1773. Scipio Moorhead.

The "S. M." of Wheatley's poem was Scipio Moorhead, an African-American artist who made this portrait of Wheatley. He was a slave who learned to draw from his master's wife, Sarah Moorhead, an art teacher. Little else is known about Scipio Moorhead, and the paintings mentioned in the poem have been lost.

## Reader's Journal

When have you been deeply affected by a piece of writing, a song, or a work of art?

# To S. M., a Young African Painter, on Seeing His Works

## PHILLIS WHEATLEY

To show the laboring bosom's deep intent,
And thought in living characters to paint,
When first thy pencil did those beauties give,
And breathing figures learnt from thee to live,
5 How did those prospects give my soul delight,
A new creation rushing on my sight?
Still, wond'rous youth! each noble path pursue,
On deathless glories fix
thine ardent view:
Still may the painter's
and the poet's fire

> What does the speaker hope for the subject of the poem?

10 To aid thy pencil, and thy verse conspire!
And may the charms of each seraphic[2] theme
Conduct thy footsteps to immortal fame!
High to the blissful wonders of the skies
Elate thy soul, and raise thy wishful eyes.
15 Thrice[3] happy, when exalted to survey
That splendid city, crowned with endless day,
Whose twice six gates[4] on radiant hinges ring:
Celestial Salem[5] blooms in endless spring.

Calm and serene thy moments glide along,
20 And may the muse[6] inspire each future song!
Still, with the sweets of
contemplation blest,
May peace with balmy
wings your soul invest!

> What words are used to describe the artist's movements? Who inspires him?

But when these shades of time are
chased away,
And darkness ends in everlasting day,
25 On what seraphic pinions[7] shall we move,
And view the landscape in the realms above?
There shall thy tongue in heavenly
murmurs flow,
And there my muse with heavenly
transport glow:
No more to tell of Damon's[8] tender sighs,
30 Or rising radiance of
Aurora's[9] eyes,
For nobler themes
demand a nobler strain,
And purer language on
the ethereal plain.
Cease, gentle muse! the solemn gloom of night
Now seals the fair creation from my sight.  ■

> What event does the speaker describe in the last lines of the poem? Why, in the last line, is she unable to see the creation?

---

1. **S. M.** Scipio Moorhead, servant to a Boston minister
2. **seraphic.** Angelic
3. **Thrice.** Triple (extremely)
4. **twice six gates.** Twelve gates to heaven
5. **Salem.** Jerusalem
6. **muse.** Any of the nine goddesses who preside over literature and the arts in Greek mythology
7. **pinions.** Wings
8. **Damon.** Mythical hero and loyal friend (to Pythias)
9. **Aurora.** Mythical goddess of dawn

---

**WORDS FOR EVERYDAY USE**

**ar • dent** (ärd´ 'nt) *adj.,* intensely enthusiastic or devoted. *Phil, an ardent animal lover, volunteers at the animal shelter.*

**e • late** (ē lāt´) *vt.,* raise the spirits of. *After weeks of rain, Lisa was elated by the warm, sunny day.*

**con • tem • pla • tion** (kän´təm plā´shən) *n.,* thoughtful inspection, study, or meditation. *The art student was engaged in rapt contemplation of the Picasso statue.*

**balm • y** (bäm´ē) *adj.,* soothing, mild, or pleasant. *On a balmy day in May, Piglet decided to go on a picnic.*

**trans • port** (trans´pôrt) *n.,* strong emotion; rapture. *What transport Satya felt when she read the letter from her boyfriend!*

**e • the • re • al** (ē thir´ē əl) *adj.,* not earthly; heavenly, celestial. *New Age music often creates an ethereal, elevated mood.*

If you were an African American living in eighteenth-century America, would your outlook be as positive as that of the speaker in the poem? Why, or why not?

# INVESTIGATE Inquire Imagine

**Recall:** GATHERING FACTS

1a. What is the speaker's emotional response to the painter's work?

2a. How does the speaker hope the painter will be rewarded for his beautiful work?

3a. When will the speaker meet the painter?

**Interpret:** FINDING MEANING

1b. What does the speaker mean when she says that the painter creates "breathing figures"? What does she mean by "A new creation"?

2b. To what subjects should the painter turn his attention, fixing his "ardent view"?

3b. How will the poet's and the painter's work change after they die and "view the landscape in the realms above"?

**Analyze:** TAKING THINGS APART

4a. What is the speaker's underlying assumption about inspiration?

**Synthesize:** BRINGING THINGS TOGETHER

4b. In what way does Phillis Wheatley follow her own advice when writing this poem?

**Evaluate:** MAKING JUDGMENTS

5a. Do you share the same perspective as Wheatley about the importance of art, the nature of inspiration, and the existence of life after death? Why, or why not?

**Extend:** CONNECTING IDEAS

5b. What several influences from her life and education guided Wheatley's hand in writing this poem?

# Understanding Literature

HEROIC COUPLET. Review the definition for **couplet** in the Handbook of Literary Terms. Which pairs of lines in this poem are heroic couplets? What makes them heroic?

ALLUSION. Review the definition for **allusion** in the Handbook of Literary Terms. Then make a chart, listing the lines from the poem that have allusions on the left and the meaning of the allusions on the right. The first example has been done for you.

| Allusions in the Poem | Meaning |
|---|---|
| "And may the muse inspire each future song" | One of the mythological Greek muses presided over lyric poetry. |

# WRITER'S JOURNAL

1. Write a **paragraph** to a classmate, explaining why you think Wheatley responds to the painting with a poem instead of a letter to express her sentiments about the painter's art.

2. Imagine that, as Phillis Wheatley, you have received a letter from another poet praising the optimism and positive spirit of your poem. Write a **letter** responding to your reader, explaining where your optimism and positive spirit come from.

3. Imagine that the speaker of the poem and the painter meet. Write a **dialogue** between other poets and painters in eighteenth-century America that covers their discussion about artistic inspiration.

# Integrating *the* LANGUAGE ARTS

## Speaking and Listening & Collaborative Learning

**INTERPRETING ART.** Form small groups. Imagine that Scipio Moorhead, the young painter to whom Wheatley's poem is addressed, has just created a painting in response to Wheatley's poem. Describe the painting, explaining its composition and how it reflects the content of the poem. As you listen to your group members' descriptions, sketch the paintings that they describe. Then compare your sketches.

## Applied English

**MEMO WRITING.** Read the Language Arts Survey 6.6, "Writing a Memo." Imagine that you are the CEO of a Fortune 500 company called American Amalgamated Motors. Your board of directors has approved a donation of $1,250,000 to the Detroit Institute of American Arts to begin a collection of works by famous African-American artists, to be called the "Scipio Moorhead Collection" in honor of the artist to whom Wheatley's poem is addressed. Write a memo to Ms. Paula Palette, director of the museum, announcing your company's decision, explaining the types of art you are willing to sponsor, and requesting a meeting to discuss the details of the arrangement. Follow proper memo form.

## Collaborative Learning

**ROLE-PLAY.** With a partner, play the roles of Phillis Wheatley and Susannah Wheatley. Phillis has just read her new poem, called "To S. M., a Young African Painter, on Seeing His Works," to Susannah. If you play the role of Susannah, ask Phillis questions about word choice, allusions, the poem's rhyme and meter scheme, the meaning of certain lines, and her beliefs about inspiration and life after death. If you play the role of Phillis, give complete answers to Susannah's questions.

## Media Literacy & Study and Research

**MULTIMEDIA SHOW.** Form groups to plan a multimedia show about African-American contributions to the arts in the twentieth century. Work with your group to create a list of African Americans in the areas of dance, poetry, music, painting, acting, sculpture, and photography, and then take notes on these artists' contributions. Decide which of each artist's pieces or performances to include in your show. Then decide how you will display each artist's pieces or performances, whether by audiotape, videotape, slides, film, or photographs. Your show must include commentary and transitional material that holds the elements together.

# DECLARATION *of* INDEPENDENCE

BY THOMAS JEFFERSON

## About *the* A U T H O R

**Thomas Jefferson** (1743–1826) was a man of many talents and achievements. Born in 1743 in Albemarle County, Virginia, Jefferson attended William and Mary College in Williamsburg, studied law, and was admitted to the bar.

Jefferson's political career began after college when he was elected to the Virginia House of Burgesses. In 1774, he wrote a pamphlet denying British authority over America. In 1775, he was sent as a delegate to the Second Continental Congress, where he drafted, with input from Benjamin Franklin, John Adams, and others, the Declaration of Independence. Jefferson then returned to the Virginia legislature, and drafted a statute guaranteeing religious freedom. In 1779, he became governor of Virginia. In 1789, he became the first secretary of state under the new Constitution. During that time, he became embroiled in a controversy with Alexander Hamilton that resulted in the formation of the American two-party political system.

In 1779, Jefferson became vice president under John Adams, and was later elected president in 1800. As president, he more than doubled the size of the country through the Louisiana Purchase, an acquisition of North American lands owned by France. After his retirement from public life, Jefferson devoted himself to planning the buildings and curriculum of the new University of Virginia. The Library of Congress was founded with some ten thousand volumes from Jefferson's private library. He died a few hours before John Adams on the fourth of July, fifty years after the signing of the Declaration of Independence.

## About *the* S E L E C T I O N

In June of 1776, Richard Lee, a delegate from Virginia, brought before the Continental Congress two resolutions, one calling for separation from Great Britain and the other calling for formation of a new government. After much debate, Congress decided to accept the resolutions and set up a committee to draft a declaration of independence. Jefferson drafted the document, adding a strong statement against slavery that was deleted from the version adopted on July 4, 1776.

## Literary T O O L S

**ALLITERATION. Alliteration** is the repetition of initial consonant sounds. Jefferson uses alliteration in one of the most famous sentences in the Declaration of Independence.

**PARALLELISM. Parallelism** is a rhetorical technique in which a writer emphasizes the equal value or weight of two or more ideas by expressing them in the same grammatical form. As you read the selection, map the way Jefferson uses parallelism in his presentation of the grievances against King George. Create a radiating circle like the one that follows. In each empty circle write an example of unlawful jurisdiction by the British, working from the section where Jefferson uses parallel structure by starting each clause with the word "For."

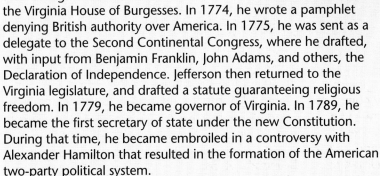

For quartering large bodies of armed troops among us

Unlawful jurisdiction by the British

## Reader's *Journal*

What rights do you have at home, school, and work?

# DECLARATION *of* INDEPENDENCE

## THOMAS JEFFERSON

*The Drafting of the Declaration of Independence,*
c.1900. Jean Leon Jerome Ferris. Private Collection.

IN CONGRESS, JULY 4, 1776

When in the course of human events, it becomes necessary for one people to dissolve the political bands which have connected them with another, and to assume, among the powers of the earth, the separate and equal station to which the laws of nature and of nature's God entitle them, a decent respect to the opinions of mankind requires that they should declare the causes which impel them to the separation.

What is the reason for the drafting of the Declaration as stated in its opening paragraph?

We hold these truths to be self-evident:—that all men are created equal; that they are endowed by their Creator with certain <u>unalienable</u> rights; that among these are life, liberty, and the pursuit of happiness. That, to secure these rights, governments are instituted among men, deriving their just powers from the consent of the governed; that, whenever any form of government becomes destructive of these ends, it is the right of the people to alter or to abolish it, and to institute a new government, laying its foundation on such principles, and organizing its powers in such form, as to them shall seem most likely to effect their safety and happiness. Prudence, indeed, will dictate that governments long established should not be changed for light and <u>transient</u> causes; and, accordingly, all experience hath shown that mankind are more disposed to suffer, while evils are sufferable, than to right themselves by abolishing the forms to which they are accustomed. But, when a long train of abuses and <u>usurpations</u>, pursuing invariably the same object, <u>evinces</u> a design to reduce them under absolute despotism,[1] it is their right, it is their duty, to throw off such government, and to provide new guards for their future security.

---

1. **despotism.** Government by a tyrant

**WORDS FOR EVERYDAY USE**

un • al • ien • a • ble (un āl´yən ə bəl) *adj.,* that which may not be taken away. *Melody argued with her parents that staying up late was an <u>unalienable</u> right.*

tran • si • ent (tran´sē ənt) *adj.,* not permanent; temporary. *Colds are <u>transient</u>; they go away after a week or so.*

u • sur • pa • tion (yü zər pā´shən) *n.,* unlawful or violent taking of power. *The prime minister was accused of <u>usurpation</u> of rights belonging to the king.*

e • vince (ē vin[t]s´) *vt.,* show plainly. *By scowling, the server <u>evinced</u> his displeasure at the small size of the tip.*

IN CONGRESS, JULY 4, 1776.

A DECLARATION

BY THE REPRESENTATIVES OF THE

UNITED STATES OF AMERICA,

IN GENERAL CONGRESS ASSEMBLED.

WHEN in the Course of human Events, it becomes necessary for one People to dissolve the Political Bands which have connected them with another, and to assume among the Powers of the Earth, the separate and equal Station to which the Laws of Nature and of Nature's God entitle them, a decent Respect to the Opinions of Mankind requires that they should declare the causes which impel them to the Separation.

We hold these Truths to be self-evident, that all Men are created equal, that they are endowed by their Creator with certain unalienable Rights, that among these are Life, Liberty, and the Pursuit of Happiness—That to secure these Rights, Governments are instituted among Men, deriving their just Powers from the Consent of the Governed, that whenever any Form of Government becomes destructive of these Ends, it is the Right of the People to alter or to abolish it, and to institute new Government, laying its Foundation on such Principles, and organizing its Powers in such Form, as to them shall seem most likely to effect their Safety and Happiness. Prudence, indeed, will dictate that Governments long established should not be changed for light and transient Causes; and accordingly all Experience hath shewn, that Mankind are more disposed to suffer, while Evils are sufferable, than to right themselves by abolishing the Forms to which they are accustomed. But when a long Train of Abuses and Usurpations, pursuing invariably the same Object, evinces a Design to reduce them under absolute Despotism, it is their Right, it is their Duty, to throw off such Government, and to provide new Guards for their future Security. Such has been the patient Sufferance of these Colonies; and such is now the Necessity which constrains them to alter their former Systems of Government. The History of the present King of Great-Britain is a History of repeated Injuries and Usurpations, all having in direct Object the Establishment of an absolute Tyranny over these States. To prove this, let Facts be submitted to a candid World.

He has refused his Assent to Laws, the most wholesome and necessary for the public Good.

He has forbidden his Governors to pass Laws of immediate and pressing Importance, unless suspended in their Operation till his Assent should be obtained; and when so suspended, he has utterly neglected to attend to them.

He has refused to pass other Laws for the Accommodation of large Districts of People, unless those People would relinquish the Right of Representation in the Legislature, a Right inestimable to them, and formidable to Tyrants only.

He has called together Legislative Bodies at Places unusual, uncomfortable, and distant from the Depository of their public Records, for the sole Purpose of fatiguing them into Compliance with his Measures.

He has dissolved Representative Houses repeatedly, for opposing with manly Firmness his Invasions on the Rights of the People.

He has refused for a long Time, after such Dissolutions, to cause others to be elected; whereby the Legislative Powers, incapable of Annihilation, have returned to the People at large for their exercise; the State remaining in the mean time exposed to all the Dangers of Invasion from without, and Convulsions within.

He has endeavoured to prevent the Population of these States; for that Purpose obstructing the Laws for Naturalization of Foreigners; refusing to pass others to encourage their Migrations hither, and raising the Conditions of new Appropriations of Lands.

He has obstructed the Administration of Justice, by refusing his Assent to Laws for establishing Judiciary Powers.

He has made Judges dependent on his Will alone, for the Tenure of their Offices, and the Amount and Payment of their Salaries.

He has erected a Multitude of new Offices, and sent hither Swarms of Officers to harrass our People, and eat out their Substance.

He has kept among us, in Times of Peace, Standing Armies, without the consent of our Legislatures.

He has affected to render the Military independent of and superior to the Civil Power.

He has combined with others to subject us to a Jurisdiction foreign to our Constitution, and unacknowledged by our Laws; giving his Assent to their Acts of pretended Legislation:

For quartering large Bodies of Armed Troops among us:

For protecting them, by a mock Trial, from Punishment for any Murders which they should commit on the Inhabitants of these States:

Such has been the patient <u>sufferance</u> of these colonies; and such is now the necessity that constrains them to alter their former systems of government. The history of the present King of Great Britain[2] is a history of repeated injuries and usurpations, all having, in direct object, the establishment of an absolute tyranny over these States. To prove this, let facts be submitted to a candid world.

He has refused his <u>assent</u> to laws the most wholesome and necessary for the public good.

He has forbidden his Governors to pass laws of immediate and pressing importance, unless suspended in their operation till his assent should be obtained; and when so suspended, he has utterly neglected to attend to them.

He has refused to pass other laws for the accommodation of large districts of people, unless these people would relinquish the right of representation in the legislature—a right <u>inestimable</u> to them, and formidable to tyrants only.

> What had the king asked the people to relinquish? What did this right mean to them? Why is such a right formidable to tyrants?

---

2. **present King of Great Britain.** King George III (1760–1820)

WORDS FOR EVERYDAY USE

suf • fer • ance (suf´ər əns) n., power to tolerate pain. *The workers' long sufferance of poor working conditions ended when they decided to go on strike.*

as • sent (ə sent´) n., agreement. *Marie nodded in assent.*

in • es • ti • ma • ble (in es´tə mə bəl) adj., too great to be measured. *Leonardo da Vinci's paintings are of inestimable value.*

He has called together legislative bodies at places unusual, uncomfortable, and distant from the depository of their public records, for the sole purpose of fatiguing them into <u>compliance</u> with his measure.

He has dissolved representative houses repeatedly, for opposing, with manly firmness, his invasions on the rights of the people.

*What has the king dissolved? What effect has this had on the people?*

He has refused, for a long time after such dissolutions, to cause others to be elected; whereby the legislative powers, incapable of annihilation, have returned to the people at large for their exercise; the State remaining, in the meantime, exposed to all dangers of invasion from without, and <u>convulsions</u> within.

He has endeavored to prevent the population of these States; for that purpose obstructing the laws for the <u>naturalization</u> of foreigners; refusing to pass others to encourage their migration hither, and raising the conditions of new appropriations of lands.

He has obstructed the administration of justice, by refusing his assent to laws for establishing judiciary powers.

He has made judges dependent on his will alone for the <u>tenure</u> of their offices, and the amount and payment of their salaries.

He has erected a multitude of new offices, and sent hither swarms of officers to harass our people and eat out their substance.

He has kept among us in times of peace, standing armies, without the consent of our legislatures.

He has affected to render the military independent of, and superior to, the civil power.

He has combined with others to subject us to a jurisdiction foreign to our constitutions, and

unacknowledged by our laws; giving his assent to their acts of pretended legislation:

For quartering large bodies of armed troops among us;

For protecting them, by a mock trial, from punishment for any murders which they should commit on the inhabitants of these States;

For cutting off our trade with all parts of the world;

For imposing taxes on us without our consent;

For depriving us, in many cases, of the benefits of trial by jury;

For transporting us beyond the seas, to be tried for pretended offences;

For abolishing the free system of English laws in a neighboring province, establishing there an arbitrary government, and enlarging its boundaries, so as to render it at once an example and fit instrument for introducing the same absolute rule into these colonies;

For taking away our charters, abolishing our most valuable laws, and altering, fundamentally, the forms of our governments;

For suspending our own legislatures, and declaring themselves invested with power to legislate for us in all cases whatsoever.

He has <u>abdicated</u> government here, by declaring us out of his protection, and waging war against us.

*What has the king declared? What destructive things has he done?*

He has plundered our seas, ravaged our coasts, burnt our towns, and destroyed the lives of our people.

He is at this time transporting large armies of foreign mercenaries[3] to complete the works of death, desolation, and tyranny, already begun

---

3. **mercenaries.** Hired soldiers

---

**WORDS FOR EVERYDAY USE**

**com • pli • ance** (kəm plīʹən[t]s) *n.*, act of giving in to wishes or demands. <u>Compliance</u> *with the tax laws is required.*

**con • vul • sion** (kən vulʹshən) *n.*, sudden, violent disturbance. *The feverish patient was shaken by* <u>convulsions</u>.

**nat • u • ral • i • za • tion** (nachʹər əl izʹā shən) *n.*, bestowal of the rights of citizenship. *Before his* <u>naturalization</u>, *Juan needed a green card to work in the United States.*

**ten • ure** (tenʹyər) *n.*, right to hold a position permanently. *The governor's* <u>tenure</u> *in office is four years.*

**ab • di • cate** (abʹdi kātʹ) *vt.*, give up a right or a responsibility. *The powerful barons forced the king to* <u>abdicate</u> *his throne.*

with circumstances of cruelty and perfidy[4] scarcely paralleled in the most barbarous ages, and totally unworthy the head of a civilized nation.

He has constrained our fellow-citizens, taken captive on the high seas, to bear arms against their country, to become the executioners of their friends and brethren, or to fall themselves by their hands.

He has excited domestic <u>insurrection</u> amongst us, and has endeavored to bring on the inhabitants of our frontiers the merciless Indian savages, whose known rule of warfare is an undistinguished destruction of all ages, sexes, and conditions.

In every state of these oppressions we have petitioned for <u>redress</u>, in the most humble terms; our repeated petitions have been answered only by repeated injury. A prince whose character is thus marked by every act which may define a tyrant is unfit to be the ruler of a free people.

Nor have we been wanting in our attentions to our British brethren. We have warned them, from time to time, of attempts by their legislature to extend an unwarrantable jurisdiction over us. We have reminded them of the circumstances of our emigration and settlement here. We have appealed to their native justice and <u>magnanimity</u>; and we have conjured them, by the ties of our common kindred, to disavow these usurpations, which would inevitably interrupt our connections and correspondence. They, too, have been deaf to the voice of justice and of consanguinity.[5] We must, therefore, <u>acquiesce</u> in the necessity which denounces our separation; and hold them, as we hold the rest of mankind, enemies in war, in peace friends.

WE, THEREFORE, THE REPRESENTATIVES OF THE UNITED STATES OF AMERICA, in General Congress assembled, appealing to the Supreme Judge of the world for the <u>rectitude</u> of our intentions, do, in the name and by the authority of the good people of these colonies, solemnly publish and declare, That these United Colonies are, and of right ought to be, FREE AND INDEPENDENT STATES; that they are absolved from all allegiance to the British crown, and that all political connection between them and the state of Great Britain is, and ought to be, totally dissolved; and that, as free and independent states, they have full power to levy war, conclude peace, contract alliances, establish commerce, and to do all other acts and things which independent states may of right do. And, for the support of this declaration, with a firm reliance on the protection of Divine Providence, we mutually pledge to each other our lives, our fortunes, and our sacred honor. ∎

*What powers do the united colonies have?*

---

4. **perfidy.** Betrayal of trust
5. **consanguinity.** Close connection; relatedness

---

**WORDS FOR EVERYDAY USE**

**in • sur • rec • tion** (in´sə rek´shən) *n.*, uprising. *In 1913, Irish patriots took over the Dublin Post Office, but British troops put down the <u>insurrection</u>.*

**re • dress** (rē´dres´) *n.*, compensation. *Mrs. Blount demanded <u>redress</u> from the driver who dented her car.*

**mag • na • nim • i • ty** (mag´nə nim´ ə tē) *n.*, state of being above pettiness. *A good leader treats the people with <u>magnanimity</u>.*

**ac • qui • esce** (ak´wē es´) *vi.*, agree without protest. *We asked the people next door to turn down their music, but they would not <u>acquiesce</u> to our request.*

**rec • ti • tude** (rek´tə tüd´) *n.*, correctness. *The judge will determine the <u>rectitude</u> of your case.*

## Respond *to the* SELECTION

What do you think Jefferson meant by "all men are created equal" when he wrote of the rights to "life, liberty, and the pursuit of happiness"?

The Declaration of Independence is unique in its insistence on inalienable rights, rights that cannot be taken away from the people, and on the notion that government derives its legitimacy from the consent of the governed.

During the debates on the adoption of the United States Constitution, its opponents repeatedly charged that the Constitution as drafted would open the way to tyranny by the central government. They demanded a "bill of rights" that would spell out the immunities of individual citizens. On September 25, 1789, the First Congress of the United States passed the first ten amendments of the Constitution, known as the Bill of Rights.

## The Bill of Rights

### Amendment 1

Congress shall make no law respecting an establishment of religion, or prohibiting the free exercise thereof; or abridging the freedom of speech, or of the press; or the right of the people peaceably to assemble, and to petition the Government for a redress of grievances.

### Amendment 2

A well-regulated militia, being necessary to the security of a free State, the right of the people to keep and bear arms shall not be infringed.

### Amendment 3

No soldier shall, in time of peace, be quartered in any house, without the consent of the owner, nor in time of war, but in a manner to be prescribed by law.

### Amendment 4

The right of the people to be secure in their persons, houses, papers, and effects, against unreasonable searches and seizures, shall not be violated, and no warrants shall issue, but upon probable cause, supported by oath or affirmation, and particularly describing the place to be searched, and the persons or things to be seized.

### Amendment 5

No person shall be held to answer for a capital, or otherwise infamous crime, unless on a presentment or indictment of a Grand Jury, except in cases arising in the land or naval forces, or in the militia, when in actual service in time of war or public danger; nor shall any person be subject for the same offense to be twice put in jeopardy of life or limb; nor shall be compelled in any criminal case to be a witness against himself, nor be deprived of life, liberty, or property, without due process of law; nor shall private property be taken for public use without just compensation.

### Amendment 6

In all criminal prosecutions, the accused shall enjoy the right to a speedy and public trial, by an impartial jury of the State and district wherein the crime shall have been committed, which district shall have been previously ascertained by law, and to be informed of the nature and cause of the accusation; to be confronted with the witnesses against him; to have compulsory process for obtaining witnesses in his favor, and to have the assistance of counsel for his defense.

### Amendment 7

In suits at common law, where the value in controversy shall exceed twenty dollars, the right of trial by jury shall be preserved, and no fact tried by a jury shall be otherwise reexamined in any court of the United States, than according to the rules of the common law.

### Amendment 8

Excessive bail shall not be required, nor excessive fines imposed, nor cruel and unusual punishments inflicted.

### Amendment 9

The enumeration in the Constitution, of certain rights, shall not be construed to deny or disparage others retained by the people.

### Amendment 10

The powers not delegated to the United States by the Constitution, nor prohibited by it to the States, are reserved to the States respectively, or to the people.

# INVESTIGATE, Inquire, Imagine

**Recall:** GATHERING FACTS

1a. What is an "unalienable" right? What rights does Jefferson consider as being unalienable?

2a. What are some of the specific grievances that the colonists had against the British monarch?

3a. With what personal statement do the signers of the Declaration conclude the document?

**Interpret:** FINDING MEANING

1b. According to the Declaration, why are governments "instituted among" people? What right does a people have when its government "becomes destructive" of the ends of securing the rights to "life, liberty, and the pursuit of happiness"?

2b. In your opinion, which is the most serious offense of the crown? Which is the least serious?

3b. What risks were the signers of the Declaration taking upon themselves?

**Analyze:** TAKING THINGS APART

4a. Into how many sections is the Declaration of Independence divided? What is the purpose of each section?

**Synthesize:** BRINGING THINGS TOGETHER

4b. The eighteenth-century English philosopher John Locke held that people are born with "natural rights" that cannot be taken from them. The eighteenth-century French philosopher Jean-Jacques Rousseau believed that government is a social contract entered into by the people for their mutual protection and well-being. What statements in the Declaration reflect these writers' beliefs? How would these two writers have received the news of the Declaration of Independence? Why?

**Evaluate:** MAKING JUDGMENTS

5a. Draw your own conclusions about how the Declaration of Independence was received by King George.

**Extend:** CONNECTING IDEAS

5b. Write a personal declaration of independence. First, state with whom you are dissolving ties. Second, provide reasons for the necessity of this dissolution. Third, declare your independence and state what you are willing to sacrifice to attain your freedom.

# Understanding Literature

**ALLITERATION.** Review the definition for **alliteration** in the Handbook of Literary Terms. What examples of alliteration can you find in the second sentence of the Declaration of Independence?

**PARALLELISM.** Review the definition for **parallelism** given in Literary Tools on page 163 and the radiating circle you completed as you read the selection. How does Jefferson use parallelism in his presentation of the grievances against King George? What effect does this parallelism have on the reader?

# Writer's Journal

1. Assume the role of a colonial journalist. Write a **news bulletin** for your fellow colonists explaining what they will be able to do on their own after declaring their independence.

2. Imagine how the lives of free and independent colonists will be different from serving as subjects of the British crown. Write an **account** of the changes that take place in one person's life.

3. Write an **editorial** stating why people should fight for the right to be "equal," according to the Declaration of Independence. Make sure you explain the difference between equality and identity.

# Integrating *the* LANGUAGE ARTS

## Language, Grammar, and Style

ACHIEVING PARALLELISM. Read the Language Arts Survey 3.38, "Achieving Parallelism." Then rewrite the following sentences, using parallel structure.

1. The Declaration of Independence was adopted by representatives of the Thirteen Colonies on July 4, 1776, announcing the separation of those colonies from Britain and to make them into the United States.

2. Previously, the colonies had sought redress from the crown and wanted reconciliation.

3. The actual writing of the Declaration was entrusted to Jefferson, and the revising giving to Franklin, Adams, and Jefferson.

4. The Declaration asserts the fundamental American ideal of government and indicted King George for willfully infringing on the rights of the colonies.

5. The stirring closing paragraph is the formal pronouncement of independence and borrowed from the resolution of independence adopted by Congress July 2, 1776.

## Study and Research

JEFFERSON AND SLAVERY. The original draft of the Declaration of Independence contained a strong statement opposing slavery. Research the original draft of the Declaration to learn what the passage against slavery stated. Then research the life of Thomas Jefferson. Does his life reflect the beliefs stated in the passage about slavery? Finally, write a short essay explaining what you have learned in your research.

## Applied English

CREDO. Imagine that you work for a nonprofit organization. Write a credo, or statement of belief, expressing your organization's most strongly held opinions and values. Use formal language and parallelism to express your beliefs effectively. You may want to read the Language Arts Survey 3.38, "Achieving Parallelism."

## Media Literacy & Collaborative Learning

TV SHOW PLOTS. The first ten amendments to the Constitution of the United States, ratified in 1791 and known collectively as the Bill of Rights, are printed on page 168. Working with other students in a small group, paraphrase each of these amendments. Then write plot summaries of real or imaginary movies and TV shows that raise issues based on the Bill of Rights and indicate the amendments to which they refer. For example, a plot summary might read: A newspaper in a small town publishes an article criticizing the mayor. The mayor orders the local police to confiscate copies of the newspaper (the First Amendment).

# Letter to John Adams, May 7, 1776

BY ABIGAIL ADAMS

## About the AUTHOR

**Abigail Adams** (1744–1818) was born in Weymouth, Massachusetts, the daughter of a minister. At the age of twenty, she married John Adams, a Boston lawyer who played important roles in the founding and governing of the United States. An ardent supporter of the American Revolution, Adams began a remarkable correspondence with her husband when, in 1774, he became a delegate to the First Continental Congress, a federal parliamentary body established by the British colonies in America.

From 1774 to 1783 (the year in which a peace treaty was signed with England), John Adams was often away from home, involved in work that included the drafting of the Declaration of Independence, the conduct of the American Revolution, and the formation of the new nation. During this time, Adams kept up a lively, fascinating correspondence with him. This correspondence offers many insights into the revolution and into daily life during the period. In her letters, Adams proved to be one of the first American champions of women's rights. She was particularly interested in expanding educational opportunities for women, which at that time were few. Adams was also an ardent opponent of slavery.

After the American Revolution, John Adams served as a diplomat in Europe, and Abigail traveled with him, living at various times in Paris, The Hague, and London. John Adams served as the first vice president of the new nation and then as its second president. During this period, Adams divided her time between the family residence in Massachusetts and the temporary capitol in Philadelphia. Her son John Quincy Adams became the sixth president of the United States.

## Reader's Journal

When did you last write a letter, and why did you write it?

## Literary TOOLS

**AIM.** A writer's **aim** is his or her purpose, or goal. People may write with the following aims: to inform; to entertain; to narrate (tell a story); to reflect; or to persuade. As you read, determine Adams's primary aim in writing to her husband.

**DICTION. Diction,** when applied to writing, refers to word choice. Ask yourself if Adams uses formal or informal diction when writing to her husband.

## ArtNote

***Abigail Adams,*** c.1800. Gilbert Stuart.

Gilbert Stuart left America before the Revolution to study art in England, where there were more opportunities for artists. When he returned to America in 1793, he found a demand for portraits of the new country's leaders. In addition to these paintings of the Adamses, Stuart made the definitive images of Washington and Jefferson.

## About the SELECTION

Abigail Adams wrote the following letter to her husband, John, then a delegate to the First Continental Congress. The letter was written shortly before the drafting of the Declaration of Independence, at a time when members of the Congress were debating whether to declare the colonies' independence from Britain.

# Letter to *John Adams,* May 7, 1776

## ABIGAIL ADAMS

**Braintree**[1]

How many are the solitary hours I spend, <u>ruminating</u> upon the past and anticipating the future whilst you, overwhelmed with the cares of state, have but few moments you can devote to any individual. All domestic pleasures and enjoyments are absorbed in the great and important duty you owe your country "for our country is, as it were, a secondary god and the first and greatest parent. It is to be preferred to parents, wives, children, friends and all things; the gods only excepted. For if our country perishes, it is as impossible to save an individual as to preserve one of the fingers of a mortified hand." Thus do I suppress every wish and silence every murmur, acquiescing in a painful separation from the companion of my youth and the friend of my heart.

*Why must the good of the country come before the needs of individuals?*

I believe it is near ten days since I wrote you a line. I have not felt in a humor to entertain you. If I had taken up my pen, perhaps some unbecoming invective might have fallen from it; the eyes of our rulers have been closed and a <u>lethargy</u> has seized almost every member. I fear a fatal security has taken possession of them. Whilst the building is in flame, they tremble at

*John Adams,* 1826. Gilbert Stuart.
National Museum of American Art, Washington, DC.

the expense of water to quench it. In short, two months have elapsed since the evacuation of Boston and very little has been done in that time to secure it or the harbor from future invasion until the people are all in a flame, and no one among us that I have heard of even mentions expense. They think universally that there has been an amazing neglect somewhere. Many have turned out as volunteers to work upon Nodles

---

1. **Braintree.** Town south of Boston

---

**WORDS FOR EVERYDAY USE**

**ru • mi • nate** (rü´mə nāt´) *vt.,* go over in the mind repeatedly; contemplate. *At eighty, Mrs. Bell often <u>ruminated</u> about the things in her life that she would have done differently.*

**leth • ar • gy** (leth´ər jē) *n.,* quality or state of being lazy. *Due to their <u>lethargy</u>, half of the students did not complete the research assignment.*

Island, and many more would go upon Nantasket if it was once set on foot. "It is a maxim of state that power and liberty are like heat and moisture; where they are well mixed everything prospers; where they are single, they are destructive."

A government of more stability is much wanted in this colony, and they are ready to receive it from the hands of the Congress, and since I have begun with maxims of state, I will add another: A people may let a king fall, yet still remain a people, but if a king lets his people slip from him, he is no longer a king. And as this is most certainly our case, why not proclaim to the world in decisive terms your own importance?

*If people lose faith in their leader, what happens?*

Shall we not be despised by foreign powers for hesitating so long at a word?

I cannot say that I think you very generous to the ladies, for whilst you are proclaiming peace and good will to men, emancipating all nations, you insist upon retaining an absolute power over wives. But you must remember that <u>arbitrary</u> power is like most other things which are very hard, very liable to be broken—and notwithstanding all your wise laws and maxims, we have it in our power not only to free ourselves but to subdue our masters, and without violence throw both your natural and legal authority at our feet—

Charm by accepting, by submitting sway
Yet have our humor most when we obey.

I thank you for several letters which I have received since I wrote last. They alleviate a tedious absence, and I long earnestly for a Saturday evening and experience a similar pleasure to that which I used to find in the return of my friend upon that day after a week's absence.

Our little ones, whom you so often recommend to my care and instruction, shall not be deficient in virtue or probity[2] if the <u>precepts</u> of a mother have their desired effect, but they would be doubly enforced could they be indulged with the example of a father constantly before them; I often point them to their sire

Engaged in a corrupted state
Wrestling with vice and faction.  ■

## The idea of a year dissolves all my philosophy.

2. **probity.** Integrity

**WORDS FOR EVERYDAY USE**

ar • bi • trary (är´bə trer ē) *adj.*, ruling by absolute authority. *The CEO's <u>arbitrary</u> decision to lay off fifty employees hurt the company.*

pre • cept (prē´sept) *n.*, command or principle. *The professor asked the student teachers to outline their educational <u>precepts</u>.*

## Respond to the SELECTION

If you were Abigail Adams, how would you feel about your husband's frequent absences as he worked to found a new nation?

# INVESTIGATE, Inquire, *Imagine*

**Recall:** GATHERING FACTS

1a. According to the opening of the letter, how does Adams spend her time? With what duties is her absent husband "overwhelmed"?

2a. According to Adams, whose "eyes . . . have been closed"? Who is suffering from a "fatal security"?

3a. When does Adams say that a king is no longer a king?

→ **Interpret:** FINDING MEANING

1b. Does Adams resent her husband's absence? Why, or why not?

2b. What metaphor does Adams use in paragraph 2 of her letter to describe the reluctance of some leaders to take action?

3b. For centuries, most British subjects believed in the Divine Right of Kings (that kings were divinely appointed). Does Adams subscribe to such a view? Why, or why not?

**Analyze:** TAKING THINGS APART

4a. The United States was the first country in the world founded on the principle that government derives its rights from "the consent of the governed" and is justified in exercising those rights only as long as the governed continue in their consent. What passages in Adams's letter show that she believes government not consented to by the governed to be illegitimate?

→ **Synthesize:** BRINGING THINGS TOGETHER

4b. What part of the American population does Adams believe is not being equally represented by its leaders? What does Adams imply she wants her husband and the other delegates to do with regard to this part of the population?

**Perspective:** LOOKING AT OTHER VIEWS

5a. As the wife of a political figure, why might Adams state that one's country is "a secondary god and the first and greatest parent"? What perspective might she have in being married to a man so influential to the founding of the nation? How different might her point of view be if she were married to a private citizen?

→ **Empathy:** SEEING FROM INSIDE

5b. If you were Adams, what would be your motive in using the metaphor of water quenching the burning building? What are you trying to get your husband to do in this passage?

# Understanding *Literature*

**AIM.** Review the definition for **aim** in Literary Tools on page 171. Then create a chart, listing, on the left, four important passages from Adams's letter and, on the right, the aim Adams's writing expresses in those passages. One example has been done for you.

| Passages | Aim |
|---|---|
| "How many are the solitary hours I spend . . . whilst you . . . have but few moments you can devote to any individual." | Adams informs her husband she misses him and understands why he is so busy. |

**DICTION.** Review the definition for **diction** in the Handbook of Literary Terms. Does Adams use formal or informal diction when addressing her husband? Is the diction she selects in keeping with the aim of her writing? What are the most personal topics Adams broaches in her letter? Does her diction change in those places?

# Writer's Journal

1. Imagine that you are a friend of Abigail Adams. Write an **e-mail message** summarizing the effect that John Adams's absence is having on his wife and children to mutual friends of yours.
2. Imagine you are John Adams. Write a **letter** back to your wife, commenting on the main points of her letter.
3. The seventeenth-century philosopher Thomas Hobbes argued that life in the "state of nature" is "solitary, poor, nasty, brutish, and short" and that a strong central authority is necessary to maintain order and ensure self-preservation. Assuming the persona of Adams, write an **opinion piece** for a philosophical journal, explaining in what respect you agree with Hobbes and in what respect you disagree.

# Integrating 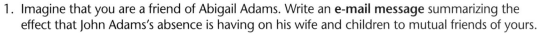 the LANGUAGE ARTS

## Language, Grammar, and Style

**COMBINING SENTENCES USING CLAUSES.** Read the Language Arts Survey 3.36, "Combining and Expanding Sentences." Then read the first sentence in paragraph 3. Write four simple sentences to express the meaning of the original compound-complex sentence from the selection.

## Speaking and Listening

**ROLE-PLAY.** Imagine that the telephone had been invented in Adams's time and that rather than write a letter, she simply called her husband. With a partner, play the roles of John and Abigail Adams, who are having a telephone conversation on May 7, 1776. If you play the role of Abigail Adams, refer to the letter for topics of conversation. If you play the role of John Adams, agree and disagree with statements your wife makes.

## Applied English

**BUSINESS LETTER.** Choose a political issue that interests you and write a **business letter** to a political figure, such as your town's mayor, your governor, your congressperson, or one of your senators, stating your position and the reasons for your views. Refer to the Language Arts Survey 6.5, "Writing a Business Letter," and write your letter in proper business letter form. (Note: A reference librarian in your school or community will be able to help you to identify the names, titles, and addresses of political figures at the local, state, and national levels.)

## Media Literacy

**BOOK JACKET.** Design a book jacket for the collected letters of Abigail Adams to her husband John. On the front, draw a picture suggestive of the content of the book. On the inside cover, write a summary of the book that will make people want to read it. You may want to use a quotation from Abigail Adams's May 7, 1776, letter in your summary.

## from *Letters from an American Farmer*
by J. Hector St. Jean de Crèvecœur

I wish I could be acquainted with the feelings and thoughts which must agitate the heart and present themselves to the mind of an enlightened[1] Englishman, when he first lands on this continent. He must greatly rejoice that he lived at a time to see this fair country discovered and settled; he must necessarily feel a share of national pride, when he views the chain of settlements which embellishes these extended shores. When he says to himself, this is the work of my countrymen, who, when convulsed by factions,[2] afflicted by a variety of miseries and wants, restless and impatient, took refuge here. They brought along with them their national genius, to which they principally owe what liberty they enjoy, and what substance they possess. Here he sees the industry of his native country displayed in a new manner, and traces in their works the embryos of all the arts, sciences, and ingenuity which flourish in Europe. Here he beholds fair cities, substantial villages, extensive fields, an immense country filled with decent houses, good roads, orchards, meadows, and bridges, where an hundred years ago all was wild, woody, and uncultivated! What a train of pleasing ideas this fair spectacle must suggest; it is a prospect which must inspire a good citizen with the most heartfelt pleasure. The difficulty consists in the manner of viewing so extensive a scene. He is arrived on a new continent; a modern society offers itself to his contemplation, different from what he had hitherto seen. It is not composed, as in Europe, of great lords who possess everything, and of a herd of people who have nothing. Here are no aristocratical families, no courts, no kings, no bishops, no ecclesiastical dominion,[3] no invisible power giving to a few a very visible one; no great manufacturers employing thousands, no great refinements of luxury. The rich and the poor are not so far removed from each other as they are in Europe. Some few towns excepted, we are all tillers of the earth, from Nova Scotia to West Florida. We are a people of cultivators, scattered over an immense territory, communicating with each other by means of good roads and navigable rivers, united by the silken bands of mild government, all respecting the laws, without dreading their power, because they are equitable. We are all animated with the spirit of an industry which is unfettered and unrestrained, because each person works for himself. If he travels through our rural districts he views not the hostile castle, and the haughty mansion, contrasted with the clay-built hut and miserable cabin, where cattle and men help to keep each other warm, and dwell in meanness, smoke, and indigence.[4] A pleasing uniformity of decent competence appears throughout our habitations. The meanest of our log-houses is a dry and comfortable habitation. Lawyer or merchant are the fairest titles our towns afford; that of a farmer is the only appellation of the rural inhabitants of our country. It must take some time ere he can reconcile himself to our dictionary, which is but short in words of dignity, and names of honor. There, on a Sunday, he sees a congregation of respectable farmers and their wives, all clad in neat homespun, well mounted, or riding in their own humble wagons. There is not among them an esquire, saving the unlettered[5] magistrate. There he sees a parson as simple as his flock, a farmer who does not riot on the labor of others. We have no princes, for whom we toil, starve, and bleed; we are the most perfect society now existing in the world. Here man is free as he ought to be; nor is this pleasing equality so transitory as many others are. Many ages will not see the shores of our great lakes replenished with inland nations, nor the unknown bounds of North America entirely peopled. Who can tell how far it extends? Who can tell the millions of men whom it will feed and contain? for no European foot has as yet traveled half the extent of this mighty continent!

The next wish of this traveler will be to know whence[6] came all these people? They are a mixture of English, Scotch, Irish, French, Dutch, Germans and Swedes. From this promiscuous breed, that race now called Americans have arisen. The eastern provinces must indeed be excepted,[7] as being the unmixed descendants of Englishmen. I have heard many wish that they had been more intermixed also: for my part, I am no wisher, and think it much better as it has happened. They exhibit a most conspicuous figure in this great and variegated picture; they too enter for a great share in the pleasing perspective displayed in these thirteen provinces.[8] I know it is fashionable to reflect on them, but respect them for what they have done; for the accuracy and wisdom with which they have settled their territory; for the decency of their manners; for their early love of letters; their ancient college,[9] the first in this hemisphere; for their industry, which to me who am but a farmer is the criterion of everything. There never was a people, situated as they are, who with so ungrateful a soil have done more in so short a time.

---

1. **enlightened.** Knowledgeable; full of understanding
2. **convulsed by factions.** Upset by disagreement among groups of citizens
3. **ecclesiastical dominion.** Religious authority over a state
4. **indigence.** Poverty
5. **unlettered.** Uneducated
6. **whence.** From where
7. **excepted.** Excluded
8. **provinces.** Colonies
9. **college.** Harvard College (founded in 1636) in Cambridge, Massachusetts

# from *Common Sense*
by Thomas Paine

From *III. Thoughts on the Present State of American Affairs*

In the following pages I offer nothing more than simple facts, plain arguments, and common sense: and have no other preliminaries to settle with the reader, than that he will divest himself of prejudice and prepossession, and suffer his reason and his feelings to determine for themselves: that he will put on, or rather that he will not put off, the true character of a man, and generously enlarge his views beyond the present day.

Volumes have been written on the subject of the struggle between England and America. Men of all ranks have embarked in the controversy, from different motives, and with various designs; but all have been ineffectual, and the period of debate is closed. Arms as the last resource decide the contest; the appeal was the choice of the King, and the continent has accepted the challenge.

◆　◆　◆

A government of our own is our natural right: and when a man seriously reflects on the precariousness of human affairs, he will become convinced that it is infinitely wiser and safer to form a constitution of our own in a cool deliberate manner, while we have it in our power, than to trust such an interesting event to time and chance. If we omit it now, some Massanello[1] may hereafter arise, who, laying hold of popular disquietudes, may collect together the desperate and the discontented, and by assuming to themselves the powers of government, finally sweep away the liberties of the continent like a deluge. Should the government of America return again into the hands of Britain, the tottering situation of things will be a temptation for some desperate adventurer to try his fortune; and in such a case, what relief can Britain give? Ere she could hear the news, the fatal business might be done; and ourselves suffering like the wretched Britons under the oppression of the conqueror. Ye that oppose independence now, ye know not what ye do: ye are opening a door to eternal tyranny by keeping vacant the seat of government. There are thousands and tens of thousands, who would think it glorious to expel from the continent that barbarous and hellish power.

# from *Crisis, No. 1*
by Thomas Paine

These are the times that try men's souls. The summer soldier and the sunshine patriot will, in this crisis, shrink from the service of their country, but he that stands it now, deserves the love and thanks of man and woman. Tyranny, like hell, is not easily conquered; yet we have this consolation with us, that the harder the conflict, the more glorious the triumph. What we obtain too cheap, we esteem too lightly: it is dearness only that gives everything its value. Heaven knows how to put a proper price upon its goods; and it would be strange

indeed if so celestial an article as freedom should not be highly rated. Britain, with an army to enforce her tyranny, has declared that she has a right (not only to tax) but "to bind us in all cases whatsoever," and if being bound in that manner is not slavery, then is there not such a thing as slavery upon earth. Even the expression is impious; for so unlimited a power can belong only to God.

Whether the independence of the continent was declared too soon, or delayed too long, I will not now enter into as an argument; my own simple opinion is, that had it been eight months earlier, it would have been much better. We did not make a proper use of last winter, neither could we, while we were in a dependent state. However, the fault, if it were one, was all our own;[2] we have none to blame but ourselves. But no great deal is lost yet. All that Howe[3] has been doing for this month past is rather a ravage than a conquest, which the spirit of the Jerseys,[4] a year ago, would have quickly repulsed, and which time and a little resolution will soon recover.

I have as little superstition in me as any man living, but my secret opinion has ever been, and still is, that God Almighty will not give up a people to military destruction, or leave them unsupportedly to perish, who have so earnestly and so repeatedly sought to avoid the calamities of war, by every decent method which wisdom could invent. Neither have I so much of the infidel[5] in me as to suppose that He has relinquished the government of the world, and given us up to the care of devils; and as I do not, I cannot see on what grounds the King of Britain can look up to heaven for help against us: a common murderer, a highwayman, or a housebreaker has as good a pretense as he.

'Tis surprising to see how rapidly a panic will sometimes run through a country. All nations and ages have been subject to them: Britain has trembled like an ague[6] at the report of a French fleet of flat-bottomed boats, and in the fourteenth century[7] the whole English army, after ravaging the kingdom of France, was driven back like men petrified with fear; and this brave exploit was performed by a few broken forces collected and headed by a woman, Joan of Arc. Would that heaven might inspire some Jersey maid to spirit up her countrymen, and save her fair fellow sufferers from ravage and ravishment! Yet panics, in some cases, have their uses; they produce as much good as hurt. Their duration is always short;

---

1. **Massanello.** Thomas Anello, or Massanello, a fisherman, became king for a day after inciting a revolt against the Spanish who were occupying his city of Naples.
2. **own.** Paine wanted an immediate declaration of independence uniting the colonies.
3. **Howe.** Lord William Howe was commander of the British Army in America from 1775 to 1778.
4. **Jerseys.** East and West Jersey were separate colonies.
5. **infidel.** Person who does not accept some particular theory, belief, etc.; used derogatorily
6. **ague.** Chill; fit of shivering
7. **fourteenth century.** Actually the fifteenth; Joan of Arc triumphed over the English in 1429.

the mind soon grows through them, and acquires a firmer habit than before. But their peculiar advantage is that they are the touchstones[1] of sincerity and hypocrisy, and bring things and men to light, which might otherwise have lain forever undiscovered. In fact, they have the same effect on secret traitors, which an imaginary apparition would have upon a private murderer. They sift out the hidden thoughts of man, and hold them up in public to the world. Many a disguised tory[2] has lately shown his head, that shall penitentially solemnize with curses the day on which Howe arrived upon the Delaware. . . .

The far and the near, the home counties and the back,[3] the rich and poor will suffer or rejoice alike. The heart that feels not now is dead: the blood of his children will curse his cowardice who shrinks back at a time when a little might have saved the whole, and made them happy. I love the man that can smile in trouble, that can gather strength from distress, and grow brave by reflection. 'Tis the business of little minds to shrink; but he whose heart is firm, and whose conscience approves his conduct, will pursue his principles unto death. My own line of reasoning is to myself as straight and clear as a ray of light. Not all the treasures of the world, so far as I believe, could have induced me to support an offensive war, for I think it murder; but if a thief breaks into my house, burns and destroys my property, and kills or threatens to kill me, or those that are in it, and to "bind me in all cases whatsoever"[4] to his absolute will, am I to suffer it? What signifies it to me, whether he who does it is a king or a common man; my countryman or not my countryman; whether it be done by an individual villain, or an army of them? If we reason to the root of things we shall find no difference; neither can any just cause be assigned why we should punish in the one case and pardon in the other. Let them call me rebel, and welcome, I feel no concern from it; but I should suffer the misery of devils were I to make a whore of my soul by swearing allegiance to one whose character is that of a sottish, stupid, stubborn, worthless, brutish man. I conceive likewise a horrid idea in receiving mercy from a being, who at the last day shall be shrieking to the rocks and mountains to cover him, and fleeing with terror from the orphan, the widow, and the slain of America.

# from "Remarks Concerning the Natives of North America"
## by Benjamin Franklin

Savages we call them, because their manners differ from ours, which we think the perfection of civility; they think the same of theirs.

Perhaps, if we could examine the manners of different nations with impartiality, we should find no people so rude, as to be without any rules of politeness; nor any so polite, as not to have some remains of rudeness.

The Indian men, when young, are hunters and warriors; when old, counselors; for all their government is by counsel of the sages;[5] there is no force, there are no prisons, no officers to compel obedience, or inflict punishment. Hence they generally study oratory, the best speaker having the most influence. The Indian women till the ground, dress the food, nurse and bring

up the children, and preserve and hand down to posterity the memory of public transactions. These employments of men and women are accounted natural and honorable. Having few artificial wants, they have abundance of leisure for improvement by conversation. Our laborious manner of life, compared with theirs, they esteem[6] slavish and base; and the learning, on which we value ourselves, they regard as frivolous and useless. An instance of this occurred at the Treaty of Lancaster, in Pennsylvania, *anno* 1744, between the government of Virginia and the Six Nations.[7] After the principal business was settled, the commissioners from Virginia acquainted the Indians by a speech, that there was at Williamsburg a college, with a fund for educating Indian youth; and that, if the Six Nations would send down half a dozen of their young lads to that college, the government would take care that they should be well provided for, and instructed in all the learning of the white people. It is one of the Indian rules of politeness not to answer a public proposition the same day that it is made; they think it would be treating it as a light matter, and that they show it respect by taking time to consider it, as of a matter important. They therefore deferred their answer till the day following; when their speaker began, by expressing their deep sense of the kindness of the Virginia government, in making them that offer; "for we know," says he, "that you highly esteem the kind of learning taught in those Colleges, and that the maintenance of our young men, while with you, would be very expensive to you. We are convinced, therefore, that you mean to do us good by your proposal; and we thank you heartily. But you, who are wise, must know that different nations have different conceptions of things; and you will therefore not take it amiss, if our ideas of this kind of education happen not to be the same with yours. We have had some experience of it; several of our young people were formerly brought up at the colleges of the northern provinces; they were instructed in all your sciences; but, when they came back to us, they were bad runners, ignorant of every means of living in the woods, unable to bear either cold or hunger, knew neither how to build a cabin, take a deer, or kill an enemy, spoke our language imperfectly, were therefore neither fit for hunters, warriors, nor counselors; they were totally good for nothing. We are however not the less obliged by your kind offer, though we decline accepting it; and, to show our grateful sense of it, if the gentlemen of Virginia will send us a dozen of their sons, we will take great care of their education, instruct them in all we know, and make *men* of them."

---

1. **touchstones.** Types of stone formerly used to test the purity of gold or silver; hence, any test for determining genuineness or value
2. **tory.** Supporter of continued allegiance to Great Britain
3. **back.** Backwoods
4. **"bind me . . . whatsoever."** On February 24, 1776, the Declaratory Act of Parliament established British authority over the American colonies.
5. **sages.** Very wise people, widely respected for their wisdom, experience, and judgment
6. **esteem.** Consider; hold to be
7. **Six Nations.** Confederation of Iroquoian peoples, comprising the Mohawk, Oneida, Onondaga, Cayuga, Seneca, and Tuscarora

# Guided Writing

## DEFENDING A VIEWPOINT

When Patrick Henry delivered his Speech in the Virginia Convention, his goal was to persuade a nation to take a certain course of action. While you may not have to write an essay or give a speech that will ultimately determine the course of world history, you are constantly using language to persuade others, and that will determine your personal history.

Persuasion is, in a sense, a writer's declaration of independent thought. The writer is attempting to get his or her readers to accept a certain viewpoint or take some action. Persuasion might be as basic as convincing your parents that you are capable of taking the family car out on a Friday night or of having a job and keeping your grades up. Of course, home is not the only place where persuasion is needed. At school you might argue for an extension on a research paper deadline, argue against a dress code that would have a negative impact on student body morale, or persuade the school administration to fund a girls' hockey team.

As you have grown and matured, you have developed more sophisticated techniques for persuasion. Think about the small children you have witnessed in the grocery store, lying on the polished floor, arms waving, feet kicking, screaming hysterically, "But I want it!" This may be a good attention-getting device, but it isn't very persuasive. You know that to persuade your audience, you must establish and maintain a clear argument and offer compelling evidence.

**WRITING ASSIGNMENT.** In this assignment, you will write a persuasive essay defending a viewpoint while considering the viewpoints of others.

## Professional Model

Patrick Henry's speech to the Virginia Convention was logical and compelling. Over two hundred years later, readers still admire Henry's skillful use of language and find his words moving and powerful.

> "How does one write persuasively?....
> There is a recipe. It includes:
>
> 1. making an assertion
>
> 2. providing at least three supports
>
> 3. ordering that support toward a crescendo
>
> 4. giving time to the opposing position
>
> 5. using images and details to persuade the reader instead of relying on emotionally loaded words that tell, rather than show."
>
> —Sheila Bender

Henry spoke to his colleagues in the Virginia Convention who disagreed with him, but who also had the power to bring about the action he desired.

As you read the professional model, look for Henry's argument and the evidence he offers for it. Also try to determine which words and phrases show the speaker's respect for the opposing viewpoint.

Critical in persuasive writing is identifying the audience; Patrick Henry certainly knew his. Who is Henry's audience? How does he acknowledge them in this opening passage and show respect for those whose opinions differ from his own?

As an orator, Patrick Henry was known for capturing the attention of his listeners. Note the use of rhetorical questions and emphatic statements. How do Henry's allusion to "the song of that siren" and his reference to what should characterize "wise men" keep his audience hooked?

Most Americans know by heart Henry's famous concluding words, "Give me liberty or give me death!" What is another passage you find memorable from Henry's Speech in the Virginia Convention?

## from Speech in the Virginia Convention by Patrick Henry

Mr. President: No man thinks more highly than I do of the patriotism, as well as abilities, of the very worthy gentlemen who have just addressed the house. But different men often see the same subject in different lights: and, therefore, I hope it will not be thought disrespectful to those gentlemen, if, entertaining, as I do, opinions of a character very opposite to theirs, I shall speak forth my sentiments freely and without reserve. This is no time for ceremony. The question before the house is one of awful moment to this country. For my own part, I consider it as nothing less than a question of freedom or slavery.

. . .

We are apt to shut our eyes against a painful truth, and listen to the song of that siren till she transforms us into beasts. Is this the part of wise men, engaged in a great and arduous struggle for liberty?

. . .

It is in vain, sir, to extenuate the matter. Gentlemen may cry, "Peace, peace"—but there is no peace. The war is actually begun! The next gale that sweeps from the north will bring to our ears the clash of resounding arms! Our brethren are already in the field! Why stand we here idle? What is it that gentlemen wish? What would they have? Is life so dear, or peace so sweet, as to be purchased at the price of chains and slavery? Forbid it, Almighty God! I know not what course others may take; but as for me, give me liberty or give me death!

## Prewriting

**WRITING WITH A PLAN.** Finding a topic that means something to you is key to writing a successful persuasive essay. Some topic ideas include:

Lowering or raising the driving age
Shortening or lengthening the school day or year
Mandating second language education in high school
Testing all high school athletes for drug use
Awarding PE credit for varsity sports
Legislating hate crimes
Banning skaters in public places
Making school mascots politically correct

Generate at least five additional topics; then, in groups of three or four, **brainstorm** even more topics for ten minutes. List at least 20 topics. From the small groups, one member should report back to the class. As each group reports, write down any topic you like, or any topics that come to mind because of something someone else has said.

Before finalizing a topic, consider another source: the media. Spend some time reading the newspaper. Watch the evening news. Listen to public radio. What stories are being reported? What issues are given editorial space? Find at least three more potential topics and add them to your list. Then, as you select your topic, remember that the best topic for you is one that lends itself well to argument and that you care and know about.

## Student Model—Graphic Organizer

Min, a student concerned about the lack of activities for teens in his town, created this graphic organizer for his ideas. After examining his graphic organizer, copy it onto your own paper and add your ideas to it.

Thesis: a teen center is good for teens and adults

| my points of support | opposition's counterpoints |
| --- | --- |
| gives teens something to do | kids have enough to do |
| gets adults involved in community | adults don't have time |
| keeps kids out of trouble | more kids and more trouble |
| more chances to socialize | some kids aren't social |

| opposition's points | my counterpoints |
| --- | --- |
| too much money | investment so kids involved |
| noisy and disturbs neighborhood | set hours and activities |
| bring gangs into the neighborhood | gangs aren't interested in center |

## Drafting

Set up a preliminary outline. This will tell you if you know enough about the topic to write about it.

The following points should be included in your essay:

- your thesis
- three points of support
- the opposition's counterpoints
- three points of the opposition's argument
- your counterpoints of the opposition's argument
- your conclusion: why your argument is superior

Once you have an outline, you are ready to write. As Atticus Finch says in *To Kill a Mockingbird,* "It's not time to worry yet"—about capturing the reader's attention in the introductory paragraph, that is. Simply put down your thesis and the points

**IDENTIFYING YOUR AUDIENCE.** You would approach a friend, a teacher, and a parent differently to ask a favor or make a convincing argument. It is important to know your audience before you try to persuade that audience.

You will have the greatest influence if you are writing to the people who have the power to affect the issue you are writing about, not to the people who already agree with you. Identify and write down the characteristics of your audience. Think about the arguments and counter-arguments that are important to them.

**FINDING YOUR VOICE.** To convince your reader that change is necessary, it is important that your honesty comes through. "Gee, Mrs. Cleaver. That's a beautiful dress," said Eddie Haskell on nearly every episode of *Leave It to Beaver.* No one, not even Mrs. Cleaver, believed he was sincere. Don't use an Eddie Haskell voice; the phoniness weakens even the strongest argument. Neither should your tone be combative: "The school day should be shortened because we don't do anything, anyway." To be convincing, you need to show the audience that you have considered all sides of the issue, and that while considering all sides, yours is the most logical one.

Write a sentence that states your opinion about the issue you are writing about. Now

*continued on page 182*

write that sentence as if you were trying to placate, or soothe, your audience rather than argue that they should change their view. Next, write the sentence as if you were forcing your view on your audience without being reasonable and logical. Notice the different word choices and sentence structures in each sentence.

What effective techniques can you use to enlist your reader's support and adopt your point of view?

- select pertinent and focused points of support
- appeal to your reader's knowledge and experiences
- use illustrations and anecdotes
- compare and contrast situations

of support in that opening paragraph. Then start each body paragraph with a topic sentence that contains a point of support. Elaborate thoroughly so that your writing clearly moves the reader along. Include the opposing viewpoint, but explain why it is not as valid as your point. It may be easier to start with your strongest point first, but ultimately in your revision you may want to reverse the order. That way the reader will remember the strongest part of your argument.

Your conclusion should reinforce the thesis, tie ideas together, and bring closure. Simply restating your thesis and main ideas will give the paper a feeling of redundancy. However you decide to conclude your essay, do it with style so that your reader has a heightened awareness, feels better informed, or wants to act.

To be effective, illustrations and layout should help your audience to quickly and clearly understand your information and viewpoint. See the Language Arts Survey 6.11, "Displaying Effective Visual Information," for more information on the use of illustrations.

## Self- and Peer Evaluation

After you finish your first draft, complete a self-evaluation of your persuasive essay. Read your draft as if you were an opponent to the thesis presented in the draft. If time allows, you may want to get one or two peer evaluations. See the Language Arts Survey 2.37–2.40 for more details about self-evaluation and peer evaluation.

As you evaluate your persuasive essay or that of a classmate, answer the following questions:

- How does the introduction compel the reader to keep reading? Is there a clear thesis statement?
- What facts, examples, and logic in the body strengthen the argument? What additions or deletions would strengthen the argument more?
- How does the body acknowledge and respond to counterpoints?
- Does the voice in the paper suggest rational, intelligent, even sophisticated thought?
- Are there transitions in and between the paragraphs?
- How might the order of the points and counterpoints be presented to be most effective?
- Do the sentences have a variety of structures and lengths?
- Which verbs are active and strong? Which verb choices could be improved? Do all verbs agree with their subjects?
- What writing conventions—paragraph structure, sentence structure, grammar, punctuation, and capitalization—could be improved to make the essay easier to read?
- How might word choice be modified to create a clearer and more convincing argument?
- How does the conclusion make the essay unforgettable?

Min drafted his persuasive essay arguing that the community should open a teen center to help kids spend their time in more meaningful ways. His friend, Kyle, played "devil's advocate" and added peer review comments from the perspective of an unconvinced city council member. The Student Model below shows a draft copy that incorporates both self- and peer-evaluation comments.

## Student Model—Draft

**A Teen Center**

*Flat opening— add something interesting?*

Teen centers are places where young people can go to play games and socialize with other kids. I think that

*maybe don't use "I." It doesn't sound as official*

having a teen center in any town is a good idea for everyone including adults, that probably won't even use the center. Besides being a fun thing for teens around the area, it may also help kids from getting into gangs or into trouble because they have somewhere to go and meet people at.

*Awkward*

Along with the opinion of having a teen center goes the opinion not to have one. In this essay I'm going to explain

*How? examine the issues?*

why we should have a teen center and counter the opposing opinion of not having one.

The reasons that I want a teen center

*ARE*

*subject & verb don't agree*

is because it is a good place for teens to go when they have nothing to do. A center for teens motivates people to be more active in their communities. It keeps many kids out of trouble, that they may be getting into without the center. With this teen center kids can socialize with other kids more often and have fun while doing it.

*good points— Any examples to add?*

"When someone reliable gives you . . . feedback, you now have some true sense of your work's effect on people, and you may now know how to approach your final draft."

—Anne Lamott

"[Writers] should declare the causes which impel them...."

—Thomas Jefferson

## Language, Grammar, and Style

**Subject-Verb Agreement**

**IDENTIFYING SUBJECT-VERB AGREEMENT.** The subject of a sentence must agree in number with the verb of the sentence.

Example: The *boys* (subject) *are* (verb) staying after school.

When there is an intervening phrase or clause, the verb still must agree with the subject.

Example: *One* (subject) of the boys *is* (verb) staying after school.

THOSE OPPOSED (SOUNDS BETTER!)

The opposition might think that the points that I just listed ~~is not valid~~ Agreement ARE because kids in any town can find things to do. They don't need a teen center that costs a lot of money, to do things that any kid could do elsewhere in town. Why would a teen center make people socialize more? If a teen has trouble socializing in the town why would he/she not have trouble socializing at the teen center? Instead of keeping kids out of gangs it might start up more gangs because kids are socializing with people they might never have before if the teen center wasn't open.

TEENS ARE THE CITY'S FUTURE ADULTS. KNOWING THE CITY HELPED THEM COULD HELP THEM CONTRIBUTE TO THE CITY

Money is a legitimate issue with the city's budget. Why shouldn't the private sector take on this responsibility?

I think many adults think, why spend money making this teen center and in the end not have many kids using it. Where the teen center is built would be another problem. The adults that live close to the teen center might REORGANIZE COUNTERPOINTS WITH POINTS disapprove because of the noise and the kids around their house, bothering them. If the kids are socializing with others at the teen center it might create more problems with gangs in town, since the teens would be socializing with kids, that before the

Why should the city be responsible for babysitting teens?
What are parents & schools doing?

TEENS ARE CITIZENS TOO!
DOESN'T THE CITY HAVE PROGRAMS FOR THE ELDERLY?

REWRITE WITHOUT "I"

teen center was built, might not have
been associated with.

The problems that I listed above
(for the opposing side) where good
points for not building a teen center,
but in this situation I think that the
*good point!*
good outweighs the bad for making the
teen center. The money and effort put
toward the teen center is very worth
while in helping kids in the town feel
like part of a "group," somewhere where
they can belong. Things like ping-pong
*any other examples?*
tables, and helpful classes for
*swimming pool?*
different hobbies, the kids would enjoy
*COUNSELORS?*
will be included in the teen center,
which is what much of the money would
be used for in building the center. The
adults living by them shouldn't have a
problem with the kids hanging around
*reorganize & tighten up?*
the center and being noisy. I'd imagine
that the teen center wouldn't stay open
throughout the night (because kids have
to sleep, too). Most of the kids using
the center would be inside using the
equipment that the center has provided
for them to use (which also pertains to
what the money would be used for). There
shouldn't be a problem with kids getting
into more gangs while hanging out at the
center. The majority of the kids using
the center is kids that want to have

A compound subject takes a plural verb.

> Example: The dog and the cat *are* sleeping.

If the compound subject refers to a single being, then it takes a singular verb.

> Example: The quarterback and the captain *has* injured his throwing hand.

> Fish and chips *is* popular in England.

Singular indefinite pronouns require singular verbs.

> Example:
> Everybody *has* given his speech.
> Nobody in the family *was* home.
> Neither of the clowns *was* funny.

Plural indefinite pronouns require plural verbs.

> Example:
> Both of the teams *were* outstanding.
> Few of the scholars *fall* asleep in class.

Some indefinite pronouns may be singular or plural.

> Example:
> All of the test *was* difficult.
> All sections of the test *were* difficult.

> Most of the year *was* boring.

> Most of the days *were* fun.
> None of the work *was* finished.
> None of the jobs *were* done.

*continued on page 186*

Read the following sentence from Patrick Henry's Speech to the Virginia Convention. Identify the subject and the verb. Explain why the subject and verb are in agreement.

The next gale that sweeps from the north will bring to our ears the clash of resounding arms!

**FIXING SUBJECT-VERB AGREEMENT ERRORS.** Look at the first draft of Min's essay. Identify and fix several errors in subject-verb agreement. Briefly explain your reasoning for your editing.

**USING SUBJECT-VERB AGREEMENT.** Underline the subject and circle the verb in each sentence in your introduction. Check each sentence for subject-verb agreement. Review the remaining sentences in your essay, checking each for subject-verb agreement.

For more information, see the Language Arts Survey 3.40, "Getting Subject and Verb to Agree."

whole hearted fun and meet new kids that have the same interests they do. I don't think that gang members think it was "cool" to hang out at a teen center. If a problem like that did arise in the future, the teen center employees could try to work with the kids and help them with their problems or if it got really bad they would just have to make a close watch on who the people are that are coming to use the teen center.

*Any better way to start this?*

~~In conclusion,~~ I think that having a

*agreement*

center for teens ~~are~~ a wonderful idea

*is*

and is very worth while. Most kids in today's lifestyle sit around the house and watch T.V. With the teen center they can play an assortment of games and at the same time socialize with other kids attending the teen center. Teens could feel like they have a place to belong and be a part of. A good way to bring  a whole community together is to have a teen center in your town.

*HILLARY CLINTON TAKES A VILLAGE QUOTE— CHECK ON THIS!*

*bring in your "good outweighs the bad" idea?*

## Revising and Proofreading

If possible, let your draft and evaluation comments rest a day before you begin editing. Think about the strengths and weaknesses the evaluation comments pinpointed. Decide what types of revision your draft could benefit from based on your responses to these comments. What additional revisions might be needed?

## Publishing and Presenting

Determine how your essay should be presented to your audience—a report, a letter, a bulletin, a speech, or a video presentation. If the final presentation is to be in print, what layout and illustrations would be most effective? If you are going to present in a speech or a video presentation, what visual props would help your audience to better understand your information and viewpoint?

## Reflecting

Compare your persuasive essay with essays by other members of the class. Discuss various writers' theses, use of evidence, and examples. Are the papers written in a way that encourages you to consider other viewpoints even if you disagree? Do the papers make you look at a topic somewhat differently than you had before?

"The language leads, and we continue to follow."

—Wright Morris

# UNIT REVIEW
## *The American Revolution*

### Words for Everyday Use

Check your knowledge of the following vocabulary words from the selections in this unit. Write short sentences using these words in context to make the meaning clear. To review the definition or usage of a word, refer to the page number listed or the Glossary of Words for Everyday Use.

| | | | |
|---|---|---|---|
| abdicate, 166 | convulsion, 166 | inviolate, 156 | subjugation, 155 |
| acquiesce, 167 | effectual, 156 | lethargy, 172 | submission, 155 |
| admonish, 149 | elate, 160 | magnanimity, 167 | sufferance, 165 |
| arbitrary, 173 | ethereal, 160 | martial, 155 | supinely, 156 |
| ardent, 160 | evade, 150 | naturalization, 166 | temporal, 154 |
| assent, 165 | evince, 160 | precept, 173 | tenure, 166 |
| avert, 155 | formidable, 156 | prostrate, 155 | transient, 164 |
| balmy, 160 | indulgence, 149 | rectitude, 167 | transport, 160 |
| compliance, 166 | inestimable, 156, 165 | redress, 167 | unalienable, 164 |
| comport, 155 | ingenious, 149 | remonstrate, 155 | usurpation, 164 |
| consultation, 150 | insidious, 155 | ruminate, 172 | venture, 150 |
| contemplation, 160 | insurrection, 167 | solace, 155 | |

### Literary Tools

Define the following terms, giving concrete examples of how they are used in the selections in this unit. To review a term, refer to the page number indicated or to the Handbook of Literary Terms.

| | | |
|---|---|---|
| aim, 171 | diction, 171 | rhetorical question, 153 |
| alliteration, 163 | Enlightenment, 153 | style, 147 |
| allusion, 159 | heroic couplet, 159 | |
| autobiography, 147 | parallelism, 163 | |

# Reflecting
## *on* YOUR READING

### Genre Studies

1. **POETRY.** Interestingly, Phillis Wheatley achieves with her poem what the subject of her poem achieves with his painting. In some ways her poem is a treatise on what an artist or poet can do. Discuss Wheatley's view of art and what an artist does.

### Thematic Studies

2. **THE SEARCH FOR FREEDOM.** Examine the writings of Henry and Jefferson. Their words were important tools in the American Revolution. Each makes a clear statement of case followed by a rallying cry. How does each define freedom? What price is it sometimes necessary to pay for freedom? Which expressions from their works would have had an emotional impact:

Discuss their statements of situation, their concept of the nature of freedom, and the power of their language.

3. **FUTURE REBELLIONS.** Even as most of America moved toward independence, some groups of Americans were overlooked. Examine Adams's letter to her husband. What seeds of future conflict do you find? What appeals does Adams give? How would you characterize her presentation?

## Historical/Biographical Studies

4. **THE EMERGING NATION.** Economic factors play an important role in history and politics. What economic factors in the Mid-Atlantic and Southern colonies made independence feasible? What other growth factors strengthened the colonies?

5. **EUROPEAN ROOTS.** The Declaration of Independence can trace its roots to the European Age of Reason and Romanticism. Name three or four philosophers, writers, or scientists whose work in Europe had influence on the colonists. Briefly describe their work and explain how it is related to the thinking of the colonists.

6. **ECONOMIC TRADITION.** Benjamin Franklin was an apprentice to his brother, a printer. Describe the impact of apprenticeship on the economy of the colonies. What were the advantages to the apprentice? What were the advantages to the business owner?

**B**ut oh! shipmates! on the

starboard hand of every woe,

there is a sure delight; and higher

the top of that delight, than the

bottom of the woe is deep.

—Herman Melville
*Moby-Dick*

*Watson and the Shark* [Detail],
John Singleton Copley.

*Watson and the Shark*. John Singleton Copley.
Museum of Fine Arts, Boston.

## ArtNote

*Watson and the Shark* depicts an incident that occurred in Havana in 1749. A fourteen-year-old sailor, Brook Watson, lost his right foot in a shark attack. John Singleton Copley (1738–1815) broke with European tradition by painting a monumental depiction of a contemporary event that happened to an ordinary person, rather than a great historical event of the aristocracy.

At first the painting appears to be very lifelike, but is the action realistic? Do you think the incident could have looked like this? What has Copley done to heighten the drama? Notice the lines of the men's arms, the oar, the spear, and how they form patterns. How does this direct your eyes? Notice the variety of reactions and how they are compressed into a single moment.

# THE NEW ENGLAND RENAISSANCE (1800–1860)

## SOCIAL EXPANSION AND DEMOCRATIZATION

After the **Louisiana Purchase** of 1803, which doubled the size of the country, the United States expanded rapidly across the continent. By 1836, the original thirteen colonies had grown into twenty-five states, stretching as far west as Arkansas. Two important technological developments helped to make that expansion seem less daunting. The invention of the telegraph by **Samuel Morse** in 1838 made it possible to communicate across distances instantly. The introduction of the steam locomotive by **John Stephens** in 1825 made possible the development of a railway system to connect towns and cities across the vast country. By the 1850s, the East

## LITERARY EVENTS

➤ = American Events

➤1800. Library of Congress established

➤1800. Mason Locke Weems's *The Life and Memorable Actions of George Washington* published

1804. Johann Christoph Friedrich von Schiller's *Wilhelm Tell* published

➤1806. Noah Webster's *Compendious Dictionary of the English Language* published

1807. William Wordsworth's *Poetry in Two Volumes* published

➤1809. Washington Irving's *Rip van Winkle* published

| 1800 | 1805 | 1810 |
|---|---|---|

➤1800. Thomas Jefferson elected president

➤1803. Louisiana Purchase

1804. Napoleon declared emperor of France; sets up Napoleonic Code

➤1804. Alexander Hamilton, Secretary of the Treasury, killed in a duel with Aaron Burr

➤1804. Thomas Jefferson reelected

➤1804. Lewis and Clarke expedition begins

➤1807. Chesapeake incident; British impress United States sailors

➤1808. James Madison elected president

## HISTORICAL EVENTS

Coast was connected to Chicago by rail and beyond that to the western side of the Mississippi. Still, while industrial transformation was well under way in various parts of the East, the rest of the country remained predominantly agricultural, with many new farms springing up in the new territories.

The 1820s, culminating in the presidency of **Andrew Jackson**, saw an ideological shift to the "common people." In many states, voting rights, which the wealthy property owners who framed the Constitution had not granted, were extended to all free men. This shift was also felt in an emerging local and national interest in the public's cultural and educational life. In the mid-1830s, **Horace Mann** of Massachusetts undertook studies that would eventually lead to more systematic methods for public education throughout the North. Many states, beginning with Massachusetts, began to offer free public education at the primary and secondary levels; by 1850, free education was widespread in the North. In addition, the **Lyceum Movement** emerged. Begun in 1826, lyceums were institutions that offered educational and inspirational lectures, debates, and entertainments in large public halls. These presentations covered a wide range of subject matter, from philosophy to anthropology to the questions of slavery and women's rights. By 1860, more than three thousand lyceums in the United States served as focal points for the transmission of ideas and culture.

## ROMANTICISM AND TRANSCENDENTALISM

In Europe, the cultural and political era of the Enlightenment was superseded by **Romanticism**. Enlightenment thinkers of the eighteenth century had stressed objectivity and the power of reason to discover the laws of the universe in an objective, scientific, systematic fashion. To the young writers of the Romantic Period, the Enlightenment emphasis on reason undervalued private, subjective experience, including human emotions and the creative imagination. The English poet and essayist Samuel Taylor Coleridge, building on his reading of German writers such as Immanuel Kant, argued that there was a higher form of reason, to be distinguished from the ordinary "understanding" by which we know things in the physical world of sense perception. This higher reason was an intuitive capacity to grasp "metaphysical" truths in the physical world, to see in nature more than the mere operation of regularity and laws, and to see in life more than the practical advancement of social systems of organization. Nature was a repository of and stimulus for such intuitions,

1811. Jane Austen's *Sense and Sensibility* published

➤1814. Francis Scott Key's "Star Spangled Banner" published

1816. Georg Hegel completes third volume of philosophy

➤1817. William Cullen Bryant's "Thanatopsis" published

1818. Mary Shelley's *Frankenstein* published

1819. Arthur Schopenhauer's *The World as Will and Idea* published

➤1820. Washington Irving's *The Sketch Book* published

| 1815 | 1820 | 1825 |

➤1812. War of 1812 against Britain

➤1812. James Madison reelected

➤1814. Bombing of Fort McHenry

➤1814. Treaty of Ghent ends War of 1812

➤1815. Battle of New Orleans; United States defeats Britain, both armies unaware of the Treaty of Ghent

1815. Battle of Waterloo; Napoleon defeated

➤1816. James Monroe elected president

➤1817. First Seminole War

1819. Florida purchased from Spain

➤1820. James Monroe reelected

➤1820. Missouri Compromise

which might transform the individual by granting him or her access to higher truths than ordinary experience and social interaction could afford. British writers of the **Romantic Era,** including Coleridge; William Wordsworth; John Keats; Percy Shelley; Mary Shelley; and George Gordon, Lord Byron praised the natural over the artificial, emotion over reason, and the individual conscience over all types of authority and external control.

European Romanticism had a profound impact on American literature. By the first decades of the nineteenth century, its influence could already be seen in the works of the American "Knickerbocker" writers such as **Washington Irving.** Centered around New York City, these writers had begun to turn their attention toward nature and to critique the ethic of material success and social advancement espoused by writers like Benjamin Franklin in the post-Revolutionary years.

The real flowering of Romanticism in American literature came in the New England literary movement called **Transcendentalism,** which gave its own distinctive inflection and variation to European Romanticism and put the United States on the world literary map to stay. At the core of Transcendentalism was a belief in a realm of spiritual or transcendent truths beyond sense perception and material existence. These truths could be intuited by humans in heightened moments of contemplation or under the influence of natural environs. Though abstract, the Transcendentalist philosophy had a number of practical implications. The Transcendentalists valued spiritual over material success and so opposed the materialism, or desire for increased wealth, that was present in the American psyche since the time of the Puritans and that was elevated to an ideal in the writings of Benjamin Franklin. Contrast, for example, the

*Progress,* 1853. Asher B. Durand. The Warner Collection, Tuscaloosa, Alabama.

Transcendentalist Ralph Waldo Emerson's "Things are in the saddle / And ride mankind" with Benjamin Franklin's "Get what you can, and what you get hold; 'Tis the stone that will turn all your lead into gold."

Because they believed each person capable of intuiting truths directly, the Transcendentalists also dismissed tradition and social convention—any authority beyond that of the individual conscience. For the first time in America, the self became something to celebrate rather than deny. Followers of Transcendentalism perceived that self-awareness was not a selfish dead end but a way to understand and open themselves to the universe. Transcendentalists believed that the soul of each individual was a microcosm of the larger world and that, by studying the self, a person could know the universe and the God who had made it. Compound words such as "self-realization," "self-expression," and "self-reliance" were coined, all with positive connotations.

Transcendentalists insisted on the unique voice of the individual and recognized that with this came the need to respect multiple, often divergent, viewpoints. Consequently, Transcendentalism as a movement lacked unity. Because of its failure to provide a collective voice, however, Transcendentalist writers saw themselves as isolated from conventional society in a way that allowed them to push individualism to a radical degree. Instead of borrowing from the traditional literary forms of their European forebears, American Transcendentalist writers committed themselves to forging new ground. America and its writers were consumed with the task of inventing themselves. Emerson wrote, for example, that "Nothing is at last sacred but the integrity of our own mind. . . . The only right is what is after my constitution, the only wrong what is against it."

Emerson's friend **Henry David Thoreau** carried out an experiment in self-reliance, in keeping with Transcendentalist philosophy, building for himself a small cabin in the woods near Walden Pond in order to live simply and in close contact with nature. Thoreau's *Walden,* a record of this experience, tells us, "If a man does not keep pace with his companions, perhaps it is because he hears a different drummer. Let him step to the music which he hears, however measured or far away." Thoreau's keen observations of nature have made his book a source of inspiration to environmentalists around the world, in addition to being one of the definitive statements of American individualism.

➤1841. Ralph Waldo Emerson's *Self-Reliance* published

➤1841. Henry Wadsworth Longfellow's *Ballads and Other Poems* published

➤1842. Edgar Allan Poe's "The Raven" published

1843. Søren Kierkegaard's *Either-Or* published

➤1843. Edgar Allan Poe's "The Pit and the Pendulum" published

1843. Charles Dickens's *A Christmas Carol* published

➤1846. Henry Wadsworth Longfellow's *The Belfry of Bruges and Other Poems* published

1847. Charlotte Brontë's *Jane Eyre* published

1847. Emily Brontë's *Wuthering Heights* published

1848. William Makepeace Thackeray's *Vanity Fair* published

| 1840 | 1845 | 1850 |
|---|---|---|

➤1840. William Henry Harrison elected president

➤1841. President Harrison dies; John Tyler succeeds him

➤1843. Dorothea Dix begins humanitarian reforms

➤1844. James Knox Polk elected president

1845. Potato famine in Ireland; immigration to United States increases

➤1846. Mexican War; United States annexes New Mexico

➤1848. Zachary Taylor elected president

➤1849. First gold rush

➤1849. Harriet Tubman escapes from slavery

Emerson was an eternal optimist in his view of nature's goodness; in the midst of the 1837 economic panic and subsequent nationwide depression, he could blithely remark that "on the bosom of this vast (natural) plenty the blight of trade & manufacture seems to me a momentary mischance." Thoreau was capable of similar optimism, though he generally was much more socially reclusive and skeptical of his peers.

Several other major writers of the period, though influenced by Transcendentalism, did not take so sanguine a view of nature. In short stories such as "Rappaccini's Daughter" and in the brilliant allegorical novel *The Scarlet Letter,* **Nathaniel Hawthorne** dealt with the darker aspects of human nature, specifically with sin and the ways in which humans deal with temptation, guilt, and revenge. Hawthorne joined a Boston-area Transcendentalist utopian community called **Brook Farm** in 1840, but left a year later in disgust and wrote a satire about it called *The Blithedale Romance.* **Louisa May Alcott** wrote her satirical short story, "Transcendental Wild Oats" as a loosely fictitious account of her own family's failed experiment to live in 1834 at Fruitlands, a Transcendentalist utopia. **Herman Melville** explored the forces of evil and obsession in his masterpiece, *Moby-Dick.* **Edgar Allan Poe** brought the horror story to its zenith, exploring the psychology of madness and terror in such works as "The Pit and the Pendulum" and "The Fall of the House of Usher." Irving, Hawthorne, and Poe were collectively responsible for the development of the modern short story, a form that Poe defined as a brief fictional work designed to create in the reader a single dominant impression or effect.

## THE WRITING PROFESSION AND SOCIAL PURPOSE

Despite their recognition by some important figures abroad, the Transcendentalists were not popular writers. Of the seven hundred copies of Thoreau's *Walden* printed in the first edition, most were eventually returned to him, unsold, by the publisher. Thoreau eventually filled orders himself by mail. It remained for later generations to recognize the quintessentially American genius that informed Transcendentalism.

Some American writers were popular, however, and there were American best-sellers in this era, notably the historical novels of **James Fenimore Cooper**, such as *Last of the Mohicans*, and Herman Melville's tales of seafaring adventure, such as *Typee* and *Omoo.* The economics of publication, however, did not yet favor writing

LITERARY
EVENTS

➤ = American Events

➤1854. Henry David Thoreau's *Walden* published

➤1852. Harriet Beecher Stowe's *Uncle Tom's Cabin* published

➤1855. Walt Whitman's *Leaves of Grass* published

➤1851. Herman Melville's *Moby-Dick* published

➤1851. Nathaniel Hawthorne's *The House of the Seven Gables* published

1857. Gustave Flaubert's *Madame Bovary* published

1859. Charles Dickens's *A Tale of Two Cities* published

➤1850. Nathaniel Hawthorne's *The Scarlet Letter* published

| 1850 | 1855 | 1860 |

➤1850. President Taylor dies; Millard Fillmore succeeds him

➤1852. Franklin Pierce elected president

➤1853. The Monroe Doctrine

➤1856. James Buchanan elected president

➤1856. "Bleeding Kansas"

HISTORICAL
EVENTS

➤1854. Kansas-Nebraska Act repeals Missouri Compromise

➤1857. Dred Scott decision

196    *UNIT FOUR / THE NEW ENGLAND RENAISSANCE*

as a source of income, even if a work was popular. It was not yet possible to make a living in America as a professional writer because, though United States copyright laws were enacted in the states in 1841, there was no international copyright protection until 1891. American books could be sold legally in England without paying royalties to the American author, and English books could be sold in America without paying royalties to the English author. The cost of publishing a book from abroad was therefore less than the cost of publishing a work by an American. To get their books published under such circumstances, American writers usually had to sell their books without any claim to royalties.

Why, then, did these individuals write? One answer is that they were committed to effecting change and believed in the power of literature to shape society. Thoreau's *Walden,* for example, is a kind of guide for living a simple life characterized by a fundamental relationship with the natural world. Emerson, too, sought to change how people live and think, to teach people how to trust their own better natures.

## New England Renaissance Poetry

Other writers of the period also had social purpose in their writing; for example, **Henry Wadsworth Longfellow**, **James Russell Lowell**, **John Greenleaf Whittie**r, and **Oliver Wendell Holmes** wrote poems on various social and political issues of the time such as slavery. These men were not social rebels, however; they were models of the respectable citizen-poet, and their poetry was highly popular. They were part of a group now known alternately as the **Fireside,** or **Schoolroom, Poets** because their work was quite popular among families reading in the evening around the fire and because their work came to be recited and memorized widely in American schoolrooms. Their most popular poems were songlike, containing regular rhythms and rhymes that made the poems easy to recite and remember. These poets offered mostly idealized, romantic, morally uplifting views of the nation and its past in lyric and narrative verse. Though the work of the Fireside Poets has often been denigrated by twentieth-century critics as unchallenging, their works helped to create greater popular interest in poetry and to elevate the status of the poet in the national imagination; indeed, Longfellow's seventy-fifth birthday was an occasion for a national celebration. The work of another poet of this era, **Edgar Allan Poe**, was similarly straightforward in its rhymes and rhythms but explored elements of the gothic, the macabre, and the mysterious.

Completely different from the Fireside or Schoolroom Poetry in almost every respect was the poetry of **Emily Dickinson**, which is generally more highly regarded by critics today. Dickinson called her poems her "letter to the world," but of the 1,775 that she wrote, only a handful were read by the world in her lifetime; the rest were discovered in a storage trunk by her sister and later published by a friend. Dickinson's poetry does not follow the regular rhythmic patterns of the Schoolroom Poets; it is full of interrupted thoughts and sudden bursts of awareness, often jarring the reader through irony and paradox into a wholly different, more unsettling view of the world. Rather than idealizing the past, Dickinson focuses on a vivid present or an uncertain future, addressing time, isolation, and death from a surprising number of perspectives. At times humorous, at other times anxious, at all times precise and compressed, Dickinson's poems are some of the most difficult and rich in American literature.

*Kindred Spirits* [Detail], Asher Brown Durand.

# ECHOES ECHOES ECHOES ECHOES ECHOES ECHOES ECHOES

## Quotations from Ralph Waldo Emerson

On accomplishment: "If a man write a better book, preach a better sermon, or make a better mouse-trap than his neighbor, tho' he build his house in the woods, the world will make a beaten path to his door."

On ambition: "Hitch your wagon to a star."

On consistency: "A foolish consistency is the hobgoblin of little minds."

On enthusiasm: "Nothing great was ever achieved without enthusiasm."

On history: "There is properly no history, only biography."

On individuality: "Whoso would be a man must be a nonconformist."

On individuality: "To believe your own thought, to believe that what is true for you in your private heart is true for all men,—that is genius."

On rewards for actions: "The reward of a thing well done, is to have done it."

On society: "Society everywhere is in conspiracy against the manhood of every one of its members."

On the histories of words: "Language is fossil poetry."

On writing: "The art of writing consists in putting two things together that are unlike and that belong together like a horse & cart."

## Quotations from Henry David Thoreau

On economics: "For more than five years I maintained myself thus solely by the labor of my hands, and I found, that by working about six weeks in a year, I could meet all the expenses of living."

On government: "I heartily accept the motto, 'That government is best which governs least.'"

On individuality: "If a man does not keep pace with his companions, perhaps it is because he hears a different drummer. Let him step to the music which he hears, however measured or far away."

On nature: "I frequently tramped eight or ten miles through the deepest snow to keep an appointment with a beech-tree, or a yellow birch, or an old acquaintance among the pines."

On nature: "I once had a sparrow alight on my shoulder for a moment while I was hoeing in a village garden, and I felt that I was more distinguished by that circumstance than I should have been by any epaulet I could have worn."

On solitude: "I never found the companion that was so companionable as solitude."

On technology: "Men have become the tools of their tools."

On the failure to follow one's dreams: "The mass of men live lives of quiet desperation."

*Watson and the Shark* [Detail], John Singleton Copley.

# *"Thanatopsis"*

### BY WILLIAM CULLEN BRYANT

## About the AUTHOR

**William Cullen Bryant** (1794–1878), born in rural Cummington, Massachusetts, had an abiding love for nature. He briefly attended Williams College in 1810 but dropped out, hoping to go to Yale. Because his father could not afford that expense, Bryant read for the law and was admitted to practice in 1815.

Heavily influenced by the English Romantic poets Thomas Gray and William Wordsworth, Bryant began to write poetry at a young age but realized that he could not afford to pursue a full-time career as a poet. Appointed justice of the peace in Great Barrington in 1820, the following year Bryant married Frances Fairchild and published a volume entitled *Poems*. The Bryants moved to New York City, where he worked as an editor of the *New York Review* and *Atheneum Magazine*. Thereafter, he became editor-in-chief and part owner of the *Evening Post*, a position that brought him wealth, fame, and influence.

Bryant championed humanitarian causes, including the abolition of slavery and of debtors' prisons. He also became a key figure in American political life, helping to form the Republican Party and to get both Andrew Jackson and Abraham Lincoln elected president. He traveled widely in Europe and in the Middle East and published letters about his experiences. Bryant continued writing into his seventies, translating Homer's epics, the *Odyssey* and the *Iliad*, and writing poems.

## About the SELECTION

Bryant probably began **"Thanatopsis"** in 1811, when he was only sixteen years old. The subject and moral outlook of the poem owe much to Thomas Gray's "Elegy Written in a Country Churchyard." The first version of the poem consisted of the present poem's lines 18–66. Bryant's father submitted this poem and another on the subject of death to the *North American Review* in 1817, and the two were mistakenly published as a single work.

In 1821, Bryant completed "Thanatopsis," framing the original lines with an introduction (lines 1–17) and a conclusion (lines 66–82). In the earlier version, the central lines had been in the poet's own voice; in the later version, the speaker is a romanticized and personified Nature. The ideas in the three parts of the poem betray the changes in the poet's thinking over the ten years of its composition. Nevertheless, the beauty of the poem's language and the grandeur of its images immediately established Bryant's literary reputation and helped to create pride in the ability of Americans to match the literary creations of the British Romantic school.

## Literary TOOLS

**BLANK VERSE. Blank verse** is unrhymed poetry written in iambic pentameter. (An iambic pentameter line consists of five feet, each containing two syllables, the first weakly stressed and the second strongly stressed.) As you read "Thanatopsis," pay attention to this regular pattern in the poem.

**ELABORATION. Elaboration,** or **amplification,** is a writing technique in which a subject is introduced and then expanded upon by means of repetition with slight changes, the addition of details, or similar devices. As you read "Thanatopsis," try to find an example of elaboration.

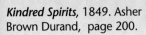

## Reader's Journal

When do you see nature as beautiful and generous, and when do you see it as violent and cruel?

## ArtNote

***Kindred Spirits***, 1849. Asher Brown Durand, page 200.

Trends in literature often have parallels in the visual arts. In the mid-1800s, a group of American landscape painters called the Hudson River School believed in the spiritual power of nature as did many of the writers during the New England Renaissance. Asher Brown Durand makes this clear by depicting fellow painter Thomas Cole on the right with writer William Cullen Bryant in a typical Hudson River School painting that he called *Kindred Spirits*. What words or phrases that Bryant uses to describe nature in "Thanatopsis" evoke the mood of Durand's landscape painting?

# Thanatopsis[1]

To him who in the love of Nature holds
<u>Communion</u> with her visible forms, she speaks
A various language; for his gayer hours
She has a voice of gladness, and a smile

5 And eloquence of beauty, and she glides
Into his darker musings, with a mild
And gentle sympathy, that steals away
Their sharpness, ere he is aware. When thoughts
Of the last bitter hour come like a <u>blight</u>

10 Over thy spirit, and sad images
Of the stern agony, and shroud, and pall,
And breathless darkness, and the narrow house,[2]
Make thee to shudder, and grow sick at heart,—
Go forth under the open sky, and list[3]

15 To Nature's teachings, while from all around—
Earth and her waters, and the depths of air,—
Comes a still voice—Yet a few days, and thee
The all-beholding sun shall see no more
In all his course; nor yet in the cold ground,

*What effect can thoughts of death have?*

*Where should the reader seek comfort?*

---

1. **Thanatopsis.** This word, coined by Bryant, means "views and thoughts on death."
2. **shroud . . . narrow house.** *Shroud*—cloth used to wrap a corpse for burial; *pall*—cloth draped over a coffin; *narrow house*—grave
3. **list.** Listen

**WORDS FOR EVERYDAY USE**

com • mun • ion (kə myün´yən) *n.,* act of sharing thoughts and actions. *In silent <u>communion</u> with the horse, the boy stared into the gray stallion's eyes.*

blight (blīt) *n.,* anything that destroys or prevents growth. *<u>Blight</u> destroyed half of the Nelsons' apple crop.*

*Kindred Spirits,* 1849. Asher Brown Durand.
The New York Public Library.

20   Where thy pale form was laid, with many tears,
      Nor in the embrace of ocean shall exist
      Thy image. Earth, that nourished thee, shall claim
      Thy growth, to be resolv'd to earth again;
      And, lost each human trace, surrend'ring up

25   Thine individual being, shalt thou go
      To mix forever with the elements,
      To be a brother to th' <u>insensible</u> rock
      And to the sluggish <u>clod</u>, which the rude swain
      Turns with his share,[4] and treads upon. The oak

30   Shall send his roots abroad, and pierce thy mould.[5]
      Yet not to thy eternal resting place
      Shalt thou retire alone—nor couldst thou wish
      Couch more magnificent. Thou shalt lie down
      With <u>patriarchs</u> of the infant world—with kings

35   The powerful of the earth—the wise, the good,
      Fair forms, and <u>hoary</u> seers of ages past,
      All in one mighty <u>sepulcher</u>.—The hills
      Rock-ribb'd and ancient as the sun,—the vales
      Stretching in <u>pensive</u> quietness between;

40   The <u>venerable</u> woods—rivers that move
      In majesty, and the complaining brooks
      That make the meadows green; and pour'd round all,
      Old ocean's grey and melancholy waste,—
      Are but the solemn decorations all

45   Of the great tomb of man. The golden sun,
      The planets, all the infinite host of heaven,

*How does the speaker describe the life cycle in relation to the earth?*

*With whom will the reader share the grave?*

---

4. **share.** Plough
5. **mould.** Form or body

**WORDS FOR EVERYDAY USE**

**in • sen • si • ble** (in sen´sə bəl) *adj.*, lacking sensation; unaware. *The marathon runners seemed <u>insensible</u> to pain.*

**clod** (kläd) *n.*, lump, such as lump of earth or clay. *A <u>clod</u> of curds floated in the butter churn.*

**pa • tri • arch** (pā´trē ärk´) *n.*, father; ruler; founder. *Johnny Carson, former* Tonight Show *host, is the <u>patriarch</u> of late-night talk shows.*

**hoar • y** (hôr´ē) *adj.*, having white or gray hair. *Noah is often shown on his ark with <u>hoary</u> hair blowing in the salt wind.*

**sep • ul • cher** (sep´əl kər) *n.*, vault for burial. *With great ceremony, the king was laid to rest in the national <u>sepulcher</u>.*

**pen • sive** (pen´siv) *adj.*, expressing deep thoughtfulness, often with some sadness. *Rodin sculpted a <u>pensive</u> look on* The Thinker's *face.*

**ven • er • a • ble** (ven´ər ə bəl) *adj.*, worthy of respect by reason of age and dignity. *The young lawyer sought the counsel of <u>venerable</u> Judge Albert J. Cooke.*

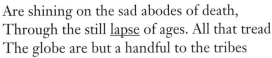

Are shining on the sad abodes of death,
Through the still <u>lapse</u> of ages. All that tread
The globe are but a handful to the tribes
50      That slumber in its bosom.—Take the wings
Of morning—and the Barcan desert[6] pierce,
Or lose thyself in the continuous woods
Where rolls the Oregan,[7] and hears no sound,
Save his own dashings—yet—the dead are there,
55      And millions in those solitudes, since first
The flight of years begin, have laid them down
In their last sleep—the dead reign there alone.—
So shalt thou rest—and what if thou shalt fall
Unnoticed by the living—and no friend
60      Take note of thy departure? All that breathe
Will share thy destiny. The gay will laugh
When thou art gone, the solemn brood of care
Plod on, and each one as before will chase
His favorite phantom; yet all these shall leave
65      Their mirth and their employments, and shall come,
And make their bed with thee. As the long train
Of ages glide away, the sons of men,
The youth in life's green spring, and he who goes
In the full strength of years, matron, and maid,
70      The bow'd with age, the infant in the smiles
And beauty of its innocent age cut off,—
Shall one by one be gathered to thy side,
By those, who in their turn shall follow them.
So live, that when thy summons comes to join
75      The innumerable caravan, that moves
To the pale realms of shade, where each shall take
His chamber in the silent halls of death,
Thou go not, like the quarry-slave at night,
Scourged to his dungeon, but sustain'd and sooth'd
80      By an unfaltering trust, approach thy grave,
Like one who wraps the drapery of his couch
About him, and lies down to pleasant dreams. ■

*What is the ratio of living to deceased?*

*What happens after someone dies?*

*What should be the reader's attitude approaching the grave?*

---

6. **Barcan desert.** Desert in northeast Libya
7. **Oregan.** Early spelling of Oregon

**WORDS FOR EVERYDAY USE**

**lapse** (laps) *n.*, gliding or passing away. *Failing to stop at the yellow light proved to be a <u>lapse</u> in judgment for Sandy.*

If you were the speaker anticipating your own imminent death, what specific comfort could you draw from the words in lines 17–82?

# INVESTIGATE Inquire, Imagine

**Recall:** GATHERING FACTS → **Interpret:** FINDING MEANING

1a. To what two moods does Nature respond? How does it respond differently to each one?

1b. What is the "last bitter hour"? What images in lines 11–12 support this view?

2a. With what pronoun in line 17 does Bryant introduce a new point of view?

2b. Who is the speaker up to line 17 of the poem? Who begins to speak in line 17?

3a. According to lines 33–37, what brings comfort at the thought of death?

3b. What does Nature tell those who fear their death will go "Unnoticed by the living"?

---

**Analyze:** TAKING THINGS APART → **Synthesize:** BRINGING THINGS TOGETHER

4a. According to the speaker, why should dying be like lying down to "pleasant dreams"?

4b. In this poem, is Nature the same as the planet Earth? If so, how? If not, how would you describe it?

---

**Evaluate:** MAKING JUDGMENTS → **Extend:** CONNECTING IDEAS

5a. Does "Thanatopsis" present an optimistic or a pessimistic view of death? Explain your answer.

5b. Consider how the biblical expression "ashes to ashes, dust to dust" might relate to the view of death expressed in the poem. Cite specific lines of the poem in your response.

# Understanding Literature

**BLANK VERSE. Blank verse** is unrhymed poetry written in iambic pentameter. (See the definition for *meter* in the Handbook of Literary Terms for an example of iambic pentameter.) Copy the first five lines of "Thanatopsis" and mark the strongly stressed syllables with accent marks. Which line is least regular?

**ELABORATION. Elaboration**, or **amplification**, is a writing technique in which a subject is introduced and then expanded upon by means of repetition with slight changes, the addition of details, or similar devices. How does this poem make use of the technique of elaboration? What is the idea that is elaborated?

# WRITER'S JOURNAL

1. Imagining that you are a literary columnist for a newspaper, write a **review** of "Thanatopsis," telling your readers what they might experience reading it.

2. Write four lines of **blank verse** for an environmental magazine that celebrates the beauty of nature.

3. The *memento mori* theme, which warned that death comes quickly and unexpectedly, is found in English and American literature throughout the centuries. Write **rap lyrics** with a *memento mori* theme to introduce "Thanatopsis" to contemporary high school students.

# Integrating *the* LANGUAGE ARTS

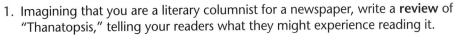

## Language, Grammar, and Style

**WORKING WITH PREPOSITIONS.** Read the Language Arts Survey 3.11, "Prepositions." Then write out the following sentences. Underline each prepositional phrase with a single underscore and each preposition with a double underscore. Each sentence has two or three examples of prepositions and prepositional phrases.

1. "Thanatopsis," the best-known poem by William Cullen Bryant, draws its title from the Greek language.

2. In Greek, *thanatopsis* means "view of death"; no one could object to this phrase as a summary of the poem.

3. Despite Bryant's upbringing in the Calvinist tradition, the poem reflects toward its topic a Wordsworthian pantheism, or nature worship.

4. Bryant seems to have been strongly impressed by the ideas of several English poets grouped by the title "graveyard school."

5. Clearly, however, the major influence on Bryant was William Wordsworth, one of the greatest English Romantic poets, who wrote about Nature as a loving friend to humanity.

## Collaborative Learning

**THINKING ALOUD ABOUT THEME.** With a partner, examine the themes of "Thanatopsis." First, locate lines in the poem that discuss the themes of life cycles, comfort, and common destiny. Then engage in a "think aloud" about each theme. In a think aloud, the speaker puts the author's meaning into his or her own words. Take turns reading the relevant lines from the poem aloud to your partner and stating what you think they mean. Finally, discuss how the themes are woven together to articulate Bryant's view of death.

## Media Literacy & Study and Research

**WRITING BRYANT'S OBITUARY.** Read several obituaries in your local newspaper and make a list of the information that is usually included. Then imagine that it is 1878 and William Cullen Bryant has just died. Write an obituary that includes his important literary contributions, as well as the information that you researched. In addition to researching obituaries, you will need to research appropriate details of Bryant's life, such as the family members he left behind.

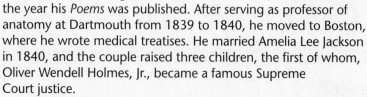

"The Chambered Nautilus" BY OLIVER WENDELL HOLMES

## Literary TOOLS

**APOSTROPHE.** An **apostrophe** is a rhetorical device by which a speaker turns from the audience as a whole to address a single person or thing. Look for an example of apostrophe in "The Chambered Nautilus."

**STANZA.** A **stanza** is a recurring pattern of grouped lines in a poem. The pattern formed by the ends of the lines in each stanza is called the *rhyme scheme.* Determine the rhyme pattern by making a chart like the one below. On the left, list the rhyming words in each stanza. On the right, give the rhyme pattern in each stanza. The first stanza has been done for you. As you read the poem, pay attention to the rhyme pattern of each stanza.

| Rhyming Words | Rhyme Pattern |
|---|---|
| feign-main; flings-wings-sings; bare-hair | *aabbbcc* |

## Reader's Journal

What do you think of and feel when you touch or listen to a seashell?

## About the AUTHOR

**Oliver Wendell Holmes** (1809–1894) was born in Cambridge, Massachusetts, and was class poet at Harvard in 1829. After studying law, he went to Paris to study medicine. He was awarded his M.D. degree from Harvard in 1836, the year his *Poems* was published. After serving as professor of anatomy at Dartmouth from 1839 to 1840, he moved to Boston, where he wrote medical treatises. He married Amelia Lee Jackson in 1840, and the couple raised three children, the first of whom, Oliver Wendell Holmes, Jr., became a famous Supreme Court justice.

From 1847 until 1882, Holmes was a professor of anatomy at Harvard, writing several important scientific papers. In the late 1850s, the *Atlantic Monthly,* which he helped found, serialized his humorous essays and printed his poems, including "The Chambered Nautilus" and "The Deacon's Masterpiece."

Holmes also wrote three novels—"medicated novels" was his term for them—that dealt with genetic and psychological determinism. (Determinism is the belief that people's ideas, thoughts, feelings, and actions are caused by hereditary and environmental forces.) From the 1860s through the 1880s, Holmes published volumes of poems and essays, as well as a biography of Ralph Waldo Emerson. Holmes was the most famous after-dinner speaker of his time, a leading figure in literary circles, and a witty writer of occasional verse.

## About the SELECTION

**"The Chambered Nautilus"** was published in the February 1858 issue of the *Atlantic Monthly* in one of Holmes's essays in *The Autocrat of the Breakfast Table.* The creature of the title is a mollusk, related to clams and octopi, that gradually builds a spiral, pearly-lined shell with a series of air-filled chambers. The creature acquired the name *nautilus* from the Greek word for "sailor," because of the belief that it had a membrane that served as a sail, by means of which it navigated the waters of the Indian and Pacific Oceans. Holmes may have conceived the idea for the poem when reading the essay "Compensation," by Ralph Waldo Emerson, which compares human development to that of a shellfish.

# The Chambered Nautilus

OLIVER
WENDELL
HOLMES

This is the ship of pearl, which, poets <u>feign</u>,

    Sails the unshadowed main[1],—

    The venturous bark[2] that flings

On the sweet summer wind its purpled wings

5    In gulfs enchanted, where the siren[3] sings,

      And coral reefs lie bare,

Where the cold sea-maids rise to sun their streaming hair.

---

1. **main.** High seas
2. **bark.** Ship
3. **siren.** A female and partly human creature in Greek mythology that lured mariners to destruction by her singing

WORDS
FOR
EVERYDAY
USE

**feign** (fān) *vt.*, pretend or imagine. *Jeremy <u>feigned</u> illness so he would not have to go to school.*

Its webs of living gauze no more <u>unfurl</u>;
    Wrecked is the ship of pearl!
10       And every chambered cell,
Where its dim dreaming life was wont to dwell,
As the frail <u>tenant</u> shaped his growing shell,
    Before thee lies revealed,—
Its irised ceiling rent, its sunless <u>crypt</u> unsealed!

15 Year after year beheld the silent toil
    That spread his <u>lustrous</u> coil;
    Still, as the spiral grew,
He left the past year's dwelling for the new,
Stole with soft step its shining archway through,
20     Built up its idle door,
Stretched in his last-found home, and knew the old no more.

Thanks for the heavenly message brought by thee,
    Child of the wandering sea,
    Cast from her lap, <u>forlorn</u>!
25 From thy dead lips a clearer note is born
Than ever Triton[4] blew from wreathéd horn!
    While on mine ear it rings,
Through the deep caves of thought I hear a voice that sings:—

Build thee more stately mansions, O my soul,
30     As the swift seasons roll!
    Leave thy low-vaulted past!
Let each new temple, nobler than the last,
Shut thee from heaven with a dome more vast,
    Till thou at length art free,
35 Leaving thine outgrown shell by life's unresting sea!

> Why is the "ship of pearl" described as "Wrecked"?

> What is the message the nautilus brings to the speaker?

---

4. **Triton.** Greek god of the sea

**WORDS FOR EVERYDAY USE**

un • furl (un fərl´) vt., unfold. _The flag <u>unfurled</u> in the wind._
ten • ant (te´nənt) n., one who rents or owns; occupant. _The new <u>tenant</u> filed a grievance against the landlord._
crypt (kript) n., underground chamber. _The bishops were buried in the <u>crypt</u> of the cathedral._
lus • trous (lus´trəs) adj., reflecting light. _The <u>lustrous</u> glow of Sue's diamond shone in the darkened room._
for • lorn (fər lôrn´) adj., forsaken or miserable. _Dickens addressed the plight of <u>forlorn</u> orphans in Oliver Twist._

## Respond to the SELECTION

If you were the speaker, how would you feel about unexpected changes in your life? Would you fear them or welcome them as opportunities for growth?

# INVESTIGATE, Inquire, Imagine

**Recall**: GATHERING FACTS

1a. What mythological allusion does the speaker make in stanza 1 about the nautilus's environment?

2a. What details does the speaker provide about the life of the nautilus in stanzas 2 and 3?

3a. What does the singing voice of stanza 4 tell its listener to build in stanza 5? Why? From what do these structures separate the soul?

**Interpret**: FINDING MEANING

1b. Remember that Holmes was a scientific person, a trained physician. Why do you suppose the speaker in Holmes's poem introduces the shellfish with imagined details instead of using a scientifically accurate description?

2b. In the first three stanzas, how does the speaker give the shellfish a personality? What are some of the details that make the audience more sympathetic toward it?

3b. What is the speaker's "outgrown shell"? When will he leave it behind?

**Analyze**: TAKING THINGS APART

4a. To whom are stanzas 1–3 addressed? stanza 4? stanza 5?

**Synthesize**: BRINGING THINGS TOGETHER

4b. Why does Holmes continually change to whom the poem is addressed? What provides the transition between stanza 4 and stanza 5? What is the theme of the poem?

**Evaluate**: MAKING JUDGMENTS

5a. In the nineteenth century, amateur and professional naturalists sought to codify the natural world. Many new specimens of plants and animals were discovered and analyzed solely in scientific terms. Imagine you were part of Holmes's nineteenth-century audience. Would you have praised or criticized Holmes's poem? Why?

**Extend**: CONNECTING IDEAS

5b. How does the speaker's attitude toward death in "The Chambered Nautilus" compare with the speaker's attitude in "Thanatopsis"? Which do you value more?

# Understanding Literature

APOSTROPHE. Review the definition for **apostrophe** in the Handbook of Literary Terms. Identify examples of apostrophe in the fourth and fifth stanzas. Who or what is being addressed? The apostrophes signal development in the content of the poem. How do the lines that follow the apostrophes differ from those before them?

STANZA. Review the definition for **stanza** in the Handbook of Literary Terms. Then examine the chart you made using the example in Literary Tools on page 206. What is the rhyme pattern for each stanza?

# WRITER'S JOURNAL

1. Imagine that you are a contemporary of Holmes. Write the poet a **letter**, explaining what insight you gleaned about life after contemplating the life of the nautilus in his poem.

2. Write the **credo** of the speaker, based on what you learned about him by reading "The Chambered Nautilus." A credo is a statement of belief, expressing one's most strongly held opinions and values.

3. Holmes's poem owes much to the mythology of the nautilus and its compartmentalized shape. Write a **paragraph** describing how these attributes of the shellfish are significant to the meaning of the poem.

# Integrating the LANGUAGE ARTS

## Language, Grammar, and Style

**PRONOUNS AND ANTECEDENTS.** Read the Language Arts Survey 3.45, "Getting Pronouns and Antecedents to Agree." Then rewrite these sentences, using pronouns correctly.

1. Long ago, people really believed in myths, but today we see it simply as literature.

2. Still, mythology says something about human nature that makes him more than just old stories.

3. In the Greek myths, sirens are "cold sea-maids," as the poem says, but to us she stands for all sorts of temptations.

4. Everybody knows that they can blame Pandora for the world's problems, for according to Greek myth, she was the one who let all the evils of the world out of a box.

5. Though different cultures call their gods of war by different names, he represents the same weaknesses in all of us—distrust and hostility toward people who are not like us.

## Collaborative Learning

**ABSTRACT.** With a partner, write an abstract of the Holmes poem. An abstract is a brief account of the main ideas presented in a work. In your abstract, try to reflect the tone of "The Chambered Nautilus."

## Applied English

**BUSINESS LETTER.** Imagine that it is 1858 and you would like to invite Oliver Wendell Holmes to speak to your literary circle. Write a letter to Holmes, requesting that he accept the honor of addressing your group after dinner. Supply important details, such as the nature of your society and the place and time of the dinner so that Holmes has the information he needs to accept or refuse your invitation. You may find it useful to read the Language Arts Survey 6.5, "Writing a Business Letter" and the Sample Letter of Request in that section.

## Study and Research

**ENCYCLOPEDIA RESEARCH.** Read the material about specialized encyclopedias in the Language Arts Survey 5.20, "Using Reference Works." Then investigate a library to find out which encyclopedias of literature, mythology, and literary terms are available in the reference department. List the title and the particular focus of each. Then look up Triton in two of these encyclopedias and compare the amount and type of information provided.

# "The *Village* BLACKSMITH"

BY HENRY WADSWORTH LONGFELLOW

## About *the* AUTHOR

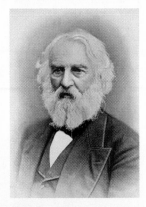

**Henry Wadsworth Longfellow** (1807–1882) was the most popular of the so-called "Fireside Poets," a group that included Ralph Waldo Emerson, John Greenleaf Whittier, James Russell Lowell, and Oliver Wendell Holmes. The name of the group derived from the fact that people often entertained one another in the evening by reading aloud by the fireside.

Longfellow was born in Portland, Maine, and attended Bowdoin College there. Following graduation and language study in Europe, Longfellow taught foreign languages first at Bowdoin and then at Harvard. Well-known works by Longfellow include "A Psalm of Life," "The Wreck of the Hesperus," "Excelsior," "The Arsenal at Springfield," *Evangeline, Song of Hiawatha,* "The Children's Hour," *The Courtship of Miles Standish,* and "Paul Revere's Ride" (one of the *Tales of a Wayside Inn*). Longfellow also edited *The Poets and Poetry of Europe,* an important anthology.

As famous in Britain as in the United States, he received honorary degrees from Oxford and Cambridge and was given a private audience with Queen Victoria. After his death, a bust of Longfellow was installed in the Poet's Corner of Westminster Abbey, making him the only American poet to be so honored.

## About *the* SELECTION

"The Village Blacksmith" was first published in an 1841 collection called *Ballads and Other Poems.* At the time of the poem's publication, Longfellow was a professor at Harvard. His poetry collections had begun to make him famous, not only in America but also in England. Sweet, romantic, didactic, and occasionally gripping in their retellings of stories from history or legend, Longfellow's poems appealed greatly to the tastes of the day. "The Village Blacksmith" is a narrative poem that tells the story of a common man, honest and hard-working, whose strength and positive attitude matched the popular notion of the ideal citizen of the young, unsophisticated country.

## Literary TOOLS

**IMAGE.** An **image** is language that creates a concrete representation of an object or an experience. Notice the images that Longfellow uses to describe the blacksmith.

**ALLITERATION.** The repetition of initial consonant sounds is called **alliteration**. Watch for examples of alliteration in this poem.

## Reader's *Journal*

What do you think you might like to do for a living? What do you imagine your work-day would be like?

## Art**Note**

*Pat Lyon at the Forge,* 1826–1827. John Neagle, page 212.

Painted portraits have always been expensive, and in the 1800s only the wealthy could afford to have one made. The story behind the heroic portrait on page 212 of a working-class person is especially unusual. The blacksmith in the picture, Pat Lyon, was imprisoned on false charges but was eventually proven innocent. He received restitution from the bank that had accused him and spent the money on this painting. The artist certainly would have portrayed him the way Lyon wanted himself to be seen. What do you think Pat Lyon is telling us about himself? What qualities does he share with the blacksmith in Longfellow's poem?

# The *Village* BLACKSMITH

HENRY WADSWORTH LONGFELLOW

*Pat Lyon at the Forge,* 1826–1827. John Neagle.
Museum of Fine Arts, Boston.

Under a spreading chestnut tree
    The village smithy[1] stands:
The smith, a mighty man is he,
    With large and sinewy[2] hands,
5    And the muscles of his brawny arms
    Are strong as iron bands.

His hair is crisp,[3] and black, and long,
    His face is like the tan;
His brow is wet with honest sweat,
10    He earns whate'er he can,
And looks the whole world in the face,
    For he owes not any man.

Week in, week out, from morn till night,
    You can hear his bellows[4] blow,
15    You can hear him swing his heavy sledge,
    With measured beat and slow,
Like a sexton[5] ringing the village bell,
    When the evening sun is low.

> What words are used to describe the strength of the smith?

> To what is the smith's swinging his sledge compared?

---

1. **smithy.** Blacksmith shop
2. **sinewy.** Muscular, strong
3. **crisp.** Curly and wiry
4. **bellows.** Fan for keeping a fire going
5. **sexton.** Church official who rings the bells

And children coming home from school
20      Look in at the open door;
They love to see the flaming forge,
        And hear the bellows roar,
And catch the burning sparks that fly
        Like chaff[6] from a threshing floor.

25   He goes on Sunday to the church,
        And sits among his boys;
He hears the parson pray and preach,
        He hears his daughter's voice
Singing in the village choir,
30   And it makes his heart rejoice.

*What does the smith
do on Sundays?
What does he hear?
How does he feel?*

It sounds to him like her mother's voice,
        Singing in Paradise!
He needs must think of her once more,
        How in the grave she lies;
35   And with his hard, rough hand he wipes
        A tear out of his eyes.

*Of what does the
smith's daughter's
voice remind him?
What effect does it
have on him?*

Toiling—rejoicing—sorrowing,
        Onward through life he goes;
Each morning sees some task begin,
40      Each evening sees it close;
Something attempted, something done,
        Has earned a night's repose.

Thanks, thanks to thee, my worthy friend.
        For the lesson thou hast taught!
45   Thus at the flaming forge of life
        Our fortunes must be <u>wrought</u>;
Thus on its sounding anvil shaped
        Each burning deed and thought.    ■

---

6. **chaff.** Husks of grain separated during threshing

**WORDS
FOR
EVERYDAY
USE**     **wrought** (rôt) *adj.*, worked; made (alt. pp. of work). *The handmade craft was carefully <u>wrought</u>.*

Which aspects of the blacksmith's life seem attractive to you? Which aspects of his life would you find difficult?

# INVESTIGATE Inquire *Imagine*

## Recall: GATHERING FACTS

1a. Why can the blacksmith "look the whole world in the face"?

2a. What has happened to the blacksmith's wife?

3a. According to the speaker, what lesson can be learned from the life of the blacksmith?

## Interpret: FINDING MEANING

1b. What does the fact that he has no debts tell you about his character?

2b. What kind of relationship does the blacksmith have with his children?

3b. How does the blacksmith's life teach that lesson?

## Analyze: TAKING THINGS APART

4a. What evidence does the poem provide that the blacksmith is hard-working?

## Synthesize: BRINGING THINGS TOGETHER

4b. Do you think that the blacksmith's job gives him high prestige in the village? Compare his job with a modern job, such as car mechanic or truck driver. How are they similar or different?

## Evaluate: MAKING JUDGMENTS

5a. Some critics think that this poem is overly sentimental and preachy. Tell why you agree or disagree with this point of view.

## Extend: CONNECTING IDEAS

5b. What qualities made the blacksmith a popular person in American culture in the nineteenth century? Are those qualities still considered desirable in the United States today? If not, what other qualities are now more important?

# Understanding *Literature*

IMAGE. Review the definition of **image** in the Handbook of Literary Terms. What images did you find that Longfellow uses to describe the blacksmith?

ALLITERATION. Read the complete definition of **alliteration** in the Handbook of Literary Terms. Identify at least two other examples of alliteration in this poem.

# WRITER'S JOURNAL

1. Imagine that the blacksmith has retired. Write a **help wanted ad** for a new blacksmith that would appear in the town newspaper.

2. Imagine that you are the blacksmith and write a **letter** to your wife who has passed away, telling her about your life without her. Tell her about how hearing your daughter's voice singing in the village choir reminds you of her and how it makes you feel.

3. Write a brief **character sketch**, or description, of the blacksmith. Include as many details as you can about the character of the blacksmith from the poem, such as how he looks, acts, and feels.

# Integrating *the* LANGUAGE ARTS

## Language, Grammar, and Style

**ADDING PREPOSITIONAL PHRASES.** Read the Language Arts Survey 3.30, "Identifying Prepositional Phrases." Then read each sentence below. Copy the sentences and underline each prepositional phrase and circle the word it modifies. Draw an arrow connecting the word and its modifying phrase. Finally, tell whether the phrase is adjectival or adverbial.

1. Under the spreading chestnut tree the village smithy stands.
2. The smith is a mighty man with large and sinewy hands.
3. On Sunday, he goes to church and sits among his boys.
4. The mother of his children is now dead and he remembers her with sadness.
5. Each deed and thought must be shaped on the sounding anvil.

## Speaking and Listening

**INTERVIEW.** Choose a person you know who has a profession that interests you. Interview him or her to find out more about the job, what kind of educational background is required, the place where the employee works, what he or she likes and doesn't like about the profession, etc. (You may ask about the salary range, but remember that it is not polite to ask a person how much money he or she makes.) Take notes during the interview and present an oral report about the profession to your classmates.

## Study and Research

**WRITING A JOB DESCRIPTION.** Research the profession of blacksmith, sometimes called a farrier, in the library or on the Internet. Write a job description for the job that details the daily tasks and responsibilities of a blacksmith. Include educational and physical qualifications, hours, special skills required, salary, and benefits.

# About the AUTHOR

**Emily Dickinson** (1830–1886) lived a private life, rarely venturing beyond her home and her close circle of family and friends, but she lived that life intensely, in vivid moments of observation and reflection captured in astonishingly original verse. Considered by many critics and writers to be the greatest of American lyric poets, she did not seek fame, for which she had considerable contempt, but rather kept her writing to herself, sharing small portions of it with her closest family members and friends. Only seven of her poems were published during her lifetime, all anonymously and without her full consent. The first volumes of her poetry, published after her death, mangled the work by "correcting" her unconventional punctuation and her purposeful deviations from grammatical propriety. Only in 1955, with the publication of *The Poems of Emily Dickinson,* edited by T. H. Johnson, did the full extent of her achievement become known.

At her death, which occurred in her house in Amherst, Massachusetts, where she was born, Dickinson had produced over one thousand poems. These explored a tremendous range of subjects in language remarkable for its wit, inventiveness, and economy of expression. Taken as a whole, her verses, most of them quite brief, present a complex self-portrait, a sort of spiritual autobiography. Her voice is alternately humble and proud, intimate and aloof, ecstatic and sorrowful, but always questioning, reflective, and intensely alive. She was a keen observer of particulars, but capable of sudden, breathtaking generalizations that synthesized these particulars into truths.

Much nonsense has been made of the few details known of her life, which because of its outward meagerness has invited much speculation. This speculation has centered on her various romantic interests and on her famed reclusiveness. She was born to a prominent Amherst family. Her closest friends were her brother, Austin; her sister, Lavinia; and Austin's wife, Susan Huntington Dickinson. Neither Emily nor Lavinia married. Emily seldom left Amherst, although she did spend one year at Mt. Holyoke Female Seminary, ten miles away, and took a trip to Washington and Philadelphia with her father. Her grandfather was one of the founders of Amherst College. Her father, Edward, served as treasurer of Amherst College, a state representative, and a state senator.

Dickinson attended Amherst Academy before spending a year at Mt. Holyoke. At home again, she delighted in reading books that might "joggle the Mind." She read a few books very deeply, especially the Bible, the plays of Shakespeare, and works by such contemporary writers as Emerson, Keats, Tennyson, and George Eliot. Early on, she befriended Benjamin Newton, a law student who encouraged her writing. His early death led to a period of spiritual crisis during which she turned for advice to a well-known minister from Philadelphia, Charles Wadsworth, who became a close friend. In the late 1850s,

Portrait of Emily Dickinson, 1848, photographer unknown. The only known photograph of Emily Dickinson, this daguerreotype was made when she was eighteen years old.

she wrote drafts of love letters to an unknown person identified in the letters as "Master," and some of her poems of the period reflect the frustrations and tensions of thwarted romantic feeling.

She corresponded with the critic Thomas Wentworth Higginson, who encouraged but failed to understand her work, and she was courted by a family friend, Judge Otis P. Lord. Perhaps because of physical problems, her last twenty-five years were spent in seclusion from all but her closest friends and family members.

# "This is my letter to the World"
# "The Soul selects her own Society—"
# "Because I could not stop for Death—"
# "I heard a Fly buzz—when I died—"

BY EMILY DICKINSON

## About the SELECTIONS

When T. H. Johnson numbered all Dickinson's known poems for his three-volume edition of *The Poems of Emily Dickinson* (1955), he used such clues as handwriting differences to infer the order of composition. **"This is my letter to the World"** was assigned number 441. It was written in the early 1860s, probably in 1862, when Dickinson was most prolific, averaging a poem a day.

In **"The Soul selects her own Society—,"** written around 1862, Dickinson might be speaking about herself. Contemporary scholars have offered various explanations for Dickinson's withdrawal from society, including thwarted love and physical disabilities. The poems themselves support the theory that her reclusiveness was the determined, willful act of someone who wished to encounter life on her own terms. This view is supported by the affirmation in "The Soul selects her own Society—" of an individual's freedom to choose associates.

Most critics agree that **"Because I could not stop for Death—"** is one of Dickinson's best poems. The writer and critic Allen Tate has written that it is "one of the greatest in the English language; it is flawless to the last detail. . . . Every image is precise and . . . fused with the central idea." The poem was written in 1863 and published in 1890 in the first collection of Dickinson's work.

As a member of a solid New England family, Emily Dickinson was immersed in the Puritan tradition, and for many years she attended church services twice each Sunday. Many of her poems deal with religious subjects, often with questions about the relationship of the individual soul to God and about immortality and the afterlife. In **"I heard a Fly buzz—when I died—,"** the speaker imagines her own death, expressing with brilliant irony her fears about the transition from this life to the next.

Emily Dickinson's bedroom, Dickinson homestead, Amherst, Massachusetts.

# This is my letter to the World

EMILY DICKINSON

This is my letter to the World
That never wrote to Me—
The simple News that Nature told—
With tender Majesty

5     Her Message is committed
To Hands I cannot see—
For love of Her—Sweet—countrymen—
Judge tenderly—of Me ∎

*Where does the poet find her subject matter?*

If you could talk with Emily Dickinson, would you tell her you judged her work tenderly? Why, or why not?

# INVESTIGATE *Inquire Imagine*

**Recall:** GATHERING FACTS

1a. What does the speaker call her poem, or her poetry in general?

2a. Which line of the poem describes those to whom the speaker's work "is committed"?

3a. Whom or what does the word "Her" refer to in line 7?

**Interpret:** FINDING MEANING

1b. What is the speaker's inspiration for her work?

2b. How does the speaker feel about having a reader for her poetry?

3b. What information or understanding might the reader gain from the speaker's poetry?

**Analyze:** TAKING THINGS APART

4a. Identify what "cannot be seen."

**Synthesize:** BRINGING THINGS TOGETHER

4b. During her lifetime, Dickinson kept her writing to herself. What light does this poem shed on her motives? Elaborate on whether or not she meant to share her work with an audience.

**Evaluate:** MAKING JUDGMENTS

5a. Why does the speaker request that she be judged "tenderly"? What fears might she have about her audience?

**Extend:** CONNECTING IDEAS

5b. When have you shared a creative effort with an audience? What were your fears? How was your work appraised? What did you learn from sharing your work with someone else?

# Understanding *Literature*

APOLOGY. An **apology** is a literary defense. Explain how this poem can be seen as an apology. What does it defend?

METER. The **meter** of a poem is its rhythmical pattern. Look over the examples of stress patterns included in the definition for *meter* in the Handbook of Literary Terms. Then copy the poem in your notebook and mark its stress pattern. The first line of the poem has been done for you.

´ ˘ ˘ ´ ˘ ´ ˘ ´
This is my letter to the World

# The Soul selects her own Society—

EMILY DICKINSON

The Soul selects her own Society—
Then—shuts the Door—
To her divine Majority—
Present no more—

5 Unmoved—she notes the Chariots—pausing—
At her low Gate—
Unmoved—an Emperor be kneeling
Upon her Mat—

I've known her—from an ample nation—
10 Choose One—
Then—close the Valves of her attention—
Like Stone—

> *What does the Soul do with her attention?*

If Emily Dickinson selected you as her friend, would you want to be part of her "society"? Why, or why not?

# INVESTIGATE, Inquire, Imagine

**Recall:** GATHERING FACTS

1a. Which of the three verbs in stanza 1 expresses a command? Explain the command and give an example of someone who might talk like this.

2a. Identify two attractions that fail to tempt the interest of the soul.

3a. In the final stanza, how does the soul block off access by anyone other than the one she has chosen?

→ **Interpret:** FINDING MEANING

1b. Does the speaker feel that she is thrown together with her friends by chance? Is she more interested in quality or quantity? How do you know?

2b. What real-life attractions might be symbolized by the "Chariots" and the "Emperor"?

3b. Do you suppose that the phrase "ample nation" in the final stanza refers to the United States or simply to a large number of people? Explain your answer.

**Analyze:** TAKING THINGS APART

4a. How many syllables does each line in the poem have? What kind of pattern can you discern?

→ **Synthesize:** BRINGING THINGS TOGETHER

4b. How does the abruptness of the syllable pattern in the final stanza contribute to the meaning of the poem?

**Evaluate:** MAKING JUDGMENTS

5a. Do you agree with Dickinson that it is better to have a few close friends than a large number of acquaintances? What are some of the benefits of being selective about one's friendships?

→ **Extend:** CONNECTING IDEAS

5b. Name a character in fiction, film, or television who is selective about his or her friendships. Describe his or her relationship with a close friend. What makes it rewarding?

# Understanding Literature

SIGHT RHYME. A **sight rhyme**, or **eye rhyme**, is a pair of words, generally at the ends of lines of verse, that are spelled similarly but pronounced differently, for example, *move/above*. Find an example of sight rhyme in this poem.

SLANT RHYME. A **slant rhyme** is substitution of assonance or consonance for true rhyme. The pairs *world/boiled* and *bear/bore* are examples. Diagram the slant rhymes in "The Soul selects her own Society—" by making a chart. On the left, write the examples of slant rhymes in the poem. On the right, explain what ideas in the poem the rhymes reinforce. One example has been done for you.

| Slant Rhymes | Explanation |
|---|---|
| "Society/Majority" | The selective "Majority" of a small group of intimates is the type of "Society" the soul selects. |

# Because I could not stop for Death—

EMILY DICKINSON

Because I could not stop for Death—
He kindly stopped for me—
The Carriage held but just Ourselves—
And Immortality.

5    We slowly drove—He knew no haste
And I had put away
My labor and my leisure too,
For His <u>Civility</u>—

We passed the School, where Children strove
10   At recess—in the Ring—
We passed the Fields of Gazing Grain—
We passed the Setting Sun—

> *What three things does the carriage pass?*

WORDS
FOR
EVERYDAY
USE

**ci • vil • i • ty** (sə vil´ə tē) *n.,* gentleness; a civilized manner. *She longed for a world of <u>civility</u> in which gentleness, cooperation, and manners would be prized.*

Or rather—He passed Us—
The Dews drew quivering and Chill—
15   For only Gossamer, my Gown—
My Tippet[1]—only Tulle[2]—

We paused before a House that seemed
A Swelling of the Ground—
The Roof was scarcely visible—
20   The Cornice[3]—in the Ground

Since then—'tis Centuries—and yet
Feels shorter than the Day
I first surmised the Horses Heads
Were toward Eternity— ■

What is this house?

---

1. **Tippet.** Short cape worn over the shoulders
2. **Tulle.** Thin netting
3. **Cornice.** Molded projection at the top of a building

**Winter Sunday in Norway, Maine,** c.1860. Artist unknown.
New York State Historical Association, Cooperstown, NY.

If you were the speaker, what would be your attitude toward life in view of your belief in immortality?

# INVESTIGATE, Inquire, Imagine

**Recall:** GATHERING FACTS

1a. How does the speaker picture Death in stanza 1? What kind of a person is he? What does he propose?

2a. Identify the three visual images the speaker notes during the carriage ride.

3a. To which sense does most of stanza 4 relate?

**Interpret:** FINDING MEANING

1b. Why do you think the speaker could not stop for Death?

2b. In what way do the three images reflect stages of life? Or, to what parts of life is the speaker saying good-bye?

3b. How does the speaker react to Death in this stanza?

**Analyze:** TAKING THINGS APART

4a. In what way does the speaker change by the end of the poem? What has happened to her? How has this change come about?

**Synthesize:** BRINGING THINGS TOGETHER

4b. What is the speaker's attitude toward death in the poem?

**Evaluate:** MAKING JUDGMENTS

5a. Critique Dickinson's use of time in the poem. Does time pass as it would during a real carriage ride? Is the concept of time developed in the poem?

**Extend:** CONNECTING IDEAS

5b. Read Dylan Thomas's poem "Do Not Go Gentle into That Good Night." Contrast Thomas's attitude toward death with the one expressed in "Because I could not stop for Death—."

# Understanding Literature

EXTENDED METAPHOR. An **extended metaphor** is a point-by-point presentation of one thing as though it were another. Explore the extended metaphor in this poem by making a chart. On the left, explain what is happening in the poem in stanzas 1–5. On the right, describe the events of the funeral procession. The first example has been done for you.

| Explanation of Extended Metaphor | Description of Funeral Procession |
| --- | --- |
| Death, like a gentleman caller, takes the speaker for a carriage ride. | The corpse is in the funeral carriage, or hearse. |

POINT OF VIEW. **Point of view** is the vantage point from which a literary work is told. Review the definition for *point of view* in the Handbook of Literary Terms. What pronouns indicate that the speaker uses the first-person point of view? What is unusual about the speaker? What is she looking back on? What might account for the calmness and humor of her description of her experience with Death?

# I heard a Fly buzz— when I died—

EMILY DICKINSON

I heard a Fly buzz—when I died—
The Stillness in the Room
Was like the Stillness in the Air—
Between the Heaves of Storm—

5    The Eyes around—had wrung them dry—
and Breaths were gathering firm
For that last Onset—when the King
Be witnessed—in the Room

I willed my Keepsakes[1]—Signed away
10   What portion of me be
Assignable—and then it was
There interposed[2] a Fly—

With Blue—uncertain stumbling Buzz—
Between the light—and me—
15   And then the Windows failed—and then
I could not see to see—

*Who else is in the room besides the speaker?*

1. **Keepsakes.** Personal items that are treasured
2. **interposed.** Appeared suddenly

If you were the dying person described in the poem, what would be your biggest fear?

# INVESTIGATE, Inquire, *Imagine*

**Recall:** GATHERING FACTS

1a. Describe the scene at the beginning of the poem.

2a. All the sentences and clauses in the poem except one follow the subject-verb pattern. Identify the clause that breaks away from that pattern. What pattern does it use?

3a. What does the speaker notice about the fly? What does she notice about the rest of the room after the fly enters?

➤ **Interpret:** FINDING MEANING

1b. Explain the figure of speech in stanza 1 that indicates something momentous is about to happen.

2b. Why does the poet vary the sentence pattern in the single clause? What effect does the unusual word order produce?

3b. How does the speaker's actual experience contradict the expectation of the people gathered around her deathbed? What fears about death does the poem explore?

**Analyze:** TAKING THINGS APART

4a. To what senses does the poem refer?

➤ **Synthesize:** BRINGING THINGS TOGETHER

4b. Summarize the mood of the speaker at the end of the poem.

**Evaluate:** MAKING JUDGMENTS

5a. In your opinion, how realistic is the moment of death as described by the speaker?

➤ **Extend:** CONNECTING IDEAS

5b. Contrast the view of death described in "I heard a Fly buzz—when I died—" with the one presented in "Because I could not stop for Death—."

# Understanding *Literature*

SYNAESTHESIA. **Synaesthesia** is a figure of speech that combines in a single expression images related to two or more different senses; for example, "blue note" suggests both sight and hearing. What example of synaesthesia do you find in stanza 4?

SYMBOL. A **symbol** is a thing that stands for or represents both itself and something else. Consider Dickinson's use of symbols in this poem by making a chart. On the left, list two symbols that appear in stanza 4 of the poem. On the right, state what the symbols represent.

# Writer's Journal

1. Reread "This is my letter to the World." Then write your own **letter** to the world, telling what you want the world to know and how you want it to regard or judge you.

2. Write an **advice column** responding to a teenager's complaint that she has many acquaintances, but no close friends. Quote part of "The Soul selects her own Society—" in framing your response.

3. Imagine that the speaker in "Because I could not stop for Death—" and the speaker in "I heard a Fly buzz—when I died—" want to debate each other about their views about death. Play the role of one of the speakers and write a **rebuttal** of the other speaker's views.

# Integrating
## *the* LANGUAGE ARTS

## Language, Grammar, and Style

**THE SUBJUNCTIVE MOOD.** Read the Language Arts Survey 3.64, "Properties of Verbs: Mood," on the subjunctive mood and the past subjunctive. Then write these sentences and underline each verb that is used in the subjunctive mood.

1. To understand Dickinson's work, it is important that the reader remember the pressures on women of her day.

2. Society required that a woman marry in order to be respected.

3. Certainly, friends would suggest that a woman accept almost any proposal, no matter how undesirable.

4. Were I a woman in Dickinson's era, I would not have been able to plan a career of my own.

5. Can you imagine Dickinson's surprise and pleasure if she were to see the great number of modern women with important careers in business, science, and the arts?

## Study and Research & Collaborative Learning

**RESEARCHING WOMEN OF THE 1800S.** With three classmates, research the role of women in the United States in the 1800s or the life of a famous woman of that time period. Famous women of the nineteenth century to consider include Nelly Bly (the first female reporter); Amelia Bloomer, Elizabeth Cady Stanton, Margaret Fuller, or Susan B. Anthony (feminists); Harriet Tubman or Sojourner Truth (civil rights leaders); or Florence Nightingale (founder of the Red Cross).

First, take notes as you do your research. Second, choose roles for the project, deciding who will rather be the secretary, the writer, the editor, or the presenter. Third, the secretary takes notes for an outline, receiving ideas from the other three group members. Then the writer uses the outline to write the paper, giving it to the editor to mark revisions. Finally, the presenter uses the outline to give a presentation to the class, and the writer submits the revised paper to your teacher.

## Vocabulary

**ETYMOLOGIES.** Read the information about etymologies in the Language Arts Survey 5.21, "Types of Dictionaries." Using a dictionary that gives etymologies, list the Latin words that *majesty, major,* and *civility* come from. Then make a list of other English words that are related to these words.

# About *the* A U T H O R

**Edgar Allan Poe** (1809–1849) led a short, troubled life, but managed in his forty years to make major contributions to literary form and criticism. Considered to be one of the two creators of the modern short story (the other being Nathaniel Hawthorne), Poe also invented detective fiction, wrote lyric poetry, and pioneered the psychological horror story. Poe's major innovation in the last of these literary forms was to use a technique of double meaning, whereby a tale could be read as being either about the supernatural or about the imaginings of a madman.

Few writers have had such enduring popularity and influence as Poe. As a critic, Poe offered a superb definition of the short story, which he thought of as a brief fictional work, the details of which are carefully chosen to create in the reader a single dominant impression.

Poe's tragic life was plagued with insecurity. His father deserted the family when Edgar was a year old. His mother died at the age of twenty-four, and Poe, two years old, was taken in by John Allan, a prosperous Richmond, Virginia, merchant. Poe briefly attended the University of Virginia and did well in his studies. He joined the army after publishing *Tamerlane and Other Poems* in 1827, and was appointed to West Point, but poor class attendance led to his expulsion from the academy. Poe's strange marriage in 1835 to his first cousin, Virginia Clemm, who was not yet fourteen, has been interpreted as his attempt to find the stable family life he lacked.

Poe later held various editorial jobs, reviewed literary works, and wrote one novel, *The Narrative of Arthur Gordon Pym*, in addition to producing numerous short stories and poems. Briefly famous and successful after the publication of his poem "The Raven," Poe nonetheless spent most of his adult life in poverty, losing one job after another due to drinking and quarrelsomeness. After his death, he was hailed as a genius, particularly in France, where he greatly influenced the Symbolist poets Paul Valéry and Charles Baudelaire. Several of his works, including his poem "The Bells," were published after his death.

Poe believed that strangeness was an essential ingredient of beauty, and his writing is often exotic. His stories and poems are populated with doomed, introspective aristocrats (Poe, like many other southerners, cherished an aristocratic ideal). Themes of death-in-life, especially of being buried alive or returning like a vampire from the grave, appear in many of his works. Poe's twilight realm between life and death and his gaudy, Gothic settings reflect the overcivilized yet deathly interior of his characters' disturbed psyches. As symbolic expressions of the unconscious, they are central to his art.

Other well-known works by Poe include the poem "Annabel Lee" and the stories "The Fall of the House of Usher," "The Masque of the Red Death," "The Black Cat," "The Cask of Amontillado," "The Purloined Letter," and "The Tell-Tale Heart."

# "The Pit and the Pendulum"

# "The Raven"

BY EDGAR ALLAN POE

## About *the* SELECTIONS

**"The Pit and the Pendulum"** is a tale of terror, a short story nightmare. Poe's stories often were set in foreign locales, rarely in familiar American locations. Removed from familiar settings, the stories take on macabre, mysterious overtones that add to their overall mood of strangeness and suspense.

The Spanish Inquisition, which lasted from the 1400s to the 1800s, provides a fitting setting for this story of a man who finds himself imprisoned for reasons he cannot understand and becomes the helpless victim of unknowable and cruel torturers. The Inquisition began as an attempt by the Catholic Church to identify and punish heretics, who refused to believe in the Church's teachings. However, the Inquisition degenerated into an excuse for those in power to persecute their enemies, as was the case with the prisoner in this tale.

**"The Raven"** was Poe's first international success. When it was published in 1845 in the *New York Evening Mirror*, the editor warned readers that "it would stick to the memory of everybody who reads it." It seems that this prophecy came true, because soon after the poem's publication, "The Raven" was read and reread by critics, poets, and students all over the world. To this day, "The Raven" is included in many anthologies; it has become a staple in the education of American students. Poe himself considered it to be one of his finest works. In 1846, he claimed that "future generations will be able to sift the gold from the dross, and 'The Raven' will be beheld, shining above them all as a diamond of the purest water."

## Literary TOOLS

**POINT OF VIEW.** The vantage point from which a story is told is called **point of view.** "The Pit and the Pendulum" is written from a first-person point of view, in which the narrator uses such pronouns as *I* and *me*. The narrator's point of view can be *limited*, in which the narrator can reveal the private, internal thoughts of himself or herself or of a single character. Point of view can also be *omniscient*, revealing the private, internal thoughts of any character. Is the narrator's point of view in "The Pit and the Pendulum" limited or omniscient?

**GOTHIC FICTION. Gothic fiction** is a style of fiction characterized by the use of medieval settings, a murky atmosphere of horror and gloom, and grotesque, mysterious, and violent incidents. Essential to Gothic fiction is a setting that evokes strong feelings of foreboding or fearful anticipation. How does the setting in "The Pit and the Pendulum" achieve this purpose?

## Reader's *Journal*

Do you enjoy taking carnival rides, going to "haunted houses," and watching or reading thrillers and horror stories? Why, or why not?

# The Pit and the Pendulum

EDGAR ALLAN POE

*The Drawbridge*, from the *Imaginary Prisons* series, c.1761.
Giovanni Battista Piranesi. Private Collection.

I was sick—sick unto death with that long agony; and when they at length unbound me, and I was permitted to sit, I felt that my senses were leaving me. The sentence—the dread sentence of death—was the last of distinct <u>accentuation</u> which reached my ears. After that, the sound of the <u>inquisitorial</u> voices seemed merged in one dreamy <u>indeterminate</u> hum. It conveyed to my soul the idea of *revolution*—perhaps from its association in fancy with the burr of a mill wheel. This only for a brief period; for presently I heard no more. Yet, for a while, I saw; but with how terrible an exaggeration! I saw the lips of the black-robed judges. They appeared to me white—whiter than the sheet upon which I trace these words—and thin even to

**WORDS FOR EVERYDAY USE**

**ac • cen • tu • a • tion** (ak sen chü ā´shən) *n.*, emphasis; clear pronunciation. *He pronounced each word with very clear <u>accentuation</u> to give emphasis.*

**in • quis • i • to • ri • al** (in kwiz´ə tôr´ē əl) *adj.*, prying. *The interviewer's questions about my personal life seemed <u>inquisitorial</u>.*

**in • de • ter • mi • nate** (in di tʉrm´nət) *adj.*, unspecific; unsettled. *The source of the sounds was <u>indeterminate</u>: they could have been coming from almost any direction.*

grotesqueness; thin with the intensity of their expression of firmness—of immovable resolution—of stern contempt of human torture. I saw that the decrees of what to me was Fate were still issuing from those lips. I saw them <u>writhe</u> with a deadly <u>locution</u>. I saw them fashion the syllables of my name; and I shuddered because no sound succeeded. I saw, too, for a few moments of delirious horror, the soft and nearly imperceptible waving of the sable draperies which enwrapped the walls of the apartment. And then my vision fell upon the seven tall candles upon the table. At first they wore the aspect of charity, and seemed white slender angels who would save me; but then, all at once, there came a most deadly nausea over my spirit, and I felt every fiber in my frame thrill as if I had touched the wire of a galvanic[1] battery, while the angel forms became meaningless specters, with heads of flame, and I saw that from them there would be no help. And then there stole into my fancy, like a rich musical note, the thought of what sweet rest there must be in the grave. The thought came gently and stealthily, and it seemed long before it attained full appreciation; but just as my spirit came at length properly to feel and entertain it, the figures of the judges vanished, as if magically, from before me; the tall candles sank into nothingness; their flames went out utterly; the blackness of darkness <u>supervened</u>; all sensations appeared swallowed up in a mad rushing descent as of the soul into Hades.[2] Then silence, and stillness, and night were the universe.

I had swooned; but still will not say that all of consciousness was lost. What of it there remained I will not attempt to define, or even to describe; yet all was not lost. In the deepest slumber—no! In delirium—no! In a swoon—no! In death—no! even in the grave all is *not* lost. Else there is no immortality for man. Arousing from the most profound of slumbers, we break the gossamer web of *some* dream. Yet in a second afterward (so frail may that web have been), we remember not that we have dreamed. In the return to life from the swoon there are two stages; first, that of the sense of mental or spiritual; secondly, that of the sense of physical, existence. It seems probable that if, upon reaching the second stage, we could recall the impressions of the first, we should find these impressions eloquent in memories of the gulf beyond. And that gulf is—what? How at least shall we distinguish its shadows from those of the tomb? But if the impressions of what I have termed the first stage, are not, at will, recalled, yet, after long interval, do they not come unbidden, while we marvel whence they come? He who has never swooned is not he who finds strange palaces and wildly familiar faces in coals that glow; is not he who beholds floating in midair the sad visions that the many may not view; is not he who ponders over the perfume of some novel flower—is not he whose brain grows bewildered with the meaning of some musical <u>cadence</u> which has never before arrested his attention.

Amid frequent and thoughtful endeavors to remember; amid <u>earnest</u> struggles to regather some token of the state of seeming nothingness into which my soul had lapsed, there have been moments when I have dreamed of success; there

<aside>What exaggerations does the prisoner see?</aside>

<aside>What sorts of visions has the prisoner experienced?</aside>

---

1. **galvanic.** Producing an electric current
2. **Hades.** In Greek mythology, home of the dead; underground

---

**WORDS FOR EVERYDAY USE**

**writhe** (rīth) *vi.,* twist as if in pain or struggling. *He tried to <u>writhe</u> his way free of the ropes that entangled him.*

**lo • cu • tion** (lō kyü´shən) *n.,* word; phrase. *She spoke with the <u>locutions</u> of her southern upbringing.*

**su • per • vene** (sü´pər vēn´) *vi.,* happen unexpectedly. *The rain <u>supervened</u> and ruined the picnic.*

**ca • dence** (kā´dən[t]s) *n.,* rhythmic flow of sound or tone. *The marching band kept time with the <u>cadence</u> of the drums.*

**ear • nest** (ʉr´nist) *adj.,* serious; intense. *The student made an <u>earnest</u> attempt to pass the test.*

have been brief, very brief periods when I have conjured up remembrances which the lucid reason of a later epoch assures me could have had reference only to that condition of seeming unconsciousness. These shadows of memory tell, indistinctly, of tall figures that lifted and bore me in silence down—down—still down—till a hideous dizziness oppressed me at the mere idea of the interminableness of the descent. They tell also of a vague horror at my heart, on account of that heart's unnatural stillness. Then comes a sense of sudden motionlessness throughout all things; as if those who bore me (a ghastly train!) had outrun, in their descent, the limits of the limitless, and paused from the wearisomeness of their toil. After this I call to mind flatness and dampness; and then all is madness—the madness of a memory which busies itself among forbidden things.

Very suddenly there came back to my soul motion and sound—the tumultuous motion of the heart, and, in my ears, the sound of its beating. Then a pause in which all is blank. Then again sound, and motion, and touch—a tingling sensation pervading my frame. Then the mere consciousness of existence, without thought—a condition which lasted long. Then, very suddenly, *thought*, and shuddering terror, and earnest endeavor to comprehend my true state. Then a strong desire to lapse into insensibility. Then a rushing revival of soul and a successful effort to move. And now a full memory of the trial, of the judges, of the sable draperies, of the sentence, of the sickness, of the swoon. Then entire forgetfulness of all that followed; of all that a later day and much earnestness of endeavor have enabled me vaguely to recall.

So far, I had not opened my eyes. I felt that I lay upon my back, unbound. I reached out my hand, and it fell heavily upon something damp and hard. There I suffered it to remain for many minutes, while I strove to imagine where and *what* I could be. I longed, yet dared not to

## The intensity of the darkness seemed to oppress and stifle me.

employ my vision. I dreaded the first glance at objects around me. It was not that I feared to look upon things horrible, but that I grew aghast lest there should be *nothing* to see. At length, with a wild desperation at heart, I quickly unclosed my eyes. My worst thoughts, then, were confirmed. The blackness of eternal night encompassed me. I struggled for breath. The intensity of the darkness seemed to oppress and stifle me. The atmosphere was intolerably close. I still lay quietly, and made effort to exercise my reason. I brought to mind the inquisitorial proceedings, and attempted from that point to deduce my real condition. The sentence had passed; and it appeared to me that a very long interval of time had since elapsed. Yet not for a moment did I suppose myself actually dead. Such a supposition, notwithstanding what we read in fiction, is altogether inconsistent with real existence;—but where and in what state was I? The condemned to death, I knew, perished usually at the autos-da-fe,[3] and one of these had been held on the very night of the day of my trial. Had I

3. **autos-da-fe.** Public ceremonies in which the inquisitors pronounced judgment and passed sentences on heretics

---

**WORDS FOR EVERYDAY USE**

**con • jure** (kän´jər) *vt.*, call up. *Certain words conjure pleasant images.*

**in • ter • mi • na • ble** (in tʉr´mi nə bəl) *adj.*, without, or seemingly without, end. *It seemed that the interminable lecture would never end.*

**en • com • pass** (en kum´pəs) *vt.*, surround. *The darkness was all around him; it encompassed him like a blanket.*

been remanded to my dungeon, to await the next sacrifice, which would not take place for many months? This I at once saw could not be. Victims had been in immediate demand. Moreover, my dungeon, as well as all the condemned cells at Toledo,[4] had stone floors, and light was not altogether excluded.

A fearful idea now suddenly drove the blood in torrents upon my heart, and for a brief period, I once more relapsed into insensibility. Upon recovering, I at once started to my feet, trembling convulsively in every fiber. I thrust my arms wildly above and around me in all directions. I felt nothing; yet dreaded to move a step, lest I should be impeded by the walls of a *tomb*. Perspiration burst from every pore, and stood in cold big beads upon my forehead. The agony of suspense grew at length intolerable, and I cautiously moved forward,

*Where does the prisoner fear he is?*

with my arms extended, and my eyes straining from their sockets, in the hope of catching some faint ray of light. I proceeded for many paces; but still all was blackness and vacancy. I breathed more freely. It seemed evident that mine was not, at least, the most hideous of fates.

And now, as I still continued to step cautiously onward, there came thronging upon my recollection, a thousand vague rumors of the horrors of Toledo. Of the dungeons there had been strange things narrated—fables I had always deemed them—but yet strange, and too ghastly to repeat, save in a whisper. Was I left to perish of starvation in this subterranean world of darkness; or what fate, perhaps even more fearful, awaited me? That the result would be death, and a death of more than customary bitterness, I knew too well the character of my judges to

*What were the rumors about Toledo?*

doubt. The mode and the hour were all that occupied or distracted me.

My outstretched hands at length encountered some solid obstruction. It was a wall, seemingly of stone masonry—very smooth, slimy, and cold. I followed it up; stepping with all the careful distrust with which certain antique narratives had inspired me. This process, however, afforded me no means of ascertaining the dimensions of my dungeon; as I might make its circuit, and return to the point whence I set out, without being aware of the fact; so perfectly uniform seemed the wall. I therefore sought the knife which had been in my pocket, when led into the inquisitorial chamber; but it was gone; my clothes had been exchanged for a wrapper of coarse serge.[5] I had thought of forcing the blade in some minute crevice of the masonry, so as to identify my point of departure. The difficulty, nevertheless, was but trivial; although, in the disorder of my fancy, it seemed at first insuperable. I tore a part of the hem from the robe and placed the fragment at full length, and at right angles to the wall. In groping my way around the prison, I could not fail to encounter this rag upon completing the circuit. So, at least I thought; but I had not counted upon the extent of the dungeon, or upon my own weakness. The ground was moist and slippery. I staggered onward for some time, when I stumbled and fell. My excessive fatigue induced me to remain prostrate; and sleep soon overtook me as I lay.

Upon awaking, and stretching forth an arm, I found beside me a loaf and a pitcher with water. I was too much exhausted to reflect upon this circumstance, but ate and drank with avidity. Shortly afterward, I resumed my tour around the prison, and with much toil, came at last

---

4. **Toledo.** Spanish city
5. **serge.** Sturdy fabric

**WORDS FOR EVERYDAY USE**

im • pede (im pēd´) *vt.,* obstruct; hinder. *The deep snow in the road impeded the progress of the car.*

in • su • per • a • ble (in sü´pər ə bəl) *adj.,* insurmountable. *The difficult tasks ahead seemed insuperable.*

a • vid • i • ty (ə vid´ə tē) *n.,* eagerness; enthusiasm. *The greedy lawyer overcharged his clients with avidity.*

upon the fragment of the serge. Up to the period when I fell I had counted fifty-two paces, and upon resuming my walk, I had counted forty-eight more;—when I arrived at the rag. There were in all, then, a hundred paces; and, admitting two paces to the yard, I presumed the dungeon to be fifty yards in circuit. I had met, however, with many angles in the wall, and thus I could form no guess at the shape of the vault; for vault I could not help supposing it to be.

How does the prisoner measure his cell?

I had little object—certainly no hope—in these researches; but a vague curiosity prompted me to continue them. Quitting the wall, I resolved to cross the area of the enclosure. At first I proceeded with extreme caution, for the floor, although seemingly of solid material, was treacherous with slime. At length, however, I took courage, and did not hesitate to step firmly; endeavoring to cross in as direct a line as possible. I had advanced some ten or twelve paces in this manner, when the remnant of the torn hem of my robe became entangled between my legs. I stepped on it, and fell violently on my face.

In the confusion attending my fall, I did not immediately apprehend a somewhat startling circumstance, which yet, in a few seconds afterward, and while I still lay prostrate, arrested my attention. It was this—my chin rested upon the floor of the prison, but my lips and the upper portion of my head, although seemingly at a less elevation than the chin, touched nothing. At the same time my forehead seemed bathed in a clammy vapor, and the peculiar smell of decayed fungus arose to my nostrils. I put forward my arm, and shuddered to find that I had fallen at the very brink of a circular

How does the prisoner discover the pit?

pit, whose extent, of course, I had no means of ascertaining at the moment. Groping about the masonry just below the margin, I succeeded in dislodging a small fragment, and let it fall into the abyss. For many seconds I hearkened to its reverberations as it dashed against the sides of the chasm in its descent; at length there was a sullen plunge into water, succeeded by loud echoes. At the same moment there came a sound resembling the quick opening, and as rapid closing of a door overhead, while a faint gleam of light flashed suddenly through the gloom, and as suddenly faded away.

I saw clearly the doom which had been prepared for me, and congratulated myself upon the timely accident by which I had escaped. Another step before my fall, and the world had seen me no more. And the death just avoided, was of that very character which I had regarded as fabulous and frivolous in the tales respecting the Inquisition. To the victims of its tyranny, there was the choice of death with its direst physical agonies, or death with its most hideous moral horrors. I had been reserved for the latter. By long suffering my nerves had been unstrung, until I trembled at the sound of my own voice, and had become in every respect a fitting subject for the species of torture which awaited me.

Shaking in every limb, I groped my way back to the wall; resolving there to perish rather than risk the terrors of the wells, of which my imagination now pictured many in various positions about the dungeon. In other conditions of mind I might have had courage to end my misery at once by a plunge into one of these abysses; but now I was the veriest of cowards. Neither could I forget what I had read of these pits—that the *sudden* extinction of life formed no part of their most horrible plan.

Agitation of spirit kept me awake for many

**WORDS FOR EVERYDAY USE**

**a • byss** (ə bis´) *n.*, bottomless hole. *The explosion formed an* abyss *in the earth that seemed to go on forever.*

long hours; but at length I again slumbered. Upon arousing, I found by my side, as before, a loaf and a pitcher of water. A burning thirst

A deep sleep
fell upon me—
a sleep like that
of death.

consumed me, and I emptied the vessel at a draught. It must have been drugged; for scarcely had I drunk, before I became irresistibly drowsy. A deep sleep fell upon me—a sleep like that of death. How long it lasted of course, I know not; but when, once again, I unclosed my eyes, the objects around me were visible. By a wild sulphurous[6] luster, the origin of which I could not at first determine, I was enabled to see the extent and aspect of the prison.

> *What happens to the prisoner after he quenches his thirst?*

In its size I had been greatly mistaken. The whole circuit of its walls did not exceed twenty-five yards. For some minutes this fact occasioned me a world of vain trouble; vain indeed! for what could be of less importance, under the terrible circumstances which environed me, than the mere dimensions of my dungeon? But my soul took a wild interest in trifles, and I busied myself in endeavors to account for the error I had committed in my measurement. The truth at length flashed upon me. In my first attempt at exploration I had counted fifty-two paces, up to the period when I fell; I must then

> *What absorbs the prisoner's interest?*

have been within a pace or two of the fragment of serge; in fact, I had nearly performed the circuit of the vault. I then slept, and upon awaking, I must have returned upon my steps—thus supposing the circuit nearly double what it actually was. My confusion of mind prevented me from observing that I began my tour with the wall to the left; and ended it with the wall to the right.

I had been deceived, too, in respect to the shape of the enclosure. In feeling my way I had found many angles, and thus deduced an idea of great irregularity; so potent is the effect of total darkness upon one arousing from lethargy or sleep! The angles were simply those of a few slight depressions, or niches, at odd intervals. The general shape of the prison was square. What I had taken for masonry seemed now to be iron, or some other metal, in huge plates, whose sutures or joints occasioned the depression. The entire surface of this metallic enclosure was rudely daubed in all the hideous and repulsive devices to which the charnel[7] superstition of the monks has given rise. The figures of fiends in aspects of menace, with skeleton forms, and other more really fearful images, overspread and disfigured the walls. I observed that the outlines of these monstrosities were sufficiently distinct, but that the colors seemed faded and blurred, as if from the effects of a damp atmosphere. I now noticed the floor, too, which was of stone. In the center yawned the circular pit from whose jaws I had escaped; but it was the only one in the dungeon.

All this I saw indistinctly and by much effort: for my personal condition had been greatly changed during slumber. I now lay upon my back, and at full length, on a species of low framework of wood. To this I was securely bound by a long strap resembling a surcingle.[8] It passed in many

> *What change has taken place?*

---

6. **sulphurous.** Similar to the color of burning sulphur, suggesting the fires of hell
7. **charnel.** Building where bodies and bones are placed
8. **surcingle.** Strap around a horse's body to hold on a saddle

*The Round Tower*, from the *Imaginary Prisons* series, c.1761. Giovanni Battista Piranesi. Private Collection.

## ArtNote

Giovanni Battista Piranesi (1720–1778) was an Italian artist who was especially interested in the archeology of ancient Rome. He came from a family of engineers, and early in his career as an artist he painted stage scenery for opera houses in Venice. All these influences combined in his dramatic and exaggerated drawings of Roman architecture. Among his most fantastic pictures are the *Carceri d'Invenzione* or "Imaginary Prisons," a book of fourteen etchings straight from Piranesi's gloomy imagination. The drawing on page 230 is also from this series. These foreboding pictures have influenced romantic, horror, and surrealist writers and artists through the centuries. How might this drawing have influenced Poe as he wrote this story?

<u>convolutions</u> about my limbs and body, leaving at liberty only my head, and my left arm to such extent that I could, by dint of much exertion, supply myself with food from an earthen dish which lay by my side on the floor. I saw, to my horror, that the pitcher had been removed. I say to my horror, for I was consumed with intolerable thirst. This thirst it appeared to be the design of my persecutors to stimulate, for the food in the dish was meat <u>pungently</u> seasoned.

Looking upward, I surveyed the ceiling of my prison. It was some thirty or forty feet overhead, and constructed much as the side walls. In one of its panels a very singular figure riveted my whole attention. It was the painted figure of Time as he is commonly represented, save that, in lieu of a scythe, he held what, at a casual glance, I supposed to be the pictured image of a huge pendulum such as we see on antique clocks. There was something, however, in the appearance of this machine which caused me to regard it more attentively. While I gazed directly upward at it (for its position was immediately over my own) I fancied that I saw it in motion. In an instant afterward the fancy was confirmed. Its sweep was brief, and of course slow. I watched it for some minutes, somewhat in fear, but more in wonder. Wearied at length with observing its dull movement, I turned my eyes upon the other objects in the cell.

A slight noise attracted my notice, and, looking to the floor, I saw several enormous rats traversing it. They had issued from the well, which lay just within view to my right. Even then, while I gazed, they came up in troops, hurriedly, with ravenous eyes, allured by the scent of the meat. From this it required much effort and attention to scare them away.

*What attracts the rats?*

| WORDS FOR EVERYDAY USE | |
|---|---|
| **con • vo • lu • tion** (kän´və lü´shən) *n.*, twist; coil; fold. *The package was securely bound with many <u>convolutions</u> of twine.* |
| **pun • gent • ly** (pun´jənt lē) *adv.*, sharply; strongly. *The air was sharp with the fragrance of the <u>pungently</u> scented candle.* |

It might have been half an hour, perhaps even an hour (for I could take but imperfect note of time), before I again cast my eyes upward. What I then saw confounded and amazed me. The sweep of the pendulum had increased in extent by nearly a yard. As a natural consequence, its velocity was also much greater. But what mainly disturbed me was the idea that it had perceptibly *descended*. I now observed—with what horror it is needless to say— that its nether extremity was formed of a crescent of glittering steel, about a foot in length from horn to horn; the horns upward, and the under edge evidently as keen as that of a razor. Like a razor also, it seemed massy and heavy, tapering from the edge into a solid and broad structure above. It was appended to a weighty rod of brass, and the whole *hissed* as it swung through the air.

> What is most frightening about the pendulum?

I could no longer doubt the doom prepared for me by monkish <u>ingenuity</u> in torture. My <u>cognizance</u> of the pit had become known to the inquisitorial agents—*the pit*, whose horrors had been destined for so bold a recusant[9] as myself— *the pit*, typical of hell, and regarded by rumor as the Ultima Thule[10] of all their punishments. The plunge into this pit I had avoided by the merest of accidents, and I knew that surprise, or entrapment into torment, formed an important portion of all the grotesquerie of these dungeon deaths. Having failed to fall, it was no part of the demon plan to hurl me into the abyss; and thus (there being no alternative) a different and a milder destruction awaited me. Milder! I half smiled in my agony as I thought of such application of such a term.

What boots it[11] to tell of the long, long hours of horror more than mortal, during which I counted the rushing oscillations of the steel!

Inch by inch—line by line—with a descent only appreciable at intervals that seemed ages— down and still down it came! Days passed—it

**I prayed— I wearied heaven with my prayer for its more speedy descent.**

might have been that many days passed—ere it swept so closely over me as to fan me with its acrid breath. The odor of the sharp steel forced itself into my nostrils. I prayed—I wearied heaven with my prayer for its more speedy descent. I grew frantically mad, and struggled to force myself upward against the

> For what does the prisoner pray?

sweep of the fearful scimitar.[12] And then I fell suddenly calm, and lay smiling at the glittering death, as a child at some rare bauble.

There was another interval of utter insensibility; it was brief; for, upon again lapsing into life there had been no perceptible descent in the pendulum. But it might have been long; for I knew there were demons who took note of my swoon, and who could have arrested the vibration at pleasure. Upon my recovery, too, I felt very—oh, inexpressibly sick and weak, as if through long <u>inanition</u>. Even amid the agonies

---

9. **recusant.** Person who refuses to obey an established authority
10. **Ultima Thule.** Farthest limit
11. **What boots it.** What good is it
12. **scimitar.** Curved sword

---

**WORDS FOR EVERYDAY USE**

in • ge • nu • i • ty (in´jə nü´ə tē) *n.*, cleverness. *The escape artist displayed his <u>ingenuity</u> by freeing himself within seconds.*

cog • ni • zance (käg´nə zəns) *n.*, knowledge. *The novice climbers had no <u>cognizance</u> of the danger they could be facing.*

in • a • ni • tion (in´ə nish´ən) *n.*, lack of strength due to lack of food. *Having not eaten for days, the patient felt weak from the <u>inanition</u>.*

of that period, the human nature craved food. With painful effort I outstretched my left arm as far as my bonds permitted, and took possession of the small remnant which had been spared me by the rats. As I put a portion of it within my lips, there rushed to my mind a half-formed thought of joy—of hope. Yet what business had *I* with hope? It was, as I say, a half-formed thought—man has many such which are never completed. I felt that it was of joy—of hope; but I felt also that it had perished in its formation. In vain I struggled to perfect—to regain it. Long suffering had nearly annihilated all my ordinary powers of mind. I was an imbecile—an idiot.

> What is happening to the prisoner's mind?

The vibration of the pendulum was at right angles to my length. I saw that the crescent was designed to cross the region of the heart. It would fray the serge of my robe—it would return and repeat its operations—again—and again. Notwithstanding its terrifically wide sweep (some thirty feet or more) and the hissing vigor of its descent sufficient to sunder these very walls of iron, still the fraying of my robe would be all that, for several minutes, it would accomplish. And at this thought I paused. I dared not go further than this reflection. I dwelt upon it with a <u>pertinacity</u> of attention—as if, in so dwelling, I could arrest *here* the descent of the steel. I forced myself to ponder upon the sound of the crescent as it should pass across the garment—upon the peculiar thrilling sensation which friction of cloth produces on the nerves. I pondered upon all this frivolity until my teeth were on edge.

Down—steadily down it crept. I took a frenzied pleasure in contrasting its downward with its lateral velocity. To the right—to the left—far and wide—with the shriek of a damned spirit; to my heart with the stealthy pace of the tiger! I

alternately laughed and howled as the one or the other idea grew predominant.

Down—certainly, relentlessly down! It vibrated within three inches of my bosom! I struggled violently, furiously, to free my left arm. This was free only from the elbow to the hand. I could reach the latter, from the platter beside me, to my mouth, with great effort, but no farther. Could I have broken the fastenings above the elbow I would have seized and attempted to arrest the pendulum. I might as well have attempted to arrest an avalanche!

Down—still unceasingly—still inevitably down! I gasped and struggled at each vibration. I shrunk convulsively at its every sweep. My eyes followed its outward or upward whirls with the eagerness of the most unmeaning despair; they closed themselves spasmodically at the descent, although death would have been a relief, oh! how unspeakable! Still I quivered in every nerve to think how slight a sinking of the machinery would precipitate that keen, glistening ax upon my bosom. It was *hope* that prompted the nerve to quiver—the frame to shrink. It was *hope*—the hope that triumphs on the rack—that whispers to the death-condemned even in the dungeons of the Inquisition.

> What lives even in the dungeon?

I saw that some ten or twelve vibrations would bring the steel in actual contact with my robe, and with this observation there suddenly came over my spirit all the keen, collected calmness of despair. For the first time during many hours—or perhaps days—I *thought*. It now occurred to me that the bandage, or surcingle, which enveloped me, was *unique*. I was tied by no separate cord. The first stroke of the razorlike crescent athwart any portion of the band, would so detach it that it might be unwound from my person by means of my left hand. But how

**WORDS FOR EVERYDAY USE**

per • ti • nac • i • ty (pʉr´tə na´sə tē) *n.*, stubbornness. *She stubbornly refused to help, showing us her usual <u>pertinacity</u>.*

fearful, in that case, the proximity of the steel! the result of the slightest struggle, how deadly! Was it likely, moreover, that the minions of the torturer had not foreseen and provided for this possibility? Was it probable that the bandage crossed my bosom in the track of the pendulum? Dreading to find my faint, and, as it seemed, my last hope frustrated, I so far elevated my head as to obtain a distinct view of my breast. The surcingle enveloped my limbs and body close in all directions—*save in the path of the destroying crescent.*

Scarcely had I dropped my head back into its original position, when there flashed upon my mind what I cannot better describe than as the unformed half of that idea of deliverance to which I have previously alluded, and of which a <u>moiety</u> only floated indeterminately through my brain when I raised food to my burning lips. The whole thought was now present—feeble, scarcely sane, scarcely definite—but still entire. I proceeded at once, with the nervous energy of despair, to attempt its execution.

For many hours the immediate vicinity of the low framework upon which I lay, had been literally swarming with rats. They were wild, bold, ravenous; their red eyes glaring upon me as if they waited but for motionlessness on my part to make me their prey. "To what food," I thought, "have they been accustomed in the well?"

They had devoured, in spite of all my efforts to prevent them, all but a small remnant of the contents of the dish. I had fallen into an habitual seesaw, or wave of the hand about the platter; and, at length, the unconscious uniformity of the movement deprived it of effect. In their voracity the <u>vermin</u> frequently fastened their sharp fangs in my fingers. With the particles of the oily and spicy <u>viand</u> which now remained, I thoroughly rubbed the bandage wherever I could reach it;

then, raising my hand from the floor, I lay breathlessly still.

At first the ravenous animals were startled and terrified at the change—at the <u>cessation</u> of movement. They shrank alarmedly back; many sought the well. But this was only for a moment. I had not counted in vain upon their <u>voracity</u>. Observing that I remained with-

**What actions are part of the prisoner's plan?**

> **They pressed— they swarmed upon me in ever accumulating heaps.**

out motion, one or two of the boldest leaped upon the framework and smelt at the surcingle. This seemed the signal for a general rush. Forth from the well they hurried in fresh troops. They clung to the wood—they overran it, and leaped in hundreds upon my person. The measured movement of the pendulum disturbed them not at all. Avoiding its strokes, they busied themselves with the <u>anointed</u> bandage. They pressed—they swarmed upon me in ever accumulating heaps. They writhed

**What do the rats do?**

upon my throat; their cold lips sought my own; I was half stifled by their thronging pressure; disgust, for which the world has no name, swelled my bosom and chilled, with a heavy clamminess, my heart. Yet one minute, and I felt that the struggle would be over. Plainly I perceived the loosening of the bandage. I knew

| | |
|---|---|
| **WORDS FOR EVERYDAY USE** | **moi • e • ty** (moi´ə tē) *n.,* half. *He divided the portion in half and shared the <u>moiety</u> with his friend.* <br> **ver • min** (vʉr´mən) *n.,* small animals regarded as pests. *Mice are considered to be <u>vermin</u> by most people.* <br> **vi • and** (vī´ənd) *n.,* article of food, especially a tasty dish. *He relished eating the last <u>viand</u> of his meal.* <br> **ces • sa • tion** (se sā´shən) *n.,* ceasing or stopping. *We were relieved with the <u>cessation</u> of the shrill sound.* <br> **vo • rac • i • ty** (vô ras´ə tē) *n.,* greediness. *The hungry dogs lunged at the food with <u>voracity</u>.* <br> **a • noint** (ə noint´) *vt.,* rub with oil. *The cook <u>anointed</u> the meat with a spicy sesame oil.* |

that in more than one place it must be already severed. With a more than human resolution I lay *still*.

Nor had I erred in my calculations—nor had I endured in vain. I at length felt that I was *free*. The surcingle hung in ribands from my body. But the stroke of the pendulum already pressed upon my bosom. It had divided the serge of the robe. It had cut through the linen beneath. Twice again it swung, and a sharp sense of pain shot through every nerve. But the moment of escape had arrived. At a wave of my hand my deliverers hurried tumultuously away. With a steady movement—cautious, sidelong, shrinking, and slow—I slid from the embrace of the bandage and beyond the reach of the scimitar. For the moment, at least, *I was free*.

> Why is the prisoner free but not free?

Free!—and in the grasp of the Inquisition! I had scarcely stepped from my wooden bed of horror upon the stone floor of the prison, when the motion of the hellish machine ceased and I beheld it drawn up, by some invisible force, through the ceiling. This was a lesson which I took desperately to heart. My every motion was undoubtedly watched. Free!—I had but escaped death in one form of agony, to be delivered unto worse than death in some other. With that thought I rolled my eyes nervously around on the barriers of iron that hemmed me in. Something unusual—some change which, at first, I could not appreciate distinctly—it was obvious, had taken place in the apartment. For many minutes of a dreamy and trembling abstraction, I busied myself in vain, unconnected conjecture. During this period, I became aware, for the first time, of the origin of the sulphurous light which illuminated the cell. It proceeded from a fissure, about half an inch in width, extending entirely around the prison at the base of the walls, which thus appeared, and were, completely separated from the floor. I endeavored, but of course in vain, to look through the aperture.

As I arose from the attempt, the mystery of the alteration in the chamber broke at once upon my understanding. I have observed that, although the outlines of the figures upon the walls were sufficiently distinct, yet the colors seemed blurred and indefinite. These colors had now assumed, and were momentarily assuming, a startling and most intense brilliancy, that gave to the spectral and fiendish portraitures an aspect that might have thrilled even firmer nerves than my own. Demon eyes, of a wild and ghastly vivacity, glared upon me in a thousand directions where none had been visible before, and gleamed with the lurid luster of a fire that I could not force my imagination to regard as unreal.

*Unreal!*—Even while I breathed there came to my nostrils the breath of the vapor of the heated iron! A suffocating odor pervaded the prison! A deeper glow settled each moment in the eyes that glared at my agonies! A richer tint of crimson diffused itself over the pictured horrors of blood. I panted! I gasped for breath! There could be no doubt of the design of my tormentors—oh! most unrelenting! oh! most demoniac of men! I shrank from the glowing metal to the center of the cell. Amid the thought of the fiery destruction that impended, the idea of the coolness of the well came over my soul like balm. I rushed to its deadly brink. I threw my straining vision below. The glare from the enkindled roof illumined its inmost recesses. Yet, for a wild moment, did my spirit refuse to comprehend the

---

**WORDS FOR EVERYDAY USE**

**ab • strac • tion** (ab strak´shən) *n.*, mental withdrawal; absent-mindedness. *She could not concentrate because her mind was in a state of abstraction.*

**con • jec • ture** (kən jek´chər) *n.*, speculation. *Based on the evidence, his conjecture was that the defendant was innocent.*

**fis • sure** (fish´ər) *n.*, deep crack. *The earthquake caused a deep fissure in the ground.*

**ap • er • ture** (ap´ər chər) *n.*, opening; hole. *A ray of sunlight came in through the aperture in the wall.*

**dif • fuse** (di fyüz´) *vt.*, spread out; pour out. *The light was diffused by the filter.*

**im • pend** (im pend´) *vi.*, be about to happen. *There was no escaping the disaster that was impending.*

**balm** (bäm) *n.*, anything healing or soothing. *The nurse applied the soothing balm to her rough, dry skin.*

meaning of what I saw. At length it forced—it wrestled its way into my soul—it burned itself in upon my shuddering reason.—Oh! for a voice to speak!—oh! horror!—oh! any horror but this! With a shriek, I rushed from the margin, and buried my face in my hands—weeping bitterly.

The heat rapidly increased, and once again I

> "Death," I said, "any death but that of the pit!"

looked up, shuddering as with a fit of the ague.[13] There had been a second change in the cell— and now the change was obviously in the form. As before, it was in vain that I, at first, endeavored to appreciate or understand what was taking place. But not long was I left in doubt. The inquisitorial <u>vengeance</u> had been hurried by my twofold escape, and there was to be no more <u>dallying</u> with the King of Terrors. The room had been square. I saw that two of its iron angles were now acute—two, consequently, obtuse. The fearful difference quickly increased with a low rumbling or moaning sound. In an instant the apartment had shifted its form into that of a lozenge. But the alteration stopped not here—I neither hoped nor desired it to stop. I could have clasped the red walls to my bosom as a garment of eternal peace. "Death," I said, "any death but that of the pit!" Fool! might I have not known that into the pit it was the object of the burning iron to urge me? Could I resist its glow? or, if even that, could I withstand its pressure? And now, flatter and flatter grew the lozenge, with a rapidity that left me no time for contemplation. Its center, and of course, its greatest width, came just over the yawning gulf. I shrank back—but the closing walls pressed me resistlessly onward. At length for my seared and writhing body there was no longer an inch of foothold on the firm floor of the prison. I struggled no more, but the agony of my soul found vent in one loud, long, and final scream of despair. I felt that I tottered upon the brink—I <u>averted</u> my eyes—.

There was a <u>discordant</u> hum of human voices! There was a loud blast as of many trumpets! There was a harsh grating as of a thousand thunders! The fiery walls rushed back! An outstretched arm caught my own as I fell, fainting, into the abyss. It was that of General Lasalle. The French army had entered Toledo. The Inquisition was in the hands of its enemies. ∎

*What form does the rescue take?*

---

13. **ague.** Fever with chills

---

**WORDS FOR EVERYDAY USE**

**venge • ance** (ven′jən[t]s) *n.*, revenge. *The victim sought <u>vengeance</u> for the wrong that was done to him.*

**dal • ly** (dal′ē) *vi.*, waste time. *The students were wasting time <u>dallying</u> in the halls.*

**a • vert** (ə vʉrt′) *vt.*, turn away. *He avoided looking at me by <u>averting</u> his eyes.*

**dis • cord • ant** (dis kôr′dənt) *adj.*, disagreeing; conflicting. *The boy heard the <u>discordant</u> voices of his parents arguing.*

## Respond *to the* SELECTION

The main character in this tale escapes from death three times. Of the three methods of death, which would have been most terrifying to you, and why?

# Inquire Imagine

**Recall:** GATHERING FACTS

1a. What does the prisoner remember about the reason why he is imprisoned?

2a. Describe the cell where the prisoner is kept.

3a. How does the prisoner escape the descending pendulum?

→ **Interpret:** FINDING MEANING

1b. What could account for the speaker's fuzzy memory of the events that led to his imprisonment?

2b. Why is there a pit in the center of the cell? Why wasn't the prisoner executed immediately?

3b. What does the prisoner's plan for escape tell you about his character? Why did it take so long for him to devise a plan for escape from the swinging blade?

---

**Analyze:** TAKING THINGS APART

4a. If Poe writes to create a single effect, what are the ingredients of setting, atmosphere, and plot that create the effect?

→ **Synthesize:** BRINGING THINGS TOGETHER

4b. Describe the single effect that Poe has created.

---

**Evaluate:** MAKING JUDGMENTS

5a. Do you think the Inquisition is justified in the methods of torture used to punish its prisoners? What does this tell you about the ethics or morality of the monarchy of Spain at that time?

→ **Extend:** CONNECTING IDEAS

5b. Tales of terror, or horror stories, have been popular throughout history and continue to be popular with modern readers. Why do you think people are attracted to the morbid and grotesque situations often presented in this genre of literature?

# Understanding Literature

**POINT OF VIEW.** Read the complete definition of **point of view** in the Handbook of Literary Terms. This story is written from a *first-person point of view* that is *limited*, meaning that the narrator can reveal only his private, internal thoughts. How does the first-person limited point of view add to the suspense in the story?

**GOTHIC FICTION.** Review the definition of **Gothic fiction** in the Handbook of Literary Terms. *Sensory details*—images of sound, sight, touch, taste, or smell—help to describe the setting and create the mood of gothic fiction. Create a chart like the example below, listing the sensory details you encountered as you read the selection. What sensory details does Poe use to create the mood of foreboding and fearful apprehension?

| SIGHT | SOUND | TOUCH | TASTE | SMELL |
|-------|-------|-------|-------|-------|
|       |       |       |       |       |

# WRITER'S JOURNAL

1. Imagine that you are the prisoner in the story and write a **journal entry** describing your experiences in the prison cell.

2. Make a **storyboard** with descriptions of the main scenes from the story, accompanied by drawings of the main character in the settings where he finds himself.

3. The lifesaving event at the end of the story, the conquest of the tormentors by the French army, and the release of the prisoner would be covered as a major news story if it happened today. Write a **press release** describing this event. The press release should offer facts and should avoid opinion. You may want to refer to the Language Arts Survey 6.9, "Delivering a Press Release."

# Integrating

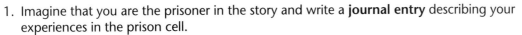

### *the* LANGUAGE ARTS

## Vocabulary

**USING CONTEXT CLUES.** Read the Language Arts Survey 1.16, "Using Context Clues to Estimate Word Meaning." Then read each of the following sentences. Write the definition of each underlined word, using context clues to deduce its meaning.

1. The prisoner searched frantically for a <u>crevice</u> in the masonry but could find no such crack or opening.

2. He had been <u>remanded</u>, or sent back, to his dungeon after the sentence was passed.

3. Pictures of <u>monstrosities</u> such as fiends, leering skeletons, and evil spirits covered the wall.

4. The prisoner was horrified to see several rats <u>traversing</u>, or traveling across, the floor.

5. The prisoner went through a period of <u>insensibility</u> and remembered nothing that happened during this time of unconsciousness.

## Collaborative Learning

**ROLE-PLAYING A TRIAL.** After doing research on the Inquisition, role-play an Inquisition trial. Try to imagine what the inquisitors might ask and how the defendant might respond. Enact the trial from the reading of the charges through the defense and the prosecution to the eventual sentencing.

## Language, Grammar, and Style

**INTERJECTIONS.** Read the Language Arts Survey 3.74, "Interjections." Then, as you read the story, make a list of all the interjections that the speaker uses. Note how Poe capitalizes and punctuates the interjections. Examples are given below.

> no!
>
> oh,
>
> Free!
>
> oh! horror!

## Media Literacy

**INTERNET ACTIVITY.** Take a virtual field trip to the Edgar Allan Poe Museum in Richmond, Virginia, at the Internet site http://www.poemuseum.org. Follow the online museum tour and write an inventory of the museum collection shown in the tour with a description of each item. Include where the item is from and how it was related to Poe's life. You may want to print some of the items in the tour and make a catalog of them, writing copy alongside each artifact. You might also explore the other links on the main page, which provide further biographical information about Poe, as well as samples of his literary work.

# The Raven

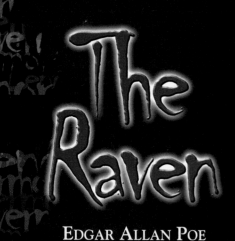

### EDGAR ALLAN POE

*The Raven*, 1959. Antonio Frasconi. National Gallery of Art, Washington, DC.

Once upon a midnight dreary, while I pondered, weak and weary,

Over many a quaint and curious volume of forgotten lore,

While I nodded, nearly napping, suddenly there came a tapping,

As of some one gently rapping, rapping at my chamber door.

5     " 'Tis some visiter," I muttered, "tapping at my chamber door—

Ah, distinctly I remember it was in the bleak December,
And each separate dying ember wrought its ghost upon the floor.
Eagerly I wished the morrow;—vainly I had tried to borrow
10   From my books surcease of sorrow—sorrow for the lost Lenore—
For the rare and radiant maiden whom the angels name Lenore—
                              Nameless here for evermore.

And the silken sad uncertain rustling of each purple curtain
Thrilled me—filled me with fantastic terrors never felt before;
15   So that now, to still the beating of my heart, I stood repeating
" 'Tis some visiter entreating entrance at my chamber door—
Some late visiter entreating entrance at my chamber door;—
                              This it is, and nothing more."

Presently my soul grew stronger; hesitating then no longer,
20   "Sir," said I, "or Madam, truly your forgiveness I implore;
But the fact is I was napping, and so gently you came rapping,
And so faintly you came tapping, tapping at my chamber door,
That I scarce was sure I heard you"—here I opened wide the door,—
                              Darkness there, and nothing more.

25   Deep into that darkness peering, long I stood there wondering, fearing,
Doubting dreaming dreams no mortal ever dared to dream before;
But the silence was unbroken, and the darkness gave no token,
And the only word there spoken was the whispered word, "Lenore!"
This I whispered, and an echo murmured back the word, "Lenore!"
30                              Merely this, and nothing more.

Then into the chamber turning, all my soul within me burning,
Soon I heard again a tapping somewhat louder than before.
"Surely," said I, "surely that is something at my window lattice;
Let me see, then, what thereat is, and this mystery explore—
35   Let my heart be still a moment and this mystery explore;—
                              'Tis the wind, and nothing more!"

Open here I flung the shutter, when, with many a flirt and flutter,
In there stepped a stately raven of the saintly days of yore;
Not the least obeisance made he; not an instant stopped or stayed he;
40   But, with mien of lord or lady, perched above my chamber door—

What is the cause of the author's sorrow?

What enters through the open window?

WORDS FOR EVERYDAY USE

sur • cease (sʉr sēs´) n., respite; end. *The winning lottery ticket brought him surcease from his financial problems.*
en • treat (en trēt´) vt., beg; implore; ask earnestly. *The employee entreated his boss for another chance.*
lat • tice (lat´is) n., shutter; openwork structure used as a screen. *In the garden there was a lovely lattice of crossed wood strips.*
o • bei • sance (ō bā´səns) n., gesture of respect. *The servant made a slight bow of obeisance to his master.*
mien (mēn) n., manner; appearance. *The attending royalty gave an aristocratic mien to the affair.*

Perched upon a bust of Pallas[1] just above my chamber door—
　　　　　　　Perched, and sat, and nothing more.

*Where does the visitor sit?*

　　　Then this ebony bird beguiling my sad fancy into smiling,
　　　By the grave and stern decorum of the countenance it wore,
45　　"Though thy crest be shorn and shaven, thou," I said, "art sure no <u>craven</u>,
　　　Ghastly grim and ancient raven wandering from the Nightly shore—
　　　Tell me what thy lordly name is on the Night's Plutonian[2] shore!"
　　　　　　　Quoth the raven, "Nevermore."

　　　Much I marvelled this ungainly fowl to hear discourse so plainly,
50　　Though its answer little meaning—little relevancy bore;
　　　For we cannot help agreeing that no sublunary[3] being
　　　Ever yet was blessed with seeing bird above his chamber door—
　　　Bird or beast upon the sculptured bust above his chamber door,
　　　　　　　With such name as "Nevermore."

*Does the speaker find the visitor's response meaningful?*

55　　But the raven, sitting lonely on the placid bust, spoke only
　　　That one word, as if his soul in that one word he did outpour.
　　　Nothing farther then he uttered—not a feather then he fluttered—
　　　Till I scarcely more than muttered, "Other friends have flown before—
　　　On the morrow *he* will leave me, as my hopes have flown before."
60　　　　　　Quoth the raven, "Nevermore."

　　　Wondering at the stillness broken by reply so aptly spoken,
　　　"Doubtless," said I, "what it utters is its only stock and store,
　　　Caught from some unhappy master whom unmerciful Disaster
　　　Followed fast and followed faster—so, when Hope he would <u>adjure</u>,
65　　Stern Despair returned, instead of the sweet Hope he dared adjure—
　　　　　　　That sad answer, "Nevermore!"

　　　But the raven still <u>beguiling</u> all my sad soul into smiling,
　　　Straight I wheeled a cushioned seat in front of bird, and bust, and door;
　　　Then upon the velvet sinking, I betook myself to linking
70　　Fancy unto fancy thinking what this <u>ominous</u> bird of yore—

*Where does the speaker sit?*

　　　What this grim, ungainly, ghastly, gaunt, and ominous bird of yore
　　　　　　　Meant in croaking "Nevermore."

---

1. **Pallas.** Greek goddess of wisdom
2. **Plutonian.** Black; relating to the underworld
3. **sublunary.** Earthly

**WORDS FOR EVERYDAY USE**

cra • ven (krā´vən) *n.*, coward. *His failure to try to stop the thief made him appear to be a <u>craven</u>.*
ad • jure (ə jer´) *vt.*, urge; beg. *I <u>adjure</u> you not to walk home alone after dark.*
be • guile (bē gīl´) *vt.*, charm; lead by deception. *The salesperson <u>beguiled</u> customers into buying useless items.*
om • i • nous (äm´ə nəs) *adj.*, forewarning evil. *The dark cloud was <u>ominous</u> of the storm on the horizon.*

Illustration to Edgar Allan Poe's *The Raven*, 1875. Edouard Manet. Museum of Fine Arts, Boston.

This I sat engaged in guessing, but no syllable expressing
To the fowl whose fiery eyes now burned into my bosom's core;
75   This and more I sat divining, with my head at ease reclining
On the cushion's velvet lining that the lamplight gloated o'er,
But whose velvet violet lining with the lamplight gloating o'er,
                      *She* shall press, ah, nevermore!

Then, methought, the air grew denser, perfumed from an unseen <u>censer</u>
80   Swung by angels whose faint foot-falls tinkled on the tufted floor.
"Wretch," I cried, "thy God hath lent thee—by these angels he hath sent thee
Respite—respite and Nepenthe[4] from thy memories of Lenore!
Let me <u>quaff</u> this kind Nepenthe and forget this lost Lenore!"
                      Quoth the raven, "Nevermore."

*Of whom is the speaker thinking?*

---

4. **Nepenthe.** Potion used to induce forgetfulness of pain or sorrow

**WORDS FOR EVERYDAY USE**

**cen • ser** (sen´sər) *n.*, container for burning incense. *The monks chanted and swung the <u>censer</u>, causing fragrant incense to rise toward the heavens.*

**quaff** (kwäf) *vi.*, drink deeply. *In his great thirst he <u>quaffed</u> the glass of water entirely.*

85  "Prophet!" said I, "thing of evil!—prophet still, if bird or devil!—
    Whether Tempter sent, or whether <u>tempest</u> tossed thee here ashore,
    Desolate, yet all <u>undaunted</u>, on this desert land enchanted—
    On this home by Horror haunted—tell me truly, I implore—
    Is there—*is* there balm in Gilead?[5]—tell me—tell me, I implore!"
90                                          Quoth the raven, "Nevermore."

    "Prophet!" said I, "thing of evil!—prophet still, if bird or devil!
    By that Heaven that bends above us—by that God we both adore—
    Tell this soul with sorrow laden if, within the distant Aidenn,[6]
    It shall clasp a sainted maiden whom the angels name Lenore—
95  Clasp a rare and radiant maiden whom the angels name Lenore."
                                            Quoth the raven, "Nevermore."

*How has the speaker's attitude toward the raven's answers changed?*

    "Be that word our sign of parting, bird or fiend!" I shrieked, upstarting—
    Get thee back into the tempest and the Night's Plutonian shore!
    Leave no black <u>plume</u> as a token of that lie thy soul hath spoken!
100 Leave my loneliness unbroken—quit the bust above my door!
    Take thy beak from out my heart, and take thy form from off my door!"
                                            Quoth the raven, "Nevermore."

    And the raven, never flitting, still is sitting, still is sitting
    On the pallid bust of Pallas just above my chamber door;
105 And his eyes have all the seeming of a demon that is dreaming,
    And the lamp-light o'er him streaming throws his shadow on the floor;
    And my soul from out that shadow that lies floating on the floor
                                            Shall be lifted—nevermore! ∎

---

5. **balm in Gilead.** Gilead is a mountainous area in the Middle East where evergreens provide medicinal resins. The question echoes Jeremiah 8:22, "Is there no balm in Gilead?"
6. **Aidenn.** Name created by Poe to suggest Eden

---

**WORDS FOR EVERYDAY USE**

tem • pest (tĕm´pəst) *n.*, violent storm. *The boat was lost at sea in the severe tempest.*
un • daunt • ed (ən dônt´əd) *adj.*, resolute in the face of danger. *The brave man's courage was undaunted.*
plume (plüm) *n.*, feather. *The peacock is known for its beautiful tail plumes.*

## Respond *to the* SELECTION

How does the appearance of the raven affect the speaker's mood? Do you think that the raven is real or is it simply imagined by the speaker?

# INVESTIGATE, Inquire, Imagine

**Recall:** GATHERING FACTS

1a. What is the speaker doing when he first hears the rapping at his door?

2a. Who or what enters the room through the open window?

3a. What is the raven's single-word answer to every question?

**Interpret:** FINDING MEANING

1b. Why does the speaker hesitate before answering the door?

2b. Describe the raven. How is it different from normal birds?

3b. The speaker soon knows how the raven will respond to his questions and commands. Why does he continue to talk to it and ask it questions?

**Analyze:** TAKING THINGS APART

4a. What are the stages of the narrator's developing anger?

**Synthesize:** BRINGING THINGS TOGETHER

4b. What does the narrator's anger have to do with the lost Lenore?

**Evaluate:** MAKING JUDGMENTS

5a. Other birds, such as the parrot, also can be trained to speak. Evaluate whether Poe's choice of the raven achieves his desired effect in this story.

**Extend:** CONNECTING IDEAS

5b. What other animal could Poe have chosen? How would a different animal have changed the poem?

# Understanding Literature

**RHYME. Rhyme** is the repetition of sounds at the ends of words. A particular kind of rhyme called *internal rhyme*, in which rhyming words appear within lines of verse, can be found in "The Raven"; for example, "Wondering at the stillness broken by reply so aptly spoken." Find at least five other examples of internal rhyme in the poem. Does the internal rhyme add to your enjoyment of the poem? Why, or why not?

**ALLITERATION.** The repetition of initial consonant sounds is called **alliteration**. Here are examples of the use of alliteration in lines 3, 11, and 12. Make a list of other examples of alliteration in other lines of the poem.

| line 3 | **n**odded **n**early **n**apping |
| line 11 | **r**are **r**adiant |
| line 12 | **s**ilken **s**ad |

**RUN-ON LINE. A run-on line** is a line of verse in which the sense or the grammatical structure does not end with the end of the line but rather is continued on one or more subsequent lines. Find two examples of run-on lines in "The Raven." Then identify two examples of the opposite of run-on lines, that is, *end-stopped lines* in which both the sense and the grammar are complete at the end of the line. What is the effect of including a variety of lines in a poem rather than only one?

# Writer's Journal

1. Write a **paragraph** describing the feelings the word *nevermore* creates in you. Why is it such a powerful word?
2. Draw a **comic strip** telling the story of "The Raven." Include details about the changing appearance and emotions of the speaker, as well as details about the setting, such as the speaker's lonely, gloomy room.
3. Talking animals have appeared in folk tales, myths, children's stories, and fantasies for centuries. Write a **dialogue** between yourself and a talking animal in which the animal repeats a word or phrase, as the raven does in the poem.

# Integrating *the* LANGUAGE ARTS

## Language, Grammar, and Style

**QUOTATION MARKS.** Read the Language Arts Survey 3.92, "Quotation Marks." For each quotation below, add the correct punctuation.

1. It is a visitor tapping at my door I said.
2. Nevermore said the enigmatic raven.
3. I said that the others had left me and that the raven would soon leave, too.
4. I pleaded Tell me if I shall ever escape from my memories of Lenore.
5. Take thy beak from out my heart, and take thy form from off my door I shrieked.

## Speaking and Listening & Collaborative Learning

**INTERVIEW.** After researching Edgar Allan Poe, choose a critical point in his life and stage an imagined interview with him. Work with a partner; one person should play Poe, and the other the interviewer. Discuss the major events in Poe's life and his plans for the future.

## Applied English

**LOST AND FOUND AD.** Write a lost and found ad, looking for the owner of the raven that appears in the poem. Describe the physical characteristics, behavior, and speech pattern of the bird.

## Study and Research

**REFERENCE WORKS.** Read the Language Arts Survey 5.20, "Using Reference Works." Find at least two types of references that contain literary information about Edgar Allan Poe. Try to find at least one traditional reference in the library, in a printed source like an encyclopedia or periodical, and one on-line reference on the Internet. To find web sites with information on Edgar Allan Poe, do a key word search using "Edgar Allan Poe." Write a reference list for the sources in which you found the information you were seeking.

# "Rappaccini's Daughter"

BY NATHANIEL HAWTHORNE

## About the AUTHOR

**Nathaniel Hawthorne** (1804–1864) was born in Salem, Massachusetts, where his ancestors had participated in the Salem witch trials and the Quaker persecution. He studied at Bowdoin College where he met Franklin Pierce and Henry Wadsworth Longfellow. For over a decade after graduation, he studied the Puritans and wrote, anonymously publishing his first novel, *Fanshawe*. He then directed his efforts to short stories and published *Twice-Told Tales*. His next collection, *Mosses from an Old Manse*, received a glowing review by Herman Melville but little financial success.

After leaving employment as a surveyor at the Salem Customs House, Hawthorne published *The Scarlet Letter*. From 1850 on, Hawthorne concentrated on writing for children, notably *The House of Seven Gables* and *The Blithedale Romance*.

Hawthorne was named American consul at Liverpool and Manchester, England, (1853–1855) by President Franklin Pierce. When he left this post, he traveled through Europe, publishing *The Marble Faun* after spending a year in Italy. When he died, he left several unfinished works.

## About the SELECTION

In 1842, Nathaniel Hawthorne and his wife moved to Emerson's former home, The Old Manse, in Concord, Massachusetts. During the following four years, Hawthorne produced many of his finest stories, publishing them individually in magazines or in the collections *Twice-Told Tales* and *Mosses from an Old Manse*.

"**Rappaccini's Daughter**" was first published in December 1844, in the *Democratic Review,* with a mock-autobiographical introduction. The story shows many of Hawthorne's characteristic traits, including strong use of symbolism, a psychological approach, and a focus on the Puritan preoccupation with evil. His skillful working of such elements demonstrates why he is credited, along with Washington Irving and Edgar Allan Poe, with the development of the modern short story.

## Literary TOOLS

**SYMBOL.** A **symbol** is a thing that stands for or represents both itself and something else. Many critics have pointed out that Nathaniel Hawthorne shared a Puritan preoccupation with good and evil. As you read the story, look for elements that might symbolize good and evil.

**ALLUSION.** An **allusion** is a rhetorical technique in which reference is made to a person, event, object, or work from history or literature. Hawthorne uses several allusions in this story.

**FANTASY.** A **fantasy** is a literary work that contains highly unrealistic elements. Use the graphic organizer below to make a radiating circle of fantastic elements that you find in "Rappaccini's Daughter."

garden of poisonous plants

FANTASTIC ELEMENTS

## Reader's Journal

How can you tell whether a friend is a bad influence or someone you can trust?

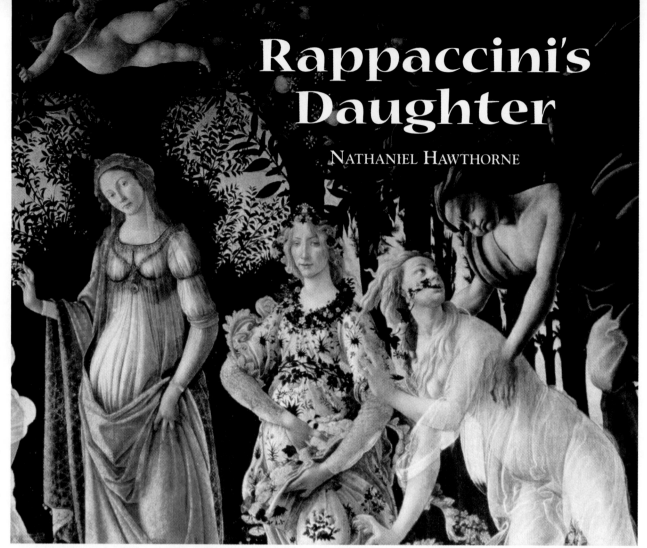

# Rappaccini's Daughter

### NATHANIEL HAWTHORNE

*The Allegory of Spring* [Detail], 1477–1478. Sandro Botticelli.

young man, named Giovanni Guasconti, came, very long ago, from the more southern region of Italy, to pursue his studies at the University of Padua. Giovanni, who had but a scanty supply of gold ducats in his pocket, took lodgings in a high and gloomy chamber of an old edifice,[1] which looked not unworthy to have been the palace of a Paduan[2] noble, and which, in fact, exhibited over its entrance the armorial bearings of a family long since extinct. The young stranger, who was not unstudied in the great poem of his country, recollected that one of the ancestors of this family, and perhaps an occupant of this very mansion, had been pictured by Dante as a partaker of the immortal agonies of his Inferno.[3] These <u>reminiscences</u> and associations, together with the tendency to heartbreak natural to a young man for the first

---

1. **edifice.** Building
2. **Paduan.** From Padua, Italy
3. **Dante . . . his Inferno.** Dante Alighieri (1265–1321), Italian poet who wrote *The Divine Comedy;* "Inferno" is that section of *The Divine Comedy* which describes hell and the suffering of the damned.

WORDS FOR EVERYDAY USE

**rem • i • nis • cence** (rem ə nis´əns) *n.,* memory or something remembered. *As an adult writer, Proust used great detail in each <u>reminiscence</u> from his youth.*

time out of his native sphere, caused Giovanni to sigh heavily, as he looked around the desolate and ill-furnished apartment.

"Holy Virgin, signor,[4]" cried old dame Lisabetta, who, won by the youth's remarkable beauty of person, was kindly endeavoring to give the chamber a habitable air, "what a sigh was that to come out of a young man's heart! Do you find this old mansion gloomy? For the love of heaven, then, put your head out of the window, and you will see as bright sunshine as you have left in Naples."

Guasconti mechanically did as the old woman advised, but could not quite agree with her that the Lombard[5] sunshine was as cheerful as that of southern Italy. Such as it was, however, it fell upon a garden beneath the window, and expended its fostering influences on a variety of plants, which seemed to have been cultivated with exceeding care.

"Does this garden belong to the house?" asked Giovanni.

"Heaven forbid, signor!—unless it were fruitful of better pot-herbs than any that grow there now," answered old Lisabetta. "No: that garden is cultivated by the own hands of Signor Giacomo Rappaccini, the famous Doctor, who, I warrant him, has been heard of as far as Naples. It is said he distils these plants into medicines that are as potent as a charm. Oftentimes you may see the signor Doctor at work, and perchance the signora[6] his daughter, too, gathering the strange flowers that grow in the garden."

The old woman had now done what she could for the aspect[7] of the chamber, and, commending the young man to the protection of the saints, took her departure.

> What causes Giovanni to sigh?

iovanni still found no better occupation than to look down into the garden beneath his window. From its appearance, he judged it to be one of those botanic gardens, which were of earlier date in Padua than elsewhere in Italy, or in the world. Or, not improbably, it might once have been the pleasure place of an opulent family; for there was the ruin of a marble fountain in the center, sculptured with rare art, but so woefully shattered that it was impossible to trace the original design from the chaos of remaining fragments. The water, however, continued to gush and sparkle into the sunbeams as cheerfully as ever. A little gurgling sound ascended to the young man's window, and made him feel as if the fountain were an immortal spirit, that sung its song unceasingly, and without heeding the vicissitudes[8] around it; while one century embodied it in marble, and another scattered the garniture[9] on the soil. All about the pool into which the water subsided, grew various plants, that seemed to require a plentiful supply of moisture for the nourishment of gigantic leaves, and, in some instances, flowers gorgeously magnificent. There was one shrub in particular, set in a marble vase in the midst of the pool, that bore a profusion of purple blossoms, each of which had the luster and richness of a gem; and the whole together made a show so resplendent that it seemed enough to

> What does Giovanni find particularly eyecatching in the garden?

---

4. **signor.** Mr., Sir; Italian title of respect
5. **Lombard.** Lombardy, region of northern Italy on the border of Switzerland
6. **signora.** Mrs., Madam; Italian title of respect
7. **aspect.** Appearance
8. **vicissitudes.** Changes
9. **garniture.** Decoration, ornament

---

**WORDS FOR EVERYDAY USE**

op • u • lent (äp′yü lənt) *adj.*, very wealthy or rich. *The celebrity was known for showing off his wealth by giving opulent parties.*

re • splend • ent (ri splen′dənt) *adj.*, shining brightly. *The sequins covered Keisha's prom dress, making her glowing and resplendent.*

illuminate the garden, even had there been no sunshine. Every portion of the soil was peopled with plants and herbs, which, if less beautiful, still bore tokens of assiduous[10] care; as if all had their individual virtues, known to the scientific mind that fostered them. Some were placed in urns, rich with old carving, and others in common garden-pots; some crept serpent-like along the ground, or climbed on high, using whatever means of ascent was offered them. One plant had wreathed itself round a statue of Vertumnus,[11] which was thus quite veiled and shrouded in a drapery of hanging foliage, so happily arranged that it might have served a sculptor for a study.

While Giovanni stood at the window, he heard a rustling behind a screen of leaves, and became aware that a person was at work in the garden. His figure soon emerged into view, and showed itself to be that of no common laborer, but a tall, emaciated, sallow, and sickly looking man, dressed in a scholar's garb[12] of black. He was beyond the middle term of life, with grey hair, a thin grey beard, and a face singularly marked with intellect and cultivation, but which could never, even in his more youthful days, have expressed much warmth of heart.

Nothing could exceed the intentness with which this scientific gardener examined every shrub which grew in his path; it seemed as if he was looking into their inmost nature, making observations in regard to their creative essence, and discovering why one leaf grew in this shape, and another in that, and wherefore such and such flowers differed among themselves in hue and perfume. Nevertheless, in spite of the deep intelligence on his part, there was no approach to intimacy between himself and these vegetable existences. On the contrary, he avoided their actual touch, or the direct inhaling of their odors, with a caution that impressed Giovanni most disagreeably; for the man's demeanor was that of one walking among malignant influences, such as savage beasts, or deadly snakes, or evil spirits, which, should he allow them one moment of license, would wreak upon him some terrible fatality. It was strangely frightful to the young man's imagination, to see this air of insecurity in a person cultivating a garden, that most simple and innocent of human toils, and which had been alike the joy and labor of the unfallen parents of the race. Was this garden, then, the Eden of the present world?—and this man, with such a perception of harm in what his own hands caused to grow, was he the Adam?[13]

The distrustful gardener, while plucking away the dead leaves or pruning the too luxuriant growth of the shrubs, defended his hands with a pair of thick gloves. Nor were these his only armor. When, in his walk through the garden, he came to the magnificent plant that hung its purple gems beside the marble fountain, he placed a kind of mask over his mouth and nostrils, as if all this beauty did but conceal a deadlier malice. But finding his task still too dangerous, he drew back, removed the mask, and called loudly, but in the infirm voice of a person affected with inward disease:

"Beatrice!—Beatrice!"

"Here am I, my father! What would you?" cried a rich and youthful voice from the window of the opposite house; a voice as rich as a tropi-

To what are the garden and gardener compared?

What does the gardener do when examining the plant that Giovanni noticed?

10. **assiduous.** Done with constant and careful attention
11. **Vertumnus.** Roman god of the changing seasons
12. **garb.** Attire; manner of dress
13. **Adam.** Name of the first man created, according to the book of Genesis in the Bible

**WORDS FOR EVERYDAY USE**

de • mean • or (di mēn´ər) *n.*, way of behaving; manner. *My brother's psychologist tells him that he must work to improve his obnoxious demeanor.*

ma • lig • nant (mə lig´nənt) *adj.*, harmful; evil. *Her intentions were so malignant that we worried she would hurt someone.*

cal sunset, and which made Giovanni, though he knew not why, think of deep hues of purple or crimson, and of perfumes heavily delectable.—"Are you in the garden?"

What images does the voice suggest to Giovanni?

"Yes, Beatrice," answered the gardener, "and I need your help."

Soon there emerged from under a sculptured portal the figure of a young girl, arrayed with as much richness of taste as the most splendid of the flowers, beautiful as the day, and with a bloom so deep and vivid that one shade more would have been too much. She looked redundant[14] with life, health, and energy; all of which attributes were bound down and compressed, as it were, and girdled tensely, in their luxuriance, by her virgin zone. Yet Giovanni's fancy must have grown morbid, while he looked down into the garden; for the impression which the fair stranger made upon him was as if here were another flower, the human sister of those vegetable ones, as beautiful as they—more beautiful than the richest of them—but still to be touched only with a glove, nor to be approached without a mask. As Beatrice came down the garden path, it was observable that she handled and inhaled the odor of several of the plants, which her father had most sedulously[15] avoided.

What does Beatrice do that her father does not?

"Here, Beatrice," said the latter,—"see how many needful offices require to be done to our chief treasure. Yet, shattered as I am, my life might pay the penalty of approaching it so closely as circumstances demand. Henceforth, I fear, this plant must be consigned to your sole charge."

"And gladly will I undertake it," cried again the rich tones of the young lady, as she bent toward the magnificent plant, and opened her arms as if to embrace it. "Yes, my sister, my splendor, it shall be Beatrice's task to nurse and serve thee; and thou shalt reward her with thy kisses and perfumed breath, which to her is as the breath of life!"

Then, with all the tenderness in her manner that was so strikingly expressed in her words, she busied herself with such attentions as the plant seemed to require; and Giovanni, at his lofty window, rubbed his eyes, and almost doubted whether it were a girl tending her favorite flower, or one sister performing the duties of affection to another. The scene soon <u>terminated</u>. Whether Doctor Rappaccini had finished his labors in the garden, or that his watchful eye had caught the stranger's face, he now took his daughter's arm and retired. Night was already closing in; oppressive exhalations seemed to proceed from the plants, and steal upward past the open window; and Giovanni, closing the lattice, went to his couch, and dreamed of a rich flower and beautiful girl. Flower and maiden were different and yet the same, and fraught[16] with some strange peril in either shape.

What does Giovanni dream?

But there is an influence in the light of morning that tends to rectify whatever errors of fancy, or even of judgment, we may have incurred during the sun's decline, or among the shadows of the night, or in the less wholesome glow of moonshine. Giovanni's first movement on starting from sleep, was to throw open the window, and gaze down into the garden which his dreams had made so fertile of mysteries. He was surprised, and a

---

14. **redundant.** Overfull, as though having more than one's share of life
15. **sedulously.** Diligently; persistently
16. **fraught.** Filled

**WORDS FOR EVERYDAY USE**

ter • mi • nate (tur´mə nāt´) *vi.,* end; stop; cease. *I wish the families would <u>terminate</u> their longstanding feud.*

little ashamed, to find how real and matter-of-fact an affair it proved to be, in the first rays of the sun, which gilded the dewdrops that hung upon leaf and blossom, and, while giving a brighter beauty to each rare flower, brought everything within the limits of ordinary experience. The young man rejoiced, that, in the heart of the barren city, he had the privilege of overlooking this spot of lovely and luxuriant vegetation. It would serve, he said to himself, as a symbolic language, to keep him in communion with nature. Neither the sickly and thought-worn Doctor Giacomo Rappaccini, it is true, nor his brilliant daughter were now visible; so that Giovanni could not determine how much of the singularity which he attributed to both, was due to their own qualities, and how much to his wonder-working fancy. But he was inclined to take a most rational view of the whole matter.

In the course of the day, he paid his respects to Signor Pietro Baglioni, professor of medicine in the University, a physician of eminent repute, to whom Giovanni had brought a letter of introduction. The professor was an elderly personage, apparently of genial nature, and habits that might almost be called jovial; he kept the young man to dinner, and made himself very agreeable by the freedom and liveliness of his conversation, especially when warmed by a flask or two of Tuscan wine. Giovanni, conceiving that men of science, inhabitants of the same city, must needs be on familiar terms with one another, took an opportunity to mention the name of Dr. Rappaccini. But the professor did not respond with so much <u>cordiality</u> as he had anticipated.

"Ill would it become a teacher of the divine art of medicine," said Professor Pietro Baglioni, in answer to a question of Giovanni, "to withhold due and well-considered praise of a physician so eminently skilled as Rappaccini. But, on the other hand, I should answer it but scantily to my conscience, were I to permit a worthy youth like yourself, Signor Giovanni, the son of an ancient friend, to imbibe <u>erroneous</u> ideas respecting a man who might hereafter chance to hold your life and death in his hands. The truth is, our worshipful Doctor Rappaccini has as much science as any member of the faculty—with perhaps one single exception—in Padua, or all Italy. But there are certain grave objections to his professional character."

"And what are they?" asked the young man.

"Has my friend Giovanni any disease of body or heart, that he is so inquisitive about physicians?" said the Professor, with a smile. "But as for Rappaccini, it is said of him—and I, who know the man well, can answer for its truth—that he cares infinitely more for science than for mankind. His patients are interesting to him only as subjects for some new experiment. He would sacrifice human life, his own among the rest, or whatever else was dearest to him, for the sake of adding so much as a grain of mustard-seed to the great heap of his accumulated knowledge."

What does Baglioni find objectionable about Rappaccini?

"Methinks he is an awful[17] man, indeed," remarked Guasconti, mentally recalling the cold and purely intellectual aspect of Rappaccini. "And yet, worshipful Professor, is it not a noble spirit? Are there many men capable of so spiritual a love of science?"

"God forbid," answered the Professor, somewhat <u>testily</u>—"at least, unless they take sounder views of the healing art than those adopted by Rappaccini. It is his theory, that all medicinal virtues are comprised within those substances

17. **awful.** Awe-inspiring

WORDS FOR EVERYDAY USE

cor • di • al • i • ty (kôr´jē al´ə tē) n., warm, friendly act or remark. *She was a woman of great <u>cordiality</u>, welcoming people to her home with a smile.*
er • ro • ne • ous (ər rō´nē əs) adj., mistaken; wrong. *The man was jailed on <u>erroneous</u> charges and was later released.*
tes • ti • ly (tes´tə lē) adv., in an irritable manner. *"I won't eat my broccoli!" the toddler said <u>testily</u>.*

which we term vegetable poisons. These he cultivates with his own hands, and is said even to have produced new varieties of poison, more horribly <u>deleterious</u> than Nature,

What is Rappaccini's particular interest?

without the assistance of this learned person, would ever have plagued the world with. That the signor Doctor does less mischief than might be expected, with such dangerous substances, is undeniable. Now and then, it must be owned, he has effected—or seemed to effect—a marvelous cure. But, to tell you my private mind, Signor Giovanni, he should receive little credit for such instances of success—they being probably the work of chance—but should be held strictly accountable for his failures, which may justly be considered his own work."

The youth might have taken Baglioni's opinions with many grains of allowance, had he known

Why might Baglioni have a motivation to lie about Rappaccini?

that there was a professional warfare of long continuance between him and Doctor Rappaccini, in which the latter was generally thought to have gained the advantage. If the reader be inclined to judge for himself, we refer him to certain black-letter tracts on both sides, preserved in the medical department of the University of Padua.

"I know not, most learned Professor," returned Giovanni, after musing on what had been said of Rappaccini's exclusive zeal for science—"I know not how dearly this physician may love his art; but surely there is one object more dear to him. He has a daughter."

"Aha!" cries the Professor with a laugh. "So now our friend Giovanni's secret is out. You have heard of this daughter, whom all the young men in Padua are wild about, though not half a dozen have ever had the good hap to see her face. I know little of the Signora Beatrice, save that Rappaccini is said to have instructed her deeply in his science, and that, young and beautiful as fame reports her, she is already qualified to fill a professor's chair. Perchance her father destines her for mine! Other absurd rumors there be, not worth talking about, or listening to. So now, Signor Giovanni, drink off your glass of Lacryma."

Guasconti returned to his lodgings somewhat heated with the wine he had quaffed,[18] and which caused his brain to swim with strange fantasies in reference to Doctor Rappaccini and the beautiful Beatrice. On his way, happening to pass by a florist's, he bought a fresh bouquet of flowers.

Ascending to his chamber, he seated himself near the window, but within the shadow thrown by the depth of the wall, so that he could look down into the garden with little risk of being discovered. All beneath his eye was a solitude. The strange plants were basking in the sunshine, and now and then nodding gently to one another, as if in acknowledgment of sympathy and kindred. In the midst, by the shattered fountain, grew the magnificent shrub, with its purple gems clustering all over it; they glowed in the air, and gleamed back again out of the depths of the pool, which thus seemed to overflow with colored radiance from the rich reflection that was steeped in it. At first, as we have said, the garden was a solitude. Soon, however,—as Giovanni had half-hoped, half-feared, would be the case,—a figure appeared beneath the antique sculptured <u>portal</u>, and came down between the rows of plants, inhaling their various perfumes, as if she were one of those beings of old classic fable, that lived upon sweet odors. On again beholding Beatrice, the young man

18. **quaffed.** Drunk

**WORDS FOR EVERYDAY USE**

**del • e • te • ri • ous** (del´ə tir´ē əs) *adj.*, harmful to health or well-being. *Too much caffeine can cause <u>deleterious</u> effects on sleep patterns.*

**por • tal** (pōr´təl) *n.*, doorway, gate, or entrance. *The <u>portal</u> to the castle was heavily guarded and the knight could find no other entrance.*

was even startled to perceive how much her beauty exceeded his recollection of it; so brilliant, so vivid in its character, that she glowed amid the sunlight, and, as Giovanni whispered to himself, positively illuminated the more shadowy intervals of the garden path. Her face being now more revealed than on the former occasion, he was struck by its expression of simplicity and sweetness; qualities that had not entered into his idea of her character, and which made him ask anew, what manner of mortal she might be. Nor did he fail again to observe, or imagine, an <u>analogy</u> between the beautiful girl and the gorgeous shrub that hung its gem-like flowers over the fountain; a resemblance which Beatrice seemed to have indulged a fantastic humor in heightening, both by the arrangement of her dress and the selection of its hues.

Approaching the shrub, she threw open her arms, as with a passionate ardor, and drew its branches into an intimate embrace; so intimate, that her features were hidden in its leafy bosom, and her glistening ringlets all intermingled with the flowers.

"Give me thy breath, my sister," exclaimed Beatrice; "for I am faint with common air! And give me this flower of thine, which I separate with gentlest fingers from the stem, and place it close beside my heart."

With these words, the beautiful daughter of Rappaccini plucked one of the richest blossoms of the shrub, and was about to fasten it in her bosom. But now, unless Giovanni's draughts of wine had bewildered his senses, a singular incident occurred. A small orange-colored reptile of the lizard or chameleon species, chanced to be creeping along the path, just at the feet of Beatrice. It appeared to Giovanni—but, at the distance from which he gazed, he could scarcely have seen anything so minute—it appeared to him, however, that a drop or two of moisture from the broken stem of the flower descended upon the lizard's head. For an instant, the reptile contorted itself violently, and then lay motionless in the sunshine. Beatrice observed this remarkable <u>phenomenon</u>,

> *What shocking incident occurs?*

and crossed herself, sadly, but without surprise; nor did she therefore hesitate to arrange the fatal flower in her bosom. There it blushed, and almost glimmered with the dazzling effect of a precious stone, adding to her dress and aspect the one appropriate charm, which nothing else in the world could have supplied. But Giovanni, out of the shadow of his window bent forward and shrank back, and murmured and trembled.

"Am I awake? Have I my senses?" said he to himself. "What is this being?—beautiful, shall I call her?—or inexpressibly terrible?"

Beatrice now strayed carelessly through the garden, approaching closer beneath Giovanni's window, so that he was compelled to thrust his head quite out of its concealment in order to gratify the intense and painful curiosity which she excited. At this moment, there came a beautiful insect over the garden wall; it had perhaps wandered through the city and found no flowers nor verdure[19] among those antique haunts of men, until the heavy perfumes of Doctor Rappaccini's shrubs had lured it from afar. Without alighting on the flowers, this winged brightness seemed to be attracted by Beatrice, and lingered in the air and fluttered about her head. Now here it could not be but that Giovanni Guasconti's eyes deceived him. Be that as it might, he fancied that while Beatrice was gazing at the insect with childish delight, it grew faint and fell at her feet!—its bright wings shivered! it was dead!—from no cause that he could

---

19. **verdure.** Green growing plants and trees

**Words For Everyday Use**

**a • nal • o • gy** (ə nal´ə jē) *n.*, similarity in some respects between things otherwise unalike. *You can draw a definite <u>analogy</u> between her treatment as a child and her behavior as an adult.*

**phe • nom • e • non** (fə näm´ə nän´) *n.*, extremely unusual or extraordinary thing or occurrence. *A total eclipse is a rare <u>phenomenon</u>.*

discern, unless it were the atmosphere of her breath. Again Beatrice crossed herself and sighed heavily, as she bent over the dead insect.

An impulsive movement of Giovanni drew her eyes to the window. There she beheld the beautiful head of the young man—rather a Grecian than an Italian head, with fair, regular features, and a glistening of gold among his ringlets—gazing down upon her like a being that hovered in mid-air. Scarcely knowing what he did, Giovanni threw down the bouquet which he had hitherto held in his hand.

"Signora," said he, "there are pure and healthful flowers. Wear them for the sake of Giovanni Guasconti!"

"Thanks, Signor," replied Beatrice, with her rich voice, that came forth as it were like a gush of music; and with a mirthful expression half childish and half woman-like. "I accept your gift, and would fain[20] recompense it with this precious purple flower; but if I toss it into the air, it will not reach you. So Signor Guasconti must even content himself with my thanks."

*What does Beatrice say she would like to give Giovanni in return? Why doesn't she?*

She lifted the bouquet from the ground, and then as if inwardly ashamed at having stepped aside from her maidenly reserve to respond to a stranger's greeting, passed swiftly homeward through the garden. But, few as the moments were, it seemed to Giovanni when she was on the point of vanishing beneath the sculptured portal, that his beautiful bouquet was already beginning to wither in her grasp. It was an idle thought; there could be no possibility of distinguishing a faded flower from a fresh one at so great a distance.

*What happens to the bouquet Giovanni gives to Beatrice?*

For many days after the incident, the young man avoided the window that looked into Doctor Rappaccini's garden, as if something ugly and monstrous would have blasted his eyesight, had he been betrayed into a glance. He felt conscious of having put himself, to a certain extent, within the influence of an unintelligible power, by the communication which he had opened with Beatrice. The wisest course would have been, if his heart were in any real danger, to quit his lodgings and Padua itself, at once; the next wiser, to have accustomed himself, as far as possible, to the familiar and day-light view of Beatrice; thus bringing her rigidly and systematically within the limits of ordinary experience. Least of all, while avoiding her sight, should Giovanni have remained so near this extraordinary being, that the proximity and possibility even of intercourse, should give a kind of substance and reality to the wild vagaries which his imagination ran riot continually in producing. Guasconti had not a deep heart—or at all events, its depths were not sounded now—but he had a quick fancy, and an ardent southern temperament, which rose every instant to a higher fever-pitch. Whether or no Beatrice possessed those terrible attributes—that fatal breath—the affinity with those so beautiful and deadly flowers—which were indicated by what Giovanni had witnessed, she had at least instilled a fierce and subtle poison into his system. It was not love, although her rich beauty was a madness to him; nor horror, even while he fancied her spirit to be imbued with the same baneful essence that seemed to pervade her physical frame; but a wild offspring of both love and horror that had each parent in it, and burned like one and shivered like the other.

20. **fain.** With eagerness; gladly

---

**WORDS FOR EVERYDAY USE**

rec • om • pense (rek´əm pens) vt., repay; reward. "To _recompense_ your hard work, I will triple your salary," Ray's boss said.

un • in • tel • li • gi • ble (un in tel´i jə bəl) adj., that which cannot be understood. The cellular phone picked up so much static that her voice was _unintelligible_.

va • ga • ry (vā´ger ē) n., odd, whimsical, or freakish idea or notion. One of his _vagaries_ was to take a hot-air balloon trip around the world.

af • fin • i • ty (ə fin´i tē) n., close relationship; connection. We share an _affinity_ for football and would not miss a game.

bane • ful (bān´fəl) adj., causing distress, death, or ruin. Hemlock is a _baneful_ substance, as Socrates would attest.

Giovanni knew not what to dread; still less did he know what to hope; *hope* and *dread* kept a continual warfare in his breast, alternately vanquishing one another and starting up afresh to renew the contest. Blessed are all simple emotions, be they dark or bright! It is the <u>lurid</u> intermixture of the two that produces the illuminating blaze of the infernal regions.

Sometimes he endeavored to <u>assuage</u> the fever of his spirit by a rapid walk through the streets of Padua, or beyond its gates; his footsteps kept time with the throbbings of his brain, so that the walk was apt to accelerate itself to a race. One day, he found himself arrested; his arm was seized by a portly personage who had turned back on recognizing the young man, and expended much breath in overtaking him.

"Signor Giovanni!—stay, my young friend!" cried he. "Have you forgotten me? That might well be the case, if I were as much altered as yourself."

It was Baglioni, whom Giovanni had avoided, ever since their first meeting, from a doubt that the professor's sagacity would look too deeply into his secrets. Endeavoring to recover himself, he stared forth wildly from his inner world into the outer one, and spoke like a man in a dream.

"Yes; I am Giovanni Guasconti. You are Professor Pietro Baglioni. Now let me pass!"

"Not yet—not yet, Signor Giovanni Guasconti," said the Professor, smiling, but at the same time scrutinizing the youth with an earnest glance.—"What; did I grow up side by side with your father, and shall his son pass me like a stranger, in these old streets of Padua? Stand still, Signor Giovanni; for we must have a word or two, before we part."

"Speedily, then, most worshipful Professor, speedily!" said Giovanni, with feverish impatience. "Does not your worship see that I am in haste?"

Now, while he was speaking, there came a man in black along the street, stooping and moving feebly, like a person in inferior health. His face was all overspread with a most sickly and sallow hue, but yet so pervaded with an expression of piercing and active intellect, that an observer might easily have overlooked the merely physical attributes, and have seen only this wonderful energy. As he passed, this person exchanged a cold and distant salutation with Baglioni, but fixed his eyes upon Giovanni with an intentness that seemed to bring out whatever was within him worthy of notice. Nevertheless, there was a peculiar quietness in the look, as if taking merely a <u>speculative</u>, not a human interest, in the young man.

> What sort of look does Rappaccini give Giovanni?

"It is Doctor Rappaccini!" whispered the Professor, when the stranger had passed.—"Has he ever seen your face before?"

"Not that I know," answered Giovanni starting at the name.

"He *has* seen you!—he must have seen you!" said Baglioni, hastily. "For some purpose or other, this man of science is making a study of you. I know that look of his! It is the same that coldly illuminates his face,

> What warning does Baglioni give Giovanni?

as he bends over a bird, a mouse, or a butterfly, which, in pursuance of some experiment, he has killed by the perfume of a flower;—a look as deep as nature itself, but without nature's warmth of love. Signor Giovanni, I will stake my life upon it, you are the subject of one of Rappaccini's experiments!"

"Will you make a fool of me?" cried Giovanni, passionately. "*That*, Signor Professor, were an <u>untoward</u> experiment."

"Patience, patience!" replied the <u>imperturbable</u> Professor.—"I tell thee, my poor Giovanni, that

---

**WORDS FOR EVERYDAY USE**

**lu • rid** (loॅor′id) *adj.*, vivid in a harsh or shocking way. *The bright lights of the casinos cast a <u>lurid</u> glow over the city.*
**as • suage** (ə swāj′) *vt.*, lessen; calm; pacify. *To <u>assuage</u> his guilt, Rob told Mia he would replace the video he had lost.*
**spec • u • la • tive** (spe′kyə lə tiv) *adj.*, theoretical. *Her idea is still <u>speculative</u>; she hasn't put it into practice yet.*
**un • to • ward** (un tō′ərd) *adj.*, improper; unseemly; not favorable. *Such <u>untoward</u> and improper behavior will not be tolerated.*
**im • per • turb • a • ble** (im pər tur′bə bəl) *adj.*, that cannot be disconnected or disturbed. *Jeff was so <u>imperturbable</u> that nothing could shake him.*

Rappaccini has a scientific interest in thee. Thou hast fallen into fearful hands! And the Signora Beatrice? What part does she act in this mystery?"

But Guasconti, finding Baglioni's pertinacity[21] intolerable, here broke away and was gone before the Professor could again seize his arm. He looked after the young man intently, and shook his head.

"This must not be," said Baglioni to himself. "The youth is the son of my old friend, and should not come to any harm from which the arcana[22] of medical science can preserve him. Besides, it is too insufferable an impertinence in Rappaccini, thus to snatch the bud out of my own hands, as I may say, and make use of him for his infernal experiments. This daughter of his! It shall be looked to. Perchance, most learned Rappaccini, I may foil you where you little dream of it!"

---

21. **pertinacity.** Stubborn persistence; obstinacy
22. **arcana.** Secrets or mysteries

*The Allegory of Spring*, 1477–1478. Sandro Botticelli. Uffizi Gallery, Florence.

## ArtNote

Botticelli ("the little barrel") was a nickname for Alessandro di Mariano Filipepi (1445–1510), an Italian Renaissance painter. He had been largely forgotten until artists in Hawthorne's time rediscovered him, seeing delicate and mysterious qualities in his work that appealed to their romantic sensibilities. Botticelli preferred mythical subjects to Christian ones. *The Allegory of Spring* is an allegory for the change from winter to spring, although scholars cannot agree on the identity of the figures or the exact meaning of the painting.

Using a dictionary of ancient Greek and Roman mythology, can you determine who these figures might be? Choose from among Cupid, the Three Graces, Mercury, Venus, Zephyr, Flora, Persephone, and Chloris. Considering the attributes of these characters, what might the painting symbolize?

Meanwhile, Giovanni had pursued a circuitous route, and at length found himself at the door of his lodgings. As he crossed the threshold, he was met by old Lisabetta, who smirked and smiled, and was evidently desirous to attract his attention; vainly, however, as the <u>ebullition</u> of his feelings had momentarily subsided into a cold and dull <u>vacuity</u>. He turned his eyes full upon the withered face that was puckering itself into a smile, but seemed to behold it not. The old dame, therefore, laid her grasp upon his cloak.

"Signor!—Signor!" whispered she, still with a smile over the whole breadth of her visage, so that it looked not unlike a grotesque carving in wood, darkened by centuries—"Listen, Signor! There is a private entrance into the garden!"

"What do you say?" exclaimed Giovanni, turning quickly about, as if an inanimate thing should start into feverish life.—"A private entrance into Doctor Rappaccini's garden!"

"Hush! hush!—not so loud!" whispered Lisabetta, putting her hand over his mouth. "Yes; into the worshipful Doctor's garden, where you may see all his fine shrubbery. Many a young man in Padua would give gold to be admitted among those flowers."

Giovanni put a piece of gold into her hand.

"Show me the way," said he.

A surmise, probably excited by his conversation with Baglioni, crossed his mind, that this interposition of old Lisabetta might perchance be connected with the

> What possibility does Giovanni consider?

intrigue, whatever were its nature, in which the Professor seemed to suppose that Doctor Rappaccini was involving him. But such a suspicion, though it disturbed Giovanni, was inadequate to restrain him. The instant he was aware of the possibility of approaching Beatrice, it seemed an absolute necessity of his existence to do so. It mattered not whether she were angel or demon; he was irrevocably within her sphere, and must obey the law that whirled him onward, in ever lessening circles, towards a result which he did not attempt to foreshadow. And yet, strange to say, there came across him a sudden doubt, whether this intense interest on his part were not <u>delusory</u>—whether it were really of so deep and positive a nature as to justify him in now thrusting himself into an incalculable position—whether it were not merely the fantasy of a young man's brain, only slightly, or not at all, connected with his heart!

He paused—hesitated—turned half about—but again went on. His withered guide led him along several obscure passages, and finally undid a door, through which, as it was opened, there came the sight and sound of rustling leaves, with the broken sunshine glimmering among them. Giovanni stepped forth, and forcing himself through the entanglement of a shrub that wreathed its tendrils over the hidden entrance, he stood beneath his own window, in the open area of Doctor Rappaccini's garden.

ow often is it the case, that, when impossibilities have come to pass, and dreams have condensed their misty substance into tangible realities, we find ourselves calm, and even coldly self-possessed, amid circumstances which it would have been a delirium of joy or agony to anticipate! Fate delights to thwart us thus. Passion will choose his own time to rush upon the scene, and lingers sluggishly behind, when an appropriate adjustment of events would seem to summon his appearance. So was it now with Giovanni. Day after day, his pulses had throbbed with feverish blood, at the improbable idea of an interview with Beatrice, and of stand-

**WORDS FOR EVERYDAY USE**

**eb • ul • li • tion** (eb´ə lish´ən) *n.*, boiling or bubbling up. *Jamie's <u>ebullition</u> could not be contained when she won the tennis match.*

**va • cu • i • ty** (va kyü´ə tē) *n.*, empty space, void, or vacuum. *Can you picture the <u>vacuity</u> of outer space and its total emptiness?*

**de • lu • so • ry** (di lü´sə rē) *adj.*, quality of seeming unreal. *His dream of winning the lottery was nothing but a <u>delusory</u> fantasy.*

ing with her, face to face, in this very garden, basking in the oriental sunshine of her beauty, and snatching from her full gaze the mystery which he deemed the riddle of his own existence. But now there was a singular and untimely equanimity within his breast. He threw a glance around the garden to discover if Beatrice or her father were present, and perceiving that he was alone, began a critical observation of the plants.

The aspect of one and all of them dissatisfied him; their gorgeousness seemed fierce, passionate, and even unnatural. There was hardly an individual shrub which a wanderer, straying by himself through a forest, would not have been startled to find growing wild, as if an unearthly face had glared at him out of the thicket. Several, also, would have shocked a delicate instinct by an appearance of artificialness, indicating that there had been such commixture, and, as it were, adultery of various vegetable species, that the production was no longer of God's making, but the monstrous offspring of man's depraved fancy, glowing with only an evil mockery of beauty. They were probably the result of experiment, which, in one or two cases, had succeeded in mingling plants individually lovely into a compound possessing the questionable and ominous character that distinguished the whole growth of the garden. In fine, Giovanni recognized but two or three plants in the collection, and those of a kind that he well knew to be poisonous. While busy with these contemplations, he heard the rustling of a silken garment, and turning, beheld Beatrice emerging from beneath the sculptured portal.

Giovanni had not considered with himself what should be his deportment; whether he should apologize for his intrusion into the garden, or assume that he was there with the privity, at least, if not the desire of Doctor Rappaccini or his daughter. But Beatrice's manner placed him at his ease, though leaving him still in doubt by what agency he had gained admittance. She came lightly along the path, and met him near the broken fountain. There was surprise in her face, but brightened by a simple and kind expression of pleasure.

*What is shocking or objectionable about the flowers' appearance?*

"You are a connoisseur in flowers, Signor," said Beatrice with a smile, alluding to the bouquet which he had flung her from the window. "It is no marvel, therefore, if the sight of my father's rare collection has tempted you to take a nearer view. If he were here, he could tell you many strange and interesting facts as to the nature and habits of these shrubs, for he has spent a lifetime in such studies, and this garden is his world."

"And yourself, lady"—observed Giovanni— "if fame says true—you, likewise, are deeply skilled in the virtues indicated by these rich blossoms, and these spicy perfumes. Would you deign[23] to be my instructress, I should prove an apter scholar than under Signor Rappaccini himself."

"Are there such idle rumors?" asked Beatrice, with the music of a pleasant laugh. "Do people say that I am skilled in my father's science of plants? What a jest is there! No; though I have grown up among these flowers, I know no more of them than their hues and perfume; and sometimes, methinks I would fain rid myself of even that small knowledge. There are many flowers here, and those not the least brilliant, that shock and offend me, when they meet my eye. But, pray, Signor, do not believe these stories about

---

23. **deign.** Condescend to do something slightly beneath one's dignity

**WORDS FOR EVERYDAY USE**

e • qua • nim • i • ty (ek´wə nim´ə tē) n., evenness of mind or temper. *Josh considered all opinions calmly and with great equanimity.*

de • praved (dē prāvd´) adj., morally bad; corrupt. *Lucy considered any but the most upright actions to be depraved.*

de • port • ment (dē pôrt´mənt) n., manner of conducting or bearing oneself. *Etiquette is a concern for the proper deportment of individuals.*

con • nois • seur (kän´ə sur´) n., person who has expert knowledge in some field. *The food critic was a knowledgeable connoisseur of fine chocolates.*

my science. Believe nothing of me save what you see with your own eyes."

What does Beatrice ask Giovanni to do?

"And must I believe all that I have seen with my own eyes?" asked Giovanni pointedly, while the recollection of former scenes made him shrink. "No, Signora, you demand too little of me. Bid me believe nothing, save what comes from your own lips."

It would appear that Beatrice understood him.

Why does Beatrice blush?

There came a deep flush to her cheek; but she looked full into Giovanni's eyes, and responded to his gaze of uneasy suspicion with a queen-like haughtiness.

"I do so bid you, Signor!" she replied. "Forget whatever you may have fancied in regard to me. If true to the outward senses, still it may be false in its essence. But the words of Beatrice Rappaccini's lips are true from the heart outward. Those you may believe!"

A <u>fervor</u> glowed in her whole aspect, and beamed upon Giovanni's consciousness like the light of truth itself. But while she spoke, there was a fragrance in the atmosphere around her, rich and delightful, though <u>evanescent</u>, yet which the young man, from an indefinable reluctance, scarcely dared to draw into his lungs. It might be the odor of the flowers. Could it be Beatrice's breath, which thus embalmed her words with a strange richness, as if by steeping them in her heart? A faintness passed like a shadow over Giovanni, and flitted away; he seemed to gaze through the beautiful girl's eyes into her transparent soul, and felt no more doubt or fear.

The tinge of passion that had colored Beatrice's manner vanished; she became gay, and appeared to derive a pure delight from her communion with the youth, not unlike what the maiden of a lonely island might have felt, conversing with a voyager from the civilized world. Evidently her experience of life had been confined within the limits of that garden. She talked now about matters as simple as the daylight or summer clouds, and now asked questions in reference to the city, or Giovanni's distant home, his friends, his mother, and his sisters; questions indicating such seclusion, and such lack of familiarity with modes and forms, that Giovanni responded as if to an infant. Her spirit gushed out before him like a fresh rill,[24] that was just catching its first glimpse of the sunlight, and wondering at the reflections of earth and sky which were flung into its bosom. There came thoughts, too, from a deep source, and fantasies of a gem-like brilliancy, as if diamonds and rubies sparkled upward among the bubbles of the fountain. Ever and anon, there gleamed across the young man's mind a sense of wonder, that he should be walking side by side with the being who had so wrought upon his imagination—whom he had idealized in such hues of terror—in whom he had positively witnessed such manifestations of dreadful attributes—that he should be conversing with Beatrice like a brother, and should find her so human and so maiden-like. But such reflections were only momentary; the effect of her character was too real, not to make itself familiar at once.

In this free intercourse, they had strayed through the garden, and now, after many turns among its avenues, were come to the shattered fountain, beside which grew the magnificent shrub with its treasury of glowing blossoms. A fragrance was diffused from it, which Giovanni recognized as identical with that which he had attributed to Beatrice's breath, but incomparably more powerful. As her eyes fell upon it,

24. **rill.** Little brook or stream

WORDS
FOR
EVERYDAY
USE

fer • vor (fur´vər) n., great warmth or emotion. *Alex has a great <u>fervor</u> for life and experiences everything fully.*
ev • a • nes • cent (ev´ə ne´sənt) adj., tending to fade; vanishing. *My dreams are <u>evanescent</u>; they vanish as soon as I wake.*

Giovanni beheld her press her hand to her bosom, as if her heart were throbbing suddenly and painfully.

"For the first time in my life," murmured she, addressing the shrub, "I had forgotten thee!"

What has Beatrice forgotten for the first time in her life?

"I remember, Signora," said Giovanni, "that you once promised to reward me with one of these living gems for the bouquet, which I had the happy boldness to fling to your feet. Permit me now to pluck it as a memorial of this interview."

He made a step towards the shrub, with extended hand. But Beatrice darted

What does Giovanni do that frightens Beatrice?

forward, uttering a shriek that went through his heart like a dagger. She caught his hand, and drew it back with the whole force of her slender figure. Giovanni felt her touch thrilling through his fibres.

"Touch it not!" exclaimed she, in a voice of agony. "Not for thy life! It is fatal!"

Then, hiding her face, she fled from him, and vanished beneath the sculptured portal. As Giovanni followed her with his eyes, he beheld the emaciated figure and pale intelligence of Doctor Rappaccini, who had been watching the scene, he knew not how long, within the shadow of the entrance.

No sooner was Guasconti alone in his chamber, than the image of Beatrice came back to his passionate musings, invested with all the witchery that had been gathering around it ever since his first glimpse of her, and now likewise imbued with a tender warmth of girlish womanhood. She was human: her nature was endowed with all gentle and feminine qualities; she was worthiest to be worshiped; she was capable, surely, on her part, of the height and heroism of love. Those

tokens, which he had hitherto considered as proofs of a frightful peculiarity in her physical and moral system, were now either forgotten, or, by the subtle sophistry[25] of passion, transmuted into a golden crown of enchantment, rendering Beatrice the more admirable, by so much as she was the more unique. Whatever had looked ugly, was now beautiful; or, if incapable of such a change, it stole away and hid itself among those shapeless half-ideas, which throng the dim region beyond the daylight of our perfect consciousness. Thus did Giovanni spend the night, nor fell asleep, until the dawn had begun to awake the slumbering flowers in Doctor Rappaccini's garden, whither his dreams doubtless led him. Up rose the sun in his due season, and flinging his beams upon the young man's eyelids, awoke him to a sense of pain. When thoroughly aroused, he became sensible of a burning and tingling agony in his hand—in his right hand—the very hand which Beatrice had grasped in her own, when he was on the point of plucking one of the gem-like flowers. On the back of that hand there was now a purple print, like that of four small fingers, and the likeness of a slender thumb upon his wrist.

What has happened to Giovanni's hand?

Oh, how stubbornly does love—or even that cunning semblance of love which flourishes in the imagination, but strikes no depth of root into the heart—how stubbornly does it hold its faith, until the moment come, when it is doomed to vanish into thin mist! Giovanni wrapt a handkerchief about his hand, and wondered what evil thing had stung him, and soon forgot his pain in a reverie of Beatrice.

After the first interview, a second was in the inevitable course of what we call fate. A third; a fourth; and a meeting with Beatrice in the garden

25. **sophistry.** Subtly deceptive reasoning or argumentation

---

**WORDS FOR EVERYDAY USE**

e • ma • ci • at • ed (ē mā´shē āt əd) adj., abnormally thin. *After being sick, my cat had lost so much weight he appeared emaciated.*

trans • mute (trans myüt´) vt., change from one form, species, or condition into another. *The caterpillar transmuted into a beautiful butterfly.*

rev • er • ie (rev´ər ē) n., dreamy thinking. *My mother woke me from my reverie, saying, "Stop daydreaming and pay attention!"*

was no longer an incident in Giovanni's daily life, but the whole space in which he might be said to live; for the anticipation and memory of that ecstatic hour made up the remainder. Nor was it otherwise with the daughter of Rappaccini. She watched for the youth's appearance, and flew to his side with confidence as unreserved as if they had been playmates from early infancy—as if they were such playmates still. If, by any unwonted[26] chance, he failed to come at the appointed moment, she stood beneath the window, and sent up the rich sweetness of her tones to float around him in his chamber, and echo and reverberate throughout his heart— "Giovanni! Giovanni! Why tarriest thou? Come down!"—And down he hastened into that Eden of poisonous flowers.

> How do Giovanni and Beatrice feel about each other?

But, with all this intimate familiarity, there was still a reserve in Beatrice's demeanor, so rigidly and invariably sustained, that the idea of infringing it scarcely occurred to his imagination. By all appreciable signs, they loved; they had looked love, with eyes that conveyed the holy secret from the depths of one soul into the depths of the other, as if it were too sacred to be whispered by the way; they had even spoken love, in those gushes of passion when their spirits darted forth in articulated breath, like tongues of long-hidden flame; and yet there had been no seal of lips, no clasp of hands, nor any slightest caress, such as love claims and hallows. He had never touched one of the gleaming ringlets of her hair; her garment—so marked was the physical barrier between them—had never been waved against him by a breeze. On the few occasions when Giovanni had seemed tempted to overstep the limit, Beatrice grew so sad, so stern, and withal wore such a look of desolate separation,

shuddering at itself, that not a spoken word was requisite to repel him. At such times, he was startled at the horrible suspicions that rose, monster-like, out of the caverns of his heart, and stared him in the face; his love grew thin and faint as the morning mist; his doubts alone had substance. But when Beatrice's face brightened again, after the momentary shadow, she was transformed at once from the mysterious, questionable being, whom he had watched with so much awe and horror; she was now the beautiful and unsophisticated girl, whom he felt that his spirit knew with a certainty beyond all other knowledge.

A considerable time had now passed since Giovanni's last meeting with Baglioni. One morning, however, he was disagreeably surprised by a visit from the Professor, whom he had scarcely thought of for whole weeks, and would willingly have forgotten still longer. Given up, as he had long been, to a pervading excitement, he could tolerate no companions, except upon condition of their perfect sympathy with his present state of feeling. Such sympathy was not to be expected from Professor Baglioni.

The visitor chatted carelessly, for a few moments, about the gossip of the city and the University, and then took up another topic.

"I have been reading an old classic author lately," said he, "and met with a story that strangely interested me. Possibly you may remember it. It is of an Indian prince, who sent a beautiful woman as a present to Alexander the Great. She was as lovely as the dawn, and gorgeous as the sunset; but what especially distinguished her was a certain rich perfume in her breath—richer than a garden of Persian roses. Alexander, as was natural to a youthful

---

26. **unwonted.** Not common or usual

**WORDS FOR EVERYDAY USE**

**in • fringe** (in frinj´) vt., violate [a rule]; vi., encroach; trespass [used with *on* or *upon*]. *By restricting our voting rights, you are infringing on our rights as citizens.*

**ar • tic • u • lat • ed** (ar tik´yü lāt´əd) adj., made up of distinct syllables or words, as human speech. *Laila spoke so clearly that everyone could understand her articulated words.*

conqueror, fell in love at first sight with this magnificent stranger. But a certain sage physician, happening to be present, discovered a terrible secret in regard to her."

"And what was that?" asked Giovanni, turning his eyes downward to avoid those of the Professor.

"That this lovely woman," continued Baglioni, with emphasis, "had been nourished with poisons from her birth upward, until her whole nature was so imbued with them, that she herself had become the deadliest poison in existence. Poison was her element of life. With that rich perfume of her breath, she blasted the very air. Her love would have been poison!—her embrace death! Is not this a marvelous tale?"

*What happens in the classic book Baglioni has been reading? Why does he relate this story to Giovanni?*

"A childish fable," answered Giovanni, nervously starting from his chair. "I marvel how your worship finds time to read such nonsense, among your graver studies."

*How does Giovanni respond to Baglioni's tale? Which of his actions reveal that he believes the professor's story?*

"By the by," said the Professor, looking uneasily about him, "what singular fragrance is this in your apartment? Is it the perfume of your gloves? It is faint, but delicious, and yet, after all, by no means agreeable. Were I to breathe it long, methinks it would make me ill. It is like the breath of a flower—but I see no flowers in the chamber."

"Nor are there any," replied Giovanni, who had turned pale as the Professor spoke; "nor, I think, is there any fragrance, except in your worship's imagination. Odors, being a sort of element combined of the sensual and the spiritual, are apt to deceive us in this manner. The recollection of a perfume—the bare idea of it— may easily be mistaken for a present reality."

"Aye; but my sober imagination does not often play such tricks," said Baglioni; "and were I to fancy any kind of odor, it would be that of some vile apothecary[27] drug, wherewith my fingers are likely enough to be imbued. Our worshipful friend Rappaccini, as I have heard, tinctures his medicaments with odors richer than those of Araby. Doubtless, likewise, the fair and learned Signora Beatrice would minister to her patients with draughts as sweet as a maiden's breath. But woe to him that sips them!"

Giovanni's face evinced many contending emotions. The tone in which the Professor alluded to the pure and lovely daughter of Rappaccini was a torture to his soul; and yet, the intimation of a view of her character, opposite to his own, gave instantaneous distinctness to a thousand dim suspicions, which now grinned at him like so many demons. But he strove hard to quell them, and to respond to Baglioni with a true lover's perfect faith.

"Signor Professor," said he, "you were my father's friend—perchance, too, it is your purpose to act a friendly part towards his son. I would fain feel nothing towards you, save respect and deference. But I pray you to observe, Signor, that there is one subject on which we must not speak. You know not the Signora Beatrice. You cannot, therefore, estimate the wrong—the blasphemy, I may even say—that is offered to her character by a light or injurious word."

"Giovanni!—my poor Giovanni!" answered the Professor, with a calm expression of pity. "I know this wretched girl far better than yourself. You shall hear the truth in respect to the poisoner Rappaccini, and his poisonous daughter. Yes; poisonous as she is beautiful! Listen; for even should you do violence to my gray hairs, it shall not silence me. That old fable of the Indian woman

27. **apothecary.** Druggist or pharmacist

**WORDS FOR EVERYDAY USE**

im • bue (im byü´) vt., fill; saturate. *Tom was* imbued *with an inner strength that carried him through many difficult times.*

e • vince (ē vin[t]s´) vt., show plainly; indicate. *The expression on Mikhail's face* evinced *anger at the new homework policy.*

has become a truth, by the deep and deadly science of Rappaccini, and in the person of the lovely Beatrice!"

Giovanni groaned and hid his face.

"Her father," continued Baglioni, "was not restrained by natural affection from offering up his child, in this horrible manner, as the victim of his insane zeal for science. For—let us do him justice—he is as true a man of science as ever distilled his own heart in an alembic.[28] What, then, will be your fate? Beyond a doubt, you are selected as the material of some new experiment. Perhaps the result is to be death—perhaps a fate more awful still! Rappaccini, with what he calls the interest of science before his eyes, will hesitate at nothing."

"It is a dream!" muttered Giovanni to himself, "surely it is a dream!"

"But," resumed the professor, "be of good cheer, son of my friend! It is not yet too late for the rescue. Possibly, we may even succeed in bringing back this miserable child within the limits of ordinary nature, from which her father's madness has estranged her. Behold this little silver vase! It was wrought by the hands of the renowned Benvenuto Cellini,[29] and is well worthy to be a lovegift to the fairest dame in Italy. But its contents are invaluable. One little sip of this antidote would have rendered the most virulent poisons of the Borgias[30] innocuous. Doubt not that it will be as <u>efficacious</u> against those of Rappaccini. Bestow the vase, and the precious liquid within it, on your Beatrice, and hopefully await the result."

*What does Baglioni give to Giovanni? What is it supposed to do?*

Baglioni laid a small, exquisitely wrought silver phial[31] on the table, and withdrew, leaving what he had said to produce its effect upon the young man's mind.

"We will thwart Rappaccini yet!" thought he, chuckling to himself, as he descended the stairs. "But, let us confess the truth of him, he is a wonderful man!—a wonderful man indeed! A vile empiric,[32] however, in his practice, and therefore not to be tolerated by those who respect the good old rules of the medical profession!"

Throughout Giovanni's whole acquaintance with Beatrice, he had occasionally, as we have said, been haunted by dark <u>surmises</u> as to her character. Yet, so thoroughly had she made herself felt by him as a simple, natural, most affectionate and guileless creature, that the image now held up by Professor Baglioni, looked as strange and incredible, as if it were not in accordance with his own original conception. True, there were ugly recollections connected with his first glimpses of the beautiful girl; he could not quite forget the bouquet that withered in her grasp, and the insect that perished amid the sunny air, by no ostensible agency, save the fragrance of her breath. These incidents, however, dissolving in the pure light of her character, had no longer the efficacy of facts, but were acknowledged as mistaken fantasies, by whatever testimony of the senses they might appear to be substantiated. There is something truer and more real, than what we can see with the eyes, and touch with the finger. On such better evidence, had Giovanni founded his confidence in Beatrice, though rather by the necessary force of her high attributes, than by any deep and generous faith, on his part. But, now, his spirit was

---

28. **alembic.** Apparatus used for distilling
29. **Benvenuto Cellini.** (1500–1578) Italian goldsmith and sculptor
30. **Borgias.** Italian family, religiously and politically influential during the Renaissance, but also known for cruelty
31. **phial.** Small bottle
32. **empiric.** Person who relies on practical experiences rather than on scientific principles

---

**WORDS FOR EVERYDAY USE**

ef • fi • ca • cious (ef´i kā´shəs) *adj.*, producing or capable of producing the desired effect. *When Devon had strep throat, his doctor prescribed an <u>efficacious</u> antibiotic.*

sur • mise (sər mīz´) *n.*, conjecture; guess. *From Shawna's strange behavior, I <u>surmised</u> she was upset.*

incapable of sustaining itself at the height to which the early enthusiasm of passion had exalted it; he fell down, grovelling among earthly doubts, and defiled therewith the pure whiteness of Beatrice's image. Not that he gave her up; he did but distrust. He resolved to institute some decisive test that should satisfy him, once for all, whether there were those dreadful peculiarities in her physical nature, which could not be supposed to exist without some corresponding monstrosity of soul. His eyes, gazing down afar, might have deceived him as to the lizard, the insect, and the flowers. But if he could witness, at the distance of a few paces, the sudden blight of one fresh and healthful flower in Beatrice's hand, there would be room for no further question. With this idea, he hastened to the florist's, and purchased a bouquet that was still gemmed with the morning dewdrops.

*What does Giovanni assume about Beatrice's outer and inner nature?*

I t was now the customary hour of his daily interview with Beatrice. Before descending into the garden, Giovanni failed not to look at his figure in the mirror; a vanity to be expected in a beautiful young man, yet, as displaying itself at that troubled and feverish moment, the token of a certain shallowness of feeling and insincerity of character. He did gaze, however, and said to himself, that his features had never before possessed so rich a grace, nor his eyes such vivacity, nor his cheeks so warm a hue of superabundant life.

"At least," thought he, "her poison has not yet <u>insinuated</u> itself into my system. I am no flower to perish in her grasp!"

With that thought, he turned his eyes on the bouquet, which he had never once laid aside from his hand. A thrill of indefinable horror shot through his frame, on perceiving that those dewy flowers were already beginning to droop; they wore the aspect of things that had been fresh and lovely, yesterday. Giovanni grew white as marble, and stood motionless before the mirror, staring at his own reflection there, as at the likeness of something frightful. He remembered Baglioni's remark about the fragrance that seemed to pervade the chamber. It must have been the poison in his breath! Then he shuddered—shuddered at himself! Recovering from his stupor, he began to watch, with curious eye, a spider that was busily at work, hanging its web from the antique cornice of the apartment, crossing and recrossing the artful system of interwoven lines, as vigorous and active a spider as ever dangled from an old ceiling. Giovanni bent towards the insect, and emitted a deep, long breath. The spider suddenly ceased its toil; the web vibrated with a tremor originating in the body of the small artisan. Again Giovanni sent forth a breath, deeper, longer, and imbued with a venomous feeling out of his heart; he knew not whether he were wicked or only desperate. The spider made a convulsive gripe with his limbs, and hung dead across the window.

*What does Giovanni realize about himself?*

"Accursed! Accursed!" muttered Giovanni, addressing himself. "Hast thou grown so poisonous, that this deadly insect perishes by the breath?"

At that moment, a rich, sweet voice came floating up from the garden:—

"Giovanni! Giovanni! It is past the hour! Why tarriest thou! Come down!"

"Yes," muttered Giovanni again. "She is the only being whom my breath may not slay! Would that it might!"

He rushed down, and in an instant, was standing before the bright and loving eyes of Beatrice. A moment ago, his wrath and despair had been

**WORDS FOR EVERYDAY USE**

in • sin • u • ate (in sin′yü āt) vt., introduce or work into gradually. *As skillfully as he could, the lawyer began to <u>insinuate</u> that the defendant had committed the robbery.*

so fierce that he could have desired nothing so much as to wither her by a glance. But, with her actual presence, there came influences which had too real an existence to be at once shaken off; recollections of the delicate and benign power of her feminine nature, which had so often enveloped him in a religious calm; recollections of many a holy and passionate outgush of her heart, when the pure fountain had been unsealed from its depths, and made visible in its transparency to his mental eye; recollections which, had Giovanni known how to estimate them, would have assured him that all this ugly mystery was but an earthly illusion, and that, whatever mist of evil might seem to have gathered over her, the real Beatrice was a heavenly angel. Incapable as he was of

*Why is Giovanni incapable of seeing Beatrice's true nature?*

such high faith, still her presence had not utterly lost its magic. Giovanni's rage was quelled into an aspect of sullen insensibility. Beatrice, with a quick spiritual sense, immediately felt that there was a gulf of blackness between them, which neither he nor she could pass. They walked on together, sad and silent, and came thus to the marble fountain, and to its pool of water on the ground, in the midst of which grew the shrub that bore gem-like blossoms. Giovanni was affrighted at the eager enjoyment—the appetite, as it were—with which he found himself inhaling the fragrance of the flowers.

"Beatrice," asked he abruptly, "whence came this shrub?"

"My father created it," answered she, with simplicity.

"Created it! created it!" repeated Giovanni. "What mean you, Beatrice?"

"He is a man fearfully acquainted with the secrets of nature," replied Beatrice; "and, at the hour when I first drew breath, this plant sprang from the soil, the offspring of his science, of his

intellect, while I was but his earthly child. "Approach it not!" continued she, observing with terror that Giovanni was drawing nearer to the shrub. "It has qualities that you little dream of. But I, dearest Giovanni,—I grew up and blossomed with the plant, and was nourished with its breath. It was my sister, and I loved it with a human affection: for—alas! hast thou not suspected it? there was an awful doom."

*How did the plant come into being? What is its relation to Beatrice?*

Here Giovanni frowned so darkly upon her that Beatrice paused and trembled. But her faith in his tenderness reassured her, and made her blush that she had doubted for an instant.

"There was an awful doom," she continued,— "the effect of my father's fatal love of science— which estranged me from all society of any kind. Until Heaven sent thee, dearest Giovanni, Oh! how lonely was thy poor Beatrice!"

"Was it a hard doom?" asked Giovanni, fixing his eyes upon her.

"Only of late have I known how hard it was," answered she tenderly. "Oh, yes; but my heart was <u>torpid</u>, and therefore quiet."

Giovanni's rage broke forth from his sullen gloom like a lightning flash out of a dark cloud.

"Accursed one!" cried he, with venomous scorn and anger. "And finding thy solitude wearisome, thou hast severed me, likewise, from all the warmth of life, and enticed me into thy region of unspeakable horror!"

*How does Giovanni behave toward Beatrice?*

"Giovanni!" exclaimed Beatrice, turning her large bright eyes upon his face. The force of his words had not found its way into her mind; she was merely wonder-struck.

"Yes, poisonous thing!" repeated Giovanni, beside himself with passion. "Thou has done it! Thou has blasted me! Thou hast filled my veins

**WORDS FOR EVERYDAY USE**

tor • pid (tôr´pəd) *adj.,* dormant; sluggish. *The townspeople were deceived by the <u>torpid</u> appearance of the flood waters.*

with poison! Thou hast made me as hateful, as ugly, as loathsome and deadly a creature as thyself,—a world's wonder of hideous monstrosity! Now—if our breath be happily as fatal to ourselves as to all others—let us join our lips in one kiss of unutterable hatred, and so die!"

"What has befallen me?" murmured Beatrice, with a low moan out of her heart. "Holy Virgin pity me, a poor heartbroken child!"

"Thou! Dost thou pray?" cried Giovanni, still with the same fiendish scorn. "Thy very prayers, as they come from thy lips, taint the atmosphere with death. Yes, yes; let us pray! Let us to church, and dip our fingers in the holy water at the portal! They that come after us will perish as by a pestilence. Let us sign crosses in the air! It will be scattering curses abroad in the likeness of holy symbols!"

"Giovanni," said Beatrice calmly, for her grief was beyond passion, "why dost thou join thyself with me thus in those terrible words? I, it is true, am the horrible thing thou namest me. But thou!—what hast thou to do, save with one other shudder at my hideous misery, to go forth out of the garden and mingle with thy race, and forget that there ever crawled on earth such a monster as poor Beatrice?"

"Dost thou pretend ignorance?" asked Giovanni, scowling upon her. "Behold! This power have I gained from the pure daughter of Rappaccini!"

There was a swarm of summer-insects flitting through the air, in search of the food promised by the flower-odors of the fatal garden. They circled round Giovanni's head, and were evidently attracted towards him by the same influence which had drawn them, for an instant, within the sphere of several of the shrubs. He sent forth a breath among them, and smiled bitterly at Beatrice, as at least a score of the insects fell dead upon the ground.

"I see it! I see it!" shrieked Beatrice. "It is my father's fatal science! No, no, Giovanni; it was not I! Never, never! I dreamed only to love thee, and be with thee a little time, and so to let thee pass away, leaving but thine image in mine heart. For, Giovanni—believe it—though my body be nourished with poison, my spirit is God's creature, and craves love as its daily food. But my father!—he has united us in this fearful sympathy. Yes; spurn me!—tread upon me!—kill me! Oh, what is death, after such words as thine? But it was not I! Not for a world of bliss would I have done it!"

Giovanni's passion had exhausted itself in its outburst from his lips. There now came across a sense, mournful, and not without tenderness, of the intimate and peculiar relationship between Beatrice and himself. They stood, as it were, in an utter solitude, which would be made none the less solitary by the densest throng of human life. Ought not, then, the desert of humanity around them to press this insulated pair close together? If they should be cruel to one another, who was there to be kind to them? Besides, thought Giovanni, might there not still be a hope of his returning within the limits of ordinary nature, and leading Beatrice—the redeemed Beatrice—by the hand? Oh, weak, and selfish, and unworthy spirit, that could dream of an earthly union and earthly happiness as possible, after such deep love had been so bitterly wronged as was Beatrice's love by Giovanni's blighting words! No, no; there could be no such hope. She must pass heavily, with that broken heart, across the borders—she must bathe her hurts in some fount of Paradise, and forget her grief in the light of immortality—and *there* be well!

But Giovanni did not know it.

"Dear Beatrice," said he, approaching her, while she shrank away, as always at his approach, but now with a different impulse—"dearest Beatrice, our fate is not yet so desperate. Behold! There is a medicine, potent, as a wise physician has assured me, and almost divine in its efficacy.

What does Beatrice say her intentions were? Does she resemble in any way the woman Giovanni has accused her of being?

What does Giovanni realize? Why is it too late?

Why is Beatrice shrinking from Giovanni now?

It is composed of ingredients the most opposite to those by which thy awful father has brought this calamity upon thee and me. It is distilled of blessed herbs. Shall we not quaff it together and thus be purified from evil?"

"Give it me!" said Beatrice, extending her hand to receive the little silver phial which Giovanni took from his bosom. She added, with a peculiar emphasis; "I will drink—but do thou await the result."

She put Baglioni's antidote to her lips; and, at the same moment, the figure of Rappaccini emerged from the portal, and came slowly towards the marble fountain. As he drew near, the pale man of science seemed to gaze with a triumphant expression at the beautiful youth and maiden, as might an artist who should spend his life in achieving a picture or a group of statuary, and finally be satisfied with his success. He paused—his bent form grew erect with conscious power, he spread out his hand over them, in the attitude of a father imploring a blessing upon his children. But those were the same hands that had thrown poison into the stream of their lives! Giovanni trembled. Beatrice shuddered nervously, and pressed her hand upon her heart.

"My daughter," said Rappaccini, "thou art no longer lonely in the world! Pluck one of those precious gems from thy sister shrub, and bid thy bridegroom wear it in his bosom. It will not harm him now! My science, and the sympathy between thee and him, have so wrought within his system, that he now stands apart from common men, as thou dost, daughter of my pride and triumph, from ordinary women. Pass on, then, through the world, most dear to one another, and dreadful to all besides!"

"My father," said Beatrice, feebly—and still, as she spoke, she kept her hand upon her heart—"wherefore didst thou inflict this miserable doom upon thy child?"

"Miserable!" exclaimed Rappaccini. "What mean you, foolish girl? Dost thou deem it misery to be endowed with[33] marvelous gifts, against which no power nor strength could avail an enemy? Misery, to be able to quell the mightiest with a breath? Misery, to be as terrible as thou art beautiful? Wouldst thou, then, have preferred the condition of a weak woman, exposed to all evil, and capable of none?"

"I would fain have been loved, not feared," murmured Beatrice, sinking down upon the ground.—"But now it matters not; I am going, father, where the evil, which thou hast striven to mingle with my being, will pass away like a dream—like the fragrance of these poisonous flowers, which will no longer taint my breath among the flowers of Eden. Farewell, Giovanni! Thy words of hatred are like lead within my heart—but they, too, will fall away as I ascend. Oh, was there not, from the first, more poison in thy nature than in mine?"

> What does Beatrice ask Giovanni?

To Beatrice—so radically had her earthly part been wrought upon by Rappaccini's skill—as poison had been life, so the powerful antidote was death. And thus the poor victim of man's ingenuity and of thwarted nature, and of the fatality that attends all such efforts of perverted wisdom, perished there, at the feet of her father and Giovanni. Just at that moment, Professor Pietro Baglioni looked forth from the window, and called loudly, in a tone of triumph mixed with horror, to the thunderstricken man of science:

"Rappaccini! Rappaccini! And is *this* the upshot of your experiment?" ∎

---

33. **endowed with.** Given

## Respond *to the* SELECTION

If you were Baglioni, who would you think is responsible for Beatrice's death? If you were Giovanni, whom would you blame? Why?

## THE REAL BEATRICE?

**R**eaders familiar with Dante's *Divine Comedy* might assume that his immortal Beatrice influenced Hawthorne when he wrote "Rappaccini's Daughter." Hawthorne does, in fact, mention Dante in the very first paragraph of his story. But there was another famous Beatrice who lived in Italy at about the time "Rappaccini's Daughter" takes place. Beatrice Cenci was the daughter of Francesco Cenci, a rich nobleman considered the most powerful man in Rome. Her abusive father kept his family virtually imprisoned and Beatrice tried several times unsuccessfully to escape. In 1599, after Francesco Cenci died after falling from a balcony under mysterious circumstances, the entire family, including Beatrice, was accused of murder. While her stepmother and brothers admitted to the act, Beatrice proclaimed her innocence until, under great torture, she confessed at last. The public protested that Beatrice, who was then twenty-two years old, should be pardoned. But Pope Clement VIII ordered the executions to be carried out and Beatrice and other members of her family were beheaded. The Vatican then inherited the Cenci fortune.

*Beatrice Cenci,* photogravure after Guido Reni painting of 1599, from Nathaniel Hawthorne's *The Marble Faun.*

Did Beatrice Cenci murder her own father? The public demanded to know how someone so young, beautiful, and reputedly good could be capable of such a horrible crime. More than two centuries later, the story of Beatrice Cenci captivated the imagination of Hawthorne and many of his nineteenth-century contemporaries, including Percy Bysshe Shelley, Honoré Balzac, and Charles Dickens. Hawthorne, in fact, may have been familiar with Percy Shelley's 1819 play *The Cenci* by the time he wrote "Rappaccini's Daughter" in 1844. He certainly knew the story by 1859, when he wrote *The Marble Faun,* in which he included a chapter entitled "Beatrice." In that chapter, an artist named Hilda becomes captivated by Guido Reni's famous portrait of Beatrice Cenci, which is said to have been painted the night before she was executed. In Hawthorne's story, no artist is allowed to copy Guido's masterpiece, but Hilda stares at it for days and paints it from memory. Hawthorne describes her copy as "the very saddest picture ever painted or conceived; it involved an unfathomable depth of sorrow, the sense of which came to the observer by a sort of intuition. It was a sorrow that removed this beautiful girl out of the sphere of humanity and set her in a far-off region, the remoteness of which—while her face is so close before us—makes us shiver as at a spectre."

Hawthorne had seen Guido Reni's portrait of Beatrice Cenci when he was living in Rome in 1858 and, like many of the expatriate American writers and artists then flocking to Italy, he was haunted by it. "Its spell is indefinable—and the painter has wrought it more like magic than anything else," he wrote in his notebook. "It is the most profoundly wrought picture in the world." Later editions of *The Marble Faun* included a photogravure (an early process that combined photography and printmaking) of the painting.

# INVESTIGATE Inquire, Imagine

## Recall: GATHERING FACTS

1a. When and in what city does the story take place? How does Giovanni Guasconti happen to be there? How does he enjoy spending his time when in his chamber?

2a. Who is Baglioni? What is his relationship with Rappaccini? How does he warn Giovanni when they meet on the street?

3a. Before Giovanni meets Beatrice, what does he see, or think he sees, that makes him fear her? After he meets her, what makes him ignore his fears until Baglioni's visit?

## Interpret: FINDING MEANING

1b. Giovanni suspects that Rappaccini has arranged for him to visit the garden. Why does he think so? What might be Rappaccini's reasons for allowing a man to visit Beatrice? for choosing Giovanni to be that man?

2b. Could Giovanni trust Baglioni's opinion of Rappaccini? Why, or why not? At the end of the story, why does Baglioni's voice suggest triumph as well as horror?

3b. During their first meeting in the garden, why does Beatrice hide her face and run away? When Giovanni suggests that both he and Beatrice drink Baglioni's antidote, why does she say, "I will drink—but do thou await the result"? Whose love is more real, Beatrice's for Giovanni or Giovanni's for Beatrice?

## Analyze: TAKING THINGS APART

4a. What things, natural and unnatural, are considered poisonous in this story? What behaviors?

## Synthesize: BRINGING THINGS TOGETHER

4b. Is Rappaccini evil? Is Baglioni, Beatrice, Lisabetta, or Giovanni himself? How do you define evil? What degree of evil does each of the characters possess?

## Evaluate: MAKING JUDGMENTS

5a. Determine how believably Hawthorne portrays Beatrice as a female character, using evidence from the text to support your response.

## Extend: CONNECTING IDEAS

5b. In popular culture and throughout history, people have accused others of being poisonous, toxic, or a "bad influence." Name examples of such people and the ways they have influenced the world around them. Then name people or groups who have countered them.

# Understanding Literature

FANTASY. Review the definition for **fantasy** in the Handbook of Literary Terms. Consult the radiating circle of fantastic elements that you completed as you read the story. Can you characterize "Rappaccini's Daughter" as a fantasy, or do realistic elements dominate the story? Explain your answer, using examples from the text.

SYMBOL. Review the definition for **symbol** in the Handbook of Literary Terms. Then consider that the lush, poisonous foliage in Rappaccini's garden might represent temptation or evil. If so, what does the fountain that flows "cheerfully" into the garden pool symbolize? Does Beatrice also represent evil, or something more complex? What might Rappaccini himself symbolize?

**ALLUSION.** Review the definition for **allusion** in the Handbook of Literary Terms. According to the Bible, God declared that "It is not good for man to be alone" and therefore created Eve to be Adam's partner in the Garden of Eden. In the final scene of "Rappaccini's Daughter," set in the poisonous garden, Rappaccini tells Beatrice that, due to his science, Giovanni is a fit partner and "thou art no longer lonely." How does this allusion to the biblical story of creation demonstrate Rappaccini's pride? What light does it throw on the nature of the evil in Rappaccini and his garden?

# WRITER'S JOURNAL

1. Imagining that you are Baglioni, write a **character reference** for Giovanni to attend the university. Consider which qualities of Giovanni are worth mentioning and which would be important to a university admissions committee.

2. Assume that you are an advice columnist and that Beatrice has written to you about how to explore the world beyond the garden or how to deal with her father. Write an **advice column** in response.

3. Write a **news story** about Beatrice Rappaccini, choosing either (1) a factual, objective report on her death and the coroner's decision to blame it on natural causes, or (2) a sensational, tabloid-style report on her ability to kill small animals with her breath, and humans with her kiss.

# Integrating
## *the* LANGUAGE ARTS

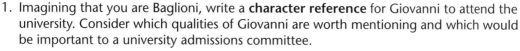

### Language, Grammar, and Style & Speaking and Listening

**PARAPHRASING HAWTHORNE.** Work with a small group of students to translate a scene from "Rappaccini's Daughter" into informal English. Refer to the Language Arts Survey 3.2, "Formal and Informal English." Take turns reading the dialogues aloud and restating the ideas in language more natural to your group. Try not to change the thoughts as you change words or word order. (Note that any translation will change the meaning somewhat. Robert Frost once wrote that "Poetry is what gets lost in the translation.") After you have finished, work with your group to enact the modern version of the scene you selected. Then discuss as a class the differences between the "translations" and Hawthorne's text.

### Applied English & Collaborative Learning

**FANTASY GARDEN CATALOG.** Work with a small group to create a two- to four-page catalog advertising fantastic plants such as those in Rappaccini's garden. Brainstorm possible variations on existing plants, or combinations of two or more species. Use your imagination to produce frightening, mysterious, or comical plants. Develop illustrations of the plants by drawing, using computer art programs, or splicing together pictures of real plants. Write a description for each plant, keeping a consistent tone, which may be academic, attention-getting, or tongue-in-cheek. Lay out the pages, pasting art and text in place. In working collaboratively, you may want to assign specific tasks to each person; for example, one person could write text, one could illustrate the plants, one could edit the text, and one could lay out the pages.

# About *the* AUTHOR

**Ralph Waldo Emerson** (1803–1882) was considered the greatest American thinker of his day. He grew up in Boston and entered Harvard at the age of fourteen, graduating with honors in 1821. Thereafter, he taught school and then studied for the ministry. In 1829, he was ordained as junior pastor of Boston's Second Church, and in the same year, he married Ellen Tucker, who died sixteen months later of tuberculosis.

With literary friends from Boston, Emerson founded a magazine, *The Dial*, which became an important vehicle for the Transcendentalist Movement, of which Emerson was a leader. The Transcendentalists, like the English Romantics, believed in a deep spiritual connection between people and nature. The Transcendentalist Movement was based on a fundamental belief in the unity of the world and God. The soul of each individual was thought to be identical with the world—a microcosm of the world itself. The doctrine of individualism developed through the belief in the identification of the individual soul with God. Emerson believed that by attending closely to one's innermost thoughts and feelings, one could glimpse the great spirit of the universe, what Emerson called the "Over-Soul."

Many accused Emerson of subverting Christianity, but his response was that for him "to be a good minister, it was necessary to leave the church." Emerson's philosophy has been called contradictory, but he held strongly to his romantic belief in personal intuition and flexibility. Such beliefs led Emerson to a radical individualism that helped to shape the American spirit. In his own words, "To believe your own thought, to believe that what is true for you in your private heart is true for all men,—that is genius."

Emerson traveled in Europe and, on returning moved to Concord, Massachusetts, which was the first rural artist's colony and the first place to offer a spiritual and cultural alternative to American materialism. There he married Lydia Jackson, with whom he had four children. During their fifty years of marriage, the Emersons entertained at home many of the leading intellectuals of the day, including their neighbors the Alcotts and Henry David Thoreau. Today, Emerson's house in Concord remains a place of literary pilgrimage. Emerson himself has become a symbol of American optimism and independent thinking. His prose-poetry has influenced a long line of American poets, including Walt Whitman, Emily Dickinson, Edwin Arlington Robinson, Wallace Stevens, Hart Crane, and Robert Frost.

# "Self-Reliance"
# "The Rhodora"

### BY RALPH WALDO EMERSON

## About *the* SELECTIONS

"**Self-Reliance**" was first published in 1841 as part of Emerson's book *Essays*. This essay is considered to be the finest expression of his beliefs on individualism. It is a combination of different ideas from a journal in which Emerson recorded his thoughts for years. Emerson used his journal as a source of ideas for his frequent lectures. He tested and perfected his style and wording before audiences, noting their reactions. He then condensed his ideas into essay form, as he does here in "Self-Reliance," for a wider audience to read and reread.

The ideas presented in the poem "**The Rhodora**" (1847) are extensions of Emerson's thoughts expressed in his long essay *Nature*, his first published book. In *Nature*, published in 1836, Emerson maintains that all natural forms, such as "a leaf, sunbeam, a landscape, the ocean," are harmonious and always beautiful. They work together to express a universal beauty and truth that transcend the beauty and truth of the natural world. Emerson held that humans can understand absolute, or universal, beauty and truth only through what can be experienced through our senses. "The Rhodora" is an eloquent statement of Emerson's belief in the value of each of nature's creations.

## Literary TOOLS

**ESSAY AND THEME.** An **essay** is a brief work of prose nonfiction. A good essay develops a single idea. A **theme** is a central idea in a literary work. Think about what Emerson's central idea is as you read the essay "Self-Reliance."

**APHORISM.** An **aphorism** is a short saying or pointed statement. An aphorism that gains currency and is passed from generation to generation is called a proverb or adage. The Greek philosopher Hippocrates first used the term in his book *Aphorisms* by writing, "Life is short, art is long, opportunity fleeting, experimenting dangerous, reasoning difficult." Look for aphorisms in Emerson's essay "Self-Reliance."

## Reader's *Journal*

Have you ever been in a situation where you had to choose between what you thought was the right course of action and the course that others thought you should take? What was your final decision?

*Distant View of Niagara Falls*, 1830. Thomas Cole. The Art Institute of Chicago.

# Self-Reliance

#### RALPH WALDO EMERSON

There is a time in every man's education when he arrives at the conviction that envy is ignorance; that imitation is suicide; that he must take himself for better, for worse, as his portion; that though the wide universe is full of good, no kernel of nourishing corn can come to him but through his toil bestowed on that plot of ground which is given to him to till.

◆ ◆ ◆

Trust thyself: every heart vibrates to that iron string. Accept the place the divine Providence has found for you; the society of your contemporaries, the connexion of events. Great men have always done so and confided themselves childlike to the genius of their age,

*Whom should you trust? What should you accept?*

betraying their perception that the Eternal was stirring at their heart, working through their hands, predominating in all their being.

◆ ◆ ◆

Society everywhere is in conspiracy against the manhood of every one of its members. Society is a joint-stock company[1] in which the members agree for the better securing of his bread to each shareholder, to surrender the liberty and culture of the eater. The virtue in most request is conformity. Self-reliance is its aversion. It loves not realities and creators, but names and customs.

Whoso would be a man must be a nonconformist. He who would gather immortal palms must not be hindered by the name of goodness, but must explore if it be goodness. Nothing is at last sacred but the integrity of our own mind.

◆ ◆ ◆

What I must do, is all that concerns me, not what the people think. This rule, equally arduous in actual and in intellectual life, may serve for the whole distinction between greatness and meanness. It is the harder, because you

*By what opinion is it easy to live? Whose opinion should you follow?*

will always find those who think they know what is your duty better than you know it. It is easy in the world to live after the world's opinion; it is easy in solitude to live after our own; but the great man is he who in the midst of the crowd keeps with perfect sweetness the independence of solitude.

◆ ◆ ◆

# *Nothing is at last sacred but the integrity of our own mind.*

◆ ◆ ◆

A foolish consistency is the hobgoblin of little minds, adored by little statesmen and philosophers and divines. With consistency a great soul has simply nothing to do. He may as well concern himself with his shadow on the wall. Out upon your guarded lips! Sew them up with packthread, do. Else, if you would be a man, speak what you think today in words as hard as cannon balls, and tomorrow speak what tomorrow thinks in hard words again, though it contradict

---

1. **joint-stock company.** Company in which joint owners hold the capital

WORDS FOR EVERYDAY USE

pre • dom • i • nate (prē däm´ə nāt´) vi., have authority or influence over others. *Her opinions predominate and everyone does what she says.*

a • ver • sion (ə vur´zhən) n., definite dislike. *Since she was allergic to nuts, she developed an aversion to them.*

ar • du • ous (är´jü əs) adj., difficult. *The farmer endured a life of arduous toil.*

every thing you said today. Ah, then, exclaim the aged ladies, you shall be sure to be misunderstood. Misunderstood! It is a right fool's word. Is it so bad then to be misunderstood? Pythagoras was misunderstood, and Socrates, and Jesus, and Luther, and Copernicus, and Galileo, and Newton, and every pure and wise spirit that ever took flesh. To be great is to be misunderstood.

*What evidence does the speaker offer to suggest that being misunderstood is not bad?*

◆  ◆  ◆

## *To be great is to be misunderstood.*

◆  ◆  ◆

I hope in these days we have heard the last of conformity and consistency. Let the words be gazetted and ridiculous henceforward.[2] Instead of the gong for dinner, let us hear a whistle from the Spartan fife.[3] Let us bow and apologize never more. A great man is coming to eat at my house. I do not wish to please him: I wish that he should wish to please me. I will stand here for humanity, and though I would make it kind, I would made it true. Let us affront and reprimand the smooth mediocrity and squalid

contentment of the times, and hurl in the face of custom, and trade, and office, the fact which is the upshot of all history, that there is a great responsible Thinker and Actor moving wherever moves a man; that a true man belongs to no other time or place, but is the center of things. Where he is, there is nature. . . . Every true man is a cause, a country, and an age; requires infinite spaces and numbers and time fully to accomplish his thought;—and posterity seem to follow his steps as a procession. A man Cæsar is born, and for ages after, we have a Roman Empire. Christ is born, and millions of minds so grow and cleave[4] to his genius, that he is confounded with virtue and the possible of man. An institution is the lengthened shadow of one man; as, the Reformation, of Luther; Quakerism, of Fox; Methodism, of Wesley; Abolition, of Clarkson.[5] Scipio,[6] Milton called, "the height of Rome;" and all history resolves itself very easily into the biography of a few stout and earnest persons. ■

---

2. **gazetted and ridiculous henceforward.** Labeled and not used from now on
3. **gong . . . fife.** The gong stands for ease and leisure, and the fife represents disciplined, alert life.
4. **cleave.** Cling; adhere
5. **Reformation . . . Clarkson.** Martin Luther (1483–1546), founder of the Reformation; George Fox (1624–1691), founder of Quakerism; John Wesley (1703–1791), founder of Methodism; and Thomas Clarkson (1760–1846), abolitionist
6. **Scipio.** (237–183 BC) Roman conqueror of Carthage, a city-state of ancient Africa

**WORDS FOR EVERYDAY USE**

squal • id (skwäl´id) *adj.*, wretched; miserable. *The destitute family lived in a squalid shack.*

## Respond *to the* SELECTION

With what quote from "Self-Reliance" do you agree most strongly, and why?

# INVESTIGATE Inquire, Imagine

**Recall:** GATHERING FACTS

1a. According to Emerson, what does each person come to realize at a certain point in his or her education?

2a. What is the virtue that society asks of each person? What should people strive for instead?

3a. Emerson says that it is easy to live your life doing what other people think is appropriate and it is also easy to act on your own beliefs when you are alone. What type of behavior does he say is difficult but essential for greatness?

**Interpret:** FINDING MEANING

1b. Why does Emerson say that envy is ignorance and imitation is suicide? What alternative does Emerson recommend?

2b. Why does Emerson advocate nonconformity? What does he mean by nonconformity?

3b. What does Emerson mean by the phrase "the independence of solitude"? Why is it something for which to strive?

**Analyze:** TAKING THINGS APART

4a. Consider some of the people Emerson says were misunderstood in their time. What qualities distinguish them from other people?

**Synthesize:** BRINGING THINGS TOGETHER

4b. Why might great people sometimes be inconsistent? Summarize Emerson's view of the importance of consistency.

**Evaluate:** MAKING JUDGMENTS

5a. Do you agree with Emerson that is it better to rely on yourself rather than upon others for your values and your principles? What are some of the benefits of being self-reliant?

**Extend:** CONNECTING IDEAS

5b. In your opinion, if society values conformity over individualism, why do nonconformists seem to have the greatest impact on society? Why can nonconformists change society so radically, as Cæsar, Jesus, and Martin Luther did? What contemporary nonconformists can you think of that have had a great impact on our culture?

# Understanding Literature

ESSAY AND THEME. Review the discussion of **essay** and **theme** in Literary Tools on page 277. Identify at least one theme that runs through this essay.

APHORISM. Review the definition of **aphorism** in the Handbook of Literary Terms. Select two quotations from Emerson that could be considered to be aphorisms and that you believe have the potential of becoming proverbs. Explain why you chose them and why you think they will speak to many generations.

# Writer's Journal

1. Read the Language Arts Survey 5.43, "Paraphrasing, Summarizing, and Quoting." Then choose two of the passages from "Self-Reliance" and rewrite them as **paraphrases**.

2. Emerson often gave lectures to groups to supplement his income. Create a **poster** advertising one of his lectures. Include the topics he will speak about. Give the potential audience good reasons for paying to see and hear him.

3. Imagine that Emerson were the writer of an advice column. Compose an appropriate **question** to pose to Emerson and then write an **answer** in the style of Emerson.

# Integrating *the* LANGUAGE ARTS

## Language, Grammar, and Style

**CORRECTING RUN-ONS.** Read the Language Arts Survey 3.34, "Correcting Sentence Run-ons." Then read each of the following sentences. If it is a run-on, rewrite it correctly.

1. Emerson trained to be a minister for years when he began his ministry he found that it had lost its meaning.

2. After visiting Europe, Emerson's spirits were revived, and he was inspired to write his first book.

3. Emerson lectured on many topics he always included a discussion of the moral principles that underlay his thinking.

4. Believing that slavery was an abomination, Emerson delivered lectures against it even when he was emotionally involved with his subject he kept his dignity.

5. Emerson's optimism is obvious in most of his works he believed that people have within themselves everything they need to know about the meaning of their own existence.

## Speaking and Listening

**ADVICE BOOKLET.** Everyone gets advice from his or her parents, relatives, teachers, coworkers, and friends. Ask friends and family for advice or rules by which to live. Assemble and organize the advice in a booklet, which you may choose to illustrate.

## Collaborative Learning

**PROVERB CHARADES.** Divide into small groups and have team members write proverbs on slips of paper, one to a slip. Then have team members take turns selecting proverbs to pantomime for the rest of your team. See how long it takes each team to guess the correct proverb. You may wish to include aphorisms from writers such as Ralph Waldo Emerson, Henry David Thoreau, or Benjamin Franklin.

## Study and Research

**BIOGRAPHY.** A biography is the story of a person's life, told by someone other than that person. Read about the life of one of the people that Emerson mentions in his essay: Scipio, Pythagoras, Socrates, Jesus, Luther, Copernicus, Galileo, Newton, Cæsar, Fox, Wesley, or Clarkson. Write a brief biography about that person, including the most memorable events in his life. You might choose a phrase from Emerson's essay as a title for your biography.

# The Rhodora

## RALPH WALDO EMERSON

*Rhododendrun*, 1895. Paul De Longpre.
Private Collection.

*On Being Asked, Whence[1] Is the Flower?*

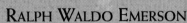

In May, when sea-winds pierced our solitudes,
I found the fresh Rhodora[2] in the woods,
Spreading its leafless blooms in a damp nook,
To please the desert and the sluggish brook.
5   The purple petals, fallen in the pool,
Made the black water with their beauty gay;
Here might the red-bird come his plumes to cool,
And court the flower that cheapens his array.
Rhodora! if the sages[3] ask thee why
10  This charm is wasted on the earth and sky,
Tell them, dear, that if eyes were made for seeing,
Then Beauty is its own excuse for being:
Why thou wert there,[4] O rival of the rose!
I never thought to ask, I never knew;
15  But, in my simple ignorance, suppose
The self-same Power that brought me there brought you. ■

*Who enjoys what the flower offers?*

---

1. **Whence.** From where
2. **Rhodora.** Deciduous plant, native to northeastern United States, that bears pink flowers in spring
3. **sages.** Wise older people
4. **thou wert there.** You were there

What natural objects found in the woods, on the mountains, at the beach, or in the meadow do you find particularly beautiful or affecting?

# INVESTIGATE Inquire, Imagine

**Recall:** GATHERING FACTS

1a. At what time of year does the speaker find the rhodora in the woods?

2a. Where is the rhodora growing? What is the rhodora's effect on the area in which it is blooming?

→ **Interpret:** FINDING MEANING

1b. Why is the rhodora especially beautiful at this time of year? Why do you think the speaker compares the rhodora to a rose?

2b. Does the speaker believe that any other person besides himself has appreciated the rhodora's beauty? Why is the isolated location of the rhodora significant to the speaker?

**Analyze:** TAKING THINGS APART

3a. According to the speaker, how can the rhodora justify its blooming alone in the woods when usually no one sees it?

→ **Synthesize:** BRINGING THINGS TOGETHER

3b. Does Emerson agree with the sages that the charm of the rhodora is wasted on the earth and sky? Why, or why not?

**Evaluate:** MAKING JUDGMENTS

4a. Do you think that the speaker is glad that he happened upon the rhodora in the woods? What do you think he gained through this encounter?

→ **Extend:** CONNECTING IDEAS

4b. Which flower do you think the speaker would find more pleasing—the rhodora blooming alone in the woods or the pampered orchid blooming in a greenhouse? Would the speaker find them equally pleasing? Explain your answer.

# Understanding Literature

**RHYME. Rhyme** is the repetition of sounds at the ends of words. Review the complete definition of *rhyme* in the Handbook of Literary Terms. Identify the rhyme scheme of "The Rhodora," labeling the sound at the end of each line with a letter of the alphabet. If the sound is the same as the one that came before, label it with the same letter. If it is a different sound, assign it a new letter. When you are done, look for the pattern or rhyme scheme. The first four lines have been done for you.

In May, when sea-winds pierced our solitudes, (a)

I found the fresh Rhodora in the woods, (a)

Spreading its leafless blooms in a damp nook, (b)

To please the desert and the sluggish brook. (b)

**ROMANTICISM. Romanticism** was a literary and artistic movement of the eighteenth and nineteenth centuries that placed value on emotion or imagination over realism, and on nature and wildness over human works. Read the complete definition of *Romanticism* in the Handbook of Literary Terms. Explain why this poem may be categorized as romantic.

# WRITER'S JOURNAL

1. Have you ever experienced a special moment in nature, for example, when you were hiking or bicycling? Try to recreate that moment in your mind and jot down a **journal entry** about the sights you saw, the sounds you heard, and the emotions you felt.

2. Imagine that you are walking in the woods on that May day with the speaker. Write a **stream-of-consciousness style paragraph** that describes what you are experiencing and thinking as you hike along. Include your thoughts on finding the rhodora by the stream. For a definition of *stream-of-consciousness writing,* refer to the Handbook of Literary Terms.

3. Write a **poem** about a natural element that has meaning for you.

# Integrating *the* LANGUAGE ARTS

## Language, Grammar, and Style

**CORRECTING MODIFIERS.** Read the Language Arts Survey 3.46, "Avoiding Dangling and Misplaced Modifiers." Then correctly rewrite each sentence below.

1. While blooming by a quiet stream, the speaker discovered a hidden rhodora.

2. Fallen into the water, the river washed the petals downstream.

3. Cooling his plumes at the brook, the rhodora's purple petals contrasted with the bird's red feathers.

4. The Transcendentalists had a lasting effect on American literature who believed that through intuition humans can know truth.

5. Even more useful than the teachings of organized religion, Emerson believed that the most direct way to enlightenment was an openness to nature.

## Study and Research & Applied English

**TECHNICAL WRITING.** Do research to find information on the rhodora. What type of flower is it? What color are its blossoms? Where does it originate? What is its Latin name? Write instructions on caring for the plant that would accompany it if it were sold in a flower shop or nursery. Include details such as how much sunlight is required, how often to water, and when it blooms.

## Critical Thinking

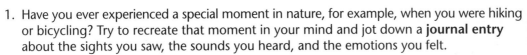

**EDITORIAL.** Write an editorial in which you state your point of view on preserving wilderness areas in your state, the United States, or another part of the world. Begin by explaining the issue you will be discussing; then give at least three reasons why you feel as you do. Conclude with a recommendation about what you believe is the correct course of action.

# from *Walden*

BY HENRY DAVID THOREAU

## Literary TOOLS

APHORISM. As you learned in Literary Tools for the selections by Emerson on page 277, an **aphorism** is a short saying or pointed statement. As you read this selection from Walden, find two aphorisms that are well known today. Then compare them to the aphorisms you found reading Emerson's "Self-Reliance." Be prepared to discuss which aphorisms you find most meaningful, and why.

TONE. **Tone** is the emotional attitude toward the reader or toward the subject implied by a literary work. In this selection, Thoreau employs a very strong attitude toward the people around him. Try to determine this tone as you read.

## About the AUTHOR

**Henry David Thoreau** (1817–1862), writer, philosopher, and naturalist, lived in Concord, Massachusetts, most of his life. He won his place in American literature by, as he put it, traveling a good deal in Concord. He made numerous trips to Maine, Cape Cod, and New Hampshire, and also traveled to Quebec, Canada, and Minnesota in an unsuccessful attempt to strengthen his tubercular lungs. Thoreau never married. He read widely and wrote constantly in his journals, using them as sources for lectures, essays, and his books *A Week on the Concord and Merrimack Rivers* (1849) and *Walden* (1854). His neighbors knew him as an educated man without an occupation. He worked as a school teacher, as a handyman at Ralph Waldo Emerson's house, and as a tutor.

Thoreau lived for two years in a cabin he built on Emerson's property at Walden Pond. During that time, he also surveyed property, wrote magazine articles, and worked in his father's pencil factory. In 1846 Thoreau spent one night in jail for refusing to pay his poll tax, in protest of the Mexican War (1846–1848). In his essay "Civil Disobedience" (1849), he clarified his position and discussed passive resistance, a method of protest that later was adopted by civil rights activists.

Thoreau's work demonstrates how the abstract ideals of individualism and libertarianism can be effectively instilled in a person's life. His most popular essays during his lifetime were *Slavery in Massachusetts* and *A Plea for Captain John Brown.* He was forty-four when he died of tuberculosis at his mother's house in Concord. Sections of his books *The Maine Woods* and *Cape Cod* were published after his death.

## Reader's *Journal*

What do you need in order to be happy?

## About the SELECTION

One of the two books that Thoreau published during his lifetime, *Walden* is drawn from the journals he kept before, during, and after his stay on Emerson's property at Walden Pond from July 4, 1845, to September 6, 1847. His first book, *A Week on the Concord and Merrimack Rivers,* the narrative of a boating trip Thoreau took with his brother, was published in 1849 but did not sell well. The unpopularity of his first book caused Thoreau to hold back his *Walden* manuscript for five years. During that time he revised and reworked the text numerous times, enriching and perfecting the work. The book firmly established his reputation as a writer as well as an outspoken individualist.

## from *Walden*

### Henry David Thoreau

#### FROM "ECONOMY"

**T**he mass of men lead lives of quiet desperation.

*What kind of lives do most people lead? What does Thoreau call resignation?*

What is called <u>resignation</u> is confirmed desperation. From the desperate city you go into the desperate country, and have to console yourself with the bravery of minks and muskrats. A stereotyped but unconscious despair is concealed even under what are called the games and amusements of mankind. There is no play in them, for this comes after work. But it is a characteristic of wisdom not to do desperate things. When we consider what, to use the words of the catechism, is the chief end of man,[1] and what are the true necessaries and means of life, it appears as if men had deliberately chosen the common mode of living because they preferred it to any other. Yet they honestly think there is no choice left. But alert and healthy natures remember that the sun rose clear. It is never too late to give up our prejudices. No way of thinking or doing, however ancient, can be trusted without proof. What every body echoes or in silence passes by as true today may turn out to be falsehood tomorrow,

*What happens to things people believe to be true?*

mere smoke of opinion, which some had trusted for a cloud that would sprinkle fertilizing rain on their fields. What old people say you cannot do you try and find that you can. Old deeds for old people, and new deeds for new. Old people did

---

1. **When . . . man.** Refers to a line from the shorter Catechism in the *New England Primer*, "What is the chief end of man? Man's chief end is to glorify God and enjoy him forever."

---

**WORDS FOR EVERYDAY USE**

**res • ig • na • tion** (rez ig nā´shən) *n.*, submission; patient acceptance. *Micah had to accept his grade with <u>resignation</u> since he could not change it.*

not know enough once, perchance, to fetch fresh fuel to keep the fire a-going; new people put a little dry wood under a pot, and are whirled round the globe with the speed of birds, in a way to kill old people, as the phrase is. Age is no better, hardly so well, qualified for an instructor as youth, for it has not profited so much as it has lost. One may almost doubt if the wisest man has learned any thing of absolute value by living. Practically, the old have no very important advice to give the young, their own experience has been so partial, and their lives have been such miserable failures, for private reasons, as they must believe; and it may be that they have some faith left which belies that experience, and they are only less young than they were. I have lived some thirty years on this planet and I have yet to hear the first syllable of valuable or even <u>earnest</u> advice from my seniors. They have told me nothing, and probably cannot tell me any thing, to the purpose. Here is life, an experiment to a great extent untried by me; but it does not avail me that they have tried it. If I have any experience which I think valuable, I am sure to reflect that this my Mentors[2] said nothing about.

*Does Thoreau believe in the wisdom of old age? Why, or why not?*

> *One may almost doubt if the wisest man has learned any thing of absolute value by living.*

◆  ◆  ◆

Near the end of March, 1845, I borrowed an axe and went down to the woods by Walden Pond, nearest to where I intended to build my house, and began to cut down some tall arrowy white pines, still in their youth, for timber. It is difficult to begin without borrowing, but perhaps it is the most generous course thus to permit your fellow-men to have an interest in your enterprise. The owner of the axe, as he released his hold on it, said that it was the apple of his eye; but I returned it sharper than I received it. It was a pleasant hillside where I worked, covered with pine woods, through which I looked out on the pond, and a small open field in the woods where pines and hickories were springing up. The ice in the pond was not yet dissolved, though there were some open spaces, and it was all dark colored and <u>saturated</u> with water. There were some slight flurries of snow during the days that I worked there, but for the most part when I came out on to the railroad, on my way home, its yellow sand heap stretched away gleaming in the hazy atmosphere, and the rails shone in the spring sun, and I heard the lark and pewee and other birds already come to commence another year with us. They were pleasant spring days, in which the winter of man's discontent was thawing as well as the earth, and the life that had lain torpid began to stretch itself. One day, when my axe had come off and I had cut a green hickory for a wedge, driving it with a stone and had placed the whole to soak in a pond hole in order to swell the wood, I saw a striped snake run into the water, and he lay on the bottom, apparently without inconvenience, as long as I staid there, or more than a quarter of an hour;

---

2. **Mentors.** Wise advisors; from Mentor, the friend of Odysseus in Homer's *Odyssey* who educated Odysseus's son

**WORDS FOR EVERYDAY USE**

ear • nest (ɤr´nist) *adj.*, serious; sincere. *If you are <u>earnest</u> about getting on the team, you must condition for it in every way possible.*

sat • u • rat • ed (sach´ə rāt´ əd) *adj.*, thoroughly soaked. *When the sponge is <u>saturated</u>, it weighs twice as much as it does when it is dry.*

perhaps because he had not yet fairly come out of the torpid state. It appeared to me that for a like reason men remain in their present low and primitive condition; but if they should feel the influence of the spring of springs arousing them, they would of necessity rise to a higher and more <u>ethereal</u> life. I had previously seen the snakes in frosty mornings in my path with portions of their bodies still numb and inflexible, waiting for the sun to thaw them. On the 1st of April it rained and melted the ice, and in the early part of the day, which was very foggy, I heard a stray goose groping about over the pond and cackling as if lost, or like the spirit of the fog.

So I went on for some days cutting and hewing timber, and also studs and rafters, all with my narrow axe, not having many communicable or scholarlike thoughts, singing to myself,—

Men say they know many things;
But lo! they have taken wings,—
The arts and sciences
And a thousand appliances
The wind that blows
Is all that any body knows.

I hewed the main timbers six inches square, most of the studs on two sides only, and the rafters and floor timbers on one side, leaving the rest of the bark on, so that they were just as straight and much stronger than sawed ones. Each stick was carefully mortised or tenoned[3] by its stump, for I had borrowed other tools by this time. My days in the woods were not very long ones, yet I usually carried my dinner of bread and butter, and read the newspaper in which it was wrapped, at noon, sitting amid the green pine boughs which I had cut off, and to my bread was imparted

*To what does Thoreau compare the condition of humans?*

some of their fragrance, for my hands were covered with a thick coat of pitch. Before I had done I was more the friend than the foe of the pine tree, though I had cut down some of them, having become better acquainted with it. Sometimes a rambler in the wood was attracted by the sound of my axe, and we chatted pleasantly over the chips which I had made.

By the middle of April, for I made no haste in my work, but rather made the most of it, my house was framed and ready for the raising. I had already bought the shanty of James Collins, an Irishman who worked on the Fitchburg Railroad, for boards. James Collins' shanty was considered an uncommonly fine one. When I called to see it he was not at home. I walked about the outside, at first unobserved from within, the window was so deep and high. It was of small dimensions, with a peaked cottage roof, and not much else to be seen, the dirt being raised five feet all around as if it were a compost heap. The roof was the soundest part, though a good deal warped and made brittle by the sun. Door-sill there was none, but a <u>perennial</u> passage for the hens under the door board. Mrs. C. came to the door and asked me to view it from the inside. The hens were driven in by my approach. It was dark, and had a dirt floor for the most part, dank, clammy, and aguish, only here a board and there a board which would not bear removal. She lighted a lamp to show me the inside of the roof and the walls, and also that the board floor extended under the bed, warning me not to step into the cellar, a sort of dust hole two feet deep. In her own words, they were "good boards overhead, good boards all around, and a good window,"—

*What is the shanty like?*

---

3. **mortised or tenoned.** Joined or fastened

**WORDS FOR EVERYDAY USE**

e • the • re • al (ē thir´ē əl) *adj.,* heavenly. *Many listeners think a harp sounds* <u>ethereal</u> *and call it a heavenly instrument.*

per • en • ni • al (pər en´ē əl) *adj.,* throughout the year; perpetual. *My father gave me a magazine subscription, saying his* <u>perennial</u> *present could be enjoyed all year.*

of two whole squares originally, only the cat had passed out that way lately. There was a stove, a bed, and a place to sit, an infant in the house where it was born, a silk parasol, gilt-framed looking-glass, and a patent new coffee mill nailed to an oak sapling, all told. The bargain was soon concluded, for James had in the mean while returned. I to pay four dollars and twenty-five cents tonight, he to vacate at five tomorrow morning, selling to nobody else meanwhile: I to take possession at six. It were well, he said, to be there early, and anticipate certain indistinct but wholly unjust claims on the score of ground rent and fuel. This he assured me was the only <u>encumbrance</u>. At six I passed him and his family on the road. One large bundle held their all,—bed, coffee-mill, looking-glass, hens, all but the cat, she took to the woods and became a wild cat, and, as I learned afterward, trod in a trap set for wood-chucks, and so became a dead cat at last.

I took down this dwelling the same morning, drawing the nails, and removed it to the pond side by small cartloads, spreading the boards on the grass there to bleach and warp back again in the sun. One early thrush gave me a note or two as I drove along the woodland path. I was informed treacherously by a young Patrick that neighbor Seeley, an Irishman, in the intervals of the carting, transferred the still tolerable, straight, and drivable nails, staples, and spikes to his pocket, and then stood when I came back to pass the time of day, and look freshly up, uncon-cerned, with spring thoughts, at the devastation; there being a dearth[4] of work, as he said. He was there to represent specta-tordom, and help make this seemingly insignificant event one with the removal of the gods of Troy.[5]

Who watches Thoreau? What effect does the spectator have on the occasion?

I dug my cellar in the side of a hill sloping to the south, where a woodchuck had formerly dug his burrow, down through sumach and black-berry roots, and the lowest stain of vegetation, six feet square by seven deep, to a fine sand where potatoes would not freeze in any winter. The sides were left shelving, and not stoned; but the sun having never shone on them, the sand still keeps its place. It was but two hours' work. I took particular pleasure in this breaking of ground, for in almost all latitudes men dig into the earth for an equable temperature. Under the most splendid house in the city is still to be found the cellar where they store their

Why is the cellar of a house so important?

roots as of old, and long after the superstructure has disappeared <u>posterity</u> remark its dent in the earth. The house is still but a sort of porch at the entrance of a burrow.

At length, in the beginning of May, with the help of some of my acquaintances, rather to improve so good an occasion for neighborliness than from any necessity, I set up the frame of my house. No man was ever more honored in the character of his raisers than I. They are des-tined, I trust, to assist at the raising of loftier structures one day. I began to occupy my house on the 4th of July, as soon as it was boarded and roofed, for the boards were carefully feather-edged and lapped, so that it was per-fectly impervious to rain;[6] but before boarding I laid the foundation of a chimney at one end, bringing two cartloads of stones up the hill from the pond in my arms. I built the chimney after my hoeing in the fall, before a fire became nec-

---

4. **dearth.** Scarcity
5. **gods of Troy.** Reference to Virgil's *Aeneid* in which Aeneas escapes with his household gods
6. **feather-edged . . . rain.** The boards' thin edges overlapped, making the roof watertight.

---

**WORDS FOR EVERYDAY USE**

en • cum • brance (en kum´brəns) *n.*, hindrance. *My dachshund is beginning to find her extra weight an encumbrance in moving quickly.*

pos • ter • i • ty (päs ter´ə tē) *n.*, succeeding generations. *Often an author honored during his or her lifetime is judged insignifi-cant by posterity.*

essary for warmth, doing my cooking in the mean while out of doors on the ground, early in the morning: which mode I still think is in some respects more convenient and agreeable than the usual one. When it stormed before my bread was baked, I fixed a few boards over the fire, and sat under them to watch my loaf, and passed some pleasant hours in that way. In those days, when my hands were much employed, I read but little, but the least scraps of paper which lay on the ground, my holder, or table-cloth, afforded me as much entertainment, in fact answered the same purpose as the Iliad.[7]

♦   ♦   ♦

FROM "WHERE I LIVED AND WHAT I LIVED FOR"

Every morning was a cheerful invitation to make my life of equal simplicity, and I may say innocence, with Nature herself. I have been as sincere a worshipper of Aurora[8] as the Greeks. I got up early and bathed in the pond; that was a religious exercise, and one of the best things which I did. They say that characters were engraven on the bathing tub of king Tching-thang to this effect: "Renew thyself completely each day; do it again, and again, and forever again."[9] I can understand that. Morning brings back the heroic ages. I was as much affected by the faint hum of a mosquito making its invisible and unimaginable tour through my apartment at earliest dawn, when I was sitting with door and windows open, as I could be by any trumpet that ever sang of fame. It was Homer's requiem; itself an Iliad and Odyssey in the air, singing its own wrath and wanderings. There was something cosmical about it, a standing advertisement, till forbidden,[10] of the everlasting vigor and fertility of the world. The morning, which is the most memorable season of the day, is the awakening hour. Then there is least somnolence in us; and for an hour, at least, some part of us awakes which slumbers all the rest of the day and night. Little is to be expected of that day, if it can be called a day, to which we are not awakened by our Genius, but by the

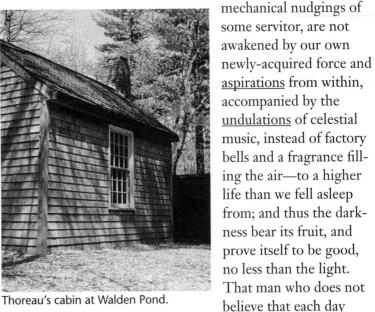

Thoreau's cabin at Walden Pond.

mechanical nudgings of some servitor, are not awakened by our own newly-acquired force and <u>aspirations</u> from within, accompanied by the <u>undulations</u> of celestial music, instead of factory bells and a fragrance filling the air—to a higher life than we fell asleep from; and thus the darkness bear its fruit, and prove itself to be good, no less than the light. That man who does not believe that each day contains an earlier, more sacred, and auroral hour than he has yet profaned, has despaired of life, and is pursuing a descending and darkening way. After a partial <u>cessation</u> of his sensuous life, the soul of man, or its organs rather, are reinvigorated each day, and his Genius tries again what noble life it can make. All memorable

---

7. **Iliad.** Greek epic by Homer
8. **Aurora.** Goddess of dawn
9. **"Renew . . . again."** From Confucius, Chinese philosopher
10. **standing . . . forbidden.** Advertisement that was to be run "till forbidden" or stopped by the advertiser

---

**WORDS FOR EVERYDAY USE**

**as • pi • ra • tion** (as pə rā´shən) n., strong ambition. *Many musicians practice long hours if they have <u>aspirations</u> of becoming famous.*

**un • du • la • tion** (un dyü lā´shən) n., act of moving in waves. *The athlete was overcome by <u>undulations</u> of pain sweeping over him.*

**ces • sa • tion** (se sā´shən) n., stopping. *Until the <u>cessation</u> of the drill, no one could hear anything.*

events, I should say, transpire in morning time and in a morning atmosphere. The Vedas[11] say, "All intelligences awake with the morning." Poetry and art, and the fairest and most memorable of the actions of men, date from such an hour. All poets and heroes, like Memnon,[12] are the children of Aurora, and emit their music at sunrise. To him whose elastic and vigorous thought keeps pace with the sun, the day is a perpetual morning. It matters not what the clocks say or the attitudes and labors of men. Morning is when I am awake and there is a dawn in me. Moral reform is the effort to throw off sleep. Why is it that men give so poor an account of their day if they have not been slumbering? They are not such poor calculators. If they had not been overcome with drowsiness they would have performed something. The millions are awake enough for physical labor; but only one in a million is awake enough for effective intellectual exertion, only one in a hundred millions to a poetic or divine life. To be awake is to be alive. I have never yet met a man who was quite awake. How could I have looked him in the face?

What meaning does Thoreau give to the word awake?

We must learn to reawaken and keep ourselves awake, not by mechanical aids, but by an infinite expectation of the dawn, which does not forsake us in our soundest sleep. I know of no more encouraging fact than the unquestionable ability of man to elevate his life by a conscious endeavor. It is something to be able to paint a particular picture, or to carve a statue, and so to make a few objects beautiful; but it is far more glorious to carve and paint the very atmosphere and medium through which we look, which morally we can do. To affect the quality of the day, that is the highest of arts. Every man is tasked to make his life, even in its details, worthy of the contemplation of his most elevated and critical hour. If we refused, or rather used up, such paltry information as we get, the oracles[13] would distinctly inform us how this might be done.

What is the "highest of arts"?

I went to the woods because I wished to live deliberately, to front only the essential facts of life, and see if I could not learn what it had to teach, and not, when I came to die, discover that I had not lived. I did not wish to live what was not life, living is so dear; nor did I wish to practice resignation, unless it was quite necessary. I wanted to live deep and suck out all the marrow of life, to live so sturdily and Spartan-like[14] as to put to rout all that was not life, to cut a broad swath and shave close, to drive life into a corner, and reduce it to its lowest terms, and, if it proved to be mean, why then to get the whole and genuine meanness of it, and publish its meanness to the world; or if it were sublime, to know it by experience, and be able to give a true account of it in my next excursion. For most men, it appears to me, are in a strange uncertainty about it, whether it is of the devil or of God, and have somewhat hastily concluded that it is the chief end of man here to "glorify God and enjoy him forever."[15]

Why did Thoreau go to the woods?

Still we live meanly, like ants; though the fable tells us that we were long ago changed into men;[16] like pygmies we fight with cranes; it is

---

11. **Vedas.** Hindu scriptures
12. **Memnon.** King killed by Achilles in the Trojan War
13. **oracles.** People in communication with the gods
14. **Spartan-like.** Without excess comforts
15. **"glorify . . . forever."** Reference to the *New England Primer*
16. **fable . . . men.** Refers to a Greek fable in which Zeus turns ants into men

WORDS FOR EVERYDAY USE

en • deav • or (en dev´ər) *n.*, effort; attempt. *Serious work has been done in the* endeavor *to promote world peace.*

pal • try (pôl´trē) *adj.*, insignificant. *The help he offered was so* paltry *that I ended up doing most of the work myself.*

error upon error, and clout upon clout, and our best virtue has for its occasion a <u>superfluous</u> and evitable wretchedness. Our life is frittered away by detail. An honest man has hardly need to count more than his ten fingers, or in extreme cases he may add his ten toes, and lump the rest. Simplicity, simplicity, simplicity! I say, let your affairs be as two or three, and not a hundred or a thousand; instead of a million count half a dozen, and keep your accounts on your thumb nail. In the midst of this chopping sea of civilized life, such are the clouds and storms and quicksands and thousand-and-one items to be allowed for, that a man has to live, if he would not founder and go to the bottom and not make his port at all, by dead reckoning, and he must be a great calculator indeed who succeeds. Simplify, simplify. Instead of three meals a day, if it be necessary eat but one, instead of a hundred dishes, five; and reduce other things in proportion. Our life is like a German Confederacy, made up of petty states, with its boundary forever <u>fluctuating</u>, so that even a German cannot tell you how it is bounded at any moment. The nation itself, with all its so called internal improvements, which, by the way, are all external and superficial, is just such an <u>unwieldy</u> and

Walden Pond, Concord, Massachusetts.

*What does Thoreau recommend?*

*What advice does Thoreau give?*

overgrown establishment, cluttered with furniture and tripped up by its own traps, ruined by luxury and heedless expense, by want of calculation and a worthy aim, as the million households in the land; and the only cure for it as for them is in a rigid economy, a stern and more than Spartan simplicity of life and elevation of purpose. It lives too fast. Men think that it is essential that the Nation have commerce, and export ice, and talk through a telegraph, and ride thirty miles an hour, without a doubt, whether they do or not; but whether we should live like baboons or like men, is a little uncertain. If we do not get out sleepers,[17] and forge rails, and devote days and nights to the work, but go to tinkering upon our lives to improve them, who will build railroads? And if railroads are not built, how shall we get to heaven in season? But if we stay at home and

*What does Thoreau think of "progress"?*

---

17. **sleepers.** Railroad ties

**WORDS FOR EVERYDAY USE**

su • per • flu • ous (sə pʉr´ flü əs) *adj.*, excessive. *After she had thanked me a dozen times, her gratitude began to seem* <u>superfluous</u>.

fluc • tu • ate (fluk´chü āt´) *vi.*, change or vary continuously. *The unpredictable stock market* <u>fluctuates</u> *from minute to minute.*

un • wield • y (un wēl´dē) *adj.*, hard to manage. *That large box is light but too* <u>unwieldy</u> *to move up the stairs alone.*

mind our business, who will want railroads? We do not ride on the railroad; it rides upon us. Did you ever think what those sleepers are that underlie the railroad? Each one is a man, an Irish-man, or a Yankee man. The rails are laid on them, and they are covered with sand, and the cars run smoothly over them. They are sound sleepers, I assure you. And every few years a new lot is laid down and run over; so that, if some have the pleasure of riding on a rail, others have the misfortune to be ridden upon. And when they run over a man that is walking in his sleep, a supernumerary[18] sleeper in the wrong position, and wake him up, they suddenly stop the cars, and make a hue and cry about it, as if this were an exception. I am glad to know that it takes a gang of men for every five miles to keep the sleepers down and level in their beds as it is, for this is a sign that they may sometime get up again.

Why should we live with such hurry and waste of life? We are determined to be starved before we are hungry. Men say that a stitch in time saves nine, and so they take a thousand stitches today to save nine tomorrow. As for work, we haven't any of any consequence. We have the Saint Vitus' dance[19] and cannot possibly keep our heads still. If I should only give a few pulls at the parish bell-rope, as for a fire, that is, without setting the bell, there is hardly a man on his farm in the outskirts of Concord, notwithstanding that press of engagements which was his excuse so many times this morning, nor a boy, nor a woman, I might almost say, but would forsake all and follow that sound, not mainly to save property from the flames, but, if we will confess the truth, much more to see it burn, since burn it must, and we, be it known, did not set it on fire,—or to see it put out, and have a hand in it, if that is done as handsomely; yes, even if it were the parish church itself. Hardly a man takes a half hour's nap after dinner, but when he wakes he holds up his head and asks "What's the news?" as if the rest of mankind had stood his sentinels. Some give

directions to be waked every half hour, doubtless for no other purpose; and then, to pay for it, they tell what they have dreamed. After a night's sleep the news is as indispensable as the breakfast. "Pray tell me any thing new that has happened to a man any where on this globe",—and he reads it over his coffee and rolls, that a man had had his eyes gouged out this morning on the Wachito River; never dreaming the while that he lives in the dark unfathomed mammoth cave of this world, and has but the rudiment of an eye himself.[20]

◆ ◆ ◆

I left the woods for as good a reason as I went there. Perhaps it seemed to me that I had several more lives to live, and could not spare any more time for that one. It is remarkable how easily and insensibly we fall into a particular route, and make a beaten track for ourselves. I had not lived there a week before my feet wore a path from my door to the pond-side; and though it is five or six years since I trod it, it is still quite distinct. It is true, I fear that others may have fallen into it, and so helped to keep it open. The surface of the earth is soft and impressible by the feet of men; and so with the paths which the mind travels. How worn and dusty, then, must be the highways of the world, how deep the ruts of tradition and conformity! I did not wish to take a cabin passage, but rather to go before the mast and on the deck of the world, for there I could best see the moonlight amid the mountains. I do not wish to go below now.

I learned this, at least, by my experiment; that if one advances confidently in the direction of his dreams, and endeavors to live the life which he has imagined, he will meet

*Why did Thoreau leave the woods? What easily happens to people?*

*What did Thoreau learn?*

---

18. **supernumerary.** Extra
19. **Saint Vitus' dance.** Refers to a nervous disorder with symptoms of jerky motions
20. **dark . . . himself.** Reference to sightless fish found in Mammoth Cave

with a success unexpected in common hours. He will put some things behind, will pass an invisible boundary; new, universal, and more liberal laws will begin to establish themselves around and within him; or old laws be expanded, and interpreted in his favor in a more liberal sense, and he will live with the license of a higher order of beings. In proportion as he simplifies his life, the laws of the universe will appear less complex, and solitude will not be solitude, nor poverty poverty, nor weakness weakness. If you have built castles in the air, your work need not be lost; that is where they should be. Now put the foundations under them.

It is a ridiculous demand which England and America make, that you shall speak so that they can understand you. Neither men nor toadstools grow so. As if that were important, and there were not enough to understand you without them. As if Nature could support but one order of understandings, could not sustain birds as well as quadrupeds, flying as well as creeping things, and *hush* and *who*, which Bright[21] can understand, were the best English. As if there were safety in stupidity alone. I fear chiefly lest my expression may not be *extra-vagant* enough, may not wander far enough beyond the narrow limits of my daily experience, so as to be adequate to the truth of which I have been convinced. *Extra vagance!* it depends on how you are yarded. The migrating buffalo, which seeks new pastures in another latitude, is not extravagant like the cow which kicks over the pail, leaps the cow-yard fence, and runs after her calf, in milking time. I desire to speak somewhere *without* bounds; like a

*If a man does not keep pace with his companions, perhaps it is because he hears a different drummer.*

man in a waking moment, to men in their waking moments; for I am convinced that I cannot exaggerate enough even to lay the foundation of a true expression. Who that has heard a strain of music feared then lest he should speak extravagantly any more forever? In view of the future or possible, we should live quite <u>laxly</u> and undefined in front, our outlines dim and misty on that side; as our shadows reveal an insensible perspiration toward the sun. The <u>volatile</u> truth of our words should continually betray the inadequacy of the residual statement. Their truth is instantly *translated*; its literal monument alone remains. The words which express our faith and piety are not definite; yet they are significant and fragrant like frankincense[22] to superior natures.

Why level downward to our dullest perception always, and praise that as common sense? The commonest sense is the sense of men asleep, which they express by snoring. Sometimes we are inclined to class those who are once-and-a-half witted with the half-witted, because we appreciate only a third part of their wit. Some would find fault with the morning-red, if they ever got up early enough. "They pretend," as I hear, "that the verses of Kabir have four different senses; illusion, spirit, intellect, and the exoteric doctrine of the Vedas;" but in this part of the world it is considered a ground for complaint if a man's writings admit of more than one interpretation. While England endeavors to cure the potato-rot, will not any endeavor to

---

21. **Bright.** Name for an ox
22. **frankincense.** Type of incense

**WORDS FOR EVERYDAY USE**

**lax • ly** (laks′lē) *adv.,* loosely; not strictly. *Jenna's parents enforce her curfew so <u>laxly</u> that she sometimes stays out all night.*

**vol • a • tile** (väl′ə təl) *adj.,* unstable; fleeting. *"Stand back," said the science teacher, "because this chemical mixture is quite <u>volatile</u>."*

cure the brain-rot, which prevails so much more widely and fatally?

I do not suppose that I have attained to obscurity, but I should be proud if no more fatal fault were found with my pages on this score than was found with the Walden ice. Southern customers objected to its blue color, which is the evidence of its purity, as if it were muddy, and preferred the Cambridge ice, which is white, but tastes of weeds. The purity men love is like the mists which envelop the earth, and not like the azure ether beyond.

Some are dinning in our ears that we Americans, and moderns generally, are intellectual dwarfs compared with the ancients, or even the Elizabethan[23] men. But what is that to the purpose? A living dog is better than a dead lion.[24] Shall a man go and hang himself because he belongs to the race of pygmies, and not be the biggest pygmy that he can? Let every one mind his own business, and endeavor to be what he was made.

What does Thoreau advocate?

Why should we be in such desperate haste to succeed, and in such desperate enterprises? If a man does not keep pace with his companions, perhaps it is because he hears a different drummer. Let him step to the music which he hears, however measured or far away. It is not important that he should mature as soon as an apple-tree or an oak. Shall he turn his spring into summer? If the condition of things which we were made for is not yet, what were any reality which we can substitute? We will not be shipwrecked on a vain reality. Shall we with pains erect a heaven of blue glass over ourselves, though when it is done we shall be sure to gaze still at the true ethereal heaven far above, as if the former were not? ∎

Title page of *Walden.*

---

23. **Elizabethan.** From the time of Queen Elizabeth I (1533–1603)
24. **A living . . . lion.** Ecclesiastes 9:4

# Respond *to the* SELECTION

Imagine you have lived like Thoreau in communion with nature in a vocation of your choice. What lessons do you think you might learn?

# INVESTIGATE, Inquire, Imagine

**Recall:** GATHERING FACTS

1a. According to Thoreau, age alone does not qualify people to be teachers of the young. Why not?

2a. Describe the area in which Thoreau built his home.

3a. Why did Thoreau decide to live in the woods for a while? Why did he decide to leave?

**Interpret:** FINDING MEANING

1b. Explain why Thoreau encourages us to examine our assumptions and "to give up our prejudices." Describe his attitudes toward what older people consider to be conventional wisdom.

2b. What evidence suggests that Thoreau was not interested in expending much money or time in building a home that others would admire?

3b. What does Thoreau mean when he urges the reader to "Simplify, simplify"?

**Analyze:** TAKING THINGS APART

4a. In what ways do you think Thoreau heard "a different drummer"?

**Synthesize:** BRINGING THINGS TOGETHER

4b. What did Thoreau learn from his experiment of life in the woods?

**Evaluate:** MAKING JUDGMENTS

5a. What is Thoreau's attitude towards work and progress? Do you agree or disagree with this philosophy? Explain your answer.

**Extend:** CONNECTING IDEAS

5b. If every person lived by Thoreau's philosophy that each person should only be concerned with his or her own business, how would the development of society be affected?

# Understanding Literature

APHORISM. Review the definition for **aphorism** in the Handbook of Literary Terms. This selection from *Walden* begins with a famous aphorism, "The mass of men lead lives of quiet desperation." The final paragraph includes what may be Thoreau's best-known statement: "If a man does not keep pace with his companions, perhaps it is because he hears a different drummer." Explain why these aphorisms are still popular today.

TONE. Read the definition of **tone** in the Handbook of Literary Terms. Consider such statements in this selection as these: "I have lived some thirty years on this planet, and I have yet to hear the first syllable of valuable or even earnest advice from my seniors"; "I have never yet met a man who was quite awake"; "Our life is frittered away by detail." What attitude toward the reader is implied with these statements? Whom does Thoreau expect to be his reader? How does he expect his reader to react to these statements?

# WRITER'S JOURNAL

1. Imagine that Thoreau has "left the woods" and wants to sell his small house there. Write a **real estate ad** accurately describing the building and highlighting its advantages. Assume you are hoping to attract a buyer with similar values as your own.

2. An **epitaph** is an inscription on a tomb or gravestone in memory of the person buried there. Write an epitaph for Henry David Thoreau.

3. Blues music uses a melancholy style to express sadness. Choose a quote from the selection and paraphrase it into a stanza or two of **blues lyrics**.

# Integrating *the* LANGUAGE ARTS

## Language, Grammar, and Style

**SIMPLIFYING SENTENCES.** Read the Language Arts Survey 3.35, "Correcting Wordy Sentences." Then revise these sentences, following Thoreau's edict to "Simplify, simplify."

1. The usual picture we get from *Walden* is that Thoreau lived a rather solitary life by himself.

2. However, many journal entries show how the neighbors who lived around Walden Pond were an important part of the writer's life.

3. For example, one neighbor lent Thoreau an axe, and he was careful to sharpen that axe before he returned the tool when he was finished with it.

4. Thoreau also notes that he had pleasant chats when he talked with people who were taking walks in his woods.

5. The passage about his contract with James Collins, in which he made a bargain with Collins to buy the boards of the Irishman's shanty, is amusing and makes the reader laugh.

## Critical Thinking

**PROBLEM SOLVING.** Read the Language Arts Survey 5.1, "Making Decisions and Solving Problems." Then analyze the selection as an example of problem solving, completing a diagram like the one in that section. If going into the woods was the action, what was the problem? What did Thoreau know already? What did he need to know? What did Thoreau expect to gain from the action? How did he evaluate and apply the results?

## Collaborative Learning

**NATURE WALK.** In Thoreau's essay "Walking," he refers to "the art of Walking" as "sauntering," which is derived "from idle people who roved about the country" in the Middle Ages. The walking that he speaks of "has nothing in it akin to taking exercise, . . . but is itself the enterprise and adventure of the day." Thoreau often wrote in his journals of the things he observed on his long walks. Plan and execute a leisurely walk in a nature area with a companion or with your class. Take notes on the experience and record them in your journal.

## Media Literacy

**ONLINE NEWSLETTER.** Inspired both by Henry David Thoreau's love of the natural world and his dislike of big government, the Thoreau Institute seeks ways to protect the environment without regulation, bureaucracy, or central control. The Institute was founded in 1975 to help environmentalists and others understand and influence public land management. Visit the **Thoreau Institute** website at http://www.walden.org and research its posted materials on Thoreau, transcendentalism, and environmental concerns. Report your findings to the class.

## from *Moby-Dick* by Herman Melville

### I.   Loomings

Call me Ishmael. Some years ago — never mind how long precisely — having little or no money in my purse, and nothing particular to interest me on shore, I thought I would sail about a little and see the watery part of the world. It is a way I have of driving off the spleen, and regulating the circulation. Whenever I find myself growing grim about the mouth; whenever it is a damp, drizzly November in my soul; whenever I find myself involuntarily pausing before coffin warehouses, and bringing up the rear of every funeral I meet; and especially whenever my hypos get such an upper hand of me, that it requires a strong moral principle to prevent me from deliberately stepping into the street, and methodically knocking people's hats off — then, I account it high time to get to sea as soon as I can. This is my substitute for pistol and ball. With a philosophical flourish Cato throws himself upon his sword; I quietly take to the ship. There is nothing surprising in this. If they but knew it, almost all men in their degree, some time or other, cherish very nearly the same feelings towards the ocean with me.

There now is your insular city of the Manhattoes, belted round by wharves as Indian isles by coral reefs — commerce surrounds it with her surf. Right and left, the streets take you waterward. Its extreme down-town is the battery, where that noble mole is washed by waves, and cooled by breezes, which a few hours previous were out of sight of land. Look at the crowds of water-gazers there.

Circumambulate the city of a dreamy Sabbath afternoon. Go from Corlears Hook to Coenties Slip, and from thence, by Whitehall, northward. What do you see? — Posted like silent sentinels all around the town, stand thousands upon thousands of mortal men fixed in ocean reveries. Some leaning against the spiles; some seated upon the pier-heads; some looking over the bulwarks of ships from China; some high aloft in the rigging, as if striving to get a still better seaward peep. But these are all landsmen; of week days pent up in lath and plaster — tied to counters, nailed to benches, clinched to desks. How then is this? Are the green fields gone? What do they here?

But look! here come more crowds, pacing straight for the water, and seemingly bound for a dive. Strange! Nothing will content them but the extremest limit of the land; loitering under the shady lee of yonder warehouses will not suffice. No. They must get just as nigh the water as they possibly can without falling in. And there they stand — miles of them — leagues. Inlanders all, they come from lanes and alleys, streets and avenues — north, east, south, and west. Yet here they all unite. Tell me, does the magnetic virtue of the needles of the compasses of all those ships attract them thither?

Once more. Say, you are in the country; in some high land of lakes. Take almost any path you please, and ten to one it carries you down in a dale, and leaves you there by a pool in the stream. There is magic in it. Let the most absent-minded of men be plunged in his deepest reveries — stand that man on his legs, set his feet a-going, and he will infallibly lead you to water, if water there be in all that region. Should you ever be athirst in the great American desert, try this experiment, if your caravan happen to be supplied with a metaphysical professor. Yes, as every one knows, meditation and water are welded for ever.

But here is an artist. He desires to paint you the dreamiest, shadiest, quietest, most enchanting bit of romantic landscape in all the valley of the Saco. What is the chief element he employs? There stand his trees, each with a hollow trunk, as if a hermit and a crucifix were within; and here sleeps his meadow, and there sleep his cattle; and up from yonder cottage goes a sleepy smoke. Deep into distant woodlands winds a mazy way, reaching to overlapping spurs of mountains bathed in their hill-side blue. But though the picture lies thus tranced, and though this pine-tree shakes down its sighs like leaves upon this shepherd's head, yet all were vain, unless the shepherd's eye were fixed upon the magic stream before him. Go visit the Prairies in June, when for scores on scores of miles you wade knee-deep among Tiger-lilies — what is the one charm wanting? — Water — there is not a drop of water there! Were Niagara but a cataract of sand, would you travel your thousand miles to see it? Why did the poor poet of Tennessee, upon suddenly receiving two handfuls of silver, deliberate whether to buy him a coat, which he sadly needed, or invest his money in a pedestrian trip to Rockaway Beach? Why is almost every robust healthy boy with a robust healthy soul in him, at some time or other crazy to go to sea? Why upon your first voyage as a passenger, did you yourself feel such a mystical vibration, when first told that you and your ship were now out of sight of land? Why did the old Persians hold the sea holy? Why did the Greeks give it a separate deity, and own brother of Jove? Surely all this is not without meaning. And still deeper the meaning of that story of Narcissus, who because he could not grasp the tormenting, mild image he saw in the fountain, plunged into it and was drowned. But that same image, we ourselves see in all rivers and oceans. It is the image of the ungraspable phantom of life; and this is the key to it all.

Now, when I say that I am in the habit of going to sea whenever I begin to grow hazy about the eyes, and begin to be over conscious of my lungs, I do not mean to have it inferred that I ever go to sea as a passenger. For to go as a passenger you must needs have a purse, and a purse is but a rag unless you have something in it. Besides, passengers get sea-sick — grow quarrelsome — don't sleep at nights — do not enjoy themselves much, as a general thing; — no, I never go as a passenger; nor, though I am something of a salt, do I ever go to sea as a Commodore, or a Captain, or a Cook. I abandon the glory and distinction of such offices to those who like them. For my part, I abominate all honorable respectable toils, trials, and tribulations of every kind whatsoever. It is quite as much as I can do to take care of myself, without taking care of ships, barques, brigs, schooners, and what not. And as for going as cook, — though I confess there is considerable glory in that, a cook being a sort of officer on ship-board — yet, somehow, I never fancied broiling fowls; — though once broiled, judiciously buttered, and judgmatically salted and peppered, there is no one who will speak more respectfully, not to say reverentially, of a broiled fowl than I will. It is out of the idolatrous dotings of the old Egyptians upon broiled ibis and roasted river horse, that you see the mummies of those creatures in their huge bake-houses the pyramids.

No, when I go to sea, I go as a simple sailor, right before the mast, plumb down into the forecastle, aloft there to the royal mast-head. True, they rather order me about some, and make me jump from spar to spar, like a grasshopper in a May meadow. And at first, this sort of thing is unpleasant enough. It touches one's sense of honor, particularly if you come of an old established family in the land, the Van Rensselaers, or Randolphs, or Hardicanutes. And more than all, if just previous to putting your hand into the tar-pot, you have been lording it as a country schoolmaster, making the tallest boys stand in awe of you. The transition is a keen one, I assure you, from a schoolmaster to a sailor, and requires a strong decoction of Seneca and the Stoics to enable you to grin and bear it. But even this wears off in time.

What of it, if some old hunks of a sea-captain orders me to get a broom and sweep down the decks? What does that indignity amount to, weighed, I mean, in the scales of the New Testament? Do you think the archangel Gabriel thinks anything the less of me, because I promptly and respectfully obey that old hunks in that particular instance? Who aint a slave? Tell me that. Well, then, however the old sea-captains may order me about — however they may thump and punch me about, I have the satisfaction of knowing that it is all right; that everybody else is one way or other served in much the same way — either in a physical or metaphysical point of view, that is; and so the universal thump is passed round, and all hands should rub each other's shoulder-blades, and be content.

Again, I always go to sea as a sailor, because they make a point of paying me for my trouble, whereas they never pay passengers a single penny that I ever heard of. On the contrary, passengers themselves must pay. And there is all the difference in the world between paying and being paid. The act of paying is perhaps the most uncomfortable infliction that the two orchard thieves entailed upon us. But *being paid*, — what will compare with it? The urbane activity with which a man receives money is really marvellous, considering that we so earnestly believe money to be the root of all earthly ills, and that on no account can a monied man enter heaven. Ah! how cheerfully we consign ourselves to perdition!

Finally, I always go to sea as a sailor, because of the wholesome exercise and pure air of the forecastle deck. For as in this world, head winds are far more prevalent than winds from astern (that is, if you never violate the Pythagorean maxim), so for the most part the Commodore on the quarter-deck gets his atmosphere at second hand from the sailors on the forecastle. He thinks he breathes it first; but not so. In much the same way do the commonalty lead their leaders in many other things, at the same time that the leaders little suspect it. But wherefore it was that after having repeatedly smelt the sea as a merchant sailor, I should now take it into my head to go on a whaling voyage; this the invisible police officer of the Fates, who has the constant surveillance of me, and secretly dogs me, and influences me in some unaccountable way — he can better answer than any one else. And, doubtless, my going on this whaling voyage, formed part of the grand programme of Providence that was drawn up a long time ago. It came in as a sort of brief interlude and solo between more extensive performances. I take it that this part of the bill must have run something like this:

"*Grand Contested Election for the Presidency of the United States.*
"Whaling Voyage by One Ishmael.
"Bloody Battle in Afghanistan."

Though I cannot tell why it was exactly that those stage managers, the Fates, put me down for this shabby part of a whaling voyage, when others were set down for magnificent parts in high tragedies, and short and easy parts in genteel comedies, and jolly parts in farces — though I cannot tell why this was exactly; yet, now that I recall all the circumstances, I think I can see a little into the springs and motives which being cunningly presented to me under various disguises, induced me to set about performing the part I did, besides cajoling me into the delusion that it was a choice resulting from my own unbiased freewill and discriminating judgment.

Chief among these motives was the overwhelming idea of the great whale himself. Such a portentous and mysterious monster roused all my curiosity. Then the wild and distant seas where he rolled his island bulk; the undeliverable, nameless perils of the whale; these, with all the attending marvels of a thousand Patagonian sights and sounds, helped to sway me to my wish. With other men, perhaps, such things would not have been inducements; but as for me, I am tormented with an everlasting itch for things remote. I love to sail forbidden seas, and land on barbarous coasts. Not ignoring what is good, I am quick to perceive a horror, and could still be social with it — would they let me — since it is but well to be on friendly terms with all the inmates of the place one lodges in.

By reason of these things, then, the whaling voyage was welcome; the great flood-gates of the wonder-world swung open, and in the wild conceits that swayed me to my purpose, two and two there floated into my inmost soul, endless processions of the whale, and, mid most of them all, one grand hooded phantom, like a snow hill in the air.

## "Transcendental Wild Oats" by Louisa May Alcott

A Chapter from an Unwritten Romance
*Independent*, 18 December 1873

On the first day of June, 184–, a large wagon, drawn by a small horse and containing a motley load, went lumbering over certain New England hills, with the pleasing accompaniments of wind, rain, and hail. A serene man with a serene child upon his knee was driving, or rather being driven, for the small horse had it all his own way. A brown boy with a William Penn style of countenance sat beside him, firmly embracing a bust of Socrates. Behind them was an energetic-looking woman, with a benevolent brow, satirical mouth, and eyes brimful of hope and courage. A baby reposed upon her lap, a mirror leaned against her knee, and a basket of provisions danced about at her feet, as she struggled with a large, unruly umbrella. Two blue-eyed little girls, with hands full of childish treasures, sat under one old shawl, chatting happily together.

In front of this lively party stalked a tall, sharp-featured man, in a long blue cloak; and a fourth small girl trudged along beside him through the mud as if she rather enjoyed it.

The wind whistled over the bleak hills; the rain fell in a despondent drizzle, and twilight began to fall. But the calm man gazed as tranquilly into the fog as if he beheld a radiant bow of promise spanning the gray sky. The cheery woman tried to cover every one but herself with the big umbrella. The brown boy pillowed his head on the bald pate of Socrates and slumbered peacefully. The little girls sang lullabies to their dolls in soft, maternal murmurs. The sharp-nosed pedestrian marched steadily on, with the blue cloak streaming out behind him like a banner; and the lively infant splashed through the puddles with a duck-like satisfaction pleasant to behold.

Thus these modern pilgrims journeyed hopefully out of the old world, to found a new one in the wilderness.

The editors of *The Transcendental Tripod* had received from Messrs. Lion & Lamb (two of the aforesaid pilgrims) a communication from which the following statement is an extract: —

"We have made arrangements with the proprietor of an estate of about a hundred acres which liberates this tract from human ownership. Here we shall prosecute our effort to initiate a Family in harmony with the primitive instincts of man.

"Ordinary secular farming is not our object. Fruit, grain, pulse, herbs, flax, and other vegetable products, receiving assiduous attention, will afford ample manual occupation, and chaste supplies for the bodily needs. It is intended to adorn the pastures with orchards, and to supersede the labor of cattle by the spade and the pruning-knife.

"Consecrated to human freedom, the land awaits the sober culture of devoted men. Beginning with small pecuniary means, this enterprise must be rooted in a reliance on the succors of an ever-bounteous Providence, whose vital affinities being secured by this union with uncorrupted field and unworldly persons, the cares and injuries of a life of gain are avoided.

"The inner nature of each member of the Family is at no time neglected. Our plan contemplates all such disciplines, cultures, and habits as evidently conduce to the purifying of the inmates.

"Pledged to the spirit alone, the founders anticipate no hasty or numerous addition to their numbers. The kingdom of peace is entered only through the gates of self-denial; and felicity is the test and the reward of loyalty to the unswerving law of Love."

This prospective Eden at present consisted of an old red farmhouse, a dilapidated barn, many acres of meadow-land, and a grove. Ten ancient apple-trees were all the "chaste supply" which the place offered as yet; but, in the firm belief that plenteous orchards were soon to be evoked from their inner consciousness, these sanguine founders had christened their domain Fruitlands.

Here Timon Lion intended to found a colony of Latter Day Saints, who, under his patriarchal sway, should regenerate the world and glorify his name for ever. Here Abel Lamb, with the devoutest faith in the high ideal which was to him a living truth, desired to plant a Paradise, where Beauty, Virtue, Justice, and Love might live happily together, without the possibility of a serpent entering in. And here his wife, unconverted but faithful to the end, hoped, and after many wanderings over the face of the earth, to find rest for herself and a home for her children.

"There is our new abode," announced the enthusiast, smiling with a satisfaction quite undampened by the drops dripping from his hat-brim, as they turned at length into a cart-path that wound along a steep hillside into a barren-looking valley.

"A little difficult of access," observed his practical wife, as she endeavored to keep her various household goods from going overboard with every lurch of the laden ark.

"Like all good things. But those who earnestly desire and patiently seek will soon find us," placidly responded the philosopher from the mud, through which he was now endeavoring to pilot the much-enduring horse.

"Truth lies at the bottom of a well, Sister Hope," said Brother Timon, pausing to detach his small comrade from a gate, whereon she was perched for a clearer gaze into futurity.

"That's the reason we so seldom get at it, I suppose," replied Mrs. Hope, making a vain clutch at the mirror, which a sudden jolt sent flying out of her hands.

"We want no false reflections here," said Timon, with a grim smile, as he crunched the fragments under foot in his onward march.

Sister Hope held her peace, and looked wistfully through the mist at her promised home. The old red house with a hospitable glimmer at its windows cheered her eyes; and, considering the weather, was a fitter refuge than the sylvan bowers some of the more ardent souls might have preferred.

The new-comers were welcomed by one of the elect precious, — a regenerate farmer, whose idea of reform consisted chiefly in wearing white cotton raiment and shoes of untanned leather. This costume, with a snowy beard, gave him a venerable, and at the same time a somewhat bridal appearance.

The goods and chattels of the Society not having arrived, the weary family reposed before the fire on blocks of wood, while Brother Moses White regaled them with roasted potatoes, brown bread and water, in two plates, a tin pan, and one mug; his table service being limited. But, having cast the forms and vanities of a depraved world behind them, the elders welcomed hardship with the enthusiasm of new pioneers, and the children heartily enjoyed this foretaste of what they believed was to be a sort of perpetual picnic.

During the progress of this frugal meal, two more brothers appeared. One a dark, melancholy man, clad in homespun, whose peculiar mission was to turn his name hind part before and use as few words as possible. The other was a bland, bearded Englishman, who expected to be saved by eating uncooked food and going without clothes. He had not yet adopted the primitive costume, however; but contented himself with meditatively chewing dry beans out of a basket.

"Every meal should be a sacrament, and the vessels used should be beautiful and symbolical," observed Brother Lamb, mildly, righting the tin pan slipping about on his knees. "I priced a silver service when in town, but it was too costly; so I got some graceful cups and vases of Britannia ware."

"Hardest things in the world to keep bright. Will whiting be allowed in the community?" inquired Sister Hope, with a housewife's interest in labor-saving institutions.

"Such trivial questions will be discussed at a more fitting time," answered Brother Timon, sharply, as he burnt his fingers with a very hot potato. "Neither sugar, molasses, milk, butter, cheese, nor flesh are to be used among us, for nothing is to be admitted which has caused wrong or death to man or beast."

"Our garments are to be linen till we learn to raise our own cotton or some substitute for woolen fabrics," added Brother Abel, blissfully basking in an imaginary future as warm and brilliant as the generous fire before him.

"Haou abaout shoes?" asked Brother Moses, surveying his own with interest.

"We must yield that point till we can manufacture an innocent substitute for leather. Bark, wood, or some durable fabric will be invented in time. Meanwhile, those who desire to carry out our idea to the fullest extent can go barefooted," said Lion, who liked extreme measures.

"I never will, nor let my girls," murmured rebellious Sister Hope, under her breath.

"Haou do you cattle'ate to treat the ten-acre lot? Ef things ain't 'tended to right smart, we shan't hev no crops," observed the practical patriarch in cotton.

"We shall spade it," replied Abel, in such perfect good faith that Moses said no more, though he indulged in a shake of the head as he glanced at hands that had held nothing heavier than a pen for years. He was a paternal old soul and regarded the younger men as promising boys on a new sort of lark.

"What shall we do for lamps, if we cannot use any animal substance? I do hope light of some sort is to be thrown upon the enterprise," said Mrs. Lamb, with anxiety, for in those days kerosene and camphene were not, and gas unknown in the wilderness.

"We shall go without till we have discovered some vegetable oil or wax to serve us," replied Brother Timon, in a decided tone, which caused Sister Hope to resolve that her private lamp should be always trimmed, if not burning.

"Each member is to perform the work for which experience, strength, and taste best fit him," continued Dictator Lion. "Thus drudgery and disorder will be avoided and harmony prevail. We shall rise at dawn, begin the day by bathing, followed by music, and then a chaste repast of fruit and bread. Each one finds congenial occupation till the meridian meal; when some deep-searching conversation gives rest to the body and development to the mind. Healthful labor again engages us till the last meal, when we assemble in social communion, prolonged till sunset, when we retire to sweet repose, ready for the next day's activity."

"What part of the work do you incline to yourself?" asked Sister Hope, with a humorous glimmer in her keen eyes.

"I shall wait till it is made clear to me. Being in preference to doing is the great aim, and this comes to us rather by a resigned willingness than a wilful activity, which is a check to all divine growth," responded Brother Timon.

"I thought so." And Mrs. Lamb sighed audibly, for during the year he had spent in her family Brother Timon had so faithfully carried out his idea of "being, not doing," that she had found his "divine growth" both an expensive and unsatisfactory process.

Here her husband struck into the conversation, his face shining with the light and joy of the splendid dreams and high ideals hovering before him.

"In these steps of reform, we do not rely so much on scientific reasoning or physiological skill as on the spirit's dictates. The greater part of man's duty consists in leaving alone much that he now does. Shall I stimulate with tea, coffee, or wine? No. Shall I consume flesh? Not if I value health. Shall I subjugate cattle? Shall I claim property in any created thing? Shall I trade? Shall I adopt a form of religion? Shall I interest myself in politics? To how many of these questions — could we ask them deeply enough and could they be heard as having relation to our eternal welfare — would the response be 'Abstain'?"

A mild snore seemed to echo the last word of Abel's rhapsody, for Brother Moses had succumbed to mundane slumber and sat nodding like a massive ghost. Forest Absalom, the silent man, and John Pease, the English member, now departed to the barn; and Mrs. Lamb led her flock to a temporary fold, leaving the founders of the "Consociate Family" to build castles in the air till the fire went out and the symposium ended in smoke.

The furniture arrived next day, and was soon bestowed; for the principal property of the community consisted in books. To this rare library was devoted the best room in the house, and the few busts and pictures that still survived many flittings were added to beautify the sanctuary, for here the family was to meet for amusement, instruction, and worship.

Any housewife can imagine the emotions of Sister Hope, when she took possession of a large, dilapidated kitchen, containing an old stove and the peculiar stores out of which food was to be evolved for her little family of eleven. Cakes of maple sugar, dried peas and beans, barley and hominy, meal of all sorts, potatoes, and dried fruit. No milk, butter, cheese, tea, or meat appeared. Even salt was considered a useless luxury and spice entirely forbidden by these lovers of Spartan simplicity. A ten years' experience of vegetarian vagaries had been good training for this new freak, and her sense of the ludicrous supported her through many trying scenes.

Unleavened bread, porridge, and water for breakfast; bread, vegetables, and water for dinner; bread, fruit, and water for supper was the bill of fare ordained by the elders. No teapot profaned that sacred stove, no gory steak cried aloud for vengeance from her chaste gridiron; and only a brave woman's taste, time, and temper were sacrificed on that domestic altar.

The vexed question of light was settled by buying a quantity of bayberry wax for candles; and, on discovering that no one knew how to make them, pine knots were introduced, to be used when absolutely necessary. Being summer, the evenings were not long, and the weary fraternity found it no great hardship to retire with the birds. The inner light was sufficient for most of them. But Mrs. Lamb rebelled. Evening was the only time she had to herself, and while the tired feet rested the skillful hands mended torn frocks and little stockings, or anxious heart forgot its burden in a book.

So "mother's lamp" burned steadily, while the philosophers built a new heaven and earth by moonlight; and through all the metaphysical mists and philanthropic pyrotechnics of that period Sister Hope played her own little game of "throwing light," and none but the moths were the worse for it.

Such farming probably was never seen before since Adam delved. The band of brothers began by spading garden and field; but a few days of it lessened their ardor amazingly. Blistered hands and aching backs suggested the expediency of permitting the use of cattle till the workers were better fitted for noble toil by a summer of the new life.

Brother Moses brought a yoke of oxen from his farm, — at least, the philosophers thought so till it was discovered that one of the animals was a cow; and Moses confessed that he "must be let down easy, for he couldn't live on garden sarse entirely."

Great was Dictator Lion's indignation at this lapse from virtue. But time pressed, the work must be done; so the meek cow was permitted to wear the yoke and the recreant brother continued to enjoy forbidden draughts in the barn, which dark proceeding caused the children to regard him as one set apart for destruction.

The sowing was equally peculiar, for, owing to some mistake, the three brethren, who devoted themselves to this graceful task, found when about half through the job that each had been sowing a different sort of grain in the same field; a mistake which caused much perplexity; as it could not be remedied; but, after a long consultation and a good deal of laughter, it was decided to say nothing and see what would come of it.

The garden was planted with a generous supply of useful roots and herbs; but, as manure was not allowed to profane the virgin soil, few of these vegetable treasures ever came up. Purslane reigned supreme, and the disappointed planters ate it philosophically, deciding that Nature knew what was best for them, and would generously supply their needs, if they could only learn to digest her "sallets" and wild roots.

The orchard was laid out, a little grafting done, new trees and vines set, regardless of the unfit season and entire ignorance of the husbandmen, who honestly believed that in the autumn they would reap a bounteous harvest.

Slowly things got into order, and rapidly rumors of the new experiment went abroad, causing many strange spirits to flock thither, for in those days communities were the fashion and transcendentalism raged wildly. Some came to look on and laugh, some to be supported in poetic idleness, a few to believe sincerely and work heartily. Each member was allowed to mount his favorite hobby and ride it to his heart's content. Very queer were some of the riders, and very rampant some of the hobbies.

One youth, believing that language was of little consequence if the spirit was only right, startled new-comers by blandly greeting them with "Good-morning, damn you," and other remarks of an equally mixed order. A second irresponsible being held that all the emotions of the soul should be freely expressed, and illustrated his theory by antics that would have sent him to a lunatic asylum, if, as an unregenerate wag said, he had not already been in one. When his spirit soared, he climbed trees and shouted; when doubt assailed him, he lay upon the floor and groaned lamentably. At joyful periods, he raced, leaped, and sang; when sad, he wept aloud; and when a great thought burst upon him in the watches of the night, he crowed like a jocund cockerel, to the great delight of the children and the great annoyance of the elders. One musical brother fiddled whenever so moved, sang sentimentally to the four little girls, and put a music-box on the wall when he hoed corn.

Brother Pease ground away at his uncooked food, or browsed over the farm on sorrel, mint, green fruit, and new vegetables. Occasionally he took his walks abroad, airily attired in an unbleached cotton *poncho*, which was the nearest approach to the primeval costume he was allowed to indulge in. At midsummer he retired to the wilderness, to try his plan where the woodchucks were without prejudices and huckleberry-bushes were hospitably full. A sunstroke unfortunately spoilt his plan, and he returned to semi-civilization a sadder and wiser man.

Forest Absalom preserved his Pythagorean silence, cultivated his fine dark locks, and worked like a beaver, setting an excellent example of brotherly love, justice, and fidelity by his upright life. He it was who helped overworked Sister Hope with her heavy washes, kneaded the endless succession of batches of bread, watched over the children, and did the many tasks left undone by the brethren, who were so busy discussing and defining great duties that they forgot to perform the small ones.

Moses White placidly plodded about, "chorin' raound," as he called it, looking like an old-time patriarch, with his silver hair and flowing beard, and saving the community from many a mishap by his thrift and Yankee shrewdness.

Brother Lion domineered over the whole concern; for, having put the most money into the speculation, he was resolved to make it pay, — as if anything founded on an ideal basis could be expected to do so by any but enthusiasts.

Abel Lamb simply revelled in the Newness, firmly believing that his dream was to be beautifully realized and in time not only little Fruitlands, but the whole earth, be turned into a

Happy Valley. He worked with every muscle of his body, for *he* was in deadly earnest. He taught with his whole head and heart; planned and sacrificed, preached and prophesied, with a soul full of the purest aspirations, most unselfish purposes, and desires for a life devoted to God and man, too high and tender to bear the rough usage of this world.

It was a little remarkable that only one woman ever joined his community. Mrs. Lamb merely followed wheresoever her husband led, — "as ballast for his balloon," as she said, in her bright way.

Miss Jane Gage was a stout lady of mature years, sentimental, amiable, and lazy. She wrote verses copiously, and had vague yearnings and graspings after the unknown, which led her to believe herself fitted for a higher sphere than any she had yet adorned.

Having been a teacher, she was set to instructing the children in the common branches. Each adult member took a turn at the infants; and, as each taught in his own way, the result was a chronic state of chaos in the minds of these much-afflicted innocents.

Sleep, food, and poetic musings were the desires of dear Jane's life, and she shirked all duties as clogs upon her spirit's wings. Any thought of lending a hand with the domestic drudgery never occurred to her; and when to the question, "Art there any beasts of burden on the place?" Mrs. Lamb answered, with a face that told its own tale, "Only one woman!" the buxom Jane took no shame to herself, but laughed at the joke, and let the stout-hearted sister tug on alone.

Unfortunately, the poor lady hankered after the flesh-pots, and endeavored to stay herself with private sips of milk, crackers, and cheese, and on one dire occasion she partook of fish at a neighbor's table.

One of the children reported this sad lapse from virtue, and poor Jane was publicly reprimanded by Timon.

"I only took a little bit of the tail," sobbed the penitent poetess.

"Yes, but the whole fish had to be tortured and slain that you might tempt your carnal appetite with that one taste of the tail. Know ye not, consumers of flesh meat, that ye are nourishing the wolf and tiger in your bosoms?"

At this awful question and the peal of laughter which arose from some of the younger brethren, tickled by the ludicrous contrast between the stout sinner, the stern judge, and the naughty satisfaction of the young detective, poor Jane fled from the room to pack her trunk and return to a world where fishes' tails were not forbidden fruit.

Transcendental wild oats were sown broadcast that year, and the fame thereof has not yet ceased in the land; for, futile as this crop seemed to outsiders, it bore an invisible harvest, worth much to those who planted in earnest. As none of the members of this particular community have ever recounted their experiences before, a few of them may not be amiss, since the interest in these attempts has never died out and Fruitlands was the most ideal of all these castles in Spain.

A new dress was invented, since cotton, silk, and wool were forbidden as the product of slave-labor, worm-slaughter, and sheep-robbery. Tunics and trowsers of brown linen were the only wear. The women's skirts were longer, and their straw hat-brims wider than the men's, and this was the only difference. Some persecution lent a charm to the costume, and the long-haired, linen-clad reformers quite enjoyed the mild martyrdom they endured when they left home.

Money was abjured, as the root of all evil. The produce of the land was to supply most of their wants, or be exchanged for the few things they could not grow. This idea had its inconveniences; but self-denial was the fashion, and it was surprising how many things one can do without. When they desired to travel, they walked, if possible, begged the loan of a vehicle, or boldly entered car or coach, and, stating their principles to the officials, took the consequences. Usually their dress, their earnest frankness, and gentle resolution won them a passage; but now and then they met with hard usage, and had the satisfaction of suffering for their principles.

On one of these penniless pilgrimages they took passage on a boat, and, when fare was demanded, artlessly offered to talk, instead of pay. As the boat was well under way and they actually had not a cent, there was no help for it. So Brothers Lion and Lamb held forth to the assembled passengers in their most eloquent style. There must have been something effective in this conversation, for the listeners were moved to take up a contribution for these inspired lunatics, who preached peace on earth and good-will to man so earnestly, with empty pockets. A goodly sum was collected; but when the captain presented it the reformers proved that they were consistent even in their madness, for not a penny would they accept, saying, with a look at the group about them, whose indifference or contempt had changed to interest and respect, "You see how well we get on without money"; and so went serenely on their way, with their linen blouses flapping airily in the cold October wind.

They preached vegetarianism everywhere and resisted all temptations of the flesh, contentedly eating apples and bread at well-spread tables, and much afflicting hospitable hostesses by denouncing their food and taking away their appetite, discussing the "horrors of shambles," and "incorporation of the brute in man," and "on elegant abstinence the sign of a pure soul." But, when the perplexed or offended ladies asked what they should eat, they got in reply a bill of fare consisting of "bowls of sunrise for breakfast," "solar seeds of the sphere," "dishes from Plutarch's chaste table," and other viands equally hard to find in any modern market.

Reform conventions of all sorts were haunted by these brethren, who said many wise things and did many foolish ones. Unfortunately, these wanderings interfered with their harvest at home; but the rule was to do what the spirit moved, so they left their crops to Providence and went a-reaping in wider and, let us hope, more fruitful fields than their own.

Luckily, the earthly providence who watched over Abel Lamb was at hand to glean the scanty crop yielded by the "uncorrupted land," which "consecrated to human freedom," had received "the sober culture of devout men."

About the time the grain was ready to house, some call of the Oversoul wafted all the men away. An easterly storm was coming up and the yellow stacks were sure to be ruined. Then Sister Hope gathered her forces. Three little girls, one boy (Timon's son), and herself, harnessed to clothes-baskets and Russia-linen sheets, were the only teams she could command; but with these poor appliances the indomitable woman got in the grain and saved the food for her young, with the instinct and energy of a mother-bird with a brood of hungry nestlings to feed.

This attempt at regeneration had its tragic as well as comic side, though the world only saw the former.

With the first frosts, the butterflies, who had sunned themselves in the new light through the summer, took flight, leaving the few bees to see what honey they had stored for winter use. Precious little appeared beyond the satisfaction of a few months of holy living.

At first it seemed as if a chance to try holy dying also was to be offered them. Timon, much disgusted with the failure of the scheme, decided to retire to the Shakers, who seemed to be the only successful community going.

"What is to become of us?" asked Mrs. Hope, for Abel was heartbroken at the bursting of his lovely bubble.

"You can stay here, if you like, till a tenant is found. No more wood must be cut, however, and no more corn ground. All I have must be sold to pay the debts of the concern, as the responsibility rests with me," was the cheering reply.

"Who is to pay us for what we have lost? I gave all I had, — furniture, time, strength, six months of my children's lives, — and all are wasted. Abel gave himself body and soul, and is almost wrecked by hard work and disappointment. Are we to have no return for this, but leave to starve and freeze in an old house, with winter at hand, no money, and hardly a friend left; for this wild scheme has alienated nearly all we had. You talk much about justice. Let us have a little, since there is nothing else left."

But the woman's appeal met with no reply but the old one: "It was an experiment. We all risked something, and must bear our losses as we can."

With this cold comfort, Timon departed with his son, and was absorbed into the Shaker brotherhood, where he soon found that the order of things was reversed, and it was all work and no play.

Then the tragedy began for the forsaken little family. Desolation and despair fell upon Abel. As his wife said, his new beliefs had alienated many friends. Some thought him mad, some unprincipled. Even the most kindly thought him a visionary, whom it was useless to help till he took more practical views of life. All stood aloof, saying, "Let him work out his own ideas, and see what they are worth."

He had tried, but it was a failure. The world was not ready for Utopia yet, and those who attempted to found it only got laughed at for their pains. In other days, men could sell all and give to the poor, lead lives devoted to holiness and high thought, and, after the persecution was over, find themselves honored as saints or martyrs. But in modern times these things are out of fashion. To live for one's principles, at all costs, is a dangerous speculation; and the failure of an ideal, no matter how humane and noble, is harder for the world to forgive and forget than bank robbery or the grand swindles of corrupt politicians.

Deep waters now for Abel, and for a time there seemed no passage through. Strength and spirits were exhausted by hard work and too much thought. Courage failed when, looking about for help, he saw no sympathizing face, no hand out-stretched to help him, no voice to say cheerily,

"We all make mistakes, and it takes many experiences to shape a life. Try again, and let us help you."

Every door was closed, every eye averted, every heart cold, and no way open whereby he might earn bread for his children. His principles would not permit him to do many things that others did; and in the few fields where conscience would allow him to work, who would employ a man who had flown in the face of society, as he had done?

Then this dreamer, whose dream was the life of his life, resolved to carry out his idea to the bitter end. There seemed no place for him here, — no work, no friend. To go begging conditions was as ignoble as to go begging money. Better perish of want than sell one's soul for the sustenance of his body. Silently he lay down upon his bed, turned his face to the wall, and waited with pathetic patience for death to cut the knot which he could not untie. Days and nights went by, and neither food nor water passed his lips. Soul and body were dumbly struggling together, and no word of complaint betrayed what either suffered.

His wife, when tears and prayers were unavailing, sat down to wait the end with a mysterious awe and submission; for in this entire resignation of all things there was an eloquent significance to her who knew him as no other human being did.

"Leave all to God," was his belief; and in this crisis the loving soul clung to this faith, sure that the Allwise Father would not desert this child who tried to live so near to Him. Gathering her children about her, she waited the issue of the tragedy that was being enacted in that solitary room, while the first snow fell outside, untrodden by the foot-prints of a single friend.

But the strong angels who sustain and teach perplexed and troubled souls came and went, leaving no trace without, but working miracles within. For, when all other sentiments had faded into dimness, all other hopes died utterly; when the bitterness of death was nearly over, when body was past any pang of hunger or thirst, and soul stood ready to depart, the love that outlives all else refused to die. Head had bowed to defeat, hand had grown weary with too heavy tasks, but heart could not grow cold to those who lived in its tender depths, even when death touched it.

"My faithful wife, my little girls, — they have not forsaken me, they are mine by ties that none can break. What right have I to leave them alone? What right to escape from the burden and the sorrow I have helped to bring? This duty remains to me, and I must do it manfully. For their sakes, the world will forgive me in time; for their sakes, God will sustain me now."

Too feeble to rise, Abel groped for the food that always lay within his reach, and in the darkness and solitude of that memorable night ate and drank what was to him the bread and wine of a new communion, a new dedication of heart and life to the duties that were left him when the dreams fled.

In the early dawn, when that sad wife crept fearfully to see what change had come to the patient face on the pillow, she found it smiling at her, saw a wasted hand outstretched to her, and heard a feeble voice cry bravely, "Hope!"

What passed in that little room is not to be recorded except in the hearts of those who suffered and endured much for love's sake. Enough for us to know that soon the wan shadow of a man came forth, leaning on the arm that never failed him, to be welcomed and cherished by the children, who never forgot the experiences of that time.

"Hope," was the watchword now; and, while the last logs blazed on the hearth, the last bread and apples covered the table, the new commander, with recovered courage, said to her husband, —

"Leave all to God — and me. He has done his part, now I will do mine."

"But we have no money, dear."

"Yes, we have. I sold all we could spare, and have enough to take us away from this snow-bank."

"Where can we go?"

"I have engaged four rooms at our good neighbor, Lovejoy's. There we can live cheaply till spring. Then for new plans and a home of our own, please God."

"But, Hope, your little store won't last long, and we have no friends."

"I can sew and you can chop wood. Lovejoy offers you the same pay as he gives his other men; my old friend, Mrs. Truman, will send me all the work I want; and my blessed brother stands by us to the end. Cheer up, dear heart, for while there is work and life in the world we shall not suffer."

"And while I have my good angel Hope, I shall not despair, even if I wait another thirty years before I step beyond the circle of the sacred little world in which I still have a place to fill."

So one bleak December day, with their few possessions piled on an ox-sled, the rosy children perched atop, and the parents trudging arm in arm behind, the exiles left their Eden and faced the world again.

"Ah me! my happy dream. How much I leave behind that never can be mine again," said Abel, looking back at the lost Paradise, lying white and chill in its shroud of snow.

"Yes, dear, but how much we bring away," answered brave-hearted Hope, glancing from husband to children.

"Poor Fruitlands! The name was as great a failure as the rest!" continued Abel, with a sigh, as a frostbitten apple fell from a leafless bough at his feet.

But the sigh changed to a smile as his wife added, in a half-tender, half-satirical tone, —

"Don't you think Apple Slump would be a better name for it, dear?"

## "Annabel Lee"
## by Edgar Allan Poe

It was many and many a year ago,
    In a kingdom by the sea
That a maiden there lived whom you may know,
    By the name of ANNABEL LEE;
5  And this maiden she lived with no other thought
    Than to love and be loved by me.

*I* was a child and *she* was a child,
    In this kingdom by the sea;
But we loved with a love that was more than love—
10    I and my ANNABEL LEE—
With a love that the wingèd seraphs of heaven
    Coveted her and me.
And this was the reason that, long ago,
    In this kingdom by the sea,
15 A wind blew out of a cloud, chilling
    My beautiful ANNABEL LEE;
So that her highborn kinsmen came
    And bore her away from me,
To shut her up in a sepulchre
20    In this kingdom by the sea.

The angels, not half so happy in heaven,
    Went envying her and me—
Yes!—that was the reason (as all men know,
    In this kingdom by the sea)
25 That the wind came out of the cloud by night,
    Chilling and killing my ANNABEL LEE.

But our love it was stronger by far than the love
    Of those who were older than we—
    Of many far wiser than we—
30 And neither the angels in heaven above,
    Nor the demons down under the sea,
Can ever dissever my soul from the soul
    Of the beautiful ANNABEL LEE:

For the moon never beams, without bringing me dreams
35    Of the beautiful ANNABEL LEE;
And the stars never rise, but I feel the bright eyes
    Of the beautiful ANNABEL LEE:
And so, all the night tide, I lie down by the side
Of my darling—my darling—my life and my bride,
40    In her sepulchre there by the sea—
    In her tomb by the sounding sea.

## "Alone"
## by Edgar Allan Poe

From childhood's hour I have not been
As others were—I have not seen
As others saw—I could not bring
My passions from a common spring—

5   From the same source I have not taken
    My sorrow—I could not awaken
    My heart to joy at the same tone—
    And all I lov'd—I lov'd alone—
    Then—in my childhood—in the dawn
10  Of a most stormy life—was drawn
    From ev'ry depth of good and ill
    The mystery which binds me still—
    From the torrent, or the fountain—
    From the red cliff of the mountain—
15  From the sun that round me roll'd
    In its autumn tint of gold—
    From the lightning in the sky
    As it pass'd me flying by—
    From the thunder, and the storm—
20  And the cloud that took the form
    (When the rest of Heaven was blue)
    Of a demon in my view—

## "Stanzas on Freedom"
## by James Russell Lowell

    Men! whose boast it is that ye
    Come of fathers brave and free,
    If there breathe on earth a slave,
    Are ye truly free and brave?
5   If ye do not feel the chain,
    When it works a brother's pain,
    Are ye not base slaves indeed,
    Slaves unworthy to be freed?

    Women! who shall one day bear
10  Sons to breathe New England air,
    If ye hear, without blush,
    Deeds to make the roused blood rush
    Like red lava through your veins,
    For your sisters now in chains—
15  Answer! are ye fit to be
    Mothers of the brave and free?

    Is true freedom but to break
    Fetters for our own dear sake,
    And, with leathern[1] hearts, forget
20  That we owe mankind a debt?
    No! true freedom is to share
    All the chains our brothers wear,
    And, with heart and hand, to be
    Earnest to make others free!

25  They are slaves who fear to speak
    For the fallen and the weak;
    They are slaves who will not choose
    Hatred, scoffing, and abuse,
    Rather than in silence shrink
30  From the truth they needs must think;
    They are slaves who dare not be
    In the right with two or three.

    ---
    1. **leathern.** Like leather; tough; hard

## "There's a certain Slant of light—"
## by Emily Dickinson

    There's a certain Slant of light,
    Winter Afternoons—
    That oppresses, like the Heft
    Of Cathedral Tunes—

5   Heavenly Hurt, it gives us—
    We can find no scar,
    But internal difference,
    Where the Meanings, are—

    None may teach it—Any—
10  'Tis the Seal Despair—
    An imperial affliction
    Sent us of the Air—

    When it comes, the Landscape listens—
    Shadows—hold their breath—
15  When it goes, 'tis like the Distance
    On the look of Death—

## "'Hope' is the thing with feathers—"
## by Emily Dickinson

    "Hope" is the thing with feathers—
    That perches in the soul—
    And sings the tune without the words—
    And never stops—at all—

5   And sweetest—in the Gale—is heard—
    And sore must be the storm—
    That could abash the little Bird
    That kept so many warm—

    I've heard it in the chilliest land—
10  And on the strangest Sea—
    Yet, never, in Extremity,
    It asked a crumb—of Me.

## "Much Madness is divinest Sense—"
## by Emily Dickinson

    Much Madness is divinest Sense—
    To a discerning Eye—
    Much Sense—the starkest Madness—
    'Tis the Majority
5   In this, as All, prevail—
    Assent—and you are sane—
    Demur—you're straightway dangerous—
    And handled with a Chain—

# Guided Writing

## DESCRIBING A GOTHIC SETTING

Wild, untamed places. Dark, brooding characters. Horror, mystery, and suspense. You have probably encountered all of these Gothic motifs in books or in the media. Why? The Gothic appeal of humanity's spiritual and emotional alienation from the natural world continues to appear in modern novels, movies, and television shows.

What is a Gothic setting? The **setting** of a literary work is the time and place in which it occurs, together with all the details used to create a sense of a particular time and place. The setting quite often emphasizes key elements of the story and the characters with which it is peopled and establishes the mood or tone. A **Gothic setting** sets the stage for horror, suspense, mystery, and magic in the mood and tone it describes. In a Gothic setting, the language that describes the landscape, scenery, buildings, furniture, clothing, weather, and season is dark, suspenseful, and mysterious.

As you read the professional model, try to determine which words and phrases help to create the Gothic mood of the story and the characters.

**WRITING ASSIGNMENT.** Here is your opportunity to exercise your creativity in matters macabre. Your assignment is to create a Gothic setting. Your setting should be one that will inspire dread, foreboding, and fearful anticipation in your readers.

## Professional Model

Edgar Allan Poe's setting for his short story "The Fall of the House of Usher," fills the reader with suspense and uneasiness.

> "The Fall of the House of Usher," by Edgar Allan Poe
>
> During the whole of a dull, dark, and soundless day in the autumn of the year, when the clouds hung oppressively low in the heavens, I had been passing alone, on horseback, through a singularly dreary tract of country; and at length found myself, as the shades of the evening drew on, within view of the melancholy House of Usher. I know not how it was—but, with the first glimpse of the building, a sense of insufferable gloom pervaded my spirit. I say insufferable; for the feeling was unrelieved by any of that half-pleasurable, because poetic, sentiment, with which the mind usually receives even the sternest natural images of the desolate or terrible. I looked upon the scene before me—

---

Gothic themes focus on humanity's attempt to supersede nature, with the result that "men have become the tools of their tools" (Thoreau) and that "things are in the saddle and ride mankind" (Emerson).

**EXAMINING THE MODEL.**
Poe included gloomy, mysterious, and unnatural details to set the scene. For example, in the first sentence he describes the day as "dull, dark, and soundless." As you read the rest of this sentence, notice the other descriptions that create a sense of dread and foreboding:

clouds hung oppressively low in the heavens
passing alone
a singularly dreary tract of country
as the shades of the evening drew on

Read the remaining sentences in the model. What other details in the passages help to create this mood? List the words and phrases that contribute to the picture of the House of Usher and the effect that it has on the passer-by.

upon the vacant eye-like windows—upon a few rank sedges—and upon a few white trunks of decayed trees—with an utter depression of soul. . . .

## Prewriting

**FINDING YOUR VOICE.** How can you tailor your voice to a Gothic setting? Remember that voice springs from the writer's investment and conviction in the theme. You can create this strong voice, even if you don't like Gothic writing, by selecting a theme that is meaningful to you.

Consider the Gothic theme "technology out of control." In what instance have you seen this? What emotions do you experience when you think about it? What should be done about it? What shouldn't be? Take a few minutes now and pour out your beliefs and feelings on paper.

**IDENTIFYING YOUR AUDIENCE.** Consider who will be reading your Gothic setting—classmates, students in other grades, or family members? What will their expectations be? What details will you need to include in order to create a sense of foreboding, suspense, and mystery for your audience?

**WRITING WITH A PLAN.** Since a Gothic setting builds the tone and supports the theme presented in a story, you may find it easier to imagine the story first and then describe the setting. Begin by considering these general common Gothic themes: man versus nature, reason and science overwhelming instinct and emotion, technology out of control. What events from everyday life can you think of that might fit within these categories?

**Brainstorming** is often a productive method for discovering a theme to develop. Begin your prewriting by brainstorming a list of the modern events that would fit Gothic themes: for example, genetic engineering, weapons of subtle and terrible power, cloned animals or people, artificial limbs and organs, or computers and technologies that seem to dominate your life. Think of common, everyday items and events that you take for granted and try making them seem strange. Imagine that you can see them through the eyes of a person from another country, another time, even another galaxy or another species.

Now pick one of these themes and choose a **character** to place in your scene, someone through whose eyes your readers will experience the story and see, feel, smell, touch, taste, and breathe the setting. You will describe the setting by telling what your character experiences through as many senses as possible.

After you have selected a character, list several places in which your story could take place. From this list, choose one place that you feel is the most mysterious, foreboding, or horrible.

Carol chose the dark side of technology as her theme. She decided to use as her character a woman who surrounded herself with technology, even replacing her friends and family with her computer. She placed her character in a small room

"Children will always be afraid of the dark, and men with minds sensitive to hereditary impulse will always tremble at the thought of the hidden and fathomless worlds of strange life which may pulsate in the gulfs beyond the stars, or press hideously upon our own globe in unholy dimensions which only the dead and the moonstruck can glimpse."

—H. P. Lovecraft

Edgar Allan Poe used the strategy of determining the outcome of his poem before writing "The Raven." Consider his reasoning.

"I first established in my mind the climax or concluding query—that query to which 'Nevermore' should be in the last place an answer—that query in reply to which this word 'Nevermore' should involve the utmost conceivable amount of sorrow and despair. Here then the poem may be said to have had its beginning —at the end where all works of art should begin . . ."

that had been converted into a computer room. Carol used the following graphic organizer to help develop the details she needed to create her setting.

Copy the graphic organizer on this page onto your own paper. Use the graphic organizer to list sensory details—images of sound, sight, touch, taste, or smell—that you can use to describe your setting and emphasize the mystery, horror, or foreboding that your story will convey.

## Student Model—Graphic Organizer

Sight
the computer
the woman's eyes black and
   lifeless
dark room
only light from the
   monitor
cables, cords
beads of sweat

Touch
cold keyboard keys
smooth table
enveloping,
   overstuffed chair

Woman in computer room

Smell
dusty
stale

Sound
the woman breathing
   harder and harder
hum of the computer
silence

Taste
taste of despair

Review the sensory details you listed in your graphic organizer. Remember that a Gothic setting relies on gloomy and unnatural details. What modifiers and verbs can you add to your details to create this mood? Try to think of words that evoke specific images and feelings. Add these words to your list of sensory details. You cannot provide every detail, but if you furnish those that are the most vivid, your readers will project themselves into the scene.

## Drafting

Write a rough draft of your piece. Do not worry at this point about the details of spelling, grammar, usage, and mechanics. Instead, simply concentrate on creating a picture of the setting with words. Place your character at the scene, mentally review the scene you want to create, and then begin writing.

It may be helpful if you think, as you write, about presenting the details of your setting in a particular order. Poe used **spatial order** as he wrote "The Pit and the Pendulum." This organization, describing details as they exist in space—from left to right, right to left, foreground to background, background to foreground, top to bottom, or bottom to top—enhances for the reader the mystery of the prisoner discovering his cell. Carol chose **order of impression**—the order in which a character is impressed or impacted by things in

---

Carol added these modifiers and verbs to her details:

beads of sweat plummeting off her head each one sounding like a bullet piercing the deathly silence

her whisper growing louder as she sobbed let me in, let me in

an almost pitch black room lit only by the light emitting from the monitor screen

the computer humming incessantly

## Language, Grammar, and Style
### Vivid Verbs and Colorful Modifiers

IDENTIFYING VIVID VERBS AND COLORFUL MODIFIERS. A verb expresses action or a state of being. An action verb expresses physical or mental activity. Some action verbs create a more vivid picture of the action. For example, *saunter* creates a more vivid picture than *walk*.

the setting—to emphasize how the elements in the setting affected her. See the Language Arts Survey 2.24, "Organizing Ideas," for additional suggestions about organizing your writing.

## Self- and Peer Evaluation

After you finish your first draft, complete a self-evaluation of your writing. If time allows, you may want to get one or two peer evaluations. See the Language Arts Survey 2.37 for more details about self-evaluation and peer evaluation.

As you evaluate your setting or that of a classmate, answer the following questions:

- Is the setting clear? Does the setting include precise, concrete details that make the setting vivid to the reader?
- Do the images of sight, sound, touch, taste, and smell used in the description create a powerful mood of foreboding, mystery, and suspense? What images could be added to make the mood even more powerful?
- Are there any unnecessary or inconsistent details that detract from the mood and should be cut? Conversely, are there any missing details that could be added to strengthen the passage emotionally?
- Are there any word choices that could be improved? What modifiers and verbs could be changed to make them more concrete, specific, evocative, and descriptive?
- Do any details in the setting seem out of order? If so, where should these details go?
- Are there any places where the writing would obviously benefit from adding metaphors, similes, or other figurative language to make the writing easier to visualize and therefore more emotionally powerful?
- Does the setting create a feeling of conviction about the topic? Are the writer's beliefs and feelings about the topic apparent?

Carol did a self-evaluation of her setting that describes the horror and suspense of technology out of control. Roger provided peer evaluation comments as well.

## Student Model—Draft

```
Amanda came into the room and drew the
immensely black curtains closed now
Amanda has closed off the light outside
and the sound off the children laughing
as they play Amanda sat down in the
enveloping, overstuffed chair. The hum
of the computers grew louder and louder
```

Look at the example below from the Professional Model.

> During the whole of a dull, dark, and soundless day in the autumn of the year, when the clouds hung oppressively low in the heavens . . .

The action verb *hung* creates a somber and heavy picture of the clouds. Another verb, such as "the clouds *were* oppressively low," would not create the same picture. Read the example below from "The Pit and the Pendulum" by Poe. Identify the vivid verb. Explain why the verb is vivid.

> They had devoured, in spite of my efforts to prevent them, all but a small remnant of the contents of the dish.

Go back to the Professional Model and identify other vivid verbs. Explain why the verbs are vivid.

**ADDING VIVID VERBS.** Look at the draft of Carol's Gothic setting. Identify verbs that could be replaced with more vivid verbs. Suggest verbs that would more vividly depict the action that is taking place.

**USING VIVID VERBS.** Underline the verbs in your own Gothic setting. Consider whether or not each verb is vivid. Replace your original verb if a more vivid verb can be used.

*continued on page 312*

I need to clean this up to make it clearer.
—Carol

The image of the cords wrapping around her feet are really great.
—Roger

Maybe you could find a more realistic image here. I don't think it would sound this way.
—Roger

The cold keyboard keys bring a feeling of relief  they are like an old friend Amanda whispers the password as she types it in …… PASSWORD DENIED shows the screen no her whisper growing louder as Amanda moaned let me in, let me in The hum of the computers grow like voice taunting her "come in if you dare" ' She typed again PASSWORD DENIED "Keep trying come in. " I'm going to get you!" The computer cords suddenly seem to come alive as they begin to wrap around her feet Amanda can't get loose. The arms of the chair that once craddeled her are now growing around her devoering her. as Amanda tried again the beads of sweat plummeting off her head each one sounding like a bullet peirceing the deathly silence

**IDENTIFYING MODIFIERS.**
Modifiers are words that modify, or change, the meaning of a word. Adjectives and adverbs are modifiers. Using precise and descriptive modifiers adds color and intensity to your writing.

Look at the example below from the Professional Model.

I looked upon the scene before me—upon the vacant eye-like windows—upon a few rank sedges—and upon a few white trunks of decayed trees . . .

## Revising and Proofreading

If possible, wait a day before you revise your setting. Review your self- and peer evaluations. Revise your writing according to these comments. Consider the details, mood, organization, voice, word choice, and readability of your setting. Think about what to take out as well as what to add or reorganize. Make the heightening of Gothic suspense, mystery, and foreboding the goal of your revision.

Proofread your revised draft for errors in spelling, grammar, punctuation, capitalization, and other details. See the Language Arts Survey 2.45 for a proofreading checklist.

## Student Model—Revised

Amanda slipped into the room and drew the immensely black curtains shut, closing off the light outside and the sound of the children laughing as they played. In the room almost pitch black—lit only by the light emanating from the monitor's screen—Amanda dropped into the enveloping, overstuffed chair. The incessant hum of the computer grew louder and louder. The cold keyboard keys, like an old friend, brought a feeling of relief. Amanda whispered her password as she typed it in. PASSWORD DENIED. "No." Amanda's whisper grew louder as she moaned, "Let me in. Let me in." The hum of the computer grew like a voice taunting her, "Come in if you dare." She typed the password again. PASSWORD DENIED. "Keep trying to come in. I'm going to get you!" Amanda heard in the hum. The computer cords, tangled around her feet, suddenly seemed to come alive. Amanda couldn't get loose. The arms of the chair that once cradled her were growing around her, devouring her. As Amanda tried again, beads of sweat plummeted off her head, disrupting the menacing hum of a forbidden place.

## Publishing and Presenting

Finally, write or print a copy of your setting. You and your classmates may want to share your descriptions by reading them aloud, recording them, or illustrating them. You might add sound effects or darken the room when you present your writing. You may also want to continue writing a story based on your description of the setting. You might even wish to attempt it in the style and language of Poe or Hawthorne.

## Reflecting

Compare your Gothic description with the Gothic works in this unit, especially selections by Hawthorne and Poe. Are the themes typical of Gothic fiction still valid or do they seem dated? Why, or why not? What has changed in American life since the New England Renaissance, and what has remained the same?

The modifiers *vacant, eye-like, rank,* and *decayed* contribute to the scene of desolation and mystery that Poe is creating.

Read the example below. Identify the modifiers that contribute to the feeling of foreboding. Explain why the modifiers develop this feeling.

> During the whole of a dull, dark, and soundless day in the autumn of the year, when the clouds hung oppressively low in the heavens, I had been passing alone, on horseback, through a singularly dreary tract of country . . .

**ADDING COLORFUL MODIFIERS.**
Look at the draft of Carol's Gothic setting. Identify places where colorful modifiers are lacking. Suggest modifiers that would increase the intensity of the writing.

**USING COLORFUL MODIFIERS.**
Examine your writing for the use of colorful modifiers. Identify and revise at least two places that would benefit from the addition of colorful modifiers. For more information, see the Language Arts Survey 3.39, "Adding Colorful Language to Sentences."

# UNIT REVIEW
## *The New England Renaissance*

........................................................................................

## Words for Everyday Use

Check your knowledge of the following vocabulary words from the selections in this unit. Write short sentences using these words in context to make the meaning clear. To review the definition or usage of a word, refer to the page number listed or the Glossary of Words for Everyday Use.

| | | | |
|---|---|---|---|
| abstraction, 240 | dally, 241 | ingenuity, 237 | resignation, 287 |
| abyss, 234 | deleterious, 257 | infringing, 266 | resplendent, 252 |
| accentuation, 230 | delusory, 262 | inquisitorial, 230 | reverie, 265 |
| adjure, 246 | demeanor, 254 | insensible, 202 | saturated, 288 |
| affinity, 259 | deportment, 263 | insinuate, 269 | sepulcher, 202 |
| analogy, 258 | depraved, 263 | insuperable, 233 | speculative, 260 |
| anoint, 239 | diffuse, 240 | interminable, 232 | squalid, 280 |
| aperture, 240 | discordant, 241 | lapse, 203 | superfluous, 293 |
| arduous, 279 | earnest, 231, 288 | lattice, 245 | supervene, 231 |
| articulated, 266 | ebulition, 262 | laxly, 295 | surcease, 245 |
| aspiration, 291 | efficacious, 268 | locution, 231 | surmise, 268 |
| assuage, 260 | emaciated, 265 | lurid, 260 | tempest, 248 |
| aversion, 279 | encompass, 232 | lustrous, 208 | tenant, 208 |
| avert, 241 | encumbrance, 290 | malignant, 254 | terminate, 255 |
| avidity, 232 | endeavor, 292 | mien, 245 | testily, 256 |
| balm, 240 | entreat, 245 | moiety, 239 | torpid, 270 |
| baneful, 259 | equanimity, 263 | obeisance, 245 | transmute, 265 |
| beguile, 246 | erroneous, 256 | ominous, 246 | undaunted, 248 |
| blight, 201 | ethereal, 289 | opulent, 252 | undulation, 291 |
| cadence, 231 | evanescent, 264 | paltry, 292 | unfurl, 208 |
| censer, 247 | evince, 267 | patriarch, 202 | unintelligible, 259 |
| cessation, 239, 291 | feign, 207 | pensive, 202 | untoward, 260 |
| civility, 222 | fervor, 264 | perennial, 289 | unwieldy, 293 |
| clod, 202 | fissure, 240 | pertinacity, 238 | vacuity, 262 |
| cognizance, 237 | fluctuate, 293 | phenomenon, 258 | vagary, 259 |
| communion, 201 | forlorn, 208 | plume, 248 | venerable, 202 |
| conjecture, 240 | hoary, 202 | portal, 257 | vengeance, 241 |
| conjure, 232 | imbue, 267 | posterity, 290 | vermin, 239 |
| connoisseur, 263 | impede, 233 | predominate, 279 | viand, 239 |
| convolution, 236 | impend, 240 | pungently, 236 | volatile, 295 |
| cordiality, 256 | imperturbable, 260 | quaff, 247 | voracity, 239 |
| craven, 246 | inanition, 237 | recompense, 259 | writhe, 231 |
| crypt, 208 | indeterminate, 230 | reminiscence, 252 | wrought, 213 |

## Literary Tools

Define the following terms, giving concrete examples of how they are used in the selections in this unit. To review a term, refer to the page number indicated or to the Handbook of Literary Terms.

| | | |
|---|---|---|
| alliteration, 211, 249 | extended metaphor, 224 | run-on line, 249 |
| allusion, 251 | eye rhyme, 221 | sight rhyme, 221 |
| amplification, 199 | fantasy, 251 | slant rhyme, 221 |
| aphorism, 277, 286 | Gothic fiction, 229 | stanza, 206 |
| apology, 219 | image, 211 | symbol, 226, 251 |
| apostrophe, 206 | meter, 219 | synaesthesia, 226 |
| blank verse, 199 | point of view, 224, 229 | theme, 277 |
| elaboration, 199 | rhyme, 249, 284 | tone, 286 |
| essay, 277 | Romanticism, 284 | |

# Reflecting

## ......on YOUR READING

## Genre Studies

1. **ROMANTIC POETRY.** Romantic poetry celebrates the value of the common person, individual liberty, the common bonds of all people, emotion over reason, and the connection of human beings to the natural world. Think about these poems: "Thanatopsis" by William Cullen Bryant; "The Village Blacksmith" by Henry Wadsworth Longfellow; "The Raven," "Annabel Lee," and "Alone" by Edgar Allan Poe; and "Stanzas on Freedom" by James Russell Lowell. What makes each of these a fine example of a Romantic poem?

2. **SHORT STORY.** The work of Nathaniel Hawthorne and Edgar Allan Poe contributed to the development of the short story as a literary form. From Poe came the idea that all aspects of the short story combine to create one *dominant impression*. Examine the two short stories from this unit by Poe and Hawthorne, "The Pit and the Pendulum" and "Rappaccini's Daughter." What dominant impression is created in each one? What details create this impression?

## Thematic Studies

3. **INDIVIDUALISM.** Much of American literature celebrates the values of individualism and self-reliance. Compare the treatment of the theme of individualism in the poems "The Soul selects her own Society—" and "This is my letter to the World" by Dickinson and "Alone" by Poe.

4. **TRANSCENDENTALISM.** Transcendentalism in New England was an outgrowth of the Romantic Era in Europe. Review the definition of *Transcendentalism* in the introduction to this unit and select passages from the essays from "Self-Reliance" by Emerson and from *Walden* by Thoreau that reflect Transcendental philosophy.

## Historical/Biographical Studies

5. **COPYRIGHT LAWS.** The lack of international copyright law until 1891 meant that American authors received no royalties for books sold in England, and English authors were paid no royalties for books sold in America. Because the cost of publishing a book from abroad was therefore less than publishing a work by an American, many American writers had to sell their books without any claim to royalties. Even though they could not support themselves by their writing, they continued to write and to create. Discuss why some people have the impulse to write and express themselves regardless of monetary gain.

6. **PUBLIC EDUCATION AND THE LYCEUM MOVEMENT.** Public education did not get its start until the mid-1830s, when Horace Mann of Massachusetts undertook studies that led to more systematic methods for free public education throughout the North. In addition, the Lyceum Movement emerged in 1826. Lyceums were institutions that offered educational and inspirational lectures, debates, and entertainments in large public halls. Divide the class into two sides and hold a lyceum style debate on the virtues of public education versus home schooling.

*Rainy Day in Camp*, 1871. Winslow Homer.
The Metropolitan Museum of Art, New York.

We here highly resolve that these dead shall not have died in vain, that this nation, under God, shall have a new birth of freedom.

—Abraham Lincoln
The Gettysburg Address

317

# SLAVERY AND THE CIVIL WAR (1850–1865)

## A HOUSE DIVIDED

Slave auction.

In the early years of the nineteenth century, the new nation developed in two different directions. The North became a center for industrial manufacturing and the export of finished goods. The South, in contrast, was almost entirely agricultural, producing rice, tobacco, cotton, and sugar and exporting many of these goods to Great Britain. To protect its export business, the North favored high tariffs on imported goods. The South, which depended on imports for finished products, naturally opposed high tariffs. The economic differences between the North and the South created enormous tensions, exacerbated by fundamental differences in lifestyle. Many people in the North lived in cities and towns and worked in factories, in mills, or on small farms. Most of the people in the South worked the land, some on small farms and some on large rice, tobacco, cotton, and sugar plantations.

## THE ISSUE OF SLAVERY

At the very inception of the United States, differences arose between Northerners and Southerners over the issue of slavery. Thomas Jefferson had included a strong antislavery statement in his draft of the Declaration of Independence, but pressure from Southern delegates led to its deletion from the declaration in its final form. As the **plantation system** developed, the South began to depend more and more on imported slaves to carry out the work of its large "factory farms." While some Southerners opposed slavery, most saw it as a necessary part of the Southern econ-

## LITERARY EVENTS

➤ = American Events

➤ 1850. Henry David Thoreau delivers his antislavery speech "Slavery in Massachusetts"

➤ 1851. Sojourner Truth delivers her speech "Ain't I a Woman?"

➤ 1852. Harriet Beecher Stowe's *Uncle Tom's Cabin* published

➤ 1852. George Aiken's stage adaptation of *Uncle Tom's Cabin* produced

➤ 1853. First African-American novel published, *Clotel*, by William Wells Brown

➤ 1855. Frederick Douglass's *My Bondage and My Freedom* published

**1850**     **1852**     **1854**

➤ 1850. Compromise of 1850 presented to Congress by Henry Clay approved

➤ 1850. Congress passed Fugitive Slave Act

➤ 1854. Kansas-Nebraska Act passed

## HISTORICAL EVENTS

➤ 1851. Women's Rights Convention held in Akron, Ohio

omy. The slave trade was ended by law in 1808, but smuggling of slaves into the United States continued until the outbreak of the Civil War in 1860. By 1830, there were approximately three million slaves of African descent in the United States. About 2,500,000 of these people were forced agricultural laborers. By 1860, the number of enslaved blacks in the country had reached almost four million.

Apologists for slavery in America have often argued that the institution was benign because owners treated their "valuable property" well; however, the truth is slavery was brutal. Slaves typically worked hard, from sunup to sundown. They were fed meagerly; lived in squalid, flea-infested shacks; were often whipped for minor "offenses" by cruel overseers; were forbidden by law to learn to read and write; were sold away from their wives, husbands, or children; and suffered the basic indignity of continual subservience to others. Thousands of slaves ran away to freedom or to find family members from whom they had been separated, and hundreds revolted against their owners. In 1800, the Virginia militia put down a revolt of over a thousand slaves near Richmond. In 1822, a free black organizer named **Denmark Vesey** was hanged for attempting to organize a slave revolt in Charleston. In 1831, **Nat Turner** succeeded in organizing a revolt that led to bloody fighting and the deaths of 160 people.

Illustration from abolitionist literature.

In the North, a strong movement emerged for the abolition, or ending by law, of slavery. The leader of the Northern abolitionists was **William Lloyd Garrison,** whose newspaper, *The Liberator,* called for an immediate end to the South's "peculiar institution." Other important antislavery publications included the first black-owned newspaper, **John Russwurm** and **Samuel Cornish's** *Freedom's Journal,* and **Frederick Douglass's** *The North Star.* The New England Anti-Slavery Society, based in Massachusetts, and the Free African Society of Philadelphia became important voices in the antislavery movement. Some abolitionists, such as **Elijah P. Lovejoy** and **Charles T. Torrey,** both Protestant ministers, died for the cause. Other abolitionists organized what became known as the **Underground Railroad,** a system of safe houses and guides for leading runaways from slave states in the South to free states in the North.

➤ 1858. Stephen C. Foster writes the song "My Old Kentucky Home"

➤ 1860. Nathaniel Hawthorne's *The Marble Faun* published
1860. George Eliot's *The Mill on the Floss* published

➤ 1859. First novel by an African-American woman published, *Our Nig* by Harriet E. Wilson

1861. Charles Dickens's *Great Expectations* published

➤ 1856. Walt Whitman's *Leaves of Grass* published

**1856**          **1858**          **1860**

➤ 1858. Lincoln-Douglass senatorial debates held

➤ 1858. Abraham Lincoln loses senate race to Stephen A. Douglass

➤ 1860. Abraham Lincoln elected president

➤ 1860. South Carolina's Ordinance of Secession

➤ 1860. Elizabeth Cady Stanton urges women's suffrage to New York State Legislature

➤ 1861. The Confederate States of America formed; Jefferson Davis named president

➤ 1861. Civil War begins; Confederates attack Fort Sumter

➤ 1861. Trent affair, British/American crisis

➤ 1857. Supreme Court upholds the right to own slaves in the Dred Scott case

➤ 1859. John Brown raids Harpers Ferry

Robert E. Lee.

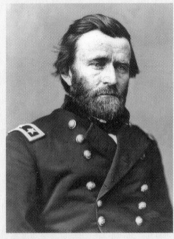

Ulysses S. Grant.

The most famous conductor on the Underground Railroad was **Harriet Tubman,** herself a runaway slave.

By the 1850s, a great deal of national energy, both political and literary, was focused on the question of slavery. At the center of concern were two issues: fugitive slave laws and the status of slavery in new territories. The **Fugitive Slave Act** of 1850 established that "good citizens" in free states could be deputized to assist federal marshals in the capture of runaway slaves. The act also imposed heavy fines for anyone assisting a runaway, a provision that greatly heightened tensions in the North, where many prominent people were involved directly or indirectly in the abolitionist movement and in the Underground Railroad. One such Northerner, **Henry David Thoreau,** in a speech called "Slavery in Massachusetts," spoke out publicly after a famous local case about the enforcement of the act, asserting that he had "lost his country." In 1852, **Harriet Beecher Stowe's** antislavery novel *Uncle Tom's Cabin* became a bestseller, helping to turn the tide of opinion in the North against slavery.

In the years preceding the Civil War, the country debated the question of whether slavery would be allowed in newly added territories such as California, New Mexico, Utah, Kansas, and Nebraska. The **Missouri Compromise** of 1820 allowed slavery only south of the 36°30' parallel. A second compromise, put forward by Senator **Henry Clay** of Kentucky in 1850, called for California to be a free state and for new territories to decide on their own whether to be free or slave; it also provided protections for slavery as it already existed in the South. This compromise was supported by **Daniel Webster** of Massachusetts, who believed it necessary in order to preserve the Union. In 1854, after much debate, the **Kansas-Nebraska Act** was passed, allowing voters in these new states to decide the issue of slavery for themselves. There followed bitter, bloody fighting in Kansas between proslavery and antislavery forces. Among the latter was a fiery militant named **John Brown.** In 1857, the Supreme Court's **Dred Scott decision** upheld the right of a slave owner to continue to own a slave, even if he moved into free territory. In the presidential election of 1857 and in the debates between senatorial candidates **Stephen Douglas** and **Abraham**

## LITERARY EVENTS

➤ = American Events

➤ 1862. Julia Ward Howe writes the lyrics of "The Battle Hymn of the Republic"

➤ 1863. Henry Wadsworth Longfellow's *Tales of a Wayside Inn* published
➤ 1863. Edward Everett Hale's "The Man Without a Country" published

➤ 1864. John Greenleaf Whittier's *In War Time* published

1865. Lewis Carroll's *Alice's Adventures in Wonderland* published
➤ 1865. Mark Twain's "The Notorious Jumping Frog of Calaveras County" published
➤ 1865. Walt Whitman's "When Lilacs Last in the Dooryard Bloom'd" published

**1862**                    **1864**                    **1865**

➤ 1862. Battle of Shiloh
➤ 1862. London refuses to recognize Confederacy
➤ 1862. Lincoln delivers Emancipation Proclamation
➤ 1862. First regiment of former slaves formed
➤ 1863. The Battle of Gettysburg

➤ 1864. General Sherman leads march to the sea, leveling a path through Georgia
➤ 1864. Lincoln reelected
➤ 1864. Geneva Conventions signed

➤ 1865. General Lee surrenders at Appomattox Court House
➤ 1865. President Lincoln assassinated by John Wilkes Booth; vice president Andrew Johnson elected president
➤ 1865. Thirteenth Amendment, prohibiting slavery, ratified

## HISTORICAL EVENTS

➤ 1863. West Virginia secedes from Virginia to join Union
➤ 1863. Draft riots in Northern cities
➤ 1863. Lincoln delivers Gettysburg Address

**Lincoln** in 1858, the issue of slavery in new territories and states was paramount. Then, in 1859, John Brown led a raid on the government arsenal at **Harpers Ferry,** West Virginia, hoping to capture weapons and to turn those over to slaves, thus beginning a slave revolt throughout the South. Brown was hanged and became a martyr to the antislavery cause, celebrated in "The Battle Hymn of the Republic."

Richmond, Virginia, at the end of the Civil War.

## SECESSION AND CIVIL WAR

When Abraham Lincoln became president in 1860, seven states—South Carolina, Mississippi, Florida, Alabama, Georgia, Louisiana, and Texas—had already voted to secede from the Union. In 1861, delegates from throughout the South met in Montgomery, Alabama, and formed the **Confederate States of America,** choosing **Jefferson Davis** of Mississippi as their new president. On April 12, 1861, Confederate troops fired on the federal stronghold at **Fort Sumter,** on Charleston Harbor, thus beginning the most troubled period in American history. Lincoln offered to put Virginian **Robert E. Lee** in charge of the Union army, but Lee, who was initially opposed to secession, declined, not wishing to fight against the people of his own state. When Virginia seceded from the Union, Lee took command of the Grand Army of the Confederacy.

Many people on both sides expected the **Civil War** to be over in a month, but it lasted five years. Union troops lost the first major campaign of the war, suffering defeat at the First Battle of Bull Run by troops under **Stonewall Jackson** and **P. G. T. Beauregard.** That defeat moved the Union to action. The Grand Army of the Potomac was organized under **George B. McClellan.** In the fighting that followed at Shiloh, New Orleans, Bull Run, Antietam, Fredericksburg, Chancellorsville, Gettysburg, Vicksburg, and Petersburg, among other places, 360,000 Union soldiers and 329,000 Confederate soldiers lost their lives, many more from disease than from battle. Union forces were at first plagued by poor leadership, but eventually, under the able direction of **Ulysses S. Grant,** the hero of the Battle of Vicksburg, they were able to bring the war to an end, invading the Confederate capital of Richmond, Virginia, in April 1865. General Robert E. Lee surrendered to Grant at **Appomattox Court House** in Virginia on April 9.

## THE LITERATURE OF ABOLITION AND PROTEST

Well before the war there existed a large and substantial body of abolitionist writing, including the work of several of the writers of the New England Renaissance such as Emerson, Thoreau, Whittier, and Lowell. Abolitionist societies, like the New England Anti-Slavery Society, sprang up as networks for support—by 1850 as many as two thousand. Publishers such as William Lloyd Garrison and Frederick Douglass made important contributions to the cause, as did novelists such as Harriet Beecher Stowe.

Though some of this literature was written by Northern whites, especially women, who were attempting in part to appeal to the family concerns of their Southern female

Walt Whitman.

counterparts, African Americans in the South developed two original forms of literature that played an important role in the abolitionist movement. First was the **spiritual,** which combined African and European music and a poetic text using religious images from the Bible to create dramatic symbols of the suffering of slaves and their hopes for deliverance. Second was the **slave narrative,** an autobiographical account of the life of a former slave, chronicling the extraordinary conditions under which he or she had lived. Ranging in length from a few pages to an entire book, hundreds of slave narratives were published in the decades before the war. These narratives were remarkable for a number of reasons, not least of which was that most of their authors had come from Southern states that by law prohibited teaching blacks to read or write. They deployed various literary strategies designed to gain sympathy without offending their primarily white audiences, many of whom were unschooled in the gorier details and horrors of slavery and not anxious to see evil in their Southern Christian counterparts. For example, Frederick Douglass's narrative, excerpted in this unit, tries repeatedly to put blame on the institution of slavery rather than on individual owners; of one owner's wife Douglass noted, "When I went there, she was a pious, warm, and tender-hearted woman. . . . Slavery soon proved its ability to divest her of these heavenly qualities."

William Wells Brown was the first African American to publish a novel. *Clotel* (1853) is the fictional account of a child born to Thomas Jefferson and a slave. This novel combined historical fiction, national legend, and the increasingly divisive subject of race to point out the disparity between the ideals of American liberty and the actual living conditions of American slaves. The first African-American woman to publish a novel was Harriet E. Wilson, who wrote *Our Nig* (1859). Wilson's novel focused on the injustices faced by free blacks in the North, which was a topic not readily acknowledged at the time.

## THE LITERATURE OF THE WAR

Much of the literature during and immediately after the war addressed itself to a concern with restoring a national identity, hoping to find threads of unity amid the horrific bloodletting, and often doing this by appealing to and honoring the courage and heroism of those who had fought. Lincoln, in the speeches excerpted in this unit, Lee, and **Walt Whitman,** in his elegy to Lincoln, honor the efforts of those in the war while insisting in various ways on a national identity and on reconciliation. As Whitman expressed it in one poem, "For my enemy is dead, a man divine as myself is dead."

In the first decades after the war, writings about the war became vehicles for achieving that reconciliation and reshaping the nation's self-image or identity. Much of this writing romanticized the war and the contributions of those who participated in it, glorifying the United States itself in the process; however, there also emerged a contrary voice in the works of **Ambrose Bierce** and **Stephen Crane.** These writers explored the darker aspects of the war, portraying courage and heroism as myths, seeing actions as the result of accident or panic under environmental pressures rather than as reflections of human strength and triumph.

# ECHOES

ECHOES ECHOES ECHOES ECHOES ECHOES ECHOES ECHOES ECHOES

## SLAVERY AND THE CIVIL WAR

A house divided against itself cannot stand. I believe this government cannot endure, permanently half slave and half free.

—Abraham Lincoln, in a speech delivered in 1858

In thinking of America, I sometimes find myself admiring her bright blue sky—her grand old woods—her fertile fields—her beautiful rivers—her mighty lakes and star-crowned mountains. But my rapture is soon checked when I remember that all is cursed with the infernal spirit of slaveholding and wrong; When I remember that with the waters of her noblest rivers, the tears of my brethren are borne to the ocean, disregarded and forgotten; That her most fertile fields drink daily of the warm blood of my outraged sisters, I am filled with unutterable loathing.

—Frederick Douglass, former slave, editor of *The North Star,* and crusader against slavery

I can anticipate no greater calamity for the country than a dissolution of the Union. It would be an accumulation of all the evils we complain of, and I am willing to sacrifice everything but honor for its preservation. . . . Secession is nothing but revolution.

—Robert E. Lee, later leader of the Confederate forces, writing about secession in a letter to his son dated January 1861

My paramount object in this struggle is to save the Union. . . . If I could save the Union without freeing any slave, I would do it; and if I could save it by freeing all the slaves, I would do it; and if I could save it by freeing some and leaving others alone, I would also do that. . . . I have here stated my purpose according to my views of official duty and I intend no modification of my oft-expressed personal wish that all men everywhere could be free.

—Abraham Lincoln, in a letter to Horace Greeley, dated August 22, 1862

Duty is the sublimest word in our language. Do your duty in all things. You cannot do more. You should never wish to do less.

—Robert E. Lee, inscribed beneath his bust in the Hall of Fame

My duty is to obey orders.

—Thomas Jonathan [Stonewall] Jackson, Confederate general

The war is over—the rebels are our countrymen again.

—Ulysses S. Grant, upon stopping his men from cheering after Lee's surrender at Appomattox Court House, April 1865

I started with this idea in my head, There's two things I've got a right to . . . death or liberty.

—Harriet Tubman, to her biographer Sarah H. Bradford, c.1868

*Rainy Day in Camp* [Detail], Winslow Homer.

## Literary TOOLS

**STEREOTYPE.** A **stereotype** is an uncritically accepted, fixed or conventional idea, particularly such an idea held about whole groups of people. Determine against what stereotype Douglass argues in this selection.

**TONE. Tone** is the emotional attitude toward the reader or toward the subject implied by a literary work. It may be expressed by word choice, imagery, and other techniques. As you read, determine the tone Douglass uses in his narrative.

## About the SELECTION

Frederick Douglass had already established himself as an orator of exceptional ability and had given many speeches about his experience under slavery when he wrote his autobiography, *Narrative of the Life of Frederick Douglass, an American Slave.* Knowing that publication of the book would reveal his identity and make him a target for slave-catchers, he went to England until money could be raised to buy his freedom.

## Reader's Journal

If you were a slave, how would you express yourself?

FROM

# Narrative of the Life of Frederick Douglass, an American Slave,

## Written by Himself

BY FREDERICK DOUGLASS

## About the AUTHOR

**Frederick Douglass** (1818–1895) was an eloquent speaker, a tireless campaigner against slavery, and a champion of civil rights for women and for persons of African descent. Born a slave in Maryland, Douglass was taught to read and write in violation of a Maryland state law prohibiting the education of African Americans. After escaping to Massachusetts in 1838, he associated with such prominent abolitionists as William Lloyd Garrison, J. G. Birney, and John Brown, and he became an influential force in the fight to end slavery.

In 1845, Douglass published the first of three autobiographies, *Narrative of the Life of Frederick Douglass, an American Slave*, in which he told of his childhood, his youth, and his escape to freedom. After traveling in Britain and Ireland, where he lectured for the abolitionist cause, Douglass returned to America. Friends helped him to buy his freedom, and he moved to Rochester, New York, where he began publishing an abolitionist newspaper, *The North Star*, later called *Frederick Douglass's Weekly* and *Frederick Douglass's Monthly*. In 1855, he published an expanded, updated version of his autobiography, *My Bondage and My Freedom,* which was followed in 1881 by a final autobiographical volume, *The Life and Times of Frederick Douglass.*

Unjustly implicated in John Brown's attack on the arsenal at Harpers Ferry, West Virginia, which Brown had hoped would instigate a slave revolt, Douglass fled to Canada and England before the Civil War. During the war, he returned to the United States where he helped to organize regiments of African-American soldiers to fight for the Northern cause, and he personally called on Abraham Lincoln, sixteenth president of the United States, to secure fair compensation for those soldiers. He also worked as a conductor on the Underground Railroad. After the war, Douglass held a number of political offices, including United States marshall and recorder of deeds for the District of Columbia, minister to Haiti, and chargé d'affaires to Santo Domingo. He also continued his political activities, lobbying for legislation to prevent discrimination of all kinds.

*Plantation Economy in the Old South,* c.1876. William Aiken Walker.
The Warner Collection, Tuscaloosa, Alabama.

FROM

# Narrative of the Life of Frederick Douglass, an American Slave,

## Written by Himself

### FREDERICK DOUGLASS

Colonel Lloyd[1] kept from three to four hundred slaves on his home plantation, and owned a large number more on the neighboring farms belonging to him. The names of the farms nearest to the home plantation were Wye Town and New Design. Wye Town was under the overseership of a man named Noah Willis. New Design was under the overseership of a Mr. Townsend. The overseers of these, and all the rest of the farms, numbering over twenty, received advice and direction from the managers of the home plantation. This was the great business place. It was the seat of government for the whole twenty farms.[2] All disputes among the overseers were settled here. . . .

Here, too, the slaves of all the other farms received their monthly allowance of food, and their yearly clothing. The men and women slaves received, as their monthly allowance of food, eight pounds of pork, or its equivalent in fish, and one bushel of corn meal. Their yearly clothing consisted of two coarse linen shirts, one pair of linen trousers, like the shirts, one jacket, one pair of trousers for winter, made of coarse negro cloth, one pair of stockings, and

> *How many slaves did Colonel Lloyd own?*

> *What happened at the "home plantation"?*

---

1. **Colonel Lloyd.** Owner of the large plantation in Maryland where Douglass was born
2. **twenty farms.** Lloyd family papers indicate only thirteen farms.

one pair of shoes; the whole of which could not have cost more than seven dollars. The allowance of the slave children was given to their mothers, or the old women having the care of them. My mother and I were separated when I was but an infant—before I knew her as my mother. It is a common custom, in the part of Maryland from which I ran away, to part children from their mothers at a very early age. Frequently, before the child has reached its twelfth month, its mother is taken from it, and hired out on some farm a considerable distance off, and the child is placed under the care of an old woman, too old for field labor. The children unable to work in the field had neither shoes, stockings, jackets, nor trousers, given to them; their clothing consisted of two coarse linen shirts per year. When these failed them, they went naked until the next allowance-day. Children from seven to ten years old, of both sexes, almost naked, might be seen at all seasons of the year.

*When was Douglass separated from his mother? What happened to children who were separated from their mothers in this way?*

The home plantation of Colonel Lloyd wore the appearance of a country village. All the mechanical operations for all the farms were performed here. The shoemaking and mending, the blacksmithing, cartwrighting, coopering,[3] weaving, and grain-grinding, were all performed by the slaves on the home plantation. The whole place wore a businesslike aspect very unlike the neighboring farms. The number of houses, too, conspired to give it advantage over the neighboring farms. It was called by the slaves the *Great House Farm*. Few privileges were esteemed higher, by the slaves of the out-farms, than that of being selected to do errands at the Great House Farm. It was associated in their minds with greatness. A representa-

tive could not be prouder of his election to a seat in the American Congress, than a slave on one of the out-farms would be of his election to do errands at the Great House Farm. They regarded it as evidence of great confidence reposed in them by their overseers; and it was on this account, as well as a constant desire to be out of the field from under the driver's lash, that they esteemed it a high privilege, one worth careful living for. He was called the smartest and most trusty fellow, who had this honor conferred upon him the most frequently. The competitors for this office sought as <u>diligently</u> to please their overseers, as the office-seekers in the political parties seek to please and deceive the people. The same traits of character might be seen in Colonel Lloyd's slaves, as are seen in the slaves of the political parties.

*How did some slaves feel about doing errands at the Great House Farm? Why?*

The slaves selected to go to the Great House Farm, for the monthly allowance for themselves and their fellow slaves, were peculiarly enthusiastic. While on their way, they would make the dense old woods, for miles around, reverberate with their wild songs, revealing at once the highest joy and the deepest sadness. They would compose and sing as they went along, consulting neither time nor tune. The thought that came up, came out—if not in the word, in the sound—and as frequently in the one as in the other. They would sometimes sing the most pathetic sentiment in the most <u>rapturous</u> tone, and the most rapturous sentiment in the most pathetic tone. Into all of their songs they would manage to weave something of the Great House Farm. Especially would they do this when leaving

---

3. **cartwrighting, coopering.** *Cartwrighting*—building carts; *coopering*—making barrels

---

**WORDS FOR EVERYDAY USE**

dil • i • gent • ly (dil´ə jənt lē) *adv.*, painstakingly, industriously. *Dad painted the garage <u>diligently</u> until it looked like new.*

rap • tur • ous (rap´ chər əs) *adj.*, full of joy or pleasure. *When Huy saw his sister, whom he had not seen since the war, he let out a <u>rapturous</u> greeting in Vietnamese.*

home. They would then sing most exultingly the following words:

> I am going away to the Great House
>     Farm!
> O, yea! O, yea! O!

This they would sing, as a chorus, to words which to many would seem unmeaning jargon, but which, nevertheless, were full of meaning to themselves. I have sometimes thought that the mere hearing of those songs would do more to impress some minds with the horrible character of slavery, than the reading of whole volumes of philosophy on the subject could do.

According to Douglass, what might some songs by slaves tell people about the character of slavery?

I did not, when a slave, understand the deep meaning of those rude and apparently incoherent songs. I was myself within the circle; so that I neither saw nor heard as those without might see and hear. They told a tale of woe which was then altogether beyond my feeble comprehension; they were tones loud, long, and deep; they breathed the prayer and complaint of souls boiling over with the bitterest anguish. Every tone was a testimony against slavery, and a prayer to God for deliverance from chains. The hearing of those wild notes always depressed my spirit, and filled me with ineffable sadness. I have frequently found myself in tears while hearing them. The mere recurrence to those songs, even now, afflicts me; and while I am writing these lines, an expression of feeling has already found its way down my cheek. To those songs I trace my first glimmering conception of the dehumanizing character of slavery. I can never get rid of that conception. Those songs still follow me, to deepen my hatred of slavery, and quicken my sympathies for my brethren in bonds. If any one wishes to be impressed with the soul-killing effects of slavery, let him go to Colonel Lloyd's plantation, and, on allowance-day, place himself in the deep pine woods; and there let him, in silence, analyze the sounds that shall pass through the chambers of his soul, and if he is not thus impressed, it will only be because "there is no flesh in his obdurate heart."

What astonished Douglass? According to him, when did slaves sing? What did their songs represent?

I have often been utterly astonished, since I came to the north, to find persons who could speak of the singing, among slaves, as evidence of their contentment and happiness. It is impossible to conceive of a greater mistake. Slaves sing most when they are most unhappy. The songs of the slave represent the sorrows of his heart; and he is relieved by them, only as an aching heart is relieved by its tears. At least, such is my experience. I have often sung to drown my sorrow, but seldom to express my happiness. Crying for joy, and singing for joy, were alike uncommon to me while in the jaws of slavery. The singing of a man cast away upon a desolate island might be as appropriately considered as evidence of contentment and happiness, as the singing of a slave; the songs of the one and of the other are prompted by the same emotion. ■

## WORDS FOR EVERYDAY USE

**in • co • her • ent** (in kō´ hir ´ənt) *adj.,* unclear; not understandable. *With her high fever, Marie's mutterings were all incoherent.*
**ob • dur • ate** (äb´dür it) *adj.,* unsympathetic; hardened. *With obdurate conviction, the judge sentenced the criminal to life in prison.*

## Respond *to the* SELECTION

If you were Douglass, what kind of a song would you have sung the day you became free? Why?

# INVESTIGATE, Inquire, Imagine

**Recall:** GATHERING FACTS

1a. How many farms and slaves did Colonel Lloyd own?

2a. What clothing did adults and young children receive each year?

3a. According to some northerners, why did the slaves sing?

➤ **Interpret:** FINDING MEANING

1b. How did Colonel Lloyd coordinate the management of his many farms?

2b. Why were young children treated less generously than adults when it came to clothing allotments?

3b. What was Douglass's assessment of slaves' singing?

---

**Analyze:** TAKING THINGS APART

4a. What were different aspects of the lives of slave children like?

➤ **Synthesize:** BRINGING THINGS TOGETHER

4b. What effect would you expect the separation of children from their mothers to have on family relationships? Why would this effect be desirable to the slaveholder?

---

**Evaluate:** MAKING JUDGMENTS

5a. Justify the comparison Douglass makes between the slaves sent for supplies on allowance-day and politicians, and the comparison between a slave and a castaway.

➤ **Extend:** CONNECTING IDEAS

5b. In what ways is the music we now call the blues similar to the singing of the slaves sent for supplies on allowance-day?

# Understanding Literature

**STEREOTYPE.** Review the definition for **stereotype** in the Handbook of Literary Terms. What stereotype about slaves does Douglass reject in his description of the slaves' singing? What is his nonstereotypical interpretation of this behavior? How does his analogy with "a man cast away upon a desolate island" reinforce his interpretation?

**TONE.** Review the definition for **tone** in the Handbook of Literary Terms. Copy and complete the graphic organizer below to understand Douglass's tone of sorrow and sympathy for the plight of slaves. Add successive circles for each example of the identified tone that you find.

# WRITER'S JOURNAL

1. Write a **letter of complaint** to a northern abolitionist, detailing your mistreatment as a slave on one of Colonel Lloyd's farms.

2. Imagine that, as a slave on the Wye Town farm, you were selected to run errands to the Great House Farm. Write a **journal entry** expressing your enthusiam and excitement about going to the Great House Farm.

3. Write **song lyrics** for the slaves of Colonel Lloyd's farm, using Douglass's analogy with "a man cast away upon a desolate island" to describe a slave's feelings.

# Integrating *the* LANGUAGE ARTS

## Language, Grammar, and Style

**APPOSITIVES.** Read the Language Arts Survey 3.77, "Appositives." Then revise these sentences, adding to each a word or phrase in apposition to the italicized word(s). Use the information provided in parentheses following each sentence to write your appositives.

1. *Frederick Douglass* worked to free slaves by speaking, writing, and serving as a conductor on the Underground Railroad. (Douglass was a famous autobiographer, speaker, and newspaper publisher.)

2. *Harriet Tubman* chose another route. (Tubman was known as the Moses of her people.)

3. After escaping from a Maryland plantation in 1849, Tubman worked with the *Underground Railroad*. (The Underground Railroad was a series of safe houses between slave states and free states.)

4. Acting as a *conductor*, Tubman was responsible for liberating about three hundred people from slavery. (A conductor was a guide.)

5. After the war, both Tubman and Douglass strongly supported the civil rights struggle and the *women's suffrage movement*. (The women's suffrage movement was an attempt to secure voting rights for women.)

## Study and Research & Collaborative Learning

**RESEARCHING AN ABOLITIONIST.** With a partner, research a person involved in abolitionism, such as Lyman Beecher, James G. Birney, John Brown, Lydia Maria Child, Charles G. Finney, William Lloyd Garrison, Angelina Grimké, Julia Ward Howe, Benjamin Lundy, Wendell Phillips, John B. Russwurm, Harriet Beecher Stowe, Arthur Tappan, Lewis Tappan, Nathaniel Taylor, Theodore D. Weld, or John Greenleaf Whittier. With your partner, present an interview between one of these people and an interviewer. The interviewer should ask specific questions about the abolitionist's beliefs and involvement in abolitionist activities based on his or her reading. The interviewee should give detailed answers based on the same research.

## Media Literacy

**SCREENPLAY.** Write a fictionalized screenplay for the selection from Douglass's autobiography. Decide on a central character to focus on, determine close-up and long camera shots, and write dialogue. In your screenplay, be sure to establish the setting, develop sympathetic characterization so that your audience will care about the slave that you portray, and delineate a conflict with another character.

## Literary TOOLS

**THEME.** A **theme** is a central idea in a literary work. Think about what the theme is in "Swing Low, Sweet Chariot" as you read its four stanzas.

**REFRAIN.** A **refrain** is a repeated line or group of words in a song or poem. Often spirituals were sung by a lone singer, with a group of people joining in for the refrain. As you read the lyrics, determine which stanza is the refrain.

## Reader's Journal

When you feel a need to escape from reality, of what real or imaginary place do you dream?

# "Swing Low, Sweet Chariot"

ANONYMOUS AFRICAN-AMERICAN SPIRITUAL

## About *the* SELECTION

By the middle of the nineteenth century, there were more than four million slaves in the United States. Most came from the west coast of Africa. West Africans, who lived in close-knit communities, often engaged in communal labor accompanied by song. In America, such traditional songs developed into the work songs and calls of laborers on plantations. These work songs typically contained repeated lines or phrases and were sung in unison by the workers or in an answer-response format.

Kept from practicing their traditional religions, many African Americans adopted Christianity. Slave owners actively encouraged the Christianizing of the slaves, some because of concern for their slaves' immortal souls, but many more out of hope that people who looked for rewards in the next life might tolerate terrible circumstances in this one. Combining elements of traditional African music, work songs, and Christian hymns, African Americans created a new kind of music known as the spiritual, a forerunner of many modern musical styles, including gospel and blues. Spirituals such as **"Swing Low, Sweet Chariot"** had Christian themes. They often retold stories from the Bible or dealt with subjects such as salvation and the afterlife. Their form was that of the traditional folk hymn, with repeated elements of the kind found in work songs. They were often sung by groups, with rhythmical accompaniments like those found in African music. Interestingly, many of the spirituals, such as "Swing Low, Sweet Chariot," were intentionally ambiguous or allegorical, dealing on one level with deliverance from earthly toil into a pleasant afterlife in heaven and on another level with deliverance from slavery.

# Swing Low, Sweet Chariot

## ANONYMOUS AFRICAN-AMERICAN SPIRITUAL

Swing low, sweet chariot,
Coming for to carry me home,
Swing low, sweet chariot,
Coming for to carry me home.

*Where does the speaker want to go?*

5    I looked over Jordan[1] and what did I see
Coming for to carry me home,
A band of angels coming after me,
Coming for to carry me home.

If you get there before I do,
10   Coming for to carry me home,
Tell all my friends I'm coming too,
Coming for to carry me home.

*What does the speaker want his or her friends to know?*

Swing low, sweet chariot,
Coming for to carry me home,
15   Swing low, sweet chariot,
Coming for to carry me home. ■

---

1. **Jordan.** According to a biblical story, the Israelites in exile had to cross the Jordan River to reach the Promised Land of Canaan.

If you were a slave, what image would you choose for consolation?

# Inquire, *Imagine*

**Recall:** GATHERING FACTS

1a. What is coming to carry the speaker home?

2a. Over what river does the singer look? What does the singer see?

3a. Who, according to stanza 3, is being addressed by the singer?

→ **Interpret:** FINDING MEANING

1b. In a religious sense, where is "home"?

2b. If this song is interpreted as being about escape from slavery, what is the symbolic implication of "a band of angels" on the other side of the river?

3b. Why are the singer's friends not with the singer at this time?

**Analyze:** TAKING THINGS APART

4a. Why might this song have been comforting to the person singing it? What feelings does the song express?

→ **Synthesize:** BRINGING THINGS TOGETHER

4b. Develop an interpretation of the spiritual as a song of hope about earthly freedom, explaining the significance of the chariot, angels, home, and the Jordan River.

**Evaluate:** MAKING JUDGMENTS

5a. How relevant is the message of this song today? Explain your answer.

→ **Extend:** CONNECTING IDEAS

5b. Here is the beginning of another famous spiritual, "Go Down, Moses":

*When Israel was in Egypt land*
*Let my people go*
*Oppressed so hard they could not stand*
*Let my people go*
*Go down, Moses, way down in Egypt land*
*Tell old Pharaoh, Let my people go*

Compare and contrast this part of "Go Down, Moses" with "Swing Low, Sweet Chariot."

# Understanding *Literature*

**THEME.** Review the definition for **theme** in the Handbook of Literary Terms. What is the theme of "Swing Low, Sweet Chariot"?

**REFRAIN.** Review the definition for **refrain** in Literary Tools on page 330. What is the refrain in "Swing Low, Sweet Chariot"? To what does the word *home* in this refrain refer?

# WRITER'S JOURNAL

1. Imagine that you are witnessing a historian interview a slave in nineteenth-century America about her feelings about "Swing Low, Sweet Chariot." Write a **dialogue** between the historian and the slave. Among other questions, the historian asks the slave why she finds comfort in the spiritual and what feelings the song expresses for her.

2. Imagine that you are an overseer on a plantation with some thoughts about the real meaning of "Swing Low, Sweet Chariot" that the slaves are singing as they work. Write a **letter** to the plantation owner, expressing your concerns about what you see as the symbolic meaning of the spiritual's lyrics.

3. Write an additional **stanza** for "Swing Low, Sweet Chariot."

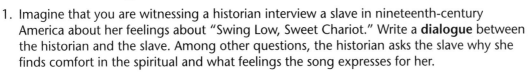

# Integrating the LANGUAGE ARTS

## Study and Research & Collaborative Learning

**RESEARCHING SPIRITUALS.** With several classmates, write a brief report on the background of spirituals. Possible topics to include are how spirituals developed, their influence on jazz or gospel music, why so many versions of any single song exist, and when spirituals became recognized. At the end of your report, add an appendix with your group's favorite spirituals. Illustrate and lay out the spirituals artistically. Be sure to include the musical notations for the songs. As you write about relevant topics, you may want to refer to the spirituals in the appendix when you need examples.

## Speaking and Listening & Collaborative Learning

**GIVING AN ORAL INTERPRETATION.** Read the Language Arts Survey 4.19, "Oral Interpretation of Poetry." Then prepare an oral interpretation of one or more spirituals and present your interpretation to a group of classmates. You may choose to sing your selections. When listening to the presentations of your group members, take notes as described in the Language Arts Survey 5.17, "Taking Notes, Outlining, and Summarizing Information."

## Literary TOOLS

**FOLK SONG.** A **folk song** is a traditional or composed song typically made up of *stanzas,* a *refrain,* and a simple melody. A *stanza* is a group of lines in a poem. A *refrain* is a phrase, line, or verse that recurs regularly at intervals throughout a poem or song, especially at the end of each stanza or division. A form of folk literature, folk songs are expressions of commonly shared ideas or feelings and may be narrative or lyric in style. As you read, try to determine the ideas or feelings that Foster expresses in "My Old Kentucky Home."

**RHYME SCHEME.** A **rhyme scheme** is a pattern of *end rhymes,* or rhymes at the ends of lines of verse. Song verse may be written with a set rhyme scheme or in *free verse,* which does not have a regular rhyme, rhythm, meter, or division into stanzas. As you read, decide whether the lyrics in this song are written with a rhyme scheme or in free verse.

## Reader's *Journal*

What was it like the first time you were separated from your family?

# "MY OLD KENTUCKY HOME"

BY STEPHEN C. FOSTER

## About *the* AUTHOR

**Stephen Collins Foster** (1826–1864) was this country's first great songwriter and has been called "America's Troubadour." His songs reflected the social consciousness of the new nation. He was born in Pittsburgh, Pennsylvania, on July 4, 1826. Foster proved his musical talent early by playing the flute at the age of four, and completed his first composition, "The Tioga Waltz," at the age of fifteen. Foster wrote more than two hundred songs, including "Oh! Susanna," "Camptown Races," "Jeanie With the Light Brown Hair," "Old Folks at Home," "Beautiful Dreamer," and many others still familiar today.

Foster originally became famous writing blackface minstrel songs, which mimicked African-American music. But as a result of living in Pittsburgh—a main hub on the Underground Railroad—and being exposed to the ideas of abolitionists like Harriet Beecher Stowe and Martin Delaney, the first African-American U.S. Army major, Foster developed a profound empathy for African Americans that is evident in his later songs.

During his lifetime Foster received only slightly over $15,000 in royalties for all of his songs, which would be worth millions today. He was nearly penniless at the time of his early death in 1864 at the age of thirty-seven. Yet his music lives on with an appeal that is not only American, but universal.

## About *the* SELECTION

**"My Old Kentucky Home"** was inspired by Harriet Beecher Stowe's abolitionist novel, *Uncle Tom's Cabin,* and expresses deep sympathy for enslaved African Americans. Written in 1858, the first draft in Foster's sketchbook of the song was entitled "Poor Uncle Tom, good night" and was written in black dialect. Prior to publication Foster dropped most of the dialect and removed the references to Uncle Tom, emphasizing the more traditional and common themes of loss of one's family, home, and childhood. "My Old Kentucky Home" is sung on national television every year on the day of the Kentucky Derby and remains the state's official song.

# MY OLD KENTUCKY HOME

## STEPHEN C. FOSTER

1. The sun shines bright in my old Kentucky home
   'tis summer, the folks there are gay.
   The corn top's ripe and the meadow's in the bloom,
   while the birds make music all the day.

2. The young folks roll on the little cabin floor,
   all merry, all happy and bright.
   By'n by, hard times come a-knockin' at the door
   then, my old Kentucky home, good night.

*What comes a-knockin' at the door?*

*Refrain:*
Weep no more, my lady,
oh, weep no more today.
We will sing one song for the old Kentucky home,
for the old Kentucky home far away.

The sun shines bright in my old Ken-tuck-y home; 'tis sum-mer, the folks there are gay. The corn top's ripe, and the mead-ow's in the bloom, while the birds make mu-sic all the day. Weep no more, my la-dy; oh, weep no more to-day. We will sing one song for the old Ken-tuck-y home, for the old Ken-tuck-y home far a way.

3. They hunt no more for the 'possum and the 'coon
   On the meadow, the hill and the shore;
   They sing no more by the glimmer of the moon
   On the bench by that old cabin door.

4. The day goes by like a shadow o'er the heart,
   with sorrow where all was delight.
   The time has come when the old friends have to part,
   Then my old Kentucky home, good night.
   *(To Refrain)*

5. The head must bow and the back will have to bend
   Wherever the poor folks may go.
   A few more days, and the trouble all will end
   in the field where the sugar canes grow.

6. A few more days for to tote the weary load;
   No matter, 'twill never be light.
   A few more days 'till we totter on the road,
   then my old Kentucky home good night.
   *(To Refrain)*

*What causes their delight to turn to sorrow?*

*What will happen in a few more days?*

**Respond** *to the*
## SELECTION

How would you deal with moving from place to place and never having a place to call home?

# Investigate Inquire, Imagine

**Recall:** GATHERING FACTS

1a. What happens when hard times come a-knockin' at the door?

2a. What are the poor folks no longer able to do?

➤ **Interpret:** FINDING MEANING

1b. To whom might the lady in the refrain refer?

2b. What causes the poor folks to have to leave their home?

**Analyze:** TAKING THINGS APART

3a. From the description given of the poor folks and their living conditions, identify to whom Foster might be referring in this poem.

➤ **Synthesize:** BRINGING THINGS TOGETHER

3b. Will the trouble really end in "a few more days"? Explain your answer.

**Perspective:** LOOKING AT OTHER VIEWS

4a. How do you think the poor folks in the song find the strength to continue, considering that they are being forced to do back-breaking work, travel from place to place, and be separated from their friends and family?

➤ **Empathy:** SEEING FROM INSIDE

4b. Has it ever seemed that your life has been ruled by circumstances beyond your control? How did your reaction compare with the way the poor folks in the song deal with their situation?

# Understanding Literature

**FOLK SONG.** Read the definition of **folk song** in the Handbook of Literary Terms. Do you think the ideas and feelings that Foster expressed in this folk song were commonly shared by people of that time period? Explain your answer.

**RHYME SCHEME.** Review the definition of **rhyme scheme** in the Handbook of Literary Terms. The rhyme scheme of a poem or verse is designated by letters, with matching letters signifying matching sounds. Write out the rhyme scheme for "My Old Kentucky Home." The first verse has been done for you.

Verse 1 *abab*

# WRITER'S JOURNAL

1. Imagine that you are one of the people Foster wrote about in his song. Write a **farewell letter** to your friends and family that you are leaving behind.

2. Write a **paraphrase** of the lyrics to "My Old Kentucky Home."

3. Choose a current topic from today's culture and write your own **folk song lyrics.** Your song should have at least two verses and a refrain, or chorus, which is a stanza that repeats after each verse. You may choose to write your lyrics in free verse or with a rhyme pattern.

# Integrating *the* LANGUAGE ARTS

## Language, Grammar, and Style

**DIALECT.** Dialect is a version of a language spoken by the people of a particular place, time, or social group. Writers often use dialect to give their works a realistic flavor. A *regional dialect* is spoken by members of a particular social group or class, or of people living in a certain regional area of the country. Make a chart listing the examples you found of dialect in this song. Write examples of dialect in the left column and an explanation in the right column. See the examples below.

| Dialect | Explanation |
| --- | --- |
| 'tis | it is |
| in the bloom | blooming |

## Study and Research

**TIME LINE.** Research the life of Stephen Foster by visiting the Internet site for the Center for American Music at the University of Pittsburgh, Foster's hometown, at http://www.library.pitt.edu/libraries/cam/cam.html. Go to "Stephen Foster Pages" and select "Stephen Foster Chronology." Read the chronology for the years from 1826 through 1864 and make a time line that includes the major events in Foster's life.

You may want to investigate other pages at this site, such as his biographical sketch, common myths about Stephen Foster, an example of a page from his sketchbook, and the complete list of his compositions.

## Applied English

**PRESS RELEASE.** Writers of public relations, or P.R., materials must capture a reader's attention and persuade the reader to buy, or feel positive about, a particular product or viewpoint. Public relations writing is also called promotional writing because its *aim* is to promote a particular thing. Imagine that you work in the public relations department for an orchestra that is performing a concert of Stephen Foster music. Write a press release to persuade the public to attend the concert. Refer to the Language Arts Survey 6.9, "Delivering a Press Release," for information on writing a press release. Include the following information in your press release:

Date of press release

Date and time of concert

Location

Name of group performing

Cost of tickets

How to purchase tickets

Why people should attend

# "The Battle Hymn of the Republic"

BY JULIA WARD HOWE

## About the AUTHOR

**Julia Ward Howe** (1819–1910), born in New York City, was a staunch abolitionist and a pioneer in the women's suffrage movement. She assisted her husband, Dr. Samuel Gridley Howe, in his philanthropic projects and in editing the *Boston Commonwealth*, an abolitionist paper. After the Civil War, she was president of the Massachusetts Women Suffrage Association and the New England Women's Suffrage Movement. The American Academy of Arts and Letters elected Howe as its first woman member.

Before and after the Civil War, Howe was much in demand as a lecturer. Although best known as author of "The Battle Hymn of the Republic," she also wrote several volumes of poetry and a memoir entitled *Reminiscences, 1819–1899*.

## About the SELECTION

After visiting a Union camp near Washington, DC in November 1861, where she saw soldiers marching off to battle, Julia Ward Howe was inspired to write **"The Battle Hymn of the Republic."** Some sources maintain that she was compelled to write the hymn after hearing Union troops sing "John Brown's body lies a-mouldering in the grave," a reference to farmer and abolitionist John Brown (1800–1859), who was hanged in Charlestown, Virginia (now West Virginia), for his fight against slavery. Howe's song was published in *The Atlantic Monthly* in February 1862 and soon became the Civil War anthem of the North. A patriotic hymn, "The Battle Hymn of the Republic" justifies the Union cause and celebrates heroic self-sacrifice.

## Literary TOOLS

**HYMN.** A **hymn** is a song or verse of praise, often religious. As you read "The Battle Hymn of the Republic," pay attention to the religious images and themes you encounter.

**ALLUSION.** An **allusion** is a rhetorical technique in which reference is made to a person, event, object, or work from history or literature. As you read "The Battle Hymn of the Republic," try to determine to what other written work the author might be alluding. Even if you do not recognize any specific allusions, try to guess based on the language you read.

## Reader's Journal

If you had to fight in a war, what thoughts would help you feel brave?

***The Second Minnesota Regiment at Mission Ridge,*** 1906. Douglas Volk.
Minnesota State Capitol, St. Paul.

# The Battle Hymn of the Republic

## JULIA WARD HOWE

Mine eyes have seen the glory
of the coming of the Lord,
He is trampling out the vintage[1]
Where the grapes of <u>wrath</u> are stored
He hath loosed his <u>fateful</u> lightning
of his terrible swift sword,
His truth is marching on.

> *According to the speaker, what can the Lord be seen doing?*

_____

1. **vintage.** Season's yield of wine from a vineyard

**WORDS FOR EVERYDAY USE**

**wrath** (rath) *n.,* strong, vengeful anger. *The captain vented his <u>wrath</u> on the enemy regiment that had killed ten of his men.*

**fate • ful** (fāt´ fəl) *adj.,* deadly. *The <u>fateful</u> winter storm claimed the lives of many travelers.*

Chorus:
Glory! Glory! Hallelujah![2]
Glory! Glory! Hallelujah!
Glory! Glory! Hallelujah!
His truth is marching on.

I have seen him in the watchfires[3] of a
hundred circling camps,
they have builded Him an altar in the evening
dews and damps[4]
I can read his righteous sentence
by the dim and <u>flaring</u> lamps;
His day is marching on.
    Chorus

I have read a firey gospel[5]
Writ in <u>burnished</u> rows of steel
As ye deal with my condemners,
So with you my grace will deal;
Let the hero born of woman
Crush the serpent with his heel;
Since God is marching on.
    Chorus

He has sounded forth the trumpet
that shall never sound retreat;
He is sifting out the hearts of men
beneath his Judgment Seat.
Oh! Be swift, my soul to answer him,
be <u>jubilant,</u> my feet!
Our God is marching on.
    Chorus

In the beauty of the lilies
Christ was born across the sea
With a glory in his bosom
That <u>transfigures</u> you and me;
As he died to make men holy
let us die to make men free,
While God is marching on.
    Chorus ■

*Where else has the speaker seen the Lord?*

*According to the speaker, what has the Lord done? What is he now doing?*

*What does the speaker say Jesus has done? What does the speaker encourage others to do?*

---

2. **Hallelujah!** Interjection of praise, joy, or thanks
3. **watchfires.** Fires lighted as a signal or for the use of a guard
4. **damps.** Mists, fogs
5. **gospel.** Message concerning Jesus, the kingdom of God, and salvation; one of the first four New Testament books in the Bible

**WORDS FOR EVERYDAY USE**

**flar • ing** (flar´ ing) *adj.*, flaming brightly or unsteadily. *The <u>flaring</u> bonfire cast flickering shadows on our faces.*

**bur • nished** (bər ´nished) *adj.*, polished; made shiny by rubbing. *<u>Burnished</u> silver sparkles like moonlight, but tarnished silver is as black as soot.*

**ju • bi • lant** (jü ´bə lənt) *adj.*, joyful, triumphant. *When our soccer team won, we let out <u>jubilant</u> shouts of celebration.*

**trans • fig • ure** (tran[t]s fi´ gyər) *vt.*, give a new and exalted or spiritual appearance to. *According to tradition, Buddha was <u>transfigured</u> while meditating under a tree.*

If you were a Union soldier, how would hearing these words make you feel about your role in the war?

# INVESTIGATE Inquire, *Imagine*

**Recall:** GATHERING FACTS  →

1a. In the first stanza of this song, what is the Lord described as doing?

2a. What words does the speaker use to describe the gospel? What does the speaker encourage the hero to do to the serpent? What is the Lord doing to the hearts of men?

3a. In the last stanza, what does the speaker say about Jesus' birth and his effect on others? What does the speaker encourage listeners to do, and for what cause?

**Interpret:** FINDING MEANING

1b. How would you characterize the way the Lord is depicted in this stanza? How might the Lord's action in the vineyard appear?

2b. What might the serpent represent? Explain what you think the speaker believes will happen to the enemies of the Republic.

3b. How does the image of Jesus in the last stanza contrast with the image of the Lord in the first stanza? What effect does this depiction have on what the speaker is asking others to do?

**Analyze:** TAKING THINGS APART  →

4a. Analyze the speaker's depiction of God in this song. According to the speaker, is God impartial in matters of war? If so, explain in what way this impartiality is revealed. If not, whose side is God on, according to the speaker, and how can you tell?

**Synthesize:** BRINGING THINGS TOGETHER

4b. Explain whether you would classify Julia Ward Howe as impartial in her depiction of the opposing forces involved in the Civil War. Explain what you think Howe's priorities were in writing this poem. In what way did the time when she wrote the song affect her depiction of the Civil War?

**Perspective:** LOOKING AT OTHER VIEWS  →

5a. Explain what attitude you believe Confederate soldiers might have adopted toward this song. What might they have thought about the speaker's portrayal of the Lord's relationship with Union troops? As an alternative to this question, explore what your attitude would be toward this song if you were a pacifist. What might you refute?

**Empathy:** SEEING FROM INSIDE

5b. Imagine what it would be like to be in a war where American fought American, and, as sometimes was the case, brother fought brother. What conflicting feelings might soldiers have experienced? Why might religious hymns, such as Howe's, have been used to ready soldiers for battle?

# Understanding *Literature*

HYMN. Review the definition for **hymn** in the Handbook of Literary Terms. What religious images and themes does Howe use in "The Battle Hymn of the Republic"?

**ALLUSION.** Review the definition for **allusion** in the Handbook of Literary Terms. You may have noticed as you read "The Battle Hymn of the Republic" that it alludes to both the Old and the New Testaments in the Bible. Identify the lines in which Howe alludes to the following biblical passages:

a. "The wine of God's wrath, poured unmixed into the cup of his anger." (Revelation 14:10)

b. "The Lord God said to the serpent . . . I will put enmity between you and the woman . . . he will strike your head." (Genesis 3:14–15)

Why do you think Howe makes biblical allusions in her lyrics?

# Writer's Journal

1. Imagine that you are a Civil War soldier who has just heard "The Battle Hymn of the Republic." Write a brief **letter** to Julia Ward Howe expressing your feelings about her song. You might also tell her a little bit about your experiences in the war.

2. Howe wrote "The Battle Hymn of the Republic" to the tune of another popular Civil War song that includes the line, "John Brown's body lies a-mouldering in the grave." Write **lyrics** to a tune you know well, making sure to select a topic that is different from the original song lyrics. Imagine that your song will be heard on a radio "Top 40" program.

3. Write a **review** of "The Battle Hymn of the Republic," imagining you are a newspaper columnist and that your readers are either pro-Union or pro-Confederate.

# Integrating
## *the* LANGUAGE ARTS

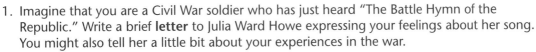

## Language, Grammar, and Style

**ARCHAIC LANGUAGE.** Archaic language consists of old or obsolete phrases such as *smote* for *hit.* When you read "The Battle Hymn of the Republic," you may have noticed that Howe wrote "Mine eyes have seen the glory," when standard usage today would dictate that we say "My eyes have seen the glory." As you read, compile a list of archaic words and the modern equivalents of these terms. Use a chart like the one that follows.

| Archaic Word or Phrase | Modern Word or Phrase |
| --- | --- |
| "Mine eyes" | My eyes |

## Study and Research & Speaking and Listening

**USING SEARCHING TOOLS.** Although "The Battle Hymn of the Republic" is probably the most widely known Civil War song, it is far from the only one. Read the Language Arts Survey 5.19, "How to Locate Library Materials." Then, working with a partner, use the library's computerized catalog to locate another Civil War song. Prepare an oral interpretation of the song, writing an introduction and any needed transitions between verses. Then read the Language Arts Survey 4.19, "Oral Interpretation of Poetry." You and your classmate do not have to sing the song if you are not comfortable doing so; you may choose to take turns expressively reading alternate verses.

# The Gettysburg Address

BY ABRAHAM LINCOLN

## About the AUTHOR

**Abraham Lincoln** (1809–1865), known to history as the Great Emancipator and responsible for preserving the Union during the Civil War, rose from obscurity to a place of reverence in the annals of American history. Born to frontier parents in a backwoods cabin in Kentucky, he nonetheless managed to school himself through voracious reading. In fact, the figure of the young Lincoln reading by candlelight in the evening has become a part of American legend. Lincoln's mother died when he was nine. His father remarried a woman who singled out Abraham for special attention and was later referred to by him as his "angel mother." A strong, lanky youth, Lincoln split rails to fence in the family farm when they moved to Illinois and then held a succession of jobs as a flatboatman, storekeeper, postmaster, and surveyor. He served as a captain in the Blackhawk War and decided to prepare himself for a career in law. Again, he schooled himself, reading law books and passing the bar exam in 1836. Moving to the Illinois capital of Springfield, he was elected to the state legislature, where he served four terms. His romance with Ann Rutledge was cut short by her death at age nineteen, and he married Mary Todd in 1842.

Abraham Lincoln and his son Tad, 1864.

In 1858, Lincoln entered the state senatorial race against Stephen A. Douglas. Lincoln lost that election, but the Lincoln–Douglas debates showed the losing candidate to be a brilliant speaker, combining learned references with homespun witticisms and steeltrap logic. In 1860, running as the candidate of the newly formed Republican party, Lincoln was elected the sixteenth president of the United States. Perhaps no other president has faced such a crisis on taking office, for immediately he was embroiled in the Civil War, brought about by the secession of Southern states from the Union to form the Confederacy. After many false starts and mistakes, Lincoln finally installed the proper command to lead his Union troops to victory. During the war, Lincoln issued the Emancipation Proclamation, freeing slaves in states then in rebellion. After the war he worked for passage of the Thirteenth Amendment, which ended slavery in the United States once and for all. In April 1865, shortly after being reelected for a second term as president, Lincoln was assassinated while watching a play at Ford's Theater in Washington.

# About the SELECTION

On November 19, 1863, Lincoln delivered his famous address at the dedication of the national cemetery at Gettysburg. Gettysburg had been the site of one of the bloodiest battles in the Civil War; in July 1863, Union and Confederate troops fought for a grueling three days on the usually peaceful farmlands of Pennsylvania. Many historians feel that this battle signified the turning point of the Civil War. However, at the time that Lincoln gave his speech, the war was still unfinished.

In light of the bitterness of the conflict, one of the most remarkable aspects of **The Gettysburg Address** is its avoidance of angry or inflammatory rhetoric that would incite listeners to further hostility against the enemy. Instead, the speech focuses on the sacrifice of the participants in the battle and the need for rededication to the principles of the nation's founders. There was a sharp contrast between this simple three-paragraph speech and the two-hour address by well-known orator Edward Everett that preceded it. In fact, Lincoln's speech was considered unimportant at the time of its delivery. The version of The Gettysburg Address that you are about to read was edited by Lincoln after he gave the speech.

---

**THE WIT AND WISDOM OF ABRAHAM LINCOLN**

**On being asked to replace a general:** "It is best not to swap horses while crossing the river."

**On charity toward one's enemies:** "Am I not destroying my enemies when I make friends of them?"

**On deception:** "You can fool all the people some of the time, and some of the people all the time, but you cannot fool all the people all of the time."

**On government:** "No man is good enough to govern another man without that other's consent."

**On personal appearance:** "The Lord prefers common-looking people. That is the reason He makes so many of them."

**On slavery:** "I intend no modification of my oft-expressed personal wish that all men everywhere should be free."

**On voting:** "The ballot is stronger than the bullet."

**To Harriet Beecher Stowe, author of the popular antislavery novel** *Uncle Tom's Cabin:* "So you're the little woman who wrote the book that made this great war!"

**On a book:** "People who like this sort of thing will find this the sort of thing they like."

**On slavery:** "In giving freedom to the slave, we assure freedom to the free,—honorable alike in what we give and what we preserve."

---

# Literary TOOLS

**PARALLELISM. Parallelism** is a rhetorical technique in which a writer emphasizes the equal value or weight of two or more ideas by expressing them in the same grammatical form. As you read, look for examples of parallelism in The Gettysburg Address.

**ANTITHESIS. Antithesis** is a rhetorical technique in which words, phrases, or ideas are strongly contrasted, often by means of a repetition of grammatical structure. Here is an example of antithesis in The Gettysburg Address: "as a final resting place for those who here gave their lives that that nation might live." As you read, look for other examples of antithesis in Lincoln's speech.

# Reader's Journal

If you were the leader of a group that needed encouragement, what would you say to inspire your followers to continue their struggle?

# The Gettysburg Address

## ABRAHAM LINCOLN

Four score and seven years ago our fathers brought forth on this continent, a new nation, conceived in Liberty, and dedicated to the proposition that all men are created equal.

Now we are engaged in a great civil war, testing whether that nation, or any nation so conceived and so dedicated, can long endure. We are met on a great battlefield of that war. We have come to dedicate a portion of that field, as a final resting place for those who here gave their lives that that nation might live. It is altogether fitting and proper that we should do this.

*What event is taking place at the time this speech is delivered? What is being tested by this event?*

But, in a larger sense, we can not dedicate—we can not consecrate—we can not hallow—this ground. The brave men, living and dead, who struggled here, have consecrated it, far above our poor power to add or detract. The world will little note, nor long remember what we say here, but it can never forget what they did here. It is for us the living, rather, to be dedicated here to the unfinished work which they who fought here have thus far so nobly advanced. It is rather for us to be here dedicated to the great task remaining before us—that from these honored dead we take increased devotion to that cause for which they gave the last full measure of devotion—that we here highly resolve that these dead shall not have died in vain—that this nation, under God, shall have a new birth of freedom—and that government of the people, by the people, for the people, shall not perish from the earth. ■

*What should people do to honor the dead?*

WORDS
FOR
EVERYDAY
USE

**score** (skôr) *n.,* set of twenty. *"We don't need one hundred eggs!" Corky exclaimed when she heard Lou order five score.*

**con • se • crate** (kän′si krāt′) *vt.,* make or declare sacred. *The bishop consecrated the church before the minister held the first service.*

## Respond *to the* SELECTION

If you were in the audience when Lincoln gave The Gettysburg Address, how would you have reacted to such a short speech about such a long war?

Lincoln's original draft of The Gettysburg Address. Library of Congress.

# INVESTIGATE, Inquire, Imagine

### Recall: GATHERING FACTS

1a. Lincoln refers to an event "Four score and seven years ago." To what date and event is he referring?

2a. Why does Lincoln say that, in a larger sense, he cannot consecrate the cemetery? Who has consecrated it better than he or the audience can?

3a. To what cause does Lincoln ask that his listeners dedicate themselves?

### Interpret: FINDING MEANING

1b. Why does Lincoln begin by referring to the principles of the founders of the United States? What emotions does he hope to evoke in his listeners?

2b. What was "the last full measure of devotion" that the soldiers demonstrated?

3b. Under what circumstances would the dead have died in vain? What can the listeners do to ensure that the deaths were not futile?

### Analyze: TAKING THINGS APART

4a. Lincoln uses the word "dedicate" six times in the course of this brief speech. Look up the word and decide which of its meanings Lincoln intended.

### Synthesize: BRINGING THINGS TOGETHER

4b. Summarize the most important message that Lincoln is trying to make.

### Evaluate: MAKING JUDGMENTS

5a. Lincoln said, "The world will little note, nor long remember what we say here." However, this speech has been repeated for over one hundred years, and many students have memorized it. Why do you think this speech has touched Americans so deeply since 1863? Assess what makes The Gettysburg Address such a memorable speech.

### Extend: CONNECTING IDEAS

5b. When the anonymous writer of "Swing Low, Sweet Chariot" and Lincoln thought about the audience for their writing, they may have wanted to evoke similar emotions. What emotions do you think each author was hoping to inspire?

# Understanding Literature

**Parallelism.** Review the definition for **parallelism** in the Handbook of Literary Terms. Lincoln uses parallelism extensively in the final sentence of the selection. For example, he repeats the modifier and noun in the series of prepositional phrases "of the people, by the people, for the people" in his description of democratic government. Make a chart listing the three examples of parallelism that begin with *that*, and paraphrase each one. The first example has been done for you.

| Examples of Parallelism | "that from these honored dead we take increased devotion to that cause for which they gave the last full measure of devotion" |
|---|---|
| Paraphrasing | that the dead may inspire us to continue the struggle for which they gave their lives |

**ANTITHESIS.** Review the definition of **antithesis** in the Handbook of Literary Terms. What other examples of antithesis did you find in Lincoln's speech?

# ŪRITER'S JOURNAL

1. Write an 1864 **prediction** for the United States based on Lincoln's stated and implied hopes for the country. For your audience, imagine the same group of people who assembled to hear The Gettysburg Address.

2. Write a **monument inscription** to accompany a monument dedicated to unknown, fallen soldiers at the Gettysburg National Cemetery.

3. Imagine that it is November 19, 1863, and that you are a Confederate spy in Gettysburg, Pennsylvania. Write a **report** intended for Confederate leaders, about the speech that Lincoln has just given.

# Integrating
## *the* LANGUAGE ARTS

## Language, Grammar, and Style

**ACHIEVING PARALLELISM.** Read the Language Arts Survey 3.38, "Achieving Parallelism." Then rewrite each of the following sentences below using parallel structure.

1. Our ancestors brought forth a new nation conceived in liberty and it was also being dedicated to the principle of equality for all people.

2. It is fitting and proper to dedicate the cemetery and setting aside a portion of it to the fallen soldiers.

3. The brave men who were fighting and died here consecrated the ground better than we can.

4. The world does not note nor will it remember what we say here.

5. We must resolve that these dead shall not have died in vain and to dedicate ourselves to the preservation of the nation.

## Language, Grammar, and Style

**USING A THESAURUS.** Rewrite The Gettysburg Address in everyday language. Use a thesaurus to find appropriate synonyms as you translate the main ideas of the speech into the language of today. You may want to read the Language Arts Survey 5.22, "Using a Thesaurus."

## Collaborative Learning & Study and Research

**RESEARCHING THE GETTYSBURG CAMPAIGN.** With two or three classmates, research an aspect of the Gettysburg campaign. You might choose from these topics: "Battle Preparations," "Pickett's Charge," "Cavalry Strategy," "Criticism of Lee and Meade," and "Turning Point of the War." First, take notes as you do your research. Second, choose roles for your group members, deciding who will be the secretary, the writer, the editor, and the presenter. Third, the secretary takes notes for an outline, receiving ideas from the other three group members. Then the writer uses the outline to write the paper, giving it to the editor to mark revisions. Finally, the presenter uses the outline to give a presentation to the class, and the writer submits the revised paper to the teacher.

# Literary
## TOOLS

**ARGUMENT.** In nonfiction writing, **argument** is the case for accepting or rejecting a proposition or course of action. As you read this speech, you will notice that Sojourner Truth mentions her opponents' arguments against women's rights as well as her arguments for women's rights. As you read, create a list of both sets of arguments. Use a chart like the following.

| Arguments Against Women's Rights Spoken at the Convention | Sojourner Truth's Arguments for Women's Rights |
| --- | --- |
| Women need to be helped into carriages | |

**REPETITION. Repetition** is a writer's conscious reuse of a sound, word, phrase, or other element. As you read, identify a phrase that Truth repeats throughout her speech.

**COLLOQUIALISM AND TONE. Colloquialism** is the use of informal language. **Tone** is the emotional attitude toward a subject implied by a literary work. As you read Truth's speech, look for the colloquial expressions that she uses and try to determine the tone.

# Reader's
## Journal

If someone belittled you for something outside your control, such as your race, sex, or religion, how do you think you would react?

# "Ain't I A Woman?"

BY SOJOURNER TRUTH

## About the
# AUTHOR

**Sojourner Truth** (c.1797–1883) was born Isabella Baumfree in Hurley, New York, the second youngest of ten or twelve children of a slave couple. Put up for auction in 1806, she worked as a slave until 1828 when she was freed under the New York State Anti-Slavery Act. She successfully fought to have one of her sons, sold illegally, returned to her, becoming the first African-American woman to take a white man to court and win.

In 1843, Isabella claimed that God told her to change her name to Sojourner Truth. Truth traveled extensively, speaking for the abolition of slavery and women's rights. Although she could neither read nor write, she became a famous preacher. By selling copies of her autobiography, *Narrative of Sojourner Truth: A Northern Slave*, she was able to support herself and buy a home in Battle Creek, Michigan. During the Civil War, she preached to make money for African-American soldiers serving in the Union army. She led an unsuccessful campaign to have land in the West set aside for freed African Americans, many of whom were poor and homeless after the war. Truth met many important figures of her day, including Abraham Lincoln, Frederick Douglass, and Harriet Beecher Stowe.

## About the
# SELECTION

Truth gave her famous **"Ain't I a Woman?"** speech at the 1851 Women's Rights Convention in Akron, Ohio. According to a review of her speech at that time, "One of the most unique and interesting speeches of the Convention was made by Sojourner Truth, an emancipated slave. It is impossible to transfer it to paper, or convey any adequate idea of the effect it produced upon the audience. Those only can appreciate it who saw her powerful form, her whole-souled, earnest gesture, and listened to her strong and truthful tones." In her colloquial speech, Truth answers opponents to women's rights with forceful arguments, including personal testimony.

# Ain't I A Woman?

## SOJOURNER TRUTH

Well, children, where there is so much racket there must be something out of kilter[1]. I think that 'twixt[2] the negroes of the South and the women at the North, all talking about rights, the white men will be in a fix pretty soon. But what's all this here talking about?

*What does Truth predict will happen because of the African Americans' and the women's call for rights?*

That man over there says that women need to be helped into carriages, and lifted over ditches, and to have the best place every-

*What did the "man over there" say about women? What fact does Truth point out?*

where. Nobody ever helps me into carriages, or over mud-puddles, or gives me any best place! And ain't I a woman? Look at me! Look at my arm! I have ploughed and planted, and gathered into barns, and no man could head[3] me! And ain't I a woman? I could work as much and eat as much as a man—when I could get it—and bear the lash as well! And ain't I a woman? I have borne thirteen children, and seen most all sold off to slavery, and when I cried out with my mother's grief, none but Jesus heard me! And ain't I a woman?

Then they talk about this thing in the head; what's this they call it? [a member of the audience whispers "intellect"] That's it, honey.

What's that got to do with women's rights or negroes' rights? If my cup won't hold but a pint, and yours holds a quart,[4] wouldn't you be mean not to let me have my little half measure full?

Then that little man in black there, he says women can't have as much rights as men, 'cause Christ wasn't a woman! Where did your Christ come from? Where did your Christ come from? From God and a woman! Man had nothing to do with Him.

If the first woman[5] God ever made was strong enough to turn the world upside down all alone, these women together ought to be able to turn it back, and get it right side up again! And now they is asking to do it, the men better let them.

*What does Truth say women ought to be able to do? What does she say men should do?*

Obliged to you for hearing me, and now old Sojourner ain't got nothing more to say. ∎

---

1. **out of kilter.** Out of order
2. **'twixt.** Between
3. **head.** Take a lead over; surpass
4. **pint . . . quart.** A pint is half a quart
5. **first woman.** In the book of Genesis in the Bible, the first woman God created was Eve who, along with the first man, Adam, was expelled from the Garden of Eden for eating the fruit of the tree of knowledge of good and evil.

---

**WORDS FOR EVERYDAY USE**

**rack • et** (raˊ kət) *n.,* confused, clattering noise; clamor. *My sister made a racket in the kitchen, banging pots and pans.*

**fix** (fiks) *n.,* position of difficulty or embarrassment. *Because Miguel had not practiced the piano in weeks, he found himself in a fix at the recital.*

---

# Respond *to the* SELECTION

Explain whether Sojourner Truth is someone you would have liked the opportunity to meet.

# INVESTIGATE, Inquire, Imagine

**Recall:** GATHERING FACTS

1a. What work has Truth done in her life? How many children did Truth have? What happened to them?

2a. What point is Truth making with her "pint" and "quart" analogy?

3a. How does Truth respond to the notion that women should not be given rights because Jesus was not a woman? What does she say "the first woman" was strong enough to do?

→ **Interpret:** FINDING MEANING

1b. What types of strength does Truth demonstrate in these examples of her life?

2b. Why doesn't Truth argue how intelligent she is to prove her point about intellect?

3b. Why does Truth use biblical women in her arguments?

---

**Analyze:** TAKING THINGS APART

4a. Based on her speech, identify Truth's feelings toward each of the following topics: women, men, and slavery.

→ **Synthesize:** BRINGING THINGS TOGETHER

4b. Hypothesize whether Truth's attitudes toward these things might have been different had she been a wealthy, white woman who never worked, married happily, and saw her children thrive.

---

**Evaluate:** MAKING JUDGMENTS

5a. Which of Truth's arguments is more effective, that women are as strong as men, or that women, as well as men, should be able to use the intelligence with which they are endowed?

→ **Extend:** CONNECTING IDEAS

5b. Truth considers the opposing side's arguments when stating her opinions. Pick a topic in which you believe strongly and list two arguments that might be used against your position. How would you respond?

---

# Understanding Literature

**ARGUMENT AND REPETITION.** Review the definitions for **argument** and **repetition** in the Handbook of Literary Terms. As you read the speech, you identified a list of arguments against and for women's rights from the Women's Convention in Akron, Ohio. What phrase does Sojourner Truth repeat to punctuate each of her arguments in favor of women's rights? Explain the effect of this repeated phrase on her argument in general.

**COLLOQUIALISM AND TONE.** Review the definitions of **colloquialism** and **tone** in the Handbook of Literary Terms. Examples of different tones that a work may have include familiar, ironic, playful, sarcastic, serious, and sincere. Identify the tone of Sojourner Truth's speech. What effect does the use of colloquial language have upon the tone? Explain whether you think Sojourner Truth's tone is well suited to her message.

# Writer's Journal

1. Write a brief **dialogue** between two people using colloquial language. You may use colloquial language of modern times, or from an earlier time.
2. Write a biographical **paragraph** about Sojourner Truth, based on what you know about her life from her speech.
3. Imagining you are Sojourner Truth, write an **advice column** response to a woman who doubts whether she deserves the same rights as men.

# Integrating *the* LANGUAGE ARTS

## Language, Grammar, and Style

**CHANGING COLLOQUIAL SPEECH.** Rewrite the following sentences, replacing underlined colloquial language with standard language. Refer to the Language Arts Survey 3.2, "Formal and Informal English."

1. '<u>Twixt</u> the racket and the hecklers, Sojourner Truth had a challenge delivering her speech at the Women's Convention in Akron, Ohio.
2. <u>Them</u> men in the back kept yelling out arguments why women shouldn't have equal rights.
3. One man actually said women shouldn't have equal rights '<u>cause</u> Christ wasn't a woman.
4. Truth's refrain was "And <u>ain't</u> I a woman?"
5. Truth should <u>of</u> learned to read and write.

## Critical Thinking

**AVOIDING FAULTY ARGUMENTS.** In her speech, Sojourner Truth finds fault with one of the arguments against women's rights, namely, "Women can't have as much rights as men, 'cause Christ wasn't a woman." This faulty argument is a type of logical fallacy known as a **non sequitur**. A **non sequitur** is a conclusion that simply does not follow from the reasons given and may have nothing to do with them. It is true that Jesus was male; the idea that women can't have rights because Jesus was male does not follow as a logical consequence. Review the Language Arts Survey 5.3, "Avoiding False Arguments and Propaganda." Then match the type of faulty argument (the letter in the left column) to a specific argument (in the right column).

| | |
|---|---|
| A. false analogy | 1. Russia's form of government was once communism. Therefore, all Russians are communists. |
| B. circularity | 2. An apple is a sweet, red fruit that grows on a tree. A strawberry is a sweet, red fruit. Therefore, it must grow on a tree. |
| C. fallacy of decomposition | 3. If you are not with us, then you are against us. |
| D. hasty generalization | 4. Our school basketball team lost every game this season. Jared is on the basketball team. He must be a terrible basketball player. |
| E. false dichotomy | 5. Sojourner Truth was the best public speaker ever because she gave the best oral presentations. |

## Literary TOOLS

**FLASHBACK.** A **flashback** is a section of a literary work that presents an event or series of events that occurred earlier than the current time in the work. Unlike traditional, straightforward narratives that present plot events chronologically, this story relies on flashbacks and journeys into the mind of the main character. Look for examples of flashback as you read the story.

**PSYCHOLOGICAL FICTION. Psychological fiction** is fiction that emphasizes the interior, subjective experiences of its characters, and especially such fiction when it deals with emotional or mental disturbance or anguish. Bierce's stories paved the way for much modern fiction with portrayals of the private psychological states of his characters. As you read, look for passages that qualify as psychological fiction.

## Reader's Journal

If you knew you were about to die, what would you think about?

# "An Occurrence at Owl Creek Bridge"

BY AMBROSE BIERCE

## About the AUTHOR

**Ambrose Bierce** (1842–c.1914), known as "Bitter Bierce," was a cynical, unhappy man with a sharp, satirical wit. Born in Ohio, he grew up in a large, poor family. An unhappy childhood followed by exposure to unimaginable brutality during the Civil War combined to create in Bierce the pessimism that became the dominant trait of his character and his fiction. After spending a year at a military academy, Bierce joined the Union army, rising to the rank of lieutenant. He was a distinguished soldier and participated in several major battles. His war experiences provided material for some of his best stories, including "An Occurrence at Owl Creek Bridge" and "Chickamuga."

After the war Bierce worked as a journalist in San Francisco, establishing himself through witty, satirical columns as a major literary figure in that rough-and-tumble frontier city. There he counted among his friends such major writers as Mark Twain and Bret Harte.

Throughout his life disaster plagued him: his marriage ended in divorce, one son was killed in a fight, and another son died of alcoholism. In 1913, Bierce traveled to Mexico, which was in civil war. There he disappeared without a trace. His greatest legacy, besides his humorous, if grotesque *The Devil's Dictionary*, was a handful of stories acclaimed today for their suspense and psychological realism.

## About the SELECTION

Bierce uses details about military customs and regulations to lend authenticity to **"An Occurrence at Owl Creek Bridge."** In its use of authentic, precisely observed details, this story is a fine early example of American Realism. It is also an early example of Naturalism, a type of writing that reveals the forces beyond people's control that determine not only their circumstances and fate, but also their characters, personalities, and subjective experiences. Although Bierce is often remembered for his bitter and caustic wit, in "An Occurrence at Owl Creek Bridge," he concentrates on telling a good story with enough twists and turns to keep the reader guessing until the last sentence.

Union soldiers guarding a railroad bridge, 1864. Library of Congress.

# An Occurrence at

## *Owl Creek Bridge*

### AMBROSE BIERCE

### I

A man stood upon a railroad bridge in northern Alabama, looking down into the swift water twenty feet below. The man's hands were behind his back, the wrists bound with a cord. A rope closely encircled his neck. It was attached to a stout cross timber above his head and the slack fell to the level of his knees. Some loose boards laid upon the sleepers[1] supporting the metals of the railway supplied a footing for him and his executioners—two private soldiers of the Federal army, directed by a sergeant who in civil life may have been a deputy sheriff. At a short remove upon the same temporary platform was an officer in the uniform of his rank, armed. He was a captain. A <u>sentinel</u> at each end of the

> What is about to happen to the man?

---

1. **sleepers.** Ties that support railroad tracks

WORDS
FOR
EVERYDAY
USE

sen • ti • nel (sen´ti nəl) *n.*, person acting as a guard. *The <u>sentinel</u> stood watch on the ramparts.*

bridge stood with his rifle in the position known as "support," that is to say, vertical in front of the left shoulder, the hammer resting on the forearm thrown straight across the chest—a formal and unnatural position, enforcing an erect carriage of the body. It did not appear to be the duty of these two men to know what was occurring at the center of the bridge; they merely blockaded the two ends of the foot planking that traversed it.

Beyond one of the sentinels nobody was in sight; the railroad ran straight away into a forest for a hundred yards, then, curving, was lost to view. Doubtless there was an outpost farther along. The other bank of the stream was open ground—a gentle <u>acclivity</u> topped with a stockade of vertical tree trunks, loopholed for rifles with a single <u>embrasure</u> through which protruded the muzzle of a brass cannon commanding the bridge. Midway of the slope between bridge and fort were the spectators—a single company of infantry in line, at "parade rest," the butts of the rifles on the ground, the barrels inclining slightly backward against the right shoulder, the hands crossed upon the stock. A lieutenant stood at the right of the line, the point of his sword upon the ground, his left hand resting upon his right. Excepting the group of four at the center of the bridge, not a man moved. The company faced the bridge, staring stonily, motionless. The sentinels, facing the banks of the stream, might have been statues to adorn the bridge. The captain stood with folded arms, silent, observing the work of his subordinates, but making no sign. Death is a dignitary who when he comes announced is to be received with formal manifestations of respect, even by those most familiar

What is Death? How should Death be received?

with him. In the code of military etiquette silence and fixity are forms of deference.

The man who was engaged in being hanged was apparently about thirty-five years of age. He was a civilian, if one might judge from his habit, which was that of a planter. His features were good—a straight nose, firm mouth, broad forehead, from which his long, dark hair was combed straight back, falling

What does the man who is about to be hanged look like? What do his clothes reveal about him? What aspect of his appearance is surprising?

behind his ears to the collar of his well-fitting frock coat. He wore a mustache and pointed beard, but no whiskers; his eyes were large and dark gray, and had a kindly expression which one would hardly have expected in one whose neck was in the hemp.[2] Evidently this was no vulgar assassin. The liberal military code makes provision for hanging many kinds of persons, and gentlemen are not excluded.

The preparations being complete, the two private soldiers stepped aside and each drew away the plank upon which he had been standing. The sergeant turned to the captain, saluted and placed himself immediately behind that officer, who in turn moved apart one pace. These movements left the condemned man and the sergeant standing on the two ends of the same plank, which spanned three of the crossties of the bridge. The end upon which the civilian stood almost, but not quite, reached a fourth. This plank had been held in place by the weight of the captain; it was now held by that of the sergeant. At a signal from the former the latter would step aside, the plank would tilt and the condemned man go down between two ties. The arrangement com-

_____
2. **hemp.** Rope made of hemp

WORDS
FOR
EVERYDAY
USE

ac • cliv • i • ty (ə klivʹə tē) n., upward slope. *Due to the <u>acclivity</u> of the land their house stood on, the Nelsons dreaded mowing the lawn.*

em • bra • sure (em brāʹzhər) n., slanted opening in a wall that increases the firing angle of a gun. *Firing through the <u>embrasure</u>, the police were protected from the criminals' barrage.*

mended itself to his judgment as simple and effective. His face had not been covered nor his eyes bandaged. He looked a moment at his "unsteadfast footing," then let his gaze wander to the swirling water of the stream racing madly beneath his feet. A piece of dancing drift-wood caught his attention and his eyes followed it down the current. How slowly it appeared to move! What a sluggish stream!

He closed his eyes in order to fix his last thoughts upon his wife and children. The water, touched to gold by the early sun, the brooding mists under the banks at some distance down the stream, the fort, the sol-diers, the piece of drift—all had dis-tracted him. And now he became conscious of a new disturbance. Striking through the thought of his dear ones was a sound which he could neither ignore nor understand, a sharp, distinct, metallic percussion like the stroke of a blacksmith's hammer upon the anvil; it had the same ringing quality. He wondered what it was, and whether immeasurably distant or near by— it seemed both. Its recurrence was regular, but as slow as the tolling of a death knell. He awaited each stroke with impatience and—he knew not why—apprehen-sion. The intervals of silence grew progressively longer; the delays became maddening. With their greater infrequency the sounds increased in strength and sharpness. They hurt his ear like the thrust of a knife; he feared he would shriek. What he heard was the ticking of his watch.

*What sound did the man seem to hear? What effect did the sound have on him? What was he actually hearing?*

He unclosed his eyes and saw again the water below him. "If I could free my hands," he thought, "I might throw off the noose and spring into the stream. By diving I could evade the bullets and, swimming vigorously, reach the bank, take to the woods and get away home.

**He closed his eyes in order to fix his last thoughts upon his wife and children.**

My home, thank God, is as yet outside their lines; my wife and little ones are still beyond the invader's farthest advance."

As these thoughts, which have here to be set down in words, were flashed into the doomed man's brain rather than evolved from it the captain nodded to the sergeant. The sergeant stepped aside.

## II

Peyton Farquhar was a well-to-do planter, of an old and highly respected Alabama family. Being a slave owner and like other slave owners a politician he was naturally an original secessionist and ardently devoted to the Southern cause. Circumstances of an imperious nature, which it is unnecessary to relate here, had prevented him from taking service with the gallant army that had fought the disastrous campaigns end-ing with the fall of Corinth, and he chafed under the inglorious restraint, longing for the release of his energies, the larger life of the soldier, the opportunity for distinction. That opportunity, he felt, would come, as it comes to all in war time. Meanwhile he did what he could. No service was too hum-ble for him to perform in aid of the South, no adventure too perilous for him to undertake if consistent with the character of a civilian who was at heart a soldier, and who in good faith and without too much qualification assented to at least a part of the frankly villainous dictum that all is fair in love and war.

*What was the man unable to do? What did he long to do?*

One evening while Farquhar and his wife were sitting on a rustic bench near the entrance to his grounds, a gray-clad soldier rode up to the gate and asked for a drink of water. Mrs. Farquhar was only too happy to serve him with her own white hands. While she was fetching the water her husband approached the dusty horseman and inquired eagerly for news from the front.

"The Yanks are repairing the railroads," said the man, "and are getting ready for another advance. They have reached the Owl Creek bridge, put it in order and built a stockade on the north bank. The commandant has issued an order, which is posted everywhere, declaring that any civilian caught interfering with the railroad, its bridges, tunnels or trains will be summarily hanged. I saw the order."

"How far is it to the Owl Creek bridge?" Farquhar asked.

"About thirty miles."

"Is there no force on this side the creek?"

"Only a picket post[3] half a mile out, on the railroad, and a single sentinel at this end of the bridge."

"Suppose a man—a civilian and student of hanging—should elude the picket post and perhaps get the better of the sentinel," said Farquhar, smiling, "what could he accomplish?"

> What does Farquhar have in mind?

The soldier reflected. "I was there a month ago," he replied. "I observed that the flood of last winter had lodged a great quantity of driftwood against the wooden pier at this end of the bridge. It is now dry and would burn like tow."[4]

The lady had now brought the water, which the soldier drank. He thanked her ceremoniously, bowed to her husband and rode away. An hour later, after nightfall, he repassed the plantation, going northward in the direction from which he had come. He was a Federal scout.

> Who is the soldier in the gray uniform? What is the importance of the revelation of his identity?

### III

As Peyton Farquhar fell straight downward through the bridge he lost consciousness and was as one already dead. From this state he was awakened—ages later, it seemed to him—by the pain of a sharp pressure upon his throat, followed by a sense of suffocation. Keen, poignant agonies seemed to shoot from his neck downward through every fiber of his body and limbs. These pains appeared to flash along well defined lines of ramification and to beat with an inconceivably rapid periodicity. They seemed like streams of pulsating fire heating him to an intolerable temperature. As to his head, he was conscious of nothing but a feeling of fullness—of congestion. These sensations were unaccompanied by thought. The intellectual part of his nature was already <u>effaced</u>; he had power only to feel, and feeling was torment. He was conscious of motion. Encompassed in a luminous cloud, of which he was now merely the fiery heart, without material substance, he swung through unthinkable arcs of <u>oscillation</u>, like a vast pendulum. Then all at once, with terrible suddenness, the light about him shot upward with the noise of a loud splash; a frightful roaring was in his ears, and all was cold and dark. The power of thought was restored; he knew that the rope had broken and he had fallen into the stream. There was no additional strangulation; the noose about his neck was already suffocating him and kept the water from his lungs. To die of hanging at the bottom of a river!—the idea seemed to him <u>ludicrous</u>. He opened his eyes in the darkness and saw above him a gleam of light, but how distant, how inaccessible! He was still sinking, for the light became fainter and fainter until it was a mere glimmer. Then it began to grow and brighten, and he knew that he was rising toward the surface—knew it with reluctance, for he was now very comfortable.

---

3. **picket post.** Troops that protect an army from a surprise attack

4. **tow.** Flammable fibers of hemp or flax

---

**WORDS FOR EVERYDAY USE**

ef • face (ə fās´) vt., erase, wipe out. *The thick coat of paint <u>effaced</u> the graffiti on the bathroom wall.*

os • cil • la • tion (äs´ə lā´shən) n., act of swinging back and forth. *The <u>oscillation</u> of the hypnotist's watch soon put the audience volunteer in a trance.*

lu • di • crous (lü´di krəs) adj., absurd, ridiculous. *It was <u>ludicrous</u> how the elephant in the cartoon was afraid of a tiny mouse.*

"To be hanged and drowned," he thought, "that is not so bad; but I do not wish to be shot. No; I will not be shot; that is not fair."

*What thought does Farquhar have as he rises to the surface of the water?*

He was not conscious of an effort, but a sharp pain in his wrist apprised him that he was trying to free his hands. He gave the struggle his attention, as an idler might observe the feat of a juggler, without interest in the outcome. What splendid effort!—what magnificent, what superhuman strength! Ah, that was a fine endeavor! Bravo! The cord fell away; his arms parted and floated upward, the hands dimly seen on each side in the growing light. He watched them with a new interest as first one and then the other pounced upon the noose at his neck. They tore it away and thrust it fiercely aside, its undulations resembling those of a watersnake. "Put it back, put it back!" He thought he shouted these words to his hands, for the undoing of the noose had been succeeded by the direst pang that he had yet experienced. His neck ached horribly; his brain was on fire; his heart, which had been fluttering faintly, gave a great leap, trying to force itself out at his mouth. His whole body was racked and wrenched with an insupportable anguish! But his disobedient hands gave no heed to the command. They beat the water vigorously with quick, downward strokes, forcing him to the surface. He felt his head emerge; his eyes were blinded by the sunlight; his chest expanded convulsively, and with a supreme and crowning agony his lungs engulfed a great draft of air, which instantly he expelled in a shriek!

> **His whole body was racked and wrenched with an insupportable anguish!**

He was now in full possession of his physical senses. They were, indeed, preternaturally[5] keen and alert. Something in the awful disturbance of his organic system had so exalted and refined them that they made record of things never before perceived. He felt the ripples upon his face and heard their separate sounds as they struck. He looked at the forest on the bank of the stream, saw the individual trees, the leaves and the veining of each leaf—saw the very insects upon them: the locusts, the brilliant-bodied flies, the gray spiders stretching their webs from twig to twig. He noted the prismatic colors in all the dewdrops upon a million blades of grass. The humming of the gnats that danced above the eddies of the stream, the beating of the dragon-flies' wings, the strokes of the water spiders' legs, like oars which had lifted their boat—all these made audible music. A fish slid along beneath his eyes and he heard the rush of its body parting the water.

*In what state are Farquhar's senses? What sensory details does he notice?*

He had come to the surface facing down the stream; in a moment the visible world seemed to wheel slowly round, himself the pivotal point, and he saw the bridge, the fort, the soldiers upon the bridge, the captain, the sergeant, the two privates, his executioners. They were in silhouette against the blue sky. They shouted and <u>gesticulated</u>, pointing at him. The captain had drawn his pistol, but did not fire; the others were unarmed. Their

---

5. **preternaturally.** Inexplicably

---

**WORDS FOR EVERYDAY USE**

ges • tic • u • late (jes tik´yü lat´) *vi.,* make gestures with hands or arms. *Late for her appointment, the woman wildly gesticulated to the taxi driver to stop.*

movements were grotesque and horrible, their forms gigantic.

Suddenly he heard a sharp report and something struck the water smartly within a few inches of his head, spattering his face with spray. He heard a second report, and saw one of the sentinels with his rifle at his shoulder, a light cloud of blue smoke rising from the muzzle. The man in the water saw the eye of the man on the bridge gazing into his own through the sights of the rifle. He observed that it was a gray eye and remembered having read that gray eyes were keenest, and that all famous marksmen had them. Nevertheless, this one had missed.

*What does Farquhar notice about the marksman? What does he fear this means? Is the superstition he had heard true?*

A counterswirl had caught Farquhar and turned him half round; he was again looking into the forest on the bank opposite the fort. The sound of a clear, high voice in a monotonous singsong now rang out behind him and came across the water with a distinctness that pierced and subdued all other sounds, even the beating of the ripples in his ears. Although no soldier, he had frequented camps enough to know the dread significance of that deliberate, drawling, <u>aspirated</u> chant; the lieutenant on shore was taking a part in the morning's work. How coldly and pitilessly—with what an even, calm intonation, presaging, and enforcing tranquillity in the men—with what accurately measured intervals fell those cruel words:

*What sound does Farquhar hear? What does he take it to mean?*

"Attention, company! . . . Shoulder arms! . . . Ready! . . . Aim! . . . fire!"

Farquhar dived—dived as deeply as he could. The water roared in his ears like the voice of

***Young Soldier,*** 1861. Winslow Homer.
Cooper-Hewitt National Design Museum, New York.

Niagara, yet he heard the dulled thunder of the volley and, rising again toward the surface, met shining bits of metal, singularly flattened, oscillating slowly downward. Some of them touched him on the face and hands, then fell away,

---

**WORDS FOR EVERYDAY USE**

**as • pi • rat • ed** (as´pə rāt´əd) *adj.,* articulated with a puff of breath before or after. *The choir director made sure the singers warmed up with <u>aspirated</u> vocalizing before the concert.*

continuing their descent. One lodged between his collar and neck; it was uncomfortably warm and he snatched it out.

As he rose to the surface, gasping for breath, he saw that he had been a long time under water; he was perceptibly farther down stream—nearer to safety. The soldiers had almost finished reloading; the metal ramrods flashed all at once in the sunshine as they were drawn from the barrels, turned in the air, and thrust into their sockets. The two sentinels fired again, independently and ineffectually.

The hunted man saw all this over his shoulder; he was now swimming vigorously with the current. His brain was as energetic as his arms and legs; he thought with the rapidity of lightning.

"The officer," he reasoned, "will not make that martinet's[6] error a second time. It is as easy to dodge a volley as a single shot. He has probably already given the command to fire at will. God help me, I cannot dodge them all!"

An appalling splash within two yards of him was followed by a loud, rushing sound, *diminuendo*,[7] which seemed to travel back through the air to the fort and died in an explosion which stirred the very river to its deeps! A rising sheet of water curved over him, fell down upon him, blinded him, strangled him! The cannon had taken a hand in the game. As he shook his head free from the commotion of the smitten water he heard the deflected shot humming through the air ahead, and in an instant it was cracking and smashing the branches in the forest beyond.

"They will not do that again," he thought; "the next time they will use a charge of grape.[8] I must keep my eye upon the gun; the smoke will apprise me—the report arrives too late; it lags behind the missile. That is a good gun."

Suddenly he felt himself whirled round and round—spinning like a top. The water, the

> Suddenly he felt himself whirled round and round—spinning like a top.

banks, the forests, the now distant bridge, fort and men—all were commingled and blurred. Objects were represented by their colors only; circular horizontal streaks of color—that was all he saw. He had been caught in a vortex and was being whirled on with a velocity of advance and gyration that made him giddy and sick. In a few moments he was flung upon the gravel at the foot of the left bank of the stream—the southern bank— and behind a projecting point which concealed him from his enemies. The sudden arrest of his motion, the abrasion of one of his hands on the gravel, restored him, and he wept with delight. He dug his fingers into the sand, threw it over himself in handfuls and audibly blessed it. It looked like diamonds, rubies, emeralds; he could think of nothing beautiful which it did not resemble. The trees upon the bank were giant garden plants; he noted a definite order in their arrangement, inhaled the fragrance of their blooms. A strange, roseate light shone through the spaces among their trunks and the wind made in their branches the music of aeolian harps.[9] He had no wish to perfect his escape—was content to remain in that enchanting spot until retaken.

> What causes Farquhar's delight and contentment?

A whiz and rattle of grapeshot among the branches high above his head roused him from his dream. The baffled cannoneer had fired him a random farewell. He sprang to his feet, rushed up the sloping bank, and plunged into the forest.

All that day he traveled, laying his course by the rounding sun. The forest seemed interminable; nowhere did he discover a break in it,

6. **martinet.** Strict disciplinarian
7. *diminuendo.* Musical term meaning a reduction in volume
8. **grape.** Cluster of small iron balls fired from a cannon
9. **aeolian harps.** Harps that produce music when air blows over the strings

not even a woodman's road. He had not known that he lived in so wild a region. There was something uncanny in the revelation.

By night fall he was fatigued, footsore, famishing. The thought of his wife and children urged him on. At last he found a road which led him in what he knew to be the right direction. It was as wide and straight as a city street, yet it seemed untraveled. No fields bordered it, no dwelling anywhere. Not so much as the barking of a dog suggested human habitation. The black bodies of the trees formed a straight wall on both sides, terminating on the horizon in a point, like a diagram in a lesson in perspective. Overhead, as he looked up through this rift in the wood, shone great golden stars looking unfamiliar and grouped in strange constellations. He was sure they were arranged in some order which had a secret and <u>malign</u> significance. The wood on either side was full of singular noises, among which—once, twice, and again, he distinctly heard whispers in an unknown tongue.

His neck was in pain and lifting his hand to it he found it horribly swollen. He knew that it had a circle of black where the rope had bruised it. His eyes felt congested; he could no longer close them. His tongue was

*What description is given of Farquhar? What image does this description bring to mind?*

swollen with thirst; he relieved its fever by thrusting it forward from between his teeth into the cold air. How softly the turf had carpeted the untraveled avenue—he could no longer feel the roadway beneath his feet!

Doubtless, despite his suffering, he had fallen asleep while walking, for now he sees another scene—perhaps he has merely recovered from a delirium. He stands at the gate of his own home. All is as he left it, and all bright and beautiful in the morning sunshine. He must have traveled the entire night. As he pushes open the gate and passes up the wide white walk, he sees a flutter of female garments; his wife, looking fresh and cool and sweet, steps down from the veranda to meet him. At the bottom of the steps she stands waiting, with a smile of ineffable joy, an attitude of matchless grace and dignity. Ah, how beautiful she is! He springs forward with extended arms. As he is about to clasp her he feels a stunning blow upon the back of the neck; a blinding white light blazes all about him with a sound like the shock of a cannon—then all is darkness and silence!

Peyton Farquhar was dead; his body, with a broken neck, swung gently from side to side beneath the timbers of the Owl Creek bridge. ∎

*What is revealed in the last paragraph about Farquhar's actions?*

**WORDS FOR EVERYDAY USE**

ma • lign (mə līn´) adj., malicious, evil. The wolf's <u>malign</u> intention was to eat Little Red Riding Hood.

# Respond to the SELECTION

If you were Farquhar, would you regret your decision to try to destroy the railroad bridge? Why, or why not?

# INVESTIGATE Inquire Imagine

**Recall:** GATHERING FACTS

1a. Describe the man on the railroad bridge and explain his situation. What is about to happen to him? How do you know?

2a. What does the gray-clad soldier tell Farquhar and his wife when he stops by their home?

3a. What happens to Farquhar at the end of the story?

**Interpret:** FINDING MEANING

1b. How did Peyton Farquhar get into this predicament? What was his crime and who is punishing him?

2b. What details suggest that Farquhar might attempt to destroy the railroad bridge?

3b. How much real time probably elapses between our introduction to Farquhar on the railroad bridge and his hanging? How much time elapses during his escape?

**Analyze:** TAKING THINGS APART

4a. How are Farquhar's experiences after his escape realistic? How are they unrealistic?

**Synthesize:** BRINGING THINGS TOGETHER

4b. Naturalism was a literary movement of the late nineteenth and early twentieth centuries that portrayed the lives of characters as being determined, or caused, by outside events or forces. In what way is Farquhar's experience naturalistic?

**Evaluate:** MAKING JUDGMENTS

5a. How effectively has the author depicted Farquhar's psychological trauma? Justify your decision from the text.

**Extend:** CONNECTING IDEAS

5b. In "An Occurrence at Owl Creek Bridge" the reader does not learn that Farquhar dies until the last paragraph. If possible, view the film version of this story and compare the written with the visual and auditory clues.

# Understanding Literature

FLASHBACK. Review the definition for **flashback** in the Handbook of Literary Terms. Then make a chart, listing the story's events in the order that you read about them on the left. On the right, list the events in chronological order. How does the flashback in this story advance the plot? What necessary information does the flashback provide?

| Reading Order | Chronological Order |
| --- | --- |
| Farquhar sits outside on the grounds of his home with his wife. | A man stands with a noose around his neck on a railroad bridge. |

PSYCHOLOGICAL FICTION. Review the definition for **psychological fiction** in Literary Tools on page 354. What parts of the story qualify it as psychological fiction?

# Writer's Journal

1. Imagine that you are the Union captain in the story. Write an entry in your **journal**, stating what happened on the Owl Creek bridge today—who you captured, why, and how you punished him.

2. Write the **military order** that the passing soldier describes to Peyton Farquhar and that was posted for Southern civilians to read.

3. Write a **dream report** about Farquhar's "escape." In other words, choose a sequence from the section that details his "escape," but make it more dreamlike or surreal, to differentiate it from reality.

# Integrating
## *the* LANGUAGE ARTS

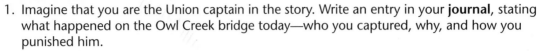

## Language, Grammar, and Style

**HELPING VERBS.** Read the Language Arts Survey 3.8, "Helping Verbs." Then underline the verbs in the following sentences.

1. It did not appear to be the duty of these two men to know what was occurring at the center of the bridge.

2. The sentinels, facing the banks of the stream, might have been statues to adorn the bridge.

3. This plank had been held in place by the weight of the captain.

4. "The Yanks are repairing the railroads," said the man, "and are getting ready for another advance."

5. The captain had drawn his pistol, but did not fire.

## Applied English

**TECHNICAL WRITING.** Ambrose Bierce gives specific details about the way each soldier is standing and holding his rifle. His description is so exact that a reader could duplicate the position of the rifle after a careful reading. Describe how to do a task with which you are familiar, such as copying a document on a computer. Read the Language Arts Survey 6.4, "Writing a Step-by-Step Procedure," for some tips on how to begin.

## Collaborative Learning & Speaking and Listening

**SENSORY DETAIL CHART.** With a couple of classmates, create a sensory detail chart for part III of "An

Occurrence at Owl Creek Bridge," when Farquhar "escapes." Reread that part of the selection, select a sense, and fill in the appropriate section of the chart. Finally, share your findings with the rest of the group so that everyone can fill in the missing sections on his or her chart.

## Media Literacy

**SCREENPLAY.** Write a screenplay for part III of the selection. Describe Farquhar's actions and in parentheses add special effects, such as lighting and music, to suggest dreamlike effects.

# FROM *"Song of Myself"*
# *"O Captain! My Captain!"*

BY WALT WHITMAN

## About *the* A U T H O R

**Walt Whitman** (1819–1892) is considered by many to be the greatest of all American poets. The son of a Long Island farmer who turned carpenter and moved his family to Brooklyn in 1823, Whitman left school at age eleven to work as an office boy. By twelve he was working in the printing office of a newspaper. By fifteen he was on his own. In his mid-teens he contributed pieces to a Manhattan newspaper and attended debating societies. After working as a journeyman printer, Whitman returned home where he taught school and continued to work on newspapers.

Later in his life, Whitman held various newspaper positions, including reviewer of books, musicals, and theater events. As a newspaper man he got to know the people of all classes. He purposefully placed himself at the center of the political battles over slavery, territorial expansion, the Mexican War, sectionalism, free trade, states' rights, worker strife, and the new market economy. He believed in the idea of using poetry as a form of political action. Through most of the 1840s and 1850s, Whitman attended the theater, concert hall, or opera house at least three times a week for the newspaper. He claimed that operas inspired him to write *Leaves of Grass*, the book of poetry for which he is most known. Always self-taught, Whitman began to write full time. His rise to fame was slow and at times his poetry drew harsh criticism. Ralph Waldo Emerson was one of the few intellectuals to praise Whitman's work, writing him a famous congratulatory letter. In an 1882 review in the *New York Examiner* one critic said: "Walt Whitman is a great poet—in his own estimation, and in that of critics who make up in noise what they lack in numbers."

During the Civil War, Whitman worked as a volunteer hospital nurse in Washington, an experience that made him well loved by the American public. *Drum-Taps* and "When Lilacs Last in the Dooryard Bloom'd" are the two great products of Whitman's wartime years. Among his best work after the war are his prose collections *Specimen Days* and *Democratic Vistas*, where he scorned

## Literary T O O L S

**ELABORATION. Elaboration**, or **amplification**, is a writing technique in which a subject is introduced and then expanded upon by means of repetition with slight changes, the addition of details, or similar devices. As you read "Song of Myself," look for examples of elaboration, as in section 6 when the child asks, "What is the grass?" The speaker responds with a series of possibilities, each of which begins with the same phrase: "I guess . . ."

**SYMBOL.** A **symbol** is a thing that stands for or represents both itself and something else. In Whitman's poem, the grass is both a conventional symbol, one with widely recognized associations, and an idiosyncratic symbol, one that assumes secondary meanings because of the special uses to which it is put by the writer. As you read "Song of Myself," find all the passages in which the grass occurs and decide what the grass symbolizes in each of these instances.

## Reader's *Journal*

What insignificant, lowly, or common thing do you value that many others do not?

# "O Captain! My Captain!"

## Literary TOOLS

**ELEGY AND STYLE.** An elegy is a long, formal poem written about death or loss. Style is the manner in which something is said or written. Traditionally, critics and scholars have referred to three levels of style: high style, for formal occasions or lofty subjects; middle style, for ordinary occasions or subjects; and low style, for extremely informal occasions or subjects. Review the full definition of style in the Handbook of Literary Terms. As you read, decide whether "O Captain! My Captain!" qualifies as an elegy. Jot down evidence to support your answer. Also decide whether the poem is written in a high, middle, or low style.

**RHYME, RHYME SCHEME, AND METER. Rhyme** is the repetition of sounds at the ends of words. A **rhyme scheme** is the pattern of end rhyme, or rhymes at the ends of lines of verse. The **meter** of a poem is its rhythmical pattern. Read the poem aloud to yourself. Jot down on paper any examples of rhyme or rhythm that you notice in your reading.

## Reader's Journal

Imagine that someone you admire greatly has died. What would you regret most about the loss of this person?

an America "canker'd, crude, superstitious and rotten"—a nation he esteemed had failed all the common laborers and favored the wealthy. Whitman worked in several government departments until he suffered a stroke in 1873. He spent the rest of his life in Camden, New Jersey, where he continued to write poems and articles. He was a major influence on later poets, inspiring them to experiment with metrical structure as well as subject matter.

## About the SELECTIONS

Whitman writes within the tradition of **Romanticism**, a literary and artistic movement of the eighteenth and nineteenth centuries that placed value on emotion and imagination rather than reason. The Romantics elevated the individual over society, nature over human works, country life over city life, common people over aristocrats, and freedom over control or authority.

**"Song of Myself"** is the first poem of *Leaves of Grass*, a single volume that Whitman spent his life writing. *Leaves of Grass* is propelled by the desire to enlighten the people and regenerate the ideals of the American republic. Unconventional in both content and technique, *Leaves of Grass* is probably the most influential volume of poems in the history of American literature. Although the book was a commercial failure, critics recognized the appearance of a bold new voice in poetry. However, some critics did not like Whitman's use of free verse in long rhythmical lines with a natural, organic structure. Two larger editions of the book appeared in 1856 and 1860. The last edition that he edited appeared in 1892.

"Song of Myself" is Whitman's effort to describe his personality, or as he put it: "one man's—the author's—identity, ardors, observations, faiths, and thoughts." The selection that follows exemplifies all the themes for which Whitman is best known: his belief that insignificant, lowly subjects are in fact worthy of poetry; his democratic celebration of the common people; and his love of natural and animal pleasure. All of these themes are summed up in the grass, the symbol central to his life work. Like all the poems in *Leaves of Grass*, "Song of Myself" is written in free verse: the poem does not fit into any planned form, and it has no regular pattern of rhyme, meter, or stanza length. To Whitman, the poet provides the energy necessary to the growth of a poem, but it develops spontaneously, in largely unpredictable ways.

**"O Captain! My Captain!"** is one of Whitman's two famous elegies, or poems of death and loss, in memory of Abraham Lincoln; the other is "When Lilacs Last in the Dooryard Bloom'd." "O Captain! My Captain!" first appeared in *Drum-Taps,* a collection of Whitman's poems that was published in 1865, the year of Lincoln's assassination. In 1867 and 1871, the poem appeared in *Leaves of Grass.* In its use of rhyme and meter and elevated diction, "O Captain! My Captain!" differs from Whitman's other poetry.

*Boy Sitting in the Grass,* c.1882. Georges Seurat.
Glasgow Art Gallery and Museum, Scotland.

FROM

# Song of Myself

## WALT WHITMAN

1

I celebrate myself, and sing myself,
And what I assume you shall assume,
For every atom belonging to me as good belongs to you.

I loafe and invite my soul,
5    I lean and loafe at my ease observing a spear of summer
      grass.

*What does the speaker celebrate? In what way is the speaker connected to the reader?*

My tongue, every atom of my blood, form'd from this soil,
    this air,
Born here of parents born here from parents the same, and
    their parents the same,
I, now thirty-seven years old in perfect health begin,
Hoping to cease not till death.

10   Creeds and schools in abeyance,
    Retiring back a while sufficed at what they are, but never
        forgotten,
    I harbor for good or bad, I permit to speak at every hazard,
    Nature without check with original energy.
    Looks down, is erect, or bends an arm on an impalpable
        certain rest,
15   Looking with side-curved head curious what will come next,
    Both in and out of the game and watching and wondering at
        it.

Backward I see in my own days where I sweated through fog
    with linguists and contenders,
I have no mockings or arguments, I witness and wait.

◆　◆　◆

6

A child said *What is the grass?* fetching it to me with full
    hands;
20   How could I answer the child? I do not know what it is
    any more than he.

*What question does the child ask? What is the speaker's first response?*

---

**WORDS FOR EVERYDAY USE**

**creed** (krēd) *n.*, statement of belief, principles, or opinions on any subject. *The creed of the organization centered around helping those in need.*

**a • bey • ance** (ə bā´əns) *n.*, temporary suspension, as of an activity or function. *Work on the highway was put in abeyance until the city could raise funds to finish building it.*

**suf • fice** (sə fīs´) *vt.*, be enough; be sufficient or adequate. *For the tip, Kim was sure five dollars would suffice.*

**har • bor** (här´bər) *vt.*, serve as, or provide, a place of protection. *He refused to harbor the runaway criminal.*

**im • pal • pa • ble** (im pal´pə bəl) *adj.*, that which cannot be felt by touching. *She could not explain the impalpable emotion that filled her when she looked at the painting.*

**lin • guist** (liŋ´gwist) *n.*, specialist in the science of language. *The linguist wrote a book about the origins of Indo-European languages.*

**con • tend • er** (kən ten´dər) *n.*, one who strives or fights in competition. *The boxer had been a contender for the heavyweight title.*

I guess it must be the flag of my <u>disposition</u>, out of hopeful
　　green stuff woven.

Or I guess it is the handkerchief of the Lord,
A scented gift and remembrancer designedly dropt,
Bearing the owner's name someway in the corners, that
　　we may see and remark, and say *Whose?*

What does the speaker
say the grass is?

25　　Or I guess the grass is itself a child, the produced babe of
　　　the vegetation.

Or I guess it is a uniform hieroglyphic,[1]
And it means, Sprouting alike in broad zones and narrow
　　zones,
Growing among black folks as among white,
Kanuck, Tuckahoe, Congressman, Cuff,[2] I give them the
　　same, I receive them the same.

30　　And now it seems to me the beautiful uncut hair of graves.

Tenderly will I use you curling grass,
It may be you transpire from the breasts of young men,
It may be if I had known them I would have loved them,
It may be you are from old people, or from offspring taken
　　soon out of their mothers' laps,
35　　And here you are the mothers' laps.

This grass is very dark to be from the white heads of old
　　mothers,
Darker than the colorless beards of old men,
Dark to come from under the faint red roofs of mouths.

O I perceive after all so many uttering tongues,
40　　And I perceive they do not come from the roofs of mouths
　　for nothing.

---

1. **hieroglyphic.** Picture or symbol representing a word, syllable, or sound, used by the ancient Egyptians and others instead of
alphabetical letters
2. **Kanuck, Tuckahoe, Congressman, Cuff.** *Kanuck*—French
Canadian; *Tuckahoe*—Virginian; *Cuff*—from the African word
*cuffee*, refers to African Americans.

**WORDS
FOR
EVERYDAY
USE**

**dis • po • si • tion** (dis´pə zi´shən) *n.,* one's customary frame of mind. *Josh's grandmother always says he has a sunny* <u>disposition</u>.

I wish I could translate the hints about the dead young
    men and women,
And the hints about old men and mothers, and the
    offspring taken soon out of their laps.

What does the speaker hear? What hints does the speaker not understand?

What do you think has become of the young and old men?
And what do you think has become of the women and
    children?

45    They are alive and well somewhere,
The smallest sprout shows there is really no death,
And if ever there was it led forward life, and does not
    wait at the end to arrest it,
And ceas'd the moment life appear'd.

What does the smallest sprout show?

All goes onward and outward, nothing collapses,
50    And to die is different from what any one supposed, and
    luckier.

&#9670;  &#9670;  &#9670;

## 7

Has any one supposed it lucky to be born?
I hasten to inform him or her it is just as lucky to die,
    and I know it.

What attitude does the speaker have toward death? Why might the speaker feel this way?

I pass death with the dying and birth with the new-wash'd
    babe, and am not contain'd between my hat and boots,

And peruse manifold objects, no two alike and every one
    good,
55    The earth good and the stars good, and their adjuncts all
    good.

I am not an earth nor an adjunct of an earth,
I am the mate and companion of people, all just as
    immortal and fathomless as myself,
(They do not know how immortal, but I know.)

What does the speaker say he is not? What does the speaker claim to be?

Every kind for itself and its own, for me mine male and
    female,
60    For me those that have been boys and that love women,

For me the man that is proud and feels how it stings to be
  slighted,
For me the sweet-heart and the old maid, for me mothers
  and the mothers of mothers,
For me lips that have smiled, eyes that have shed tears,
For me children and the begetters of children.

65    Undrape! you are not guilty to me, nor stale nor discarded,
I see through the broadcloth and gingham[3] whether or no,
And am around, tenacious, acquisitive, tireless, and cannot
  be shaken away.

♦   ♦   ♦

### 31

I believe a leaf of grass is no less than the journey-work of
  the stars,
And the pismire[4] is equally perfect, and a grain of sand, and
  the egg of the wren,
70    And the tree-toad is a chief-d'oeuvre[5] for the highest,
And the running blackberry would adorn the parlors of
  heaven,
And the narrowest hinge in my hand puts to scorn all
  machinery,
And the cow crunching with depress'd head surpasses any
  statue,
And a mouse is miracle enough to stagger sextillions[6] of
  infidels.

75    I find I incorporate gneiss,[7] coal, long-threaded moss, fruits,
  grains, esculent[8] roots,
And am stucco'd with quadrupeds and birds all over,

---

3. **broadcloth and gingham.** *Broadcloth*—fine wool, cotton, or
silk; *gingham*—cotton cloth that is woven in checks or plaids
4. **pismire.** Ant
5. **chief-d'oeuvre.** Master or culminating work
6. **sextillions.** Number represented by one followed by twenty-
one zeros
7. **gneiss.** Metamorphic rock with minerals arranged in layers
8. **esculent.** Edible

**WORDS FOR EVERYDAY USE**

**in • fi • del** (in´fə del´) *n.*, person who does not believe in a particular religion. *The crusaders set off to convert the infidels to Christianity.*

**quad • ru • ped** (kwä´drü ped´) *n.*, animal, especially a mammal, with four feet. *In science class we studied quadrupeds and bipeds.*

And have distanced what is behind me for good reasons,
But call any thing back again when I desire it.

In vain the speeding or shyness,
80  In vain the plutonic rocks[9] send their old heat against my
        approach,
In vain the mastodon retreats beneath its own powder'd
        bones,
In vain objects stand leagues off and assume manifold
        shapes,
In vain the ocean settling in hollows and the great monsters
        lying low,
In vain the buzzard houses herself with the sky,
85  In vain the snake slides through the creepers and logs,
In vain the elk takes to the inner passes of the woods,
In vain the razor-bill'd auk[10] sails far north to Labrador,[11]
I follow quickly, I ascend to the nest in the <u>fissure</u> of the
        cliff.

♦   ♦   ♦

32

I think I could turn and live with animals, they are so placid
        and self-contain'd,
90  I stand and look at them long and long.

They do not sweat and whine about their condition,
They do not lie awake in the dark and weep for their sins,
They do not make me sick discussing their duty to God,
Not one is dissatisfied, not one is demented with the
        mania of owning things,
95  Not one kneels to another, nor to his kind that lived
        thousands of years ago,
Not one is respectable or unhappy over the whole earth.

*Why would the speaker like to live with the animals? In what ways are they different from humans?*

---

9. **plutonic rocks.** Rocks formed far below the surface of the
earth
10. **auk.** Shore bird of northern seas with a heavy body, a short
tail, and short wings used as paddles
11. **Labrador.** Region along the Atlantic coast of northeastern
Canada

**WORDS
FOR
EVERYDAY
USE**
 fis • sure (fish´ər) n., long, narrow, deep cleft or crack. A *fissure* appeared in the building's foundation after the earthquake.

52

The spotted hawk swoops by and accuses me, he complains
    of my gab and my <u>loitering</u>.

I too am not a bit tamed, I too am untranslatable,
I sound my <u>barbaric</u> yawp[12] over the roofs of the world.

100    The last scud of day holds back for me,
It flings my likeness after the rest and true as any on the
    shadow'd wilds,
It coaxes me to the vapor and the dusk.

I depart as air, I shake my white locks at the runaway sun,
I effuse my flesh in eddies, and drift it in lacy <u>jags</u>.

105    I bequeath myself to the dirt to grow from the grass I
    love,
If you want me again look for me under your boot-soles.

You will hardly know who I am or what I mean,
But I shall be good health to you nevertheless,
And filter and fibre your blood.·

110    Failing to fetch me at first keep encouraged,
Missing me one place search another,
I stop somewhere waiting for you.

    ■

---

12. **yawp.** Loud, harsh cry or call

*Where should you look to see the speaker? What will the speaker do for the people he is addressing?*

**WORDS FOR EVERYDAY USE**

**loi • ter • ing** (loi´tər iŋ) *n.*, lingering in an aimless way. *The convenience store frowns on <u>loitering</u>.*
**bar • bar • ic** (bär bar´ik) *adj.*, wild, crude, and unrestrained. *Their <u>barbaric</u> treatment of prisoners was chronicled after the war.*
**jag** (jag) *n.*, sharp, toothlike projection. *The <u>jags</u> on the saw were sharp enough to cut through metal.*

## Respond *to the* SELECTION

Whitman says that he could "turn and live with animals." What do you think are the advantages and disadvantages to this proposition?

# Inquire, Imagine

## Recall: GATHERING FACTS

1a. How does Whitman respond to the question, "What is the grass?" Why does he want to treat the grass tenderly?

2a. What does Whitman say about dying in sections 6 and 7?

3a. What are the common and insignificant things that Whitman describes in section 31? To what does he compare each "lowly" thing?

## Interpret: FINDING MEANING

1b. How is the grass the great equalizer?

2b. What are Whitman's hopes for his own death?

3b. What do Whitman's comparisons indicate about his feelings for commonplace things?

## Analyze: TAKING THINGS APART

4a. A *catalog* is a list of people or things. Identify what Whitman catalogs in the poem.

## Synthesize: BRINGING THINGS TOGETHER

4b. Why does Whitman catalog these things?

## Evaluate: MAKING JUDGMENTS

5a. Do you agree with Whitman that death is a force that unites people with both nature and other human beings? What validity do his ideas have?

## Extend: CONNECTING IDEAS

5b. Compare Whitman's and Thoreau's views on the value of "lowly" things and individuality.

# Understanding Literature

**ELABORATION.** Review the definition for **elaboration** in Literary Tools on page 365. Besides section 6, find another example of elaboration. How does Whitman elaborate? What is the purpose of the elaboration?

**SYMBOL.** Review the definition for **symbol** in the Handbook of Literary Terms. Then make a chart. On the left, list quotations about grass in the poem. On the right, explain what the grass symbolizes. One example has been done for you.

| Quotations | What the Grass Symbolizes |
|---|---|
| The speaker observes "a spear of summer grass." | The grass symbolizes the speaker's individuality and connectedness with the natural world and other living things. |

***Off Mount Desert Island***, 1856. Fitz Hugh Lane.
Brooklyn Museum of Art.

# O Captain! My Captain!

## WALT WHITMAN

O Captain! my Captain! our fearful trip is done,
The ship has weather'd every rack,[1] the prize we sought
   is won,
The port is near, the bells I hear, the people all <u>exulting</u>,
While follow eyes the steady keel,[2] the vessel grim[3] and
   daring;

*What has the speaker's voyage been like? Was it successful?*

---

1. **rack.** Wrenching or upheaval, as by storm
2. **keel.** Beam along the bottom of a ship that supports the frame
3. **grim.** Fierce in action

WORDS FOR EVERYDAY USE

ex • ult (ig´ zəlt) *vi.,* be extremely joyful. *After the long drought, the farmer <u>exulted</u> at the advent of the rain.*

5   But O heart! heart! heart!
        O the bleeding drops of red,
            Where on the deck my Captain lies,
                Fallen cold and dead.

*What has happened to the captain of the ship?*

    O Captain! my Captain! rise up and hear the bells;
10  Rise up—for you the flag is flung—for you the bugle <u>trills</u>,
    For you bouquets and ribbon'd wreaths—for you the shores
        a-crowding,
    For you they call, the swaying mass, their eager faces
        turning;
        Here Captain! dear father!
            This arm beneath your head!
15          It is some dream that on the deck,
                You've fallen cold and dead.

*According to the speaker, why are the people on shore celebrating?*

    My Captain does not answer, his lips are pale and still,
    My father does not feel my arm, he has no pulse nor will,
    The ship is anchor'd safe and sound, its voyage closed and
        done,
20  From fearful trip the victor ship comes in with object won;
        Exult O shores, and ring O bells!
            But I with mournful <u>tread</u>,
                Walk the deck my Captain lies,
                    Fallen cold and dead.                          ■

---

**WORDS FOR EVERYDAY USE**

**trill** (tril) *vi.*, play or sing with a quaver. *We were moved by the notes the opera singer <u>trilled</u>.*
**tread** (tred) *n.*, manner of stepping. *My <u>tread</u> was soft on the stairs because I did not want to wake my family.*

---

## Respond *to the* SELECTION

If you were the speaker, standing on the ship near the captain, what would you want to say to the people celebrating on shore?

# INVESTIGATE, Inquire, Imagine

**Recall:** GATHERING FACTS

1a. In the first stanza, what is done? What is won? What are people on shore doing? What has happened to the captain?

2a. In the second stanza, what does the speaker ask the captain to do? What does the speaker explain as "some dream"?

3a. In the last stanza, what does the speaker note about his captain? What does the speaker do as the shores exult and the bells ring?

➤ **Interpret:** FINDING MEANING

1b. How does the mood in stanza 1 change?

2b. What is the speaker experiencing psychologically in stanza 2?

3b. What kind of relationship did the speaker have with the captain?

**Analyze:** TAKING THINGS APART

4a. Identify contrasting details in the poem. What do these details reveal about the speaker's physical and emotional relationship to the people on shore?

➤ **Synthesize:** BRINGING THINGS TOGETHER

4b. Is this poem more about the way the death of a leader affects the speaker personally or more about the way the death of a leader affects a nation? What evidence would you use to defend your position?

**Evaluate:** MAKING JUDGMENTS

5a. Evaluate whether "O Captain! My Captain!" is a fitting tribute to a slain president. Consider the historical context of the poem in formulating your response.

➤ **Extend:** CONNECTING IDEAS

5b. Compare the style of "O Captain! My Captain!" to Whitman's poem "When Lilacs Last in the Dooryard Bloom'd" on page 387. Why did Whitman choose a more formal style for "O Captain! My Captain!"? Which poem is more effective?

# Understanding Literature

ELEGY AND STYLE. Review definitions of **elegy** and **style** in the Handbook of Literary Terms. In what style do you believe "O Captain! My Captain!" was written—high, middle, or low? Explain the reasoning behind your choice. Using the evidence you listed as you read the story, explain whether you think that this poem can be classified as an elegy.

RHYME, RHYME SCHEME, AND METER. Review the definitions for **rhyme**, **rhyme scheme**, and **meter** in the Handbook of Literary Terms. Many of Whitman's poem's were free verse—they did not make use of regular rhyme schemes and patterns of rhythm. This poem is unusual for Whitman in that he used regular rhyme and meter. What is this poem's rhyme scheme? Using the handbook as a guide, determine the type of feet used most often in the following lines:

> The ship has weather'd every rack, the prize we sought is won,

> The port is near, the bells I hear, the people all exulting.

Why do you think Whitman chose to use more regular rhyme and rhythm in this poem than in some of his other works?

# Writer's Journal

1. Imagine that Walt Whitman carried a card, or **"poetic license,"** giving himself permission to do unconventional things. Using "Song of Myself" as a reference, write five things that you think Whitman would put on the card by completing the line "As a poet, I give myself permission to . . ."

2. An article written about Whitman's poetry in 1882 described Whitman and "O Captain! My Captain!" in the following way: "He will be known fifty years hence—if he is known at all, which we more than half-doubt—only as the author of 'My Captain,' on the whole, probably, the most stirring lyric that the Civil War produced." Imagine that you were alive when Whitman's poem was first published and that you had read this assessment of Whitman and the poem. Write an **editorial**, either supporting this assessment or challenging it in some way.

3. Whitman celebrated behavior that was "lawless as snowflakes." His disregard for conventional poetic subjects and forms made him unacceptable to genteel society in his day. Create a **wanted poster** for Walt Whitman. Include a description of his appearance and a list of the crimes for which society wants to imprison him.

# Integrating the LANGUAGE ARTS

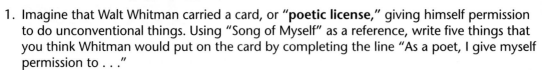

## Language, Grammar, and Style

**USING EXCLAMATION POINTS.** Read the Language Arts Survey 3.86, "End Marks." While phrases like "O Captain!" and "O heart! heart! heart!" that make generous use of exclamation points sometimes appear in formal poetry, exclamation points should be used sparingly in most writing. Rewrite the following sentences, changing periods to exclamation points where needed.

1. I had an uneasy feeling about our voyage.
2. Foreseeing that the captain would die if he took another step, I cried out, "Stop."
3. What a brave man the captain was.
4. Look at the blood on the captain's uniform.
5. Let us hold a funeral procession for the captain.

## Media Literacy & Study and Research

**RESEARCHING WHITMAN ON THE INTERNET.** The quote about Walt Whitman and "O Captain! My Captain!" that appears in the second Writer's Journal assignment first appeared in an article entitled "The Poetry of the Future," in the January 19, 1882, edition of the *New York Examiner*. There is a wealth of information about writers of all periods available on the Internet. Much can be learned about an author by discovering what his or her contemporaries wrote in articles many years ago. Walt Whitman's contemporaries, for example, were intensely divided about his work; a few praised him lavishly, but many were shocked and appalled by his poetry. Using the Internet, locate an article written about Whitman's writing during the nineteenth century. As you conduct your online search, make a list of sites that you find particularly informative. After you read the article you have chosen, write a summary outlining its main points.

# "Do not weep, maiden, for war is kind"

# "A Man Said to the Universe"

BY STEPHEN CRANE

## About the AUTHOR

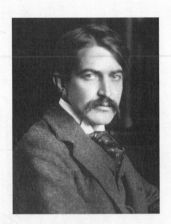

**Stephen Crane** (1871–1900) lived only twenty-eight years, but in that time he established himself as a great American fiction writer and poet. A literary pioneer, Crane applied to fiction his belief that human beings are pawns, moved by forces beyond their control to take actions beyond their understanding. This idea that nature—the forces of heredity and environment—causes humans to think, believe, feel, and act as they do is known in philosophy as Determinism and in literary theory as Naturalism. To the Determinist or Naturalist, free will is an illusion, because the decisions that people believe they are making freely are in fact the inevitable consequences of the forces acting upon them.

Crane was born in Newark, New Jersey, the youngest of fourteen children. His father, a Methodist minister, died when Crane was nine years old. Crane attended Syracuse University, but left after one semester. In 1893, Crane finished revising his novel *Maggie: A Girl of the Streets,* the draft of which he had finished while at Syracuse. Shocked by the novel's grim realism, publishers rejected the book, and Crane paid for its publication himself. In 1894, Crane's masterful novel about the Civil War, *The Red Badge of Courage,* was published serially in a magazine, and Crane began work as a reporter. In 1895, the novel was released in book form, and Crane's reputation was established. That same year, Crane issued the first volume of his experimental free verse, *The Black Rider.* This was followed by another volume of poetry, *War Is Kind,* in 1899.

Crane's experiences as a reporter in Mexico, the American West, and Florida provided material for a number of short stories, including "The Blue Hotel" and "The Open Boat." As a reporter, Crane covered the Greco-Turkish War and the Spanish-American War, seeing firsthand the cruelties of battle about which he had written so eloquently. Before his death, Crane spent some time in England, where he met many famous writers, including H. G. Wells, Joseph Conrad, and Henry James. By that time, he was severely ill with tuberculosis. He died at a health spa in Badenweiler, Germany.

## About the SELECTIONS

**"Do not weep, maiden, for war is kind"** illustrates typical characteristics of Crane's poetry—irony, realistic details, and a conversational tone, all expressed in free verse void of traditional patterns of rhyme, rhythm, and stanza form. Crane's poetry was influenced by late nineteenth- and early twentieth-century **Naturalism**, a philosophical perspective and literary movement that viewed human action as strictly determined by biological and environmental forces. In **"A Man Said to the Universe,"** Crane presents an imaginary dialogue that perfectly illustrates the worldview of the Naturalists.

## Literary TOOLS

IRONY. **Irony** is a difference between appearance and reality. In **verbal irony**, something is said that implies its opposite. As you read, make a chart showing the verbal irony in the poem "Do not weep, maiden, for war is kind." In the left column, write phrases or sentences that demonstrate verbal irony. In the right column, explain why they are ironic. One example has been done for you.

| Verbal Irony | Explanation |
|---|---|
| "War is kind." | This sentence is ironic because war is clearly unkind. |

FREE VERSE. **Free verse** is poetry that avoids use of regular rhyme, meter, or division into stanzas. As you read, decide what elements in the poem show that it is intended to be read as natural speech.

## Reader's *Journal*

What would you do to comfort someone who had lost a loved one?

# Do not weep, maiden, for war is kind

## STEPHEN CRANE

Do not weep, maiden, for war is kind.
Because your lover threw wild hands toward the sky
And the affrighted steed ran on alone,
Do not weep.
5     War is kind.

> *What happens to the lover?*

    Hoarse, booming drums of the regiment,
    Little souls who thirst for fight,
    These men were born to drill and die.
    The unexplained glory flies above them,
10     Great is the Battle-God, great, and his Kingdom—
    A field where a thousand corpses lie.

Do not weep, babe, for war is kind.
Because your father tumbled in the yellow trenches,
Raged at his breast, gulped and died,
15 Do not weep.
War is kind.

> *Does the speaker believe in the "virtue of slaughter" and the "excellence of killing"? What makes you think so?*

    Swift blazing flag of the regiment,
    Eagle with crest of red and gold,
    These men were born to drill and die.
20     Point for them the virtue of slaughter,
    Make plain to them the excellence of killing
    And a field where a thousand corpses lie.

Mother whose heart hung humble as a button
On the bright splendid shroud of your son,
25 Do not weep.
War is kind.

  ■

If you were a soldier, what causes would you consider worth dying for?

INVESTIGATE

# Inquire *Imagine*

**Recall:** GATHERING FACTS

1a. What three people are addressed by the speaker of the poem?

2a. What scenarios does the speaker describe at the beginning of stanzas 1, 3, and 5?

3a. What feelings do the phrases "Little souls who thirst for fight," "the virtue of slaughter," "a field where a thousand corpses lie," and "the excellence of killing" evoke in the reader?

→ **Interpret:** FINDING MEANING

1b. What do the three addressed people have in common?

2b. How is the shared refrain of stanzas 1, 3, and 5 ironic?

3b. What type of attitude does the speaker mock in stanzas 2 and 4? What kind of poetry does he use to mock this attitude?

**Analyze:** TAKING THINGS APART

4a. How does the poet use alliteration to reinforce a mock heroic interpretation of his poem?

→ **Synthesize:** BRINGING THINGS TOGETHER

4b. What is the main message that Crane makes about war?

**Evaluate:** MAKING JUDGMENTS

5a. Why do you think Crane ends with a stanza focused on a person rather than the regiment of stanzas 2 and 4?

→ **Extend:** CONNECTING IDEAS

5b. If you were the parent of a child killed in battle, how would you react to each of the following?

- a letter from the army informing you of your child's death
- a letter of condolence from the president
- a request to contribute your time and talents to the war effort
- a request to help pay for a war memorial

# Understanding *Literature*

IRONY. Review the definition for **irony** in the Handbook of Literary Terms. How many examples of *verbal irony* were you able to illustrate in the chart you completed as you read the poem? Why do you think Crane chose to use verbal irony to express his feelings about war?

FREE VERSE. Review the definition for **free verse** in the Handbook of Literary Terms. Free verse tends to sound more like ordinary speech than traditional verse does. What elements in this poem show that it is intended as speech, or one side of an imaginary conversation?

When writing free verse, poets often invent their own unique structures, or organizational patterns, to replace traditional rhyming stanzas. What is the structure of this poem? What do stanzas 1, 3, and 5 have in common? Why might stanzas 2 and 4 be more traditional in their use of poetic devices, such as a regular meter and rhyme, than stanzas 1, 3, and 5?

# Literary
## TOOLS

**IRONY. Irony** is a difference between appearance and reality. As you read the poem, determine what makes it ironic.

**DIALOGUE. Dialogue** is conversation involving two or more people or characters. As you read the poem, consider how the conversation might be continued, in keeping with the attitudes of two characters.

## Reader's
### Journal

Have you ever experienced a moment when you felt that the natural world was unresponsive to your needs? Relate that experience.

## ArtNote

***Aurora Borealis,*** 1865.
Frederic Church.

Until 1864, the outcome of the Civil War was still in doubt, but several battles late in that year marked the beginning of the end. In December, the aurora borealis, or "northern lights," appeared in the night sky: a spectacular light display caused by charged particles from the sun sweeping Earth's magnetic field. Many Americans took it as a celestial message that the war was coming to an end. Frederic Church (1826–1900) used the aurora as his metaphor for the war. Would Church have agreed with Crane's sentiments about the importance of human action to the universe?

***Aurora Borealis,*** 1865. Frederic Church.
National Museum of American Art, Washington, DC.

# A Man Said to the Universe

### STEPHEN CRANE

A man said to the universe,
"Sir, I exist!"
"However," replied the universe,
"The fact has not created in me
A sense of obligation." ■

## Respond *to the*
## SELECTION

If you were the man in the poem, how would you respond to the universe's reply?

# INVESTIGATE

# Inquire, Imagine

**Recall:** GATHERING FACTS

1a. Who are the two participants in the dialogue?

2a. What does each participant say to the other?

**Interpret:** FINDING MEANING

1b. What can you infer about the emotional life of the man who speaks in this poem?

2b. According to this poem, what relationship exists between the universe and human beings?

**Analyze:** TAKING THINGS APART

3a. *Personification* is a figure of speech in which an idea, animal, or thing is described as if it were a person. How does the speaker personify the universe?

**Synthesize:** BRINGING THINGS TOGETHER

3b. Why does the man reach out to the universe?

**Perspective:** LOOKING AT OTHER VIEWS

4a. In "A Man Said to the Universe," Crane's dialogue presents the worldview of the Naturalists. Illustrate an alternate worldview by framing a different response by the universe, one that the Romantics would have held. The Romantics, during the eighteenth and nineteenth centuries, placed value on emotion or imagination over reason, the individual over society, nature and wildness over human works, the country over the town, common people over aristocrats, and freedom over control or authority.

**Empathy:** SEEING FROM INSIDE

4b. Describe a time in your life when you felt no sense of obligation for another human being. If you were to relive that experience, what could you have done to help that person?

# Understanding Literature

**IRONY.** Review the definition for **irony** in the Handbook of Literary Terms. Why is it ironic that Crane personifies the universe in the poem?

**DIALOGUE.** Review the definition for **dialogue** in the Handbook of Literary Terms. Then make a chart to indicate other exchanges the man and the universe might have. For example, if such a conversation were to continue, you could imagine the other types of topics that could arise, such as, human love, the beauty of nature, and the meaning of life. On the left, write what the man would say to the universe if the conversation continued. On the right, write what the universe would say in response. It is important that both characters stay in character. One example has been done for you.

| What the Man Said | What the Universe Said |
| --- | --- |
| "My love is unrequited." | "That's life." |

# WRITER'S JOURNAL

1. Write the **vows** a more sympathetic universe might take with the man. Complete the universe's sentence "I promise to . . ."

2. Write a **contract** between the man and the universe that meets the man's needs.

3. Write a **mock heroic poem** in the style of "Do not weep, maiden for war is kind" about a deed of valor. You might want to try using regular meter and rhyme. Select a deed of questionable valor to make your ironic tone more clear.

# Integrating *the* LANGUAGE ARTS

## Language, Grammar, and Style

**HYPHENS AND PROOFREADING FOR CAPITALIZATION.** Read the Language Arts Survey 3.93, "Hyphens and Dashes," and 3.94, "Editing for Capitalization Errors." Then rewrite the following sentences, including correct capitalization and hyphenation.

1. In 1890 Stephen Crane told his mother, "I'm moving to new york city."

2. Among his many accomplishments, Crane was a short story and freelance writer.

3. Henry Fleming is the hero of *The Red Badge of Courage*, Crane's most famous novel, set during the civil war.

4. Ahead of his time, Crane anticipated several strains of twentieth century poetry with *The Black Rider* and *War is Kind*.

5. Crane depicted the American west in his short stories, which are considered among the finest in English.

## Study and Research & Media Literacy

**ONLINE BOOK REVIEW.** Several online newspapers and bookstores allow readers to post reviews of the literature they have read. Write your own review of another work by Stephen Crane, such as *The Red Badge of Courage*, "The Blue Hotel," "The Open Boat," or "The Bride Comes to Yellow Sky." Then write an online review and post it on the Internet. You may want to compare your review to others that are already posted. Which make you want to read the selection? Which are the most informative? Which are the most engaging?

## Media Literacy

**WAR CORRESPONDENT.** Imagine that you are a war correspondent who witnessed the deaths of the lover and father and the funeral of the son depicted in "Do not weep, maiden, for war is kind." Write an article describing all three events, elaborating on the details.

## from *Incidents in the Life of a Slave Girl, Seven Years Concealed*

by Harriet Jacobs (Linda Brent)

### I.

### CHILDHOOD.

I was born a slave; but I never knew it till six years of happy childhood had passed away. My father was a carpenter, and considered so intelligent and skillful in his trade, that, when buildings out of the common line were to be erected, he was sent for from long distances, to be head workman. On condition of paying his mistress two hundred dollars a year, and supporting himself, he was allowed to work at his trade, and manage his own affairs. His strongest wish was to purchase his children; but, though he several times offered his hard earnings for that purpose, he never succeeded. In complexion my parents were a light shade of brownish yellow, and were termed mulattoes.[1] They lived together in a comfortable home; and, though we were all slaves, I was so fondly shielded that I never dreamed I was a piece of merchandise, trusted to them for safe keeping, and liable to be demanded of them at any moment. I had one brother, William, who was two years younger than myself—a bright, affectionate child. I had also a great treasure in my maternal grandmother, who was a remarkable woman in many respects. She was the daughter of a planter in South Carolina, who, at his death, left her mother and his three children free, with money to go to St. Augustine, where they had relatives. It was during the Revolutionary War; and they were captured on their passage, carried back, and sold to different purchasers. Such was the story my grandmother used to tell me; but I do not remember all the particulars. She was a little girl when she was captured and sold to the keeper of a large hotel. I have often heard her tell how hard she fared during childhood. But as she grew older she envinced[2] so much intelligence, and was so faithful, that her master and mistress could not help seeing it was for their interest to take care of such a valuable piece of property. She became an indispensable personage in the household, officiating in all capacities, from cook and wet nurse[3] to seamstress. She was much praised for her cooking; and her nice crackers became so famous in the neighborhood that many people were desirous of obtaining them. In consequence of numerous requests of this kind, she asked permission of her mistress to bake crackers at night, after all the household work was done; and she obtained leave to do it, provided she would clothe herself and her children from the profits. Upon these terms, after working hard all day for her mistress, she began her midnight baking, assisted by her two oldest children. The business proved profitable; and each year she laid by a little, which was saved for a fund to purchase her children. Her master died, and the property was divided among his heirs. The widow had her dower[4] in the hotel which she continued to keep open. My grandmother remained in her service as a slave; but her children were divided among her master's children. As she had five, Benjamin, the youngest one, was sold, in order that each heir might have an equal portion of dollars and cents. There was so little difference in our ages that he seemed more like my brother than my uncle. He was a bright, handsome lad, nearly white; for he inherited the complexion my grandmother had derived from Anglo-Saxon ancestors. Though only ten years old, seven hundred and twenty dollars were paid for him. His sale was a terrible blow to my grandmother; but she was naturally hopeful, and she went to work with renewed energy, trusting in time to be able to purchase some of her children. She had laid up three hundred dollars, which her mistress one day begged as a loan, promising to pay her soon. The reader probably knows that no promise or writing given to a slave is legally binding; for, according to Southern laws, a slave, being property, can hold no property. When my grandmother lent her hard earnings to her mistress, she trusted solely to her honor. The honor of a slaveholder to a slave!

To this good grandmother I was indebted for many comforts. My brother Willie and I often received portions of the crackers, cakes, and preserves, she made to sell; and after we ceased to be children we were indebted to her for many more important services.

Such were the unusually fortunate circumstances of my early childhood. When I was six years old, my mother died; and then, for the first time, I learned, by the talk around me, that I was a slave. My mother's mistress was the daughter of my grandmother's mistress. She was the foster sister of my mother; they were both nourished at my grandmother's breast. In fact, my mother had been weaned[5] at three months old, that the babe of the mistress might obtain sufficient food. They played together as children; and, when they became women, my mother was a most faithful servant to her whiter foster sister. On her death-bed her mistress promised that her children should never suffer for any thing; and during her lifetime she kept her word. They all spoke kindly of my dead mother, who had been a slave merely in name, but in nature was noble and womanly. I grieved for her, and my young mind was troubled with the thought who would now take care of me and my little brother. I was told that my home was now to be with her mistress; and I found it a happy one. No toilsome or disagreeable duties were imposed on me. My mistress was so kind to me that I was always glad to do her bidding, and proud to labor for her as much as my young years would permit. I would sit by her side for hours, sewing diligently, with a heart as free from care as that of any free-born white child.

---

1. **mulattoes.** Persons of mixed white and African-American ancestry
2. **evinced.** Displayed clearly
3. **wet nurse.** Woman who cares for and suckles infants not her own
4. **dower.** Part of or interest in the real estate of a deceased husband given by law to his widow
5. **weaned.** Accustomed a child to take food otherwise than by nursing

When she thought I was tired, she would send me out to run and jump; and away I bounded, to gather berries or flowers to decorate her room. Those were happy days—too happy to last. The slave child had no thought for the morrow; but there came that blight, which too surely waits on every human being born to be a chattel.[1]

When I was nearly twelve years old, my kind mistress sickened and died. As I saw the cheek grow paler, and the eye more glassy, how earnestly I prayed in my heart that she might live! I loved her; for she had been almost like a mother to me. My prayers were not answered. She died, and they buried her in the little churchyard, where, day after day, my tears fell upon her grave.

I was sent to spend a week with my grandmother. I was now old enough to begin to think of the future; and again and again I asked myself what they would do with me. I felt sure I should never find another mistress so kind as the one who was gone. She had promised my dying mother that her children should never suffer for any thing; and when I remembered that, and recalled her many proofs of attachment to me, I could not help having some hopes that she had left me free. My friends were almost certain it would be so. They thought she would be sure to do it, on account of my mother's love and faithful service. But, alas! we all know that the memory of a faithful slave does not avail[2] much to save her children from the auction block.

After a brief period of suspense, the will of my mistress was read, and we learned that she had bequeathed[3] me to her sister's daughter, a child of five years old. So vanished our hopes. My mistress had taught me the precepts[4] of God's Word: "Thou shalt love thy neighbor as thyself." "Whatsoever ye would that men should do unto you, do ye even so unto them." But I was her slave, and I suppose she did not recognize me as her neighbor. I would give much to blot out from my memory that one great wrong. As a child, I loved my mistress; and, looking back on the happy days I spent with her, I try to think with less bitterness of this act of injustice. While I was with her, she taught me to read and spell; and for this privilege, which so rarely falls to the lot of a slave, I bless her memory.

She possessed but few slaves; and at her death those were all distributed among her relatives. Five of them were my grandmother's children, and had shared the same milk that nourished her mother's children. Notwithstanding my grandmother's long and faithful service to her owners, not one of her children escaped the auction block. These God-breathing machines are no more, in the sight of their masters, than the cotton they plant, or the horses they tend.

## from "A House Divided"
by Abraham Lincoln

SPEECH DELIVERED AT SPRINGFIELD, ILLINOIS, AT THE CLOSE OF THE REPUBLICAN STATE CONVENTION. JUNE 16, 1858

If we could first know where we are, and whither we are tending, we could better judge what to do, and how to do it.

We are now far into the *fifth* year, since a policy was initiated, with the *avowed* object, and *confident* promise, of putting an end to slavery agitation.

Under the operation of that policy, that agitation has not only, *not ceased*, but has *constantly augmented*.

In my opinion, it *will* not cease, until a *crisis* shall have been reached, and passed—

"A house divided against itself cannot stand."[5]

I believe this government cannot endure, permanently half *slave* and half *free*.

I do not expect the Union to be *dissolved*—I do not expect the house to *fall*—but I *do* expect it will cease to be divided.

It will become *all* one thing, or *all* the other.

Either the *opponents* of slavery, will arrest the further spread of it, and place it where the public mind shall rest in the belief that it is in course of ultimate extinction; or its *advocates* will push it forward, till it shall become alike lawful in *all* the States, *old* as well as *new*—North as well as *South*.

## Letter to Mrs. Bixby
by Abraham Lincoln

Executive Mansion, Washington,
November 21, 1864

Mrs. Bixby, Boston, Massachusetts:

Dear Madam:

I have been shown in the files of the War Department a statement of the Adjutant–General of Massachusetts that you are the mother of five sons who have died gloriously on the field of battle. I feel how weak and fruitless must be any words of mine which should attempt to beguile you from the grief of a loss so overwhelming. But I cannot refrain from tendering to you the consolation that may be found in the thanks of the Republic they died to save. I pray that our Heavenly Father may assuage the anguish of your bereavement, and leave you only the cherished memory of the loved and lost, and the solemn pride that must be yours to have laid so costly a sacrifice upon the altar of freedom.

Yours very sincerely and respectfully,

Abraham Lincoln

## from the Second Inaugural Address
by Abraham Lincoln

On the occasion corresponding to this four years ago, all thoughts were anxiously directed to an impending civil war. All dreaded it—all sought to avert it. While the inaugural address was being delivered from this place, devoted altogether to

---

1. **chattel.** Movable property
2. **avail.** Be of advantage or result in
3. **bequeathed.** Gave or left by will, especially personal property
4. **precepts.** Principles
5. **"A house . . . stand."** Biblical reference to Mark 3:25, "If a house be divided against itself, that house cannot stand."

*saving* the Union without war, insurgent agents were in the city seeking to *destroy* it without war—seeking to dissol[v]e the Union, and divide effects, by negotiation. Both parties deprecated war; but one of them would *make* war rather than let the nation survive; and the other would *accept* war rather than let it perish. And the war came.

One eighth of the whole population were colored slaves, not distributed generally over the Union, but localized in the Southern part of it. These slaves constituted a peculiar and powerful interest. All knew that this interest was, somehow, the cause of the war. To strengthen, perpetuate, and extend this interest was the object for which the insurgents would rend the Union, even by war; while the government claimed no right to do more than to restrict the territorial enlargement of it. Neither party expected for the war, the magnitude, or the duration, which it has already attained. Neither anticipated that the *cause* of the conflict might cease with, or even before, the conflict itself should cease. Each looked for an easier triumph, and a result less fundamental and astounding. Both read the same Bible, and pray to the same God; and each invokes His aid against the other. It may seem strange that any men should dare to ask a just God's assistance in wringing their bread from the sweat of other men's faces; but let us judge not that we be not judged. The prayers of both could not be answered; that of neither has been answered fully. The Almighty has his own purposes. "Woe unto the world because of offenses! for it must needs be that offenses come; but woe to that man by whom the offense cometh!" If we shall suppose that American Slavery is one of those offenses which, in the providence of God, must needs come, but which, having continued through His appointed time, He now wills to remove, and that He gives to both North and South, this terrible war, as the woe due to those by whom the offense came, shall we discern therein any departure from those divine attributes which the believers in a Living God always ascribe to Him? Fondly do we hope—fervently do we pray—that this mighty scourge of war may speedily pass away. Yet, if God wills that it continue, until all the wealth piled by the bond-man's two hundred and fifty years of unrequited toil[1] shall be sunk, and until every drop of blood drawn with the lash, shall be paid by another drawn with the sword, as was said three thousand years ago, so still it must be said "the judgments of the Lord, are true and righteous altogether."

With malice toward none; with charity for all; with firmness in the right, as God gives us to see the right, let us strive on to finish the work we are in; to bind up the nation's wounds; to care for him who shall have borne the battle, and for his widow, and his orphan—to do all which may achieve and cherish a just and lasting peace, among ourselves, and with all nations.

## Farewell to His Army
by Robert E. Lee

Headquarters, Army Northern Virginia,
April 10, 1865

After four years of arduous service, marked by unsurpassed courage and fortitude, the Army of Northern Virginia has been compelled to yield to overwhelming numbers and resources. I need not tell the survivors of so many hard-fought battles, who have remained steadfast to the last, that I have consented to this result from no distrust of them; but, feeling that valor and devotion could accomplish nothing that could compensate for the loss that would have attended the continuation of the contest, I have determined to avoid the useless sacrifice of those whose past services have endeared them to their countrymen. By the terms of the agreement, officers and men can return to their homes, and remain there until exchanged.[2]

You will take with you *the satisfaction that proceeds from the consciousness of duty faithfully performed*; and I earnestly pray that a merciful God will extend to you his blessing and protection. With an unceasing admiration of your constancy and devotion to your country, and a grateful remembrance of your kind and generous consideration of myself, I bid you an affectionate farewell.

## from "When Lilacs Last in the Dooryard Bloom'd"
by Walt Whitman

1

When lilacs last in the dooryard bloom'd,
And the great star[3] early droop'd in the western sky in
   the night,
I mourn'd, and yet shall mourn with ever-returning
   spring.
Ever-returning spring, trinity sure to me you bring,
5 Lilac blooming perennial and drooping star in the west,
And thought of him I love.

2

O powerful western fallen star!
O shades of night—O moody, tearful night!
O great star disappear'd—O the black murk that hides
   the star!
10 O cruel hands that hold me powerless—O helpless soul
   of me!
O harsh surrounding cloud that will not free my soul.

6

Coffin that passes through lanes and streets,
Through day and night with the great cloud darkening
   the land,
35 With the pomp of the inloop'd flags with the cities
   draped in black,

---

1. **bond-man's . . . toil.** Refers to the period of slavery in which the slaves were not requited or paid for their labor
2. **exchanged.** Discharged from military service
3. **great star.** Refers to Venus but comes to be associated with Lincoln

With the show of the States themselves as of crape-veil'd
    women standing,
With processions long and winding and the flambeaus[1]
    of the night,
With the countless torches lit, with the silent sea of faces
    and the unbared heads,
With the waiting depot, the arriving coffin, and the
    sombre faces,
40  With dirges through the night, with the thousand voices
    rising strong and solemn,
With all the mournful voices of the dirges pour'd
    around the coffin,
The dim-lit churches and the shuddering organs—where
    amid these you journey,
With the tolling tolling bells' perpetual clang,
Here, coffin that slowly passes,
45  I give you my sprig of lilac.

7

(Nor for you, for one alone,
Blossoms and branches green to coffins all I bring,
For fresh as the morning, thus would I chant a song for
    you O sane and sacred death.

All over bouquets of roses,
50  O death, I cover you over with roses and early lilies,
But mostly and now the lilac that blooms the first,
Copious I break, I break the sprigs from the bushes,
With loaded arms I come, pouring for you,
For you and the coffins all of you O death.)

## "When I Heard the Learn'd Astronomer"
### by Walt Whitman

When I heard the learn'd astronomer,
When the proofs, the figures, were ranged in columns
    before me,
When I was shown the charts and diagrams, to add,
    divide, and measure them,
When I sitting heard the astronomer where he lectured
    with much applause in the lecture-room,
5  How soon unaccountable I became tired and sick,
Till rising and gliding out I wander'd off by myself,
In the mystical moist night-air, and from time to time,
Look'd up in perfect silence at the stars.

## from *Up from Slavery*
### by Booker T. Washington

In those days, and later as a young man, I used to try to picture in my imagination the feelings and ambitions of a white boy with absolutely no limit placed upon his aspirations and activities. I used to envy the white boy who had no obstacles placed in the way of his becoming a Congressman, Governor, Bishop, or President by reason of the accident of his birth or race. I used to picture the way that I would act under such circumstances; how I would begin at the bottom and keep rising until I reached the highest round of success.

In later years, I confess that I do not envy the white boy as I once did. I have learned that success is to be measured not so much by the position that one has reached in life as by the obstacles which he has overcome while trying to succeed. Looked at from this standpoint, I almost reach the conclusion that often the Negro boy's birth and connection with an unpopular race is an advantage, so far as real life is concerned. With few exceptions, the Negro youth must work harder and must perform his task even better than a white youth in order to secure recognition. But out of the hard and unusual struggle which he is compelled to pass, he gets a strength, a confidence, that one misses whose pathway is comparatively smooth by reason of birth and race.

From any point of view, I had rather be what I am, a member of the Negro race, than be able to claim membership with the most favored of any other race. I have always been made sad when I have heard members of any race claiming rights and privileges, or certain badges of distinction, on the ground simply that they were members of this or that race, regardless of their own individual worth or attainments. I have been made to feel sad for such persons because I am conscious of the fact that mere connection with what is known as a superior race will not permanently carry an individual forward unless he has individual worth, and mere connection with what is regarded as an inferior race will not finally hold an individual back if he possesses intrinsic, individual merit. Every persecuted individual and race should get much consolation out of the great human law, which is universal and eternal, that merit, no matter under what skin found, is in the long run, recognized and rewarded. This I have said here, not to call attention to myself as an individual, but to the race to which I am proud to belong.

## ABOLITIONIST VOICES

### from *An Appeal in Favor of That Class of Americans Called Africans*
### by Lydia Maria Child

We first debase the nature of man by making him a slave, and then very coolly tell him that he must always remain a slave because he does not know how to use freedom. We first crush people to the earth, and then claim the right of trampling on them forever, because they are prostrate. Truly, human selfishness never invented a rule which worked out so charmingly both ways!

---

1. **flambeaus.** Torches

## from *Freedom Journal*, March 16, 1827
### by John B. Russwurm

Education being an object of the highest importance to the welfare of society, we shall endeavor to present just and adequate views of it, and to urge upon our brethren the necessity and expediency of training their children . . . It is surely time that we should awake from this lethargy of years, and make a concentrated effort for the education of our youth. We form a spoke in the human wheel, and it is necessary that we should understand our dependence on the different parts, and theirs on us, in order to perform our part with propriety.

The interesting fact that there are *five hundred thousand* free persons of color, one half of whom might peruse, and the whole benefitted by the publication of the Journal; that no publication, as yet, has been devoted exclusively to their improvement—that many selections from approved standard authors, which are within the reach of few, may occasionally be made—and more important still, that this large body of our citizens have no public channel—all serve to prove the real necessity, at present, for the appearance of the FREEDOM'S JOURNAL.

## from Editorial in *The Liberator*, January 1, 1831
### by William Lloyd Garrison

I am aware that many object to the severity of my language, but is there not cause for severity? I will be harsh as truth, and as uncompromising as justice. On this subject, I do not wish to think, or speak, or write, with moderation. No! No! Tell a man whose house in on fire to sound a moderate alarm . . . but urge me not to use moderation in cause like the present . . .

I am in earnest—I will not equivocate—I will not excuse—I will not retreat a single inch—AND I WILL BE HEARD.

## from *Appeal to the Christian Women of the Southern States*
### by Angelina Grimké

Man, who was created in the image of his Maker, never can properly be termed a thing, though the laws of the Slave States do call him a "chattel personal"[1]; Man, I assert, never was put under the feet of men by the first charter of human rights which was given by God . . . It has been justly remarked that "God never made a slave," he made man upright, his back was not made to carry burdens, nor his neck to wear a yoke, and the man must be crushed within him, before his back can be fitted to the burden of perpetual slavery; and that his back is not fitted to it, is manifest by the insurrections that so often disturb the peace and security of slaveholding countries . . . Slavery always has, and always will produce insurrections wherever it exists, because it is a violation of the natural order of things, and no human power can much longer perpetuate it.

## from *Slavery*
### by William Ellery Channing

I come now to what is to my own mind the great argument against seizing and using a man as property. He cannot be property in the sight of God and justice, because his a Rational, Moral, Immortal Being; because created in God's image, and therefore in the highest sense his child; because created to unfold godlike faculties, and to govern himself by a Divine Law written on his heart, and republished in God's Word. His whole nature forbids that he should be seized as property. From his very nature it follows, that so to seize him is to offer an insult to his Maker, and to inflict aggravated social wrong. . . .

No man, who seriously considers what human nature is, and what it was made for, can think of setting up a claim to a fellow-creature. What! own a spiritual being, a being made to know and adore God, and who is to outlive the sun and stars? What! chain to our lowest uses a being made for truth and virtue? convert into a brute instrument that intelligent nature, on which the idea of Duty has dawned, and which is a nobler type of God than all outward creation! Should we not deem it a wrong which no punishment could expiate, were one of our children seized as property, and driven by the ship to toil? And shall God's child, dearer to him than an only son to a human parent, be thus degraded?

## from *Argument before the Supreme Court in the Case of Wharton Jones v. John Vanzandt, 1846*
### by Salmon P. Chase

The law of the Creator, which invests every human being with an inalienable title to freedom, cannot be repealed by any inferior law, which asserts that man is property. Such a law may be enforced by power; but the exercise of the power must be confined within the jurisdiction of the state, which establishes the law. It cannot be enforced—it can have no operation whatever—in any other jurisdiction. The very moment a slave passes beyond the jurisdiction of the state, in which he is held as such, he ceases to be a slave; not because any law or regulation of the state which he enters confers freedom upon him, but because he continues to be a man and leaves behind him the law of force, which made him a slave.

---

1. **"chattel personal."** Movable item of personal property

# Guided Writing

"There is properly no history, only biography."

—Ralph Waldo Emerson

Recent popular biographical narratives such as Sarah and Elizabeth Delany's *Having Our Say* and Tom Brokaw's *The Greatest Generation* attest to the appeal of a personal story well told.

## BIOGRAPHICAL NARRATIVE

People *are* history. No political, social, cultural incident occurs in the absence of people making it and watching it happen. We can read about these incidents in a newspaper or history book, but learning about them from the people who made or watched them happen gives us, perhaps, the most meaningful picture of all. Why? The people know at a personal level the significance of how the incident shapes and changes lives.

The people in your community have made or watched important incidents happen, too. Behind each of these incidents —whether large or small—is a person with a story to tell. Who is this person and what is his or her story?

**WRITING ASSIGNMENT.** For this assignment, you have the opportunity to find this person and capture—through a combination of narration, biography, and oral history—his or her story about an incident.

## Professional Model

from *Incidents in the Life of a Slave Girl* by Linda Brent

**EXAMINING THE MODEL.** Brent's poignant account of her grandmother's life in slavery personalizes what it meant to be a slave. Readers today still marvel at the grandmother's courage, strength, and determination as she endured the hardships and shame of slavery.

How does Brent place the reader in her grandmother's world? The specific details she relates, capturing the facts and emotions, clarify her experience for the reader. Her expression—caring, hopeful,

> I had also a great treasure in my maternal grandmother, who was a remarkable woman in many respects. . . . She was a little girl when she was captured and sold to the keeper of a large hotel. I have often heard her tell how hard she fared during childhood. But as she grew older she evinced so much intelligence, and was so faithful, that her master and mistress could not help seeing it was for their interest to take care of such a valuable piece of property.
>
> . . .
>
> Her master died, and the property was divided among his heirs. The widow had her dower in the hotel which she continued to keep open. My grandmother remained in her service as a slave; but her children were divided among her master's children. As she had five, Benjamin, the youngest one, was sold, in order that each heir might have an equal portion of dollars and cents. . . . His sale was a terrible blow to my grandmother; but she was naturally hopeful,

and she went to work with renewed energy, trusting in time to be able to purchase some of her children.

. . .

She [Brent's mistress] possessed but few slaves; and at her death those were all distributed among her relatives. Five of them were my grandmother's children, and had shared the same milk that nourished her mother's children. Notwithstanding my grandmother's long and faithful service to her owners, not one of her children escaped the auction block. These God-breathing machines are no more, in the sight of their masters, than the cotton they plant, or the horses they tend.

## Prewriting

**FINDING YOUR VOICE.** Brent's voice is reflected through her personality, her attitude toward her grandmother and those who would read her narrative, her word choice, and sentence structure. She wanted her reader to know her grandmother's story. If you convey to the person you are interviewing sincere interest in the narrative and if you focus on the writing that follows, your voice as biographer will be honest, effective, and engaging. The use of quotations will allow the voice of your subject to come through clearly, strongly, even poetically.

**IDENTIFYING YOUR AUDIENCE.** Narrative writing that zooms in on a biographical incident is meant for sharing. With whom will you share this story? Classmates, certainly, but your teacher may want your writing to be made even more public. The writing you and your classmates do may be integrated with a social studies unit, segmented by decade and based on community or subject history. Or, your narrative may complement a publication or an exhibit presently being planned by your local historical society or museum. Your local TV or radio station or newspaper may wish to film an interview or broadcast or publish what you write. Whatever form the finished product takes, it is enormously satisfying to contribute something of enjoyment or benefit to others while preserving history.

**WRITING WITH A PLAN.** Before selecting a person to interview, make a list of older people you know or know of. Your science teacher's husband just retired from a career as NFL referee. A friend's grandmother appeared in several Broadway productions. A neighbor cultivates prize-winning roses and recently had a variety named in his honor. A friend's older sister was in the first class at West Point to graduate women.

Decide whose experiences and background interest you most. Also, consider the amount of time you have to complete the assignment and the availability of this person. Once you have made your selection, arrange a specific time and place for the

forsaken—makes it real. When Brent states that slaves were "God-breathing machines no more, in the sight of their masters, than the cotton they plant, or the horses they tend," the reader knows the truth of this statement because Brent so carefully and purposefully expressed the details of the event.

As you gear up for the interview at hand, refer to the Language Arts Survey 4.14, "Conducting an Interview," and 4.2, "Active versus Passive Listening."

"It is [the writer's] privilege to help man endure by lifting his heart, by reminding him of the courage and honor and hope and pride and compassion and pity and past."

—*William Faulkner*

interview to occur. Make sure that the time is adequate so that neither of you feels rushed. Of course, courtesy requires that the person you are interviewing be informed of the particulars of the assignment: the purpose, the completion date, and the anticipated exposure.

Prepare well. Compose a list of questions beginning with those that establish the person's identity with name, age (if relevant), title, background, and present status or occupation. Proceed with who, what, where, when, why, and how questions that you trust will elicit from the person all relevant details about the biographical incident. Determine how you will record the interview. Will you take notes by hand or use a laptop word processor/computer? Do you have access to a tape recorder? Be sure to arrive ready to face your subject. Here's a checklist: two or three pens and paper, two formatted disks, a charged battery or power cord, one or more blank tapes, and lots of enthusiasm. Consider inviting a friend or family member to sit in on the interview, helping you transcribe during and verifying information later. If your subject just starts talking and is distracted with your questions, go with it. Some of the best material can come from a tangent. If, however, it seems that you need to redirect your interviewee, politely restate your original question to clarify his or her answer. You can always double-check or note the details as the interview winds down.

## Student Model—Graphic Organizer

Greg chose to interview his high school German teacher, who had told her class a little about her early childhood in war-torn Prussia, her marriage to an American GI, her move to the United States, and her career as a foreign language teacher.

Interview Checklist
- list of questions
- two or three pens and a pad of paper
- laptop word processor/ computer and two formatted disks
- tape recorder and one or more blank tapes
- charged battery or power cord
- a friend to help with the interview

For help in preparing your questions, refer to the Language Arts Survey 2.14, "Questioning: Using the 5 *Ws* and an *H*."

**Biographical Narrative Interview Organizer**

**Interview with:** *my German language teacher, Mrs. Renete Eads*
**Date:** *Feb. 19*
**Time:** *3 p.m.*
**Place:** *high school classroom*

**Permission to take notes, tape record, print, and publish:** *given*

**My goal for the interview:** *learn about Mrs. Eads's German background and adopted American identity*

**The incident:**
*coming to and living in America*

**Incident's significance to this person:**
*lived in East Prussia and Germany when she was young*
*difference in living there and here*
*becoming more American than German*

**Questions for the interview:**
*What was it like living in Germany?*
*What is your earliest memory?*
*How did you come to America?*
*How does living in America compare to your life in Germany?*
*What special memories of teaching do you have?*

**Mementos:**
*picture of the house in Colorado Springs*

**Direct quotations:**
*"I've probably walked the distance of the world on this classroom floor."*

**Main ideas, key words, and observations:**
*the way she looks when she talks about being a young girl in Germany*
*sadness when she talks about her husband dying*

> "If you would not be forgotten as soon as you are dead, either write things worth reading or do things worth writing."
>
> —Benjamin Franklin

## Drafting

Review your notes and, if you used a tape recorder, listen to the taped interview several times until the story is clear and complete in your mind. You may want to transcribe or type out parts of the recording. If a third party joined the interview, visit with that person about what you both heard. As you continue working with your interview material, highlight or otherwise note fragments or inaccuracies. Then check back with the interviewee as necessary. Stay true to the factual account, but feel free to add descriptive words and phrases to sharpen sensory details. Begin by introducing the subject and indicating the focus; then launch into telling the incident in chronological order. Draw on your notes, the recording, and your observations. Include direct quotations, perhaps even some dialogue, and interesting details.

After the biographical narrative is complete, conclude with a short paragraph. You could update the reader on the months or years in the life of the person that followed the incident, explain his or her present situation, comment on the value to yourself as interviewer and writer, and/or suggest the insight the incident may have given to the reader. What is this person's niche in history that you have just succeeded in capturing?

Taking a photo?
- Close-ups are best.
- Eliminate background clutter.

Using an old photo or news clipping?
- Protect and preserve!
- Make a copy and return the original.

## Self- and Peer Evaluation

After you finish your first draft, complete a self-evaluation. Adjust as you deem necessary. Form a group with two or three classmates, exchange and read each others' narratives, and share constructive criticism. Consider these questions as you evaluate narratives:

- What, if anything, makes the narrative inviting, interesting, and purposeful? What would make it more appealing to the reader?
- What makes up the beginning, middle, and end? Where are the gaps?
- How does the subject come alive for the reader? What details does the reader still need?
- What sensory details create a vivid picture of the story's events, characters, or places? What could be improved?
- What, if anything, could be eliminated because it contributes nothing to the narrative or detracts from the focus?
- What indicates that the writer values the person's character, experience, or contribution?
- How do word choice and tone contribute to writing that is honest, effective, and engaging?
- What errors with run-on sentences or comma splices mar the flow? How might sentence variety be improved?
- What makes the conclusion satisfying or not satisfying?

## Student Model—Draft

> Renati Eads
>
> In the waning years of WWII a little girl named Renati was born in Konigsburg, East Prussia. She stayed there ~~until~~ her first birthday when she and her family fled to Berlin. They were fleeing from the Russian army. Her
>
> *Did she say what this was like?*
> father secured housing for her mother,
> *two*
> ~~2~~ brothers, and herself. Shortly after this Renati's father died leaving her mother responsible for raising their three children. Renati's mother cleaned

*This would make a good intro*

*Some of this stuff sounds stiff—too formal—not very friendly*

houses to support her family. The wages
she received were not great, but what
she did earn she used to put together
some sort of semblance of Christmas in
1945. She also provided Renati with her
first memory. It was Christmas of 1945.
— sentence string
~~and~~ Renati was almost 2 years old, her
Her
~~and~~ brothers were entertaining her with
shadow puppets on the wall when her
mother called them to come get their
present. It was a carved wooden duck
and a ramp. They quickly found out that
if they put the duck at the top of the
ramp, he would waddle down it.

four          five
When Renati was about ~~4~~ or ~~5~~ she spent
her days running around with her
comma splice
brothers and their friends, they would
ing
play in the rubble mountains search, for
metal to sell to the stores. They spent
the money they made on candy. During
the airlift in 1948, she was out playing
in the street hoping to catch one of
the small packages of candy that the
ped                    comma splice
men would drop, from the airplanes, ~~when~~
As
she was jumping from one snow drift to
another, she tore her stockings. ~~As~~ she
sat there crying with a bloody knee ~~and~~

Lots of long sentences—Can you shorten some up?

Need to fix run-on
sentence

All the details here
make this good—I
can almost see this.

> more worried about what her mother would do to her for tearing her only stockings ^*than hurt* a jeep pulled up and two GIs hopped out. They cleaned up her knee and gave her a small package. When they left ^, she opened the wrapping and smelled it, it smelled sweet, she licked it, it tasted sweet, and so she tore off a little piece and started chewing and chewing, and chewing. It was Wrigley's gum. *had she ever had gum before?*

*comma splices*

*comma splice*

> The details here really make this memorable. This is my favorite part.

## Language, Grammar, and Style

### Writing Effective Sentences

**IDENTIFYING EFFECTIVE SENTENCES.** In a rush to get things down, a writer sometimes runs sentences together by connecting them with one conjunction after another. Such a pattern is a type of run-on called a sentence string.

**Run-on:**

Lydia Maria Child was a Northern abolitionist and she edited and helped to publish Linda Brent's story and Linda Brent is the pen name for Harriet Brent Jacobs.

**Revised:**

Lydia Maria Child, a Northern abolitionist, edited and helped to publish *Incidents in the Life of a Slave Girl* for Harriet Brent Jacobs, who used the pen name Linda Brent.

## Revising and Proofreading

Following a revision based on self- and peer evaluation, stay away from it for a day or two, if possible. When you pick it up again, read it aloud, marking changes and corrections. Reread, continuing to tinker and polish until you are pleased with the finished narrative. Prepare a final text that is free of mechanical and grammatical errors.

## Student Model—Revised

> In the waning years of WWII a little girl named Renati was born in Konigsburg, East Prussia. She stayed there until her first birthday when she and her family fled to Berlin to escape the advancing Russian army. Her father found an apartment with nothing more than two beds, lawn chairs, and cardboard for windows for her mother, two brothers, and herself. Shortly after this, Renati's father died, leaving them alone. Renati's mother worked hard cleaning houses to support her family. "I remember my mother coming home each day, so tired but so determined to take care of us," Renati recalls. The wages her mother earned were not great, but some of what she

earned provided Renati with her first memory. It was Christmas of 1945. Renati was almost two years old. Her brothers were entertaining her with shadow puppets on the wall when her mother called them to come get their present—a carved wooden duck and a ramp. Over and over, they put the duck at the top of the ramp and watched him waddle down.

When Renati was about five, she spent her days with her brothers and their friends. She remembers, "We played in the rubble mountains that were created by the Allied bombing. We searched for metal to sell, never really thinking about the destruction under our feet. Instead, we saw the rubble as something challenging to climb on." They spent their money on candy. One day during the airlift in 1948, she was out playing in the street hoping to catch one of the small packages of candy that the men dropped from the airplanes. As she was jumping from one snow drift to another, she tore her stockings. She sat there crying with a bloody knee, more worried about what her mother would do to her for tearing her only stockings than hurt. A jeep pulled up and two GIs hopped out. They cleaned up her knee and gave her a small package. When they left, she opened the wrapping and smelled it. It smelled sweet. She licked it. It tasted sweet. She tore off a little piece and started chewing and chewing and chewing. It was Wrigley's gum, something new to Renati.

As a teenager, Renati spent late afternoons learning life skills at the German Youth Club, which was organized by the American army. When she was eighteen, she moved to Paris for two years after she had completed business college. In 1964 she moved back to Berlin where she met her future husband Danny. She met him at his workplace, the AFN, an American radio station. When they started dating, Danny took her to see many of the famous groups who visited the station, such as Herman's Hermits.

Another run-on error, called a comma splice, occurs when two or more sentences are inadequately joined with one or more commas.

**Comma Splice:**

Abraham Lincoln wrote a letter in 1864 to a Mrs. Bixby, she had lost five sons in the Civil War.

**Revised:**

In 1864 Abraham Lincoln wrote a letter to a Mrs. Bixby, whose five sons had been killed in the Civil War.

Still another problem with sentence structure is a sentence fragment, a phrase or clause that does not express a complete thought but has been punctuated as though it did.

**Sentence Fragment:**

Filled with the desire to read and write. Booker T. Washington worked as a janitor while he attended Hampton Normal and Agricultural Institute.

**Revised:**

Filled with the desire to read and write, Booker T. Washington worked as a janitor while he attended Hampton Normal and Agricultural Institute.

FIXING SENTENCES. Fixing errors in sentence structure not only cleans up the writing, but also improves its flow.

continued on page 398

Greg found the following errors in his sentences.

It was Christmas of 1945 and Renati was almost 2 years old her and brothers were entertaining her with shadow puppets on the wall when her mother called them to come get their present.

When Renati was about 4 or 5 she spent her days running around with her brothers, they would play in the rubble mountains searching for metal to sell to the stores.

After Danny had finished his four years in the service in Feb 1967.

When they left she opened the wrapping and smelled it, it smelled sweet, she licked it, it tasted sweet, and so she tore off a little piece and started chewing and chewing, and chewing.

On your own paper, correct each of the errors in Greg's sentences.

**USING EFFECTIVE SENTENCES.**
Reread the sentences in your draft, checking your writing for common sentence strings, comma splices, and fragments. Correct any errors that you find. Experiment with using a variety of sentence structures. For more information, see the Language Arts Survey 3.36,

"This was so exciting for me—a German girl with an American soldier going to see the music stars of the time. What a dream," Renati says. Eventually they married and moved to Garmisch-Partenkirschen in Bavaria. Their first child, Scarlet, was born there in 1966.

After Danny finished his four years in the service in February 1967, they moved to Colorado Springs, Colorado. He became the program director at the local radio station. They had their second child, Chris. Sadly, Danny died October 27, 1970. Renati was in the same predicament as her mother—widowed and raising two children. "I remember feeling the same as my mother, so tired every day, but so determined to take care of my children," Renati sighs. She realized she needed a higher education to get a job that would provide for her family. She enrolled in the University of Colorado at Boulder, taking courses by night and selling Avon during the day. She also received money from renting the house Danny had bought for his family in Colorado Springs.

In 1973 she moved back to Germany, but after two years she missed the United States so much that she returned to Boulder. She earned her teaching degree in 1977 and took a job with West High School in Denver. In 1978 Renati started at the newly opened Skyline High School. She has worked there for 21 years and is one of the few originals left. "I've probably walked the distance of the world on this classroom floor," she says. Her years at Skyline are full of happy memories, but perhaps the most special to her is becoming a US citizen on Feb 7, 1998. Looking back from Skyline, to Boulder, to meeting her American husband, to her first experiences with the Americans after the war, Renati readily relates, "Over the years, I know I have become more American than German."

## Publishing and Presenting

Your narrative writing may be made public in some fashion, by itself or as part of a collection. Remember to give the person you interviewed a final copy and, if the narrative appeared elsewhere, a copy of that publication. Of course, save the biographical narrative for yourself. It will undoubtedly be something you continue to take pride in and value as the years go by. Also, you never know when a publishing opportunity may arise. Greg and his classmates published their stories in an online e-zine that they designed. In doing so, they made sure they obtained permission from each person they interviewed.

"Combining and Expanding Sentences," and 3.35, "Correcting Wordy Sentences."

Before releasing your final copy for publication, be sure you have written permission from the person you interviewed.

# UNIT REVIEW
## *Slavery and the Civil War*

## Words for Everyday Use

Check your knowledge of the following vocabulary words from the selections in this unit. Write short sentences using these words in context to make the meaning clear. To review the definition or usage of a word, refer to the page number listed or the Glossary of Words for Everyday Use.

| | | |
|---|---|---|
| abeyance, 368 | fissure, 372 | obdurate, 327 |
| acclivity, 356 | fix, 351 | oscillation, 358 |
| aspirated, 360 | flaring, 341 | quadruped, 371 |
| barbaric, 373 | gesticulate, 359 | racket, 351 |
| burnished, 341 | harbor, 368 | rapturous, 326 |
| consecrate, 346 | impalpable, 368 | score, 346 |
| contender, 368 | incoherent, 327 | sentinel, 355 |
| creed, 368 | infidel, 371 | suffice, 368 |
| diligently, 326 | jag, 373 | transfigure, 341 |
| disposition, 369 | jubilant, 341 | tread, 376 |
| efface, 358 | linguist, 368 | trill, 376 |
| embrasure, 356 | loitering, 373 | wrath, 340 |
| exult, 375 | ludicrous, 358 | |
| fateful, 340 | malign, 362 | |

## Literary Tools

Define the following terms, giving concrete examples of how they are used in the selections in this unit. To review a term, refer to the page number indicated or to the Handbook of Literary Terms.

| | | |
|---|---|---|
| allusion, 339 | folk song, 334 | repetition, 350 |
| antithesis, 345 | free verse, 380 | rhyme, 366 |
| argument, 350 | hymn, 339 | rhyme scheme, 334, 366 |
| colloquialism, 350 | irony, 380, 382 | stereotype, 324 |
| dialogue, 382 | meter, 366 | symbol, 365 |
| elaboration, 365 | parallelism, 345 | theme, 330 |
| elegy, 366 | psychological fiction, 354 | tone, 324, 350 |
| flashback, 354 | refrain, 330 | |

# Reflecting
## ............................*on* YOUR READING

## Genre Studies

1. **SPEECHES.** A good speech is written in simple, direct language that appeals to the emotions and interests of its audience. With these criteria in mind, answer the following question: What qualities make The Gettysburg Address and "Ain't I a Woman?" excellent speeches? Why are these speeches remembered?

2. **SPIRITUALS.** Many spirituals are ambiguous. Explain what ambiguity is. Then explain how and why ambiguity is used in spirituals such as "Swing Low, Sweet Chariot" in this unit and "Follow the Drinking Gourd" in Unit 1.

## Thematic Studies

3. **NATURALISM.** Naturalism is the philosophical belief that people's actions, thoughts, feelings, and values result not from the free action of the will but rather are caused, or determined, by external forces or by heredity. What makes Ambrose Bierce's "An Occurrence at Owl Creek Bridge" an example of Naturalism?

4. **ROMANTICISM.** Romanticism was a literary and artistic movement of the eighteenth and nineteenth centuries that placed value on emotion or imagination over reason, the individual over society, nature and wildness over human works, the country over the town, common people over artistocrats, and freedom over control or authority. Analyze how Whitman's "Song of Myself" fits into the romantic tradition.

## Historical/Biographical Studies

5. **ABRAHAM LINCOLN.** Study The Gettysburg Address, the quotations from Lincoln on the "Echoes" page at the end of the unit introduction, and the poem about Lincoln by Whitman ("O Captain! My Captain!"). What sort of person do you think Lincoln was, based on these materials? What were his concerns, both moral and political? Why is Lincoln so greatly revered today?

6. **SLAVERY AND ITS AFTERMATH.** Based on the unit introduction, the selection from Douglass's *Narrative,* and the spiritual "Swing Low, Sweet Chariot," answer the following questions: What was the institution of slavery like for the enslaved? What hardships did it impose? How did enslaved people feel about the institution of slavery? Why was it important for ex-slaves to become educated? What difficulties did ex-slaves encounter?

Every part of this soil is sacred in the estimation of my people. Every hillside, every valley, every plain and grove, has been hallowed by some sad or happy event in days long vanished. Even the rocks, which seem to be dumb and dead as they swelter in the sun along the silent shore, thrill with memories of stirring events connected with the lives of my people, and the very dust upon which you now stand responds more lovingly to their footsteps than to yours.

—Chief Seattle of the
Suquamish and Duwamish

*Ram's Head, White Hollyhock–Hills,*
1935. Georgia O'Keeffe.
Brooklyn Museum of Art.

## ArtNote

*Ram's Head, White Hollyhock–Hills,* 1935. Georgia O'Keeffe. Brooklyn Museum of Art.

Georgia O'Keeffe (1887–1986) was among the circle of early Modern artists in New York that included her husband, Alfred Stieglitz, an influential photographer, publisher, and gallery owner. O'Keeffe preferred the West to New York and brought an austere, modern style to the forms and colors of the New Mexico desert. A highly independent artist, O'Keeffe rejected the notion that her work represented a female sensibility: "The men liked to put me down as the best woman painter. I think I'm one of the best painters."

Compare O'Keeffe's painting on page 402 with the Stieglitz photograph on page 407. They exhibit some of the same aspects of a modern approach to art, but there are differences, too. How does each artist present the perspective, or point of view, the placement of the objects, the subject matter, and the use of light in each work?

# FRONTIERS (1860–1900)

## AN EXPANDING NATION

Without doubt, the Civil War was the most costly event in the history of the United States. Fought on American soil between Americans, it wrought destruction throughout the South, cost the federal government more than fifteen billion dollars, and resulted in an estimated 618,000 deaths of Union and Confederate soldiers. In five years' time, the country lost an entire generation of its male youth. After the war, an exhausted nation set about the painful business of **Reconstruction**, setting the conditions under which rebellious states would be readmitted to the Union.

Many Civil War veterans, having traveled away from home for the first time in their lives, developed a taste for freewheeling adventure, a willingness to strike out for places unknown. Some headed west to homestead or to seek their fortunes. They were joined by thousands of settlers moving from lands along the Mississippi River and by recent European immigrants who, finding little hope in the increasingly crowded cities of the East, looked to the frontier for a better life. In a few decades, people of European descent had established homes across the American West, from the prairie lands of Nebraska to the coasts of California. In the course of this **Westward Expansion,** Americans developed a self-reliance that gave substance to what might otherwise have been a merely theoretical belief in freedom and democracy. By the end of the century, most of the United States territories from the Atlantic to the Pacific had become states with the exceptions of Oklahoma, New Mexico, and Arizona.

## PIONEERS, PROSPECTORS, AND RANCHERS

The Westward Expansion, begun early in the century, was encouraged by the **Homestead Act** of 1862, which, for a fee of ten dollars, granted 160 acres of federal

## LITERARY EVENTS

➤ = American Events

➤1870. Ralph Waldo Emerson's "Civilization" published

➤1869. Louisa May Alcott's *Little Women* and Bret Harte's "The Outcasts of Poker Flat" published

➤1868. Bret Harte's "The Luck of Roaring Camp" published

➤1866. Walt Whitman's "O Captain! My Captain!" published

1866. Feodor Dostoyevsky's *Crime and Punishment* published

| 1860 | 1865 | 1870 |
|------|------|------|

## HISTORICAL EVENTS

➤1860. Navajos attack Fort Defiance, New Mexico; Pony Express begins

➤1861. Kansas enters Union

➤1862. Cochise leads Apaches in raids; Sioux uprising under Little Crow; Homestead Act; Congress funds construction of transcontinental railroads

➤1863. Nez Percé forced to sign treaty and give up land; Kit Carson resettles Navajos and Apaches

➤1864. Navajos set off on "long walk" to Bosque Redondo prison camp; Cheyenne, Arapahoe, Apache, Comanche, and Kiawa massacred at Sand Creek

➤1866. Reconstruction begins in South

➤1867. Alaska purchased, Nebraska admitted to Union

➤1868. Attempt to impeach President Johnson; Ulysses S. Grant elected president

➤1869. Union Pacific and Central Pacific Railroads link

➤1870. First African-American legislators take seats at Washington, DC

# ArtNote

*Nat Love*

During the cattle drives of the late 1800s, more than a third of all cowboys were of African, Mexican or Native American heritage. Some historians estimate that one in four cowboys was a former slave. Among them was Nat Love, who earned the nickname "Deadwood Dick" for his extraordinary achievements at a rodeo in Deadwood, South Dakota in 1876. According to legend, he roped, saddled and rode a wild stallion in nine minutes, five minutes faster than his competition, and shot 15 straight bull's eyes. The following year the first of many "Deadwood Dick" dime novels appeared, but author Edward Wheeler made the character a white man.

Nat Love, alias "Deadwood Dick."

land in the Western Territories to anyone who would live on that land for five years. This expansion was a continuation of efforts begun in the 1820s by adventurous settlers following the routes carved out by traders and trappers. Throughout the period from the 1820s to the 1870s, pioneers loaded their belongings and their dreams onto covered wagons and headed west along the Mormon, Oregon, California, Santa Fe, and Old Spanish trails. By the 1840s, many Americans had come to believe that it was their **"Manifest Destiny,"** in the words of one newspaperman, to cover the continent from coast to coast. The expansion was fueled, as well, by dreams of striking it rich prospecting for gold and silver. The discovery of gold in 1848 at Sutter's Mill, on California's Sacramento River, was the first of many **"gold rushes"** that led to the building of boom towns—Sacramento, San Francisco, Boise, Silver City, Virginia City, Carson City, Denver, Pueblo, Tucson, Tombstone, Custer City, and Deadwood. These towns became legendary for their rough-and-tumble lawlessness, giving rise to the legends of the **"Wild West,"** with its

➤1883. James Whitcomb Riley's *The Old Swimmin' Hole and 'Leven More Poems* published

➤1881. Helen Maria Fiske Hunt Jackson's *A Century of Dishonor* published

1879. Henrik Ibsen's *A Doll's House* published

➤1879. Henry James's *Daisy Miller* published

1877. Leo Tolstoy's *Anna Karenina* published

1876. Mark Twain's *Tom Sawyer* published

1885. Émile Zola's *Germinal* published

1872. George Eliot's *Middlemarch* published

➤1884. Mark Twain's *The Adventures of Huckleberry Finn* published

**1875**      **1880**      **1885**

➤1871. Indian Appropriation Act makes Native Americans wards of the federal government; Cochise forced to surrender; Chicago fire

➤1876. Colorado admitted to Union; Chiricahua leader Geronimo terrorizes white settlers; Battle of Little Big Horn

➤1880. James Abram Garfield elected president

➤1881. Garfield assassinated; Chester Alan Arthur succeeds as president

➤1884. Grover Cleveland elected president

➤1872. Ulysses S. Grant reelected president; Victoria Woodhull runs for president; Susan B. Anthony arrested for trying to vote

➤1877. Electoral commission appoints Rutherford B. Hayes president; Nez Percé captured fleeing to Canada

➤1882. Chinese Exclusion Act; first immigration restrictions

➤1875. Comanche chief Quanah Parker ends his resistance; Tennessee enacts first "Jim Crow" law

gamblers, gunfighters, prospectors, and other colorful characters, including Calamity Jane, Deadwood Dick, Wild Bill Hickock, Annie Oakley, Billy the Kid, and Jesse James.

Cattle ranching, begun in Texas, became a big business throughout the Western Plains. Ranchers would herd their cattle together and drive them over great distances to new railway stops that would take the cattle back east, to Chicago, the center of the developing stockyard and meatpacking industry. The ranch owner and the cowboy drover were added to the West's long list of colorful stock characters. Ellsworth, Dodge City, and Abilene were among the greatest of the western cattle towns.

Geronimo (first row, third from the right) after his capture in 1886.

## THE DISPLACEMENT OF NATIVE AMERICANS

While the nineteenth century was one of new frontiers for settlers of European descent, it was one of heartbreak and trial for Native Americans, who were forced from their ancestral lands, killed in numerous "Indian Wars," and confined to reservations, often undesirable sections of the country far from their original homes. The **Indian Removal Act** passed by Congress in 1830 gave the president of the United States the power to require that all native peoples east of the Mississippi move west. This power was used by President Andrew Jackson, over the objections of the Supreme Court, to remove Cherokee peoples from Georgia and Tennessee

LITERARY
EVENTS

➤ = American Events

➤1891. Ambrose Bierce's *Tales of Soldiers and Civilians* published
1891. Thomas Hardy's *Tess of the d'Urbervilles*, and
    Oscar Wilde's *The Picture of Dorian Gray* published

➤1890. *Poems by Emily Dickinson*
    published posthumously

➤1886. William Dean Howells's *Indian Summer* published
1886. Robert Louis Stevenson's *The Strange Case of Dr. Jekyll
    and Mr. Hyde* published

➤1896. Sarah Orne Jewett's "Country
    of the Pointed Firs" published

➤1895. Stephen Crane's *The
    Red Badge of Courage* published

➤1899. Kate Chopin's
    *The Awakening* published

➤1894. Mark Twain's *Pudd'nhead Wilson* published

➤1893. Frederick Jackson Turner's "The Significance
    of the Frontier in American History" published

1890                          1895                          1900

HISTORICAL
EVENTS

➤1886. Haymarket riots; Geronimo captured

➤1889. North Dakota, South Dakota,
    Montana, and Washington admitted
    to Union

➤1890. Battle of Wounded Knee
    ends Native American resistance;
    Sherman Anti-Trust Act

➤1892. Grover Cleveland elected

➤1893. Hawaii annexationists
    overthrow Queen Liliuokalani

➤1895. Booker T.
    Washington's Atlanta
    Compromise

➤1896. Utah admitted to Union; William
    McKinley elected president

➤1897. United States annexes Hawaii

➤1898. Spanish-American War; Louisiana
    adopts "grandfather clause,"
    restricting African-American voters

1899. Great Britain
    begins the Boer War;
    Philippine insurrection

**406**  *UNIT SIX / FRONTIERS*

to the newly established Indian Territory in what is now Oklahoma. Escorted by federal troops, thirteen thousand Cherokee were put on a forced march, now known as the **"Trail of Tears"** because of the deaths of some four thousand of their number en route. The Cherokee were one of many peoples who had either to fight or to submit to being moved to reservations.

The building of railroads led to widespread slaughter of the herds of Great Plains buffalo that provided sustenance to the Native Americans of that region. As new settlers moved westward, they continually revised their ideas about what lands would belong to Native Americans "for as long as the waters run," breaking numerous treaties and promises. Some Native American groups fought back. The 1860s and 1870s saw warfare between United States troops and native groups throughout the West, with much brutality and carnage on both sides. In 1864, a massacre of over four hundred Cheyenne men, women, and children led to all-out war between the United States government and the combined forces of the Cheyenne, the Lakota, and other Plains peoples. In 1876, the Lakota defeated Lieutenant George Armstrong Custer at the **Battle of Little Big Horn,** killing the 264 men in his company. In 1886, federal troops overpowered and captured **Geronimo,** the leader of the Chiricahua Apaches, who had fought long and successfully against the invaders of his people's land in the Southwest. In 1887, they captured **Chief Joseph** of the Nez Percé after his people's long-attempted flight to freedom in Canada. That same year, Congress passed the **Dawes Act,** which granted citizenship to Native Americans after twenty-five years but took away Native American reservation lands for use by settlers, offering in exchange small plots for heads of families. In 1889, in another of a string of broken promises, the United States Congress opened up much of Indian Territory to new settlement. In a single day, the entire territory was settled. In 1890, at **Wounded Knee,** South Dakota, federal troops massacred more than two hundred—mostly unarmed— Sioux in what was to be the last action of the Indian Wars.

## IMMIGRATION, THE GROWTH OF CITIES, AND INDUSTRIALISM

The last forty years of the nineteenth century was a time of unprecedented change in American cities. Between 1880 and 1900, nine million immigrants arrived in the United States from Europe. Previous immigration had been made up, for the most part, of northern Europeans. The new wave of immigration brought southern and eastern Europeans, as well as Asians, thus greatly diversifying the United States population. This trend would continue and expand in the first two decades of the next century.

Another important trend during these years was the growth of cities. By 1900, fully 40 percent of the United States population lived in urban centers. Many of these people were recent immigrants, many were newly free African Americans from rural areas of the South, and many more were white citizens moving from farms to find jobs in America's booming industrial centers. American industry had benefited from technological developments made during the Civil War era, and a class of millionaire industrialists had emerged with monopolistic control of meatpacking, rail-

*The Steerage,* 1907. Alfred Stieglitz.

roads, and the production of oil and steel. The fabulous wealth of these often unscrupulous industrialists, satirized in Mark Twain's **The Gilded Age,** which he co-authored with Charles Dudley Warner, stood in sharp contrast with the poverty and

A "dime novel."

terrible working conditions of the average laborer. At the turn of the century, the so-called **"muckraker"** journalists Ida Tarbell and Lincoln Steffans would make careers of exposing unscrupulous practices among business people and corrupt political officials.

## THE EXPANDING LITERARY FRONTIER

The literature of the early nineteenth century in America was dominated by Romanticism and concentrated in New England. The great authors of the period were primarily scholarly, moralistic gentlemen, and public tastes ran to the sentimental and nostalgic. Expansion across the frontier in the late nineteenth century was accompanied by an equally dramatic expansion of literary frontiers. Significant writers appeared across the breadth of the nation, in the Midwest, the South, and the West. Many of these writers were women, such as **Sarah Orne Jewett**, **Kate Chopin**, and **Mary Wilkins Freeman**. Many were journalists and adventurers, such as **Mark Twain**, **Bret Harte**, **Ambrose Bierce**, and **Stephen Crane**. One of the greatest writers of the period, **Henry James**, spent much of his life in Europe, chronicling the lives of newly wealthy Americans living abroad. The characters in the fiction of the day became correspondingly diverse, including gunfighters and ranchers, runaway slaves and Civil War soldiers, steamboat captains and con artists, Cajuns and Creoles, pioneer women and children, millionaire tycoons and the desperate urban poor. "Dime novels" were a cheap, popular form of literature, similar to today's comic books. The impossibly exaggerated exploits of Jesse James, Deadwood Dick, and others were "tall tales" that created the enduring legends of the Wild West. The literature of the period fulfilled the vision of Walt Whitman: "I hear America singing, the varied carols I hear."

## REGIONALISM AND LOCAL COLOR

One outgrowth of this diversity was **Regionalism**, or **local color** writing. The mostly female readers of the many new magazines in the East developed an intense interest in the lives and lifestyles of persons living in such faraway, exotic parts of the country as the Louisiana bayou, the Mississippi River valley, and the western boom towns. Journalists and others rushed to fill the demand. Soon, most regions of the country were represented by local colorists who created often humorous pieces about the odd characters scattered across the newly conquered continent. One of the first of these local color writers was Bret Harte, who wrote stories from San Francisco such as "The Luck of Roaring Camp" and "The Outcasts of Poker Flat," beginning a fascination with the West in American popular culture. **Samuel Clemens**, who took the pseudonym Mark Twain, traveled widely throughout the country, posting short stories and humorous sketches about peoples and places as diverse as the con artists, steamboat captains, and riverboat gamblers of the Mississippi River, the natives and missionaries of the Sandwich Islands (later Hawaii), and the denizens of western mining camps, as in his tall tale "The Notorious Jumping Frog of Calaveras County." Kate Chopin and **George Washington Cable** wrote of the people of the Louisiana bayou country. **Joel Chandler Harris** wrote dialectal pieces based on the oral traditions of African Americans in the South. **Edward Eggleston** and **James Whitcomb Riley** wrote of the Hoosiers of backwoods Indiana. Sarah Orne Jewett and Mary Wilkins Freeman wrote of backwoods New England.

## THE EMERGENCE OF REALISM

The presentation in fiction of local dialect and varied, unsavory characters were two expressions of a new and dominant mode in American fiction of the late nineteenth century—**Realism.** The early-nineteenth-century Romantics of New England had tended to present idealized materials designed to inspire lofty emotions. The Realists, in contrast, drew portraits from life, often shocking more sensitive readers with their grim depictions of realities, as the country itself had been shocked by the grim realities of the Civil War. Ambrose Bierce wrote devastatingly bitter, unsentimental portrayals of the horrors of the war, including such masterful short stories as "Chickamauga" and "An Occurrence at Owl Creek Bridge." Twain, widely known for his satirical humor, often involving exaggerated, colorful characters, also showed elements of Realism. Because of its realistic use of a variety of dialects and its quintessentially American theme of the individual's quest for freedom, Twain's *The Adventures of Huckleberry Finn* is often considered the greatest of American novels. Ernest Hemingway wrote, for example, that "All modern American literature comes from one book by Mark

***Huckleberry Finn and Jim,*** 1936. Thomas Hart Benton. Missouri State Capitol.

Twain called *Huckleberry Finn.*" The great champion of Realism was the novelist **William Dean Howells**, who, as editor of *Harper's Weekly, Harper's Monthly,* and the *North American Review,* promoted the works of Mark Twain and Henry James. In novels such as *The Rise of Silas Lapham, Annie Kilburn, A Hazard of New Fortunes,* and *Quality of Mercy,* Howells presented the breakdown of traditional values and the misery of the poor that he observed in urban America. Several authors applied the penetrating accuracy of Realism to the interior lives of their characters, pioneering what became known as **Psychological Realism.** Among these, though very different in attitude, experience, style, and subject matter, are Ambrose Bierce in stories such as "An Occurrence at Owl Creek Bridge," Kate Chopin in works such as "The Story of an Hour" and *The Awakening,* **Charlotte Perkins Gilman** in her feminist horror tale "The Yellow Wallpaper," and **Henry James** in novels such as *Portrait of a Lady* and *The Turn of the Screw.*

## THE RISE OF NATURALISM

**Naturalism** was an extension and refinement of Realism, based on the theories of the French novelist **Émile Zola.** Inspired by nineteenth-century naturalists such as Charles Darwin and Thomas Huxley, Zola held that people's actions and beliefs resulted not from free will but from the arbitrary, outside forces of heredity and environment. He believed that, like a naturalist studying the causes of behavior in animals, the novelist could write "scientific" fiction that demonstrated the exact causes of human behavior. In the United States, Naturalism found its champion in Stephen Crane. In novels like *The Red Badge of Courage* and stories like "The Open Boat," "The Blue Hotel," and "A Mystery of Heroism," Crane showed human beings to be pawns manipulated by the cruel, indifferent forces of nature and society, a philosophy expressed succinctly in his poem "A Man Said to the Universe." Crane's Naturalism, however, was tempered by his belief that in such an indifferent universe, people must stick together with acts of kindness and compassion to counter the terrible forces to which they are subjected. At the turn of the century, Naturalism was to become a dominant mode in American fiction, realized in the works of such writers as **Frank Norris,** author of *McTeague*

Jack London.

and *The Octopus;* **Jack London,** author of "To Build a Fire" and *The Call of the Wild,* and **Theodore Dreiser,** author of *Sister Carrie* and *An American Tragedy.*

# ECHOES

## QUOTATIONS FROM MARK TWAIN

**On flattery:** "I can live for two months on a good compliment."

**On golf:** "Golf is a good walk spoiled."

**On grief and joy:** "Grief can take care of itself, but to get the full value from joy you must have somebody to divide it with."

**On his own writing:** "You don't know about me without you have read a book by the name of *The Adventures of Tom Sawyer;* but that ain't no matter. That book was made by Mr. Mark Twain, and he told the truth, mainly."

**On humans:** "Man is the only animal that blushes. Or needs to."

**On the desire to teach others to be good:** "To be good is noble, but to teach others how to be good is nobler—and less trouble."

**On obedience:** "Of all God's creatures there is only one that cannot be made the slave of the lash. That one is the cat. If man could be crossed with the cat it would improve man, but it would deteriorate the cat."

**On parents:** "When I was a boy of fourteen, my father was so ignorant I could hardly stand to have the old man around. But when I got to be twenty-one, I was astonished at how much he had learned in seven years."

**On politeness:** "Good breeding consists in concealing how much we think of ourselves and how little we think of the other person."

**On school:** "I have never let my schooling interfere with my education."

**On success:** "All you need in this life is ignorance and confidence, and then success is sure."

**On literature:** "A classic is something that everybody wants to have read but nobody wants to read."

**On reading:** "The man who does not read good books has no advantage over the man who can't read them."

**On speaking:** "It usually takes more than three weeks to prepare a good impromptu speech."

**On sermonizing:** "Few sinners are saved after the first twenty minutes of a sermon."

**On writing humor:** "There are several kinds of stories, but only one difficult kind—the humorous."

**On nonsense literature:** "It takes a heap of sense to write good nonsense."

**On conciseness:** "A successful book is not made of what is in it, but what is left out of it.

**In response to a false report of his death:** "The reports of my death are greatly exaggerated."

# "The Notorious Jumping Frog of Calaveras County"

BY MARK TWAIN

## About the AUTHOR

**Mark Twain** (1835–1910) was the pseudonym of Samuel Langhorne Clemens. Clemens took the name from a nautical term for "the second mark," referring to water that was two fathoms deep, or a safe depth for a boat, a term that he encountered as a riverboat pilot. Born in Florida, Missouri, Twain grew up in the nearby river town of Hannibal. At the age of twenty-one, he headed to New Orleans to depart for a trip to the Amazon. The plan fell apart, but Twain found a position as an apprentice riverboat pilot, a prestigious job that fulfilled a childhood dream. Before the Civil War, trade was lucrative on the Mississippi. When the war interrupted that trade and Twain was forced to find another job, he went west and took a job as a reporter for the *Sacramento Union.*

Twain began to write his most famous books in 1870. *The Adventures of Tom Sawyer* (1876), *Life on the Mississippi* (1883), and *Adventures of Huckleberry Finn* (1883) all draw from his experiences on the Mississippi River. *Huckleberry Finn,* often referred to as the great American novel, tells the story of a boy named Huck who, together with an escaped slave named Jim, travels down the Mississippi on a raft. Alternately funny and serious, the book is an implicit indictment of racism, showing that beneath outward differences, people have similar feelings and dreams.

In the 1890s, Twain suffered a series of misfortunes, including the death of a daughter, the illness of another daughter and of his wife, and monetary loss due to failed speculative investments. The writings of Twain's last years are bitterly directed at the hypocrisies of his fellow human beings. Twain's severest criticisms, included in *The War Prayer* and *Letters from Earth*, were not published until long after his death. Born on the day of the appearance of Halley's comet, Twain died on the day of its reappearance seventy-two years later.

## Literary TOOLS

**DIALECT.** A **dialect** is a version of a language spoken by the people of a particular place, time, or social group. As you read the story, try to understand the Western dialect Twain employs.

**FRAME TALE.** A **frame tale** is a story that provides a vehicle for the telling of other stories. As you read the story, decide what the frame tale is.

## About the SELECTION

**"The Notorious Jumping Frog of Calaveras County"** is Twain's retelling of a popular nineteenth-century tall tale. A **tall tale** is a lighthearted and humorous story that contains highly exaggerated, unrealistic events. Twain first became known nationally when the story was published in the *Saturday Press* in 1865. The story is also an outstanding example of regional writing. It portrays the entertainments of simple, uneducated men living in a frontier mining camp in California. The setting is a perfect arena for Twain to display his gift for capturing regional dialects. To commemorate the story, a frog-jumping contest is still held in Calaveras County today.

## Reader's Journal

What story have you exaggerated to impress your listeners?

# The Notorious Jumping Frog of Calaveras County

## MARK TWAIN

In compliance with the request of a friend of mine, who wrote me from the East, I called on good-natured, <u>garrulous</u> old Simon Wheeler, and inquired after my friend's friend, Leonidas W. Smiley, as requested to do, and I hereunto <u>append</u> the result. I have a lurking suspicion that *Leonidas W.* Smiley is a myth; that my friend never knew such a personage; and that he only <u>conjectured</u> that if I asked old Wheeler about him, it would remind him of his infamous *Jim* Smiley, and he would go to work and bore me to death with some exasperating reminiscence of him as long and as tedious as it should be useless to me. If that was the design, it succeeded.

*Why does the narrator visit Simon Wheeler?*

*What does the narrator suspect about Leonidas W. Smiley?*

I found Simon Wheeler dozing comfortably by the barroom stove of the <u>dilapidated</u> tavern in the decayed mining camp of Angel's, and I noticed that he was fat and bald-headed, and had an expression of winning gentleness and simplicity upon his tranquil countenance. He roused up, and gave me good-day. I told him a friend of mine had commissioned me to make some inquiries about a cherished companion of his boyhood named *Leonidas* W. Smiley—*Rev. Leonidas W.* Smiley, a young minister of the Gospel, who he had heard was at one time a resident of Angel's Camp. I added that if Mr. Wheeler could tell me anything about this Rev. Leonidas W. Smiley, I would feel under many obligations to him.

---

**WORDS FOR EVERYDAY USE**

**gar • ru • lous** (gar´ə ləs) *adj.*, talking much or too much. *The garrulous shopkeeper told us his entire life story.*

**ap • pend** (ə pend´) *vt.*, attach or affix. *My mother appended a note to the refrigerator, telling me to start dinner.*

**con • jec • ture** (kən jek´chər) *vi.*, guess. *I conjecture that the magician will pull a rabbit out of his hat.*

**di • lap • i • dat • ed** (də lap´ ə dāt´ id) *adj.*, falling to pieces or into disrepair. *The dilapidated fishing shack was finally torn down.*

# Art Note

**Caricature of Mark Twain,** 1800s.
W. J. Welch, page 412.

A caricature is a drawing that pokes fun at a person by exaggerating his or her physical features or personal traits. It often has a visual pun—in this case, Twain is literally "riding" on his first literary success, the notorious jumping frog of Calaveras County.

Simon Wheeler backed me into a corner and blockaded me there with his chair, and then sat down and reeled off the monotonous narrative which follows this paragraph. He never smiled, he never frowned, he never changed his voice from the gentle-flowing key to which he tuned his initial sentence, he never betrayed the slightest suspicion of enthusiasm; but all through the <u>interminable</u> narrative there ran a vein of impressive earnestness and sincerity, which showed me plainly that, so far from his imagining that there was anything ridiculous or funny about his story, he regarded it as a really important matter, and admired its two heroes as men of transcendent genius in *finesse*.[1] I let him go on in his own way, and never interrupted him once.

Rev. Leonidas W. H'm, Reverend Le—well, there was a feller here once by the name of *Jim* Smiley, in the winter of '49—or maybe it was the spring of '50—I don't recollect exactly, somehow, though what makes me think it was one or the other is because I remember the big flume[2] warn't finished when he first come to the camp; but any way, he was the curiousest man about always betting on anything that turned up you ever see, if he could get anybody to bet on the other side; and if he couldn't he'd change sides. Any way that suited the other man would suit *him*—any way just so's he got a bet, *he* was satisfied. But still he was lucky, uncommon lucky; he most always come out winner. He was always ready and laying for a chance; there couldn't be no solit'ry thing mentioned but that feller'd offer to bet on it, and take ary side you please, as I was just telling you. If there was a horse-race, you'd find him flush[3] or you'd find him busted[4] at the end of it; if there was a dog-fight, he'd bet on it; if there was a cat-fight, he'd bet on it; if there was a chicken-fight, he'd bet on it; why, if there was two birds setting on a fence, he would bet you which one would fly first, or if there was a camp-meeting,[5] he would be there reg'lar to bet on Parson Walker, which he judged to be the best <u>exhorter</u> about here, and so he was too, and a good man. If he even see a straddle-bug[6] start to go anywheres, he would bet you how long it would take him to get to—to wherever he was going to, and if you took him up, he would foller that straddle-bug to Mexico but what he would find out where he was bound for and how long he was on the road. Lots of the boys here has seen that Smiley, and can tell you about him. Why, it never made no difference to *him*—he'd bet on *any* thing—the dangdest feller. Parson Walker's wife laid very sick once, for a good while, and it seemed as if they warn't going to save her; but one morning he come in, and Smiley up and asked him how she was, and he said she was

> *What is curious about Jim Smiley?*

---

1. **transcendent . . . finesse.** Extraordinary skill, cunning, or artfulness
2. **flume.** Artificial channel for carrying water to furnish power or transport objects
3. **flush.** Well supplied with money
4. **busted.** Penniless
5. **camp-meeting.** Religious gathering at a camp or mining community
6. **straddle-bug.** Long-legged insect

**WORDS FOR EVERYDAY USE**

in • ter • mi • na • ble (in tʉr´mi nə bəl) *adj.*, without, or apparently without, end. *The <u>interminable</u> lecture on genetics bored Julian to tears.*

ex • hor • ter (eg zôrt´ər) *n.*, one who urges earnestly, by advice or warning. *Dad is an <u>exhorter</u> who wants to steer us away from mistakes.*

exhort

considable better—thank the Lord for his inf'nite mercy—and coming on so smart that with the blessing of Prov'dence she'd get well yet; and Smiley, before he thought says, "Well, I'll resk two-and-a-half she don't anyway."

Thish-yer Smiley had a mare—the boys called her the fifteen-minute nag, but that was only in fun, you know, because of course she was faster than that—and he used to win money on that horse, for all she was so slow and always had the asthma, or the distemper, or the consumption, or something of that kind. They used to give her two or three hundred yards start, and then pass her under way; but always at the fag end[7] of the race she'd get excited and desperate-like, and come <u>cavorting</u> and straddling up, and scattering her legs around limber, sometimes in the air, and sometimes out to one side among the fences, and kicking up m-o-r-e dust and raising m-o-r-e racket with her coughing and sneezing and blowing her nose—and *always* fetch up at the stand just about a neck ahead, as near as you could cipher it down.

And he had a little small bull-pup, that to look at him you'd think he warn't worth a cent but to set around and look <u>ornery</u> and lay for a chance to steal something. But as soon as money was up on him he was a different dog; his underjaw'd begin to stick out like the fo'castle[8] of a steamboat, and his teeth would uncover and shine like the furnaces. And a dog might tackle him and bully-rag him, and bite him, and throw him over his shoulder two or three times, and Andrew Jackson—which was the name of the pup—Andrew Jackson would never let on but what *he* was satisfied, and hadn't expected nothing else—and the bets being doubled and doubled on the other side all the time, till the money was all up; and then all of a sudden he would grab that other dog jest by the j'int of his hind leg and freeze to it—not chaw, you understand, but only just grip and hang on till they throwed up the sponge, if it was a year. Smiley always come out winner on that pup, till he harnessed a dog once that didn't have no hind legs, because they'd been sawed off in a circular saw, and when the thing had gone along far enough, and the money was all up, and he come to make a snatch for his pet holt[9] he see in a minute how he's been imposed on, and how the other dog had him in the door, so to speak, and he 'peared surprised, and then he looked sorter discouraged-like, and didn't try no more to win the fight, and so he got shucked out bad. He give Smiley a look, as much as to say his heart was broke, and it was *his* fault, for putting up a dog that hadn't no hind legs for him to take holt of, which was his main dependence in a fight, and then he limped off a piece and laid down and died. It was a good pup, was that Andrew Jackson, and would have made a name for hisself if he'd lived, for the stuff was in him and he had genius—I know it, because he hadn't no opportunities to speak of, and it don't stand to reason that a dog could make such a fight as he could under them circumstances if he hadn't no talent. It always makes me feel sorry when I think of that last fight of his'n, and the way it turned out.

Well, thish-yer Smiley had rat-terriers[10] and chicken cocks,[11] and tomcats and all them kind of things, till you couldn't rest, and you couldn't fetch nothing for him to bet on but he'd match

> In what way does the dog without hind legs have an advantage over Andrew Jackson?

---

7. **fag end.** Last part
8. **fo'castle.** Upper deck of a boat; part of a bow that protrudes
9. **pet holt.** Favorite hold
10. **rat-terriers.** Small, aggressive dogs
11. **chicken cocks.** Roosters trained to fight each other

---

**WORDS FOR EVERYDAY USE**

ca • vort (kə vôrt´) *vi.*, leap about, prance. *Full of energy, the filly <u>cavorted</u> in the meadow.*

or • ner • y (ôr´nər ē) *adj.*, having an ugly or mean disposition. *It was difficult for Chris to get along with such an <u>ornery</u> teacher as Mr. Kellett.*

you. He ketched a frog one day, and took him home, and said he cal'lated to educate him; and so he never done nothing for three months but set in his back yard and learn that frog to jump. And you bet you he *did* learn him, too. He'd give him a little punch behind, and the next minute you'd see that frog whirling in the air like a doughnut—see him turn one summerset, or maybe a couple, if he got a good start, and come down flat-footed and all right, like a cat. He got him up so in the matter of ketching flies, and kep' him in practice so constant, that he'd nail a fly every time as fur as he could see him. Smiley said all a frog wanted was education, and he could do 'most anything—and I believe him. Why, I've seen him set Dan'l Webster down here on this floor—Dan'l Webster was the name of the frog—and sing out, "Flies, Dan'l, flies!" and quicker'n you could wink he'd spring straight up and snake a fly off'n the counter there, and flop down on the floor ag'in as solid as a gob of mud, and fall to scratching the side of his head with his hind foot as indifferent as if he hadn't no idea he'd been doin' any more'n any frog might do. You never see a frog so modest and straightfor'ard as he was, for all he was so gifted. And when it come to fair and square jumping on a dead level, he could get over more ground at one straddle than any animal of his breed you ever see. Jumping on a dead level was his strong suit, you understand; and when it come to that, Smiley would ante up money on him as long as he had a red.[12] Smiley was monstrous proud of his frog, and well he might be, for fellers that had traveled and been everywheres all said he laid over any frog that ever *they* see.

Well, Smiley kep' the beast in a little lattice box, and he used to fetch him down-town sometimes and lay for a bet. One day a feller—a stranger in the camp, he was—come acrost him with his box, and says:

"What might it be that you've got in the box?"

And Smiley says, sorter indifferent-like, "It might be a parrot, or it might be a canary, maybe, but it ain't—it's only just a frog."

And the feller took it, and looked at it careful, and turned it round this way and that, and says, "H'm—so 'tis. Well, what's *he* good for?"

"Well," Smiley says, easy and careless, "he's good enough for *one* thing, I should judge—he can outjump any frog in Calaveras county."

The feller took the box again, and took another long, particular look, and give it back to Smiley, and says, very deliberate, "Well," he says, "I don't see no p'ints about that frog that's any better'n any other frog."

"Maybe you don't," Smiley says. "Maybe you understand frogs and maybe you don't understand em; maybe you've had experience, and maybe you ain't only a amature, as it were. Anyways, I've got *my* opinion, and I'll resk forty dollars that he can outjump any frog in Calaveras county."

And the feller studied a minute, and then says, kinder sad like, "Well, I'm only a stranger here, and I ain't got no frog; but if I had a frog, I'd bet you."

And then Smiley says. "That's all right—that's all right—if you'll hold my box a minute, I'll go and get you a frog." And so the feller took the box and put up his forty dollars along with Smiley's, and set down to wait.

So he set there a good while thinking and thinking to hisself, and then he got the frog out and prized his mouth open and took a teaspoon and filled him full of quailshot[13]—filled him pretty near up to his chin—and set him on the

> What is amusing or ironic about calling a frog modest?

> What does the stranger do to Dan'l Webster?

---

12. **red.** Red cent; a very small amount of money
13. **quailshot.** Lead pellets used for hunting quail

floor. Smiley he went to the swamp and slopped around in the mud for a long time, and finally he ketched a frog, and fetched him in, and give him to this feller, and says:

"Now, if you're ready, set him alongside of Dan'l, with his forepaws just even with Dan'l's, and I'll give the word." Then he says, "One—two—three—*git!*" and him and the feller touched up the frogs from behind, and the new frog hopped off lively, but Dan'l give a heave, and hysted up his shoulders—so—like a Frenchman, but it warn't no use—he couldn't budge; he was planted as solid as a church, and he couldn't no more stir than if he was anchored out. Smiley was a good deal surprised, and he was disgusted too, but he didn't have no idea what the matter was, of course.

The feller took the money and started away; and when he was going out at the door, he sorter jerked his thumb over his shoulder—so—at Dan'l, and says, again very deliberate, "Well," he says, "*I* don't see no p'ints about that frog that's any better'n any other frog."

Smiley he stood scratching his head and looking down at Dan'l a long time, and at last he says, "I do wonder what in the nation that frog throw'd off for—I wonder if there ain't something the matter with him—he 'pears to look mighty baggy, somehow." And he ketched Dan'l by the nap of the neck, and hefted him, and says, "Why blame my cats if he don't weigh five pound!" and turned him upside down and he belched out a double handful of shot. And then he see how it was, and he was the maddest man—he set the frog down and took out after that feller, but he never ketched him. And—

Here Simon Wheeler heard his name called from the front yard, and got up to see what was wanted. And turning to me as he moved away, he said: "Just set where you are, stranger, and rest easy—I ain't going to be gone a second."

But, by your leave, I did not think that a continuation of the history of the enterprising <u>vagabond</u> *Jim* Smiley would be likely to afford me much information concerning the *Rev. Leonidas W.* Smiley, and so I started away.

At the door I met the sociable Wheeler returning, and he button-holed[14] me and recommenced;

"Well, thish-yer Smiley had a yaller one-eyed cow that didn't have no tail, only jest a short stump like a bannanner, and—"

However, lacking both time and inclination, I did not wait to hear about the <u>afflicted</u> cow, but took my leave. ∎

---

14. **button-holed.** Made a person listen to one, as if by grabbing his or her coat by a buttonhole

**WORDS FOR EVERYDAY USE**

vag • a • bond (vag´ ə bänd´) *n.*, wandering, idle, disreputable, or shiftless person. *The <u>vagabond</u> slept on a park bench.*

af • flic • ted (ə flikt´ əd) *adj.*, suffering from an illness or other painful physical condition. *Nicole's grandmother is <u>afflicted</u> with painful arthritis.*

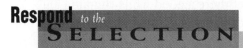
**Respond** to the
**SELECTION**

If you were the narrator, would you be bored or interested by Simon Wheeler's story? Why?

# INVESTIGATE Inquire, Imagine

**Recall:** GATHERING FACTS

1a. Why does the narrator go to see Simon Wheeler? About whom does Simon Wheeler tell his story?

2a. What two animals besides the frog does Jim Smiley use for gambling?

3a. What does Smiley bet the stranger?

**Interpret:** FINDING MEANING

1b. What is the narrator's response to Wheeler's story? Why might the narrator have this response?

2b. Why do Smiley's animals almost always win?

3b. Why does Dan'l Webster lose the contest?

**Analyze:** TAKING THINGS APART

4a. What elements make this story humorous?

**Synthesize:** BRINGING THINGS TOGETHER

4b. What tale would Simon Wheeler have related about the cow if he had been given the chance?

**Evaluate:** MAKING JUDGMENTS

5a. Is Jim Smiley a gifted or an addicted gambler? Explain your response.

**Extend:** CONNECTING IDEAS

5b. Read a tall tale about Paul Bunyan. Then compare and contrast it to "The Notorious Jumping Frog of Calaveras County."

# Understanding Literature

**DIALECT.** Review the definition for **dialect** in Literary Tools on page 411. Then make a chart. On the left, write five sentences from the story that use regional dialect. On the right, write equivalent sentences in standard, formal English. One example has been done for you. After you have completed the chart, explain how Simon Wheeler and the narrator use English differently.

| Regional Dialect | Standard English |
| --- | --- |
| 1. "He most always come out a winner." | 1. He almost always won. |

**FRAME TALE.** Review the definition for **frame tale** in Literary Tools on page 411. What is the frame tale in "The Notorious Jumping Frog of Calaveras County"? What is Simon Wheeler's attitude toward his story about Jim Smiley? What is the frame narrator's attitude toward Wheeler's story? How does the attitude of the frame narrator toward Simon's story affect the story as a whole?

# WRITER'S JOURNAL

1. Imagine that you are Jim Smiley writing a **memoir** for fellow gamblers about your gambling experiences. Write the last chapter, in which you relate your worst failure.

2. Using the regional accent he employs, write a **letter** to Simon Wheeler about your week's activities.

3. Write a **summary** for a tall tale about the cow that Wheeler mentions at the end of the story. Imagine that you are Mark Twain submitting an idea for a follow-up story in the *Saturday Press* and that your reader is the magazine's editor.

# Integrating
## *the* LANGUAGE ARTS

### Language, Grammar, and Style

**ADDING MODIFIERS.** Read the Language Arts Survey 3.65, "Modifiers—Adverbs and Adjectives," 3.66, "Adjectives," and 3.67, "Adverbs." Then identify as adjectives or adverbs the underlined modifiers in the following sentences from "The Notorious Jumping Frog of Calaveras County."

1. . . . I called on <u>good-natured</u>, <u>garrulous</u>, <u>old</u> Simon Wheeler. . . .

2. I found Simon Wheeler dozing <u>comfortably</u> by the barroom stove. . . .

3. Simon Wheeler . . . sat down and reeled off the <u>monotonous</u> narrative that follows this paragraph.

4. . . . he said she was <u>considerable</u> (considerably) better. . . .

5. Smiley was <u>monstrous</u> (monstrously) proud of his frog. . . .

### Speaking and Listening & Collaborative Learning

**ORAL INTERPRETATION.** Working with a partner, select an excerpt from one of Mark Twain's pieces of fiction or some of his humorous quotations and prepare it as an oral interpretation. Write an introduction for the material and any needed transitions. Decide how you will interpret your selection. In other words, what tone, facial expressions, and gestures will you employ? Then, imagining that you are Mark Twain, present your work to your partner. Refer to the Language Arts Survey 4.1, "Verbal and Nonverbal Communication."

### Applied English

**TALL TALE.** A **tall tale** is a story, often lighthearted or humorous, that contains highly exaggerated, unrealistic elements. Imagine that you are a fiction writer. Write your own tall tale, perhaps based on a tradition, funny personal experience, or lesson you've learned. Develop a humorous sequence of events. You may want to use nonstandard language for humorous effect.

# "The Outcasts of Poker Flat"

BY BRET HARTE

## About the AUTHOR

Bret Harte (1836–1902) was the pen name of Francis Brett Harte, who gave many Easterners their first glimpse of the Old West in his amusing stories, full of local color and characterized by unusual juxtapositions of characters and surprise endings. Though associated with the West, Harte was born in Albany, New York. After his father died, he moved in 1854 to California. There, he married and gathered the material he would later use in his stories, riding shotgun on Wells Fargo stagecoaches and prospecting like so many other Californians during the Gold Rush. Settling in San Francisco, he worked as a typesetter and then as a writer for the *Californian*. In 1861, he took a job as editor of the *Overland Monthly*, in which he published the work that would make him famous, including the stories "The Luck of Roaring Camp," "The Outcasts of Poker Flat," and the poem "Plain Language from Truthful James." Becoming well known in literary circles, he socialized with such San Francisco luminaries as Ambrose Bierce and Mark Twain.

Harte's regionalism met with an eager audience back East, so eager that the *Atlantic Monthly* in Boston offered him the then astronomical sum of ten thousand dollars to write twelve pieces for the magazine. Harte left for Boston, but the pieces that he produced under his contract were mediocre, and his fame subsided. Thereafter, Harte produced several collections of stories, two novels, and two plays, but none equaled his earlier work. He served as a United States diplomat in Prussia and in Scotland and then settled in London, England, where he lived for the rest of his life. Harte is known for his stories about life on America's Western frontier, especially his amusing explorations of the people and the landscape of northern California's High Sierras, the Gold Rush region.

## Reader's *Journal*

In your opinion, who are the outcasts in our society?

## Literary TOOLS

SENTIMENTALITY. **Sentimentality** is an excessive expression of emotion. As you read, look for moments of sentimentality in the story.

STEREOTYPICAL OR STOCK CHARACTER. A **stereotypical**, or **stock character** is one who does not deviate from conventional expectations of such a character. Identify the stock characters you find in the story.

## About the SELECTION

**"The Outcasts of Poker Flat"** is an example of nineteenth-century regional literature. Regional writers portray what is special about a particular part of the country. They write about the specific landscape, people, values, and modes of life of a region. Regionalists explore issues that are common to all human beings, but they do so only by way of writing about a particular time and place.

In "The Outcasts of Poker Flat," Harte treats the conflict between a society and its "outcasts," those people whose behavior is unacceptable to the moral values that the majority at least pretend to uphold. Harte explores this timeless conflict by describing the fate of some typical characters from the American frontier. Today these characters are familiar to anyone who watches Western movies, but in the nineteenth century they were new, and Harte was one of the first to describe them.

# The Outcasts of Poker Flat

## Bret Harte

As Mr. John Oakhurst, gambler, stepped into the main street of Poker Flat on the morning of the twenty-third of November, 1850, he was conscious of a change in its moral atmosphere from the preceding night. Two or three men, conversing earnestly together, ceased as he approached, and exchanged significant glances. There was a Sabbath lull in the air, which, in a settlement unused to Sabbath influences, looked <u>ominous</u>.

Mr. Oakhurst's calm, handsome face betrayed small concern of these indications. Whether he was conscious of any <u>predisposing</u> cause, was another question. "I reckon they're after somebody," he reflected; "likely it's me." He returned to his pocket the handkerchief with which he had been whipping away the red dust of Poker Flat from his neat boots, and quietly discharged his mind of any further <u>conjecture</u>.

In point of fact, Poker Flat was "after somebody." It had lately suffered the loss of several thousand dollars, two valuable horses, and a prominent citizen. It was experiencing a spasm of virtuous reaction, quite as lawless and ungovernable as any of the acts that had provoked it. A secret committee[1] had determined

*To what are the citizens of Poker Flat reacting?*

to rid the town of all improper persons. This was done permanently in regard of two men who were then hanging from the boughs of a sycamore in the gulch, and temporarily in the banishment of certain other objectionable characters. I regret to say that some of these were ladies. It is but due to the sex, however, to state that their impropriety was professional, and it was only in such easily established standards of evil that Poker Flat ventured to sit in judgment.

Mr. Oakhurst was right in supposing that he was included in this category. A few of the committee had urged hanging him as a possible example, and a sure method of reimbursing themselves from his pockets of the sums he had won from them. "It's agin justice," said Jim Wheeler, "to let this yer young man from Roaring Camp—an entire stranger—carry away our money." But a crude sentiment of equity residing in the breasts of those who had been fortunate enough to win from Mr. Oakhurst, overruled this narrower local prejudice.

*Why do vigilantes resent Oakhurst?*

---

1. **secret committee.** Vigilance committee; group that helps maintain order and punish crime when processes of law are not effective

**Words For Everyday Use**

⌄ **om • i • nous** (äm´ə nəs) *adj.,* threatening. *The dark clouds in the sky looked <u>ominous</u>.*

⌄ **pre • dis • pose** (prē dis pōz´) *vt.,* give a tendency. *Parents who read to their children <u>predispose</u> them to be enthusiastic about reading for the rest of their lives.*

⌄ **con • jec • ture** (kən jek´chər) *n.,* prediction based on guesswork. *The detective's <u>conjecture</u> regarding the murderer's whereabouts led to his arrest.*

*Vigilante Ways,* Olaf Carl Seltzer.
Thomas Gilcrease Institute of American History and Art, Tulsa.

Mr. Oakhurst received his sentence with philosophic calmness, none the less coolly, that he was aware of the hesitation of his judges. He was too much of a gambler not to accept Fate. With him life was at best an uncertain game, and he recognized the usual percentage in favor of the dealer.

A body of armed men accompanied the deported wickedness of Poker Flat to the outskirts of the settlement. Besides Mr. Oakhurst, who was known to be a coolly desperate man, and for whose intimidation the armed escort was intended, the expatriated party consisted of a young woman familiarly known as "The Duchess"; another, who had gained the infelicitous title of "Mother Shipton,"[2] and "Uncle Billy," a suspected sluice[3] robber and confirmed drunkard. The cavalcade provoked no comments from the spectators, nor was any word uttered by the escort. Only when the gulch which marked the uttermost limit of Poker Flat was reached, the leader spoke briefly and to the point. The exiles were forbidden to return at the peril of their lives.

As the escort disappeared, their pent-up feelings found vent in a few hysterical tears from "The Duchess," some bad language from Mother Shipton, and a Partheian[4] volley of expletives from Uncle Billy. The philosophic Oakhurst alone remained silent. He listened calmly to Mother Shipton's desire to cut somebody's heart out, to the repeated statements of "The Duchess" that she would die in the road, and to the alarming oaths that seemed to be bumped out of Uncle Billy as he rode forward.

> *Who are the other deportees?*

> **"The spot was singularly wild and impressive."**

With the easy good-humor characteristic of his class, he insisted upon exchanging his own ridinghorse, "Five Spot," for the sorry mule which the Duchess rode. But even this act did not draw the party into any closer sympathy. The young woman readjusted her somewhat draggled plumes with a feeble, faded coquetry; Mother Shipton eyed the possessor of "Five Spot" with malevolence, and Uncle Billy included the whole party in one sweeping anathema.

The road to Sandy Bar—a camp that not having as yet experienced the regenerating influences of Poker Flat, consequently seemed to offer some invitation to the emigrants—lay over a steep mountain range. It was distant, a day's severe journey. In that advanced season, the party soon passed out of the moist, temperate regions of the foot-hills, into the dry, cold, bracing air of the Sierras.[5] The trail was narrow and difficult. At noon the Duchess, rolling out of her saddle upon the ground, declared her intention of going no further, and the party halted.

The spot was singularly wild and impressive. A wooded amphitheater, surrounded on three sides by precipitous cliffs of naked granite, sloped gently toward the crest of another precipice that overlooked the valley. It was undoubtedly the most suitable spot for a camp, had camping been advisable. But Mr. Oakhurst

---

2. **Mother Shipton.** (1488–1560) Known as a witch and believed to have been taken by the devil and to have born him an imp
3. **sluice.** Trough used to separate gold from other materials
4. **Partheian.** Like the Partheians, an ancient people from Asia known for firing shots while in retreat
5. **Sierras.** Mountains in California

---

**WORDS FOR EVERYDAY USE**

**ex • pa • tri • at • ed** (eks pā´trē āt´id) *adj.*, driven from one's land. *The expatriated American writer lived in Paris in the 1920s.*

**in • fe • lic • i • tous** (in fə lis´ə təs) *adj.*, unfortunate, unsuitable. *When questioned about the hard times he'd been through, the cowboy said he was born under an infelicitous star.*

**cav • al • cade** (kav´əl kād´) *n.*, procession (of horses). *The king's cavalcade rushed into battle.*

**co • quet • ry** (kō´kə trē) *n.*, flirting. *Due to her coquetry, Estelle's social calendar was full.*

**a • nath • e • ma** (ə nath´ə mə) *n.*, curse. *The angry workers cast anathemas upon the mine owner.*

**pre • cip • i • tous** (prē sip´ə təs) *adj.*, steep. *Climbing the precipitous hills in the Lake District, Nancy grew dizzy.*

knew that scarcely half the journey to Sandy Bar was accomplished, and the party were not equipped or provisioned for delay.

Why is it unwise to halt the journey?

This fact he pointed out to his companions curtly, with a philosophic commentary on the folly of "throwing up their hand before the game was played out." But they were furnished with liquor, which in this emergency stood them in place of food, fuel, rest and prescience. In spite of his <u>remonstrances</u>, it was not long before they were more or less under its influence. Uncle Billy passed rapidly from a <u>bellicose</u> state into one of stupor, the Duchess became maudlin, and Mother Shipton snored. Mr. Oakhurst alone remained erect, leaning against a rock, calmly surveying them.

Mr. Oakhurst did not drink. It interfered with a profession which required

Why does Oakhurst not drink?

coolness, impassiveness and presence of mind, and, in his own language, he "couldn't afford it." As he gazed at his recumbent fellow-exiles, the loneliness begotten of his pariah-trade,[6] his habits of life, his very vices, for the first time seriously oppressed him. He bestirred himself in dusting his black clothes, washing his hands and face, and other acts characteristic of his studiously neat habits, and for a moment forgot his annoyance. The thought of deserting his weaker and more pitiable companions never perhaps occurred to him. Yet he could not help feeling the want of that excitement, which singularly enough was most conducive to that calm <u>equanimity</u> for which he was notorious. He looked at the gloomy walls that rose a thousand feet sheer above the circling pines around him; at the sky, ominously clouded; at the valley below, already deepening into shadow. And doing so, suddenly he heard his own name called.

A horseman slowly ascended the trail. In the fresh, open face of the newcomer, Mr. Oakhurst recognized Tom Simson, otherwise known as "The Innocent" of Sandy Bar. He had met him some months before over a "little game," and had, with perfect equanimity, won the entire fortune—amounting to some forty dollars—of that <u>guileless</u> youth. After the game was finished, Mr. Oakhurst drew the youthful speculator behind the door and thus addressed him: "Tommy, you're a good little man, but you can't gamble worth a cent. Don't try it over again." He then handed him his money back, pushed him gently from the room, and so made a devoted slave of Tom Simson.

There was a remembrance of this in his boyish and enthusiastic greeting of Mr. Oakhurst. He had started, he said, to go to Poker Flat to seek his fortune. "Alone?" No, not exactly alone; in fact—a giggle--he had run away with Piney Woods. Didn't Mr. Oakhurst remember Piney? She that used to wait on the table at the Temperance House? They had been engaged a long time, but old Jake Woods had objected, and so they had run away, and

Where are Tom Simson and Piney Woods going?

were going to Poker Flat to be married, and here they were. And they were tired out, and how lucky it was they had found a place to camp and company. All this The Innocent delivered rapidly, while Piney—a stout, comely damsel of fifteen—emerged from behind the pine tree, where she had been blushing unseen, and rode to the side of her lover.

---

6. **pariah-trade.** Profession scorned by others

**WORDS FOR EVERYDAY USE**

**re • mon • strance** (ri män[t]' stren[t]s) *n.,* protest, objection. *Despite the <u>remonstrances</u> of the striking workers, some employees crossed the picket line.*

**bel • li • cose** (bel´i kōs) *adj.,* hostile, eager to fight. *The <u>bellicose</u> customer demanded to speak with the manager.*

**e • qua • nim • i • ty** (ek´wə nim´ə tē) *n.,* evenness of temper; quality of remaining calm. *A good soldier retains his <u>equanimity</u> under enemy fire.*

**guile • less** (gīl´lis) *adj.,* without deceit. *The <u>guileless</u> child softened the heart of the cynical man.*

Mr. Oakhurst seldom troubled himself with sentiment. Still less with propriety. But he had a vague idea that the situation was not felicitous. He retained, however, his presence of mind sufficiently to kick Uncle Billy, who was about to say something, and Uncle Billy was sober enough to recognize in Mr. Oakhurst's kick a superior power that would not bear trifling. He then endeavored to <u>dissuade</u> Tom Simson from delaying further, but in vain. He even pointed out the fact that there was no provision, nor means of making a camp. But, unluckily, "The Innocent" met this objection by assuring the party that he was provided with an extra mule loaded with provisions, and by the discovery of a rude attempt at a loghouse near the trail. "Piney can stay with Mrs. Oakhurst," said The Innocent, pointing to the Duchess, "and I can shift for myself."

Nothing but Mr. Oakhurst's admonishing foot saved Uncle Billy from bursting into a roar of laughter. As it was, he felt compelled to retire up the canyon until he could recover his gravity. There he confided the joke to the tall pine trees, with many slaps of his leg, <u>contortions</u> of his face, and the usual profanity. But when he returned to the party, he found them seated by a fire—for the air had grown strangely chill and the sky overcast—in apparently amicable conversation. Piney was actually talking in an impulsive, girlish fashion to the Duchess, who was listening with an interest and animation she had not shown for many days. The Innocent was holding forth, apparently with equal effect, to Mr. Oakhurst and Mother Shipton, who was actually relaxing into amiability. "Is this yer a d——d picnic?" said Uncle Billy, with inward scorn, as he surveyed the sylvan group, the glancing fire-light and the tethered animals in the foreground. Suddenly an idea mingled with the alcoholic fumes that disturbed his brain. It was apparently of a <u>jocular</u> nature, for he felt impelled to slap his leg again and cram his fist into his mouth.

As the shadows crept slowly up the mountain, a slight breeze rocked the tops of the pine trees, and moaned through their long and gloomy aisles. The ruined cabin, patched and covered with pine boughs, was set apart for the ladies. As the lovers parted, they unaffectedly exchanged a parting kiss, so honest and sincere that it might have been heard above the swaying pines. The frail Duchess and the malevolent Mother Shipton were probably too stunned to remark upon this last evidence of simplicity, and so turned without a word to the hut. The fire was replenished, the men lay down before the door, and in a few minutes were asleep.

Mr. Oakhurst was a light sleeper. Toward morning he awoke benumbed and cold. As he stirred the dying fire, the wind, which was now blowing strongly, brought to his cheek that which caused the blood to leave it—snow!

He started to his feet with the intention of awakening the sleepers, for there was no time to lose. But turning to where Uncle Billy had been lying he found him gone. A suspicion leaped to his brain and a curse to his lips. He ran to the spot where the mules had been tethered; they were no longer there. The tracks were already rapidly disappearing in the snow.

The momentary excitement brought Mr. Oakhurst back to the fire with his usual calm. He did not waken the sleepers. The Innocent slumbered peacefully, with a smile on his good-humored, freckled face; the virgin Piney slept beside her frailer sisters as sweetly as though

> Why does Oakhurst urge Simson not to delay?

> Who departs from the camp? What does he take?

**WORDS FOR EVERYDAY USE**

*or. persvade*

**dis • suade** (di swād´) vt., talk out of. *The man tried to <u>dissuade</u> the boys from swimming in the contaminated pond.*

**con • tor • tion** (kən tôr´shən) n., twisting out of shape. *The circus performer's bodily <u>contortions</u> amazed the audience.*

**joc • u • lar** (jäk´yə lər) adj., humorous. *Only a person with such a <u>jocular</u> temperament could keep a positive outlook in such trying circumstances.*

attended by celestial guardians, and Mr. Oakhurst, drawing his blanket over his shoulders, stroked his mustachios and waited for the dawn. It came slowly in a whirling mist of snowflakes, that dazzled and confused the eye. What could be seen of the landscape appeared magically changed. He looked over the valley, and summed up the present and future in two words—"Snowed in!"

A careful inventory of the provisions, which, fortunately for the party, had been stored within the hut, and so escaped the <u>felonious</u> fingers of Uncle Billy, disclosed the fact that with care and prudence they might last ten days longer. "That is," said Mr. Oakhurst, *sotto voce*[7] to The Innocent, "if you're willing to board us. If you ain't—and perhaps you'd better not—you can wait till Uncle Billy gets back with provisions." For some occult reason, Mr. Oakhurst could not bring himself to disclose Uncle Billy's rascality, and so offered the hypothesis that he had wandered from the camp and had accidentally stampeded the animals. He dropped a warning to the Duchess and Mother Shipton, who of course knew the facts of their associate's defection. "They'll find out the truth about us all, when they find out anything," he added, significantly, "and there's no good frightening them now."

Tom Simson not only put all his worldly store at the disposal of Mr. Oakhurst, but seemed to enjoy the prospect of their enforced seclusion. "We'll have a good camp for a week, and then the snow'll melt, and we'll all go back together." The cheerful gayety of the young man and Mr. Oakhurst's calm infected the others. The Innocent, with the aid of pine boughs, <u>extemporized</u> a thatch for the roofless cabin, and the Duchess directed Piney in the rearrangement of the interior with a taste and tact that opened the blue eyes of that provincial maiden to their fullest extent. "I reckon now you're used to fine things at Poker Flat," said Piney. The Duchess turned away sharply to conceal something that reddened her cheeks through its professional tint, and Mother Shipton requested Piney not to "chatter." But when Mr. Oakhurst returned from a weary search for the trail, he heard the sound of happy laughter echoed from the rocks. He stopped in some alarm, and his thoughts first naturally reverted to the whiskey—which he had prudently *cachéd*.[8] "And yet it don't somehow sound like whiskey," said the gambler. It was not until he caught sight of the blazing fire through the still blinding storm, and the group around it, that he settled to the conviction that it was "square fun."

Whether Mr. Oakhurst had *cachéd* his cards with the whiskey as something debarred the free access of the community, I cannot say. It was certain that, in Mother Shipton's words, he "didn't say cards once" during that evening. Haply the time was beguiled by an accordion, produced somewhat <u>ostentatiously</u> by Tom Simson, from his pack. Notwithstanding some difficulties attending the manipulation of this instrument, Piney Woods managed to pluck several reluctant melodies from its keys, to an accompaniment by The Innocent on a pair of bone castanets. But the crowning festivity of the evening was reached

> "They'll find out the truth about us all, when they find out anything."

What kind of outlook does Simson have?

---

7. **sotto voce.** In an undertone, so as not to be overheard
8. **cachéd.** Hidden

**WORDS FOR EVERYDAY USE**

*think felony!*

✓ **fe • lo • ni • ous** (fə lōˊnē əs) *adj.*, of a criminal. *Judd's <u>felonious</u> actions resulted in a juvenile court hearing.*

**ex • tem • po • rize** (eks temˊpə rīzˊ) *vt.*, contrive in a makeshift way to meet a pressing need. *The volunteers <u>extemporized</u> a puppet show to cheer the children at the shelter.*

✓ **os • ten • ta • tious • ly** (äs ten tāˊshəs lē) *adv.*, so as to attract attention. *Mr. Knier hung the Christmas lights <u>ostentatiously</u>.*

in a rude camp-meeting hymn, which the lovers, joining hands, sang with

How do the snowbound campers pass the time?

great earnestness and <u>vociferation</u>. I fear that a certain defiant tone and Covenanter's swing[9] to its chorus, rather than any devotional quality, caused it to speedily infect the others, who at last joined in the refrain:

> *"I'm proud to live in the service of the Lord*
>
> *And I'm bound to die in His army."*[10]

The pines rocked, the storm eddied and whirled above the miserable group, and the flames of their altar leaped heavenward, as if in token of the vow.

At midnight the storm abated, the rolling clouds parted, and the stars glittered keenly above the sleeping camp. Mr. Oakhurst, whose professional habits had enabled him to live on the smallest possible amount of sleep, in dividing the watch with Tom Simson, somehow managed to take upon himself the greater part of that duty. He excused himself to The Innocent, by saying that he had "often been a week without sleep." "Doing what?" asked Tom. "Poker!" replied Oakhurst, sententiously; "when a man gets a streak of luck—he don't get tired. The luck gives in first. Luck," continued the gambler, reflectively, "is a mighty queer thing. All you know about it for certain is that it's bound to change. And it's finding out when it's going to change that makes you. We've had a streak of bad luck since we left Poker Flat—you come along and slap you get into it, too. If you can hold your cards right along you're all right. For," added the gambler, with cheerful irrelevance,

> *"I'm proud to live in the service of the Lord,*
>
> *And I'm bound to die in His army."*

The third day came, and the sun, looking through the white-curtained valley, saw the outcasts divide their slowly decreasing store of provisions for the morning meal. It was one of the peculiarities of that mountain climate that its rays diffused a kindly warmth over the wintry landscape, as if in regretful commiseration of the past. But it revealed drift on drift of snow piled high around the hut; a hopeless, uncharted, trackless sea of white lying below the rocky shores to which the castaways still clung. Through the marvelously clear air, the smoke of the pastoral village of Poker Flat rose miles away. Mother Shipton saw it, and from a remote pinnacle of her rocky fastness, hurled in that direction a final malediction. It was her last <u>vituperative</u> attempt, and perhaps for that reason was invested with a certain degree of sublimity. It did her good, she privately informed the Duchess. "Just you go out there and cuss, and see." She then set herself to the task of amusing "the child," as she and the Duchess were pleased to call Piney. Piney was no chicken, but it was a soothing and ingenious theory of the pair to thus account for the fact that she didn't swear and wasn't improper.

When night crept up again through the gorges, the reedy notes of the accordion rose and fell in fitful spasms and longdrawn gasps by the flickering campfire. But music failed to fill entirely the aching void

What do the outcasts need?

left by insufficient food, and a new diversion was proposed by Piney—story-telling. Neither

---

9. **Covenanter's swing.** Sung with a vigorous rhythm with a martial beat, as done by the covenanters, a group of Scottish Presbyterians who wished to separate from the Church of England

10. **"I'm proud . . . His army."** Refrain of the early American spiritual "Service of the Lord"

---

**WORDS FOR EVERYDAY USE**

**vo • cif • er • a • tion** (vō sif´ ər ā´shən) *n.,* shouting. *The protestors outside the White House started their slogans with angry* <u>vociferation</u>.

**vi • tu • per • a • tive** (vī tü´ pə rā´tiv) *adj.,* abusive; viciously fault-finding. *The wrestler's* <u>vituperative</u> *comments to his opponent were considered normal in the ring.*

Mr. Oakhurst nor his female companions caring to relate their personal experiences, this plan would have failed, too, but for The Innocent. Some months before he had chanced upon a stray copy of Mr. Pope's[11] ingenious translation of the Iliad. He now proposed to narrate the principal incidents of that poem—having thoroughly mastered the argument and fairly forgotten the words—in the current vernacular of Sandy Bar. And so for the rest of that night the Homeric demi-gods again walked the earth. Trojan bully and wily Greek wrestled in the winds, and the great pines in the canyon seemed to bow to the wrath of the son of Peleus.[12] Mr. Oakhurst listened with quiet satisfaction. Most especially was he interested in the fate of "Ash-heels,"[13] as The Innocent persisted in denominating the "swift-footed Achilles."

> And so for the rest of that night the Homeric demi-gods again walked the earth.

> How does Simson distract the outcasts' attention?

So with small food and much of Homer and the accordion, a week passed over the heads of the outcasts. The sun again forsook them, and again from leaden skies the snow-flakes were sifted over the land. Day by day closer around them drew the snowy circle, until at last they looked from their prison over drifted walls of dazzling white, that towered twenty feet above their heads. It became more and more difficult to replenish their fires, even from the fallen trees beside them, now half-hidden in the drifts. And yet no one complained. The lovers turned from the dreary prospect and looked into each other's eyes, and were happy. Mr. Oakhurst settled himself coolly to the losing game before him. The Duchess, more cheerful than she had been, assumed the care of Piney.

Only Mother Shipton—once the strongest of the party—seemed to sicken and fade. At midnight on the tenth day she called Oakhurst to her side. "I'm going," she said, in a voice of querulous weakness, "but don't say anything about it. Don't waken the kids. Take the bundle from under my head and open it." Mr. Oakhurst did so. It contained Mother Shipton's rations for the last week, untouched. "Give 'em to the child," she said, pointing to the sleeping Piney. "You've starved yourself," said the gambler. "That's what they call it," said the woman querulously, as she lay down again, and turning her face to the wall, passed quietly away.

> What is happening to Mother Shipton? What has she been doing?

The accordion and the bones were put aside that day, and Homer was forgotten. When the body of Mother Shipton had been committed to the snow, Mr. Oakhurst took The Innocent aside, and showed him a pair of snow-shoes, which he had fashioned from the old packsaddle. "There's one chance in a hundred to save her yet," he said, pointing to Piney; "but it's there," he added pointing toward Poker Flat. "If you can reach there in two days she's safe." "And you?" asked Tom Simson. "I'll stay here," was the curt reply.

The lovers parted with a long embrace. "You are not going, too," said the Duchess, as she saw Mr. Oakhurst apparently waiting to

---

11. **Mr. Pope's.** (1688–1744) English poet Alexander Pope. His translation of Homer's *Iliad* was written in heroic couplets.
12. **son of Peleus.** Achilles (ak il´ēz), chief hero on the Greek side of the Trojan War
13. **Ash-heels.** The speaker means Achilles, whose only vulnerable spot was his heel, a fact emphasized by the mispronunciation

---

**WORDS FOR EVERYDAY USE**

quer • u • lous (kwer´yü ləs) *adj.*, full of complaint. *At the grocery store a querulous patron asked for faster service.*

*Yosemite Winter Scene,* 1872. Albert Bierstadt.
Berkeley Art Museum.

accompany him. "As far as the canyon," he replied. He turned suddenly, and kissed the Duchess, leaving her pallid face aflame, and her trembling limbs rigid with amazement.

Night came, but not Mr. Oakhurst. It brought the storm again and the whirling snow. Then the Duchess, feeding the fire, found that some one had quietly piled beside the hut enough fuel to last a few days longer. The tears rose to her eyes, but she hid them from Piney.

The women slept but little. In the morning, looking into each other's faces, they read their fate. Neither spoke; but Piney, accepting the position of the stronger, drew near and placed her arm around the Duchess's waist. They kept this attitude for the rest of the day. That night the storm reached its greatest

*What do Piney and the Duchess understand?*

fury, and rending asunder the protecting pines, invaded the very hut.

Toward morning they found themselves unable to feed the fire, which gradually died away. As the embers slowly blackened, the Duchess crept closer to Piney, and broke the silence of many hours: "Piney, can you pray?" "No, dear," said Piney, simply. The Duchess, without knowing exactly why, felt relieved, and putting her head upon Piney's shoulder, spoke no more. And so reclining, the younger and purer pillowing the head of her soiled sister upon her virgin breast, they fell asleep.

The wind lulled as if it feared to waken them. Feathery drifts of snow, shaken from the long pine boughs, flew like white-winged birds, and settled about them as they slept. The moon through the rifted clouds looked down upon what had been the camp. But all human stain,

# ArtNote

*Yosemite Winter Scene,* 1872. Albert Bierstadt, page 428.

Albert Bierstadt (1830–1902) carried on the Hudson River School landscape tradition in the West. Although photography was now possible, the technology at that time could not capture the color, scale, and detail that painting could. Bierstadt's paintings became important to the early environmental movement and the preservation of the Sierra wilderness, but they also made the area a popular tourist attraction. Ambrose Bierce complained that Bierstadt's paintings "incited unpleasant people to visit California."

all trace of earthly travail, was hidden beneath the spotless mantle mercifully flung from above.

They slept all that day and the next, nor did they waken when voices and footsteps broke the silence of the camp. And when pitying fingers brushed the snow from their wan faces, you could scarcely have told from the equal peace that dwelt upon them, which was she that had sinned. Even the Law of Poker Flat recognized this, and turned away, leaving them still locked in each other's arms.

But at the head of the gulch, on one of the largest pine trees, they found the deuce of clubs pinned to the bark with a bowie knife. It bore the following, written in pencil, in a firm hand:

†
BENEATH THIS TREE
LIES THE BODY
OF
JOHN OAKHURST,
WHO STRUCK A STREAK OF BAD LUCK
ON THE 23ʀᴅ OF NOVEMBER, 1850,
AND
HANDED IN HIS CHECKS
ON THE 7ᴛʜ DECEMBER, 1850
†

And pulseless and cold, with a Derringer[14] by his side and a bullet in his heart, though still calm as in life, beneath the snow, lay he who was at once the strongest and yet the weakest of the outcasts of Poker Flat. ■

> *What has Oakhurst done?*

---

14. **Derringer.** Short-barreled pocket pistol, invented by Henry Derringer

# Respond *to the* SELECTION

If you were Oakhurst and knew you would soon be dead, what would your regrets be?

# INVESTIGATE, Inquire, Imagine

**Recall:** GATHERING FACTS

1a. Why are the outcasts thrown out of Poker Flat?

2a. Whom do the outcasts meet on the road to Sandy Bar? Why are the two young people traveling to Poker Flat?

3a. What does Oakhurst discover has happened in the middle of the night?

➤ **Interpret:** FINDING MEANING

1b. Why does the narrator say that the towns-people's decision to banish the outcasts is "as lawless and ungovernable as any of the acts that had provoked it"? What makes Oakhurst "at once the strongest and yet the weakest of the outcasts of Poker Flat"?

2b. What do the names of the two young people tell the reader about them? Is the elopement of the young people wise or unwise?

3b. Why does Oakhurst lie to the young people about Uncle Billy's theft? Why might the truth frighten the young people?

**Analyze:** TAKING THINGS APART

4a. Identify the three main groups of people in the story.

➤ **Synthesize:** BRINGING THINGS TOGETHER

4b. What would have happened to the outcasts if they had made it to Sandy Bar? Would they have continued their old lives or refashioned themselves?

**Evaluate:** MAKING JUDGMENTS

5a. Decide whether or not the townspeople of Poker Flat are justified in throwing out some of the community's members.

➤ **Extend:** CONNECTING IDEAS

5b. Identify at least three stock characters on television sitcoms. Describe the characteristics that make them stock characters.

# Understanding Literature

**SENTIMENTALITY.** Review the definition for **sentimentality** in the Handbook of Literary Terms. Is the senti-mentality of "The Outcasts of Poker Flat" found in the *exposition* (introduction), the *complication* (high point of the conflict), or the *resolution* (end of the conflict) of the story? How do the outcasts act sentimentally?

**STEREOTYPICAL OR STOCK CHARACTER.** Read the definition for **stereotypical** or **stock character** in the Handbook of Literary terms under "stereotype." Make a chart listing the characters in the story and their stereotypes. In the left column, write the names of the outcasts. In the right column, explain what stock characters they embody and their traits. One example has been done for you.

| Outcasts | Stock Characters |
|----------|------------------|
| Oakhurst | The Gambler: calm, cool, detached. |

# WRITER'S JOURNAL

1. An **epitaph** is an inscription or verse written in commemoration of someone who has died, such as the words written on the playing card left at the grave of Oakhurst. Write an **epitaph** for someone who has died.

2. Write a **character sketch** describing each of the characters you plan to include in a modern-day screenplay you are writing. Use stock characters that appear in contemporary fiction, movies, or television. Give both a name and a type to each character, for example, Dirty Harry: tough-guy Police Detective. Then tell what actors you would choose to play the title roles. Imagine that your reader is a Hollywood studio executive.

3. Write a sentimental **conclusion** to Tom Simson's life after he learns of Piney's death.

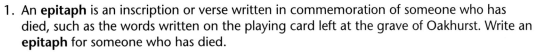

# Integrating
## *the* LANGUAGE ARTS

## Language, Grammar, and Style

**SEMICOLONS AND DASHES.** Read the Language Arts Survey 3.88, "Semicolons," and 3.93, "Hyphens and Dashes." Then rewrite the following sentences, inserting semicolons or dashes where they are needed.

1. The outcasts included Mr. John Oakhurst, gambler, the Duchess and Mother Shipton, ladies of ill repute, and Uncle Billy, thief.

2. Mr. Oakhurst did not drink it interfered with his ability to remain cool, collected, and impassive when playing cards.

3. The Innocent explained why he ran away from Sandy Bar, while Piney a stout, attractive young woman of fifteen emerged from hiding.

4. Music failed to fill entirely the aching void left by insufficient food in the camp, and a new diversion was proposed by Piney storytelling.

5. Mr. Oakhurst accepted Fate however, he was not prepared for such an ignominious end.

## Collaborative Learning

**WRITING A PARODY.** A parody is a literary work that imitates another work for humorous, often satirical, purposes. Work with other students to plan a parody of a piece of Western fiction. Begin by coming up with a list of stock characters from Westerns, such as the fearless Sheriff, the silent Gunslinger, and the sophisticated Eastern Lady. Then make up humorous names, dress, and habits for them. Create a setting, naming the town in which these characters live. Draw a map of main street and name the businesses and other places there. Next, create a plot by thinking of a conflict, or struggle, that might arise in the town. Here are some possibilities:

1. A mysterious Man in Black arrives in town, walks into the local saloon, and challenges any and all comers to a pea-shooting contest.

2. The cattlemen of the town become angry when a llama rancher starts buying up range land and fencing it in to create farms for his animals.

3. The Jones Brothers—five strapping sons of a local rancher whose collective I.Q. equals that of a cabbage—all fall in love with the lovely Miss Elvira Hornswaggle.

Finally, brainstorm a list of events involving your characters that show the conflict being introduced, developed, and resolved. See if you can come up with a humorous, surprise ending for your story.

# "I will Fight No More Forever"

BY IN-MUT-TOO-YAG-LAT-LAT, CHIEF JOSEPH OF THE NEZ PERCÉ

## About the AUTHOR

**In-mut-too-yah-lat-lat** (c.1840–1904), or Thunder Traveling over the Mountains, known in English as **Chief Joseph,** is remembered as a valiant leader who attempted to preserve the way of life of his people, the Nez Percé, in the face of overwhelming odds. He was born in Wallowa Valley, the ancestral home of the Nez Percé, in what the United States government then called Oregon Territory. His father, a Nez Percé chief, had been converted to Christianity, and Joseph himself attended a school run by missionaries. In the first part of the nineteenth century, relations between the Nez Percé and the persons of European descent in their midst were fairly good. However, relations became strained with increasing white settlement. At that time, the United States government negotiated treaties with some Nez Percé to obtain land rights for the settlers, but the Nez Percé did not consider the negotiators to be their legitimate representatives.

In 1877, Chief Joseph was preparing to move with his people to a reservation in Idaho when he learned of an attack that had been made by three Native Americans on some settlers. Fearing reprisals, Joseph decided to flee with his people to Canada. Pursued by troops of the United States Army, this group of men, women, and children traveled over a thousand miles, often meeting and defeating their pursuers in combat. Surrounded by United States troops and recognizing that his weakened, small band had the means neither to escape nor to continue fighting, Chief Joseph surrendered in October of 1877, only forty miles from the Canadian border and freedom. The Nez Percé under Chief Joseph were further decimated by sickness after their removal to a temporary reservation in what is now Oklahoma. In 1885, those who remained were sent to the Colville Indian Reservation in Washington State.

## About the SELECTION

**"I Will Fight No More Forever"** is the surrender speech of In-mut-too-yah-lat-lat, known to persons of European descent as Chief Joseph. In-mut-too-yah-lat-lat was chief of the Wal-lam-wat-kin band of the Chute-pa-lu. To the French who first encountered them, the Chute-pa-lu were known as the "Nez Percé," a name that refers to the custom of piercing the nose for personal adornment. The speech was delivered on October 5, 1877, when Chief Joseph surrendered to General Nelson Miles. Chief Joseph was told that, after the surrender, his people would be returned to their homeland. That promise, like so many others made to Native Americans, was not kept.

# I will Fight No More Forever

## CHIEF JOSEPH

**Literary**
**T O O L S**

**ORAL TRADITION.** An **oral tradition** is a work, a motif, an idea, or a custom that is passed by word of mouth from generation to generation. As you read Chief Joseph's speech, determine which lines make the speech memorable.

**SPEECH. Speech** is the public communication or expression of thoughts in spoken words intended to inspire listeners to some action. As you read the speech, consider what Chief Joseph is asking his listeners to do.

**Reader's**
*Journal*

How would you feel if you were forced to give up your home?

Tell General Howard[1] I know his heart. What he told me before, I have in my heart. I am tired of fighting. Our chiefs are killed. Looking Glass is dead. Toohoolhoolzote[2] is dead. The old men are all dead. It is the young men who say yes and no. He who led on the young men is dead. It is cold and we have no blankets. The little children are freezing to death. My people, some of them, have run away to the hills and have no blankets, no food; no one knows where they are—perhaps freezing to death. I want to have time to look for my children and see how many I can find. Maybe I shall find them among the dead. Hear me, my chiefs. I am tired; my heart is sick and sad. From where the sun now stands I will fight no more forever. ■

*What does Chief Joseph want time to do? What does he expect to find?*

---

1. **General Howard.** Oliver Howard (1830–1909), who conducted the operation against Chief Joseph and the Nez Percé (1877)
2. **Looking Glass . . . Toohoolhoolzote.** Two Nez Percé leaders

*Battle of Little Big Horn,* 1890–1900. Kicking Bear.
Southwest Museum, Los Angeles.

## ArtNote

*Battle of Little Big Horn,* 1890–1900. Kicking Bear.

Kicking Bear (1848–?), a religious leader and warrior of the Lakota Nation, fought at the Battle of Little Big Horn, also called "Custer's Last Stand." Using a traditional style of Plains Indian painting, Kicking Bear recorded this eyewitness account of the last great Lakota victory in defense of their homeland. Rather than portraying one scene from a single perspective, this "pictograph" tells a narrative with pictures. Pictographs helped storytellers recall important events in tribal history.

## INSIGHTS

### Broken Promises

In April of 1879, Chief Joseph provided the following account of his attempt to achieve justice for his people by political means: "At last I was granted permission to come to Washington. . . . I am glad we came. I have shaken hands with a great many friends, but there are some things I want to know which no one seems able to explain. . . . I cannot understand why so many chiefs are allowed to talk in so many different ways, and promise so many different things. I have seen the Great Father Chief, the next Great Chief, the Commissioner Chief, the Law Chief, and many other law chiefs,[1] and they all say they are my friends and that I shall have justice; but while their mouths all talk right, I do not understand why nothing is done for my people. I have heard talk and talk, but nothing is done. Good words do not last long unless they amount to something. Words do not pay for my dead people. They do not pay for my country, now overrun by white men. They do not protect my father's grave. They do not pay for all my horses and cattle. Good words will not give me back my children. . . . It makes my heart sick when I remember all the good words and all the broken promises. . . . All men were made by the same Great Spirit Chief. They are all brothers. The earth is the mother of all people, and all people should have equal rights upon it."

---

1. **Great Father Chief . . . other law chiefs.** President Theodore Roosevelt, various members of his administration, and various members of Congress

If you were Chief Joseph, how would you feel about the broken promises made by white politicians? Explain your answer.

# INVESTIGATE *Inquire, Imagine*

**Recall**: GATHERING FACTS

1a. How does Chief Joseph feel at the time of his surrender?

2a. What has happened to all of the people's leaders, the chiefs, and the old men?

3a. What is the condition of the children?

**Interpret**: FINDING MEANING

1b. Why does Chief Joseph surrender?

2b. Who has taken the place of the old leaders? What is dangerous about having the chiefs dead and the young men in charge?

3b. What is most important for him to do?

**Analyze**: TAKING THINGS APART

4a. Distinguish a way in which Chief Joseph would feel his situation eased.

**Synthesize**: BRINGING THINGS TOGETHER

4b. Why does Chief Joseph mention the sun?

**Evaluate**: MAKING JUDGMENTS

5a. What makes Chief Joseph's speech touching and memorable?

**Extend**: CONNECTING IDEAS

5b. Refer to Insights: Broken Promises on page 434. Then reread the opening paragraphs of the Declaration of Independence on page 164. What similarities and differences exist between Chief Joseph's beliefs and those expressed by Thomas Jefferson?

# Understanding *Literature*

ORAL TRADITION. Review the definition for **oral tradition** in the Handbook of Literary Terms. Then make a chart. On the left, copy memorable lines from the speech. On the right, explain why they are memorable and could easily be repeated by future generations of the Nez Percé. One example has been done for you.

| Memorable Lines | Explanation |
|---|---|
| "Looking Glass is dead. Toohoolhoolzote is dead." | These lines are memorable because they make the listener recall the glorious deeds of these dead warriors and leaders. They also have parallel structure, making them easy to remember. |

SPEECH. Review the definition for **speech** in Literary Tools on page 433. Who is the audience of Chief Joseph's speech? What is the purpose of the speech?

# Writer's Journal

1. Working from Insights on page 434, write a **paragraph** explaining what happened to Chief Joseph's tribe after his surrender.
2. Imagine you are Chief Joseph. Write his **wish list**.
3. Write a **treaty** that grants land rights in the state of Washington to the Nez Percé.

# Integrating *the* LANGUAGE ARTS

## Language, Grammar, and Style

**USING THE ACTIVE VOICE.** Read the Language Arts Survey 3.37, "Making Passive Sentences Active." Then rewrite the following sentences using the active voice. Make any other necessary changes.

1. The Five Civilized Tribes (Cherokee, Creek, Seminole, Choctaw, and Chickasaw) were moved by the Federal government in the 1820s.
2. Beginning in 1830 specific lands were designated for Native Americans by the President.
3. Land was officially set aside for Native Americans in 1834 by the United States government.
4. Native Americans were given land in the Indian Territory by the government; it was located in present-day Oklahoma, as well as Kansas and Nebraska.
5. Oklahoma was settled by whites in 1889, which eventually led to the extension of the territory.

## Speaking and Listening

**PUBLIC SPEAKING.** Read the Language Arts Survey 4.1, "Verbal and Nonverbal Communication," and 4.18, "Guidelines for Giving a Speech." Then form pairs and deliver Chief Joseph's surrender speech to your partner. The partner should write comments on your volume, pitch, enunciation, pace, stress, and tone. Then switch roles.

## Study and Research

**NATIVE AMERICAN TREATIES.** Research a Native American treaty. Relate its original terms and whether or not the American government broke the treaty. Tell whether the tribe still lives on the same territory as stipulated by the treaty or if it moved. If it has moved, report why. You might also report on any current litigation, for example, a dispute over fishing and gaming rights that dates back to the treaty. Consider researching a Native American tribe in your region.

## Applied English

**ADDRESS TO A JURY.** Imagine that you are an attorney representing the Nez Percé. Write an address to a jury, stating what Chief Joseph's people have lost and how they should be compensated by the United States government.

# "A White Heron"

BY SARAH ORNE JEWETT

## About the AUTHOR

**Sarah Orne Jewett** (1849–1909) was born in South Berwick, Maine, the daughter of a small-town country doctor. When she was young, she often traveled with her father when he made house calls to his patients in the country. Inspired by the work of Harriet Beecher Stowe, she published her first short story as a teenager in the *Atlantic Monthly*, a well-known national magazine. In the fiction she wrote when she grew older, she described and celebrated rural Maine and its people. Her novel *A Country Doctor* tells of a young woman from New England who takes the then unheard-of step of refusing to marry to pursue a career in medicine. Jewett is best known for her collections of short stories, including *Deephaven* (1877), *A White Heron* (1886), *The King of Folly Island* (1888), *A Native of Winby* (1893), and her finest work, *The County of the Pointed Firs* (1896).

## About the SELECTION

**"A White Heron,"** which appeared in a collection by the same name, is an example of regional literature. The nineteenth-century regionalists wrote at a time when the United States was being rapidly industrialized. Instead of being allowed to produce material goods at home, people needed to work in factories on machines provided there. Industrialization was accompanied by the movement of large numbers of people from the country to the city, where they could find work. Ancient, old-growth forests were being cut down to plant farms to feed city dwellers, and the wild animals that inhabited these places were losing their natural habitats. Like much regional literature, "A White Heron" can be seen as a protest against these events. It encourages the reader to develop an intimate relationship with a place. Above all, it describes a conflict felt during frontier days by people who lived off the land: the conflict between a desire to conquer the natural world and the need to relate to it on its own terms. This conflict is still being worked out in our own time.

## Literary TOOLS

**CONFLICT.** A **conflict** is a struggle between two forces in a literary work. In "A White Heron," the central conflict is *internal*, occurring within Sylvia. As you read, determine the conflict within Sylvia.

**MOTIF.** A **motif** is any element that recurs in one or more works of literature. Each time the motif occurs it means something slightly different because it occurs in different moments in the story.

As you read the story, make a chart like the one below. On the left, summarize passages that refer to the bird motif. On the right, state the significance of the passages, or what you learn about Sylvia and the young man. One example has been done for you.

| Bird Motif | Significance |
|---|---|
| The birds make "sleepy twitters." | Because Sylvia is sleepy like the birds, the reader learns that she is one with nature. |

## Reader's Journal

What secret have you kept, and why did you keep it?

# A White Heron

## SARAH ORNE JEWETT

*Louisiana Heron.* Rodney Busch. Private Collection.

### I

The woods were already filled with shadows one June evening, just before eight o'clock, though a bright sunset still glimmered faintly among the trunks of the trees. A little girl was driving home her cow, a plodding, <u>dilatory</u>, provoking creature in her behavior, but a valued companion for all that. They were going away from whatever light there was, and striking deep into the woods, but their feet were familiar with the path, and it was no matter whether their eyes could see it or not.

There was hardly a night the summer through when the old cow could be found waiting at the pasture bars; on the contrary, it was her greatest pleasure to hide herself away among the high huckleberry bushes, and though she wore a loud bell she had made the discovery that if one stood perfectly still it would not ring. So Sylvia had to hunt for her until she found her, and call Co'! Co'! with never an answering Moo, until her childish patience was quite spent. If the creature had not given good milk and plenty of it, the case would have seemed very different to her owners. Besides, Sylvia had all the time there was, and very little use to make of it. Sometimes in pleasant weather it was a consolation to look upon the cow's pranks as an intelligent attempt to play hide and seek, and as the child had no playmates she lent herself to this amusement with a good deal of zest. Though this chase had been so long that the wary animal herself had given an unusual signal of her whereabouts, Sylvia had only laughed when she came upon Mistress

> *Why does Sylvia look upon the cow as a playmate?*

**WORDS FOR EVERYDAY USE**

**dil • a • to • ry** (dil´ə tôr´ē) *adj.*, causing delay. *The child's tantrum was a <u>dilatory</u> tactic to avoid going to bed.*

**438**   *UNIT SIX / FRONTIERS*

Moolly at the swamp-side, and urged her affectionately homeward with a twig of birch leaves. The old cow was not inclined to wander farther, she even turned in the right direction for once as they left the pasture, and stepped along the road at a good pace. She was quite ready to be milked now, and seldom stopped to browse. Sylvia wondered what her grandmother would say because they were so late. It was a great while since she had left home at half past five o'clock, but everybody knew the difficulty of making this errand a short one. Mrs. Tilley had chased the hornéd torment[1] too many summer evenings herself to blame anyone else for lingering, and was only thankful as she waited that she had Sylvia, nowadays, to give such valuable assistance. The good woman suspected that Sylvia loitered occasionally on her own account; there never was such a child for straying about out-of-doors since the world was made! Everybody said that it was a good change for a little maid who had tried to grow for eight years in a crowded manufacturing town, but, as for Sylvia herself, it seemed as if she never had been alive at all before she came to live at

*How does Sylvia feel about living on the farm?*

the farm. She thought often with wistful compassion of a <u>wretched</u> geranium that belonged to a town neighbor.

"'Afraid of folks,'" old Mrs. Tilley said to herself, with a smile, after she had made the unlikely choice of Sylvia from her daughter's houseful of children, and was returning to the farm. "'Afraid of folks,' they said! I guess she won't be troubled no great with 'em up to the old place!" When they reached the door of the lonely house and stopped to unlock it, and the cat came to purr loudly, and rub against them, a deserted pussy, indeed, but fat with young robins, Sylvia whispered that this was a beauti-

ful place to live in, and she never should wish to go home.

The companions followed the shady woodroad, the cow taking slow steps, and the child very fast ones. The cow stopped long at the brook to drink, as if the pasture were not half a swamp, and Sylvia stood still and waited, letting her bare feet cool themselves in the <u>shoal</u> water, while the great twilight moths struck softly against her. She waded on through the brook as the cow moved away, and listened to the thrushes with a heart that beat fast with pleasure. There was a stirring in the great boughs overhead. They were full of little birds and beasts that seemed to be wide awake, and going about their world, or else saying good-night to each other in sleepy twitters. Sylvia herself felt sleepy as she walked along. However, it was not much farther to the house, and the air was soft and sweet. She was not often in the woods so late as this, and it made her feel as if she were a part of the gray shadows and the moving leaves. She was just thinking how long it seemed since she first came to the farm a year ago, and wondering if everything went on in the noisy town just the same as when she was there; the thought of the great red-faced boy who used to chase and frighten her made her hurry along the path to escape from the shadow of the trees.

Suddenly this little woods-girl is horror-stricken to hear a clear whistle not very far away. Not a bird's whistle, which would have a sort of friendliness, but a boy's

*What sound surprises Sylvia in the woods? Why is she "horror-stricken" to hear this sound?*

whistle, determined, and somewhat aggressive. Sylvia left the cow to whatever sad fate might

---

1. **hornéd torment.** Exasperating cow

**WORDS FOR EVERYDAY USE**

**wretch • ed** (rech´id) *adj.*, miserable. *Cold, hunger, thirst, and lack of sleep made the soldiers feel <u>wretched</u>.*

**shoal** (shōl) *adj.*, shallow. *Hunting for frogs, the heron walked along the edge of the <u>shoal</u> pond.*

await her, and stepped discreetly aside into the bushes, but she was just too late. The enemy had discovered her, and called out in a very cheerful and persuasive tone, "Halloa, little girl, how far is it to the road?" and trembling Sylvia answered almost <u>inaudibly</u>, "A good ways."

She did not dare to look boldly at the tall young man, who carried a gun over his shoulder, but she came out of her bush and again followed the cow, while he walked alongside. "I have been hunting for some birds," the stranger said kindly, "and I have lost my way, and need a friend very much. Don't be afraid," he added <u>gallantly</u>. "Speak up and tell me what your name is, and whether you think I can spend the night at your house, and go out gunning early in the morning."

Sylvia was more alarmed than before. Would not her grandmother consider

Why is Sylvia alarmed?

her much to blame? But who could have foreseen such an accident as this? It did not seem to be her fault, and she hung her head as if the stem of it were broken, but managed to answer "Sylvy," with much effort when her companion again asked her name.

Mrs. Tilley was standing in the doorway when the trio came into view. The cow gave a loud moo by way of explanation.

"Yes, you'd better speak up for yourself, you old trial! Where'd she tucked herself away this time, Sylvy?" But Sylvia kept an awed silence; she knew by instinct that her grandmother did not comprehend the <u>gravity</u> of the situation. She must be mistaking the stranger for one of the farmer-lads of the region.

The young man stood his gun beside the door, and dropped a lumpy gamebag beside it; then he bade Mrs. Tilley goodevening, and repeated his wayfarer's story, and asked if he could have a night's lodging

"Put me anywhere you like," he said. "I must be off early in the morning, before day; but I am very hungry, indeed. You can give me some milk at any rate, that's plain."

"Dear sakes, yes," responded the hostess, whose long slumbering hospitality seemed to be easily awakened. "You might fare better if you went out to the main road a mile or so, but you're welcome to what we've got. I'll milk right off, and you make yourself at home. You can sleep on husks or feathers," she <u>proffered</u> graciously. "I raised them all myself. There's good pasturing for geese just below here towards the ma'sh. Now step round and set a plate for the gentleman, Sylvy!" And Sylvia promptly stepped. She was glad to have something to do, and she was hungry herself.

It was a surprise to find so clean and comfortable a little dwelling in this New England wilderness. The young man had known the horrors of its most primitive housekeeping, and the dreary <u>squalor</u> of that level of society which does not rebel at the companionship of hens. This was the best thrift of an old-fashioned farmstead, though on such a small scale that it seemed like a <u>hermitage</u>. He listened eagerly to the old woman's quaint talk, he watched Sylvia's pale face and shining gray eyes with ever growing enthusiasm, and insisted that this was the best supper he had eaten for a month, and afterward the new-

**WORDS FOR EVERYDAY USE**

**in • au • di • bly** (in ô´də blē) *adv.*, not loudly enough to be heard. *The student answered <u>inaudibly</u>, so the teacher asked him to speak up.*

**gal • lant • ly** (gal´ənt lē) *adv.*, politely, nobly. *The prince <u>gallantly</u> threw down his cloak so the princess could step over the puddle.*

**grav • i • ty** (grav´i tē) *n.*, seriousness. *The <u>gravity</u> of the mayor's speech created silence in the auditorium.*

**prof • fer** (präf´ər) *vt.*, offer. *<u>Proffering</u> food to the homeless gave the rich man a deep sense of satisfaction.*

**squal • or** (skwäl´ər) *n.*, filth and misery. *The journalist found it difficult to describe the <u>squalor</u> of the street in Calcutta where the missionary worked.*

**her • mi • tage** (hʉr´mi tij) *n.*, place where a person can live away from others. *Withdrawing to his <u>hermitage</u> was the monk's solution to his problems.*

made friends sat down in the doorway together while the moon came up.

Soon it would be berry-time, and Sylvia was a great help at picking. The cow was a good milker, though a plaguy thing to keep track of, the hostess gossiped frankly, adding presently that she had buried four children, so Sylvia's mother, and a son (who might be dead) in California were all the children she had left. "Dan, my boy, was a great hand to go gunning," she explained sadly. "I never wanted for pa'tridges or gray squer'ls while he was to home. He's been a great wand'rer, I expect, and he's no hand to write letters. There, I don't blame him, I'd ha' seen the world myself if it had been so I could.

"Sylvia takes after him," the grandmother continued affectionately, after a minute's pause. "There ain't a foot o' ground she don't know her way over, and the wild creaturs counts her one o' themselves. Squer'ls she'll tame to come an' feed right out o' her hands, and all sorts o' birds. Last winter she got the jay-birds to bangeing[2] here, and I believe she'd 'a' scanted herself[3] of her own meals to have plenty to throw out amongst 'em, if I hadn't kep' watch. Anything but crows, I tell her, I'm willin' to help support—though Dan he had a tamed one o' them that did seem to have reason same as folks. It was round here a good spell after he went away. Dan an' his father they didn't hitch,—but he never held up his head ag'in after Dan had dared him an' gone off."

The guest did not notice this hint of family sorrows in his eager interest in something else.

In what is the guest interested?

"So Sylvy knows all about birds, does she?" he exclaimed, as he looked round at the little girl who sat, very <u>demure</u> but increasingly sleepy, in the moonlight. "I am making a collection of birds myself. I have been at it ever since I was a boy." (Mrs. Tilley smiled.) "There are two or three very rare ones I have been hunting for these five years. I mean to get them on my own ground if they can be found."

"Do you cage 'em up?" asked Mrs. Tilley doubtfully, in response to this enthusiastic announcement.

"Oh, no, they're stuffed and preserved, dozens and dozens of them," said the <u>ornithologist</u>, "and I have shot or snared every one myself. I caught a glimpse of a white heron three miles from here on Saturday, and I have followed it in this direction. They have never been found in this district at all. The little white heron, it is," and he turned again to look at Sylvia with the hope of discovering that the rare bird was one of her acquaintances.

Why has the young man come to the district where Sylvia and her grandmother live?

But Sylvia was watching a hop-toad in the narrow footpath.

"You would know the heron if you saw it," the stranger continued eagerly. "A queer tall white bird with soft feathers and long thin legs. And it would have a nest perhaps in the top of a high tree, made of sticks, something like a hawk's nest."

Sylvia's heart gave a wild beat; she knew that strange white bird, and had once stolen softly near where it stood in some bright green swamp grass, away over at the other side of the woods. There was an open place where the sunshine always seemed strangely yellow and hot, where tall, nodding rushes grew, and her grandmother had warned her that she might sink in the soft black mud underneath and never be

---

2. **bangeing.** Hanging around
3. **'a' scanted herself.** Would have deprived herself

**WORDS FOR EVERYDAY USE**

**de • mure** (di myür´) *adj.*, modest; shy. *Celia and Kim were too polite and <u>demure</u> to ask the celebrity for his autograph.*

**or • ni • thol • o • gist** (ôr´nə thäl´ə jist) *n.*, one who studies birds. *<u>Ornithologists</u> gathered at the convention to discuss the loss of species habitat.*

heard of more. Not far beyond were the salt marshes just this side the sea itself, which Sylvia wondered and dreamed about, but never had seen, whose great voice could sometimes be heard above the noise of the woods on stormy nights.

"I can't think of anything I should like so much as to find that heron's nest," the handsome stranger was saying. "I would give ten dollars to anybody who could show it to me," he added desperately, "and I mean to spend my whole vacation hunting for it if need be. Perhaps it was only migrating, or had been chased out of its own region by some bird of prey."

Mrs. Tilley gave amazed attention to all this, but Sylvia still watched the toad, not divining, as she might have done at some calmer time, that the creature wished to get to its hole under the doorstep, and was much hindered by the unusual spectators at that hour of the evening. No amount of thought, that night, could decide how many wished-for treasures the ten dollars, so lightly spoken of, would buy.

The next day the young sportsman hovered about the woods, and Sylvia kept him company, having lost her first fear of the friendly lad, who proved to be most kind and sympathetic. He told her many things about the birds and what they knew and where they lived and what they did with themselves. And he gave her a jackknife, which she thought as great a treasure as if she were a desert-islander. All day long he did not once make her troubled or afraid except when he brought down some unsuspecting singing creature from its bough. Sylvia would have liked him vastly better without his

How does Sylvia feel about the young man killing birds?

gun; she could not understand why he killed the very birds he seemed to like so much. But as the day waned, Sylvia still watched the young man with loving admiration. She had never seen anybody so charming and delightful; the woman's heart, asleep in the child, was vaguely thrilled by a dream of love. Some premonition of that great power stirred and swayed these young creatures who traversed the solemn woodlands with soft-footed silent care. They stopped to listen to a bird's song; they pressed forward again eagerly, parting the branches,—speaking to each other rarely and in whispers; the young man going first and Sylvia following, fascinated, a few steps behind, with her gray eyes dark with excitement.

She grieved because the longed-for white heron was elusive, but she did not lead

Is Sylvia hoping to help find the white heron?

the guest, she only followed, and there was no such thing as speaking first. The sound of her own unquestioned voice would have terrified her,—it was hard enough to answer yes or no when there was need of that. At last evening began to fall, and they drove the cow home together, and Sylvia smiled with pleasure when they came to the place where she heard the whistle and was afraid only the night before.

## II

Half a mile from home, at the farther edge of the woods, where the land was highest, a great pine tree stood, the last of its generation. Whether it was left for a boundary mark, or for what reason, no one could say; the woodchoppers who had felled its mates were dead and gone long ago, and a whole forest of sturdy trees, pines and oaks and maples, had grown again. But the stately head of this old pine towered above them all and made a landmark for

---

**WORDS FOR EVERYDAY USE**

**prem • o • ni • tion** (prē´ mə ni´ shən) *n.,* feeling that something will happen. *Mrs. Alexander had a premonition of disaster and canceled her booking on the ship.*

sea and shore miles and miles away. Sylvia knew it well. She had always believed that whoever climbed to the top of it could see the ocean; and the little girl had often laid her hand on the great rough trunk and looked up wistfully at those dark boughs that the wind always stirred, no matter how hot and still the air might be below. Now she thought of the tree with a new excitement, for why, if one climbed it at break of day, could not one see all the world, and easily discover from whence the white heron flew, and mark the place, and find the hidden nest?

What a spirit of adventure, what wild ambition! What fancied triumph and delight and glory for the later morning when she could make known the secret! It was almost too real and too great for the childish heart to bear.

All night the door of the little house stood open and the whippoorwills came and sang upon the very step. The young sportsman and his old hostess were sound asleep, but Sylvia's great design kept her broad awake and watching. She forgot to think of sleep. The short summer night seemed as long as the winter darkness, and at last when the whippoorwills ceased, and she was afraid the morning would after all come too soon, she stole out of the house and followed the pasture path through the woods, hastening toward the open ground beyond, listening with a sense of comfort and companionship to the drowsy twitter of a half-awakened bird, whose perch she had jarred in passing. Alas, if the great wave of human interest which flooded for the first time this dull little life should sweep away the satisfactions of an existence heart to heart with nature and the dumb life of the forest!

There was the huge tree asleep yet in the paling moonlight, and small and silly Sylvia began with utmost bravery to mount to the top of it, with tingling, eager blood coursing the channels of her whole frame, with her bare feet and fingers, that pinched and held like bird's claws to the monstrous ladder reaching up, up, almost to the sky itself. First she must mount the white oak tree that grew alongside, where she was almost lost among the dark branches and the green leaves heavy and wet with dew; a bird fluttered off its nest, and a red squirrel ran to and fro and scolded pettishly at the harmless housebreaker. Sylvia felt her way easily. She had often climbed there, and knew that higher still one of the oak's upper branches chafed against the pine trunk, just where its lower boughs were set close together. There, when she made the dangerous pass from one tree to the other, the great enterprise would really begin.

She crept out along the swaying oak limb at last, and took the daring step across into the old pine tree. The way was harder than she thought; she must reach far and hold fast, the sharp dry twigs caught and held her and scratched her like angry talons, the pitch made her thin little fingers clumsy and stiff as she went round and round the tree's great stem, higher and higher upward. The sparrows and robins in the woods below were beginning to wake and twitter to the dawn, yet it seemed much lighter there aloft in the pine tree, and the child knew that she must hurry if her project were to be of any use.

The tree seemed to lengthen itself out as she went up, and to reach farther and farther upward. It was like a great main-mast to the voyaging earth; it must truly have been amazed that morning through all its ponderous frame as it felt this determined spark of human spirit winding its way from higher branch to branch. Who knows how steadily the least twigs held

> **What keeps Sylvia awake?**

**WORDS FOR EVERYDAY USE**

**course** (kôrs) vi., move swiftly; flow through. *The overflowing river coursed through the streets of the town.*

**pon • der • ous** (pän'dər əs) adj., very heavy. *Archie's ponderous thoughts filled him with depression.*

themselves to advantage this light, weak creature on her way! The old pine must have loved his new dependent. More than all the hawks, and bats, and moths, and even the sweet-voiced thrushes, was the brave, beating heart of the solitary gray-eyed child. And the tree stood still and frowned away the winds that June morning while the dawn grew bright in the east.

Sylvia's face was like a pale star, if one had seen it from the ground, when the last thorny bough was past, and she stood trembling and tired but wholly triumphant, high in the tree-top. Yes, there was the sea with the dawning sun making a golden dazzle over it, and toward that glorious east flew two hawks with slow-moving pinions. How low they looked in the air from that height when one had only seen them before far up, and dark against the blue sky. Their gray feathers were as soft as moths; they seemed only a little way from the tree, and Sylvia felt as if she too could go flying away among the clouds. Westward, the woodlands and farms reached miles and miles into the distance; here and there were church steeples, and white villages; truly it was a vast and awesome world!

The birds sang louder and louder. At last the sun came up bewilderingly bright. Sylvia could see the white sails of ships out at sea, and the clouds that were purple and rose-colored and yellow at first began to fade away. Where was the white heron's nest in the sea of green branches, and was this wonderful sight and pageant of the world the only reward for having climbed to such a giddy height? Now look down again, Sylvia, where the green marsh is set among the shining birches and dark hemlocks; there where you saw the white heron once you will see him again; look, look! a white spot of him like a single floating feather comes up from the dead hemlock and grows larger, and rises, and comes close at last, and goes by the landmark pine with steady sweep of wing and outstretched slender neck and crested head. And wait! wait! do not move a foot or a finger, little girl, do not send an arrow of light and consciousness from your two eager eyes, for the heron has perched on a pine bough not far beyond yours, and cries back to his mate on the nest, and plumes his feathers for the new day!

The child gives a long sigh a minute later when a company of shouting catbirds comes also to the tree, and vexed by their fluttering and lawlessness the solemn heron goes away. She knows his secret now, the wild, light, slender bird that floats and wavers, and goes back like an arrow presently to his home in the green world beneath. Then Sylvia, well satisfied, makes her perilous way down again, not daring to look far below the branch she stands on, ready to cry sometimes because her fingers ache and her lamed feet slip. Wondering over and over again what the stranger would say to her, and what he would think when she told him how to find his way straight to the heron's nest.

"Sylvy, Sylvy!" called the busy old grandmother again and again, but nobody answered, and the small husk bed was empty and Sylvia had disappeared.

The guest waked from a dream, and remembering his day's pleasure hurried to dress himself that might it sooner begin. He was sure from the way the shy little girl looked once or twice yesterday that she had at least seen the white heron, and now she must really be made to tell. Here she comes now, paler than ever, and her worn old

> What "day's pleasure" is the young man anticipating?

**WORDS FOR EVERYDAY USE**

pin • ion (pin′yən) n., part of a bird's wing. *Clipping the hawk's pinions kept it from flying away.*

vex (veks) vt., annoy. *The hungry moles vexed the gardener by eating his turnips.*

frock is torn and tattered, and smeared with pine pitch. The grandmother and the sportsman stand in the door together and question her, and the splendid moment has come to speak of the dead hemlock tree by the green marsh.

But Sylvia does not speak after all, though the old grandmother fretfully rebukes her, and the young man's kind, appealing eyes are looking straight in her own. He can make them rich with money; he has promised it, and they are poor now. He is so well worth making happy, and he waits to hear the story she can tell.

No, she must keep silence! What is it that suddenly forbids her and makes her dumb? Has she been nine years growing and now, when the great world for the first time puts out a hand to her, must she thrust it aside for a bird's sake? The murmur of the pine's green branches is in her ears, she remembers how the white heron came flying through the golden air and how they watched the sea and the morning together, and Sylvia cannot speak; she cannot tell the heron's secret and give its life away.

> What does Sylvia do about telling the location of the white heron's nest?

Dear loyalty, that suffered a sharp pang as the guest went away disappointed later in the day, that could have served and followed him and loved him as a dog loves! Many a night Sylvia heard the echo of his whistle haunting the pasture path as she came home with the loitering cow. She forgot even her sorrow at the sharp report of his gun and the sight of thrushes and sparrows dropping silent to the ground, their songs hushed and their pretty feathers stained and wet with blood. Were the birds better friends than their hunter might have been,—who can tell? Whatever treasures were lost to her, woodlands and summertime, remember! Bring your gifts and graces and tell your secrets to this lonely country child! ∎

**WORDS FOR EVERYDAY USE**

**re • buke** (ri byük´) *vt.*, blame or scold in a sharp way. *The teacher rebuked the students for not doing their homework.*

## Respond *to the* SELECTION

If you were Sylvia, would you have led the man to the heron? Why, or why not?

# INVESTIGATE, *Inquire*, *Imagine*

**Recall:** GATHERING FACTS

1a. Why does Sylvia's grandmother, Mrs. Tilley, bring Sylvia rather than one of Sylvia's brothers or sisters to the farm?

2a. Whom does Sylvia meet on the way home? What is he doing on the road?

3a. Why does Sylvia climb the landmark pine tree?

→ **Interpret:** FINDING MEANING

1b. Why is Sylvia particularly suited to take care of the cow?

2b. Why does the young man want to know where the white heron nests?

3b. How does Sylvia's attitude toward the young man change in the course of the story?

**Analyze:** TAKING THINGS APART

4a. Identify the different ways in which the young man is described and explain what each description says about him.

→ **Synthesize:** BRINGING THINGS TOGETHER

4b. How are societal roles for men and women different in this story? In other words, what can the men do that the women cannot?

**Evaluate:** MAKING JUDGMENTS

5a. Does Sylvia make the right decision in not telling the young man where the white heron nests? Why, or why not?

→ **Extend:** CONNECTING IDEAS

5b. Consider the dialogue, setting, and characters in "A White Heron." If a writer were going to write a regional short story about where you live, how would the characters speak? Where would the story be set? What types of characters would the writer draw?

# Understanding *Literature*

**CONFLICT.** Review the definition for **conflict** in the Handbook of Literary Terms. With what internal conflict does Sylvia struggle? What are some other conflicts within the story? What is the relation between these minor conflicts and the main conflict?

**MOTIF.** Review the definition for **motif** in the Handbook of Literary Terms and the motif chart you completed for Literary Tools on page 437. In what ways does the bird motif shed light on the relationship Sylvia and the young man have with nature?

# WRITER'S JOURNAL

1. Write a **letter** to Sylvia, telling her whether you would have responded in a similar or different way to the young man's request to find the white heron's nest. Connect your response to your own relationship with animals.

2. Imagine that you are Sylvia. Write a **birdwatching log** in which you describe your observations of the white heron.

3. Write a **paragraph** describing an internal or an external conflict with which you have struggled, and detailing how it was resolved.

# Integrating
## *the* LANGUAGE ARTS

## Language, Grammar, and Style

**CORRECTING RUN-ONS.** Read the Language Arts Survey 3.34, "Correcting Sentence Run-ons." Then rewrite the following run-on sentences. Correct each one either by making it into two or three separate sentences or by adding a comma and a coordinating conjunction. If the sentence is not a run-on, copy it as it is.

1. Regional writers write about a particular part of the country they focus on what makes the region special.
2. Sarah Orne Jewett wrote about rural Maine, she was brought up in the area.
3. The story "A White Heron" is about a shy young country girl who loves the creatures in the woods because they are the companions with whom she plays, these creatures bring her great happiness.
4. The young man in "A White Heron" treats the creatures of the woods as something to study, Sylvia treats them as companions.
5. Sarah Orne Jewett was a nineteenth-century "feminist" writer, other nineteenth-century feminists include Kate Chopin and Mary E. Wilkins Freeman.

## Applied English

**POLICE REPORT.** Imagine that the young man in the story is in trouble with the police for hunting rare birds. Fill out a police report by submitting such details as the young man's appearance, habits, occupation, background, beliefs, and personality. Keep the following questions in mind as you write your report:

1. What does the young man look like? What does he wear?
2. What does the young man do for work and for play?
3. How does the young man speak?
4. What are the major personality traits of the young man?
5. How do the other people view the young man?
6. What has the young man said that indicates his beliefs?

## Study and Research

**RESEARCHING ENDANGERED SPECIES.** Research a topic related to endangered species in the United States and make a visual presentation to the class. You might want to show where an endangered species lives; tell a success story of an animal that has been saved; research a conflict between industry and an endangered species, such as the timber industry and the spotted owl in the Pacific Northwest; or research how to become active in preserving endangered species. In providing a visual to accompany your presentation, you might make a map, an illustration, or a list. You may want to use the Internet to locate up-to-date information on the topic you choose. The Audubon Society at www.audubon.org/ is a good place to start.

# "Woman's Right to Suffrage"

BY SUSAN B. ANTHONY

## Literary TOOLS

**RHETORIC. Rhetoric** is the art of speaking or writing effectively. It involves the study of the ways that speech and writing affect or influence audiences. As you read, think about how an audience in 1872 might have reacted to this speech.

**ARGUMENT.** In nonfiction writing, an **argument** is the case for accepting or rejecting a proposition or course of action. Argument is a form of rhetorical expression that is intended to convince or persuade. What is the central argument of Susan B. Anthony's speech? How does Anthony support her main argument?

As you read, make a cluster chart showing the main points Anthony uses to support her argument that women should have the right to vote. The first one has been done for you.

> Citizens are persons entitled to vote

> Women Should Have the Right to Vote

## Reader's Journal

Have you ever been discriminated against? How did you react?

## About the AUTHOR

**Susan B. Anthony** (1820–1906) was born on February 15, 1820, in Adams, Massachusetts, into a Quaker family with a long history of activist traditions. After teaching for fifteen years, she organized the first women's temperance association, the Daughters of Temperance. The temperance movement organized efforts to persuade people to abstain from drinking alcoholic beverages.

Elizabeth Cady Stanton and Susan B. Anthony

Anthony met Elizabeth Cady Stanton at a temperance meeting in 1851, and from that time until Stanton's death in 1902, they were associated as the leaders of the women's movement in the United States and were bound by a close personal friendship.

From 1868 to 1870, Anthony and Stanton published the New York liberal weekly newspaper, *The Revolution,* which called for equal pay and rights for women. In 1898, Anthony used the cash value on her life insurance to meet the University of Rochester's financial demands for the admission of women. She has been called "The Invincible" and "The Napoleon of the women's rights movement." She lived by her own motto, "Failure is impossible."

## About the SELECTION

Susan B. Anthony gave her well-known speech, **"Woman's Right to Suffrage,"** after her arrest for casting an illegal vote in the presidential election of 1872. Without allowing Anthony to testify during the trial, the judge found her guilty and fined her $100, which she refused to pay. Not discouraged, Anthony continued to fight for women's suffrage. She published three volumes of the *History of Woman Suffrage,* a collection of writings supporting a woman's right to vote. In 1905 Anthony met with President Theodore Roosevelt in Washington, DC, about submitting a suffrage amendment to Congress. Her lifetime goal was accomplished fourteen years after her death in 1906, by the passage of the Nineteenth Amendment, also known as the Susan B. Anthony amendment, giving women the right to vote in 1920.

# Woman's Right to Suffrage

## SUSAN B. ANTHONY

Friends and fellow citizens: I stand before you tonight under <u>indictment</u> for the <u>alleged</u> crime of having voted at the last presidential election, without having a lawful right to vote. It shall be my work this evening to prove to you that in thus voting, I not only committed no crime, but, instead, simply exercised my citizen's rights, guaranteed to me and all United States citizens by the National Constitution, beyond the power of any state to deny.

> *For what alleged crime is Anthony under indictment?*

The <u>preamble</u> of the Federal Constitution says:

"We, the people of the United States, in order to form a more perfect union, establish justice, insure domestic tranquillity, provide for the common defense, promote the general welfare, and secure the blessings of liberty to ourselves and our <u>posterity</u>, do ordain and establish this Constitution for the United States of America."

It was we, the people; not we, the white male citizens; nor yet we, the male citizens; but we, the whole people, who formed the Union. And we formed it, not to give the blessings of liberty, but to secure them; not to the half of ourselves and the half of our posterity, but to the whole people—women as well as men. And it is a downright <u>mockery</u> to talk to women of their enjoyment of the blessings of liberty while they are denied the use of the only means of securing them provided by this democratic-republican government—the ballot.

> *What does Anthony say is the only means of securing the blessings of liberty for women?*

For any state to make sex a qualification that must ever result in the <u>disfranchisement</u> of one entire half of the people, is to pass a bill of attainder,[1] or, an ex post facto law,[2] and is therefore a violation of the supreme law of the land. By it the blessings of liberty are forever withheld from women and their female posterity.

---

1. **bill of attainder.** Act of legislature finding a person guilty of treason or felony without trial
2. **ex post facto law.** Law made after the fact

**WORDS FOR EVERYDAY USE**

in • dict • ment (in dīt´mənt) *n.*, state of being charged with a crime or offense. *He was under <u>indictment</u> for breaking the law.*

al • leged (ə lejd´, ə le´jəd) *adj.*, accused but not proven or convicted. *Robert lost his job for his <u>alleged</u> theft of merchandise.*

pre • am • ble (prē´am bəl) *n.*, introductory statement. *The statute contained a <u>preamble</u> that declared its intent.*

pos • ter • i • ty (pä ster´ə tē) *n.*, all future generations. *A nuclear war could threaten the <u>posterity</u> of the human race.*

mock • er • y (mä´kə rē) *n.*, insulting or ridiculing action or speech. *The negative news article made a <u>mockery</u> of the incident.*

dis • fran • chise • ment (dis fran´chīz mənt) *n.*, depriving of a legal right or privilege. *A driver with several citations for drunk driving may experience the <u>disfranchisement</u> of his or her driver's license.*

To them this government has no just powers <u>derived</u> from the consent of the governed. To them this government is not a democracy. It is not a republic. It is an <u>odious</u> <u>aristocracy</u>; a hateful <u>oligarchy</u> of sex; the most hateful aristocracy ever established on the face of the globe; an oligarchy of wealth, where the rich govern the poor. An oligarchy of learning, where the educated govern the ignorant, or even an oligarchy of race, where the Saxon rules the African, might be endured; but this oligarchy of sex, which makes father, brothers, husband, sons, the oligarchs over the mother and sisters, the wife and daughters, of every household—which ordains all men sovereigns, all women subjects, carries dissension, discord, and rebellion into every home of the nation.

Webster, Worcester, and Bouvier[3] all define a citizen to be a person in the United States, entitled to vote and hold office.

*What is the definition of a citizen?*

The only question left to be settled now is: Are women persons? And I hardly believe any of our opponents will have the hardihood[4] to say they are not. Being persons, then, women are citizens; and no state has a right to make any law, or to enforce any old law, that shall <u>abridge</u> their privileges or <u>immunities</u>. Hence, every discrimination against women in the constitutions and laws of the several states is today null and void, precisely as is every one against Negroes. ∎

---

3. **Webster, Worcester, and Bouvier.** Daniel Webster (1782–1852), American statesman, lawyer, and orator; Noah Worcester (1758–1837), American Congregational clergyman; John Bouvier (1787–1851), American writer on law
4. **hardihood.** Boldness or daring

---

**WORDS FOR EVERYDAY USE**

**de • rive** (di rīv´) *vt.*, take, receive, or make, usually from a specified source. *Juan's sense of responsibility, derived from the lessons of his parents, made him a good employee.*

**o • di • ous** (ō´dē əs) *adj.*, exciting or deserving hatred. *During war, soldiers are forced to commit odious acts.*

**ar • is • toc • ra • cy** (ar ə stä´ krə sē) *n.*, government ruled by a small privileged class. *A government that is not democratic might be considered an aristocracy.*

**ol • i • gar • chy** (ä´ lə gär kē) *n.*, government in which a small group exercises control, especially for corrupt and selfish purposes. *The corrupt government of the revolutionaries was thought to be an oligarchy.*

**a • bridge** (ə brij´) *vt.*, reduce in scope. *Attempts to abridge the right of free speech have usually failed.*

**im • mu • ni • ties** (i myü´ nə tēs) , *n., pl.*, rights that are protected. *The defendants were granted certain immunities for testifying.*

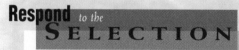

**Respond** *to the* **SELECTION**

How have you tried to achieve something you believed in?

## The Susan B. Anthony Dollar

On October 10, 1978, President Jimmy Carter signed into law the Susan B. Anthony Dollar Act, authorizing the United States Mint to manufacture small-sized dollars, dated 1979 to 1981. The historical significance of Susan B. Anthony's portrait on the silver dollar lies in her contributions to the women's movement. The coin symbolizes the long and difficult struggle of American women to obtain equal rights, a struggle to which Susan B. Anthony dedicated her life.

The United States Mint and the Treasury Department originally intended the new dollar coin to carry a "Flowing Hair Liberty" instead of Anthony's portrait. A political controversy erupted when Representative Mary Rose Oakar introduced a bill providing for the portrait of Susan B. Anthony. For more than 115 years, the only female images to appear on coins had been allegorical female figures known simply as "Miss Liberty." The only male figures to appear on currency had all been United States presidents. Despite opposition, both houses of Congress approved the use of Anthony's portrait.

The Anthony dollar quickly earned the nickname the "mini-dollar," since it was 30 percent smaller than its predecessor, the Eisenhower dollar. The creation of a smaller coin was primarily an economic consideration. The Treasury Department estimated that replacing the Eisenhower dollar with mini-dollars would result in savings of 4.5 million dollars. Even greater savings were projected by replacing circulating paper dollar notes with the mini-dollar coin, since the dollar coin would have a 15-year estimated service life, while a $1 note had only an 18-month life span. It was also intended to broaden the scope of the vending machine industry and increase efficiency of automated coin returns for cashiers. Its eleven-sided inner border was designed to provide physical recognition for the visually challenged.

The American Banker's Association opposed the production of the coin, however, fearing that the Treasury did not have an adequate plan to promote the circulation of the coin. While representatives of the vending-machine industry endorsed the concept of a smaller dollar coin, they failed to convert equipment to accommodate the new coin.

Hindsight proved the bankers' concerns to be justified when the coin failed to catch on with the public. Many people rejected the Anthony dollar because they confused it with the quarter, and the majority of vending machines did not accept the new coin. Production of Susan B. Anthony dollars ceased in 1981.

By the late 1990s, the reserves of the Susan B. Anthony dollar were running low and the U.S. Mint determined that a new dollar coin was needed. In December 1997, Congress passed a law entitled "The United States Dollar Coin Act of 1997," to create a new dollar coin. To learn about the process of selecting and designing the new Sacagawea dollar coin, visit http://www.usmint.gov/, the Internet site of the United States Mint.

# INVESTIGATE Inquire, Imagine

**Recall:** GATHERING FACTS

1a. What is Anthony attempting to prove in this speech?

2a. What part of the Federal Constitution does Anthony quote?

3a. In denying women the right to vote, does Anthony believe that the government is deriving its power from "the consent of the governed," in other words, with the agreement of the people being governed? Support your answer.

→ **Interpret:** FINDING MEANING

1b. Why was it considered a crime for Anthony to vote in the 1872 presidential election?

2b. What point is Anthony trying to make by quoting the Constitution?

3b. What does Anthony mean when she states that the government is not a democracy or a republic?

**Analyze:** TAKING THINGS APART

4a. Identify the types of oligarchies that Anthony mentions in the fourth paragraph of her speech. What type of oligarchy does she believe to be the most unacceptable?

→ **Synthesize:** BRINGING THINGS TOGETHER

4b. In the closing of her speech, Anthony declares "every discrimination against women" null and void, "precisely as is every one against Negroes." Explain how the discrimination against African Americans at that time could be compared to the discrimination against women that Anthony speaks about.

**Perspective:** LOOKING AT OTHER VIEWS

5a. Why do you think Anthony is willing to be arrested for her convictions and risk imprisonment by refusing to pay the fine imposed by the judge?

→ **Empathy:** SEEING FROM INSIDE

5b. How would you react if you lost your rights as a citizen, including the basic right to vote in a public election? Would you be willing to risk arrest to fight for your rights, as Susan B. Anthony did? Why, or why not?

# Understanding Literature

**RHETORIC.** Review the definition of **rhetoric** in the Handbook of Literary Terms. If you were in the audience when Anthony gave this speech, would you have been persuaded by her rhetoric? Do you think you would have agreed or disagreed with her argument? Support your answer.

**ARGUMENT.** Review the definition of **argument** in the Handbook of Literary Terms. After completing your cluster chart, do you think that Anthony effectively supports her argument? Give evidence for your response.

# Writer's Journal

1. Write a **newspaper editorial** stating your opinion about the arrest of the women voters in the 1872 election, that would be published in the Rochester newspaper the week after the arrests.

2. Imagine that you are Susan B. Anthony and write an **appeal** to the judge, explaining why you refuse to pay the $100 fine that you have been sentenced for voting in the election.

3. Choose a topic that you feel strongly about and write a short **persuasive speech** to deliver to your class.

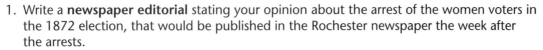

# Integrating
## *the* LANGUAGE ARTS

## Language, Grammar, and Style

**INVERTING SENTENCES FOR EMPHASIS.** Review the Language Arts Survey 3.26, "Working with Inverted Sentences." One way to add emphasis to sentences is to invert the sentence—to change the usual order of its parts. In her speech, Susan B. Anthony inverts the following sentence for emphasis:

INVERTED ORDER "To them this government is not a democracy."

REGULAR ORDER This government is not a democracy to them.

Invert the order in the following sentences:

1. I stand before you tonight.
2. I committed no crime.
3. It is not a republic.

4. We the people formed the Union.
5. A citizen is entitled to vote and hold office.

## Critical Thinking

**DEDUCTIVE REASONING.** Susan B. Anthony uses **deductive reasoning** to prove her argument. In logic, deduction is a form of inference in which particular conclusions are reached by reasoning from certain general principles assumed to be true. For example, if we know that all men have two legs and that John is a man, it is logical to deduce that John has two legs. This may be illustrated as:

*If A is true and B is true, then C is true.*

Anthony deduces that if we know that the definition of citizen is a person in the United States entitled to vote and hold office, and that women are persons, it then holds true that women are entitled to vote. Write down at least five other examples of deductive reasoning and share them with the class.

## Media Literacy

**ON-LINE TOUR.** The house where Susan B. Anthony lived from 1866 until her death in 1906 is now a museum in Rochester, New York, called the **Susan B. Anthony House.** It was in this house that Anthony was arrested for voting in the 1872 election, and it was where she did much of her organizing and writing during the most political period of her life. Visit the site at http://www.susanbanthonyhouse.org/ and take the Online Tour. By touring the house, you will learn many details about Susan B. Anthony's life and the impact she had on American history. Make a list of the important historical events that are associated with the house.

# "The Story of an Hour"

BY KATE CHOPIN

## Literary TOOLS

**IRONY. Irony** is a difference between appearance and reality. *Dramatic irony* occurs when a situation appears one way to the reader of the story and another way to the characters. As you read, look for an example of dramatic irony.

**REVERSAL. A reversal** is a dramatic change in the direction of events in a drama or narrative, especially a change in the fortunes of the protagonist.

As you read, make a sequence chart showing Mrs. Mallard's changing feelings after she learns of her husband's "death." One example has been done for you. Circle the two reversals that happen in the story.

| Mrs. Mallard is informed of her husband's death. | → | She feels grief and weeps with "wild abandonment." |
|---|---|---|

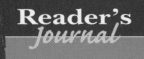

## Reader's *Journal*

When have you experienced an emotion that was considered inappropriate by your friends, family, or coworkers?

## About *the* AUTHOR

**Kate Chopin** (1851–1904), born Kate O'Flaherty, was raised in St. Louis. When she was four years old, her father died in a train wreck. She was brought up by her French-speaking Creole mother, her grandmother, and her great-grandmother, who was a fine storyteller. Until the age of seventeen, she attended a Catholic school called the St. Louis Academy of the Sacred Heart. At eighteen, she met a twenty-five-year-old banker named Oscar Chopin, whom she married. The Chopins moved to New Orleans, her husband's hometown, and before she was thirty years old, Kate Chopin gave birth to six children. When her husband's cotton business failed, the couple moved to Cloutierville in Natchitoches Parish, Louisiana.

Chopin's family physician in St. Louis recognized the quality of the writing in Chopin's letters from Louisiana and urged her to write as an outlet for her emotions. Many of the stories that Chopin was to write in later years dealt with the lives of the Creoles and Cajuns whom she came to know in Louisiana. When her husband suddenly died of swamp fever, Chopin moved back to St. Louis and began her literary career. She wrote two novels, over one hundred short stories, poetry, book reviews, and literary criticism, all while raising her six children. Chopin's second novel, *The Awakening* (1899), met with much censorship in its time but is today considered a masterpiece, having received renewed critical attention in the twentieth century because of its strong feminist message.

## About *the* SELECTION

Kate Chopin began her career as a regional writer, like Sarah Orne Jewett. In her fiction, she carefully portrayed the landscape of the Gulf Islands and the people of Louisiana—the French Creoles of New Orleans and the rural Cajuns of Natchitoches. Besides being a regionalist, however, Kate Chopin was a pioneering feminist writer. **"The Story of an Hour"** is a fine example of Chopin's feminist fiction.

# The Story of an Hour

## KATE CHOPIN

*Madame Paul Escudier,* 1882. John Singer Sargent.
Private Collection.

K nowing that Mrs. Mallard was afflicted
with a heart trouble, great care was taken
to break to her as gently as possible the news of
her husband's death.

It was her sister Josephine who told her, in
broken sentences; veiled hints that revealed in
half concealing. Her husband's friend Richards
was there, too, near her. It was he who had
been in the newspaper office when intelligence
of the railroad disaster was received, with
Brently Mallard's name leading the list of
"killed." He had only taken the time to assure
himself of its truth by a second telegram, and
had hastened to forestall any less careful, less
tender friend in bearing the sad message.

She did not hear the story as many women
have heard the same, with a paralyzed inability
to accept its significance.
She wept at once, with
sudden, wild abandon-
ment, in her sister's arms.
When the storm of grief
had spent itself she went away to her room
alone. She would have no one follow her.

*What is Mrs. Mallard's immediate reaction to news of her husband's death?*

There stood, facing the open window, a comfortable, roomy armchair. Into this she sank,
pressed down by a physical exhaustion that
haunted her body and seemed to reach into her
soul.

She could see in the open square before her
house the tops of trees that were all aquiver
with the new spring life. The delicious breath
of rain was in the air. In the street below a ped-
dler was crying his wares. The notes of a distant

song which someone was singing reached her faintly, and countless sparrows were twittering in the eaves.

There were patches of blue sky showing here and there through the clouds that had met and piled one above the other in the west facing her window.

She sat with her head thrown back upon the cushion of the chair, quite motionless except when a sob came up into her throat and shook her, as a child who has cried itself to sleep continues to sob in its dreams.

She was young, with a fair, calm face, whose lines bespoke repression and even a certain strength. But now there was a dull stare in her eyes, whose gaze was fixed away off yonder on one of those patches of blue sky. It was not a glance of reflection but rather indicated a suspension of intelligent thought.

There was something coming to her and she was waiting for it, fearfully. What was it? She did not know: it was too subtle and elusive to name. But she felt it, creeping out of the sky, reaching toward her through the sounds, the scents, the color that filled the air.

Now her bosom rose and fell <u>tumultuously</u>. She was beginning to recognize this thing that was approaching to possess her, and she was striving to beat it back with her will—as powerless as her two white slender hands would have been.

When she abandoned herself, a little whispered word escaped her slightly parted lips. She said it over and over under her breath: "free,

free, free!" The vacant stare and the look of terror that had followed it went from her eyes. They stayed keen and bright. Her pulses beat fast, and the coursing blood warmed and relaxed every inch of her body.

*What is the thought that possesses her?*

She did not stop to ask if it were or were not a monstrous joy that held her. A clear and exalted perception enabled her to dismiss the suggestion as trivial.

She knew that she would weep again when she saw the kind, tender hands folded in death; the face that had never looked save with love upon her, fixed and gray and dead. But she saw beyond that bitter moment a long procession of years to come that would belong to her absolutely. And she opened and spread her arms out to them in welcome.

There would be no one to live for her during those coming years; she would live for herself. There would be no powerful will bending hers in that blind persistence with which men and women believe they have a right to impose a private will upon a fellow creature. A kind intention or a cruel intention made the act seem no less a crime as she looked upon it in that brief moment of illumination.

And yet she had loved him—sometimes. Often she had not. What did it matter! What could love, the unsolved mystery, count for in face of this possession of self-assertion which she suddenly recognized as the strongest impulse of her being!

| WORDS FOR EVERYDAY USE | **tu • mul • tu • ous • ly** (tü mul´ chü əs lē) *adv.*, wildly. *The hurricane made the sea rage <u>tumultuously</u>.* |
| --- | --- |

# WRITER'S JOURNAL

1. Write a **tombstone inscription** for Mrs. Mallard that her friends and family will read. Include a reference to how she died.

2. Imagine that you are Mrs. Mallard and that you are sitting alone in your room, thinking about the death of your husband and about your future life. Write the **journal entry** that she might have written at that time. Be sure to write about your future plans.

3. Write a **paragraph** for your teacher exploring the love-hate relationship Mrs. Mallard has with her husband.

# Integrating
## *the* LANGUAGE ARTS

## Language, Grammar, and Style

**COMBINING SENTENCES.** Read the Language Arts Survey 3.36, "Combining and Expanding Sentences." Then combine the following pairs of sentences using single words, phrases, or clauses. You may also delete some words.

1. She sank into the armchair. She was pressed down by a physical exhaustion that haunted her body and seemed to reach into her soul.

2. She sat with her head thrown back upon the cushion of the chair. She was quite motionless.

3. There was something coming to her. She was waiting for it.

4. Her pulses beat fast. The coursing blood warmed and relaxed every inch of her body.

## Study and Research

**WRITING BIOGRAPHICAL CRITICISM.** Biographical criticism attempts to analyze elements of literary works by relating them to events in the lives of their authors. Research the life of Kate Chopin. Then write a short paper discussing the ways in which Chopin's life experience affected her fiction. For example, her father died in a train wreck, just as Mr. Brently Mallard is reported to have died in a "railroad disaster" in "The Story of an Hour."

## Study and Research & Applied English

**WRITING A PERSONALS AD.** Research gender roles at the turn of the century. Then, pretending it is 1900, write an ad for the Personals section of the local newspaper seeking a conventional spouse. You might want to tell what physical characteristics, dress, manners, educational background, financial situation, and interests you require.

## "I Am Alone"
### by Cochise of the Apache

This for a very long time has been the home of my people; they came from the darkness, few in numbers and feeble. The country was held by a much stronger and more numerous people, and from their stone houses we were quickly driven. We were a hunting people, living on the animals that we could kill. We came to these mountains about us; no one lived here, and so we took them for our home and country. Here we grew from the first feeble band to be a great people, and covered the whole country as the clouds cover the mountains. Many people came to our country. First the Spanish, with their horses and their iron shirts, their long knives[1] and guns, great wonders to my simple people. We fought some, but they never tried to drive us from our homes in these mountains. After many years the Spanish soldiers were driven away and the Mexican ruled the land. With these little wars came, but we were now a strong people and we did not fear them. At last in my youth came the white man, your people. Under the counsels of my grandfather, who had for a very long time been the head of the Apaches, they were received with friendship. Soon their numbers increased and many passed through my country to the great waters of the setting sun.[2] Your soldiers came and their strong houses[3] were all through my country. I received favors from your people and did all that I could in return and we lived at peace. At last your soldiers did me a very great wrong, and I and my whole people went to war with them. At first we were successful and your soldiers were driven away and your people killed and we again possessed our land. Soon many soldiers came from the north and from the west, and my people were driven to the mountain hiding places; but these did not protect us, and soon my people were flying from one mountain to another, driven by the soldiers, even as the wind is now driving the clouds. I have fought long and as best I could against you. I have destroyed many of your people, but where I have destroyed one white man many have come in his place; but where an Indian has been killed, there has been none to come in his place, so that the great people that welcomed you with acts of kindness to this land are now but a feeble band that fly before your soldiers as the deer before the hunter, and must all perish if this war continues. I have come to you, not from any love for you or for your great father in Washington, or from any regard for his or your wishes, but as a conquered chief, to try to save alive the few people that still remain to me. I am the last of my family, a family that for very many years have been the leaders of this people, and on me depends their future, whether they shall utterly vanish from the land or that a small remnant remain for a few years to see the sun rise over these mountains, their home. I here pledge my word, a word that has never been broken, that if your great father will set aside a part of my own country, where I and my little band can live, we will remain at peace with your people forever. If from his abundance he will give food for my women and children, whose protectors his soldiers have killed, with blankets to cover their nakedness, I will receive them with gratitude. If not, I will do my best to feed and clothe them, in peace with the white man. I have spoken.

## from *Life on the Mississippi*
### by Mark Twain

When I was a boy, there was but one permanent ambition among my comrades in our village[4] on the west bank of the Mississippi River. That was, to be a steamboatman. We had transient ambitions of other sorts, but they were only transient.

When a circus came and went, it left us all burning to become clowns; the first Negro minstrel show that came to our section left us all suffering to try that kind of life; now and then we had a hope that if we lived and were good, God would permit us to be pirates. These ambitions faded out, each in its turn; but the ambition to be a steamboatman always remained.

Once a day a cheap, gaudy packet[5] arrived upward from St. Louis, and another downward form Keokuk.[6] Before these events, the day was glorious with expectancy; after them, the day was a dead and empty thing. Not only the boys, but the whole village, felt this. After all these years I can picture that old time to myself now, just as it was then: the white town drowsing in the sunshine of a summer's morning; the streets empty, or pretty nearly so; one or two clerks sitting in front of the Water Street stores, with their splint-bottomed chairs tilted back against the wall, chins on breasts, hats slouched over their faces, asleep—with shingle shavings enough around to show what broke them down; a sow and a litter of pigs loafing along the sidewalk, doing a good business in watermelon rinds and seeds; two or three lonely little freight piles scattered about the levee; a pile of skids[7] on the slope of the stone-paved wharf, and the fragrant town drunkard asleep in the shadow of them; two or

---

1. **horses . . . knives.** Spaniards introduced horses to the Americas. Metal armor and swords are referred to here.
2. **great . . . sun.** Pacific Ocean
3. **strong houses.** Forts
4. **our village.** Hannibal, Missouri
5. **packet.** Boat on a regular route
6. **Keokuk.** Town in southeastern Iowa
7. **skids.** Wooden platforms

three wood flats[1] at the head of the wharf, but nobody to listen to the peaceful lapping of the wavelets against them; the great Mississippi, the majestic, the magnificent Mississippi, rolling its mile-wide tide along, shining in the sun; the dense forest away on the other side; the point above the town, and the point below, bounding the river-glimpse and turning it into a sort of sea, and withal a very still and brilliant and lonely one. Presently a film of dark smoke appears above one of those remote points; instantly a Negro drayman,[2] famous for his quick eye and prodigious voice, lifts up the cry, "S-t-e-a-m-boat a-comin'!" and the scene changes! The town drunkard stirs, the clerks wake up, a furious clatter of drays follows, every house and store pours out a human contribution, and all in a twinkling the dead town is alive and moving. Drays, carts, men, boys, all go hurrying from many quarters to a common center, the wharf. Assembled there, the people fasten their eyes upon the coming boat as upon a wonder they are seeing for the first time. And the boat *is* rather a handsome sight, too. She is long and sharp and trim and pretty; she has two tall, fancy-topped chimneys, with a gilded device of some kind swung between them; a fanciful pilothouse, all glass and gingerbread, perched on top of the texas deck[3] behind them; the paddle-boxes are gorgeous with a picture or with gilded rays above the boat's name; the boiler, the hurricane deck, and the texas deck are fenced and ornamented with clean white railings; there is a flag gallantly flying from the jackstaff;[4] the furnace doors are open and the fires glaring bravely; the upper decks are black with passengers; the captain stands by the big bell, calm, imposing, the envy of all; great volumes of the blackest smoke are rolling and tumbling out of the chimneys—a husbanded grandeur created with a bit of pitch pine just before arriving at a town; the crew are grouped on the forecastle;[5] the broad stage is run far out over the port bow, and an envied deckhand stands picturesquely on the end of it with a coil of rope in his hand; the pent steam is screaming through the gauge cocks; the captain lifts his hand, a bell rings, the wheels stop; then they turn back, churning the water to foam, and the steamer is at rest. Then such a scramble as there is to get aboard, and to get ashore, and to take in freight and to discharge freight, all at one and the same time; and such a yelling and cursing as the mates facilitate it all with! Ten minutes later the steamer is under way again, with no flag on the jackstaff and no black smoke issuing from the chimneys. After ten more minutes the town is dead again, and the town drunkard asleep by the skids once more.

My father was a justice of the peace, and I supposed he possessed the power of life and death over all men and could hang anybody that offended him. This was distinction enough for me as a general thing; but the desire to be a steamboatman kept intruding, nevertheless. I first wanted to be a cabin boy, so that I could come out with a white apron on and shake a tablecloth over the side, where all my old comrades could see me; later I thought I would rather be the deckhand who stood on the end of the stage plank with the coil of rope in his hand, because he was particularly conspicuous. But these were only daydreams—they were too heavenly to be contemplated as real possibilities. By and by one of our boys went away. He was not heard of for a long time. At last he turned up as apprentice engineer or striker on a steamboat. This thing shook the bottom out of all my Sunday-school teachings. That boy had been notoriously worldly, and I just the reverse; yet he was exalted to this eminence, and I left in obscurity and misery. There was nothing generous about this fellow in his greatness. He would always manage to have a rusty bolt to scrub while his boat tarried at our town, and he would sit on the inside guard and scrub it, where we could all see him and envy him and loathe him. And whenever his boat was laid up he would come home and swell around the town in his blackest and greasiest clothes, so that nobody could help remembering that he was a steamboatman; and he used all sorts of steamboat technicalities in his talk, as if he were so used to them that he forgot common people could not understand them. He would speak of the labboard[6] side of a horse in an easy, natural way that would make one wish he was dead. And he was always talking about "St. Looey" like an old citizen; he would refer casually to occasions when he "was coming down Fourth Street," or when he was "passing by the Planter's House," or when there was a fire and he took a turn on the brakes of "the old Big Missouri"; and then he would go on and lie about how many towns the size of ours were burned down there that day. Two or three of the boys had long been persons of consideration among us because they had been to St. Louis once and had a vague general knowledge of its wonders, but the day of their glory was over now. They lapsed into a humble silence, and learned to disappear when the ruthless cub engineer approached. This fellow had money, too, and hair oil. Also an ignorant silver watch and a showy brass watch chain. He wore a leather belt and used no suspenders. If ever a youth was cordially admired and hated by his comrades, this one was. No girl could withstand his charms. He cut out every boy in the village. When his boat blew up at last, it diffused a tranquil contentment among us such as we had not known for months. But when he came home the next week, alive, renowned, and appeared in church all battered up and bandaged, a shining hero, stared at and wondered over by everybody, it seemed to us that the partiality of Providence for an undeserving reptile had reached a point where it was open to criticism.

This creature's career could produce but one result, and it speedily followed. Boy after boy managed to get on the river. The minister's son became an engineer. The doctor's and the postmaster's sons became mud clerks; the wholesale liquor dealer's son became a barkeeper on a boat; four sons

---

1. **flats.** Flat-bottomed boats
2. **drayman.** Driver of a low cart called a dray
3. **texas deck.** Deck next to the officers' cabins
4. **jackstaff.** Rope running up and down a mast
5. **forecastle.** Front of the upper deck
6. **labboard.** Left side of a ship

of the chief merchant, and two sons of the county judge, became pilots. Pilot was the grandest position of all. The pilot, even in those days of trivial wages, had a princely salary—from a hundred and fifty to two hundred and fifty dollars a month, and no board to pay. Two months of his wages would pay a preacher's salary for a year. Now some of us were left disconsolate. We could not get on the river—at least our parents would not let us.

So by and by I ran away. I said I never would come home again till I was a pilot and could come in glory. But somehow I could not manage it. I went meekly aboard a few of the boats that lay packed together like sardines at the long St. Louis wharf, and very humbly inquired for the pilots, but got only a cold shoulder and short words from mates and clerks. I had to make the best of this sort of treatment for the time being, but I had comforting daydreams of a future when I should be a great and honored pilot, with plenty of money, and could kill some of these mates and clerks and pay for them.

## from *The Art of Fiction*
by Henry James

I remember an English novelist, a woman of genius, telling me that she was much commended for the impression she had managed to give in one of her tales of the nature and way of life of the French Protestant youth. She had been asked where she learned so much about this recondite[1] being, she had been congratulated on her peculiar opportunities. These opportunities consisted in her having once, in Paris, as she ascended a staircase, passed an open door where, in the household of a *pasteur*,[2] some of the young Protestants were seated at table round a finished meal. The glimpse made a picture; it lasted only a moment, but that moment was experience. She had got her direct personal impression, and she turned out her type. She knew what youth was, and what Protestantism, she also had the advantage of having seen what it was to be French, so that she converted these ideas into a concrete image and produced a reality. Above all, however, she was blessed with the faculty which when you give it an inch takes an ell,[3] and which for the artist is a much greater source of strength than any accident of residence or of place in the social scale.

The power to guess the unseen from the seen, to trace the implication of things, to judge the whole piece by the pattern, the condition of feeling life in general so completely that you are well on your way to knowing any particular corner of it—this cluster of gifts may also be said to constitute experience, and they occur in country and in town, and in the most differing stages of education. If experience consists of impressions, it may be said that impressions *are* experience, just as (have we not seen it?) they are the very air we breathe.

Therefore, if I should certainly say to a novice, "Write from experience and experience only," I should feel that this was rather a tantalizing monition[4] if I were not careful immediately to add, "Try to be one of the people on whom nothing is lost!"

---

1. **recondite.** Profound, extraordinary
2. *pasteur.* Minister
3. **ell.** Former unit of measure in England, equal to forty-five inches
4. **monition.** Warning

# Guided Writing

## APPLICATION ESSAY

Have you been thinking ahead to getting out of high school since the first day of your ninth-grade year? Graduation day is not too far away. But hold the mortarboard and gown for just a minute. Once you exit your high school's doors, where are you headed? Right now is the time to make sure that as the high school doors close behind you, you have taken the right step so that college or other doors open before you.

What lies beyond high school for you—college, a special job training program, an apprenticeship, a wilderness adventure program, the military, or a touring group? Any one of these paths may require you to write an essay to secure the place you want for yourself. Such a personal statement—another term for an application essay—informs a selection committee about you: what you value and believe in and what you can do.

Just as the universe in Crane's poem needs proof that the man is of some significance, so too the college, university, or program to which you will be applying needs proof of who you really are, not only your personality, ambitions, and character, but also your doubts, weaknesses, and concerns.

**WRITING ASSIGNMENT.** Write an application essay or personal statement that reveals your skills, experience, and goals. Your well-written essay may be precisely what stands out, putting you ahead of others or moving you above the cutoff line.

## Student Model—Revised

by Maria Martinez

I never learned my times tables. To this day I count "8, 16, 24" to figure out three times eight. I am not swift in math and never cared until someone told me I would need math skills to be a veterinarian. Then I was devastated. I have always wanted to be a vet. But after struggling with basic arithmetic and beginning algebra, I gave up my dream. Then a year ago, my grandfather

> "A man said to the universe,
> 'Sir, I exist!'
> 'However,' replied the universe,
> 'The fact has not created in me
> A sense of obligation.'"
>
> —Stephen Crane

### Reflecting

Put yourself in the position of the college or program director studying applications from students who share similar grades, praise from teachers, involvement in school activities, and desire to do well at the next stage of their life. What will the director need to see in an essay in order to take notice of it and see you as a unique applicant? What might have the opposite effect, causing the reader to think that the essay sounds like all the others? How might what seems interesting or boring to you be different for an adult on a selection committee? Anticipating the effect your essay will have on a college or program director will help you at every stage of this writing.

**EXAMINING THE MODEL.** Maria chose to write a narrative to explain how she determined to overcome a personal obstacle and work toward her dream. Why might this topic be appealing to the college or program director who will read the essay? What positive points does the essay demonstrate about Maria? Which ideas and details would help the reader notice this essay and see Maria as a unique applicant? Consider Maria's voice and use of language. In what ways does she show respect for her audience by writing intelligently, creatively, yet concisely?

showed me why that dream was worth fighting for.

I had never spent much time with my grandfather before he called me last winter. "I need some help on the farm," he said. My grandad had a pasture full of pregnant ewes. "I can't do it without you," he said, but I didn't see how I could help. I didn't know the first thing about sheep. I boarded a train to eastern Oregon and rode through the Gorge in the falling snow and past the deer in the canyons until the train pulled into Pendleton, where my grandfather stood waiting with his big smile.

That first night, he took me out to the lambing shed and showed me the ewes giving birth. I had never seen a lamb slide out in a shiny sack and plop on the ground. My grandfather picked up a newborn by the back feet. He showed me how to apply iodine to the lambs' bellies after birth and how to help the lambs suckle. I could barely sleep that night, thinking of everything he expected me to know.

After breakfast the next morning, I joined him out in the barn. The first job was to sew up a ewe with a prolapsed uterus. He used a large flat needle and thread that looked like shoelaces. I thought this was all fine until my grandfather told me to give the ewe a shot of penicillin. I said, "I don't know how," but I was thinking I couldn't jam that sharp point inside her. He ignored my protests and showed me how many cc's of antibiotics to put in the needle. After that, he just expected me to figure amounts.

Snow kept falling. Some of the lambs got so cold we had to run a tube down their throats and feed them. I had to estimate body weight and feed 10cc of colostrum per pound. I was afraid I would put in too much milk. My grandfather watched the first time, not saying much. He just pushed the lamb's head back so the tube went in straight.

Then he left me alone. By the end of the week, I had tubed over two dozen lambs and not one of them died.

Before I left, I made my grandfather promise to take care of a premature lamb we had under lights in the shed. I didn't want to leave him or the sheep. All the way home on the train I was looking at my beat-up hands and thinking, If I can do this, I can figure out how to use numbers. I'm going to be a vet after all.

"... it is the audience which makes the arts. A climate of appreciation is essential to its flowering, and the higher the expectations of the public, the better the performance of the artist."

—Marya Mannes

## Prewriting

**FINDING YOUR VOICE.** Voice is absolutely critical to the success of an application essay and ultimately achieving your goal of program or college acceptance. The way you handle the language will reflect your unique personality as well as your attitude toward the topic and the audience. In the case of an application essay, voice may determine if your essay even gets read beyond the opening paragraph. Feel what you write; don't report it. Don't just tell it; show it.

**IDENTIFYING YOUR AUDIENCE.** While you probably don't know precisely who the audience is, whether it's a person, a committee, a board, or a panel, know that the audience is educated adults. They know and appreciate good writing, but they do not have an abundance of time. They expect that you have done your homework about their program or school. They are human and ready to listen to you. However, they may have little or no patience for cynicism, flippancy, joke telling, and topic deviation. You will need to develop a balance between creatively expressing information about yourself and maintaining a formal, respectful attitude.

**WRITING WITH A PLAN.** Before you start writing, you must know what you're going to write about. In some cases, applicants are given a specific writing prompt. You might be directed to write about someone from history you wish you'd met. Or you might be asked to put just one thing in a time capsule to be opened in another thousand years that would show what life was like at the beginning of the millennium.

On the other hand, the application form may simply ask you to tell about yourself. To get started, take a personal inventory. Perhaps this could be done in the form of freewriting. Set a timer for ten minutes; then write nonstop about your strengths or positive qualities. When the timer goes off, reset it, then switch and write about your weaknesses or negative

Avoid trite phrases and empty words or phrases such as "really," "special," "unique," "interesting," "each and every," "meaningful," "nowadays," "last but not least," "very," "a lot," and "etc."

> "I celebrate myself,
> and sing myself,
> And what I assume
> you shall assume,
> For every atom
> belonging to me as
> good belongs to
> you."
>
> —Walt Whitman

qualities. After the twenty minutes of writing, read through what you've written. What came more easily for you—the positive or the negative? Would others describe you in the same way you describe yourself? What successes, failures, activities, and/or experiences come to mind to illustrate one or more of these qualities?

If nothing inspires you yet, consider these categories and topics:

- Then and now: a friend who no longer is, a first impression that changed, a bad habit you no longer have, a teacher you once resented but grew to respect
- Regret or hindsight: a choice, a decision, words, a relationship
- Double vision: a time you were glad you were gifted with a certain ability and a time you weren't, a time you tried to learn something but didn't, a time you were misled

Regardless of its subject, your application essay should be structured. Before you settle on a structure, determine your thesis or focus. What do you wish to communicate to the reader? Write one sentence that makes that statement—for example, the most influential person in your life, the incident that caused you to grow up in an instant, the time you realized life won't allow "do overs." Then consider what structure will work best to develop that focus:

- Narrative—tell a story about something significant that happened to you
- Comparison—show how you are now alike or unlike the person you were at a previous time in your life
- Cause/Effect—explain how one thing affects another
- Problem/Solution—offer one or more solutions for a problem
- Argumentation—assert and support a position or an opinion

For more information, see the Language Arts Survey 2.9, "Gathering Ideas."

## Language, Grammar, and Style

### Extending Effective Use of Phrases and Clauses

**IDENTIFYING EFFECTIVE USE OF PHRASES AND CLAUSES.** Sentence variety and expansion through the effective use of phrases and clauses is a great way to maintain interest and flow in your writing. Even simple sentences perk up with the addition of adjectives, adverbs, and verbs.

For example, "Marta wants to go to college" is a direct, but somewhat plain sentence. Adding an adverb, an adjective, and another verb phrase gives the sentence a more interesting structure and fills it with more information. Now it reads, "Marta desperately wants to go to a liberal arts college and <u>major in art history</u>."

You can expand sentences with many types of phrases and clauses.

## Student Model—Graphic Organizer

Maria, who chose to write a narrative, used the following graphic organizer to develop her ideas for her essay.

> *Goal:*
> *to show that even though I struggle with some things, I'm not going to let them stop me from achieving my dreams*

| Introduction: how the experience started | Body: what happened during the experience | Conclusion: the outcome of the experience |
| --- | --- | --- |
| my grandfather needed help with the sheep | I had to give shots | I realized that if I could learn all this |
| he asked me to come | I had to measure cc's and figure out how many cc's to give according to how much they weighed | stuff about caring for the sheep that I could learn whatever else I needed to know. |
| mom said I could | I did it; I saved animals | I guess the whole experience gave me confidence |
| how I had given up on being a vet | | |

**Thesis:** *If I can figure out how to take care of the lambs and the ewes, I can figure out how to use numbers. I'm going to be a vet after all.*

**Specific details, descriptions, dialogue, or quotations to include:**
not knowing times tables, counting by 8s
" I can't do it without you."
train ride — snow, deer, my grandfather waiting
lambing shed
sack around the lambs
iodining the lambs
getting them to suckle
the needle and the thread — like a shoelace
figuring cc's
estimating body weight, multiplying pounds and cc's
the preemie lamb
tubing lambs
my hands

If you are writing a narrative, copy the graphic organizer on your own paper and complete it. See the Language Arts Survey 2.13, "Clustering," and 2.16, "Completing Venn Diagrams" for examples of graphic organizers that use different organizational patterns.

## Drafting

After you have your thesis and pattern of development, it's time to write. The application may stipulate that the essay should be a certain length, not more than five hundred words, for example. If there is not a suggested length, plan on no more than two pages. Follow the structure you generated in your graphic organizer. Write simply, sincerely, and clearly. Provide specifics—details, descriptions, dialogue, or quotations—as needed. Use a thesaurus, but don't overdo it by either trying to

**Verb Phrase**
A verb phrase includes a verb and the words that modify it.

**Example**
Marta <u>desperately wants to go to a liberal arts college</u> and <u>major in art history</u>.

**Appositive Phrase**
An appositive phrase is an appositive—pronoun placed beside another noun or pronoun to identify or explain it—with words that modify it.

**Example**
Marta, <u>president of her school's art club,</u> wants to go to a liberal arts college and major in art history.

**Prepositional Phrase**
A preposition and its modifiers make up a prepositional phrase. Prepositional phrases can modify noun clauses or verb clauses, therefore functioning as adjectives or adverbs.

**Example—Adjective Prepositional Phrase**
Marta, president <u>of her school's art club,</u> wants to go <u>to a liberal arts college in the Midwest</u> and major in art history.

**Example—Adverb Prepositional Phrase**
<u>After a year or two of college,</u> Rod hopes to sign on with Up With People.

*continued on page 468*

## Verbal Phrases

Verbal phrases include several types of phrases in which verbs are used as other parts of speech. These include gerunds, participles, present or past participle verbs used as adjectives, and infinitives. See examples in the Language Arts Survey 3.80, "Verbals: Participles, Gerunds, and Infinitives."

## Subordinate Clause

Like phrases, a subordinate clause can be added to a sentence. A subordinate clause has a subject as well as a verb and probably one or more phrases, but it cannot stand alone.

### Example

Though she's decided to write about her experience of getting lost on London's Underground, Jill can't figure out how to get started.

If you find that you too frequently use simple sentences, try subordinating ideas and combining sentences.

### Example

High school seniors should attend College Night.

They can talk to representatives there.

The representatives are from all the in-state colleges and universities.

High school seniors should attend College Night, where they can talk to representatives from all the in-state colleges and universities.

impress the reader with an elevated vocabulary or by using words that are unnatural for your voice and style.

## Self- and Peer Evaluation

When you have a complete draft, do a self-evaluation. Your draft may also benefit from an evaluation by an adult member of your community—a parent or relative, a teacher, a guidance counselor, or an employer. Consider the following questions:

- What is the purpose of the essay? How does the thesis make the purpose clear?
- How well does the introduction appeal to the reader?
- What is the structure? Where is the structure evident? Where is it missing, unclear, or confusing?
- What specifics enhance development or detract from development? What specifics have been left out?
- What makes the writing fresh, interesting, and effective? Look for sentence variety and active verbs.
- What makes the conclusion satisfying or not satisfying?
- What does the writing say about the writer?
- What is the overall impact? Summarize the essay's contents and the impression it makes. Based solely on the essay, should the student be accepted into the college or program? Why, or why not?

## Student Model—Draft

*this is abrupt—*

To this day I will count "8, 16, 24" to ~~never~~ figure out three times eight. *because I never learned times tables* I am not swift in math. I never cared until someone told me you had to do math to be a veterinarian. Then I was devastated. It's all I ever wanted to be *a vet* from the time I was small. ~~A vet.~~ *how?*

*did you try?* And then math got in the way. But two years ago my dream came back when *my dream* *reach / fight for* my *arithmetic* *algebra* *I struggled* grandfather showed me how to get beyond my fear. *would talking about a dream be better than a fear?*

I had never spent much time with my grandfather before he called me that

winter. He said "he needed some help on
the farm" and wanted to know if I could
get time off school to come. ~~My mom~~
~~swears she had nothing to do with it,~~
~~but I thought it odd that she agreed to~~
~~let me miss school right after the~~
~~holiday break. She told me it was time~~
~~to know my grandfather, that he was~~
~~getting old and that~~ (sometimes life *interesting*
*but is it needed?*
gives you lessons you can't always
learn in school) I said yes I would go.

*I boarded a*
~~I was nervous taking the~~ train to
*and rode* *basically already says this in 2nd ¶*
eastern Oregon. ~~It had been years since~~
~~I had seen my grandfather and I didn't~~
~~even know what he looked like anymore~~
*move*
I didn't know anything about sheep and
I couldn't see how I could help him on
the farm) ~~The snow was falling and the~~
*who is "we"?*
~~ground was covered in deep drifts.~~ We
*move to ✱* *in the falling snow and past ✗*
saw (deer in the canyons past the Gorge,
*through*
~~standing next to the track watching us.~~
*until the train*
~~And then we~~ pulled into Pendleton ~~and I~~
*where*
~~could see right away w~~ho my grandfather
~~was. He had black hair with grey on the~~
*stood waiting with a*
~~sides,~~ brown eyes, and a big smile ~~like~~
~~my mom's~~
*shorten this? Combine sentences?*
    That first night, my grandfather took
me out to the lambing shed and showed
me ~~all~~ the ewes ~~that were~~ giving birth.
He showed me ~~how to lead the ewes into~~
*what was*
~~the barn and~~ how to help the lambs *that like?*

---

**FIXING SENTENCES BY EXPANDING OR COMBINING.** Expand the following sentences by adding words, phrases, and clauses or by combining with subordinate clauses. Work through at least three expansions for each. The first one has been done for you.

1. Joel is looking for a summer job. Joel is Ana's boyfriend.

Expansion/Combination 1): Joel, who is Ana's boyfriend, is looking for a summer job.

Expansion 2): Joel, Ana's boyfriend, is looking for a summer job as a camp counselor.

Expansion 3): After he tutored in the elementary school during the past year, Ana's boyfriend Joel decided to apply to be a camp counselor this summer.

2. I am taking an ACT/SAT prep class. The class is held here at school.

3. Some colleges require interviews. Private colleges, in particular, want to visit with applicants.

4. The counseling office has college information. The information includes videotapes and visitation dates.

*continued on page 470*

5. Physical fitness is essential. Military academies especially require physical fitness.

**USING A VARIETY OF SENTENCES.** Read through the draft of your college application essay looking for sentence variety in length and structure. Find at least three sentences where you can use combining and/or expanding techniques to make the sentences in your essay more interesting and readable.

suckle. ~~He showed me~~ *and* how to iodine the lambs' bellies after birth ~~and how to feed the ewes their alfalfa and corn.~~ I could barely sleep that night thinking of all the things he wanted me to know.

We ate breakfast early in the morning. Then it was out to the barn *to* ~~begin helping my grandfather.~~ The first job ~~of the day~~ was to sew up a prolapsed ewe. My grandfather used a large flat needle and thread that looked like shoelaces to ~~sew the uterus inside.~~ *good description* thought this was all fine until my grandfather told me to give the ewe a shot of penicillin. ~~I started to say I couldn't do that but~~ *said "I don't know how" but was thinking I couldn't* he just ignored ~~that~~ *my protests* and showed me how many cc's of antibiotics I should put in the needle and how to stick it in. After that, he just expected me to figure amounts ○— *good long sentence*

The snow kept falling ~~and~~ some of the lambs got so cold we had to run a tube down their throat and feed them warm colostrum ~~from a ewe.~~ I had to estimate body weight and feed 10cc of colostrum per pound. ←

~~I thought I couldn't tube a lamb.~~ I was afraid I would drown it or put in too much milk. The first time my *combine* grandfather stood and watched. He didn't say much. He pushed the lamb's head back so the tube went in straight and when he saw that everything was *informal?* going OK he left me alone. By the end of the week, I had tubed over two dozen lambs and not one of them died.

Before I left I made my grandfather promise to take care of a premature ~~bummer~~ lamb we had under lights in the shed. ~~He promised. Then I hanged on him too long until he had to peel off my hands~~ because I didn't want to leave *shorten?* him or the sheep.

But all the way home on the train I was looking at my beat-up *good!* hands and thinking, if I can do this, I can do math. I'm going to be a vet after all.

"As turning the logs will make a dull fire burn, so change of studies a dull brain."

—Henry Wadsworth Longfellow

## Publishing and Presenting

Print or type your final copy on standard white paper. Be sure your final copy is dated, identifies you as the author, and includes any necessary information from the college or program application.

## Revising and Proofreading

Openly consider your self-evaluation and the evaluation you may have received from others. Plan your revision after making decisions about how best to improve your essay. Use your word processor's grammar and spell checker and your "self-checker." Proofread over and over for even one error, for example, a homonym such as "their" instead of "there." One error could result in the paper being placed in the rejected stack and ultimately cost you acceptance. When you enclose the essay with the application, feel confident that it's clear, specific, and correct, and that it shows your effort and commitment.

# UNIT REVIEW

*Frontiers*

## Words for Everyday Use

Check your knowledge of the following vocabulary words from the selections in this unit. Write short sentences using these words in context to make the meaning clear. To review the definition or usage of a word, refer to the page number listed or the Glossary of Words for Everyday Use.

abridge, 450
afflicted, 416
alleged, 449
anathema, 422
append, 412
aristocracy, 450
bellicose, 423
cavalcade, 422
cavort, 414
conjecture, 412, 421
contortion, 424
coquetry, 422
course, 443
demure, 441
derive, 450
dilapidated, 412
dilatory, 438
disfranchisement, 449
dissuade, 424
equanimity, 423
exhorter, 413

expatriated, 422
extemporize, 425
felonious, 425
gallantly, 440
garrulous, 412
gravity, 440
guileless, 423
hermitage, 440
immunities, 450
importunity, 457
inaudibly, 440
indictment, 449
infelicitous, 422
interminable, 413
jocular, 424
mockery, 449
odious, 450
oligarchy, 450
ominous, 421
ornery, 414
ornithologist, 441

ostentatiously, 425
pinion, 444
ponderous, 443
posterity, 449
preamble, 449
precipitous, 422
predispose, 421
premonition, 442
proffer, 440
querulous, 427
rebuke, 445
remonstrance, 423
shoal, 439
squalor, 440
tumultuously, 456
vagabond, 416
vex, 444
vituperative, 426
vociferation, 426
wretched, 439

## Literary Tools

Define the following terms, giving concrete examples of how they are used in the selections in this unit. To review a term, refer to the page number indicated or to the Handbook of Literary Terms.

argument, 448
conflict, 437
dialect, 411
frame tale, 411
irony, 454

motif, 437
oral tradition, 433
reversal, 454
rhetoric, 448
sentimentality, 419

speech, 433
stereotypical or stock
    character, 419

# Reflecting

## on YOUR READING

## Genre Studies

1. **SHORT STORY.** Review the definition of *point of view* in the Handbook of Literary Terms. Examine the point of view used in the short stories in this unit. Which stories use the same point of view?

2. **SPEECHES.** Speakers have different aims when they give a speech. A writer's aim is his or her purpose, or goal. Read the expanded definition of *aim* in the Handbook of Literary Terms. Then determine Chief Joseph's and Susan B. Anthony's aims in giving their speeches.

## Thematic Studies

3. **FRONTIERS.** The name of this unit is "Frontiers." For every geographical frontier there is an interior psychological frontier. Choose characters from three separate works and explain how each character crosses an interior frontier.

4. **RITE OF PASSAGE.** A rite-of-passage story chronicles moving from childhood to adulthood. Examine Sylvia in "A White Heron" and Tom and Piney in "The Outcasts of Poker Flat." What decisions mark their maturation?

5. **REALISM.** Realism is the attempt to render in art an accurate portrayal of reality. Compare and contrast the realism in "The Outcasts of Poker Flat" and "The Story of an Hour."

## Historical/Biographical Studies

6. **DIALECT.** Note the use of dialect in both the Harte and Twain selections. What does it tell you about the expansion of America? What else might this tell you about the social strata of the country? What might the impact of the dialect be on readers in other countries?

7. **REGIONALISM.** Selections in this unit come from different regions of the United States. How is life portrayed in each region? How do the characters make a living? What do these works reveal about different areas of the United States in the nineteenth century?

**Physical Culture,**
1913. Francis Picabia.
Philadelphia Museum of Art.

# Make it new.

—Ezra Pound

## ArtNote

*Physical Culture,* 1913.
Francis Picabia, page 474.

With easier travel and mounting global crises, the twentieth century brought a new phenomenon: the international artist. Spanish-born Francis Picabia (1879–1953) traveled between New York, Paris, Barcelona, and Zurich participating in many art movements. His abstract paintings, which combine aspects of Cubism and Futurism, were featured in the 1913 Armory Show in New York, a museum exhibition which abruptly and spectacularly brought Modern art to America.

The invention of photography freed artists from the need to make representational pictures. Modern art became less concerned with describing reality and began making new realities and new possibilities. What does it mean when Modern art is said to be "art for art's sake"?

# THE MODERN ERA (1900–1945)

## A CENTURY OF CHANGE

When **William Faulkner** delivered his Nobel Prize acceptance address in 1950, he asked his audience to remember "the old verities and truths of the heart." He wanted to make the point that however much the world might change, some things— such as the human capacity for courage, compassion, sacrifice, honor, and pride—remain the same.

Like other artists living in the twentieth century, Faulkner had to come to grips with change, for at no other time had the basic conditions of life changed so rapidly and so completely. Think, for example, of the effects on everyday life of electric lights, mass merchandising, mass media such as television and the movies, transportation by automobiles and airplanes, and instant communication by telephone anywhere in the world. Or consider the effects of antibiotics and anesthesia, weapons of mass destruction, suburban housing and skyscrapers, labor unions, women in the work force, the population explosion, the concentration of people in cities, and the development of such political ideologies as Communism and Fascism. Take these things away now, and our lives would be scarcely recognizable, yet all these developments took place in a few decades.[1]

## THE FIRST WORLD WAR

One of the defining events of the first half of the twentieth century was **World War I.** Before the war, the United States was isolationist, involved in its own concerns. Writing before the war tended to be traditional and regional, providing portraits of life in the many different milieus found throughout the country.

---

1. Some developments, such as the telephone, the concentration of people in cities, and the appearance of women in the work force, had their origins in the nineteenth century but did not become truly significant until the twentieth century.

## LITERARY EVENTS

➤ = American Events

➤1905. Edith Wharton's *The House of Mirth* published
➤1904. O. Henry's *Cabbages and Kings* published
➤1903. Jack London's *The Call of the Wild* published
➤1902. Jack London's "To Build a Fire" published
➤1901. Booker T. Washington's *Up from Slavery* published
1900. Sigmund Freud's *Interpretation of Dreams* published
➤1900. Theodore Dreiser's *Sister Carrie* published

➤1912. James Weldon Johnson's *The Autobiography of an Ex-Colored Man* published
➤1912. Amy Lowell's *A Dome of Many-Coloured Glass* published

| 1900 | 1905 | 1910 |
|------|------|------|

➤1901. President McKinley assassinated; Theodore Roosevelt succeeds
➤1904. President Roosevelt reelected
➤1908. William Taft elected president
➤1910. NAACP founded
➤1912. Woodrow Wilson elected president
1912. The *Titanic* sinks

## HISTORICAL EVENTS

Edgar Lee Masters's *Spoon River Anthology,* with its depictions of people from a small village in Illinois; **Edwin Arlington Robinson's** poems of life in New England; and **Jack London's** adventure tales of the great North country are examples of **regionalism.**

World War I began in 1914, but the United States delayed entering the conflict until 1917, primarily because Americans viewed the war as a European concern. The war changed the life and culture of the United States. The breakdown of traditional European society and the loss of ten million lives in Europe from modern armaments led to a widespread belief among intellectuals and artists that the old order was passing away and that something altogether new would take its place.

Trench warfare in World War I.

## THE LOST GENERATION

To some of the writers who fought or participated in the war, such as **John Dos Passos, Ernest Hemingway,** and **E. E. Cummings,** the old rhetoric which made combat heroic and glorious seemed hollow. Many writers saw the emerging society as chaotic, destructive, and increasingly meaningless. Particularly after the war, they felt that traditional expressions of order or meaning no longer applied; they felt, in some way, that the real America had been lost or distorted, and they came to feel a sense of dislocation, or "alienation," a sense of being cut off from the past. One American writer living in Paris, **Gertrude Stein,** would label this group of postwar writers the **"lost generation."**

Their sense of dislocation and alienation led writers of the lost generation to question many fundamental tenets of the American dream, including the idea immortalized in Benjamin Franklin's autobiography and in nineteenth-century Horatio Alger stories

➤1913. William Carlos Williams's *The Tempers* published

➤1917. T. S. Eliot's *Prufrock and Other Observations* published and Edna St. Vincent Millay's *Renascence and Other Poems* published

1915. Franz Kafka's *The Metamorphosis* published

➤1915. Carl Sandburg's *Chicago Poems* and Edgar Lee Masters's *Spoon River Anthology* published

➤1919. Sherwood Anderson's *Winesburg, Ohio* published

➤1920. Sinclair Lewis's *Main Street* published

➤1923. Wallace Stevens's *Harmonium* and William Carlos Williams's *Spring and All* published

➤1925. Theodore Dreiser's *An American Tragedy,* F. Scott Fitzgerald's *The Great Gatsby,* and Ezra Pound's *The Cantos (I)* published

➤1914. Robert Frost's *North of Boston* published

1922. James Joyce's *Ulysses* published

➤1922. T. S. Eliot's *The Wasteland* published

**1915**      **1920**      **1925**

➤1916. President Wilson reelected

➤1917. U.S. declares war on Germany

1917. Bolshevik revolution in Russia

1918. Armistice signed

1914. World War I begins

1914. Mahatma Gandhi returns to India; begins nonviolent resistance

1919. Versailles Peace Conference

➤1919. Prohibition begins

➤1920. Warren G. Harding elected president

1921. Southern Ireland gains dominion status

1922. Benito Mussolini heads fascist Italy

➤1923. President Harding dies; Calvin Coolidge succeeds

➤1924. President Coolidge reelected

1915. German U-boat sinks *Lusitania*

Edith Wharton.

that through hard work, industry, and self-reliance any American could grasp a piece of the dream. In an age dominated by massive social forces, individuals seemed increasingly dominated by their environs and dehumanized by the numbing and squalid work conditions of modern industry and by the living conditions of modern cities, which swelled with the infusion of poor immigrants.

## THE JAZZ AGE AND THE NEW YORK LITERARY SCENE

Increasingly during the 1920s, the so-called **Jazz Age**, conflicts developed between an older, conservative generation and a materially prosperous but alienated younger generation. Young people demonstrated their rebelliousness by flouting Prohibition, the law passed in 1919 that prohibited the manufacture or sale of alcohol, and by frequenting "speak-easies" or "juke joints" and listening to jazz music. According to the stereotype, this was the era of the flapper, the gangster, the Charleston, and goldfish-swallowing college students in raccoon coats.

Rebelliousness among young people clearly affected the literary scene in New York City. New York was a literary center, the home of a number of publishing houses, newspapers, and magazines. **Edith Wharton** chronicled the breakdown of the traditional ways of life of the wealthy citizens of old New York in such novels as *The Age of Innocence,* written in 1920. In the 1920s and 1930s, New York became a center for avant-garde, bohemian writers, artists, and intellectuals, many of whom lived and worked in the area of lower Manhattan known as Greenwich Village. Here the Greenwich Village Theatre produced the plays of **Eugene O'Neill**, and **Thomas Wolfe** wrote his most famous novel, *Look Homeward, Angel.* During the twenties, thirties, and forties, a group of New York writers and artists, including the humorists **Dorothy Parker** and **Robert Benchley** and the playwright **George S. Kaufman**, met regularly in the dining room of the Algonquin Hotel, forming what has become known as the **Algonquin Round Table.**

## THE GREAT DEPRESSION AND THIRTIES RADICALISM

In 1925, the chief chronicler of the Jazz Age, **F. Scott Fitzgerald**, produced a novel, *The Great Gatsby,* replete with disillusionment and ambivalence about the morality of the

## LITERARY EVENTS

➤ = American Events

➤1932. William Faulkner's *Light in August* published

➤1933. Gertrude Stein's *The Autobiography of Alice B. Toklas* published

➤1931. Pearl Buck's *The Good Earth* published

1930. Virginia Woolf's *A Room of One's Own* published

➤1930. Katherine Ann Porter's *Flowering Judas* published

➤1926. Ernest Hemingway's *The Sun Also Rises* and Langston Hughes's *Weary Blues* published

➤1934. F. Scott Fitzgerald's *Tender Is the Night* published

| 1930 | 1935 | 1940 |
|---|---|---|

## HISTORICAL EVENTS

➤1929. Stock market collapses; Great Depression begins

➤1928. Herbert Hoover elected president

➤1932. Franklin D. Roosevelt elected president

1933. Adolf Hitler becomes dictator of Germany

➤1934. Prohibition ends

1936. World War II begins in Europe

➤ 1941. Japanese attack Pearl Harbor; U.S. enters Word War II

➤ 1942. Japanese Americans placed in internment camps

➤ 1944. D-Day invasion; President Roosevelt reelected

ideal "self-made man" in American society. After the financial collapse of 1929, which initiated the period known as the **Great Depression,** many other writers would take such moral and ethical questioning further, examining basic American ideals of individualism and free-market capitalism. During the twenties and thirties, many American writers adopted socialist or communist ideals based on the theories of **Karl Marx,** the German political theorist who argued that the exploitation of workers would lead to the collapse of capitalism and to the establishment of states in which workers controlled the means of production. To many, the Great Depression, which put millions of Americans out of work, seemed proof that the unbridled capitalism of millionaire industrialists, such as **Andrew Carnegie, J. P. Morgan**, and **John D. Rockefeller,** offered little hope for the average worker. In the midst of the Great Depression, hunger, labor unrest in the cities, union organizing, and anarchist bombings seemed to indicate that the United States was headed toward a socialist revolution.

Ernest Hemingway.

That such a revolution did not occur can be attributed to later disillusionment with the totalitarian turn of the Russian communist state under Joseph Stalin, to cyclical economic recovery, and to President **Franklin D. Roosevelt's New Deal** policies, which provided Social Security, welfare, unemployment insurance, and federally funded jobs. In Oklahoma in the 1930s, severe droughts that caused the area to be known as the **Great Dust Bowl** intensified the effects of the depression and led to a great migration of workers to California. The story of one family's migration is eloquently told in **John Steinbeck's** novel *The Grapes of Wrath.* Other critics of American culture in the first half of the century included **Upton Sinclair,** whose book *The Jungle* offered a scathing exposé of the meatpacking industry; **Sinclair Lewis,** whose novels *Babbitt* and *Elmer Gantry* depicted the worst excesses of materialism— the hypocrisy and greed of small-town real estate dealers and showman preachers; and **Richard Wright,** whose *Native Son* depicts the explosive results of discrimination against African Americans. Some American writers and intellectuals with socialist sympathies fought against fascism in the Spanish Civil War, in 1936–1937, only to turn from socialism on learning of Stalin's brutal purges of political opponents and his treaty with Germany's Adolf Hitler.

## THE EXPATRIATES

For writers like Fitzgerald, Hemingway, **Ezra Pound, Edna St. Vincent Millay, T. S. Eliot**, and Gertrude Stein, the effort to find more authentic beliefs and forms of expression went beyond the United States. In the teens and twenties, a number of important American writers were living in Paris and London, comprising an identifiable group of **expatriates** that often gathered in salons and cafes to exchange ideas about

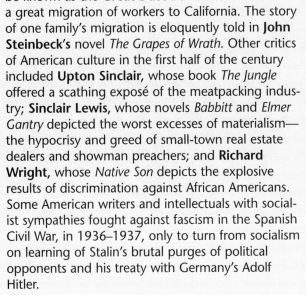

*Migrant Mother, Nipomo, California,* 1938. Dorothea Lange.

Pablo Picasso.

art, literature, and society. Some of these writers, such as Pound and Eliot, believed the United States to be inhospitable to high culture. Their views reflected a division between popular culture, with its westerns, romances, and adventure stories, and the highbrow culture now referred to as Modernism.

## MODERNISM IN AMERICAN LITERATURE

**Modernism** was an international literary and artistic movement characterized by a rejection of the artistic conventions of the past. As such, it was a response to the perceived breakdown of modern culture. This breakdown was reflected graphically in the Cubist paintings of **Pablo Picasso, Georges Braque,** and others, who rendered people, places, and objects as stylized, abstract collections of forms such as cubes. In literature, Modernism found expression in many experiments in form, including **free verse,** such as that of T. S. Eliot and E. E. Cummings, and **stream-of-consciousness** prose, such as that of William Faulkner in novels that presented the unedited thoughts and impressions passing through characters' minds.[2] Stream-of-consciousness writing was one example of the **subjectivism** of Modernist literature, its tendency to treat reality not as absolute and orderly but as depending upon the point of view of the observer. Modernist works tended to be written in the first person, revealing an individual's momentary thoughts, feelings, or perceptions. Paradoxically, this rendering of subjective experience was often done by omitting conventional commentary about the subjective states of characters. The **Imagist** poetry of Ezra Pound, **Amy Lowell, William Carlos Williams, H. D. (Hilda Doolittle),** and others sought to present single moments of sense perception without reference to the emotions or opinions of the author, narrator, or speaker. Williams formulated this aesthetic in a famous phrase, "no ideas but in things." Modernist writing, including the work of Pound, Eliot, and **Wallace Stevens,** tended to be alienating, understated, ironic, impersonal, lacking in transitions between ideas, and full of odd juxtapositions and sophisticated references, or allusions. If Modernism had a credo, it was probably Ezra Pound's "make it new."

Eliot and Pound saw art as a way to order and give coherence to the decay they saw, but most Modernist writers were tentative about the meanings they discovered. **Irony** became a signature technique of Modernist literature, indicating a retreat from a new social vision into the cold comfort of a purely literary or imaginative order. That comfort was usually limited, and much of the writing of this group conveyed a sense of hopelessness.

## CHANGES IN THE ROLES OF WOMEN

Although the twenties and thirties were years of turmoil and disillusionment for many, one bright spot was the expanded role of women in American society. In 1920 women won the right to vote. Increasingly, they were able to attend college and enter the world of work outside the home. Some of the male writers of the period targeted

---

2. While Faulkner was a Modernist in his radical experiments in form, he was a traditionalist in his upholding of older values and in his concentration on regional subject matter.

women's participation in the literary and artistic world as alienating and disorienting and engaged in what some scholars have called a "war of words." A mild example of this is Eliot's narrator in "The Love Song of J. Alfred Prufrock" who mocks these "new women" in the line "In the room, the women come and go, talking of Michelangelo." The women are portrayed as overcasual in their approach to serious art, treating it as small talk.

The increased role of women in the arts and literature is one of the most dramatic changes to occur during the twentieth century. Of course, the United States had already produced some important women writers, from Anne Bradstreet and Phillis Wheatley in the eighteenth century to Emily Dickinson, Sarah Jewett, and Kate Chopin in the nineteenth. However, the twentieth century has been the golden age of American women writers, one that includes Edith Wharton, **Eudora Welty, Kay Boyle, Willa Cather, Katherine Anne Porter, Zora Neale Hurston, Amy Lowell, Marianne Moore,** Edna St. Vincent Millay, **Shirley Jackson,** Dorothy Parker, **Lillian Hellman, Gina Berriault, Elizabeth Bishop, May Swenson, Denise Levertov, Gwendolyn Brooks, Anne Sexton, Sylvia Plath, Lucille Clifton, Nikki Giovanni, Adrienne Rich, Tillie Olsen, Alice Walker, Louise Erdrich, Maxine Kumin, Lorraine Hansberry, Amy Bloom, Joyce Carol Oates, Anne Tyler, Marsha Norman,** and **Beth Henley,** to name but a few.

Edna St. Vincent Millay.

## ALTERNATIVE LITERARY RESPONSES: REGIONALISM, NEW CRITICISM, AND THE HARLEM RENAISSANCE

During the twenties and thirties, some writers responded to feelings of discontent and hopelessness by probing for sources of renewal in the United States itself. Though often using ideas and techniques of Modernism, they are distinguished from the Modernists in their use of traditional forms and in their expression of traditional values. Prominent among these writers were various postwar **regionalists,** who wrote an "American" literature about the local, rural areas in which they had settled. Sometimes these writers found strength and hope in their works, other times only what poet **Robert Frost** called "a momentary stay against confusion." Such regional writers included Frost, who wrote deceptively simple verses set in rural New England; **Sherwood Anderson,** who had lived for years in Ohio and wrote of the people of a mythical *Winesburg, Ohio;* and Zora Neale Hurston, who wrote novels about the African-American experience in the rural South. The novels of William Faulkner, though Modernist in their experimentation with plot structure and point of view, were nonetheless traditional in their use of a regional setting (Faulkner's mythical Yoknapatawpha County, Mississippi) and in their espousal of the lost values of an older time. Southern regionalism is also found in the works of **Tennessee Williams,** Eudora Welty, **Truman Capote, Flannery O'Connor, Carson McCullers,** and Katherine Anne Porter.

One of the most significant regional literary movements was that of the **Fugitives**—led by Southern writers **John Crowe Ransom, Allen Tate,** and **Robert Penn Warren.** This southern literary school rejected "northern" urban, commercial values which they felt had taken over America. The Fugitives called for a return to the land and to American traditions that could be found in the South. The movement took its name from a literary magazine, *The Fugitive,* published from 1922 to 1925 at Vanderbilt University in Nashville, Tennessee, and with which Ransom, Tate, and Warren were all associated.

The Fugitive writers were also associated with **New Criticism,** an approach to understanding literature through close readings and attentiveness to formal patterns (of

Jewish resistance fighters are taken to death camps after the battle of the Warsaw Ghetto, 1943.

imagery, metaphors, metrics, sounds, and symbols) and their suggested meanings. Ransom, leading theorist of the Fugitive movement, published *The New Criticism* in 1941, establishing New Criticism as an alternative to earlier methods of criticism which were based on history and biography. New Criticism became the dominant American critical approach in the 1940s and 1950s.

Another important alternative to the attitude and approach of the expatriate Modernists was the politically committed work of the **Harlem Renaissance** in upper Manhattan in the late teens and twenties. The Harlem Renaissance involved not only an explosion of diversely creative work by black artists, writers, and performers, but also a new direction for literature as a force for creating community. See Unit 8, The Harlem Renaissance, which discusses at length the contributions made by writers and artists during this period.

## WORLD WAR II

World War I was supposed to be the war to end all wars. Events at mid-century would show how wrong that notion was. The Great Depression of the 1930s was a worldwide phenomenon, and citizens of several countries in Europe reacted by placing their hopes in the hands of ultranationalist leaders—Francisco Franco in Spain, Benito Mussolini in Italy, and Adolf Hitler in Germany. Expounding mystical, pseudoscientific theories of "racial purity" and a belief that the so-called "Aryan race" was destined to rule the world, Hitler initiated a campaign to conquer Europe, beginning with an invasion of Poland. The United States was reluctant to enter the war, doing so only after Germany's ally, Japan, attacked the American naval base at Pearl Harbor, Hawaii, on December 7, 1941. **World War II** lasted until 1945, when the Allied Forces of the United States, Britain, and France captured the German capital of Berlin and the United States dropped atomic bombs on the Japanese cities of Hiroshima and Nagasaki. Only after the war did the full extent of the atrocities committed by Hitler's Nazis become known, when it was revealed that Germany had conducted a systematic campaign to exterminate millions of Jews, Gypsies, and others in death camps such as Auschwitz, Treblinka, and Buchenwald.

# ECHOES

## THE MODERN ERA

Literature is news that STAYS news.
> —Ezra Pound, from *The ABC of Reading*

She ran the whole gamut of emotions from A to B.
> —Dorothy Parker, on a performance by an actress

[L]ove and the imagination are of a piece.
> —William Carlos Williams, coda to "Asphodel, That Greeny Flower"

Writing free verse is like playing tennis with the net down.
> —Robert Frost, from his Speech to the Milton Academy

All good books are alike in that they are truer than if they had really happened.
> —Ernest Hemingway

All of us failed to match our dreams of perfection. So I rate us on the basis of our splendid failure to do the impossible.
> —William Faulkner

Poetry is not a turning loose of emotion, but an escape from emotion; it is not the expression of personality, but an escape from personality. But, of course, only those who have personality and emotions know what it means to want to escape from these things.
> —T. S. Eliot

An essayist is a lucky person who has found a way to discourse without being interrupted.
> —Charles Poore

A rose is a rose is a rose is a rose.
> —Gertrude Stein

The only thing we have to fear is fear itself—nameless, unreasoning, unjustified terror which paralyzes needed efforts to convert retreat into advance.
> —Franklin Delano Roosevelt, Inaugural Address, Mar. 4, 1933

"It Don't Mean a Thing (If It Ain't Got That Swing)."
> —Edward K. (Duke) Ellington, song title

We never know what we have lost, or what we have found.
We are only ourselves, and that promise.
Continue to walk in the world. Yes, love it!
> —Robert Penn Warren

So we beat on, boats against the current, borne back ceaselessly into the past.
> —F. Scott Fitzgerald, from *The Great Gatsby*

*Physical Culture* [Detail], Francis Picabia.

## Literary TOOLS

**FREE VERSE.** Free verse is poetry that avoids use of regular rhyme, meter, or division into stanzas. Free verse tends to sound more like ordinary speech than traditional verse does. As you read, look for elements in this poem that show that it is intended to sound like speech.

**TONE.** Tone is the emotional attitude toward the reader or toward the subject implied by a literary work. As you read, try to identify the speaker's tone in this poem.

## Reader's Journal

Think about an elderly person you know. What attitude toward life does he or she express?

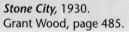

## ArtNote

**Stone City,** 1930.
Grant Wood, page 485.

Grant Wood (1892–1942) belonged to a group of midwestern artists called the Regionalists, whose work shares similarities to the regionalism in literature occurring at the same time. These artists were strongly opposed to the influence of the dominant European Modern styles, Impressionism and Cubism, and looked to older forms of painting. Wood based his style on the clean, realistic look of 17th–century Dutch painters and the simplicity of American folk painting. This Iowa landscape on page 485 is very "stylized," meaning it produces an unnatural pattern for describing shapes and surfaces: for instance, the way Wood paints smooth, rounded trees. What other paintings in this book could be called "stylized"?

From *Spoon River Anthology*

# "Lucinda Matlock"

BY EDGAR LEE MASTERS

## About *the* AUTHOR

**Edgar Lee Masters** (1868–1950) was born in Garnett, Kansas, but grew up in two small Illinois towns, Petersburg and Lewiston. Life in such small towns inspired his best-known work, *Spoon River Anthology* (1915). Masters briefly attended Knox College in Galesburg, Illinois, before studying law in his father's office and passing the bar. In 1891, he moved to Chicago, where he worked as a bill collector for the Edison Company until he was able to build a successful law practice. He later formed a law firm in which Clarence Darrow, the great criminal defense lawyer, was a partner. All the while, he was writing poems, having some published and many rejected.

When an editor sent him a copy of *Select Epigrams from the Greek Anthology,* a collection of classical epigrams—short, often witty sayings, many of which were originally used on gravestones— Masters began using the concise style of the epigram in his own work. Harriet Monroe, editor of *Poetry: A Magazine of Verse,* discovered his work in this style and helped him get the work published as *Spoon River Anthology.* The book was an instant and undreamed-of success. Masters gave up law and moved to New York City in the 1920s. His writing career included novels, plays, and biographies, but none of his other work ever achieved the recognition of *Spoon River Anthology.*

## About *the* SELECTION

"Lucinda Matlock" is from *Spoon River Anthology*, a collection of **epitaphs** (verse written to be inscribed on a tomb or to be read in commemoration of someone who has died). The speaker in these poems addresses the reader from beyond the grave, telling about the lives they lived. First serialized in the St. Louis *Mirror* in 1914–1915 under Masters's pseudonym, Webster Ford, the epitaphs in *Spoon River Anthology* tell stories reminiscent of the life stories of people whom Masters knew in Petersburg and Lewiston, Illinois, near the Spoon River. Many of the names that Masters used in his anthology can be found on tombstones in the Lewiston cemetery.

*Stone City,* 1930. Grant Wood. Joslyn Museum, Omaha, Nebraska.

# Lucinda Matlock

## EDGAR LEE MASTERS

I went to the dances at Chandlerville,
And played snap-out[1] at Winchester.
One time we changed partners,
Driving home in the moonlight of middle June,

---

1. **snap-out.** Parlor game

5     And then I found Davis.
We were married and lived together for seventy years,
Enjoying, working, raising the twelve children,
Eight of whom we lost
Ere[2] I had reached the age of sixty.
10    I spun, I wove, I kept the house, I nursed the sick,
I made the garden, and for holiday
Rambled over the fields where sang the larks,
And by Spoon River gathering many a shell,
And many a flower and medicinal weed—
15    Shouting to the wooded hills, singing to the green valleys.
At ninety-six I had lived enough, that is all,
And passed to a sweet repose.[3]
What is this I hear of sorrow and weariness,
Anger, discontent and drooping hopes?
20    Degenerate sons and daughters,
Life is too strong for you—
It takes life to love Life.

■

---

2. **Ere.** Before
3. **repose.** Rest

Imagine that you are Lucinda Matlock. What things might you have liked to be different in your life?

# INVESTIGATE Inquire Imagine

**Recall:** GATHERING FACTS

1a. Whom did Lucinda marry? How many years did she spend with him?

2a. At what age did Lucinda decide that she "had lived enough"?

3a. What does Lucinda call her sons and daughters?

**Interpret:** FINDING MEANING

1b. What kind of life did Lucinda have with her husband?

2b. For what is "sweet repose" a euphemism?

3b. Why is life "too strong" for her sons and daughters?

---

**Analyze:** TAKING THINGS APART

4a. What qualities may have enabled Lucinda to live to be ninety-six?

**Synthesize:** BRINGING THINGS TOGETHER

4b. What was Lucinda Matlock's philosophy of life?

---

**Evaluate:** MAKING JUDGMENTS

5a. Is Lucinda's criticism of the younger generation warranted?

**Extend:** CONNECTING IDEAS

5b. Some people argue that each successive generation is weaker than the last. What truth, if any, do you see in this statement? How would you explain differences in strength between your generation, your parents', and your grandparents'?

---

# Understanding Literature

**FREE VERSE.** Review the definition for **free verse** in Literary Tools on page 484. What elements in this poem show that it is intended to sound like speech?

**TONE.** Review the definition for **tone** in the Handbook of Literary Terms. Then reread the poem and make a chart. On the left, write lines that demonstrate the speaker's tone toward nature, weakness and sorrow, and life. On the right, explain what tone the lines reveal. One example has been done for you.

| Lines | Tone |
|---|---|
| "Shouting to the wooded hills, singing to the green valleys." | The speaker celebrates nature with a joyful, thankful tone. |
|  |  |

# WRITER'S JOURNAL

1. Write a **tombstone inscription** for Lucinda Matlock. Be sure to include an expression of her attitude toward life.

2. A eulogy is a formal statement remembering someone who died. Write a **eulogy** for Lucinda Matlock, to be read at her funeral. In addition to the activities she did in life, mention how she touched others' lives.

3. Imagine that you are Lucinda Matlock. Write a **letter** to the younger generation, explaining to them how you expect their attitudes to change, and why.

# Integrating *the* LANGUAGE ARTS

## Language, Grammar, and Style

**CLICHÉS AND EUPHEMISMS.** Read the Language Arts Survey 1.23, "Clichés and Euphemisms." Identify the cliché or euphemism in each of the following sentences. Then rewrite the sentences, replacing the clichés and euphemisms with more original or more direct language.

1. Martin told Gwen that the company had given him a golden parachute.
2. The minister told Sasha that time heals all wounds.
3. Paul looked out the window and saw that it was raining cats and dogs.
4. Mrs. Smythe asked for the location of the powder room.
5. Deirdre told me her grandmother had passed on.

## Speaking and Listening & Collaborative Learning

**ORAL INTERPRETATION.** Select a poem from *Spoon River Anthology* for each person in your small group. You may want to review the Language Arts Survey 4.19, "Oral Interpretation of Poetry." Then sit in a circle and take turns reading aloud the epitaphs. As you listen to the speaker before you, take notes on the character he or she presents. Then write a transition to present a logical bridge to your selection. The first presenter should write a general introduction to the selections. Finally, videotape your presentations, including transitional statements and the introduction, and play the videotape for the class.

## Study and Research

**DESIGNING AN INTERNET SITE.** Imagine that your job is to design an Internet site for Edgar Lee Masters that includes a biographical time line and virtual tour along the real Spoon River. With a partner, research Edgar Lee Masters and the Spoon River in the library. Next, design a time line and write the text you would include for the virtual tour. If possible, select and photocopy photos you would include on your site. Place the time line, photos, and text for the virtual tour on poster board and explain your planned Internet site to the class.

# "Patterns"

BY AMY LOWELL

## About the AUTHOR

**Amy Lowell** (1874–1925) was born in Brookline, Massachusetts, into one of the state's wealthiest families, whose members had played prominent roles in public life since the American Revolution. Their status was immortalized in the 1910 doggerel, "And this is good old Boston, / The home of the bean and the cod, / Where the Lowells talk to the Cabots, / And the Cabots talk only to God." The Lowell men attended Harvard and then went on to run or found businesses or major institutions. The Lowell women raised children and had roles in the social and philanthropic life of Boston. While Amy Lowell understood the importance of being a Lowell, temperamentally she was miscast for the role assigned her by gender. She wanted an independent life, which fortunately she had the money to achieve.

Lowell's desire to contribute to public life found its outlet when, at the age of thirty-eight, she launched her public literary career by publishing her poetry in *A Dome of Many-Coloured Glass.* She soon adopted the Imagist style, becoming its chief spokesperson. The Imagists sought to create poems free of "authorial intervention," ones that presented precisely observed sensory experiences and left to the reader the interpretation of those experiences. Lowell greatly admired the poet John Keats and wrote a massive two-volume biography of him during the 1920s. She was awarded the Pulitzer Prize in poetry posthumously in 1926 for *What's O'Clock* (1925). Her other works include *Sword Blades and Poppy Seed* (1914); *Men, Women, and Ghosts* (1916); *Can Grande's Castle* (1918); *Pictures of the Floating World* (1919); and *Legends* (1921).

## Literary TOOLS

**THEME.** A **theme** is a central idea in a literary work. Decide what themes are central to the selection as you read "Patterns."

**REPETITION. Repetition** is a writer's conscious reuse of a sound, word, phrase, sentence, or other element. As you read the poem, decide what idea is reinforced by the repetition of dropping water and leaves.

## About the SELECTION

**"Patterns,"** from *The Collected Poems of Amy Lowell,* presents a poetic counterpoint, the news of death against a backdrop of formulated beauty. Without preaching, the poem becomes a compelling antiwar statement. As an Imagist, Lowell sought to break from the tyranny of form; this poem portrays war as one such devastating form.

## Reader's Journal

Think of a time you received some bad news. Describe your surroundings that day.

*Trees in Bloom,* 1912. Piet Mondrian. Private Collection.

# Patterns

AMY LOWELL

I walk down the garden-paths,
And all the daffodils
Are blowing, and the bright blue squills.
I walk down the patterned garden-paths
5  In my stiff, brocaded[1] gown.
With my powdered hair and jeweled fan,
I too am a rare
Pattern. As I wander down
The garden-paths.

> To what does the speaker compare herself?

---

1. **brocaded.** Embroidered

10    My dress is richly figured,[2]
And the train[3]
Makes a pink and silver stain
On the gravel, and the thrift
Of the borders.

15    Just a plate of current fashion,
Tripping by in high-heeled, ribboned shoes.
Not a softness anywhere about me,
Only whalebone[4] and brocade.
And I sink on a seat in the shade

20    Of a lime-tree. For my passion
Wars against the stiff brocade.
The daffodils and squills
Flutter in the breeze
As they please.

25    And I weep;
For the lime-tree is in blossom
And one small flower had dropped upon my bosom.

And the plashing of waterdrops
In the marble fountain

30    Comes down the garden-paths.
The dripping never stops.
Underneath my stiffened gown
Is the softness of a woman bathing in a marble basin,[5]
A basin in the midst of hedges grown

35    So thick, she cannot see her lover hiding,
But she guesses he is near,
And the sliding of the water
Seems the stroking of a dear
Hand upon her.

40    What is Summer in a fine brocaded gown!
I should like to see it lying in a heap upon the ground.
All the pink and silver crumpled up on the ground.

I would be the pink and silver as I ran along the paths,
And he would stumble after,

45    Bewildered by my laughter.
I should see the sun flashing from his sword hilt[6] and the buckles on his shoes. I
would choose
To lead him in a maze along the patterned paths,

*What are some elements of the "current fashion"?*

*What conflict is occurring?*

*What feeling does the speaker convey?*

---

2. **figured.** Patterned
3. **train.** Trailing fabric on a gown
4. **whalebone.** Used as base for corsets
5. **basin.** Sink
6. **hilt.** Handle

A bright and laughing maze for my heavy-booted lover.
50 Till he caught me in the shade,
And the buttons of his waistcoat bruised my body as he clasped me
Aching, melting, unafraid.
With the shadows of the leaves and the sundrops,
And the plopping of the waterdrops,
55 All about us in the open afternoon—
I am very like to swoon
With the weight of this brocade,
For the sun sifts through the shade.
Underneath the fallen blossom
60 In my bosom,
Is a letter I have hid.

*What does the speaker have hidden?*

It was brought to me this morning by a rider from the Duke.[7]
"Madam, we regret to inform you that Lord Hartwell
Died in action Thursday se'nnight."[8]
65 As I read it in the white, morning sunlight,
The letters squirmed like snakes.
"Any answer, Madam," said my footman.
"No," I told him.
"See that the messenger takes some refreshment.
70 No, no answer."
And I walked into the garden,
Up and down the patterned paths,
In my stiff, correct brocade.
The blue and yellow flowers stood up proudly in the sun,
75 Each one.
I stood upright too,
Held rigid to the pattern
By the stiffness of my gown.
Up and down I walked,
80 Up and down.

*What news has the speaker received?*

In a month he would have been my husband.
In a month, here, underneath this lime,
We would have broke the pattern;
He for me, and I for him,
85 He as Colonel, I as Lady,
On this shady seat.
He had a whim
That sunlight carried blessing.

*Who was Lord Hartwell?*

---

7. **the Duke.** John Churchill, Duke of Marlborough
(1650–1722), military commander in the War of Spanish
Succession (1701–1714)
8. **se'nnight.** Seven days and nights

And I answered, "It shall be as you have said."
90   Now he is dead.

In Summer and in Winter I shall walk
Up and down
The patterned garden-paths
In my stiff, brocaded gown.
95   The squills and daffodils
Will give place to pillared roses, and to asters, and to snow.
I shall go
Up and down,
In my gown.
100   Gorgeously arrayed,
Boned and stayed.
And the softness of my body will be guarded from embrace
By each button, hook, and lace.
For the man who should loose me is dead,
105   Fighting with the Duke in Flanders,
In a pattern called a war.
Christ! What are patterns for?

*What happened to Lord Hartwell?*

■

## Respond *to the* SELECTION

Imagine that you are the speaker. How would you have imagined your future before you received news of your fiancé's death?

# INVESTIGATE *Inquire*, *Imagine*

**Recall:** GATHERING FACTS

1a. In what season does the poem take place?

2a. What does the speaker recall about softness?

3a. What does the speaker carry hidden in her bosom?

→ **Interpret:** FINDING MEANING

1b. What irony occurs between the events and the time of year?

2b. Why does the speaker wish to see her gown "lying in a heap upon the ground"?

3b. What is the speaker figuratively burying in her bosom?

**Analyze:** TAKING THINGS APART

4a. Identify the patterns described in the poem.

→ **Synthesize:** BRINGING THINGS TOGETHER

4b. In what ways are the patterns confining to the speaker?

**Evaluate:** MAKING JUDGMENTS

5a. *Foreshadowing* is the act of presenting materials that hint at events to occur later in a literary work. The poem uses foreshadowing to hint at the news of Lord Hartwell's death. Which example of foreshadowing do you find the most effective? Why?

→ **Extend:** CONNECTING IDEAS

5b. Imagine that a scientist and a poet are debating the question that the speaker asks at the end of the poem: "What are patterns for?" Summarize the views of each.

# Understanding *Literature*

**THEME.** Review the definition for **theme** in the Handbook of Literary Terms. What themes are central to the selection?

**REPETITION.** Review the definition for **repetition** in Literary Tools on page 489. What idea is reinforced by the repeated images of dropping water and leaves? Use the cluster chart below to list examples of this repetition.

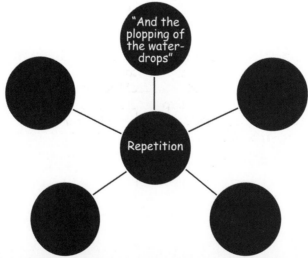

# Writer's Journal

1. Imagine that you are the speaker and that you have not yet received the bad news about Lord Hartwell. Write a **letter** to him, being sure to include memories of the time you spent together as well as your hopes for the future.

2. Imagine that you are the speaker and that you have just received news of Lord Hartwell's death. Write a **journal entry** envisioning your future without him.

3. Write a **paragraph** describing how the patterns of nature, love, and death portrayed in the poem are interconnected.

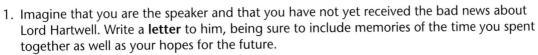

# Integrating *the* LANGUAGE ARTS

## Language, Grammar, and Style

**PREPOSITIONAL PHRASES.** Read the Language Arts Survey 3.30, "Identifying Prepositional Phrases." Then expand each of the sentences below by adding a prepositional phrase.

1. The gardener knelt slowly.
2. Daffodils, tulips, and irises bloomed.
3. The rains washed the garden path.
4. The fountain had been carved from marble.
5. She enjoyed the sound of the water splashing.

## Study and Research & Collaborative Learning

**RESEARCHING PATTERNS IN ART.** Form small groups of three or four students. As a group, research various patterns in different art forms, such as textiles, ceramics, paintings, and photographs. Conduct your research in the library or at your local art museum. Organize and assign tasks among group members. Compose three or four sets of patterns and then present them to the class.

## Critical Thinking

**COMPARING AND CONTRASTING.** Read the Language Arts Survey 5.10, "Comparing and Contrasting." Then make two columns on a piece of paper, one headed "Patterns of Joy" and the other headed "Patterns of Sorrow." List the patterns of joy and sorrow as described in the poem within the boxes of the chart that you have created.

| Patterns of Joy | Patterns of Sorrow |
| --- | --- |
|  |  |
|  |  |

# "GRASS"

BY CARL SANDBURG

## Literary TOOLS

**PERSONIFICATION. Personification** is a figure of speech in which an idea, animal, or thing is described as if it were a person. As you read, decide what is personified in this poem.

**PARALLELISM. Parallelism** is a rhetorical technique in which a writer emphasizes the equal value or weight of two or more ideas by expressing them in the same grammatical form. Identify instances of parallelism in "Grass."

## About the SELECTION

Although he was a veteran of the Spanish-American War, Sandburg hated warfare. The following simple poem, **"Grass,"** is one of the most eloquent antiwar poems ever written, all the more so because of its simplicity. The poem alludes, or refers, to several battlefields— Austerlitz and Waterloo from the Napoleonic Wars, Gettysburg from the American Civil War, and Ypres and Verdun from World War I.

## About the AUTHOR

**Carl Sandburg** (1878–1967) was born in Galesburg, Illinois, the son of an immigrant Swedish blacksmith. He is often considered the poet of America's common people. During his life he was a populist, journalist, folk singer, poet, and biographer. Sandburg left school after the eighth grade and held a variety of jobs until he was twenty, when he enlisted as a volunteer in the Spanish-American War. When he came home, he attended Lombard College in Illinois but left in 1902 without graduating. His poems were first published in 1904, the year he began his journalism career at the Galesburg newspaper. In 1914, some of his poems were published in the magazine *Poetry,* and two years later, his first book of verse was published. During these years he held a variety of political jobs and wrote editorials for the *Milwaukee Leader* and other newspapers. He wrote for the *Chicago Daily News* from 1922 to 1930.

Sandburg collected and wrote songs as well as poems and as a young man had traveled the United States reading his work and singing his songs to the accompaniment of a guitar. *Always the Young Strangers* (1952) is his autobiographical account of these early years. After World War II, he took his readings to the college campus circuit. He was awarded two Pulitzer Prizes, one for his *Complete Poems* (1950), and the other for his biography *Abraham Lincoln: The War Years* (1939). In later years, Sandburg enjoyed extraordinary acclaim. Several schools in Illinois were named for him, and he was awarded the Presidential Medal of Freedom in 1964. Sandburg wrote several children's stories. In addition to these and his books of biography, his works include *Chicago Poems* (1914), *Cornhuskers* (1918), *Smoke and Steel* (1920), *Slabs of the Sunburnt West* (1922), and *The People, Yes* (1936). Sandburg also compiled collections of folk songs, most notably *The American Songbag* (1927).

## Reader's Journal

Have you ever visited a historical site where a famous person lived, a battle was fought, or a treaty was signed? How is the site different now? What emotions did visiting the site evoke in you?

# GRASS

## CARL SANDBURG

Pile the bodies high at Austerlitz and Waterloo.[1]
Shovel them under and let me work—
      I am the grass; I cover all.

      And pile them high at Gettysburg[2]
5      And pile them high at Ypres and Verdun.[3]
Shovel them under and let me work.
Two years, ten years; and passengers ask the conductor:
      What place is this?
      Where are we now?

10      I am the grass.
      Let me work.   ■

*What work does the grass do?*

---

1. **Austerlitz and Waterloo.** Northern European battle sites in the Napoleonic Wars
2. **Gettysburg.** Civil War battlefield in southern Pennsylvania where Confederate soldiers fought and lost
3. **Ypres and Verdun.** World War I battle sites in northern France where French soldiers fought and lost

## Respond *to the* SELECTION

Since the time of this poem, what battles and wars has the grass begun to cover?

# Inquire, *Imagine*

**Recall:** GATHERING FACTS

1a. Who is speaking in this poem?

2a. What do the passengers ask the conductor?

**Interpret:** FINDING MEANING

1b. What work does the grass do?

2b. What change occurs on the battlefields, over time, as a result of the work of the grass?

**Analyze:** TAKING THINGS APART

3a. What does the grass state and implore? What does the grass want to do?

**Synthesize:** BRINGING THINGS TOGETHER

3b. Explain why Sandburg personifies the grass.

**Evaluate:** MAKING JUDGMENTS

4a. The speaker of this poem does not think that soldiers and battles will be remembered forever. Do you agree with the attitude toward soldiers and battles the speaker expresses?

**Extend:** CONNECTING IDEAS

4b. Compare and contrast Walt Whitman's view of the grass in lines 30–50 of "Song of Myself" with Carl Sandburg's view in "Grass." Make a Venn diagram to show which views the poets share and which they do not. Then explain what the Venn diagram shows.

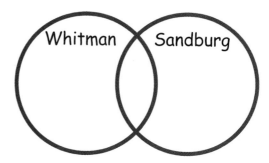

# Understanding *Literature*

**PERSONIFICATION.** Review the definition for **personification** in the Handbook of Literary Terms. What is personified in this poem?

**PARALLELISM.** Review the definition for **parallelism** in the Handbook of Literary Terms. What examples of parallelism can you find in this poem?

# Writer's Journal

1. Imagine that you are the grass. Write a **monument inscription** about what you have seen at Gettysburg for the tourists that visit the battlefield.

2. Imagine that you are a veteran of the Battle of Gettysburg. Write a **letter** to the national parks board arguing why the battlefield should not be covered with grass.

3. **Free verse** is poetry that avoids use of regular rhyme, meter, or division into stanzas. Write a **free verse poem** expressing your feelings about war for a classmate to read.

# Integrating *the* LANGUAGE ARTS

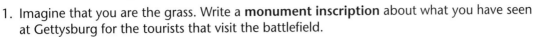

## Language, Grammar, and Style

**ACHIEVING PARALLELISM.** Read the Language Arts Survey 3.38, "Achieving Parallelism." Then rewrite the following sentences using parallel structure.

1. At Austerlitz, Napoleon won his most brilliant victory and had defeated the Russian and Austrian armies.

2. The Waterloo campaign was marked by confusion and miscalculating on all sides.

3. Both commanding generals of the Battle of Gettysburg have been criticized for their conduct—Lee for his authorization of Pickett's charge; Meade failed to organize his forces for a counterattack.

4. During the third battle of Ypres, the British advanced only five miles and were losing 300,000 men.

5. The battle of Verdun was one of the longest and bloodier engagements of World War I.

## Speaking and Listening & Collaborative Learning

**ORAL INTERPRETATION.** Form small groups of three or four students. As a group, select several of Carl Sandburg's poems that show him as the poet of America's common people. Take turns reading the poems. Listen to the presenter ahead of you and take notes on his or her poem. Then write a transition that connects that poem to yours. The first presenter should write a general introduction for the selected poems. Finally, videotape your presentations, including transitions and the introduction, and show the videotape to the class.

## Applied English

**SCRIPT.** Imagine that you are a tour guide at the Waterloo battlefield in Wallonia, the French-speaking part of Belgium. Research the Battle of Waterloo and write a script for the tourists that you can use as you give tours. If you use the Internet for your research, you may visit the website of the **Belgium Travel Network** at http://www.trabel.com/waterloo/waterloo.htm.

# Literary T O O L S

**DRAMATIC MONOLOGUE.** A **dramatic monologue** is a poem that presents the speech of a single character in a dramatic situation. The speech is one side of an imagined conversation. Identify the dramatic situation J. Alfred Prufrock is in as you read the poem.

**ALLUSION.** An **allusion** is a figure of speech in which a reference is made to a person, event, object, or work from history or literature. As you read the poem, identify as many allusions as you can.

# About *the* SELECTION

Eliot wrote **"The Love Song of J. Alfred Prufrock"** in 1910–1911 while a graduate student at Harvard. The poem, a dramatic monologue, presents the "conversation with himself" of J. Alfred Prufrock, a middle-aged man who hesitates to speak directly to the woman he loves. First published in *Poetry* magazine in 1915, the poem was later collected in *Prufrock and Other Observations and Poems.* In many ways, this poem is typical of Eliot's work, which is **elliptical,** leaving out nonessential details, and highly **allusive,** making reference to people, events, objects, or works from history or literature.

# "The Love Song of J. Alfred Prufrock"

BY T. S. ELIOT

## About *the* A U T H O R

**T(homas) S(tearns) Eliot** (1888–1965) was born in St. Louis, Missouri. He attended Milton Academy and Harvard University. In 1910, the year in which he earned his master's degree, he wrote one of his most famous poems, "The Love Song of J. Alfred Prufrock," a poem that was for its day radically experimental. During the pre-World War I period, Eliot attended the Sorbonne in Paris and studied Asian languages and religion. In 1915, following the outbreak of war, he moved to Oxford. A disappointment to his family, he supplemented his allowance by working as a bank teller. At the end of a difficult marriage to Vivian Haigh-Wood, Eliot received intensive psychiatric treatment for depression.

Then, with the help of another expatriate poet, Ezra Pound, he published "Prufrock" and caught the attention of the literary world. In 1922, again aided by Pound, Eliot published an even more challenging poem, "The Waste Land"—a view of the moral bankruptcy of the interwar period poised against what Eliot saw as the superior values of the past. In 1928, shortly after embracing British citizenship, Eliot became a member of the Church of England. He married Valerie Fletcher in 1957. In addition to his invaluable poetic achievements, Eliot made successful contributions to other literary forms, including plays and literary criticism. In 1948, he was awarded the Nobel Prize for literature. *The Complete Poems and Plays of T. S. Eliot* was published in 1969.

## Reader's *Journal*

Have you ever hesitated to tell someone how you felt about him or her? Explain why you hesitated and what you would have said if you had been able to speak frankly.

# The Love Song of J. Alfred Prufrock

## T. S. Eliot

*S'io credessi che mia risposta fosse*
*a persona che mai tornasse al mondo,*
*questa fiamma staria senza più scosse.*
*Ma per ciò che giammai di questo fondo*
*non tornò vivo alcun, s'i'odo il vero,*
*senza tema d'infamia ti rispondo.*[1]

---

1. **S'io . . . rispondo.** Epigraph from Dante's *Inferno*, Canto XXVII, lines 61–66. The speaker is one of the damned telling of his torment: "If I believed that my response would be / to somebody who would ever return to the world, / this flame would be without more movement. / But since nobody has returned from this depth alive, / if I hear the truth, / without fear of infamy, I answer you."

Let us go then, you and I,
When the evening is spread out against the sky
Like a patient etherised upon a table;
Let us go, through certain half-deserted streets,
5     The muttering retreats
Of restless nights in one-night cheap hotels
And sawdust restaurants with oyster-shells:
Streets that follow like a tedious argument
Of insidious intent
10    To lead you to an overwhelming question . . .
Oh, do not ask, "What is it?"
Let us go and make our visit.
In the room the women come and go
Talking of Michelangelo.[2]

15    The yellow fog that rubs its back upon the window-panes,
The yellow smoke that rubs its muzzle on the window-panes,
Licked its tongue into the corners of the evening,
Lingered upon the pools that stand in drains,
Let fall upon its back the soot that falls from chimneys,
20    Slipped by the terrace, made a sudden leap,
And seeing that it was a soft October night,
Curled once about the house, and fell asleep.

> *What curls around the house and falls asleep? What does the color suggest?*

And indeed there will be time
For the yellow smoke that slides along the street
25    Rubbing its back upon the window-panes;
There will be time, there will be time
To prepare a face to meet the faces that you meet;
There will be time to murder and create,
And time for all the works and days of hands
30    That lift and drop a question on your plate;
Time for you and time for me,
And time yet for a hundred indecisions,
And for a hundred visions and revisions,
Before the taking of a toast and tea.

35    In the room the women come and go
Talking of Michelangelo.

---

2. **Michelangelo.** (1475–1564) Italian sculptor, painter, architect, and poet

**WORDS FOR EVERYDAY USE**

e • ther • ize or Brit. e • ther • ise (ē´thə rīz´) *vt.*, render groggy or numb. *Dr. Bramwell etherized her patients before surgery.*

te • di • ous (tē´dē əs) *adj.*, long and tiresome. *We found the politician's dry, lengthy speech tedious.*

in • sid • i • ous (in sid´ē əs) *adj.*, deceitful. *We found it insidious that, though promising prompt delivery, the company did not deliver the product for six weeks.*

lin • ger (liŋ´gər) *vi.*, remain or stay longer than usual. *Daphne lingered after the lecture to ask the teacher a question.*

And indeed there will be time
To wonder, "Do I dare?" and, "Do I dare?"
Time to turn back and descend the stair,
40    With a bald spot in the middle of my hair—
(They will say: "How his hair is growing thin!")
My morning coat, my collar mounting firmly to the chin,
My necktie rich and modest, but <u>asserted</u> by a simple pin—
(They will say: "But how his arms and legs are thin!")
45    Do I dare
Disturb the universe?
In a minute there is time
For decisions and revisions which a minute will reverse.

For I have known them all already, known them all—
50    Have known the evenings, mornings, afternoons,
I have measured out my life with coffee spoons;
I know the voices dying with a dying fall
Beneath the music from a farther room.
        So how should I <u>presume</u>?

55    And I have known the eyes already, known them all—
The eyes that fix you in a <u>formulated</u> phrase,
And when I am formulated, sprawling on a pin,
When I am pinned and wriggling on the wall,
Then how should I begin
60    To spit out all the butt-ends of my days and ways?
        And how should I presume?

And I have known the arms already, known them all—
Arms that are braceleted and white and bare
(But in the lamplight, downed with light brown hair!)
65    Is it perfume from a dress
That makes me so <u>digress</u>?
Arms that lie along a table, or wrap about a shawl.
        And should I then presume?
        And how should I begin?

◆    ◆    ◆

70    Shall I say, I have gone at dusk through narrow streets
And watched the smoke that rises from the pipes

> Why might the speaker "turn back and descend the stair"?

> Does the speaker believe his life has been bold or fast-paced? Explain.

> In what way does Prufrock describe himself?

**WORDS FOR EVERYDAY USE**

**as • sert** (ə surt´) *vt.*, declare; affirm. *The puppy <u>asserted</u> its independence and ran down the block.*

**pre • sume** (pri züm´) *vi.*, dare; venture; take upon oneself. *I did not <u>presume</u> to raise my hand, even though I was quite sure of the answer.*

**for • mu • lat • ed** (fôr´ myə lāt´əd) *adj.*, systematical; precise. *His response seemed <u>formulated</u>, as he had planned his words earlier that morning.*

**di • gress** (dī gres´) *vi.*, deviate from the main topic in speaking or writing. *Cathy's story was hard to follow because she <u>digressed</u> often.*

Of lonely men in shirt-sleeves, leaning out of windows? . . .

I should have been a pair of ragged claws
Scuttling across the floors of silent seas.

◆   ◆   ◆

75    And the afternoon, the evening, sleeps so peacefully!
      Smoothed by long fingers,
      Asleep . . . tired . . . or it <u>malingers</u>,
      Stretched on the floor, here beside you and me.
      Should I, after tea and cakes and ices,
80    Have the strength to force the moment to its crisis?
      But though I have wept and fasted, wept and prayed,
      Though I have seen my head (grown slightly bald)
      brought in upon a platter,
      I am no prophet[3]—and here's no great matter;
      I have seen the moment of my greatness flicker,
85    And I have seen the eternal Footman hold my coat, and snicker,
      And in short, I was afraid.

      And would it have been worth it, after all,
      After the cups, the marmalade, the tea,
      Among the porcelain, among some talk of you and me,
90    Would it have been worth while,
      To have bitten off the matter with a smile,
      To have squeezed the universe into a ball
      To roll it towards some overwhelming question,
      To say: "I am Lazarus,[4] come from the dead,
95    Come back to tell you all, I shall tell you all"—
      If one, settling a pillow by her head,
          Should say: "That is not what I meant at all.
          That is not it, at all."

      And would it have been worth it, after all,
100   Would it have been worth while,
      After the sunsets and the dooryards and the sprinkled streets,
      After the novels, after the teacups, after the skirts that trail along
          the floor—

What is the "crisis" to which the speaker refers? Of what is he afraid?

---

3. **I am no prophet.** The head of the prophet John the Baptist
was brought to Princess Salome on a platter.
4. **Lazarus.** In John 11:1–44, Lazarus is resurrected.

WORDS FOR EVERYDAY USE

ma • lin • ger (mə liŋ´gər) vi., pretend illness. *The employee was fired because he frequently <u>malingered</u>, calling in sick even when he was in fine health.*

And this, and so much more?—
105 It is impossible to say just what I mean!
But as if a magic lantern threw the nerves in patterns on a
 screen:
Would it have been worth while
If one, settling a pillow or throwing off a shawl,
And turning toward the window, should say:
110   "That is not it at all,
   That is not what I meant, at all."

*What causes frustration? What patterns are projected?*

◆　◆　◆

No! I am not Prince Hamlet, nor was meant to be;
Am an attendant lord, one that will do
To swell a progress,[5] start a scene or two,
115 Advise the prince; no doubt, an easy tool,
<u>Deferential</u>, glad to be of use,
Politic, cautious, and meticulous;
Full of high sentence,[6] but a bit <u>obtuse</u>;
At times, indeed, almost ridiculous—
120 Almost, at times, the Fool.

*Does the speaker believe he is a hero, a main character, or a minor character? Explain.*

I grow old . . . I grow old . . .
I shall wear the bottoms of my trousers rolled.

Shall I part my hair behind? Do I dare to eat a peach?
I shall wear white flannel trousers, and walk upon the beach.
125 I have heard the mermaids singing, each to each.

I do not think that they will sing to me.

I have seen them riding seaward on the waves
Combing the white hair of the waves blown back
When the wind blows the water white and black.

130 We have lingered in the chambers of the sea
By sea-girls wreathed with seaweed red and brown
Till human voices wake us, and we drown. ■

---

5. **progress.** Procession
6. **sentence.** Opinions

**WORDS FOR EVERYDAY USE**

**def • er • en • tial** (def´ə ren´shəl) *adj.*, respectful. *Mr. Bloomquist was <u>deferential</u> to his clients.*

**ob • tuse** (əb tüs´) *adj.*, slow to understand or perceive; insensitive. *People who persist in polluting the environment act as if they are <u>obtuse</u>.*

If you were J. Alfred Prufrock and could find the courage, what would you say to the woman you love?

# INVESTIGATE Inquire, *Imagine*

## Recall: GATHERING FACTS

1a. In the first section of the poem (lines 1–74), where is the speaker going? Whom is he going to visit? What time of day is it? What actions is the speaker considering?

2a. In the second section of the poem (lines 75–111), what action is the speaker considering?

3a. In the third section of the poem (lines 112–132), does the speaker consider large or insignificant actions?

## Interpret: FINDING MEANING

1b. How does the speaker view himself physically and emotionally? What details in stanza 3 emphasize the difficulty the speaker has in committing himself to word or action?

2b. Of what is the speaker afraid? What does the speaker confess to himself?

3b. Why does the speaker not think that the mermaids "will sing to me"? What happens when Prufrock begins to picture himself in a romantic scene? In what sense does reality intrude upon his daydreams?

## Analyze: TAKING THINGS APART

4a. Identify the sea imagery used in the poem and what it reveals about the speaker's psychological state.

## Synthesize: BRINGING THINGS TOGETHER

4b. Explain in what ways "The Love Song of J. Alfred Prufrock" is a psychological study of a modern man.

## Evaluate: MAKING JUDGMENTS

5a. How accurate is "The Love Song of J. Alfred Prufrock" as a portrayal of a modern person?

## Extend: CONNECTING IDEAS

5b. When you experience a moment of self-doubt, what strategies are effective in building a more confident picture of yourself?

# Understanding *Literature*

DRAMATIC MONOLOGUE. Review the definition of **dramatic monologue** in Literary Tools on page 500. In what dramatic situation is J. Alfred Prufrock? What does Prufrock reveal about himself in the dramatic monologue that makes him sympathetic or unsympathetic?

ALLUSION. Review the definition of **allusion** in the Handbook of Literary Tools. Make a chart listing the allusions and explaining their meaning in the poem. One example has been done for you.

| Lines | Allusions | Meaning |
|---|---|---|
| Epigram | Canto 27, lines 61–66, of the *Inferno,* book one of *The Divine Comedy,* by the Italian poet Dante Alighieri. | The use of this passage implies that the "love song" is not sung in this world. Like Guido da Montefeltro, who is tortured in the eighth circle of hell for the sin of fraud through evil counsel, Prufrock is guilty of fraud because he has perverted human reason to pointless fantasy. |

# WRITER'S JOURNAL

1. Write a **letter** to J. Alfred Prufrock, telling him how he exaggerates his shortcomings and building up his self-confidence.
2. Using a couple of the allusions in "The Love Song of J. Alfred Prufrock," imagine yourself as Prufrock and write a **dream description** for a psychiatrist about a dream that you might have.
3. A **parody** is a literary work that imitates another work for humorous, often satirical, purposes. Write a **parody**, in free verse, on the topic of hesitation for a classmate to read.

# Integrating
## *the* LANGUAGE ARTS

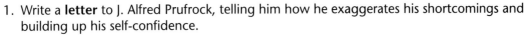

## Language, Grammar, and Style

**REPLACING LINKING VERBS WITH ACTION VERBS.** Read the Language Arts Survey 3.10, "Linking Verbs," and 3.60, "Action Verbs and State of Being Verbs." Then, revise each of the following sentences, using action verbs in place of linking verbs.

1. Eliot's "The Love Song of J. Alfred Prufrock" is melancholy.
2. Prufrock gives the reader an invitation to walk through "certain half-deserted streets."
3. Prufrock is a man with many worries, including concerns about his baldness.
4. Prufrock's hesitations are sources of frustration for the reader.
5. Prufrock is, at times, the Fool.

## Study and Research & Collaborative Learning

**RESEARCHING ALLUSIONS.** T. S. Eliot employs allusions that are expected to evoke in his readers echoes of other works and other ideas with the purpose of enriching the context of the poem and the original source. With a partner, research the original texts below, noting where you located each source. Then explain how Eliot changed the references for his own purposes and what point these allusions make in the stated lines of the poem.

| | | |
|---|---|---|
| Hesiod | "Works and Days" | Line 29 |
| William Shakespeare | Act 1, scene 1, line 4, of *Twelfth Night* | Line 52 |
| Emily Dickinson | "I cannot live with you" | Line 89 |
| Andrew Marvell | "To His Coy Mistress" | Line 92 |

## Speaking and Listening

**THINK ALOUD.** A "think aloud" is an oral activity in which you freely associate your ideas about a selection. With a partner, conduct a "think aloud" of "The Love Song of J. Alfred Prufrock." Alternate stanzas with your partner. Be sure to express as many thoughts as you have about the passages for which you are responsible. When you are the listening partner, offer positive comments and open-ended questions.

## Media Literacy

**SITUATION COMEDY.** Write a situation comedy episode about a man with J. Alfred Prufrock's psychological profile, changing the tragic elements to humorous ones.

# "MENDING WALL"

# "Home Burial"

BY ROBERT FROST

## Literary TOOLS

SYMBOL. A **symbol** is a thing that stands for or represents both itself and something else. As you read "Mending Wall," decide what the wall symbolizes.

CHARACTER. A **character** is a figure who participates in the action of a literary work. A *protagonist,* or *main character,* is the central figure in a literary work. An *antagonist* is a character who is pitted against a protagonist. Think about the characteristics of the speaker's neighbor as you read "Mending Wall." Is he the protagonist or the antagonist?

## Reader's Journal

Why do you think people build walls between themselves and others?

## About the AUTHOR

**Robert Frost** (1874–1963) was without question the most popular American poet of the twentieth century. Born in San Francisco, Frost moved to New England with his mother when his father died. He graduated at the top of his high school class, sharing the position of valedictorian with Elinor White, whom he later married. At the age of seventeen, he published his first poem. After a brief stint at Dartmouth, he worked as a bobbin boy in a cotton mill, a cobbler, a schoolteacher, and a journalist. Later, he entered Harvard but left after two years to try farming. In 1912, Frost took his family to England, and it was there that his poetry first found a major audience with the publication of *A Boy's Will* (1913) and *North of Boston* (1914).

After he returned to the United States, Frost began to achieve financial stability from the sale of his books. He taught and lectured at various colleges, including Dartmouth, Amherst, Harvard, and the University of Michigan. He was awarded Pulitzer Prizes in 1924, 1931, 1937, and 1943 and received honorary degrees from many universities. In 1961, he recited his poem "The Gift Outright" at the inauguration of John F. Kennedy, thirty-fifth president of the United States. In his later years, Frost also made several goodwill trips for the U.S. State Department.

Frost's many popular works, most of which deal with the character, people, and landscape of New England, include *Mountain Interval* (1916), *New Hampshire* (1923), *West-Running Brook* (1928), *A Way Out* (1929), *Collected Poems* (1930), *A Further Range* (1936), *A Witness Tree* (1942), *Steeple Bush* (1947), and *In the Clearing* (1962). Frost also wrote two plays in blank verse, *A Masque of Reason* (1945) and *A Masque of Mercy* (1947). Although rooted in New England subject matter, Frost's work goes beyond mere regionalism. The careful local observations and homely details of his poems often have deeper symbolic meanings. The poems are concerned with people's tragedies and fears, their reactions to the complexities of life, and their ultimate acceptance of life's burdens.

## "Home Burial"

### About the SELECTIONS

Robert Frost had a rare talent that enabled him to produce poetry simple and clear enough to appeal to a large audience and yet intellectually rich enough to appeal to sophisticated literary critics. Frost wrote often of the nature and people of his adopted home of New England. He wrote in the language of ordinary speech and didn't care for modern free verse, which he likened to "playing tennis without a net." Instead, he wrote in conventional forms, including **blank verse** made up of unrhymed iambic pentameter lines, as in **"Mending Wall"** and **"Home Burial."** (An iambic pentameter line has ten alternating weakly stressed and strongly stressed syllables: "And spills the upper boulders in the sun.")

Many of Frost's finest poems, such as the narrative poem "The Death of the Hired Man," in the Selections for Additional Reading on page 594, are **dramatic monologues** or **dramatic dialogues**. Such poems present a situation in which one or two people speak, sometimes to an imaginary audience.

### Literary TOOLS

**METAPHOR.** A **metaphor** is a figure of speech in which one thing is spoken or written about as if it were another. As you read the poem, look for the lines in which the man expresses his grief after digging the child's grave and determine what the lines mean metaphorically.

**DICTION. Diction,** when applied to writing, refers to word choice. Much of a writer's style or voice is determined by his or her diction, the types of words that are chosen, whether formal or informal, simple or complex, contemporary or archaic, ordinary or unusual, standard or dialectical. Find examples characteristic of the wife's diction as you read.

### Reader's Journal

Describe a failure of communication you experienced with someone you care about.

Robert Frost receives a congressional medal for his contribution to American literature from President Kennedy in 1962.

# MENDING WALL

## ROBERT FROST

Something there is that doesn't love a wall,
That sends the frozen-ground-swell[1] under it,
And spills the upper boulders in the sun,
And makes gaps even two can pass abreast.
5   The work of hunters is another thing:
I have come after them and made repair
Where they have left not one stone on a stone,
But they would have the rabbit out of hiding,
To please the yelping dogs. The gaps I mean,
10   No one has seen them made or heard them made,
But spring mending-time we find them there.
I let my neighbor know beyond the hill;
And on a day we meet to walk the line
And set the wall between us once again.

> *What do the speaker and his neighbor do together?*

---

1. **frozen-ground-swell.** Winter ground heaves

15       We keep the wall between us as we go.
              To each the boulders that have fallen to each.
              And some are loaves and some so nearly balls
              We have to use a spell to make them balance:
              "Stay where you are until our backs are turned!"
20       We wear our fingers rough with handling them.
              Oh, just another kind of outdoor game.
              One on a side. It comes to little more;
              There where it is we do not need the wall:
              He is all pine and I am apple orchard.
25       My apple trees will never get across
              And eat the cones under his pines, I tell him.
              He only says, "Good fences make good neighbors."
              Spring is the mischief in me, and I wonder
              If I could put a notion in his head:
30       "*Why* do they make good neighbors? Isn't it
              Where there are cows? But here there are no cows.
              Before I built a wall I'd ask to know
              What I was walling in or walling out,
              And to whom I was like to give offense.
35       Something there is that doesn't love a wall,
              That wants it down." I could say "Elves" to him,
              But it's not elves exactly, and I'd rather
              He said it for himself. I see him there
              Bringing a stone grasped firmly by the top
40       In each hand, like an old-stone savage armed.
              He moves in darkness as it seems to me,
              Not of woods only and the shade of trees.
              He will not go behind his father's saying,
              And he likes having thought of it so well
45       He says again, "Good fences make good neighbors." ∎

**Respond** *to the*
## SELECTION

Do you agree that good fences make good neighbors? Why, or why not?

# INVESTIGATE Inquire, Imagine

**Recall:** GATHERING FACTS

1a. What is the wall like in the spring? What has torn down the wall? Why does the speaker contact his neighbor?

2a. What does the speaker tell his neighbor as they repair the wall that is a reason not to build the fence? What quote does the speaker's neighbor repeat?

3a. What would the speaker like to know before he builds a wall?

**Interpret:** FINDING MEANING

1b. The speaker says, "Something there is that doesn't love a wall." What doesn't? Which character makes an attempt at friendship? How does he make this attempt? What is ironic about the wall?

2b. Why might the neighbor want to have a wall where one is not absolutely necessary? What does the neighbor's desire for a wall tell you about him?

3b. How does the neighbor look, according to the speaker? What reveals that the speaker doesn't totally trust his neighbor?

**Analyze:** TAKING THINGS APART

4a. Identify the clues that reveal the relationship between the speaker and his neighbor.

**Synthesize:** BRINGING THINGS TOGETHER

4b. Considering the nature of their relationship, who do you think makes a better neighbor, and why?

**Evaluate:** MAKING JUDGMENTS

5a. How effective is the speaker in getting the neighbor to consider a new perspective about the wall?

**Extend:** CONNECTING IDEAS

5b. Besides walls or fences, what other things keep neighbors apart?

# Understanding Literature

**SYMBOL.** Review the definition for **symbol** in the Handbook of Literary Terms. What does the wall in the poem symbolize? Why does the speaker question the value of walls?

**CHARACTER.** Review the definition for **character** in the Handbook of Literary Terms. Then fill in the character chart below for the speaker's neighbor. One example has been done for you. Is the speaker's neighbor the protagonist or the antagonist?

| Physical Appearance | Dress | Habits/Mannerisms/ Behaviors | Relationships with Other People | Other |
|---|---|---|---|---|
| "an old-stone savage armed" | | | | |

**Stairway to the Studio,** 1924. Charles Sheeler.
Philadelphia Museum of Art.

# Home Burial[1]

## ROBERT FROST

He saw her from the bottom of the stairs
Before she saw him. She was starting down,
Looking back over her shoulder at some fear.
She took a doubtful step and then undid it
5     To raise herself and look again. He spoke
Advancing toward her: "What is it you see
From up there always—for I want to know."
She turned and sank upon her skirts at that,
And her face changed from terrified to dull.
10   He said to gain time: "What is it you see,"
Mounting[2] until she <u>cowered</u> under him.
"I will find out now—you must tell me, dear."
She, in her place, refused him any help
With the least stiffening of her neck and silence.

---

1. **Home Burial.** Reference to the custom of keeping a family cemetery on one's property
2. **Mounting.** Climbing

**WORDS FOR EVERYDAY USE**

**cow • er** (kou´ər) *vi.,* crouch or shrink back in fear. *The child <u>cowered</u> before his angry parent.*

15    She let him look, sure that he wouldn't see,
Blind creature; and awhile he didn't see.
But at last he murmured, "Oh," and again, "Oh."

"What is it—what?" she said.

                      "Just that I see."

20    "You don't," she challenged. "Tell me what it is."

"The wonder is I didn't see at once.
I never noticed it from here before.
I must be wonted to it[3]—that's the reason.
The little graveyard where my people are!
25    So small the window frames the whole of it.
Not so much larger than a bedroom, is it?
There are three stones of slate and one of marble,
Broad-shouldered little slabs there in the sunlight
On the sidehill. We haven't to mind *those*.
30    But I understand: it is not the stones,
But the child's mound—"

                "Don't, don't, don't, don't," she cried.

She withdrew shrinking from beneath his arm
That rested on the banister, and slid downstairs;
35    And turned on him with such a daunting[4] look,
He said twice over before he knew himself:
"Can't a man speak of his own child he's lost?"

"Not you!—Oh, where's my hat? Oh, I don't need it!
I must get out of here. I must get air.—
40    I don't know rightly whether any man can."

"Amy! Don't go to someone else this time.
Listen to me. I won't come down the stairs."
He sat and fixed his chin between his fists.
"There's something I should like to ask you, dear."

45    "You don't know how to ask it."
                        "Help me, then."

Her fingers moved the latch for all reply.

What does the man see?

---

3. **wonted to it.** Used to it
4. **daunting.** Challenging

"My words are nearly always an offense.
I don't know how to speak of anything
50   So as to please you. But I might be taught
I should suppose. I can't say I see how.
A man must partly give up being a man
With womenfolk. We could have some arrangement
By which I'd bind myself to keep hands off
55   Anything special you're a-mind to name.
Though I don't like such things twixt those that love.
Two that don't love can't live together without them.
But two that do can't live together with them."
She moved the latch a little. "Don't—don't go.
60   Don't carry it to someone else this time.
Tell me about it if it's something human.
Let me into your grief. I'm not so much
Unlike other folks as your standing there
Apart would make me out. Give me my chance.
65   I do think, though, you overdo it a little.
What was it brought you up to think it the thing
To take your mother-loss of a first child
So inconsolably—in the face of love.
You'd think his memory might be satisfied—"

70   "There you go sneering now!"

                              "I'm not, I'm not!
You make me angry. I'll come down to you.
God, what a woman! And it's come to this,
A man can't speak of his own child that's dead."

75   "You can't because you don't know how to speak.
If you had any feelings, you that dug
With your own hand—how could you?—his little grave;
I saw you from that very window there,
Making the gravel leap and leap in air,
80   Leap up, like that, like that, and land so lightly
And roll back down the mound beside the hole.
I thought, Who is that man? I didn't know you.
And I crept down the stairs and up the stairs
To look again, and still your spade kept lifting.
85   Then you came in. I heard your rumbling voice
Out in the kitchen, and I don't know why,
But I went near to see with my own eyes.
You could sit there with the stains on your shoes
Of the fresh earth from your own baby's grave

Does the man think he and his wife should agree to not speak about some things? Why, or why not?

90      And talk about your everyday concerns.
        You had stood the spade up against the wall
        Outside there in the entry, for I saw it."

        "I shall laugh the worst laugh I ever laughed.
        I'm cursed. God, if I don't believe I'm cursed."

Why does the man feel bitter?

95      "I can repeat the very words you were saying:
        'Three foggy mornings and one rainy day
        Will rot the best birch fence a man can build.'
        Think of it, talk like that at such a time!
        What had how long it takes a birch to rot
100     To do with what was in the darkened parlor?
        You *couldn't* care! The nearest friends can go
        With anyone to death, comes so far short
        They might as well not try to go at all.
        No, from the time when one is sick to death,
105     One is alone, and he dies more alone.
        Friends make pretense of following to the grave,
        But before one is in it, their minds are turned
        And making the best of their way back to life
        And living people, and things they understand.
110     But the world's evil. I won't have grief so
        If I can change it. Oh, I won't, I won't!"

Why does Amy think friends might as well not go to the burial?

        "There, you have said it all and you feel better.
        You won't go now. You're crying. Close the door.
        The heart's gone out of it: why keep it up?
115     Amy! There's someone coming down the road!"

        "*You*—oh, you think the talk is all. I must go—
        Somewhere out of this house. How can I make you—"

        "If—you—do!" She was opening the door wider.
        "Where do you mean to go? First tell me that.
120     I'll follow and bring you back by force. I *will!*—"  ∎

Where does the man think his wife is going?

**Respond** *to the*
# SELECTION

If you were the wife, what would keep you from understanding your husband's grief?

## Letter to *The Amherst Student*

### by Robert Frost

*T*he Letter to The Amherst Student, *a college newspaper, appeared on March 25, 1935, and was written in response to the paper's congratulating Frost on reaching his sixtieth birthday. He took the occasion of this response to provide some words of wisdom, his message to the young people of the Modern Age.*

It is very, very kind of the *Student* to be showing sympathy with me for my age. But sixty is only a pretty good age. It is not advanced enough. The great thing is to be advanced. Now ninety would be really well along and something to be given credit for.

But speaking of ages, you will often hear it said that the age of the world we live in is particularly bad. I am impatient of such talk. We have no way of knowing that this age is one of the worst in the world's history. Arnold[1] claimed the honor for the age before this. Wordsworth[2] claimed it for the last but one. And so on back through literature. I say they claimed the honor for their ages. They claimed it rather for themselves. It is immodest of a man to think of himself as going down before the worst forces ever mobilized by God.

All ages of the world are bad—a great deal worse anyway than Heaven. If they weren't the world might just as well be Heaven at once and have it over with. One can safely say after from six to thirty thousand years of experience that the evident design is a situation here in which it will always be about equally hard to save your soul. Whatever progress may be taken to mean, it can't mean making the world any easier a place in which to save your soul—or if you dislike hearing your soul mentioned in open meeting, say your decency, your integrity.

Ages may vary a little. One may be a little worse than another. But it is not possible to get outside the age you are in to judge it exactly. Indeed it is as dangerous to try to get outside of anything as large as an age as it would be to engorge a donkey. Witness the many who in the attempt have suffered a dilation from which the tissues and the muscles of the mind have never been able to recover natural shape. They can't pick up anything delicate or small any more. They can't use a pen. They have to use a typewriter. And they gape in agony. They can write huge shapeless novels, huge gobs of raw sincerity bellowing with pain and that's all that they can write.

Fortunately we don't need to know how bad the age is. There is something we can always be doing without reference to how good or bad the age is. There is at least so much good in the world that it admits of form and the making of form. And not only admits of it, but calls for it. We people are thrust forward out of the suggestions of form in the rolling clouds of nature. In us nature reaches its height of form and through us exceeds itself. When in doubt there is always form for us to go on with. Anyone who has achieved the least form to be sure of it, is lost to the larger excruciations. I think it must stroke faith the right way. The artist [,] the poet [,] might be expected to be the most aware of such assurance. But it is really everybody's sanity to feel it and live by it. Fortunately, too, no forms are more engrossing [,] gratifying, comforting, staying than those lesser ones we throw off, like vortex rings of smoke, all our individual enterprise and needing nobody's co-operation; a basket, a letter, a garden, a room, an idea, a picture, a poem. For these we haven't to get a team together before we can play.

The background in hugeness and confusion shading away from where we stand into black and utter chaos; and against the background any small man-made figure of order and concentration. What pleasanter than that this should be so? Unless we are novelists or economists we don't worry about this confusion; we look out on [it] with an instrument or tackle it to reduce it. It is partly because we are afraid it might prove too much for us and our blend of democratic-republican-socialist-communist-anarchist party. But it is more because we like it, we were born to it, born used to it and have practical reasons for wanting it there. To me any little form I assert upon it is velvet,[3] as the saying is, and to be considered for how much more it is than nothing. If I were a Platonist[4] I should have to consider it, I suppose, for how much less it is than everything. ∎

---

1. **Arnold.** Matthew Arnold (1822–1888) was one of the foremost poets and critics of the Victorian Age in England.
2. **Wordsworth.** William Wordsworth (1770–1850) was one of the leading poets of the Romantic Movement in England.
3. **is velvet.** Literally, like velvet cloth, soft and comfortable; figuratively, a luxury, something that brings comfort
4. **Platonist.** A follower of Plato, the ancient Greek philosopher who believed that things in the world were but reflections or imitations of pure forms that existed in the transcendent realm of ideas. Plato didn't think much of art, which he considered an imitation of nature and thus, to him, an imitation of an imitation of ideal form.

# INVESTIGATE Inquire, Imagine

**Recall:** GATHERING FACTS

1a. What does the husband see before his wife sees him? What does the husband come to understand she sees?

2a. What kind of "creature" does the wife think her husband is (line 16)?

3a. What are the husband's words "nearly always" to his wife (line 48)?

→ **Interpret:** FINDING MEANING

1b. How might the wife's actions have been different if she had seen her husband watching her at the top of the stair?

2b. Why does the wife challenge the husband to tell her what he sees? What doesn't the wife understand about her husband?

3b. How does the husband demonstrate he cares about fixing the rupture in their marriage?

**Analyze:** TAKING THINGS APART

4a. What differences exist in how the husband and wife express their grief about the death of their infant son? How has the death of their child ruptured their marriage?

→ **Synthesize:** BRINGING THINGS TOGETHER

4b. Predict what will happen to the husband and wife beyond the end of the poem.

**Evaluate:** MAKING JUDGMENTS

5a. Compare the styles of grieving of the husband and the wife. Which is more understandable?

→ **Extend:** CONNECTING IDEAS

5b. If you were a friend of the couple, what obstacles in their characters and relationship would you have to help them overcome in order to have a healthy marriage?

# Understanding Literature

**METAPHOR.** Review the definition for **metaphor** in the Handbook of Literary Terms. Consider the following lines in "Home Burial": "I can repeat the very words you were saying: / 'Three foggy mornings and one rainy day / Will rot the best birch fence a man can build.'" How are these lines an expression of the man's sense of loss? Does his wife understand that they are such an expression? What does she think that they mean? What has happened to the communication between the man and woman?

**DICTION.** Review the definition for **diction** in the Handbook of Literary Terms. Then make a chart. On the left, write examples of the wife's speech. On the right, identify the type of diction the quotations exemplify.

| What the Wife Says | Type of Diction |
|---|---|
| "I saw you from that very window there, / Making the gravel leap and leap in air, / Leap up, like that, like that, and land so lightly / And roll back down the mound beside the hole." | The wife is excited and upset, and the repetitious diction of these lines reflects that mood. |

# WRITER'S JOURNAL

1. Imagine you are the speaker in "Mending Wall." Write a **letter** to your neighbor, stating what you think makes for good neighbors besides a fence.

2. Imagine that you are a therapist for the husband and wife in "Home Burial." Write a **monologue** giving the couple suggestions on how to improve their communication about their grief over their child's death. Provide separate suggestions for the husband and the wife.

3. Imagine that you are Robert Frost. Write a **paragraph** for *The Amherst Student* explaining what writing a poem means to you. Imagine the paragraph is the last paragraph of the Letter to *The Amherst Student* in which Frost clearly summarizes his philosophy about creativity and form.

# Integrating
## *the* LANGUAGE ARTS

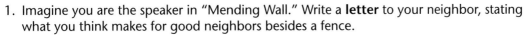

## Language, Grammar, and Style

**THE FUNCTIONS OF SENTENCES.** Read the Language Arts Survey 3.17, "Functions of Sentences." Then, decide what the function is of each of the following sentences from the selections. Write the classification of each sentence.

1. Something there is that doesn't love a wall.
2. "Tell me what it is."
3. "Can't a man speak of his own child he's lost?"
4. There is at least so much good in the world that it admits of form and the making of form.
5. "There you go sneering now!"

## Speaking and Listening & Collaborative Learning

**CONFLICT RESOLUTION.** Read the Language Arts Survey 4.7, "Communicating with Another Person." With a partner, play the roles of a husband and wife having an argument. It might be about how to discipline one of their children, how to spend money, or where to go for a family vacation. Decide what your beginning positions are, then discuss the problem, and offer suggestions until you finally resolve the conflict.

## Media Literacy

**TIME LINE.** Read Frost's biography on the Internet. One site that provides poets' biographies is the **Academy of American Poets** at www.poets.org. Then make a time line of key personal and literary events in Frost's life.

## Study and Research

**MODERNIST PAINTING.** Research a modernist painting that interests you. You might get ideas by looking at the modernist art in this unit. Then make a poster. On the poster, write a description of what makes the painting modernist and attach a copy of the painting. Copies can be photocopied from art books or found on postcards or posters available in art supply shops, frame shops, museum stores, and bookstores.

# "The Snow Man"

# "Thirteen Ways of Looking at a Blackbird"

BY WALLACE STEVENS

## About the AUTHOR

**Wallace Stevens** (1879–1955) was born and raised in Reading, Pennsylvania. His day-to-day life was conventional. After spending three years at Harvard, he went to work for the *New York Herald Tribune,* but not liking this work, he left and went to the New York Law School. He was admitted to the bar in 1904 and maintained a private law practice until 1908, when he joined the legal staff of an insurance company. In 1916, he joined the Hartford Accident and Indemnity Company and moved to Hartford, Connecticut. In 1934, he was made a vice president of the company, a position he held until his death. Few of his colleagues knew that he wrote poetry. Five years before his death, he told a reporter, "It gives a man character as a poet to have this daily contact with a job."

Stevens began writing poetry in high school and had some of his poetry published in the *Harvard Advocate.* His debut in a larger arena began, however, with the publication of some of his work in the magazine *Poetry* in 1914. *Harmonium,* his first volume, was published in 1923. While he lived in New York, Stevens was briefly involved in literary circles, but he dropped out of these after moving to Hartford. Unlike other poets of the time, he was not interested in political and social causes, so although he maintained an active correspondence with some literary figures like William Carlos Williams and Marianne Moore, his work as a poet did not drive the course of his life. His *Collected Poems* (1954) won a Pulitzer Prize and the National Book Award. Among his other works are *Ideas of Order* (1935), *The Man with the Blue Guitar* (1937), *Parts of a World* (1942), and *The Auroras of Autumn* (1950).

## About the SELECTIONS

These two selections were published in Stevens's first book of poems, *Harmonium,* which includes some of his finest work. The poems, while very different in subject matter, both treat a common theme found in much of Stevens's poetry: the nature of perception and its relationship to the imagination. The first poem, **"The Snow Man,"** deals with what is known as the pathetic fallacy, the tendency of people to interpret nature in human ways and attribute to it human feelings and motivations. The second, **"Thirteen Ways of Looking at a Blackbird,"** shows how the same object of perception, in this case a blackbird, can yield different meanings, depending on the attitude and imagination of the perceiver.

## Literary TOOLS

**PATHETIC FALLACY.** The **pathetic fallacy** is the tendency to attribute human emotions to nonhuman things, particularly to things in the natural world. As you read the "The Snow Man," decide what Stevens's attitude toward nature is.

## ArtNote

*Winter Chaos—Blizzard.* Marsden Hartley (1877–1943) was born in Maine and often used its rugged landscape as his subject. Inspired by transcendalist writers Emerson, Thoreau, and Whitman, Hartley sought to represent a spiritual power in nature with his paintings. What feelings do you think winter evoked for Marsden Hartley?

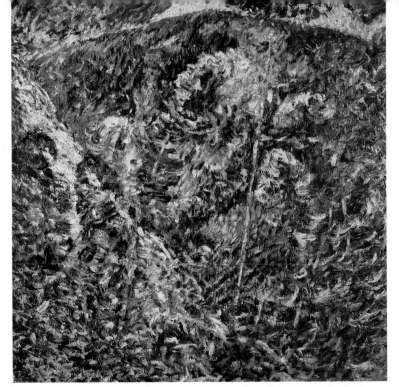

*Winter Chaos—Blizzard*, c.1909–1911. Marsden Hartley.

# The Snow man

## WALLACE STEVENS

One must have a mind of winter
To regard the frost and the boughs
Of the pine-trees crusted with snow;

5     And have been cold a long time
To behold the junipers shagged with ice,
The spruces rough in the distant glitter

Of the January sun; and not to think
Of any misery in the sound of the wind,
In the sound of a few leaves,

10    Which is the sound of the land
Full of the same wind
That is blowing in the same bare place

For the listener, who listens in the snow,
And, nothing himself, beholds
15    Nothing that is not there and the nothing that is. ∎

*What must one have in order to observe winter and not think of misery "in the sound of the wind"?*

*What is the "sound of the land"?*

## Reader's Journal

What feelings do spring, summer, fall, and winter evoke in you?

INVESTIGATE

# Inquire, *Imagine*

**Recall:** GATHERING FACTS

1a. What time of year does this poem describe? What details are used in the description of the poem's setting?

2a. What kind of mind does the speaker say a person must have not to think that there is misery in the sound of the wind and the leaves?

3a. What does the poem say that the snowman is? What does the snowman behold?

→ **Interpret:** FINDING MEANING

1b. How do the details of the setting make you respond?

2b. What characteristics would a "mind of winter" have?

3b. What comment is the speaker making about the differences between people and objects in nature?

**Evaluate:** MAKING JUDGMENTS

4a. How effectively does Stevens depict winter and the emotions associated with it?

→ **Extend:** CONNECTING IDEAS

4b. Stevens centers his poem around a snowman to show that, unlike humans, natural objects cannot perceive. If Stevens were to apply the concept of this poem to fall, spring, and summer, around what might he center each seasonal poem?

# Understanding *Literature*

PATHETIC FALLACY. Review the definition for **pathetic fallacy** in the Handbook of Literary Terms. Then consider this small poem:

> Other People's Sorrow
>
> In its extemity,
> on the farthest hill,
> the willow weeps
> alone.
> —Robin Lamb

In this poem, a willow tree is imagined as weeping and as being alone. The title of the poem invites the reader to compare the isolation of the willow to the isolation of a person who is feeling sorrow. How does Stevens's depiction of the snowman differ from Lamb's depiction of the willow? What do people sometimes see in nature that is not there, according to "The Snow Man"? In what sense is there "nothing" in nature until it is perceived by a human being?

*Raven in Moonlight,* 1943. Morris Graves.
North Carolina Museum of Art, Raleigh.

# Thirteen Ways of Looking at a Blackbird

## WALLACE STEVENS

## Literary
### TOOLS

**IMAGE AND IMAGERY.** An **image** is language that creates a concrete representation of an object or an experience. An image is also the vivid mental picture created in the reader's mind by that language. The images in a literary work are referred to, collectively, as the work's **imagery**. As you read "Thirteen Ways of Looking at a Blackbird," think about what the primary image throughout the poem is.

**ABSTRACT AND CONCRETE.** An **abstract** word or phrase is one that refers to something that cannot be directly perceived by the senses. *Freedom, power,* and *dignity* are examples of abstract terms. A **concrete** word or phrase is one that describes something that can be directly perceived by one or more of the five senses. Examples of concrete terms include *rainbow, lark,* and *scorpion.* Look for concrete and abstract terms as you read "Thirteen Ways of Looking at a Blackbird."

## Reader's
### Journal

When you think of blackbirds, what images come to mind?

I

Among twenty snowy mountains,
The only moving thing
Was the eye of the blackbird.

*What was the "only moving thing"?*

II

I was of three minds,
5  Like a tree
In which there are three blackbirds.

### III

The blackbird whirled in the autumn winds.
It was a small part of the pantomime.

### IV

A man and a woman
10  Are one.
A man and a woman and a blackbird
Are one.

### V

I do not know which to prefer,
The beauty of inflections
15  Or the beauty of innuendoes,[1]
The blackbird whistling
Or just after.

### VI

Icicles filled the long window
With barbaric[2] glass.
20  The shadow of the blackbird
Crossed it, to and fro.
The mood
Traced in the shadow
An indecipherable cause.

### VII

25  O thin men of Haddam,[3]
Why do you imagine golden birds?
Do you not see how the blackbird
Walks around the feet
Of the women about you?

### VIII

30  I know noble accents
And lucid, inescapable rhythms;
But I know, too,
That the blackbird is involved
In what I know.

*What does the speaker know?*

---

1. **innuendoes.** Hints
2. **barbaric.** Wild
3. **Haddam.** Town in Connecticut

---

**WORDS FOR EVERYDAY USE**

**pan • to • mime** (pan´tə mīm´) *n.*, gesture without speech. *The action of silent movies was like a pantomime, highly dependent on gestures.*

**in • flec • tion** (in flek´shən) *n.*, change in pitch or tone of voice. *The sharp inflection in our mother's voice clued us in that she was angry.*

**in • de • ci • pher • a • ble** (in dē sī´fər ə bəl) *adj.*, incapable of being interpreted. *The message was indecipherable; even the experts could not understand it.*

**lu • cid** (lü´sid) *adj.*, easily understood. *Because of the professor's excellent explanation, the chapter on the causes of World War I was lucid to Josh.*

IX

35  When the blackbird flew out of sight,
    It marked the edge
    Of one of many circles.

X

    At the sight of blackbirds
    Flying in a green light,
40  Even the bawds of <u>euphony</u>
    Would cry out sharply.

XI

    He rode over Connecticut
    In a glass coach.
    Once, a fear pierced him,
45  In that he mistook
    The shadow of his equipage[4]
    For blackbirds.

XII

    The river is moving.
    The blackbird must be flying.

XIII

50  It was evening all afternoon.
    It was snowing
    And it was going to snow.
    The blackbird sat
    In the cedar-limbs. ■

*Why did it seem like "evening all afternoon"?*

---

4. **equipage.** Refers to his coach

**WORDS FOR EVERYDAY USE**

eu • pho • ny (yü´fə nē) *n.,* pleasing or sweet sound. *The <u>euphony</u> of the symphony relaxed Sophie.*

# Respond *to the* SELECTION

Which of the "Thirteen Ways of Looking at a Blackbird" do you find most interesting? Why?

# Inquire, *Imagine*

**Recall:** GATHERING FACTS

1a. In stanza 1, what does the speaker see "Among twenty snowy mountains"?

2a. In stanza 2, to what does the speaker compare three blackbirds?

3a. In stanza 3, what did the blackbird do in the autumn winds?

4a. In stanza 4, what groups of things are described as being "one"?

5a. In stanza 5, what two aspects of human speech does the speaker of the poem compare to a blackbird whistling and "just after"?

6a. In stanza 6, what scene is described?

7a. In stanza 7, what do the men of Haddam look like? What do they imagine? What question does the speaker put to them?

8a. In stanza 8, what does the speaker know?

➤ **Interpret:** FINDING MEANING

1b. What kind of eyesight would a person need to be able to see the eye of a blackbird move "Among twenty snowy mountains"? In what way is the perceptive power of the imagination greater than the perceptive power of the senses?

2b. In what circumstance might a person be "of three minds"?

3b. What is the "pantomime" referred to in stanza 3?

4b. In what circumstances are a man and a woman often spoken of as being "one"? Some critics have suggested that stanza 4 is a kind of joke in which the speaker demonstrates the absurdity of thinking of two people as one. If that reading of the stanza is accepted, why does the speaker say that "A man and a woman and a blackbird / Are one"? Suppose that the stanza is not a joke but is meant to be taken seriously. How might a man, a woman, and a blackbird become one? What does this imply about the blackbird?

5b. How is an inflection like a blackbird whistling? How is an innuendo like "just after"?

6b. What mood, or feeling, does the scene create? Why might the speaker consider a natural world that would create such a mood "indecipherable"? Where does the mood come from?

7b. What might the "golden birds" represent? What kind of image is the blackbird walking around women's feet? How does nature violate people's dreams? Does the speaker favor dreams or the real world?

8b. A poet is someone who has command of "noble accents / And lucid, inescapable rhythms." However, such a person does not necessarily come by these on his or her own. What role does nature play in teaching the poet his or her trade?

9a. In stanza 9, what did the blackbird touch when it flew out of sight?

9b. The point at which the blackbird disappears from sight marks the limits of the speaker's physical perception. What lies beyond the limits of the circle of one's physical perception? What can one perceive beyond one's physical senses? On what is the imagination dependent?

10a. In stanza 10, who would cry out "At the sight of blackbirds / Flying in a green light"?

10b. Imagine a poet who normally writes only euphonious, pleasant-sounding verse. What kinds of subjects might force such a poet to "cry out sharply"?

11a. In stanza 11, what does the man ride in? What causes him to feel fear?

11b. What kind of life does the man live? Of what might the blackbirds be an omen? What does the glass coach symbolize?

12a. In stanza 12, what is moving? What must be flying?

12b. The ancient Greek philosopher Heraclitus wrote that "You can never step into the same river twice." What similar statement about the nature of the world is made by the speaker in stanza 12?

13a. In stanza 13, what does the afternoon look like? What is unchanging?

13b. How might the speaker feel? In what sense are both the speaker and the blackbird "waiting it out"?

**Analyze:** TAKING THINGS APART

14a. Blackbirds are generally associated with isolation, sadness, and despair. Identify stanzas in which these emotions are expressed.

**Synthesize:** BRINGING THINGS TOGETHER

14b. Why does Stevens show thirteen different ways of looking at blackbirds?

# Understanding *Literature*

IMAGE AND IMAGERY. Review the definitions for **image** and **imagery** in Literary Tools on page 523. What primary image is used throughout the poem? How does the winter setting in many of the poem's stanzas contribute to the poem's imagery?

ABSTRACT AND CONCRETE. Review the definitions for **abstract** and **concrete** in the Handbook of Literary Terms. Then make a chart to classify the terms found in stanza 5 as abstract or concrete.

One example has been done for you.

| Abstract | Concrete |
|---|---|
| beauty |  |
|  |  |
|  |  |

# WRITER'S JOURNAL

1. Write an **introduction** for a public television feature on "Thirteen Ways of Looking at a Blackbird." Give an example of how Stevens demonstrates that the nature of perception is related to the imagination.

2. Write a **paragraph** for Wallace Stevens describing a season of your choice. Use the pathetic fallacy to attribute human emotions and motivations to elements of the season.

3. Choose a concrete thing, such as an oak tree, a garden, a beach, a pair of sneakers, or a backpack. Then write a **poem** with three stanzas to share with a classmate, having each stanza demonstrate a different perspective of the thing you chose.

# Integrating *the* LANGUAGE ARTS

## Vocabulary

**BASE WORDS AND PREFIXES.** Read the Language Arts Survey 1.19, "Learning Base Words, Prefixes, and Suffixes." Then, on your own paper, underline the base word once and the prefix twice in each of the following words from "Thirteen Ways of Looking at a Blackbird." Next write the meaning of each word, consulting this text or a dictionary.

1. inflections    2. innuendoes    3. indecipherable    4. inescapable

## Speaking and Listening & Collaborative Learning

**ORAL INTERPRETATION.** A common theme in Wallace Stevens's poetry is the nature of perception and its relationship to the imagination. For everyone in your small group, select a Stevens poem that deals with this theme. You may want to review the Language Arts Survey 4.19, "Oral Interpretation of Poetry." Then sit in a circle and take turns reading aloud the poems. As you listen to the speaker before you, take notes on the poem he or she presents. Then write a transition to present a logical segue to your selection. The first presenter should write a general introduction to the selections. Finally, videotape your presentations, including transitional statements and the introduction, and play the videotape for the class.

## Study and Research

**RESEARCHING POETRY CRITICISM.** Locate and read Wallace Stevens's long poem "Notes toward a Supreme Fiction," in which he elaborates on the poet's role in creating the fictions necessary to transform and harmonize the world. Then compare and contrast Stevens's views with those expressed by Robert Frost in his letter to *The Amherst Student.* You may want to review using comparison and contrast order in the Language Arts Survey 2.24, "Organizing Ideas."

# *"this is just to say"*

# "**The Red Wheelbarrow**"

BY WILLIAM CARLOS WILLIAMS

## About *the* AUTHOR

**William Carlos Williams** (1883–1963) was born in Rutherford, New Jersey. After graduating from high school, he began studying to become a dentist, but he soon switched to medicine. In college he met and became friends with Ezra Pound, who would become one of the most influential American literary figures, and Hilda Doolittle, who later achieved fame as the poet and novelist, H. D. These relationships fed his interest in literature and poetry and changed his career plans even as he was completing his medical internship in New York City and doing postgraduate study in Leipzig, Germany.

In 1912, Williams married and settled in Rutherford, where he began his medical practice. Specializing in pediatrics, Williams delivered thousands of babies, made house calls, and gained a reputation as a dedicated, old-fashioned doctor. He lived and practiced medicine in Rutherford for the rest of his life. It was an occupation that supported his poetry and his other writing. He was active in local politics and helped found several small magazines. In the 1930s and 1940s, he occasionally supported leftist causes, which later resulted in his not receiving the post of consultant in poetry at the Library of Congress. A heart attack in 1948 and a series of strokes later caused him to cede his medical practice to one of his two sons, and by 1961 he had stopped writing because of his health. Williams was awarded the National Book Award in 1950, the Bollingen Prize in 1953, and the Pulitzer Prize in 1962 for *Pictures from Brueghel,* among other honors. His other works include *Spring and All* (1923), *The Edge of the Knife* (1932), *The Wedge* (1944), and an epic poem with a city as its hero, *Paterson* (1946–1958).

## About *the* SELECTIONS

A map of Williams's lifelong journey in pursuit of the American idiom can be read in these two poems. **"The Red Wheelbarrow,"** one of Williams's earlier poems, reflects the impact of **Imagism**, a movement that championed the use of free verse and concise images, or word pictures. In 1924, Williams rejected free verse and began his experimentation with controlled measure, eventually developing his signature "variable feet," or, as Williams called them, "loose verses." Williams said, "The iamb is not the normal measure of American speech. The foot has to be expanded or contracted in terms of actual speech. The key to modern poetry is measure, which must reflect the flux of modern life." **"This Is Just to Say"** was published in 1934, while Williams was still refining and experimenting with his verse.

## Literary TOOLS

**SPEAKER AND TONE.** The **speaker** is the character who speaks in a poem—the voice assumed by the writer. **Tone** is the emotional attitude toward the reader or toward the subject implied by a literary work. As you read, determine what tone the speaker uses toward the person he is addressing.

**RHYTHM AND METER. Rhythm** is the pattern of beats or stresses in a line of verse or prose. The **meter** of a poem is its rhythmical pattern. Try to figure out the stress pattern of the poem as you read.

## Reader's *Journal*

Did you ever wish to borrow something? Write the note you would leave behind if you took the item without asking.

# *This Is Just to Say*

## WILLIAM CARLOS WILLIAMS

I have eaten
the plums
that were in
the icebox[1]

5    and which
you were probably
saving
for breakfast

Forgive me
10   they were delicious
so sweet
and so cold   ■

*What has the speaker done?*

*What does the speaker ask of the owner of the plums?*

---

1. **icebox.** Refrigerator

If you were the owner of the plums, would you forgive the speaker? Why, or why not?

# INVESTIGATE Inquire Imagine

**Recall**: GATHERING FACTS

1a. What has the speaker eaten?

2a. How does the speaker say that the plums tasted?

→ **Interpret**: FINDING MEANING

1b. Whom is the speaker addressing in the poem?

2b. Why does the speaker ask for forgiveness?

**Analyze**: TAKING THINGS APART

3a. Identify the emotions that the title, "This Is Just to Say," connotes.

→ **Synthesize**: BRINGING THINGS TOGETHER

3b. Does the title indicate that the poem will be formal or informal?

**Evaluate**: MAKING JUDGMENTS

4a. If you were the speaker, what type of reaction would you expect from the owner of the plums?

→ **Extend**: CONNECTING IDEAS

4b. If you were the owner of the plums, would you want to trust the speaker again? Why, or why not?

# Understanding Literature

**SPEAKER AND TONE.** Review the definitions for **speaker** and **tone** in the Handbook of Literary Terms. What tone does the speaker use toward the person he is addressing?

**RHYTHM AND METER.** Review the definitions for **rhythm** and **meter** in the Handbook of Literary Terms. Then copy the poem in your notebook and mark its stress pattern. The first line of the poem has been done for you.

**Stress Pattern**

ˇ ˇ ˇ ´ ˇ

I have eaten

## Literary TOOLS

**IMAGE AND IMAGERY.** An **image** is language that creates a concrete representation of an object or an experience. An image is also the vivid mental picture created in the reader's mind by that language. The images in a literary work are referred to, collectively, as the work's **imagery**. As you read, think about what senses the images refer to.

**SPEAKER AND EFFECT.** The **speaker** is the character who speaks, or narrates, a poem—the voice assumed by the writer. The **effect** of a literary work is the general impression or emotional impact that it achieves. As you read, think about how the speaker sees the image, and consider the effect the poem creates upon the reader.

## Reader's Journal

When you close your eyes, what image do you see?

# The Red Wheelbarrow

## WILLIAM CARLOS WILLIAMS

so much depends
upon

a red wheel
barrow

5    glazed with rain
water

beside the white
chickens    ■

## Respond to the SELECTION

What other senses, besides sight, can you associate with the imagery in this poem?

# INVESTIGATE *Inquire, Imagine*

**Recall**: GATHERING FACTS

1a. With what is the red wheelbarrow glazed?

2a. Beside what do the white chickens stand?

→ **Interpret**: FINDING MEANING

1b. How does the presence of the rainwater emphasize the momentariness of the image? What moment is captured in the poem?

2b. What colors are part of the image? What do the colors add to the poem? Why is "so much depends / upon" the most important phrase in the poem?

**Analyze**: TAKING THINGS APART

3a. What details are provided about the red wheelbarrow?

→ **Synthesize**: BRINGING THINGS TOGETHER

3b. Why does so much depend upon the red wheelbarrow?

# Understanding *Literature*

**IMAGE AND IMAGERY.** Review the definitions for **image** and **imagery** in Literary Tools on page 532. List the images in this poem. To which senses do these images appeal? What setting is created by the images?

**SPEAKER AND EFFECT.** Review the definitions for **speaker** and **effect** in the Handbook of Literary Terms. With what kind of eye does the speaker see the image? What effect, or general impression, does the poem create within the reader?

# WRITER'S JOURNAL

1. Imagine that you are the owner of the plums in "This Is Just to Say." Write a **note** to the speaker, explaining what you were saving the plums for and why you do or do not forgive the speaker.

2. Write a **poem** to someone you have offended. Model the poem after "This Is Just to Say": start with "I have" plus a past participle, stating what you have just done. Conclude by asking forgiveness.

3. Write an imagistic **poem** in free verse about an ordinary object, such as a blue shoe, a yellow notebook, a green lamp, or a black telephone. Describe the object and connect it to another object. You may want to use "The Red Wheelbarrow" as a model.

# Integrating the LANGUAGE ARTS

## Language, Grammar, and Style

**CAPITALIZING TITLES OF LITERARY WORKS.** Read the Language Arts Survey 3.99, "Titles of Artworks and Literary Works." Then rewrite the following sentences, correcting the capitalization errors in each one.

1. William Carlos Williams's early poetry shows the influences of the various poetic trends of the time, such as metaphorical imagism in *poems* (1909) and *the tempers* (1913).

2. He uses free-verse expressionism in *al que quiere!* (1917), *kora in hell* (1920), and *sour grapes* (1921).

3. In his five-volume, impressionistic, philosophical poem, *paterson* (1946–58), Williams uses the experience of life in an American city in New Jersey to voice his feelings on the duty of the poet.

4. Williams was awarded the Pulitzer Prize in 1962 for *pictures from brueghel*.

5. Williams's essays include those in *in the american grain* (1925), *selected essays* (1954), and *embodiment of knowledge* (1974).

## Study and Research

**BIBLIOGRAPHY CARDS.** Read the Language Arts Survey 5.40, "Making Bibliographies and Bibliography Cards." Then, locate one each of the following resources on the topic of William Carlos Williams. Write one bibliography card for each resource.

1. a book with one author

2. a book with an editor but no single author

3. a poem, short story, essay, or chapter in a collection of works by one author

4. an introduction, preface, foreword, or afterword written by someone other than the author(s) of a work

5. an article in an encyclopedia, dictionary, or other alphabetically organized reference work

The best place to look for this information is your local library. If your library has an online catalog, you can conduct your research on the Internet. If not, you might try a broad approach, searching the Internet as a whole for resources. Visit a search engine and enter the keywords "william carlos williams" + "bibliography" or "william carlos williams" + "works cited."

## Study and Research & Media Literacy

**RESEARCHING ON THE INTERNET.** Read articles about William Carlos Williams on the Internet. One site that you will find useful is the **Edmunds Community College William Carlos Williams** page at http://web.edcc.edu/gvb/ wcw.html. Then write four thesis statements for four different compositions you could write about Williams. You may want to read the Language Arts Survey 2.25, "Writing a Thesis Statement," before you begin.

# "somewhere i have never travelled, gladly beyond"

BY E. E. CUMMINGS

## About the AUTHOR

E(dward) E(stlin) Cummings (1894–1962) was born in Cambridge, Massachusetts. His father was a Congregationalist minister and a Harvard faculty member. Cummings graduated from Harvard in 1915 and earned an M.A. in 1916. When the United States entered World War I, Cummings joined the ambulance corps in France but was imprisoned by the French for his outspoken letters home. *The Enormous Room* (1922) is his prose account of the experience. Intervention by his father in the form of a letter to President Woodrow Wilson freed him, and Cummings found the experience of being made a prisoner by one's own side outrageous, yet funny.

After the war, he made a life primarily in Greenwich Village in New York City, working full time as a poet and painter. Prizes, royalties, commissions, and a small allowance from his mother supported his independence. Cummings's work is known for its radical innovations in punctuation, capitalization, spelling, and grammar. Some of his poems seem literally to explode into fragments across the page, for he often arranged letters, words, and phrases in unique ways to make a visual as well as a verbal impact. In keeping with his innovative style, Cummings often had his name printed in all lowercase letters: *e. e. cummings*.

His works include four volumes of well-received poetry in the 1920s and a book of collected poems toward the end of the 1930s. During the 1950s, he lectured and read on the college campus circuit. In 1950, he was honored with a fellowship from the Academy of American Poets for "great achievement" over a period of years. He received a special citation from the National Book Award Committee in 1955 and the Bollingen Prize for poetry at Yale in 1957.

## Reader's Journal

Have you ever looked deeply into the eyes of someone else? What did you think you saw in that person's eyes?

## Literary TOOLS

**SYNTAX AND INVERSION. Syntax** is the pattern of arrangement of words in a statement. An **inversion** is a poetic technique in which the normal order of words in an utterance is altered. As you read, decide what the normal order of words in the first two lines of the poem would be without inversion.

**REPETITION. Repetition** is a writer's conscious reuse of a sound, word, phrase, sentence, or other element. Make a chart. On the left, write examples of repetition that play on the words *open* and *close*. On the right, write the meaning of these lines. One example has been done for you.

| Repetition | Meaning |
| --- | --- |
| "in your most frail gesture are things which enclose me" | the least action on the part of the subject envelops the speaker |

## About the SELECTION

Following the prolific first decade of his work, Cummings published in 1931 the volume of verse *w[viva]* which included "**somewhere i have never travelled,gladly beyond.**" When Cummings wrote the selection, he was stretching to the limits his capacity for experimentation with poetic form. Seeking to catch the aliveness of the moment, Cummings manipulated typography, imagery, structure, diction, punctuation, grammar, syntax, rhyme, meter, and verse form.

## E. E. Cummings

somewhere i have never travelled,gladly beyond
any experience,your eyes have their silence:
in your most frail gesture are things which enclose me,
or which i cannot touch because they are too near

*In what are things that enclose the speaker?*

5    your slightest look easily will unclose me
though i have closed myself as fingers,
you open always petal by petal myself as Spring opens
(touching skilfully,mysteriously)her first rose

or if your wish be to close me,i and
10   my life will shut very beautifully,suddenly,
as when the heart of this flower imagines
the snow carefully everywhere descending;

nothing which we are to perceive in this world equals
the power of your intense fragility:whose texture

*What has so much power over the speaker?*

15   compels me with the colour of its countries,
rendering death and forever with each breathing

(i do not know what it is about you that closes
and opens; only something in me understands
the voice of your eyes is deeper than all roses)
20   nobody,not even the rain,has such small hands

How does the speaker feel about the person he is addressing? When have you felt this way about somebody?

# Inquire, Imagine

## Recall: GATHERING FACTS

1a. What does the speaker say "your eyes" have?

2a. What will easily "unclose" the speaker, even if he has closed himself "as fingers"? To what is the closing of the speaker compared?

3a. What equals "the power of your intense fragility"? What does the speaker understand about "the voice of your eyes"?

## Interpret: FINDING MEANING

1b. Where has the speaker never traveled? What does it mean for eyes to "have their silence"?

2b. In the metaphor "you open always petal by petal," to what does the speaker compare the subject of the poem? To what does he compare himself? What power does the subject of the poem hold over the speaker? If the subject closes the speaker, what happens to their relationship?

3b. What does the use of the word *countries* suggest about the nature of the subject's personality? Does this person have traditionally masculine or feminine attributes?

## Analyze: TAKING THINGS APART

4a. Identify the various things to which the speaker compares the person addressed.

## Synthesize: BRINGING THINGS TOGETHER

4b. Why is it paradoxical that the speaker refers to the "frail gestures," "intense fragility," and "small hands" of the beloved?

## Perspective: LOOKING AT OTHER VIEWS

5a. Considering the perspective of the speaker, how do you think the person addressed feels about him? What effect does the person being addressed have on the speaker? Give evidence to support your response.

## Empathy: SEEING FROM INSIDE

5b. If you were the speaker, how would you react to each of the following from the person addressed in this poem?

- a Valentine
- a broken date
- an invitation to a dance
- a rebuke

# Understanding Literature

SYNTAX AND INVERSION. Review the definitions of **syntax** and **inversion** in the Handbook of Literary Terms. Cummings begins the poem with two modifying phrases, delaying until the middle of the second line the appearance of the noun that is modified—*eyes*. How are the words in the first two lines inverted? How would the first two lines read if Cummings had followed the usual order of words in a sentence, placing the subject first?

REPETITION. Review the definition of **repetition** in Literary Tools on page 535 and the related graphic organizer you completed. What is the effect of the repetition of the words *open* and *close*?

# Writer's Journal

1. Imagine that you are the person whom the speaker addresses in the poem. Write the speaker a **letter** expressing your feelings of love toward him.

2. Write a **greeting card message** for the person whom the speaker addresses in the poem. Expand on the metaphor of spring expressed in stanza 2.

3. Write a **poem** about a subject other than love, experimenting with syntax and punctuation.

# Integrating *the* LANGUAGE ARTS

## Language, Grammar, and Style

**ADDING MODIFIERS.** Read the Language Arts Survey 3.39, "Adding Colorful Language to Sentences." Then rewrite the following sentences about E. E. Cummings's life, adding appropriate modifiers. Reread About the Author on page 535 to find your answers.

1. E. E. Cummings's father was a minister and a faculty member.
2. The poet spent time in a prison.
3. *The Enormous Room* is his account of the experience.
4. E. E. Cummings arranged letters, words, and phrases in ways that make an impact.
5. His works include volumes of poetry written in the 1920s and a book of poems published toward the end of the 1930s.

## Study and Research & Media Literacy

**RESEARCHING ON THE INTERNET.** Below is the text of an E. E. Cummings poem transcribed into paragraph form. Rewrite the poem in poetic form, using what you consider to be logical line and stanza breaks, capitalization, and punctuation. Then compare your version of the poem to E. E. Cummings's original poem, which you can find on the **Poets' Corner** Internet site at http://www.poets-corner.org. Finally, write a paragraph analyzing how the poet uses language experimentally in the poem.

"In just-spring when the world is mud-luscious the little lame balloon man whistles far and wee and Eddie and Bill come running from marbles and piracies and it's spring when the world is puddle-wonderful the queer old balloon man whistles far and wee and Betty and Isbel come dancing from hop-scotch and jump-rope, and it's spring and the goat-footed balloon man whistles far and wee."

## Speaking and Listening & Collaborative Learning

**DOING A "THINK ALOUD."** Select an E. E. Cummings poem for you and your partner to examine together. One partner begins by freely associating ideas about the first half of the poem. Whom or what is the poem about? What is happening in the poem? What might the poem mean? Express as many of your thoughts as possible, focusing on specific elements or proofs within the text. The listening partner encourages the "think aloud" by offering positive comments and open-ended questions. Halfway through the poem, switch roles.

# "A Wagner Matinee"

BY WILLA CATHER

## About the AUTHOR

**Willa Cather** (1873–1947) was born in Virginia. When she was ten her family moved to Nebraska, where her father was a frontier farmer and owner of a farm loan and mortgage business. Cather graduated from the University of Nebraska in 1895. She began writing in college, reviewing books, plays, and music for the *Nebraska Journal*.

In the late 1890s and early 1900s, she lived in Pittsburgh, Pennsylvania, and worked as a newspaper and magazine writer and editor before teaching high school English and Latin. In 1906, she moved to New York City and joined *McClure's* magazine, first as a contributing editor from 1906 to 1908 and then as managing editor from 1908 to 1912.

Her early work about the Nebraska prairie and its pioneers made her famous. She is also remembered for her powerful female figures, who are often unconventional, as was Cather herself.

Her first novel, *Alexander's Bridge* (1912), was published when Cather was thirty-nine. Her other works include the poetry collection *April Twilights* (1903), the short story collections *The Troll Garden* (1912), and the novels *O Pioneers!* (1913), *The Song of the Lark* (1915), *My Ántonia* (1918), *A Lost Lady* (1923), *The Professor's House* (1925), and *Death Comes for the Archbishop* (1926).

Cather was awarded the Pulitzer Prize for the novel *One of Ours* (1922) and the Howells Medal from the American Academy and Institute of Arts and Letters in 1930 for *Death Comes for the Archbishop*. *My Ántonia* is widely considered to be her finest work.

## Reader's Journal

What emotions do you feel when listening to your favorite piece of music?

## Literary TOOLS

**NARRATOR AND POINT OF VIEW.** A **narrator** is one who tells a story. **Point of view** is the vantage point from which a story is told. In this story, written in *first-person point of view*, the narrator is limited in his knowledge. In first-person point of view, the narrator uses words such as *I* and *we*. In *limited* point of view, the narrator can reveal the private, internal thoughts of himself or herself or of a single character. As you read, think about how the narrator misjudging his aunt early on affects his point of view.

**SIMILE.** A **simile** is a comparison using *like* or *as*. For example, if you say, "My friend is as slow as a snail," you are using a simile. Look for similes as you read and determine what things are being compared.

## About the SELECTION

In **"A Wagner Matinee,"** Cather juxtaposes the pioneer world of Red Willow, Nebraska, and the musical world of Boston. Cather's method of writing from firsthand experience, particularly about growing up in Red Cloud, Nebraska, is well known and typical of her work. Music was one of Cather's passionate interests. In "A Wagner Matinee," she created the character of Aunt Georgiana, a woman who studied music at the Boston Conservatory. A martyr in the eyes of her nephew, Aunt Georgiana "inexplicably" gives up her musical life for a life on the silent Nebraska frontier.

***First Row Orchestra,*** 1951. Edward Hopper.
Hirshhorn Museum, Washington, DC.

# A Wagner Matinee

## WILLA CATHER

I received one morning a letter, written in pale ink on glassy, blue-lined note-paper, and bearing the postmark of a little Nebraska village. This communication, worn and rubbed, looking as if it had been carried for some days in a coat pocket that was none too clean, was from my Uncle Howard, and informed me that his wife had been left a small legacy[1] by a bachelor relative, and that it would be necessary for her to go to Boston to attend to the settling of the estate. He requested me to meet her at the station and render her whatever services might be necessary. On examining the date indicated as that of her arrival, I found it to be no later than tomorrow. He had characteristically delayed writing until, had I been away from home for a day, I must have missed my aunt altogether.

The name of my Aunt Georgiana opened before me a gulf of recollection so wide and deep that, as the letter dropped from my hand, I felt suddenly a stranger to all the present conditions of my existence, wholly ill at ease and out of place amid the familiar surroundings of

> Who wrote the letter to the narrator? Who is coming to visit? When is the visitor coming? What is the narrator asked to do?

---

1. **legacy.** Inheritance

my study. I became, in short, the gangling farmer-boy my aunt had known, scourged with chilblains[2] and bashfulness, my hands cracked and sore from the corn husking. I sat again before her parlor organ, fumbling the scale with my stiff, red fingers, while she, beside me, made canvas mittens for the huskers.

The next morning, after preparing my land-lady for a visitor, I set out for the station. When the train arrived I had some difficulty in finding my aunt. She was the last of the passengers to alight, and it was not until I got her into the carriage that she seemed really to recognize me. She had come all the way in a day coach; her linen duster[3] had become black with soot and her black bonnet grey with dust during the journey. When we arrived at my boarding-house the landlady put her to bed at once, and I did not see her again until the next morning.

Whatever shock Mrs. Springer experienced at my aunt's appearance, she considerately concealed. As for myself, I saw my aunt's battered figure with that feeling of awe and respect with which we behold explorers who have left their ears and fingers north of Franz-Joseph-Land, or their health somewhere along the Upper Congo.[4] My Aunt Georgiana had been a music teacher at the Boston Conservatory, somewhere back in the latter sixties.[5] One summer, while visiting in the little village among the Green Mountains where her ancestors had dwelt for generations, she had kindled the callow fancy of my uncle, Howard Carpenter, then an idle, shiftless boy of twenty-one. When she returned to her duties in Boston, Howard followed her, and the upshot of this infatuation was that she eloped with him, eluding the reproaches of her family and the criticism of her friends by going with him to the Nebraska frontier.[6] Carpenter, who, of course, had no money, took up a homestead in Red Willow County, fifty miles from the railroad. There they had measured off their land themselves, driving across the prairie in a wagon, to the wheel of which they had tied a red cotton handkerchief, and counting its revolutions. They built a dug-out in the red hillside, one of those cave dwellings whose inmates so often reverted to primitive conditions. Their water they got from the lagoons where the buffalo drank, and their slender stock of provisions[7] was always at the mercy of bands of roving Indians. For thirty years my aunt had not been farther than fifty miles from the homestead.

How was the land measured? What did Georgiana and Howard build? Where did they get their water?

I owed to this woman most of the good that ever came my way in my boyhood, and had a reverential affection for her. During the years when I was riding herd for my uncle, my aunt, after cooking the three meals—the first of which was ready at six o'clock in the morning—and putting the six children to bed, would often stand until midnight at her ironing board, with me at the kitchen table beside her, hearing me recite Latin declensions and conjugations, gently shaking me when my drowsy head sank down

How did Aunt Georgiana help the narrator with his studies? What did she teach the narrator? What musical instrument did they have?

---

2. **scourged with chilblains.** Tormented by blisters on hands and feet
3. **duster.** Lightweight coat
4. **north of Franz-Joseph-Land . . . Congo.** *Franz-Joseph-Land*—group of tiny islands in the Arctic Ocean; *Congo*—river in central Africa
5. **sixties.** 1860s
6. **Nebraska frontier.** Western border of Nebraska; uncharted territory
7. **provisions.** Supplies

WORDS FOR EVERYDAY USE

**cal • low** (kal´ō) *adj.*, lacking adult sophistication. *Not appreciating her children's callow tastes in videocassettes, Mrs. Bratton went to the video rental store alone.*

**in • fat • u • a • tion** (in fa´ chü ā´ shən) *n.*, foolish or shallow love or affection. *Justin's infatuation with the movie star ended when he met Beth.*

**re • vert** (ri vurt´) *vi.*, return to a former practice or state. *Some young children revert to baby talk when they want attention.*

**rev • er • en • tial** (rev´ə ren´ shəl) *adj.*, showing a feeling of deep respect, love, and awe. *Julia's reverential feelings for the pastor stemmed from the fact that he had baptized, confirmed, and married her.*

over a page of irregular verbs. It was to her, at her ironing or mending, that I read my first Shakespeare, and her old textbook on mythology was the first that ever came into my empty hands. She taught me my scales and exercises[8] on the little parlor organ which her husband had bought her after fifteen years during which she had not so much as seen a musical instrument. She would sit beside me by the hour, darning and counting, while I struggled with the "Joyous Farmer." She seldom talked to me about music, and I understood why. Once when I had been doggedly beating out some easy passages from an old score of *Euryanthe* I had found among her music books, she came up to me and, putting her hands over my eyes, gently drew my head back upon her shoulder, saying tremulously, "Don't love it so well, Clark, or it may be taken from you."

Why do you think Aunt Georgiana told the narrator not to love the music so well?

When my aunt appeared on the morning after her arrival in Boston, she was still in a semisomnambulant[9] state. She seemed not to realize that she was in the city where she had spent her youth, the place longed for hungrily half a lifetime. She had been so wretchedly train-sick throughout the journey that she had no recollection of anything but her discomfort, and, to all intents and purposes, there were but a few hours of nightmare between the farm in Red Willow County and my study on Newbury Street. I had planned a little pleasure for her that afternoon, to repay her for some of the glorious moments she had given me when we used to milk together in the straw-thatched cowshed and she, because I was more than usually tired, or because her husband had spoken sharply to me, would tell me of the splendid performance of the *Huguenots* she had seen in Paris, in her youth.

What "little pleasure" does the narrator plan for the afternoon?

At two o'clock the Symphony Orchestra was to give a Wagner[10] program, and I intended to take my aunt; though, as I conversed with her, I grew doubtful about her enjoyment of it. I suggested our visiting the Conservatory and the Common[11] before lunch, but she seemed altogether too timid to wish to venture out. She questioned me absently about various changes in the city, but she was chiefly concerned that she had forgotten to leave instructions about feeding half-skimmed milk to a certain weakling calf, "old Maggie's calf, you know, Clark," she explained, evidently having forgotten how long I had been away. She was further troubled because she had neglected to tell her daughter about the freshly-opened kit of mackerel[12] in the cellar, which would spoil if it were not used directly.

I asked her whether she had ever heard any of the Wagnerian operas, and found that she had not, though she was perfectly familiar with their respective situations, and had once possessed the piano score of *The Flying Dutchman*. I began to think it would be best to get her back to Red Willow County without waking her, and regretted having suggested the concert.

From the time we entered the concert hall, however, she was a trifle less passive and inert, and for the first time seemed to perceive her surroundings. I had felt some trepidation lest she might become aware of her queer, country clothes, or might experience some painful embarrassment at stepping suddenly into the

---

8. **scales and exercises.** Musical scales and practice pieces
9. **semisomnambulant.** Like one who is sleepwalking
10. **Wagner** (väg´ner). German composer Richard Wagner (1813–1883)
11. **the Common.** Boston Common, park in a historic section of Boston
12. **kit of mackerel.** Container of pickled fish

**WORDS FOR EVERYDAY USE**

**trem • u • lous • ly** (trem´yü ləs lē) *adv.*, in a trembling or quivering manner. *Lou's voice wavers tremulously whenever he gives a speech.*

**re • spec • tive** (ri spek´tiv) *adj.*, as relates individually to each of two or more persons or things. *The boxers returned to their respective corners of the ring.*

world to which she had been dead for a quarter of a century. But, again, I found how superficially I had judged her. She sat looking about her with eyes as impersonal, almost as stony, as those with which the granite Rameses[13] in a museum watches the froth and fret that ebbs and flows about his pedestal. I have seen this same aloofness in old miners who drift into the Brown hotel at Denver, their pockets full of bullion, their linen soiled, their <u>haggard</u> faces unshaven; standing in the thronged corridors as solitary as though they were still in a frozen camp on the Yukon.

*How does Aunt Georgiana react to being in the concert hall? About what is the narrator concerned?*

The matinee audience was made up chiefly of women. One lost the contour of faces and figures, indeed any effect of line whatever, and there was only the color of bodices past counting, the shimmer of fabrics soft and firm, silky and sheer; red, mauve, pink, blue, lilac, purple, ecru, rose, yellow, cream, and white, all the colors that an impressionist[14] finds in a sunlit landscape, with here and there the dead shadow of a frock coat. My Aunt Georgiana regarded them as though they had been so many daubs of tube-paint on a palette.

*Who comprises the matinee audience? How are they dressed?*

When the musicians came out and took their places, she gave a little stir of anticipation, and looked with quickening interest down over the rail at that invariable grouping, perhaps the first wholly familiar thing that had greeted her eye since she had left old Maggie and her weakling calf. I could feel how all those details sank into her soul, for I had not forgotten how they had sunk into mine when I came fresh from ploughing forever and forever between green aisles of corn, where, as in a treadmill, one might walk from daybreak to dusk without perceiving a shadow of change. The clean profiles of the musicians, the gloss of their linen, the dull black of their coats, the beloved shapes of the instruments, the patches of yellow light on the smooth, varnished bellies of the cellos and the bass viols in the rear, the restless, wind-tossed forest of fiddle necks and bows—I recalled how, in the first orchestra I ever heard, those long bow-strokes seemed to draw the heart out of me, as a conjurer's stick[15] reels out yards of paper ribbon from a hat.

The first number was the *Tannhauser* <u>overture</u>. When the horns drew out the first strain of the Pilgrim's chorus, Aunt Georgiana clutched my coat sleeve. Then it was I first realized that for her this broke a silence of thirty years. With the battle between the two motives, with the frenzy of the Venusberg theme and its ripping of strings, there came to me an overwhelming sense of the waste and wear we are so powerless to combat; and I saw again the tall, naked house on the prairie, black and grim as a wooden fortress; the black pond where I had learned to swim, its margin pitted with sun-dried cattle tracks; the rain gullied clay banks about the naked house, the four dwarf ash seedlings where the dishcloths were always hung to dry before the kitchen door. The world there was the flat world of the ancients; to the east, a cornfield that stretched to daybreak; to the west, a corral that reached to sunset; between, the conquests of peace, dearer-bought than those of war.

*How does Aunt Georgiana react to the music? What awareness comes to the narrator?*

---

13. **Rameses.** Name of a number of Egyptian kings who ruled from *circa* 1315 BC to *circa* 1090 BC
14. **impressionist.** Painter, writer, or composer who seeks to render impressions and moods in which the chief aim is to capture a momentary glimpse of a subject
15. **conjurer's stick.** Magician's wand

---

**WORDS FOR EVERYDAY USE**

**hag • gard** (ha´gərd) *adj.*, having a worn or emaciated appearance. *Years of working the third shift had left Mr. Tufone with a* <u>haggard</u> *expression that showed his fatigue.*

**o • ver • ture** (ō´vər chər) *n.*, musical introduction to an opera or other long musical work. *The* <u>overture</u> *introduced the themes of the opera.*

The overture closed, my aunt released my coat sleeve, but she said nothing. She sat staring dully at the orchestra. What, I wondered, did she get from it? She had been a good pianist in her day, I knew, and her musical education had been broader than that of most music teachers of a quarter of a century ago. She had often told me of Mozart's operas and Meyerbeer's and I could remember hearing her sing, years ago, certain melodies of Verdi. When I had fallen ill with a fever in her house, she used to sit by my cot in the evening—when the cool, night wind blew in through the faded mosquito netting tacked over the window and I lay watching a certain bright star that burned red above the cornfield—and sing "Home to our mountains, O, let us return!" in a way fit to break the heart of a Vermont boy near dead of homesickness already.

*What did Aunt Georgiana do when the narrator was sick? What effect did her action have on the narrator?*

I watched her closely through the <u>prelude</u> to *Tristan and Isolde*, trying vainly to conjecture what that seething turmoil of strings and winds might mean to her, but she sat mutely staring at the violin bows that drove obliquely downward, like the pelting streaks of rain in a summer shower. Had this music any message for her? Had she enough left to at all comprehend this power which had kindled the world since she had left it? I was in a fever of curiosity, but Aunt Georgiana sat silent upon her peak in Darien.[16] She preserved this utter <u>immobility</u> throughout the number from *The Flying Dutchman*, though her fingers worked mechanically upon her black dress, as if, of themselves, they were recalling the piano score they had once played. Poor hands! They had been stretched and twisted into mere tentacles to hold and lift and knead with—on one of them a thin, worn band that had once been a wedding ring. As I pressed and gently quieted one of those groping hands, I remembered with quivering eyelids their services for me in other days.

Soon after the tenor began the "Prize Song," I heard a quick drawn breath and turned to my aunt. Her eyes were closed, but the tears were glistening on her cheeks, and I think, in a moment more, they were in my eyes as well. It never really died, then—the soul which can suffer so <u>excruciatingly</u> and so <u>interminably</u>; it withers to the outward eye only; like that strange moss which can lie on a dusty shelf half a century and yet, if placed in water, grows green again. She wept so throughout the development and elaboration of the melody.

*How does the tenor's solo affect Aunt Georgiana? the narrator? What insight into the human soul does the narrator have?*

During the intermission before the second half, I questioned my aunt and found that the "Prize Song" was not new to her. Some years before there had drifted to the farm in Red Willow County a young German, a tramp cow-puncher, who had sung in the chorus at Bayreuth[17] when he was a boy, along with the other peasant boys and girls. Of a Sunday morning he used to sit on his gingham-sheeted bed in the hands' bedroom which opened off the kitchen, cleaning the

*How does Aunt Georgiana know the "Prize Song"? Who used to sing it? What became of the singer?*

---

16. **peak in Darien.** Mountain in Panama (formerly called the Isthmus of Darien) where Cortés was said to have looked westward at the Pacific Ocean, a new discovery for Europeans
17. **Bayreuth.** Site of international music festivals in Germany

---

**WORDS FOR EVERYDAY USE**

**pre • lude** (prel´yüd; prä´lüd) *n.*, first movement of an opera; introduction. *The <u>prelude</u> of the opera preceded the famous soprano solo.*

**im • mo • bil • i • ty** (im´mō bil´i tē) *n.*, state of being fixed or unmovable. *The <u>immobility</u> of the house owners in Western Springs to decide on a price resulted in Mary and Ted buying a different house.*

**ex • cru • ci • at • ing • ly** (eks krü´shē āt´iŋ lē) *adv.*, in a painful or agonizing manner. *Physical therapy was <u>excruciatingly</u> painful, and Joyce wondered if she would ever again walk without pain.*

**in • ter • mi • na • bly** (in tʉr´mi nə blē) *adv.*, endlessly. *The lecture went on <u>interminably</u>; we thought it would never end.*

leather of his boots and saddle, singing the "Prize Song," while my aunt went about her work in the kitchen. She had hovered over him until she had prevailed upon him to join the country church, though his sole fitness for this step, in so far as I could gather, lay in his boyish face and his possession of this divine melody. Shortly afterward, he had gone to town on the Fourth of July, been drunk for several days, lost his money at a faro[18] table, ridden a saddled Texas steer on a bet, and disappeared with a fractured collar-bone. All this my aunt told me huskily, wanderingly, as though she were talking in the weak lapses of illness.

"Well, we have come to better things than the old *Trovatore* at any rate, Aunt Georgie?" I queried, with a well meant effort at <u>jocularity</u>.

Her lip quivered and she hastily put her handkerchief up to her mouth. From behind it she murmured, "And you have been hearing this ever since you left me, Clark?" Her question was the gentlest and saddest of <u>reproaches</u>.

The second half of the program consisted of four numbers from the *Ring*, and closed with Siegfried's funeral march. My aunt wept quietly, but almost continuously, as a shallow vessel overflows in a rain-storm. From time to time her dim eyes looked up at the lights, burning softly under their dull glass globes.

The deluge of sound poured on and on; I never knew what she found in the shining current of it; I never knew how far it bore her, or past what happy islands. From the trembling of her face I could well believe that before the last number she had been carried out where the myriad[19] graves are, into the grey, nameless burying grounds of the sea; or into some world of death vaster yet, where, from the beginning of the world, hope has lain down with hope and dream with dream and, renouncing, slept.

> Where does the narrator believe the music transports Aunt Georgiana?

The concert was over; the people filed out of the hall chattering and laughing, glad to relax and find the living level again, but my kinswoman made no effort to rise. The harpist slipped the green felt cover over his instrument; the flute-players shook the water from their mouthpieces; the men of the orchestra went out one by one, leaving the stage to the chairs and music stands, empty as a winter cornfield.

I spoke to my aunt. She burst into tears and sobbed pleadingly. "I don't want to go, Clark, I don't want to go!"

I understood. For her, just outside the concert hall, lay the black pond with the cattle-tracked bluffs; the tall, unpainted house, with weather-curled boards, naked as a tower; the crook-backed ash seedlings where the dishcloths hung to dry; the gaunt, moulting[20] turkeys picking up refuse about the kitchen door. ∎

> Why does Aunt Georgiana want to stay in the concert hall?

---

18. **faro.** Gambling game
19. **myriad.** Numerous
20. **moulting.** Shedding feathers

**WORDS FOR EVERYDAY USE**

**joc • u • lar • i • ty** (jäk´yü lar´ə tē) *n.*, humor, joking. *My uncle's <u>jocularity</u> was contagious, and soon everyone was laughing.*

**re • proach** (ri prōch´) *n.*, blaming or reproving; rebuke. *Our science teacher thought no one was above <u>reproach</u> when a Bunsen burner started a fire.*

# Respond *to the* SELECTION

Imagine that you are Aunt Georgiana. Explain what music means to you.

# INVESTIGATE, Inquire, Imagine

**Recall:** GATHERING FACTS

1a. What is the reason for Aunt Georgiana's visit to Boston?

2a. What jobs did the narrator perform for his aunt and uncle on their farm?

3a. What pleasure does the narrator plan for his aunt?

**Interpret:** FINDING MEANING

1b. Why does the name "Aunt Georgiana" open before the narrator "a gulf of recollection so wide and deep"? What facts emphasize the hardship of Aunt Georgiana's life on the Nebraska frontier?

2b. What actions on the part of Aunt Georgiana emphasize that the narrator owes to her "most of the good" that came his way in boyhood?

3b. Why doesn't Aunt Georgiana want to leave the concert hall?

**Analyze:** TAKING THINGS APART

4a. Identify Aunt Georgiana's life experiences with music.

**Synthesize:** BRINGING THINGS TOGETHER

4b. Considering the types of experiences Aunt Georgiana has had, what kind of relationship between music and the human soul does Cather describe in this story? What evidence in the selection supports your conclusion?

**Evaluate:** MAKING JUDGMENTS

5a. Which setting, rural Nebraska or cosmopolitan Boston, is described more effectively? Give details to support your answer.

**Extend:** CONNECTING IDEAS

5b. Describe a time you had to give up something you loved, and explain what that loss meant to you.

# Understanding Literature

NARRATOR AND POINT OF VIEW. Review the definitions for **narrator** and **point of view** in the Handbook of Literary Terms. The narrator is aware of his limitations and acknowledges his misjudgment of Aunt Georgiana. In what ways does the narrator misjudge or underestimate his aunt? How does this affect the *first-person point of view* of the narrator? Is Clark a reliable narrator?

SIMILE. Review the definition for **simile** in the Handbook of Literary Terms. Then make a chart. On the left, list the similes you find in the story. On the right, explain the comparisons. One example has been done for you.

| Similes | Explanations |
|---|---|
| "It never really died, then—the soul which can suffer so excruciatingly and so interminably; it withers to the outward eye only; like that strange moss which can lie on a dusty shelf half a century and yet, if placed in water, grows green again." | Both the soul and moss suffer and wither, but can be replenished under the right conditions. |

# WRITER'S JOURNAL

1. Imagine that you are Aunt Georgiana. Write a **letter** to your nephew, Clark, thanking him for taking you to the Wagner matinee, explaining what the concert experience has meant to you.

2. Imagine that you are Clark's uncle. Write a **journal entry** dating back to when you founded your homestead. Talk about the house you built, how you measured the land, and the work you do each day.

3. Aunt Georgiana warned her nephew when he was a boy, "Don't love it so well, Clark, or it may be taken from you." Write a **monologue** in which Aunt Georgiana finishes her thought by sharing her own experience.

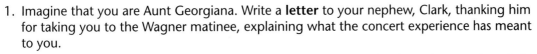

# Integrating
## *the* LANGUAGE ARTS

## Language, Grammar, and Style

**DANGLING AND MISPLACED MODIFIERS.** Read the Language Arts Survey 3.46, "Avoiding Dangling and Misplaced Modifiers." Then, on your own paper, rewrite each sentence, correcting the dangling or misplaced modifiers.

1. Carefully folded in half, he removed the important letter from the envelope.
2. The young woman moved to the silent and faraway plains who wished to avoid her family's reproach.
3. To keep from feeling homesick, the cow herd occupied most of the young boy's time.
4. Before moving to the Nebraska frontier, Boston had been Georgiana's home while studying music at the conservatory.
5. Having left her music career behind, he understood why she seldom talked to him about music.

## Vocabulary

**BASE WORDS AND SUFFIXES.** Read the Language Arts Survey 1.19, "Learning Base Words, Prefixes, and Suffixes." On your own paper, underline the base word once and the suffix twice in each of the following words from "A Wagner Matinee." Next, look up each suffix in a dictionary and write two additional words that end with the same suffix.

1. reverential
2. mythology
3. martyrdom
4. glistening
5. immobility

## Study and Research

**RESEARCHING SETTING ON THE INTERNET.** "Willa Cather drew on her home town of Red Cloud, Nebraska for descriptions found in her novels." Using this as the thesis statement for a composition, research Willa Cather and Red Cloud, Nebraska, on the Internet to find supporting facts. One site that you will find useful is the **Willa Cather Pioneer Memorial** Internet site, at http://www.willacather.org. You may want to review the Language Arts Survey 2.24, "Organizing Ideas," before you begin writing.

# "The Sensible Thing"

BY F. SCOTT FITZGERALD

## About *the* AUTHOR

The fiction and life of **F. Scott Fitzgerald** (1896–1940) embodied the "Jazz Age," a phrase coined by Fitzgerald himself to capture the excitement and glamour of America in the 1920s. For Fitzgerald, this decade represented the American Dream, a time when one might hope to gain wealth and thereby achieve happiness.

Fitzgerald was born and raised in St. Paul, Minnesota, and later attended Princeton University. After three years at Princeton, he left school and joined the army. While he was stationed in Montgomery, Alabama, he met his wife, Zelda Sayre. After being discharged from the army, Fitzgerald went to New York to make his fortune. There F. Scott and Zelda became known as madcap socialites. The Fitzgeralds moved to France in 1921, living in Paris and on the French Riviera, where they became part of a celebrated circle of American expatriates. After 1930, Zelda was frequently hospitalized for schizophrenia. Besides his wife's mental problems, financial difficulties plagued Fitzgerald in his later years. He died of a heart attack at the age of forty-four.

Part of the interest in Fitzgerald's work stems from the fact that the carefree, gin-drinking socialites in his fiction mirror his own life. In 1920, his first novel, *This Side of Paradise,* was published, followed by *The Beautiful and Damned* (1922), and his masterpiece, considered by some literary critics as the greatest American novel, *The Great Gatsby* (1925). After publishing *Tender Is the Night* (1934), Fitzgerald moved to Hollywood and turned to screenwriting. He published four short story collections: *Flappers and Philosophers* (1920), *Tales of the Jazz Age* (1922), *All the Sad Young Men* (1926), and *Taps at Reveille* (1935). In addition to being a shrewd social observer, Fitzgerald is also known for his literary artistry; his style of narrative point of view is often imitated.

## About *The* SELECTION

**"The Sensible Thing"** was first published in the magazine *Liberty* in 1924 and then in a collection of short stories called *All the Sad Young Men* (1926). Fitzgerald's readers were drawn to his carefully crafted plots, which often revolved around the themes of love and loss. In "The Sensible Thing," the story's protagonist, George O'Kelly, experiences a reversal of fortune much as Fitzgerald had done in 1919 and 1920 when he achieved early success as a writer. Also like Fitzgerald, George O'Kelly recaptures his beloved, only to find that love is not repeatable. In this story Fitzgerald introduces common themes that return in *The Great Gatsby* and other stories.

"The Sensible Thing" was developed into an acclaimed independent short film that was featured as the premier episode of Public Broadcasting's television series *American Storytellers* in 1999.

## Literary
### T O O L S

**REVERSAL.** A **reversal** is a dramatic change in the direction of events in a drama or narrative, especially a change in the fortunes of the protagonist. As you read, look for the reversal that happens in this story. How has O'Kelly's life changed in a year?

**CHARACTER.** A **character** is a person who figures in the action of a literary work. A *dynamic character* is one who changes in the course of the action. As you read the story, pay attention to how George O'Kelly changes.

## Reader's
### Journal

If you went away for a year, what adjustments would you anticipate having to make upon your return?

# The Sensible Thing

## F. SCOTT FITZGERALD

At the Great American Lunch Hour young George O'Kelly straightened his desk deliberately and with an assumed air of interest. No one in the office must know that he was in a hurry, for success is a matter of atmosphere, and it is not well to advertise the fact that your mind is separated from your work by a distance of seven hundred miles.

But once out of the building he set his teeth and began to run, glancing now and then at the gay noon of early spring which filled Times Square and <u>loitered</u> less than twenty feet over the heads of the crowd. The crowd all looked slightly upward and took deep March breaths, and the sun dazzled their eyes so that scarcely any one saw any one else but only their own reflection on the sky.

George O'Kelly, whose mind was over seven hundred miles away, thought that all outdoors was horrible. He rushed into the subway, and for ninety-five blocks bent a <u>frenzied</u> glance on a car-card[1] which showed vividly how he had only one chance in five of keeping his teeth for ten years. At 137th Street he broke off his study of commercial art, left the subway, and began to run again, a tireless, anxious run that brought him this time to his home—one room in a high, horrible apartment-house in the middle of nowhere.

*Why is George's mind "over seven hundred miles away"?*

There it was on the bureau, the letter—in sacred ink, on blessed paper—all over the city, people, if they listened, could hear the beating of George O'Kelly's heart. He read the commas, the blots, and the thumb-smudge on the margin—then he threw himself hopelessly upon his bed.

He was in a mess, one of those terrific messes which are ordinary incidents in the life of the poor, which follow poverty like birds of prey. The poor go under or go up or go wrong or even go on, somehow, in a way the poor have—but George O'Kelly was so new to poverty that had any one denied the uniqueness of his case he would have been astounded.

Less than two years ago he had been graduated with honors from The Massachusetts Institute of Technology and had taken a position with a

*What degree did George earn? From which university?*

firm of construction engineers in southern Tennessee. All his life he had thought in terms of tunnels and skyscrapers and great squat dams and tall, three-towered bridges, that were like dancers holding hands in a row, with heads as tall as cities and skirts of cable strand. It had seemed romantic to George O'Kelly to change the sweep of rivers and the shape of mountains so that life could <u>flourish</u> in the old bad lands of the world where it had never taken root before. He loved steel, and there was always steel near him in his dreams, liquid steel, steel in bars, and blocks and beams and formless plastic masses, waiting for him, as paint and canvas to his hand. Steel inexhaustible, to be made lovely and austere in his imaginative fire . . .

At present he was an insurance clerk at forty dollars a week with his dream slipping fast behind him. The dark little girl who had made this mess, this terrible and intolerable mess, was waiting to be sent for in a town in Tennessee.

In fifteen minutes the woman from whom he sublet his room knocked and asked him with maddening kindness if, since he was home, he would have some lunch. He shook his head, but the interruption aroused him, and getting up from the bed he wrote a telegram.

"Letter depressed me have you lost your nerve you are foolish and just upset to think of breaking off why not marry me immediately sure we can make it all right—"

He hesitated for a wild minute, and then added in a hand that could scarcely be recognized as his own: "In any case I will arrive tomorrow at six o'clock."

When he finished he ran out of the apartment and down to the telegraph office near the subway stop. He possessed in this world not

---

1. **car-card.** An advertisement in a subway car

WORDS FOR EVERYDAY USE

**loi • ter** (loi´tər) *vi.*, to remain in an area for no obvious reason. *The boys <u>loitered</u> in the lobby after the movie.*

**fren • zied** (fren´zēd) *adj.*, marked by emotional agitation. *Chandra gave a <u>frenzied</u> look to her friend when she couldn't get the subway car door to open.*

**flour • ish** (flʉr´ish) *vi.*, thrive. *The flowers <u>flourished</u> in the sunshine.*

quite one hundred dollars, but the letter showed that she was "nervous" and this left him no choice. He knew what "nervous" meant—that she was emotionally depressed, that the prospect of marrying into a life of poverty and struggle was putting too much strain upon her love.

Why does George feel he must send a telegram to his girlfriend?

George O'Kelly reached the insurance company at his usual run, the run that had become almost second nature to him, that seemed best to express the tension under which he lived. He went straight to the manager's office.

"I want to see you, Mr. Chambers," he announced breathlessly.

"Well?" Two eyes, eyes like winter windows, glared at him with <u>ruthless</u> impersonality.

"I want to get four days' vacation."

"Why, you had a vacation just two weeks ago!" said Mr. Chambers in surprise.

"That's true," admitted the distraught young man, "but now I've got to have another."

Why does George talk to his boss? What happens? How does George feel?

"Where'd you go last time? To your home?"

"No, I went to—a place in Tennessee."

"Well, where do you want to go this time?"

"Well, this time I want to go to—a place in Tennessee."

"You're consistent, anyhow," said the manager dryly. "But I didn't realize you were employed here as a travelling salesman."

"I'm not," cried George desperately, "but I've got to go."

"All right," agreed Mr. Chambers, "but you don't have to come back. So don't!"

> **"I think I'd have gone crazy if you'd said that I could come back."**

"I won't." And to his own astonishment as well as Mr. Chambers' George's face grew pink with pleasure. He felt happy, <u>exultant</u>—for the first time in six months he was absolutely free. Tears of gratitude stood in his eyes, and he seized Mr. Chambers warmly by the hand.

"I want to thank you," he said with a rush of emotion. "I don't want to come back. I think I'd have gone crazy if you'd said that I could come back. Only I couldn't quit myself, you see, and I want to thank you for—for quitting for me."

He waved his hand <u>magnanimously</u>, shouted aloud, "You owe me three days' salary but you can keep it!" and rushed from the office. Mr. Chambers rang for his stenographer to ask if O'Kelly had seemed queer lately. He had fired many men in the course of his career, and they had taken it in many different ways, but none of them had thanked him—ever before.

## II

Jonquil Cary was her name, and to George O'Kelly nothing had ever looked so fresh and pale as her face when she saw him and fled to him eagerly along the station platform. Her arms were raised to him, her mouth was half parted for his kiss, when she held him off suddenly and lightly and, with a touch of embarrassment, looked around. Two boys, somewhat younger than George, were standing in the background.

"This is Mr. Carddock and Mr. Holt," she announced cheerfully. "You met them when you were here before."

Disturbed by the transition of a kiss into an introduction and suspecting some hidden

---

**WORDS FOR EVERYDAY USE**

**ruth • less** (rüth´ləs) *adj.,* merciless. *Jim's teacher gave a harsh and <u>ruthless</u> critique of his piano recital.*

**ex ul • tant** (ig zəl´tənt) *adj.,* filled with great joy. *The <u>exultant</u> shouts of the children told him that they had won their game.*

**mag • nan • i • mous • ly** (mag na´nə məs lē) *adv.,* showing nobility of feeling or generosity of mind. *Mr. Cheever <u>magnanimously</u> donated a million dollars to the charity.*

had recognized so surely in her eyes back in the station, had been <u>dissipated</u> by the intrusion of the ride. Something that he had looked forward to had been rather casually lost, and he was brooding on this as he said good night stiffly to the two young men. Then his ill-humor faded as Jonquil drew him into a familiar embrace under the dim light of the front hall and told him in a dozen ways, of which the best was without words, how she had missed him. Her emotion reassured him, promised his anxious heart that everything would be all right.

They sat together on the sofa, overcome by each other's presence, beyond all except fragmentary endearments. At the supper hour Jonquil's father and mother appeared and were glad to see George. They liked him, and had been interested in his engineering career when he had first come to Tennessee over a year before. They had been sorry when he had given it up and gone to New York to look for something more immediately profitable, but while they deplored the <u>curtailment</u> of his career they sympathized with him and were ready to recognize the engagement. During dinner they asked about his progress in New York.

"Everything's going fine," he told them with enthusiasm. "I've been promoted—better salary."

He was miserable as he said this—but they were all *so* glad.

"They must like you," said Mrs. Cary, "that's certain—or they wouldn't let you off twice in three weeks to come down here."

"I told them they had to," explained George hastily; "I told them if they didn't I wouldn't work for them any more."

significance, George was more confused when he found that the automobile which was to carry them to Jonquil's house belonged to one of the two young men. It seemed to put him at a disadvantage. On the way Jonquil chattered between the front and back seats, and when he tried to slip his arm around her under cover of the twilight she compelled him with a quick movement to take her hand instead.

> What troubles George when he arrives at the train station in Tennessee?

"Is this street on the way to your house?" he whispered. "I don't recognize it."

"It's the new boulevard. Jerry just got this car today, and he wants to show it to me before he takes us home."

When, after twenty minutes, they were deposited at Jonquil's house, George felt that the first happiness of the meeting, the joy he

**WORDS FOR EVERYDAY USE**

**dis • si • pate** (di´sə pāt) *vi.,* break up; scatter; vanish. *The showers <u>dissipated</u>, and the sun broke through the clouds.*

**cur • tail • ment** (kər tā[ə]l´mənt) *n.,* abrupt ending. *The <u>curtailment</u> of the bridge game was due to the impending storm.*

"But you ought to save your money," Mrs. Cary reproached him gently. "Not spend it all on this expensive trip."

Dinner was over—he and Jonquil were alone and she came back into his arms.

"So glad you're here," she sighed. "Wish you never were going away again, darling."

"Do you miss me?"

"Oh, so much, so much."

"Do you—do other men come to see you often? Like those two kids?"

The question surprised her. The dark velvet eyes stared at him.

"Why, of course they do. All the time. Why—I've told you in letters that they did, dearest."

This was true—when he had first come to the city there had been already a dozen boys around her, responding to her picturesque fragility with adolescent worship, and a few of them perceiving that her beautiful eyes were also sane and kind.

"Do you expect me never to go anywhere"—Jonquil demanded, leaning back against the sofa-pillows until she seemed to look at him from many miles away—"and just fold my hands and sit still—forever?"

"What do you mean?" he blurted out in a panic. "Do you mean you think I'll never have enough money to marry you?"

"Oh, don't jump at conclusions so, George."

"I'm not jumping at conclusions. That's what you said."

George decided suddenly that he was on dangerous grounds. He had not intended to let anything spoil this night. He tried to take her again in his arms, but she resisted unexpectedly, saying:

"It's hot. I'm going to get the electric fan."

When the fan was adjusted they sat down again, but he was in a supersensitive mood and involuntarily he plunged into the specific world he had intended to avoid.

"When will you marry me?"

"Are you ready for me to marry you?"

All at once his nerves gave way, and he sprang to his feet.

"Let's shut off that damned fan," he cried, "it drives me wild. It's like a clock ticking away all the time I'll be with you. I came here to be happy and forget everything about New York and time—"

He sank down on the sofa as suddenly as he had risen. Jonquil turned off the fan, and drawing his head down into her lap began stroking his hair.

"Let's sit like this," she said softly, "just sit quiet like this, and I'll put you to sleep. You're all tired and nervous and your sweetheart'll take care of you."

"But I don't want to sit like this," he complained, jerking up suddenly, "I don't want to sit like this at all. I want you to kiss me. That's the only thing that makes me rest. And anyways I'm not nervous—it's you that's nervous. I'm not nervous at all."

To prove that he wasn't nervous he left the couch and plumped himself into a rocking-chair across the room.

"Just when I'm ready to marry you you write me the most nervous letters, as if you're going to back out, and I have to come rushing down here—"

> **"Do you mean you think I'll never have enough money to marry you?"**

---

**WORDS FOR EVERYDAY USE**

**pic • tur • esque** (pik chə resk´) *adj.*, charming or quaint in appearance. *The picturesque Swiss village sat on the edge of Lake Geneva.*

"You don't have to come if you don't want to."

"But I *do* want to!" insisted George.

It seemed to him that he was being very cool and logical and that she was putting him deliberately in the wrong. With every word they were drawing farther and farther apart—and he was unable to stop himself or to keep worry and pain out of his voice.

But in a minute Jonquil began to cry sorrowfully and he came back to the sofa and put his arms around her. He was the comforter now, drawing her head close to his shoulder, murmuring old familiar things until she grew calmer and only trembled a little, <u>spasmodically</u>, in his arms. For over an hour they sat there, while the evening pianos thumped their last cadences into the street outside. George did not move, or think, or hope, lulled into numbness by the <u>premonition</u> of disaster. The clock would tick on, past eleven, past twelve, and then Mrs. Cary would call down gently over the banister—beyond that he saw only tomorrow and despair.

### III

*I*n the heat of the next day the breaking-point came. They had each guessed the truth about the other, but of the two she was the more ready to admit the situation.

"There's no use going on," she said miserably, "you know you hate the insurance business, and you'll never do well in it."

"That's not it," he insisted stubbornly; "I hate going on alone. If you'll marry me and come with me and take a chance with me, I can make good at anything, but not while I'm worrying about you down here."

She was silent a long time before she answered, not thinking—for she had seen the end—but only waiting, because she knew that every word would seem more cruel than the last. Finally she spoke:

"George, I love you with all my heart, and I don't see how I can ever love any one else but you. If you'd been ready for me two months ago I'd have married you—now I can't because it doesn't seem to be the sensible thing."

> *Why won't Jonquil marry George?*

He made wild accusations—there was some one else—she was keeping something from him!

"No, there's no one else."

This was true. But reacting from the strain of this affair she had found relief in the company of young boys like Jerry Holt, who had the merit of meaning absolutely nothing in her life.

George didn't take the situation well, at all. He seized her in his arms and tried literally to kiss her into marrying him at once. When this failed, he broke into a long monologue of self-pity, and ceased only when he saw that he was making himself despicable in her sight. He threatened to leave when he had no intention of leaving, and refused to go when she told him that, after all, it was best that he should.

For a while she was sorry, then for another while she was merely kind.

"You'd better go now," she cried at last, so loud that Mrs. Cary came downstairs in alarm.

"Is something the matter?"

"I'm going away, Mrs. Cary," said George brokenly. Jonquil had left the room.

> ## *"Perhaps after all this is the sensible thing—"*

**WORDS FOR EVERYDAY USE**

spas • mod • i • cal • ly (spaz mä´dik lē) *adv.,* intermittently. *The child braked <u>spasmodically</u> as she tried out her new bike.*

pre • mo • ni • tion (prē mə ni´shən) *n.,* anticipation of an event without conscious reason. *Julia had a <u>premonition</u> that Chad would break up with her on their next date.*

"Don't feel so badly, George." Mrs. Cary blinked at him in helpless sympathy—sorry and, in the same breath, glad that the little tragedy was almost done. "If I were you I'd go home to your mother for a week or so. Perhaps after all this is the sensible thing—"

"Please don't talk," he cried. "Please don't say anything to me now!"

Jonquil came into the room again, her sorrow and her nervousness alike tucked under powder and rouge and hat.

"I've ordered a taxicab," she said impersonally. "We can drive around until your train leaves."

She walked out on the front porch. George put on his coat and hat and stood for a minute exhausted in the hall—he had eaten scarcely a bite since he had left New York. Mrs. Cary came over, drew his head down and kissed him on the cheek, and he felt very ridiculous and weak in his knowledge that the scene had been ridiculous and weak at the end. If he had only gone the night before—left her for the last time with a decent pride.

> Why does George regret not leaving Jonquil earlier?

The taxi had come, and for an hour these two that had been lovers rode along the less-frequented streets. He held her hand and grew calmer in the sunshine, seeing too late that there had been nothing all along to do or say.

"I'll come back," he told her.

"I know you will," she answered, trying to put a cheery faith into her voice. "And we'll write each other—sometimes."

"No," he said, "we won't write. I couldn't stand that. Some day I'll come back."

> At the train station, what does George say he will do?

"I'll never forget you, George."

They reached the station, and she went with him while he bought his ticket. . . .

"Why, George O'Kelly and Jonquil Cary!"

It was a man and a girl whom George had known when he had worked in town, and Jonquil seemed to greet their presence with relief. For an <u>interminable</u> five minutes they all stood there talking; then the train roared into the station, and with ill-concealed agony in his face George held out his arms toward Jonquil. She took an uncertain step toward him, faltered, and then pressed his hand quickly as if she were taking leave of a chance friend.

"Good-by, George," she was saying, "I hope you have a pleasant trip."

"Good-by, George. Come back and see us all again."

Dumb, almost blind with pain, he seized his suitcase, and in some dazed way got himself aboard the train.

Past clanging street-crossings, gathering speed through wide suburban spaces toward the sunset. Perhaps she too would see the sunset and pause for a moment, turning, remembering, before he faded with her sleep into the past. This night's dusk would cover up forever the sun and the trees and the flowers and laughter of his young world.

## IV

On a damp afternoon in September of the following year a young man with his face burned to a deep copper glow got off a train at a city in Tennessee. He looked around anxiously, and seemed relieved when he found that there was no one in the station to meet him. He taxied to the best hotel in the city where he registered with some satisfaction as George O'Kelly, Cuzco, Peru.

**WORDS FOR EVERYDAY USE**

in • ter • mi • na • ble (in tər´mi nə bəl; in tərm´nə bəl) adj., seeming to have no end. The <u>interminable</u> wait to be selected for a team depressed Lori.

Up in his room he sat for a few minutes at the window looking down into the familiar street below. Then with his hand trembling faintly he took off the telephone receiver and called a number.

"Is Miss Jonquil in?"

"This is she."

"Oh—" His voice after overcoming a faint tendency to waver went on with friendly formality.

"This is George O'Kelly. Did you get my letter?"

"Yes. I thought you'd be in today."

Her voice, cool and unmoved, disturbed him, but not as he had expected. This was the voice of a stranger, unexcited, pleasantly glad to see him—that was all. He wanted to put down the telephone and catch his breath.

"I haven't seen you for—a long time." He succeeded in making this sound offhand. "Over a year."

He knew how long it had been—to the day.

"It'll be awfully nice to talk to you again.

"I'll be there in about an hour."

He hung up. For four long seasons every minute of his leisure had been crowded with anticipation of this hour, and now this hour was here. He had thought of finding her married, engaged, in love—he had not thought she would be unstirred at his return.

> When George returns to Tennessee, of what is he afraid? Are his fears justified?

There would never again in his life, he felt, be another ten months like these he had just gone through. He had made an admittedly remarkable showing for a young engineer—stumbled into two unusual opportunities, one in Peru, whence he had just returned, and another, consequent upon it, in New York, whither he was bound. In this short time he had risen from poverty into a position of unlimited opportunity.

He looked at himself in the dressing-table mirror. He was almost black with tan, but it was a romantic black, and in the last week, since he had had time to think about it, it had given him considerable pleasure. The hardiness of his frame, too, he appraised with a sort of fascination. He had lost part of an eyebrow somewhere, and he still wore an elastic bandage on his knee, but he was too young not to realize that on the steamer many women had looked at him with unusual tributary interest.

His clothes, of course, were frightful. They had been made for him by a Greek tailor in Lima—in two days. He was young enough, too, to have explained this <u>sartorial</u> deficiency to Jonquil in his otherwise <u>laconic</u> note. The only further detail it contained was a request that he should *not* be met at the station.

George O'Kelly, of Cuzco, Peru, waited an hour and a half in the hotel, until, to be exact, the sun had reached a midway position in the sky. Then, freshly shaven and talcum-powdered toward a somewhat more Caucasian hue, for vanity at the last minute had overcome romance, he engaged a taxicab and set out for the house he knew so well.

He was breathing hard—he noticed this but he told himself that it was excitement, not emotion. He was here; she was not married—that was enough. He was not even sure what he had to say to her. But this was the moment of his life that he felt he could least easily have dispensed with. There was no triumph, after all, without a girl concerned, and if he did not lay his spoils at her feet he could at least hold them for a passing moment before her eyes.

The house loomed up suddenly beside him, and his first thought was that it had assumed a

---

**WORDS FOR EVERYDAY USE**

**sar • tor • ial** (sär tōr´ē əl) *adj.*, of or relating to clothes. *"Not another <u>sartorial</u> purchase,"* exclaimed Sandra's mother when Sandra came downstairs in a new outfit.

**la • con • ic** (lə kä´nik) *adj.*, concise. *The defendant's <u>laconic</u> response was so short that the attorney asked him to elaborate.*

strange unreality. There was nothing changed—only everything was changed. It was smaller and it seemed shabbier than before—there was no cloud of magic hovering over its roof and issuing from the windows of the upper floor. He rang the door-bell and an unfamiliar colored maid appeared. Miss Jonquil would be down in a moment. He wet his lips nervously and walked into the sitting-room—and the feeling of unreality increased. After all, he saw, this was only a room, and not the enchanted chamber where he had passed those <u>poignant</u> hours. He sat in a chair, amazed to find it a chair, realizing that his imagination had distorted and colored all these simple familiar things.

Then the door opened and Jonquil came into the room—and it was as though everything in it suddenly blurred before his eyes. He had not remembered how beautiful she was, and he felt his face grow pale and his voice diminish to a poor sigh in his throat.

She was dressed in pale green, and a gold ribbon bound back her dark, straight hair like a crown. The familiar velvet eyes caught his as she came through the door, and a spasm of fright went through him at her beauty's power of inflicting pain.

He said "Hello," and they each took a few steps forward and shook hands. Then they sat in chairs quite far apart and gazed at each other across the room.

"You've come back," she said, and he answered just as tritely: "I wanted to stop in and see you as I came through."

He tried to neutralize the tremor in his voice by looking anywhere but at her face. The obligation to speak was on him, but, unless he immediately began to boast, it seemed that there was nothing to say. There had never been anything casual in their previous relations—it didn't seem possible that people in this position would talk about the weather.

"This is ridiculous," he broke out in sudden embarrassment. "I don't know exactly what to do. Does my being here bother you?"

"No." The answer was both <u>reticent</u> and impersonally sad. It depressed him.

"Are you engaged?" he demanded.

"No."

"Are you in love with some one?"

She shook her head.

"Oh." He leaned back in his chair. Another subject seemed exhausted—the interview was not taking the course he had intended.

"Jonquil," he began, this time on a softer key, "after all that's happened between us, I wanted to come back and see you. Whatever I do in the future I'll never love another girl as I've loved you."

This was one of the speeches he had rehearsed. On the steamer it had seemed to have just the right note—a reference to the tenderness he would always feel for her combined with a non-committal attitude toward his present state of mind. Here with the past around him, beside him, growing minute by minute more heavy on the air, it seemed theatrical and stale.

She made no comment, sat without moving, her eyes fixed on him with an expression that might have meant everything or nothing.

> **"Whatever I do in the future I'll never love another girl as I've loved you."**

**WORDS FOR EVERYDAY USE**

**poi • gnant** (poi′ nyənt) *adj.*, deeply affecting the feelings. *Lance's <u>poignant</u> farewell look told Amy that he didn't want to leave her.*

**ret • i • cent** (re′tə sənt) *adj.*, reserved or uncommunicative in speech. *The normally talkative child made such <u>reticent</u> comments that his parents knew that the field trip had not gone well.*

"You don't love me any more, do you?" he asked her in a level voice.

"No."

When Mrs. Cary came in a minute later, and spoke to him about his success—there had been a half-column about him in the local paper—he was a mixture of emotions. He knew now that he still wanted this girl, and he knew that the past sometimes comes back—that was all. For the rest he must be strong and watchful and he would see.

"And now," Mrs. Cary was saying, "I want you two to go and see the lady who has the chrysanthemums. She particularly told me she wanted to see you because she'd read about you in the paper."

They went to see the lady with the chrysanthemums. They walked along the street, and he recognized with a sort of excitement just how her shorter footsteps always fell in between his own. The lady turned out to be nice, and the chrysanthemums were enormous and extraordinarily beautiful. The lady's gardens were full of them, white and pink and yellow, so that to be among them was a trip back into the heart of summer. There were two gardens full, and a gate between them; when they strolled toward the second garden the lady went first through the gate.

And then a curious thing happened. George stepped aside to let Jonquil pass, but instead of going through she stood still and stared at him for a minute. It was not so much the look, which was not a smile, as it was the moment of silence. They saw each other's eyes, and both took a short, faintly accelerated breath, and then they went on into the second garden. That was all.

The afternoon waned. They thanked the lady and walked home slowly, thoughtfully, side by side. Through dinner too they were silent. George told Mr. Cary something of what had happened in South America, and managed to let it be known that everything would be plain sailing for him in the future.

Then dinner was over, and he and Jonquil were alone in the room which had seen the beginning of their love affair and the end. It seemed to him long ago and inexpressibly sad. On that sofa he had felt agony and grief such as he would never feel again. He would never be so weak or so tired and miserable and poor. Yet he knew that that boy of fifteen months before had had something, a trust, a warmth that was gone forever. The sensible thing—they had done the sensible thing. He had traded his first youth for strength and carved success out of despair. But with his youth, life had carried away the freshness of his love.

"You won't marry me, will you?" he said quietly.

Jonquil shook her dark head.

"I'm never going to marry," she answered.

He nodded.

"I'm going on to Washington in the morning," he said.

"Oh—"

"I have to go. I've got to be in New York by the first, and meanwhile I want to stop off in Washington."

"Business!"

"No-o," he said as if reluctantly. "There's some one there I must see who was very kind to me when I was so—down and out."

This was invented. There was no one in Washington for him to see—but he was watching Jonquil narrowly, and he was sure that she winced a little, that her eyes closed and then opened wide again.

"But before I go I want to tell you the things that happened to me since I saw you, and, as maybe we won't meet again, I wonder if—if just this once you'd sit in my lap like you used to. I wouldn't ask except since there's no one else—yet—perhaps it doesn't matter."

She nodded, and in a moment was sitting in his lap as she had sat so often in that vanished spring. The feel of her head against his shoulder, of her familiar body, sent a chock of emotion over him. His arms holding her had a tendency to tighten around her, so he leaned back and began to talk thoughtfully into the air.

He told her of a despairing two weeks in New York which had terminated with an attractive if not very profitable job in a construction plant in Jersey City. When the Peru business had first presented itself it had not seemed an extraordinary opportunity. He was to be third assistant engineer on the expedition, but only ten of the American party, including eight rodmen and surveyors, had ever reached Cuzco. Ten days later the chief of the expedition was dead of yellow fever. That had been his chance, a chance for anybody but a fool, a marvelous chance—

"A chance for anybody but a fool?" she interrupted innocently.

"Even for a fool," he continued. "It was wonderful. Well, I wired New York—"

"And so," she interrupted again, "they wired that you ought to take a chance?"

"Ought to!" he exclaimed, still leaning back. "That I *had* to. There was no time to lose—"

"Not a minute?"

"Not a minute."

"Not even time for—" she paused.

"For what?"

"Look."

> **"A chance for anybody but a fool?"**

He bent his head forward suddenly, and she drew herself to him in the same moment, her lips half open like a flower.

"Yes," he whispered into her lips. "There's all the time in the world. . . ."

All the time in the world—his life and hers. But for an instant as he kissed her he knew that though he searched through eternity he could never recapture those lost April hours. He might press her close now till the muscles knotted on his arms—she was something desirable and rare that he had fought for and made his own—but never again an intangible whisper in the dusk, or on the breeze of night. . . .

Well, let it pass, he thought; April is over, April is over. There are all kinds of love in the world, but never the same love twice. ∎

*What does George learn about love at the end of the story?*

## Respond *to the* SELECTION

Do you think George and Jonquil should marry now? Why, or why not?

# INVESTIGATE, *Inquire, Imagine*

**Recall:** GATHERING FACTS

1a. During George's absence, how does Jonquil spend her time?

2a. What does Jonquil see as "the sensible thing"?

3a. What does George realize about his relationship with Jonquil during their reunion the following year?

→ **Interpret:** FINDING MEANING

1b. Is George or Jonquil more faithful to their love?

2b. Why does George feel "ridiculous and weak" after Jonquil ends their relationship?

3b. What commitment do George and Jonquil make to each other at the end of the story?

**Analyze:** TAKING THINGS APART

4a. Identify the two reversals of fortune that George experiences.

→ **Synthesize:** BRINGING THINGS TOGETHER

4b. George changes considerably in the course of this story. What is the relationship between change and growth?

**Evaluate:** MAKING JUDGMENTS

5a. Which love is stronger, the love George and Jonquil feel for each other at the beginning of the story or at the end of the story?

→ **Extend:** CONNECTING IDEAS

5b. The story ends with George realizing that there is "never the same love twice." Do you agree with this statement? Why, or why not?

# Understanding *Literature*

**REVERSAL.** Review the definition of **reversal** in the Handbook of Literary Terms. What is the reversal that happens to George O'Kelly professionally? How has George's life changed in a year?

**CHARACTER.** Review the definition for **character** in the Handbook of Literary Terms. Then fill in the chart below to describe George's character when he returns to Tennessee. What makes George a *dynamic character?*

| Physical Appearance | Dress | Habits/ Mannerisms/ Behaviors | Relationships with Other People | Other |
|---|---|---|---|---|
| tan, rugged appearance (indicating George has learned to work outdoors, which he formerly hated) | | | | |

# WRITER'S JOURNAL

1. Imagine that George O'Kelly has written a letter to an advice columnist explaining his financial and emotional problems when he lives in New York. Play the role of the columnist and write an **advice column** telling George what he should do.

2. Imagine that you are Jonquil at the moment she learns that George is coming back into town. Write a **journal entry** explaining why you broke up with George, how you feel about him now, and what you hope will happen during your reunion.

3. Write **jazz lyrics** about love, such as the changing love George feels for Jonquil at the end of the story.

# Integrating
## *the* LANGUAGE ARTS

## Vocabulary

**USING CONTEXT CLUES.** Identify five words in the selection that are unfamiliar to you and use context clues to decipher their meanings. Before you begin, read the Language Arts Survey 1.16, "Using Context Clues to Estimate Word Meaning." Write your own definitions for the unfamiliar words. Then check your definitions with the words' actual definitions in a dictionary and make any necessary corrections to your definitions.

## Applied English

**WRITING A LETTER OF RESIGNATION.** Imagine that you are George O'Kelly, but that instead of talking to Mr. Chambers you want to resign with a letter. Write Mr. Chambers a letter of resignation, stating why you're resigning, giving the date your resignation is effective, thanking him for your employment experience, and requesting a letter of recommendation. You might want to review the Language Arts Survey 6.5, "Writing a Business Letter," before you begin writing.

entertainment, historical events, and the economy. First, take notes as you do your research. Second, choose roles for your group members, deciding who will be the secretary, the writer, the editor, and the presenter. Third, the secretary takes notes for an outline, receiving ideas from the other three group members. Then the writer uses the outline to write the paper, giving it to the editor to mark revisions. Finally, the presenter uses the outline to give a presentation to the class, and the writer submits the revised paper to the teacher.

## Study and Research & Collaborative Learning

**RESEARCHING THE 1920s.** With two or three classmates, research an aspect of the Roaring Twenties or the Jazz Age. You might choose from these topics: prohibition and speakeasies, music and dance, other forms of

## Study and Research

**RESEARCHING ON THE INTERNET.** Look for quotations by F. Scott Fitzgerald on the Internet. Then make a daily calendar for this month with a notable Fitzgerald quote for each day. Be sure to cite which work of fiction each quote comes from.

## Literary
## T O O L S

IRONY. **Irony** is a difference between appearance and reality. In *irony of situation,* one of the forms of irony, an event occurs that violates the expectations of the characters or the reader. As you read, look for the two major examples of irony of situation in the short story.

STREAM-OF-CONSCIOUSNESS WRITING. **Stream-of-consciousness writing** is literary work that attempts to render the flow of feelings, thoughts, and impressions within the minds of characters. Look for examples of stream-of-consciousness writing as you read.

## About *the*
## S E L E C T I O N

Like all of the other short stories published in the 1930 collection *Flowering Judas,* "**The Jilting of Granny Weatherall**" was first published in a magazine. While Porter's earliest audience was quite small, comprising mostly writers who read obscure magazines, it was nonetheless enthusiastic about her perfection of style and the short story form.

## Reader's
*Journal*

What do you think you will be like when you are old?

# "The Jilting of Granny Weatherall"

BY KATHERINE ANNE PORTER

## About *the*
## A U T H O R

**Katherine Anne Porter** (1890–1980) was born Callie Porter in Indian Creek, Texas. Her mother died when she was about two, and her father moved the family to live with his mother, who raised them in a house that Porter recalled as "full of books" and extreme poverty. When Porter was eleven her grandmother died; when she was sixteen, she married so she could leave home. It was a short union, and by 1916 she began her writing career as a reporter. She worked for newspapers in Dallas and Fort Worth, Texas, and Denver, Colorado.

Porter moved to Greenwich Village in New York City in 1918 and then spent the years between 1918 and 1924 living mainly in Mexico, freelancing and becoming involved in revolutionary politics. "Maria Conception," her first fiction story, was written while she was in Mexico. Published in *Century* magazine in 1922, it won her critical acclaim.

Porter lived a life filled with travel, activity, many jobs, and four marriages. She was a self-supporting woman with expensive tastes, so even though she considered herself a "serious writer," she didn't want to give up lucrative freelance offers, which had the effect of limiting her literary production. In 1931, Porter used a Guggenheim Fellowship to return to Mexico for several years. In the 1950s she lectured and was a writer-in-residence at college campuses. *Collected Stories* (1965) received a National Book Award, the Pulitzer Prize, and the Gold Medal for fiction of the National Institute of Arts and Letters.

Among her other works are *Flowering Judas* (1929), *Noon Wine* (1937), *Pale Horse, Pale Rider* (1939), *The Leaning Tower* (1944), and her only novel, *Ship of Fools,* begun in 1931, but not published until 1962. *Ship of Fools* was made into a film and brought her a great deal of money.

*New England Woman (Mrs. Jedediah H. Richards),* 1895. Cecilia Beaux.
The Pennsylvania Academy of the Fine Arts, Philadelphia.

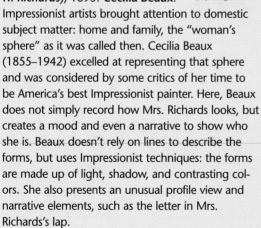

## Art**Note**

***New England Woman (Mrs. Jedediah H. Richards),*** 1895. **Cecilia Beaux.**
Impressionist artists brought attention to domestic subject matter: home and family, the "woman's sphere" as it was called then. Cecilia Beaux (1855–1942) excelled at representing that sphere and was considered by some critics of her time to be America's best Impressionist painter. Here, Beaux does not simply record how Mrs. Richards looks, but creates a mood and even a narrative to show who she is. Beaux doesn't rely on lines to describe the forms, but uses Impressionist techniques: the forms are made up of light, shadow, and contrasting colors. She also presents an unusual profile view and narrative elements, such as the letter in Mrs. Richards's lap.

# The Jilting of Granny Weatherall

## KATHERINE ANNE PORTER

**S**he flicked her wrist neatly out of Doctor Harry's pudgy careful fingers and pulled the sheet up to her chin. The brat ought to be in knee breeches. Doctoring around the country with spectacles on his nose! "Get along now, take your schoolbooks and go. There's nothing wrong with me."

Doctor Harry spread a warm paw like a cushion on her forehead where the forked green vein danced and made her eyelids twitch. "Now, now, be a good girl, and we'll have you up in no time."

"That's no way to speak to a woman nearly eighty years old just because she's down. I'd have you respect your elders, young man."

"Well, Missy, excuse me," Doctor Harry patted her cheek. "But I've got to warn you, haven't I? You're a marvel, but you must be careful or you're going to be good and sorry."

"Don't tell me what I'm going to be. I'm on my feet now, morally speaking. It's Cornelia. I had to go to bed to get rid of her."

Her bones felt loose, and floated around in her skin, and Doctor Harry floated like a balloon around the foot of the bed. He floated and pulled down his waistcoat and swung his glasses on a cord. "Well, stay where you are, it certainly can't hurt you."

"Get along and doctor your sick," said Granny Weatherall. "Leave a well woman alone. I'll call for you when I want you. . . . Where were you forty years ago when I pulled through milk leg[1] and double pneumonia? You weren't even born. Don't let Cornelia lead you on," she shouted, because Doctor Harry appeared to float up to the ceiling and out. "I pay my own bills, and I don't throw my money away on nonsense!"

*How old is Granny Weatherall? Approximately how old is Doctor Harry?*

She meant to wave good-bye, but it was too much trouble. Her eyes closed of themselves, it was like a dark curtain drawn around the bed. The pillow rose and floated under her, pleasant as a hammock in a light wind. She listened to the leaves rustling outside the window. No, somebody was swishing newspapers: no, Cornelia and Doctor Harry were whispering together. She leaped broad awake, thinking they whispered in her ear.

"She was never like this, *never* like this!" "Well, what can we expect?" "Yes, eighty years old. . . ."

Well, and what if she was? She still had ears. It was like Cornelia to whisper around doors. She always kept things secret in such a public way. She was always being tactful and kind. Cornelia was dutiful: that was the trouble with her. Dutiful and good: "So good and dutiful," said Granny, "that I'd like to spank her." She saw herself spanking Cornelia and making a fine job of it.

"What'd you say, Mother?"

Granny felt her face tying up in hard knots.

"Can't a body think, I'd like to know?"

"I thought you might want something."

"I do. I want a lot of things. First off, go away and don't whisper."

She lay and drowsed, hoping in her sleep that the children would keep out and let her rest a minute. It had been a long day. Not that she was tired. It was always pleasant to snatch a minute now and then. There was always so much to be done, let me see: tomorrow.

Tomorrow was far away and there was nothing to trouble about. Things were finished somehow when the time came: thank God there was always a little margin over for peace: then a person could spread out the plan of life and tuck in the edges orderly. It was good to have everything clean and folded away, with the hair brushes and tonic bottles sitting straight on the white embroidered linen: the day started without fuss and the pantry shelves laid out with rows of jelly glasses and brown jugs and white stonechina jars with blue whirligigs and words painted on them: coffee, tea, sugar, ginger, cinnamon, allspice: and the bronze clock with the lion on top nicely dusted off. The dust that lion could collect in twenty-four hours! The box in the attic with all those letters tied up, well, she'd have to go through that tomorrow. All those letters— George's letters and John's letters and her letters to them both—lying around for the children to find afterwards made her uneasy. Yes, that would be tomorrow's business. No use to let them know how silly she had been once.

*What does Granny Weatherall need to do tomorrow?*

*Tomorrow was far away and there was nothing to trouble about.*

While she was rummaging around she found death in her mind and it felt clammy and unfa-

---

1. **milk leg.** Painful swelling of the leg

**WORDS FOR EVERYDAY USE**

**rum • mage** (rumˈij) *vt.,* search through thoroughly; ransack. *Mr. Sorenson rummaged around in the garage until he found the drill he had borrowed from his neighbor.*

miliar. She had spent so much time preparing for death there was no need for bringing it up again. Let it take care of itself now. When she was sixty she had felt very old, finished, and went around making farewell trips to see her children and grandchildren, with a secret in her mind: This is the very last of your mother, children! Then she made her will and came down with a long fever. That was all just a notion like a lot of other things, but it was lucky too, for she had once for all got over the idea of dying for a long time. Now she couldn't be worried. She hoped she had better sense now. Her father had lived to be one hundred and two years old and had drunk a noggin of strong hot toddy on his last birthday. He told the reporters it was his daily habit, and he owed his long life to that. He had made quite a scandal and was very pleased about it. She believed she'd just plague Cornelia a little.

*What had she done twenty years ago?*

"Cornelia! Cornelia!" No footsteps, but a sudden hand on her cheek. "Bless you, where have you been?"

"Here, mother."

"Well, Cornelia, I want a noggin of hot toddy."

"Are you cold, darling?"

"I'm chilly, Cornelia. Lying in bed stops the circulation. I must have told you that a thousand times."

Well, she could just hear Cornelia telling her husband that Mother was getting a little childish and they'd have to humor her. The thing that most annoyed her was that Cornelia thought she was deaf, dumb, and blind. Little hasty glances and tiny gestures tossed around her and over her head saying, "Don't cross her, let her have her way, she's eighty years old," and she sitting there as if she lived in a thin glass cage. Sometimes Granny almost made up her mind to pack up and move back to her own house where nobody could

*What does Cornelia do that bothers her mother?*

remind her every minute that she was old. Wait, wait, Cornelia, till your own children whisper behind your back!

In her day she had kept a better house and had got more work done. She wasn't too old yet for Lydia to be driving eighty miles for advice when one of the children jumped the track, and Jimmy still dropped in and talked things over: "Now, Mammy, you've a good business head, I want to know what you think of this? . . ." Old. Cornelia couldn't change the furniture around without asking. Little things, little things! They had been so sweet when they were little. Granny wished the old days were back again with the children young and everything to be done over. It had been a hard pull, but not too much for her. When she thought of all the food she had cooked, and all the clothes she had cut and sewed, and all the gardens she had made— well, the children showed it. There they were, made out of her, and they couldn't get away from that. Sometimes she wanted to see John again and point to them and say, Well, I didn't do so badly, did I? But that would have to wait. That

*Who is John? What does Granny Weatherall want him to know?*

was for tomorrow. She used to think of him as a man, but now all the children were older than their father, and he would be a child beside her if she saw him now. It seemed strange and there was something wrong in the idea. Why, he couldn't possibly recognize her. She had fenced in a hundred acres once, digging the post holes herself and clamping the wires with just a negro boy to help. That changed a woman. John would be looking for a young woman with the peaked Spanish comb in her hair and the painted fan. Digging post holes changed a woman. Riding country roads in the winter when women had their babies was another thing: sitting up nights with sick

*What kinds of things has Granny done?*

horses and sick children and hardly ever losing one. John, I hardly ever lost one of them! John would see that in a minute, that would be something he could understand, she wouldn't have to explain anything!

It made her feel like rolling up her sleeves and putting the whole place to rights again. No matter if Cornelia was determined to be everywhere at once, there were a great many things left undone on this place. She would start tomorrow and do them. It was good to be strong enough for everything, even if all you made melted and changed and slipped under your hands, so that by the time you finished you almost forgot what you were working for. What was it I set out to do? she asked herself intently, but she could not remember. A fog rose over the valley, she saw it marching across the creek swallowing the trees and moving up the hill like an army of ghosts. Soon it would be at the near edge of the orchard, and then it was time to go in and light the lamps. Come in, children, don't stay out in the night air.

Lighting the lamps had been beautiful. The children huddled up to her and breathed like little calves waiting at the bars in the twilight. Their eyes followed the match and watched the flame rise and settle in a blue curve, then they moved away from her. The lamp was lit, they didn't have to be scared and hang on to mother any more. Never, never, never more. God, for all my life I thank Thee. Without Thee, my God, I could never have done it. Hail Mary, full of grace.

I want you to pick all the fruit this year and see that nothing is wasted. There's always someone who can use it. Don't let good things rot for want of using. You waste life when you waste good food. Don't let things get lost. It's bitter to lose things. Now, don't let me get to thinking, not when I am tired and taking a little nap before supper. . . .

The pillow rose about her shoulders and pressed against her heart and the memory was being squeezed out of it: oh, push down the pillow, somebody: it would smother her if she tried to hold it. Such a fresh breeze blowing and such a green day with no threats in it. But he had not come, just the same.

> *What does a woman do when she has put on the white veil and set out the white cake for a man and he doesn't come?*

What does a woman do when she has put on the white veil and set out the white cake for a man and he doesn't come? She tried to remember. No, I swear he never harmed me but in that. He never harmed me but in that . . . and what if he did? There was the day, the day, but a whirl of dark smoke rose and covered it, crept up and over into the bright field where everything was planted so carefully in orderly rows. That was hell, she knew hell when she saw it. For sixty years she had prayed against remembering him and against losing her soul in the deep pit of hell, and now the two things were mingled in one and the thought of him was a smoky cloud from hell that moved and crept in her head when she had just got rid of Doctor Harry and was trying to rest a minute. Wounded vanity, Ellen, said a sharp voice in the top of her mind. Don't let your wounded vanity get the upper hand of you. Plenty of girls get <u>jilted</u>. You were jilted, weren't you? Then stand up to it. Her eyelids wavered and let in streamers of blue-gray light like tissue paper over her eyes. She must get up and pull the shades down or she'd never sleep. She was in bed again and the

---

**WORDS FOR EVERYDAY USE**

**jilt** (jilt) *vt.*, reject; cast off. *Carol <u>jilted</u> her friends when she ran into Bill at the fair.*

shades were not down. How could that happen? Better turn over, hide from the light, sleeping in the light gave you nightmares. "Mother, how do you feel now?" and a stinging wetness on her forehead. But I don't like having my face washed in cold water!

Hapsy? George? Lydia? Jimmy? No, Cornelia, and her features were swollen and full of little puddles. "They're coming, darling, they'll all be here soon." Go wash your face, child, you look funny.

Instead of obeying, Cornelia knelt down and put her head on the pillow. She seemed to be talking but there was no sound. "Well, are you tongue-tied? Whose birthday is it? Are you going to give a party?"

Cornelia's mouth moved urgently in strange shapes. "Don't do that, you bother me, daughter."

"Oh, no, Mother. Oh, no. . . ."

Nonsense. It was strange about children. They disputed your every word. "No what, Cornelia?"

"Here's Doctor Harry."

"I won't see that boy again. He just left five minutes ago."

"That was this morning, Mother. It's night now. Here's the nurse."

"This is Doctor Harry, Mrs. Weatherall. I never saw you look so young and happy!"

"Ah, I'll never be young again—but I'd be happy if they'd let me lie in peace and get rested."

She thought she spoke up loudly, but no one answered. A warm weight on her forehead, a warm bracelet on her wrist, and a breeze went on whispering, trying to tell her something. A shuffle of leaves in the everlasting hand of God, He blew on them and they danced and rattled. "Mother, don't mind, we're going to give you a little hypodermic."[2] "Look here, daughter, how do ants get in this bed? I saw sugar ants yesterday." Did you send for Hapsy too?

It was Hapsy she really wanted. She had to go a long way back through a great many rooms to find Hapsy standing with a baby on her arm. She seemed to herself to be Hapsy also, and the baby on Hapsy's arm was Hapsy and himself and herself, all at once, and there was no surprise in the meeting. Then Hapsy melted from within and turned flimsy as gray gauze and the baby was a gauzy shadow, and Hapsy came up close and said, "I thought you'd never come," and looked at her very searchingly and said, "You haven't changed a bit!" They leaned forward to kiss, when Cornelia began whispering from a long way off. "Oh, is there anything you want to tell me? Is there anything I can do for you?"

Yes, she had changed her mind after sixty years and she would like to see George. I want you to find George. Find him and be sure to tell him I forgot him. I want him to know I had my husband just the same and my children and my house like any other woman. A good house too and a good husband that I loved and fine children out of him. Better than I hoped for even. Tell him I was given back everything he took away and more. Oh, no, oh, God, no, there was something else besides the house and the man and the children. Oh, surely they were not all? What was it? Something not given back. . . . Her breath crowded down under her ribs and grew into a monstrous frightening shape with cutting edges; it bored up into her head, and the agony was unbelievable: Yes, John, get the Doctor now, no more talk, my time has come.

When this one was born it should be the last. The last. It should have been born first, for it was the one she had truly wanted. Everything came in good time. Nothing left out, left over. She was strong, in three days she would be as well as ever. Better. A woman needed milk in her to have her full health.

*Who is Hapsy? What are Granny Weatherall's feelings for her? What happened to her?*

*Has Granny Weatherall's life been complete?*

---

2. **hypodermic.** Injection

"Mother, do you hear me?"

"I've been telling you—"

"Mother, Father Connolly's here."

"I went to Holy Communion only last week. Tell him I'm not so sinful as all that."

"Father just wants to speak to you."

He could speak as much as he pleased. It was like him to drop in and inquire about her soul as if it were a teething baby, and then stay on for a cup of tea and a round of cards and gossip. He always had a funny story of some sort, usually about an Irishman who made his little mistakes and confessed them, and the point lay in some absurd thing he would blurt out in the confessional showing his struggles between native piety and original sin. Granny felt easy about her soul. Cornelia, where are your manners? Give Father Connolly a chair. She had her secret comfortable understanding with a few favorite saints who cleared a straight road to God for her. All as surely signed and sealed as the papers for the new Forty Acres. Forever . . . heirs and assigns[3] forever. Since the day the wedding cake was not cut, but thrown out and wasted. The whole bottom dropped out of the world, and there she was blind and sweating with nothing under her feet and the walls falling away. His hand had caught her under the breast, she had not fallen, there was the freshly polished floor with the green rug on it, just as before. He had cursed like a sailor's parrot and said, "I'll kill him for you." Don't lay a hand on him, for my sake leave something to God. "Now, Ellen, you must believe what I tell you. . . ."

So there was nothing, nothing to worry about any more, except sometimes in the night one of the children screamed in a nightmare, and they both hustled out shaking and hunting for the matches and calling, "There, wait a minute, here we are!" John, get the doctor now. Hapsy's

*Who came to her aid on the day she was jilted?*

*Her eyes opened very wide and the room stood out like a picture she had seen somewhere.*

time has come. But there was Hapsy standing by the bed in a white cap. "Cornelia, tell Hapsy to take off her cap. I can't see her plain."

Her eyes opened very wide and the room stood out like a picture she had seen somewhere. Dark colors with the shadows rising towards the ceiling in long angles. The tall black dresser gleamed with nothing on it but John's picture, enlarged from a little one, with John's eyes very black when they should have been blue. You never saw him, so how do you know how he looked? But the man insisted the copy was perfect, it was very rich and handsome. For a picture, yes, but it's not my husband. The table by the bed had a linen cover and a candle and a crucifix. The light was blue from Cornelia's silk lampshades. No sort of light at all, just frippery. You had to live forty years with kerosene lamps to appreciate honest electricity. She felt very strong and she saw Doctor Harry with a rosy nimbus[4] around him.

"You look like a saint, Doctor Harry, and I vow that's as near as you'll ever come to it."

"She's saying something."

"I heard you, Cornelia. What's all this carrying on?"

"Father Connolly's saying—"

Cornelia's voice staggered and bumped like a cart in a bad road. It rounded corners and turned back again and arrived nowhere. Granny stepped up in the cart very lightly and reached for the reins, but a man sat beside her and she knew him by his hands, driving the cart. She did not look in his face, for she knew without seeing, but looked instead down the road where the trees leaned over and bowed to each other and a thousand birds were singing a Mass. She felt like singing too, but she put her hand in the bosom of her dress and pulled out a rosary, and Father

---

3. **assigns.** People to whom property is transferred
4. **nimbus.** Halo; circle of light around the head of a saint or divinity

Connolly murmured Latin in a very solemn voice and tickled her feet.[5] My God, will you stop that nonsense? I'm a married woman. What if he did run away and leave me to face the priest by myself? I found another a whole world better. I wouldn't have exchanged my husband for anybody except St. Michael himself, and you may tell him that for me with a thank you in the bargain.

Light flashed on her closed eyelids, and a deep roaring shook her. Cornelia, is that lightning? I hear thunder. There's going to be a storm. Close all the windows. Call the children in. "Mother, here we are, all of us." "Is that you, Hapsy?" "Oh, no, I'm Lydia. We drove as fast as we could." Their faces drifted above her, drifted away. The rosary fell out of her hands and Lydia put it back. Jimmy tried to help, their hands fumbled together, and Granny closed two fingers around Jimmy's thumb. Beads wouldn't do, it must be something alive. She was so amazed her thoughts ran round and round. So, my dear Lord, this is my death and I wasn't even thinking about it. My children have come to see me die. But I can't, it's not time. Oh, I always hated surprises. I wanted to give Cornelia the amethyst set—Cornelia, you're to have the amethyst set, but Hapsy's to wear it when she wants, and, Doctor Harry, do shut up. Nobody sent for you. Oh, my dear Lord, do wait a minute. I meant to do something about the Forty Acres, Jimmy doesn't need it and Lydia will later on, with that worthless husband of hers. I meant

> Is Granny Weatherall ready to die?

to finish the altar cloth and send six bottles of wine to Sister Borgia for her dyspepsia. I want to send six bottles of wine to Sister Borgia, Father Connolly, now don't let me forget.

Cornelia's voice made short turns and tilted over and crashed. "Oh, Mother, oh, Mother, oh Mother. . . ."

"I'm not going, Cornelia. I'm taken by surprise. I can't go."

You'll see Hapsy again. What about her? "I thought you'd never come." Granny made a long journey outward, looking for Hapsy. What if I don't find her? What then? Her heart sank down and down, there was no bottom to death, she couldn't come to the end of it. The blue light from Cornelia's lampshade drew into a tiny point in the center of her brain, it flickered and winked like an eye, quietly it fluttered and <u>dwindled</u>. Granny lay curled down within herself, amazed and watchful, staring at the point of light that was herself: her body was now only a deeper mass of shadow in an endless darkness and this darkness would curl around the light and swallow it up. God, give a sign!

For the second time there was no sign. Again no bridegroom and the priest in the house. She could not remember any other sorrow because this grief wiped them all away. Oh, no, there's nothing more cruel than this— I'll never forgive it. She stretched herself with a deep breath and blew out the light. ∎

> Who jilts Granny Weatherall this time?

---

5. **murmured . . . feet.** Administered the last rites, a sacrament in the Catholic church for a person who is dying

---

**WORDS FOR EVERYDAY USE**

**dwin • dle** (dwin´dəl) vt., languish; fade. *When the light <u>dwindled</u> at sunset, we lit candles.*

---

**Respond** *to the* **SELECTION**

If you were Granny Weatherall, would you finally forgive George for jilting you on your wedding day? Why, or why not?

# INVESTIGATE Inquire, Imagine

## Recall: GATHERING FACTS

1a. What explanation for being in bed does Granny Weatherall give to the doctor?

2a. How had Granny Weatherall prepared herself for death when she was sixty years old?

3a. What does Granny Weatherall remember most about her first wedding day?

→ ## Interpret: FINDING MEANING

1b. What traits describe Granny Weatherall before she became ill?

2b. Why doesn't Granny Weatherall worry now about death?

3b. Why does Granny Weatherall mingle the thought of the bridegroom with the thought of losing her soul in hell?

## Analyze: TAKING THINGS APART

4a. Identify two times when Granny Weatherall was jilted. What do the two jiltings have in common? Which jilting is the hardest for her to take?

→ ## Synthesize: BRINGING THINGS TOGETHER

4b. Why is Granny Weatherall an appropriate name for the character in this story?

## Evaluate: MAKING JUDGMENTS

5a. To what degree do the past and future influence Granny Weatherall's thinking?

→ ## Extend: CONNECTING IDEAS

5b. Compare the experiences of death of Granny Weatherall and the speaker in Emily Dickinson's "I heard a Fly buzz—when I died—" (Unit 4).

# Understanding Literature

IRONY. Review the definition for **irony** in the Handbook of Literary Terms. What are two major examples of *irony of situation* in this short story? How are the expectations of Granny Weatheralll violated in each case?

STREAM-OF-CONSCIOUSNESS WRITING. Review the definition for **stream-of-consciousness writing** in the Handbook of Literary Terms. Then make a chart. On the left, list examples of stream-of-consciousness in the story. On the right, explain what the examples mean. One example has been done for you.

| Stream-of-Consciousness Writing | Explanation |
|---|---|
| "It was Hapsy she really wanted. . . . They leaned forward to kiss. . . ." | Granny remembers her dead daughter; in her confused mind she is also Hapsy and Hapsy's baby is Hapsy. |

# WRITER'S JOURNAL

1. Imagine you are Granny Weatherall. Write a **will**, stating what possessions you are leaving to family members and friends.
2. Write an imaginary **dialogue** between Granny Weatherall and George. Have Granny discuss her feelings at being jilted, and have George explain why he changed his mind about marrying her.
3. Imagine you are the young Granny Weatherall. Write a **letter** to George or John (one of the letters she doesn't want her children to find).

# Integrating *the* LANGUAGE ARTS

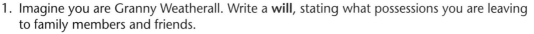

## Language, Grammar, and Style

**PRECISE NOUNS.** Read the Language Arts Survey 3.39, "Adding Colorful Language to Sentences." Then rewrite each of the following sentences, replacing the vague nouns with precise nouns.

1. The children had left their toys on the porch.
2. Every fall, she lined the shelves with jars of food and spices.
3. Illnesses plagued the children throughout the horrible winter.
4. After finishing the chore, she came into the house and fixed dinner.
5. Years ago, the jilted bride was left behind with the vestiges of the day.

## Speaking and Listening

**NONVERBAL COMMUNICATION.** Read the Language Arts Survey 4.1, "Verbal and Nonverbal Communication." Then describe how each emotion listed below might be communicated through eye contact, facial expressions, gestures, body language, or proximity.

1. bewilderment
2. shock
3. determination
4. surprise
5. sorrow

## Media Literacy

**OBITUARY.** Write an obituary for Granny Weatherall, including details that will communicate to your readers what was unique or characteristic about her, as well as facts about her life.

## Study and Research

**LIBRARY RESEARCH.** Investigate the reference section of your local library to find critical analyses of Katherine Anne Porter and her work, specifically of the story "The Jilting of Granny Weatherall." Ask your librarian for guidance. For general critical information, your librarian might steer you to the following reference books: *American Writers: A Collection of Literary Biographies; Great Women Writers;* or *Modern American Women Writers.* For more specific criticism, he or she might recommend *Library of Literary Criticism: Modern American Literature; Short Story Criticism;* or *Reference Guide to Short Fiction.* Select one critical analysis and write a summary of it. You may also explain whether you agree or disagree with its author.

# Literary TOOLS

**INTERNAL MONOLOGUE.** An **internal monologue** presents the private sensations, thoughts, and emotions of a character. As you read, think about what the older waiter's internal monologue reveals about his feelings about human existence.

**CHARACTERIZATION AND DIALOGUE.** **Characterization** is the use of literary techniques to create a character. **Dialogue** is conversation involving two or more people or characters. As you read, determine which characteristics of the younger waiter are revealed through dialogue.

## About the SELECTION

Between 1923 and 1933, Hemingway wrote all of his major short stories, including **"A Clean, Well-Lighted Place,"** which was published in the 1933 collection *Winner Take Nothing.* Five years later, *The Fifth Column* and the *First Forty-Nine Stories,* which compiled three collections—*In Our Time, Men Without Women,* and *Winner Take Nothing*—established Hemingway as one of America's most admired writers of short fiction. Written with Hemingway's characteristic spare prose, "A Clean, Well-Lighted Place" unfolds primarily through dialogue. In the selection, two waiters at a Spanish café discuss one of their regular clients, an elderly man who likes to sit late at night at a table on the café terrace. A careful listener, Hemingway vitalized the writing of dialogue by stripping verbal exchange to its essentials, producing the illusion of actual speech.

# "A Clean, Well-Lighted Place"

BY ERNEST HEMINGWAY

## About the AUTHOR

**Ernest Hemingway** (1899–1961) was born and raised in Oak Park, Illinois, one of six children. His father was a successful doctor, his mother a music teacher. After high school, Hemingway began his writing career as a reporter at the *Kansas City Star.* When World War I broke out and an eye problem prevented him from joining the United States Army, he served as an ambulance driver with the Italian army.

After the war he returned to Europe as a journalist and also began his serious writing career. There he was part of the large community of expatriate artists and writers—Gertrude Stein, Sherwood Anderson, Ezra Pound, and F. Scott Fitzgerald among others.

Seriously injured in a 1953 plane crash in Africa, he never fully recovered his mental health or productivity. He committed suicide in 1961 in Idaho after years of suffering from despair and paranoia.

Hemingway won a Pulitzer Prize in 1953 for *The Old Man and the Sea* (1952) and a Nobel Prize for literature in 1954. He was a prolific writer whose works include *The Sun Also Rises* (1926), *A Farewell to Arms* (1929), *Death in the Afternoon* (1932), *The Green Hills of Africa* (1935), *The Snows of Kilimanjaro* (1936), *To Have and Have Not* (1937), *The Fifth Column* (play, 1938), *For Whom the Bell Tolls* (1940), *A Moveable Feast* (posthumously in 1964), and *Islands in the Stream* (posthumously in 1970), *The Garden of Eden* (posthumously in 1986), and *True at First Light* (posthumously in 1999).

## Reader's *Journal*

What special place do you go to when you want to be alone?

*Cafe Terrace at Night,* 1888. Vincent van Gogh.
Kröller-Müller Museum, Otterlo, Netherlands.

I t was late and every one had left the café except an old man who sat in the shadow the leaves of the tree made against the electric light. In the day time the street was dusty, but at night the dew settled the dust and the old man liked to sit late because he was deaf and now at night it was quiet and he felt the difference. The two waiters inside the café knew that the old man was a little drunk, and while he was a good client they knew that if he became too drunk he would leave without paying, so they kept watch on him.

"Last week he tried to commit suicide," one waiter said.

"Why?"

"He was in despair."

"What about?"

"Nothing."

"How do you know it was nothing?"

"He has plenty of money."

They sat together at a table that was close against the wall near the door of the café and looked at the terrace where the tables were all empty except where the old man sat in the shadow of the leaves of the tree that moved slightly in the wind. A girl and a soldier went by in the street. The street light shone on the brass number on his collar. The girl wore no head covering and hurried beside him.

"The guard will pick him up," one waiter said.

"What does it matter if he gets what he's after?"

"He had better get off the street now. The guard will get him. They went by five minutes ago."

*What does the waiter think caused the man's despair?*

The old man sitting in the shadow rapped on his saucer with his glass. The younger waiter went over to him.

"What do you want?"

The old man looked at him. "Another brandy," he said.

"You'll be drunk," the waiter said. The old man looked at him. The waiter went away.

"He'll stay all night," he said to his colleague. "I'm sleepy now. I never get into bed before three o'clock. He should have killed himself last week."

The waiter took the brandy bottle and another saucer from the counter inside the café and marched out to the old man's table. He put down the saucer and poured the glass full of brandy.

*What does the waiter say to the old man? Why?*

"You should have killed yourself last week," he said to the deaf man. The old man motioned with his finger. "A little more," he said. The waiter poured on into the glass so that the brandy slopped over and ran down the stem into the top saucer of the pile. "Thank you," the old man said. The waiter took the bottle back inside the café. He sat down at the table with his colleague again.

"He's drunk now," he said.

"He's drunk every night."

"What did he want to kill himself for?"

"How should I know."

"How did he do it?"

"He hung himself with a rope."

"Who cut him down?"

"His niece."

"Why did they do it?"

"Fear for his soul."

*How did the old man attempt suicide? Who rescued him? Why?*

"How much money has he got?"

"He's got plenty."

"He must be eighty years old."

"Anyway I should say he was eighty."

"I wish he would go home. I never get to bed before three o'clock. What kind of hour is that to go to bed?"

"He stays up because he likes it."

"He's lonely. I'm not lonely. I have a wife waiting in bed for me."

"He had a wife once too."

"A wife would be no good to him now."

"You can't tell. He might be better with a wife."

"His niece looks after him."

"I know. You said she cut him down."

"I wouldn't want to be that old. An old man is a nasty thing."

"Not always. This old man is clean. He drinks without spilling. Even now, drunk. Look at him."

"I don't want to look at him. I wish he would go home. He has no regard for those who must work."

The old man looked from his glass across the square, then over at the waiters.

"Another brandy," he said, pointing to his glass. The waiter who was in a hurry came over.

"Finished," he said, speaking with that omission of syntax stupid people employ when talking to drunken people or foreigners. "No more tonight. Close now."

"Another," said the old man.

"No. Finished." The waiter wiped the edge of the table with a towel and shook his head.

The old man stood up, slowly counted the saucers, took a leather coin purse from his pocket and paid for the drinks, leaving half a peseta[1] tip.

The waiter watched him go down the street, a very old man walking unsteadily but with dignity.

"Why didn't you let him stay and drink?" the unhurried waiter asked. They were putting up the shutters. "It is not half past two."

"I want to go home to bed."

"What is an hour?"

"More to me than to him."

"An hour is the same."

"You talk like an old man yourself. He can buy a bottle and drink at home."

---

1. **peseta.** Spanish currency

"It's not the same."

"No, it is not," agreed the waiter with a wife. He did not wish to be unjust. He was only in a hurry.

On what do the two waiters agree?

"And you? You have no fear of going home before your usual hour?"

"Are you trying to insult me?"

"No, hombre,[2] only to make a joke."

"No," the waiter who was in a hurry said, rising from pulling down the metal shutters. "I have confidence. I am all confidence."

"You have youth, confidence, and a job," the older waiter said. "You have everything."

"And what do you lack?"

"Everything but work."

"You have everything I have."

"No. I have never had confidence and I am not young."

"Come on. Stop talking nonsense and lock up."

"I am of those who like to stay late at the café," the older waiter said. "With all those who do not want to go to bed. With all those who need a light for the night."

"I want to go home and into bed."

"We are of two different kinds," the older waiter said. He was now dressed to go home. "It is not only a question of youth and confidence although those things are very beautiful. Each night I am reluctant to close up because there may be some one who needs the café."

With whom does the older waiter sympathize?

"Hombre, there are bodegas[3] open all night long."

"You do not understand. This is a clean and pleasant café. It is well lighted. The light is very good and also, now, there are shadows of the leaves."

"Good night," said the younger waiter.

"Good night," the other said. Turning off the electric light he continued the conversation with himself. It is the light of course but it is necessary that the place be clean and pleasant. You do not want music. Certainly you do not want music. Nor can you stand before a bar with dig-nity although that is all that is provided for these hours. What did he fear? It was not fear or dread. It was a nothing that he knew too well. It was all a nothing and a man was nothing too. It

How would you describe the older waiter's outlook on life?

was only that and light was all it needed and a certain cleanness and order. Some lived in it and never felt it but he knew it all was nada[4] y pues nada y nada y pues nada. Our nada who art in nada, nada be thy name thy kingdom nada thy will be nada in nada as it is in nada. Give us this nada our daily nada and nada us our nada as we nada our nadas and nada us not into nada but deliver us from nada; pues nada. Hail nothing full of nothing, nothing is with thee.[5] He smiled and stood before a bar with a shining steam pressure coffee machine.

"What's yours?" asked the barman.

"Nada."

"Otro loco mas,"[6] said the barman and turned away.

"A little cup," said the waiter.

The barman poured it for him.

"The light is very bright and pleasant but the bar is unpolished," the waiter said.

The barman looked at him but did not answer. It was too late at night for conversation.

"You want another copita?"[7] the barman asked.

"No, thank you," said the waiter and went out. He disliked bars and bodegas. A clean, well-lighted café was a very different thing. Now, without thinking further, he would go home to his room. He would lie in the bed and finally, with daylight, he would go to sleep. After all, he said to himself, it is probably only insomnia. Many must have it. ■

---

2. **hombre.** Man
3. **bodegas.** Bars; taverns
4. **nada.** Nothing
5. **Our nada . . . thee.** The waiter is replacing words in two common prayers with *nada* or *nothing*.
6. **Otro loco mas.** Another crazy one
7. **copita.** Cup

If you were the waiter waiting on the elderly deaf man, would you patiently wait for him to finish drinking, or would you hurry him to leave in order to close the café? Why?

# INVESTIGATE Inquire Imagine

**Recall:** GATHERING FACTS

1a. What does one waiter tell the other the elderly, deaf client tried to do last week?

2a. What reason does the younger waiter give the older waiter for not letting the elderly man stay longer in the café?

3a. What does the older waiter think he lacks?

**Interpret:** FINDING MEANING

1b. What attitude does the younger waiter express when stating the old man's despair was over "nothing"?

2b. Why does the younger waiter tell the older waiter, "You talk like an old man yourself"?

3b. Why would the older waiter not mind staying another hour at the café?

**Analyze:** TAKING THINGS APART

4a. Identify the characteristics of the café that make it appealing to the older waiter and the elderly, deaf customer.

**Synthesize:** BRINGING THINGS TOGETHER

4b. What feelings do the older waiter and the elderly, deaf client have in common?

**Evaluate:** MAKING JUDGMENTS

5a. Which waiter do you find to be a more sympathetic character? Why?

**Extend:** CONNECTING IDEAS

5b. The young waiter says, "An old man is a nasty thing." Compare the portrayal of old age in Hemingway's story with that in "The Jilting of Granny Weatherall." What does old age represent to Hemingway and Porter?

# Understanding Literature

INTERNAL MONOLOGUE. Review the definition for **internal monologue** in the Handbook of Literary Terms. In the following passage from the selection, the reader is allowed to step inside the mind of the older waiter and overhear his private thoughts:

> It is the light of course but it is necessary that the place be clean and pleasant. . . . What did he fear? It was not fear or dread. It was a nothing that he knew too well. It was all a nothing and a man was nothing too. It was only that and light was all it needed and a certain cleanness and order. . . . Our nada who art in nada, nada be thy name thy kingdom nada. . . .

How does the waiter feel about human existence?

**CHARACTERIZATION AND DIALOGUE.** Review the definitions for **characterization** and **dialogue** in the Handbook of Literary Terms. Then make a chart. On the left, copy dialogue by the younger waiter that reveals aspects of his personality. On the right, explain what aspects of his personality are revealed. One example has been done for you.

| Dialogue | Explanation |
|---|---|
| "He has plenty of money." | In assuming that wealthy people have no reason for feeling despair, the younger waiter reveals his lack of empathy for the client's despair and suicide attempt. |

# WRITER'S JOURNAL

1. Imagine that you are the elderly, deaf client. Write a **journal entry** in which you explain why you enjoy the café you frequent.

2. Imagine that the older waiter went home early and that the younger waiter stayed late at the café. Write a **monologue** to be performed for your class in which the younger waiter reveals his feelings about life.

3. With a partner, play the roles of the older waiter and the elderly, deaf client. Pass a notebook between yourselves to engage in a **dialogue**, asking and answering questions.

# Integrating *the* LANGUAGE ARTS

## Speaking and Listening

**ACTIVE LISTENING.** Read the Language Arts Survey 4.2, "Active versus Passive Listening." Then identify some of the word repetitions in the dialogue between the two waiters that signal feedback or understanding. Identify those places in the dialogue where you think a statement is misunderstood.

## Media Literacy

**RADIO ADVERTISEMENT.** Write a radio advertisement for the café described in "A Clean, Well-Lighted Place." Give the café a name and describe its best features. Decide what age group to appeal to, and create a slogan appropriate for that age group.

## Study and Research

**RESEARCHING ON THE INTERNET.** Imagine that you are writing a biography of Ernest Hemingway. Use the Internet to locate places to which you would need to travel to complete your research. Two sites that you may find useful are the **Hemingway Days Festival** site at http://www.hemingwaydays. com/hemhome.htm and the **Ernest Hemingway Foundation of Oak Park**, at http://www.heming-way.org. Write an itinerary listing each location you would need to visit, what you would research there, and the dates you would spend in each location.

## Literary TOOLS

**COLLAGE.** In literature, a **collage** is a work that incorporates or brings together an odd assortment of materials, such as allusions, quotations, bits of song, dialogue, foreign words, mythical or folkloric elements, headlines, and pictures or other graphic devices. Make a chart. On the left, quote different materials used in "Newsreel LXVIII." On the right, list the types of materials used. One example has been done for you.

| Quotes | Materials |
|--------|-----------|
| "Wall Street Stunned" | Headlines (newspaper) |

## About the SELECTION

*The Big Money* is the third volume in John Dos Passos's trilogy *U.S.A.* **"Newsreel LXVIII"** focuses on issues related to the Great Depression of the 1930s, a time when millions of Americans were without work and facing severe economic hardship. At the time, strong and sometimes violent conflicts arose between those who felt that government should help and those who felt that it should not.

# FROM *THE BIG MONEY,* "Newsreel LXVIII"
## THE THIRD VOLUME IN THE TRILOGY *U.S.A.*

BY JOHN DOS PASSOS

## About the AUTHOR

**John Dos Passos** (1896–1970) was born in Chicago and educated at Harvard University. After graduating from college, he went to Europe and served in World War I as an ambulance driver and a medic. His wartime experiences provided the basis for *One Man's Initiation: 1917* (1919) and *Three Soldiers* (1921). In his first great novel *Manhattan Transfer* (1925) and in his three-volume *U.S.A.* (1938), Dos Passos created epic portraits of American life by telling many interrelated or parallel stories.

U.S.A., which consists of *The 42nd Parallel, 1919,* and *The Big Money,* is Dos Passos's major contribution to Modernism, the twentieth-century artistic movement characterized by experiments in form, impersonality, and extensive use of allusion. In the three *U.S.A.* volumes, Dos Passos created personal commentaries called "The Camera Eye." He also created a new fictional form, the newsreel, modeled on the newsreels that, prior to the introduction of television, were shown before featured films in movie houses. Dos Passos's newsreels were collages, reminiscent of the work of such Modernist painters as Picasso and Braque. They contained bits and pieces of the popular culture, including headlines, advertising slogans, jingles, common sayings of the time, and excerpts from conversations and speeches. The total effect was to create an overall portrait of the country in the early part of this century.

## Reader's *Journal*

What headlines, song lyrics, phrases from TV ads, announcements over the school P.A. system, and billboard slogans have you been exposed to today? What do they tell you about contemporary American culture?

*Difficult*, c.1942. Kurt Schwitters.
Albright-Knox Art Gallery, Buffalo, New York.

FROM *THE BIG MONEY*

# Newsreel LXVIII

JOHN DOS PASSOS

## ArtNote

*Difficult*, c.1942. Kurt Schwitters.

Kurt Schwitters (1887–1948)
was a German artist associated with the Dada
movement. Attacking the traditional culture that
caused World War I and the rise of fascism, the
Dadaists used collage methods in poetry, visual
art, and performance to destroy linear, rational
thinking in the arts. Schwitters would walk the
streets filling his pockets with trash: ". . . everything that had been thrown away—all this he
loved, and restored to an honored place in life
by means of his art," according to fellow Dada
artist Hans Richter. This collage contains items
he picked up in England, where he fled to
escape the Nazis. In what ways does Schwitters's
technique resemble the technique of John Dos
Passos in "Newsreel LXVIII"?

WALL STREET STUNNED

*This is not Thirtyeight, but it's old Ninetyseven*
*You must put her in Center on time*[1]

MARKET SURE TO RECOVER FROM SLUMP

DECLINE IN CONTRACTS

POLICE TURN MACHINE GUNS ON
COLORADO MINE STRIKERS KILL 5 WOUND 40

sympathizers appeared on the scene just as
thousands of office workers were pouring out of
the buildings at the lunch hour. As they raised

---

1. **This is not . . . on time.** This is a line from the railroad ballad "The Wreck of the Old Ninety-Seven," which immortalized
the wreck of train number 97 on the Southern Railway in
Danville, Virginia, in 1909. One recording of such a railroad ballad sold over a million copies in the 1920s, making it one of the
earliest pop singles.

"*NEWSREEL LXVIII*"   **579**

their <u>placard</u> high and started an <u>indefinite</u> march from one side to the other, they were jeered and hooted not only by the office workers but also by workmen on a building under construction

Who jeers and hoots at the sympathizers?

NEW METHODS OF SELLING SEEN

RESCUE CREWS TRY TO UPEND

ILL-FATED CRAFT

WHILE WAITING FOR <u>PONTOONS</u>

*He looked 'round an' said to his black greasy*
*fireman*
*Jus' shovel in a little more coal*
*And when we cross that White Oak Mountain*
*You can watch your Ninety-seven roll*

I find your column interesting and need advice. I have saved four thousand dollars which I want to invest for a better income. Do you think I might buy stocks?

POLICE KILLER FLICKS CIGARETTE AS HE GOES

TREMBLING TO DOOM

PLAY AGENCIES IN RING OF SLAVE GIRL MARTS

MAKER OF LOVE <u>DISBARRED</u> AS LAWYER

*Oh the right wing clothesmakers*
*And the Socialist fakers*
*They make by the workers . . .*
*Double cross*

*They preach Social-ism*
*But practice Fasc-ism*
*To keep capitalism*
*By the boss*[2]

MOSCOW CONGRESS OUSTS OPPOSITION

*It's a mighty rough road from Lynchburg to*
*Danville*
*An' a line on a three mile grade*
*It was on that grade he lost his average*
*An' you see what a jump he made*

MILL THUGS IN MURDER RAID

here is the most dangerous example of how at the decisive moment the bourgeois <u>ideology</u> liquidates class <u>solidarity</u> and turns a friend of the workingclass of yesterday into a most miserable <u>propagandist</u> for imperialism[3] today

RED[4] PICKETS FINED FOR PROTEST HERE

*We leave our home in the morning*
*We kiss our children goodbye*

OFFICIALS STILL HOPE FOR

RESCUE OF MEN

*He was goin' downgrade makin' ninety miles*
*an hour*
*When his whistle broke into a scream*
*He was found in the wreck with his hand on*
*the throttle*
*An' was scalded to death with the steam*

---

2. **Oh the . . . By the boss.** Socialist labor-union protest song that is interspersed throughout the work
3. **imperialism.** Policy or practice of seeking to dominate the economic or political affairs of underdeveloped areas or weaker countries
4. **red.** Political radical or reactionary, especially a communist

**WORDS FOR EVERYDAY USE**

**plac • ard** (plaˊ kärd; plaˊ kərd) *n.*, notice for display in a public place; sign. *The <u>placard</u> directed us to the festival entrance.*

**in • def • i • nite** (in defˊə nit) *adj.*, having no exact limits. *George prepared food for an <u>indefinite</u> number of guests, since he wasn't sure how many people would show up for his party.*

**pon • toon** (pän tünˊ) *n.*, flat-bottomed boat; floating object used for support. *The airplane was able to land on water by floating on its <u>pontoons</u>.*

**dis • bar** (dis bärˊ) *vt.*, deprive (a lawyer) of the right to practice law. *The lawyer was <u>disbarred</u> for embezzling funds from his client.*

**i • de • ol • o • gy** (īˊdē älˊə gē) *n.*, doctrine, opinion, or way of thinking. *Communism and capitalism are economic <u>ideologies</u> that propose very different ways of distributing wealth.*

**sol • i • dar • i • ty** (sälˊə darˊə tē) *n.*, combination or agreement of all elements or individuals. *Due to their <u>solidarity</u>, the striking pilots were able to force management to meet their demands.*

**prop • a • gan • dist** (präpˊə ganˊdist) *n.*, one who spreads ideas for a particular cause. *The <u>propagandist</u> issued statements encouraging Americans to buy the expensive running shoes.*

RADICALS FIGHT WITH CHAIRS
AT UNITY MEETING

PATROLMEN PROTECT REDS

U.S. CHAMBER OF COMMERCE
URGES CONFIDENCE

REAL VALUES UNHARMED

*While we slave for the bosses*
  *Our children scream an' cry*
*But when we draw our*
  *money*
*Our grocery bills to pay*

> What two opinions of economics are juxtaposed?

PRESIDENT SEES PROSPERITY NEAR

*Not a cent to spend for clothing*
  *Not a cent to lay away*

STEAMROLLER IN ACTION
AGAINST MILITANTS

MINERS BATTLE SCABS[5]

*But we cannot buy for our children*
  *Our wages are too low*
*Now listen to me you workers*
  *Both you women and men*
*Let us win for them the victory*
  *I'm sure it ain't no sin*

CARILLON PEALS IN SINGING TOWER[6]

the President declared it was impossible to view the increased advantages for the many without smiling at those who a short time ago expressed so much fear lest our country might come under the control of a few individuals of great wealth.

HAPPY CROWDS THRONG CEREMONY

on a tiny island nestling like a green jewel in the lake that mirrors the singing tower, the President today partici-

> How does the imagery in this passage, or "clip," compare with the imagery in the rest of the newsreel? Explain.

pated in the dedication of a bird sanctuary and its pealing carillon, fulfilling the dream of an immigrant boy

*The Camera Eye (51)*

at the head of the valley in the dark of the hills on the broken floor of a lurchedover[7] cabin a man halfsits halflies propped up by an old woman two wrinkled girls that might be young      chunks of coal flare in the hearth flicker in his face white and sagging as dough      blacken the cavedin mouth the taut throat the belly swelled enormous with the wound he got working on the minetipple[8]

the barefoot girl brings him a tincup of water the woman wipes sweat off his streaming face with a dirty denim sleeve      the firelight flares in his eyes stretched big with fever in the women's scared eyes and in the blanched faces of the foreigners

without help in the valley <u>hemmed</u> by dark strike-silent hills the man will die (my father died we know what it is like to see a man die) the women will lay him out on the <u>rickety</u> cot the miners will bury him

in the jail it's light too hot the steamheat hisses we talk through the greenpainted iron bars to a tall white mustachioed old man some smiling miners in shirtsleeves a boy      faces

---

5. **scabs.** Derogatory term for workers who refuse to join a union, or who work for lower wages or under different conditions than those accepted by the union; workers who refuse to strike, or who take the place of a striking worker

6. **carillon . . . singing tower.** *Carillon*—set of stationary bells, each producing one tone of the chromatic scale; *singing tower*—the Spring Tower erected in Florida; President Calvin Coolidge spoke at the dedication of the tower in 1929.

7. **lurchedover.** Dos Passos has run the words *lurched* and *over* together. The selection contains several more run-together words.

8. **minetipple.** Equipment that tips cars in a coal mine to unload the coal

---

**WORDS FOR EVERYDAY USE**

**hem** (hem) *adj.*, encircle; surround. *Hemmed in by a wall, the mansion kept intruders out.*

**rick • e • ty** (rik´it ē) *adj.*, shaky. *The rickety fire escape was replaced.*

white from mining have already the <u>tallowy</u> look of jailfaces

foreigners what can we say to the dead? foreigners what can we say to the jailed? the representative of the political party talks fast through the bars join up with us and no other union we'll send you tobacco candy solidarity our lawyers will write briefs

*What does the party representative say the party will do for the prisoners?*

speakers will shout your names at meetings they'll carry your names on cardboard on pick-etlines     the men in jail shrug their shoulders smile thinly our eyes look in their eyes through the bars

what can I say?     (in another continent I have seen the faces looking out through the barred basement windows behind the ragged sentry's boots I have seen before day the strag-gling footsore prisoners herded through the streets limping between bayonets     heard the volley

I have seen the dead lying out in those distant deeper valleys)     what can we say to the jailed?

in the law's office we stand against the wall the law is a big man with eyes angry in a big pump-kinface     who sits and

*Who is "the law"?*

stares at us <u>meddling</u> foreigners through the door the deputies crane with their guns     they stand guard at the mines

they blockade the miners' soupkitchens they've cut off the road up the valley     the hiredmen with guns stand ready to shoot (they have made us foreigners in the land where we were born they are the conquering army that has filtered into the country unnoticed they have taken the hilltops by stealth they levy toll they stand at the minehead     they stand at the polls     they stand by when the bailiffs carry the furniture of the family evicted from the city tenement out on the sidewalk they are there when the bankers foreclose[9] on a farm they are ambushed and ready to shoot down the strikers marching behind the flag up the switch-back road to the mine     those that the guns spare they jail)

the law stares across the desk out of angry eyes his face reddens in splotches like a gobbler's neck with the strut of the power of submachine guns

*What powers does "the law" have? Who supports "the law"?*

sawedoffshotguns teargas and vomitinggas the power that can feed you or leave you to starve

sits easy at his desk his back is covered he feels strong behind him he feels the prosecuting-attorney the judge an owner himself the politi-cal boss the minesuperintendent the board of directors     the president of the utility the manipulator of the holdingcompany

he lifts his hand towards the telephone
the deputies crowd in the door
we have only words against     ∎

---

9. **foreclose.** Legally force someone to sell their farm because they are unable to pay their debts

---

**WORDS FOR EVERYDAY USE**

**tal • low • y** (tal´ō ē) *adj.*, fatty and pale. <u>Tallowy</u> clumps of congealed lard floated on the dishwater.

**med • dling** (med´liŋ) *adj.*, interfering; concerning oneself with other people's affairs without being asked. *Christopher's <u>meddling</u> personality would not allow him to stay out of other people's problems.*

If you were a mine worker in the 1930s, do you think Dos Passos would be sympathetic to your poor working conditions? Why, or why not?

# INVESTIGATE *Inquire Imagine*

**Recall:** GATHERING FACTS

1a. What events led to the death of the train operator?

2a. What did the workers say they wanted for their families?

3a. Why does "the law" have so much power?

➔ **Interpret:** FINDING MEANING

1b. How did the train operator's death symbolize what was happening at the time to other American workers?

2b. Why couldn't workers buy what their families needed?

3b. "The law" underlines the conflict between what two groups in American society?

**Analyze:** TAKING THINGS APART

4a. Identify the principal themes that are raised throughout "Newsreel LXVIII."

➔ **Synthesize:** BRINGING THINGS TOGETHER

4b. What overall point do the materials selected by Dos Passos make?

**Evaluate:** MAKING JUDGMENTS

5a. How effective is the newsreel structure in presenting a portrait of life at a particular time?

➔ **Extend:** CONNECTING IDEAS

5b. Use the notes you took in the Reader's Journal to create your own collage about life in contemporary American society. You might want to carry a notebook around with you for a day to add material to your collage.

# Understanding *Literature*

COLLAGE. Review the definition for **collage** in the Handbook of Literary Terms and the chart you made in Literary Tools on page 578. Which material used by Dos Passos in "Newsreel LXVIII" has the most impact in stating the selection's theme?

# WRITER'S JOURNAL

1. After researching the 1930s in the library or on the Internet, write three additional **headlines** to add to the Dos Passos newsreel.

2. Write an additional **verse** to the workers' song, expressing what the workers want their bosses to do for them.

3. Imagine you are the injured mine worker described in "The Camera Eye." Write a **letter to the editor** describing your accident and your living conditions. Tell the editor what needs to be changed in the mines and in the lives of the mine workers.

# Integrating the LANGUAGE ARTS

## Language, Grammar, and Style

**APOSTROPHES.** Read the Language Arts Survey 3.90, "Apostrophes." Then rewrite the sentences below to correct errors in the use of apostrophes.

1. John Dos Passos *U.S.A.* depicts a moment in Americas history.

2. In each of his newsreel's, Dos Passos was able to capture a moment, including it's vivid contradictions.

3. Dos Passoss vision was molded by his wartime experiences and by the Great Depression.

4. Were fortunate to have been born after the Great Depression, arent we?

5. Todays society is no less troubled, and its clear that many of the same problems exist today.

## Media Literacy

**COLLAGE.** Using the collage structure, create an impression of the year in which you were born by selecting headlines, editorials, letters to newspaper columnists, letters to the editor, song lyrics, advertisements, and images of people in various situations. Try to follow the approach used in "Newsreel LXVIII," juxtaposing elements in a thoughtful and thought-provoking way. Do research in the library to gather materials for your collage. Try to use as wide a variety of materials as possible. You may want to refer to the Research Skills section in the Language Arts Survey 5.18–5.29 for tips on effective research strategies.

## Study and Research

**RESEARCHING ON THE INTERNET.** Use the Internet to locate a book and an article critiquing John Dos Passos's *U.S.A.* One site that you may find helpful is **PAL: Perspectives in American Literature: A Research and Reference Guide** at http://www.csustan.edu/english/reuben/home.html. Click on the link to view an alphabetical list of American authors, then click on John Dos Passos's name to view an extensive bibliography of literature by and about Don Passos. Then make a bibliography card for the book and the article. Refer to the Language Arts Survey 5.40, "Making Bibliographies and Bibliography Cards," to review how to make bibliography cards.

# Nobel Prize Acceptance Speech
# "Darl" from As I Lay Dying

### BY WILLIAM FAULKNER

## About the AUTHOR

**William Faulkner** (1897–1962) was born in New Albany, Mississippi, to a prominent Southern family and spent most of his life in Oxford, Mississippi. He dropped out of high school and, except for one year as a student at the University of Mississippi, had no further formal education. His first novel, *Soldier's Pay* (1926), published through the help of acclaimed fiction writer Sherwood Anderson, earned him an advance of two hundred dollars each on his next two novels. Recalling those events, he is reported to have said, "I liked that money," and to have noted that Anderson "worked only in the morning," which seemed to him "a mighty easy way to earn money." Whether or not it was easy, Faulkner spent most of his adult life earning his living as a writer.

Most of his many novels are set in mythical Yoknapatawpha County, Mississippi, and tell stories related to the decline of traditional Southern ways of life. Long, sonorous sentences with abundant details are one of the hallmarks of Faulkner's style. He also experimented considerably with **point of view**, telling the stories in some of his novels from the points of view of several different characters, including that of a mentally challenged man in *The Sound and the Fury* (1929) and those of a mentally deficient poor white family in *As I Lay Dying* (1930). Much of Faulkner's fiction employed a **stream-of-consciousness** mode, presenting characters' random thoughts, feelings, and impressions in **interior monologues**.

In addition to his novels, Faulkner wrote screenplays, the most notable of which are his adaptations of Ernest Hemingway's *To Have and Have Not* and Raymond Chandler's *The Big Sleep*. Faulkner's work was recognized in 1950 with a Nobel Prize for literature and two Pulitzer Prizes in 1954 and 1962, among other awards and honors. Other works by Faulkner include *The Marble Faun* (poetry, 1924), *Mosquitoes* (1927), *Sartoris* (1929), *Sanctuary* (1931), *Light in August* (1932), *Absalom, Absalom!* (1936), *Go Down, Moses* (1942), and *Intruder in the Dust* (1948).

## Literary TOOLS

**AIM.** A writer's **aim** is his or her purpose or goal. As you read, decide what Faulkner's aim was in writing his Nobel Prize Acceptance Speech.

**ALLITERATION. Alliteration** is the repetition of initial consonant sounds. As you read Faulkner's speech, look for examples of alliteration.

## About the SELECTIONS

Faulkner received the Nobel Prize for literature in 1950 for his powerful and artistically unique contribution to the modern American novel. The brief address that he delivered on accepting the prize presents a noble view of the role to be played by imaginative literature in the modern age.

Faulkner's novel *As I Lay Dying* is an excellent example of his distinctive narrative structures—the use of multiple points of view and the inner psychological voices of the characters. Faulkner tells the darkly comic tale of the death of Addie Bundren, the matriarch of the Bundren family, through the eyes of each family member, including Addie herself.

## Reader's Journal

In general, what do you gain when you read literature?

William Faulkner, right, receiving the 1950 Nobel Prize for literature.

# Nobel Prize Acceptance Speech

## WILLIAM FAULKNER

I feel that this award was not made to me as a man, but to my work—a life's work in the agony and sweat of the human spirit, not for glory and least of all for profit, but to create out of the materials of the human spirit something which did not exist before. So this award is only mine in trust.[1] It will not be difficult to find a dedication for the money part of it <u>commensurate</u> with the purpose and significance of its origin. But I would like to do the same with the acclaim too, by using this moment as a pinnacle from which I might be

---

1. **in trust.** In another's care

**WORDS FOR EVERYDAY USE**

com • men • su • rate (kə men´shü r it) *adj.*, equal in measure or size; proportionate. *Jemma decided to quit her job because the pay was not <u>commensurate</u> with her experience.*

listened to by the young men and women already dedicated to the same anguish and <u>travail</u>, among whom is already that one who will some day stand here where I am standing.

Our tragedy today is a general and universal physical fear so long sustained by now that we can even bear it. There are no longer problems of the spirit. There is only the question: When will I be blown up? Because of this, the young man or woman writing today has forgotten the problems of the human heart in conflict with itself which alone can make good writing because only that is worth writing about, worth the agony and the sweat.

> What have young writers forgotten today?

He must learn them again. He must teach himself that the basest of all things is to be afraid; and, teaching himself that, forget it forever, leaving no room in his workshop for anything but the old <u>verities</u> and truths of the heart, the old universal truths lacking which any story is <u>ephemeral</u> and doomed—love and honor and pity and pride and compassion and sacrifice. Until he does so, he labors under a curse. He writes not of love but of lust, of defeats in which nobody loses anything of value, of victories without hope

> What is "the basest of all things"?

and, worst of all, without pity or compassion. His griefs grieve on no universal bones, leaving no scars. He writes not of the heart but of the glands.

Until he relearns these things, he will write as though he stood among and watched the end of man. I decline to accept the end of man. It is easy enough to say that man is immortal simply because he will <u>endure</u>: that when the last ding-dong of doom has clanged and faded from the last worthless rock hanging tideless in the last red and dying evening, that even then there will still be one more sound: that of his puny inexhaustible voice, still talking. I refuse to accept this. I believe that man will not merely endure: he will <u>prevail</u>. He is immortal, not because he alone among creatures has an inexhaustible voice, but because he has a soul, a spirit capable of compassion and sacrifice and endurance. The poet's, the writer's, duty is to write about these things. It is his privilege to help man endure by lifting his heart, by reminding him of the courage and honor and hope and pride and compassion and pity and sacrifice which have been the glory of his past. The poet's voice need not merely be the record of man, it can be one of the props, the pillars to help him endure and prevail. ∎

---

**WORDS FOR EVERYDAY USE**

**trav • ail** (trə vāl´) *n.*, very hard work; toil. *The image of the struggling artist suffering many <u>travails</u> to produce great art is a relatively recent popular myth.*

**ver • i • ty** (ver´ə tē) *n.*, principle or belief taken to be fundamentally and permanently true. *Ancient Greek tragedies continue to be produced today because they contain timeless <u>verities</u> regarding the human condition.*

**e • phem • er • al** (e fem´ər əl) *adj.*, short-lived; transitory. *Japanese haiku is renowned for capturing <u>ephemeral</u> emotions in very few words.*

**en • dure** (en dür´) *vi.*, continue in existence; last, remain. *Tina was sure her love for her husband would <u>endure</u> through old age.*

**pre • vail** (prē vāl´) *vi.*, gain advantage or mastery; be victorious; triumph. *Jerry's opinions <u>prevailed</u> at the meeting because he presented logical arguments.*

---

**Respond** *to the* **SELECTION**

Do you think that humanity will endure or prevail? Why, or why not?

# from As I Lay Dying
# "Darl"

## WILLIAM FAULKNER

As the novel begins, Addie Bundren, a Mississippi farm woman, is dying. During the course of the book, her husband, Anse; her four sons, Cash, Darl, Jewel, and Vardaman; her daughter, Dewey Dell; and various neighbors reveal through words and actions their relationship to Addie, who has made Anse promise to take her to Jefferson to be buried.

Pa stands beside the bed. From behind his leg Vardaman peers, with his round head and his eyes round and his mouth beginning to open. She looks at pa; all her failing life appears to drain into her eyes, urgent, irremediable.[1] "It's Jewel she wants," Dewey Dell says.

"Why, Addie," pa says, "him and Darl went to make one more load. They thought there was time. That you would wait for them, and that three dollars and all . . ." He stoops laying his hand on hers. For a while yet she looks at him, without reproach, without anything at all, as if her eyes alone are listening to the irrevocable cessation of his voice. Then she raises herself, who has not moved in ten days. Dewey Dell leans down, trying to press her back.

"Ma," she says; "ma."

She is looking out the window, at Cash stooping steadily at the board in the failing light, laboring on toward darkness and into it as though the stroking of the saw illumined its own motion, board and saw engendered.[2]

"You, Cash," she shouts, her voice harsh, strong, and unimpaired. "You, Cash!"

He looks up at the gaunt face framed by the window in the twilight. It is a composite picture of all time since he was a child. He drops the saw and lifts the board for her to see, watching the window in which the face has not moved. He drags a second plank into position and slants the two of them into their final juxtaposition,[3] gesturing toward the ones yet on the ground, shaping with his empty hand in pantomime[4] the finished box. For a while still she looks down at him from the composite picture, neither with censure nor approbation.[5] Then the face disappears.

She lies back and turns her head without so much as glancing at pa. She looks at Vardaman; her eyes, the life in them, rushing suddenly upon them; the two flames glare up for a steady instant. Then they go out as though someone had leaned down and blown upon them.

"Ma," Dewey Dell says; "ma!" Leaning above the bed, her hands lifted a little, the fan still moving like it has for ten days, she begins to keen. Her voice is strong, young, tremulous and clear, rapt with its own timbre and volume, the fan still moving steadily up and down, whispering the useless air. Then she flings herself across Addie Bundren's knees, clutching her, shaking her with the furious strength of the young before sprawling suddenly across the handful of rotten bones that Addie Bundren left, jarring the whole bed into a chattering sibilance[6] of mat-

---

1. **irremediable.** Not remediable; not able to be cured
2. **engendered.** Assumed form; originated
3. **juxtaposition.** State of being side by side
4. **pantomime.** Communication conveyed by bodily movements only
5. **censure nor approbation.** Condemnation or approval
6. **sibilance.** A hissing sound

tress shucks, her arms outflung and the fan in one hand still beating with expiring breath into the quilt.

From behind pa's leg Vardaman peers, his mouth full open and all color draining from his face into his mouth, as though he has by some means fleshed his own teeth in himself, sucking. He begins to move slowly backward from the bed, his eyes round, his pale face fading into the dusk like a piece of paper pasted on a failing wall, and so out of the door.

Pa leans above the bed in the twilight, his humped silhouette partaking of that owl-like quality of awry-feathered, disgruntled outrage within which lurks a wisdom too profound or too inert for even thought.

"Durn them boys," he says.

*Jewel, I say. Overhead the day drives level and gray, hiding the sun by a flight of gray spears. In the rain the mules smoke a little, splashed yellow with mud, the off one clinging in sliding lunges to the side of the road above the ditch. The tilted lumber gleams dull yellow, water-soaked and heavy as lead, tilted at a steep angle into the ditch above the broken wheel; about the shattered spokes and about Jewel's ankles a runnel of yellow neither water nor earth swirls, curving with the yellow road neither of earth nor water, down the hill dissolving into a streaming mass of dark green neither of earth nor sky. Jewel, I say.*

**Entrance to Frank Tengle's Bedroom, Hale County, Alabama,** 1936. Walker Evans. Library of Congress.

Cash comes to the door, carrying the saw. Pa stands beside the bed, humped, his arms dangling. He turns his head, his shabby profile, his chin collapsing slowly as he works the snuff against his gums.

"She's gone," Cash says.

"She taken and left us," pa says. Cash does not look at him.

"How nigh are you done?" pa says. Cash does not answer. He enters, carrying the saw. "I reckon you better get at it," pa says. "You'll have to do the best you can, with them boys gone off that-away." Cash looks down at her face. He is not listening to pa at all. He does not approach the bed. He stops in the middle of the floor, the saw against his leg, his sweating arms powdered lightly with sawdust, his face composed. "If you get in a tight, maybe some of them'll get here tomorrow and help you," pa says. "Vernon could." Cash is not listening. He is looking down at her peaceful, rigid face fading into the dusk as though darkness were a precursor[7] of the ultimate earth, until at last the face seems to float detached upon it, lightly as the reflection of a dead leaf. "There is Christians enough to help you," pa says. Cash is not listening. After a while he turns

---

7. **precursor.** Something that comes before; forerunner

without looking at pa and leaves the room. Then the saw begins to snore again. "They will help us in our sorrow," pa says.

The sound of the saw is steady, competent, unhurried, stirring the dying light so that at each stroke her face seems to wake a little into an expression of listening and of waiting, as though she were counting the strokes. Pa looks down at the face, at the black sprawl of Dewey Dell's hair, the outflung arms, the clutched fan now motionless on the fading quilt. "I reckon you better get supper on," he says.

Dewey Dell does not move.

"Git up, now, and put supper on," pa says. "We got to keep our strength up. I reckon Doctor Peabody's right hungry, coming all this way. And Cash'll need to eat quick and get back to work so he can finish it in time."

Dewey Dell rises, heaving to her feet. She looks down at the face. It is like a casting of fading bronze upon the pillow, the hands alone still with any semblance of life: a curled, gnarled inertness; a spent yet alert quality from which weariness, exhaustion, travail has not yet departed, as though they doubted even yet the actuality of rest, guarding with horned and penurious[8] alertness the cessation which they know cannot last.

Dewey Dell stoops and slides the quilt from beneath them and draws it up over them to the chin, smoothing it down, drawing it smooth. Then without looking at pa she goes around the bed and leaves the room.

*She will go out where Peabody is, where she can stand in the twilight and look at his back with such an expression that, feeling her eyes and turning, he will say: I would not let it grieve me, now. She was old, and sick too. Suffering more than we knew. She couldn't have got well. Vardaman's*

*getting big now, and with you to take good care of them all. I would try not to let it grieve me. I expect you'd better go and get some supper ready. It dont have to be much. But they'll need to eat, and she looking at him, saying You could do so much for me if you just would. If you just knew. I am I and you are you and I know it and you dont know it and you could do so much for me if you just would and if you just would then I could tell you and then nobody would have to know it except you and me and Darl[9]*

Pa stands over the bed, dangle-armed, humped, motionless. He raises his hand to his head, scouring his hair, listening to the saw. He comes nearer and rubs his hand, palm and back, on his thigh and lays it on her face and then on the hump of quilt where her hands are. He touches the quilt as he saw Dewey Dell do, trying to smoothe it up to the chin, but disarranging it instead. He tries to smoothe it again, clumsily, his hand awkward as a claw, smoothing at the wrinkles which he made and which continue to emerge beneath his hand with perverse ubiquity,[10] so that at last he desists, his hand falling to his side and stroking itself again, palm and back, on his thigh. The sound of the saw snores steadily into the room. Pa breathes with a quiet, rasping sound, mouthing the snuff against his gums. "God's will be done," he says. "Now I can get them teeth."

*Jewel's hat droops limp about his neck, channelling water onto the soaked towsack tied about his shoulders as, ankle-deep in the running ditch, he pries with a slipping two-by-four, with a piece of rotting log for fulcrum, at the axle. Jewel, I say, she is dead, Jewel. Addie Bundren is dead* ■

---

8. **penurious.** Marked by severe poverty

9. *If you just knew...Darl.* Dewey Dell (who is not married) is pregnant, and nobody in the family knows this except for Darl.

10. **ubiquity.** Omnipresence; the state of being or seeming to be everywhere

# INVESTIGATE, Inquire, Imagine

**Recall:** GATHERING FACTS

1a. With what acknowledgment did Faulkner accept the Nobel Prize?

2a. According to the first sentence of the address, what did Faulkner attempt to do in his fiction?

3a. Why will people prevail, according to Faulkner?

**Interpret:** FINDING MEANING

1b. What does Faulkner believe is the relationship between people's souls and writing?

2b. Why did Faulkner say that the award was "only [his] in trust"? To whom does he address his comments? What does he want to communicate to these people?

3b. What is a writer's duty?

---

**Analyze:** TAKING THINGS APART

4a. Identify the elements that, according to Faulkner, must be included in a story if it is not to be ephemeral and doomed.

**Synthesize:** BRINGING THINGS TOGETHER

4b. Speaking a few years after the end of World War II and the dropping of atomic bombs on Hiroshima and Nagasaki, Faulkner said, "There are no longer problems of the spirit. There is only the question: When will I be blown up?" Do you feel that the threat of nuclear attack is as serious today as it was when Faulkner gave his address in 1950? Why, or why not? Why do you think Faulkner wanted his listeners not to live in fear, but rather to remember the "old verities and truths of the heart"?

---

**Evaluate:** MAKING JUDGMENTS

5a. In the nuclear age, is Faulkner's assertion that "man will not merely endure: he will prevail" a realistic one? Explain your answer.

**Extend:** CONNECTING IDEAS

5b. Does Robert Frost's Letter to *The Amherst Student* on page 517 support or contradict Faulkner's views about the modern age, spirituality, and the value of literature? Explain your answer.

---

# Understanding Literature

**AIM.** Review the definition for **aim** in the Handbook of Literary Terms. What do you think was Faulkner's aim in writing his Nobel Prize acceptance speech?

**ALLITERATION.** Review the definition of **alliteration** in the Handbook of Literary Terms. Make a chart showing Faulkner's use of alliteration in his Nobel address. On the left, quote examples of alliteration from the speech. On the right, explain what ideas are emphasized by the alliteration. One example has been done for you. What is the most memorable example of alliteration in the speech?

| Alliteration | Explanation |
|---|---|
| "not **m**ade to **m**e as a **m**an" | Faulkner feels the Nobel Prize was not awarded to him personally, but to him as a writer. |

# Writer's Journal

1. Write a **paragraph** explaining what you think Faulkner means when he says that "the young man or woman writing today has forgotten the problems of the human heart in conflict with itself." Do you agree with this statement? Why, or why not?

2. Imagine that a young writer wrote to Faulkner for advice about whether he should continue writing. Write the **letter** that Faulkner could have written to the young writer.

3. Write a **character sketch** about one of the characters in "Darl." Feel free to write about other characteristics that you think the character may possess that are not necessarily pointed out in the selection.

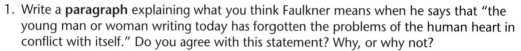

# Integrating the LANGUAGE ARTS

## Language, Grammar, and Style

**COLORFUL ADJECTIVES.** Read the Language Arts Survey 3.66, "Adjectives," and 3.39, "Adding Colorful Language to Sentences." Then identify all the adjectives, along with the nouns that they modify, in the following sentence from Faulkner's speech:

"It is easy enough to say that man is immortal simply because he will endure: that when the last ding-dong of doom has clanged and faded from the last worthless rock hanging tideless in the last red and dying evening, that even then there will still be one more sound: that of his puny inexhaustible voice, still talking."

## Speaking and Listening & Collaborative Learning

**ACCEPTANCE SPEECH.** Imagine that you are presented with an award for an activity in which you participate or a job that you do. Write an acceptance speech and deliver it to a partner or a small group. You might want to include thanks to specific people, an explanation of why you participate in your chosen activity, and your beliefs. Like Faulkner, you might also choose to give advice to those who will follow you. Review the Language Arts Survey 4.15, "Giving a Speech."

## Media Literacy

**MOVIE REVIEW.** Watch a movie based on a Faulkner novel or short story. You might consider *Today We Live* (based on the story "Turn About"), *Intruder in the Dust, The Sound and the Fury, Sanctuary,* or *The Reivers.* Then write a movie review, commenting on the quality of the screenplay, the caliber of the actors' performances, and the director's vision and execution of that vision. You might want to read several movie reviews before you begin writing.

A new version of *As I Lay Dying*, from which "Darl" is excerpted, was filmed in 1998 and stars Sean Penn.

## Study and Research

**RESEARCHING ON THE INTERNET.** Use the Internet to locate news items about William Faulkner. One site you might find useful is **Faulkner News** at http://www.mcsr.olemiss.edu/~egjbp/faulkner/news/index.html. Then lay out a page of a newsletter dedicated to Faulkner, including articles on such items as new films made from his novels, conferences, commemorative events, and articles and books about the author and his work.

## "Richard Cory"
### by Edwin Arlington Robinson

Whenever Richard Cory went down town,
We people on the pavement looked at him:
He was a gentleman from sole to crown,
Clean favored, and imperially slim.

5  And he was always quietly arrayed,
And he was always human when he talked;
But still he fluttered pulses when he said,
"Good-morning," and he glittered when he walked.

And he was rich—yes, richer than a king—
10  And admirably schooled in every grace:
In fine, we thought that he was everything
To make us wish that we were in his place.

So on we worked, and waited for the light,
And went without the meat, and cursed the bread;
15  And Richard Cory, one calm summer night,
Went home and put a bullet through his head.

## "Petit, the Poet," from *Spoon River Anthology*
### by Edgar Lee Masters

Seeds in a dry pod, tick, tick, tick,
Tick, tick, tick, like mites[1] in a quarrel—
Faint iambics that the full breeze wakens—
But the pine tree makes a symphony thereof.
5  Triolets, villanelles, rondels, rondeaus,[2]
Ballades by the score with the same old thought:
The snows and the roses of yesterday are vanished,
And what is love but a rose that fades?
Life all around me here in the village:
10  Tragedy, comedy, valor[3] and truth,
Courage, constancy, heroism, failure—
All in the loom, and oh what patterns!
Woodlands, meadows, streams and rivers—
Blind to all of it all my life long.
15  Triolets, villanelles, rondels, rondeaus,
Seeds in a dry pod, tick, tick, tick,
Tick, tick, tick, what little iambics,
While Homer and Whitman[4] roared in the pines?

## "In a Station of the Metro"[5]
### by Ezra Pound

The apparition of these faces in the crowd;
Petals on a wet, black bough.

## "The Flower-Fed Buffaloes"
### by Vachel Lindsay

The flower-fed buffaloes of the spring
In the days of long ago,
Ranged[6] where the locomotives sing
And the prairie flowers lie low:—
5  The tossing, blooming, perfumed grass
Is swept away by the wheat,
Wheels and wheels and wheels spin by
In the spring that still is sweet.
But the flower-fed buffaloes of the spring
10  Left us, long ago.
They gore[7] no more, they bellow no more,
They trundle around the hills no more:—
With the Blackfeet, lying low,
With the Pawnees,[8] lying low,
15  Lying low.

## "Euclid Alone Has Looked on Beauty Bare"
### by Edna St. Vincent Millay

Euclid alone has looked on Beauty bare.
Let all who prate of Beauty hold their peace,
And lay them prone upon the earth and cease
To ponder on themselves, the while they stare
5  At nothing, intricately drawn nowhere
In shapes of shifting lineage; let geese
Gabble and hiss, but heroes seek release
From dusty bondage into luminous air.
O blinding hour, O holy, terrible day,
10  When first the shaft into his vision shone
Of light anatomized! Euclid alone
Has looked on Beauty bare. Fortunate they
Who, though once only and then but far away,
Have heard her massive sandal set on stone.

---

1. **mites.** Small insects
2. **Triolets, villanelles, rondels, rondeaus.** Types of poems
3. **valor.** Courage
4. **Homer and Whitman.** *Homer*—Ancient Greek poet; *Whitman*—Walt Whitman (1819–1892), American poet, one of the first to write in free verse
5. **In a Station of the Metro.** In a Paris subway station
6. **Ranged.** Roamed, feeding on the prairie grass
7. **gore.** Attack with their horns
8. **Blackfeet . . . Pawnees.** Refers to two Native American peoples of the western United States

## "The Death of the Hired Man"
## by Robert Frost

Mary sat musing on the lamp-flame at the table,
Waiting for Warren. When she heard his step,
She ran on tiptoe down the darkened passage
To meet him in the doorway with the news
5  And put him on his guard. "Silas is back."
She pushed him outward with her through the door
And shut it after her. "Be kind," she said.
She took the market things from Warren's arms
And set them on the porch, them drew him down
10  To sit beside her on the wooden steps.

"When was I ever anything but kind to him?
But I'll not have the fellow back," he said.
"I told him so last haying,[1] didn't I?
If he left then, I said, that ended it.
15  What good is he? Who else will harbor him
At his age for the little he can do?
What help he is there's no depending on.
Off he goes always when I need him most.
He thinks he ought to earn a little pay,
20  Enough at least to buy tobacco with,
So he won't have to beg and be beholden.[2]
'All right,' I say, 'I can't afford to pay
Any fixed wages, though I wish I could.'
'Someone else can.' 'Then someone else will have to.'
25  I shouldn't mind his bettering himself
If that was what it was. You can be certain,
When he begins like that, there's someone at him
Trying to coax him off with pocket money—
In haying time, when any help is scarce.
30  In winter he comes back to us. I'm done."

"Sh! not so loud: he'll hear you," Mary said.

"I want him to: he'll have to soon or late."

"He's worn out. He's asleep beside the stove.
When I came up from Rowe's I found him here,
35  Huddled against the barn-door fast asleep,
A miserable sight, and frightening, too—
You needn't smile—I didn't recognize him—
I wasn't looking for him—and he's changed.
Wait till you see."

40          "Where did you say he'd been?"

"He didn't say. I dragged him to the house,
And gave him tea and tried to make him smoke.
I tried to make him talk about his travels.
Nothing would do: he just kept nodding off."

45  "What did he say? Did he say anything?"

"But little."

"Anything? Mary, confess
He said he'd come to ditch the meadow for me."

"Warren!"

50          "But did he? I just want to know."

"Of course he did. What would you have him say?
Surely you wouldn't grudge the poor old man
Some humble way to save his self-respect.
He added, if you really care to know,
55  He meant to clear the upper pasture, too.
That sounds like something you have heard before?
Warren, I wish you could have heard the way
He jumbled everything. I stopped to look
Two or three times—he made me feel so queer—
60  To see if he was talking in his sleep.
He ran on Harold Wilson—you remember—
The boy you had in haying four years since.
He's finished school, and teaching in his college.
Silas declares you'll have to get him back.
65  He says they two will make a team for work:
Between them they will lay this farm as smooth!
The way he mixed that in with other things.
He thinks young Wilson a likely lad, though daft
On education—you know how they fought
70  All through July under the blazing sun,
Silas up on the cart to build the load,
Harold along beside to pitch it on."

"Yes, I took care to keep well out of earshot."

"Well, those days trouble Silas like a dream.
75  You wouldn't think they would. How some things linger!
Harold's young college-boy's assurance piqued him.
After so many years he still keeps finding
Good arguments he sees he might have used.
I sympathize. I know just how it feels
80  To think of the right thing to say too late.
Harold's associated in his mind with Latin.
He asked me what I thought of Harold's saying
He studied Latin, like the violin,
Because he liked it—that an argument!
85  He said he couldn't make the boy believe
He could find water with a hazel prong—
Which showed how much good school had ever
      done him.
He wanted to go over that. But most of all
He thinks if he could have another chance
90  To teach him how to build a load of hay—"

"I know, that's Silas' one accomplishment.
He bundles every forkful in its place,
And tags and numbers it for future reference,

---

1. **haying.** Harvest, gathering of hay
2. **beholden.** Indebted to anyone

So he can find and easily dislodge it
95 In the unloading. Silas does that well.
He takes it out in bunches like big birds' nests.
You never see him standing on the hay
He's trying to lift, straining to lift himself."

"He thinks if he could teach him that he'd be
100 Some good perhaps to someone in the world.
He hates to see a boy the fool of books.
Poor Silas, so concerned for other folk,
And nothing to look backward to with pride,
And nothing to look forward to with hope,
105 So now and never any different."
Part of a moon was falling down the west,
Dragging the whole sky with it to the hills.
Its light poured softly in her lap. She saw it
And spread her apron to it. She put out her hand
110 Among the harplike morning-glory strings,
Taut with the dew from garden bed to eaves,
As if she played unheard some tenderness
That wrought on him beside her in the night.
"Warren," she said, "he has come home to die:
115 You needn't be afraid he'll leave you this time."

"Home," he mocked gently.

"Yes, what else but home?
It all depends on what you mean by home.
Of course he's nothing to us, any more
120 Than was the hound that came a stranger to us
Out of the woods, worn out upon the trail."
"Home is the place where, when you have to go there,
They have to take you in."

"I should have called it
125 Something you somehow haven't to deserve."

Warren leaned out and took a step or two,
Picked up a little stick, and brought it back
And broke it in his hand and tossed it by.
"Silas has better claim on us you think
130 Than on his brother? Thirteen little miles
As the road winds would bring him to his door.
Silas has walked that far no doubt today.
Why doesn't he go there? His brother's rich,
A somebody—director in the bank."

135 "He never told us that."

"We know it though."

"I think his brother ought to help, of course.
I'll see to that if there is need. He ought of right
To take him in, and might be willing to—
140 He may be better than appearances.
But have some pity on Silas. Do you think
If he had any pride in claiming kin

Or anything he looked for from his brother,
He'd keep so still about him all this time?"

145 "I wonder what's between them."

"I can tell you.
Silas is what he is—we wouldn't mind him—
But just the kind that kinsfolk can't abide.
He never did a thing so very bad.
150 He don't know why he isn't quite as good
As anybody. Worthless though he is,
He won't be made ashamed to please his brother."

"*I* can't think Si ever hurt anyone."

"No, but he hurt my heart the way he lay
155 And rolled his old head on that sharp-edged chair-back.
He wouldn't let me put him on the lounge.
You must go in and see what you can do.
I made the bed up for him there tonight.
You'll be surprised at him—how much he's broken.
160 His working days are done; I'm sure of it."

"I'd not be in a hurry to say that."

"I haven't been. Go, look, see for yourself.
But, Warren, please remember how it is:
He's come to help you ditch the meadow.
165 He has a plan. You mustn't laugh at him.
He may not speak of it, and then he may.
I'll sit and see if that small sailing cloud
Will hit or miss the moon."

It hit the moon.
170 Then there were three there, making a dim row,
The moon, the little silver cloud, and she.
Warren returned—too soon, it seemed to her,
Slipped to her side, caught up her hand and waited.

"Warren?" she questioned.

175    "Dead," was all he answered.


## "An Old Man's Winter Night"
by Robert Frost

All out-of-doors looked darkly in at him
Through the thin frost, almost in separate stars,
That gathers on the pane in empty rooms.
What kept his eyes from giving back the gaze
5 Was the lamp tilted near them in his hand.
What kept him from remembering what it was
That brought him to that creaking room was age.
He stood with barrels round him—at a loss.
And having scared the cellar under him

10 In clomping here, he scared it once again
   In clomping off—and scared the outer night,
   Which has its sounds, familiar, like the roar
   Of trees and crack of branches, common things,
   But nothing so like beating on a box.
15 A light he was to no one but himself
   Where now he sat, concerned with he knew what,
   A quiet light, and then not even that.
   He consigned[1] to the moon—such as she was,
   So late-arising—to the broken moon,
20 As better than the sun in any case
   For such a charge, his snow upon the roof,
   His icicles along the wall to keep;
   And slept. The log that shifted with a jolt
   Once in the stove, disturbed him and he shifted,
25 And eased his heavy breathing, but still slept.
   One aged man—one man—can't keep a house,
   A farm, a countryside, or if he can,
   It's thus he does it of a winter night.

## "Disillusionment of Ten O'Clock"
by Wallace Stevens

The houses are haunted
By white night-gowns.
None are green,
Or purple with green rings,
5 Or green with yellow rings,
Or yellow with blue rings.
None of them are strange,
With socks of lace
And beaded ceintures.[2]
10 People are not going
To dream of baboons and periwinkles.[3]
Only, here and there, an old sailor,
Drunk and asleep in his boots,
Catches tigers
15 In red weather.

## "Wind and Silver"
by Amy Lowell

Greatly shining,
The Autumn moon floats in the thin sky;
And the fish-ponds shake their backs and flash their
    dragon scales
As she passes over them.

## "A Lover"
by Amy Lowell

If I could catch the green lantern of the firefly
I could see to write you a letter.

## "anyone lived in a pretty how town"
by E. E. Cummings

anyone lived in a pretty how town
(with up so floating many bells down)
spring summer autumn winter
he sang his didn't he danced his did

5 Women and men(both little and small)
cared for anyone not at all
they sowed their isn't they reaped their same
sun moon stars rain

children guessed(but only a few
10 and down they forgot as up they grew
autumn winter spring summer)
that noone loved him more by more

when by now and tree by leaf
she laughed his joy she cried his grief
15 bird by snow and stir by still
anyone's any was all to her

someones married their everyones
laughed their cryings and did their dance
(sleep wake hope and then)they
20 said their nevers they slept their dream

stars rain sun moon
(and only the snow can begin to explain
how children are apt to forget to remember
with up so floating many bells down)

25 one day anyone died i guess
(and noone stooped to kiss his face)
busy folk buried them side by side
little by little and was by was

all by all and deep by deep
30 and more by more they dream their sleep
noone and anyone earth by april
wish by spirit and if by yes.

Women and men(both dong and ding)
summer autumn winter spring
35 reaped their sowing and went their came
sun moon stars rain

## "Sophistication" from *Winesburg, Ohio*
by Sherwood Anderson

It was early evening of a day in the late fall and the
Winesburg County Fair had brought crowds of country

---

1. **consigned.** Put in care of
2. **ceintures.** Sashes; belts
3. **periwinkles.** Tiny, pale blue-violet sea snails

people into town. The day had been clear and the night came on warm and pleasant. On the Trunton Pike, where the road after it left town stretched away between berry fields now covered with dry brown leaves, the dust from passing wagons arose in clouds. Children, curled into little balls, slept on the straw scattered on wagon beds. Their hair was full of dust and their fingers black and sticky. The dust rolled away over the fields and the departing sun set it ablaze with colors.

In the main street of Winesburg, crowds filled the stores and the sidewalks. Night came on, horses whinnied, the clerks in the stores ran madly about, children became lost and cried lustily, an American town worked terribly at the task of amusing itself.

Pushing his way through the crowds in Main Street, young George Willard concealed himself in the stairway leading to Doctor Reefy's office and looked at the people. With feverish eyes he watched the faces drifting past under the store lights. Thoughts kept coming into his head and he did not want to think. He stamped impatiently on the wooden steps and looked sharply about. "Well, is she going to stay with him all day? Have I done all this waiting for nothing?" he muttered.

George Willard, the Ohio village boy, was fast growing into manhood, and new thoughts had been coming into his mind. All that day, amid the jam of people at the Fair, he had gone about feeling lonely. He was about to leave Winesburg to go away to some city where he hoped to get work on a city newspaper, and he felt grown up. The mood that had taken possession of him was a thing known to men and unknown to boys. He felt old and a little tired. Memories awoke in him. To his mind his new sense of maturity set him apart, made him a half-tragic figure. He wanted someone to understand the feeling that had taken possession of him after his mother's death.

There is a time in the life of every boy when he for the first time takes the backward view of life. Perhaps that is the moment when he crosses the line into manhood. The boy is walking through the streets of his town. He is thinking of the future and of the figure he will cut in the world. Ambitions and regrets awake within him. Suddenly something happens; he stops under a tree and waits as for a voice calling his name. Ghosts of old things creep into his consciousness; the voices outside of himself whisper a message concerning the limitations of life. From being quite sure of himself and his future, he becomes not at all sure. If he be an imaginative boy a door is torn open and for the first time he looks out upon the world, seeing, as though they marched in procession before him, the countless figures of men who before his time have come out of nothingness into the world, lived their lives and again disappeared into nothingness. The sadness of sophistication has come to the boy. With a little gasp he sees himself as merely a leaf blown by the wind through the streets of his village. He knows that in spite of all the stout talk of his fellows he must live and die in uncertainty, a thing blown by the winds, a thing destined like corn to wilt in the sun. He shivers and looks eagerly about. The eighteen years he has lived seem but a moment, a breathing space in the long march of humanity. Already he hears death calling. With all his heart he wants to come close to some other human, touch someone with his hands, be touched by the hand of another. If he prefers that the other be a woman, that is because he believes that a woman will be gentle, that she will understand. He wants, most of all, understanding.

When the moment of sophistication came to George Willard, his mind turned to Helen White, the Winesburg banker's daughter. Always he had been conscious of the girl growing into womanhood as he grew into manhood. Once on a summer night when he was eighteen, he had walked with her on a country road and in her presence had given way to an impulse to boast, to make himself appear big and significant in her eyes. Now he wanted to see her for another purpose. He wanted to tell her of the new impulses that had come to him. He had tried to make her think of him as a man when he knew nothing of manhood, and now he wanted to be with her and to try to make her feel the change he believed had taken place in his nature.

As for Helen White, she also had come to a period of change. What George felt, she in her young woman's way felt also. She was no longer a girl and hungered to reach into the grace and beauty of womanhood. She had come home from Cleveland, where she was attending college, to spend a day at the Fair. She also had begun to have memories. During the day she sat in the grandstand with a young man, one of the instructors from the college, who was a guest of her mother's. The young man was of a pedantic[1] turn of mind, and she felt at once he would not do for her purpose. At the Fair she was glad to be seen in his company as he was well dressed and a stranger. She knew that the fact of his presence would create an impression. During the day she was happy, but when night came on she began to grow restless. She wanted to drive the instructor away, to get out of his presence. While they sat together in the grandstand and while the eyes of former schoolmates were upon them, she paid so much attention to her escort that he grew interested. "A scholar needs money. I should marry a woman with money," he mused.

Helen White was thinking of George Willard even as he wandered gloomily through the crowds thinking of her. She remembered the summer evening when they had walked together and wanted to walk with him again. She thought that the months she had spent in the city, the going to theaters and the seeing of great crowds wandering in lighted thoroughfares, had changed her profoundly. She wanted him to feel and be conscious of the change in her nature.

The summer evening together that had left its mark on the memory of both the young man and woman had, when looked at quite sensibly, been rather stupidly spent. They had walked out of town along a country road. Then they had stopped by a fence near a field of young corn, and George had taken off his coat and let it hang on his arm. "Well, I've stayed here in Winesburg—yes—I've not yet gone away but I'm growing up," he had said. "I've been reading books and I've been thinking. I'm going to try to amount to something in life."

---

1. **pedantic.** Making a show of knowledge

"Well," he explained, "that isn't the point. Perhaps I'd better quit talking."

The confused boy put his hand on the girl's arm. His voice trembled. The two started to walk back along the road toward town. In his desperation George boasted, "I'm going to be a big man, the biggest that ever lived here in Winesburg," he declared. "I want you to do something. I don't know what. Perhaps it is none of my business. I want you to try to be different from other women. You see the point. It's none of my business, I tell you. I want you to be a beautiful woman. You see what I want."

The boy's voice failed, and in silence the two came back into town and went along the street to Helen White's house. At the gate he tried to say something impressive. Speeches he had thought out came into his head, but they seemed utterly pointless: "I thought—I used to think—I had it in my mind you would marry Seth Richmond. Now I know you won't," was all he could find to say as she went through the gate and toward the door of her house.

On the warm fall evening as he stood in the stairway and looked at the crowd drifting through Main Street, George thought of the talk beside the field of young corn and was ashamed of the figure he had made of himself. In the street the people surged up and down like cattle confined in a pen. Buggies and wagons almost filled the narrow thoroughfare. A band played and small boys raced along the sidewalk, diving between the legs of men. Young men with shining red faces walked awkwardly about with girls on their arms. In a room above one of the stores, where a dance was to be held, the fiddlers tuned their instruments. The broken sounds floated down through an open window and out across the murmur of voices and the loud blare of the horns of the band. The medley of sounds got on young Willard's nerves. Everywhere, on all sides, the sense of crowding, moving life closed in about him. He wanted to run away by himself and think. "If she wants to stay with that fellow she may. Why should I care? What difference does it make to me?" he growled and went along Main Street and through Hern's grocery into a side street.

George felt so utterly lonely and dejected that he wanted to weep, but pride made him walk rapidly along, swinging his arms. He came to Wesley Moyer's livery barn and stopped in the shadows to listen to a group of men who talked of a race Wesley's stallion, Tony Tip, had won at the Fair during the afternoon. A crowd had gathered in front of the barn, and before the crowd walked Wesley, prancing up and down and boasting. He held a whip in his hand and kept tapping the ground. Little puffs of dust arose in the lamplight. "Hey, quit your talking," Wesley claimed. "I wasn't afraid; I knew I had him beat all the time. I wasn't afraid."

Ordinarily George Willard would have been intensely interested in the boasting of Moyer the horseman. Now it made him angry. He turned and hurried away along the street. "Old windbag," he sputtered. "Why does he want to be bragging? Why don't he shut up?"

George went into a vacant lot, and as he hurried along, fell over a pile of rubbish, a nail protruding from an empty barrel tore his trousers. He sat down on the ground and swore. With a pin he mended the torn place and then arose and went on. "I'll go to Helen White's house; that's what I'll do. I'll walk right in. I'll say that I want to see her. I'll walk right in and sit down, that's what I'll do," he declared, climbing over a fence and beginning to run.

On the veranda of Banker White's house, Helen was restless and distraught. The instructor sat between the mother and daughter. His talk wearied the girl. Although he had not been raised in an Ohio town, the instructor began to put on the airs of the city. He wanted to appear cosmopolitan.[1] "I like the chance you have given to me to study the background out of which most of our girls come," he declared. "It was good of you, Mrs. White, to have me down for the day." He turned to Helen and laughed. "Your life is still bound up with the life of the town?" he asked. "There are people here in whom you are interested?" To the girl his voice sounded pompous and heavy.

Helen arose and went into the house. At the door leading to a garden at the back, she stopped and stood listening. Her mother began to talk. "There is no one here fit to associate with a girl of Helen's breeding," she said.

Helen ran down a flight of stairs at the back of the house and into the garden. In the darkness she stopped and stood trembling. It seemed to her that the world was full of meaningless people saying words. Afire with eagerness she ran through a garden gate, and turning a corner by the banker's barn, went into a little side street. "George! Where are you, George?" she cried, filled with nervous excitement. She stopped running, and leaned against a tree to laugh hysterically. Along the dark little street came George Willard, still saying words. "I'm going to walk right into her house. I'll go right in and sit down," he declared as he came up to her. He stopped and stared stupidly. "Come on," he said and took hold of her hand. With hanging heads they walked away along the street under the trees. Dry leaves rustled under foot. Now that he had found her, George wondered what he had better do and say.

At the upper end of the fair ground, in Winesburg, there is a half-decayed old grandstand. It has never been painted and the boards are all warped out of shape. The fair ground stands on top of a low hill rising out of the valley of Wine Creek, and from the grandstand one can see at night, over a cornfield, the lights of the town reflected against the sky.

George and Helen climbed the hill to the fair ground, coming by the path past Waterworks Pond. The feeling of loneliness and isolation that had come to the young man in the crowded streets of his town was both broken and intensified by the presence of Helen. What he felt was reflected in her.

In youth there are always two forces fighting in people. The warm unthinking little animal struggles against the thing

---

1. **cosmopolitan.** Having worldwide rather than narrow experience or sophistication

that reflects and remembers, and the older, the more sophisticated thing had possession of George Willard. Sensing his mood, Helen walked beside him filled with respect. When they got to the grandstand, they climbed up under the roof and sat down on one of the long benchlike seats.

There is something memorable in the experience to be had by going into a fair ground that stands at the edge of a Middle Western town on a night after the annual fair has been held. The sensation is one never to be forgotten. On all sides are ghosts, not of the dead, but of living people. Here, during the day just passed, have come the people pouring in from the town and the country around. Farmers with their wives and children and all the people from the hundreds of little frame houses have gathered within these board walls. Young girls have laughed and men with beards have talked of the affairs of their lives. The place has been filled to overflowing with life. It has itched and squirmed with life and now it is night and the life has all gone away. The silence is almost terrifying. One conceals oneself standing silently beside the trunk of a tree, and what there is of a reflective tendency in his nature is intensified. One shudders at the thought of the meaninglessness of life while at the same instant, and if the people of the town are his people, one loves life so intensely that tears come into the eyes.

In the darkness under the roof of the grandstand, George Willard sat beside Helen White and felt very keenly his own insignificance in the scheme of existence. Now that he had come out of town where the presence of the people stirring about, busy with a multitude of affairs, had been so irritating, the irritation was all gone. The presence of Helen renewed and refreshed him. It was as though her woman's hand was assisting him to make some minute readjustment of the machinery of his life. He began to think of the people in the town where he had always lived with something like reverence. He had reverence for Helen. He wanted to love and to be loved by her, but he did not want at the moment to be confused by her womanhood. In the darkness he took hold of her hand, and when she crept close put a hand on her shoulder. A wind began to blow and he shivered. With all his strength he tried to hold and to understand the mood that had come upon him. In that high place in the darkness the two oddly sensitive human atoms held each other tightly and waited. In the mind of each was the same thought. "I have come to this lonely place and here is this other," was the substance of the thing felt.

In Winesburg the crowded day had run itself out into the long night of the late fall. Farm horses jogged away along lonely country roads, pulling their portion of weary people. Clerks began to bring samples of goods in off the sidewalks and lock the doors of stores. In the Opera House a crowd had gathered to see a show, and further down Main Street the fiddlers, their instruments tuned, sweated and worked to keep the feet of youth flying over a dance floor.

In the darkness in the grandstand Helen White and George Willard remained silent. Now and then the spell that held them was broken and they turned and tried in the dim light to see into each other's eyes. They kissed, but that impulse did not last. At the upper end of the fair ground a half dozen men worked over horses that had raced during the afternoon. The men had built a fire and were heating kettles of water. Only their legs could be seen as they passed back and forth in the light. When the wind blew, the little flames of the fire danced crazily about.

George and Helen arose and walked away into the darkness. They went along a path past a field of corn that had not yet been cut. The wind whispered among the dry corn blades. For a moment during the walk back into town, the spell that had held them was broken. When they had come to the crest of Waterworks Hill they stopped by a tree, and George again put his hands on the girl's shoulders. She embraced him eagerly, and then again they drew quickly back from that impulse. They stopped kissing and stood a little apart. Mutual respect grew big in them. They were both embarrassed, and to relieve their embarrassment, dropped into the animalism of youth. They laughed and began to pull and haul at each other. In some way chastened and purified by the mood they had been in they became, not man and woman, not boy and girl, but excited little animals.

It was so they went down the hill. In the darkness they played like two splendid young things in a young world. Once, running swiftly forward, Helen tripped George and he fell. He squirmed and shouted. Shaking with laughter, he rolled down the hill. Helen ran after him. For just a moment she stopped in the darkness. There is no way of knowing what woman's thoughts went through her mind but, when the bottom of the hill was reached and she came up to the boy, she took his arm and walked beside him in dignified silence. For some reason they could not have explained, they had both got from their silent evening together the thing needed. Man or boy, woman or girl, they had for a moment taken hold of the thing that makes the mature life of men and women in the modern world possible.

## from *The Grapes of Wrath*
by John Steinbeck

### Chapter I

To the Red Country and part of the gray country of Oklahoma, the last rains came gently, and they did not cut the scarred earth. The plows crossed and recrossed the rivulet marks. The last rains lifted the corn quickly and scattered weed colonies and grass along the sides of the roads so that the gray country and the dark red country began to disappear under a green cover. In the last part of May the sky grew pale and the clouds that had hung in high puffs for so long in the spring were dissipated. The sun flared down on the growing corn day after day until a line of brown spread along the edge of each green bayonet. The clouds appeared, and went away, and in a while they did not try any more. The weeds grew darker green to protect themselves, and they did not spread any more. The surface of the earth crusted, a thin hard crust, and as the sky became pale, so the earth became pale, pink in the red country and white in the gray country.

In the water-cut gullies the earth dusted down in dry little streams. Gophers and ant lions started small avalanches. And as the sharp sun struck day after day, the leaves of the young corn became less stiff and erect; they bent in a curve at first, and then, as the central ribs of strength grew weak, each leaf tilted downward. Then it was June, and the sun shone more fiercely. The brown lines on the corn leaves widened and moved in on the central ribs. The weeds frayed and edged back toward their roots. The air was thin and the sky more pale; and every day the earth paled.

In the roads where the teams moved, where the wheels milled the ground and the hooves of the horses beat the ground, the dirt crust broke and the dust formed. Every moving thing lifted the dust into the air: a walking man lifted a thin layer as high as his waist, and a wagon lifted the dust as high as the fence tops, and an automobile boiled a cloud behind it. The dust was long in settling back again.

When June was half gone, the big clouds moved up out of Texas and the Gulf, high heavy clouds, rainheads. The men in the fields looked up at the clouds and sniffed at them and held wet fingers up to sense the wind. And the horses were nervous while the clouds were up. The rainheads dropped a little spattering and hurried on to some other country. Behind them the sky was pale again and the sun flared. In the dust there were drop craters where the rain had fallen, and there were clean splashes on the corn, and that was all.

A gentle wind followed the rain clouds, driving them on northward, a wind that softly clashed the drying corn. A day went by and the wind increased, steady, unbroken by gusts. The dust from the roads fluffed up and spread out and fell on the weeds beside the fields, and fell into the fields a little way. Now the wind grew strong and hard and it worked at the rain crust in the corn fields. Little by little the sky was darkened by the mixing dust, and the wind felt over the earth, loosened the dust, and carried it away. The wind grew stronger. The rain crust broke and the dust lifted up out of the fields and drove gray plumes into the air like sluggish smoke. The corn threshed the wind and made a dry, rushing sound. The finest dust did not settle back to earth now, but disappeared into the darkening sky.

The wind grew stronger, whisked under stones, carried up straws and old leaves, and even little clods, marking its course as it sailed across the fields. The air and the sky darkened and through them the sun shone redly, and there was a raw sting in the air. During a night the wind raced faster over the land, dug cunningly among the rootlets of the corn, and the corn fought the wind with its weakened leaves until the roots were freed by the prying wind and then each stalk settled wearily sideways toward the earth and pointed the direction of the wind.

The dawn came, but no day. In the gray sky a red sun appeared, a dim red circle that gave a little light, like dusk; and as that day advanced, the dusk slipped back toward darkness, and the wind cried and whimpered over the fallen corn.

Men and women huddled in their houses, and they tied handkerchiefs over their noses when they went out, and wore goggles to protect their eyes.

When the night came again it was black night, for the stars could not pierce the dust to get down, and the window lights could not even spread beyond their own yards. Now the dust was evenly mixed with the air, an emulsion of dust and air. Houses were shut tight, and cloth wedged around doors and windows, but the dust came in so thinly that it could not be seen in the air, and it settled like pollen on the chairs and tables, on the dishes. The people brushed it from their shoulders. Little lines of dust lay at the door sills.

In the middle of that night the wind passed on and left the land quiet. The dust-filled air muffled sound more completely than fog does. The people, lying in their beds, heard the wind stop. They awakened when the rushing wind was gone. They lay quietly and listened deep into the stillness. Then the roosters crowed, and their voices were muffled, and the people stirred restlessly in their beds and wanted the morning. They knew it would take a long time for the dust to settle out of the air. In the morning the dust hung like fog, and the sun was red as ripe new blood. All day the dust sifted down from the sky, and the next day it sifted down. An even blanket covered the earth. It settled on the corn, piled up on the tops of the fence posts, piled up on the wires; it settled on roofs, blanketed the weeds and trees.

The people came out of their houses and smelled the hot stinging air and covered their noses from it. And the children came out of the houses, but they did not run or shout as they would have done after a rain. Men stood by their fences and looked at the ruined corn, drying fast now, only a little green showing through the film of dust. The men were silent and they did not move often. And the women came out of the houses to stand beside their men—to feel whether this time the men would break. The women studied the men's faces secretly, for the corn could go, as long as something else remained. The children stood near by, drawing figures in the dust with bare toes, and the children sent exploring senses out to see whether men and women would break. The children peeked at the faces of the men and women, and then drew careful lines in the dust with their toes. Horses came to the watering troughs and nuzzled the water to clear the surface dust. After a while the faces of the watching men lost their bemused perplexity and became hard and angry and resistant. Then the women knew that they were safe and that there was no break. Then they asked, What'll we do? And the men replied, I don't know. But it was all right. The women knew it was all right, and the watching children knew it was all right. Women and children knew deep in themselves that no misfortune was too great to bear if their men were whole. The women went into the houses to their work, and the children began to play, but cautiously at first. As the day went forward the sun became less red. It flared down on the dust-blanketed land. The men sat in the doorways of their houses; their hands were busy with sticks and little rocks. The men sat still—thinking—figuring.

# Guided Writing

> "Quite a lot of people remember and they tell their children and their children and their grandchildren remember.... And if it's good enough it lasts forever."
>
> —Ernest Hemingway

## WRITING AN ANNOTATED BIBLIOGRAPHY

Patrick asked his father to edit the story he had written. After reviewing the manuscript carefully, the father returned it to his son. "But, Papa," Patrick cried in dismay, "you've only changed one word."

"If it's the right word," said Ernest Hemingway, "that's a lot." Hemingway prized the apt and simple word. He also prized the immortality of great writers. We remember Hemingway—and many other writers—for their contributions to exploring and understanding humanity through literature.

**WRITING ASSIGNMENT.** Your assignment is to write an annotated bibliography based on your research on an American author from the modern era. Your annotated bibliography will focus on the literary, social, or personal aspects of the author's life.

## Professional Model

### Edna St. Vincent Millay: Liberated Woman Poet
by Cherie A. Boen

Gould, Jean. *The Poet and Her Book: A Biography of Edna St. Vincent Millay.* New York: Dodd, Mead & Company, 1969.

Gould recounts Millay's life in great detail from her early childhood to her death. The author makes some attempts to connect Millay's work with her life, but mostly she concentrates on the people and places of the poet's life. What a life it was! Edna St. Vincent Millay (who was called Vincent) was truly liberated. In her post-college years, she was very interested in theater—she wrote for and appeared on the stage with the Provincetown Players. She moved to Greenwich Village right after college. There she became the center of the literary scene—she knew everyone. After many relationships, Millay married Eugen Jan Boissevain; apparently, she always used her maiden name. As she grew older, her poetry gradually lost its appeal. She had recurring illness through her adult life (she went directly from her wedding to a hospital for surgery), finally suffering a nervous breakdown right after World War II. Her poetry started falling from favor in the mid-thirties.

Gould obviously admires Millay; even her most outrageous behavior is portrayed in a favorable light. The

An **annotated bibliography** is a list of citations of books, articles, and documents. Each citation is followed by an **annotation,** a brief (usually 150 words or less) descriptive and evaluative paragraph. The purpose of an annotation is to inform the reader of the relevance, accuracy, and quality of the source cited. Expect to include 6–8 sources in your complete annotated bibliography: 3–5 conventional, or print, sources and 1–3 online sources.

An annotated bibliography may serve a number of **purposes,** including but not limited to:

- review of the literature
- illustration of the quality of research you've done
- demonstration of the types of sources available
- description of other topics that may be of interest
- indication of other areas of research

*continued on page 602*

**EXAMINING THE MODEL.** Note the way the Professional Model not only summarizes each work but gives specific information to help the reader understand and assess its accuracy and relevance. While these entries are arranged alphabetically by author, they are also discussed in relationship to each other.

Boen compares the first two entries by saying Gurko's book is "not as detailed as Gould's, but it quotes Millay's work copiously as it attempts to establish links between life and poetry." When Boen cites a chapter from a book by Nina Miller, she notes that "the focus is sharper and her impact more clearly portrayed than in the two biographies previously cited." What does Boen say is the "most obvious difference" between this and the two biographies? What strengths does Nina Miller's chapter on Millay present that the books do not? How does this method of comparing sources help a reader use an annotated bibliography for research?

extensive bibliography mentions many sources that can be pursued. Finding specific details is extremely easy because the biography has an extensive index. The book reads like a novel, but the writer's bias makes it seem dated.

Gurko, Miriam. *Restless Spirit: The Life of Edna St. Vincent Millay.* New York: Thomas Y. Cromwell Company, 1962.

Gurko's major focus is to establish relationships between Edna St. Vincent Millay's poetry and the events of her life. The biography itself is not as detailed as Gould's, but it quotes Millay's work copiously as it attempts to establish links between life and poetry. (Gurko seldom discusses Millay's other writing.) The most interesting material contained is a comparison between the passionate work of Millay with the cool, distant poetry of T. S. Eliot. With the publication of *The Wasteland*, the entire poetry world changed, and Millay's poetry began to lose popularity.

Clear short chapters make finding specific information easy; the book contains both a bibliography and an index, but neither is as detailed as those in the Gould biography.

Miller, Nina. "Edna St. Vincent Millay," *Making Love Modern: The Intimate Public World of New York's Literary Women.* New York: Oxford University Press, 1999.

Miller's chapter on Edna St. Vincent Millay discusses her impact on the New York literary scene of the twenties and thirties. In the 1920s Millay was the most read and quoted poet in America. Because the book concentrates on Millay's New York influence, the focus is sharper and her impact more clearly portrayed than in the two biographies previously cited.

The most obvious difference between this and the two biographies is the scholarship. The two biographies (from the 1960s) appear willing to overlook anything that might be distasteful. The focused scholarship of *Making Love Modern* makes the material more credible. Not only does Millay have her own chapter, but materials about her are found throughout the book. It also has an extensive bibliography and table of contents. Millay was an icon, but she was a harbinger of a new order of women and women writers.

## Prewriting

**IDENTIFYING YOUR AUDIENCE.** Authors are interesting people. They often have a unique and insightful way of looking at people and events and often lead interesting lives. Are you writing for other students and giving them interesting details about a writer, or are you writing for a teacher to demonstrate your knowledge of the author's works and ability to analyze literature? As you write, keep two goals for your audience in mind. One goal is to demonstrate your knowledge of the author and his or her works. A second goal is to create interest about the author's life, contributions, and accomplishments.

**FINDING YOUR VOICE.** Informative writing doesn't have to be dry. The examples, words, style, and tone that you choose will communicate your interest in the author. Similarly, informative writing does not need to be overly complex. Look at the example below. What similarities and differences do you find between the two sentences?

> This process concentrates on weighing your current high school requirements for admission to college and establishing a targeted schedule and financial goal. Further, it provides a monitor of your progress allowing revisions to be made when necessary.

> You need to balance your high school needs with your long-term educational goals and monitor your progress along the way.

Both sentences are about educational planning, but one is clear and the other is overly complex, wordy, and obscure. As you develop your annotations, work to maintain a clear, to-the-point voice in your writing. In addition, your annotations should be objective and authoritative, and therefore be written in the third person.

**WRITING WITH A PLAN.** Your task is to produce an annotated bibliography that you could use to write a report or critical essay about one aspect of a writer's life or work. But while an annotated bibliography can lead to a research paper, it also stands on its own and offers helpful information to others interested in your topic.

The first step in writing the bibliography is to settle on an author in the modern era whose work you enjoy, one you want to know and understand even more. The writer may or may not be included in this unit. You may not yet have any idea where you want to go with your research. The next steps will help you focus.

Ask a series of questions that will lead you to different kinds of information. For example, you might ask questions about an author's background: where did he grow up, what lifestyle did she live, what education did he have? You can ask what critics have said about this author. You can ask about causes the writer may have championed. You can investigate what else the author has written and what awards he or she may have received. This will open up several directions you might want to take. You will quickly be able to see what interests you and what sources are available.

The next step is to go online and to the library to find what research materials are available. For each print citation, write down the title, author, publishing company, place of publication,

> "What is written without effort is in general read without pleasure."
> —Samuel Johnson

**What legacy does an author leave?**
- characters and images that live on after a book is closed
- themes and issues worthy of contemplation and debate
- literary pictures of society, culture, and history

## Language, Grammar, and Style

### Documenting Online and Conventional Sources

Providing exact listings of sources for scholarly works is important for several reasons. The writer establishes credibility in the mind of the reader based upon reputation and validity. The reader needs to be able to verify the objectivity, authenticity, and accuracy of the sources. Finally, a properly ordered and detailed citation provides a clear trail for the researcher to follow back to the source. The Modern Language Association provides detailed guidelines for properly citing sources.

**IDENTIFYING DOCUMENTATION.** Look at the bibliography entries below and identify what type of source each entry documents (whether it's an anthology, magazine, electronic source, etc.). Then identify the elements included in each citation (volume, edition, author, editor, title, etc.).

Deloria, Vine Jr. "Indians Today, the Real and Unreal," <u>Native American Literature: An Anthology</u>. Ed. Lawana Trout. Lincolnwood, Illinois: NTC Publishing Group, 1998.

<u>The Robert Frost Web Site</u>. Ed. "Uncle" Danny Clayton and Jay & Sue D. Michalowski. 20 April 1999. 29 August 2000 <http://www.robertfrost.org/indexgood.html>.

date of publication, and the call number. You should also include its title. Record the names of articles in magazines, along with the magazine titles and dates. For each electronic source, write down the Internet address, the date you accessed it, and the date it is copyrighted. Find the actual sources to see what information is covered. Your first look at the material is to scan it, not to read carefully. That will come later, after you've found your focus. Decide which areas are most interesting to you; see what connections you can make. Decide on your title. Go back to the sources, read them carefully and make your annotations.

Marta decided to research modern American writer F. Scott Fitzgerald. She asked the focus questions above and decided she was most interested in finding out about how the author's background influences his writing.

Marta created this graphic organizer to help keep her focus as she did the research on F. Scott Fitzgerald.

## Student Model—Graphic Organizer

| Author |
| --- |
| F. Scott Fitzgerald |

| Citation | Citation | Citation |
| --- | --- | --- |
| Lehan, Richard. <u>The Great Gatsby: The Limits of Wonder.</u> Boston: G.K. Hall & Co., 1990. Professor at U. of Wisconsin | Fitzgerald, F. Scott. <u>The Great Gatsby.</u> New York: Charles Scribner's Sons, 1942. Use quotes about ash heaps, valley of ashes, p. 69 Rush from emptiness, p.118 | Bruccoli, Matthew J. "Getting It Right: The Publishing Process and the Correction of Factual Errors—with Reference to <u>The Great Gatsby.</u>" February 20, 1997. 30 October 1999. <http:www.sc.edu/essays/right.html> |
| Gives chronology of F.'s life Sense of loss (use quote p. 10) Two kinds of seeing concept: visionary & moral observer Values: "moral carelessness"/Gatsby's obsession | | noted scholar on Fitzgerald calls F. an "impressionistic realist" who uses style and tone to evoke emotions most in this source is not usable for this bib., but is interesting. Much deals with the editing process F. used. |

| Focus Statement |
| --- |
| Early life experiences influence Fitzgerald's theme in <u>The Great Gatsby.</u> |

| Citation | Citation | Citation |
| --- | --- | --- |
| | | |
| | | |

Copy the graphic organizer on your own paper and complete it as you do your research. After you have finished, you will have what you need to write complete annotated citations in your bibliography.

## Drafting

Gather your materials and your graphic organizer. Remember to be brief and to include only directly significant information and write in an efficient manner. Focus on the item's usefulness for your investigation, any conclusions the authors have drawn, and your reaction to those conclusions. Summarize the work.

When you are actually writing the annotation, you should comment on and evaluate your sources, not just list them. Overall, your annotated bibliography should demonstrate that you have knowledge about or an understanding of your topic by showing a particular perspective toward, angle on, or interpretation of your topic. The commentary should contain all or some of the following elements: explaining the main purpose of the work; briefly describing the contents; indicating the possible audience for the work; noting any special features; warning of any defect, weakness, or suspected bias. Prepare the basic bibliographical entries by arranging the information about the works according to the Modern Language Association (MLA). Finally, title your annotated bibliography based on your focus statement.

## Self- and Peer Evaluation

After you finish your first draft, complete a self-evaluation of your writing. As you look over your work, ask yourself these questions:

- Who is the audience for this annotated bibliography? In what ways does it suit this audience?
- Read the title. What is the purpose of the annotated bibliography? If it is too broad or too narrow, how could the focus be adjusted?
- How well do the annotations support the purpose?
- What details and relevant information are included to explain the contents of the citation? Where is this information the strongest? the weakest?
- Where does the writer support evaluative comments about the citation with examples?
- Where is there a need for additional facts or information?
- Which annotation has the most purposeful organization? Which has the weakest? Why?
- Which sentences contain the best examples of appropriate, descriptive, and precise word choice and effective sentence structure?
- Where are there errors in mechanics in the bibliographic references?

Saino, Elaine. "Welty and Her World: Weldon Kees." Eudora Welty Newsletter. 23.2 (Winter 1999): 49–55.

**FIXING DOCUMENTATION ERRORS.** Are all the sources correctly punctuated? Are the titles of books, periodicals, and websites underlined or in italics? Remember that there are different rules for different media as well as for different variations of a specific medium. Correct any errors that you find, using the Language Arts Survey 5.40, "Making Bibliographies and Bibliography Cards" as a guide. Look at one of Marta's bibliographic entries below. Identify the errors in her entry.

Lehan, Richard. The Great Gatsby: the Limits of Wonder. Boston; G.K. Hall & Co.

**USING DOCUMENTATION EFFECTIVELY.** Compile your own sources for an annotated bibliography, noting pertinent information for each source, and order them using the proper format for the type of publication. As you review your work, check for errors. Fix them before submitting your final copy.

For more information, see the Language Arts Survey 5.36, "Documenting Sources."

*continued on page 606*

Note that your citations should be listed alphabetically. If an entry has no author or editor, alphabetize by title. Do not include articles such as *an*, *the*, and *a* when you alphabetize.

## Student Model—Draft

Here is an excerpt from Marta's annotated bibliography.

> Lehan, Richard. *The Great Gatsby: The Limits of Wonder.* Boston: G.K. Hall & Co., 1990.
>
> *Professor at U. of Wisconsin*
> *Book shows scholarly work*
> *Can you qualify the author?*
>
> Lehan gives examples of how the twenties may in many ways be thought of as Gatsby's America. He referred to Fitzgerald's own sense of loss at the end of the decade, the end of an American era as "exactly the same emotion that he delineated so brilliantly in The Great Gatsby."
>
> *(You shift from present to past)*
> *italicize*
>
> The novel presents two kinds of seeing. One is the visionary, Jay Gatsby, who is on a quest for the great American dream. The other, Nick Carraway, stands as a moral observer. Nick sees what is
>
> *both*
>
> pathetic and grand in Gatsby and in America. He also sees a carelessness in the other characters in the novel, perhaps demonstrating the carelessness of American society in the twenties. He notices power run amok, rampant selfishness, and moral abandonment.
>
> *Order here?*
>
> *Put this sentence last to show a better flow*

## Revising and Proofreading

Review the focus of your research and your self- and peer evaluations. Does each annotation give enough examples to show how the citation relates to your research focus? Does your annotation clearly give information about the source? Decide which revisions are needed. Check the form of the citation for complete content and proper order and punctuation.

Proofread your revised draft for errors in spelling, grammar, punctuation, capitalization, and other details. For more information, see the Language Arts Survey 2.45, "A Proofreading Checklist."

## Student Model—Revised

The American Dream: An Empty Promise to F. Scott Fitzgerald

Lehan, Richard. *The Great Gatsby: The Limits of Wonder.* Boston: G.K. Hall & Co., 1990.

Lehan, a former professor at the University of Wisconsin, provides an index and extensive bibliography.

Lehan notes two kinds of seeing in *Gatsby*. One is of the visionary, Jay Gatsby, who is on a quest for the great American dream. The other, Nick Carraway, stands as a moral observer. Nick sees what is pathetic and grand in Gatsby and in America. He also sees carelessness in the other characters in the novel, showing the carelessness of American society in the twenties. He notices power run amok, rampant selfishness, and moral abandonment. He gives examples of how the twenties may in many ways be thought of as Gatsby's America. He refers to Fitzgerald's own sense of loss at the end of the decade, the end of an American era as "exactly the same emotion that he delineated so brilliantly in *The Great Gatsby*."

## Publishing and Presenting

Create a classroom anthology of annotated bibliographies. Share Internet sites with other students so others can go online with their comments and questions. You may want to devote a day to going online to explore the Internet sites the papers include. See your school librarian about setting up a file of favorite authors for students to access.

## Reflecting

Consider the value of researching an author whom you admire. How has your appreciation for this writer changed? In what ways do you now see him or her differently than before? What about your thoughts about the art and craft of research? What have you learned about yourself as a writer and a researcher? How has your own work with writing an annotated bibliography helped you read and respond to other annotated bibliographies by your peers?

# UNIT REVIEW
## *The Modern Era*

## Words for Everyday Use

Check your knowledge of the following vocabulary words from the selections in this unit. Write short sentences using these words in context to make the meaning clear. To review the definition or usage of a word, refer to the page number listed or the Glossary of Words for Everyday Use.

assert, 503
callow, 541
commensurate, 586
cower, 513
curtailment, 552
deferential, 505
digress, 503
disbar, 580
dissipate, 552
dwindle, 569
endure, 587
ephemeral, 587
etherize, 502
euphony, 525
excruciatingly, 544
exultant, 551
flourish, 550
formulated, 503
frenzied, 550
haggard, 543
hem, 581
ideology, 580
immobility, 544

indecipherable, 524
indefinite, 580
infatuation, 541
inflection, 524
insidious, 502
interminable, 555
interminably, 544
jilt, 566
jocularity, 545
laconic, 556
linger, 502
loiter, 550
lucid, 524
magnanimously, 551
malinger, 504
meddling, 582
obtuse, 505
overture, 543
pantomime, 524
picturesque, 553
placard, 580
poignant, 557
pontoon, 580

prelude, 544
premonition, 554
presume, 503
prevail, 587
propagandist, 580
reproach, 545
respective, 542
reticent, 557
reverential, 541
revert, 541
rickety, 581
rummage, 564
ruthless, 551
sartorial, 556
solidarity, 580
spasmodically, 554
tallowy, 582
tedious, 502
travail, 587
tremulously, 542
verity, 587

## Literary Tools

Define the following terms, giving concrete examples of how they are used in the selections in this unit. To review a term, refer to the page number indicated or the Handbook of Literary Terms.

abstract, 523
aim, 585
alliteration, 585
allusion, 500
character, 508, 549
characterization, 572
collage, 578
concrete, 523
dialogue, 572
diction, 509
dramatic monologue, 500
effect, 532

free verse, 484
image, 523, 532
imagery, 523, 532
internal monologue, 572
inversion, 535
irony, 562
metaphor, 509
meter, 530
narrator, 539
parallelism, 496
pathetic fallacy, 521
personification, 496

point of view, 539
repetition, 489, 535
reversal, 549
rhythm, 530
simile, 539
speaker, 530, 532
stream-of-consciousness
   writing, 562
symbol, 508
syntax, 535
theme, 489
tone, 484, 530

# Reflecting
## *on* YOUR READING

## Genre Studies

1. **IMAGIST POETRY.** Poetry is a concentrated form of writing, and Imagist poetry is extremely concentrated, presenting single moments of sense perception without reference to the emotions or opinions of the author, narrator, or speaker. Select two Imagist poems from this unit and discuss the subject and message conveyed.

2. **NONFICTION.** Describe the preoccupations of the modern age as revealed in "Newsreel LXVIII" and Faulkner's Nobel Prize Acceptance Speech. What attitude does each author convey toward these preoccupations?

## Thematic Studies

3. **ALIENATION.** Two world wars and a society rapidly changing yielded feelings of alienation and anxiety. Select three poems from this unit that deal with the theme of alienation. Explore the differences and similarities in the treatment of this theme in the poems you select.

4. **VIEWING THE PAST.** The main characters in "Lucinda Matlock" and "The Jilting of Granny Weatherall" look back on their lives. What philosophy of life do their reflections reveal? What major disappointment has each character experienced? What impact has the disappointment made in their lives?

## Historical/Biographical Studies

5. **SOCIOECONOMICS.** Aunt Georgiana in "A Wagner Matinee" and George O'Kelly in "The Sensible Thing" are impacted by their socioeconomic status. Explain how socioeconomic realities affect the outcome of their lives. What socioeconomic bracket does each character belong to? What are these characters prevented from doing due to socioeconomic considerations? How would their lives be different if they belonged to a different station in life?

*Aspects of Negro Life: From Slavery through Reconstruction,* 1934.
Aaron Douglas. Schomberg Center for Research in Black Culture, New York.

I, too, am America.

—Langston Hughes

## ArtNote

**Aspects of Negro Life: From Slavery through Reconstruction**, 1934. Aaron Douglas.

In this painting, Aaron Douglas (1899–1979) tells the history of African Americans in the 19th century by compressing into a single image several events: slavery, civil war, emancipation, racist terrorism, and northern migration. Douglas developed his distinctive style from the flat, geometric figures found in African, Egyptian, and Greek art. He said his method was also based on the form of African-American spirituals: "stark...simplified and abstract." The flat shapes are given vibrancy by juxtaposing warm and cool colors and the waves of light that radiate from key sections. A central figure unifies the composition. What is the meaning of this figure? What do you think he is saying?

# THE HARLEM RENAISSANCE (1920–1936)

## THE RISE OF AFRICAN-AMERICAN LITERATURE

The literary achievement of African Americans was one of the most striking developments of the post-Civil War era. In the writings of **Booker T. Washington, W. E. B. Du Bois, James Weldon Johnson, Charles Waddell Chesnutt, Paul Laurence Dunbar**, and others, the roots of African-American writing took hold, notably in the forms of autobiography, protest literature, sermons, poetry, and song. These early writers laid the foundation for and strongly influenced the African-American writers that followed during the early part of the twentieth century.

## BACKGROUND AND BEGINNINGS

The roots of the Harlem Renaissance reach back to the Reconstruction period, when Southern African Americans tried to claim the education, economic opportunity, and political liberty that slavery had long denied to them. To help with this cause, the Freedmans' Bureau, a temporary Federal bureau for the improvement, protection, and employment of freed slaves, was organized in 1865 and lasted until 1872.

Though many scholars disagree about exactly when the Harlem Renaissance began and ended, many consider **World War I** a starting point. Strict immigration laws were enacted during this time, and many recent European immigrants returned to their home countries to take part in the war. This exodus resulted in new employment opportunities in the Northern industrial cities, including opportunities for African Americans. Between 1915 and 1918, so many Southern blacks moved north that their relocation has become known as **The Great Migration**.

Other scholars believe that the Renaissance began at the end of World War I, when African-American troops returned to America. After fighting bravely for democracy in

## LITERARY EVENTS

➤ = American Events

➤ 1919. Benjamin Brawley's *The Negro in Literature and Art in the United States* published

➤ 1920. Claude McKay's *Spring in New Hampshire* published
➤ 1920. W. E. B. Du Bois's *Darkwater* published
➤ 1920. Eugene O'Neill's *The Emperor Jones*, starring Charles Gilpin, produced

➤ 1923. Jean Toomer's *Cane* published
➤ 1923. *Opportunity: A Journal of Negro Life*, founded by Urban League and edited by Charles S. Johnson

| 1918 | 1920 | 1922 |
|---|---|---|

## HISTORICAL EVENTS

➤ 1919. March of 369th Regiment up Fifth Avenue to Harlem
1919. First Pan African Congress organized by W. E. B. Du Bois, Paris
➤ 1919. Race riots in Washington DC, Chicago, Charleston, Knoxville, and Omaha
➤ 1919. Race Relations Commission founded
➤ 1919. Beginning of Prohibition

➤ 1920. Universal Negro Improvement Association (UNIA) Convention held
➤ 1920. Founding by Marcus Garvey of African Orthodox Church
➤ 1920. Warren G. Harding elected president
➤ 1920. James Weldon Johnson appointed first African-American officer of NAACP
1921. Second Pan African Congress

➤ 1922. First anti-lynching legislation approved by House of Representatives
➤ 1923. Third Pan African Congress
➤ 1923. Opening of the Cotton Club
➤ 1923. Arrest of Marcus Garvey for mail fraud; five-year prison sentence
➤ 1923. Death of President Harding; succession of Calvin Coolidge

Europe, these men expected America's respect. Political leader W. E. B. Du Bois wrote, "We return. We return from fighting. We return fighting. Make way for Democracy! We saved it in France, and by the Great Jehovah, we will save it in the United States of America, or know the reason why." Instead of being welcomed home, however, these soldiers returned to a wave of racist persecution. An estimated 300 lynchings occurred between 1919 and 1923.

In response, African Americans began to mobilize politically. In doing so, they experienced widespread sympathy and support from progressive white people. Some scholars argue that this wave of activism sparked the Harlem Renaissance. Some also argue that a better term would be "Negro Renaissance" because New Orleans, Atlanta, Chicago, Kansas City, and Washington, DC were also experiencing African-American political action and artistic creativity. But it was Harlem, a two-square-mile neighborhood of New York City, that caught the world's attention.

*True Sons of Freedom*, 1918. Charles Gustine.
Library of Congress.

## THE HARLEM RENAISSANCE IN LITERATURE

During the high-spirited 1920s, Harlem, the black community situated uptown in New York City, generated great passion and creativity. Never before had so much African-American artistic productivity bloomed in so short a time. Writers, poets, philosophers, musicians, visual artists, and filmmakers gathered to form a large and diverse talent base whose achievements reflected and challenged societal conventions.

Although comprehensive in its scope of creative forms, the Harlem Renaissance was foremost a period of literature. Sometimes supported financially by the **National Association for the Advancement of Colored People (NAACP)**, formed earlier in the century, African-American writing became part of an organized movement to give voice to the oppression African Americans experienced and to the cultural heritage and traditions they shared.

➤ 1924. Jessie Redmon Fauset's novel *There Is Confusion* published
➤ 1924. Countee Cullen winner of first prize in Witter Bynner Poetry Competition
➤ 1924. Du Bois's *The Gift of Black Folk* published

➤ 1926. Langston Hughes's volume of poetry *The Weary Blues* published
➤ 1926. Alain Locke's anthology *The New Negro* published

➤ 1925. Langston Hughes, Countee Cullen, and Zora Neale Hurston winners of *Opportunity*'s first literary awards
➤ 1925. Countee Cullen winner of first prize at first *Crisis* awards ceremony
➤ 1925. Countee Cullen's first volume of poetry, *Color*, published

➤ 1929. Negro Experimental Theater, Negro Art Theater, and National Colored Players founded
➤ 1929. Wallace Thurman's play *Harlem* opens at the Apollo Theater

➤ 1928. Nella Larsen's novel *Quicksand* published

**1924**     **1926**     **1928**

➤ 1924. Reelection of Calvin Coolidge

➤ 1925. American Negro Labor Congress held in Chicago

➤ 1927. Marcus Garvey deported

➤ 1928. Herbert Hoover elected president

➤ 1929. Black Thursday, October 19, Stock Exchange crash; beginning of Great Depression

*Harlem Couple,* 1933. James Van Der Zee.
Sheldon Memorial Art Gallery, Lincoln, Nebraska.

W. E. B. Du Bois believed that African Americans could not achieve social equality by emulating white ideals, that equality could be achieved only by teaching black racial pride with an emphasis on an African cultural heritage. Du Bois described the leaders of the Harlem Renaissance as the **Talented Tenth**, a few privileged professionals and intellectuals who were nearly all second-generation college graduates. The Talented Tenth created a new ideology of racial assertiveness that was to be embraced by influential African Americans, a group that included educated doctors, lawyers, and businessmen.

The poet **Countee Cullen,** a native of Harlem who was briefly married to W. E. B. Du Bois's daughter, wrote accomplished rhymed poetry in accepted forms that white audiences could also appreciate. He did not believe that a poet should allow race to dictate the style and subject matter of a poem. Like Cullen, **Jean Toomer** envisioned an American identity that would transcend race. Perhaps for this reason he brilliantly employed poetic traditions of rhyme and meter and did not seek out new "black" forms for his poetry.

In his 1925 book *The New Negro,* **Alain Locke** envisioned Harlem as a "race capital" where African-American culture, consciousness, and identity might find adequate social expression and stimulation. Such a center, Locke believed, could serve as a vital source for the future advancement of African Americans and "a new democracy in American culture." At the other end of the spectrum were African Americans who rejected the United States entirely and followed **Marcus Garvey's** "Back to Africa" movement.

The social purpose behind African-American literature of this time influenced its choice of techniques and styles: it sought to reach the entire community, not merely its most highly educated members. Important writers of the Harlem Renaissance who

## LITERARY EVENTS

➤ = American Events

➤ 1931. James Weldon Johnson's history *Black Manhattan* published
➤ 1931. Arna Bontemps's novel *God Sends Sunday* published

➤ 1932. Wallace Thurman's second novel, *Infants of the Spring,* published

➤ 1933. Claude McKay's second novel, *Banana Bottom,* published

| 1930 | 1931 | 1932 | 1933 |

## HISTORICAL EVENTS

➤ 1932. Franklin D. Roosevelt elected president
➤ 1932. Beginning of mass defection of African Americans from the Republican party

➤ 1933. End of National Negro Business League

➤ 1930. Universal Holy Temple of Tranquillity founded
➤ 1930. Islam Temple opened in Detroit by Black Muslims

wrote for the masses include **Countee Cullen, Jean Toomer, Langston Hughes, Zora Neale Hurston, Claude McKay, Dorothy West, James Weldon Johnson, Jessie Redmon Fauset, Arna Bontemps, and Nella Larsen.**

During this era, not only books but organizational periodicals proved to be important. These publications acted as the medium of intellectual discourse and grew steadfastly throughout the Renaissance. In particular, *The Crisis*, magazine of the NAACP and edited by Jessie Redmon Fauset, and *Opportunity: A Journal of Negro Life*, founded by the National Urban League and edited by **Charles S. Johnson,** became voices for the era's great thinkers. Periodicals could address time-sensitive issues more quickly than books, while distributing ideas to a growing audience.

## THE JAZZ AGE

During the Harlem Renaissance, artistic experimentation was not limited to literature. It also found expression in music. **Eubie Blake's** catchy "I'm Just Wild About Harry" was among the many tunes that carried a lively ragtime style that heralded jazz. **William Grant Still** began to come into his own as a classical composer. The Harlem Renaissance also ushered in one of the most charismatic performers, **Josephine Baker,** who has continued to be admired as a legendary singer long after her death. The sounds of African-American jazz invigorated and popularized American music, and jazz musicians and composers like **Duke Ellington** and **Cab Calloway** became beloved stars at home and abroad. **Bessie Smith** and other blues singers presented bold, witty, emotionally raw lyrics. African-American spirituals became widely appreciated as uniquely beautiful religious music.

Cab Calloway, 1934.

➤ 1934. Zora Neale Hurston's first novel,
*Jonah's Gourd Vine,* published
➤ 1934. Langston Hughes's story collection
*The Ways of White Folks* published

➤ 1936. Arna Bontemps's novel
*Black Thunder* published

**1934**        **1935**        **1936**

➤ 1934. Ending of Prohibition

➤ 1935. Harlem Race Riot on March 19
➤ 1935. Fifty percent of Harlem's families
unemployed

1936. Beginning of World War II
in Europe

## THEATER AND FILM

Many young African-American actors performed in the Lafayette and Lincoln theaters, including **Ethel Waters** and **Noble Sissle**. Harlem's first theater group was also founded at the Lafayette in 1916. **Charles Gilpin**, considered one of the most prominent black actors of the time, founded the **Lafayette Players**. Other theater groups born during the Harlem Renaissance included the **Harlem Experimental Theater**, the **Krigwa Players**, the **Negro Art Theater**, the **Utopia Players**, and the **Harlem Community Players**. The majority of these groups were amateur and produced classics or melodramas on middle-class life. Although some of their plays dealt with black life and culture, few were written by African Americans.

Two highly successful plays focusing on the black experience were written by white playwright **Eugene O'Neill**: "The Emperor Jones" (1920) and "All God's Chillun Got Wings" (1924). "The Emperor Jones" brought fame to two black actors, **Charles Gilpin** and **Paul Robeson**, and allowed them to play more serious roles. Although most successful plays were being written by whites, African-American performers were finally getting an unprecedented chance to do respectable and serious drama.

While live performers, visual artists, and writers of the Harlem Renaissance have often been honored, filmmakers of the period have been frequently overlooked. Pioneer filmmaker **Oscar Micheaux's** films, including "Within Our Gates" (1919), and **Paul Robeson's** movie debut, "Body and Soul" (1924), resisted the trend of escapist fare and addressed complex themes, including class issues and inter- and intraracial conflict.

Cover of *Opportunity* magazine, 1926. Aaron Douglas. Schomberg Center for Research in Black Culture, New York.

## VISUAL ARTS

Many African-American visual artists across the country became prominent at this time. Those most closely associated with the Harlem Renaissance were **Aaron Douglas, Palmer Hayden, Archibald Motley, William H. Johnson, Malvin Grey Johnson, Augusta Savage,** and **James Van Der Zee.** Aaron Douglas's illustrations for magazines such as *Crisis* and *Opportunity,* and his book covers for the leading Harlem writers made his style the "look" of the Harlem Renaissance. James Van Der Zee photographed many of the defining images of Harlem's middle class.

African-American painters and sculptors developed a wide range of styles, based on the art of Africa and ancient Egypt, American folk art, and representational and abstract European art. African tribal art in particular, previously dismissed as "primitive," began to be appreciated for its intelligence and beauty. Even among white artists, attention shifted to African art, and Cubists and Expressionists began to base their radical new forms on traditional African sculpture.

Support for African-American artists came from the **Harmon Foundation** and the **Colored Men's Branch of the YMCA**, both of which organized nationwide competitions and exhibitions, and from prosperous African-American businessmen and women who collected art. African-American artists were at last freed from the expectations of white patrons and the pressure to mimic the styles of white artists.

*Saturday Night Street Scene,* 1936. Archibald J. Motley, Jr. Private Collection.

## The End of the Renaissance

The Great Depression hit urban African Americans, including those in Harlem, very hard. When jobs were eliminated, jobs for African Americans were often cut first, and Harlem's concentration of talent was scattered away from the city. Almost 50 percent of the families in Harlem were out of work, while a mere 9 percent received government relief jobs. The combination of poverty and racial tension led to a race riot on the evening of March 19, 1935. Ten thousand enraged Harlemites marched down Lenox Avenue, destroying two million dollars of white-owned property. The riot left three African Americans dead, thirty people hospitalized, and more than one hundred in jail. **The Harlem Race Riot** is considered by many scholars to mark the end of the Harlem Renaissance.

But the gains of the Harlem Renaissance were not lost. African Americans had proven themselves to be as talented and capable of excellence as any other American citizens. The Harlem Renaissance created a new consciousness in both white and black Americans; its importance lies in the legacy of new American art forms and in the socioeconomic changes it helped to advance. The rich heritage of the Harlem Renaissance lives on, not just in the modern African-American creative world, but also in the entirety of American art and literature.

# ECHOES

## THE HARLEM RENAISSANCE

Harlem has the same role to play for the New Negro as Dublin has had for the New Ireland or Prague for the New Czechoslovakia.

—Alain Leroy Locke

But who is going to write the intimate...tale of the New Negro, the years of plenty? The golden legend of the amazing young crowd who gathered in Harlem and almost succeeded in doing for New York what the pre-Raphaelites did for London...?

—Arna Bontemps to Countee Cullen

Your people have exhibited a degree of loyalty and patriotism that should command the admiration of the whole nation.

—President Woodrow Wilson to congregation of African-American clergy

Where is the black man's Government? Where is his King and his kingdom? Where is his President, his country, and his ambassador, his army, his navy, his men of big affairs? I could not find them. I will help to make them.

—Marcus Mosiah Garvey

My destiny, is to travel a different road.

—Claude McKay

In time, for though the sun is setting on
A song-lit race of slaves, it has not yet set;
Though late, O soil, it is not too late yet
To catch thy plaintive soul, leaving, soon gone,
Leaving, to catch thy plaintive soul soon gone.

—from *Cane*, Jean Toomer

And some of us have songs to sing
Of jungle beast and fires;
And some of us are solemn grown
With pitiful desires
    And there are those who feel the pull
    Of seas beneath the skies;
        And some there be who want to croon
        of Negro lullabies.
            We claim no part with racial dearth,
            We want to sing the songs of birth!

—from "To Usward," Gwendolyn Bennet

First, the language of Harlem is not alien; it is not Italian or Yiddish; it is English. Harlem talks American, reads American, thinks American.

—James Weldon Johnson

To know how much there is to know is the beginning of learning to live.

—Dorothy West

I have no separate feeling about being an American citizen and colored. I am merely a fragment of the Great Soul that surges within the boundaries. My country, right or wrong.

—Zora Neale Hurston

We have tomorrow
Bright before us
Like a flame.
Yesterday, a night-gone thing
A sun-down name.
And dawn today
Broad arch above the road we came.
We march!

—Langston Hughes

*Aspects of Negro Life: From Slavery through Reconstruction* [Detail], Aaron Douglas.

# "We Wear the Mask"

BY PAUL LAURENCE DUNBAR

## About the AUTHOR

**Paul Laurence Dunbar** (1872–1906), the first African American to gain national eminence as a poet, is considered a precursor to the Harlem Renaissance. He was born in Dayton, Ohio, the son of former slaves. His father, Joshua, was a United States Army soldier and plasterer, and his mother, Matilda, was a laundry worker. Although his mother had no formal education, she taught Dunbar to read when he was four. He reported that both his parents were "fond of books" and read aloud to the family in the evenings as they sat around the fire. Dunbar said that he made his first attempt at rhyming when he was about six and found a poem by Wordsworth. He thought it had been written by a man in Dayton of the same name. The idea that someone he knew wrote poetry impressed his young mind and "after that I rhymed continually," he said.

Dunbar wrote in his free time, began submitting poems to local newspapers, and in 1893 printed *Oak and Ivy*. He gained national recognition in 1896 with the publication of *Lyrics of Lowly Life* and a full-page, enthusiastic review of *Majors and Minors* (1895) in *Harper's Weekly.* That launched him as a reader on the lecture circuit in the United States and in Europe and eventually landed him a series of jobs at the Library of Congress, where he worked until sickness forced him to leave. His works include *The Uncalled* (novel, 1896), *Lyrics of the Hearthside* (1899), *Uncle Eph's Christmas* (one-act musical, 1900), *The Sport of the Gods* (novel, 1902), *Lyrics of Love and Laughter* (1903), and *Lyrics of Sunshine and Shadow* (1905).

## About the SELECTION

While Dunbar's reputation rests on his poems and short stories written in African-American dialect, Dunbar himself considered his nondialectical work to be his best. At the time Dunbar wrote his poems the use of dialect was very popular; consequently and regrettably, many of Dunbar's poems not written in dialect were neglected. In its formal language and use of rhyme, **"We Wear the Mask"** shows the influence of poets Robert Burns and James Whitcomb Riley, both of whom Dunbar admired.

## Literary TOOLS

**SPEAKER.** The **speaker** is the character who speaks in or narrates a poem—the voice assumed by the writer. The speaker in this poem uses the pronoun *we*, not *I*. As you read the poem, decide for whom the speaker is speaking.

**RHYME SCHEME.** A **rhyme scheme** is a pattern of end rhymes, or rhymes at the ends of lines of verse. The rhyme scheme of a poem is designated by letters, with matching letters signifying matching sounds.

## Reader's Journal

When do you hide your feelings from others?

## ArtNote

*Les Fétiches,* 1938. Lois Mailou Jones, page 620.

Lois Mailou Jones (1905– ) taught art at Howard University from 1930 to 1977, influencing generations of artists. Like other African-American artists of the Harlem Renaissance era, she had to fight prejudice in the art world. Jones won many awards for her superior painting skills but often had to have white friends enter her paintings in their names.

The painting on page 620 which depicts a variety of tribal masks Jones had seen in museums, reveals the artist's early interest in African art. The painting marked the beginning of Jones's in-depth, lifelong study of African art. Could Jones's celebration of traditional African masks extend the mask metaphor of Paul Laurence Dunbar's poem, or are the themes of the painting and the poem opposed to each other?

*Les Fétiches,* 1938. Lois Mailou Jones. National Museum of American Art, Washington, DC.

# We Wear the Mask

### PAUL LAURENCE DUNBAR

We wear the mask that grins and lies,
It hides our cheeks and shades our eyes—
This debt we pay to human guile;[1]
With torn and bleeding hearts we smile,
5    And mouth with myriad[2] subtleties.

Why should the world be otherwise,
In counting all our tears and sighs?
Nay, let them only see us, while
      We wear the mask.

10    We smile, but, O great Christ, our cries
To thee from tortured souls arise.
We sing, but oh the clay is vile[3]
Beneath our feet, and long the mile;
But let the world dream otherwise,
15        We wear the mask! ∎

*What does the mask show? What does it hide?*

*What contradictions are apparent in stanza 3?*

---

1. **guile.** Secretiveness; sneakiness
2. **myriad.** Large number; of a varied nature
3. **vile.** Offensive

Imagine that you are the speaker in the poem. Describe the kinds of emotions you hide when wearing the mask.

# INVESTIGATE Inquire Imagine

**Recall:** GATHERING FACTS

1a. What "grins and lies"? What is paid "to human guile"?

2a. What does the speaker suggest is not counted by the world?

3a. From what kind of souls do the cries mentioned in the poem arise?

→ **Interpret:** FINDING MEANING

1b. Who is the "we" mentioned in the poem? Who is the "them"? Does the speaker express a positive or negative attitude toward human duplicity?

2b. Why does the speaker suggest "Nay, let them only see us, while / We wear the mask"?

3b. Whom is the speaker addressing in the third stanza?

**Analyze:** TAKING THINGS APART

4a. For what is the mask a metaphor in the poem?

→ **Synthesize:** BRINGING THINGS TOGETHER

4b. Why do people wear the mask?

**Evaluate:** MAKING JUDGMENTS

5a. Do you think the use of the mask is justified by the speaker?

→ **Extend:** CONNECTING IDEAS

5b. Identify a character in film, literature, or on TV who wears a mask. From whom is the character trying to keep his feelings hidden? How successful is he or she? What do you think would happen if the character revealed his or her true feelings?

# Understanding Literature

**SPEAKER.** Review the definition for **speaker** in the Handbook of Literary Terms. For whom is the speaker speaking? Explain. How might your interpretation of the poem change if you decided that the speaker were speaking for the entire human race? Who, then, would be the "we"? Who would be the "them"?

**RHYME SCHEME.** Review the definition for **rhyme scheme** in the Handbook of Literary Terms. Then determine the rhyme scheme of each stanza. The rhyme scheme of the first stanza is given as an example. Which rhyme is not exact? Which lines in each stanza do not rhyme with any other lines?

| | |
|---|---|
| We wear the mask that grins and lies, | *a* |
| It hides our cheeks and shades our eyes— | *a* |
| This debt we pay to human guile; | *b* |
| With torn and bleeding hearts we smile, | *b* |
| And mouth with myriad subtleties. | *c* |

# Writer's Journal

1. Imagine that you are the speaker. Write a **journal entry** describing what type of personality you aspire to display with your mask.

2. The poem says that the wearer of the mask has a tortured soul. Write a **paragraph** describing one scenario that results in suffering for the mask wearer.

3. The speaker says the wearer of the mask speaks with "myriad subtleties." Imagine that you wear the mask at work. Write a **letter** to your boss listing your common utterances and explaining what they really mean.

# Integrating *the* LANGUAGE ARTS

## Language, Grammar, and Style

**WORKING WITH NAMERS.** Read the Language Arts Survey 3.49, "Namers—Nouns and Pronouns." Then rewrite the following sentences, underlining the namers and identifying whether they function as subjects or objects. If a namer is an object, specify whether it is a direct object, indirect object, object of a preposition, or object of an infinitive. For more information, see the Language Arts Survey 3.6, "Identifying the Parts of Speech," and 3.22, "Sentence Completers for Action Verbs: Direct and Indirect Objects."

1. Paul Laurence Dunbar wrote novels, poems, and short stories.

2. *Lyrics of Lowly Life* made him famous.

3. Writing gave Dunbar a sense of personal satisfaction.

4. He liked to use African-American dialect to reflect realistic speech patterns.

5. His death at such a young age was tragic.

## Speaking and Listening

**ROLE-PLAY.** Have a dialogue with a partner. One student will take on the persona of a character wearing a mask. The other student should try to get the character to disclose his or her true feelings and to explain why he or she feels compelled to wear a mask.

## Media Literacy

**USING THE INTERNET.** Using the Internet, locate a poem by Dunbar that uses dialect. Then rewrite the poem in standard English. Discuss which version of the poem is more powerful and explain why. One site you will find useful is http://www.udayton.edu/~dunbar.

# "Yet Do I Marvel"

## Literary TOOLS

**SONNET.** A **sonnet** is a fourteen-line poem that follows one of a number of different rhyme schemes. The rhyme scheme of a *Shakespearean, English,* or *Elizabethan sonnet* is *abab cdcd efef gg.* Like the Shakespearean sonnet, "Yet Do I Marvel" can be divided into four parts: three **quatrains,** or four-line stanzas, and a final *couplet,* or two-line stanza. As you look at the poem, determine how the rhyme scheme varies slightly from that of a Shakespearean sonnet.

**ALLUSION.** An **allusion** is a figure of speech in which a reference is made to a person, event, object, or work from history or literature. As you read, make a chart. On the left, list the allusions from the selection. On the right, describe the allusions. One example has been done for you.

| Allusions | Descriptions |
|-----------|--------------|
| Tantalus  | Condemned to spend eternity in the underworld, eternally thirsty and hungry. |

## Reader's Journal

Have you ever marveled at a seemingly unexplainable event or occurrence? What was the event and how did you try to understand it?

# "Yet Do I Marvel"
# "Any Human to Another"

BY COUNTEE CULLEN

## About the AUTHOR

**Countee Cullen** (1903–1946) was born Countee Leroy Porter in New York City. In 1918, he was adopted by Reverend Frederick Cullen, a Methodist minister. He attended New York public schools, graduated Phi Beta Kappa with a B.A. from New York University in 1925, and took an M.A. at Harvard in 1926. He married twice. His first marriage to Yolande Du Bois, daughter of W. E. B. Du Bois, black educator and sociologist, lasted two years.

Like many African Americans of his time, Cullen shaped the expression of his talents in reaction to racism in the society in which he lived. Recalling an incident in 1930 when he was barred from eating in a restaurant at the New York Central terminal in Buffalo, New York, he later said, "There may have been many things in my life that have hurt me, and I find that the surest relief from these hurts is in writing. Most things I write, I do for the sheer love of the music in them. Somehow or other, however, I find my poetry of itself treating of the Negro, of his joys and his sorrows, mostly of the latter, and of the heights and the depths of emotion which I feel as a Negro."

From 1926 to 1928, Cullen was assistant editor of *Opportunity: Journal of Negro Life,* the magazine of the National Urban League, where he wrote "The Dark Tower," a column of reflections and literary criticism. He taught French at Frederick Douglass Junior High School in New York City from 1934 to 1945 and wrote and published children's stories. Cullen was proud of being African American, of his "ebony muse," but not surprisingly, he was bitter about the African-American experience in America. Best known for his poems about racial issues, he was nonetheless criticized by his contemporaries for the mildness of his attacks on racial injustice. Cullen was a middle-class New Yorker who wanted to be a traditional poet, and his ideas about poetry were counter to those of other writers of the Harlem Renaissance.

Among other awards and honors, Cullen received a Guggenheim Fellowship in 1929 to complete *The Black Christ and Other Poems*

(1929). His works include *Color* (poetry, 1925), *Caroling Dusk: An Anthology of Verse by Negro Poets* (1927), *Copper Sun* (1927), *The Ballad of the Brown Girl* (1928), *One Way to Heaven* (novel, 1932), and *On These I Stand* (1947).

In 1995, a monument honoring Countee Cullen was created by sculptor Meredith Bergmann for an exhibition at the Woodlawn Cemetery in New York where Cullen is buried. A bronze-colored Countee Cullen is portrayed reaching out to a bust of himself in the classic representation of a poet: a white marble-colored bust crowned with a laurel wreath. His other hand holds his book *Color*. The two portraits of the poet are made of brown and white cement, imitating the colors of the two most traditional sculpture media: bronze and marble. By making both pieces out of cement the artist is telling us that we are all made of the same stuff regardless of our "color." This sentiment echoes Cullen's words:

> "And when your body's death gives birth
>      To soil for spring to crown
> Men will not ask if that rare earth
>      Was white flesh once or brown"

## About the SELECTIONS

"**Yet Do I Marvel**" appeared in *On These I Stand* (1947), the collection considered to include Cullen's best poetry. The final lines of the selection are among the most famous of all produced by the poets of the Harlem Renaissance.

"**Any Human to Another**" appeared in *The Medea and Some Poems* (1935). A lyric poem, it addresses the sorrow that afflicts all humans and the need to share and alleviate one another's pain.

*Countee Cullen Monument,* 1995. Meredith Bergmann.
New York Public Library.

---

## "Any Human to Another"

### Literary TOOLS

**SIMILE.** A **simile** is a comparison using *like* or *as*. As you read "Any Human to Another," look for the similes.

**THEME.** A **theme** is a central idea in a literary work. As you read, make a cluster chart about what the speaker learns about sorrow.

> Sorrow pierces "not me alone"
>
> SORROW

### Reader's Journal

With whom do you share your pain when you are hurt by events in this world?

# Yet Do I Marvel

## COUNTEE CULLEN

**Rise, Shine for Thy Light Has Come,** c.1930.
Aaron Douglas. The Gallery of Art,
Howard University, Washington, DC.

I doubt not God is good, well-meaning,
    kind,
And did He stoop to quibble could tell why
The little buried mole continues blind,
Why flesh that mirrors Him must some day die,
5  Make plain the reason tortured Tantalus[1]
Is baited by the fickle fruit, declare
If merely brute <u>caprice</u> dooms Sisyphus[2]
To struggle up a never-ending stair.
Inscrutable[3] His ways are, and immune
10  To catechism[4] by a mind too strewn
With petty cares to slightly understand
What awful brain compels His awful hand.
Yet do I marvel at this curious thing:
To make a poet black, and bid him sing! ◼

*What kind of God does
the speaker envision?*

*What does the speaker
say about understanding
the motivations of God?*

---

1. **Tantalus.** King in Greek mythology who was doomed in Hades to
stand in water that receded from him when he was thirsty and under
branches of fruit that he could not reach when hungry
2. **Sisyphus.** King whose doom in Hades was to roll a heavy stone
uphill only to have it always roll down again
3. **Inscrutable.** That cannot be easily understood
4. **catechism.** Close questioning; religious debate or discussion

WORDS
FOR
EVERYDAY
USE
    **ca • price** (kə prēs´) *n.,* whim; change in way of thinking. *Due to the <u>caprices</u> of the weather, we brought along rain gear.*

In lines 3–8, the speaker offers examples of tragic circumstances in the world and in stories from world mythology. What examples might the speaker give of love, generosity, and kindness in the world?

# INVESTIGATE, Inquire, Imagine

**Recall:** GATHERING FACTS

1a. What tragic circumstances of the world in stories from mythology does the speaker mention in lines 3–8?

2a. What comparison does the speaker make between the mind of God and the mind of a human?

**Interpret:** FINDING MEANING

1b. What does the speaker not doubt, despite the existence of pain?

2b. How does the speaker respond to the old argument that a just God would not allow pain or injustice to continue?

**Analyze:** TAKING THINGS APART

3a. At what does the speaker marvel? What paradox does the speaker seem to see in "this curious thing"?

**Synthesize:** BRINGING THINGS TOGETHER

3b. Why is it curious that a black poet would be bid to sing?

**Evaluate:** MAKING JUDGMENTS

4a. Do you agree with the explanation the speaker offers that God has reasons for the existence of cruelty, pain, death, and injustice in the world? Why, or why not?

**Extend:** CONNECTING IDEAS

4b. What current events or personal incidents can you think of that mirror the injustices in lines 3–8 that the speaker talks about?

# Understanding Literature

SONNET. Review the definition for **sonnet** in the Handbook of Literary Terms. How does the rhyme scheme of the selection differ from that of a Shakespearean sonnet?

ALLUSION. Review the definition for **allusion** in the Handbook of Literary Terms. Then refer to the chart that you made in Literary Tools on page 624. What purpose is served by the allusions to these two myths? Of what kinds of experiences are the myths examples?

*Can Fire in the Park,* 1946. Beauford Delaney. National Museum of American Art, Washington, DC.

# ANY Human to Another

COUNTEE CULLEN

The ills I sorrow at
Not me alone
Like an arrow,
Pierce to the marrow,
5  Through the fat
And past the bone.

Your grief and mine
Must intertwine
Like sea and river,
10  Be fused and mingle,
Diverse yet single,
Forever and forever.

According to the speaker, what must be joined?

Let no man be so proud
And confident,
15  To think he is allowed
A little tent
Pitched in a meadow
Of sun and shadow
All his little own.

20  Joy may be shy, unique,
Friendly to a few,
Sorrow never scorned to speak
To any who
Were false or true.

Whom does sorrow touch?

25  Your every grief
Like a blade
Shining and unsheathed
Must strike me down.
Of bitter aloes[1] wreathed,
30  My sorrow must be laid
On your head like a crown. ■

Where must the speaker lay his sorrow?

---

1. **aloes.** Succulent plants known for their medicinal quality

**WORDS FOR EVERYDAY USE**

**scorn** (skôrn) *vt.,* reject or dismiss as contemptible or unworthy. *The year he turned thirteen, Jeff scorned to dress up for Halloween, saying it was "kid stuff."*

What types of pain do you think the speaker is talking about?

# INVESTIGATE Inquire, Imagine

**Recall:** GATHERING FACTS

1a. In stanza 1, what does the speaker observe about sorrow?

2a. What happens to individual suffering, according to stanza 2?

3a. According to the final stanza, what expectation does the speaker have of others' pain?

→ **Interpret:** FINDING MEANING

1b. To what does the speaker compare his sorrow?

2b. When "Your grief and mine" are intertwined, does a person's individual experience diminish?

3b. How should a person transfer his or her sorrow?

**Analyze:** TAKING THINGS APART

4a. Identify that which all people share, according to the speaker.

→ **Synthesize:** BRINGING THINGS TOGETHER

4b. Why is joy selective, addressing only "a few"?

**Evaluate:** MAKING JUDGMENTS

5a. Do the speaker's views offer a healthy psychological perspective?

→ **Extend:** CONNECTING IDEAS

5b. The English poet John Donne said that "No man is an island, entire of itself." What stanza in "Any Human to Another" does this sentiment echo?

# Understanding Literature

SIMILE. Review the definition for **simile** in the Handbook of Literary Terms. To what are "The ills I sorrow at" compared in stanza 1? To what is "Your every grief" compared in the final stanza? What characteristics do the subject and object of both comparisons have in common?

THEME. Review the definition for **theme** in the Handbook of Literary Terms. Then refer to the cluster chart you made in Literary Tools on page 625. What do you think is the theme of "Any Human to Another"?

# WRITER'S JOURNAL

1. Write a **journal entry** describing your "petty cares" today.

2. Imagine you are Countee Cullen. Write a **letter** to your readers explaining why you entitled your poem "Any Human to Another."

3. Write **blues lyrics** that are based on an aspect of the African-American experience.

# Integrating
## *the* LANGUAGE ARTS

## Language, Grammar, and Style

**USING CONTEXT CLUES.** Read the Language Arts Survey 1.16, "Using Context Clues to Estimate Word Meaning." Then use context clues to identify the meaning of "awful" in line 12 of "Yet Do I Marvel" and "unsheathed" in line 27 of "Any Human to Another."

## Speaking and Listening & Media Literacy

**ORAL INTERPRETATION.** Using the Internet, find poems by contemporaries of Countee Cullen who participated in the Harlem Renaissance but who are not represented in this textbook. One site you will find useful is The University of South Carolina's Harlem Renaissance page at http://www.unc.edu/courses/eng81br1/harlem.html. Divide into small groups and select a poem for everyone in your group.

You may want to review the Language Arts Survey 4.19, "Oral Interpretation of Poetry." Then sit in a circle and take turns reading the poems aloud. As you listen to the speaker before you, take notes on his or her poem. Then write a transition to present a logical segue to your selection. The first presenter can write a general introduction to all the selections by focusing on common themes in Harlem Renaissance poetry. Finally, videotape your presentations, including transitional statements and the introduction, and play the videotape for the class.

## Literary TOOLS

**TONE. Tone** is the emotional attitude toward the reader or toward the subject implied by a literary work. As you read, pay attention to how the tone changes in each stanza.

**METER AND RHYME.** The **meter** of a poem is its rhythmical pattern. A poem is made up of rhythmical units, called *feet*. Types of feet include *iambic, trochaic, anapestic, dactylic,* and *spondaic.* (For definitions of these terms, see the entry on *meter* in the Handbook of Literary Terms.) **Rhyme** is the repetition of sounds at the ends of words. One type of rhyme, **end rhyme**, is the use of rhyming words at the ends of lines. A **sight rhyme**, or **eye rhyme**, is a pair of words, generally at the ends of lines of verse, that are spelled similarly but pronounced differently. As you look at "The Tropics in New York," try to figure out its meter and rhyme scheme.

## Reader's Journal

Describe a time you felt homesick. What did you miss most about home?

# "THE TROPICS IN NEW YORK"

BY CLAUDE MCKAY

## About *the* AUTHOR

**Claude McKay** (1890–1948), who also wrote under the pseudonym Eli Edwards, was born in Jamaica, in the West Indies, to poor farm workers. He was educated by his brother and by an Englishman who was a specialist in Jamaican folklore. His first two collections of poems, written in native dialect, were published in England in 1912. These collections earned him prize money that helped him to emigrate to the United States that year. He studied at Booker T. Washington's Tuskegee Institute and at Kansas State College. After moving to Harlem in 1914, he worked at odd jobs, and pursued his writing.

McKay was a prominent figure in the Harlem Renaissance who was radicalized by the racial prejudice he witnessed and experienced. He left America to live in Europe but returned after the publication of his award-winning novel *Home to Harlem* (1928), one of the first bestsellers by an African-American writer. By the 1940s, he had repudiated his earlier radicalism and become a naturalized citizen. McKay's "If We Must Die," written as a response to the Harlem race riots of 1919, is considered a major impetus behind the Civil Rights movement that began after World War II and the poem was entered into the United States Congressional Record.

In 1942, McKay joined the Catholic Church and for the last five years of his life lived in Chicago doing research for the National Catholic Youth Organization. His works include *Songs of Jamaica* (poetry, 1912), *Harlem Shadows* (poetry, 1922), *Banjo* (1929), *Banana Bottom* (1933), *Gingertown* (short stories, 1932), *A Long Way from Home* (autobiography, 1937), and *Harlem: Negro Metropolis* (sociological study, 1940).

## About *the* SELECTION

Perhaps reflective of McKay's own experience of emigrating to the United States from Jamaica, the speaker in **"The Tropics in New York"** is reminded of his former life in the tropics and longs for its old and familiar ways.

Harlem, 1927.

# THE *Tropics* IN NEW YORK

CLAUDE MCKAY

Bananas ripe and green, and ginger-root,
    Cocoa in pods and alligator pears,
And tangerines and mangoes and grapefruit,
    Fit for the highest prize at parish fairs,

5    Set in the window, bringing memories
        Of fruit-trees laden by low-singing rills,[1]
And dewy dawns, and mystical blue skies
        In benediction[2] over nun-like hills.

My eyes grew dim, and I could no more gaze;
10    A wave of longing through my body swept,
And, hungry for the old, familiar ways,
        I turned aside and bowed my head and wept. ∎

*What does the speaker see in the window? What memories do these things bring?*

*For what does the speaker grow hungry? Why does the fruit have such an effect on him?*

1. **rills.** Small brooks
2. **benediction.** Blessing

In the poem sight triggers memories. What sights, sounds, or smells remind you of another place or time?

# INVESTIGATE, Inquire, *Imagine*

**Recall:** GATHERING FACTS

1a. What fruits are "fit for the highest prize at parish fairs"?

2a. What sweeps through the speaker's body?

➤ **Interpret:** FINDING MEANING

1b. What images recall the past for the speaker?

2b. How does the speaker feel toward "the old, familiar ways"?

**Analyze:** TAKING THINGS APART

3a. Identify two types of hunger.

➤ **Synthesize:** BRINGING THINGS TOGETHER

3b. Which type of hunger is the speaker of this poem experiencing? How do you know?

**Perspective:** LOOKING AT OTHER VIEWS

4a. What effect, or emotional impact, do the images in the poem create for the speaker?

➤ **Empathy:** SEEING FROM INSIDE

4b. If you were the speaker, what would you do to reconnect with your tropical homeland and make your homesickness diminish?

# Understanding *Literature*

**TONE.** Review the definition for **tone** in the Handbook of Literary Terms. What is the tone in each stanza? Is the tone in stanza 1 similar to the tone in stanza 3? Explain.

**METER AND RHYME.** Review the definitions for **meter** and **rhyme** in the Handbook of Literary Terms. Then fill in the chart below to indicate the poem's rhyme scheme. The rhyme scheme of the first stanza has been provided. What rhyme scheme does the poem repeat in each stanza? What example of *sight rhyme* did you find? What is the poem's meter?

| Stanza | Rhyme Scheme |
|--------|--------------|
| 1 | *abab* |
| 2 | |
| 3 | |

# Writer's Journal

1. Imagine that you are a tourist in Jamaica. Write a **postcard** describing the landscape in front of you.
2. The speaker expresses his hunger for the "old, familiar ways." Write a **paragraph** contrasting the speaker's life in New York with the life he left behind in Jamaica. You may rely on your imagination to fill in details.
3. Write a **lyric poem** in which the speaker is an American living abroad who feels nostalgic for the United States. What sight might trigger his or her memories of home? Use Claude McKay's poem as a model. You may or may not want your poem to rhyme.

# Integrating the LANGUAGE ARTS

## Language, Grammar, and Style

USING THE ACTIVE VOICE. Rewrite the following sentences using the active voice. Read the Language Arts Survey 3.37, "Making Passive Sentences Active," before you begin.

1. The fruits at the fruit stand were admired by the speaker.
2. Prizes were awarded by the judges at the parish fair.
3. The tree was filled with bananas.
4. The speaker was flooded with memories of Jamaica.
5. The speaker was overcome with longing for the "old, familiar ways."

## Language, Grammar, and Style

USING COLORFUL MODIFIERS. Read the Language Arts Survey 3.39, "Adding Colorful Language to Sentences." Then identify some modifiers in the poem and note what mood the adjectives lend to each noun and to the overall selection.

## Collaborative Learning

MEMORY AND THE SENSES. In "The Tropics in New York," sight triggers a memory in the speaker. What other senses can trigger memories? With a partner, make a chart of the five senses and list things that trigger memory for each sense. Then select one of the senses and write a paragraph describing the process of triggering memory.

# Literary
## TOOLS

**PERSONIFICATION. Personification** is a figure of speech in which an idea, animal, or thing is described as if it were a person. Look for examples of personification as you read "Storm Ending."

**METAPHOR AND SIMILE.** A **metaphor** is a figure of speech in which one thing is spoken or written about as if it were another. A **simile** is a comparison using *like* or *as*. These figures of speech invite the reader to make a comparison between the two things. The two "things" involved are the writer's actual subject, the *tenor* of the metaphor, and another thing to which the subject is likened, the *vehicle* of the metaphor. As you read, make a chart of the metaphors and similes in the poem. On the left, write the tenor and on the right, write the vehicle. One example has been done for you.

| Tenor | Vehicle |
| --- | --- |
| 1. thunder | flower |
| 2. | |
| 3. | |

# Reader's
## Journal

What do you see, hear, touch, taste, and smell during a storm?

# "Storm Ending"

BY JEAN TOOMER

## About *the* AUTHOR

**Jean Toomer** (1896–1967), writer, poet, and playwright, was born in Washington, DC, the son of a Georgian farmer. Though he passed for white during certain periods of his life, he was raised in a predominantly African-American community and attended African-American high schools. Of his college education, which ended in 1917, Toomer said, "Neither the universities of Wisconsin or New York gave me what I wanted, so I quit them." He turned to writing poetry and prose, which he published in such periodicals as *Broom, The Liberator,* and *The Little Review.* A stint in Georgia as a teacher inspired *Cane* (1923), a book of prose poetry in which an African American struggles to discover his selfhood in various African-American communities. Toomer was praised for uniting "folk culture and the elite culture of the white avant-garde." With the publication of *Cane,* Toomer was considered a promising black writer.

After *Cane,* Toomer continued writing prodigiously, but most of his work was rejected by publishers. He turned to the spiritual teachings of Gurdjieff and taught his principles first in Harlem, then in Chicago. Toomer became a Quaker and lived the last ten years of his life as a recluse. His writing centers around his longing for racial unity, as illustrated by his long poem "Blue Meridian." In 1931 he published *Essentials,* a book of aphorisms and apothegms. Many of Toomer's short stories and poems are included in anthologies.

## About *the* SELECTION

In **"Storm Ending"** Toomer describes a storm using such figures of speech as metaphor, simile, and personification. Typical of his verse, "Storm Ending" does not employ new African-American poetic forms, but rather follows established poetic traditions.

*Mountain Blossoms, Volda,* c.1936–1937. William H. Johnson.
National Museum of American Art, Washington, DC.

# Storm Ending

## JEAN TOOMER

Thunder blossoms gorgeously above our heads,
Great, hollow, bell-like flowers,
Rumbling in the wind,
Stretching clappers[1] to strike our ears . . .
5    Full-lipped flowers
Bitten by the sun
Bleeding rain
Dripping rain like golden honey—
And the sweet earth flying from the thunder. ■

*What is "great" and "hollow"?*

*What flies from the thunder?*

---

1. **clappers.** Metal pieces suspended inside bells that strike the sides when
the bell is swung

Imagine you are the speaker. How do you feel about the storm?

# INVESTIGATE *Inquire, Imagine*

**Recall:** GATHERING FACTS

1a. What "blossoms gorgeously above our heads"?

2a. What do the clouds look like?

➤ **Interpret:** FINDING MEANING

1b. What does the speaker think of the thunder clouds?

2b. Why does the rain "bleed"?

**Analyze:** TAKING THINGS APART

3a. Identify the senses that the speaker refers to in the poem.

➤ **Synthesize:** BRINGING THINGS TOGETHER

3b. Why does the speaker pay more attention to how the storm looks than to how it sounds?

**Perspective:** LOOKING AT OTHER VIEWS

4a. Which aspect of the storm has the most impact on the speaker?

➤ **Empathy:** SEEING FROM INSIDE

4b. If you were the speaker, would you seek shelter from the storm or stand out in it?

# Understanding *Literature*

**PERSONIFICATION.** Review the definition for **personification** in the Handbook of Literary Terms. How is personification used in the poem? How are these examples of personification connected?

**METAPHOR AND SIMILE.** Review the definitions for **metaphor** and **simile** in the Handbook of Literary Terms and the chart you completed for Literary Tools on page 636. Which figure of speech is amplified in the poem?

# WRITER'S JOURNAL

1. Write a **paragraph** describing in your own words what the storm looks like.
2. Write a **dialogue** in which two people discuss the weather on the day of the storm.
3. Images in the poem evoke the senses of sight and sound. Write **two new lines to the poem** that add another sense—touch, taste, or smell.

# Integrating *the* LANGUAGE ARTS

## Language, Grammar, and Style

**SEMICOLONS AND DASHES.** Read the Language Arts Survey 3.88, "Semicolons," and 3.93, "Hyphens and Dashes." Then rewrite the following sentences, adding semicolons and dashes. (Note: recall that semicolons can be used to combine two sentences into one.)

1. Jean Toomer was a delivery boy, soda clerk, salesman, shipyard worker, and librarian assistant however, he did not let his jobs interfere with his writing.
2. The Gurdjieff doctrine taught unity through group interactions transcendence through meditation and mastery of self through yoga.
3. Toomer eventually left Harlem to live above the boundaries of race.
4. While he was searching for answers, Toomer expressed the cry of one caught in the modern human condition. His work was a reminder of modern man's isolation.
5. Later he insisted on dogmatically pointing the way his way.

## Media Literacy

**WEATHER REPORT.** Review weather reports on the Internet to analyze how they are written. You might want to copy an example or two to use as a model. Then videotape a weather report for the day of the storm described in the poem. When you make your videotape, be sure to dress professionally and to use a map of your region that you can point to during your presentation.

## Study and Research

**RESEARCHING ARTISTS OF THE HARLEM RENAISSANCE.** Select an artist from the Harlem Renaissance and research his or her contributions to the movement. You might choose a writer, a painter, a singer, or a musician. Then write a composition outlining what you have learned. Before you begin writing, you may want to read the Language Arts Survey 2.24–2.30, "Organizing Ideas."

## Art Note

*Mountain Blossoms, Volda,* c.1936–1937. William H. Johnson, page 637.

William H. Johnson (1901–1970) began his career in the early days of the Harlem Renaissance, but spent most of that period in Europe. There, he painted Expressionist landscapes influenced by Vincent van Gogh and Edvard Munch, such as this one made in Norway. When he returned to New York in 1938, Johnson began painting in a completely new style that he identified as "primitive." This style was inspired by the rural life Johnson experienced while living in Denmark and North Africa and especially while growing up in South Carolina.

There are many differences between *Mountain Blossoms, Volda* (page 637), and Johnson's later painting *Sowing,* done in 1940 (page 649). One difference is the way Johnson applied the paint with his brush. A thick buildup of paint that leaves visible brushmarks is called *impasto.* Looking carefully at the way the paint was applied, can you identify which of the two paintings exhibits *impasto*? How do Johnson's different choices affect the way you feel about each painting?

## "The Negro Speaks of Rivers"

### Literary T O O L S

**REFRAIN AND EFFECT.** A **refrain** is a line or group of lines repeated in a poem or song. The **effect** of a literary work is the general impression or emotional impact that it achieves. As you read, locate the refrains used in "The Negro Speaks of Rivers" and decide the effect of the refrains.

**SIMILE.** A **simile** is a comparison using *like* or *as*. This figure of speech invites the reader to make a comparison between two things. The two "things" involved are the writer's actual subject, the *tenor* of the simile, and another thing to which the subject is likened, the *vehicle* of the simile. As you read, look for the similes in the poem.

### Reader's *Journal*

What experiences have you had with rivers?

## "The Negro Speaks of Rivers"

## "I, too, sing America"

BY LANGSTON HUGHES

## About *the* A U T H O R

**Langston Hughes** (1902–1967) was born in Joplin, Missouri, and lived for most of his childhood in Lawrence, Kansas, with his maternal grandmother, whose first husband had been one of the African Americans killed in John Brown's raid on the arsenal at Harpers Ferry. Hughes was thirteen when she died, at which time he went to live with his mother. He graduated from high school in Cleveland, Ohio, and then spent more than a year with his father in Mexico. It was there that he wrote the poem "The Negro Speaks of Rivers," which would later gain him recognition as a writer.

Hughes studied for a year at Columbia University, leaving in 1920. For the next several years, he traveled, taking whatever jobs he found. During this peripatetic period, he continued to write. His work began to be published in important African-American periodicals like *Opportunity* and *The Crisis.* He accepted a scholarship from Lincoln University in Pennsylvania and graduated in 1929. While there, he wrote his first novel, *Not without Laughter* (1930). Political activism in the 1930s resulted in his later being called to testify before the House Un-American Activities Committee in 1953 and listed as a security risk by the FBI until 1959.

Hughes was a prolific, versatile writer and is especially well known for his famous fictional character Jesse B. Semple, or "Simple." Awards and honors recognizing his work include Rosenwald and Guggenheim fellowships and a grant from the American Academy of Arts and Letters. His works include *The Weary Blues* (1926), *The Negro Artist and the Racial Mountain* (essay, 1926), *The Ways of White Folks* (stories, 1934), *Shakespeare in Harlem* (1942), *Simple Speaks His Mind* (1950), *First Book of Negroes* (anthology, 1952), *First Book of Jazz* (anthology, 1955), *Simple Stakes a Claim* (1957), *First Book of Negro Folklore* (anthology, 1958).

## About The SELECTIONS

Before graduating from Lincoln University in Pennsylvania, Hughes had published his first collection of verse, *The Weary Blues*. Included in that 1926 collection was **"The Negro Speaks of Rivers"** and **"I, too, sing America."** During the 1920s, while writing these poems, Hughes worked to unite the elements of blues with formal poetry.

Langston Hughes worked as a busboy even as he was gaining national attention as a writer, 1925.

## Literary TOOLS

**TONE. Tone** is the emotional attitude toward the reader or toward the subject implied by a literary work. As you read, identify the tone of the poem.

**POINT OF VIEW. Point of view** is the vantage point from which a story is told. Stories and poems are typically written from a *first-person point of view*, in which the narrator uses words such as *I* and *we*; from a *second-person point of view* in which the narrator uses *you*; or from a *third-person point of view*, in which the narrator uses words such as *he, she, it,* and *they*. As you read, make a cluster chart of the words that indicate the point of view of the poem. One example has been done for you.

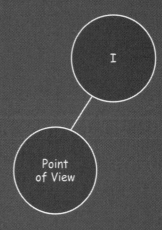

## Reader's Journal

When have you been left out of a group? How did you react?

***Blue Lagoon.*** John Wesley Hardrick. Indiana State Museum.

# The Negro Speaks of Rivers

LANGSTON HUGHES

I've known rivers:
I've known rivers ancient as the world and older than the
    flow of human blood in human veins.

My soul has grown deep like the rivers.

5    I bathed in the Euphrates when dawns were young.
I built my hut near the Congo and it lulled me to sleep.
I looked upon the Nile[1] and raised the pyramids above it.
I heard the singing of the Mississippi when Abe Lincoln
    went down to New Orleans, and I've seen its muddy
10    bosom turn all golden in the sunset.

I've known rivers:
Ancient, dusky rivers.

My soul has grown deep like the rivers. ∎

*What is significant about the rivers?*

*To what aspect of the rivers does the speaker compare his soul?*

---

1. **Euphrates . . . Nile.** *Euphrates*—river that flows through Turkey, Syria, and Iraq; *Congo*—river in central Africa; *Nile*—river in northeastern Africa

How does the speaker of this poem feel about his or her heritage? Do you have a similar attitude toward your own heritage? Why, or why not?

# INVESTIGATE Inquire Imagine

**Recall:** GATHERING FACTS

1a. What has the speaker known?

2a. What specific rivers does the speaker mention in the poem?

3a. What has happened to the speaker's soul?

**Interpret:** FINDING MEANING

1b. Who is the speaker in this poem?

2b. What accomplishments and experiences are associated with each of the rivers in the poem?

3b. What has caused the speaker's soul to deepen?

**Analyze:** TAKING THINGS APART

4a. Identify two sentences in the selection that build on the simple sentence "I've known rivers."

**Synthesize:** BRINGING THINGS TOGETHER

4b. What is the speaker saying about the age and experience of Africans and people of African descent?

**Evaluate:** MAKING JUDGMENTS

5a. Decide whether the use of "rivers" is an effective vehicle for the theme of the poem.

**Extend:** CONNECTING IDEAS

'5b. Compare and contrast the black experience in "We Wear the Mask" and "The Negro Speaks of Rivers."

# Understanding Literature

**REFRAIN AND EFFECT.** Review the definitions for **refrain** and **effect** in the Handbook of Literary Terms. What refrains are used in the poem? What is the effect of the refrains?

**SIMILE.** Review the definition for **simile** in the Literary Tools on page 640. Then fill in the chart below with two similes from the selection. Indicate the *tenor* and the *vehicle*. One example has been done for you. How is the soul like a river? What qualities do the two parts share?

| Simile | Tenor | Vehicle |
|---|---|---|
| 1. My soul has grown deep like the rivers.<br>2. | soul | rivers |

# I, too, sing America

**Langston Hughes**, 1925. Winold Reiss.
National Portrait Gallery, Washington, DC.

## LANGSTON HUGHES

I, too, sing America.

I am the darker brother.
They send me to eat in the kitchen
When company comes,
But I laugh,
And eat well,
And grow strong.

*Where does the speaker eat when company comes?*

Tomorrow,
I'll be at the table
When company comes.
Nobody'll dare
Say to me,
"Eat in the kitchen,"
Then.

*Where will the speaker eat tomorrow when company comes?*

Besides,
They'll see how beautiful I am
And be ashamed—

I, too, am America.  ■

## Respond *to the* SELECTION

Imagine the speaker of the poem is alive today. What social progress would he note since the poem was written during the 1920s?

# INVESTIGATE Inquire Imagine

**Recall:** GATHERING FACTS

1a. What does the speaker sing?

2a. Who sends the speaker to eat in the kitchen when company comes?

3a. What will change tomorrow?

→ **Interpret:** FINDING MEANING

1b. What does it mean to "sing America"?

2b. Who are "they"?

3b. What does eating at the table symbolize?

**Analyze:** TAKING THINGS APART

4a. Identify the details in the poem that suggest a view of America as one family.

→ **Synthesize:** BRINGING THINGS TOGETHER

4b. Why does the speaker identify himself with America?

**Perspective:** LOOKING AT OTHER VIEWS

5a. In what ways, if any, is the speaker's lack of anger understandable?

→ **Empathy:** SEEING FROM INSIDE

5b. Imagine you are the speaker and things have changed. Do you still harbor feelings of resentment against "them" for their years of discrimination against you?

# Understanding Literature

TONE. Review the definition for **tone** in the Handbook of Literary Terms. What is the tone of the poem?

POINT OF VIEW. Review the definition for **point of view** in the Handbook of Literary Terms and the graphic organizer you made for Literary Tools on page 641. What is the point of view of the poem? Is the speaker describing his own experience, or does he speak for others?

# WRITER'S JOURNAL

1. Eating in the kitchen symbolizes segregation and discrimination in "I, too, sing America." Write a **free verse poem** that uses another symbol to express segregation and discrimination.

2. Write **two lines of the poem** "The Negro Speaks of Rivers," adding two rivers and events to the middle stanza to deepen the expression of the African-American experience. For example, what river did many slaves cross to gain freedom in the North?

3. In "The Negro Speaks of Rivers," the speaker says "My soul has grown deep like the rivers." Write a **character sketch** of a person with such a soul. How does this person hold himself or herself? How does this person treat others? What struggles is this person engaged in? What dreams does this person have for his or her race? What sacrifices are made by this person to achieve his or her goals?

# Integrating *the* LANGUAGE ARTS

## Language, Grammar, and Style

**ACHIEVING PARALLELISM.** Read the Language Arts Survey 3.38, "Achieving Parallelism." Then revise the sentences below by correcting the faulty parallel structure.

1. Langston Hughes attended high school in Cleveland and to publish fiction and poetry in his high school magazine.

2. For more than twenty years, Hughes wrote for the *Chicago Defender*, in which he introduced the character "Simple" and to make him the heart of his column.

3. Hughes said "I've known rivers" and his soul has grown deep like the rivers.

4. In 1932, the year Hughes lived and was working in the former Soviet Union, he wrote his most radical poetry.

5. Hughes published dozens of books of fiction, nonfiction, and poetry and was translating books by Lorca, Mistral, Guillen, and Roumain.

## Study and Research

**USING REFERENCE WORKS.** Read the Language Arts Survey 5.20, "Using Reference Works." Then, for each subject in the following list, identify the type of reference work in which you can find out what you need to know.

1. location of the Congo River

2. history of the Nile River

3. news story about the most recent Mississippi River flood

4. quotations about rivers

5. name of the river with which the Euphrates unites

## Collaborative Learning

**WRITING A BLUES POEM.** The blues is a central feature of Langston Hughes's poetry. He published "The Negro Speaks of Rivers" and "I, too, sing America" in a poetry collection called *The Weary Blues*. Here is a poem by Hughes that takes its inspiration from blues music:

"Homesick Blues"
De railroad bridge's
A sad song in de air.
De railroad bridge's
A sad song in de air.
Ever time de trains pass
I wants to go somewhere. . . .

With a partner, write your own blues poem. Then read it to the class. You might want to set your poem to blues music.

## Collaborative Learning & Study and Research

**RESEARCHING AFRICAN CIVILIZATIONS.** With two or three classmates, research an ancient African civilization, such as the Songhai Empire in Niger. First, take notes as you do your research. Second, choose roles for your group members, deciding who will be the secretary, the writer, the editor, and the presenter. Third, the secretary takes notes for an outline, receiving ideas from the other group members. Then the writer uses the outline to write the paper, giving it to the editor to mark revisions. Finally, the presenter uses the outline to give a presentation to the class, and the writer submits the revised paper to the teacher.

# Literary
## TOOLS

**SPEAKER.** The **speaker** is the character who speaks in a poem—the voice assumed by the writer. As you read, decide who is the speaker of "A Black Man Talks of Reaping."

**RHYME.** **Rhyme** is the repetition of sounds at the ends of words. One type of rhyme, *end rhyme*, is the use of rhyming words at the ends of lines. As you read, try to figure out the rhyme scheme of each stanza.

## About *the*
# SELECTION

In his novels and poetry, Bontemps portrayed the lives and struggles of African Americans, a theme that can be seen in his poem **"A Black Man Talks of Reaping."** In this poem he uses the metaphor of farming to express the bitterness felt by blacks in a racist America. The message of the poem is that black Americans have labored long and hard only to look on while white Americans reap, or harvest, the benefits.

## Reader's
### *Journal*

Have you ever worked hard at something only to see someone else reap the benefits of your efforts? How did you respond to the experience?

# "A Black Man Talks of Reaping"

BY ARNA BONTEMPS

## About *the*
# AUTHOR

**Arna (Wendell) Bontemps** (1902–1973) was born in Alexandria, Louisiana. His father was a brick mason and his mother a teacher. Arna was the nickname given him by his grandmother. He had a comfortable childhood, although his family relocated from Louisiana to Los Angeles after some racial harassment of his father. In 1923, Bontemps graduated from Pacific Union College. He married Alberta Johnson in 1926, and they had six children. A teacher, librarian, anthologist, poet, novelist, playwright, biographer, and author of children's fiction, Bontemps dealt in his work almost exclusively with black life and culture. Active in writers' organizations and in the American Library Association, he also served as a member of the Metropolitan Nashville Board of Education. In 1943, he earned an M.A. from the University of Chicago. He worked as a high school teacher and principal, as well as a freelance writer, before serving as Librarian of Fisk University from 1943 to 1965. He also taught at the University of Chicago and Yale University.

Much of Bontemps's writing, in all genres, reflects his attempts to reconcile his respect for the richness of African-American folk culture with his repudiation of negative ethnic stereotypes. His works for adults include *God Sends Sunday* (1931); *Popo and Fifina: Children of Haiti* (1932), written with Langston Hughes; *Black Thunder* (1935); *Drums at Dusk* (1939); *St. Louis Woman* (1946), a dramatization written with Countee Cullen; *Story of the Negro* (1948); and *One Hundred Years of Negro Freedom* (1961). His works for children include *Sam Patch* (1951), written with Jack Conroy; and *Famous Negro Athletes* (1964). Among the many awards and honors he received in recognition of his writing were *The Crisis* magazine's poetry prize (1926), the Alexander Pushkin Poetry Prize (1926 and 1927), the short story prize of the journal *Opportunity* (1932), Julius Rosenwald fellowships (1938–1939, 1942–1943), a Newbery Honor (for outstanding children's book, 1949), a Guggenheim Fellowship for creative writing (1949–1950), and a Jane Addams Children's Book Award (1956).

*Sowing,* c.1940. William H. Johnson. National Museum of American Art, Washington, DC.

# A Black Man
## Talks of Reaping[1]
### ARNA BONTEMPS

I have sown[2] beside all waters in my day.
I planted deep, within my heart the fear
that wind or fowl would take the grain away.
I planted safe against this stark, lean year.

*How has the speaker done this year?*

5    I scattered seed enough to plant the land
in rows from Canada to Mexico
but for my reaping only what the hand
can hold at once is all that I can show.

*How does the speaker estimate his labors?*

Yet what I sowed and what the orchard yields
10   my brother's sons are gathering stalk and root:
small wonder then my children glean[3] in fields
they have not sown, and feed on bitter fruit. ∎

---

1. **Reaping.** Harvesting
2. **sown.** Planted
3. **glean.** Pick up bits of grain or produce left behind after a harvest

Imagine that you are the speaker in the poem, who has seen his children "glean in fields / they have not sown, and feed on bitter fruit." What emotions would arise in you as you watched your children eat what others had left behind in the fields?

# INVESTIGATE, Inquire, *Imagine*

**Recall: GATHERING FACTS**

1a. What does the planter fear?

2a. How much seed has the speaker sown?

3a. Who is gathering what the speaker sowed and "what the orchard yields"?

➤ **Interpret: FINDING MEANING**

1b. What does the speaker mean when he says "I planted safe against this stark, lean year"?

2b. What does the speaker have to show for all his hard work?

3b. Why do the speaker's children "feed on bitter fruit"?

**Analyze: TAKING THINGS APART**

4a. Identify what you think the theme of the poem is.

➤ **Synthesize: BRINGING THINGS TOGETHER**

4b. Summarize in your own words what the speaker wants.

**Evaluate: MAKING JUDGMENTS**

5a. Do you agree that the speaker deserves to be better compensated for his work? Why, or why not?

➤ **Extend: CONNECTING IDEAS**

5b. How does the tone of "A Black Man Talks of Reaping" compare to the tone of "The Negro Speaks of Rivers"? How do Bontemps and Hughes differ in their views of the African-American experience?

# Understanding *Literature*

**SPEAKER.** Review the definition for **speaker** in the Handbook of Literary Terms. Who is the speaker of the poem? What is the speaker's experience with reaping? How might his view of reaping be different from that of a white man?

**RHYME.** Review the definition for **rhyme** in the Handbook of Literary Terms. Then fill in a chart like the one on the next page, noting the rhyme scheme for each stanza of the poem. The first stanza has been done for you. What is the rhyme scheme for each stanza of the poem?

| Stanza | Rhyme Scheme |
|---|---|
| Stanza 1:<br>I have sown beside all waters in my day.<br>I planted deep, within my heart the fear<br>that wind or fowl would take the grain away.<br>I planted safe against this stark, lean year. | *a*<br>*b*<br>*a*<br>*b* |

# Writer's Journal

1. Imagine that you are the speaker. Write a **journal entry** expressing what your children have and what you want them to have.

2. Imagine you are one of the speaker's children. Write a **letter** to your father expressing the life lessons you have learned from watching him work.

3. The speaker uses farming as an allegory for the labor market. Write a **paragraph** explaining how African Americans have fared differently from whites in the American economy.

# Integrating *the* LANGUAGE ARTS

## Language, Grammar, and Style

**CAPITALIZATION.** Read about capitalization in the Language Arts Survey 3.94–3.99, "Editing for Capitalization Errors." Then rewrite the following sentences, inserting correct capitalization.

1. An important literary movement of the twentieth century took place in upper manhattan.

2. There was an explosion of african-american artists, writers, and performers.

3. The harlem renaissance had as much to do with building community as with promoting the arts.

4. Although Arna Bontemps was born in the south, his writing identified him with this movement.

5. He won the jane addams children's book award in 1956.

## Study and Research

**RESEARCHING TENANT FARMING.** Research the history of tenant farming in the South. Then write a composition comparing the experiences of African-American tenant farmers to the experiences of the speaker in "A Black Man Talks of Reaping." You may want to read the Language Arts Survey 2.24–2.30, "Organizing Ideas" before you begin.

## Speaking and Listening

**DIALOGUE.** With a partner, play the roles of the speaker in the poem and one of his children. If you play the role of the child, ask your father how he has lived his life, what his goals are, and what's happening to him right now. If you play the role of the speaker, answer your child's questions with responses based on the poem and express what your hopes are for him or her.

# "The Richer, the Poorer"

BY DOROTHY WEST

## Literary
### T O O L S

**THEME.** A **theme** is a central idea in a literary work. As you read "The Richer, the Poorer," think about what you consider to be the story's theme.

**MOTIVATION.** A **motivation** is a force that moves a character to think, feel, or behave in a certain way. As you read, decide what motivates Lottie to be frugal.

## Reader's
### *Journal*

Are you a spender or a saver? Relate a conflict you have experienced because of how you view money.

## About *the* AUTHOR

**Dorothy West** (c.1909–1998), novelist, short story writer, editor, and journalist, was born and educated in Boston. West wrote her first story at the age of seven; by the time she was fourteen, she had won several writing competitions sponsored by the *Boston Post*. At eighteen, wider recognition followed when her story "The Typewriter" won a prize from *Opportunity*, a journal published by the National Urban League. After attending Boston University and the Columbia School of Journalism, West settled in Harlem, where she founded the magazine *Challenge* (and later, *New Challenge*). By publishing the work of her friends and colleagues—Langston Hughes, Countee Cullen, Richard Wright, Arna Bontemps, Zora Neale Hurston, Wallace Thurman, and Claude McKay—she brought into focus the great talent of the Harlem Renaissance. When the periodical failed, West participated in the Federal Writers' Project until the mid-1940s.

In her writings, West explores the important issues of race and class within the African-American community. She probes deeply into the minds of her characters, who face moral, psychological, and social confinement. Her first novel, *The Living Is Easy*, published in 1948, is a semi-autobiographical account depicting middle-class' blacks' pursuit of false values that result in economic and psychological imprisonment. Her second novel, *The Wedding*, published in 1995, became a two-part television miniseries produced by Oprah Winfrey.

## About *the* SELECTION

**"The Richer, the Poorer"** tells the story of two sisters who have lived their lives very differently and who, coming to live together in their old age, offer important lessons to each other. The short story appeared in West's collection of short stories *The Richer, the Poorer,* which was published in 1995.

# The Richer, The Poorer

## DOROTHY WEST

Over the years Lottie had urged Bess to prepare for her old age. Over the years Bess had lived each day as if there were no other. Now they were both past sixty, the time for summing up. Lottie had a bank account that had never grown <u>lean</u>. Bess had the clothes on her back, and the rest of her worldly possessions in a battered suitcase.

> *How is Lottie different from her sister?*

Lottie had hated being a child, hearing her parents' skimping and scraping. Bess had never seemed to notice. All she ever wanted was to go outside and play. She learned to skate on borrowed skates. She rode a borrowed bicycle. Lottie couldn't wait to grow up and buy herself the best of everything.

As soon as anyone would hire her, Lottie put herself to work. She minded babies, she ran errands for the old.

She never touched a penny of her money, though her child's mouth watered for ice cream and candy. But she could not bear to share with Bess, who never had anything to share with her. When the dimes began to add up to dollars, she lost her taste for sweets.

By the time she was twelve, she was clerking after school in a small variety store. Saturdays she worked as long as she was wanted. She decided to keep her money for clothes. When she entered high school, she would wear a wardrobe that neither she nor anyone else would be able to match.

***Anna Washington Derry,*** 1927.
Laura Wheeler Waring.
National Museum of American Art, Washington, DC.

But her freshman year found her unable to indulge so frivolous a <u>whim</u>, particularly when her admiring instructors advised her to think seriously of college. No one in her family had ever gone to college, and certainly Bess would never get there. She would show them all what she could do, if she put her mind to it.

She began to bank her money, and her bankbook became her most private and precious possession.

In her third year of high school she found a job in a small but expanding restaurant, where she cashiered from the busy hour until closing. In her last year of high school the business increased so rapidly that Lottie was faced with

WORDS
FOR
EVERYDAY
USE

**lean** (lēn) *adj.,* lacking capital. *The writer spent his <u>lean</u> years living in an attic that he rented for three hundred dollars a month.*
**whim** (hwim) *n.,* fancy; eccentric and often sudden idea. *On a <u>whim</u>, Todd borrowed his brother's motorcycle and rode out to the lake.*

the choice of staying in school or working full time.

*Why didn't Lottie go to college?*

She made her choice easily. A job in hand was worth two in the future.

Bess had a <u>beau</u> in the school band, who had no other ambition except to play a horn. Lottie expected to be settled with a home and family while Bess was still waiting for Harry to earn enough to buy a marriage license.

That Bess married Harry straight out of high school was not surprising. That Lottie never married at all was not really surprising either. Two or three times she was halfway persuaded, but to give up a job that paid well for a home-making job that paid nothing was a risk she was incapable of taking.

Bess's married life was nothing for Lottie to envy. She and Harry lived like <u>gypsies</u>, Harry playing in second-rate bands all over the country, even getting himself and Bess stranded in Europe. They were often in rags and never in riches.

Bess grieved because she had no child, not having sense enough to know she was better off without one. Lottie was certainly better off without nieces and nephews to feel sorry for. Very likely Bess would have dumped them on her doorstep.

That Lottie had a doorstep they might have been left on was only because her boss, having bought a second house, offered Lottie his first house at a price so low and

*How did Lottie get her house?*

terms so reasonable that it would have been like losing money to refuse.

She shut off the rooms she didn't use, letting them go to rack and ruin.[1] Since she ate her meals out, she had no food at home, and did not encourage callers, who always expected a cup of tea.

Her way of life was mean and <u>miserly</u>, but she did not know it. She thought she lived frugally in her middle years so that she could live in comfort and ease when she most needed peace of mind.

The years, after forty, began to race. Suddenly Lottie was sixty, and retired from her job by her boss's son, who had no sentimental feeling about keeping her on until she was ready to quit.

She made several attempts to find other employment, but her <u>dowdy</u> appearance made her look old and inefficient. For the first time in her life Lottie would gladly have worked for nothing, to have some place to go, something to do with her day.

Harry died abroad, in a third-rate hotel, with Bess weeping as hard as if he had left her a fortune. He had left her nothing but his horn. There wasn't even money for her passage home.

Lottie, trapped by the blood tie, knew she would not only have to send for her sister, but take her in when she returned. It

*When Bess's husband dies, leaving her stranded abroad, what realization does Lottie come to?*

didn't seem fair that Bess should reap the harvest of Lottie's lifetime of self-denial.

It took Lottie a week to get a bedroom ready, a week of hard work and hard cash. There was everything to do, everything to replace or paint. When she was through the room looked so fresh and new that Lottie felt she deserved it more than Bess.

She would let Bess have her room, but the mattress was so lumpy, the carpet so worn, the curtains so threadbare that Lottie's conscience pricked her. She supposed she would have to redo that room, too, and went about doing it with an eagerness that she mistook for haste.

---

1. **rack and ruin.** Destruction; disrepair

---

**Words For Everyday Use**

**beau** (bō) *n.,* boyfriend. *Sylvia waited for her <u>beau</u> to claim most of the dances on her dance card.*

**gyp • sy** (jip´sē) *n.,* wanderer; member of an itinerant people who live chiefly in Asia, Europe, and North America. *After three months of living like a <u>gypsy</u> in Europe, Claire was happy to come home.*

**mi • ser • ly** (mī´zər lē) *adj.,* characterized by stinginess. *The Ghost of Christmas Past intended to change Scrooge's <u>miserly</u> ways.*

**dow • dy** (dou´dē) *adj.,* unbecoming in appearance. *The television makeover transformed Gloria's <u>dowdy</u> appearance.*

When she was through upstairs, she was shocked to see how dismal downstairs looked by comparison. She tried to ignore it, but with nowhere to go to escape it, the contrast grew more intolerable.

She worked her way from kitchen to parlor, persuading herself she was only putting the rooms to rights to give herself something to do. At night she slept like a child after a long and happy day of playing house. She was having more fun than she had ever had in her life. She was living each hour for itself.

> How does Lottie feel about refurbishing her house?

There was only a day now before Bess would arrive. Passing her gleaming mirrors, at first with vague awareness, then with painful clarity, Lottie saw herself as others saw her, and could not stand the sight.

She went on a spending spree from the specialty shops to beauty salon, emerging transformed into a woman who believed in miracles.

She was in the kitchen basting a turkey when Bess rang the bell. Her heart raced, and she wondered if the heat from the oven was responsible.

She went to the door, and Bess stood before her. Stiffly she suffered Bess's embrace, her heart racing harder, her eyes suddenly smarting from the onrush of cold air.

"Oh, Lottie, it's good to see you," Bess said, but saying nothing about Lottie's splendid appearance. Upstairs Bess, putting down her shabby suitcase, said, "I'll sleep like a rock tonight," without a word of praise for her lovely room. At the <u>lavish</u> table, top-heavy with turkey, Bess said, "I'll take light and dark, both," with no marveling at the size of the bird, or that there was turkey for two elderly women, one of them too poor to buy her own bread.

With the glow of good food in her stomach, Bess began to spin stories. They were rich with places and people, most of them lowly, all of them magnificent. Her face reflected her telling, the joys and sorrows of her remembering, and above all, the love she lived by that enhanced the poorest place, the humblest person.

Then it was that Lottie knew why Bess had made no mention of her finery, or the shining room, or the twelve-pound turkey. She had not even seen them. Tomorrow she would see the room as it really looked, and Lottie as she really looked, and the warmed-over turkey in its second-day glory. Tonight she saw only what she had come seeking, a place in her sister's home and heart.

She said, "That's enough about me. How have the years used you?"

"It was me who didn't use them," said Lottie <u>wistfully</u>. "I saved for them. I saved for them. I forgot the best of them would go without my ever spending a day or a dollar enjoying them. That's my life story in those few words, a life never lived.

> What does Lottie say is the story of her life?

"Now it's too near the end to try."

Bess said, "To know how much there is to know is the beginning of learning to live. Don't count the years that are left us. At our time of life it's the days that count. You've too much catching up to do to waste a minute of a waking hour feeling sorry for yourself."

Lottie grinned, a real wide-open grin, "Well to tell the truth, I felt sorry for you. Maybe if I had any sense I'd feel sorry for myself, after all. I know I'm too old to kick up my heels, but I'm going to let you show me how. If I land on my head, I guess it won't matter; I feel <u>giddy</u> already, and I like it."  ∎

> What does Lottie resolve to do?

---

**WORDS FOR EVERYDAY USE**

**lav • ish** (la´ vish) *adj.*, abundant; excessive. *Mr. Hilpisch's <u>lavish</u> gifts to his family were received with laughter and surprise.*

**wist • ful • ly** (wist´ fə lē) *adv.*, expressing yearning or desire mixed with melancholy. *Mom said <u>wistfully</u>, "My beautiful wedding dress has yellowed with age."*

**gid • dy** (gi´ dē) *adj.*, lightheartedly silly. *Justin was pleased with Carol's <u>giddy</u> laughter at his jokes.*

If you were Lottie, filled with resolve to finally enjoy life, what would you do first with your sister?

# INVESTIGATE Inquire Imagine

**Recall:** GATHERING FACTS

1a. Why is Lottie better prepared financially for old age than Bess?

2a. As Lottie grows up, what becomes her most precious possession?

3a. When Lottie buys a house, what does she do with the rooms she feels she doesn't need?

→ **Interpret:** FINDING MEANING

1b. What formative events caused Lottie to begin saving?

2b. Why does Lottie resent Bess?

3b. In what way does Lottie's closing rooms of the house mirror what she is doing to herself?

---

**Analyze:** TAKING THINGS APART

4a. Identify the ways in which Lottie has denied herself happiness.

→ **Synthesize:** BRINGING THINGS TOGETHER

4b. Why does Lottie tell Bess, "I know I'm too old to kick up my heels, but I'm going to let you show me how"?

---

**Evaluate:** MAKING JUDGMENTS

5a. Which sister has the better philosophy of life, Lottie or Bess?

→ **Extend:** CONNECTING IDEAS

5b. What is your philosophy of life as it relates to money management?

---

# Understanding Literature

**THEME.** Review the definition for **theme** in the Handbook of Literary Terms. What do you believe is the story's theme?

**MOTIVATION.** Review the definition for **motivation** in the Handbook of Literary Terms. Then fill out the radiating circle below to explore the motivating reasons behind Lottie's frugality.

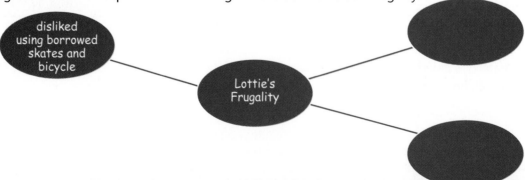

disliked using borrowed skates and bicycle

Lottie's Frugality

# WRITER'S JOURNAL

1. Imagine you are Lottie. Write a **letter** to your sister Bess telling her what you resent about her.

2. Imagine that you are Bess and that you are still abroad. Write Lottie a **postcard** describing what you have been up to. Explain why you will be coming to visit your sister.

3. Imagine you are Lottie. Write a **journal entry** explaining the transformation of your life philosophy. How did you used to live? How do you want to live now? Name specific things you would like to do.

# Integrating
### *the* LANGUAGE ARTS

## Language, Grammar, and Style

**TONE.** Read the Language Arts Survey 3.3, "Register, Tone, and Voice." Rewrite the following sentences from "The Richer, the Poorer" to give each a completely different tone from what it has now.

1. As soon as anyone would hire her, Lottie put herself to work.

2. She would show them all what she could do, if she put her mind to it.

3. Lottie expected to be settled with a home and family, while Bess was still waiting for Harry to earn enough to buy a marriage license.

4. Lottie, trapped by the blood tie, knew she would not only have to send for her sister, but take her in when she returned.

5. She would let Bess have her room, but the mattress was so lumpy, the carpet so worn, the curtains so threadbare that Lottie's conscience pricked her.

## Speaking and Listening & Collaborative Learning

**DEBATE.** Form two groups in which one side argues the benefits of working hard and saving money for the future and the other side argues the benefits of spending freely in order to enjoy life to the fullest in the present. Point out the disadvantages of the opposite behavior. Even if you don't believe in the position assigned to your group, imagine arguments from the point of view of someone who does.

## Collaborative Learning

**WRITING CREATIVELY.** Lottie takes responsibility for her life by saving for her old age. Write about a fictitious character who takes responsibility for his or her life in another way. Characters you might consider include a single mother, a homeless man, a rock star, and a teen without a job. You might choose to write a story, a play, a poem, or lyrics for a song. When you have finished, share your creative writing in a small group or with the class.

# Literary TOOLS

**ARCHETYPE.** An **archetype** is an inherited, often unconscious, ancestral memory or motif that recurs throughout history or literature. One archetypal theme found throughout literature is the fall from a state of innocence to a state of experience. An early work in which this theme occurs is the story of Adam and Eve in the book of Genesis in the Bible. As you read, note how this archetype relates to Hurston's life.

**SYMBOL AND THEME.** A **symbol** is a thing that stands for or represents something else. A **theme** is a central idea in a literary work. As you read, pay careful attention to a symbol Hurston uses at the end—a bag filled with different objects. Make a cluster chart listing the contents of the bag. One example has been done for you. What do the contents of the bag symbolize?

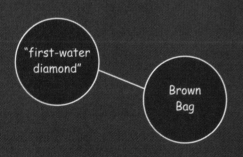

"first-water diamond"

Brown Bag

# Reader's Journal

When have you maintained a positive attitude to get through a difficult experience?

## "How It Feels to Be Colored Me"

BY ZORA NEALE HURSTON

# About the AUTHOR

**Zora Neale Hurston** (c.1901–1960), writer and folklorist, was born and raised in the African-American town of Eatonville, Florida. Educated at Howard University, Barnard College, and Columbia University, Hurston began her career as a folklorist. *Mules and Men* (1935), one of her best-known folklore collections, was based on her field research in the American South. *Tell My Horse* (1938) describes folk customs in Haiti and Jamaica.

As a novelist, Hurston is noted for her storytelling abilities, use of metaphoric language, and celebration of Southern African-American culture. Her writing influenced the Harlem Renaissance writers of the 1930s, as well as later African-American writers, such as Ralph Ellison, Alice Walker, and Toni Morrison. *Their Eyes Were Watching God* (1937), her most famous novel, is widely read in college classes. Other novels include *Jonah's Gourd Vine* (1934); *Moses, Man of the Mountain* (1939); and *Seraph on the Suwanee* (1948). A prolific writer, Hurston also wrote short stories, plays, journal articles, and an autobiography, *Dust Tracks on a Road* (1942).

Hurston died in a county welfare home and was buried in an unmarked grave. Interest in her has only recently been revived after decades of neglect by the literary community. A new generation of African-American writers is recognizing her contributions to African-American literature. Many of Hurston's writings were republished in the 1970s, and in 1995 a two-volume set of her work, some previously unpublished, was released. In 1999 her writing from the 1930s Florida Federal Writer's Project was published in *Go Gator and Muddy the Water*, edited by Pamela Bordelon.

# About the SELECTION

Published in 1928 in *World Tomorrow*, the essay **"How It Feels to Be Colored Me"** provides a remarkably contemporary view of what it feels like for one woman to be African American. The author uses personal anecdotes to discuss the issues of prejudice, discrimination, and equality in American society.

**Woman Dancing in the Rain (Josephine Baker),**
1929. Paul Colin. National Portrait Gallery, Washington, DC.

# How It Feels to Be Colored Me

ZORA NEALE HURSTON

I am colored but I offer nothing in the way of <u>extenuating</u> circumstances except the fact that I am the only Negro in the United States whose grandfather on the mother's side was *not* an Indian chief.

I remember the very day that I became colored. Up to my thirteenth year I lived in the little Negro town of Eatonville, Florida. It is exclusively a colored town. The only white people I knew passed through the town going to or coming from Orlando. The native whites rode dusty horses, the Northern tourists chugged down the sandy village road in automobiles. The town knew the Southerners and never stopped cane chewing[1] when they passed. But the Northerners were something else again. They were peered at cautiously from behind curtains by the timid. The more

> What does Hurston say happened to her one day?

---

1. **cane chewing.** Chewing sugar cane; may also have a connotation similar to *chewing the fat*, meaning "making friendly, familiar conversation"

**WORDS FOR EVERYDAY USE**

ex • ten • u • at • ing (ik sten′ yə wāt iŋ) *adj.*, lessening the seriousness of [a crime] by making, or serving as, an excuse. *The defense attorney argued that the defendant's desire to reform should be considered an <u>extenuating</u> circumstance in the case.*

venturesome would come out on the porch to watch them go past and got just as much pleasure out of the tourists as the tourists got out of the village.

The front porch might seem a daring place for the rest of the town, but it was a gallery seat[2] to me. My favorite place was atop the gate-post. Proscenium box[3] for a born first-nighter.[4] Not only did I enjoy the show, but I didn't mind the actors knowing that I liked it. I usually spoke to them in passing. I'd wave at them and when they returned my salute, I would say something like this: "Howdy-do-well-I-thank-you-where-you-goin'?" Usually the automobile or the horse paused at this, and after a queer exchange of compliments, I would probably "go a piece of the way" with them, as we say in far-thest Florida. If one of my family happened to come to the front in time to see me, of course negotiations would be rudely broken off. But even so, it is clear that I was the first "welcome-to-our-state," Floridian, and I hope the Miami Chamber of Commerce will please take notice.

During this period, white people differed from colored to me only in that they rode through town and never lived there. They liked to hear me "speak pieces"[5] and sing and wanted to see me dance the parse-me-la, and gave me generously of their small silver for doing these things, which seemed strange to me for I wanted to do

*Where did Hurston grow up? In what way did the town residents' reaction to the two groups of white people differ?*

*What did Hurston do when Northerners passed through town?*

*What distinction did Hurston make between white people and the African Americans she knew? What did Hurston do for the white people?*

them so much that I needed bribing to stop. Only they didn't know it. The colored people gave no dimes. They deplored any joyful tendencies in me, but I was their Zora nevertheless. I belonged to them, to the nearby hotels, to the county—everybody's Zora.

But changes came in the family when I was thirteen, and I was sent to school in Jacksonville. I left Eatonville, the town of the oleanders,[6] as Zora. When I disembarked from the river-boat at Jacksonville, she was no more. It seemed that I had suffered a sea change.[7] I was not Zora of Orange County any more, I was a little colored girl. I found it out in certain ways. In my heart as well as in the mirror, I became a fast[8] brown—warranted not to rub nor run.

But I am not tragically colored. There is no great sorrow dammed up in my soul, nor lurking behind my eyes. I do not mind at all. I do not belong to the sobbing school of Negrohood who hold that nature somehow has given them a lowdown dirty deal and whose feelings are all hurt about it. Even in the helter-skelter skirmish that is my life, I have seen that

*What transformation did Hurston undergo at thirteen?*

*How does Hurston feel about being "colored"?*

2. **gallery seat.** Seat in the highest balcony in a theater, commonly having the cheapest seats
3. **proscenium box.** Compartment of theater seats having a good view of the proscenium or stage
4. **born first-nighter.** Someone born to attend the opening night of plays at theaters; a true lover of theater
5. **speak pieces.** Recite familiar examples of poetry or prose
6. **oleanders.** Evergreen shrubs with fragrant white to red flowers
7. **suffered a sea change.** Allusion to these lines from Shakespeare's *The Tempest:* "But doth suffer a sea change / Into something rich and strange"
8. **fast.** Firmly fixed

**WORDS FOR EVERYDAY USE**

**ven • ture • some** (ven[t]'shər səm) *adj.,* daring; inclined to incur risk or danger. *In the novel* Tom Sawyer, *a group of venturesome children explore an old mine.*

**de • plore** (di plōr') *vt.,* regret strongly; consider unfortunate or deserving of criticism. *Before the Civil War, many abolitionists deplored slavery and spoke out against it.*

**dis • em • bark** (dis əm bärk') *vi.,* leave a ship to go ashore. *The captain of the ship told us to watch our step as we disembarked.*

**hel • ter-skel • ter** (hel' tər skel'tər) *adj.,* marked by a lack of order or plan; haphazard. *The many toys strewn about the girls' room contributed to its helter-skelter appearance.*

**skir • mish** (skər'mish) *n.,* minor fight in war; minor dispute or contest between opposing parties. *The skirmish between British soldiers and Massachusetts townspeople in Concord and Lexington started the American Revolutionary War.*

the world is to the strong regardless of a little pigmentation more or less. No, I do not weep at the world—I am too busy sharpening my oyster knife.[9]

Someone is always at my elbow reminding me that I am the granddaughter of slaves. It fails to register[10] depression with me. Slavery is sixty years in the past. The operation was successful and the patient is doing well, thank you. The terrible struggle that made me an American out of a potential slave said "On the line!" The Reconstruction said "Get set!"; and the generation before said "Go!" I am off to a flying start and I must not halt in the stretch to look behind and weep. Slavery is the price I paid for civilization, and the choice was not with me. It is a bully[11] adventure and worth all that I have paid through my ancestors for it. No one on earth ever had a greater chance for glory. The world to be won and nothing to be lost. It is thrilling to think—to know that for any act of mine, I shall get twice as much praise or twice as much blame. It is quite exciting to hold the center of the national stage, with the spectators not knowing whether to laugh or to weep.

*What fact about being an African American does Hurston find exciting?*

The position of my white neighbor is much more difficult. No brown specter pulls up a chair beside me when I sit down to eat. No dark ghost thrusts its leg against mine in bed. The game of keeping what one has is never so exciting as the game of getting.

I do not always feel colored. Even now I often achieve the unconscious Zora of Eatonville before the Hegira.[12] I feel

*When does Hurston feel most "colored"?*

most colored when I am thrown against a sharp white background.

For instance at Barnard.[13] "Beside the waters of the Hudson" I feel my race. Among the thousand white persons, I am a dark rock surged upon, overswept by a creamy sea. I am surged upon and overswept, but through it all, I remain myself. When covered by the waters, I am; and the ebb but reveals me again.

Sometimes it is the other way around. A white person is set down in our midst, but the contrast is just as sharp for me. For instance, when I sit in the drafty basement that is The New World Cabaret[14] with a white person, my color comes. We enter chatting about any little nothing that we have in common and are seated by the jazz waiters. In the abrupt way that jazz orchestras have, this one plunges into a number. It loses no time in circumlocutions, but gets right down to business. It constricts the thorax[15] and splits the heart with its tempo[16] and narcotic harmonies. This orchestra grows rambunctious, rears on its hind legs and attacks the tonal veil with primitive fury, rending it, clawing it until it breaks through to the jungle beyond. I follow those heathen[17]—follow them exultingly. I dance

*How does Hurston describe the jazz music?*

---

9. **oyster knife.** Knife used to pry open the shellfish
10. **register.** Make or convey an impression of
11. **bully.** Excellent or first-rate
12. **Hegira.** Journey undertaken to escape from a dangerous or undesirable situation; the flight of Muhammad from Mecca in AD 622
13. **Barnard.** College in New York City
14. **New World Cabaret.** Jazz club
15. **thorax.** Part of the body between the neck and abdomen
16. **tempo.** Rate of speed of a musical piece
17. **heathen.** Uncivilized people

---

**WORDS FOR EVERYDAY USE**

**ebb** (eb) *n.,* flowing back of the tide toward the sea. *The ebb of the ocean exposed a sandy stretch of sea treasures.*

**cir • cum • lo • cu • tion** (sər kəm lō kyü′shən) *n.,* use of an unnecessarily large number of words to express an idea. *The union workers were already committed to the strike and did not want to hear their leader's circumlocutions.*

**ram • bunc • tious** (ram bəŋk′shəs) *adj.,* marked by uncontrollable enthusiasm; unruly. *The babysitter could not control the rambunctious children who ran through the house in a whirlwind of motion.*

**ex • ult • ing • ly** (ig zəlt′iŋ lē) *adv.,* in a joyful manner. *The congregation sang the Easter hymn exultingly.*

wildly inside myself; I yell within, I whoop; I shake my assegai[18] above my head, I hurl it true to the mark *yeeeeooww!* I am in the jungle and living in the jungle way. My face is painted red and yellow and my body is painted blue. My pulse is throbbing like a war drum. I want to slaughter something—give pain, give death to what, I do not know. But the piece ends. The men of the orchestra wipe their lips and rest their fingers. I creep back slowly to the veneer we call civilization with the last tone and find the white friend sitting motionless in his seat, smoking calmly.

> How does Hurston describe herself at the New World Cabaret?

"Good music they have here," he remarks, drumming the table with his fingertips.

Music! The great blobs of purple and red emotion have not touched him. He has only heard what I felt. He is far away and I see him but dimly across the ocean and the continent that have fallen between us. He is so pale with his whiteness then and I am *so* colored.

At certain times I have no race, I am *me*. When I set my hat at a certain angle and saunter down Seventh Avenue, Harlem City, feeling as snooty as the lions in front of the Forty-Second Street Library, for instance. So far as my feelings are concerned, Peggy Hopkins Joyce on the Boule Mich[19] with her gorgeous raiment, stately carriage, knees knocking together in a most aristocratic manner, has nothing on me. The cosmic Zora emerges. I belong to no race nor time. I am the eternal feminine with its string of beads.

> When is Hurston unconscious of her race? How does she see herself?

I have no separate feeling about being an American citizen and colored. I am merely a fragment of the Great Soul that surges within the boundaries. My country, right or wrong.

Sometimes, I feel discriminated against, but it does not make me angry. It merely astonishes me. How *can* any deny themselves the pleasure of my company! It's beyond me.

> What is Hurston's reaction when she feels discriminated against?

But in the main, I feel like a brown bag of miscellany propped against a wall. Against a wall in company with other bags, white, red and yellow. Pour out the contents, and there is discovered a jumble of small things priceless and worthless. A first-water diamond,[20] an empty spool, bits of broken glass, lengths of string, a key to a door long since crumbled away, a rusty knifeblade, old shoes saved for a road that never was and never will be, a nail bent under the weight of things too heavy for any nail, a dried flower or two, still a little fragrant. In your hand is the brown bag. On the ground before you is the jumble it held—so much like the jumble in the bags, could they be emptied, that all might be dumped in a single heap and the bags refilled without altering the content of any greatly. A bit of colored glass more or less would not matter. Perhaps that is how the Great Stuffer of Bags filled them in the first place—who knows? ■

> To what does Hurston compare herself? In what ways are the bags of different colors alike?

---

18. **assegai.** Slender hardwood spear tipped with iron used in southern Africa
19. **Peggy Hopkins Joyce on the Boule Mich.** A famous beauty of the 1920s walking down the Boulevard Saint Michel, a fashionable street in Paris
20. **first-water diamond.** Diamond of the highest quality and purest luster

---

**WORDS FOR EVERYDAY USE**

**ve • neer** (və nir') *n.,* superficial or deceptively attractive appearance, display, or effect. *Although the host made some very cutting remarks at dinner, the guests retained a veneer of politeness.*

**saun • ter** (sôn' tər; sän' tər) *vi.,* walk about in an idle or leisurely manner. *Confident of his performance, Miguel sauntered to the front of the room to turn in his college board exam before the time was up.*

**rai • ment** (rā'mənt) *n.,* clothing. *In Europe, purple was usually reserved for the raiment of kings.*

**car • riage** (kar'ij) *n.,* manner of bearing the body; posture. *The gentleman's carriage on horseback was stately and dignified.*

**mis • cel • la • ny** (mi'sə lā' nē) *n.,* mixture of various things. *The miscellany of items spread across Leon's desk prevented me from finding the plane tickets.*

## from "The Resurrection of Zora Neale Hurston and Her Work"

by Alice Walker

*An address delivered at the First Annual Zora Neale Hurston Festival, Eatonville, Florida, January 26,1990.*

I had read Robert Hemenway's thoughtful and sensitive biography of Zora Neale Hurston, after loving and teaching her work for a number of years, and I could not bear that she did not have a known grave. After all, with her pen she had erected a monument to the African-American and African-AmerIndian common people both she and I are descended from. After reading Hurston, anyone coming to the United States would know exactly where to go to find the remains of a culture that kept Southern black people going through centuries of white oppression. They could find what was left of the music; they could find what was left of the speech; they could find what was left of the dancing (I remember wanting to shout with joy to see that Zora, in one of her books, mentioned the "moochie," a dance that scandalized—and titillated—the elders in my community when I was a very small child, and that I had never seen mentioned anywhere); they could find what was left of the work, the people's relationship to the earth and to animals; they could find what was left of the orchards, the gardens, and the fields; they could find what was left of the prayer.

I will never forget reading Zora and seeing for the first time, written down, the prayer that my father, and all the old elders before him, prayed in church. The one that thanked God that the cover on his bed the night before was not winding sheet, nor his bed itself his cooling board. When I read this prayer, I saw again the deeply sincere praying face of my father, and relived my own awareness of his passion, his gratitude for life, and his humbleness.

Nor will I forget finding a character in Zora's work called Shug. It is what my "outside" grandmother, my grandfather's lover and mother of two of my aunts, was called. It is also the nickname of an aunt, Malsenior, for whom I was named. On any page in Zora's work I was

Zora Neale Hurston.

likely to see something or someone I recognized; reading her tales of adventure and risk became an act of self-recognition and affirmation I'd experienced but rarely before.

Reading her, I saw for the first time my own specific culture, and recognized it as such, with its humor always striving to be equal to its pain, and I felt as if, indeed, I had been given a map that led to the remains of my literary country. The old country, as it were. Her characters spoke the language I'd heard the elders speaking all my life. Her work chronicled the behavior of the elders I'd witnessed. And she did not condescend to them, and she did not apologize for them, and she was them, delightedly. ■

Do Hurston's feelings about her ethnic heritage surprise you in any way? Explain why or why not.

# INVESTIGATE, Inquire Imagine

**Recall:** GATHERING FACTS

1a. What does Hurston say happened to her when she moved to Jacksonville?

2a. What is Hurston's reaction when someone reminds her that she is the granddaughter of a slave? What does she think is thrilling? According to Hurston, whose position is more difficult than her own?

3a. When does Hurston feel most colored? What example does she provide of a time when she feels this way? What other example does she provide of a situation when it is "the other way around"?

**Interpret:** FINDING MEANING

1b. What forces did Hurston become aware of when she went away to school?

2b. What does Hurston mean by the statement "I am not tragically colored"? In what way does her attitude toward her position as the granddaughter of a slave support this statement? Why does she believe the position of white people is more difficult than her own?

3b. Explain why both examples make Hurston aware of her race.

**Analyze:** TAKING THINGS APART

4a. Identify the different attitudes toward race that Hurston reveals in this essay.

**Synthesize:** BRINGING THINGS TOGETHER

4b. Why does Hurston see the bags of different colors as all being essentially alike? What inner resources do her attitudes about color reveal?

**Evaluate:** MAKING JUDGMENTS

5a. Do you find Hurston's attitude toward her race and toward discrimination outdated, or do you think it holds true today? Using evidence from the text, state whether or not you think Hurston's attitude about race is healthy.

**Extend:** CONNECTING IDEAS

5b. What other attitudes about race and discrimination have you encountered in literature, films, or everyday life? In what way do these attitudes compare and contrast with Hurston's?

# Understanding Literature

ARCHETYPE. Review the definition for **archetype** in Literary Tools on page 658. What fall from innocence to experience did Hurston undergo? Explain to what extent, if any, she ascribes tragic consequences to this event.

SYMBOL AND THEME. Review the definitions for **symbol** and **theme** in the Handbook of Literary Terms and the graphic organizer you made for Literary Tools on page 658. What do the bags of different colors Hurston mentions at the end of the selection represent? What do their contents represent? What or who does the "Great Stuffer of Bags" symbolize? Considering such symbolism, what do you believe is the theme of this selection?

# Writer's Journal

1. Write a personal **anecdote**, focusing on what it means to be you by describing a specific aspect of your background, upbringing, or personality.

2. Imagine you are the thirteen-year-old Hurston in Jacksonville. Write a **journal entry** in which you describe how you once saw yourself and how you see yourself through others' eyes now.

3. Write a **paragraph** describing your reaction to a musical experience.

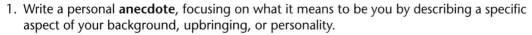

# Integrating *the* LANGUAGE ARTS

## Vocabulary

**CONNOTATION AND DENOTATION.** You may have noticed that in this selection Hurston uses terms for African Americans that are considered to be inappropriate or offensive today, namely *colored* and *Negro*. These terms were replaced by the term *black* in the 1970s, and today, the term *African American* is more commonly used. These words all have connotations that have changed over time. Because English is a fluid language, not only are new words constantly being added and deleted, but shifts in denotation and connotation of established words occur over time. Review the Language Arts Survey 1.24, "Connotation and Denotation." A pair of words with essentially the same denotation is provided in each numbered item below. Choose which word has the more positive connotation and which the more negative connotation.

1. thin; skinny

2. obese; stout

3. stingy; frugal

4. easygoing; lazy

5. lie; fabrication

## Media Literacy

**EVALUATING INTERNET SITES.** Working in small groups, use the Internet to research four sites that discuss Zora Neale Hurston's work. Read the information in each site. Then rate each site. Which is the most interesting? the most informative? the best constructed? the most accurate? Once you have compiled your evaluations, work together to chart your results, making your assessment as visually appealing as possible. Present your work to the class. See the Language Arts Survey 5.35, "How to Understand Internet Sites," for more information.

## Study and Research

**THE PARTS OF A DICTIONARY DEFINITION.** In this essay, Hurston uses the word *hegira*, meaning "a journey undertaken to escape from a dangerous or undesirable situation." Review the Language Arts Survey 1.17, "Using a Dictionary." Then write out the dictionary entry for *hegira*, labeling each part.

## from *The Souls of Black Folk*
### by W. E. B. Du Bois

Easily the most striking thing in the history of the American Negro since 1876[1] is the ascendancy of Mr. Booker T. Washington. It began at the time when war memories and ideals were rapidly passing; a day of astonishing commercial development was dawning; a sense of doubt and hesitation overtook the freedmen's sons,—then it was that his leading began. Mr. Washington came, with a simple definite program, at the psychological moment when the nation was a little ashamed of having bestowed so much sentiment on Negroes, and was concentrating its energies on Dollars. His program of industrial education, conciliation of the South, and submission and silence as to civil and political rights, was not wholly original; the Free Negroes from 1830 up to war-time had striven to build industrial schools, and the American Missionary Association had from the first taught various trades; and Price[2] and others had sought a way of honorable alliance with the best of the Southerners. But Mr. Washington first indissolubly linked these things; he put enthusiasm, unlimited energy, and perfect faith into this program, and changed it from a bypath into a veritable Way of Life. And the tale of the methods by which he did this is a fascinating study of human life.

It startled the nation to hear a Negro advocating such a program after many decades of bitter complaint; it startled and won the applause of the South, it interested and won the admiration of the North; and after a confused murmur of protest, it silenced if it did not convert the Negroes themselves.

To gain the sympathy and cooperation of the various elements comprising the white South was Mr. Washington's first task; and this, at the time Tuskegee[3] was founded, seemed, for a black man, well-nigh impossible. And yet ten years later it was done in the word spoken at Atlanta: "In all things purely social we can be as separate as the five fingers, and yet one as the hand in all things essential to mutual progress." This "Atlanta Compromise"[4] is by all odds the most notable thing in Mr. Washington's career. The South interpreted it in different ways: the radicals received it as a complete surrender of the demand for civil and political equality; the conservatives, as a generously conceived working basis for mutual understanding. So both approved it, and today its author is certainly the most distinguished Southerner since Jefferson Davis, and the one with the largest personal following.

Next to this achievement comes Mr. Washington's work in gaining place and consideration in the North. Others less shrewd and tactful had formerly essayed to sit on these two stools and had fallen between them, but as Mr. Washington knew the heart of the South from birth and training, so by singular insight he intuitively grasped the spirit of the age which was dominating the North. And so thoroughly did he learn the speech and thought of triumphant commercialism, and the ideals of material prosperity, that the picture of a lone black boy poring over a French grammar amid the weeds and dirt of a neglected home soon seemed to him the acme of absurdities.[5] One wonders what Socrates and St. Francis of Assisi[6] would say to this.

And yet this very singleness of vision and thorough oneness with his age is a mark of the successful man. It is as though Nature must needs make men narrow in order to give them force. So Mr. Washington's cult has gained unquestioning followers, his work has wonderfully prospered, his friends are legion, and his enemies are confounded. Today he stands as the one recognized spokesman of his ten million fellows, and one of the most notable figures in a nation of seventy millions. One hesitates, therefore, to criticize a life which, beginning with so little, has done so much. And yet the time is come when one may speak in all sincerity and utter courtesy of the mistakes and shortcomings of Mr. Washington's career, as well as of his triumphs, without being thought captious or envious, and without forgetting that it is easier to do ill than well in the world.

The criticism that has hitherto met Mr. Washington has not always been of this broad character. In the South especially has he had to walk warily to avoid the harshest judgments,—and naturally so, for he is dealing with the one subject of deepest sensitiveness to that section. Twice— once when at the Chicago celebration of the Spanish-American War he alluded to the color-prejudice that is "eating away the vitals of the South," and once when he dined with President Roosevelt[7]—has the resulting

---

1. **1876.** In 1876, Reconstruction following the Civil War ended, federal troops withdrew from the South, and African Americans lost political power.
2. **Price.** Thomas Frederick Price (1860–1919), editor, Roman Catholic priest, and founder of the American Missionary Association
3. **Tuskegee.** Tuskegee Institute, a vocational school for African Americans founded in 1881 by Booker T. Washington
4. **Atlanta Compromise.** Washington's speech at the Atlanta Exposition of 1895 essentially traded the political, civil, and social rights of African Americans for the promise of jobs and vocational-training schools.
5. **acme of absurdities.** Refers to a passage in *Up From Slavery* in which Washington describes nonpractical knowledge as absurd
6. **Socrates and St. Francis of Assisi.** *Socrates*—(c.470–399 BC) Greek philosopher; *St. Francis of Assisi*—(c.AD 1182–1226) founder of the Franciscan orders and leader of movements to reform the church
7. **he dined with President Roosevelt.** Theodore Roosevelt (1858–1919) asked Washington to dine with him in 1901, causing much controversy and criticism around the country.

Southern criticism been violent enough to threaten seriously his popularity. In the North the feeling has several times forced itself into words, that Mr. Washington's counsels of submission overlooked certain elements of true manhood, and that his educational program was unnecessarily narrow. Usually, however, such criticism has not found open expression, although, too, the spiritual sons of the Abolitionists have not been prepared to acknowledge that the schools founded before Tuskegee, by men of broad ideals and self-sacrificing spirit, were wholly failures or worthy of ridicule. While, then, criticism has not failed to follow Mr. Washington, yet the prevailing public opinion of the land has been but too willing to deliver the solution of a wearisome problem into his hands, and say, "If that is all you and your race ask, take it."

Among his own people, however, Mr. Washington has encountered the strongest and most lasting opposition, amounting at times to bitterness, and even today continuing strong and insistent even though largely silenced in outward expression by the public opinion of the nation. Some of this opposition is, of course, mere envy; the disappointment of displaced demagogues and the spite of narrow minds. But aside from this, there is among educated and thoughtful colored men in all parts of the land a feeling of deep regret, sorrow, and apprehension at the wide currency and ascendancy which some of Mr. Washington's theories have gained. These same men admire his sincerity of purpose, and are willing to forgive much to honest endeavor which is doing something worth the doing. They cooperate with Mr. Washington as far as they conscientiously can; and, indeed, it is no ordinary tribute to this man's tact and power that, steering as he must between so many diverse interests and opinions, he so largely retains the respect of all.

But the hushing of the criticism of honest opponents is a dangerous thing. It leads some of the best of the critics to unfortunate silence and paralysis of effort, and others to burst into speech so passionately and intemperately as to lose listeners. Honest and earnest criticism from those whose interests are most nearly touched,—criticism of writers by readers, of government by those governed, of leaders by those led,—this is the soul of democracy and the safeguard of modern society. If the best of the American Negroes receive by outer pressure a leader whom they had not recognized before, manifestly there is here a certain palpable gain. Yet there is also irreparable loss,—a loss of that peculiarly valuable education which a group receives when by search and criticism it finds and commissions its own leaders. The way in which this is done is at once the most elementary and the nicest problem of social growth. History is but the record of such group leadership; and yet how infinitely changeful is its type and character! And of all types and kinds, what can be more instructive than the leadership of a group within a group?—that curious double movement where real progress may be negative and actual advance be relative retrogression. All this is the social student's inspiration and despair.

Now in the past the American Negro has had instructive experience in the choosing of group leaders, founding thus a peculiar dynasty which in the light of present conditions is worthwhile studying. When sticks and stones and beasts form the sole environment of a people, their attitude is largely one of determined opposition to and conquest of natural forces. But when to earth and brute is added an environment of men and ideas, then the attitude of the imprisoned group may take three main forms,—a feeling of revolt and revenge; an attempt to adjust all thought and action to the will of the greater group; or, finally, a determined effort at self-realization and self-development despite environing opinion. The influence of all of these attitudes at various times can be traced in the history of the American Negro, and in the evolution of his successive leaders.

Before 1750, while the fire of African freedom still burned in the veins of the slaves, there was in all leadership or attempted leadership but the one motive of revolt and revenge,—typified in the terrible Maroons, the Danish blacks, and Cato of Stono,[1] and veiling all the Americas in fear of insurrection. The liberalizing tendencies of the latter half of the eighteenth century brought, along with kindlier relations between black and white, thoughts of ultimate adjustment and assimilation. Such aspiration was especially voiced in the earnest songs of Phyllis, in the martyrdom of Attucks, the fighting of Salem and Poor, the intellectual accomplishments of Banneker and Derham, and the political demands of the Cuffes.[2]

Stern financial and social stress after the war cooled much of the previous humanitarian ardor. The disappointment and impatience of the Negroes at the persistence of slavery and serfdom voiced itself in two movements. The slaves in the South, aroused undoubtedly by vague rumors of the Haytian revolt, made three fierce attempts at insurrection,—in 1800 under Gabriel in Virginia, in 1822 under Vesey in Carolina, and in 1831 again in Virginia under the terrible Nat Turner.[3] In the Free States, on the other hand, a new and curious attempt at self-development was made. In Philadelphia and New York color prescription led to a with-

---

1. **Maroons . . . Stono.** *Maroons*—fugitive slaves or their descendants; *Danish blacks*—slaves in the Danish West Indies who revolted in 1733; *Cato of Stono*—leader of a slave revolt in South Carolina
2. **Phyllis . . . the Cuffes.** *Phillis Wheatley*—(c.1753–1784) African-American poet; *Crispus Attucks*—(c.1723–1770) slain leader of the Boston Massacre; *Peter Salem*—(d.1816) African-American patriot killed in the battle of Bunker Hill; *Benjamin Banneker*—(1731–1800) African-American mathematician; *James Derham*—(1762–?) first recognized African-American physician; *Paul Cuffe*—(1759–1817) organizer of a movement to resettle African Americans in African colonies
3. **Gabriel . . . Turner.** *Gabriel*—(c.1775–1800) conspired to attack Richmond, Virginia; *Denmark Vesey*—(c.1767–1822) led an unsuccessful uprising in 1822; *Nat Turner*—(1800–1831) led the Southampton insurrection in 1831, in which one hundred slaves and sixty-one whites were killed.

drawal of Negro communicants from white churches and the formation of a peculiar socio-religious institution among the Negroes known as the African Church,—an organization still living and controlling in its various branches over a million of men.

Walker's[1] wild appeal against the trend of the times showed how the world was changing after the coming of the cotton-gin. By 1830, slavery seemed hopelessly fastened on the South, and the slaves thoroughly cowed into submission. The free Negroes of the North, inspired by the mulatto immigrants from the West Indies, began to change the basis of their demands; they recognized the slavery of slaves, but insisted that they themselves were freemen, and sought assimilation and amalgamation with the nation on the same terms with other men. Thus, Forten and Purvis of Philadelphia, Shad of Wilmington, Du Bois of New Haven, Barbadoes[2] of Boston, and others, strove singly and together as men, they said, not as slaves; as "people of color," not as "Negroes." The trend of the times, however, refused them recognition save in individual and exceptional cases, considered them as one with all the despised blacks, and they soon found themselves striving to keep even the rights they formerly had of voting and working and moving as freemen. Schemes of migration and colonization arose among them; but these they refused to entertain, and they eventually turned to the Abolition movement as a final refuge.

Here, led by Remond, Nell, Wells-Brown, and Douglass,[3] a new period of self-assertion and self-development dawned. To be sure, ultimate freedom and assimilation was the ideal before the leaders, but the assertion of the manhood rights of the Negro by himself was the main reliance, and John Brown's raid was the extreme of its logic. After the war and emancipation, the great form of Frederick Douglass, the greatest of American Negro leaders, still led the host. Self-assertion, especially in political lines, was the main program, and behind Douglass came Elliot, Bruce, and Langston, and the Reconstruction politicians, and, less conspicuous but of greater social significance Alexander Crummell and Bishop Daniel Payne.[4]

Then came the Revolution of 1876, the suppression of the Negro votes, the changing and shifting of ideals, and the seeking of new lights in the great night. Douglass, in his old age, still bravely stood for the ideals of his early manhood,—ultimate assimilation *through* self-assertion, and on no other terms. For a time Price arose as a new leader, destined, it seemed, not to give up, but to restate the old ideals in a form less repugnant to the white South. But he passed away in his prime. Then came the new leader. Nearly all the former ones had become leaders by the silent suffrage of their fellows, had sought to lead their own people alone, and were usually, save Douglass, little known outside their race. But Booker T. Washington arose as essentially the leader not of one race but of two,—a compromiser between the South, the North, and the Negro. Naturally the Negroes resented, at first bitterly, signs of compromise which surrendered their civil and political rights, even though this was to be

exchanged for larger chances of economic development. The rich and dominating North, however, was not only weary of the race problem, but was investing largely in Southern enterprises, and welcomed any method of peaceful cooperation. Thus, by national opinion, the Negroes began to recognize Mr. Washington's leadership; and the voice of criticism was hushed.

Mr. Washington represents in Negro thought the old attitude of adjustment and submission; but adjustment at such a peculiar time as to make his program unique. This is an age of unusual economic development, and Mr. Washington's program naturally takes an economic cast, becoming a gospel of Work and Money to such an extent as apparently almost completely to overshadow the higher aims of life. Moreover, this is an age when the more advanced races are coming in closer contact with the less developed races, and the race-feeling is therefore intensified; and Mr. Washington's program practically accepts the alleged inferiority of the Negro races. Again, in our own land, the reaction from the sentiment of wartime has given impetus to race-prejudice against Negroes, and Mr. Washington withdraws many of the high demands of Negroes as men and American citizens. In other periods of intensified prejudice all the Negro's tendency to self-assertion has been called forth; at this period a policy of submission is advocated. In the history of nearly all other races and peoples the doctrine preached at such crises has been that manly self-respect is worth more than lands and houses, and that a people who voluntarily surrender such respect, or cease striving for it, are not worth civilizing.

---

1. **Walker's.** *David Walker*—(1785–1830) author of an inflammatory antislavery pamphlet
2. **Forten . . . Barbadoes.** *James Forten*—(1766–1842) African-American philanthropist and civic leader; *Robert Purvis*—(1810–1898) founder of the American Anti-Slavery Society and president of the Underground Railroad; *Abraham Shadd*—African-American abolitionist and activist; *Alexander Du Bois*—(1803–1887) W. E. B. Du Bois's grandfather, co-founder of the Negro Episcopal Parish of St. Luke; *James G. Barbadoes*—(c.1796–1841) delegate to the first National Negro Convention
3. **Remond . . . Douglass.** *Charles Lenox Remond*—(1810–1873) African-American leader; *William Cooper Nell*—(1816–1874) first African American to acquire a governmental position (clerk in the post office), abolitionist, writer, and advocate for equal education; *William Wells Brown*—(c.1816–1884) publisher of *Clotel*, the first novel and play by an African American; *Fredrick Douglass*—(1817–1895) African-American abolitionist and diplomat
4. **Elliot . . . Payne.** *Robert Brown Elliot*—(1842–1884) African-American South Carolina congressman in the United States House of Representatives; *Blanche K. Bruce*—(1841–1898) first African-American man to serve a full term in the United States Senate (1875–1881); *John Mercer Langston*—(1829–1897) African-American congressman, lawyer, diplomat, educator; *Alexander Crummell*—(1819–1898) clergyman of the protestant Episcopal Church, missionary in Liberia for twenty years and then in Washington, DC; *Daniel Alexander Payne*—(1811–1893) bishop of the African Methodist Episcopal Church and president of Wilberforce University (1863–1876)

In answer to this, it has been claimed that the Negro can survive only through submission. Mr. Washington distinctly asks that black people give up, at least for the present, three things,—

First, political power,

Second, insistence on civil rights,

Third, higher education of Negro youth,—and concentrate all their energies on industrial education, the accumulation of wealth, and the conciliation of the South. This policy has been courageously and insistently advocated for over fifteen years, and has been triumphant for perhaps ten years. As a result of this tender of the palm-branch, what has been the return? In these years there have occurred:

1. The disfranchisement of the Negro.

2. The legal creation of a distinct status of civil inferiority for the Negro.

3. The steady withdrawal of aid from institutions for the higher training of the Negro.

These movements are not, to be sure, direct results of Mr. Washington's teachings; but his propaganda has, without a shadow of doubt, helped their speedier accomplishment. The question then comes: Is it possible, and probable, that nine millions of men can make effective progress in economic lines if they are deprived of political rights, made a servile caste, and allowed only the most meager chance for developing their exceptional men? If history and reason give any distinct answer to these questions, it is an emphatic *No.* And Mr. Washington thus faces the triple paradox of his career:

1. He is striving nobly to make Negro artisans businessmen and property-owners; but it is utterly impossible, under modern competitive methods, for workingmen and property-owners to defend their rights and exist without the right of suffrage.

2. He insists on thrift and self-respect, but at the same time counsels a silent submission to civic inferiority such as is bound to sap the manhood of any race in the long run.

3. He advocates common-school and industrial training, and depreciates institutions of higher learning; but neither the Negro common schools, nor Tuskegee itself, could remain open a day were it not for teachers trained in Negro colleges, or trained by their graduates.

This triple paradox in Mr. Washington's position is the object of criticism by two classes of colored Americans. One class is spiritually descended from Toussaint the Savior,[1] through Gabriel, Vesey, and Turner, and they represent the attitude of revolt and revenge; they hate the white South blindly and distrust the white race generally, and so far as they agree on definite action, think that the Negro's only hope lies in emigration beyond the borders of the United States. And yet, by the irony of fate, nothing has more effectually made this program seem hopeless than the recent course of the United States toward weaker and darker peoples in the West Indies, Hawaii, and the Philippines,—for where in the world may we go and be safe from lying and brute force?

The other class of Negroes who cannot agree with Mr. Washington has hitherto said little aloud. They deprecate the sight of scattered counsels, of internal disagreement; and especially they dislike making their just criticism of a useful and earnest man an excuse for a general discharge of venom from small-minded opponents. Nevertheless, the questions involved are so fundamental and serious that it is difficult to see how men like the Grimkes, Kelly Miller, J. W. E. Bowen,[2] and other representatives of this group, can much longer be silent. Such men feel in conscience bound to ask of this nation three things:

1. The right to vote.

2. Civic equality.

3. The education of youth according to ability.

They acknowledge Mr. Washington's invaluable service in counselling patience and courtesy in such demands; they do not ask that ignorant black men vote when ignorant whites are debarred, or that any reasonable restrictions in the suffrage should not be applied; they know that the low social level of the mass of the race is responsible for much discrimination against it, but they also know, and the nation knows, that relentless color-prejudice is more often a cause than a result of the Negro's degradation; they seek the abatement of this relic of barbarism, and not its systematic encouragement and pampering by all agencies of social power from the Associated Press to the Church of Christ. They advocate, with Mr. Washington, a broad system of Negro common schools supplemented by thorough industrial training; but they are surprised that a man of Mr. Washington's insight cannot see that no such educational system ever has rested or can rest on any other basis than that of the well-equipped college and university, and they insist that there is a demand for a few such institutions throughout the South to train the best of the Negro youth as teachers, professional men, and leaders.

This group of men honor Mr. Washington for his attitude of conciliation toward the white South; they accept the "Atlanta Compromise" in its broadest interpretation; they recognize, with him, many signs of promise, many men of high purpose and fair judgment, in this section; they know that no easy task has been laid upon a region already tottering under heavy burdens. But, nevertheless, they insist that the way to truth and right lies in straightforward honesty, not in indiscriminate flattery; in praising those of the South who do well and criticizing uncompromisingly those who do ill; in taking advantage of the opportunities at hand and urging their fellows to do the same, but at the same time in remembering that only a firm adherence to their higher

---

1. **Toussaint the Savior.** *Pierre-Dominique Toussaint*—(c.1743–1803), Haitian general and liberator

2. **Grimkes . . . Bowen.** *Archibald Grimke*—(1849–1930) and *Francis Grimke*—(1850–1937), civic leaders concerned with African-American affairs; *Kelly Miller*—(1863–1939) dean of Howard University, lecturer on African-American issues; *John Wesley Edward Bowen*—(1855–?) clergyman and educator

ideals and aspirations will ever keep those ideals within the realm of possibility. They do not expect that the free right to vote, to enjoy civic rights, and to be educated will come in a moment; they do not expect to see the bias and prejudices of years disappear at the blast of a trumpet; but they are absolutely certain that the way for a people to gain their reasonable rights is not by voluntarily throwing them away and insisting that they do not want them; that the way for a people to gain respect is not by continually belittling and ridiculing themselves that, on the contrary, Negroes must insist continually, in season and out of season, that voting is necessary to modern manhood, that color discrimination is barbarism, and that black boys need education as well as white boys.

In failing thus to state plainly and unequivocally the legitimate demands of their people, even at the cost of opposing an honored leader, the thinking classes of American Negroes would shirk a heavy responsibility,—a responsibility to themselves, a responsibility to the struggling masses, a responsibility to the darker races of men whose future depends so largely on this American experiment, but especially a responsibility to this nation,—this common Fatherland. It is wrong to encourage a man or a people in evil-doing, it is wrong to aid and abet a national crime simply because it is unpopular not to do so. The growing spirit of kindliness and reconciliation between the North and South after the frightful differences of a generation ago ought to be a source of deep congratulation to all, and especially to those whose mistreatment caused the war; but if that reconciliation is to be marked by the industrial slavery and civic death of those same black men, with permanent legislation into a position of inferiority, then those black men, if they are really men, are called upon by every consideration of patriotism and loyalty to oppose such a course by all civilized methods, even though such opposition involves disagreement with Mr. Booker T. Washington. We have no right to sit silently by while the inevitable seeds are sown for a harvest of disaster to our children black and white.

First, it is the duty of black men to judge the South discriminatingly. The present generation of Southerners are not responsible for the past, and they should not be blindly hated or blamed for it. Furthermore, to no class is the indiscriminate endorsement of the recent course of the South toward Negroes more nauseating than to the best thought of the South. The South is not "solid"; it is a land in the ferment of social change, wherein forces of all kinds are fighting for supremacy; and to praise the ill the South is today perpetrating is just as wrong as to condemn the good. Discriminating and broad-minded criticism is what the South needs,—needs it for the sake of her own white sons and daughters, and for the insurance of robust, healthy mental and moral development.

Today even the attitude of the Southern whites toward the blacks is not, as so many assume, in all cases the same; the ignorant Southerner hates the Negro, the workingmen fear his competition, the money-makers wish to use him as a laborer, some of the educated see a menace in his upward development, while others—usually the sons of the masters—wish to help him to rise. National opinion has enabled this last class to maintain the Negro common schools, and to protect the Negro partially in property, life, and limb. Through the pressure of the money-makers, the Negro is in danger of being reduced to semi-slavery, especially in the country districts; the workingmen, and those of the educated who fear the Negro, have united to disfranchise him, and some have urged his deportation; while the passions of the ignorant are easily aroused to lynch and abuse any black man. To praise this intricate whirl of thought and prejudice is nonsense; to inveigh indiscriminately against "the South" is unjust; but to use the same breath in praising Governor Aycock, exposing Senator Morgan, arguing with Mr. Thomas Nelson Page, and denouncing Senator Ben Tillman,[1] is not only sane, but the imperative duty of thinking black men.

It would be unjust to Mr. Washington not to acknowledge that in several instances he has opposed movements in the South which were unjust to the Negro; he sent memorials to the Louisiana and Alabama constitutional conventions, he has spoken against lynching, and in other ways has openly or silently set his influence against sinister schemes and unfortunate happenings. Notwithstanding this, it is equally true to assert that on the whole the distinct impression left by Mr. Washington's propaganda is, first, that the South is justified in its present attitude toward the Negro because of the Negro's degradation; secondly, that the prime cause of the Negro's failure to rise more quickly is his wrong education in the past; and, thirdly, that his future rise depends primarily on his own efforts. Each of these propositions is a dangerous half-truth. The supplementary truths must never be lost sight of: first, slavery and race-prejudice are potent if not sufficient causes of the Negro's position; second, industrial and common-school training were necessarily slow in planting because they had to await the black teachers trained by higher institutions,—it being extremely doubtful if any essentially different development was possible, and certainly a Tuskegee was unthinkable before 1880; and, third, while it is a great truth to say that the Negro must strive and strive mightily to help himself, it is equally true that unless his striving be not simply seconded, but rather aroused and encouraged, by the initiative of the richer and wiser environing group, he cannot hope for great success.

In his failure to realize and impress this last point, Mr. Washington is especially to be criticized. His doctrine has tended to make the whites, North and South, shift the

---

1. **Governor Aycock . . . Ben Tillman.** *Charles Brantley Aycock*—(1859–1905) governor of North Carolina; *Edwin Denison Morgan*—governor of New York (1859–1863) and United States senator; *Thomas Nelson Page*—(1853–1922) novelist who glamorized the Southern plantation; *Benjamin Ryan Tillman*—(1847–1918) United States senator who presented the views of Southern extremists

burden of the Negro problem to the Negro's shoulders and stand aside as critical and rather pessimistic spectators; when in fact the burden belongs to the nation, and the hands of none of us are clean if we bend not our energies to righting these great wrongs.

The South ought to be led, by candid and honest criticism, to assert her better self and do her full duty to the race she has cruelly wronged and is still wronging. The North—her co-partner in guilt—cannot salve her conscience by plastering it with gold. We cannot settle this problem by diplomacy and suaveness, by "policy" alone. If worse come to worst, can the moral fiber of this country survive the slow throttling and murder of nine millions of men?

The black men of America have a duty to perform, a duty stern and delicate,—a forward movement to oppose a part of the work of their greatest leader. So far as Mr. Washington preaches Thrift, Patience, and Industrial Training for the masses, we must hold up his hands and strive with him, rejoicing in his honors and glorying in the strength of this Joshua called of God and of man to lead the headless host. But so far as Mr. Washington apologizes for injustice, North or South, does not rightly value the privilege and duty of voting, belittles the emasculating effects of caste distinctions, and opposes the higher training and ambition of our brighter minds,—so far as he, the South or the Nation, does this,—we must unceasingly and firmly oppose them. By every civilized and peaceful method we must strive for the rights which the world accords to men, clinging unwaveringly to those great words which the sons of the Fathers would fain forget: "We hold these truths to be self-evident: That all men are created equal; that they are endowed by their Creator with certain inalienable rights; that among these are life, liberty, and the pursuit of happiness."

## from *Their Eyes Were Watching God*
## by Zora Neale Hurston

It was a spring afternoon in West Florida. Janie had spent most of the day under a blossoming pear tree in the back-yard. She had been spending every minute that she could steal from her chores under that tree for the last three days. That was to say, ever since the first tiny bloom had opened. It had called her to come and gaze on a mystery. From barren brown stems to glistening leaf-buds; from the leaf-buds to snowy virginity of bloom. It stirred her tremendously. How? Why? It was like a flute song forgotten in another existence and remembered again. What? How? Why? This singing she heard that had nothing to do with her ears. The rose of the world was breathing out smell. It followed her through all her waking moments and caressed her in her sleep. It connected itself with other vaguely felt mat-

ters that had struck her outside observation and buried themselves in her flesh. Now they emerged and quested about her consciousness.

She was stretched on her back beneath the pear tree soaking in the alto chant of the visiting bees, the gold of the sun and the panting breath of the breeze when the inaudible voice of it all came to her. She saw a dust-bearing bee sink into the sanctum of a bloom; the thousand sister-calyxes arch to meet the love embrace and the ecstatic shiver of the tree from root to tiniest branch creaming in every blossom and frothing with delight. So this was a marriage! She had been summoned to behold a revelation. Then Janie felt a pain remorseless sweet that left her limp and languid.

After a while she got up from where she was and went over the little garden field entire. She was seeking confirmation of the voice and vision, and everywhere she found and acknowledged answers. A personal answer for all other creations except herself. She felt an answer seeking her, but where? When? How? She found herself at the kitchen door and stumbled inside. In the air of the room were flies tumbling and singing, marrying and giving in marriage. When she reached the narrow hallway she was reminded that her grandmother was home with a sick headache. She was lying across the bed asleep so Janie tipped on out of the front door. Oh to be a pear tree—*any* tree in bloom! With kissing bees singing of the beginning of the world! She was sixteen. She had glossy leaves and bursting buds and she wanted to struggle with life but it seemed to elude her. Where were the singing bees for her? Nothing on the place nor in her grandma's house answered her. She searched as much of the world as she could from the top of the front steps and then went on down to the front gate and leaned over to gaze up and down the road. Looking, waiting, breathing short with impatience. Waiting for the world to be made.

Through pollinated air she saw a glorious being coming up the road. In her former blindness she had known him as shiftless Johnny Taylor, tall and lean. That was before the golden dust of pollen had beglamored his rags and her eyes.

In the last stages of Nanny's sleep, she dreamed of voices. Voices far-off but persistent, and gradually coming nearer. Janie's voice. Janie talking in whispery snatches with a male voice she couldn't quite place. That brought her wide awake. She bolted upright and peered out of the window and saw Johnny Taylor lacerating her Janie with a kiss.

"Janie!"

The old woman's voice was so lacking in command and reproof, so full of crumbling dissolution,—that Janie half believed that Nanny had not seen her. So she extended herself outside of her dream and went inside of the house. That was the end of her childhood.

# Guided Writing

## WRITING A LYRIC POEM

Take a survey among your friends. How many music CDs do they have? Several? Hundreds? Likely, you and your friends listen to music daily—in your cars, in your rooms, while you study, while you work, while you relax, while you sleep. The appeal of music is the combination of words, sound, and rhythm that touches hearts and minds.

The same aspects of good music—words, sound, and rhythm—are present in lyric poetry. In addition to being highly musical, a lyric poem focuses on expressing the emotions of its speaker, often using figurative language and rhythmic and rhyming patterns. Thus, like music, the appeal of lyric poetry is the combination of words, sound, and rhythm that touches hearts and minds.

**WRITING ASSIGNMENT.** In this assignment, you will write a lyric poem that expresses your emotions about a particular subject.

### Professional Model
"A Black Man Talks of Reaping" by Arna Bontemps

> I have sown beside all waters in my day.
> I planted deep, within my heart the fear
> that wind or fowl would take the grain away.
> I planted safe against this stark, lean year.
>
> I scattered seed enough to plant the land
> in rows from Canada to Mexico
> but for my reaping only what the hand
> can hold at once is all that I can show.
>
> Yet what I sowed and what the orchard yields
> my brother's sons are gathering stalk and root:
> small wonder then my children glean in fields
> they have not sown, and feed on bitter fruit.

**EXAMINING THE MODEL.** In simple yet beautiful language, Arna Bontemps expresses the sorrow and bitterness of a man who has worked hard all his life, planting "seeds" which he hoped

"For me poems usually begin with 'true things'—people, experiences, quotes—but quickly ride off into that other territory of imagination, which lives alongside us as much as we will allow in a world that likes to pay too much attention to 'facts' sometimes."

—Naomi Shihab Nye

would become fruit for his children to enjoy—only to find that others benefited from his labor and he was left with nothing. Because Bontemps chose to express these thoughts and emotions in a lyric poem, he carefully chose words and structured their rhythm to accentuate his expression.

Consider why Bontemps chose to begin the sentences in the first two stanzas with "I." Note how this parallel structure cues the reader to focus on the speaker's accomplishments. Read the first two stanzas aloud. Notice how the parallel structure creates a distinct rhythm that seems to flow along with the speaker's thoughts. In the last stanza, however, the sentence structure becomes more complex, and the melodious rhythm nearly disappears. What change in thought accompanies this change in structure?

Say out loud the words in the poem with long vowel sounds—*sown, deep, take, away.* How do their smooth, low tones capture the sound of mournful frustration? This, too, changes in the last stanza. "Yet what . . ." has a biting sound as do the clipped vowels and harsh consonants in the phrases "stalk and root" and "bitter fruit." These harsh sounds in the final stanza contrast with the smoothness found in the first two stanzas. What mood is conveyed in the final stanza?

Finally, Bontemps chose a rhythm and rhyme scheme for his poem. Notice that each line of the poem consists of ten beats. This particular rhythm, or **meter**, is known as pentameter. The **rhyme scheme** of the poem is *abab, cdcd,* and *efef.* In other words, every other line in each stanza rhymes.

Through the use of parallel structure, careful word choice, rhythm, and rhyme, Bontemps greatly increases the impact of his poem. This example shows that a poem's ability to communicate the speaker's feelings lies not only in *what* the poet says, but in *how* he or she says it.

## Prewriting

**IDENTIFYING YOUR AUDIENCE.** A poet first writes not for others, but for him- or her*self,* in order to discover what he or she knows, thinks, and feels about a subject. Sometimes, after the words are on paper, the poet realizes that the poem is saying something original, saying something in a new way. Then, like a little kid who has just made something, the poet has to show the poem to someone else. For this writing assignment, write first for yourself, but be prepared to share with your peers.

**FINDING YOUR VOICE.** Bontemps's voice—his use of language to reflect his attitude toward his topic and audience—comes through clearly in the simple language, word choice, repetition of sentence structure, and tone. To find your voice, you have to express yourself about something that is important to you. What are your sources of passion? joy? sadness? Take a few

"Sit down right now. Write whatever's running through you . . . Don't try to control it. Stay present with whatever comes up, and keep your hand moving."
—Natalie Goldberg

In his book *The Dyer's Hand* W. H. Auden says: "The questions that interest me most when reading a poem are two: 1. Here is a verbal contraption. How does it work? 2. What kind of guy inhabits this poem?"

Asking these questions can help you begin to develop taste, critical judgment, a knowledge of the craft of writing poetry, and a sense of humanity.

"For me a poem doesn't always start at the beginning. The idea may be a word, a phrase, or a whole sentence that eventually turns up anywhere in the poem, depending on what I do with it and how much I revise to say exactly what I want to say."

—Margaret Hillert

minutes and freewrite about these. You may discover (or rediscover) the forces that move you. Express them and you'll express your voice.

Sound like yourself. You don't need to sound stiff and formal, unless you want to sound that way. At the same time, your voice might not ring true if you are trying to sound like someone that you are not.

## Student Model—Graphic Organizer

**WRITING WITH A PLAN.** Create a cluster chart to get your ideas going. Start with the phrase "I have . . ." and put this at the center of your paper. Then branch out from there writing down whatever comes to mind. See where it goes. Try for thirty items. Some will relate, some won't, but don't worry about it right now. Some items will list things ("I have a baby sister"), but some will be experiences ("I have seen the space shuttle take off"). Others may be statements of beliefs or philosophy such as: "I have a love of the quiet."

For example, Neil's cluster chart included the following details:

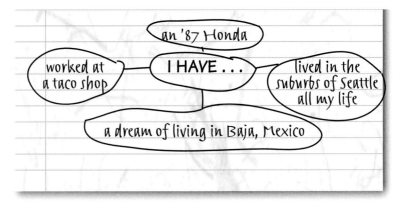

After you have exhausted yourself of ideas, go back through the list to see if you can see a pattern forming. If there are several items that relate, this may be your topic. You don't need to use all the items—in fact, you should not use all the items. If, however, there are a couple that seem to connect, they probably mean something to you. This is an activity of self-discovery, and one of the best ways of discovering is by writing things down. So, start with one of your "I haves" and freewrite for ten minutes or so. Don't be concerned with organization, order, or mechanics. Don't focus on only writing facts; you are writing poetry now, not journalism, so use your poetic license to associate your ideas with images. If there are things you don't know or don't remember, make up what you need to make up.

Neil started writing a nostalgic piece about his old Honda, but then his imagination took off. His description of an old car began to express thoughts about family and America.

I have an '87 Honda Civic, rust brown—
except for the rear fender that has
natural rust, no paint—with over 246K
miles and the speedometer broke the
day after I got it 14 months, two
weeks and three days ago. The
windshield is cracked. The interior is
vinyl, but a high quality vinyl that
in the winter stays cold and in the
summer hot. The dash split, right next
to the speedometer so I keep a five
dollar bill, folded 8 times hid there
in the crack. When I fill the gas tank,
the car's value doubles. It sits on
the street, collecting the sap from
the maple while my dad's Explorer
dreams of exploring more than the
commute to work and Mom's Acura which
never goes farther than the gourmet
store where she can find the cinnamon
she likes and which is very accurate
share the garage. The transmission
grinds, the main seal leaks, the
starter sometimes doesn't, the duct
tape that holds the left front
headlight needs to be replaced, but it
gets me to school, it gets me to Joe's
Tacos to work so I can pay the
insurance, to Wes's house where we
chill for hours. Someday it will get
me out of here. It is my ride and
there are better looking cars around
but none that were purchased with the
sweat of my brow as it dripped into
soft shelled tacos.

## Drafting

After you have something down, start putting the information into some type of structure. Think about order, but don't worry about rhymes or meter yet. Instead, try to break lines at natural places. If you are working on a computer, use the return key to do this; also be willing to delete. If you are writing in longhand, concentrate on how the lines fall as you write them out. Cross out, move, and rewrite lines until they sound right.

Neil's freewriting, which began as a paragraph, started to take on the sound and rhythm of a poem when he inserted line breaks that divided the writing into thoughts.

"A poem compresses much into a small space and adds music, thus heightening its meaning."

—E. B. White

## Language, Grammar, and Style

**Effective Language**
IDENTIFYING EFFECTIVE LANGUAGE. Different types of writing require different qualities to be effective. The effectiveness of some writing depends on its having the appropriate **tone**, whether formal or informal. **Register**—the use of an appropriate voice for the audience, can determine effectiveness, too. Not so in poetry. Poetry gives you the freedom to use any tone or voice you choose, and to say practically anything you want. It can also be freer in the ordering of words and the use of punctuation.

But poetry has its own set of rules. Most importantly, since poetry packs a lot of meaning into very few words, your language must be concise. At the same time, your language

*continued on page 676*

must be imaginative and should move the reader through its musical sound. To create an effective poem, therefore, requires a bit of thought.

Recall that poets spend a lot of time on revision. The finished product may be only a few stanzas in length, but you can bet that it took many months to get that poem "just so." So you need to play around with your poem. Cut your lines down to the fewest words possible to make your language concise. Add figures of speech like metaphor, simile, and personification. Try changing the words to create different rhymes. Use sound techniques like alliteration, assonance, consonance, and onomatopoeia.

Also recall that whether the poem is effective or not is for the most part subjective. As you revise, trust your own ear and your own senses to decide what sounds right.

Read the following lines from Neil's first draft and final draft, listening for idea, rhythm, and sound. Which language choices are most effective? How do the changes in the final draft reflect a more effective use of language in terms of word choice, rhythm, and rhyme?

## First Draft

while my dad's Explorer
   dreams of exploring more
   than the commute to work
   and Mom's Acura which
   never goes farther than the
   gourmet store
where she can find the
   cinnamon she likes
and which is very accurate
   share the garage.

## Student Model—Draft

My '87 Honda Civic,
rust brown—except for the rear fenders
that are natural rust, no paint—with
   over 246K miles and
the speedometer broke the day after I
   got it
14 months, two weeks and three days
   ago.
The windshield is cracked.
The interior is vinyl, but a high
   quality vinyl
that in the winter stays cold and in
   the summer hot.
The dash split, right next to the
   speedometer
so I keep a five dollar bill, folded 8
   times hid there in the crack.
When I fill the gas tank, the car's
   value doubles.

It sits on the street, collecting the
   sap from the maple
while my dad's Explorer dreams of
   exploring more than the commute to
   work and Mom's Accura which
never goes farther than the gourmet
   store
where she can find the cinnamon she
   likes
share the garage.
The transmission grinds,
the main seal leaks,
the starter sometimes doesn't,
the duct tape that holds the left front
   headlight needs to be replaced,
but it gets me to school,
it gets me to Joe's Tacos to work so I
   can pay the insurance,
to my friend Wes's house where we chill
   for hours.
Someday it will get me out of here.

It is my ride and
there are better looking cars around
but none that were purchased
with the sweat of my brow
as it dripped into
soft shelled tacos.

Poets like to play, especially with words. Now is your chance to start. Read the lines of your draft as you have separated them. Do the lines say what you want them to say? Are there ideas or expressions that you think are missing or that aren't needed? Would some thoughts and expressions have more impact if they appeared in a different place in the poem? Experiment with adding, removing, and reorganizing the lines.

Listen to the words. How do the words sound together? Are there any extra syllables or words that could be cut or added? Recall how Bontemps used words like *sown* and *deep,* with long vowel sounds, to accentuate the mood of sorrow. Are there word changes you could make to further develop a sound that matches your thoughts? Would the use of rhyme add to the poem, or detract from it by forcing you to use words that aren't quite right? Play with the words. If you decide to rhyme your poem, keep in mind that you can use a number of different rhyme schemes—*abab,* or every other line; *abba, abcabc,* and so on. You can also use **slant rhyme,** rhyme which is not exact. *Rave/rove* and *rot/rock* are two examples.

Now, listen to the rhythm and flow of the lines. Do any of the lines sound too short or too long? Would running several lines together reinforce the intent of a thought? Would breaking lines into smaller sections emphasize a point? You may wish to use pentameter, or ten beats per line, as in Bontemps's poem. This creates a very even, strict rhythm and may require you to mix and match words until you get it right. But even if you use pentameter, you can depart from it in some lines if it helps your poem. Fuss and finesse until the thoughts in the poem move the way you want them.

## Self- and Peer Evaluation

Read your poem out loud, listening for the effect. Have your classmates listen and read with you and let them offer suggestions. Sometimes the reader and listener can see and hear things that are going on that the writer hasn't even considered. Complete a self-evaluation and peer evaluation using the following questions.

- What thoughts and emotions does the poem reflect? What reaction does this poem stir in the reader?
- Where might the poem further develop the thoughts and emotions? Where might the expression be toned down?
- Which words seem to purposely resound with the poem's ideas? Which words might be replaced with a more purposeful word choice?
- Where is the best flow of language? Where does the rhythm move the reader? What changes might speed up an appropriate line or slow a reader down to more fully grasp the meaning? What changes might create a more effective rhyme or even meter?

**Final Draft**
while my dad's Explorer
   dreams to explore
more than the commute to
   work.
Mom's Acura voyages to the
   store,
in quest of her gourmet
   spice, where the clerk
smiles and secretly smirks.

**FIXING INEFFECTIVE LANGUAGE.**
Evaluate these lines from Neil's first draft for their effectiveness. Suppose Neil were trying to convey a sense of anxiety over some of the car's problems and a sense of satisfaction that the car still does what he requires. What changes in organization, word choice, and rhythm would you make?

The transmission grinds,
the main seal leaks,
the starter sometimes
   doesn't,
the duct tape that holds the
   left front headlight needs
   to be replaced,
but it gets me to school,
it gets me to Joe's Tacos to
   work so I can pay the
   insurance,
to my friend Wes's house
   where we chill for hours.
Someday it will get me out
   of here.

**USING EFFECTIVE LANGUAGE.**
Read your poem with a critical eye as to the effectiveness of the language. Find at least two places where a change in organization, word choice, or rhythm would improve the effectiveness of the language.

## Student Model—Revised

Neil added and deleted some ideas, moved lines and even entire stanzas around, and worked to get the words right. He decided to rhyme every other line, so he adjusted both words and placement. Notice that in some places he did not stick to the *abab* rhyme scheme, and in other places he used slant rhyme instead of exact rhyme. Since Neil wanted to create an even rhythm, or meter, he worked until he had ten beats per line in the second stanza, and alternating ten beats in the first and third stanzas. Notice that in the final stanza, Neil used shorter lines.

What is the rhyme scheme of the first stanza? What tone, or attitude does Neil communicate?

Note how Neil changed and reworded this stanza to create rhyme and a meter of ten beats per line. Do you think the rhyme works here, or does it seem forced?

How does Neil use parallel structure in the final stanza? What mood is conveyed in this final stanza?

My '87 Honda rests on the street,
collecting sap from the oak
on "the best block in town," although
  discreet,
while my dad's Explorer dreams to explore
more than the commute to work.
Mom's Acura voyages to the store,
in quest of her gourmet spice, where the
  clerk
smiles and secretly smirks.

200K miles and more to go
Rust brown—except for the rear fender, see
the speedometer broke while I drove slow
I was just bringing it home tenderly
14 months, two weeks and three days ago.
Chip on the windshield where a rock
  attacked,
Seats of vinyl, such fine quality so
in winter they're cold (a heater is
  lacked).
The dash is split, but this causes no
  troubles—
I keep a five-dollar bill in the crack.
Fill the gas tank, and the car's value
  doubles.

It is my ride—lady killer it's not,
but I earned it, I can say with pride
from the very sweat of my brow's knot
as it dripped into hard-shelled tacos,
  fried.

The transmission grinds,
the main seal leaks a pool,
the starter whines,
but it gets me to school.
It gets me to Joe's Tacos (my career)
it gets me to my friend's place,
where we chill, just dreaming of the day
it will get us out of here.

## Revising and Proofreading

Neil isn't happy with his poem yet. Although he has tightened the rhythm and language of the poem, there are some rough spots that he recognizes, but it takes a long time to get the words right. He realizes, though, that words and lines can be changed, so each time he reads the poem over the next couple of weeks, he will probably make some minor changes.

## Publishing and Presenting

Poetry is best when shared. A videotaped or audiotaped reading gives you an opportunity to share your poem with many and to keep an oral record of it. Or consider reading to a small group of students. Creating a poetry poster is another way to present your poem. Start by printing your poem in a way that suggests the content and the feeling of the poem. Add art, designs, or colors that draw out the ideas. Display your poster in the classroom or publish it in the school newspaper or literary magazine.

"Sometimes I've spent weeks looking for precisely the right word. It's like having a tiny marble in your pocket; you can feel it. Sometimes you find a word and say, 'No, I don't think this is precisely it . . .' Then you discard it, and take another and another until you get it right."

—Eve Merriam

# UNIT REVIEW
## *The Harlem Renaissance*

## Words for Everyday Use

Check your knowledge of the following vocabulary words from the selections in this unit. Write short sentences using these words in context to make the meaning clear. To review the definition or usage of a word, refer to the page number listed or the Glossary of Words for Everyday Use.

| | | |
|---|---|---|
| beau, 654 | exultingly, 661 | rambunctious, 661 |
| caprice, 626 | giddy, 655 | saunter, 662 |
| carriage, 662 | gypsy, 654 | scorn, 629 |
| circumlocution, 661 | helter-skelter, 660 | skirmish, 660 |
| deplore, 660 | lavish, 655 | veneer, 662 |
| disembark, 660 | lean, 653 | venturesome, 660 |
| dowdy, 654 | miscellany, 662 | whim, 653 |
| ebb, 661 | miserly, 654 | wistfully, 655 |
| extenuating, 659 | raiment, 662 | |

## Literary Tools

Define the following terms, giving concrete examples of how they are used in the selections in this unit. To review a term, refer to the page number indicated or to the Handbook of Literary Terms.

| | | |
|---|---|---|
| allusion, 624 | personification, 636 | sonnet, 624 |
| archetype, 658 | point of view, 641 | speaker, 619, 648 |
| effect, 640 | refrain, 640 | symbol, 658 |
| metaphor, 636 | rhyme, 632, 648 | theme, 625, 652, 658 |
| meter, 632 | rhyme scheme, 619 | tone, 632, 641 |
| motivation, 652 | simile, 625, 636, 640 | |

# Reflecting
## *on* YOUR READING

## Genre Studies

1. **ESSAY.** Zora Neale Hurston uses anecdotes in her essay "How It Feels to Be Colored Me." An anecdote is a usually short narrative of an interesting, amusing, or biographical incident. What social purpose is revealed by Hurston's use of anecdotes in this essay?

2. **LYRIC POETRY.** Lyric poetry is highly musical verse that expresses the emotions of a speaker. Compare and contrast the emotional experiences of the speakers in "Yet Do I Marvel" (Countee Cullen) and "A Negro Speaks of Rivers" (Langston Hughes).

# Thematic Studies

3. **IDENTITY.** Discuss the statements of identity in "We Wear the Mask," "The Tropics in New York," "I, too, sing America," "A Black Man Talks of Reaping," "The Richer, the Poorer," and "How It Feels to Be Colored Me."

4. **ARTISTIC EXPRESSION.** Select one of the illustrations in the unit. Discuss how the theme and mood of the art are related to the theme and mood of the writing. Create or describe your artistic expression of this piece of writing.

# Historical/Biographical Studies

5. **SOCIOECONOMICS.** What role does money play in Lottie's life ("The Richer, the Poorer") and in the life of the speaker of "A Black Man Talks of Reaping"? What goals does each have? How are these goals thwarted by financial considerations? What financial reward does the future hold for Lottie and the speaker of "A Black Man Talks of Reaping"?

6. **OPPRESSION.** The Harlem Renaissance developed in part to give voice to the oppression African Americans experienced. What forms of oppression are evident in the selections from this unit?

*New York Movie,* 1939. Edward Hopper.
The Museum of Modern Art, New York.

I am the opposite of the stage musician. He gives you illusion that has the appearance of truth. I give you truth in the pleasant disguise of illusion.

—Tennessee Williams

Thorton Wilder giving a public reading of his play *Our Town,* 1952.

# MODERN DRAMA (1900–1945)

Although mainstream American literature found a voice uniquely its own in the period surrounding the Civil War, serious American drama lagged behind for more than a half-century. Not until after World War I, in the work of **Eugene O'Neill**, did American drama begin to assert importance in world literature.

Throughout the 1920s and into the 1950s, O'Neill (1888–1953) dominated the American stage with such plays as *Beyond the Horizon, Anna Christie, Strange Interlude, Emperor Jones, The Hairy Ape, The Iceman Cometh, A Moon for the Misbegotten,* and *Long Day's Journey into Night.* Known for their brooding realism and symbolic expressionism, his plays explore motifs of love, death, frustration, illusion, and fate. A four-time winner of the Pulitzer Prize for drama, O'Neill received the Nobel Prize for literature in 1936.

During the Depression of the 1930s came plays of social protest, many of them critical of the excesses of American capitalism and of the international growth of fascism. Representative playwrights of the decade were **Clifford Odets, Sidney Kingsley, Robert Sherwood, Lillian Hellman,** and **Maxwell Anderson.**

Immediately following World War II, two American playwrights, **Arthur Miller** (1915–  ) and **Tennessee [Thomas Lanier] Williams** (1911–1983), skyrocketed to prominence. In 1947 Miller's *All My Sons* appeared on Broadway, followed by *Death of a Salesman* (1949), *The Crucible* (1953), *A View from the Bridge* (1955), and *After the Fall* (1964). Frequently revived since their initial productions, Miller's plays are noted for fusing naturalism and symbolism into psycho-dramas of illusion and betrayal. After *The Glass Menagerie* (1945), regarded as "a memory play," opened in New York, Williams went on to write numerous naturalistic dramas famed for their lyricism, sexuality, and violence. These include *A Streetcar Named Desire, Cat on a Hot Tin Roof* (1955), *Suddenly Last Summer* (1958), and *The Night of the Iguana* (1961).

Bridging the pre- and post-World War II period was the work of **Thornton Wilder** (1897–1975), whose plays, rooted in commonplace human realities, continue to delight audiences: *Our Town* opened on Broadway in 1938 and was followed by *The Skin of Our Teeth* (1942) and *The Matchmaker* (1956).

Later **Edward Albee** (1928–  ) would write dramas marked by allegorical confrontations and surrealistic techniques, among them, *The Zoo Story* (1958), *Who's Afraid of Virginia Woolf?* (1962), *Tiny Alice* (1965), and *A Delicate Balance* (1966).

In recent decades a number of American playwrights—**David Rabe, Sam Shepard, August Wilson, Arthur Kopit, Le Roi Jones [Imamu Amiri Baraka], Ed Bullins, David Mamet, Christopher Durang, Marsha Norman, Ntozake Shange,** and **Wendy Wasserstein**—have dealt in their plays with such contemporary American problems as rootlessness, violence, and sexism, or with the realities of the African-American urban experience. Because of rising production costs, the work of these playwrights has often been staged off Broadway or even off off Broadway.

At the beginning of the new millennium, the strength and vitality of American drama seems ensured, thanks to a backlog of enduring plays, to the growth and energy of community and regional theaters, to experimental theaters off Broadway, and to the extraordinary talent of numerous young playwrights.

# ECHOES

## MODERN DRAMA

Drama is life with the dull bits cut out.
—Alfred Hitchcock

The ever importunate murmur, "Dramatize it, dramatize it!"
—Henry James

Everything written is as good as it is dramatic. It need not declare itself in form, but it is drama or nothing.
—Robert Frost

All theories of what a good play is, or how a good play should be written, are futile. A good play is a play which when acted upon the boards makes an audience interested and pleased. A play that fails in this is a bad play.
—Maurice Baring

All perform their tragic play,
There struts Hamlet, there is Lear.
—William Butler Yeats

To know, one must be an actor as well as a spectator.
—Aldous Huxley

On the stage, it is always *now;* the personages are standing on that razor-edge, between the past and the future . . . ; the words are rising to their lips in immediate spontaneity. A novel is what *took place* . . . .
—Thornton Wilder

The theatre has given me a chance not only to live my own life but a million others.
—Margo Jones

. . . I think the playwright's only obligation is one of integrity. He must have something he believes in, and express this belief with the full strength of his talent.
—Elmer Rice

For the theater, one needs long arms . . . . An *artiste* with short arms can never, never make a fine gesture.
—Sarah Bernhardt

. . . I am trying to account as best I can for the realistic surface of life as well as Man's intense need to symbolize the meaning of what he experiences.
—Arthur Miller

I don't have to tell you that speech on the stage is not the speech of life, not even the written speech.
—Lillian Hellman

. . . I sense that there is a relationship . . . between a dramatic structure, the form and sound and shape of a play, and the equivalent structure in music.
—Edward Albee

It's one of the tragic ironies of the theatre that only one man in it can count on steady work—the night watchman.
—Tallulah Bankhead

*New York Movie* [Detail], Edward Hopper.

# The Glass Menagerie

BY TENNESSEE WILLIAMS

## About the AUTHOR

**Tennessee Williams** (1911–1983) was the pen name of one of America's finest dramatists. Born Thomas Lanier Williams, he grew up in Mississippi and St. Louis. Williams began writing early, publishing his first short story at the age of fourteen. He attended the University of Washington and the University of Iowa and then worked at various jobs in Chicago, St. Louis, New Orleans, and California. In 1939, his *American Blues,* a collection of short plays, was produced in New York to enthusiastic reviews. However, his next play, *Battle of Angels,* later rewritten and retitled *Orpheus Descending,* failed when it was produced in Boston. *The Glass Menagerie,* produced in 1944 and a tremendous success, was followed by *A Streetcar Named Desire* (1947), *Summer and Smoke* (1948), *Camino Real* (1953), *Cat on a Hot Tin Roof* (1955), *Suddenly Last Summer* (1958), *Sweet Bird of Youth* (1959), and *The Night of the Iguana* (1962). Williams also wrote the novella *The Roman Spring of Mrs. Stone* (1950) and his *Memoirs* (1975).

Williams's plays often deal with troubled, emotionally intense social misfits and are often set in the post-Civil War, or antebellum, South. Because of the intensity of emotion in these plays and because of their powerfully evocative settings, they are often referred to as examples of **Southern Gothic**. Williams was also a pioneering American Expressionist. **Expressionism** was an artistic movement of the early and mid-twentieth century that sought to express emotions by exaggerating the artistic medium itself. Expressionist painters tended to use heavy strokes of the brush or palette knife and vivid, intense colors. Expressionist dramatists often exaggerated the elements of spectacle and the literary techniques in their works, using lighting, sound, properties, and elements of the stage set for symbolic purposes.

## About the SELECTION

The closest companion of Williams's youth, his sister Rose, provided the model for the central character in the play that was to be his first major success, ***The Glass Menagerie****.* This largely autobiographical play, originally called *The Gentleman Caller,* deals with a socially isolated young woman, Laura, whose intense fragility is symbolized by her collection of glass figurines. Laura's nickname, "Blue Roses," recalls the name of Williams's sister, Rose, and evokes numerous connotations: oddness and rarity (because blue roses do not actually occur in nature), fragility and weakness (because of the association of the color blue with the blue veins that show so clearly against the white skin of a sickly, anemic person), and sadness (because of the use of the word *blues* to describe a melancholic or depressed state). Such strong symbolism is characteristic of Williams's work and that of other Expressionist writers. The character Tom in the play, a young writer, is something of a self-portrait, and critics have often expressed the idea that Williams wrote the play because of the guilt that he felt for abandoning his sister Rose, who ended up in a mental institution. Williams's sister, like Laura, collected glass figures, and this remembered detail became an evocative image in his work. Williams wrote of his fascination with his sister's glass collection, "They were mostly little glass animals. By poetic association they came to represent, in my memory, all the softest

emotions that belong to recollection of things past. They stood for all the small and tender things that relieve the austere pattern of life and make it endurable to the sensitive."

First staged in Chicago in 1944, *The Glass Menagerie* was an immediate success, opening in New York the following year. Since that time the play has been produced many times on Broadway and by theater companies throughout the world. Several film versions of the play have been produced, one in 1950 starring Jane Wyman and Arthur Kennedy, one in 1973 starring Katherine Hepburn and Sam Waterston, and one in 1987 starring Joanne Woodward and John Malkovich. The last of these versions was directed by Paul Newman.

Stage production of *A Streetcar Named Desire,* 1947.

## Literary TOOLS

**STAGE DIRECTIONS. Stage directions** are notes included in a play, in addition to the dialogue, for the purpose of describing how something should be performed on stage. As you read the stage directions for act 1, scene 1, pay attention to what Williams says about the economic and social setting in which the characters live.

**EXPRESSIONISM. Expressionism** is the name given to a twentieth-century movement in literature and art that reacted against *Realism* in favor of an exaggeration of the elements of the artistic medium itself, in an attempt to express ideas or feelings. As you read the stage directions, determine what elements of the setting are unrealistic and calculated to create emotional responses in the audience.

## Reader's Journal

Would you call yourself more of an extrovert or more of an introvert? Why?

The Glass Menagerie

# TENNESSEE WILLIAMS

## CAST OF CHARACTERS

AMANDA WINGFIELD
LAURA WINGFIELD

TOM WINGFIELD
JIM O'CONNOR

## ACT 1, SCENE 1

*The Wingfield apartment is in the rear of the building, one of those vast hive-like <u>conglomerations</u> of cellular living-units that flower as warty growths in overcrowded urban centers of lower middle-class population and are <u>symptomatic</u> of the impulse of this largest and fundamentally enslaved section of American society to avoid fluidity and differentiation and to exist and function as one <u>interfused</u> mass of automatism. The apartment faces an alley and is entered by a fire-escape, a structure whose name is a touch of accidental poetic truth, for all of these huge buildings are always burning with the slow and <u>implacable</u> fires of human desperation. The fire-escape is included in the set—that is, the landing of it and steps descending from it. (Note that the stage* L. *alley may be entirely omitted, since it is never used except for* TOM'S *first entrance, which can take place stage* R.) *The scene is memory and is therefore nonrealistic. Memory takes a lot of poetic license. It omits some details, others are exaggerated, according to the emotional value of the articles it touches, for memory is seated predominantly in the heart. The interior is therefore rather dim and poetic.* (CUE #1. *As soon as the house lights dim, dance-hall music heard on-stage* R. *Old popular music of, say 1915–1920 period. This continues until* TOM *is at fire-escape landing, having lighted cigarette, and begins speaking.*)

**What does the author say about memory?**

AT RISE: *At the rise of the house curtain, the audience is faced with the dark, grim rear wall of the Wingfield tenement. (The stage set proper is screened out by a gauze curtain, which suggests the front part, outside, of the building.) This building, which runs parallel to the footlights, is flanked on both sides by dark, narrow alleys which run into murky canyons of tangled clotheslines, garbage cans and the sinister lattice-work of neighboring fire-escapes. (The alleys are actually in darkness, and the objects just mentioned are not visible.) It is up and down these side alleys that exterior entrances and exits are made, during the play. At the end of* TOM'S *opening commentary, the dark tenement wall slowly reveals (by means of a transparency) the interior of the ground-floor Wingfield apartment. (Gauze curtain, which suggests front part of building, rises on the interior set.) Downstage is the living-room, which also serves as a sleeping room for* LAURA, *the day-bed unfolding to make her bed. Just above this is a small stool or table on which is a telephone. Up-stage,* C., *and divided by a wide arch or second proscenium[1] with transparent faded portieres (or second curtain, "second curtain" is actually the inner gauze curtain between the living-room and the dining-room, which is up-stage of it), is the dining-room. In an old-fashioned whatnot in the living-room are seen scores of transparent glass*

---

1. **proscenium.** Plane, including the arch and the curtain, separating the stage proper from the audience

**WORDS FOR EVERYDAY USE**

**con • glom • er • a • tion** (kən gläm´ər ā´shən) *n.*, collection or mixture. *During the Elizabethan period, the theater entertained a <u>conglomeration</u> of classes.*

**symp • to • mat • ic** (simp´tə mat´ik) *adj.*, indicative; that constitutes a condition. *Sneezing and watery eyes are <u>symptomatic</u> of allergies.*

**in • ter • fused** (in tər fyüzd´) *adj.*, combined, blended. *Snorkeling among the coral reefs, we were awed by the color of the water <u>interfused</u> with light.*

**im • pla • ca • ble** (im plā´kə bəl) *adj.*, cannot be appeased or pacified. *The <u>implacable</u> tourist insisted someone at the hotel desk speak to her in English.*

*animals. A blown-up photograph of the father hangs on the wall of the living-room, facing the audience, to the* L. *of the archway. It is the face of a very handsome young man in a doughboy's*[2] *First World War cap. He is gallantly smiling,* ineluctably *smiling, as if to say, "I will be smiling forever." (Note that all that is essential in connection with dance-hall is that the window be shown lighting lower part of alley. It is not necessary to show any considerable part of dance-hall.) The audience hears and sees the opening scene in the dining-room through both the transparent fourth wall (this is the gauze curtain which suggests outside of building) of the building and the transparent gauze portieres of the dining-room arch. It is during this revealing scene that the fourth wall slowly ascends, out of sight. This transparent exterior wall is not brought down again until the very end of the play, during* TOM's *final speech. The narrator is an undisguised convention of the play. He takes whatever license with dramatic convention as is convenient to his purposes.*

TOM *enters, dressed as a merchant sailor, from alley, stage* L. *(i.e., stage* R. *if* L. *alley is omitted), and strolls across the front of the stage to the fire-escape. (*TOM *may lean against grillwork of this as he lights cigarette.) There he stops and lights a cigarette. He addresses the audience.*

**TOM.** I have tricks in my pocket—I have things up my sleeve—but I am the opposite of the stage magician. He gives you illusion that has the appearance of truth. I give you truth in the pleasant disguise of illusion. I take you back to an alley in St. Louis. The time that quaint period when the huge middle class of America was matriculating from a school for the blind. Their eyes had failed them, or they had failed their eyes, and so they were having their fingers pressed

> What does Tom, the narrator, say about the nature of truth and illusion in this play?

forcibly down on the fiery Braille alphabet of a dissolving economy.—In Spain there was revolution.—Here there was only shouting and confusion and labor disturbances, sometimes violent, in otherwise peaceful cities such as Cleveland—Chicago—Detroit. . . . That is the social background of this play. . . . The play is memory. (MUSIC CUE #2.) Being a memory play, it is dimly lighted, it is sentimental, it is not realistic.—In memory everything seems to happen to music.—That explains the fiddle in the wings. I am the narrator of the play, and also a character in it. The other characters in the play are my mother, Amanda, my sister, Laura, and a gentleman caller who appears in the final scenes. He is the most realistic character in the play, being an emissary from a world that we were somehow set apart from.—But having a poet's weakness for symbols, I am using this character as a symbol—as the long-delayed but always expected something that we live for.—There is a fifth character who doesn't appear other than in a photograph hanging on the wall. When you see the picture of this grinning gentleman, please remember this is our father who left us a long time ago. He was a telephone man who fell in love with long distance—so he gave up his job with the telephone company and skipped the light fantastic out of town. . . . The last we heard of him was a picture postcard from the Pacific coast of Mexico, containing a message of two words—"Hello—Good-bye!" and no address.

> What do you think is meant by "a memory play"? What is memory associated with in this play?

> Of what is the gentleman caller a symbol?

> Where is Tom and Laura's father?

---

2. **doughboy.** World War I United States infantryman

---

**WORDS FOR EVERYDAY USE**

in • e • luc • ta • bly (in´ē luk´tə blē) *adv.,* in an inescapable or unavoidable manner. *In a Greek drama, fate* ineluctably *draws protagonists to their doom.*

ma • tric • u • late (mə trik´yü lāt´) *vt.,* enroll. *Durrell* matriculated *at the University of Wisconsin.*

em • is • sar • y (em´i ser´ē) *n.,* person or agent sent on a mission. *The* emissary *from the king of Spain requested an audience with Queen Elizabeth I to discuss the king's marriage proposal.*

*(LIGHTS UP IN DINING-ROOM. TOM exits R. He goes off downstage, takes off his sailor overcoat and skull-fitting knitted cap and remains off-stage by dining-room R. door for his entrance cue. AMANDA's voice becomes audible through the portieres—i.e., gauze curtains separating dining-room and living-room. AMANDA and LAURA are seated at a drop-leaf table. AMANDA is sitting in C. chair and LAURA in L. chair. Eating is indicated by gestures without food or utensils. AMANDA faces the audience. The interior of the dining-room has lit up softly and through the scrim[3]—gauze curtains—we see AMANDA and LAURA seated at the table in the upstage area.)*

**AMANDA.**   You know, Laura, I had the funniest experience in church last Sunday. The church was crowded except for one pew way down front and in that was just one little woman. I smiled very sweetly at her and said, "Excuse me, would you mind if I shared this pew?" "I certainly would," she said, "this space is rented." Do you know that is the first time that I ever knew that the Lord rented space. *(Dining-room gauze curtains open automatically.)* These Northern Episcopalians! I can understand the Southern Episcopalians, but these Northern ones, no. *(TOM enters dining-room R., slips over to table and sits in chair R.)* Honey, don't push your food with your fingers. If you have to push your food with something, the thing to use is a crust of bread. You must chew your food. Animals have secretions in their stomachs which enable them to digest their food without <u>mastication</u>, but human beings must chew their food before they swallow it down, and chew, chew. Oh, eat leisurely. Eat leisurely. A well-cooked meal has many delicate flavors that have to be held in the mouth for appreciation, not just gulped down. Oh, chew, chew—chew! *(At this point the scrim curtain—if the director decides to use it—the one suggesting exte-rior wall, rises here and does not come down again until just before the end of the play.)* Don't you want to give your salivary glands a chance to function?

**TOM.**   Mother, I haven't enjoyed one bite of my dinner because of your constant directions on how to eat it. It's you that makes me hurry through my meals with your hawk-like attention to every bite I take. It's disgusting—all this discussion of animal's secretion—salivary glands—mastication! *(Comes down to armchair in living-room R., lights cigarette.)*

**AMANDA.**   Temperament like a Metropolitan star! You're not excused from this table.

**TOM.**   I'm getting a cigarette.

**AMANDA.**   You smoke too much.

**LAURA**   *(Rising)*. Mother, I'll bring in the coffee.

**AMANDA.**   No, no, no, no. You sit down. I'm going to be the servant today and you're going to be the lady.

**LAURA.**   I'm already up.

**AMANDA.**   <u>Resume</u> your seat. Resume your seat. You keep yourself fresh and pretty for the gentlemen callers. *(LAURA sits.)*

> Why does Amanda tell Laura to remain seated? How does Laura feel about her mother's expectations?

**LAURA.**   I'm not expecting any gentlemen callers.

**AMANDA**   *(Who has been gathering dishes from table and loading them on tray)*. Well, the nice thing about them is they come when they're least expected. Why, I remember one Sunday afternoon in Blue Mountain when your mother was a girl . . .

---

3. **scrim.** Hanging of light cloth as a semitransparent curtain in a theatrical production

---

**WORDS FOR EVERYDAY USE**

**mas • ti • ca • tion** (mas´ti kā´shən) *n.*, chewing. *"With good dental hygiene," the dentist said, "you can enjoy <u>mastication</u> with your own teeth for the rest of your life."*

**re • sume** (ri züm´) *vt.*, take, get, or occupy again. *The car alarm <u>resumed</u> ringing just as we were drifting off to sleep again.*

Film version of *The Glass Menagerie*, 1950.

*(Goes out for coffee,* U. R.*)*

**TOM.**  I know what's coming now! *(*LAURA *rises.)*

**LAURA.**  Yes. But let her tell it. *(Crosses to* L. *of day-bed, sits.)*

**TOM.**  Again?

**LAURA.**  She loves to tell it.

**AMANDA**  *(Entering from* R. *in dining-room and coming down into living-room with tray and coffee).* I remember one Sunday afternoon in Blue Mountain when your mother was a girl she received—seventeen—gentlemen callers! *(*AMANDA *crosses to* TOM *at armchair* R.*, gives him coffee, and crosses* C. LAURA *comes to her, takes cup, resumes her place on* L. *of day-bed.* AMANDA *puts tray on small table* R. *of day-bed, sits* R. *on day-bed. Inner curtain closes, light dims out.)* Why sometimes there weren't chairs enough to accommodate them all and we had to send the servant over to the parish house to fetch the folding chairs.

> What event in her life does Amanda enjoy remembering?

**TOM.**  How did you entertain all those gentlemen callers? *(*TOM *finally sits in armchair* R.*)*

**AMANDA.**  I happened to understand the art of conversation!

**TOM.**  I bet you could talk!

**AMANDA.**  Well, I could. All the girls in my day could, I tell you.

**TOM.**  Yes?

**AMANDA.**  They knew how to entertain their gentlemen callers. It wasn't enough for a girl to be possessed of a pretty face and a graceful figure—although I wasn't slighted in either respect. She also needed to have a nimble wit and a tongue to meet all occasions.

**TOM.**  What did you talk about?

**AMANDA.**  Why, we'd talk about things of importance going on in the world! Never anything common or coarse or vulgar. My callers were gentlemen—all! Some of the most <u>prominent</u> men on the Mississippi Delta—planters and sons of planters! There was young Champ Laughlin. (MUSIC CUE #3.) He later

**WORDS FOR EVERYDAY USE**

**prom • i • nent** (präm´ə nənt) *adj.,* widely and favorably known. *The most <u>prominent</u> celebrities appeared on her talk show.*

became Vice-President of the Delta Planters' Bank. And Hadley Stevenson; he was drowned in Moon Lake.—My goodness, he certainly left his widow well provided for—a hundred and fifty thousand dollars in government bonds. And the Cutrere Brothers—Wesley and Bates. Bates was one of my own bright particular beaus! But he got in a quarrel with that wild Wainwright boy and they shot it out on the floor of Moon Lake Casino. Bates was shot through the stomach. He died in the ambulance on his way to Memphis. He certainly left his widow well provided for, too—eight or ten thousand acres, no less. He never loved that woman; she just caught him on the rebound. My picture was found on him the night he died. Oh and that boy, that boy that every girl in the Delta was setting her cap for! That beautiful (MUSIC FADES OUT.) brilliant young Fitzhugh boy from Greene County!

**TOM.** What did he leave his widow?

**AMANDA.** He never married! What's the matter with you—you talk as though all my old admirers had turned up their toes to the daisies!

**TOM.** Isn't this the first you've mentioned that still survives?

**AMANDA.** He made an awful lot of money. He went North to Wall Street and made a fortune. He had the Midas touch—everything that boy touched just turned to gold! (*Gets up.*) And I could have been Mrs. J.

> What does Amanda regret?

Duncan Fitzhugh—mind you! (*Crosses* L. C.) But—what did I do?—I just went out of my way and picked your father! (*Looks at picture on* L. *wall. Goes to small table* R. *of day-bed for tray.*)

**LAURA** (*Rises from day-bed*). Mother, let me clear the table.

**AMANDA** (*Crossing* L. *for* LAURA's *cup, then crossing* R. *for* TOM's). No, dear, you go in front and study your typewriter chart. Or practice your shorthand a little. Stay fresh and pretty! It's almost time for our gentlemen callers to start arriving. How many do you suppose we're going to entertain this afternoon? (TOM *opens curtains between dining-room and living-room for her. These close behind her, and she exits into kitchen* R. TOM *stands* U. C. *in living-room.*)

**LAURA** (*To* AMANDA, *off-stage*). I don't believe we're going to receive any, Mother.

**AMANDA** (*Off-stage*). Not any? Not one? Why, you must be joking! Not one gentleman caller? What's the matter? Has there been a flood or a tornado?

**LAURA** (*Crossing to typing table*). It isn't a flood. It's not a tornado, Mother. I'm just not popular like you were in Blue Mountain. Mother's afraid that I'm going to be an old maid. (MUSIC CUE #4.) (*Lights dim out.* TOM *exits* U. C. *in blackout.* LAURA *crosses to* menagerie R.)

> What reason does Amanda give for the lack of gentlemen callers? What does Laura see as the reason? How do you think her mother's joking and prodding might make Laura feel?

---

**WORDS FOR EVERYDAY USE**

me • nag • er • ie (mə naj´ər ē) n., collection of wild or strange animals kept in enclosures for exhibition. *The heiress owned a private* menagerie *that rivaled the local zoo.*

---

**Respond** to the **SELECTION**

If you were the son or daughter of Amanda Wingfield, how would you feel about your mother? Why?

# INVESTIGATE, Inquire, Imagine

**Recall:** GATHERING FACTS

1a. What does the narrator, Tom, say a stage magician does? Why does Tom say the play is "not realistic"?

2a. What does Amanda tell Tom and Laura to do?

3a. What memory from her past does Amanda relate? What question does she pose to Laura after dinner?

**Interpret:** FINDING MEANING

1b. How does Tom differ from a stage magician? What are Tom's roles in the play?

2b. What kind of mother is Amanda?

3b. About what is Amanda nostalgic? What does she want for her daughter?

---

**Analyze:** TAKING THINGS APART

4a. In what ways does Amanda Wingfield live in a world of illusion? How accurate is her memory and her assessment of the present?

**Synthesize:** BRINGING THINGS TOGETHER

4b. Describe Amanda's socioeconomic status as it was in the past and as it is in the present.

---

**Evaluate:** MAKING JUDGMENTS

5a. Do you agree with Laura that it is a good idea to let Amanda recount the memory of her seventeen gentlemen callers? Why, or why not?

**Extend:** CONNECTING IDEAS

5b. What strategies have you seen people use to escape a present that does not live up to their wishes?

---

# Understanding Literature

**STAGE DIRECTIONS.** Review the definition for **stage directions** in the Handbook of Literary Terms. Reread the stage directions at the opening of the play, before the entrance of the narrator. What is the social class of the people who live in the "overcrowded urban centers" described in those stage directions? What "poetic truth" is expressed by the term *fire-escape*?

**EXPRESSIONISM.** Review the definition for **Expressionism** in the Handbook of Literary Terms. Then make a chart. On the left, list several significant elements of setting in the play that are calculated to create emotional responses in the audience. On the right, explain the meaning the elements are intended to convey. One example has been done for you.

| Elements of Setting | Explanation |
|---|---|
| The Wingfields enter their apartment from a fire escape. | The fire escape, a physical symbol, is used to represent various aspects of being trapped or of having a method of escape. |

*New York House Fronts,* 1938. Walker Evans. Library of Congress.

# Literary
## T O O L S

**IRONY.** **Irony** is a difference between appearance and reality. As you read, think about why Amanda's reference to her husband is ironic in view of her plans for Laura.

**CHARACTER.** A **character** is a person who figures in the action of a literary work. Assess Laura's character as you read the scene.

# Reader's
*Journal*

When have you disappointed a parent? What happened?

## ACT 1, SCENE 2

*Scene is the same. Lights dim up on living-room.*

LAURA *discovered by menagerie, polishing glass. Crosses to phonograph, plays record. She times this business so as to put needle on record as* MUSIC CUE #4 *ends. Enter* AMANDA *down alley* R. *Rattles key in lock.* LAURA *crosses guiltily to typewriter and types. (Small typewriter table with typewriter on it is still on stage in living-room* L.) AMANDA *comes into room* R. *closing door. Crosses to arm-chair, putting hat, purse and gloves on it. Something has happened to* AMANDA. *It is written in her face: a look that is grim and hopeless and a little absurd. She has on one of those cheap or imitation velvety-looking cloth coats with imitation fur collar. Her hat is five or six years old, one of those dreadful cloche[4] hats that were worn in the late twenties and she is clasping an enormous black patent-leather pocketbook with nickel clasps and initials. This is her fulldress outfit, the one she usually wears to the* D.A.R.[5] *She purses her lips, opens her eyes very wide, rolls them upward and shakes her head. Seeing her mother's expression,* LAURA *touches her lips with a nervous gesture.*

**LAURA.** Hello, Mother, I was just . . .

**AMANDA.** I know. You were just practicing your typing, I suppose. *(Behind chair* R.)

---

4. **cloche.** Close-fitting, bell-shaped hat
5. **D.A.R.** Daughters of the American Revolution, a civic organization

**LAURA.** Yes.

**AMANDA.** Deception, deception, deception!

**LAURA** *(Shakily)*. How was the D.A.R. meeting, Mother?

**AMANDA** *(Crosses to* LAURA*)*. D.A.R. meeting!

**LAURA.** Didn't you go to the D.A.R. meeting, Mother?

**AMANDA** *(Faintly, almost inaudibly)*. No, I didn't go to any D.A.R. meeting. *(Then more forcibly.)* I didn't have the strength—I didn't have the courage. I just wanted to find a hole in the ground and crawl in it and stay there the rest of my entire life.

*(Tears type charts, throws them on floor.)*

**LAURA** *(Faintly)*. Why did you do that, Mother?

**AMANDA** *(Sits on* R. *end of day-bed)*. Why? Why? How old are you, Laura?

**LAURA.** Mother, you know my age.

**AMANDA.** I was under the impression that you were an adult, but evidently I was very much mistaken.

*(She stares at* LAURA.*)*

**LAURA.** Please don't stare at me, Mother! *(*AMANDA *closes her eyes and lowers her head. Pause.)*

**AMANDA.** What are we going to do? What is going to become of us? What is the future? *(Pause.)*

**LAURA.** Has something happened, Mother? Mother, has something happened?

**AMANDA.** I'll be all right in a minute. I'm just bewildered—by life . . .

**LAURA.** Mother, I wish that you would tell me what's happened!

> How does Amanda say she feels? What effect does she hope to produce in Laura?

**AMANDA.** I went to the D.A.R. this afternoon, as you know; I was to be <u>inducted</u> as an officer. I stopped off at Rubicam's Business College to tell them about your cold and to ask how you were progressing down there.

**LAURA.** Oh . . .

**AMANDA.** Yes, oh—oh—oh. I went straight to your typing instructor and introduced myself as your mother. She didn't even know who you were. Wingfield, she said? We don't have any such scholar enrolled in this school. I assured her she did. I said my daughter Laura's been coming to classes since early January. "Well, I don't know," she said, "unless you mean that terribly shy little girl who dropped out of school after a few days' attendance?" "No," I said, "I don't mean that one. I mean my daughter, Laura, who's been coming here every single day for the past six weeks!" "Excuse me," she said. And she took down the attendance book and there was your name, unmistakable, printed, and all the dates you'd been absent. I still told her she was wrong. I still said, "No, there must have been some mistake! There must have been some mix-up in the records!" "No," she said, "I remember her perfectly now. She was so shy and her hands trembled so that her fingers couldn't touch the right keys! When we gave a speed-test—she just broke down completely—was sick at the stomach and had to be carried to the washroom! After that she never came back. We telephoned the house every single day and never got any answer." *(Rises from day-bed, crosses* R. C.*)* That was while I was working all day long down at that department store, I suppose, demonstrating those— *(With hands indicates brassiere.)* Oh! I felt so

> Why is Amanda angry with her daughter?

> In what way does Laura's former teacher describe her?

---

**WORDS FOR EVERYDAY USE**

**in • duct** (in dukt´) *vt.*, place in official position. *Theresa was <u>inducted</u> into the club with much ceremony.*

weak I couldn't stand up! (*Sits in armchair.*) I had to sit down while they got me a glass of water! (LAURA *crosses up to phonograph.*) Fifty dollars' tuition. I don't care about the money so much, but all my hopes for any kind of future for you—gone up the spout, just gone up the spout like that. (LAURA *winds phonograph up.*) Oh, don't do that, Laura!—Don't play that victrola![6]

**LAURA.** Oh! (*Stops phonograph, crosses to typing table, sits.*)

**AMANDA.** What have you been doing every day when you've gone out of the house pretending that you were going to business college?

**LAURA.** I've just been going out walking.

**AMANDA.** That's not true!

**LAURA.** Yes, it is, Mother, I just went walking.

**AMANDA.** Walking? Walking? In winter? Deliberately courting pneumonia in that light coat? Where did you walk to, Laura?

**LAURA.** All sorts of places—mostly in the park.

**AMANDA.** Even after you'd started catching that cold?

**LAURA.** It was the lesser of two evils, Mother. I couldn't go back. I threw up on the floor!

**AMANDA.** From half-past seven till after five every day you mean to tell me you walked around in the park, because you wanted to make me think that you were still going to Rubicam's Business College?

**LAURA.** Oh, Mother, it wasn't as bad as it sounds. I went inside places to get warmed up.

**AMANDA.** Inside where?

**LAURA.** I went in the art museum and the bird-houses at the Zoo. I visited the penguins every day! Sometimes I did without lunch and went to the movies. Lately I've been spending most of my afternoons in the Jewelbox, that big glass house where they raise the tropical flowers.

> How has Laura been spending her time?

**AMANDA.** You did all that to deceive me, just for deception! Why? Why? Why? Why?

**LAURA.** Mother, when you're disappointed, you get that awful suffering look on your face, like the picture of Jesus' mother in the Museum! (*Rises.*)

**AMANDA.** Hush!

**LAURA** (*Crosses R. to menagerie*). I couldn't face it. I couldn't. (MUSIC CUE #5.)

**AMANDA** (*Rising from day-bed*). So what are we going to do now, honey, the rest of our lives? Just sit down in this house and watch the parades go by? Amuse ourselves with the glass menagerie? Eternally play those worn-out records your father left us as a painful reminder of him? (*Slams phonograph lid.*) We can't have a business career. (END MUSIC CUE #5.) No, we can't do that—that just gives us indigestion. (*Around R. day-bed.*) What is there left for us now but dependency all our lives? I tell you, Laura, I know so well what happens to unmarried women who aren't prepared to occupy a position in life. (*Crosses L., sits on day-bed.*) I've seen such pitiful cases in the South—barely tolerated spinsters living on some brother's wife or a sister's husband—tucked away in some mousetrap of a room—encouraged by one in-law to go on and visit the next in-law—little bird-like women—without any nest—eating the crust of humility all their lives! Is that the future that we've mapped out for ourselves? I swear I don't see any other alternative. And I don't think that's a very pleasant alternative. Of course—some girls *do* marry. My goodness, Laura, haven't you ever liked some boy?

> What does Amanda say they can't do now that Laura has failed at business school?

> What sort of future does Amanda envision?

> What does Amanda ask Laura? Why does she ask her this?

**LAURA.** Yes, Mother, I liked one once.

---

6. **victrola.** Record player

**AMANDA.** You did?

**LAURA.** I came across his picture a while ago.

**AMANDA.** He gave you his picture too? (*Rises from day-bed, crosses to chair* R.)

**LAURA.** No, it's in the year-book.

**AMANDA** (*Sits in armchair*). Oh—a high-school boy.

**LAURA.** Yes. His name was Jim. (*Kneeling on floor, gets year-book from under menagerie.*) Here he is in "The Pirates of Penzance."

**AMANDA** (*Absently*). The what?

**LAURA.** The operetta the senior class put on. He had a wonderful voice. We sat across the aisle from each other Mondays, Wednesdays and Fridays in the auditorium. Here he is with a silver cup for debating! See his grin?

**AMANDA.** So he had a grin, too! (*Looks at picture of father on wall behind phonograph. Hands year-book back.*)

**LAURA.** He used to call me—Blue Roses.

**AMANDA.** Blue Roses? What did he call you a silly name like that for?

**LAURA** (*Still kneeling*). When I had that attack of pleurosis[7]—he asked me what was the matter when I came back. I said pleurosis—he thought that I said "Blue Roses." So that's what he always called me after that. Whenever he saw me, he'd holler, "Hello, Blue Roses!" I didn't care for the girl that he went out with. Emily Meisenbach. Oh, Emily was the best-dressed girl at Soldan.

But she never struck me as being sincere . . . I read in a newspaper once that they were engaged. (*Puts year-book back on a shelf of glass menagerie.*) That's a long time ago—they're probably married by now.

**AMANDA.** That's all right, honey, that's all right. It doesn't matter. Little girls who aren't cut out for business careers sometimes end up married to very nice young men. And I'm just going to see that you do that, too!

> What does Amanda set as her goal?

**LAURA.** But, Mother—

**AMANDA.** What is it now?

**LAURA.** I'm—crippled!

**AMANDA.** Don't say that word! (*Rises, crosses to* C. *Turns to* LAURA.) How many times have I told you never to say that word! You're not crippled, you've just got a slight defect. (LAURA *rises.*) If you lived in the days when I was a girl and they had long graceful skirts sweeping the ground, it might have been considered an asset. When you've got a slight disadvantage like that, you've just got to <u>cultivate</u> something else to take its place. You have to cultivate charm—or vivacity—or *charm*! (*Spotlight on photograph. Then dim out.*) That's the only thing your father had plenty of—charm! (AMANDA *sits on day-bed.* LAURA *crosses to armchair and sits.*) (MUSIC CUE #6.) (*Blackout.*)

---

7. **pleurosis.** Inflammation of the lungs

**WORDS FOR EVERYDAY USE**

**cul • ti • vate** (kul´tə vāt) *vt.*, acquire and develop. *Jeremy <u>cultivated</u> his interest in jazz by buying CDs and going to jazz clubs.*

**Respond** *to the* **SELECTION**

If you were Laura, what could you have done to allay your fears so you could succeed at business college?

# INVESTIGATE *Inquire* *Imagine*

**Recall:** GATHERING FACTS ➔

1a. What does Amanda discover when she stops by the business school? Why is she distraught?

2a. According to Amanda, what alternative to having a career does a young woman have?

3a. After expressing her worries about Laura's future, what does Amanda ask her daughter? How does Laura respond? Why did the boy call Laura "Blue Roses"?

**Interpret:** FINDING MEANING

1b. What happened to Laura when she went to the business college? Why did she drop out? What does she spend her days doing? What do these details reveal about Laura's personality and character?

2b. Does Laura seem capable of finding a husband?

3b. What does the nickname "Blue Roses" signify? What does it underline about Laura's personality?

**Analyze:** TAKING THINGS APART ➔

4a. In what ways has Amanda changed since scene 1?

**Synthesize:** BRINGING THINGS TOGETHER

4b. Predict what Amanda might do to find a husband for Laura.

**Perspective:** LOOKING AT OTHER VIEWS ➔

5a. What relationship in Laura's high school years seems to have had the most impact on her? Why?

**Empathy:** SEEING FROM INSIDE

5b. If you were Laura, how would you prepare for a gentleman caller?

# Understanding *Literature*

IRONY. Review the definition for **irony** in the Handbook of Literary Terms. At the end of the scene, Amanda mentions her husband. What became of this man? What makes it ironic that Amanda should pin her hopes on Laura's having a gentleman caller and then immediately think of her husband's picture? What does this sequence of events suggest about the fulfillment of Amanda's hopes for Laura?

CHARACTER. Review the definition for **character** in the Handbook of Literary Terms. Then make a chart like the one below describing Laura's character traits. Fill in the chart with examples from scenes 1 and 2 of the play. One example has been done for you. What do Laura's pastimes at home reveal about her character?

| Physical Appearance | Dress | Habits/Mannerisms/ Behaviors | Relationships with Other People | Other |
|---|---|---|---|---|
| physical disability | | | | |

**SYMBOL.** A **symbol** is a thing that stands for or represents both itself and something else. Think about what the glass menagerie symbolizes as you read.

**CONFLICT.** A **conflict** is a struggle between two forces in a literary work. A struggle that takes place between a character and some outside force is called an *external conflict*. A struggle that takes place within a character is called an *internal conflict*. As you read, determine what Tom's conflicts are in this scene.

## Reader's
### *Journal*

What dreams do you have for the future?

***New York House Fronts*** [Detail], 1938. Walker Evans.

### ACT **1**, SCENE **3**

SCENE: *The same. Lights up again but only on* R. *alley and fire-escape landing, rest of the stage dark.* (*Typewriter table and typewriter have been taken offstage.*) *Enter* TOM, *again wearing merchant sailor overcoat and knittedcap, in alley* R. *As* MUSIC CUE #6 *ends,* TOM *begins to speak.*

TOM  (*Leans against grill of fire-escape, smoking*). After the <u>fiasco</u> at Rubicam's Business College, the idea of getting a gentleman caller for my sister Laura began to play a more and more important part in my mother's calculations. It became an obsession. Like some archetype[8] of the universal unconscious, the image of the gentleman caller haunted our small apartment. An evening at home rarely passed without some allusion to this image, this spectre, this hope. . . . And even when he wasn't mentioned, his presence hung in my mother's preoccupied look and in my sister's frightened, apologetic manner. It hung like a sentence passed upon the Wingfields! But my mother was a woman of action as well as words. (MUSIC CUE #7.) She began to take logical steps in the planned direction. Late that winter and in the early spring—realizing that extra money would be needed to properly feather the nest and plume the bird—she began a vigorous campaign on the telephone, roping in subscribers to one of those

*What does Tom say about his mother's plan? How does it change his mother and sister? Does he see this plan as realistic?*

8. **archetype.** Original pattern; prototype

**WORDS FOR EVERYDAY USE**

**fi • as • co** (fē as´kō) *n.*, complete failure. *Jeff's ownership of a cinema cafe turned into a complete fiasco.*

magazines for matrons called "The Homemaker's Companion," the type of journal that features the serialized <u>sublimations</u> of ladies of letters who think in terms of delicate cup-like breasts, slim, tapering waists, rich creamy thighs, eyes like wood-smoke in autumn, fingers that soothe and caress like soft, soft strains of music. Bodies as powerful as Etruscan[9] sculpture. *(He exits down* R. *into wings. Light in alley* R. *is blacked out, and a head-spot falls on* AMANDA, *at phone in living-room.* MUSIC CUE #7 *ends as* TOM *stops speaking.)*

**AMANDA.** Ida Scott? *(During this speech* TOM *enters dining-room* U. R. *unseen by audience, not wearing overcoat or hat. There is an unlighted reading lamp on table. Sits* C. *of dining-room table with writing materials.)* This is Amanda Wingfield. We missed you at the D.A.R. last Monday. Oh, first I want to know how's your sinus condition? You're just a Christian martyr. That's what you are. You're just a Christian martyr. Well, I was just going through my little red book, and I saw that your subscription to the "Companion" is about to expire just when that wonderful new serial by Bessie Mae Harper is starting. It's the first thing she's written since "Honeymoon for Three." Now, that was unusual, wasn't it? Why, Ida, this one is even lovelier. It's all about the horsey set on Long Island and a debutante is thrown from her horse while taking him over the jumps at the—regatta. Her spine—her spine is injured. That's what the horse did—he stepped on her. Now, there is only one surgeon in the entire world that can keep her from being completely paralyzed, and that's the man she's engaged to be married to and he's tall and he's blond and he's handsome. That's unusual, too, huh? Oh, he's not perfect. Of course he has a weakness. He has the most terrible weakness in the entire world. He just drinks too much. What? Oh, no,

Honey, don't let them burn. You go take a look in the oven and I'll hold on . . . Why, that woman! Do you know what she did? She hung up on me. *(Dining-room and living-room lights dim in. Reading lamp lights up at same time.)*

**LAURA.** Oh, Mother, Mother, Tom's trying to write. *(Rises from armchair where she was left at curtain of previous scene, goes to curtain between dining-room and living-room, which is already open.)*

**AMANDA.** Oh! So he is. So he is. *(Crosses from phone, goes to dining-room and up to* TOM.*)*

**TOM** *(At table).* Now what are you up to?

**AMANDA.** I'm trying to save your eyesight. *(Business with lamp.)* You've only got one pair of eyes and you've got to take care of them. Oh, I know that Milton was blind, but that's not what made him a genius.

> What does Tom enjoy doing? In what way does this activity and his mother's personality conflict?

**TOM.** Mother, will you please go away and let me finish my writing?

**AMANDA** *(Squares his shoulders).* Why can't you sit up straight? So your shoulders don't stick through like sparrows' wings?

**TOM.** Mother, please go busy yourself with something else. I'm trying to write.

**AMANDA** *(Business with* TOM).* Now, I've seen a medical chart, and I know what that position does to your internal organs. You sit up and I'll show you. Your stomach presses against your lungs, and your lungs press against your heart, and that poor little heart gets discouraged because it hasn't got any room left to go on beating for you.

**TOM.** What in hell! . . . *(Inner curtains between living-room and dining-room close. Lights dim down in dining-room.* LAURA *crosses, stands* C. *of*

---

9. **Etruscan.** Of a culture that flourished on the Italian peninsula before the Romans

---

**WORDS FOR EVERYDAY USE**

sub • li • ma • tion (sub´lə ma´shən) *n.,* expression of socially or personally unacceptable impulses in constructive, acceptable forms. *The still life of food on Paul's dining room wall was a <u>sublimation</u> of his desire to eat while on his diet.*

*curtains in living-room listening to following scene between* TOM *and* AMANDA.)

AMANDA.    Don't you talk to me like that—

TOM.    —am I supposed to do?

AMANDA.    What's the matter with you? Have you gone out of your senses?

TOM.    Yes, I have. You've driven me out of them.

AMANDA.    What is the matter with you lately, you big—big—idiot?

TOM.    Look, Mother—I haven't got a thing, not a single thing left in this house that I can call my own.

AMANDA.    Lower your voice!

TOM.    Yesterday you confiscated my books! You had the nerve to——

AMANDA.    I did. I took that horrible novel back to the library—that awful book by that insane Mr. Lawrence.[10] I cannot control the output of a diseased mind or people who <u>cater</u> to them, but I won't allow such filth in my house. No, no, no, no, no!

TOM.    House, house! Who pays the rent on the house, who makes a slave of himself to—!

AMANDA.    Don't you dare talk to me like that! (LAURA *crosses* D. L. *to back of armchair.*)

TOM.    No, *I* mustn't say anything! I've just got to keep quiet and let you do all the talking.

AMANDA.    Let me tell you something!

TOM.    I don't want to hear any more.

AMANDA.    You will hear more—(LAURA *crosses to phonograph.*)

TOM    (*Crossing through curtains between dining-room and living-room. Goes up stage of door* R. *where, in a dark spot, there is supposedly a closet*). Well, I'm not going to listen. I'm going out. (*Gets out coat.*)

AMANDA    (*Coming through curtains into living-room, stands* C.). You are going to listen to me, Tom Wingfield. I'm tired of your impudence.—And another thing—I'm right at the end of my patience!

TOM    (*Putting overcoat on back of armchair and crossing back to* AMANDA). What do you think I'm at the end of, Mother? Aren't I supposed to have any patience to reach the end of? I know, I know. It seems unimportant to you, what I'm *doing*—what I'm trying to do—having a difference between them! You don't think that.

AMANDA.    I think you're doing things that you're ashamed of, and that's why you act like this. (TOM *crosses to day-bed and sits.*) I don't believe that you go every night to the movies. Nobody goes to the movies night after night. Nobody in their right minds goes to the movies as often as you pretend to. People don't go to the movies at nearly midnight and movies don't let out at two A.M. Come in stumbling, muttering to yourself like a maniac. You get three hours' sleep and then go to work. Oh, I can picture the way you're doing down there. Moping, doping, because you're in no condition.

TOM.    That's true—that's very, very true. I'm in no condition!

AMANDA.    How dare you jeopardize your job? Jeopardize our security? How do you think we'd manage—? (*Sits armchair* R.)

TOM.    Look, Mother, do you think I'm *crazy* about the *warehouse?* You think I'm in love with the Continental Shoemakers? You think I want to spend fifty-five years of my life down there in that—*celotex interior!* with *fluorescent tubes?!* Honest to God, I'd rather somebody picked up

---

10.  **Mr. Lawrence.** D. H. Lawrence (1858–1930) was a poet and novelist whose writings were considered outrageous by some of his contemporaries.

**WORDS FOR EVERYDAY USE**

**ca • ter** (kāt´ər) *vi.,* take special pains in seeking to gratify another's needs or desires. *In deciding on a trip to Florida, we did not <u>cater</u> to Raymond's wishes to spend a week in the mountains.*

a crow-bar and battered out my brains—than go back mornings! But I *go!* Sure, every time you come in yelling that bloody *Rise and Shine! Rise and shine!!* I think how lucky dead people are. But I get up. *(Rises from day-bed.)* I *go!* For sixty-five dollars a month I give up all that I dream of doing and being *ever*! And you say that is all I think of. Oh, God! Why, Mother, if self is all I ever thought of, Mother, *I'd be where he is—GONE! (Crosses to get overcoat on back of armchair.)* As far as the system of transportation reaches! *(AMANDA rises, crosses to him and grabs his arm.)* Please don't grab at me, Mother!

How does Tom feel about his job? Why does he continue doing it? What has "doing the right thing" made him give up?

**AMANDA**  *(Following him).* I'm not grabbing at you. I want to know where you're going now.

**TOM**  *(Taking overcoat and starts crossing to door* R.*)* I'm going to the movies!

**AMANDA**  *(Crosses* C.*).* I don't believe that lie!

**TOM**  *(Crosses back to* AMANDA*).* No? Well, you're right. For once in your life you're right. I'm not going to the movies. I'm going to opium dens! Yes, Mother, opium dens, dens of vice and criminals' hang-outs, Mother. I've joined the Hogan gang. I'm a hired assassin, I carry a tommy-gun in a violin case! I run a string of cathouses in the valley! They call me Killer, Killer Wingfield, I'm really leading a double life. By day I'm a simple, honest warehouse worker, but at night I'm a dynamic <u>czar</u> of the under-world. Why, I go to gambling casinos and spin away a fortune on the roulette table! I wear a patch over one eye and a false moustache, some-times I wear green whiskers. On those occasions they call me—El Diablo![11] Oh, I could tell you things to make you sleepless! My enemies plan to dynamite this place some night! Some night they're going to blow us all sky-high. And will I be glad! Will I be happy! And so will you be. You'll go up—up—over Blue Mountain on a broomstick! With seventeen gentlemen callers. You ugly babbling old witch! *(He goes through a series of violent, clumsy movements, seizing his over-coat, lunging to* R. *door, pulling it fiercely open. The women watch him,* <u>aghast</u>. *His arm catches in the sleeve of the coat as he struggles to pull it on. For a moment he is* <u>pinioned</u> *by the bulky garment. With an out-raged groan he tears the coat off again, splitting the shoulder of it, and hurls it across the room. It strikes against the shelf of* LAURA's *glass collection, there is a tinkle of shattering glass.* LAURA *cries out as if wounded.)*

What happens to the glass menagerie?

**LAURA.**  My glass!—menagerie . . . *(She covers her face and turns away.* MUSIC CUE #8 *through to end of scene.)*

**AMANDA**  *(In an awful voice).* I'll never speak to you again as long as you live unless you apolo-gize to me! *(AMANDA exits through living-room curtains.* TOM *is left with* LAURA. *He stares at her stu-pidly for a moment. Then he crosses to shelf holding glass menagerie. Drops awkwardly on his knees to collect fallen glass, glancing at* LAURA *as if he would speak, but couldn't. Blackout.* TOM, AMANDA, *and* LAURA *exit in blackout.)*

What feelings for his sister are revealed by Tom's actions?

---

11. **El Diablo.** Spanish for "the devil"

---

**WORDS FOR EVERYDAY USE**

**czar** (zar) *n.*, emperor. *The Russian <u>czar</u> was an absolute monarch.*

**a • ghast** (ə gast´) *adj.*, feeling great horror or dismay. *When Sheila dropped my favorite figure, I looked at her, <u>aghast</u>!*

**pin • ion** (pin´yən) *vt.*, disable or impede. *They <u>pinioned</u> the prize parrot's wings so that it could not fly away.*

## Respond to the SELECTION

If you were Tom, would you follow your dreams or carry out your familial duties? Why?

# INVESTIGATE, Inquire, Imagine

**Recall:** GATHERING FACTS

1a. What new job does Amanda undertake?

2a. What does Tom do for a living? What is his role in the financial stability of the family? About what do Tom and Amanda argue?

3a. What happens at the end of the scene to Laura's menagerie?

→ **Interpret:** FINDING MEANING

1b. How does Amanda intrude on Tom's privacy?

2b. What does Tom want to do with himself? What does he fear will happen if he continues working at Continental Shoemakers?

3b. How would Tom's plans for his future harm Laura?

**Analyze:** TAKING THINGS APART

4a. Analyze why Laura is physically present in this scene even though she hardly speaks.

→ **Synthesize:** BRINGING THINGS TOGETHER

4b. What is the significance of the shattered glass animals?

**Evaluate:** MAKING JUDGMENTS

5a. Which character possesses the most determination—Amanda, Tom, or Laura? Why?

→ **Extend:** CONNECTING IDEAS

5b. What could Tom and Laura do to equal their mother's determination?

# Understanding Literature

SYMBOL. Review the definition for **symbol** in the Handbook of Literary Terms. Of what is the glass menagerie in the play a symbol? What similarities do the menagerie and Laura have?

CONFLICT. Review the definition of **conflict** in the Handbook of Literary Terms, reviewing the distinction between *external conflict* and *internal conflict.* Then make a chart like the one below. On the left, write examples of Tom's conflicts in scene 3. On the right, identify whether each example demonstrates an external or an internal conflict. One example has been done for you.

| Conflicts | Type of Conflict |
|---|---|
| Tom is trying to write but is interrupted by his mother. | External |

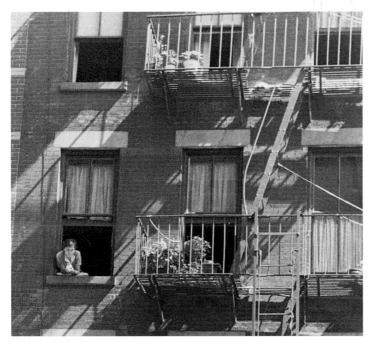

*New York House Fronts* [Detail], 1938. Walker Evans.

## Literary
### T O O L S

**SYMBOL.** A **symbol** is a thing that stands for or represents both itself and something else. As you read this scene, determine what the magician's trick symbolizes for Tom.

**CHARACTER.** A **character** is a person who figures in the action of a literary work. Assess Tom's character as you read this scene.

## Reader's
*Journal*

From what have you wanted to escape?

### ACT 1, SCENE 4

*The interior is dark. Faint light in alley* R. *A deep-voiced bell in a church is tolling the hour of five as the scene commences.*

  TOM *appears at the top of* R. *alley. After each solemn boom of the bell in the tower he shakes a little toy noisemaker or rattle as if to express the tiny spasm of man in contrast to the sustained power and dignity of the Almighty. This and the unsteadiness of his advance make it evident that he has been drinking. As he climbs the few steps to the fire-escape landing light steals up inside.* LAURA *appears in night-dress, entering living-room from* L. *door of dining-room, observing* TOM's *empty bed (day-bed) in the living-room.* TOM *fishes in his pockets for door-key, removing a <u>motley</u> assortment of articles in the search, including a perfect shower of movie-ticket stubs and an empty bottle. At last he finds the key, but just as he is about to insert it, it slips from his fingers. He strikes a match and crouches below the door.*

**TOM**   *(Bitterly).* One crack—and it falls through! (LAURA *opens door* R.)

**LAURA.**   Tom! Tom, what are you doing?

**WORDS FOR EVERYDAY USE**   **mot • ley** (mät´lē) *adj.,* composed of many different elements. *The junk drawer held a <u>motley</u> collection of gadgets, rubber bands, and bills.*

**TOM.** Looking for a door-key.

**LAURA.** Where have you been all this time?

**TOM.** I have been to the movies.

**LAURA.** All this time at the movies?

**TOM.** There was a very long program. There was a Garbo picture and a Mickey Mouse and a travelogue and a newsreel[12] and a preview of coming attractions. And there was an organ solo and a collection for the milk-fund—simultaneously—which ended up in a terrible fight between a fat lady and an usher!

**LAURA** *(Innocently).* Did you have to stay through everything?

**TOM.** Of course! And, oh, I forgot! There was a big stage show! The headliner on this stage show was Malvolio the Magician. He performed wonderful tricks, many of them, such as pouring water back and forth between pitchers. First it turned to wine and then it turned to beer and then it turned to whiskey. I know it was whiskey it finally turned into because he needed somebody to come up out of the audience to help him, and I came up—both shows! It was Kentucky Straight Bourbon. A very generous fellow, he gave souvenirs. *(He pulls from his back pocket a shimmering rainbow-colored scarf.)* He gave me this. This is his magic scarf. You can

> What does Tom give Laura? Why does he give this to her?

have it, Laura. You wave it over a canary cage and you get a bowl of gold-fish. You wave it over the gold-fish bowl and they fly away canaries. . . . But the wonderfullest trick of all was the coffin trick. We nailed him into a coffin and he got out of the coffin without removing one nail. *(They enter.)* There is a trick that would come in handy for me— get me out of this 2 by 4 situation! *(Flops onto day-bed and starts removing shoes.)*

> To what trick does Tom compare his desire to get out of his situation?

**LAURA.** Tom—shhh!

**TOM.** What're you shushing me for?

**LAURA.** You'll wake up Mother.

**TOM.** Goody goody! Pay'er back for all those "Rise an' Shines." *(Lies down groaning.)* You know it don't take much intelligence to get yourself into a nailed-up coffin, Laura. But who in hell ever got himself out of one without removing one nail? *(As if in answer, the father's grinning photograph lights up.* LAURA *exits up* L. *Lights fade except for blue glow in dining-room. Pause after lights fade, then clock chimes six times. This is followed by the alarm clock. Dim in fore-stage.)*

---

12. **travelogue and a newsreel.** *Travelogue*—film about a foreign place; *newsreel*—short motion picture of recent news events; both were formerly shown as part of the program in movie theaters.

**Respond** *to the*
## SELECTION

If you were Tom, what concerns would you have about your family if you left?

# INVESTIGATE, Inquire, Imagine

**Recall**: GATHERING FACTS

1a. How does Tom behave when he returns home?

2a. According to Tom, what was "the wonderfullest trick of all" performed by Malvolio the Magician?

3a. What lights up at the end of this scene?

→ **Interpret**: FINDING MEANING

1b. Why does Tom drink?

2b. Why is Tom so impressed by the magic trick of escaping from a coffin without removing a nail? What similarities are there between the trick and what Tom would have to do to get himself out of his current situation?

3b. What event does this illumination foreshadow?

**Analyze**: TAKING THINGS APART

4a. Identify Tom's feelings for his sister, Laura, and tell how he demonstrates those feelings.

→ **Synthesize**: BRINGING THINGS TOGETHER

4b. Summarize how Tom resembles his father.

**Perspective**: LOOKING AT OTHER VIEWS

5a. Tom treats Laura as a child and does not reveal his intentions to her. How would the scene be different if Tom confided in Laura his plans of going away?

→ **Empathy**: SEEING FROM INSIDE

5b. If you were Laura, how would you be affected by Tom's strange behavior in this scene?

# Understanding Literature

**SYMBOL.** Review the definition for **symbol** in the Handbook of Literary Terms. What does the coffin of which Tom speaks symbolize for him? What "trick" does Tom want to be able to perform? What "nails" would he have to remove in order to perform this trick? Why does Tom think that it would take magic for him to be able to do that?

**CHARACTER.** Review the definition for **character** in the Handbook of Literary Terms. Then make a chart like the one below to assess Tom's character traits. Fill in the chart with examples from scenes 1 through 4 of the play. One example has been done for you. How do Tom's dreams contrast with his mother's?

| Physical Appearance | Dress | Habits/Mannerisms/ Behaviors | Relationships with Other People | Other |
|---|---|---|---|---|
| | merchant sailor uniform | | | |

SETTING. The **setting** of a literary work is the time and place in which it occurs, together with all the details used to create a sense of a particular time and place. Writers create a setting by various means. In drama, the setting is often revealed by the stage set and the costumes, though it may be revealed through what the characters say about their environs. In its widest sense, setting includes the general social, political, moral and psychological conditions in which characters find themselves. As you read this scene, think about what realities the characters in the play are escaping.

CLICHÉ. A **cliché** is an overused or unoriginal expression such as *quiet as a mouse* or *couch potato*. As you read this scene, notice the clichés Amanda uses.

*New York House Fronts* [Detail], 1938.
Walker Evans.

### ACT 1, SCENE 5

*Scene is the same. Immediately following. The churchbell is heard striking six. At the sixth stroke the alarm clock goes off in* AMANDA's *room off* R. *of dining-room and after a few moments we hear her calling, "Rise and shine! Rise and shine!* LAURA, *go tell your brother to rise and shine!"*

**TOM** *(Sitting up slowly in day-bed).* I'll rise—but I won't shine. *(The light increases.)*

**AMANDA** *(Offstage).* Laura, tell your brother his coffee is ready. (LAURA, *fully dressed, a cape over her shoulders, slips into living-room.* TOM *is still in bed, covered with blanket, having taken off only shoes and coat.)*

**LAURA.** Tom!—It's nearly seven. Don't make Mother nervous. *(He stares at her stupidly. Beseechingly.)* Tom, speak to Mother this morning. Make up with her, apologize, speak to her!

**TOM** *(Putting on shoes).* She won't to me. It's her that started not speaking.

**LAURA.** If you just say you're sorry she'll start speaking.

**TOM.** Her not speaking—is that such a tragedy?

**LAURA.** Please—please!

**AMANDA** *(Calling offstage* R. *from kitchen).* Laura, are you going to do what I asked you to do, or do I have to get dressed and go out myself?

**LAURA.** Going, going—soon as I get on my coat! *(She rises and crosses to door* R.) Butter and what else?

*(To* AMANDA.)

**AMANDA** *(Offstage)*. Just butter. Tell them to charge it.

**LAURA.** Mother, they make such faces when I do that.

**AMANDA** *(Offstage)*. Sticks and stones can break our bones, but the expression on Mr. Garfinkel's face won't harm us! Tell your brother his coffee is getting cold.

**LAURA** *(At door* R.). Do what I asked you, will you, will you, Tom? *(He looks sullenly away.)*

**AMANDA.** Laura, go now or just don't go at all!

**LAURA** *(Rushing out* R.). Going—going! *(A second later she cries out. Falls on fire-escape landing.* TOM *springs up and crosses to door* R. AMANDA *rushes anxiously in from dining-room, puts dishes on dining-room table.* TOM *opens door* R.)

> What do Tom and Amanda do when Laura falls? What feelings are revealed by their actions?

**TOM.** Laura?

**LAURA.** I'm all right. I slipped, but I'm all right. *(Goes up* R. *alley, out of sight.)*

**AMANDA** *(On fire-escape)*. I tell you if anybody falls down and breaks a leg on those fire-escape steps, the landlord ought to be sued for every cent he——*(Sees* TOM.) Who are you? *(Leaves fire-escape landing, crosses to dining-room and returns with bowls, coffee cup, cream, etc. Puts them on small table* R. *of day-bed, crosses to armchair, sits. Counts 3.* MUSIC CUE #9. *As* TOM *reenters* R., *listlessly* *for his coffee, she turns her back to him, as she sits in armchair. The light on her face with its aged but childish features is cruelly sharp, satirical as a Daumier print.*[13] TOM *glances* *sheepishly* *but*

*sullenly at her averted figure and sits on day-bed next to the food. The coffee is scalding hot, he sips it and gasps and spits it back in the cup. At his gasp,* AMANDA *catches her breath and half turns. Then catches herself and turns away.* TOM *blows on his coffee, glancing sidewise at his mother. She clears her throat.* TOM *clears his. He starts to rise. Sinks back down again, scratches his head, clears his throat again.* AMANDA *coughs.* TOM *raises his cup in both hands to blow on it, his eyes staring over the rim of it at his mother for several moments. Then he slowly sets the cup down and awkwardly and hesitantly rises from day-bed.)*

**TOM** *(Hoarsely)*. I'm sorry, Mother. I'm sorry for all those things I said. I didn't mean it. I apologize.

**AMANDA** *(Sobbingly)*. My devotion has made me a witch and so I make myself hateful to my children!

**TOM.** No, you don't.

**AMANDA.** I worry so much, I don't sleep, it makes me nervous!

**TOM** *(Gently)*. I understand that.

**AMANDA.** You know I've had to put up a solitary battle all these years. But you're my right hand bower! Now don't fail me. Don't fall down.

> What has Amanda's life been like? Why does she depend on her son?

**TOM** *(Gently)*. I try, Mother.

**AMANDA** *(With great enthusiasm)*. That's all right! You just keep on trying and you're bound to succeed. Why, you're—you're just full of natural endowments! Both my children are—they're very precious children and I've got an

---

13. **Daumier print.** Lithograph by Honoré Daumier (1808–1879), artist famed for his caricatures and satires

| **WORDS FOR EVERYDAY USE** | **list • less • ly** (list´lis lē) *adv.,* in a disinterested manner. *It was such a hot day that I lay* *listlessly* *in the hammock.*<br>**sheep • ish • ly** (shēp´ish lē) *adv.,* in an embarrassed manner. *Steve looked at me* *sheepishly* *when I pointed out his socks did not match.*<br>**en • dow • ment** (en dou´mənt) *n.,* gift of nature; inherent talent. *Wit and writing skill were only two of Samuel Johnson's* *endowments*. |
|---|---|

awful lot to be thankful for; you just must promise me one thing.

(MUSIC CUE #9 *stops.*)

**TOM.** What is it, Mother?

**AMANDA.** Promise me you're never going to become a drunkard!

**TOM.** I promise, Mother. I won't ever become a drunkard!

**AMANDA.** That's what frightened me so, that you'd be drinking! Eat a bowl of Purina.

**TOM.** Just coffee, Mother.

**AMANDA.** Shredded Wheat Biscuit?

**TOM.** No, no, Mother, just coffee.

**AMANDA.** You can't put in a day's work on an empty stomach. You've got ten minutes—don't gulp! Drinking too-hot liquids makes cancer of the stomach. . . . Put cream in.

**TOM.** No, thank you.

**AMANDA.** To cool it.

**TOM.** No! No, thank you, I want it black.

**AMANDA.** I know, but it's not good for you. We have to do all that we can to build ourselves up. In these trying times we live in, all that we have to cling to is—each other. . . . That's why it's so important to—Tom, I—I sent out your sister so I could discuss something with you. If you hadn't spoken I would have spoken to you. *(Sits down.)*

**TOM** *(Gently).* What is it, Mother, that you want to discuss?

**AMANDA.** Laura! (TOM *puts his cup down slowly.* MUSIC CUE #10.)

**TOM.** Oh.—Laura . . .

**AMANDA** *(Touching his sleeve).* You know how Laura is. So quiet but—still water runs deep! She notices things and I think she—broods about them. (TOM *looks up.*) A few days ago I came in and she was crying.

**TOM.** What about?

**AMANDA.** You.

**TOM.** Me?

**AMANDA.** She has an idea that you're not happy here.

(MUSIC CUE #10 *stops.*)

**TOM.** What gave her that idea?

**AMANDA.** What gives her any idea? However, you do act strangely. (TOM *slaps cup down on small table.*) I—I'm not criticizing, understand that! I know your ambitions do not lie in the warehouse, that like everybody in the whole wide world—you've had to—make sacrifices, but—Tom—Tom—life's not easy, it calls for— Spartan endurance!

> What is hard for Amanda to admit?

There's so many things in my heart that I cannot describe to you! I've never told you but I— loved your father . . .

**TOM** *(Gently).* I know that, Mother.

**AMANDA.** And you—when I see you taking after his ways! Staying out late—and—well, you had been drinking the night you were in that— terrifying condition! Laura says that you hate the apartment and that you go out nights to get away from it! Is that true, Tom?

> Why is Laura upset?

**TOM.** No. You say there's so much in your heart that you can't describe to me. That's true of me, too. There's so much in my heart that I can't describe to you! So let's respect each other's—

**AMANDA.** But why—why, Tom—are you always so restless? Where do you go to, nights?

---

**WORDS FOR EVERYDAY USE**

**Spar • tan** (spartʹən) *adj.,* like the Spartans; warlike, stoical, and disciplined. *The coach complimented the Spartan attitude of the team after their victory.*

**TOM.** I—go to the movies.

**AMANDA.** Why do you go to the movies so much, Tom?

**TOM.** I go to the movies because—I like adventure. Adventure is something I don't have much of at work, so I go to the movies.

**AMANDA.** But, Tom, you go to the movies entirely too much!

**TOM.** I like a lot of adventure. (AMANDA *looks baffled, then hurt. As the familiar* inquisition *resumes he becomes hard and impatient again.* AMANDA *slips back into her* querulous *attitude toward him.*)

**AMANDA.** Most young men find adventure in their careers.

**TOM.** Then most young men are not employed in a warehouse.

**AMANDA.** The world is full of young men employed in warehouses and offices and factories.

**TOM.** Do all of them find adventure in their careers?

**AMANDA.** They do or they do without it! Not everybody has a craze for adventure.

**TOM.** Man is by instinct a lover, a hunter, a fighter, and none of those instincts are given much play at the warehouse!

**AMANDA.** Man is by instinct! Don't quote instinct to me! Instinct is something that people have got away from! It belongs to animals! Christian adults don't want it!

**TOM.** What do Christian adults want, then, Mother?

**AMANDA.** Superior things! Things of the mind and the spirit! Only animals have to satisfy instincts! Surely your aims are somewhat higher than theirs! Than monkeys—pigs——

**TOM.** I reckon they're not.

**AMANDA.** You're joking. However, that isn't what I wanted to discuss.

**TOM** *(Rising).* I haven't much time.

**AMANDA** *(Pushing his shoulders).* Sit down.

**TOM.** You want me to punch in red at the warehouse, Mother?

**AMANDA.** You have five minutes. I want to talk about Laura.

**TOM.** All right! What about Laura?

**AMANDA.** We have to be making some plans and provisions for her. She's older than you, two years, and nothing has happened. She just drifts along doing nothing. It frightens me terribly how she just drifts along.

**TOM.** I guess she's the type that people call home girls.

**AMANDA.** There's no such type, and if there is, it's a pity! That is unless the home is hers, with a husband!

**TOM.** What?

**AMANDA** *(Crossing* D. R. *to armchair).* Oh, I can see the handwriting on the wall as plain as I see the nose in front of my face! It's terrifying! More and more you remind me of your father! He was out all *(Sits in armchair)* hours without explanation!—Then left! Good-bye! And me with the bag to hold. I saw that letter you got from the Merchant Marine. I know what you're dreaming of. I'm not standing here blindfolded. Very well, then. Then do it! But not till there's somebody to take your place.

**TOM.** What do you mean?

**AMANDA.** I mean that as soon as Laura has got

> Under what circumstances does Amanda say Tom can free himself from the responsibility of supporting his family?

---

**WORDS FOR EVERYDAY USE**

in • qui • si • tion (in´kwə zish´ən) *n.,* severe or intensive questioning. *An* inquisition *of the employees ensued when money was discovered missing.*

quer • u • lous (kwer´yü ləs) *adj.,* full of complaint; peevish. *Amy's* querulous *questioning angered her boyfriend.*

somebody to take care of her, married, a home of her own, independent— why, then you'll be free to go wherever you please, (*Rises, crosses to* TOM.) on land, on sea, whichever way the wind blows you! But until that time you've got to look out for your sister. (*Crosses* R. *behind armchair.*) I don't say me because I'm old and don't matter! I say for your sister because she's young and dependent. I put her in business college—a dismal failure! Frightened her so it made her sick at the stomach! I took her over to the Young People's League at the church. Another fiasco. She spoke to nobody, nobody spoke to her. (*Sits armchair.*) Now all she does is fool with those pieces of glass and play those worn-out records. What kind of a life is that for a girl to lead?

**TOM.** What can I do about it?

**AMANDA.** Overcome selfishness! Self, self, self is all that you ever think of! (TOM *springs up and crosses* R. *to get his coat and put it on. It is ugly and bulky. He pulls on a cap with earmuffs.*) Where is your muffler? Put your wool muffler on! (*He snatches it angrily from the hook and tosses it around his neck and pulls both ends tight.*) Tom! I haven't said what I had in mind to ask you.

**TOM.** I'm too late to——

**AMANDA** (*Catching his arm—very* importunately. *Then shyly*). Down at the warehouse, aren't there some—nice young men?

**TOM.** No!

**AMANDA.** There must be—some . . .

**TOM.** Mother——(*Gesture.*)

**AMANDA.** Find out one that's clean-living—doesn't drink and—ask him out for sister!

> What does Amanda ask Tom to do?

**TOM.** What?

**AMANDA.** For sister! To meet! Get acquainted!

**TOM** (*Stamping to door* R.). Oh, my go-osh!

**AMANDA.** Will you? (*He opens door.* Imploringly.) Will you? (*He starts out.*) Will you? Will you, dear? (TOM *exits up alley* R. AMANDA *is on fire-escape landing.*)

**TOM** (*Calling back*). Yes!

**AMANDA** (*Re-entering* R. *and crossing to phone.* MUSIC CUE #11). Ella Cartwright? Ella, this is Amanda Wingfield. First, first, how's that kidney trouble? Oh, it has? It has come back? Well, you're just a Christian martyr, you're just a Christian martyr. I was noticing in my little red book that your subscription to the "Companion" has run out just when that wonderful new serial by Bessie Mae Harper was starting. It's all about the horsey set on Long Island. Oh, you have? You have read it? Well, how do you think it turns out? Oh, no. Bessie Mae Harper never lets you down. Oh, of course, we have to have complications. You have to have complications—oh, you can't have a story without them—but Bessie Mae Harper always leaves you with such an uplift—— What's the matter, Ella? You sound so mad. Oh, because it's seven o'clock in the morning. Oh, Ella, I forgot that you never got up until nine. I forgot that anybody in the world was allowed to sleep as late as that. I can't say any more than I'm sorry, can I? Oh, you will? You're going to take that subscription from me anyhow? Well, bless you, Ella, bless you, bless you, bless you. (MUSIC CUE #11 faces into MUSIC CUE #11-A, *dance music, and continues into next scene. Dim out lights.* MUSIC CUE #11-A.)

---

**WORDS FOR EVERYDAY USE**

**dis • mal** (diz´məl) *adj.*, causing gloom or misery. *The dismal weather in London spoiled the Smiths' vacation.*

**im • por • tu • nate • ly** (im pôr´chü nit lē) *adv.*, in an annoyingly urgent or persistent manner. *Alicia got the bicycle she wanted after importunately begging her parents for weeks.*

**im • plor • ing • ly** (im plôr´iŋ lē) *adv.*, in a beseeching manner. *My brother looked at me imploringly until I agreed to take him to the movie.*

If you were Laura, how would you feel about your family fixing you up with a suitor?

# INVESTIGATE Inquire Imagine

**Recall:** GATHERING FACTS

1a. What does Laura want Tom to do? How is Amanda acting toward Tom at the beginning of this scene? Why?

2a. Amanda is afraid that Tom is becoming like someone else. Who is that person? How did she feel about him?

3a. What does Amanda want Tom to delay doing? What specific request does she make of him at the end of the scene?

**Interpret:** FINDING MEANING

1b. How does Amanda treat Tom once they are talking to each other again?

2b. What similarity does Amanda see between Tom and her husband?

3b. What is Amanda's plan for her family?

**Analyze:** TAKING THINGS APART

4a. How do Amanda's and Tom's views of human nature differ?

**Synthesize:** BRINGING THINGS TOGETHER

4b. Does Laura seem to subscribe to Tom's or Amanda's vision of human nature? Explain.

**Evaluate:** MAKING JUDGMENTS

5b. Do you think Tom is justified in wanting to leave home? Why, or why not?

**Extend:** CONNECTING IDEAS

5b. How do other characters in fiction, on TV, and in movies oppose their parents' world? What risks do they take? How often are they successful?

# Understanding Literature

**SETTING.** Review the definition for **setting** in the Handbook of Literary Terms. *The Glass Menagerie* is a play about people's dreams for the future. From what realities are the characters in the play escaping? What must Tom do if he is to confront reality and realize his dreams, rather than simply continuing to escape by going to the movies?

**CLICHÉ.** Review the definition for **cliché** in the Handbook of Literary Terms. Then make a chart. On the left, list clichés that Amanda uses. On the right, paraphrase the clichés. One example has been done for you.

| Clichés | Paraphrases |
| --- | --- |
| rise and shine | get up and greet the day with enthusiasm |
|  |  |

**DIALOGUE. Dialogue** is conversation involving two or more people or characters. Plays are made up of dialogue and stage directions. As you read this scene, determine what the dialogue reveals about Amanda and Tom and how they communicate with each other.

**SYMBOL.** A **symbol** is a thing that stands for or represents both itself and something else. Think about all the symbols in act 1 and decide what they represent.

## Reader's
### Journal

When you invite a guest home, what kinds of plans do you make?

*New York House Fronts* [Detail], 1938. Walker Evans.

## ACT 1, SCENE 6

SCENE: *The same.—Only* R. *alley lighted, with dim light.*

**TOM** *(Enters down* R. *and stands as before, leaning against grill-work, with cigarette, wearing merchant sailor coat and cap).* Across the alley was the Paradise Dance Hall. Evenings in spring they'd open all the doors and windows and the music would come outside. Sometimes they'd turn out all the lights except for a large glass sphere that hung from the ceiling. It would turn slowly about and filter the dusk with delicate rainbow colors. Then the orchestra would play a waltz or a tango, something that had a slow and sensuous rhythm. The young couples would come outside, to the relative privacy of the alley. You could see them kissing behind ashpits and telephone poles. This was the compensation for lives that passed like mine, without change or adventure. Changes and adventure, however, were <u>imminent</u> this year. They were waiting around the corner for all these dancing kids. Suspended in the mist over Berchtesgaden,[14] caught in the folds of Chamberlain's

---

14. **Berchtesgaden.** Town in southern Germany that was destroyed by an Allied air attack in 1945

**WORDS FOR EVERYDAY USE**

**im • mi • nent** (im´ə nənt) *adj.,* likely to happen without delay. *Since Marty and Chris had different opinions about the strike, an argument was imminent.*

umbrella. In Spain there was Guernica![15] Here there was only hot swing music and liquor, dance halls, bars, and movies, and sex that hung in the gloom like a chandelier and flooded the world with brief, deceptive rainbows. . . . While these unsuspecting kids danced to "Dear One, The World Is Waiting for the Sunrise." All the world was really waiting for <u>bombardments</u>. (MUSIC #11-A *stops. Dim in dining-room: faint glow.* AMANDA *is seen in dining-room.*)

**AMANDA.** Tom, where are you?

**TOM** *(Standing as before).* I came out to smoke. *(Exit* R. *into the wings, where he again changes coats and leaves hat.)*

**AMANDA** *(*TOM *re-enters and stands on fire-escape landing, smoking. He opens door for* AMANDA, *who sits on hassock on landing).* Oh, you smoke too much. A pack a day at fifteen cents a pack. How much would that be in a month? Thirty times fifteen? It wouldn't be very much. Well, it would be enough to help towards a night-school course in accounting at the Washington U! Wouldn't that be lovely?

**TOM.** I'd rather smoke.

**AMANDA.** I know! That's the tragedy of you. This fire-escape landing is a poor excuse for the porch we used to have. What are you looking at?

**TOM.** The moon.

**AMANDA.** Is there a moon this evening?

**TOM.** It's rising over Garfinkel's Delicatessen.

**AMANDA.** Oh! So it is! Such a little silver slipper of a moon. Have you made a wish on it?

**TOM.** Um-mm.

**AMANDA.** What did you wish?

**TOM.** That's a secret.

**AMANDA.** All right, I won't tell you what I wished, either. I can keep a secret, too. I can be just as mysterious as you.

**TOM.** I bet I can guess what you wished.

**AMANDA.** Why, is my head transparent?

**TOM.** You're not a sphinx.

**AMANDA.** No, I don't have secrets. I'll tell you what I wished for on the moon. Success and happiness for my precious children. I wish for that whenever there's a moon, and when there isn't a moon, I wish for it, too.

> What does Amanda wish for her children?

**TOM.** I thought perhaps you wished for a gentleman caller.

**AMANDA.** Why do you say that?

**TOM.** Don't you remember asking me to fetch one?

**AMANDA.** I remember suggesting that it would be nice for your sister if you brought home some nice young man from the warehouse. I think that I've made that suggestion more than once.

**TOM.** Yes, you have made it repeatedly.

**AMANDA.** Well?

**TOM.** We are going to have one.

**AMANDA.** *What?*

**TOM.** A gentleman caller!

**AMANDA.** You mean you have asked some nice young man to come over? *(Rising from stool, facing* TOM.)*

**TOM.** I've asked him to dinner.

**AMANDA.** You really did?

**TOM.** I did.

**AMANDA.** And did he accept?

---

15. **Guernica.** City in northern Spain that was heavily bombed by the Germans in 1937

**WORDS FOR EVERYDAY USE**

bom • bard • ment (bäm bard´mənt) *n.,* attack by bombs. *Londoners took refuge in shelters during the <u>bombardment</u> by German planes.*

**TOM.** He did!

**AMANDA.** He did?

**TOM.** He did.

**AMANDA.** Well, isn't that lovely!

**TOM.** I thought that you would be pleased.

**AMANDA.** It's definite, then?

**TOM.** Oh, very definite.

**AMANDA.** How soon?

**TOM.** Pretty soon.

**AMANDA.** How soon?

**TOM.** Quite soon.

**AMANDA.** How soon?

**TOM.** Very, very soon.

**AMANDA.** Every time I want to know anything you start going on like that.

**TOM.** What do you want to know?

**AMANDA.** Go ahead and guess. Go ahead and guess.

**TOM.** All right, I'll guess. You want to know when the gentleman caller's coming—he's coming tomorrow.

**AMANDA.** Tomorrow? Oh, no, I can't do anything about tomorrow. I can't do anything about tomorrow.

**TOM.** Why not?

**AMANDA.** That doesn't give me any time.

**TOM.** Time for what?

**AMANDA.** Time for preparations. Oh, you should have phoned me the minute you asked him—the minute he accepted!

**TOM.** You don't have to make any fuss.

**AMANDA.** Of course I have to make a fuss! I can't have a man coming into a place that's all sloppy. It's got to be thrown together properly. I certainly have to do some fast thinking by tomorrow night, too.

**TOM.** I don't see why you have to think at all.

How does Amanda feel about Tom's news? In what way does her speech betray this emotion?

**AMANDA.** That's because you just don't know. (*Enter living-room, crosses to* C. *Dim in living-room.*) You just don't know, that's all. We can't have a gentleman caller coming into a pig-sty! Now, let's see. Oh, I've got those three pieces of wedding silver left. I'll polish that up. I wonder how that old lace tablecloth is holding up all these years? We can't wear anything. We haven't got it. We haven't got anything to wear. We haven't got it. (*Goes back to door* R.)

**TOM.** Mother! This boy is no one to make a fuss over.

**AMANDA** (*Crossing to* C.). I don't know how you can say that when this is the first gentleman caller your little sister's ever had! I think it's pathetic that that little girl has never had a single gentleman caller! Come on inside! Come on inside!

Why is Amanda so excited about this gentleman caller?

**TOM.** What for?

**AMANDA.** I want to ask you a few things.

**TOM** (*From doorway* R.). If you're going to make a fuss, I'll call the whole thing off. I'll call the boy up and tell him not to come.

**AMANDA.** No! You mustn't ever do that. People hate broken engagements. They have no place to go. Come on inside. Come on inside. Will you come inside when I ask you to come inside? Sit down. (TOM *comes into living-room.*)

**TOM.** Any particular place you want me to sit?

**AMANDA.** Oh! Sit anywhere. (TOM *sits armchair* R.) Look! What am I going to do about that? (*Looking at day-bed.*) Did you ever see anything look so sad? I know, I'll get a bright piece of cretonne.[16] That won't cost much. And I made payments on a floor lamp. So I'll have that sent out! And I can put a bright cover on the chair. I wish I had time to paper the walls. What's his name?

**TOM.** His name is O'Connor.

---

16. **cretonne.** Heavy, printed cotton used for slipcovers

**AMANDA.** O'Connor—he's Irish and tomorrow's Friday—that means fish. Well, that's all right, I'll make a salmon loaf and some mayonnaise dressing for it. Where did you meet him? *(Crosses to day-bed and sits.)*

**TOM.** At the warehouse, of course. Where else would I meet him?

**AMANDA.** Well, I don't know. Does he drink?

**TOM.** What made you ask me that?

**AMANDA.** Because your father did.

**TOM.** Now, don't get started on that!

**AMANDA.** He drinks, then.

**TOM.** No, not that I know of.

**AMANDA.** You have to find out. There's nothing I want less for my daughter than a man who drinks.

**TOM.** Aren't you being a little bit <u>premature</u>? After all, poor Mr. O'Connor hasn't even appeared on the scene yet.

**AMANDA.** But he will tomorrow. To meet your sister. And what do I know about his character? *(Rises and crosses to* TOM *who is still in armchair, smooths his hair.)*

**TOM** *(Submitting grimly).* Now what are you up to?

**AMANDA.** I always did hate that cowlick. I never could understand why it won't sit down by itself.

**TOM.** Mother, I want to tell you something and I mean it sincerely right straight from my heart. There's a lot of boys who meet girls which they don't marry!

> What does Tom try to tell his mother?

**AMANDA.** You know you always had me worried because you could never stick to a subject.

*(Crosses to day-bed.)* What I want to know is what's his position at the warehouse?

**TOM.** He's a shipping clerk.

**AMANDA.** Oh! Shipping clerk! Well, that's fairly important. That's where you'd be if you had more get-up. How much does he earn? *(Sits on day-bed.)*

**TOM.** I have no way of knowing that for sure. I judge his salary to be approximately eighty-five dollars a month.

**AMANDA.** Eighty-five dollars? Well, that's not princely.

**TOM.** It's twenty dollars more than I make.

**AMANDA.** I know that. Oh, how well I know that! How well I know that! Eighty-five dollars a month. No. It can't be done. A family man can never get by on eighty-five dollars a month.

**TOM.** Mother, Mr. O'Connor is not a family man.

> Does Amanda listen? What does she do instead?

**AMANDA.** Well, he might be some time in the future, mightn't he?

**TOM.** Oh, I see . . . Plans and provisions.

**AMANDA.** You are the only young man that I know of who ignores the fact that the future becomes the present, the present the past, and the past turns into everlasting regret if you don't plan for it.

> Why does Amanda say you have to plan for the future?

**TOM.** I will think that over and see what I can make of it!

**AMANDA.** Don't be <u>supercilious</u> with your mother! Tell me some more about this—What do you call him? Mr. O'Connor, Mr. O'Connor. He must have another name besides Mr.——?

---

**WORDS FOR EVERYDAY USE**

pre • ma • ture (prē´mə tür´) *adj.*, too early. *The <u>premature</u> infant was placed in an incubator.*

su • per • cil • i • ous (sü´pər sil´ē əs) *adj.*, disdainful, contemptuous. *The queen adopted a <u>supercilious</u> attitude toward anyone who was less than an archduke.*

**TOM.** His full name is James D. O'Connor. The D. is for Delaney.

**AMANDA.** Delaney? Irish on both sides and he doesn't drink?

**TOM** *(Rises from armchair).* Shall I call him up and ask him? *(Starts toward phone.)*

**AMANDA** *(Crossing to phone).* No!

**TOM.** I'll call him up and tell him you want to know if he drinks. *(Picks up phone.)*

**AMANDA** *(Taking phone away from him).* No, you can't do that. You have to be <u>discreet</u> about that subject. When I was a girl in Blue Mountain if it was (TOM *sits on* R. *of day-bed*) suspected that a young man was drinking and any girl was receiving his attentions—if any girl *was* receiving his attentions, she'd go to the minister of his church and ask about his character—or her father, if her father was living, then it was his duty to go to the minister of his church and ask about his character, and that's how young girls in Blue Mountain were kept from making tragic mistakes. *(Picture dims in and out.)*

**TOM.** How come you made such a tragic one?

**AMANDA.** Oh, I don't know how he did it, but that face fooled everybody. All he had to do was grin and the world was bewitched. *(Behind day-bed, crosses to armchair.)* I don't know of anything more tragic than a young girl just putting herself at the mercy of a handsome appearance, and I hope Mr. O'Connor is not too goodlooking.

**TOM.** As a matter of fact he isn't. His face is covered with freckles and he has a very large nose.

**AMANDA.** He's not right-down homely?

**TOM.** No. I wouldn't say right-down—homely—medium homely, I'd say.

**AMANDA.** Well, if a girl had any sense she'd look for character in a man anyhow.

**TOM.** That's what I've always said, Mother.

**AMANDA.** You've always said it—you've always said it! How could you've always said it when you never even thought about it?

**TOM.** Aw, don't be so suspicious of me.

**AMANDA.** I am. I'm suspicious of every word that comes out of your mouth, when you talk to me, but I want to know about this young man. Is he up and coming?

**TOM.** Yes. I really do think he goes in for self-improvement.

**AMANDA.** What makes you think it?

**TOM.** He goes to night school.

**AMANDA.** Well, what does he do there at night school?

**TOM.** He's studying radio engineering and public speaking.

**AMANDA.** Oh! Public speaking! Oh, that shows, that shows that he intends to be an executive some day—and radio engineering. Well, that's coming . . . huh?

**TOM.** I think it's here.

**AMANDA.** Well, those are all very illuminating facts. *(Crosses to back of armchair.)* Facts that every mother should know about any young man calling on her daughter, seriously or not.

**TOM.** Just one little warning, Mother. I didn't tell him anything about Laura. I didn't let on we had dark <u>ulterior</u> motives. I just said, "How about coming home to dinner some time?" and he said, "Fine," and that was the whole conversation.

**AMANDA.** I bet it was, too. I tell you, sometimes you can be as eloquent as an oyster.

---

**WORDS FOR EVERYDAY USE**

**dis • creet** (di skrēt´) *adj.,* careful about what one says and does. *We were <u>discreet</u> so Susan would not find out about the surprise party we were planning for her.*

**ul • te • ri • or** (ul tir´ē ər) *adj.,* further; more remote; undisclosed; concealed. *We suspected the <u>ulterior</u> motives of the salesman when he offered us donuts with a smile.*

However, when he sees how pretty and sweet that child is, he's going to be, well, he's going to be very glad he was asked over here to have some dinner. *(Sits in armchair.)*

**TOM.** Mother, just one thing. You won't expect too much of Laura, will you?

*What warning does Tom give about Laura?*

**AMANDA.** I don't know what you mean. *(TOM crosses slowly to AMANDA. He stands for a moment, looking at her. Then—)*

**TOM.** Well, Laura seems all those things to you and me because she's ours and we love her. We don't even notice she's crippled any more.

**AMANDA.** Don't use that word.

**TOM.** Mother, you have to face the facts; she is, and that's not all.

**AMANDA.** What do you mean "that's not all"? *(TOM kneels by her chair.)*

**TOM.** Mother—you know that Laura is very different from other girls.

**AMANDA.** Yes, I do know that, and I think that difference is all in her favor, too.

*Who views Laura's predicament and character more honestly? Who views her with blind devotion?*

**TOM.** Not quite all—in the eyes of others—strangers—she's terribly shy. She lives in a world of her own and those things make her seem a little peculiar to people outside the house.

**AMANDA.** Don't use that word peculiar.

**TOM.** You have to face the facts.—She is.

**AMANDA.** I don't know in what way she's peculiar. *(MUSIC CUE #12, till curtain. TOM pauses a moment for music, then—)*

**TOM.** Mother, Laura lives in a world of little glass animals. She plays old phonograph records—and—that's about all——*(TOM rises slowly, goes quietly out the door R., leaving it open, and exits slowly up the alley. AMANDA rises, goes on to fire-escape landing R., looks at moon.)*

**AMANDA.** Laura! Laura! *(LAURA answers from kitchen R.)*

**LAURA.** Yes, Mother.

**AMANDA.** Let those dishes go and come in front! *(LAURA appears with dish towel. Gaily.)* Laura, come here and make a wish on the moon!

**LAURA** *(Entering from kitchen R. and comes down to fire-escape landing)*. Moon—moon?

**AMANDA.** A little silver slipper of a moon. Look over your left shoulder, Laura, and make a wish! *(LAURA looks faintly puzzled as if called out of sleep. AMANDA seizes her shoulders and turns her at an angle on the fire-escape landing.)* Now! Now, darling, wish!

**LAURA.** What shall I wish for, Mother?

**AMANDA** *(Her voice trembling and her eyes suddenly filling with tears)*. Happiness! And just a little bit of good fortune! *(The stage dims out.)*

**CURTAIN**

**End of Act One**

**Respond** *to the* **SELECTION**

If you were Amanda, how would you feel if Jim did not like Laura?

# INVESTIGATE Inquire Imagine

**Recall:** GATHERING FACTS

1a. What news does Tom give his mother at the beginning of the scene?

2a. What plans does Amanda make?

3a. What warning does Amanda give Tom?

→ **Interpret:** FINDING MEANING

1b. Why is Amanda excited about Tom's news?

2b. What is irrational about Amanda's plans to refurbish the apartment?

3b. Why would these words of Amanda's be better spent on Laura than on Tom?

---

**Analyze:** TAKING THINGS APART

4a. Identify what Tom reveals about Jim O'Connor to Amanda.

→ **Synthesize:** BRINGING THINGS TOGETHER

4b. Why does Amanda set all her hopes for Laura on Jim O'Connor?

---

**Evaluate:** MAKING JUDGMENTS

5a. Who sees Laura more realistically, Tom or Amanda? Explain.

→ **Extend:** CONNECTING IDEAS

5b. How might Laura react if she ran into Jim O'Connor on the street?

---

# Understanding Literature

**DIALOGUE.** Review the definition for **dialogue** in Literary Tools on page 714. How does Tom talk to Amanda after she learns a gentleman caller will be coming? Then how does Amanda talk to Tom? Does the dialogue reveal that Tom, or that Amanda, is more realistic about the gentleman caller's visit?

**SYMBOL.** Review the definition for **symbol** in the Handbook of Literary Terms. Then make a chart. On the left, list the symbols in act 1. On the right, explain the meaning of these symbols. One example has been done for you.

| Symbols | Meaning |
|---|---|
| Laura's tripping and falling on her way out to Garfinkle's Delicatessen | Laura's tripping and falling symbolizes her inability to operate on the most minimal level in the real world; she is unable to secure even the most basic of her needs. |
| | |

*New York House Fronts* [Detail], 1938. Walker Evans.

# Literary
## T O O L S

**CHARACTER.** A **character** is a person who figures in the action of a literary work. A *static character* is one who does not change during the course of the action. A *dynamic character* is one who does change. As you read this scene, decide whether Amanda is a static or a dynamic character and determine her primary characteristics.

# Reader's
## Journal

What does being successful mean to you?

## ACT 2, SCENE 7

SCENE: *The same.*

*Inner curtains closed between dining-room and living-room. Interiors of both rooms are dark as at beginning of play.* TOM *has on the same jacket and cap as at first. Same dance-hall music as* CUE #1, *fading as* TOM *begins.*

**TOM** (*Discovered leaning against grill on fire-escape landing, as before, and smoking*). And so the following evening I brought Jim home to dinner. I had known Jim slightly in high school. In high school, Jim was a hero. He had tremendous Irish good nature and vitality with the scrubbed and polished look of white chinaware. He seemed to move in a continual spotlight. He was a star in basketball, captain of the debating club, president of the senior class and the glee club, and he sang the male lead in the annual light opera. He was forever running or bounding, never just walking. He seemed always just at the point of defeating the law of gravity. He was shooting with such <u>velocity</u> through his adolescence that you would just logically expect him to arrive at nothing short of the White House by the time he was thirty. But Jim apparently ran into more <u>interference</u> after his graduation from high school because his speed had definitely slowed. And so, at this particular time in our lives he was holding

*What was Jim like in high school? What did people expect of him?*

| WORDS FOR EVERYDAY USE | **ve • loc • i • ty** (və läs´ə tē) *n.*, quickness or rapidity of motion or action. *The bay mare ran with such <u>velocity</u> that she was sure to win the race.* |
|---|---|
| | **in • ter • fer • ence** (in´ter fir´ens) *n.*, something that comes into collision or opposition. *His child's <u>interference</u> prevented Allan from finishing his project.* |

a job that wasn't much better than mine. He was the only one at the warehouse

What happened to Jim after high school?

with whom I was on friendly terms. I was valuable to Jim as someone who could remember his former glory, who had seen him win basketball games and the silver cup in debating. He knew of my secret practice of retiring to a cabinet of the washroom to work on poems whenever business was slack in the warehouse. He called me Shakespeare. And while the other boys in the warehouse regarded me with suspicious hostility, Jim took a humorous attitude toward me. Gradually his attitude began to affect the other boys and their hostility wore off. And so, after a time they began to smile at me too, as people smile at some oddly fashioned dog that trots across their path at some distance. I knew that Jim and Laura had known each other in high school because I had heard my sister Laura speak admiringly of Jim's voice. I didn't know if Jim would remember her or not. Because in high school Laura had been as <u>unobtrusive</u> as Jim had been astonishing. And, if he did remember Laura, it was not as my sister, for when I asked him home to dinner, he smiled and said, "You know, a funny thing, Shakespeare, I never thought of you as having folks!" Well, he was about to discover that I did . . . (MUSIC CUE #13. TOM *exits* R. *Interior living-room lights dim in.* AMANDA *is sitting on small table* R. *of day-bed sewing on hem on* LAURA's *dress.* LAURA *stands facing the door* R. AMANDA *has worked like a Turk in preparation for the gentleman caller. The results are astonishing. The new floor lamp with its rose-silk shade is in place,* R. *of living-room next to wall, a colored paper lantern conceals the broken light fixture in the ceiling, chintz*[17] *covers are on chairs and sofa, a pair of new sofa pillows make their initial appearance.* LAURA *stands in the middle of room with lifted arms while* AMANDA *crouches before her, adjusting the hem of the new dress,* <u>devout</u> *and ritualistic. The dress is colored and designed by memory. The arrangement of* LAURA's *hair is changed; it is softer and more becoming. A fragile, unearthly prettiness has come out in* LAURA; *she is like a piece of translucent glass touched by light, given a momentary radiance, not actual, not lasting.* AMANDA, *still seated, is sewing* LAURA's *dress.* LAURA *is standing* R. *of* AMANDA.)

**AMANDA.** Why are you trembling so, Laura?

**LAURA.** Mother, you've made me so nervous!

**AMANDA.** Why, how have I made you nervous?

**LAURA.** By all this fuss! You make it seem so important.

**AMANDA.** I don't understand you at all, honey. Every time I try to do anything for you that's the least bit different you just seem to set yourself against it. Now take a look at yourself. (LAURA *starts for door* R.) No, wait! Wait just a minute—I forgot something. (*Picks two powder puffs from day-bed.*)

**LAURA.** What is it?

**AMANDA.** A couple of improvements. (*Business with powder puffs.*) When I was a girl we had round little lacy things like that and we called them "Gay Deceivers."

**LAURA.** I won't wear them!

**AMANDA.** Of course you'll wear them.

**LAURA.** Why should I?

**AMANDA.** Well, to tell you the truth, honey, you're just a little bit flat-chested.

**LAURA.** You make it seem like we were setting a trap.

---

17. **chintz.** Cotton cloth printed in color with flower designs or other patterns

**WORDS FOR EVERYDAY USE**

un • ob • tru • sive (un əb trü´siv) *adj.,* not calling attention to itself. *The student was <u>unobtrusive</u> in his plain clothes and quiet demeanor.*

de • vout (di vout´) *adj.,* showing reverence. *In ancient Canaanite civilization, many people were <u>devout</u> and faithful followers of the fertility god Ba'al.*

**AMANDA.** We are. All pretty girls are a trap and men expect them to be traps. Now look at yourself in that glass. (*LAURA crosses* R. *Looks at mirror, invisible to audience, which is in darkness up* R. *of* R. *door.*) See? You look just like an angel on a postcard. Isn't that lovely? Now you just wait. I'm going to dress myself up. You're going to be astonished at your mother's appearance. (END OF MUSIC CUE. *End of music cue leads into dance music, which then leads in* MUSIC CUE #14, *a few lines below, at stage direction.* AMANDA *exits through curtains upstage off* L. *in dining-room.* LAURA *looks in mirror for a moment. Removes "Gay Deceivers," hides them under mattress of day-bed. Sits on small table* R. *of day-bed for a moment, goes out to fire-escape landing, listens to dance music, until* AMANDA's *entrance.* AMANDA, *off.*) I found an old dress in the trunk. But what do you know? I had to do a lot to it but it broke my heart when I had to let it out. Now, Laura, just look at your mother. Oh, no! Laura, come look at me now! (*Enters dining-room* L. *door. Comes down through living-room curtain to living-room* C. MUSIC CUE. #14.)

**LAURA** (*Re-enters from fire-escape landing. Sits on* L. *arm of armchair*). Oh, Mother, how lovely! (AMANDA *wears a girlish frock. She carries a bunch of jonquils.*)

**AMANDA** (*Standing* C., *holding flowers*). It used to be. It used to be. It had a lot of flowers on it, but they got awful tired so I had to take them all off. I led the cotillion[18] in this dress years ago. I won the cake-walk[19] twice at Sunset Hill, and I wore it to the Governor's ball in Jackson. You should have seen your mother. You should have seen your mother how she just sashayed around (*Crossing around* L. *of day-bed back to* C.) the ballroom, just like that. I had it on the day I met your father. I had malaria fever, too. The change of climate from East Tennessee to the Delta—weakened my resistance. Not enough to be dangerous, just enough to make me restless and giddy. Oh, it was lovely. Invitations poured in from all over. My mother said, "You can't go any place because you have a fever. You have to stay in bed." I said I wouldn't and I took quinine[20] and kept on going and going. Dances every evening and long rides in the country in the afternoon and picnics. That country—that country—so lovely—so lovely in May, all lacy with dogwood and simply flooded with jonquils. My mother said, "You can't bring any more jonquils in this house." I said, "I will," and I kept on bringing them in anyhow. Whenever I saw them I said, "Wait a minute, I see jonquils," and I'd make my gentlemen callers get out of the carriage and help me gather some. To tell you the truth, Laura, it got to be a kind of a joke. "Look out," they'd say, "here comes that girl and we'll have to spend the afternoon picking jonquils." My mother said, "You can't bring any more jonquils in the house, there aren't any more vases to hold them." "That's quite all right," I said, "I can hold some myself." Malaria fever, your father and jonquils. (AMANDA *puts jonquils in* LAURA's *lap and goes out on to fire-escape land-*

*To what does Laura object? What does her mother say in response about the relationship between men and women? Do you agree with Amanda's statement? Why, or why not?*

*Of what does Amanda's dress remind her? Why might she always think back to this time?*

*What three things are united in Amanda's memory? In what way are her associations bitterly humorous?*

---

18. **cotillion.** Formal ball, especially one at which debutants are presented
19. **cake-walk.** Elaborate, strutting dance
20. **quinine.** Bitter medicine used to treat malaria

WORDS FOR EVERYDAY USE

**sa • shay** (sa shāʹ) *vi.,* move or walk in such a way as to attract attention. *Julia* sashayed *across the stage to show the egotism of her character.*

*ing.* MUSIC CUE #14 *stops. Thunder heard.)* I hope they get here before it starts to rain. I gave your brother a little extra change so he and Mr. O'Connor could take the service car home. *(*LAURA *puts flowers on armchair* R., *and crosses to door* R.)

**LAURA.** Mother!

**AMANDA.** What's the matter now? *(Reentering room.)*

**LAURA.** What did you say his name was?

**AMANDA.** O'Connor. Why?

**LAURA.** What is his first name?

**AMANDA** *(Crosses to armchair* R.). I don't remember—Oh, yes, I do too—it was—Jim! *(Picks up flowers.)*

**LAURA.** Oh, Mother, not Jim O'Connor!

**AMANDA.** Yes, that was it, it was Jim! I've never known a Jim that wasn't nice. *(Crosses* L., *behind day-bed, puts flowers in vase.)*

**LAURA.** Are you sure his name was Jim O'Connor?

**AMANDA.** Why, sure I'm sure. Why?

**LAURA.** Is he the one that Tom used to know in high school?

**AMANDA.** He didn't say so. I think he just got to know him—*(Sits on day-bed.)* at the warehouse.

**LAURA.** There was a Jim O'Connor we both knew in high school. If that is the one that Tom is bringing home to dinner——Oh, Mother, you'd have to excuse me, I wouldn't come to the table!

**AMANDA.** What's this now? What sort of silly talk is this?

**LAURA.** You asked me once if I'd ever liked a boy. Don't you remember I showed you this boy's picture?

**AMANDA.** You mean the boy in the year-book?

**LAURA.** Yes, that boy.

Why can't Laura sit at the table with Jim O'Connor?

**AMANDA.** Laura, Laura, were you in love with that boy?

**LAURA** *(Crosses to* R. *of armchair).* I don't know, Mother. All I know is that I couldn't sit at the table if it was him.

**AMANDA** *(Rises, crosses* L. *and works up* L. *of day-bed).* It won't be him! It isn't the least bit likely. But whether it is or not, you will come to the table—you will not be excused.

**LAURA.** I'll have to be, Mother.

**AMANDA** *(Behind day-bed).* I don't intend to humor your silliness, Laura, I've had too much from you and your brother, both. So just sit down and compose yourself till they come. Tom has forgotten his key, so you'll *have* to let them in when they arrive.

**LAURA.** Oh, Mother—*you* answer the door! *(Sits chair* R.)

**AMANDA.** How can I when I haven't even finished making the mayonnaise dressing for the salmon?

**LAURA.** Oh, Mother, please answer the door, don't make me do it! *(Thunder heard off-stage.)*

**AMANDA.** Honey, do be reasonable! What's all this fuss about—just one gentleman caller—that's all—just one! *(Exits through living-room curtains.* TOM *and* JIM *enter alley* R., *climb fire-escape steps to landing and wait outside of closed door. Hearing them approach,* LAURA *rises with a panicky gesture. She retreats to living-room curtains. The doorbell rings.* LAURA *catches her breath and touches her throat. More thunder heard off-stage.)*

**AMANDA** *(Off-stage).* Laura, sweetheart, the door!

**LAURA.** Mother, please, you go to the door! *(Starts for door* R., *then back.)*

**AMANDA** *(Off-stage, in a fierce whisper).* What is the matter with you, you silly thing? *(Enters through living-room curtains, and stands by day-bed.)*

Does Amanda understand why Laura is afraid? What words does she use to describe her daughter's behavior?

**LAURA.** Please you answer it, please.

**AMANDA.** Why have you chosen this moment to lose your mind? You go to that door.

**LAURA.** I can't.

**AMANDA.** Why can't you?

**LAURA.** Because I'm sick. (*Crosses to* L. *end of day-bed and sits.*)

**AMANDA.** You're sick! Am I sick? You and your brother have me puzzled to death. You can never act like normal children. Will you give me one good reason why you should be afraid to open a door? You go to that door. Laura Wingfield, you march straight to that door!

**LAURA** (*Crosses to door* R.). Yes, Mother.

**AMANDA** (*Stopping* LAURA). I've got to put courage in you, honey, for living. (*Exits through living-room curtains, and exits* R. *into kitchen.* LAURA *opens door.* TOM *and* JIM *enter.* LAURA *remains hidden in hall behind door.*)

What reason does Amanda say she has for forcing Laura to open the door?

**TOM.** Laura—(LAURA *crosses* C.) this is Jim. Jim, this is my sister Laura.

**JIM.** I didn't know that Shakespeare had a sister! How are you, Laura?

**LAURA** (*Retreating stiff and trembling. Shakes hands*). How—how do you do?

**JIM.** Well, I'm okay! Your hand's *cold*, Laura! (TOM *puts hats on phone table.*)

**LAURA.** Yes, well—I've been playing the victrola. . . .

**JIM.** Must have been playing classical music on it. You ought to play a little hot swing music to warm you up. (LAURA *crosses to phonograph.* TOM *crosses up to* LAURA. LAURA *starts phonograph—looks at* JIM. *Exits through living-room curtains and goes off* L.)

**JIM.** What's the matter?

**TOM.** Oh—Laura? Laura is—is terribly shy. (*Crosses and sits on day-bed.*)

**JIM** (*Crosses down* C.). Shy, huh? Do you know it's unusual to meet a shy girl nowadays? I don't believe you ever mentioned you had a sister?

Does Tom seem willing to take part in bringing Jim together with his sister?

**TOM.** Well, now you know I have one. You want a piece of the paper?

**JIM** (*Crosses to* TOM). Uh-huh.

**TOM.** Comics?

**JIM.** Comics? Sports! (*Takes paper. Crosses, sits chair* R.) I see that Dizzy Dean is on his bad behavior.

**TOM** (*Starts to door* R. *Goes out*). Really?

**JIM.** Yeah. Where are *you* going? (*As* TOM *reaches steps* R. *of fire-escape landing.*)

**TOM** (*Calling from fire-escape landing*). Out on the terrace to smoke.

**JIM** (*Rises, leaving newspaper in arm-chair, goes over to turn off victrola. Crosses* R. *Exits to fire-escape landing*). You know, Shakespeare—I'm going to sell you a bill of goods!

**TOM.** What goods?

**JIM.** A course I'm taking.

**TOM.** What course?

**JIM.** A course in public speaking! You know you and me, we're not the warehouse type.

**TOM.** Thanks—that's good news. What has public speaking got to do with it?

**JIM.** It fits you for—executive positions!

**TOM.** Oh.

**JIM.** I tell you it's done a helluva lot for me.

**TOM.** In what respect?

**JIM.** In all respects. Ask yourself: what's the difference between you and me and the guys in the office down front? Brains?—No!— Ability?—No! Then what? Primarily, it amounts to just one single thing——

**TOM.** What is that one thing?

**JIM.** Social <u>poise</u>! The ability to square up to somebody and hold your own on any social level!

**AMANDA** (Off-stage). Tom?

**TOM.** Yes, Mother?

**AMANDA.** Is that you and Mr. O'Connor?

**TOM.** Yes, Mother.

**AMANDA.** Make yourselves comfortable.

**TOM.** We will.

**AMANDA.** Ask Mr. O'Connor if he would like to wash his hands?

**JIM.** No, thanks, ma'am—I took care of that down at the warehouse. Tom?

**TOM.** Huh?

**JIM.** Mr. Mendoza was speaking to me about you.

**TOM.** Favorably?

**JIM.** What do you think?

**TOM.** Well——

**JIM.** You're going to be out of a job if you don't wake up.

**TOM.** I'm waking up——

**JIM.** Yeah, but you show no signs.

**TOM.** The signs are interior. I'm just about to make a change. I'm right at the point of committing myself to a future that doesn't include the warehouse or Mr. Mendoza, or even a night school course in public speaking.

**JIM.** Now what are you gassing[21] about?

**TOM.** I'm tired of the movies.

**JIM.** The movies!

**TOM.** Yes, movies! Look at them. (He waves his hands.) All of those glamorous people—having adventures—hogging it all, gobbling the whole thing up! You know what happens? People go to

*What quality does Jim value? Which characters have this quality? Which characters lack it?*

the *movies* instead of *moving.* Hollywood characters are supposed to have all the adventures for everybody in America, while everybody in America sits in a dark room and watches them having it! Yes, until there's a war. That's when adventure becomes available to the masses! Everyone's dish, not only Gable's![22] Then the people in the dark room come out of the dark room to have some adventures themselves—goody—goody! It's our turn now to go to the South Sea Island—to make a safari—to be exotic, far off! . . . But I'm not patient. I don't want to wait till then. I'm tired of the movies and I'm about to move!

*What does Tom see as the problem with movies?*

**JIM** (*Incredulously*). Move?

**TOM.** Yes.

**JIM.** When?

**TOM.** Soon!

**JIM.** Where? Where?

**TOM.** I'm starting to boil inside. I know I seem dreamy, but inside—well, I'm boiling! Whenever I pick up a shoe I shudder a little, thinking how short life is and what I am doing!—Whatever that means, I know it doesn't mean shoes—except as something to wear on a traveler's feet! (*Gets card from inside coat pocket.*) Look!

**JIM.** What?

**TOM.** I'm a member.

**JIM** (*Reading*). The Union of Merchant Seamen.

*What has Tom joined? Where has he acquired the money?*

**TOM.** I paid my dues this month, instead of the electric light bill.

---

21. **gassing.** Talking in an idle or boastful way
22. **Gable's.** Clark Gable (1901–1960), leading star in Hollywood films who often played a rough, adventurous, romantic hero

**WORDS FOR EVERYDAY USE**

**poise** (poiz) *n.*, ease and dignity of manner. *Dominick's <u>poise</u> hid his nervousness at addressing the school assembly.*

**in • cred • u • lous • ly** (in krē´ jə ləs lē) *adv.*, in a doubting or skeptical manner. *"I won the lottery? You must be joking," she said <u>incredulously</u>.*

**JIM.** You'll regret it when they turn off the lights.

**TOM.** I won't be here.

**JIM.** Yeah, but how about your mother?

**TOM.** I'm like my father. See how he grins? And he's been absent going on sixteen years.

**JIM.** You're just talking, you drip. How does your mother feel about it?

> To whom does Tom feel that he is similar? What desire makes the two similar?

**TOM.** Sh! Here comes Mother! Mother's not acquainted with my plans!

**AMANDA** *(Off-stage).* Tom!

**TOM.** Yes, Mother?

**AMANDA** *(Off-stage).* Where are you all?

**TOM.** On the terrace, Mother.

**AMANDA** *(Enters through living-room curtain and stands* C.*).* Why don't you come in? *(They start inside. She advances to them.* TOM *is distinctly shocked at her appearance. Even* JIM *blinks a little. He is making his first contact with girlish Southern* vivacity *and in spite of the night-school course in public speaking is somewhat thrown off the beam*[23] *by the unexpected outlay of social charm. Certain responses are attempted by* JIM *but are swept aside by* AMANDA's *gay laughter and chatter.* TOM *is embarrassed*

> In what way does Amanda appear before Jim and Tom? Why do the two men react differently to her presence?

*but after the first shock* JIM *reacts very warmly. Grins and chuckles, is altogether won over.* TOM *and* JIM *come in, leaving door open.)*

**TOM.** Mother, you look so pretty.

**AMANDA.** You know, that's the first compliment you ever paid me. I wish you'd look pleasant when you're about to say something pleasant, so I could expect it. Mr. O'Connor? *(*JIM *crosses to* AMANDA.*)*

**JIM.** How do you do?

**AMANDA.** Well, well, well, so this is Mr. O'Connor? Introduction's entirely unnecessary. I've heard so much about you from my boy. I finally said to him, "Tom, good gracious, why don't you bring this paragon to supper finally? I'd like to meet this nice young man at the warehouse! Instead of just hearing you sing his praises so much?" I don't know why my son is so standoffish—that's not Southern behavior. Let's sit down. *(*TOM *closes door; crosses* U. R.*, stands.* JIM *and* AMANDA *sit on day-bed,* JIM, R., AMANDA L.*)* Let's sit down, and I think we could stand a little more air in here. Tom, leave the door open. I felt a nice fresh breeze a moment ago. Where has it gone to? Mmmm, so warm already! And not quite summer, even. We're going to burn up when summer really gets started. However, we're having—we're having a very light supper. I think light things are better fo'—for this time of year. The same as light clothes are. Light clothes and light food are what warm weather calls fo'. You know our blood get so thick during th' winter—it takes a while fo' us to adjust ourselves—when the season changes. . . . It's come so quick this year. I wasn't prepared. All of a sudden—Heavens! Already summer!—I ran to the trunk an'—pulled out this light dress—terribly old! Historical almost! But feels so good—so good and cool, why, y' know——

**TOM.** Mother, how about our supper?

**AMANDA** *(Rises, crosses* R. *to* TOM*).* Honey, you go ask sister if supper is ready! You know that sister is in full charge of supper. Tell her you hungry boys are waiting for it. *(*TOM *exits through curtains and off* L. AMANDA *turns to* JIM.*)* Have you met Laura?

---

23. **off the beam.** Off-balance or in the wrong direction

---

**WORDS FOR EVERYDAY USE**

**vi • vac • i • ty** (vī vas´ə tē) *n.,* liveliness of spirit; animation. *Lana's vivacity made her very popular with all the groups at school.*

**par • a • gon** (par´ə gän´) *n.,* model or pattern of perfection or excellence. *Because Will was such a talented calculus student, his teacher described him as a paragon of mathematical ability.*

**JIM.**  Well, she came to the door.

**AMANDA.**  She let you in?

**JIM.**  Yes, ma'am.

**AMANDA**  *(Crossing to armchair and sitting).* She's very pretty.

**JIM.**  Oh, yes ma'am.

**AMANDA.**  It's rare for a girl as sweet an' pretty as Laura to be domestic! But Laura is, thank heavens, not only pretty but also very domestic. I'm not at all. I never was a bit. I never could make a thing but angel-food cake. Well, in the South we had so many servants. Gone, gone, gone. All <u>vestige</u> of gracious living! Gone completely! I wasn't prepared for what the future brought me. All of my gentlemen callers were sons of planters and so of course I assumed that I would be married to one and raise my family on a large piece of land with plenty of servants. But man proposes—and woman accepts the proposal!—To vary that old, old saying a little bit—I married no planter! I married a man who worked for the telephone company!—That gallantly smiling gentleman over there! *(Points to picture.)* A telephone man who—fell in love with long-distance!—Now he travels and I don't even know where!—But what am I going on for about my—<u>tribulations</u>? Tell me yours—I hope you don't have any! Tom?

**TOM**  *(Re-enters through living-room curtains from off L.).* Yes, Mother.

**AMANDA.**  What about that supper?

**TOM.**  Why, supper is on the table. *(Inner curtains between living-room and dining-room open. Lights dim up in dining-room, dim out in living-room.)*

**AMANDA.**  Oh, so it is. *(Rises, crosses up to table C. in dining-room and chair C.)* How lovely. Where is Laura?

**TOM**  *(Going to chair L. and standing).* Laura is not feeling too well and thinks maybe she'd better not come to the table.

**AMANDA.**  Laura!

**LAURA**  *(Off-stage. Faintly).* Yes, Mother? *(*TOM *gestures re:* JIM.*)*

**AMANDA.**  Mr. O'Connor. *(*JIM *crosses up L. to table and to chair L. and stands.)*

**JIM.**  Thank you, ma'am.

**AMANDA.**  Laura, we can't say grace till you come to the table.

**LAURA**  *(Enters U. L., obviously quite faint, lips trembling, eyes wide and staring. Moves unsteadily toward dining-room table).* Oh, Mother, I'm so sorry. *(*TOM *catches her as she feels faint. He takes her to day-bed in living-room.)*

**AMANDA**  *(As* LAURA *lies down).* Why, Laura, you are sick, darling! Laura—rest on the sofa. Well! *(To* JIM.*)* Standing over the hot stove made her ill!—I told her that it was just too warm this evening, but——*(To* TOM.*)* Is Laura all right now?

**TOM.**  She's better, Mother. *(Sits chair L. in dining-room. Thunder off-stage.)*

**AMANDA**  *(Returning to dining-room and sitting at table, as* JIM *does).* My goodness, I suppose we're going to have a little rain! Tom, you say grace.

**TOM.**  What?

**AMANDA.**  What do we generally do before we have something to eat? We say grace, don't we?

**TOM.**  For these and all Thy mercies—God's Holy Name be praised. *(Lights dim out.* MUSIC CUE #15.*)*

> What happens when Laura comes to the table. Why might she apologize to her mother and not the others?

| WORDS FOR EVERYDAY USE | |
|---|---|
| | **ves • tige** (ves´tij) *n.,* trace, mark, or sign of something that once existed but has passed away. *The worn marble columns were the only <u>vestige</u> of Roman civilization that Claudia saw.* |
| | **trib • u • la • tion** (trib´yü lā´shən) *n.,* great misery or distress. *Job's <u>tribulations</u> brought Emma to tears.* |

If you were Laura, whose life philosophy would you admire more, Tom's or Jim's?

# INVESTIGATE Inquire Imagine

**Recall:** GATHERING FACTS

1a. Why does Laura say she won't be able to come to the table when she learns who the gentleman caller will be?

2a. What is Jim's nickname for Tom? Why does he call him that?

3a. What course is Jim taking in night school? Why?

**Interpret:** FINDING MEANING

1b. How does Laura feel toward Jim? How do you know? In what ways are Jim and Laura different?

2b. What attitude does Jim have toward Tom's writing? What comment is the playwright making about the role of the artist in a society driven by material success?

3b. Is Jim O'Connor the sort of man whom Amanda would want to have as a suitor for Laura? Why, or why not?

**Analyze:** TAKING THINGS APART

4a. Identify ways in which Laura fails to meet Amanda's expectations for her.

**Synthesize:** BRINGING THINGS TOGETHER

4b. Why does Laura rush to the phonograph after opening the door?

**Evaluate:** MAKING JUDGMENTS

5a. Decide whether Tom is going to realize his dreams.

**Extend:** CONNECTING IDEAS

5b. In your opinion, if society values Jim O'Connor's belief in materialistic success over Tom's belief in artistic success, why do so many people dedicate themselves to an artistic life?

# Understanding Literature

CHARACTER. Review the definition for **character** in Literary Tools on page 721. Is Amanda a *static* or a *dynamic character?* Make a cluster chart to show the characteristics of Amanda. One example has been done for you. When you are finished with the cluster chart, underline the characteristics that demonstrate what type of character Amanda is (static or dynamic).

Amanda

nostalgic about her past

**THEME.** A **theme** is a central idea in a literary work. As you read, decide what theme Williams develops about the modern world.

**SYMBOL.** A **symbol** is a thing that stands for or represents both itself and something else. As you read, decide what the symbols of act 2 are and what they represent.

## Reader's
### *Journal*

Whom in your peer group do you look up to? Why?

*New York House Fronts* [Detail], 1938.
Walker Evans.

## ACT 2, SCENE 8

SCENE:    *The same. A half-hour later. Dinner is coming to an end in dining-room.*

AMANDA, TOM *and* JIM *sitting at table as at end of last scene. Lights dim up in both rooms, and* MUSIC CUE #15 *ends.*

**AMANDA**    *(Laughing, as* JIM *laughs too).* You know, Mr. O'Connor, I haven't had such a pleasant evening in a very long time.

> By the end of the dinner, how do Amanda and Jim get along? Why might they get along so well?

**JIM**    *(Rises).* Well, Mrs. Wingfield, let me give you a toast. Here's to the old South.

**AMANDA.**    The old South. *(Blackout in both rooms.)*

**JIM.**    Hey, Mr. Light Bulb!

**AMANDA.**    Where was Moses when the lights went out? Do you know the answer to that one, Mr. O'Connor?

> What happens to the lights? Why?

**JIM.**    No, ma'am, what's the answer to that one?

**AMANDA.**    Well, I heard one answer, but it wasn't very nice. I thought you might know another one.

**JIM.**    No, ma'am.

**AMANDA.**    It's lucky I put those candles on the table. I just put them on for <u>ornamentation</u>, but it's nice when they prove useful, too.

**JIM.** Yes, ma'am.

**AMANDA.** Now, if one of you gentlemen can provide me with a match we can have some illumination.

**JIM** (*Lighting candles. Dim in glow for candles*). I can, ma'am.

**AMANDA.** Thank you.

**JIM** (*Crosses back to* R. *of dining-room table*). Not at all, ma'am.

**AMANDA.** I guess it must be a burnt-out fuse. Mr. O'Connor, do you know anything about a burnt-out fuse?

**JIM.** I know a little about them, ma'am, but where's the fuse box?

**AMANDA.** Must you know that, too? Well it's in the kitchen. (JIM *exits* R. *into kitchen.*) Be careful. It's dark. Don't stumble over anything. (*Sound of crash off-stage.*) Oh, my goodness, wouldn't it be awful if we lost him! Are you all right, Mr. O'Connor?

**JIM** (*Off-stage*). Yes, ma'am, I'm all right.

**AMANDA.** You know, electricity is a very mysterious thing. The whole universe is mysterious to me. Wasn't it Benjamin Franklin who tied a key to a kite? I'd like to have seen that—he might have looked mighty silly. Some people say that science clears up all the mysteries for us. In my opinion they just keep on adding more. Haven't you found it yet?

**JIM** (*Re-enters* R.). Yes, ma'am. I found it all right, but them fuses look okay to me. (*Sits as before.*)

**AMANDA.** Tom.

**TOM.** Yes, Mother?

**AMANDA.** That light bill I gave you several days ago. The one I got the notice about?

**TOM.** Oh—yeah. You mean last month's bill?

**AMANDA.** You didn't neglect it by any chance?

**TOM.** Well, I——

**AMANDA.** You did! I might have known it!

**JIM.** Oh, maybe Shakespeare wrote a poem on that light bill, Mrs. Wingfield?

**AMANDA.** Maybe he did, too. I might have known better than to trust him with it! There's such a high price for negligence in this world today.

**JIM.** Maybe the poem will win a ten-dollar prize.

**AMANDA.** We'll just have to spend the rest of the evening in the nineteenth century, before Mr. Edison[24] found that Mazda lamp!

**JIM.** Candle-light is my favorite kind of light.

**AMANDA.** That shows you're romantic! But that's no excuse for Tom. However, I think it was very nice of them to let us finish our dinner before they plunged us into everlasting darkness. Tom, as a penalty for your carelessness you can help me with the dishes.

**JIM** (*Rising.* TOM *rises*). Can I be of some help, ma'am?

**AMANDA** (*Rising*). Oh, no, I couldn't allow that.

**JIM.** Well, I ought to be good for *something*.

**AMANDA.** What did I hear?

**JIM.** I just said, "I ought to be good for something."

---

24. **Mr. Edison.** American inventor of the incandescent lamp

WORDS
FOR
EVERYDAY
USE

or • na • men • ta • tion (ôr´na men tā´shən) *n.*, decoration. *The crystal goblets in the hutch were antiques and served as <u>ornamentation</u> in the dining room.*

**AMANDA.** That's what I thought you said. Well, Laura's all by her lonesome out front. Maybe you'd like to keep her company. I can give you this lovely old candelabrum[25] for light. (JIM *takes candles.*) It used to be on the altar at the Church of the Heavenly Rest, but it was melted a little out of shape when the church burnt down. The church was struck by lightning one spring, and Gypsy Jones who was holding a revival meeting in the village, said that the church was struck by lightning because the Episcopalians had started to have card parties right in the church.

*What does Amanda suggest that Jim do?*

**JIM.** Is that so, ma'am?

**AMANDA.** I never say anything that isn't so.

**JIM.** I beg your pardon.

**AMANDA** (*Pouring wine into glass—hands it to* JIM). I'd like Laura to have a little dandelion wine. Do you think you can hold them both?

**JIM.** I can try, ma'am.

**AMANDA** (*Exits* U. R. *into kitchen*). Now, Tom, you get into your apron.

**TOM.** Yes, Mother. (*Follows* AMANDA. JIM *looks around, puts wine-glass down, takes swig from wine decanter, replaces it with thud, takes wine-glass—enters living-room. Inner curtains close as dining-room dims out.* LAURA *sits up nervously as* JIM *enters. Her speech at first is low and breathless from the almost* <u>intolerable</u> *strain of being alone with a stranger. In her speeches in this scene, before* JIM's *warmth overcomes her paralyzing shyness,* LAURA's *voice is thin and breathless as though she has just run up a steep flight of stairs.*)

**JIM** (*Entering holding candelabra with lighted candles in one hand and glass of wine in other, and stands*). How are you feeling now? Any better? (JIM's *attitude is gently humorous. In playing this scene it should be stressed that while the incident is apparently unimportant, it is to* LAURA *the climax of her secret life.*)

**LAURA.** Yes, thank you.

**JIM** (*Gives her glass of wine*). Oh, here, this is for you. It's a little dandelion wine.

**LAURA.** Thank you.

**JIM** (*Crosses* C.). Well, drink it—but don't get drunk. (*He laughs heartily.*) Say, where'll I put the candles?

**LAURA.** Oh, anywhere . . .

**JIM.** Oh, how about right here on the floor? You got any objections?

**LAURA.** No.

**JIM.** I'll spread a newspaper under it to catch the drippings. (*Gets newspaper from armchair. Puts candelabra down on floor* C.) I like to sit on the floor. (*Sits on floor.*) Mind if I do?

**LAURA.** Oh, no.

**JIM.** Would you give me a pillow?

**LAURA.** What?

**JIM.** A pillow!

*What do Laura's brief responses reveal about her feelings? Is she comfortable? overwhelmed? nervous? annoyed?*

**LAURA.** Oh . . . (*Puts wine-glass on telephone table, hands him pillow, sits* L. *on day-bed.*)

**JIM.** How about you? Don't you like to sit on the floor?

**LAURA.** Oh, yes.

**JIM.** Well, why don't you?

**LAURA.** I—will.

**JIM.** Take a pillow! (*Throws pillow as she sits on floor.*) I can't see you sitting way over there. (*Sits on floor again.*)

---

25. **candelabrum.** Large, branched candleholder

---

**WORDS FOR EVERYDAY USE**

**in • tol • er • a • ble** (in täl´ər ə bəl) *adj.,* too severe, painful, or cruel to be endured. *Oliver found the loud, pounding music to be* <u>intolerable</u>, *so he left the concert.*

**LAURA.** I can—see you.

**JIM.** Yeah, but that's not fair. I'm right here in the <u>limelight</u>. (LAURA *moves a little closer to him.*) Good! Now I can see you! Are you comfortable?

**LAURA.** Yes. Thank you.

**JIM.** So am I. I'm comfortable as a cow! Say, would you care for a piece of chewing-gum? (*Offers gum.*)

**LAURA.** No, thank you.

**JIM.** I think that I will indulge. (*Musingly unwraps it and holds it up.*) Gee, think of the fortune made by the guy that invented the first piece of chewing gum! It's amazing, huh? Do you know that the Wrigley Building is one of the sights of Chicago?—I saw it summer before last at the Century of Progress.[26] Did you take in the Century of Progress?

**LAURA.** No, I didn't.

**JIM.** Well, it was a wonderful <u>exposition</u>, believe me. You know what impressed me most? The Hall of Science. Gives you an idea of what the future will be like in America. Oh, it's more wonderful than the present time is! Say, your brother tells me you're shy. Is that right, Laura?

**LAURA.** I—don't know.

> *What description of Laura does Jim suggest? How does he feel about such a girl?*

**JIM.** I judge you to be an old-fashioned type of girl. Oh, I think that's a wonderful type to be. I hope you don't think I'm being too personal—do you?

**LAURA.** Mr. O'Connor?

**JIM.** Huh?

**LAURA.** I believe I *will* take a piece of gum, if you don't mind. (JIM *peels gum—gets on knees, hands it to* LAURA. *She breaks off a tiny piece.* JIM *looks at what remains, puts it in his mouth, and sits*

*again.*) Mr. O'Connor, have you—kept up with your singing?

**JIM.** Singing? Me?

**LAURA.** Yes. I remember what a beautiful voice you had.

**JIM.** You heard me sing?

**LAURA.** Oh, yes! Very often. . . . I—don't suppose—you remember me—at all?

**JIM** (*Smiling doubtfully*). You know, as a matter of fact I did have an idea I'd seen you before. Do you know it seemed almost like I was about to remember your name. But the name I was about to remember—wasn't a name! So I stopped myself before I said it.

> *What shared memory establishes a connection between Laura and Jim?*

**LAURA.** Wasn't it—Blue Roses?

**JIM** (*Grinning*). Blue Roses! Oh, my gosh, yes—Blue Roses! You know, I didn't connect you with high school somehow or other. But that's where it was, it was high school. Gosh, I didn't even know you were Shakespeare's sister! Gee, I'm sorry.

**LAURA.** I didn't expect you to.—You barely knew me!

**JIM.** But, we did have a speaking acquaintance.

**LAURA.** Yes, we—spoke to each other.

**JIM.** Say, didn't we have a class in something together?

**LAURA.** Yes, we did.

**JIM.** What class was that?

**LAURA.** It was—singing—chorus!

**JIM.** Aw!

---

26. **Century of Progress.** World's Fair held in Chicago in 1933

**WORDS FOR EVERYDAY USE**

**lime • light** (līm′ līt′) *n.*, prominent or conspicuous position, as if under a spotlight. *Jessica wanted to become an actress because she loved being in the* <u>limelight</u>.

**ex • po • si • tion** (eks′pə zish′ən) *n.*, large, public exhibition or show, often international in scope. *The Crystal Palace was one of the first* <u>expositions</u>, *or world's fairs.*

**LAURA.** I sat across the aisle from you in the auditorium Mondays, Wednesdays, and Fridays.

**JIM.** Oh, yeah! I remember now—you're the one who always came in late.

**LAURA.** Yes, it was so hard for me, getting upstairs. I had that brace on my leg then—it clumped so loud!

**JIM.** I never heard any clumping.

*What made high school hard for Laura? Did other people notice this difficulty?*

**LAURA** (*Wincing at recollection*). To me it sounded like—thunder!

**JIM.** I never even noticed.

**LAURA.** Everybody was seated before I came in. I had to walk in front of all those people. My seat was in the back row. I had to go clumping up the aisle with everyone watching!

**JIM.** Oh, gee, you shouldn't have been self conscious.

**LAURA.** I know, but I was. It was always such a relief when the singing started.

**JIM.** I remember now. And I used to call you Blue Roses. How did I ever get started calling you a name like that?

**LAURA.** I was out of school a little while with pleurosis. When I came back you asked me what was the matter. I said I had pleurosis and you thought I said Blue Roses. So that's what you always called me after that!

**JIM.** I hope you didn't mind?

**LAURA.** Oh, no—I liked it. You see, I wasn't acquainted with many—people . . .

**JIM.** Yeah. I remember you sort of stuck by yourself.

**LAURA.** I never did have much luck at making friends.

**JIM.** Well, I don't see why you wouldn't.

**LAURA.** Well, I started out badly.

**JIM.** You mean being——?

**LAURA.** Well, yes, it—sort of—stood between me . . .

**JIM.** You shouldn't have let it!

**LAURA.** I know, but it did, and I——

**JIM.** You mean you were shy with people!

**LAURA.** I tried not to be but never could——

**JIM.** Overcome it?

**LAURA.** No, I—never could!

**JIM.** Yeah. I guess being shy is something you have to work out of kind of gradually.

**LAURA.** Yes—I guess it——

**JIM.** Takes time!

**LAURA.** Yes . . .

**JIM.** Say, you know something, Laura? (*Rises to sit on day-bed* R.) People are not so dreadful when you know them. That's what you have to remember! And everybody has problems, not just you but practically everybody has problems. You think of yourself as being the only one who is disappointed. But just look around you and what do you see—a lot of people just as disappointed as you are. You take me, for instance. Boy, when I left high school I thought I'd be a lot further along at this time than I am now. Say, you remember that wonderful write-up I had in "The Torch"?

*In what way is Jim disappointed?*

**LAURA.** Yes, I do! (*She gets year-book from under pillow* L. *of day-bed.*)

**JIM.** Said I was bound to succeed in anything I went into! Holy Jeez! "The Torch"! (*She opens book, shows it to him and sits next to him on day-bed.*)

---

**WORDS FOR EVERYDAY USE**

**wince** (win[t]s) *vi.*, shrink or draw back slightly, usually with a grimace, as in pain, embarrassment, or alarm. *The blisters on Don's feet made him* wince *with every step.*

**LAURA.** Here you are in "The Pirates of Penzance"!

**JIM.** "The Pirates"! "Oh, better far to live and die under the brave black flag I fly!" I sang the lead in that operetta.

**LAURA.** So beautifully!

**JIM.** Aw . . .

**LAURA.** Yes, yes—beautifully—beautifully!

**JIM.** You heard me then, huh?

**LAURA.** I heard you all three times!

**JIM.** No!

**LAURA.** Yes.

**JIM.** You mean all three performances?

**LAURA.** Yes!

**JIM.** What for?

**LAURA.** I—wanted to ask you to—autograph my program. *(Takes program from book.)*

**JIM.** Why didn't you ask me?

**LAURA.** You were always surrounded by your own friends so much that I never had a chance.

**JIM.** Aw, you should have just come right up and said, "Here is my——"

**LAURA.** Well, I—thought you might think I was——

**JIM.** Thought I might think you was—what?

**LAURA.** Oh——

**JIM** *(With reflective <u>relish</u>).* Oh! Yeah, I was <u>beleaguered</u> by females in those days.

**LAURA.** You were terribly popular!

**JIM.** Yeah . . .

**LAURA.** You had such a—friendly way——

*On what period in their lives—past, present, or future—do Laura and Jim seem to be focused? Do they have the same feelings about this period? Why might Jim be focused on it? Laura?*

**JIM.** Oh, I was spoiled in high school.

**LAURA.** Everybody liked you!

**JIM.** Including you?

**LAURA.** I—why, yes, I—I did, too. . . .

**JIM.** Give me that program, Laura. *(She does so, and he signs it.)* There you are—better later than never!

**LAURA.** My—what a—surprise!

**JIM.** My signature's not worth very much right now. But maybe some day—it will increase in value! You know, being disappointed is one thing and being discouraged is something else. Well, I may be disappointed but I am not discouraged. Say, you finished high school?

**LAURA.** I made bad grades in my final examinations.

**JIM.** You mean you dropped out?

**LAURA** *(Rises).* I didn't go back. *(Crosses R. to menagerie. JIM lights cigarette still sitting on day-bed. LAURA puts year-book under menagerie. Rises, picks up unicorn[27]—small glass object—her back to JIM. When she touches unicorn, MUSIC CUE #16-A.)* How is Emily Meisenbach getting along?

**JIM.** That kraut-head!

**LAURA.** Why do you call her that?

**JIM.** Because that's what she was.

**LAURA.** You're not still—going with her?

**JIM.** Oh, I never even see her.

**LAURA.** It said in the Personal section that you were—engaged!

**JIM.** Uh-huh. I know, but I wasn't impressed by that—propaganda!

---

27. **unicorn.** According to legend, the mythical unicorn could only be tamed by a young, unmarried woman.

---

**WORDS FOR EVERYDAY USE**

rel • ish (rel´ish) *n.*, pleasure; enjoyment. *I look forward with <u>relish</u> to a vacation on the beach.*

be • lea • guer (bē lē´gər) *vt.*, besiege by encircling. *The Vikings <u>beleaguered</u> the castle with the intent of starving out the Saxons.*

**LAURA.** It wasn't the truth?

**JIM.** It was only true in Emily's optimistic opinion!

**LAURA.** Oh . . . (*Turns R. of* JIM. JIM *lights a cigarette and leans* <u>indolently</u> *back on his elbows, smiling at* LAURA *with a warmth and charm which lights her inwardly with altar candles. She remains by the glass menagerie table and turns in her hands a piece of glass to cover her tumult.* CUT MUSIC CUE #16-A.)

**JIM.** What have you done since high school? Huh?

**LAURA.** What?

**JIM.** I said what have you done since high school?

**LAURA.** Nothing much.

**JIM.** You must have been doing something all this time.

**LAURA.** Yes.

**JIM.** Well, then, such as what?

**LAURA.** I took a business course at business college . . .

**JIM.** You did? How did that work out?

**LAURA** (*Turns back to* JIM). Well, not very—well . . . I had to drop out, it gave me—indigestion. . . .

**JIM** (*Laughs gently*). What are you doing now?

**LAURA.** I don't do anything—much. . . . Oh, please don't think I sit around doing nothing! My glass collection takes a good deal of time. Glass is something you have to take good care of.

**JIM.** What did you say—about glass?

**LAURA** (*She clears her throat and turns away again,* <u>acutely</u> *shy*). Collection, I said—I have one.

**JIM** (*Puts out cigarette. Abruptly*). Say! You know what I judge to be the trouble with you? (*Rises from day-bed and crosses R.*) Inferiority complex! You know what that is? That's what they call it when a fellow low-rates himself! Oh, I understand it because I had it, too. Uh-huh! Only my case was not as aggravated as yours seems to be. I had it until I took up public speaking and developed my voice, and learned that I had an <u>aptitude</u> for science. Do you know that until that time I never thought of myself as being outstanding in any way whatsoever!

**LAURA.** Oh, my!

**JIM.** Now I've never made a regular study of it—(*Sits armchair R.*) mind you, but I have a friend who says I can analyze people better than doctors that make a profession of it. I don't claim that's necessarily true, but I can sure guess a person's psychology. Excuse me, Laura. (*Takes out gum.*) I always take it out when the flavor is gone. I'll just wrap it in a piece of paper. (*Tears a piece of paper off the newspaper under candelabrum, wraps gum in it, crosses to day-bed, looks to see if* LAURA *is watching. She isn't. Crosses around day-bed.*) I know how it is when you get it stuck on a shoe. (*Throws gum under day-bed, crosses around L. of day-bed. Crosses R. to* LAURA.) Yep—that's what I judge to be your principal trouble. A lack of confidence in yourself as a person. Now I'm basing that fact on a number of your remarks and on certain observations I've made. For instance, that clumping you thought was so awful in high school. You say that you dreaded to go upstairs? You see what you did? You

> What problem does Jim say that he and Laura share? Do you agree with his assessment of Laura? of himself?

> What does Jim do with his gum? What does this action reveal about him?

**WORDS FOR EVERYDAY USE**

**in • do • lent • ly** (inˊdə lənt lē) *adv.*, lazily. *While Mr. Miller prepared dinner, his wife lay* <u>indolently</u> *on the couch.*

**a • cute • ly** (ə kyütˊlē) *adv.*, sharply, painfully, or severely. *Kim was* <u>acutely</u> *embarrassed during her demonstration speech.*

**ap • ti • tude** (apˊtə tüdˊ) *n.*, natural tendency or inclination. *Jay showed an* <u>aptitude</u> *for math at an early age.*

dropped out of school, you gave up an education all because of a little clump, which as far as I can see is practically non-existent! Oh, a little physical defect is all you have. It's hardly noticeable even! Magnified a thousand times by your imagination! You know what my strong advice to you is? You've got to think of yourself as *superior* in some way! *(Crosses L. to small table R. of day-bed. Sits.* LAURA *sits in armchair.)*

**LAURA.** In what way would I think?

**JIM.** Why, man alive, Laura! Look around you a little and what do you see? A world full of common people! All of 'em born and all of 'em going to die! Now, which of them has one-tenth of your strong points! Or mine! Or anybody else's for that matter? You see, everybody excels in some one thing. Well—some in many! You take me, for instance. My interest happens to lie in electrodynamics.[28] I'm taking a course in radio engineering at night school, on top of a fairly responsible job at the warehouse. I'm taking that course *and* studying public speaking.

> What does Jim really think about himself?

**LAURA.** Ohhhh. My!

**JIM.** Because I believe in the future of television! I want to be ready to go right up along with it. *(Rises, crosses R.)* I'm planning to get in on the ground floor. Oh, I've already made the right connections. All that remains now is for the industry itself to get under way—full steam! You know, *knowledge*—ZSZZppp! *Money*—Zzzzzzpp! *POWER*! Wham! That's the cycle democracy is built on! *(Pause.)* I guess you think I think a lot of myself!

**LAURA.** No—o-o-o, I don't.

**JIM** *(Kneels at armchair R.).* Well, now how about you? Isn't there some one thing that you take more interest in than anything else?

**LAURA.** Oh—yes . . .

**JIM.** Well, then, such as what?

**LAURA.** Well, I do—as I said—have my—glass collection . . . *(*MUSIC CUE #16-A.*)*

**JIM.** Oh, you do. What kind of glass is it?

**LAURA** *(Takes glass ornament off shelf.)* Little articles of it, ornaments mostly. Most of them are little animals made out of glass, the tiniest little animals in the world. Mother calls them the glass menagerie! Here's an example of one, if you'd like to see it! This is one of the oldest, it's nearly thirteen. *(Hands it to* JIM.*)* Oh, be careful—if you breathe, it breaks! *(*THE BELL SOLO SHOULD BEGIN HERE. *This is last part of* CUE #16-A *and should play to end of record.)*

**JIM.** I'd better not take it. I'm pretty clumsy with things.

**LAURA.** Go on, I trust you with him! *(*JIM *takes horse.)* There—you're holding him gently! Hold him over the light, he loves the light! *(*JIM *holds horse up to light.)* See how the light shines through him?

> Why does Laura give Jim the glass unicorn to hold? How does she feel about the unicorn?

**JIM.** It sure does shine!

**LAURA.** I shouldn't be partial, but he is my favorite one.

**JIM.** Say, what kind of a thing is this one supposed to be?

**LAURA.** Haven't you noticed the single horn on his forehead?

**JIM.** Oh, a unicorn, huh?

**LAURA.** Mmmm-hmmmmm!

**JIM.** Unicorns, aren't they extinct in the modern world?

**LAURA.** I know!

**JIM.** Poor little fellow must feel kind of lonesome.

**LAURA.** Well, if he does he doesn't complain about it. He stays on a shelf with some horses that don't

> Does Laura talk about her glass animals as if they were objects or companions?

---

28. **electrodynamics.** Branch of physics dealing with electric currents and magnetic forces

have horns and they all seem to get along nicely together.

**JIM.** They do. Say, where will I put him?

**LAURA.** Put him on the table. (JIM *crosses to small table* R. *of day-bed, puts unicorn on it.*) They all like a change of scenery once in a while!

**JIM** (C., *facing upstage, stretching arms*). They do. (MUSIC CUE #16-B: *Dance Music.*) Hey! Look how big my shadow is when I stretch.

**LAURA** (*Crossing to* L. *of day-bed*). Oh, oh, yes—it stretched across the ceiling!

**JIM** (*Crosses to door* R., *exits, leaving door open, and stands on fire-escape landing. Sings to music.* [*Popular record of day for dance-hall.*] *When* JIM *opens door, music swells*). It's stopped raining. Where does the music come from?

**LAURA.** From the Paradise Dance Hall across the alley.

**JIM** (*Re-entering room, closing door* R., *crosses to* LAURA). How about cutting the rug[29] a little, Miss Wingfield? Or is your program filled up? Let me take a look at it. (*Crosses back* C. *Music, in dance hall, goes into a waltz. Business here with imaginary dance-program card.*) Oh, say! Every dance is taken! I'll just scratch some of them out. Ahhhh, a waltz! (*Crosses to* LAURA.)

**LAURA.** I—can't dance!

**JIM.** There you go with that inferiority stuff!

**LAURA.** I've never danced in my life!

**JIM.** Come on, try!

**LAURA.** Oh, but I'd step on you!

**JIM.** Well, I'm not made out of glass.

**LAURA.** How—how do we start?

**JIM.** You hold your arms out a little.

**LAURA.** Like this?

**JIM.** A little bit higher. (*Takes* LAURA *in arms.*) That's right. Now don't tighten up, that's the principal thing about it—just relax.

**LAURA.** It's hard not to.

**JIM.** Okay.

**LAURA.** I'm afraid you can't budge me.

**JIM** (*Dances around* L. *of day-bed slowly*). What do you bet I can't?

**LAURA.** Goodness, yes, you can!

**JIM.** Let yourself go, now, Laura, just let yourself go.

**LAURA.** I'm——

**JIM.** Come on!

**LAURA.** Trying!

**JIM.** Not so stiff now—easy does it!

**LAURA.** I know, but I'm——!

**JIM.** Come on! Loosen your backbone a little! (*When they get to up-stage corner of day-bed—so that the audience will not see him lift her—*JIM'*s arm tightens around her waist and he swings her around* C. *with her feet off floor about 3 complete turns before they hit the small table* R. *of day-bed. Music swells as* JIM *lifts her.*) There we go! (JIM *knocks glass horse off table.* MUSIC FADES.)

**LAURA.** Oh, it doesn't matter——

**JIM** (*Picks horse up*). We knocked the little glass horse over.

**LAURA.** Yes.

**JIM** (*Hands unicorn to* LAURA). Is he broken?

**LAURA.** Now he's just like all the other horses.

**JIM.** You mean he lost his——?

**LAURA.** He's lost his horn. It doesn't matter. Maybe it's a blessing in disguise.

**JIM.** Gee, I bet you'll never forgive me. I bet that was your favorite piece of glass.

**LAURA.** Oh, I don't have favorites—(*Pause*) much. It's no tragedy. Glass breaks so easily. No matter how careful you are. The traffic jars the shelves and things fall off them.

**JIM.** Still I'm awfully sorry that I was the cause of it.

> What happens to the unicorn? What does Laura say about her favorite piece being broken? How do you think she really feels?

---

29. **cutting the rug.** Dancing

**LAURA.** I'll just imagine he had an operation. The horn was removed to make him feel less—freakish! *(Crosses* L., *sits on small table.)* Now he will feel more at home with the other horses, the ones who don't have horns. . . .

*What does Laura imagine the horn made the unicorn feel? Is this a feeling with which she is familiar?*

**JIM** *(Sits on arm of armchair* R., *faces* LAURA). I'm glad to see that you have a sense of humor. You know—you're—different than anybody else I know? *(*MUSIC CUE #17.*)* Do you mind me telling you that? I mean it. You make me feel sort of—I don't know how to say it! I'm usually pretty good at expressing things, but—this is something I don't know how to say! Did anybody ever tell you that you were pretty? *(Rises, crosses to* LAURA.*)* Well, you are! And in a different way from anyone else. And all the nicer because of the difference. Oh, boy, I wish that you were my sister. I'd teach you to have confidence in yourself. Being different is nothing to be ashamed of. Because other people aren't such wonderful people. They're a hundred times one thousand. You're one times one! They walk all over the earth. You just stay here. They're as common as—weeds, but—you, well you're— *Blue Roses!*

*What does Jim say about Laura? Why is she special?*

**LAURA.** But blue is—wrong for—roses . . .

**JIM.** It's right for you!—You're pretty!

**LAURA.** In what respect am I pretty?

**JIM.** In all respects—your eyes—your hair. Your hands are pretty! You think I'm saying this because I'm invited to dinner and have to be nice. Oh, I could do that! I could say lots of things without being sincere. But I'm talking to you sincerely. I happened to notice you had this inferiority complex that keeps you from feeling comfortable with people. Somebody ought to build your confidence up—way up! and make you proud instead of shy and turning away and—blushing——(JIM *lifts* LAURA *up on small table on "way up."*) Somebody ought to—(Lifts

her down.) somebody ought to kiss you, Laura! *(They kiss.* JIM *releases her and turns slowly away, crossing a little* D. R. *Then, quietly, to himself: As* JIM *turns away,* MUSIC ENDS.*)* Gee, I shouldn't have done that—that was way off the beam. *(Gives way* D. R. *Turns to* LAURA. LAURA *sits on small table.)* Would you care for a cigarette? You don't smoke, do you? How about a mint? Peppermint—Life-Saver? My pocket's a regular drug-store. . . . Laura, you know, if I had a sister like you, I'd do the same thing as Tom. I'd bring fellows home to meet you. Maybe I shouldn't be saying this. That may not have been the idea in having me over. But what if it was? There's nothing wrong with that.—The only trouble is that in my case—I'm not in a position to——I can't ask for your number and say I'll phone. I can't call up next week end— ask for a date. I thought I had better explain the situation in case you—misunderstood and I hurt your feelings . . .

*What does Jim say that hurts Laura? Has he misled her in any way?*

**LAURA** *(Faintly)*. You—won't—call again?

**JIM** *(Crossing to* R. *of day-bed, and sitting)*. No, I can't. You see, I've—got strings on me. Laura, I've—been going steady! I go out all the time with a girl named Betty. Oh, she's a nice quiet home girl like you, and Catholic and Irish, and in a great many ways we—get along fine. I met her last summer on a moonlight boat trip up the river to Alton, on the *Majestic.* Well—right away from the start it was—love! Oh, boy, being in love has made a new man of me! The power of love is pretty tremendous! Love is something that—changes the whole world. It happened that Betty's aunt took sick and she got a wire and had to go to Centralia. So naturally when Tom asked me to dinner—naturally I accepted the invitation, not knowing—I mean—not knowing. I wish that you would—say something. (LAURA *gives* JIM *unicorn.)* What are you doing that for? You mean you want me to have him? What for?

*What does Laura give Jim? Why does she give this to him? Is this an appropriate gesture? Why, or why not?*

**LAURA.** A—souvenir. (*She crosses* R. *to menagerie.* JIM *rises.*)

**AMANDA** (*Off-stage*). I'm coming, children. (*She enters into dining-room from kitchen* R.) I thought you'd like some liquid refreshment. (*Puts tray on small table. Lifts a glass.*) Mr. O'Connor, have you heard that song about lemonade? It's "Lemonade, lemonade, Made in the shade and stirred with a spade—And then it's good enough for any old maid!"

> Given what has occurred, in what way is Amanda's song ironic?

**JIM.** No, ma'am, I never heard it.

**AMANDA.** Why are you so serious, honey? (*To* LAURA.)

**JIM.** Well, we were having a serious conversation.

**AMANDA.** I don't understand modern young people. When I was a girl I was gay about everything.

**JIM.** You haven't changed a bit, Mrs. Wingfield.

**AMANDA.** I suppose it's the gaiety of the occasion that has rejuvenated me. Well, here's to the gaiety of the occasion! (*Spills lemonade on dress.*) Oooo! I baptized myself. (*Puts glass on small table* R. *of day-bed.*) I found some cherries in the kitchen, and I put one in each glass.

**JIM.** You shouldn't have gone to all that trouble, ma'am.

**AMANDA.** It was no trouble at all. Didn't you hear us cutting up[30] in the kitchen? I was so outdone with Tom for not bringing you over sooner, but now you've found your way I want you to come all the time—not just once in a while—but all the time. Oh, I think I'll go back in that kitchen. (*Starts to exit* U. C.)

**JIM.** Oh, no, ma'am, please don't go, ma'am. As a matter of fact, I've got to be going.

**AMANDA.** Oh, Mr. O'Connor, it's only the shank of the evening![31] (JIM *and* AMANDA *stand* U. C.)

**JIM.** Well, you know how it is.

**AMANDA.** You mean you're a young working man and have to keep workingmen's hours?

**JIM.** Yes, ma'am.

**AMANDA.** Well, we'll let you off early this time, but only on the condition that you stay later next time, much later—— What's the best night for you? Saturday?

**JIM.** Well, as a matter of fact, I have a couple of time-clocks to punch, Mrs. Wingfield, one in the morning and another one at night!

**AMANDA.** Oh, isn't that nice, you're so ambitious! You work at night, too?

**JIM.** No, ma'am, not work but—Betty!

**AMANDA** (*Crosses* L. *below day-bed*). Betty? Who's Betty?

**JIM.** Oh, just a girl. The girl I go steady with!

**AMANDA.** You mean it's serious? (*Crosses* D. L.)

**JIM.** Oh, yes, ma'am. We're going to be married the second Sunday in June.

**AMANDA** (*Sits on day-bed*). Tom didn't say anything at all about your going to be married?

**JIM.** Well, the cat's not out of the bag at the warehouse yet. (*Picks up hat from telephone table.*) You know how they are. They call you Romeo and stuff like that.—It's been a wonderful evening, Mrs. Wingfield. I guess this is what they mean by Southern hospitality.

**AMANDA.** It was nothing. Nothing at all.

> What is Amanda's response when Jim thanks her for her hospitality? Why is this comment appropriate given the evening's outcome?

**JIM.** I hope it don't seem like I'm rushing off. But I promised Betty I'd pick her up at the Wabash depot an' by the time I get my jalopy[32] down there her train'll be in. Some women are pretty upset if you keep them waiting.

---

30. **cutting up.** Clowning, joking
31. **shank of the evening.** Early part of the evening
32. **jalopy.** Old, ramshackle car

**AMANDA.** Yes, I know all about the tyranny of women! Well, good-bye, Mr. O'Connor. *(AMANDA puts out hand. JIM takes it.)* I wish you happiness—and good fortune. You wish him that, too, don't you, Laura?

**LAURA.** Yes, I do, Mother.

**JIM** *(Crosses L. to LAURA).* Good-bye, Laura. I'll always treasure that souvenir. And don't you forget the good advice I gave you. So long, Shakespeare! *(Up C.)* Thanks, again, ladies.— Good night! *(He grins and ducks jauntily out R.)*

**AMANDA** *(Faintly).* Well, well, well. Things have a way of turning out so badly——*(LAURA crosses to phonograph, puts on record.)* I don't believe that I would play the victrola. Well, well—well, our gentleman caller was engaged to be married! Tom!

**TOM** *(Off).* Yes, Mother?

**AMANDA.** Come out here. I want to tell you something very funny.

**TOM** *(Entering through R. kitchen door to dining-room and into living-room, through curtains, D. C.).* Has the gentleman caller gotten away already?

**AMANDA.** The gentleman caller made a very early departure. That was a nice joke you played on us, too!

**TOM.** How do you mean?

**AMANDA.** You didn't mention that he was engaged to be married.

**TOM.** Jim? Engaged?

**AMANDA.** That's what he just informed us.

**TOM.** I'll be jiggered! I didn't know.

**AMANDA.** That seems very peculiar.

**TOM.** What's peculiar about it?

**AMANDA.** Didn't you tell me he was your best friend down at the warehouse?

**TOM.** He is, but how did I know?

**AMANDA.** It seems very peculiar you didn't know your best friend was engaged to be married!

**TOM.** The warehouse is the place where I work, not where I know things about people!

**AMANDA.** You don't know things anywhere! You live in a dream; you manufacture illusions! *(TOM starts for R. door.)* Where are you going? Where are you going? Where are you going?

> What does Amanda say about Tom?

**TOM.** I'm going to the movies.

**AMANDA** *(Rises, crosses up to TOM).* That's right, now that you've had us make such fools of ourselves. The effort, the preparations, all the expense! The new floor lamp, the rug, the clothes for Laura! All for what? To entertain some other girl's fiancé! Go to the movies, go! Don't think about us, a mother deserted, an unmarried sister who's crippled and has no job! Don't let anything interfere with your selfish pleasure! Just go, go, go—to the movies!

> Why is Amanda angry with Tom? Is she more angry with the expense incurred or in the sad situation of both mother and daughter?

**TOM.** All right, I will, and the more you shout at me about my selfish pleasures, the quicker I'll go, and I won't go to the movies either. *(Gets hat from phone table, slams door R., and exits up alley R.)*

**AMANDA** *(Crosses up to fire-escape landing, yelling).* Go, then! Then go to the moon—you selfish dreamer! *(MUSIC CUE #18. INTERIOR LIGHT dims out. Re-enters living-room, slamming*

---

**WORDS FOR EVERYDAY USE**

**jaun • ti • ly** (jônt´ə lē) *adv.,* in a confident, carefree manner. *Drew tipped his hat jauntily to the ladies.*

R. *door.* TOM's *closing speech is timed with the interior* <u>*pantomime*</u>. *The interior scene is played as though viewed through soundproof glass, behind outer scrim curtain.* AMANDA, *standing, appears to be making a comforting speech to* LAURA *who is huddled on* R. *side of day-bed. Now that we cannot hear the mother's speech, her silliness is gone and she has dignity and tragic beauty.* LAURA's *hair hides her face until at the end of the speech she lifts it to smile at her mother.* AMANDA's *gestures are slow and graceful, almost dance-like, as she comforts her daughter.* TOM, *who has meantime put on, as before, the jacket and cap, enters down* R. *from off-stage, and again comes to fire-escape landing, stands as he speaks. Meantime lights are upon* AMANDA *and* LAURA, *but are dim.)*

**TOM.** I didn't go to the moon. I went much farther. For time is the longest distance between two places. . . . I left Saint Louis. I descended these steps of this fire-escape for the last time and followed, from then on, in my father's footsteps, attempting to find in motion what was lost in space. . . . I travelled around a great deal. The cities swept about me like dead leaves, leaves that were brightly colored but torn away from the branches. I would have stopped, but I was pursued by something. It always came upon me unawares, taking me altogether by surprise. Perhaps it was a familiar bit of music. Perhaps it was only a piece of transparent glass. . . . Perhaps I am walking along a street at night, in some strange city, before I have found companions, and I pass the lighted window of a shop where perfume is sold. The window is filled with pieces of colored glass, tiny transparent bottles in delicate colors, like bits of a shattered rainbow. Then all at once my sister touches my shoulder. I turn around and look into her eyes . . . . Oh, Laura, Laura, I tried to leave you behind me, but I am more faithful than I intended to be! I reach for a cigarette, I cross the street, I run into a movie or a bar. I buy a drink, I speak to the nearest stranger—anything that can blow your candles out!—for nowadays the world is lit by lightning! Blow out your candles, Laura . . . (LAURA *blows out candles still burning in candelabrum and the whole interior is blacked out.)* And so—good-bye! *(Exits up alley* R. *Music continues to the end.)* ∎

> What does Tom say about his sister? What image does he use to describe her?

**CURTAIN**

**END OF PLAY**

**WORDS FOR EVERYDAY USE**

**pan • to • mime** (pan′tə mīm) *n.,* dramatic presentation without words. *Kim related her experience as a* <u>*pantomime*</u> *since she had laryngitis.*

## Respond *to the* SELECTION

If you were Tom, would you have left? Why, or why not?

# INVESTIGATE, Inquire, *Imagine*

**Recall:** GATHERING FACTS

1a. What happens to the lights in the apartment? Why?

2a. What does Amanda ask Jim to do while she and Tom take care of the dishes?

3a. How does Laura react to Jim?

**Interpret:** FINDING MEANING

1b. How does being plunged in darkness affect the final scene of the play? What situation is thereby created for Jim and Laura? What might this darkness represent?

2b. Why does Amanda want to leave Jim and Laura alone together? In what sense is this "apparently unimportant" event the climax of Laura's "secret life"?

3b. How does Laura view Jim? What impact does the news of his engagement have on Laura?

**Analyze:** TAKING THINGS APART

4a. How does Laura introduce Jim to her inner world?

**Synthesize:** BRINGING THINGS TOGETHER

4b. How does the significance of the unicorn change in this scene?

**Evaluate:** MAKING JUDGMENTS

5a. Considering the characters Tom, Amanda, Laura, and Jim, evaluate whether each views life realistically or unrealistically. Then rank the degree of realism each character possesses.

**Extend:** CONNECTING IDEAS

5b. Jim tells Laura she has an inferiority complex. Imagine that you are Laura's friend. What could you do and say that might help Laura get over her inferiority complex?

# Understanding *Literature*

THEME. Review the definition for **theme** in the Handbook of Literary Terms. Jim, who is taking night classes and who wishes to become an executive, epitomizes those people who aspire to a material success. What sort of person is Jim? Would you describe him as optimistic or pessimistic? What indications does the play give that Jim is shallow, thoughtless, and egotistical? Jim says, "You know, *knowledge*—ZSZZppp! *Money*—Zzzzzzpp! POWER! Wham! That's the cycle democracy is built on!" Do you agree with him? Why, or why not? What has happened to the old, gracious way of life that Amanda remembers? At the end of the play, Tom says, "I speak to the nearest stranger—anything that can blow your [Laura's] candles out!—for nowadays the world is lit by lightning!" How is Tom's phrase "lit by lightning" related to Jim's statements about television and electricity? Is someone like Laura suited to life in the modern world? What theme does Williams develop by drawing this comparison between Jim and Laura?

SYMBOL. Review the definition for **symbol** in the Handbook of Literary Terms. Then make a chart. On the left, list the symbols in act 2. On the right, explain the meaning of these symbols. One example has been done for you.

| Symbols | Meaning |
|---|---|
| the lightning that now lights the world, referred to by Tom at the end of the play | The lightning is symbolic of the stronger, less fragile forces that dominate the modern world. |

# Writer's Journal

1. According to the sociologist Erik Erickson, young people go through an identity crisis, a stage in which they attempt to break away from childhood and establish their own adult identities. This period in a person's life is often characterized by turmoil and uncertainty and sometimes involves conflicts with parents. In this play, Tom experiences an identity crisis and decides to break away for good from his family. Write a **journal entry** from Tom's point of view explaining how he views himself and why he feels he must break away to be the person he wants to be.

2. Choose either Laura, Tom, or Amanda as the main character of the play. Write a **character sketch** of the character you select, and argue why he or she is the main character.

3. A **soliloquy** is a speech delivered by a lone character that reveals the speaker's thoughts and feelings. Imagine that the narrator is Amanda instead of Tom and write her soliloquy at the end of the play.

# Integrating *the* LANGUAGE ARTS

## Study and Research

**RESEARCHING SETTING.** Research the setting of another play by Tennessee Williams to examine how setting figures in his work. What socioeconomic groups do his characters come from? What information is revealed in the stage directions? What are the characters' dreams? In what moral and cultural context do their conflicts emerge? Write a composition comparing or contrasting the setting of the play you choose with the setting of *The Glass Menagerie*. You may find it useful to review the Language Arts Survey 2.24, "Organizing Ideas."

## Collaborative Learning & Speaking and Listening

**ACTING.** With other students in your class, stage a scene from *The Glass Menagerie* for the rest of the class to see.

**ACTING.** With other students in your class, select a cutting from a modern drama selection such as *Our Town*, *Spoon River Anthology*, *Long Day's Journey into Night*, or *The Crucible*. Write an introduction for your cutting; decide what gestures, facial expressions, and body language to use; and rehearse. Then act out the cutting for the rest of the class to see.

## Media Literacy

**FILM REVIEW.** View a film version of *The Glass Menagerie* and write a film review. In your review, include answers to these questions:

a. Is the film version true to the play? What differences exist in the film version and in the script that you have read? Do these differences make the play better or worse? Why?

b. Which are the best performances in the film? Which are the worst? Why?

c. What aspects of the play are emphasized in the film?

d. Does the film live up to the playwright's expressed intention of creating a "memory play"? Do its scenes have the dreamlike quality described in the playwright's stage directions? If so, how are these effects achieved? If not, what might the director and set designers have done to give the film such a quality?

You may want to read some examples of film reviews before you begin writing.

# Guided Writing

## EVALUATING A PLAY OR FILM

Deciding which movie to see is a lot like picking a restaurant. There are so many things to consider: the atmosphere, the service, the specific recipes, the preparation, the presentation, even the type of food for which you're in the mood. In a movie, there are many considerations too: the setting and the camera work, the actors, the director, and the plot. Is the movie a drama or a comedy or an action/adventure? Do you want to be inspired, scared, or thrilled?

Just as two people might try the same restaurant, even the same meal, and have different opinions, so two people can see the same movie and come away with different reactions. This might be because they have different tastes, but often it is because they're looking at different things and have different perspectives.

No doubt, you have read opposite reactions to the same movie by two critics. How do you decide which one is right? One way would be to look at the evidence and examples the critics give and consider the logic of their conclusions.

**WRITING ASSIGNMENT.** In this assignment, you will review a film or play, arguing whether or not a performance is worth seeing. Your review will also include a response to a critique from another reviewer.

## Student Model—Revised
by Kelly McElroy

> *The Glass Menagerie* is a film adaptation
> of a play by Tennessee Williams. The
> entire film takes place in a small
> apartment in St. Louis during the
> 1930s, and the story is that of four
> characters: Amanda (Joanne Woodward),
> her grown son Tom (John Malkovich) and
> daughter Laura (Karen Allen), and a
> Gentleman Caller (James Naughton). This

> "True opinions are a fine thing and do all sorts of good so long as they stay in their place; but they will not stay long. They run away from a man's mind, so they are not worth much until you tether them by working out the reason. Once they are tied down, they become knowledge, and are stable."
>
> —Plato

**Looking for a review?**
Magazines, newspapers, and Internet sites are good sources for movie and play reviews.

"The greatest deception men suffer is from their own opinions."

—Leonardo da Vinci

version was made in 1987, and is directed by Paul Newman.

Reviews of this version of *The Glass Menagerie* tend to focus on Allen's Laura, the disabled daughter, or Malkovich as Tom, who both narrates and participates in the story. However, in this version Woodward as Amanda is the most effective character.

In one scene early in the film, Amanda provokes Tom to argue with her. He insults her caustically, and storms from the house. The next morning, Laura convinces him to apologize for his behavior. The son's anger has paralyzed Amanda; she fixates on how her affections have been wasted, in a way. Her life is nothing without her kids and she can't take it when they rebuff her. Tom has made it clear that her involvement in his life frustrates him and he explodes. He apologizes for these explosions, and, as the actors share a moment of silence, we wonder if Amanda has taken his reactions to heart, if she will change her nagging.

However, "you can't teach an old dog new tricks" applies here. Amanda instantly starts bothering Tom for drinking his coffee black and being so selfish. Amanda wants Tom to promise he will stay with the family until Laura has found a husband, a goal that seems unlikely in the near future. She just wants to know that her children will be taken care of, and although Tom can take care of himself, Laura is more dependent.

The details in this scene make it striking. Woodward has developed an effective voice for her character; Amanda's voice creeps higher as she becomes distressed, displaying her impatience and frustration with life. Her accent also varies, almost as if Amanda is trying to accentuate her Southern gentility, trying to remind herself and those around her that she really is still a debutante.

To earn some extra money, Amanda sells magazine subscriptions to a ladies' journal, the *Homemaker's Companion*, over the phone. These scenes show Woodward sitting at a desk talking them into renewing. The audience feels as if we are spying on her during this embarrassing task. Amanda knows that her efforts are somewhat fruitless, that she really won't earn that much for her children, but she tries nonetheless. The women she calls are friendly acquaintances, and Amanda is putting these relationships at risk by asking for money in a time when money is tight. Woodward shows this in the tightness of her face as one woman hangs up and the tears when another woman agrees to renew. Amanda says repeatedly "Bless you," to the woman.

Tom finally finds a friend to come to dinner, to be a Gentlemen Caller, and thus potential suitor, for Laura. The night when he is to come, Amanda works on Laura, who is dragging her feet, to dress up for the occasion. Then, Amanda prepares herself. This gentle,

- find the reviewer's thesis
- identify the arguments for the thesis
- analyze the supporting evidence

Where are there inconsistencies in the review? With what points do you disagree?

- list major scenes in the plot
- describe characters and their performances
- describe costumes, scenery, lighting, music, special effects
- identify common themes

Discuss your response . . .

- review the film or play's overall effect
- consider the value of the plot and theme and how well they are developed
- state your personal reactions
- raise questions and criticisms
- weigh the parts and the whole

sentimental scene proves Hal Hinson, of the *Washington Post*, wrong when he said, "Woodward leaves out the tragic dimension to the character; her Amanda isn't moving—she's a prattling bore." Her stories of being desired by Southern gentlemen captivate both Laura and the audience. The stories, and Woodward's glazed eyes and small smile, tell us that Amanda longs for the past, practically lives in her Blue Mountain days. When Tom brings his friend to dinner, Amanda plans to relive her own youth, as well as trying to better her daughter's life.

Amanda has two purposes in life: consciously, she attempts to secure a good life for her children, and on a less cognizant level, she tries to relive the gaiety and carelessness of her past. Joanne Woodward's Amanda longs for the past, but worries of the future.

**EXAMINING THE MODEL.** Read the student model review above. Summarize the thesis in one sentence and then list the arguments supporting it along with the evidence. Make special note of any inconsistencies or specific points with which you disagree. Is the review convincing? Why, or why not? Do you agree or disagree with it? For whom do you think the review was written and for what purpose? How could this review be improved? Does the writer use any slang, dialect, colloquialisms, or jargon?

## Prewriting

**IDENTIFYING YOUR AUDIENCE.** Professional reviews can be written many different ways. Some reviews have a casual tone and use the first person, as if the writer is recommending the film or play to a friend. Other reviews that appear in theater journals have a formal, even academic tone. For this assignment, assume that a panel of English teachers from your school will evaluate your essay. You will need to use formal, standard English persuasively and effectively, presenting your position reasonably and logically. Since a critical essay—your review—is an objective analysis, you should write in the third-person, avoiding the use of *I*. In addition, you will need to prove the reliability of your logic and evidence by documenting your sources.

**FINDING YOUR VOICE.** A review, or critique, presents a judgment about a movie or play. While you want to state a definite opinion, keep in mind that your opinion should be stated with care and precision, not indiscriminately. Your personality and attitude toward the movie or play, as well as your choice of words, sentence structure, and tone, reflect your voice. If you keep this in mind as you state your definite opinion about whether the movie or play is worth seeing, your voice as a reviewer will be precise, persuasive, and reasonable.

Look at the two examples below. Which provides a better example of a precise, persuasive, and reasonable voice? How do the two examples differ in personality, attitude, word choice, sentence structure, and tone?

> No one should bother spending money on a ticket for this play.

> Each person can decide how to spend his or her entertainment dollars. This play's lack of plot and shallow acting suggest that money would be better spent someplace else.

**WRITING WITH A PLAN.** Choose a movie or play that you have seen before and that you would like to review. Then find a review of it that disagrees with your thinking about certain aspects of it. Summarize the thesis of the review in one sentence and then list the arguments along with supporting evidence the review's author cites. Note any inconsistencies or points with which you disagree.

Now view the film or play objectively, analyzing it as you watch. Take notes, listing major scenes, personal reactions, and common themes. Also write comments about any questions or criticism that may arise. If possible, view the film or play more than once. Focus the purpose and position of your review. Most reviews assume that the reader has not seen the film and provide enough context so that the audience will understand the points they are making.

Your review should argue critically and persuasively against the position of the professional review. It must have an introduction, supporting paragraphs, and a conclusion. The introduction should state the name of the film, briefly describe it, and state the thesis—your position on the movie. Your review must be logical and organized presenting an opposing opinion supported by concrete evidence—facts, reasons, examples, quotes, statistics, or comparisons that objectively support your thesis. Each supporting paragraph should focus on a specific

> "The difference between the almost right word and the right word is really a large matter—'tis the difference between the lightning-bug and the lightning."
>
> —Mark Twain

**Searching for an introduction?**
Wisely, many writers focus on crafting a captivating introduction after completing a rough draft. Finding an effective introduction is easier after you know what your essay says.

idea and provide convincing evidence and arguments to support or refute that idea. The conclusion should restate the title, reassert your thesis, and provide a summary statement about your support.

To identify a thesis, consider issues, actions, or characters about the movie or play that bother, perplex, or intrigue you. Now develop some questions to explore:

- What is the play or film trying to convey? Is it successful?
- What do you like or dislike?
- What are its strengths and weaknesses?
- How do the characters develop?
- Is the dialogue believable?
- What do you think of the acting/directing/special effects?
- When, if ever, does the play or film drag?
- What scenes are unnecessary or problematic?
- What more could or should have been done?

As you consider answers to these questions, formulate a thesis statement that provides a basis and direction for your review.

Next, give yourself a starting point and break the assignment into manageable parts by putting together a graphic organizer and a plan. This plan can range from a brief sketch of main points to a detailed point-by-point outline complete with paragraphs and topic sentences. The idea is to provide yourself with a rough map of where the essay will go, making a diagram of your thoughts to sharpen and define your purpose. At this point you can also give your review a working title.

## Student Model—Graphic Organizer

After deciding on a thesis, Kelly started filling in this graphic organizer to gather and organize information for her review.

> *Review:* Woodward's Compelling Performance in *The Glass Menagerie*
> *Movie or play:* *The Glass Menagerie*
> *Production information:* film adaptation of Tennessee Williams's play 1987 version directed by Paul Newman.
> Amanda—Joanne Woodward, Tom—John Malkovich, Laura—Karen Allen, Gentleman Caller—James Naughton
>
> *Notes about professional review:*
> focuses on Tom and Laura
> doesn't think Woodward brings out Amanda's character
> calls her a "prattling bore"
>
> *Viewing notes:*
> opening shot establishes melancholy, junked-up apartment building
> sad wind instrument music
> Tom talks directly to camera; explains play, characters, and some symbols
> gentle colors

## Language, Grammar, and Style

### Extending Effective Use of Standard, Formal English

**IDENTIFYING STANDARD, FORMAL ENGLISH.** Standard English is the type of language used in formal works of scholarship, public ceremonies, speeches, and in other types of creative writing. Informal English is that which is spoken in everyday life, the language of common conversation. It is used in personal notes, letters, and e-mails, some newspapers and magazines, and some types of creative writing, especially those including dialogue. It is more forgiving of grammatical structure and is enriched by colloquialism, dialect, and slang, which provide color and flavor. Standard English is preferred in some instances because it is objective and universally accessible, both geographically and historically: regardless of the era or region, it will be understood. For more

*Laura is set up in first 10 minutes as being lonely "I'm not expecting any gentlemen callers."*

*Synopsis:*
*The film takes place in a small apartment in St. Louis during the 1930s. Characters include Amanda, Tom, Laura, and a Gentleman Caller. Amanda, the mother, wishes to make sure her children have a good future, particularly Laura, who is physically disabled and extremely shy. Tom persuades a friend to come to dinner as a potential suitor for his sister. Before the dinner party, the characters are developed, showing how Amanda, Laura, and Tom interact. The film centers around this dinner party.*

**My thesis:** *Amanda is the most effective character and Woodward does an excellent job portraying her.*

*Information needed to support:*
*scenes that show Amanda is an essential character in the film*
*scenes that show Woodward does a great acting job*

*Supporting facts, reasons, specific examples, quotes, references, statistics, comparisons, or anecdotes:*
*A quote I really disagree with: "Woodward leaves out the tragic dimension to the character; her Amanda isn't moving—she's a prattling bore." (Hinson, Hal, "The Glass Menagerie." The Washington Post, November 11, 1987, p.D1.)*

# Drafting

Although you have prepared a graphic organizer with your basic points, it is likely that the process of composing an initial draft will alter your original plans somewhat. Your first draft will help you clarify the issues.

**ORGANIZE YOUR REVIEW.** General information about the film or play is essential at the beginning of a review. Try to incorporate several facts that the reader needs to know into clear, concise statements. Ask yourself what your audience knows already, and what it needs to know in order to understand the context for your thesis. Try to strengthen your role as reviewer by establishing as much evidence of your expertise as possible. For example, refer to other works by the same director or other works in the same genre that you have seen.

**PROVIDE A SYNOPSIS.** Limit the synopsis to less than one-fourth of your paper. Keep in mind that you only wish to reveal enough basic knowledge concerning the film so that your criticism will have a foundation.

**BEGIN THE CRITICAL PORTION OF YOUR REVIEW.** Support your opinion of the film with facts and evidence from the work. This section of the review is the most important, and it is also where

information, see the Language Arts Survey 3.2, "Formal and Informal English."

Explain how the following contrasting examples either represent formal or informal English.

> Beverly asked her cousin if he would like to accompany them to the shopping complex.

> Bev asked her cousin if he wanted to hang out with them at the mall.

**FIXING INCONSISTENT USE OF STANDARD ENGLISH.** Look at the following examples from a draft of Kelly's essay.

> Her life is nothing without her kids and she can't take it when they rebuff her.

> However, "you can't teach an old dog new tricks" applies here.

> These scenes show Woodward sitting at a desk talking them into renewing their subscriptions.

> The night when he is to arrive, Amanda works on Laura, who is dragging her feet, to dress up for the occasion.

Try to identify several errors in formal language or places in which the tone isn't consistent with the scholarly, dispassionate, well-reasoned tone that this critical essay should strive to capture. Suggest remedies for these flaws.

*continued on page 752*

For more help on fixing errors and weaknesses in formal English, see the Language Arts Survey 3.48, "Correcting Common Usage Problems."

**Using Standard English.**
Review your essay for instances of standard, formal English and informal English. Look carefully; colloquialisms, slang, and jargon are often difficult to spot because they occur so frequently in everyday language. Revise any instances of informal English that you find.

you have the most freedom as a critic. Explain and give support for why you disagree with the other review.

**Finally, Summarize Your Support.** Make a statement that pulls together your points of support. Encourage your reader to adopt your view. Give credit for your sources. List them at the end of the review, following proper style for documentation. For more information, see the Language Arts Survey 5.36, "Documenting Sources."

## Self- and Peer Evaluation
After you finish your first draft, complete a self-evaluation using the following questions. If time permits, form a group with two or three classmates, exchange and read each others' reviews, and share constructive criticism.

- What point is the review trying to convey? How successfully does the review make the point?
- What does the reviewer identify as the movie or film's strengths and weaknesses? What support is provided? How convincing is the support?
- How does each aspect of the support relate to the thesis? What support is either missing or not needed?
- What organizational changes could be made to provide coherence and continuity?
- What changes might improve the precision, persuasiveness, and reasonableness of the voice?
- How objectively and logically is information from the professional view integrated?
- How convincing is the conclusion? What additions or deletions would make it more convincing?
- What colloquialisms, slang, or jargon needs to be replaced with more carefully chosen, concrete, and vivid words?
- Where might the audience express concern over mechanics, sentence fluency, and the use of first or second person?

## Revising and Proofreading
If possible, allow some time to think about your draft and your evaluation comments. Reconsider your audience, the thesis, the reasoning behind it, and the evidence you have provided. Decide which comments will most improve your review, and then revise. Finally, proofread your writing, cleaning up any grammar, spelling, and punctuation errors. Refer to the Language Arts Survey 2.45, "A Proofreading Checklist."

## Publishing and Presenting
Prepare a neat final text in an essay format. To distinguish your review, add a cover page with a picture and relevant quotation from the movie or play and the title of your essay.

## Reflecting

You can judge a play or film in many different ways. You can look at the parts of the work itself and weigh its intrinsic merits: character, theme, causes, contrasts, and symbols. For example, an actor or actress may give a powerful performance, portraying a character so well that the expressions, dialogue, and scene may cause the viewer to rethink the scene over and over again. Or you can consider it in terms of the author against the backdrop of the culture and measure its extrinsic significance: psychology, biography, philosophy, history, or structure. For example, the theme presented in the play or film may cause the viewer to reconsider his or her thinking about current society, humanity's past, or humanity's future. Which approach do you find the most helpful for making sense of the movies and plays you see? Does it apply to other works of art, such as novels, paintings, and music?

"Everything written is as good as it is dramatic. It need not declare itself in form, but it is drama or nothing."

—Robert Frost

# UNIT REVIEW
## *Modern Drama*

## Words for Everyday Use

Check your knowledge of the following vocabulary words from the selections in this unit. Write short sentences using these words in context to make the meaning clear. To review the definition or usage of a word, refer to the page number listed or the Glossary of Words for Everyday Use.

acutely, 736
aghast, 703
aptitude, 736
beleaguer, 735
bombardment, 715
cater, 702
conglomeration, 689
cultivate, 698
czar, 703
devout, 722
discreet, 718
dismal, 712
emissary, 690
endowment, 709
exposition, 733
fiasco, 700
imminent, 714
implacable, 689
imploringly, 712
importunately, 712

incredulously, 726
indolently, 736
induct, 696
ineluctably, 690
inquisition, 711
interference, 721
interfused, 689
intolerable, 732
jauntily, 741
limelight, 733
listlessly, 709
mastication, 691
matriculate, 690
menagerie, 693
motley, 705
ornamentation, 731
pantomime, 742
paragon, 727
pinion, 703
poise, 726

premature, 717
prominent, 692
querulous, 711
relish, 735
resume, 691
sashay, 723
sheepishly, 709
Spartan, 710
sublimation, 701
supercilious, 717
symptomatic, 689
tribulation, 728
ulterior, 718
unobtrusive, 722
velocity, 721
vestige, 728
vivacity, 727
wince, 734

## Literary Tools

Define the following terms, giving concrete examples of how they are used in the selections in this unit. To review a term, refer to the page number indicated or to the Handbook of Literary Terms.

character, 695, 705, 721
cliché, 708
conflict, 700
dialogue, 714

Expressionism, 687
irony, 695
setting, 708
stage directions, 687

symbol, 700, 705, 714, 730
theme, 730

# Reflecting
## ........... *on* YOUR READING

## Genre Studies

1. **EXPRESSIONIST DRAMA.** *The Glass Menagerie* is an example of Expressionist drama. In such drama, literary and dramatic elements such as the set design and symbolism are often heightened or exaggerated. What elements of this setting are exaggerated and unrealistic? Why? What symbolism does Williams use and for what purposes?

## Thematic Studies

2. **NOSTALGIA.** What role does nostalgia play in *The Glass Menagerie*? Which character has a sentimental yearning for the past? How does this character's nostalgia interfere with living in the present and planning for the future? Does Williams view nostalgia as helpful or harmful?

## Historical/Biographical Studies

3. **MODERN DRAMA.** What characteristics of modern drama are evident in *The Glass Menagerie?* How are they developed by Williams? Review the introduction to modern drama on page 684.

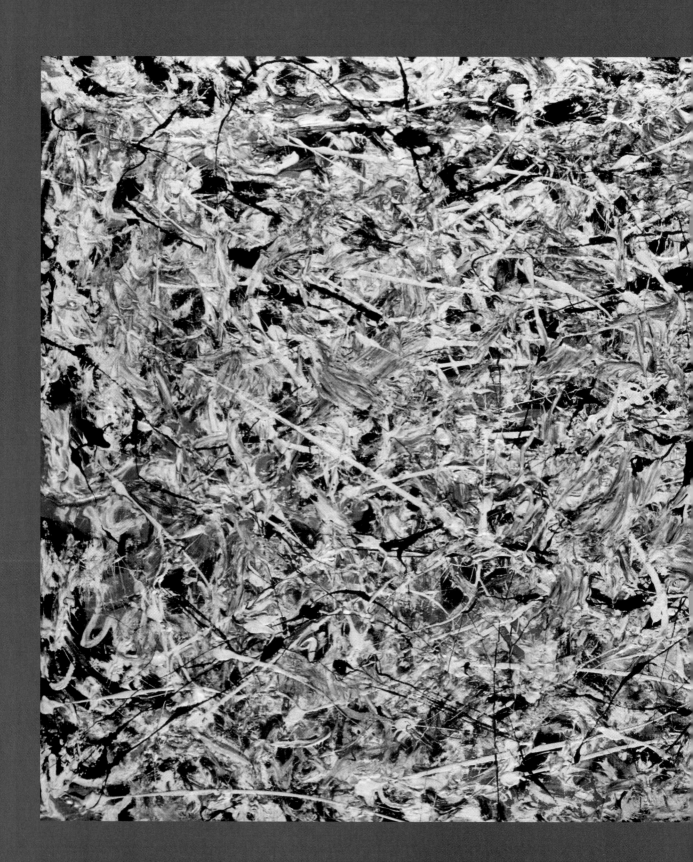

*White Light,* 1954. Jackson Pollock.
Museum of Modern Art, New York.

America is woven of many strands; I would recognize them and let it so remain . . . Our fate is to become one, and yet many.

—Ralph Ellison

## ArtNote

*White Light,* 1954. Jackson Pollock.

The works of Jackson Pollock (1912–1956) were called "drip paintings" because of Pollock's technique. Pollock placed the canvas on the floor and dripped paint from a stick or poured it directly from the can. It was an entirely new way of painting on canvas, although Pollock acknowledged it was influenced by the sandpainting techniques of the Navajo tribe. Pollock's style also represented a new way of thinking about art. He advised the viewer not to "look for something" in the painting, but to approach it as a sensory experience. Consequently, a Pollock painting is huge, eight feet high or more, and the viewer has the feeling of being surrounded and pulled in by it. Art critics also speak of his work as having an "all over" composition. What do you think that means?

# POSTWAR LITERATURE (1945–1960)

## THE POLITICS

The period following **World War II** was a time of relative prosperity in the United States and was characterized by social and political conservatism in most of the population. The ideological, political, and economic tensions after the war between the USSR and Eastern Europe on the one hand and the USA and Western Europe on the other created what became known as the **Cold War,** which lasted from 1945 to 1989. Throughout the forties and fifties, tensions escalated between the United States and the Communist "Eastern Bloc," especially after such events as the detonation of an atomic bomb by the Soviet Union in 1949 and the Soviet repression of an uprising in Hungary in 1956. In 1957, the Soviet Union launched the first orbital satellite, *Sputnik,* raising fears that the United States was falling behind technologically and initiating the **Space Race** that would result in the landing of United States astronauts on the moon in 1969. The U.S. involvement in the **Korean War** (1950–1953), against North Korea and its ally Communist China, led the United States to commit itself to defense against communism in other parts of Southeast Asia, thus laying the groundwork for war in Vietnam.

When war hero **Dwight David Eisenhower** was elected president in 1952, **Richard M. Nixon,** a strong anticommunist, became his vice president. The country's economy was strong, and employment was high. The mood of the country was conservative, and marked by a revulsion to communism and all it represented. Anyone expressing liberal views risked being called "pinko" or "commie." Herbert Fillbrick of *I Led Three Lives* was television's hero, a counterspy who rooted out burrowed communists in American society. When **Senator Joseph McCarthy** of Wisconsin accused the former Truman administration of hiding and promoting communists to high government posts, the country was ready to listen. Hollywood had already blacklisted ten directors and

## LITERARY EVENTS

➤ = American Events

➤ 1945. Richard Wright's *Black Boy* published

➤ 1946. Robert Penn Warren's *All the King's Men* published

➤ 1946. Eugene O'Neill's *The Iceman Cometh* produced

➤ 1947. Tennessee Williams's *A Streetcar Named Desire* produced

➤ 1948. Norman Mailer's *The Naked and the Dead* published

➤ 1948. T. S. Eliot wins the Nobel Prize

| 1945 | 1946 | 1947 | 1948 |
| --- | --- | --- | --- |

1945. World War II ends

➤ 1945. Jackie Robinson hired as the first African-American ball player in the major leagues

➤ 1947. Transistor invented

➤ 1948. Truman elected president; he ends segregation in the armed forces

➤ 1948. Paperback books become popular

## HISTORICAL EVENTS

➤ 1946. First electronic calculator produced

➤ 1946. Dr. Benjamin Spock's *Baby and Child Care* published

producers for their affiliation with the Communist Party. **Dashiell Hammett,** the writer of the mysteries *The Thin Man* and *The Maltese Falcon,* served prison time for refusing to identify communist sympathizers. In 1954, McCarthy changed his focus of accusations to the United States Army. After many accusations based on flimsy evidence and many ruined lives, the *Army v. McCarthy* hearings ended with the Senate condemning McCarthy for his unseemly and destructive behavior. The hearings were over, but the wounds from this "witch hunt" would remain, as they had after the Salem witch trials in 1692. The McCarthy hearings inspired **Arthur Miller's** *The Crucible,* a drama first produced in 1952 that used the story of the Salem witch trials to demonstrate how mass hysteria and guilt by association destroy the systems of justice. **Elia Kazan's** film *On the Waterfront,* on the other hand, seemed to

Senator Joseph McCarthy, 1954.

support the McCarthy hearings by giving the message that one should "sing" or "rat on" one's corrupt friends to the authorities. Although the worst of the anticommunist paranoia in the United States ended with the deterioration of the McCarthy hearings, the Cold War would last until 1989, with the destruction of the Berlin Wall in East Germany and the thundering collapse of Communist governments in Eastern Europe.

## THE SOCIAL SCENE

When World War II ended, the surviving soldiers came home, most of them eager to put war behind them and return to or start families in a house with a white picket fence and at least a one-car garage. Their goal was to find a good job in a business or factory that was now converting to peacetime production. Most women returned to their homes and became housewives and mothers while the men became breadwinners. The days of "Rosie the Riveter" were gone; the "baby boom" was here. The cities sprawled outward into suburbia, made possible by the production of newer and better cars from General Motors, Ford, and Chrysler Corporation. President Eisenhower had little trouble in 1956

➤ 1949. Arthur Miller's *Death of a Salesman* produced

➤ 1949. Carson McCullers's *Member of the Wedding* published

➤ 1949. Ezra Pound wins the Bollinger Prize and is jailed for broadcasting pro-Mussolini propaganda

➤ 1950. Ray Bradbury's *The Martian Chronicles* published

➤ 1950. Clifford Odets's *The Country Girl* produced

➤ 1950. William Inge's *Come Back Little Sheba* produced

➤ 1950. William Faulkner wins the Nobel Prize

➤ 1951. J. D. Salinger's *Catcher in the Rye* published

➤ James Jones's *From Here to Eternity* published

➤ 1952. Ralph Ellison's *The Invisible Man* published

➤ 1952. John Steinbeck's *East of Eden* published

➤ 1952. Ernest Hemingway's *The Old Man and the Sea* published

➤ 1952. Bernard Malamud's *The Natural* published

**1949** | **1950** | **1951** | **1952**

1949. Communists take over China

➤ 1949. 45 rpm records introduced

1950. Korean War begins

➤ 1950. Tri-color picture tube invented

➤ 1950. Althea Gibson becomes the first African-American to play in the U.S. grass court tennis championships at Forest Hills, New York

➤ 1950. Ralph Bunche wins the Nobel Peace Prize

➤ 1951. Hydrogen bomb tested

➤ 1951. Fifty-one Americans indicted as communists

➤ 1951. Color TV introduced in New York

➤ 1951. David Reisman's *The Lonely Crowd* published

➤ 1952. Eisenhower elected president

➤ 1952. Buckminster Fuller builds a geodesic dome

Car advertisement, 1955.

persuading Congress to levy more than 33 billion dollars for an interstate highway system to cross America from east to west and from north to south. The mobile society was on its way. Motor inns and motels such as Holiday Inn and Howard Johnson's emerged alongside fast food drive-in restaurants such as A&W and drive-in movie theaters. The automobile was, more than ever, a sign of success. Tiny suburban homes were abandoned to young families starting out, while established, more affluent families began moving ever outward to multi-bedroom homes with two-car garages and larger lawns. Every night on black and white television, the middle class watched **Steve Allen** on *The Tonight Show,* and on Sunday nights the family gathered for **Ed Sullivan's** *Toast of the Town,* a variety show of singers, mimes, magicians, and emerging recording stars such as **Elvis Presley** and, in the early 1960s, **The Beatles.** It was the time of *Father Knows Best, I Love Lucy,* and *Ozzie and Harriet,* situation comedies that set ideals for families that were difficult to live up to. Television also had the effect of shrinking the globe, bringing foreign lands almost instantaneously into the living room.

In 1954 **Bill Haley and the Comets** issued the 45 rpm recording of "Rock around the Clock." Shortly thereafter in a Memphis studio, Elvis Presley recorded "Hound Dog," "Blue Suede Shoes," and "Don't Be Cruel" to establish rock and roll, a new music that was a mixture of blues and country. **Pat Boone** was the all-American boy. Parents read their children *The Cat in the Hat* by Dr. Seuss and learned to parent from *Baby and Child Care* by **Dr. Benjamin Spock. Marilyn Monroe,** the blonde bombshell, married **Joe DiMaggio,** Mr. Baseball, in 1954, then playwright Arthur Miller in 1956. Under the surface prosperity was a turmoil within, a pervading loneliness that **David Reisman** described in *The Lonely Crowd* in 1951. *Rebel without a Cause,* a film starring **James Dean,** depicted an alienated young man's search for meaningful friendships in an adult world that had abandoned him. Similarly in **J. D. Salinger's** 1951 novel *The Catcher in the Rye*, Holden Caulfield pronounced the adult world "phony."

# LITERARY EVENTS

➤ = American Events

➤ 1953. William Inge's *Picnic* produced
➤ 1953. James Baldwin's *Go Tell It on the Mountain* published
➤ 1953. Arthur Miller's *The Crucible* produced

➤ 1954. Ernest Hemingway wins the Nobel Prize

➤ 1955. Tennessee Williams's *Cat on a Hot Tin Roof* produced

➤ 1956. Saul Bellows's *Seize the Day* published

| 1953 | 1954 | 1955 | 1956 |

➤ 1953. Salk vaccine against polio introduced
➤ 1953. DNA discovered to be a double helix
1953. Korean armistice announced; Soviet Union develops hydrogen bomb
➤ 1953. Joseph McCarthy accuses the Truman administration of aiding communists

1955. Warsaw pact established
1955. Big Four summit takes place in Geneva
➤ 1955. Jasper Johns and Robert Rauschenberg introduce the pop art movement

➤ 1956. Bus boycott takes place in Montgomery, Alabama
1956. Egyptian President Nasser nationalizes the Suez Canal
➤ 1956. Elvis Presley has a number one hit on the charts
1956. Hungarian Revolt squelched

# HISTORICAL EVENTS

➤ 1954. Supreme Court orders school integration
➤ 1954. Bill Haley and the Comets' hit "Rock Around the Clock" becomes number one

## CIVIL RIGHTS MOVEMENT

As the white middle class prospered and moved out to the suburbs, many African Americans were left in the old and decaying inner cities. Inner-city neighborhoods became areas of increased poverty and unemployment and a backdrop for rising social unrest. By the mid-1950s the Civil Rights movement had begun. On December 1, 1955, when **Rosa Parks** in Montgomery, Alabama, refused to give up her seat to a white man and move farther back on the city bus, she was arrested. Soon, under the leadership of **Martin Luther King, Jr.,** blacks boycotted public transportation. The fight for equal rights had begun. Almost a year later, the Supreme Court decided that the bus segregation laws in Montgomery were unconstitutional. The boycott had become

Students arrive at integrated Little Rock Central High protected by the army, 1957.

the Movement. However, the first blow to racial segregation had come in 1954 with the Supreme Court decision under **Chief Justice Earl Warren** in the ***Brown v. The Topeka Board of Education*** lawsuit. The court had then decided unanimously that the *Plessy v. Ferguson* decision a half century earlier to maintain "separate but equal" schools was inherently unequal and thus unconstitutional. In 1957, this decision was tested in Little Rock, Arkansas, when nine black students attempted to enter the all-white public high school to the jeers and assaults of an angry public. A few weeks later, Little Rock Central High School was integrated with the assistance of media scrutiny and federal troops. The Civil Rights movement was well under way and would continue throughout the 1960s. During this period several black writers emerged, most notably **Richard Wright** with *Black Boy* (1945); **Ralph Ellison** with *Invisible Man* (1952); **James Baldwin** with *Go Tell It on the Mountain* (1953); **Gwendolyn Brooks** through her poetry collection *Bronzeville Boys and Girls* (1956); and **Lorraine Hansberry** with her drama *A Raisin in the Sun* (1958).

---

➤ 1957. Jack Kerouac's *On the Road* published

➤ 1957. Bernard Malamud's *The Assistant* published

➤ 1957. Eugene O'Neill's *Long Day's Journey into Night* produced

➤ 1958. Leon Uris's *Exodus* published

1958. Harold Pinter's *The Birthday Party* produced

➤ 1959. Truman Capote's *Breakfast at Tiffany's* published

➤ 1959. Tennessee Williams's *Sweet Bird of Youth* produced

➤ 1959. Lorraine Hansberry's *A Raisin in the Sun* produced on Broadway

➤ 1960. Harper Lee's *To Kill a Mockingbird* published

➤ 1960. Lillian Hellman's *Toys in the Attic* produced

➤ 1960. John Updike's *Rabbit, Run* published

**1957**   **1958**   **1959**   **1960**

1957. European Common Market established

➤ 1957. Troops desegregate schools in Little Rock, Arkansas

1957. Soviet Union launches *Sputnik*

➤ 1958. *Explorer I* satellite launched

➤ 1958. Dr. Seuss's *Cat in the Hat* published

1959. Fidel Castro takes over in Cuba

1959. Soviets send rocket past the moon

➤ 1959. Alaska becomes the forty-ninth state

➤ 1959. School opens in Little Rock, Arkansas, under court order

➤ 1960. Kennedy elected president

➤ 1960. U-2 spy incident occurs

➤ 1960. Vance Packard's *The Waste Makers* published

# THE LITERARY SCENE

The postwar period was a time of great literary creativity. The war itself gave rise to many fine literary works, including Norman Mailer's *The Naked and the Dead* and James Jones's *From Here to Eternity.* Many of the finest American writers of the early to mid-century period were at the height of their powers during this time, including **William Faulkner, John Steinbeck,** and **Katherine Anne Porter.** Faulkner won the Nobel Prize for literature in 1950 and Hemingway followed, winning it in 1952. In that same year Steinbeck wrote *East of Eden,* one of his finest works.

**John Hersey,** in *Hiroshima* (1946), created a new genre that combined journalism and literature. Joining literary techniques and the factual air of reporting to describe real events, *Hiroshima* began what some critics call the genre of the **"nonfiction novel."** It has been called the most significant piece of journalism in modern times.

Among Jewish writers who reflected their experience of the Holocaust and life in America were **Saul Bellow** through his novels *The Adventures of Augie March* (1953) and *Henderson, the Rain King* (1959) and his novella *Seize the Day* (1956); **Bernard Malamud** through his novels *The Natural* (1952) and *The Assistant* (1957), and his short story "The Magic Barrel" (1954); and **Isaac Bashevis Singer** through his short story collection *Gimpel the Fool* (1953) and his many novels, including *The Family Moskat* (1950). In 1978 Singer won the Nobel Prize for literature.

City Lights Book Store.

In the South **John Crowe Ransom** had fathered the **Fugitive School,** which rebelled against Northern materialism and against science and progress. Postwar writers from this school included **Robert Penn Warren** and **Allan Tate.** Other writers who emerged from the South included **Flannery O'Connor, Walker Percy,** and **Eudora Welty.** Additional major fiction writers starting to gain prominence in the fifties included **Truman Capote, John Cheever, John O'Hara,** and **John Updike.**

The postwar period also saw a flowering of American drama in work by new dramatists such as Arthur Miller, **Tennessee Williams,** and **William Inge,** as well as new work by established dramatists such as **Eugene O'Neill** and **Lillian Hellman.**

Among the poets, **Wallace Stevens, T. S. Eliot, Robert Frost, Carl Sandburg, Marianne Moore, E. E. Cummings,** and **William Carlos Williams** reached their peak during the postwar years. Eliot had served as mentor for most poets in the three previous decades, proposing that poetry should be "an escape from emotion and personality." In 1947, Eliot won the Nobel Prize for literature. In the 1950s, such poets as **Robert Lowell** and **Randall Jarrell** followed Eliot's lead by maintaining a stable poetic tradition of precise rhyme and rhythm.

Still, poetry was remarkably diverse. E. E. Cummings experimented with parts of speech, capitalization, and punctuation to explore the essence of language. Influenced by William Carlos Williams, who believed there should "be no ideas except in things," **Charles Olson** started the **Black Mountain School** in North Carolina. His "projective verse" experimented with the rhythms and sounds of words in lines based on breath pauses. These poets focused on the extraordinary versatility and power of words which in combination created a thing in itself, an artifact. Notable poets in the Black Mountain School were **Robert Creeley** and **Robert Duncan.**

In sharp contrast to those who objected to emotion and personality in literature, the new **confessional poets** such as **John Berryman** and Robert Lowell used haunting, stark images to reveal intensely personal experience. These writers set the tone for the 1960s and for writers to follow, such as Sylvia Plath and Anne Sexton. Berryman and Lowell wrote of their inner demons, strained and broken marriages, and alcoholism. **Theodore Roethke**, a new romantic, based much of his poetry on his childhood experience, using his father's greenhouse as metaphor.

Inspired by **Abstract Expressionism,** as **Wallace Stevens** continued to be, the New York poets **John Ashbery, Frank O'Hara,** and **Kenneth Koch** experimented with new perceptions and poetic forms. They tried to duplicate in words what the expressionist artists accomplished in paint. Most controversial was the counterculture that developed on the West Coast in San Francisco during the mid-1950s. **Kenneth Rexroth,** a radical poet and intellectual, opened his upstairs apartment over Jack's Record Cellar to the new "literati," who challenged the social malaise and traditional forms of the time. In 1953 **Lawrence Ferlinghetti** and **Peter Martins** opened the City Lights Book Store, the first all-paperback bookstore in the United States and a haven for writers. In 1955 at the Six Gallery poetry reading, **Allen Ginsberg** gave a dramatic reading of his poem "Howl," a spontaneous composition written to jazz rhythms that challenged every aspect of American life and language. Soon his poem and those of many of the **"Beat Generation,"** as **Jack Kerouac** dubbed it, were in bookstores throughout America. Based on existential and Eastern philosophy, beat poems strove to cut through superficial facades, denouncing and reviling thoughtless conformism, to embrace life itself. Among the Beats, as the poets came to be called, were **Gary Snyder,** Jack Kerouac, **Michael McClure,** Lawrence Ferlinghetti, **Gregory Corso,** and Kenneth Rexroth.

At the same time, the **Kingston Trio** was bringing to public attention the folk songs of **Woody Guthrie, Pete and Peggy Seeger,** and **Peter, Paul, and Mary.** With the Kingston Trio's recording of "Tom Dooley," folk music became the craze of the late 1950s and continued through the 1960s. The youth of America joined the "folk song army," as **Tom Lehrer** sang in one of his brilliant satirical songs about American life. College campuses hummed with the strumming of guitars and banjoes. Dozens of folk singers and groups arose until much of the younger generation was singing Guthrie's "This Land Is Your Land." Folk music, and not the jazz accompaniment of the "Beat" protests, would become the voice of the youth protest movement—of the "hippies" and flower children—in the years to come.

The postwar era was a time of prosperity and stability, but underneath ran a current of distrust, disapproval, and disillusionment with the status quo. The literary scene included traditionalists, experimenters, and iconoclasts. The **"Silent Generation,"** as it came to be called, spoke with a loud voice.

Folksinging group Peter, Paul, and Mary.

# ECHOES ECHOES ECHOES ECHOES ECHOES ECHOES ECHOES ECHOES ECHOES

## POSTWAR LITERATURE

Without alienation, there can be no politics.
—Arthur Miller

Most of us are about as eager to be changed as we were to be born, and go through our changes in a similar state of shock.
—James Baldwin

The very essence of literature is the war between emotion and intellect, between life and death. When literature becomes too intellectual—when it begins to ignore the passions, the emotions—it becomes sterile, silly, and actually without substance.
—Isaac Bashevis Singer

We know what a person thinks not when he tells us what he thinks, but by his actions.
—Isaac Bashevis Singer

For every man who lives without freedom, the rest of us must face the guilt.
—Lillian Hellman, from *Watch on the Rhine*

The past, with its pleasures, its rewards, its foolishness, its punishments, is there for each of us forever, and it should be.
—Lillian Hellman, from *Scoundrel Time*

Don't look back. Something may be gaining on you.
—Satchel [Leroy] Paige

I wake to sleep, and take my waking slow.
I feel my fate in what I cannot fear.
I learn by going where I have to go.
—Theodore Roethke, from *The Waking*

The excursion is the same when you go looking for your sorrow as when you go looking for your joy.
—Eudora Welty, from *The Wide Net*

Fear tastes like a rusty knife and do not let her get into your house. Courage tastes of blood. Stand up straight. Admire the world. Relish the love of a gentle woman. Trust in the Lord.
—John Cheever, from *The Wapshot Chronicle*

Art attempts to find in the universe, in matter as well as in the facts of life, what is fundamental, enduring, essential.
—Saul Bellow

Does one's integrity ever lie in what he is not able to do? I think that usually it does, for free will does not mean one will, but many wills conflicting in one man. Freedom cannot be conceived simply.
—Flannery O'Connor, from *Wiseblood*

Thanks to the interstate highway system, it is now possible to travel across the country from coast to coast without seeing anything.
—Charles Kuralt

To love so well the world that we may believe, in the end, in God.
—Robert Penn Warren

*Documents II* [Detail], Jackson Pollock.

# "COMMANDER LOWELL"

BY ROBERT LOWELL

## About *the* AUTHOR

**Robert Lowell** (1917–1977), poet, playwright, and translator, was born in Boston to parents who could both trace their ancestors back to early New England families. Educated at Harvard University and Kenyon College, Lowell befriended Randall Jarrell and John Crowe Ransom while an undergraduate. Both writers were active in defining the New Criticism, which focused on verbal nuances and thematic structure of poems rather than on biographical or social backgrounds.

In 1940 Lowell converted for a short time to Roman Catholicism. The conflict between his Bostonian upbringing and Catholicism is portrayed in his first volume of verse, *Land of Unlikeness* (1944). In *Lord Weary's Castle*, which won the Pulitzer Prize in 1947, rebellion against "Old Law, imperialism, militarism, capitalism, Calvinism, Authority, the Father, the 'proper Bostonians,' [and] the rich" is a dominant theme. In the mid-1960s Lowell turned to plays to develop the theme of the individual's relation to history. His translation of Aeschylus's *Prometheus Bound* (1969) also appeared during this period. Lowell's experiences of political activism during the Vietnam War are described in the sonnets of *Notebook 1967–68*. One of three volumes of poetry published in 1973, *The Dolphin*, which won Lowell a second Pulitzer Prize, professes that love makes freedom meaningful and allows for human growth. His last collection of poetry, *Day by Day* (1977), is an elegiac and deeply personal volume that provides quick glimpses at Lowell's family and friends, the horrors of his manic-depressive illness, and the joys of his recoveries.

## Reader's *Journal*

What is it about your parents' behavior that sets them apart from their peers?

## Literary TOOLS

**SLANT RHYME.** A **slant rhyme**, **half rhyme**, **near rhyme**, or **off rhyme** is substitution of assonance or consonance for true rhyme. As you read, look for examples of slant rhyme.

**CHARACTERIZATION. Characterization** is the use of literary techniques to create a character. Writers use three major techniques to create characters: direct description, portrayal of characters' behavior, and representations of characters' internal states. How is Commander Lowell characterized in this poem?

## About *the* SELECTION

**"Commander Lowell,"** a critical portrait of the poet's father, appeared in 1959 in his collection of poetry, *Life Studies*. *Life Studies* gives glimpses into the themes of Lowell's childhood. The collection, with its "confessional" poems, had an enormous influence on the future of poetry in the United States.

Although best known for *Life Studies,* Lowell established his true greatness as an American poet in the astonishing variety of his work. He wrote both intricate and tightly patterned poems that incorporated traditional meter and rhyme, as well as autobiographical poetry structured in much looser forms and meters. According to his friend Peter Taylor, Lowell's interest in personal development and history and politics were one and the same, a search for "oneness in himself and a oneness in the world."

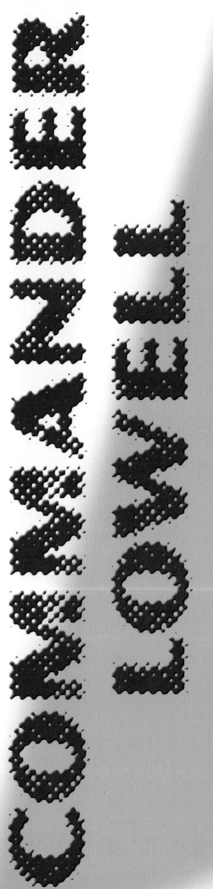

**COMMANDER LOWELL**

*Inspection*, 1943. Edward Steichen.

## ROBERT LOWELL

There were no undesirables or girls in my set,
when I was a boy at Mattapoisett—
only Mother, still her Father's daughter.
Her voice was still electric
with a hysterical, unmarried panic,
when she read to me from the Napoleon book.

> Who reads to the
> narrator from the
> Napoleon book?

Long-nosed Marie Louise
Hapsburg in the frontispiece[1]
had a downright Boston bashfulness,
where she groveled to Bonaparte, who scratched his navel,
and bolted his food—just my seven years tall!
And I, bristling and manic,
skulked in the attic,
and got two hundred French generals by name,
from *A* to *V* —from Augereau to Vandamme.
I used to dope myself asleep,
naming those unpronounceables like sheep.

Having a naval officer
for my Father was nothing to shout
about to the summer colony at "Matt."
He wasn't at all "serious,"
when he showed up on the golf course,
wearing a blue serge jacket and numbly cut white ducks he'd bought
at a Pearl Harbor commissariat . . .
and took four shots with his putter to sink his putt.
"Bob," they said, "golf's a game you really ought to know how
     to play,
if you play at all."
They wrote him off as "naval,"
naturally supposed his sport was sailing.
Poor Father, his training was engineering!
Cheerful and cowed
among the seadogs[2] at the Sunday yacht club,
he was never one of the crowd.

*Since the narrator's father wasn't good at golf, what did his friends assume he was good at? Why?*

"Anchors aweigh," Daddy boomed in his bathtub,
"Anchors aweigh,"
when Lever Brothers offered to pay
him double what the Navy paid.
I nagged for his dress sword with gold braid,
and cringed because Mother, new
caps on all her teeth, was born anew

*Why did Commander Lowell leave the Navy?*

---

1. **frontispiece.** Illustration preceding and usually facing the
title page of a book or magazine
2. **seadogs.** Veteran sailors

**WORDS FOR EVERYDAY USE**

**grov • el** (grä´vəl) *vi.*, give oneself over to what is base or unworthy. *Mr. Stevens groveled in self-pity when he was overlooked for a promotion.*

**skulk** (skəlk) *vi.*, hide or conceal oneself, often out of cowardice or fear. *The burglar skulked in the bushes, waiting for the lights of the Davies' house to go out.*

**cowed** (koud) *adj.*, intimidated. *Cowed by the good voices in the choir, Jim hid in the back.*

at forty. With seamanlike <u>celerity</u>
Father left the Navy,
and deeded Mother his property.

He was soon fired. Year after year,
he still hummed "Anchors aweigh" in the tub—
whenever he left a job,
he bought a smarter car.
Father's last employer
was Scudder, Stevens and Clark, Investment Advisors
himself his only client.
While Mother dragged to bed alone,
read Menninger,[3]
and grew more and more suspicious,
he grew defiant.
Night after night,
*à la clarté déserte de sa lampe,*[4]
he slid his ivory Annapolis slide rule
across a pad of graphs—
piker speculations![5] In three years
he squandered sixty thousand dollars.

Smiling on all,
Father was once successful enough to be lost
in the mob of ruling-class Bostonians.
As early as 1928,
he owned a house converted to oil,
and redecorated by the architect
of St. Mark's School. . . . Its main effect
was a drawing room, "longitudinal as Versailles,"
its ceiling, roughened with oatmeal, was blue as the sea.
And once
nineteen, the youngest ensign[6] in his class,
he was "the old man" of a gunboat on the Yangtze.[7] ■

What did Commander Lowell buy whenever he left a job?

When had Commander Lowell been successful?

---

3. **Menninger.** Karl Menninger (1893–1966), American psychiatrist and author of *The Human Mind* and *Man Against Himself*
4. *à la clarté déserte de sa lampe.* By the deserted light of the lamp (French)
5. **piker speculations.** Investments made with small amounts of money
6. **ensign.** Commissioned officer in the navy ranking above a chief warrant officer and below a lieutenant junior grade
7. **Yangtze.** River in China that flows into the China Sea

WORDS
FOR
EVERYDAY
USE

ce • ler • i • ty (sə ler′ ə t ē) *n.*, rapidity of motion or action. *With <u>celerity</u> June ran to the door to greet her prom date.*

If you were the narrator, how would you react to the tensions in your household?

# INVESTIGATE Inquire, *Imagine*

**Recall:** GATHERING FACTS

1a. How does the narrator "dope" himself asleep as a boy?

2a. How well does Commander Lowell play golf?

3a. How successful is Commander Lowell in business?

**Interpret:** FINDING MEANING

1b. Why do you think the narrator is so intrigued with French generals?

2b. Why is it important for the narrator to show that his father plays golf so poorly?

3b. What does the Commander's failure at business lend to his characterization?

**Analyze:** TAKING THINGS APART

4a. Analyze the narrator's attitude toward his father.

**Synthesize:** BRINGING THINGS TOGETHER

4b. Why does the narrator's mother grow "suspicious"?

**Perspective:** LOOKING AT OTHER VIEWS

5a. How does Commander Lowell see himself?

**Empathy:** SEEING FROM INSIDE

5b. If you were the narrator, would you be proud of your father? Why, or why not?

# Understanding *Literature*

**SLANT RHYME.** Review the definition for **slant rhyme** in the Handbook of Literary Terms. What examples of slant rhyme did you find in the poem?

**CHARACTERIZATION.** Review the definition for **characterization** in the Handbook of Literary Terms. Then complete the following chart to describe the character of Commander Lowell. One example has been done for you. How does the poet create the character of the Commander?

| Physical Appearance | Dress | Habits/ Mannerisms/ Behaviors | Relationships with Other People | Other |
|---|---|---|---|---|
| | blue serge jacket and white ducks; dress sword with gold braid | | | |

# WRITER'S JOURNAL

1. Imagine that you are the narrator as a boy. Write a **journal entry** detailing your observations of your parents' behavior and emotions.

2. Imagine you are a reporter for the weekly newspaper at Mattapoisett. Write an **obituary** for Commander Lowell. You might want to read several examples of obituaries in your local newspaper before you begin.

3. Imagine that you are a former fellow naval officer of Commander Lowell. Write him a **letter** advising him how to regain control of his life.

# Integrating
## *the* LANGUAGE ARTS

## Language, Grammar, and Style

**CONCRETE AND ABSTRACT NOUNS.** Read the Language Arts Survey 3.52, "Concrete Nouns and Abstract Nouns." Then identify the concrete and abstract nouns in the following lines from "Commander Lowell."

1. Her voice was still electric / with a hysterical, unmarried panic. . . .
2. Long-nosed Marie Louise / Hapsburg in the frontispiece / had a downright Boston bashfulness. . . .
3. Poor Father, his training was Engineering!
4. With seamanlike celerity, / Father left the Navy, / and deeded Mother his property.
5. In three years / he squandered sixty thousand dollars.

## Speaking and Listening

**INTERVIEW.** Interview a classmate about one of his or her parents or adult relatives. Ask questions that reveal the person's hopes, dreams, and disappointments. Then write a portrait in verse of this person, using "Commander Lowell" as a model.

## Applied English

**RÉSUMÉ.** Write a résumé for Commander Lowell, including his experiences in the navy and in business. You will need to invent the names of the companies he worked for and other details. Before you begin, you may want to review the résumé in the Language Arts Survey 6.8, "Writing a Résumé."

# "THE DEATH OF THE BALL TURRET GUNNER"

BY RANDALL JARRELL

## About the AUTHOR

**Randall Jarrell** (1914–1965), poet, novelist, and literary critic, was born in Nashville, Tennessee. He attended both Vanderbilt University, where he became an instructor in English, and Kenyon College. During World War II he served in the U.S. Army Air Force. Jarrell translated his experiences of war into two volumes of poetry, *Little Friend, Little Friend* (1945) and *Losses* (1948), in which he examined the lives of individual fighting men in compassionate detail, indicting the evil of war. According to many critics, these collections remain unsurpassed as American poetic contributions to the literature of World War II. Jarrell was also a renowned literary critic.

In subsequent poems Jarrell turned his attention to the "dailiness of life" in civilian America. He was particularly interested in the role of women in society, whom he saw as trapped or victimized. *The Woman at the Washington Zoo* received the National Book Award for Poetry in 1961. Other themes included loneliness and fear of aging and death. Childhood is the subject of his last book of poems, *The Lost World* (1965). His only novel, *Pictures from an Institution* (1954), is an affectionate satire of academic life. Jarrell was killed while walking beside a highway in North Carolina.

## About the SELECTION

**"The Death of the Ball Turret Gunner"** was published in *Little Friend, Little Friend* (1945), one of Jarrell's collections of war poetry. It is perhaps the best-known American poem about World War II. Jarrell explained the ball turret and gave insight into understanding this poem: "A ball turret was a plexiglass sphere set into the belly of a B-17 or B-24, and inhabited by two .50 caliber machine guns and one man, a short small man. When this gunner tracked with his machine guns a fighter attacking his bomber from below, he revolved with the turret; hunched upsidedown in his little sphere, he looked like the fetus in the womb. The fighters which attacked him were armed with cannon firing explosive shells. The hose was a steam hose."

## Literary TOOLS

**AIM.** A writer's **aim** is his or her purpose, or goal. People may write with the following aims: to inform (expository/informational writing); to tell a story, either true or invented, about an event or sequence of events (narrative writing); to reflect (personal/expressive writing); to share a perspective by using an artistic medium, such as fiction or poetry, to entertain, enrich, or enlighten (imaginative writing); to persuade readers or listeners to respond in some way, such as to agree with a position, change a view on an issue, reach an agreement, or perform an action (persuasive/argumentative writing). As you read, decide Jarrell's aim in writing "The Death of the Ball Turret Gunner."

**TONE.** **Tone** is the emotional attitude toward the reader or toward the subject implied by a literary work. As you read, determine the poet's tone toward the subject.

## Reader's Journal

What demands does the government make on your life?

# THE DEATH OF THE BALL TURRET GUNNER

### RANDALL JARRELL

From my mother's sleep I fell into the State,
And I hunched in its belly till my wet fur froze.
Six miles from earth, loosed from its dream of life,
I woke to black flak[1] and the nightmare fighters.
When I died they washed me out of the turret with a hose. ■

How high up is the plane?

What happens to the ball turret gunner?

---

1. **black flak.** Antiaircraft bullet shells

If you were the speaker, would you think you had died for the glory of the State? Explain.

# INVESTIGATE Inquire Imagine

**Recall:** GATHERING FACTS

1a. To what does the word "State" refer?

2a. What causes the "wet fur" to freeze?

3a. How is the gunner removed from the ball turret?

→ **Interpret:** FINDING MEANING

1b. What does it mean when the speaker says "I fell into the State"?

2b. What is the "wet fur"?

3b. What happens to the plane?

**Analyze:** TAKING THINGS APART

4a. Identify the metaphor in line 2.

→ **Synthesize:** BRINGING THINGS TOGETHER

4b. How is this metaphor extended at the end of the poem?

**Perspective:** LOOKING AT OTHER VIEWS

5a. How does the speaker view his experience? Where would he prefer to be?

→ **Empathy:** SEEING FROM INSIDE

5b. If you were the speaker, would you think you were fighting a "good war," as World War II was sometimes called? Why, or why not?

# Understanding Literature

AIM. Review the definition for **aim** in the Handbook of Literary Terms. What is Jarrell's aim in writing this poem?

TONE. Review the definition of **tone** in the Handbook of Literary Terms. What is the poet's tone toward the subject of the poem?

# Writer's Journal

1. Write a **telegram** announcing the gunner's death to his family.
2. Imagine you are the gunner. Write a **journal entry** contrasting your "dream of life" with your "nightmare."
3. Write a **paragraph** explaining Jarrell's attitude toward war. State whether or not "The Death of the Ball Turret Gunner" is an antiwar poem.

# Integrating the LANGUAGE ARTS

## Language, Grammar, and Style

**HELPING VERBS.** Read the Language Arts Survey 3.8, "Helping Verbs." Write out the following sentences, underlining the helping verbs.

1. While World War II was taking place, Jarrell served as a pilot and instructor.
2. He did not appear to have nice things to say about weak poets.
3. He did promote the art of poetry.
4. He had been working in the English departments of many colleges and universities.
5. Jarrell might have written more books if he had not died tragically.

## Collaborative Learning & Speaking and Listening

**DEBATE.** Form two small groups to debate U.S. participation in wars overseas. One group should argue that the United States has a duty to become involved in certain types of conflicts in other parts of the world. As a part of their argument, this group should describe the circumstances in which such U.S. involvement is necessary. The other group should maintain an isolationist posture, arguing that the U.S. should never become involved in overseas conflicts. Before you begin the debate, your class should brainstorm and discuss the times in recent history in which the United States became involved in a conflict abroad.

## Applied English

**CITATION FOR BRAVERY.** Imagine you are the ball turret gunner's commanding officer. Write a citation for bravery for the gunner to be awarded to him posthumously. In your citation, describe a heroic act that the ball turret gunner performed.

# "TO BLACK WOMEN"

### BY GWENDOLYN BROOKS

## About the AUTHOR

**Gwendolyn Brooks** (1917–2000) was born in Topeka, Kansas, and raised in the "Bronzeville" section of Chicago, Illinois. She attended Englewood High School and Wilson Junior College. Brooks began writing poetry at age seven and published her earliest work in the *Chicago Defender.* Her first book of poetry, *A Street in Bronzeville,* appeared in 1945. In 1950, Brooks received the Pulitzer Prize for her second book of poetry, *Annie Allen* (1949), becoming the first African American to receive this prestigious award. Brooks's first two books of poetry and her novel *Maude Martha* (1953) all draw upon her experiences growing up in the Chicago inner city. Other works by Brooks include *The Bean Eaters* (1960), a collection of poetry; *Bronzeville Boys and Girls* (1956), a children's book; and *Report from Part One* (1972), an autobiographical work. In 1969, Brooks was named poet laureate of the state of Illinois. In 1985, she was appointed Poetry Consultant to the Library of Congress, the first African-American woman to hold that position. Her *Winnie* (1988) is a book of poetry inspired by the South African leader Winnie Mandela, wife of Nelson Mandela, the anti-apartheid activist who became president of South Africa's first black majority government. Gwendolyn Brooks lived in Chicago until her death on December 3, 2000.

## About the SELECTION

The Civil Rights movement of the late 1950s and 1960s made enormous strides toward achieving equality of rights for African Americans in the United States. An important part of that movement was the call by activists such as Eldridge Cleaver, Bobby Seale, Huey Newton, Malcolm X, and others for Black Pride—pride in the traditions, history, and culture of the African-American people. Gwendolyn Brooks was an important voice for Black Pride, and especially for pride among African-American women, reminding the world of her sisters' struggles, triumphs, and potential in poems such as **"To Black Women."**

## Literary TOOLS

**INTERNAL RHYME. Internal rhyme** is the use of rhyming words within lines. As you read, find an example of internal rhyme in stanzas 3 and 4.

**PARALLELISM. Parallelism** is a rhetorical technique in which a writer emphasizes the equal value or weight of two or more ideas by expressing them in the same grammatical form, as in Abraham Lincoln's reference in The Gettysburg Address to "government of the people, by the people, for the people." As you read, make a chart. On the left, write examples of parallelism in the poem. On the right, write what ideas the parallelism underlines. One example has been done for you.

| Parallelism | Ideas |
|---|---|
| "no hallelujahs, no hurrahs . . . no handshakes, / no neon . . . no smiling faces" | examples of how the sisters are not recognized |

## Reader's Journal

When have you felt unrecognized for some talent or quality that you have?

*Gemini Etching,* 1969. Lou Mills.

# TO BLACK WOMEN

GWENDOLYN BROOKS

Sisters,
where there is cold silence—
no hallelujahs, no hurrahs at all, no handshakes,
no neon red or blue, no smiling faces—

5    prevail.
Prevail across the editors[1] of the world!
who are obsessed, self-honeying and self-crowned
in the seduced arena.

It has been a
10   hard trudge, with fainting, bandaging and death.
There have been startling confrontations.
There have been tramplings. Tramplings
of monarchs[2] and of other men.

But there remain large countries in your eyes.
15   Shrewd sun.
The civil balance.
The listening secrets.

And you create and train your flowers still.  ■

What do "sisters" face?
What does the speaker
tell them to do?

Why has it been a hard
trudge?

---

1. **editors.** Those who revise and make corrections in written
statements of thought
2. **monarchs.** Kings, queens; rulers of nations, who have
absolute authority

**WORDS FOR EVERYDAY USE**

**pre • vail** (prē vāl´) vi., triumph. *Despite all their setbacks, the team prevailed in the regional competition.*

**ob • sessed** (əb sest´) adj., greatly preoccupied or troubled. *Leroy was obsessed with his appearance and constantly preened in front of the mirror.*

**Respond** *to the* **SELECTION**

Imagine you are the speaker. Describe one of the "confrontations" to which you are referring.

# INVESTIGATE, Inquire, Imagine

## Recall: GATHERING FACTS

1a. To whom is this poem addressed? What does the speaker tell these people to do in line 5? What adjectives does the speaker use to describe "the editors of the world"?

2a. What sorts of trials or struggles are mentioned in stanza 2?

3a. What can be found in the women's eyes?

## Interpret: FINDING MEANING

1b. What conditions listed in stanza 1 would make life difficult for the people mentioned in line 1? Editors are people who make decisions about what ideas and writings will be published or broadcast. Does the speaker believe that the "editors of the world" pay proper attention to the voices of her "sisters"? Why, or why not?

2b. To what might the "It" at the beginning of line 9 refer?

3b. Which line in stanza 3 suggests that the women have large, unexplored potential? that they help others to achieve harmony and community? that they are intelligent and warm? that they pay attention to other people and therefore know many things that others do not know?

## Analyze: TAKING THINGS APART

4a. Identify the symbol used in the final stanza. What does it represent?

## Synthesize: BRINGING THINGS TOGETHER

4b. Why do the women "create and train" their "flowers"?

## Evaluate: MAKING JUDGMENTS

5a. To what degree does the speaker speak for other African-American women?

## Extend: CONNECTING IDEAS

5b. Compare and contrast the tone, or attitude, of "To Black Women" with the attitudes in Langston Hughes's "The Negro Speaks of Rivers" (page 643) and in Arna Bontemps's "A Black Man Talks of Reaping" (page 649).

# Understanding Literature

INTERNAL RHYME. Review the definition for **internal rhyme** in Literary Tools on page 775. What word in stanza 3 rhymes with what word in the final line?

PARALLELISM. Review the definition for **parallelism** in the Handbook of Literary Terms. Which example of parallelism do you find the most compelling? Why?

# Writer's Journal

1. Imagine that you are the speaker. Write a **journal entry** explaining why you feel a sense of solidarity with your "sisters."

2. Imagine that you are one of the "sisters" in the poem. Write a **letter** to the speaker describing your personal experiences of having trudged "with fainting, bandaging and death."

3. Imagine that you are an African-American man. Write a **lyric poem** for an African-American friend that encourages your brother in the struggle for racial equality. You might choose to use Brooks's poem as a model, changing the feminine images to masculine ones.

# Integrating *the* LANGUAGE ARTS

## Vocabulary

**BASE WORDS AND PREFIXES.** Read the Language Arts Survey 1.19, "Learning Base Words, Prefixes, and Suffixes," and 1.21, "Exploring Word Origins and Word Families." The word *monarch* comes from *mono*, meaning "one," and *arch*, meaning "to rule." Use a dictionary to find the meanings of the following words that use either the prefix *mono* or the root *arch*.

1. monopoly
2. monotone
3. monochromatic
4. monogamy
5. monologue
6. monotheism
7. archangel
8. archbishop
9. archenemy
10. matriarch

## Collaborative Learning

**A CELEBRATION OF AFRICAN-AMERICAN WOMEN POETS.** Work with a small group of students in your class to plan a celebration of the work of the many great African-American women poets in the American literary tradition. Write an introduction for each poet, then select a poem to share with your group or the class. Read the Language Arts Survey 4.19, "Oral Interpretation of Poetry." You may choose from this list of poets:

Maya Angelou
Gwendolyn Brooks
Lucille Clifton
Rita Dove
Mari Evans
Nikki Giovanni
Frances Harper
Sonia Sanchez
Ntozake Shange
Alice Walker
Margaret Walker
Phillis Wheatley

## Media Literacy

**BIBLIOGRAPHY.** About the Author on page 775 does not contain a complete list of Gwendolyn Brooks's published works. Using the Internet, compile a complete bibliography for Brooks, listing the title and year of publication of each work. One site that you will find useful is the website of the Academy of American Poets at http://www.poets.org.

# Literary TOOLS

**ELEGY.** An **elegy** is a poem or verse that laments the dead. As you read, determine the feelings of the speaker for Jane, the subject of the poem.

**METAPHOR.** A **metaphor** is a figure of speech in which one thing is spoken or written about as if it were another. It invites the reader to make a comparison between the two things. As you read, make a chart. On the left, write the metaphor that Roethke uses. On the right, write what Jane and the thing being compared have in common. One example has been done for you.

| Metaphor | Commonalities |
|---|---|
| "A wren, happy, tail into the wind." | Jane and the wren are both in motion, leading active lives. |

## About the SELECTION

**"Elegy for Jane,"** which first appeared in Roethke's poetry collection *The Waking* in 1953, is one of several elegies written by the poet. The use of natural imagery in the poem, especially that of birds, fish, and plants, is common in Roethke's work.

# "ELEGY for JANE"

BY THEODORE ROETHKE

## About the AUTHOR

**Theodore Roethke** (1908–1963), poet, was born in Saginaw, Michigan. His father and uncle owned greenhouses, which taught the young boy a reverence for nature. The greenhouse appeared as a frequent subject in his poetry. Roethke once wrote that the greenhouse "is . . . my symbol for the whole of life, a womb, a heaven-on-earth."

Roethke attended the University of Michigan, where he was a reputed athlete. He dropped out of law school there and went to Harvard for graduate work. After graduation, he supported himself by teaching English at different universities. He was known for his public readings, which were enormously successful with students. Struggling to balance his vocation with his avocation, poetry, Roethke exhausted himself and suffered from mental breakdowns. Diagnosed with manic-depressive illness, he spent time in mental institutions. Roethke belied the stereotype of the conventional poet: a bear-like man, he weighed over two hundred pounds.

Roethke's first book, *Open House*, which appeared in 1941, was reviewed by the poet W. H. Auden, who said that Roethke had the ability to transform personal humiliation into something beautiful. The volume introduced the rich music, bitter wit, and dramatic themes that would characterize his work. The "greenhouse" lyrics of *The Lost Son and Other Poems* (1948) reveal the poet's empathy and search for oneness with all animate life: "I can hear, underground, that sucking and sobbing, / In my veins, in my bones I feel it." *Praise to the End* (1951) presented a sequence of dramatic pieces. Other collections of poetry included *The Waking* (1953), which won the Pulitzer Prize, *Words for the Wind: The Collected Verse* (1958), and *The Far Field* (1964). The publication of *Collected Poems*, published posthumously in 1966, brought renewed interest in Roethke, who counted himself "among the happy poets."

## Reader's Journal

Remember a time when you lost someone or something very important to you. What were your strongest images of that person or thing?

*Message,* 1943. Morris Graves. Seattle Art Museum.

# ELEGY for JANE

## THEODORE ROETHKE

MY STUDENT,
THROWN BY A HORSE

I remember the neckcurls,
    limp and damp as
    <u>tendrils</u>;
And her quick look, a sidelong pickerel[1] smile;
And how, once startled into talk, the light
    syllables leaped for her,
And she balanced in the delight of her thought,
A wren, happy, tail into the wind,
Her song trembling the twigs and small branches.
The shade sang with her;
The leaves, their whispers turned to kissing;
And the mold sang in the bleached valleys under
    the rose.

Oh, when she was sad, she cast herself down
    into such a pure depth,
Even a father could not find her;
Scraping her cheek against straw;

*What does the speaker remember about Jane?*

Stirring the clearest water.

My sparrow, you are not here,
Waiting like a fern, making a spiny shadow.
The sides of wet stones cannot <u>console</u> me,
Nor the moss, wound with
    the last light.

*Why is the speaker inconsolable?*

If only I could nudge you from this sleep,
My maimed darling, my skittery[2] pigeon.
Over this damp grave I speak the words of my
    love:
I, with no rights in this
    matter,
Neither father nor lover. ■

*Why does the speaker feel he does not have the right to love Jane?*

---

1. **pickerel.** Large-eyed like a pickerel, a type of fish
2. **skittery.** Coy; easily frightened

**WORDS FOR EVERYDAY USE**

ten • dril (ten′drəl) *n.,* something that curls in a spiral. *The <u>tendrils</u> of the vine wrapped delicately around the nearby branch.*
con • sole (kən sōl′) *vt.,* comfort. *Nothing could <u>console</u> Chiara when she lost her puppy.*

The speaker says, "The sides of wet stones cannot console me, / Nor the moss, wound with the last light." Where does the speaker look for consolation?

# INVESTIGATE, Inquire, *Imagine*

**Recall:** GATHERING FACTS

1a. What effect does the wren's song have?

2a. What emotion of Jane's is described in the second stanza?

3a. In the last stanza, what does the speaker want to do?

→ **Interpret:** FINDING MEANING

1b. What impact did Jane have on people?

2b. Who was able to console Jane when she was sad?

3b. How does the speaker picture Jane in the last stanza?

**Analyze:** TAKING THINGS APART

4a. Compare and contrast the last three lines of the first stanza with the last three lines of the final stanza. Consider line length and tone.

→ **Synthesize:** BRINGING THINGS TOGETHER

4b. Why does the speaker "speak" in the final stanza?

**Evaluate:** MAKING JUDGMENTS

5a. Judge whether the speaker has the right to speak about his love for Jane, even if he is outside her family.

→ **Extend:** CONNECTING IDEAS

5b. Think about the different relationships in your life, such as those you have with your parents, your siblings, friends, coworkers, teachers, or classmates. What emotions do you associate with each relationship? What boundaries exist in each type of relationship? In other words, which emotions are appropriate, and which are out of place?

# Understanding *Literature*

**ELEGY.** Review the definition for **elegy** in the Handbook of Literary Terms. What makes this poem an elegy? What do the first two stanzas describe? What do the last two stanzas describe?

**METAPHOR.** Review the definition for **metaphor** in the Handbook of Literary Terms. Then review the chart you made in Literary Tools on page 780. What metaphors does Roethke use to describe Jane? What do the metaphors together say about Jane?

# WRITER'S JOURNAL

1. Write a **sympathy note** to the speaker. Use details about Jane in your note.
2. Write an **obituary** for Jane. Use information about her gathered from the poem and invent other details about her life to include information essential to an obituary. You might want to read several obituaries before you begin.
3. Write an **elegy** in verse for someone you have lost or would hate to lose.

# Integrating *the* LANGUAGE ARTS

## Language, Grammar, and Style

**ADDING MODIFIERS.** Read the Language Arts Survey 3.39, "Adding Colorful Language to Sentences." Then rewrite each of the following sentences, adding an appropriate adjective or adverb. Some sentences may require more than one modifier.

1. Jane's neckcurls hung.
2. She gave me a look.
3. Her syllables leaped.

4. The wren had its tail into the wind.
5. I speak words over this grave.

## Study and Research & Applied English

**ROETHKE NATURE GUIDE.** Working in small groups, identify natural elements that Roethke refers to in his poetry, such as specific birds, plants, and fish. For this activity, familiarize yourself with more of Roethke's poetry. Then, using online and print sources, collect pictures and descriptions of these natural elements. Finally, create a nature guide to Roethke's poetry. To accompany each picture, label the element and write down both a poem in which the element is mentioned and a scientific description of the element.

## Speaking and Listening & Collaborative Learning

**ORAL INTERPRETATION.** The elegy—a poem about loss—is one of the oldest forms of literature. Some famous elegies in American literature include Walt Whitman's "O Captain, My Captain!" and "When Lilacs Last in the Dooryard Bloom'd" and John Crowe Ransom's "Bells for John Whiteside's Daughter." Hold a class poetry reading in which each student reads a different elegy of his or her choosing. You might ask your teacher to help you select an appropriate piece. Before you prepare your reading, review the Language Arts Survey 4.19, "Oral Interpretation of Poetry." Then sit in a circle and take turns reading the elegies. Finally, hold a discussion about the similarities and differences between the poems.

## Literary T O O L S

**SYMBOL.** A **symbol** is a thing that stands for or represents both itself and something else. As you read, identify what might be symbolized by the Christ-like stance of Mr. Shiftlet at the beginning of the story and the "turnip" storm at the end.

**SOUTHERN GOTHIC. Southern Gothic** is writing containing elements of horror, suspense, mystery, or magic, produced in or set in the southern United States. In "The Life You Save May Be Your Own," the element of Southern Gothic horror is partially found in the deformities of the characters and setting. As you read, make a cluster chart in which you list these deformities. One example has been done for you.

> The farm is in a "desolate spot" and has fallen into disrepair.

> Deformities

## Reader's *Journal*

What qualities do you need to see in a stranger before you can trust him or her?

# "The LIFE YOU SAVE May Be YOUR OWN"

BY FLANNERY O'CONNOR

## About *the* A U T H O R

**(Mary) Flannery O'Connor** (1925–1964), short story writer and novelist, was born in Savannah, Georgia. At age twelve she moved with her family to Milledgeville, Georgia, where her family had lived since before the Civil War. She knew from an early age that she wanted to write, and after graduating from the Georgia State College for Women, she left her home state to study writing at the University of Iowa. Her first story, "The Geranium," was published while she was there. To gain some perspective on contemporary culture, she moved to a writer's colony called Yaddo in Saratoga Springs, New York, and then to New York City and Connecticut.

Like her father, O'Connor contracted disseminated lupus. At age twenty-five, she returned to Milledgeville to live with her mother on the family dairy farm called "Andalusia," where she wrote and raised peacocks. Her disease increasingly confined her and, within five years, she was able to walk only with crutches. Her darkest fiction was written after the onset of her illness, and the themes of human limitations and mortality became more and more prominent. But she did not allow her illness to destroy her enjoyment of life, her sense of humor, or her ability to work. She kept up a lively and extensive correspondence with friends, other authors, and readers until her death at age thirty-nine. O'Connor's first novel, *Wise Blood*, was published in 1952. This was followed by a collection of short stories, *A Good Man Is Hard to Find* (1953), a second novel, *The Violent Bear It Away* (1960), and a second short story collection, *Everything That Rises Must Converge* (1965).

## About *the* S E L E C T I O N

Peopled by con men, criminals, the maimed, deformed, and the insane, O'Connor's stories have been called "dark," "grotesque," "bizarre," and even "comic." The characters in **"The Life You Save May Be Your Own"** include a man with an amputated arm and a young woman who is deaf and mentally handicapped. The central concern in this story and in much of O'Connor's fiction is the abstract idea of good and evil. A devout Roman Catholic throughout her life, the author believed in a spiritual center and an acceptance of divine grace in people's lives.

# The LIFE YOU SAVE May Be YOUR OWN

FLANNERY O'CONNOR

*Sharecropper,* 1937. Jerry Bywaters. Dallas Museum of Art.

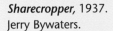

## ArtNote

*Sharecropper,* 1937.
Jerry Bywaters.

Jerry Bywaters (1906–1989) studied with the great Mexican painter Diego Rivera, from whom he learned not only the mural style, but also the importance of making art for a mass audience. Bywaters belonged to the Texas Regionalists, who were influenced by Grant Wood's Midwest Regionalism. What similarities can you see in the work of Jerry Bywaters and Grant Wood?

The old woman and her daughter were sitting on their porch when Mr. Shiftlet came up their road for the first time. The old woman slid to the edge of her chair and leaned forward, shading her eyes from the piercing sunset with her hand. The daughter could not see far in front of her and continued to play with her fingers. Although the old woman lived in this desolate spot with only her daughter and she had never seen Mr. Shiftlet before, she could tell, even from a distance, that he was a tramp and no one to be afraid of. His left coat sleeve was folded up to show there was only half an arm

How is Mr. Shiftlet described?

in it and his gaunt figure <u>listed</u> slightly to the side as if the breeze were pushing him. He had on a black town suit and a brown felt hat that was turned up in the front and down in the back and he carried a tin tool box by a handle. He came on, at an amble, up her road, his face turned toward the sun which appeared to be balancing itself on the peak of a small mountain.

The old woman didn't change her position until he was almost into her yard; then she rose with one hand fisted on her hip. The daughter, a large girl in a short blue organdy dress, saw him all at once and jumped up and began to stamp and point and make excited speechless sounds.

Mr. Shiftlet stopped just inside the yard and set his box on the ground and tipped his hat at her as if she were not in the least afflicted; then he turned toward the old woman and swung the hat all the way off. He had long black slick hair that hung flat from a part in the middle to beyond the tips of his ears on either side. His face descended in forehead for more than half its length and ended suddenly with his features just balanced over a jutting steel-trap jaw. He seemed to be a young man but he had a look of composed dissatisfaction as if he understood life thoroughly.

"Good evening," the old woman said. She was about the size of a cedar fence post and she had a man's gray hat pulled down low over her head.

The tramp stood looking at her and didn't answer. He turned his back and faced the sunset. He swung both his whole and his short arm up slowly so that they indicated an expanse of

> He seemed to be a young man but he had a look of composed dissatisfaction as if he understood life thoroughly.

sky and his figure formed a crooked cross. The old woman watched him with her arms folded across her chest as if she were the owner of the sun, and the daughter watched, her head thrust forward and her fat helpless hands hanging at the wrists. She had long pink-gold hair and eyes as blue as a peacock's neck.

He held the pose for almost fifty seconds and then he picked up his box and came on to the porch and dropped down on the bottom step.

"Lady," he said in a firm nasal voice, "I'd give a fortune to live where I could see me a sun do that every evening."

"Does it every evening," the old woman said and sat back down. The daughter sat down too and watched him with a cautious sly look as if he were a bird that had come up very close. He leaned to one side, rooting[1] in his pants pocket, and in a second he brought out a package of chewing gum and offered her a piece. She took it and unpeeled it and began to chew without taking her eyes off him. He offered the old woman a piece but she only raised her upper lip to indicate she had no teeth.

Mr. Shiftlet's pale sharp glance had already passed over everything in the yard—the pump near the corner of the house and the big fig tree that three or four chickens were preparing to roost in—and had moved to a shed where he saw the square rusted back of an automobile. "You ladies drive?" he asked.

What does Mr. Shiftlet do when he faces the sun?

What does Mr. Shiftlet see in the shed?

---

1. **root.** Dig

**WORDS FOR EVERYDAY USE**

list (list) *vi.,* tilt to one side. *The ship <u>listed</u> as it sailed into port.*

"That car ain't run in fifteen year," the old woman said. "The day my husband died, it quit running."

"Nothing is like it used to be, lady," he said. "The world is almost rotten."

"That's right," the old woman said. "You from around here?"

"Name Tom T. Shiftlet," he murmured, looking at the tires.

"I'm pleased to meet you," the old woman said. "Name Lucynell Crater and daughter Lucynell Crater. What you doing around here, Mr. Shiftlet?"

He judged the car to be about a 1928 or '29 Ford. "Lady," he said, and turned and gave her his full attention, "lemme tell you something. There's one of these doctors in Atlanta that's taken a knife and cut the human heart—the human heart," he repeated, leaning forward, "out of a man's chest and held it in his hand," and he held his hand out, palm up, as if it were slightly weighted with the human heart, "and studied it like it was a day-old chicken, and lady," he said, allowing a long significant pause in which his head slid forward and his clay-colored eyes brightened, "he don't know no more about it than you or me."

> What does Mr. Shiftlet say about the doctor who cut the human heart?

"That's right," the old woman said.

"Why, if he was to take that knife and cut into every corner of it, he still wouldn't know no more than you or me. What you want to bet?"

"Nothing," the old woman said wisely. "Where you come from, Mr. Shiftlet?"

He didn't answer. He reached into his pocket and brought out a sack of tobacco and a package of cigarette papers and rolled himself a cigarette, expertly with one hand, and attached it in a hanging position to his upper lip. Then he took a box of wooden matches from his pocket and struck one on his shoe. He held the burning match as if he were studying the mystery of flame while it traveled dangerously toward his skin. The daughter began to make loud noises and to point to his hand and shake her finger at him, but when the flame was just before touching him, he leaned down with his hand cupped over it as if he were going to set fire to his nose and lit the cigarette.

He flipped away the dead match and blew a stream gray into the evening. A sly look came over his face. "Lady," he said, "nowadays, people'll do anything anyways. I can tell you my name is Tom T. Shiftlet and I come from Tarwater, Tennessee, but you never have seen me before: how you know I ain't lying? How you know my name ain't Aaron Sparks, lady, and I come from Singleberry, Georgia, or how you know it's not George Speeds and I come from Lucy, Alabama, or how you know I ain't Thompson Bright from Toolafalls, Mississippi?"

"I don't know nothing about you," the old woman muttered, irked.

"Lady," he said, "people don't care how they lie. Maybe the best I can tell you is, I'm a man; but listen lady," he said and paused and made his tone more <u>ominous</u> still, "what is a man?"

The old woman began to gum a seed. "What you carry in that tin box, Mr. Shiftlet?" she asked.

"Tools," he said, put back. "I'm a carpenter."

"Well, if you come out here to work, I'll be able to feed you and give you a place to sleep but I can't pay. I'll tell you that before you begin," she said.

> What does old Lucynell offer Mr. Shiftlet?

There was no answer at once and no particular expression on his face. He leaned back

---

**WORDS FOR EVERYDAY USE**

om • i • nous (ä' mə nəs) *adj.,* foreboding or foreshowing evil or menace. *The <u>ominous</u> rumblings from the volcano alerted the vacationers to leave the island.*

against the two-by-four that helped support the porch roof. "Lady," he said slowly, "there's some men that some things mean more to them than money." The old woman rocked without comment and the daughter watched the trigger that moved up and down in his neck. He told the old woman then that all most people were interested in was money, but he asked what a man was made for. He asked her if a man was made for money, or what. He asked her what she thought she was made for but she didn't answer, she only sat rocking and wondered if a one-armed man could put a new roof on her garden house. He asked a lot of questions that she didn't answer. He told her that he was twenty-eight years old and had lived a varied life. He had been a gospel singer, a foreman on the railroad, an assistant in an undertaking parlor, and he had come over the radio for three months with Uncle Roy and his Red Creek Wranglers. He said he had fought and bled in the Arm Service of his country and visited every foreign land and that everywhere he had seen people that didn't care if they did a thing one way or another. He said he hadn't been raised thataway.

> What does Mr. Shiftlet call the military?

A fat yellow moon appeared in the branches of the fig tree as if it were going to roost there with the chickens. He said that a man had to escape to the country to see the world whole and that he wished he lived in a desolate place like this where he could see the sun go down every evening like God made it to do.

"Are you married or are you single?" the old woman asked.

There was a long silence. "Lady," he asked finally, "where would you find you an innocent woman today? I wouldn't have any of this trash I could just pick up."

The daughter was leaning very far down, hanging her head almost between her knees, watching him through a triangular door she had made in her overturned hair; and she suddenly fell in a heap on the floor and began to whimper. Mr. Shiftlet straightened her out and helped her get back in the chair.

"Is she your baby girl?" he asked.

"My only," the old woman said, "and she's the sweetest girl in the world. I wouldn't give her up for nothing on earth. She's smart too. She can sweep the floor, cook, wash, feed the chickens, and hoe. I wouldn't give her up for a casket of jewels."

"No," he said kindly, "don't ever let any man take her away from you."

"Any man come after her," the old woman said, " 'll have to stay around the place."

Mr. Shiftlet's eye in the darkness was focused on a part of the automobile bumper that glittered in the distance. "Lady," he said, jerking his short arm up as if he could point with it to her house and yard and pump, "there ain't a broken thing on this plantation that I couldn't fix for you, one-arm jackleg[2] or not. I'm a man," he said with a <u>sullen</u> dignity, "even if I ain't a whole one. I got," he said, tapping his knuckles on the floor to emphasize the immensity of what he was going to say, "a moral intelligence!" and his face pierced out of the darkness into a shaft of doorlight and he stared at her as if he were astonished himself at this impossible truth.

> What does Mr. Shiftlet tell old Lucynell that he possesses?

The old woman was not impressed with the phrase. "I told you you could hang around and

---

2. **jackleg.** One who is not properly trained or competent for a job

---

WORDS FOR EVERYDAY USE

**sul • len** (sə′ lən) *adj.*, gloomily or resentfully silent. *Her brother's <u>sullen</u> expression tipped off Amanda that now was not the time to ask for a favor.*

788    UNIT TEN / POSTWAR LITERATURE

work for food," she said, "if you don't mind sleeping in that car yonder."

"Why listen, Lady," he said with a grin of delight, "the monks of old slept in their coffins!"

"They wasn't as advanced as we are," the old woman said.

The next morning he began on the roof of the garden house while Lucynell, the daughter, sat on a rock and watched him work. He had not been around a week before the change he had made in the place was apparent. He had patched the front and back steps, built a new hog pen, restored a fence, and taught Lucynell, who was completely deaf and had never said a word in her life, to say the word "bird." The big rosy-faced girl followed him everywhere, saying "Burrttddt ddbirrrttdt," and clapping her hands. The old woman watched from a distance, secretly pleased. She was <u>ravenous</u> for a son-in-law.

*What does Mr. Shiftlet accomplish in less than a week? What is wrong with young Lucynell?*

*What does old Lucynell want?*

Mr. Shiftlet slept on the hard narrow back seat of the car with his feet out the side window. He had his razor and a can of water on a crate that served him as a bedside table and he put up a piece of mirror against the back glass and kept his coat neatly on a hanger that he hung over one of the windows.

In the evenings he sat on the steps and talked while the old woman and Lucynell rocked violently in their chairs on either side of him. The old woman's three mountains were black against the dark blue sky and were visited off

> **Mr. Shiftlet said that the trouble with the world was that nobody cared, or stopped and took any trouble.**

and on by various planets and by the moon after it had left the chickens. Mr. Shiftlet pointed out that the reason he had improved this plantation was because he had taken a personal interest in it. He said he was even going to make the automobile run.

He had raised the hood and studied the mechanism and he said he could tell that the car had been built in the days when cars were really built. You take now, he said, one man puts in one bolt and another man puts in another bolt and another man puts in another bolt so that it's a man for a bolt. That's why you have to pay so much for a car: you're paying all those men. Now if you didn't have to pay but one man, you could get you a cheaper car and one that had had a personal interest taken in it, and it would be a better car. The old woman agreed with him that this was so.

Mr. Shiftlet said that the trouble with the world was that nobody cared, or stopped and took any trouble. He said he never would have been able to teach Lucynell to say a word if he hadn't cared and stopped long enough.

"Teach her to say something else," the old woman said.

"What you want her to say next?" Mr. Shiftlet asked.

The old woman's smile was broad and toothless and suggestive. "Teach her to say 'sugarpie,'" she said.

Mr. Shiftlet already knew what was on her mind.

The next day he began to <u>tinker</u> with the automobile and that evening he told her that if she would buy a fan belt, he would be able to make the car run.

---

**WORDS FOR EVERYDAY USE**

**rav • en • ous** (ra′ və nəs) *adj.,* eager or greedy for food, satisfaction, or gratification. *After the game, the team was <u>ravenous</u> for pizza.*

**tin • ker** (tiŋ′ kər) *vi.,* repair, adjust, or work with something in an unskilled or experimental manner. *Dad <u>tinkered</u> with the clock because it was running fast.*

The old woman said she would give him the money. "You see that girl yonder?" she asked, pointing to Lucynell who was sitting on the floor a foot away, watching him, her eyes blue even in the dark. "If it was ever a man wanted to take her away, I would say, 'No man on earth is going to take that sweet girl of mine away from me!' but if he was to say, 'Lady, I don't want to take her away, I want her right here,' I would say, 'Mister, I don't blame you none. I wouldn't pass up a chance to live in a permanent place and get the sweetest girl in the world myself. You ain't no fool,' I would say."

Why does old Lucynell give Mr. Shiftlet money?

"How old is she?" Mr. Shiftlet asked casually.

"Fifteen, sixteen," the old woman said. The girl was nearly thirty but because of her innocence it was impossible to guess.

"It would be a good idea to paint it too," Mr. Shiftlet remarked. "You don't want it to rust out."

"We'll see about that later," the old woman said.

The next day he walked into town and returned with the parts he needed and a can of gasoline. Late in the afternoon, terrible noises issued from the shed and the old woman rushed out of the house, thinking Lucynell was somewhere having a fit. Lucynell was sitting on a chicken crate, stamping her feet and screaming, "Burrddttt! bddurrddtttt!" but her fuss was drowned out by the car. With a volley of blasts it emerged from the shed, moving in a fierce and stately way. Mr. Shiftlet was in the driver's seat, sitting very erect. He had an expression of serious modesty on his face as if he had just raised the dead.

That night, rocking on the porch, the old woman began her business at once. "You want you an innocent woman, don't you?" she

"No man on earth is going to take that sweet girl of mine away from me!"

asked sympathetically. "You don't want none of this trash."

"No'm, I don't," Mr. Shiftlet said.

"One that can't talk," she continued, "can't sass you back or use foul language. That's the kind for you to have. Right there," and she pointed to Lucynell sitting cross-legged in her chair, holding both feet in her hands.

"That's right," he admitted. "She wouldn't give me any trouble."

"Saturday," the old woman said, "you and her and me can drive into town and get married."

Mr. Shiftlet eased his position on the steps.

"I can't get married right now," he said. "Everything you want to do takes money and I ain't got any."

"What you need with money?" she asked.

"It takes money," he said. "Some people'll do anything anyhow these days, but the way I think, I wouldn't marry no woman that I couldn't take on a trip like she was somebody. I mean take her to a hotel and treat her. I wouldn't marry the Duchesser Windsor,"[3] he said firmly, "unless I could take her to a hotel and give her something good to eat.

What would it take for Mr. Shiftlet to marry young Lucynell? What does old Lucynell tell Mr. Shiftlet he'll get if he marries her daughter? What else does she tell him?

"I was raised thataway and there ain't a thing I can do about it. My old mother taught me how to do."

"Lucynell don't even know what a hotel is," the old woman muttered. "Listen here, Mr. Shiftlet," she said, sliding forward in her chair, "you'd be getting a permanent house and a deep well and the most innocent girl in the world. You don't need no money. Lemme tell you

---

3. **Duchesser Windsor.** Duchess of Windsor, the title given to Wallis Warfield Simpson when she married Edward, duke of Windsor; he abdicated the British throne in order to marry her in 1937.

something: there ain't any place in the world for a poor disabled friendless drifting man."

The ugly words settled in Mr. Shiftlet's head like a group of buzzards in the top of a tree. He didn't answer at once. He rolled himself a cigarette and lit it and then he said in an even voice, "Lady, a man is divided into two parts, body and spirit."

The old woman clamped her gums together.

"A body and a spirit," he repeated. "The body, lady, is like a house: it don't go anywhere; but the spirit, lady, is like a automobile: always on the move, always . . ."

"Listen, Mr. Shiftlet," she said, "my well never goes dry and my house is always warm in the winter and there's no mortgage on a thing about this place. You can go to the courthouse and see for yourself. And yonder under that shed is a fine automobile." She laid the bait carefully. "You can have it painted by Saturday. I'll pay for the paint."

In the darkness, Mr. Shiftlet's smile stretched like a weary snake waking up by a fire. After a second he recalled himself and said, "I'm only saying a man's spirit means more to him than anything else. I would have to take my wife off for the weekend without no regards at all for cost. I got to follow where my spirit says to go."

> What does Mr. Shiftlet say is the most important thing to a man?

"I'll give you fifteen dollars for a weekend trip," the old woman said in a crabbed[4] voice. "That's the best I can do."

"That wouldn't hardly pay for more than the gas and the hotel," he said. "It wouldn't feed her."

"Seventeen-fifty," the old woman said. "That's all I got so it isn't any use you trying to milk me. You can take a lunch."

Mr. Shiftlet was deeply hurt by the word "milk." He didn't doubt that she had more money sewed up in her mattress but he had already told her he was not interested in her money. "I'll make that do," he said and rose and walked off without treating with her further.

On Saturday the three of them drove into town in the car that the paint had barely dried on and Mr. Shiftlet and Lucynell were married in the Ordinary's[5] office while the old woman witnessed. As they came out of the courthouse, Mr. Shiftlet began twisting his neck in his collar. He looked <u>morose</u> and bitter as if he had been insulted while someone held him. "That didn't satisfy me none," he said. "That was just something a woman in an office did, nothing but paper work and blood tests. What do they know about my blood? If they was to take my heart and cut it out," he said, "they wouldn't know a thing about me. It didn't satisfy me at all."

> What happens on Saturday?

"It satisfied the law," the old woman said sharply.

"The law," Mr. Shiftlet said and spit. "It's the law that don't satisfy me."

He had painted the car dark green with a yellow band around it just under the windows. The three of them climbed in the front seat and the old woman said, "Don't Lucynell look pretty? Looks like a baby doll." Lucynell was dressed up in a white dress that her mother had uprooted from a trunk and there was a Panama hat on her head with a bunch of red wooden cherries on the brim. Every now and then her <u>placid</u> expression was changed by a sly isolated little thought like a shoot of green in the desert. "You got a prize!" the old woman said.

---

4. **crabbed.** Forbiddingly gloomy; ill-tempered
5. **Ordinary.** Official of the court

WORDS FOR EVERYDAY USE

mo • rose (mə rōs′) adj., having a sullen and gloomy disposition. Jolene was <u>morose</u> because she failed her driver's test.

pla • cid (pla′ səd) adj., calm or free of disturbance. Greg enjoyed waterskiing on the <u>placid</u> lake.

Mr. Shiftlet didn't even look at her.

They drove back to the house to let the old woman off and pick up the lunch. When they were ready to leave, she stood staring in the window of the car, with her fingers clenched around the glass. Tears began to seep sideways out of her eyes and run along the dirty creases in her face. "I ain't ever been parted with her for two days before," she said.

Mr. Shiftlet started the motor.

"And I wouldn't let no man have her but you because I seen you would do right. Good-by, Sugarbaby," she said, clutching at the sleeve of the white dress. Lucynell looked straight at her and didn't seem to see her there at all. Mr. Shiftlet eased the car forward so that she had to move her hands.

The early afternoon was clear and open and surrounded by pale blue sky. Although the car would go only thirty miles an hour, Mr. Shiftlet imagined a terrific climb and dip and swerve that went entirely to his head so that he forgot his morning bitterness. He had always wanted an automobile but he had never been able to afford one before. He drove very fast because he wanted to make Mobile by nightfall.

Occasionally he stopped his thoughts long enough to look at Lucynell in the seat beside him. She had eaten the lunch as soon as they were out of the yard and now she was pulling the cherries off the hat one by one and throwing them out the window. He became depressed in spite of the car. He had driven about a hundred miles when he decided that

<aside>Why does Mr. Shiftlet stop?</aside>

she must be hungry again and at the next small town they came to, he stopped in front of an aluminum-painted eating place called The Hot Spot and took her in and ordered her a plate of ham and grits. The ride had made her sleepy and as soon as she got up on the stool, she rested her head on the counter and shut her eyes. There was no one in The Hot Spot but Mr. Shiftlet and the boy behind the counter, a pale youth with a greasy rag hung over his shoulder. Before he could dish up the food, she was snoring gently.

"Give it to her when she wakes up," Mr. Shiftlet said. "I'll pay for it now."

The boy bent over her and stared at the long pink-gold hair and the half-shut sleeping eyes. Then he looked up and stared at Mr. Shiftlet. "She looks like an angel of Gawd," he murmured.

<aside>What does the boy behind the counter call young Lucynell?</aside>

"Hitch-hiker," Mr. Shiftlet explained. "I can't wait. I got to make Tuscaloosa."

The boy bent over again and very carefully touched his finger to a strand of the golden hair and Mr. Shiftlet left.

He was more depressed than ever as he drove on by himself. The late afternoon had grown hot and <u>sultry</u> and the country had flattened out. Deep in the sky a storm was preparing very slowly and without thunder as if it meant to drain every drop of air from the earth before it broke. There were times when Mr. Shiftlet preferred not to be alone. He felt too that a man with a car had a responsibility to others and he kept his eye out for a hitch-hiker. Occasionally he saw a sign that warned: "Drive carefully. The life you save may be your own."

<aside>How does Mr. Shiftlet feel when he leaves Lucynell behind at The Hot Spot?</aside>

<aside>What sign does Mr. Shiftlet see as he drives?</aside>

> "Drive carefully. The life you save may be your own."

WORDS FOR EVERYDAY USE

**sul • try** (səl′ trē) *adj.*, very hot and humid. *The <u>sultry</u> weather found Sonja on her hammock with a cool glass of lemonade.*

The narrow road dropped off on either side into dry fields and here and there a shack or a filling station stood in a clearing. The sun began to set directly in front of the automobile. It was a reddening ball that through his windshield was slightly flat on the bottom and top. He saw a boy in overalls and a gray hat standing on the edge of the road and he slowed the car down and stopped in front of him. The boy didn't have his hand raised to thumb the ride, he was only standing there, but he had a small cardboard suitcase and his hat was set on his head in a way to indicate that he had left somewhere for good. "Son," Mr. Shiftlet said, "I see you want a ride."

The boy didn't say he did or he didn't but he opened the door of the car and got in, and Mr. Shiftlet started driving again. The child held the suitcase on his lap and folded his arms on top of it. He turned his head and looked out the window away from Mr. Shiftlet. Mr. Shiftlet felt oppressed. "Son," he said after a minute, "I got the best old mother in the world so I reckon you only got the second best."

The boy gave him a quick dark glance and then turned his face back out the window.

"It's nothing so sweet," Mr. Shiftlet continued, "as a boy's mother. She taught him his first prayers at her knee, she give him love when no other would, she told him what was right and what wasn't, and she seen that he done the right thing.

"Son," he said, "I never rued[6] a day in my life like the one I rued when I left that old mother of mine."

*What does Mr. Shiftlet regret?*

The boy shifted in his seat but he didn't look at Mr. Shiftlet. He unfolded his arms and put one hand on the door handle.

"My mother was a angel of Gawd," Mr. Shiftlet said in a very strained voice. "He took her from heaven and giver to me and I left her." His eyes were instantly clouded over with a mist of tears. The car was barely moving.

The boy turned angrily in the seat. "You go to the devil!" he cried. "My old woman is a flea bag and yours is a stinking pole cat!"[7] and with that he flung the door open and jumped out with his suitcase into the ditch.

Mr. Shiftlet was so shocked that for about a hundred feet he drove along slowly with the door still open. A cloud, the exact color of the boy's hat and shaped like a turnip, had descended over the sun, and another, worse looking, crouched behind the car. Mr. Shiftlet felt that the rottenness of the world was about to engulf him. He raised his arm and let it fall again to his breast. "Oh Lord!" he prayed. "Break forth and wash the slime from this earth!"

*What does Mr. Shiftlet feel is about to engulf him?*

The turnip continued slowly to descend. After a few minutes there was a <u>guffawing</u> peal of thunder from behind and fantastic raindrops, like tin-can tops, crashed over the rear of Mr. Shiftlet's car. Very quickly he stepped on the gas and with his stump sticking out the window he raced the galloping shower into Mobile. ■

*What follows Mr. Shiftlet to Mobile?*

---

6. **rue.** Feel remorse or regret
7. **pole cat.** Type of weasel

WORDS FOR EVERYDAY USE

guf • faw • ing (gə fô′ iŋ) *adj.*, laughing loudly and coarsely. *The <u>guffawing</u> old-timers thought it was the funniest joke they had ever heard.*

If you were old Lucynell, what would you think had happened when Mr. Shiftlet failed to return with your daughter?

# Inquire, Imagine

**Recall:** GATHERING FACTS

1a. What things can the old woman observe about Mr. Shiftlet the first time she sees him?

2a. What does Mr. Shiftlet look at during his conversations with the old woman?

3a. How does Mr. Shiftlet exploit old Lucynell? How does old Lucynell exploit Mr. Shiftlet?

➤ **Interpret:** FINDING MEANING

1b. Why do the old woman's initial observations lead her to believe that Mr. Shiftlet is "no one to be afraid of"?

2b. Why does Mr. Shiftlet marry young Lucynell?

3b. What sign does Mr. Shiftlet sees as he drives to Mobile? Why is it the title of the story?

**Analyze:** TAKING THINGS APART

4a. Examine Mr. Shiftlet's statements about the world and the honesty and integrity of the people in it. How does he portray himself? Compare and contrast his statements about himself with his actions.

➤ **Synthesize:** BRINGING THINGS TOGETHER

4b. Why does the author have Mr. Shiftlet buy Lucynell a meal at The Hot Spot and reveal that he cries at the thought of his mother?

**Evaluate:** MAKING JUDGMENTS

5a. If the characters in "The Life You Save May Be Your Own" are on a continuum from innocence to evil, where would you place each character?

➤ **Extend:** CONNECTING IDEAS

5b. Philosophers, theologians, and social scientists have, throughout the years, disagreed over the basic nature of man. Some believe that human nature is inherently good, while others believe human nature to be inherently evil and in need of restraint, discipline, and improvement. What do you think Flannery O'Connor believed about human nature? What do you personally believe, and why?

# Understanding Literature

SYMBOL. Review the definition for **symbol** in the Handbook of Literary Terms. What do you think the Christ-like stance of Mr. Shiftlet at the beginning of the story and the "turnip" storm at the end symbolize?

SOUTHERN GOTHIC. Review the definition for **Southern Gothic** in the Handbook of Literary Terms. Then review the cluster chart you made in Literary Tools on page 784. What do the deformities of the characters reveal about human nature?

# WRITER'S JOURNAL

1. Imagine that you are a small-town newspaper reporter assigned to write a story about the girl found abandoned in the Hot Spot Restaurant. You have interviewed the boy who works behind the counter and have spoken to local authorities who were called there. Now, write a short **article** about the incident. Give a description of the girl and use quotes from the people you interviewed.

2. Imagine that you are Mr. Shiftlet and that you have arrived in Mobile. Write a **letter** to old Lucynell explaining your actions.

3. Imagine that you are old Lucynell. Write a **journal entry** trying to justify why you wanted your daughter to go off with Mr. Shiftlet.

# Integrating *the* LANGUAGE ARTS

## Language, Grammar, and Style

**SUBJECT/VERB AGREEMENT.** Read the Language Arts Survey 3.40, "Getting Subject and Verb to Agree." Then rewrite the following sentences from the story, using correct subject/verb agreement. Make any other necessary corrections.

1. He don't know no more about it than you or me.
2. Lady, there's some men that some things mean more to them than money.
3. They wasn't as advanced as we are!
4. The body, lady, is like a house: it don't go anywhere.
5. It's the law that don't satisfy me.

## Speaking and Listening & Collaborative Learning

**NONVERBAL COMMUNICATION.** With a partner, play the roles of Mr. Shiftlet and old Lucynell in the first section of the story where they meet each other. To add appropriate nonverbal communication to the interpretation of your character, consider the character's motives and personality. You might want to review the Language Arts Survey 4.1, "Verbal and Nonverbal Communication," before you begin.

## Media Literacy

**NEWSPAPER ADVERTISEMENT.** Imagine that you are old Lucynell and want a hired hand to make some repairs around your farm. Write a newspaper advertisement in which you specify the tasks that need to get done and explain your method of payment. Newspaper advertisements often use abbreviated language. You might want to review the Classified section of your local newspaper to get ideas before you begin.

# Literary
## T O O L S

**ARCHETYPE.** An **archetype** is an inherited, often unconscious, ancestral memory or motif that recurs throughout history and literature. The story of the journey, in which someone sets out on a path, experiences adventures, and emerges wiser, is considered archetypal. As you read, decide what human emotion makes it possible for Phoenix to surmount the obstacles of her journey.

**CHARACTER.** A **character** is a person who figures in the action of a literary work. A *one-dimensional character, flat character,* or *caricature* is one who exhibits a single dominant quality or *character trait.* A *three-dimensional, full,* or *rounded character* is one who exhibits the complexity of traits associated with actual human beings. Is Phoenix a one-dimensional character or a three-dimensional character?

# About *the* SELECTION

One of Welty's most popular stories, **"A Worn Path"** appeared in *A Curtain of Green,* her first collection, in 1941. Like many of Welty's stories, "A Worn Path" explores the intricacies of the inner life and the small heroisms of an ordinary character. In the story, Phoenix Jackson makes an archetypal journey in which she demonstrates determination, generosity, and resourcefulness.

# "A Worn Path"

BY EUDORA WELTY

# About *the* AUTHOR

**Eudora Welty** (1909–2001), short story writer, novelist, and book reviewer, was born in Jackson, Mississippi. Writing about her sheltered upbringing, Welty says in her brief autobiography, *One Writer's Beginnings* (1984): "A sheltered life can be a daring life as well. For all serious daring starts from within."

After studying at the Mississippi State College for Women, the University of Wisconsin, and Columbia's Graduate School of Business, Welty returned to Jackson, where she worked for newspapers and a radio station. She then served as publicity agent for President Franklin Roosevelt's Works Progress Administration, the agency formed to provide work for people during the Great Depression. As she traveled through the state for the WPA, Welty took her now-famous photographs of poverty in rural Mississippi. These images inspired Welty's first collection of short stories, *A Curtain of Green* (1941). In her next collection, *The Wide Net and Other Stories* (1943), Welty again shared stories of small-town Mississippi, finding in them the timeless themes and patterns of myth.

In her first novel, *Delta Wedding* (1946), Welty explores the experience and values of women characters and honors the community and harmony created by mothers for their families. *The Optimist's Daughter* (1972), focusing on a daughter's care for her aging father, won the Pulitzer Prize. The novel brought renewed attention to Welty's writing, as well as requests for interviews and speaking engagements. Book reviews that she wrote over a span of forty years were published in *A Writer's Eye* (1994).

Welty's legacy is a fictional chronicle of Mississippi life that affirms the sustaining power of community and family life at the same time as it observes the need for solitude. Working with the twin themes of "love and separateness," Welty celebrates the love of men and women, the many dimensions and stages of women's lives, and the fleeting joys of childhood.

# Reader's *Journal*

What journey have you taken that held personal significance for you?

# A Worn Path

*Georgia Landscape,* c.1934. Hale Woodruff. National Museum of American Art, Washington, DC.

## EUDORA WELTY

It was December—a bright frozen day in the early morning. Far out in the country there was an old Negro woman with her head tied in a red

**When does Phoenix Jackson make her journey?**

rag, coming along a path through the pine-woods. Her name was Phoenix Jackson. She was very old and small and she walked slowly in the dark pine shadows, moving a little from side to side in her steps, with the balanced heaviness and lightness of a <u>pendulum</u> in a grandfather clock. She carried a thin, small cane made from an umbrella, and with this she kept tapping the frozen earth in front of her. This made a grave and persistent noise in the still air, that seemed meditative like the chirping of a solitary little bird.

She wore a dark striped dress reaching down to her shoe tops, and an equally long apron of bleached sugar sacks, with a full pocket: all neat and tidy, but every time she took a step she might have fallen over her shoelaces, which dragged from her unlaced shoes. She looked straight ahead. Her eyes were blue with age. Her skin had a

> *What is wrong with Phoenix's shoes?*

pattern all its own of numberless branching wrinkles and as though a whole little tree stood in the middle of her forehead, but a golden color ran underneath, and the two knobs of her cheeks were illumined by a yellow burning under the dark. Under the red rag her hair came down on her neck in the frailest of ringlets, still black, and with an odor like copper.

Now and then there was a <u>quivering</u> in the thicket. Old Phoenix said, "Out of my way, all you foxes, owls, beetles, jack rabbits, coons and wild animals! . . . Keep out from

> *To whom is Phoenix speaking?*

under these feet, little bob-whites. . . . Keep the big wild hogs out of my path. Don't let none of those come running my direction. I got a long way." Under her small black-freckled hand her cane, <u>limber</u> as a buggy whip, would switch at the brush as if to <u>rouse</u> up any hiding things.

> " Something always take a hold of me on this hill—pleads I should stay."

On she went. The woods were deep and still. The sun made the pine needles almost too bright to look at, up where the wind rocked. The cones dropped as light as feathers. Down in the hollow was the morning dove—it was not too late for him.

The path ran up a hill. "Seem like there is chains about my feet, time I get this far," she said, in the voice of argument old people keep to use with themselves. "Something always take a hold of me on this hill—pleads I should stay."

After she got to the top she turned and gave a full, severe look behind her where she had come. "Up through pines," she said at length. "Now down through oaks."

Her eyes opened their widest, and she started

> *Why does Phoenix stop?*

down gently. But before she got to the bottom of the hill a bush caught her dress.

Her fingers were busy and intent, but her skirts were full and long, so that before she could pull them free in one place they were caught in another. It was not possible to allow the dress to tear. "I in the thorny bush," she said. "Thorns, you doing your appointed work. Never want to let folks pass, no sir. Old eyes thought you was a pretty little *green* bush."

Finally, trembling all over, she stood free, and after a moment dared to stoop for her cane.

"Sun so high!" she cried, leaning back and looking, while the thick tears went over her eyes. "The time getting all gone here."

At the foot of this hill was a place where a log was laid across the creek.

---

**WORDS FOR EVERYDAY USE**

**pen • du • lum** (pen' jə ləm) *n.*, body suspended from a fixed point so as to swing freely to and fro under the action of gravity and commonly used to regulate movements (as of clockwork). *The sharp, descending <u>pendulum</u> threatened the narrator's life in the Edgar Allan Poe story "The Pit and the Pendulum."*

**quiv • er • ing** (kwiv' riŋ) *n.*, shaking or moving characterized by a slight trembling motion. *The <u>quivering</u> of Grandpa's hands is due to Parkinson's disease.*

**lim • ber** (lim' bər) *adj.*, having a supple and resilient quality. *After a few warm-up exercises, Mr. Hogan felt as <u>limber</u> as a twenty-year-old.*

**rouse** (rouz) *vi.*, awaken or stir up. *The slamming of the kitchen door <u>roused</u> the birds, and they flew up into the trees.*

"Now comes the trial," said Phoenix.

Putting her right foot out, she mounted the log and shut her eyes. Lifting her skirt, leveling her cane fiercely before her, like a festival figure in some parade, she began to march across. Then she opened her eyes and she was safe on the other side.

> How does Phoenix cross the log that covers the creek?

"I wasn't as old as I thought," she said.

But she sat down to rest. She spread her skirts on the bank around her and folded her hands over her knees. Up above her was a tree in a pearly cloud of mistletoe. She did not dare to close her eyes, and when a little boy brought her a plate with a slice of marble-cake on it she spoke to him. "That would be acceptable," she said. But when she went to take it there was just her own hand in the air.

> What does the little boy offer Phoenix in her daydream?

So she left that tree, and had to go through a barbed-wire fence. There she had to creep and crawl, spreading her knees and stretching her fingers like a baby trying to climb the steps. But she talked loudly to herself: she could not let her dress be torn now, so late in the day, and she could not pay for having her arm or her leg sawed off if she got caught fast where she was.

> Why does Phoenix take such care in crossing through the barbed-wire fence?

At last she was safe through the fence and risen up out in the clearing. Big dead trees, like black men with one arm, were standing in the purple stalks of the withered cotton field. There sat a buzzard.

"Who you watching?"

In the furrow she made her way along.

"Glad this not the season for bulls," she said, looking sideways, "and the good Lord made his snakes to curl up and sleep in the winter. A pleasure I don't see no two-headed snake coming around that tree, where it come once. It took a while to get by him, back in the summer."

She passed through the old cotton and went into a field of dead corn. It whispered and shook and was taller than her head. "Through the maze now," she said, for there was no path.

Then there was something tall, black, and skinny there, moving before her.

At first she took it for a man. It could have been a man dancing in the field. But she stood still and listened, and it did not make a sound. It was as silent as a ghost.

"Ghost," she said sharply, "who be you the ghost of? For I have heard of nary death close by."

But there was no answer—only the ragged dancing in the wind.

She shut her eyes, reached out her hand, and touched a sleeve. She found a coat and inside that an emptiness, cold as ice.

> What is Phoenix afraid of in the cornfield?

"You scarecrow," she said. Her face lighted. "I ought to be shut up for good," she said with laughter. "My senses is gone. I too old. I the oldest people I ever know. Dance, old scarecrow," she said, "while I dancing with you."

She kicked her foot over the furrow, and with mouth drawn down, shook her head once or twice in a little strutting way. Some husks blew down and whirled in streamers about her skirts.

Then she went on, parting her way from side to side with the cane, through the whispering field. At last she came to the end, to a wagon track where the silver grass blew between the red ruts. The quail were walking around like pullets, seeming all dainty and unseen.

---

**WORDS FOR EVERYDAY USE**

pul • let (pu˘' lət) *n.*, young hen. *The farmer put the pullets in the chicken coop for safety.*

"Walk pretty," she said. "This the easy place. This the easy going."

She followed the track, swaying through the quiet bare fields, through the little strings of trees silver in their dead leaves, past cabins silver from weather, with the doors and windows boarded shut, all like old women under a spell sitting there. "I walking in their sleep," she said, nodding her head vigorously.

In a ravine she went where a spring was silently flowing through a hollow log. Old Phoenix bent and drank. "Sweet-gum makes the water sweet," she said, and drank more. "Nobody know who made this well, for it was here when I was born."

The track crossed a swampy part where the moss hung as white as lace from every limb. "Sleep on, alligators, and blow your bubbles." Then the track went into the road.

Deep, deep the road went down between the high green-colored banks. Overhead the live-oaks met, and it was as dark as a cave.

A black dog with a lolling tongue came up out of the weeds by the ditch. She was meditating, and not ready, and when he came at her she only hit him a little with her cane. Over she went in the ditch, like a little puff of milkweed.

*What does the dog do to Phoenix?*

Down there, her senses drifted away. A dream visited her, and she reached her hand up, but nothing reached down and gave her a pull. So she lay there and presently went to talking. "Old woman," she said to herself, "that black dog come up out of the weeds to stall your off, and now there he sitting on his fine tail, smiling at you."

A white man finally came along and found her—a hunter, a young man, with his dog on a chain.

*Who pulls Phoenix out of the ditch?*

"Well, Granny!" he laughed. "What are you doing there?"

"Lying on my back like a June-bug waiting to be turned over, mister," she said, reaching up her hand.

He lifted her up, gave her a swing in the air, and set her down. "Anything broken, Granny?"

"No sir, them old dead weeds is springy enough," said Phoenix, when she had got her breath. "I thank you for your trouble."

"Where do you live, Granny?" he asked, while the two dogs were growling at each other.

"Away back yonder, sir, behind the ridge. You can't even see it from here."

"On your way home?"

"No sir, I going to town."

"Why, that's too far! That's as far as I walk when I come out myself, and I get something for my trouble." He patted the stuffed bag he carried, and there hung down a little closed claw. It was one of the bob-whites, with its beak hooked bitterly to show it was dead. "Now you go on home, Granny!"

"I bound to go to town, mister," said Phoenix. "The time come around."

He gave another laugh, filling the whole landscape. "I know you old colored people! Wouldn't miss going to town to see Santa Claus!"

But something held old Phoenix very still. The deep lines in her face went into a fierce and different radiation. Without warning, she had seen with her own eyes a flashing nickel fall out of the man's pocket onto the ground.

"How old are you, Granny?" he was saying.

"There is no telling, mister," she said, "no telling."

Then she gave a little cry and clapped her hands and said, "Git on away from here, dog! Look! Look at that dog!" She laughed as if in

---

**WORDS FOR EVERYDAY USE**

ra • vine (rə vēn′) n., small, narrow, steep-sided valley larger than a gully and smaller than a canyon. *The wheel fell off the carriage and tumbled down into the ravine.*

admiration. "He ain't scared of nobody. He a big black dog." She whispered, "Sic him!"

"Watch me get rid of that cur," said the man. "Sic him, Pete! Sic him!"

Phoenix heard the dogs fighting, and heard the man running and throwing sticks. She even heard a gunshot. But she was slowly bending forward by that time, further and further forward, the lids stretched down over her eyes, as if she were doing this in her sleep. Her chin was lowered almost to her knees. The yellow palm of her hand came out from the fold of her apron. Her fingers slid down and along the ground under the piece of money with the grace and care they would have in lifting an egg from under a setting hen. Then she slowly straightened up, she stood erect, and the nickel was in her apron pocket. A bird flew by. Her lips moved: "God watching me the whole time. I come to stealing."

*Of what action is Phoenix ashamed?*

The man came back, and his own dog panted about them. "Well, I scared him off that time," he said, and then he laughed and lifted his gun and pointed it at Phoenix.

*How does the hunter threaten Phoenix?*

She stood straight and faced him.

"Doesn't the gun scare you?" he said, still pointing it.

"No, sir, I seen plenty go off closer by, in my day, and for less than what I done," she said, holding utterly still.

He smiled, and shouldered the gun. "Well, Granny," he said, "you must be a hundred years old, and scared of nothing. I'd give you a dime if I had any money with me. But you take my advice and stay home, and nothing will happen to you."

"I bound to go on my way, mister," said Phoenix. She inclined her head in the red rag. Then they went in different directions, but she could hear the gun shooting again and again over the hill.

She walked on. The shadows hung from the oak trees to the road like curtains. Then she smelled wood-smoke, and smelled the river, and she saw a steeple and the cabins on their steep steps. Dozens of little black children whirled around her. There ahead was Natchez shining. Bells were ringing. She walked on.

In the paved city it was Christmas time. There were red and green electric lights strung and criss-crossed everywhere, and all turned on in the daytime. Old Phoenix would have been lost if she had not distrusted her eyesight and depended on her feet to know where to take her.

*Why is the city of Natchez decorated with red and green electric lights?*

She paused quietly on the sidewalk where people were passing by. A lady came along in the crowd, carrying an armful of red-, green- and silver-wrapped presents; she gave off perfume like the red roses in hot summer, and Phoenix stopped her.

"Please, missy, will you lace up my shoe?" She held up her foot.

*What does Phoenix ask a woman on the street?*

"What do you want, Grandma?"

"See my shoe," said Phoenix. "Do all right for out in the country, but wouldn't look right to go in a big building."

"Stand still then, Grandma," said the lady. She put her packages down on the sidewalk beside her and laced and tied both shoes tightly.

"Can't lace 'em with a cane," said Phoenix. "Thank you, missy. I doesn't mind asking a nice lady to tie up my shoe, when I gets out on the street."

Moving slowly and from side to side, she went into the big building, and into a tower of steps, where she walked up and around and around until her feet knew to stop.

> " *God watching me the whole time. I come to stealing.* "

She entered a door, and there she saw nailed up on the wall the document that had been stamped with the gold seal and framed in the gold frame, which matched the dream that was hung up in her head.

How does Phoenix know she's reached the right location?

"Here I be," she said. There was a fixed and ceremonial stiffness over her body.

"A charity case, I suppose," said an attendant who sat at the desk before her.

But Phoenix only looked above her head. There was sweat on her face, the wrinkles in her skin shone like a bright net.

"Speak up, Grandma," the woman said. "What's your name? We must have your history, you know. Have you been here before? What seems to be the trouble with you?"

Old Phoenix only gave a twitch to her face as if a fly were bothering her.

"Are you deaf?" cried the attendant.

But then the nurse came in.

"Oh, that's just old Aunt Phoenix," she said. "She doesn't come for herself—she has a little grandson. She makes these trips just as regular as clockwork. She lives away back off the Old Natchez Trace." She bent down. "Well, Aunt Phoenix, why don't you just take a seat? We won't keep you standing after your long trip." She pointed.

The old woman sat down, bolt upright in the chair.

"Now, how is the boy?" asked the nurse.

Old Phoenix did not speak.

"I said, how is the boy?"

But Phoenix only waited and stared straight ahead, her face very solemn and withdrawn into rigidity.

"Is his throat any better?" asked the nurse. "Aunt Phoenix, don't you hear me? Is your grandson's throat any better since the last time you came for the medicine?"

With her hands on her knees, the old woman waited, silent, erect and motionless, just as if she were in armor.

"You mustn't take up our time this way, Aunt Phoenix," the nurse said. "Tell us quickly about your grandson, and get it over. He isn't dead, is he?"

> *" Tell us quickly about your grandson, and get it over. He isn't dead, is he?"*

At last there came a flicker and then a flame of comprehension across her face, and she spoke.

Why does Phoenix refuse to answer the nurse's questions?

"My grandson. It was my memory had left me. There I sat and forgot why I made my long trip."

"Forgot?" The nurse frowned. "After you came so far?"

Then Phoenix was like an old woman begging a dignified forgiveness for waking up frightened in the night. "I never did go to school, I was too old at the Surrender,"[1] she said in a soft voice. "I'm an old woman without an education. It was my memory fail me. My little grandson, he is just the same, and I forgot it in the coming."

"Throat never heals, does it?" said the nurse, speaking in a loud, sure voice to old Phoenix. By now she had a card with something written on it, a little list. "Yes. Swallowed lye. When was it?—January—two-three years ago—"

What is wrong with Phoenix's grandson?

Phoenix spoke unasked now. "No, missy, he not dead, he just the same. Every little while his throat begin to close up again, and he not able to swallow. He not get his breath. He not able to help himself. So the time come around, and I go on another trip for the soothing medicine."

---

1. **Surrender.** Surrender of the South to the North at the end of the Civil War in 1865

"All right. The doctor said as long as you came to get it, you could have it," said the nurse. "But it's an obstinate case."

Why did Phoenix make the journey?

"My little grandson, he sit up there in the house all wrapped up, waiting by himself," Phoenix went on. "We is the only two left in the world. He suffer and it don't seem to put him back at all. He got a sweet look. He going to last. He wear a little patch quilt and peep out holding his mouth open like a little bird. I remembers so plain now. I not going to forget him again, no, the whole enduring time. I could tell him from all the others in creation."

"All right." The nurse was trying to hush her now. She brought her a bottle of medicine. "Charity," she said, making a check mark in a book.

Old Phoenix held the bottle close to her eyes, and then carefully put it into her pocket.

"I thank you," she said.

"It's Christmas time, Grandma," said the attendant. "Could I give you a few pennies out of my purse?"

"Five pennies is a nickel," said Phoenix stiffly.

"Here's a nickel," said the attendant.

Phoenix rose carefully and held out her hand. She received the nickel and then fished the other nickel out of her pocket and laid it beside the new one. She stared at her palm closely, with her head on one side.

Then she gave a tap with her cane on the floor.

"This is what come to me to do," she said. "I going to the store and buy my child a little windmill they sells, made out of paper. He going to find it hard to believe there such a thing in the world. I'll march myself back where he waiting, holding it straight up in this hand."

What does Phoenix decide to buy with her ten cents?

She lifted her free hand, gave a little nod, turned around, and walked out of the doctor's office. Then her slow step began on the stairs, going down. ∎

# Respond *to the* SELECTION

Imagine you are Phoenix. What would you tell people you live for?

## "Is Phoenix Jackson's Grandson Really Dead?"

by Eudora Welty

A story writer is more than happy to be read by students; the fact that these serious readers think and feel something in response to his work he finds life-giving. At the same time he may not always be able to reply to their specific questions in kind. I wondered if it might clarify something, for both the questioners and myself, if I set down a general reply to the question that comes to me most often in the mail, from both students and their teachers, after some classroom discussion. The unrivaled favorite is this: "Is Phoenix Jackson's grandson really dead?"

It refers to a short story I wrote years ago called "A Worn Path," which tells of a day's journey an old woman makes on foot from deep in the country into town and into a doctor's office on behalf of her little grandson; he is at home, periodically ill, and periodically she comes for his medicine; they give it to her as usual, she receives it and starts the journey back.

I had not meant to mystify readers by withholding any fact; it is not a writer's business to tease. The story is told through Phoenix's mind as she undertakes her errand. As the author at one with the character as I tell it, I must assume that the boy is alive. As the reader, you are free to think as you like, of course: the story invites you to believe that no matter what happens, Phoenix for as long as she is able to walk and can hold to her purpose will make her journey. The *possibility* that she would keep on even if he were dead is there in her devotion and its single-minded, single-track errand. Certainly the *artistic* truth, which should

> *The path is the thing that matters.*

be good enough for the fact, lies in Phoenix's own answer to that question. When the nurse asks, "He isn't dead, is he?" she speaks for herself: "He still the same. He going to last."

The grandchild is the incentive. But it is the journey, the going of the errand, that is the story, and the question is not whether the grandchild is in reality alive or dead. It doesn't affect the outcome of the story or its meaning from start to finish. But it is not the question itself that has struck me as much as the idea, almost without exception implied in the asking, that for Phoenix's grandson to be dead would somehow make the story "better."

It's *all right,* I want to say to the students who write to me, for things to be what they appear to be, and for words to mean what they say. It's all right, too, for words and appearances to mean more than one thing—ambiguity is a fact of life. A fiction writer's responsibility covers not only what he presents as the facts of a given story but what he chooses to stir up as their implications; in the end, these implications, too, become facts, in the larger, fictional sense. But it is not all right, not in good faith, for things *not* to mean what they say.

The grandson's plight was real and it made the truth of the story, which is the story of an errand of love carried out. If the child no longer lived, the truth would persist in the "wornness" of the path. But his being dead can't increase the truth of the story, can't affect it one way or the other. I think I signal this, because the end of the story has been reached before old Phoenix gets home again: she simply starts back. To the question "Is the grandson really dead?" I could reply that it doesn't make any difference. I could also say that I did not make him up in order to let him play a trick on Phoenix. But my best answer would be: "*Phoenix is alive.*"

The origin of a story is sometimes a trustworthy clue to the author—or can provide him with the clue—to its key image; maybe in this case it will do the same for the reader. One day I saw a solitary old woman like Phoenix. She was walking; I saw her, at middle distance, in a winter country landscape, and watched her slowly make her way across my line of vision. That sight of her made me write the story. I invented an errand for her, but that only seemed a living part of the figure she was herself: what errand other than for someone else could be making her go? And her going was the first thing, her persisting in her landscape was the real thing, and the first and the real were what I wanted and worked to keep. I brought her up close enough, by imagination, to describe her face, make her present to the eyes, but the full-length figure moving across the winter fields was the indelible one and the image to keep, and the perspective extending into the vanishing distance the true one to hold in mind.

I invented for my character, as I wrote, some passing adventures—some dreams and harassments and a small triumph or two, some jolts to her pride, some flights of fancy to console her, one or two encounters to scare her, and a moment that gave her cause to feel ashamed, a moment to dance and preen—for it had to be a *journey,* and all these things belonged to that, parts of life's uncertainty.

A narrative line is in its deeper sense, of course, the tracing out of a meaning and the real continuity of a story lies in this probing forward. The real dramatic force of a story depends on the strength of the emotion that has set it going. The emotional value is the measure of the reach of the story. What gives any such content to "A Worn Path" is not its circumstances but its *subject:* the deep-grained habit of love.

What I hoped would come clear was that in the whole surround of this story, the world it threads through, the only certain thing at all is the worn path. The habit of love cuts through confusion and stumbles or contrives its way out of difficulty, it remembers the way even when it forgets, for a dumbfounded moment, its reason for being. The path is the thing that matters.

*Her* victory—old Phoenix's—is when she sees the diploma in the doctor's office, when she finds "nailed up on the wall the document that had been stamped with the gold seal and framed in the gold frame, which matched the dream that was hung up in her head." The return with the medicine is just a matter of retracing her own footsteps. It is the part of the journey, and of the story, that can now go without saying.

In the matter of function, old Phoenix's way might even do as a sort of parallel to your way of work if you are a writer of stories. The way to get there is the all-important, all-absorbing problem, and this problem is your reason for undertaking the story. Your only guide, too, is your sureness about your subject, about what this subject is. Like Phoenix, you work all your life to find your way, through all the obstructions and the false appearances and the upsets you may have brought on yourself, to reach a meaning—using inventions of your imagination, perhaps helped out by your dreams and bits of good luck. And finally too, like Phoenix, you have to assume that what you are working in aid of is life, not death.

But you would make the trip anyway—wouldn't you?—just on hope. ∎

# Inquire, *Imagine*

**Recall:** GATHERING FACTS

1a. When does Phoenix begin her journey?

2a. Through which areas does Phoenix walk?

3a. Why is the woman who ties Phoenix's shoes carrying presents?

→ **Interpret:** FINDING MEANING

1b. How old is Phoenix? How do you know?

2b. Which obstacle in Phoenix's journey poses the greatest threat to her?

3b. What associations with the Christmas story can you make to Phoenix's journey?

**Analyze:** TAKING THINGS APART

4a. Identify the obstacles that Phoenix runs into during her journey and describe how she overcomes each one.

→ **Synthesize:** BRINGING THINGS TOGETHER

4b. Why does Welty wait until the end of the story to reveal why the journey was made?

**Evaluate:** MAKING JUDGMENTS

5a. When a work of literature is ambiguous, it can be interpreted in more than one way. Is Phoenix's grandson dead or alive? Cite examples from the text to support your viewpoint.

→ **Extend:** CONNECTING IDEAS

5b. Think of a historic or literary journey with which you are familiar. Compare and contrast the motives of the historic or literary character for making the journey with those of Phoenix for making her journey to Natchez. Whose journey was more selfless? more difficult?

# Understanding *Literature*

ARCHETYPE. Review the definition for **archetype** in the Handbook of Literary Terms. What human emotion makes it possible for Phoenix to surmount the obstacles of her journey?

CHARACTER. Review the definition for **character** in the Handbook of Literary Terms. Fill out the chart below with details about Phoenix's character. What do you learn about Phoenix's character from her encounters with the bramblebush, the imaginary boy who offers her marble cake, the scarecrow, the hunter, and the woman who ties her shoe? What character trait does Phoenix demonstrate by getting the medicine and a paper windmill for her grandson?

| Physical Appearance | Dress | Habits/ Mannerisms/ Behaviors | Relationships with Other People | Other |
|---|---|---|---|---|
| | long dark striped dress; long, neat, tidy apron of bleached sugar sacks; untied shoes | | | |

# WRITER'S JOURNAL

1. Imagine you are Phoenix Jackson's grandson. Write a **thank-you note** to your grandmother for the medicine and gift she brought you.

2. Imagine you are the young white hunter in the story. Write a **letter** to a friend describing your interactions with the old African-American woman you met. Be sure to explain why you helped her and then pointed your gun at her. Why were your feelings and behavior toward her so ambivalent?

3. Imagine you are Phoenix Jackson, having returned home with the medicine and the paper windmill. Write a **journal entry** describing your adventures, how you feel now that the journey is over, and telling your grandson's reactions to the gifts you brought him. You might choose to use Phoenix's dialect in the journal entry.

# Integrating the LANGUAGE ARTS

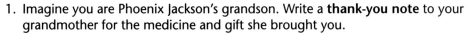

## Vocabulary

**USING DICTIONARIES.** Phoenix Jackson makes a journey in "A Worn Path." There are many synonyms for *journey: pilgrimage, expedition, odyssey, trek,* and *trip.* Read the Language Arts Survey 1.17, "Using a Dictionary." Then look up the definition for each of these words, including *journey.* Finally, write two paragraphs. In the first paragraph, describe a journey that you have made, giving its purpose, duration, difficulties, and lessons learned. Be sure to identify it correctly as a journey, pilgrimage, expedition, odyssey, trek, or trip. In the second paragraph, based on how the author presented the story, decide which word best describes Phoenix's journey. Explain your decision, citing examples from the selection.

## Speaking and Listening

**ROLE-PLAY.** With a partner, play the roles of Phoenix Jackson and her grandson. Imagine that Phoenix has just returned from Natchez. The grandson should ask questions about his grandmother's adventures, and Phoenix should answer in detail. You might want to attempt imitating Phoenix's dialect.

## Study and Research & Media Literacy

**RESEARCHING ON THE INTERNET.** Use the Internet to locate news items about Eudora Welty, for example, adaptations of her work, interviews with Welty or Welty scholars, forthcoming conferences about Welty, awards given to the author, reviews of her writing, and winners of the Eudora Welty Writing Contest for high school students. One site you will find useful is the Mississippi Writers Page at http://www.olemiss.edu/depts/english/ms-writers. Then lay out a page of a newsletter dedicated to Welty, including articles on the topics you find most interesting. You might even decide to write your own review of "A Worn Path." Finally, share your newsletter with the class.

# Literary
## T O O L S

**MOTIVATION.** A **motivation** is a force that moves a character to think, feel, or behave in a certain way. As you read, decide how Leo Finkle's motivations change as the story progresses.

**ANTIHERO.** An **antihero** is a central character who lacks all the qualities traditionally associated with heroes. As you read, make a cluster chart to list Leo Finkle's characteristics that classify him as an antihero.

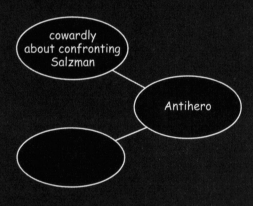

cowardly about confronting Salzman

Antihero

# About
## the
## S E L E C T I O N

**"The Magic Barrel"** appeared in the short story collection of the same name, published in 1958. Containing influences of Yiddish folktales and Hasidic traditions, most of the stories in this collection depict the search for hope and meaning within the grim entrapment of poor urban settings. Scholars have noted that the stories in the collection also owe a debt to Hawthorne: like Hawthorne, Malamud combines "reality and the dream, the natural and supernatural."

# "The Magic Barrel"

BY BERNARD MALAMUD

# About
## the
## A U T H O R

**Bernard Malamud** (1914–1986), short story writer and novelist, was born in Brooklyn, New York, to Russian Jewish immigrants who owned a grocery store. Educated at the City College of New York and Columbia University, where he earned his B.A. and Master's degree, he taught high school and then college English until shortly before his death. Affected by World War II, he began investigating his Jewish identity and started reading about Jewish tradition and history. His works commonly employ literary conventions drawn from earlier Jewish literature. His first novel, *The Natural* (1952), a fable about a baseball player who is gifted with miraculous powers, deals with the nature of heroic figures. *The Assistant* (1957), which describes the relationship between a young Gentile hoodlum and an old Jewish grocer, affirms the redemptive value of maintaining faith in the goodness of the human soul. *The Fixer* (1966), which won the National Book Award and the Pulitzer Prize, tells the story of a Jewish handyman unjustly imprisoned for the murder of a Christian boy in Czarist Russia. Other novels include *A New Life* (1961) and *God's Grace* (1982).

Malamud's renown as the best-known spokesman of the Jewish experience in America rests on his short stories, which transcend their ethnic origin to tell universal tales of men and women searching for love and coping with moral responsibility. He said the most important task of the writer is "to recapture his image as human being as each of us in his secret heart knows it to be." Using emotional, metaphorical language, Malamud presents magical events that often interlace the grim reality of his characters' lives. His most celebrated collection of short stories, *The Magic Barrel* (1958), received the National Book Award and earned him a Ford Fellowship. Other short story collections include *Pictures of Fidelman: An Exhibition* (1969) and *The Stories of Bernard Malamud* (1983). *The People and Uncollected Stories* was published posthumously in 1989.

# Reader's
*Journal*

When have you sought outside help to attain a goal?

# The Magic Barrel

*The Wedding*, Marc Chagall. Gosudarstrennaja Tretjakovsk Galerja, Moscow.

## BERNARD MALAMUD

# ArtNote

***The Wedding***, Marc Chagall,
page 809.

Although he spent most of his life in Paris and
America, Marc Chagall (1887–1985) always
depicted the Jewish villages of his native Russia. He
was looking back with nostalgia at a way of life that
was being eliminated throughout Europe by the
Holocaust and Russian pogroms. Chagall usually
depicted the delirious ecstasy of newlyweds, but in
the painting on page 809 there is a tinge of sadness. How would you compare the mood conveyed
by this painting to that of Malamud's story?

Not long ago there lived in uptown New York, in a small, almost meager room, though crowded with books, Leo Finkle, a rabbinical student at the Yeshiva University.[1] Finkle, after six years of study, was to be ordained in June and had been advised by an acquaintance that he might find it easier to win himself a congregation if he were married. Since he had no present prospects of marriage, after two tormented days of turning it over in his mind, he called in Pinye Salzman, a marriage broker whose two-line advertisement he had read in the *Forward*.[2]

*Where does the rabbinical student live? What is his room like?*

*Whose advertisement had Finkle read in the Forward?*

The matchmaker appeared one night out of the dark fourth-floor hallway of the graystone rooming house where Finkle lived, grasping a black, strapped portfolio that had been worn thin with use. Salzman, who had been long in the business, was of slight but dignified build, wearing an old hat, and an overcoat too short and tight for him. He smelled frankly of fish, which he loved to eat, and although he was missing a few teeth, his presence was not dis-pleasing, because of an amiable manner curiously contrasted with mournful eyes. His voice, his lips, his wisp of beard, his bony fingers were animated, but give him a moment of repose and his mild blue eyes revealed a depth of sadness, a characteristic that put Leo a little at ease although the situation, for him, was inherently tense.

He at once informed Salzman why he had asked him to come, explaining that his home was in Cleveland, and that but for his parents, who had married comparatively late in life, he was alone in the world. He had for six years devoted himself almost entirely to his studies, as a result of which, understandably, he had found himself without time for a social life and the company of young women. Therefore he thought it the better part of trial and error—of embarrassing fumbling—to call in an experienced person to advise him on these matters. He remarked in passing that the function of the marriage broker was ancient and honorable, highly approved in the Jewish community, because it made practical the necessary without hindering joy. Moreover, his own parents had been brought together by a matchmaker. They had made, if not a financially profitable marriage—since neither had possessed any worldly goods to speak of—at least a successful one in the sense of their everlasting devotion to each other. Salzman listened in embarrassed surprise, sensing a sort of apology. Later, however, he experienced a glow of

*What couple does Leo know that met through a matchmaker? How could he tell their marriage was a success?*

---

1. **Yeshiva University.** University in New York City offering both theological and secular courses
2. ***Forward.*** *The Jewish Daily Forward*, New York City newspaper written in the Yiddish language

---

**WORDS FOR EVERYDAY USE**

**mea • ger** (mē´gər) *adj.*, not rich or bountiful; inadequate. *The portions at the restaurant were so meager that we left hungry.*

**or • dain** (ôr dān´) *vt.*, officially give someone the authority and duties of a minister, priest, or rabbi. *Marla was excited when, after years of study at divinity school, she was ordained a minister.*

**in • her • ent • ly** (in hir´ ənt lē) *adv.*, characteristically; naturally. *Some philosophers maintain that people are inherently good.*

pride in his work, an emotion that had left him years ago, and he heartily approved of Finkle.

The two went to their business. Leo had led Salzman to the only clear place in the room, a table near a window that overlooked the lamp-lit city. He seated himself at the matchmaker's side but facing him, attempting by an act of will to suppress the unpleasant tickle in his throat. Salzman eagerly unstrapped his portfolio and removed a loose rubber band from a thin packet of much-handled cards. As he flipped through them, a gesture and sound that physically hurt Leo, the student pretended not to see and gazed steadfastly out the window. Although it was still February, winter was on its last legs, signs of which he had for the first time in years begun to notice. He now observed the round white moon, moving high in the sky through a cloud <u>menagerie</u>, and watched with half-open mouth as it penetrated a huge hen, and dropped out of her like an egg laying itself. Salzman, though pretending through eyeglasses he had just slipped on, to be engaged in scanning the writing on the cards, stole occasional glances at the young man's distinguished face, noting with pleasure the long, severe scholar's nose, brown eyes heavy with learning, sensitive yet <u>ascetic</u> lips, and a certain, almost hollow quality of the dark cheeks. He gazed around at shelves upon shelves of books and let out a soft, contented sigh.

When Leo's eyes fell upon the cards, he counted six spread out in Salzman's hand.

"So few?" he asked in disappointment.

"You wouldn't believe me how much cards I got in my office," Salzman replied. "The drawers are already filled to the top, so I keep them now in a barrel, but is every girl good for a new rabbi?"

Leo blushed at this, regretting all he had revealed of himself in a curriculum vitae[3] he had sent to Salzman. He had thought it best to acquaint him with his strict standards and specifications, but in having done so, he felt he had told the marriage broker more than was absolutely necessary.

He hesitantly inquired, "Do you keep photographs of your clients on file?"

> What does Leo want to see?

"First comes family, amount of dowry, also what kind promises," Salzman replied, unbuttoning his tight coat and settling himself in the chair. "After come pictures, rabbi."

"Call me Mr. Finkle. I'm not yet a rabbi."

Salzman said he would, but instead called him doctor, which he changed to rabbi when Leo was not listening too attentively.

Salzman adjusted his horn-rimmed spectacles, gently cleared his throat and read in an eager voice the contents of the top card:

"Sophie P. Twenty four years. Widow one year. No children. Educated high school and two years college. Father promises eight thousand dollars. Has wonderful wholesale business. Also real estate. On the mother's side comes teachers, also one actor. Well known on Second Avenue."

Leo gazed up in surprise. "Did you say a widow?"

"A widow don't mean spoiled, rabbi. She lived with her husband maybe four months. He was a sick boy she made a mistake to marry him."

"Marrying a widow has never entered my mind."

> Why does Leo reject Sophie P.?

"This is because you have no experience. A widow, especially if she is young and healthy

---

3. **curriculum vitae.** Summary of one's personal history and professional qualifications; a résumé

---

**WORDS FOR EVERYDAY USE**

me • nag • er • ie (mə naj´ ər ē) *n.*, collection of wild or exotic animals. *In Tennessee Williams's play, Laura Wingfield's prized <u>menagerie</u> is made of glass.*

as • cet • ic (ə set´ik) *adj.*, self-denying; austere. *The monks lived an <u>ascetic</u> lifestyle, denying themselves most of civilization's pleasures.*

like this girl, is a wonderful person to marry. She will be thankful to you the rest of her life. Believe me, if I was looking now for a bride, I would marry a widow."

Leo reflected, then shook his head.

> ❝Believe me, if I was looking now for a bride, I would marry a widow.❞

Salzman hunched his shoulders in an almost imperceptible gesture of disappointment. He placed the card down on the wooden table and began to read another:

"Lily H. High school teacher. Regular. Not a substitute. Has savings and new Dodge car. Lived in Paris one year. Father is successful dentist thirty-five years. Interested in professional man. Well Americanized family. Wonderful opportunity."

"I knew her personally," said Salzman. "I wish you could see this girl. She is a doll. Also very intelligent. All day you could talk to her about books and theater and what not. She also knows current events."

"I don't believe you mentioned her age?"

"Her age?" Salzman said, raising his brows. "Her age is thirty-two years."

Leo said after a while, "I'm afraid that seems a little too old."

Salzman let out a laugh. "So how old are you, rabbi?"

"Twenty-seven."

"So what is the difference, tell me, between twenty-seven and thirty-two? My own wife is seven years older than me. So what did I suffer?—Nothing. If Rothschild's[4] daughter wants to marry you, would you say on account her age, no?"

"Yes," Leo said dryly.

Salzman shook off the no in the yes. "Five years don't mean a thing. I give you my word that when you will live with her for one week you will forget her age. What does it mean five years—that she lived more and knows more than somebody who is younger? On this girl, God bless her, years are not wasted. Each one that it comes makes better the bargain."

"What subjects does she teach in high school?"

"Languages. If you heard the way she speaks French, you will think it is music. I am in the business twenty-five years, and I recommend her with my whole heart. Believe me, I know what I'm talking, rabbi."

"What's on the next card?" Leo said abruptly.

Salzman reluctantly turned up the third card:

"Ruth K. Nineteen years. Honor student. Father offers thirteen thousand cash to the right bridegroom. He is a medical doctor. Stomach specialist with marvelous practice. Brother in law owns own garment business. Particular people."

Salzman looked as if he had read his trump card.

"Did you say nineteen?" Leo asked with interest.

"On the dot."

"Is she attractive?" He blushed. "Pretty?"

---

4. **Rothschild's.** The Rothschilds were once a very wealthy Jewish family of international bankers and business leaders.

WORDS FOR EVERYDAY USE

im • per • cep • ti • ble (im´ pər sep´ tə bəl) adj., not able to be detected by the senses or the mind. *Adam's progress in spelling was so slow as to be imperceptible.*

Salzman kissed his finger tips. "A little doll. On this I give you my word. Let me call the father tonight and you will see what means pretty."

But Leo was troubled. "You're sure she's that young?"

"This I am positive. The father will show you the birth certificate."

"Are you positive there isn't something wrong with her?" Leo insisted.

"Who says there is wrong?"

"I don't understand why an American girl her age should go to a marriage broker."

A smile spread over Salzman's face.

"So for the same reason you went, she comes."

Leo flushed. "I am pressed for time."

Salzman, realizing he had been tactless, quickly explained. "The father came, not her. He wants she should have the best, so he looks around himself. When we will locate the right boy he will introduce him and encourage. This makes a better marriage than if a young girl without experience takes for herself. I don't have to tell you this."

"But don't you think this young girl believes in love?" Leo spoke uneasily.

Salzman was about to guffaw but caught himself and said soberly, "Love comes with the right person, not before."

Leo parted dry lips but did not speak. Noticing that Salzman had snatched a glance at the next card, he cleverly asked, "How is her health?"

"Perfect," Salzman said, breathing with difficulty. "Of course, she is a little lame on her right foot from an auto accident that it happened to her when she was twelve years, but nobody notices on account she is so brilliant and also beautiful."

*What is wrong with Ruth K.?*

Leo got up heavily and went to the window. He felt curiously bitter and upbraided himself for having called in the marriage broker.

Finally, he shook his head.

"Why not?" Salzman persisted, the pitch of his voice rising.

"Because I detest stomach specialists."

"So what do you care what is his business? After you marry her do you need him? Who says he must come every Friday night in your house?"

Ashamed of the way the talk was going, Leo dismissed Salzman, who went home with heavy, melancholy eyes.

Though he had felt only relief at the marriage broker's departure, Leo was in low spirits the next day. He explained it as arising from Salzman's failure to produce a suitable bride for him. He did not care for his type of clientele. But when Leo found himself hesitating whether to seek out another matchmaker, one more polished than Pinye, he wondered if it could be—his protestations to the contrary, and although he honored his father and mother—that he did not, in essence, care for the match-making institution? This thought he quickly put out of mind yet found himself still upset. All day he ran around in the woods—missed an important appointment, forgot to give out his laundry, walked out of a Broadway cafeteria without paying and had to run back with the ticket in his hand; had even not recognized his landlady in the street when she passed with a friend and courteously called out, "A good evening to you, Doctor Finkle." By nightfall, however, he had regained sufficient calm to sink his nose into a book and there found peace from his thoughts.

*What does Leo wonder about himself after Salzman failed to find him a suitable bride?*

Almost at once there came a knock on the door. Before Leo could say enter, Salzman, commercial cupid, was standing in the room. His face was gray and meager, his expression hungry, and he looked as if he would expire on his feet. Yet the marriage broker managed, by some trick of the muscles, to display a broad smile.

"So good evening. I am invited?"

Leo nodded, disturbed to see him again, yet unwilling to ask the man to leave.

Beaming still, Salzman laid his portfolio on the table. "Rabbi, I got for you tonight good news."

"I've asked you not to call me rabbi. I'm still a student."

"Your worries are finished. I have for you a first-class bride."

"Leave me in peace concerning this subject," Leo pretended lack of interest.

"The world will dance at your wedding."

"Please, Mr. Salzman, no more."

"But first must come back my strength," Salzman said weakly. He fumbled with the portfolio straps and took out of the leather case an oily paper bag, from which he extracted a hard, seeded roll and a small, smoked white fish. With a quick motion of his hand he stripped the fish out of its skin and began <u>ravenously</u> to chew. "All day in a rush," he muttered.

Leo watched him eat.

"A sliced tomato you have maybe?" Salzman hesitantly inquired.

"No."

The marriage broker shut his eyes and ate. When he had finished he carefully cleaned up the crumbs and rolled up the remains of the fish, in the paper bag. His spectacled eyes roamed the room until he discovered, amid some piles of books, a one-burner gas stove. Lifting his hat he humbly asked, "A glass tea you got, rabbi?"

Conscience-stricken, Leo rose and brewed the tea. He served it with a chunk of lemon and two cubes of lump sugar, delighting Salzman.

After he had drunk his tea, Salzman's strength and good spirits were restored.

"So tell me, rabbi," he said amiably, "you considered some more the three clients I mentioned yesterday?"

"There was no need to consider."

"Why not?"

"None of them suits me."

"What then suits you?"

Leo let it pass because he could give only a confused answer.

Without waiting for a reply, Salzman asked, "You remember this girl I talked to you—the high school teacher?"

"Age thirty-two?"

But, surprisingly, Salzman's face lit in a smile. "Age twenty-nine."

Leo shot him a look. "Reduced from thirty-two?"

> What information about Lily H. does Salzman revise?

"A mistake," Salzman <u>avowed</u>. "I talked today with the dentist. He took me to his safety deposit box and showed me the birth certificate. She was twenty-nine years last August. They made her a party in the mountains where she went for her vacation. When her father spoke to me the first time I forgot to write the age and I told you thirty-two, but now I remember this was a different client, a widow."

"The same one you told me about? I thought she was twenty-four?"

"A different. Am I responsible that the world is filled with widows?"

"No, but I'm not interested in them, nor for that matter, in school teachers."

Salzman pulled his clasped hands to his breast. Looking at the ceiling he devoutly exclaimed, "Yiddishe kinder,[5] what can I say to somebody that he is not interested in high

---

5. **Yiddishe kinder.** Jewish children (Yiddish); Salzman is both calling Leo a child and lamenting the loss of the more traditional values Leo's parents' generation held.

---

WORDS FOR EVERYDAY USE

**rav • e • nous • ly** (rav´ ə nəs lē) *adv.*, in a greedy or wildly hungry manner. *After reading* Emma, *Sheila* <u>ravenously</u> *devoured the rest of Jane Austen's novels.*

**a • vow** (ə vou´) *vt.*, admit frankly. *"I made a mistake," Frank* <u>avowed</u> *after he was caught cheating on a test.*

school teachers? So what then you are interested?"

Leo flushed but controlled himself.

"In what else will you be interested," Salzman went on, "if you not interested in this fine girl that she speaks four languages and has personally in the bank ten thousand dollars? Also her father guarantees further twelve thousand. Also she has a new car, wonderful clothes, talks on all subjects, and she will give you a first-class home and children. How near do we come in our life to paradise?"

"If she's so wonderful, why wasn't she married ten years ago?"

"Why?" said Salzman with a heavy laugh. "—Why? Because she is *partikiler*.[6] This is why. She wants the *best*."

Leo was silent, amused at how he had entangled himself. But Salzman had aroused his interest in Lily H., and he began seriously to consider calling on her. When the marriage broker observed how intently Leo's mind was at work on the facts he had supplied, he felt certain they would soon come to an agreement.

Late Saturday afternoon, conscious of Salzman, Leo Finkle walked with Lily Hirschorn along Riverside Drive. He walked briskly and erectly, wearing with distinction the black fedora he had that morning taken with <u>trepidation</u> out of the dusty hat box on his closet shelf, and the heavy black Saturday coat he had thoroughly whisked clean. Leo also owned a walking stick, a present from a distant relative, but quickly put temptation aside and did not use it. Lily, petite and not unpretty, had on something signifying the approach of spring. She was au courant,[7] animatedly, with all sorts of subjects, and he weighed her words and found her surprisingly sound—score another for Salzman, whom he uneasily sensed to be somewhere around, hiding perhaps high in a tree along the street, flashing the lady signals with a pocket mirror; or perhaps a cloven-hoofed Pan,[8] piping <u>nuptial</u> ditties as he danced his invisible way before them, strewing wild buds on the walk and purple grapes in their path, symbolizing fruit of a union, though there was of course still none.

Lily startled Leo by remarking, "I was thinking of Mr. Salzman, a curious figure, wouldn't you say?"

Not certain what to answer, he nodded.

She bravely went on, blushing, "I for one am grateful for his introducing us. Aren't you?"

He courteously replied, "I am."

"I mean," she said with a little laugh—and it was all in good taste, or at least gave the effect of being not in bad—"do you mind that we came together so?"

He was not displeased with her honesty, recognizing that she meant to set the relationship aright, and understanding that it took a certain amount of experience in life, and courage, to want to do it quite that way. One had to have some sort of past to make that kind of beginning.

He said that he did not mind. Salzman's function was traditional and honorable—valuable for what it might achieve, which, he pointed out, was frequently nothing.

Lily agreed with a sigh. They walked on for a while and she said after a long silence, again with a nervous laugh, "Would you mind if I asked you something a little bit personal? Frankly, I find

---

6. *partikiler.* Particular; having high standards
7. **au courant.** In keeping with the times; up-to-date (French)
8. **Pan.** Greek god of fields, forests, wild animals, flocks, and shepherds, represented as a man with the legs of a goat who plays a flutelike instrument

**Words For Everyday Use**

**trep • i • da • tion** (trep´ ə dā´shən) *n.*, anxiety; nervousness. *How many people do you know who face the unknown with a vague but insistent <u>trepidation</u>?*

**nup • tial** (nup´ shəl) *adj.*, concerning marriage or a wedding. *Some of Shakespeare's comedies end in <u>nuptial</u> plans.*

the subject fascinating." Although Leo shrugged, she went on half embarrassedly, "How was it that you came to your calling? I mean was it a sudden passionate inspiration?"

> What does Lily Hirschorn want to know about Leo?

Leo, after a time, slowly replied, "I was always interested in the Law."

"You saw revealed in it the presence of the Highest?"

He nodded and changed the subject. "I understand that you spent a little time in Paris, Miss Hirschorn?"

"Oh, did Mr. Salzman tell you, Rabbi Finkle?" Leo winced but she went on, "It was ages ago and almost forgotten. I remember I had to return for my sister's wedding."

And Lily would not be put off. "When," she asked in a trembly voice, "did you become enamored of God?"

He stared at her. Then it came to him that she was talking not about Leo Finkle, but of a total stranger, some mystical figure, perhaps even passionate prophet that Salzman had dreamed up

> What does Leo realize Salzman has done in his interview with Lily Hirschorn?

for her—no relation to the living or dead. Leo trembled with rage and weakness. The trickster had obviously sold her a bill of goods, just as he had him, who'd expected to become acquainted with a young lady of twenty-nine, only to behold, the moment he laid eyes upon her strained and anxious face, a woman past thirty-five and aging rapidly. Only his self control had kept him this long in her presence.

"I am not," he said gravely, "a talented religious person," and in seeking words to go on, found himself possessed by shame and fear. "I think," he said in a strained manner, "that I came to God not because I loved Him, but because I did not."

This confession he spoke harshly because its unexpectedness shook him.

Lily wilted. Leo saw a profusion of loaves of bread go flying like ducks high over his head, not

> What confession on the part of Leo makes Lily "wilt"?

unlike the winged loaves by which he had counted himself to sleep last night. Mercifully, then, it snowed, which he would not put past Salzman's machinations.

He was infuriated with the marriage broker and swore he would throw him out of the room the minute he reappeared. But Salzman did not come that night, and when Leo's anger had subsided, an unaccountable despair grew in its place. At first he thought this was caused by his disappointment in Lily, but before long it became evident that he had involved himself with Salzman without a true knowledge of his own intent. He gradually realized—with an emptiness that seized him with six hands— that he had called in the broker to find him a bride because he was incapable

> What does Leo realize about himself?

of doing it himself. This terrifying insight he had derived as a result of his meeting and conversation with Lily Hirschorn. Her probing questions had somehow irritated him into revealing—to himself more than her—the true nature of his relationship to God, and from that it had come upon him, with shocking force, that apart from his parents, he had never loved anyone. Or perhaps it went the other way, that he did not love God so well as he might, because he had not loved man. It seemed to Leo that his whole life stood starkly revealed and he saw himself for the first time as he

> Upon reflection, how does Leo begin to view himself?

---

**WORDS FOR EVERYDAY USE**

**pro • fu • sion** (prō fyü´ zhən) *n.*, large number; abundance. *The dandelions grew in such* profusion *in the Kelters' front lawn that their lawn appeared yellow, not green.*

**mach • i • na • tion** (mak ə nā´ shən) *n.*, clever plot or scheme. *Machiavelli wrote persuasively about the art of political* machination *in The Prince.*

truly was—unloved and loveless. This bitter but somehow not fully unexpected revelation brought him to a point of panic, controlled only by extraordinary effort. He covered his face with his hands and cried.

The week that followed was the worst of his life. He did not eat and lost weight. His beard darkened and grew ragged. He stopped attending seminars and almost never opened a book. He seriously considering leaving the Yeshiva, although he was deeply troubled at the thought of the loss of all his years of study—saw them like pages torn from a book, strewn over the city—and at the devastating effect of this decision upon his parents. But he had lived without knowledge of himself, and never in the Five Books[9] and all the Commentaries—mea culpa[10]—had the truth been revealed to him. He did not know where to turn, and in all this desolating loneliness there was no *to whom*, although he often thought of Lily but not once could bring himself to go downstairs and make the call. He became touchy and irritable, especially with his landlady, who asked him all manner of personal questions; on the other hand, sensing his own disagreeableness, he waylaid her on the stairs and apologized <u>abjectly</u>, until mortified, she ran from him. Out of this, however, he drew the consolation that he was a Jew and that a Jew suffered. But gradually, as the long and terrible week drew to a close, he regained his composure and some idea of purpose in life: to go on as planned. Although he was imperfect, the ideal was not. As for his quest of a bride, the thought of continuing afflicted him with anxiety and heartburn, yet perhaps with this new knowledge of himself he would be more successful than in the past. Perhaps love would now come to him and a bride to

that love. And for this sanctified seeking who needed a Salzman?

The marriage broker, a skeleton with haunted eyes, returned that very night. He looked, withal, the picture of frustrated expectancy—as if he had steadfastly waited the week at Miss Lily Hirschorn's side for a telephone call that never came.

Casually coughing, Salzman came immediately to the point: "So how did you like her?"

Leo's anger rose and he could not refrain from chiding the matchmaker: "Why did you lie to me, Salzman?"

Salzman's pale face went dead white, the world had snowed on him.

"Did you not state that she was twenty-nine?" Leo insisted.

"I gave you my word—"

"She was thirty-five, if a day. *At least thirty-five.*"

"Of this don't be too sure. Her father told me—"

"Never mind. The worst of it was that you lied to her."

"How did I lie to her, tell me?"

"You told her things about me that weren't true. You made me out to be more, consequently less than I am. She had in mind a totally different person, a sort of semimystical Wonder Rabbi."

"All I said, you was a religious man."

"I can imagine."

Salzman sighed. "This is my weakness that I have," he confessed. "My wife says to me I shouldn't be a salesman, but when I have two fine people that they would be wonderful to be married, I am so happy that I talk too much."

---

9. **Five Books.** The Pentateuch, or Five Books of Moses, consists of Genesis, Exodus, Leviticus, Numbers, and Deuteronomy.
10. **mea culpa.** I am to blame (Latin)

---

**WORDS FOR EVERYDAY USE**

ab • ject • ly (ab´ jekt´ lē) *adv.,* miserably; in a manner that shows utter hopelessness or resignation. *The homeless man, standing <u>abjectly</u> at the intersection, held a sign begging for money.*

He smiled wanly. "This is why Salzman is a poor man."

Leo's anger left him. "Well, Salzman, I'm afraid that's all."

The marriage broker fastened hungry eyes on him.

"You don't want any more a bride?"

"I do," said Leo, "but I have decided to seek her in a different way. I am no longer interested in an arranged marriage. To be frank, I now admit the necessity of premarital love. That is, I want to be in love with the one I marry."

> **"Love, I have said to myself, should be a by-product of living and worship rather than its own end."**

"Love?" said Salzman, astounded. After a moment he remarked, "For us, our love is our life, not for the ladies. In the ghetto they—"

"I know, I know," said Leo. "I've thought of it often. Love, I have said to myself, should be a by-product of living and worship rather than its own end. Yet for myself I find it necessary to establish the level of my need and fulfill it."

Salzman shrugged but answered, "Listen, rabbi, if you want love, this I can find for you also. I have such beautiful clients that you will love them the minute your eyes will see them."

Leo smiled unhappily. "I'm afraid you don't understand."

But Salzman hastily unstrapped his portfolio and withdrew a manila packet from it.

"Pictures," he said, quickly laying the envelope on the table.

What does Salzman bring on this visit?

Leo called after him to take the pictures away, but as if on the wings of the wind, Salzman had disappeared.

March came. Leo had returned to his regular routine. Although he felt not quite himself yet—lacked energy—he was making plans for a more active social life. Of course it would cost something, but he was an expert in cutting corners; and when there were no corners left he would make circles rounder. All the while Salzman's pictures had lain on the table, gathering dust. Occasionally as Leo sat studying, or enjoying a cup of tea, his eyes fell on the manila envelope, but he never opened it.

The days went by and no social life to speak of developed with a member of the opposite sex—it was difficult, given the circumstances of his situation. One morning Leo toiled up the stairs to his room and stared out the window at the city. Although the day was bright his view of it was dark. For some time he watched people in the street below hurrying along and then turned with a heavy heart to his little room. On the table was the packet. With a sudden <u>relentless</u> gesture he tore it open. For a half-hour he stood by the table in a state of excitement, examining the photographs of the ladies Salzman had included. Finally, with a deep sigh he put them down. There were six, of varying degrees of attractiveness, but look at them long enough and they all became Lily Hirschorn: all past their prime, all starved behind bright smiles, not a true personality in the lot. Life, despite their frantic yoohooings, had passed them by; they were pictures in a briefcase that stank of fish. After a while, however, as Leo attempted to

---

**WORDS FOR EVERYDAY USE**

**re • lent • less** (ri lent´ləs) *adj.*, harsh; pitiless. *Tony's parents' <u>relentless</u> questioning about the accident forced him to admit his friend was driving their car.*

return the photographs into the envelope, he found in it another, a snapshot of the type taken by a machine for a quarter. He gazed at it a moment and let out a cry.

Her face deeply moved him. Why, he could at first not say. It gave him the impression of youth—spring flowers, yet age—a sense of having been used to the bone, wasted; this came from the eyes, which were hauntingly familiar yet absolutely strange. He had a vivid impression that he had met her before, but try as he might he could not place her although he could almost recall her name, as if he had read it in her own handwriting. No, this couldn't be; he would have remembered her. It was not, he affirmed, that she had an extraordinary beauty—no, though her face was attractive enough; it was that *something* about her moved him. Feature for feature, even some of the ladies of the photographs could do better; but she leaped forth to his heart—had *lived*, or wanted to—more than just wanted, perhaps regretted how she had lived—had somehow deeply suffered: it could be seen in the depths of those reluctant eyes, and from the way the light enclosed and shone from her, and within her, opening realms of possibility: this was her own. Her he desired. His head ached and eyes narrowed with the intensity of his gazing, then as if an obscure fog had blown up in the mind, he experienced fear of her and was aware that he had received an impression, somehow, of evil. He shuddered, saying softly, it is thus with us all. Leo brewed some tea in a small pot and sat sipping it without sugar, to calm himself. But before he had finished drinking, again with excitement he examined the face and found it good: good for Leo Finkle. Only such a one could understand him and help him seek whatever he was seeking. She might, perhaps, love him. How she had happened to be among the discards in Salzman's barrel he could never guess, but he knew he must urgently go find her.

Where is Leo going?

Leo rushed downstairs, grabbed up the Bronx telephone book, and searched for Salzman's home address. He was not listed, nor was his office. Neither was he in the Manhattan book. But Leo remembered having written down the address on a slip of paper after he had read Salzman's advertisement in the "personals" column of the *Forward*. He ran up to his room and tore through his papers, without luck. It was <u>exasperating</u>. Just when he needed the matchmaker he was nowhere to be found. Fortunately Leo remembered to look in his wallet. There on a card he found his name written and a Bronx address. No phone number was listed, the reason—Leo now recalled—he had originally communicated with Salzman by letter. He got on his coat, put a hat on over his skull cap and hurried to the subway station. All the way to the far end of the Bronx he sat on the edge of his seat. He was more than once tempted to take out the picture and see if the girl's face was as he remembered it, but he <u>refrained</u>, allowing the snapshot to remain in his inside coat pocket, content to have her so close. When the train pulled into the station he was waiting at the door and bolted out. He quickly located the street Salzman had advertised.

The building he sought was less than a block from the subway, but it was not an office building, nor even a loft, nor a store in which one could rent office space. It was a very old tenement house. Leo found Salzman's name in pencil on a soiled tag under the bell and climbed three dark flights to his apartment. When he knocked, the door was opened by a

---

**WORDS FOR EVERYDAY USE**

**ex • as • per • at • ing** (eg zas´pər āt iŋ) *adj.*, irritating; annoying. *"It's <u>exasperating</u> training this puppy," thought Darla.*

**re • frain** (ri frān´) *vi.*, hold back; keep oneself from doing something. *While observing Ramadan, practicing Muslims <u>refrain</u> from eating during daylight hours.*

thin, asthmatic, gray-haired woman, in felt slippers.

"Yes?" she said, expecting nothing. She listened without listening. He could have sworn he had seen her, too, before but knew it was an illusion.

"Salzman—does he live here? Pinye Salzman," he said, "the matchmaker?"

She stared at him a long minute. "Of course."

He felt embarrassed. "Is he in?"

"No." Her mouth, though left open, offered nothing more.

"The matter is urgent. Can you tell me where his office is?"

"In the air." She pointed upward.

"You mean he has no office?" Leo asked.

"In his socks."

He peered into the apartment. It was sunless and dingy, one large room divided by a half-open curtain, beyond which he could see a sagging metal bed. The near side of a room was crowded with rickety chairs, old bureaus, a three-legged table, racks of cooking utensils, and all the <u>apparatus</u> of a kitchen. But there was no sign of Salzman or his magic barrel, probably also a figment of the imagination. An odor of frying fish made Leo weak to the knees.

"Where is he?" he insisted. "I've got to see your husband."

At length she answered, "So who knows where he is? Every time he thinks a new thought he runs to a different place. Go home, he will find you."

"Tell him Leo Finkle."

She gave no sign she had heard.

He walked downstairs, depressed.

But Salzman, breathless, stood waiting at his door.

Leo was astounded and overjoyed. "How did you get here before me?"

"I rushed."

"Come inside."

They entered. Leo fixed tea, and a sardine sandwich for Salzman. As they were drinking he reached behind him for the packet of pictures and handed them to the marriage broker.

Salzman put down his glass and said expectantly, "You found somebody you like?"

"Not among these."

The marriage broker turned away.

"Here is the one I want." Leo held forth the snapshot.

Salzman slipped on his glasses and took the picture into his trembling hand. He turned ghastly and let out a groan.

"What's the matter?" cried Leo.

"Excuse me. Was an accident this picture. She isn't for you."

Salzman frantically shoved the manila packet into his portfolio. He thrust the snapshot into his pocket and fled down the stairs.

Leo, after momentary paralysis, gave chase and cornered the marriage broker in the <u>vestibule</u>. The landlady made hysterical outcries but neither of them listened.

"Give me back the picture, Salzman."

"No." The pain in his eyes was terrible.

"Tell me who she is then."

"This I can't tell you. Excuse me."

He made to depart, but Leo, forgetting himself, seized the matchmaker by his tight coat and shook him frenziedly.

"Please," sighed Salzman. "*Please.*"

Leo ashamedly let him go. "Tell me who she is," he begged. "It's very important for me to know."

"She is not for you. She is a wild one—wild, without shame. This is not a bride for a rabbi."

**WORDS FOR EVERYDAY USE**

ap • pa • ra • tus (ap´ə rat´əs) *n.*, materials and tools needed for a specific purpose. *Rube Goldberg was a cartoonist famous for designing comically complex <u>apparatuses</u>.*

ves • ti • bule (ves´tə byül´) *n.*, hallway or small room at the entrance of a building. *The umbrella stand was located in the <u>vestibule</u> of the apartment.*

"What do you mean wild?"

"Like an animal. Like a dog. For her to be poor was a sin. This is why to me she is dead now."

"In God's name, what do you mean?"

"Her I can't introduce to you," Salzman said.

"Why are you so excited?"

"Why, he asks," Salzman said, bursting into tears. "This is my baby, my Stella, she should burn in hell."

Leo hurried up to bed and hid under the covers. Under the covers he thought his life through. Although he soon fell asleep he could not sleep her out of his mind. He woke, beating his breast. Though he prayed to be rid of her, his prayers went unanswered. Through days of torment he endlessly struggled not to love her; fearing success, he escaped it. He then concluded to convert her to goodness, himself to God. The idea alternately nauseated and exalted him.

He perhaps did not know that he had come to a final decision until he encountered Salzman in a Broadway cafeteria. He was sitting alone at a rear table, sucking the bony remains of a fish. The marriage broker appeared <u>haggard</u>, and transparent to the point of vanishing.

Salzman looked up at first without recognizing him. Leo had grown a pointed beard and his eyes were weighted with wisdom.

"Salzman," he said, "love has at last come to my heart."

"Who can love from a picture?" mocked the marriage broker.

Who is the young woman that Leo likes from the picture?

"It is not impossible."

"If you can love her, then you can love anybody. Let me show you some new clients that they just sent me their photographs. One is a little doll."

"Just her I want," Leo murmured.

"Don't be a fool, doctor. Don't bother with her."

"Put me in touch with her, Salzman," Leo said humbly. "Perhaps I can be of service."

Salzman had stopped eating and Leo understood with emotion that it was now arranged.

Leaving the cafeteria, he was, however, afflicted by a tormenting suspicion that Salzman had planned it all to happen this way.

What suspicion does Leo have after Salzman agrees to let him meet Stella?

Leo was informed by letter that she would meet him on a certain corner, and she was there one spring night, waiting under a street lamp. He appeared, carrying a small bouquet of violets and rosebuds. Stella stood by the lamppost, smoking. She wore white with red shoes, which fitted his expectations, although in a troubled moment he had imagined the dress red, and only the shoes white. She waited uneasily and shyly. From afar he saw that her eyes—clearly her father's—were filled with desperate innocence. He pictured, in her, his own redemption. Violins and lit candles revolved in the sky. Leo ran forward with flowers outthrust.

Around the corner, Salzman, leaning against a wall, chanted prayers for the dead. ∎

What does Leo see in Stella?

WORDS FOR EVERYDAY USE

**hag • gard** (hag´ərd) *adj.,* having a wasted or exhausted look. *Elwood looked <u>haggard</u> after working a double shift.*

"THE MAGIC BARREL"   821

Imagine you are Leo Finkle. What feelings do you have as you approach Stella under the lamppost?

# INVESTIGATE *Inquire, Imagine*

**Recall:** GATHERING FACTS

1a. What kind of services does Pinye Salzman sell? What is the nature of Leo Finkle's business with Pinye Salzman?

2a. Who are the women Salzman initially suggests as potential brides? What characteristics do they have? Which one does Finkle actually meet?

3a. What does Finkle find in the photographs Salzman leaves behind? What impact does one of the photographs have on him?

**Interpret:** FINDING MEANING

1b. Why does Leo Finkle think he needs a bride?

2b. How does Finkle feel about Salzman after talking to Lily Hirschorn?

3b. The photograph Finkle finds touches important emotions inside him. What are these feelings? What elements in the photograph contribute to the effect?

**Analyze:** TAKING THINGS APART

4a. Identify the thoughts that lead to Leo's emotional crisis and inability to study for a week.

**Synthesize:** BRINGING THINGS TOGETHER

4b. Does Stella appear to be the woman in whom Leo can find his own redemption?

**Evaluate:** MAKING JUDGMENTS

5a. Do you think Salzman's ultimate intent is to keep Stella from Leo or to bring them together intentionally? Support your answer with examples from the story.

**Extend:** CONNECTING IDEAS

5b. Research the matchmaking traditions of another culture, such as the "picture brides" of Japan in the early twentieth century. Then write a paragraph comparing and contrasting that culture's tradition with the Jewish matchmaking tradition described in "The Magic Barrel." Which tradition seems the more humane and workable to you? What do you think is the most effective way to meet a proper mate?

# Understanding *Literature*

**MOTIVATION.** Review the definition for **motivation** in the Handbook of Literary Terms. How do Leo Finkle's motivations change as the story progresses?

**ANTIHERO.** Review the definition for **antihero** in the Handbook of Literary Terms and the cluster chart you made for Literary Tools on page 808. What characteristics of an antihero does Finkle possess? Which is his worst flaw? Why?

# ꟽRITER'S JOURNAL

1. Imagine that you are twenty-seven, the same age as Leo Finkle, and you have not yet found a mate. Write a **personals ad** describing yourself, the qualities you have to offer, and what you are looking for in a prospective mate.

2. Imagine that you are Pinye Salzman. Write a **letter** to your daughter, Stella, telling her what you think of her and describing the man you would like her to meet.

3. Write a **paragraph** or two describing what Leo Finkle's life is like two years after the story ends.

# Integrating the LANGUAGE ARTS

## Language, Grammar, and Style

**DIALECT.** Dialect is a version of a language spoken by the people of a particular place, time, or social group. The use of dialect helps writers create vivid characters by placing those characters in a social, temporal, or geographic context. Salzman frequently speaks in grammatically incorrect English, employing Yiddish (a form of dialect spoken by Jewish people) phrases, such as *Yiddishe kinder*. While Salzman's English follows the grammatical rules of Yiddish, Leo's English is more standard, emphasizing the fact that Salzman is more closely connected to traditional Jewish culture. Put the following sentences spoken by Salzman into standard English, correcting grammar and syntax. Before you begin, read the Language Arts Survey 3.5, "Dialects of English."

1. "You wouldn't believe me how much cards I got in my office."

2. "Let me call the father tonight and you will see what means pretty."

3. "Of course, she is a little lame on her right foot from an auto accident that it happened to her when she was twelve years, but nobody notices on account she is so brilliant and also beautiful."

4. "Rabbi, I got for you tonight good news."

5. "A glass tea you got, rabbi?"

## Study and Research

**JEWISH TRADITIONS.** Research a Jewish tradition other than matchmaking. Then prepare an oral presentation to give to a small group or the class. You might want to include visuals in your presentation. Consult your librarian or card catalog for possible topics. Before your visit to the library, you may want to review the Language Arts Survey 5.19, "How to Locate Library Materials."

## Media Literacy

**WRITING THESIS STATEMENTS.** Using the Internet, find some reviews or criticism of Bernard Malamud's work and read them. Then write thesis statements for four compositions you could develop about Malamud's fiction. Before you begin writing, you may want to review the Language Arts Survey 2.25, "Writing a Thesis Statement."

## Literary TOOLS

**AIM.** A writer's **aim** is his or her purpose, or goal. People may write with the following aims: to inform (expository/informational writing); to tell a story, either true or invented, about an event or sequence of events (narrative writing); to reflect (personal/expressive writing; to share a perspective by using an artistic medium, such as fiction or poetry, to entertain, enrich, or enlighten (imaginative writing); to persuade readers or listeners to respond in some way, such as to agree with a position, change a view on an issue, reach an agreement, or perform an action (persuasive/argumentative writing). As you read, determine what the author's aim is.

**AUTOBIOGRAPHY.** An **autobiography** is the story of a person's life, written by that person. As you read, decide what the autobiography reveals about the author's character.

## Reader's Journal

What story has made you want to read more by a certain author?

# from *Black Boy*

BY RICHARD WRIGHT

## About the AUTHOR

**Richard Wright** (1908–1960), novelist, short story writer, poet, and essayist, was born on a farm near Natchez, Mississippi. He had a difficult childhood of poverty, emotional neglect, and frequent relocations. His father abandoned the family in 1914 and, for a time, Wright and his brother stayed in an orphanage. His mother, frequently ill, was forced to depend on relatives. Wright read widely, getting books from Memphis's "whites only" public library by forging a note from a white patron. In 1925, he graduated as valedictorian of his high school class in Jackson.

After moving to Chicago, Wright found work with the Federal Writers' Project and joined a Communist literary society. His concern with the social roots of racial oppression led him to join the Communist Party in 1932. In 1937 Wright moved to New York to become Harlem editor of the *Daily Worker. Uncle Tom's Children*, a collection of short stories published in 1938, portrays the oppression of African Americans in the South. With the financial support of a Guggenheim Fellowship, Wright completed *Native Son* (1940), one of the first best-sellers written by an African-American author.

## About the SELECTION

Wright's autobiography, ***Black Boy,*** published in 1945, is considered by many critics to be his most important work. According to Ralph Ellison, the autobiography "is filled with blues-tempered echoes of railroad trains, the names of Southern towns and cities, estrangements, fights and flights, deaths and disappointments, charged with physical and spiritual hungers and pain." *Black Boy* was originally seen as primarily an attack on Southern white supremacist society, but later critics described it as the development of a young writer's sensibility, in which race was only a factor. In the following selection, Wright seeks refuge in fiction, much to the dismay of his grandmother.

from
# Black Boy

RICHARD WRIGHT

## ArtNote

**Black Ghetto**, c.1968–1970. David C.
Driskell. Fisk University, Nashville, Tennessee.

David C. Driskell (b.1931) said of this painting: "The composition is an autobiographical reflection of my own childhood, one in which I look out into the larger world from beyond my narrowly confined abode. . . . The figure of the young boy is all but hemmed in and orderly, contained by the rectangular format of the painting." How does this compare to Richard Wright's experiences as a child?

To help support the household my grandmother boarded a colored schoolteacher, Ella, a young woman with so remote and dreamy and silent a manner that I was as much afraid of her as I was attracted to her. I had long wanted to ask her to tell me about the books that she was always reading, but could never

> What did Wright's grandmother do to help support the household?

quite <u>summon</u> enough courage to do so. One afternoon I found her sitting alone upon the front porch reading.

"Ella," I begged, "please tell me what you are reading."

"It's just a book," she said <u>evasively</u>, looking about with <u>apprehension</u>.

"But what's it about?" I asked.

"Your grandmother wouldn't like it if I talked to you about novels," she told me.

What is Ella reading on the front porch?

I detected a note of sympathy in her voice.

"I don't care," I said loudly and bravely.

"Shhh—You mustn't say things like that," she said.

"But I want to know."

"When you grow up, you'll read books and know what's in them," she explained.

"But I want to know now."

She thought a while, then closed the book.

"Come here," she said.

I sat at her feet and lifted my face to hers.

"Once upon a time there was an old, old man named Bluebeard," she began in a low voice.

She whispered to me the story of *Bluebeard and His Seven Wives* and I ceased to see the porch, the sunshine, her face, every-thing. As her words fell upon my new ears, I <u>endowed</u> them with a reality that welled up from somewhere within me. She told how Bluebeard had <u>duped</u> and married his seven wives, how he had loved and slain them, how he had hanged them up by their hair in a dark closet. The tale made the world

What story does Ella tell Wright?

What effect does the story have on Wright?

around me be, throb, live. As she spoke, reality changed, the look of things altered, and the world became peopled with magical presences. My sense of life deepened and the feel of things was different, somehow. Enchanted and <u>enthralled</u>, I stopped her constantly to ask for details. My imagination blazed. The sensations the story aroused in me were never to leave me. When she was about to finish, when my inter-est was keenest, when I was lost to the world around me, Granny stepped briskly onto the porch.

"You stop that, you evil gal!" she shouted. "I want none of that Devil stuff in my house!"

How does Wright's grandmother react to the storytelling?

Her voice jarred me so that I gasped. For a moment I did not know what was happening.

"I'm sorry, Mrs. Wilson," Ella stammered, rising. "But he asked me—"

"He's just a foolish child and you know it!" Granny blazed.

Ella bowed her head and went into the house.

"But, Granny, she didn't finish," I protested, knowing that I should have kept quiet.

She bared her teeth and slapped me across my mouth with the back of her hand.

"You shut your mouth," she hissed. "You don't know what you're talking about!"

"But I want to hear what happened!" I wailed, dodging another blow that I thought was coming.

"That's the Devil's work!" she shouted.

My grandmother was as nearly white as a Negro can get without being white, which means that she was white. The sagging flesh of her face quivered; her eyes, large, dark, deep-

---

**WORDS FOR EVERYDAY USE**

**sum • mon** (sə′ mən) *vt.*, call forth. *The host <u>summoned</u> the bingo winners to come to the front of the hall.*

**eva • sive • ly** (i vā′ siv lē) *adv.*, in a manner intended to evade. *"I was resting," the defendant answered <u>evasively</u> when questioned about his whereabouts.*

**ap • pre • hen • sion** (a pri hen[t]′ shən) *n.*, suspicion or fear. *With <u>apprehension</u> Nigel took his place at the podium.*

**en • dow** (in dou′) *vt.*, provide with something freely or naturally. *I <u>endowed</u> my description of summer camp with humor.*

**dupe** (düp) *vt.*, deceive by underhanded means. *Bridget <u>duped</u> her brother into lending her his car by saying a friend was in the hospital.*

**en • thralled** (in thrôld′) *adj.*, held spellbound. *<u>Enthralled</u>, the spectators never took their eyes off the magician.*

set, wide apart, glared at me. Her lips narrowed to a line. Her high forehead wrinkled. When she was angry her eyelids drooped halfway down over her pupils, giving her a baleful aspect.

"But I liked the story," I told her.

"You're going to burn in hell," she said with such furious conviction that for a moment I believed her.

Not to know the end of the tale filled me with a sense of emptiness, loss. I hungered for the sharp, frightening, breathtaking, almost painful excitement that the story had given me, and I vowed that as soon as I was old enough I would buy all the novels there were and read them to feed that thirst for violence that was in me, for intrigue, for plotting, for secrecy, for bloody murders. So profoundly responsive a chord had the tale struck in me that the threats of my mother and grandmother had no effect whatsoever. They read my insistence as mere obstinacy, as foolishness, something that would quickly pass; and they had no notion how desperately serious the tale had made me. They could not have known that Ella's whispered story of deception and murder had been the first experience in my life that had elicited from me a total emotional response. No words or punishment could have possibly made me doubt. I had tasted what to me was life, and I would have more of it, somehow someway. I realized that they could not understand what I was feeling and I kept quiet. But when no one was looking I would slip into Ella's room and steal a book and take it back of the barn and try to read it. Usually I could not decipher enough words to make the story have meaning. I burned to learn to read novels and I tortured my mother into telling me the meaning of every strange word I saw, not because the word itself had any value, but because it was the gateway to a forbidden and enchanting land. ∎

> *What does Wright vow?*

> *Why does Wright ask his mother the meaning of every strange word he sees?*

> I had tasted what to me was life, and I would have more of it, somehow someway.

| WORDS FOR EVERYDAY USE | |
|---|---|
| | **bale • ful** (bā[ə]l′ fəl) *adj.,* sinister. *The actor's baleful look told the audience that his character was turning into Mr. Hyde.* |
| | **in • trigue** (in trēg′) *n.,* secret scheme. *Brad could not keep the intrigue at the bank quiet.* |
| | **de • cep • tion** (di sep′ shən) *n.,* the act of misleading by a false appearance or statement. *Mrs. Burchard's deception about her real age fooled the neighborhood.* |
| | **elic • it** (i li′ sət) *vt.,* draw forth or bring out. *Dad elicited the support of the neighbors for a neighborhood watch program.* |
| | **de • ci • pher** (dē sī′ fər) *vt.,* make out the meaning of. *Scotland Yard deciphered the spy's message.* |

## Respond *to the* SELECTION

Wright says that hearing the story of Bluebeard was the first experience in his life that had elicited a "total emotional response." At what time in your life have you experienced a total emotional response?

# INVESTIGATE *Inquire Imagine*

**Recall:** GATHERING FACTS

1a. What kind of manner did Ella have?

2a. What did Wright want Ella to do?

3a. Who interrupted the story? Why?

➤ **Interpret:** FINDING MEANING

1b. What fascinated Wright about Ella?

2b. What enabled Wright to imagine so vividly the story Ella told him?

3b. What kinds of stories do you think the grandmother would have permitted?

---

**Analyze:** TAKING THINGS APART

4a. Identify evidence from Wright's childhood that suggested he would grow up to be a writer.

➤ **Synthesize:** BRINGING THINGS TOGETHER

4b. Why didn't the threats of Wright's grandmother and mother have any effect on him whatsoever?

---

**Perspective:** LOOKING AT OTHER VIEWS

5a. Imagine you are Wright's grandmother. Describe your feelings when you catch Ella telling your grandson a story. What are you afraid of? From what do you want to protect your grandson? What kind of man do you want him to grow up to be?

➤ **Empathy:** SEEING FROM INSIDE

5b. When no one was looking, Wright slipped into Ella's room and stole a book in order to try to read it. Was Wright's behavior understandable? Why, or why not? If you had been Wright, what other ways would you have found to explore the world of fiction?

---

# Understanding *Literature*

**AIM.** Review the definition of **aim** in the Handbook of Literary Terms. What is Wright's aim in writing *Black Boy?* Give examples from the selection that support your answer.

**AUTOBIOGRAPHY.** Review the definition of **autobiography** in the Handbook of Literary Terms. Then make a chart. On the left, list quotes from the selection that reveal aspects of Wright's character. On the right, explain what you learned about Wright's character. One example has been done for you. Which of Wright's personality traits do you find the most compelling?

| Quotes | Wright's Character |
|---|---|
| "I don't care," I said loudly and bravely. | He was brave in being willing to risk his grandmother's disapproval. |

# WRITER'S JOURNAL

1. Imagine you are Wright. Write a **journal entry** explaining what hearing the story of *Bluebeard and His Seven Wives* meant to you.

2. Imagine you are Wright's grandmother. Write a **letter** to your grandson explaining why you consider fiction to be "the Devil's work." Tell him what you would prefer him to read.

3. Wright writes: ". . . I tortured my mother into telling me the meaning of every strange word I saw, not because the word itself had any value, but because it was the gateway to a forbidden and enchanting land." Write a **paragraph** hypothesizing (making an informed guess about) how Wright gained access to that land as he grew older.

# Integrating *the* LANGUAGE ARTS

## Language, Grammar, and Style

**WORKING WITH NAMERS.** Read the Language Arts Survey 3.49–3.58. Then identify each namer in the following sentences and note whether it is a common noun, proper noun, or personal pronoun.

1. Richard Wright lived with his mother and grandmother.
2. The author was insistent that Ella tell him a story.
3. That he loved fiction was clear to Ella.
4. Learning the meanings of words became Wright's new passion.
5. To understand Ella's novels was his goal.

## Study and Research

**BIBLIOGRAPHY CARDS.** Read the Language Arts Survey 5.40, "Making Bibliographies and Bibliography Cards." Then find five of the following types of resources on the topic of Richard Wright and his work. Write one bibliography card for each resource. You may find a list of resources on the Internet at PBS Online's Richard Wright page: http://www.pbs.org/rwbb.

1. book with one author
2. book with an editor but no single author
3. selection from an anthology
4. introduction, preface, foreword, or afterword
5. encyclopedia entry

## Media Literacy

**RICHARD WRIGHT AND THE SOUTHERN EXPERIENCE.** Imagine that you are a high school English teacher designing a course on African-American literature and theater. Using the Internet, make a list of videos that you can use to teach your course and write a critique of each one. One site that you will find useful is California Newsreel at http://www.newsreel.org. For more information, see the Language Arts Survey 5.32, "How to Evaluate a Film."

## Literary T O O L S

**EFFECT.** The **effect** of a literary work is the general impression or emotional impact that it achieves. As you read, determine the effect this selection produces.

**IRONY.** Irony is a difference between appearance and reality. In *verbal irony,* a statement is made that implies its opposite. In *irony of situation,* an event occurs that violates the expectations of the characters, the reader, or the audience. As you read, make a chart. On the left list examples of irony in the selection. On the right describe which type of irony is being used. One example has been done for you.

| Examples of Irony | Type of Irony |
| --- | --- |
| Miss Sasaki is seriously injured when books, which are symbols of civilization, fall on her | irony of situation |

## Reader's *Journal*

When has something good or bad happened to you just because you varied your routine?

# "A Noiseless Flash" from *Hiroshima*   BY JOHN HERSEY

## About *the* A U T H O R

**John Hersey** (1914–1993), novelist, short story and nonfiction writer, was born in China to missionary parents. He graduated from Yale and the University of Cambridge, England, where he studied English literature. After serving as a private secretary for novelist Sinclair Lewis, Hersey became a journalist for *Time* and *Life* magazines, for which he covered World War II in both the Asian and European theaters. His first two books, *Men on Bataan* (1942) and *Into the Valley* (1943), are examples of skillful war reporting. His novel *A Bell for Adano* (1944) won the Pulitzer Prize. Set in an Italian village occupied by American troops during World War II, it reveals both his faith in humanity and his fears for the future of democracies threatened by ambitious and egotistic leaders.

With *Hiroshima* (1946), Hersey created a new genre that combined journalism and literature. According to Hersey, "Fiction is a clarifying agent. It makes truth plausible. . . . [A]mong all the means of communication now available, imaginative literature comes closer than any other to being able to give an impression of the truth." In *The Wall* (1950), Hersey employed the device of a fictitious personal diary to tell the story of the murder of 500,000 Polish Jews in Warsaw during World War II. Much of Hersey's fictional output is also historical and political. *The Conspiracy* (1972) uses an incident in ancient Roman history to explore the contemporary problems of political corruption and individual freedom.

## About *The* S E L E C T I O N

On August 6, 1945, the United States dropped an atomic bomb on the city of Hiroshima, Japan, in order to bring an end to World War II. The city was largely destroyed, and more than 70,000 people are believed to have been killed. Thousands more who survived the initial blast died of radiation sickness. **"A Noiseless Flash"** from *Hiroshima* portrays the story of six individuals who survived the atomic bombing of Hiroshima.

Combining literary techniques and the factual air of reporting to describe a real event, *Hiroshima* began what some critics call the genre of the "nonfiction novel." In 1946 it appeared in *The New Yorker,* which dedicated a whole issue to the book. *Hiroshima* has been called the most significant piece of journalism in modern times.

# A Noiseless Flash

## JOHN HERSEY

At exactly fifteen minutes past eight in the morning, on August 6, 1945, Japanese time, at the moment when the atomic bomb flashed above Hiroshima, Miss Toshiko Sasaki, a clerk in the personnel department of the East Asia Tin works, had just sat down at her place in the plant office and was turning her head to speak to the girl at the next desk. At that same moment, Dr. Masakazu Fujii was settling down cross-legged to read the Osaka *Asahi* on the porch of his private hospital, overhanging one of the seven deltaic[1] rivers which divide Hiroshima; Mrs. Hatsuyo Nakamura, a tailor's widow, stood by the window of her kitchen, watching a neighbor tearing down his house because it lay in the path of an air-raid-defense fire lane; Father Wilhelm Kleinsorge, a German priest of the Society of Jesus, reclined in his underwear on a cot on the top floor of his order's three-story mission house, reading a Jesuit magazine, *Stimmen der Zeit;*[2] Dr. Terufumi Sasaki, a young member of the surgical staff of the city's large, modern Red Cross Hospital, walked along one of the hospital corridors with a blood specimen for a Wassermann test[3] in his hand; and the Reverend Mr. Kiyoshi Tanimoto, pastor of the Hiroshima Methodist Church, paused at the door of a rich man's house in Koi, the city's western suburb, and prepared to unload a handcart full of things he had evacuated from town in fear of the massive B-29 raid which everyone expected Hiroshima to suffer. A hundred thousand people were killed by the atomic bomb, and these six were among the survivors. They still wonder why they lived when so many others died. Each of them counts many small items of chance or <u>volition</u>—a step taken in time, a decision to go indoors, catching one streetcar instead of the next—that spared him. And now each knows that in the act of survival he lived a dozen lives and saw more death than he ever thought he would see. At the time, none of them knew anything.

The Reverend Mr. Tanimoto got up at five o'clock that morning. He was alone in the parsonage,[4] because for some time his wife had been commuting with their year-old baby to spend nights with a friend in Ushida, a suburb

> What were the residents of Hiroshima expecting?

> How many people were killed by the atomic bomb?

> To what does each of the six credit his or her survival?

---

1. **deltaic.** Related to the triangular deposits at the mouth of a river
2. ***Stimmen der Zeit.*** German for "Voices of the Time"
3. **Wassermann test.** Blood test used to diagnose syphilis
4. **parsonage.** Home that a church provides for its pastor

WORDS FOR EVERYDAY USE

vo • li • tion (vō li' shən) *n.,* choice or decision made. *Margot had to drag Omar to the conference, but he stayed of his own <u>volition</u>.*

to the north. Of all the important cities of Japan, only two, Kyoto and Hiroshima, had been visited in strength by *B-san*, or Mr. B, as the Japanese, with a mixture of respect and unhappy familiarity, called the B-29; and Mr. Tanimoto, like all his neighbors and friends, was almost sick with anxiety. He had heard uncomfortably detailed accounts of mass raids on Kure, Iwakuni, Tokuyama, and other nearby towns; he was sure Hiroshima's turn would come soon. He had slept badly the night before, because there had been

> *Why had Mr. Tanimoto not slept well?*

several air raid warnings. Hiroshima had been getting such warnings almost every night for weeks, for at that time the B-29s were using Lake Biwa, northeast of Hiroshima, as a <u>rendezvous</u> point, and no matter what city the Americans planned to hit, the Superfortresses streamed in over the coast near Hiroshima. The frequency of the warnings and the continued <u>abstinence</u> of Mr. B with respect to Hiroshima had made its citizens jittery; a rumor was going around that the Americans were saving something special for the city.

Mr. Tanimoto is a small man, quick to talk, laugh, and cry. He wears his black hair parted in the middle and rather long; the prominence of the frontal bones just above his eyebrows and the smallness of his mustache, mouth, and chin give him a strange, old-young look, boyish and yet wise, weak and yet fiery. He moves nervously and fast, but with a restraint which suggests that he is a cautious, thoughtful man. He showed, indeed, just those qualities in the uneasy days before the bomb fell.

> *What actions of Mr. Tanimoto showed his "cautious, thoughtful" nature?*

Besides having his wife spend the nights in Ushida, Mr. Tanimoto had been carrying all the portable things from his church, in the close-packed residential district called Nagaragawa, to a house that belonged to a rayon manufacturer in Koi, two miles from the center of town. The rayon man, a Mr. Matsui, had opened his then unoccupied estate to a large number of his friends and acquaintances, so that they might evacuate whatever they wished to a safe distance from the probable target area. Mr. Tanimoto had had no difficulty in moving chairs, hymnals, Bibles, altar gear, and church records by pushcart himself, but the organ console and an upright piano required some aid. A friend of his named Matsuo had, the day before, helped him get the piano out to Koi; in return, he had promised this day to assist Mr. Matsuo in hauling out a daughter's belongings. That is why he had risen so early.

> *Why had Mr. Tanimoto risen early on the day of the bombing?*

Mr. Tanimoto cooked his own breakfast. He felt awfully tired. The effort of moving the piano the day before, a sleepless night, weeks of worry and unbalanced diet, the cares of his parish—all combined to make him feel hardly adequate to the new day's work. There was another thing, too: Mr. Tanimoto had studied theology at Emory College, in Atlanta, Georgia; he had graduated in 1940; he spoke excellent English; he dressed in American clothes; he had corresponded with many American friends right up to the time the war began; and among a people obsessed with a fear of being spied upon—perhaps almost obsessed himself—he found himself growing increasingly uneasy. The police had questioned him several times, and just a few days before, he had heard that an influential acquaintance, a Mr. Tanaka, a retired officer of the Toyo Kisen Kaisha steamship line, an anti-Christian, a man famous

---

**WORDS FOR EVERYDAY USE**

**ren • dez • vous** (rän′ di vü) *adj.,* planned meeting. *At Valley Fair we decided to set a <u>rendezvous</u> point in case we were separated in the crowd.*

**ab • sti • nence** (ab′ stə nən[t]s) *n.,* habitual going without. *Dora's <u>abstinence</u> from dairy products helped her lose ten pounds.*

in Hiroshima for his showy <u>philanthropies</u> and notorious for his personal tyrannies, had been telling people that Tanimoto should not be trusted. In compensation, to show himself publicly a good Japanese, Mr. Tanimoto had taken on the chairmanship of his local *tonarigumi*, or Neighborhood Association, and to his other duties and concerns this position had added the business of organizing air raid defense for about twenty families.

What rumors have arisen about Mr. Tanimoto? What did he do to try to disprove the rumors?

Before six o'clock that morning, Mr. Tanimoto started for Mr. Matsuo's house. There he found that their burden was to be a *tansu*, a large Japanese cabinet, full of clothing and household goods. The two men set out. The morning was perfectly clear and so warm that the day promised to be uncomfortable. A few minutes after they started, the air raid siren went off—a minute-long blast that warned of approaching planes but indicated to the people of Hiroshima only a slight degree of danger, since it sounded every morning at this time, when an American weather plane came over. The two men pulled and pushed the handcart through the city streets. Hiroshima was a fanshaped city, lying mostly on the six islands formed by the seven estuarial rivers[5] that branch out from the Ota River; its main commercial and residential districts, covering about four square miles in the center of the city, contained three-quarters of its population, which had been reduced by several evacuation programs from a wartime peak of 380,000 to about 245,000. Factories and other residential districts, or suburbs, lay compactly around the edges of the city. To the south were the

docks, an airport, and the island-studded Inland Sea. A rim of mountains runs around the other three sides of the delta. Mr. Tanimoto and Mr. Matsuo took their way through the shopping center, already full of people, and across two of the rivers to the sloping streets of Koi, and up them to the outskirts and foothills. As they started up a valley away from the tight-ranked houses, the all-clear sounded. (The Japanese radar operators, detecting only three planes, supposed that they comprised a reconnaissance.[6]) Pushing the handcart up to the rayon man's house was tiring, and the men, after they had maneuvered their load into the driveway and to the front steps, paused to rest awhile. They stood with a wing of the house between them and the city. Like most homes in this part of Japan, the house consisted of a wooden frame and wooden walls supporting a heavy tile roof. Its front hall, packed with rolls of bedding and clothing, looked like a cool cave full of fat cushions. Opposite the house, to the right of the front door, there was a large, <u>finicky</u> rock garden. There was no sound of planes. The morning was still; the place was cool and pleasant.

**Then a tremendous flash of light cut across the sky.**

Then a tremendous flash of light cut across the sky. Mr. Tanimoto has a distinct recollection that it traveled from east to west, from the city toward the hills. It seemed a sheet of sun. Both he and Mr. Matsuo reacted in terror—and both had time to react (for they were 3,500 yards, or two miles,

What does Mr. Tanimoto remember of the flash? What did it seem like? How far was he from the center of the explosion?

---

5. **estuarial rivers.** Rivers that meet the sea
6. **reconnaissance.** Exploratory military survey of enemy territory

---

**WORDS FOR EVERYDAY USE**

phi • lan • thro • py (fə lan[t]′ thrə pē) *n.*, act or gift of dispensing aid or funds set aside for humanitarian purposes. *One of Carnegie's principal <u>philanthropies</u> was establishing public libraries.*

fin • ick • y (fi′ ni kē) *adj.*, excessively nice or exacting in taste or standards. *Mrs. Bucket's <u>finicky</u> preparations resulted in an exquisite candlelight supper.*

from the center of the explosion). Mr. Matsuo dashed up the front steps into the house and dived among the bedrolls and buried himself there. Mr. Tanimoto took four or five steps and threw himself between two big rocks in the garden. He bellied up very hard against one of them. As his face was against the stone, he did not see what happened. He felt a sudden pressure, and then splinters and pieces of board and fragments of tile fell on him. He heard no roar. (Almost no one in Hiroshima recalls hearing any noise of the bomb. But a fisherman in his sampan[7] on the Inland Sea near Tsuzu, the man with whom Mr. Tanimoto's mother-in-law and sister-in-law were living, saw the flash and heard a tremendous explosion; he was nearly twenty miles from Hiroshima, but the thunder was greater than when the B-29s hit Iwakuni, only five miles away.)

> What did most of the residents of Hiroshima hear when the bomb went off?

When he dared, Mr. Tanimoto raised his head and saw that the rayon man's house had collapsed. He thought a bomb had fallen directly on it. Such clouds of dust had risen that there was a sort of twilight around. In panic, not thinking for the moment of Mr. Matsuo under the ruins, he dashed out into the street. He noticed as he ran that the concrete wall of the estate had fallen over—toward the house rather than away from it. In the street, the first thing he saw was a squad of soldiers who had been burrowing into the hillside opposite, making one of the thousands of dugouts in which the Japanese apparently intended to resist invasion, hill by hill, life for life; the soldiers were coming out of the hole, where they should have been safe, and blood was running from their heads, chests, and backs. They were silent and dazed.

Under what seemed to be a local dust cloud, the day grew darker and darker.

At nearly midnight, the night before the bomb was dropped, an announcer on the city's radio station said that about two hundred B-29s were approaching southern Honshu[8] and advised the population of Hiroshima to evacuate to their designated "safe areas." Mrs. Hatsuyo Nakamura, the tailor's widow, who lived in the section called Noboricho and who had long had a habit of doing as she was told, got her three children—a ten-year-old boy, Toshio, an eight-year-old girl, Yaeko, and a five-year-old girl, Myeko—out of bed and dressed them and walked with them to the military area known as the East Parade Ground, on the northeast edge of the city. There she unrolled some mats and the children lay down on them. They slept until about two, when they were awakened by the roar of the planes going over Hiroshima.

As soon as the planes had passed, Mrs. Nakamura started back with her children. They reached home a little after two-thirty and she immediately turned on the radio, which, to her distress, was just then broadcasting a fresh warning. When she looked at the children and saw how tired they were, and when she thought of the number of trips they had made in past weeks, all to no purpose, to the East Parade Ground, she decided that in spite of the instructions on the radio, she simply could not face starting out all over again. She put the children in their bedrolls on the floor, lay down herself at three o'clock, and fell asleep at once, so soundly that when the planes passed over later, she did not waken to their sound.

> Why didn't Mrs. Nakamura return to the East Parade Ground despite the warning she heard on the radio?

The siren jarred her awake at about seven. She arose, dressed quickly, and hurried to the house of Mr. Nakamoto, the head of her Neighborhood Association, and asked him what she should do. He said that she should remain at home unless an urgent warning—a series of

---

7. **sampan.** Small, flat-bottomed, Asian boat
8. **Honshu.** Largest island of Japan

intermittent blasts of the siren—was sounded. She returned home, lit the stove in the kitchen, set some rice to cook, and sat down to read that morning's Hiroshima *Chugoku*. To her relief, the all-clear sounded at eight o'clock. She heard the children stirring, so she went and gave each of them a handful of peanuts and told them to stay on their bedrolls, because they were tired from the night's walk. She had hoped that they would go back to sleep, but the man in the house directly to the south began to make a terrible hullabaloo of hammering, wedging, ripping, and split- ting. The prefectural[9] govern- ment, convinced, as everyone in Hiroshima was, that the city would be attacked soon, had begun to press with threats and warnings for the completion of wide fire lanes, which, it was hoped, might act in conjunction with the rivers to localize any fires started by an incendiary raid; and the neighbor was reluc- tantly sacrificing his home to the city's safety. Just the day before, the pre- fecture had ordered all able-bodied girls from the secondary schools to spend a few days help- ing to clear these lanes, and they started work soon after the all-clear sounded.

Why was Mrs. Nakamura's neighbor destroying his house?

Mrs. Nakamura went back to the kitchen, looked at the rice, and began watching the man next door. At first, she was annoyed with him for making so much noise, but then she was moved almost to tears by pity. Her emotion was specifically directed toward her neighbor, tearing down his home, board by board,

For whom did Mrs. Nakamura feel pity?

at a time when there was so much unavoidable destruction, but undoubtedly she also felt a generalized, community pity, to say nothing of self-pity. She had not had an easy time. Her husband, Isawa, had gone into the Army just after Myeko was born, and she had heard nothing from or of him for a long time, until, on March 5, 1942, she received a seven-word telegram: "Isawa died an honorable death at Singapore." She learned later that he had died on February 15th, the day Singapore fell, and that he had been a corporal. Isawa had been a not particularly prosperous tailor, and his only capital was a Sankoku sewing machine. After his death, when his allotments[10] stopped coming, Mrs. Nakamura got out the machine and began to take in piecework herself, and since then had supported the children, but poorly, by sewing.

As Mrs. Nakamura stood watching her neigh- bor, everything flashed whiter than any white she had ever seen. She did not notice what happened to the man next door; the reflex of a mother set her in motion toward her children. She had taken a single step (the house was 1,350 yards, or three-quarters of a mile, from the center of the explosion) when something picked her up and she seemed to fly into the next room over the raised sleeping platform, pursued by parts of her house.

What did Mrs. Nakamura think of when the explosion came? What happened to her?

> **As Mrs. Nakamura stood watching her neighbor, everything flashed whiter than any white she had ever seen.**

---

9. **prefectural.** Relating to a district governed by a chief officer
10. **allotments.** Monetary payments provided by the government

---

**WORDS FOR EVERYDAY USE**

in • ter • mit • tent (in tər mi′ tənt) *adj.*, coming and going at intervals, not continuous. *We could occasionally hear the announcer between the intermittent blasts of static.*

hul • la • ba • loo (hə lə bə lü′) *n.*, confused noise. *Mr. Auriemma shouted to be heard over the hullabaloo in the gym.*

in • cen • di • ar • y (in sen′ dē er ē) *adj.*, relating to or involving deliberate burning of property. *During the riots in the inner city, residents were most afraid of incendiary crime.*

Hiroshima, the day after the atomic bomb was dropped.

Timbers fell around her as she landed, and a shower of tiles <u>pommelled</u> her; everything became dark, for she was buried. The debris did not cover her deeply. She rose up and freed herself. She heard a child cry, "Mother, help me!," and saw her youngest—Myeko, the five-year-old—buried up to her breast and unable to move. As Mrs. Nakamura started frantically to claw her way toward the baby, she could see or hear nothing of her other children.

In the days right before the bombing, Dr. Masakazu Fujii, being prosperous, <u>hedonistic</u>, and at the time not too busy, had been allowing himself the luxury of sleeping until nine or nine-thirty, but fortunately he had to get up early the morning the bomb was dropped to see a house guest off on a train. He rose at six, and half an hour later walked with his friend to the station, not far away, across two of the rivers. He was back home by seven, just as the siren sounded its sustained warning. He ate breakfast and then, because the morning was already hot, undressed down to his underwear and went out on the porch to read the paper. This porch—in fact, the whole building—was curiously constructed. Dr. Fujii was the proprietor of a peculiarly Japanese institution: a private, single-doctor hospital. This building, perched beside and over the water of the Kyo River, and next to the bridge of the same name, contained thirty rooms for thirty patients and their kinfolk—for, according to Japanese custom, when a person falls sick and goes to a hospital, one or more members of his family go and live there with him, to cook for him, bathe, massage, and read to him, and to offer <u>incessant</u>

> How was Dr. Fujii's building constructed?

**WORDS FOR EVERYDAY USE**

**pom • mel** (pə′məl) vt., pound or beat. After the punk <u>pommelled</u> him and took his wallet, Steve went to the police station to file a report.

**he • do • nis • tic** (hē dən is′tik) adj., relating to or characterized by pleasure. Kleo planned to devote himself to a <u>hedonistic</u> lifestyle during vacation.

**in • ces • sant** (in se′ sənt) adj., continuing or following without interruption. The <u>incessant</u> noise of the drum beating gave Tanja a headache.

familial sympathy, without which a Japanese patient would be miserable indeed. Dr. Fujii had no beds—only straw mats—for his patients. He did, however, have all sorts of modern equipment: an x-ray machine, diathermy apparatus,[11] and a fine tiled laboratory. The structure rested two-thirds on the land, one-third on piles over the tidal waters of the Kyo. This overhang, the part of the building where Dr. Fujii lived, was queer-looking, but it was cool in summer and from the porch, which faced away from the center of the city, the prospect of the river, with pleasure boats drifting up and down it, was always refreshing. Dr. Fujii had occasionally had anxious moments when the Ota and its mouth branches rose to flood, but the piling was apparently firm enough and the house had always held.

Why was Dr. Fujii's hospital built with room for patients' kinfolk?

Dr. Fujii had been relatively idle for about a month because in July, as the number of untouched cities in Japan dwindled and as Hiroshima seemed more and more inevitably a target, he began turning patients away, on the ground that in case of a fire raid he would not be able to evacuate them. Now he had only two patients left—a woman from Yano, injured in the shoulder, and a young man of twenty-five recovering from burns he had suffered when the steel factory near Hiroshima in which he worked had been hit. Dr. Fujii had six nurses to tend his patients. His wife and children were safe; his wife and one son were living outside Osaka, and another son and two daughters were in the country on Kyushu.[12] A niece was living with him, and a maid and a manservant. He had little to do and did not mind, for

Why had Dr. Fujii been turning away patients? How many patients and staff did Dr. Fujii have at the time of the bombing?

he had saved some money. At fifty, he was healthy, convivial, and calm, and he was pleased to pass the evenings drinking whiskey with friends, always sensibly and for the sake of conversation. Before the war, he had *affected* brands imported from Scotland and America; now he was perfectly satisfied with the best Japanese brand, Suntory.

Dr. Fujii sat down cross-legged in his underwear on the spotless matting of the porch, put on his glasses, and started reading the Osaka *Asahi*. He liked to read the Osaka news because his wife was there. He saw the flash. To him—faced away from the center and looking at his paper—it seemed a brilliant yellow. Startled, he began to rise to his feet. In that moment (he was 1,550 yards from the center), the hospital leaned behind his rising and, with a terrible ripping noise, toppled into the river. The Doctor, still in the act of getting to his feet, was thrown forward and around and over; he was buffeted and gripped; he lost track of everything, because things were so speeded up; he felt the water.

Dr. Fujii hardly had time to think that he was dying before he realized that he was alive, squeezed tightly by two long timbers in a V across his chest, like a morsel suspended between two huge chopsticks—held upright, so that he could not move, with his head miraculously above water and his torso and legs in it. The remains of his hospital were all around him in a mad assortment of splintered lumber and materials for the relief of pain. His left shoulder hurt terribly. His glasses were gone.

What image does Hersey use to describe Dr. Fujii after he has been tossed into the water from the impact of the blast? Why is this image appropriate?

---

11. **diathermy apparatus.** Equipment for heat treatments
12. **Kyushu.** Southernmost of the main islands of Japan

WORDS FOR EVERYDAY USE

con • viv • i • al (kən viv′ yəl) *adj.,* relating to feasting, drinking, and good company. *"Eat, drink, and be merry" describes Leslie's convivial attitude toward life.*

buf • fet (bə′ fət) *vt.,* batter or drive by force. *During the storm, the ship was buffeted by heavy winds and sank.*

Father Wilhelm Kleinsorge, of the Society of Jesus, was, on the morning of the explosion, in rather frail condition. The Japanese wartime diet had not sustained him, and he felt the strain of being a foreigner in an increasingly xenophobic Japan; even a German, since the defeat of the Fatherland,[13] was unpopular. Father Kleinsorge had, at thirty-eight, the look of a boy growing too fast—thin in the face, with a prominent Adam's apple, a hollow chest, dangling hands, big feet. He walked clumsily, leaning forward a little. He was tired all the time. To make matters worse, he had suffered for two days, along with Father Cieslik, a fellow-priest, from a rather painful and urgent diarrhea, which they blamed on the beans and black ration bread they were obliged to eat. Two other priests then living in the mission compound, which was in the Noboricho section—Father Superior LaSalle and Father Schiffer—had happily escaped this affliction.

*What factors contributed to Father Kleinsorge's weakened condition?*

Father Kleinsorge woke up about six the morning the bomb was dropped, and half an hour later—he was a bit tardy because of his sickness—he began to read Mass in the mission chapel, a small Japanese-style wooden building which was without pews, since its worshipers knelt on the usual Japanese matted floor, facing an altar graced with splendid silks, brass, silver, and heavy embroideries. This morning, a Monday, the only worshipers were Mr. Takemoto, a theological student living in the mission house; Mr. Fukai, the secretary of the diocese;[14] Mrs. Murata, the mission's devoutly Christian housekeeper; and his fellow-priests. After Mass, while Father Kleinsorge was reading the Prayers of Thanksgiving, the siren sounded. He stopped the service and the missionaries retired across the compound to the bigger building. There, in his room on the ground floor, to the right of the front door, Father Kleinsorge changed into a military uniform which he had acquired when he was teaching at the Rokko Middle School in Kobe and which he wore during air raid alerts.

*Aside from moving to a bigger building, what did Father Kleinsorge do when the siren sounded?*

After an alarm, Father Kleinsorge always went out and scanned the sky, and in this instance, when he stepped outside, he was glad to see only the single weather plane that flew over Hiroshima each day about this time. Satisfied that nothing would happen, he went in and breakfasted with the other Fathers on substitute coffee and ration bread, which, under the circumstances, was especially repugnant to him. The Fathers sat and talked a while, until, at eight, they heard the all-clear. They went then to various parts of the building. Father Schiffer retired to his room to do some writing. Father Cieslik sat in his room in a straight chair with a pillow over his stomach to ease his pain, and read. Father Superior LaSalle stood at the window of his room, thinking. Father Kleinsorge went up to a room on the third floor, took off all his clothes except his underwear, and stretched out on his right side on a cot and began reading his *Stimmen der Zeit*.

After the terrible flash—which, Father Kleinsorge later realized, reminded him of something he had read as a boy about a large meteor col-

*Of what did the flash of the explosion remind Father Kleinsorge?*

---

13. **defeat of the Fatherland.** Germany surrendered in May, 1945.
14. **diocese.** Territorial jurisdiction of a bishop

---

**WORDS FOR EVERYDAY USE**

**xe • no • pho • bic** (zē nə fō′ bik) *adj.,* fearful of or showing hatred toward foreigners. *My xenophobic neighbor did not welcome the immigrants who moved in next door.*

**theo • log • i • cal** (thē ə lä′ ji kəl) *adj.,* of or relating to theology, or the study of religious faith, practice, and experience. *The theological magazine was published by a Catholic press.*

**re • pug • nant** (ri pug′ nənt) *adj.,* exciting distaste or aversion. *The idea of conceding defeat was repugnant to our team.*

liding with the earth—he had time (since he was 1,400 yards from the center) for one thought: A bomb has fallen directly on us. Then, for a few seconds or minutes, he went out of his mind.

Father Kleinsorge never knew how he got out of the house. The next things he was conscious of were that he was wandering around in the mission's vegetable garden in his underwear, bleeding slightly from small cuts along his left flank; that all the buildings round about had fallen down except the Jesuits' mission house, which had long before been braced and double-braced by a priest named Groppe, who was terrified of earthquakes; that the day had turned dark; and that Murata-*san*, the housekeeper, was nearby, crying over and over, "*Shu Jesusu, awaremi tamia!* Our Lord Jesus, have pity on us!"

*What might have accounted for the safety of the Jesuits' mission house?*

**Then, for a few seconds or minutes, he went out of his mind.**

**O**n the train on the way into Hiroshima from the country, where he lived with his mother, Dr. Terufumi Sasaki, the Red Cross Hospital surgeon, thought over an unpleasant nightmare he had had the night before. His mother's home was in Mukaihara, thirty miles from the city, and it took him two hours by train and tram[15] to reach the hospital. He had slept uneasily all night and had wakened an hour earlier than usual, and, feeling sluggish and slightly feverish, had debated whether to go to the hospital at all; his sense of duty finally forced him to go, and he had started out on an earlier train than he took most mornings. The dream had particularly frightened him because it was so closely associated, on the surface at least, with a disturbing actuality. He was only twenty-five years old and had just completed his training at the Eastern Medical University, in Tsingtao,[16] China. He was something of an idealist and was much distressed by the inade-quacy of medical facilities in the country town where his mother lived. Quite on his own, and without a permit, he had begun visiting a few sick people out there in the evenings, after his eight hours at the hospital and four hours' commuting. He had recently learned that the penalty for practicing without a permit was severe; a fellow-doctor whom he had asked about it had given him a serious scolding. Nevertheless, he had continued to practice. In his dream, he had been at the bedside of a country patient when the police and the doctor he had consulted burst into the room, seized him, dragged him outside, and beat him up cruelly. On the train, he just about decided to give up the work in Mukaihara, since he felt it would be impossible to get a permit, because the authorities would hold that it would conflict with his duties at the Red Cross Hospital.

*How did Dr. Sasaki spend his evenings in Mukaihara? What was dangerous about his occupation?*

At the terminus,[17] he caught a streetcar at once. (He later calculated that if he had taken his customary train that morning, and if he had had to wait a few minutes for the streetcar, as often happened, he would have been close to the center at the time of the explosion and would surely have perished.) He arrived at the hospital at seven-forty and reported to the chief surgeon. A few minutes later, he went to a room on the first floor and drew blood from the arm of a man in order to perform a Wassermann test. The laboratory containing the incubators for the test was on the third floor. With the blood specimen in his left hand, walking in a kind if distraction he had felt all morning, probably because of the dream and

---

15. **tram.** Streetcar
16. **Tsingtao.** Large Chinese city on the Yellow River, which was occupied by Japan during World War II
17. **terminus.** Station at the end of a transportation line

The Industrial Promotion Hall, left in this condition after the atomic blast, is now the Hiroshima Peace Memorial.

his restless night, he started along the main corridor on his way toward the stairs. He was one step beyond an open window when the light of the bomb was reflected, like a gigantic photograph flash, in the corridor. He ducked down on one knee and said to himself, as only a Japanese would, "Sasaki, *gambare!* Be brave!" Just then (the building was 1,650 yards from the center), the blast ripped through the hospital. The glasses he was wearing flew off his face; the bottle of blood crashed against one wall, his Japanese slippers zipped out from under his feet—but otherwise, thanks to where he stood, he was untouched.

*What probably saved Dr. Sasaki's life?*

Dr. Sasaki shouted the name of the chief surgeon and rushed around to the man's office and found him terribly cut by glass. The hospital was in horrible confusion: heavy partitions and ceilings had fallen on patients, beds had overturned, windows had blown in and cut people, blood was spattered on the walls and floors, instruments were everywhere, many of the patients were running about screaming, many more lay dead. (A colleague working in the laboratory to which Dr. Sasaki had been walking was dead; Dr. Sasaki's patient, whom he had just left and who a few moments before had been dreadfully afraid of syphilis, was also dead.) Dr. Sasaki found himself the only doctor in the hospital who was unhurt.

*Who is the only doctor who was unhurt in the explosion?*

Dr. Sasaki, who believed that the enemy had hit only the building he was in, got bandages and began to bind the wounds of those inside the hospital; while outside, all over Hiroshima, maimed and dying citizens turned their unsteady steps toward the Red Cross Hospital to begin an invasion that was to make Dr. Sasaki forget his private nightmare for a long, long time.

Miss Toshiko Sasaki, the East Asia Tin Works clerk, who is not related to Dr. Sasaki, got up at three o'clock in the morning on the day the bomb fell. There was extra housework to do. Her eleven-month-old brother, Akio, had come down the day before with a serious stomach upset; her mother had taken him to the Tamura Pediatric Hospital and was staying there with him. Miss Sasaki, who was about twenty, had to cook breakfast for her father, a brother, a sister, and herself, and—since the hospital, because of the war, was unable to provide food—to prepare a whole day's meals for her mother and the baby, in time for her father, who worked in a factory making rubber earplugs for artillery crews, to take the food by on his way to the plant. When she had finished and had cleaned and put away the cooking things, it was nearly seven. The family lived in Koi, and she had a forty-five-minute trip to the tin works, in the section of town called Kannonmachi. She was in charge of the personnel records in the factory. She left Koi at seven, and as soon as she reached the plant, she went with some of the other girls from the personnel department to the factory auditorium. A prominent local Navy man, a former employee, had committed suicide the day before by throwing himself under a train—a death considered honorable enough to warrant a memorial service, which was to be held at the tin works at ten o'clock that morning. In the large hall, Miss Sasaki and the others made suitable preparations for the meeting. This work took about twenty minutes.

Miss Sasaki went back to her office and sat down at her desk. She was quite far from the windows, which were off to her left, and behind her were a couple of tall bookcases containing all the books of the factory library, which the personnel department had organized. She settled herself at her desk, put some things in a drawer, and shifted papers. She thought that before she began to make entries in her lists of new employees, discharges, and departures for the Army, she would chat for a moment with the girl at her right. Just as she turned her head away from the windows, the room was filled with a blinding light. She was paralyzed by fear, fixed still in her chair for a long moment (the plant was 1,600 yards from the center).

Everything fell, and Miss Sasaki lost consciousness. The ceiling dropped suddenly and the wooden floor above collapsed in splinters and the people up there came down and the roof above them gave way; but principally and first of all, the bookcases right behind her swooped forward and the contents threw her down, with her left leg horribly twisted and breaking underneath her. There, in the tin factory, in the first moment of the atomic age, a human being was crushed by books. ∎

*Why did Miss Sasaki get up so early on the day the bomb fell?*

*How was Miss Sasaki injured?*

# Respond *to the* SELECTION

Hersey says, "And now each [of the survivors] knows that in the act of survival he lived a dozen lives and saw more death than he ever thought he would see." Describe the different emotions one might feel after surviving an atomic bombing.

# Inquire, *Imagine*

## Recall: GATHERING FACTS

1a. Whom does Hersey identify in the opening paragraph? What was each person doing when the atomic bomb flashed above Hiroshima?

2a. What difficulties did Father Kleinsorge face that the other survivors did not share? What did Father Kleinsorge do when the air raid sirens sound?

3a. What nightmare did Dr. Sasaki have the night before the bombing?

## Interpret: FINDING MEANING

1b. Why does Hersey focus on six individuals? Why does he give the distance away from the city center of each of the survivors?

2b. Why did Father Kleinsorge change his clothes?

3b. What relieved Dr. Sasaki of his nightmare? Describe his new living nightmare.

## Analyze: TAKING THINGS APART

4a. Identify the images Hersey uses to describe the explosion of the atomic bomb, as seen by each of the survivors.

## Synthesize: BRINGING THINGS TOGETHER

4b. Hersey combines literary techniques with factual reporting to describe the impact of the nuclear blast on six survivors' lives. Many reporters would have contented themselves with factual reporting and a few quotes from survivors. Assess Hersey's use of literary techniques and their effect on his account.

## Evaluate: MAKING JUDGMENTS

5a. Hersey observed that journalism "allows the reader to witness history; fiction gives its readers an opportunity to live it." Assess this statement in relation to the selection you have just read.

## Extend: CONNECTING IDEAS

5b. Dr. Fujii built rooms for patients' kinfolk to accommodate the Japanese custom of allowing for relatives to attend the sick. Make a cross-cultural comparison between how the sick are cared for in Japanese and U.S. hospitals.

# Understanding *Literature*

EFFECT. Review the definition for **effect** in the Handbook of Literary Terms. What effect does this selection produce? How does the author achieve this effect? What emotions did you experience while reading this account?

IRONY. Review the definition for **irony** in the Handbook of Literary Terms. Then look at the chart you made in Literary Tools on page 830. Which example of irony in the selection is the most powerful? Why?

# Writer's Journal

1. Imagine that you are one of the survivors identified in this selection. Write a **journal entry** explaining what you have experienced.

2. Write a **letter** to the people of Hiroshima either justifying or apologizing for the nuclear attack on their city.

3. Write a **paragraph** discussing whether Hersey employs objective or subjective reporting in *Hiroshima*. Cite examples from the selection to support your assessment.

# Integrating *the* LANGUAGE ARTS

## Language, Grammar, and Style

**APPOSITIVE PHRASES.** Read about appositive phrases in the Language Arts Survey 3.77, "Appositives." Then write out the appositive phrases used in the following sentences from *Hiroshima*. Some sentences may have more than one appositive phrase.

1. [W]hen the atomic bomb flashed above Hiroshima, Miss Toshiko Sasaki, a clerk in the personnel department of the East Asia Tin works, had just sat down at her place in the plant office and was turning her head to speak to the girl at the next desk.

2. Mrs. Hatsuyo Nakamura, a tailor's widow, stood by the window of her kitchen, watching a neighbor tearing down his house because it lay in the path of an air-raid-defense fire lane.

3. Father Wilhelm Kleinsorge, a German priest of the Society of Jesus, reclined in his underwear on a cot on the top floor of his order's three-story mission house, reading a Jesuit magazine, *Stimmen der Zeit*.

4. Dr. Terufumi Sasaki, a young member of the surgical staff of the city's large, modern Red Cross Hospital, walked along one of the hospital corridors with a blood specimen for a Wassermann test in his hand.

5. The Reverend Mr. Kiyoshi Tanimoto, pastor of the Hiroshima Methodist Church, paused at the door of a rich man's house in Koi, the city's western suburb, and prepared to unload a handcart full of things he had evacuated from town in fear of the massive B-29 raid which everyone expected Hiroshima to suffer.

## Media Literacy & Study and Research

**NEWSPAPER ARTICLE.** Imagine it is August 7, 1945, the day after the nuclear bombing in Hiroshima. Write a newspaper article that a Japanese journalist might have written. Be sure to include what part of the city the bomb exploded in, how many people you estimate have died, how many more were wounded, and the reaction of the citizens and the government to the bombing. You will need to do some research in the library to provide accurate facts for your article.

## Study and Research & Speaking and Listening

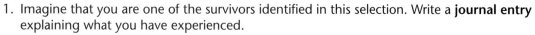

**DEBATE.** Research the historic decision to drop the bomb on Hiroshima and Nagasaki. Then form two groups. One group defends the decision to drop the bomb, and the other group presents arguments against it.

### from *Invisible Man*
### by Ralph Ellison

When I reached the door of Mr. Emerson's office it occurred to me that perhaps I should have waited until the business of the day was under way, but I disregarded the idea and went ahead. My being early would be, I hoped, an indication of both how badly I wanted work, and how promptly I would perform any assignment given me. Besides, wasn't there a saying that the first person of the day to enter a business would get a bargain? Or was that said only of Jewish business? I removed the letter from my brief case. Was Emerson a Christian or a Jewish name?

Beyond the door it was like a museum. I had entered a large reception room decorated with cool tropical colors. One wall was almost covered by a huge colored map, from which narrow red silk ribbons stretched tautly from each division of the map to a series of ebony pedestals, upon which sat glass specimen jars containing natural products of the various countries. It was an importing firm. I looked around the room, amazed. There were paintings, bronzes, tapestries, all beautifully arranged. I was dazzled and so taken aback that I almost dropped my brief case when I heard a voice say, "And what would your business be?"

I saw the figure out of a collar ad: ruddy face with blond hair faultlessly in place, a tropical weave suit draped handsomely from his broad shoulders, his eyes gray and nervous behind clear-framed glasses.

I explained my appointment. "Oh, yes," he said. "May I see the letter, please?"

I handed it over, noticing the gold links in the soft white cuffs as he extended his hand. Glancing at the envelope he looked back at me with a strange interest in his eyes and said, "Have a seat, please. I'll be with you in a moment."

I watched him leave noiselessly, moving with a long hip-swinging stride that caused me to frown. I went over and took a teakwood chair with cushions of emerald-green silk, sitting stiffly with my brief case across my knees. He must have been sitting there when I came in, for on a table that held a beautiful dwarf tree I saw smoke rising from a cigarette in a jade ash tray. An open book, something called *Totem and Taboo*, lay beside it. I looked across to a lighted case of Chinese design which held delicate-looking statues of horses and birds, small vases and bowls, each set upon a carved wooden base. The room was quiet as a tomb—

until suddenly there was a savage beating of wings and I looked toward the window to see an eruption of color, as though a gale had whipped up a bundle of brightly colored rags. It was an aviary of tropical birds set near one of the broad windows, through which, as the clapping of wings settled down, I could see two ships plying[1] far out upon the greenish bay below. A large bird began a song, drawing my eyes to the throbbing of its bright blue, red and yellow throat. It was startling and I watched the surge and flutter of the birds as their colors flared for an instant like an unfurled oriental fan. I wanted to go and stand near the cage for a better view, but decided against it. It might seem unbusinesslike. I observed the room from the chair.

These folks are the Kings of the Earth! I thought, hearing the bird make an ugly noise. There was nothing like this at the college museum—or anywhere else that I had ever been. I recalled only a few cracked relics from slavery times: an iron pot, an ancient bell, a set of ankle-irons and links of chain, a primitive loom, a spinning wheel, a gourd for drinking, an ugly ebony African god that seemed to sneer (presented to the school by some traveling millionaire), a leather whip with copper brads,[2] a branding iron with the double letter . . . Though I had seen them very seldom, they were vivid in my mind. They had not been pleasant and whenever I had visited the room I avoided the glass case in which they rested, preferring instead to look at photographs of the early days after the Civil War, the times close to those blind Barbee[3] had described. And I had not looked even at these too often.

I tried to relax; the chair was beautiful but hard. Where had the man gone? Had he shown any antagonism when he saw me? I was annoyed that I had failed to see him first. One had to watch such details. Suddenly there came a harsh cry from the cage, and once more I saw a mad flashing as though the birds had burst into spontaneous flame, fluttering and beating their wings maliciously against the bamboo bars, only to settle down just as suddenly when the door opened and the blond man stood beckoning, his hand

---

1. **plying.** Sailing regularly back and forth
2. **brads.** Wire nails of uniform thickness with small heads
3. **Barbee.** The character Homer A. Barbee appeared earlier in the novel and gave a speech at the narrator's college about the period after the Emancipation during which the narrator's college was founded.

upon the knob. I went over, tense inside me. Had I been accepted or rejected?

There was a question in his eyes. "Come in, please," he said.

"Thank you," I said, waiting to follow him.

"*Please,*" he said with a slight smile.

I moved ahead of him, sounding the tone of his words for a sign.

"I want to ask you a few questions," he said, waving my letter at two chairs.

"Yes, sir?" I said.

"Tell me, what is it that you're trying to accomplish?" he said.

"I want a job, sir, so that I can earn enough money to return to college in the fall."

"To your old school?"

"Yes, sir."

"I see." For a moment he studied me silently. "When do you expect to graduate?"

"Next year, sir. I've completed my junior classes . . ."

"Oh, you have? That's very good. And how old are you?"

"Almost twenty, sir."

"A junior at nineteen? You *are* a good student."

"Thank you, sir," I said, beginning to enjoy the interview.

"Were you an athlete?" he asked.

"No, sir . . ."

"You have the build," he said, looking me up and down. "You'd probably make an excellent runner, a sprinter."

"I've never tried, sir."

"And I suppose it's silly even to ask what you think of your Alma Mater?"[1] he said.

"I think it's one of the best in the world," I said, hearing my voice surge with deep feeling.

"I know, I know," he said, with a swift displeasure that surprised me.

I became alert again as he mumbled something incomprehensible about "nostalgia for Harvard yard."

"But what if you were offered an opportunity to finish your work at some other college," he said, his eyes widening behind his glasses. His smile had returned.

"*Another* college?" I asked, my mind beginning to whirl.

"Why, yes, say some school in New England . . ."

I looked at him speechlessly. Did he mean Harvard? Was this good or bad. Where was it leading? "I don't know, sir," I said cautiously. "I've never thought about it. I've only a year more, and, well, I know everyone at my old school and they know me . . ."

I came to a confused halt, seeing him look at me with a sigh of resignation. What was on his mind? Perhaps I had been too frank about returning to the college, maybe he was against our having a higher education . . . But hell, he's only a secretary . . . Or *is* he?

"I understand," he said calmly. "It was presumptuous of me to even suggest another school. I guess one's college is really a kind of mother and father . . . a sacred matter."

"Yes, sir. That's it," I said in hurried agreement.

His eyes narrowed. "But now I must ask you an embarrassing question. Do you mind?"

"Why, no, sir," I said nervously.

"I don't like to ask this, but it's quite necessary . . ." He leaned forward with a pained frown. "Tell me, did you *read* the letter which you brought to Mr. Emerson? This," he said, taking the letter from the table.

"Why, no, sir! It wasn't addressed to me, so naturally I wouldn't think of opening it . . ."

"Of course not, I know you wouldn't," he said, fluttering his hand and sitting erect. "I'm sorry and you must dismiss it, like one of those annoying personal questions you find so often nowadays on supposedly impersonal forms."

I didn't believe him. "But was it opened, sir? Someone might have gone into my things . . ."

"Oh, no, nothing like that. Please forget the question . . . And tell me, please, what are your plans after graduation?"

"I'm not sure, sir. I'd like to be asked to remain at the college as a teacher, or as a member of the administrative staff. And . . . Well . . ."

"Yes? And what else?"

"Well—er, I guess I'd really like to become Dr. Bledsoe's[2] assistant . . ."

"Oh, I see," he said, sitting back and forming his mouth into a thin-lipped circle. "You're very ambitious."

"I guess I am, sir. But I'm willing to work hard."

"Ambition is a wonderful force," he said, "but sometimes it can be blinding . . . On the other hand, it can make you successful—like my father . . ." A new edge came into his voice and he frowned and looked down at his hands, which were trembling. "The only trouble with ambition is that it sometimes blinds one to realities . . . Tell me, how many of these letters do you have?"

"I had about seven, sir," I replied, confused by his new turn. "They're—"

---

1. **Alma Mater.** College or school that one attended
2. **Dr. Bledsoe.** President of the college that the narrator has been asked to leave. Bledsoe has, however, provided the narrator with letters of "introduction" to help him find a job.

"*Seven!*" He was suddenly angry.

"Yes, sir, that was all he gave me . . ."

"And how many of these gentlemen have you succeeded in seeing, may I ask?"

A sinking feeling came over me. "I haven't seen any of them personally, sir."

"And this is your last letter?"

"Yes, sir, it is, but I expect to hear from the others . . . They said—"

"Of course you will, and from all seven. They're all loyal Americans."

There was unmistakable irony in his voice now, and I didn't know what to say.

"Seven," he repeated mysteriously. "Oh, don't let me upset you," he said with an elegant gesture of self-disgust. "I had a difficult session with my analyst last evening and the slightest thing is apt to set me off. Like an alarm clock without control— Say!" he said, slapping his palms against his thighs. "What on earth does that mean?" Suddenly he was in a state. One side of his face had begun to twitch and swell.

I watched him light a cigarette, thinking, What on earth is this all about?

"Some things are just too unjust for words," he said, expelling a plume of smoke, "and too ambiguous for either speech or ideas. By the way, have you ever been to the Club Calamus?"

"I don't think I've ever heard of it, sir," I said.

"You haven't? It's very well known. Many of my Harlem friends go there. It's a rendezvous for writers, artists and all kinds of celebrities. There's nothing like it in the city, and by some strange twist it has a truly continental flavor."

"I've never been to a night club, sir. I'll have to go there to see what it's like after I've started earning some money," I said, hoping to bring the conversation back to the problem of jobs.

He looked at me with a jerk of his head, his face beginning to twitch again.

"I suppose I've been evading the issue again—as always. Look," he burst out impulsively. "Do you believe that two people, two strangers who have never seen one another before can speak with utter frankness and sincerity?"

"Sir?"

"Oh, damn! What I mean is, do you believe it possible for us, the two of us, to throw off the mask of custom and manners that insulate man from man, and converse in naked honesty and frankness?"

"I don't know what you mean exactly, sir," I said.

"Are you sure?"

"I . . ."

"Of course, of course. If I could only speak plainly! I'm confusing you. Such frankness just isn't possible because all our motives are impure. Forget what I just said. I'll try to put it this way—and remember this, please . . ."

My head spun. He was addressing me, leaning forward confidentially, as though he'd known me for years, and I remembered something my grandfather had said long ago: *Don't let no white man tell you his business, 'cause after he tells you he's liable to git shame he tole it to you and then he'll hate you. Fact is, he was hating you all the time . . .*

". . . I want to try to reveal a part of reality that is most important to you—but I warn you, it's going to hurt. No, let me finish," he said, touching my knee lightly and quickly removing his hand as I shifted my position.

"What I want to do is done very seldom, and, to be honest, it wouldn't happen now if I hadn't sustained a series of impossible frustrations. You see—well, I'm a thwarted . . . Oh, damn, there I go again, thinking only of myself . . . We're both frustrated, understand? Both of us, and I want to help you . . ."

"You mean you'll let me see Mr. Emerson?"

He frowned. "Please don't seem so happy about it, and don't leap to conclusions. I want to help, but there is a tyranny involved . . ."

"A *tyranny?*" My lungs tightened.

"Yes. That's a way of putting it. Because to help you I must disillusion you . . ."

"Oh, I don't think I mind, sir. Once I see Mr. Emerson, it'll be up to me. All I want to do is speak to him."

"*Speak* to him," he said, getting quickly to his feet and mashing his cigarette into the tray with shaking fingers. "No one speaks *to* him. *He* does the speaking—" Suddenly he broke off. "On second thought, perhaps you'd better leave me your address and I'll mail you Mr. Emerson's reply in the morning. He's really a very busy man."

His whole manner had changed.

"But you said . . ." I stood up, completely confused. Was he having fun with me? "Couldn't you let me talk to him for just five minutes?" I pleaded. "I'm sure I can convince him that I'm worthy of a job. And if there's someone who has tampered with my letter, I'll prove my identity . . . Dr. Bledsoe would—"

"Identity! My God! Who has any identity any more anyway? It isn't so perfectly simple. Look," he said with an anguished gesture. "Will you trust me?"

"Why, yes, sir, I trust you."

He leaned forward. "Look," he said, his face working violently, "I was trying to tell you that I know many things about you—not you personally, but fellows like you. Not much, either, but still more than the average. With us it's still Jim and Huck Finn.[1] A number of my friends are jazz musicians, and I've been around. I know the conditions under which you live—Why go back, fellow? There is so much you could do here where there is more freedom. You won't find what you're looking for when you return anyway; because so much is involved that you can't possibly know. Please don't misunderstand me; I don't say all this to impress you. Or to give myself some kind of sadistic catharsis. Truly, I don't. But I do know this world you're trying to contact—all its virtues and all its unspeakables—Ha, yes, unspeakables. I'm afraid my father considers me one of the unspeakables . . . I'm Huckleberry, you see . . ."

He laughed drily as I tried to make sense of his ramblings. *Huckleberry?* Why did he keep talking about that kid's story? I was puzzled and annoyed that he could talk to me this way because he stood between me and a job, the campus . . .

"But I only want a job, sir," I said. "I only want to make enough money to return to my studies."

"Of course, but surely you suspect there is more to it than that. Aren't you curious about what lies behind the face of things?"

"Yes, sir, but I'm mainly interested in a job."

"Of course," he said, "but life isn't that simple . . ."

"But I'm not bothered about all the other things, whatever they are, sir. They're not for me to interfere with and I'll be satisfied to go back to college and remain there as long as they'll allow me to."

"But I want to help you do what is best," he said. "What's *best*, mind you. Do you wish to do what's best for yourself?"

"Why, yes, sir. I suppose I do . . ."

"Then forget about returning to the college. Go somewhere else . . ."

"You mean leave?"

"Yes, forget it . . ."

"But you said that you would help me!"

"I did and I am—"

"But what about seeing Mr. Emerson?"

"Oh, God! Don't you see that it's best that you do *not* see him?"

Suddenly I could not breathe. Then I was standing, gripping my brief case. "What have you got against me?" I blurted. "What did I ever do to you? You never intended to let me see him. Even though I presented my letter of introduction. Why? Why? I'd never endanger *your* job—"

"No, no, no! Of course not," he cried, getting to his feet. "You've misunderstood me. You mustn't do that! God, there's too much misunderstanding. Please don't think I'm trying to prevent you from seeing my—from seeing Mr. Emerson out of prejudice . . ."

"Yes, sir, I do," I said angrily. "I was sent here by a friend of his. You read the letter, but still you refuse to let me see him, and now you're trying to get me to leave college. What kind of man are you, anyway? What have you got against me? You, a northern white man!"

He looked pained. "I've done it badly," he said, "but you must believe that I am trying to advise you what is best for you." He snatched off his glasses.

"But *I* know what's best for me," I said. "Or at least Dr. Bledsoe does, and if I can't see Mr. Emerson today, just tell me when I can and I'll be here . . ."

He bit his lips and shut his eyes, shaking his head from side to side as though fighting back a scream. "I'm sorry, really sorry that I started all of this," he said, suddenly calm. "It was foolish of me to try to advise you, but please, you mustn't believe that I'm against you . . . or your race. I'm your friend. Some of the finest people I know are Neg—Well, you see, Mr. Emerson is my father."

"Your father!"

"My father, yes, though I would have preferred it other-wise. But he is, and I could arrange for you to see him. But to be utterly frank, I'm incapable of such cynicism. It would do you no good."

"But I'd like to take my chances, Mr. Emerson, sir . . . This is very important to me. My whole career depends upon it."

"But you *have* no chance," he said.

"But Dr. Bledsoe sent me here," I said, growing more excited. "I must have a chance . . ."

"Dr. Bledsoe," he said with distaste. "He's like my . . . he ought to be horsewhipped! Here," he said, sweeping up the letter and thrusting it crackling toward me. I took it, looking into his eyes that burned back at me.

"Go on, read it," he cried excitedly. "Go on!"

"But I wasn't asking for this," I said.

"Read it!"

My dear Mr. Emerson:

The bearer of this letter is a former student of ours (I say *former* because he shall never, under any circumstances, be enrolled as a student here again) who has

---

1. **Jim and Huck Finn.** Characters in the novel *The Adventures of Huckleberry Finn*, by Mark Twain

been expelled for a most serious defection from our strictest rules of deportment.

Due, however, to circumstances the nature of which I shall explain to you in person on the occasion of the next meeting of the board, it is to the best interests of the college that this young man have no knowledge of the finality of his expulsion. For it is indeed his hope to return here to his classes in the fall. However, it is to the best interests of the great work which we are dedicated to perform, that he continue undisturbed in these vain hopes while remaining as far as possible from our midst.

This case represents, my dear Mr. Emerson, one of the rare, delicate instances in which one for whom we held great expectations has gone grievously astray, and who in his fall threatens to upset certain delicate relationships between certain interested individuals and the school. Thus, while the bearer is no longer a member of our scholastic family, it is highly important that his severance with the college be executed as painlessly as possible. I beg of you, sir, to help him continue in the direction of that promise which, like the horizon, recedes ever brightly and distantly beyond the hopeful traveler.

Respectfully, I am your
humble servant,

A. Hebert Bledsoe

I raised my head. Twenty-five years seemed to have lapsed between his handing me the letter and my grasping its message. I could not believe it, tried to read it again. I could not believe it, yet I had a feeling that it all had happened before. I rubbed my eyes, and they felt sandy as though all the fluids had suddenly dried.

"I'm sorry," he said. "I'm terribly sorry."

"What did I do? I always tried to do the right thing . . ."

"*That* you must tell me," he said. "To what does he refer?"

"I don't know, I don't know . . ."

"But you must have done *something*."

"I took a man for a drive, showed him into the Golden Day[1] to help him when he became ill . . . I don't know . . ."

I told him falteringly of the visit to Trueblood's[2] and the trip to the Golden Day and of my expulsion, watching his mobile face reflecting his reaction to each detail.

"It's little enough," he said when I had finished. "I don't understand the man. He is very complicated."

"I only wanted to return and help," I said.

"You'll never return. You can't return now," he said. "Don't you see? I'm terribly sorry and yet I'm glad that I gave in to the impulse to speak to you. Forget it; though that's advice which I've been unable to accept myself, it's still good advice. There is no point in blinding yourself to the truth. Don't blind yourself . . ."

I got up, dazed, and started toward the door. He came behind me into the reception room where the birds flamed in the cage, their squawks like screams in a nightmare.

He stammered guiltily, "Please, I must ask you never to mention this conversation to anyone."

"No," I said.

"I wouldn't mind, but my father would consider my revelation the most extreme treason . . . You're free of him now. I'm still his prisoner. You have been freed, don't you understand? I've still my battle." He seemed near tears.

"I won't," I said. "No one would believe me. I can't myself. There must be some mistake. There must be . . ."

I opened the door.

"Look, fellow," he said. "This evening I'm having a party at the Calamus. Would you like to join my guests? It might help you—"

"No, thank you, sir. I'll be all right."

"Perhaps you'd like to be my valet?"

I looked at him. "No, thank you, sir," I said.

"Please," he said. "I really want to help. Look, I happen to know of a possible job at Liberty Paints. My father has sent several fellows there . . . You should try—"

I shut the door.

The elevator dropped me like a shot and I went out and walked along the street. The sun was very bright now and the people along the walk seemed far away. I stopped before a gray wall where high above me the headstones of a church graveyard arose like the tops of buildings. Across the street in the shade of an awning a shoeshine boy was dancing for pennies. I went on to the corner and got on a bus and went automatically to the rear. In the seat in front of me a dark man in a panama hat kept whistling a tune between his teeth.

My mind flew in circles, to Bledsoe, Emerson and back again. There was no sense to be made of it. It was

---

1. **Golden Day.** Tavern
2. **Trueblood's.** Farm of a local African American near the narrator's college

a joke. Hell, it couldn't be a joke. Yes, it is a joke . . . Suddenly the bus jerked to a stop and I heard myself humming the same tune that the man ahead was whistling, and the words came back:

> O well they picked poor Robin clean
> O well they picked poor Robin clean
> Well they tied poor Robin to a stump
> Lawd, they picked all the feathers round
>   from Robin's rump
> Well they picked poor Robin clean.

Then I was on my feet, hurrying to the door, hearing the thin, tissue-paper-against-the-teeth-of-a-comb whistle following me outside at the next stop. I stood trembling at the curb, watching and half expecting to see the man leap from the door to follow me, whistling the old forgotten jingle about a bare-rumped robin. My mind seized upon the tune. I took the subway and it still droned through my mind after I had reached my room at Men's House and lay across the bed. What was the who-what-when-why-where of poor old Robin? What had he done and who had tied him and why had they plucked him and why had we sung of his fate? It was for a laugh, for a laugh, all the kids had laughed and laughed, and the droll tuba player of the old Elk's band had rendered it solo on his helical horn; with comical flourishes and doleful phrasing, "*Boo boo boo booooo*, Poor Robin clean"—a mock funeral dirge . . . But who was Robin and for what had he been hurt and humiliated?

Suddenly I lay shaking with anger. It was no good. I thought of young Emerson. What if he'd lied out of some ulterior motive of his own? Everyone seemed to have some plan for me, and beneath that some more secret plan. What was young Emerson's plan—and why should it have included me? Who was I anyway? I tossed fitfully. Perhaps it was a test of my good will and faith—But that's a lie, I thought. It's a lie and you know it's a lie. I had seen the letter and it had practically ordered me killed. By slow degrees . . .

"My dear Mr. Emerson," I said aloud. "The Robin bearing this letter is a former student. Please hope him to death, and keep him running. Your most humble and obedient servant, A. H. Bledsoe . . ."

Sure, that's the way it was, I thought, a short, concise verbal *coup de grace*,[1] straight to the nape of the neck. And Emerson would write in reply? Sure: "Dear Bled, have met Robin and shaved tail. Signed, Emerson."

I sat on the bed and laughed. They'd sent me to the rookery, all right. I laughed and felt numb and weak, knowing that soon the pain would come and that no matter what happened to me I'd never be the same. I felt numb and I was laughing. When I stopped, gasping for breath, I decided that I would go back and kill Bledsoe. Yes, I thought, I owe it to the race and to myself. I'll kill him.

And the boldness of the idea and the anger behind it made me move with decision. I had to have a job and I took what I hoped was the quickest means. I called the plant young Emerson had mentioned, and it worked. I was told to report the following morning. It happened so quickly and with such ease that for a moment I felt turned around. Had they planned it this way? But no, they wouldn't catch me again. This time *I* had made the move.

I could hardly get to sleep for dreaming of revenge.

---

1. *coup de grace*. Death blow

# Guided Writing

## PROBLEM-SOLUTION ESSAY

"You write where you are. It's the only thing you have to give. And if you are fortunate enough, there is a spark that will somehow ignite a work so that it touches almost anyone who reads it. "

—Gloria Naylor

At noon, a tall junior named Mike laughs with friends across the street from Wilson High School. Five minutes into the lunch period, the vice-principal crosses the street and singles Mike out for detention.

Wilson High has a closed-campus policy and this is the third time Mike has been reprimanded for leaving the school property. Mike says there were dozens of other students with him when the vice-principal approached and none of them were caught. When his mother asks him why he gets in trouble, Mike answers that the vice-principal doesn't like his clothes or hair. Any way you look at it, Mike has a problem.

Like most problems we face, Mike's dilemma has many solutions. In this case, Mike wrote the vice-principal a letter defining the problem as one of discrimination and proposing that the closed-campus rule either be applied equally or forgotten altogether. Others might argue that the problem has more to do with Mike's own behavior, but such differences in opinion are what make problems so intriguing.

In this unit, you have read postwar literature dealing with racism, war, and poverty. These issues still face us as we enter the twenty-first century. So do new problems that develop from changes in the ways we think and live. Fortunately, we possess a unique human intelligence and ability to solve problems or at least to lessen their impact. Much of real-world writing, such as letters, reports, and memos, deals with understanding problems and finding solutions.

A **problem-solution essay** is a form of persuasive writing that analyzes an issue and proposes a well-considered solution.

**WRITING ASSIGNMENT.** Write a problem-solution essay in which you look closely at a problem in your life, take a stand, and suggest ways to solve the problem.

## Student Model—Revised
### by Allison Stewart

Allison Stewart, an eleventh-grade student at Grant High School, wrote about a problem facing students in her school district. As you read the model, see if you can identify the key issue of the problem and what action she suggests schools take.

> Four male students, all juniors, cluster around one of the Internet-ready computers against the wall. They

are as far away from the scrutiny of the librarian as is possible. They snicker and make knowing gestures to one another. Their faces redden as their bodies convulse with laughter. A nearby freshman abandons her work and leaves the library. Does this scene look familiar to you? While it is true that the Internet offers the largest single source of information in high schools, some damage occurs because of its unrestricted use. This access to information can lead to dangerous and unhealthy behaviors. Because of the potential for harm, I believe Internet access at school should be restricted by installing a computer program to block out inappropriate web sites.

Adult theme web sites are a growing, moneymaking industry and the people who post them work to make their sites accessible. This ease of access can be a problem for anyone who has a computer, especially young people at school. When you consider that nearly all schools have Internet access, you can see how widespread the problem is. Some of the web sites that students log onto contain material that is in no way related to school activities. Sites like these are, at the least, a waste of time.

But more than taking time away from learning, some adult theme sites are offensive and destructive because they promote violence, racism, hatred, pornography, and drug use. Web sites with this material are harmful to the students viewing them as well as everyone sitting around them.

A common argument from high school students is that they have seen all this information before. It comes as no surprise. But to many students, it is a surprise. Some of the information in these sites can conflict with students' moral, religious, and ethical beliefs. It makes them feel uncomfortable and takes their focus away from learning.

This problem of inappropriate access, either on purpose or by accident, can be solved by having

**EXAMINING THE MODEL.** In her essay, Allison defines the problem and states a solution. To her, inappropriate material on the Internet is damaging enough to warrant restricting access to certain sites. What arguments did she use to support her proposition? In what ways do you agree with her? In what ways do you disagree? How well does she address the concerns that a reader might have? She intended her audience to be other students. What words and sentences sound natural and reasonable to you?

Internet block programs installed in all school computers. Web sites would be limited to subjects that are in harmony with generally accepted subject matter.

With any type of limitation, you risk restricting access to useful information. This could be seen as a problem, since the Internet does contain much updated material. For example, if a health teacher assigned a report about the dangerous effects of marijuana on the human immune system, web sites on the drug might be restricted. This is a small drawback. If you restrict sites, you will lose some advantages of the Internet. But high school students can benefit from this obstacle by exploring other sources of information.

By installing an Internet block program, adult theme and other inappropriate web sites will be abolished from the school system. The learning environment will be healthier and safer. I think restricting access to violent and inappropriate sites might even help reduce the chance of another shooting or bombing in schools.

Remember that a thesis is a main idea that is supported by an essay.

## Prewriting

WRITING WITH A PLAN. Pick a problem that you know and care about. Your best writing will flow from this. Choose an issue that is arguable and is as yet unsolved. It needn't be a major controversy. Small, local issues can have just as much meaning. You can talk about a policy or rule we should adopt or why we should stop doing something. Whatever you choose, make it real.

Once you have an issue to discuss, begin your writing by simply gathering as many ideas as you can. A good way to do this is to find another person to talk with about your topic. Have a conversation that asks and answers questions. What is the problem? Who is harmed most by this problem? What examples can you provide of the problem? Why should anyone care about this issue? What solutions come readily to mind? What new problems might come from these solutions? If you keep a pad of paper nearby, you can jot good ideas as they arise. This "talk-write" technique is a powerful way to start the ideas flowing.

Allison used the graphic organizer below to help her create more ideas and see new connections.

## Student Model—Graphic Organizer

### Statement of Problem or Thesis Statement

**Problem:** Students using Internet at school to access inappropriate material.

| Harmful effects | Causes of problem |
|---|---|
| wastes time | profit motive |
| some sites promote violence, racism, and other destructive behaviors | propaganda motive |
| chat rooms could introduce students to dangerous people | unsuspecting, unsophisticated students |
| schools liable | |
| exposes kids to illegal activities | |
| may offend morals and ethics | |
| misinformation | |
| takes away from learning | |
| makes other students uncomfortable | |
| harmful to students | |

### Possible solutions

get rid of all computers

have more teachers or aides watching students

trust kids or warn kids not to surf those sites

restrict access with blocker programs

### Reasons why my solution will work

students won't have access to questionable sites at school

students won't be able to get around adults to reach sites

doesn't rely on students' compliance

### Arguments against your solution

young people see all that stuff anyway in movies, on the news

kids are not affected by it

teenagers are old enough to understand and sort through the information

students have a right to look

### Responses to arguments

many students <u>haven't</u> seen or been exposed to the level of material on Internet

some kids believe and do the things they read in these web sites

the school has a responsibility to see that students study appropriate topics from reliable sources

if young people want to check out those sites they can do it on their own time instead of making people at school feel uncomfortable

Copy the graphic organizer and complete it for your own issue. List all the harmful effects from the problem. Next, list the causes of the problem. The next category includes all the possible solutions you can think of. Once you've identified possible solutions, think about which solutions will eliminate or reduce the effects of the problem and which solutions will get at the causes of the problem. Solutions that get at the causes are the ones you will want to advocate. Circle the strongest solution. In the next area, list the reasons it will work. Now list arguments others may have to this solution. Answer why those objections aren't valid, or how, if they are valid, they won't be significant. Use your graphic organizer as a blueprint for your essay.

## Language, Grammar, and Style

### Effective Use of Transitions

**IDENTIFYING TRANSITIONS.** Transition words and phrases help the reader follow what you are trying to say. They connect one idea to another and give your writing coherence and unity. Repeated nouns, synonyms, and pronouns can also serve as transitions. For examples of transition words and phrases, see the Language Arts Survey 2.35, "Using Transitions Effectively."

It is not enough to scatter transitions around and hope they help. You want to choose the right transition to show a specific connection between ideas.

The following two sentences from Allison's rough draft didn't make a lot sense as they stood. The reader had to stop and wonder what the connection was.

**Example**:
It comes as no surprise. To many students, it is a surprise.

Look what happens when a simple transition word showing contrast is added:

It comes as no surprise. <u>But</u> to many students, it is a surprise.

Search through Allison's final draft and see if you can find other places where she used transition words to guide the reader along.

**IDENTIFYING YOUR AUDIENCE.** Because you are writing about a real and pressing issue, you may want to share your essay with parents, teachers, administrators, readers of the city newspaper, or other people in the community. How might the age or interests of your readers affect the examples you use or the information you present? After determining the age and interests of your readers, consider their background and opinions on the topic and adjust your language and arguments accordingly. You will not use all the available arguments in your paper. Use the ones you think most appealing to your audience.

**FINDING YOUR VOICE.** If you argue a position on an issue that you care about, your natural voice, personality, and attitude will come through in your writing. Sometimes, because you care a lot about your topic, your natural voice may sound strident. Then, again, you may find your voice too accommodating; in order to avoid offending someone, you might risk sounding too tentative. For the problem-solution essay, strive to use your most reasonable voice to convince readers your solution is viable. How can you adjust your voice so that your arguments will be well received? Try rewriting the sentences below so that they reflect your own, most reasonable voice.

Unless you are a complete idiot, you should know that jet skis make too much noise.

If you are a decent, law-abiding American citizen, you will uphold the fabric of our community and save our country from moral corruption by voting for this law.

This is just my opinion; you may not agree with me and that is all right because your opinion is just as good as mine.

### Drafting

Consider the information on your graphic organizer to help you determine your thesis, the statement that identifies the key issue of the problem and presents a thoughtful solution.

Look at Allison's thesis: "Because of the potential for harm, I believe Internet access at school should be restricted by installing a computer program to block out inappropriate web sites." From that statement we know that she will probably define inappropriate web sites, outline some of their harmful effects, and explain why the program blocks are the best solution. That's what a good thesis does: it gives the reader the plan for the paper.

Now use your thesis and the information on your graphic organizer to write your first draft, exploring the problem and your solution. Don't focus on mechanics or style at this point. Focus on finding out what it is you think and what you want to say.

Look over your draft. Add an introduction that hooks your reader into your paper with an anecdote, a surprising fact, or an unusual observation. Check to make sure you have included your thesis statement. Often, the thesis statement is the last sentence in the introductory paragraph.

For the body of your paper, give specific reasons to support your opinion. Back up these reasons with facts, statistics, examples or quotes from experts. Let your reader know that you are aware of other points of view and have considered other solutions and rejected them. That way your reader is more likely to accept your solution as the best. Include any background information your reader may need to understand.

Strive for a conclusion that is clearly tied to the problem you have defined in your essay. Use your natural voice, reasonable and committed, but don't be afraid to show strong conviction.

## Reflecting

Writing a problem-solution essay involves learning to see an issue from all sides and learning to imagine and understand opposing viewpoints. Consider these questions as you reflect on your experience. How did your arguments change as you wrote? Why do you think that happened? What did you learn about the topic that you hadn't thought of before? How did opposing arguments help you formulate your own solution?

## Self- and Peer Evaluation

Once you have a satisfactory rough draft, complete a self-evaluation of your writing. If you can, find another student you suspect holds a different opinion than yours and seek that student's feedback. The true test of your arguments will come from opposition.

- Who is the intended audience for this essay? Would you guess this audience is friendly or hostile toward the message? How does the information relate to that audience?
- What is the problem and for whom is it a problem? How well did the writer explain why it is a problem?
- What background does the essay give about the problem? Where might the reader need more or less information?
- Which sentence most clearly describes the writer's solution to the problem?
- What are the main arguments or points in each paragraph?
- Which supporting reasons are illustrated with facts, examples, or details and which are lacking these? How could the weak reasons be improved?
- Where, if anywhere, do ideas suddenly stop or seem disconnected from the ideas around them? Where can you find logical links between sentences and paragraphs? Which transitions could help connect them?
- How would you describe your voice? Does it fit the intended audience? Are there any places where the voice does not sound true or reasonable? How could you improve those sections?

Another type of transition connects ideas by repeating or echoing phrases or words between sentences and paragraphs. Find the words that Allison uses in the last sentence of a paragraph and repeats in the first sentence of the next paragraph.

**Example:**
Some of the web sites that students log onto contain material that is in no way related to school activities. Sites like these are, at the least, a waste of <u>time</u>.

But more than taking <u>time</u> away from learning, some adult theme sites are offensive and destructive because they promote violence, racism, hatred, pornography, and drug use.

By repeating the word *time* and paraphrasing *waste*, the second paragraph shows a clear connection to the first. The reader is told that a new argument will now be added to the concept of wasting time.

The echo transition guides your reader from one point to another, and your reader will call it good writing when he or she can follow you perfectly. Standard transition words can also link two paragraphs, although you may find these transition words can sound too abrupt. For variety and a more subtle approach, try the echo transition for a paragraph hook.

*continued on page 856*

**FIXING TRANSITIONS.** Use transition words or phrases to connect these two sentences from Allison's rough draft. Think about the connection between the sentences and choose a transition that shows it.

This could be seen as a problem, since the Internet does contain much updated material. If a health teacher assigned a report about the dangerous effects of marijuana on the human immune system, web sites on the drug might be restricted.

Now try connecting the following paragraphs by using an echo transition. Paraphrase or repeat words from the end of one paragraph in the beginning of the next:

Because of the potential for harm, I believe Internet access at school should be restricted by installing a computer program to block out inappropriate web sites.

Adult theme web sites are a growing moneymaking industry and the people who post them work to make their sites accessible.

Look at Allison's self- and peer evaluations for the first three paragraphs of her rough draft.

## Student Model—Draft

*Maybe a scene where kids are messing around w/a site?*

One of my classmates tells me, "I believe that anyone and everyone is entitled to the right to look up anything at school." In Patrick's point of view, this is a strong argument for why the Internet should not be restricted to students. The Internet offers the largest single source of information in high schools. But this opportunity for information can lead to dangerous and unhealthy behaviors. Because of the potential for harm, I believe Internet access at school should be restricted by installing a computer program that blocks out inappropriate web sites.

*weak intro— "I" states the opposite of your thesis*

*—Good, clear thesis*

*Other harmful effects you can add here?*

*These inappropriate* *use echo transition*

Adult theme web sites are a growing, money-making industry and the people who post them work to make their sites accessible. This ease of access can be a problem for anyone who has a computer, especially young people at school. Some of the web sites that students log onto contain material that is in no way related to school activities. Sites like these are, at the least, a waste of time.

*—Any idea of how many schools are wired for Internet? That would show how big a problem*

*Transition? what?*

Some are offensive and destructive because they promote violence, racism, hatred, pornography, and drug use. Web sites with this material are harmful to the students viewing them as well as everyone sitting around them. Schools have a responsibility to the students who attend. They are even legally liable. *Who is your anticipated audience? Not all will be swayed by this argument*

## Revising and Proofreading

Look over your self- and peer evaluations and use the responses from them as a starting point for making decisions about revising your draft. Omit unnecessary words and add explanations and transitions where you need them. Make sure that you have included all the important ideas from your graphic organizer. Strive for clear, uncluttered language that builds a strong argument. When your revision says what you want it to say, proofread it. Check your spelling, grammar, punctuation, and other details.

A good way to finish a paper is to read it aloud and listen for problems. Run-on sentences and other technical glitches are easy to spot when you read aloud.

For more information, see the Language Arts Survey 2.45, "A Proofreading Checklist."

## Publishing and Presenting

If you have written about a real problem, you will want to publish and present your piece to your intended audience. For example, if you have an essay on a school problem, consider submitting it to the school or local newspaper, the PTA, school board, or student council. Prepare your piece for presentation to this real audience.

**USING TRANSITIONS EFFECTIVELY.** Find and underline a section in your writing where you move from one idea to the next, someplace where you are making a shift. Do you have a transition there? How could you improve the flow by using either standard transition words or an echo transition between paragraphs? Add them as needed throughout your paper, reading your work aloud to see how it sounds. Demonstrate five effective transitions in your paper by highlighting them in a copy of your final paper.

"It always comes back to the same necessity: go deep enough and there is a bedrock of truth, however hard."

—May Sarton

# UNIT REVIEW
## *Postwar Literature (1945–1960)*

## Words for Everyday Use

Check your knowledge of the following vocabulary words from the selections in this unit. Write short sentences using these words in context to make the meaning clear. To review the definition or usage of a word, refer to the page number listed or the Glossary of Words for Everyday Use.

abjectly, 817
abstinence, 832
apparatus, 820
apprehension, 826
ascetic, 811
avow, 814
baleful, 827
buffet, 837
celerity, 768
console, 781
convivial, 837
cowed, 767
deception, 827
decipher, 827
dupe, 826
elicit, 827
endow, 826
enthralled, 826
evasively, 826
exasperating, 819
finicky, 833
grovel, 767
guffawing, 793

haggard, 821
hedonistic, 836
hullabaloo, 835
imperceptible, 812
incendiary, 835
incessant, 836
inherently, 810
intermittent, 835
intrigue, 827
limber, 798
list, 786
machination, 816
meager, 810
menagerie, 811
morose, 791
nuptial, 815
obsessed, 777
ominous, 787
ordain, 810
pendulum, 798
philanthropy, 833
placid, 791
pommel, 836

prevail, 777
profusion, 816
pullet, 799
quivering, 798
ravenous, 789
ravenously, 814
ravine, 800
refrain, 819
relentless, 818
rendezvous, 832
repugnant, 838
rouse, 798
skulk, 767
sullen, 788
sultry, 792
summon, 826
tendril, 781
theological, 838
tinker, 789
trepidation, 815
vestibule, 820
volition, 831
xenophobic, 838

## Literary Tools

Define the following terms, giving concrete examples of how they are used in the selections in this unit. To review a term, refer to the page number indicated or to the Handbook of Literary Terms.

aim, 771, 824
antihero, 808
archetype, 796
autobiography, 824
character, 796
characterization, 765
effect, 830

elegy, 780
half rhyme, 765
internal rhyme, 775
irony, 830
metaphor, 780
motivation, 808
near rhyme, 765

off rhyme, 765
parallelism, 775
slant rhyme, 765
Southern Gothic, 784
symbol, 784
tone, 771

# Reflecting
## ........... *on* YOUR READING

## Genre Studies

1. **POETRY.** In "Commander Lowell" and "Elegy for Jane," characterization is used to draw a portrait of a character. Writers use three major techniques to create characters: direct description, portrayal of characters' behavior, and representations of characters' internal states. Describe the techniques of characterization used for each poem and explain why the poets decided to use the techniques they did. What kind of character does each poet draw?

2. **SHORT STORY.** "The Life You Save May Be Your Own," "A Worn Path," and "The Magic Barrel" use the third-person point of view. Review **point of view** in the Handbook of Literary Terms. Then, tell which stories use a limited point of view and which use an omniscient point of view. How would each story have been different if the other point of view were used?

## Thematic Studies

3. **RELATIONSHIPS.** "To Black Women" and the selection from *Black Boy* discuss relationships that are important to the narrators. What is the nature of the relationships described in these two works? What do the narrators get from their relationships? Are the relationships presented as beneficial or harmful to the narrators?

4. **LOVE.** What types of love are portrayed in "A Worn Path" and "The Magic Barrel"? What are the goals of the lover in each? How is the beloved portrayed? What is the lover willing to do for the beloved? Which example of love is more altruistic, or selfless?

## Historical/Biographical Studies

5. **WORLD WAR II AND ITS AFTERMATH.** Reflect on "Commander Lowell," "The Death of the Ball Turret Gunner," "To Black Women," and "A Noiseless Flash." What social realities are reflected in these writings from Unit 10? What historic events are referenced?

*Marilyn Diptych*, 1962. Andy Warhol.
Tate Gallery, London.

I write of one life only. My own. If my story is true, I trust it will resonate with significance for other lives.

—Richard Rodriguez

## ArtNote

*Marilyn Diptych*, 1962. Andy Warhol, page 860–861.

Andy Warhol (1930–1987) began his career in advertising, an experience which influenced the work he later exhibited in art galleries. In his depiction of 1950s movie star Marilyn Monroe, Warhol repeats her photograph until it disintegrates. What is Warhol saying about the effect the mass media has on our perception of celebrities?

# EARLY CONTEMPORARY LITERATURE (1960–1980)

## THE TURBULENT SIXTIES

When **John F. Kennedy** defeated **Richard Nixon** in 1960, becoming the youngest man ever to hold the office of president, it seemed to many that a new age had dawned. Kennedy, a committed cold warrior, supported a covert operation to invade **Fidel Castro's** Cuba, the **Bay of Pigs Invasion**. The invasion failed and further increased tensions with the Soviets, leading in 1962 to the **Cuban Missile Crisis**, in which Kennedy warned the Soviets to remove newly installed nuclear missiles from Cuba or face war. The threat of nuclear war seemed, for a few days, all too real. Thereafter, the Soviet Union, Great Britain, and the United States negotiated the first of many treaties related to limitations on the testing and use of nuclear arms. However, the arms race continued unabated, with each side following a policy of "mutually assured destruction" to prevent the other from making a first strike.

In the 1950s, race relations had become a central issue in the United States following the 1954 decision in which the Supreme Court ruled separate but unequal schools unconstitutional. This ruling was followed in 1955 by a successful boycott, led by the **Reverend Martin Luther King, Jr.**, of segregated buses in Montgomery, Alabama. Kennedy supported the **Civil Rights movement**, sending federal troops in 1962 and 1963 to ensure enrollment of African-American students in two Southern universities. Late in 1963, the popular President Kennedy was assassinated in Dallas, Texas. This act and the subsequent assassinations of Martin Luther King, Jr. and Robert Kennedy left the United States in a state of shock.

Kennedy's successor, **Lyndon Johnson**, carried on his predecessor's civil rights policies, pressing for the passage of the **Civil Rights Act** of 1964, which protected against discrimination in accommodations and employment and tied federal funding of education to desegregation of schools. The Voting Rights Act of 1965 followed, protecting

## LITERARY EVENTS

➤ = American Events

➤ 1960. John Updike's *Rabbit, Run* and Anne Sexton's *To Bedlam and Half Way Back* published

➤ 1961. Joseph Heller's *Catch 22* published

➤ 1962. Rachel Carson's *Silent Spring* published

➤ 1963. Sylvia Plath's *The Bell Jar* published

➤ 1964. Saul Bellow's *The Zog* published

➤ 1965. *The Autobiography of Malcolm X* published

➤ 1966. Katherine Anne Porter's *Collected Short Stories* published

1967. Gabriel García Márquez's *One Hundred Years of Solitude* published

**1960**          **1964**          **1968**

## HISTORICAL EVENTS

➤ 1960. John F. Kennedy elected president

➤ 1961. United States severs relations with Cuba; Bay of Pigs invasion fails; Berlin Wall erected

➤ 1962. Cuban Missile Crisis

➤ 1964. President Johnson reelected

➤ 1963. President Kennedy assassinated; Lyndon B. Johnson sworn in as president; Martin Luther King, Jr., delivers his "I Have a Dream" speech

➤ 1965. Vietnam War begins; Malcolm X is killed

➤ 1967. Thurgood Marshall becomes first African-American Supreme Court justice

➤ 1968. Robert F. Kennedy assassinated

➤ 1968. Martin Luther King, Jr. assassinated

➤ 1969. Neil Armstrong walks on the moon

against discrimination at the polls. In spite of these measures, major race riots occurred in several American cities in 1965, 1967, and 1968.

After defeating **Barry Goldwater** in the presidential election of 1964, Johnson initiated a legislative program designed to build what he called the **"Great Society,"** using his considerable political skills to push through a series of social welfare measures, including bills related to housing, health care for the elderly, and education. The political life of the United States since the Johnson era has been dominated by debates over such legislation, with conservatives supporting greater defense spending and less spending on domestic programs, and liberals supporting less spending on defense and greater spending on domestic programs.

Despite his political accomplishments, Johnson was to have a troubled administration because of involvement in a widely unpopular war in the Southeast Asian country of Vietnam. In 1964 an attack on United States ships led to the Gulf of Tonkin Resolution, committing the country to a "police action," commonly referred to as the **Vietnam War**, that proved to be extremely divisive, fomenting antiwar demonstrations throughout the United States.

Martin Luther King, Jr. (left) and Malcolm X (right), 1964.

These demonstrations were part of a larger "counterculture" rebellion among American youth who, relatively prosperous themselves because of their parents' material gains during the fifties, challenged the war and traditional "materialistic" values. The 1960s were a time of revolution. Young people were breaking out of the molds that were cast by their parents' era. This revolution of the baby boomer generation found that one effective outlet for their ideas was music. **The Woodstock Music and Art Fair** in 1969 drew more than 450,000 people to a pasture in Sullivan County, New York. For four days, the site became a countercultural mini-nation that closed the New York State Thruway and created one of the nation's worst traffic jams. It also inspired passage of local and state laws to ensure that nothing like it would ever happen again.

The extreme styles of dress and speech that characterized the so-called "hippie movement" soon passed into oblivion, along with the more radical politics of the period. However, the Civil Rights movement and the Vietnam War protests transformed the

1970. John Fowles's *The French Lieutenant's Woman* published

➤ 1976. Alex Haley's *Roots* and Alice Walker's *Meridian* published

➤ 1971. John Gardner's *Grendel* published

➤ 1978. John Cheever's *Falconer* published

**1972**          **1976**          **1980**

➤ 1972. Watergate affair; Nixon reelected

➤ 1976. Jimmy Carter elected president

➤ 1979. Iran takes United States citizens hostage

➤ 1973. Vietnam War ends

➤ 1974. Nixon resigns; Gerald Ford becomes president

U.S. soldiers in Vietnam, 1968.

entire nation by demonstrating the power of grassroots political organizing to bring about change. This lesson was especially instrumental to those concerned about the environment and women's rights.

## A CONCERN FOR THE ENVIRONMENT

In the early twentieth century, many Americans, accustomed to a vast land rich with seemingly endless resources, believed that the earth was infinitely renewable. As industry boomed, people accepted without question skies blackened from smokestack emissions and rivers fouled with industrial waste. When the Cuyahoga River in Ohio caught fire from burning chemical waste in the 1930s and again in the 1950s, people didn't think to protest; they barely even noticed.

During the 1960s, public attitudes began to change. **Rachel Carson,** a marine biologist, published *Silent Spring* in 1962. The book, an unexpected bestseller, spoke eloquently and insistently about a future without birds (hence the title) and told of the long-term effects of highly toxic pesticides such as DDT and other chemicals used in farming, industry, and households. In 1968, *Apollo 8* astronauts, returning from their pioneering orbital flight around the moon, photographed for the first time the planet Earth as a whole. This image of the Earth — small, fragile, beautiful, and unique — quickly made an impact on millions of people. In 1969, industrial runoff in the Cuyahoga River again caught fire. This time the public reaction was immediate and intense.

At the same time, public demonstrations against the Vietnam War fostered the idea that organized protest about the environment could create change. U.S. Senator **Gaylord Nelson** of Wisconsin announced that a "national environmental teach-in" would occur in the spring of 1970. The first **Earth Day** was held April 22, with an estimated 20 million people demonstrating peacefully nationwide. Ecology flags began to wave across the nation along with peace signs. Groundbreaking federal legislation followed. **The U.S. Environmental Protection Agency** was established in 1970, followed by the Clean Air Act, the Clean Water Act of 1972, and the Endangered Species Act of 1973.

## THE WOMEN'S MOVEMENT

Paralleling protests for civil rights, the environment, and U.S. withdrawal from Vietnam was the call for equal rights for women. Called at times the "women's movement" or "women's lib," this renewed interest in feminism was reflected and spearheaded by the founding of *Ms.* magazine in 1971. That same year **Gloria Steinem,** along with **Betty Friedan, Bella Abzug,** and **Shirley Chisholm,** helped found the **National Women's Political Caucus.** Interest in all things related to women flourished. As with everything else in American society, gender roles fell under question. Upper-middle-class women began forming "women's groups," meeting to discuss issues of importance to them and larger society. The literary canon, among other things, was analyzed and criticized, and many texts by women were unearthed from the past, published, and promoted. Feminist literary criticism became a popular way to analyze text.

## POLITICS IN THE SEVENTIES

Following the turbulent Democratic National Convention in Chicago in 1968, Richard Nixon, a Republican from California, was elected by a landslide. The Nixon administration pursued a policy of détente, or improved relations, with the Soviet Union, negotiating the first of a series of **Strategic Arms Limitation Treaties** (SALT) with the Soviets. Relations with China also improved following President Nixon's visit there in 1972. In 1973, after the signing of a peace treaty, the United States withdrew from Vietnam. Then, in 1974, following charges of a coverup of improprieties during the 1972 election campaign, including a break-in at the **Watergate** hotel in Washington, DC, President Nixon resigned, to be succeeded by **Gerald Ford.**

The first moon landing, 1969.

The Ford administration faced difficult economic problems, not the least of which was an oil embargo during the Yom Kippur War that caused fuel prices to soar. Ford lost the 1976 election campaign to **Jimmy Carter** of Georgia. The Carter administration followed a policy of promoting human rights around the world and succeeded in bringing Israel and Egypt, traditional enemies in the Middle East, to the negotiating table. However, domestic economic troubles, coupled with the administration's inability to deal with the **Iran Hostage Crisis,** in which Islamic fundamentalists in Tehran, Iran, took over the American Embassy and held its occupants hostage, led to Carter's defeat by Ronald Reagan in 1980.

## AMERICAN LITERATURE AND THE EARLY CONTEMPORARY PERIOD

The alienation and stress underlying the 1950s found outward expression in the 1960s in the United States in the Civil Rights movement, feminism, antiwar protests, minority activism, and the arrival of a counterculture whose effects are still evident in American society and its literature.

The 1960s were a time of radical experimentation in all the arts in the United States. Boundaries between literature, painting, sculpture, music, and dance broke down with the development of "happenings," spontaneous expressions of creative freedom that were precursors of the performance art of the late 1970s and beyond. Emerging during this period were a number of experimental literary forms, including found poems, made up primarily or exclusively of bits of language collected from the culture at large, from billboards, graffiti, subway posters, and other materials. Concrete poems, designed to appeal to the eye, also enjoyed a vogue during this time. Many poets of the period, notably **Robert Lowell, Anne Sexton, Sylvia Plath**, and **John Berryman**, wrote what is known as **confessional poetry,** extremely personal verse that described intimate, often troubled experiences. During the political agitation surrounding the sixties and early seventies, a number of antiwar poets emerged, including **Robert Bly** and **Denise Levertov;** and many African-American poets, such as **Leroi Jones (Imamu Amiri Baraka), Nikki Giovanni, Gwendolyn Brooks,** and **Mari Evans**, produced compelling work related to problems of race and discrimination.

The 1960s were marked by a blurring of the line between fiction and fact, novels and reportage, that continues today. **Truman Capote,** who had dazzled readers with such novels as *Breakfast at Tiffany's* (1958), stunned audiences with *In Cold Blood*

Janis Joplin performing in San Francisco, c.1969.

(1966), a riveting analysis of a brutal mass murder in the American heartland that, although labeled as nonfiction, read like detective fiction. At the same time, the **"New Journalism"** emerged—volumes of nonfiction reportage that relied heavily on techniques of fiction or that frequently manipulated the facts, reshaping them to add to the drama and immediacy of the story being reported. **Tom Wolfe's** *The Electric Kool-Aid Acid Test* (1968), extolling the countercultural antics of novelist **Ken Kesey, Hunter S. Thompson's** *Fear and Loathing in Las Vegas* (1972), and **Norman Mailer's** *Miami and the Siege of Chicago* (1968) became landmarks of a new approach to reportage in which the subjective was honored above the objective.

As the 1960s set off a series of turbulent events and the 1970s set out to make sense of them, literary works reflected it all. Ken Kesey wrote his darkly comic *One Flew Over the Cuckoo's Nest* (1962), depicting a mental hospital in which the staff are more disturbed than the patients. **John Barth** in *Lost in the Funhouse* (1968) regarded the interior self as supreme to the external world; **Richard Brautigan** in *Trout Fishing in America* (1967) played with whimsical fantasy; and **John Irving** stood social conventions on their head in *The World According to Garp* (1978). In 1969 Kurt Vonnegut, Jr. wrote one of the greatest antiwar novels, *Slaughterhouse Five,* centering on the infamous firebombing of Dresden, Germany, during World War II.

At the same time, some writers were deeply concerned with an absence in this society of morals and ethics. **Walker Percy,** a physician in Louisiana, emerged in his forties with such novels as *The Moviegoer* (1962), *The Last Gentleman* (1966), and *The Second Coming (*1980), all of which examine civilization and its discontents with a wry but moral eye. **Joan Didion** wrote about the decadent purposelessness of Hollywood in *Play It As It Lays* (1970). **John Gardner,** a professor of English at the State University of New York at Binghamton, was the most eloquent proponent for the importance of ethical values in literature. Using a realistic but innovative approach, Gardner strove in such works as *Grendel* (1971), *Nickel Mountain* (1973), and *October Light* (1976) to show that moral acts and values can lead to a life worth living. His controversial nonfiction work, *On Moral Fiction* (1978), argued that some of the most acclaimed authors were distracting themselves with empty experimentation. Gardner called instead for fiction that reflected ethical values that would make sense of the human condition.

In the late 1960s and mid-1970s, **Tim O'Brien** and others began chronicling what they had experienced in the Vietnam War. The memoirs of O'Brien's first year as an infantryman, *If I Die in a Combat Zone* (1979), provided an intelligent perspective to help Americans understand how the war had divided their country. O'Brien's *Going After Cacciato* (1978), considered by some critics to be the best novel about the Vietnam War, won the National Book Award.

## The Emergence of Women and Multicultural Writers

Women's literature began to thrive during the feminist movement, when the literary canon began to shift away from works exclusively by male writers. At the same time, not all women writers of distinction considered themselves feminists or limited themselves to topics conventionally considered "women's issues." Distinguished women writers of the 1960s and 1970s included **Carolyn Kizer, Adrienne Rich, Maxine Kumin,** Anne Sexton, **Denise Levertov, Alice Walker,** Gloria Steinem, and **Audre Lorde.**

While women of all ethnic backgrounds were gaining prominence in 1970s literary circles, black women made perhaps the most drastic inroads of all. In the early 1970s, Alice Walker and other African-American writers rediscovered the work of Zora Neale Hurston, a Harlem Renaissance writer whose work had fallen into oblivion. As renewed interest in feminist criticism took hold, Hurston's novel *Their Eyes Were Watching God* (1937) provided a new direction; rather than being a novel of social protest against racism and racial discrimination, it examined the inner dynamics of black culture and chronicled the awakening of its main character Janey into her identity as a woman and an individual.

The 1960s and 1970s saw black women writers from the 1940s, including **Gwendolyn Brooks, Margaret Walker, Ann Petry,** and **Paule Marshall,** continue to be productive. **Toni Morrison** published her first novel, *The Bluest Eye* (1970), and followed it with *Sula* (1973), and *Song of Solomon* (1977). **Toni Cade Bambara** published *Gorilla, My Love* (1972), among other works of fiction, and **Maya Angelou** came out with *I Know Why the Caged Bird Sings* (1970). Dramatist **Ntozake Shange's** play, *for colored girls who have considered suicide/when the rainbow is enuf* (1976), was popular on Broadway and **Jamaica Kincaid** emerged with her novel *At the Bottom of the River* (1978).

Multicultural literature as a whole began to gain public attention following the lead of African-American writers. During the 1970s, universities across the country began to establish ethnic studies programs. Deconstruction, applied to political as well as literary texts, constantly questioned the nature of "reality." The interest in **multiculturalism** from writers of all ethnic backgrounds would expand in the 1980s and 1990s as one of the most defining elements of contemporary literature.

## The New Regionalism and the Small Press Phenomenon

Although regional traditions flourished long before the **New Regionalism** of the 1970s, literature immediately after World War II was centered in New York City. While Southern writers like William Faulkner, Eudora Welty, and Flannery O'Connor reflected regional concerns, they still depended on large commercial publishing houses in Manhattan to promote their work.

By the 1970s, the publishing industry was becoming decentralized by hundreds of **small literary presses** and what were then known as **"little magazines."** Funded by colleges and universities or simply by loyal readers, writers, and editors, these alternative publishers were able to promote new regional and experimental works in ways the big commercial publishing houses could or would not. Literary presses gave new writers a forum for their work while allowing established writers the chance to publish experimental or unique work that mainstream publishers would not risk printing. As literary presses gained in prominence and popularity, they helped promote recognition of authors from all sectors of American society—including women and multiethnic writers. Literary presses published thousands of new works, and anthologies like the *Pushcart Prize: Best of the Small Presses,* begun in 1976 by **Bill Henderson,** became important showcases of strong new work by new and established writers alike.

# ECHOES

## EARLY CONTEMPORARY LITERATURE

I have a dream . . . that my four little children will one day live in a nation where they will not be judged by the color of their skin but by the content of their character.

    —Martin Luther King, Jr.

The first problem for all of us, men and women, is not to learn, but to unlearn.

    —Gloria Steinem, "A New Egalitarian Life Style" *New York Times,* August 26, 1971

And so, my fellow Americans, ask not what your country can do for you; ask what you can do for your country.

    —John F. Kennedy

Yes Celie, she say. Everything want to be loved. Us sing and dance, make faces and give flower bouquets, trying to be loved. You ever notice that trees do everything to git attention we do, except walk?

    —Alice Walker, from *The Color Purple*

It's not just the kids. It's lawyers, doctors, scientists, mothers. Maybe this is one area where the generation gap doesn't exist. We're all working toward the same goals. We're Earth Housekeepers.

    —Ora Citron, University of Southern California student, at the first Earth Day in 1970

Well-dressed people ask me sometimes, with their teeth bared, as though they were about to bite me, if I believe in a redistribution of wealth. I can only reply that it doesn't matter what I think, that wealth is already being redistributed every hour, often in ways which are absolutely fantastic.

    —Kurt Vonnegut, Jr.

The whole New Critical period I went through, and the scholarly period that followed it, betrayed me, I think, into an excessive concern with significance.

—John Gardner

Well, this is no age of gold. It is only what it is. Can we do no more than complain about it? We writers have better choices. We can either shut up because the times are too bad, or continue because we have an instinct to make books, a talent to enjoy, which even these disfigured times cannot obliterate.

    —Saul Bellow

Why is it that scientists, who know a good deal about the world, know less about language than the backside of the moon, even though language is the one observable behavior which most clearly sets a man apart from the beasts and the one activity in which all men, scientists included, engage more than in any other?

    —Walker Percy

*Marilyn Diptych* [Detail], Andy Warhol.

# "Constantly risking absurdity"

BY LAWRENCE FERLINGHETTI

## About the AUTHOR

**Lawrence Ferlinghetti** (c.1919– ), poet and publisher, was born in Yonkers, New York. He earned a doctoral degree in poetry at the Sorbonne in Paris with a dissertation entitled "The City as Symbol in Modern Poetry: In Search of a Metropolitan Tradition." In 1951 Ferlinghetti settled in San Francisco, where he started a magazine called *City Lights*, named after a 1931 Charlie Chaplin movie. He also started a bookstore on the ground floor, a center for "beat" writers, now one of the most famous bookstores in the world. Popular during the 1950s, the Beat Generation of poets and writers were influenced by existentialism and Eastern philosophy. They adopted rhythms of simple American speech and progressive jazz.

Ferlinghetti was a central figure in the Beat movement of the 1950s and 1960s with his message for people to free themselves from conventional traditions in both life and art. His collections of poetry include *A Coney Island of the Mind* (1958), *Starting from San Francisco* (1967), and *Open Eye, Open Heart* (1974).

## About the SELECTION

In **"Constantly risking absurdity"** Ferlinghetti uses the metaphor of the tightrope acrobat to ponder the poet's profession. The poem was published in 1958 in Ferlinghetti's poetry collection *A Coney Island of the Mind*.

## Reader's Journal

What risks have you taken in your life?

## Literary TOOLS

**FREE VERSE. Free verse** is poetry that avoids use of regular rhyme, meter, or division into stanzas. As you read the poem, think about what the line structure of the poem imitates.

**SIMILE AND METAPHOR.** A **simile** is a comparison using *like* or *as*. A **metaphor** is a figure of speech in which one thing is spoken or written about as if it were another. As you read, make a cluster chart to list words and phrases that reflect tightrope walking, which the poet uses as a metaphor for his profession. One example has been done for you.

"performs above the heads of his audience"

Tightrope Walking

## ArtNote

*Aerial Act*, 1940. Louis Schanker.

Woodblock printing is a method that is thousands of years old. A flat block is carved into the required shape, and ink is applied and pressed onto paper. A different block is used for each color. What visual qualities of woodblock printing make it a good choice for an abstract artist like Louis Schanker (1903–1981), whose *Aerial Act* appears on page 870? In what ways does this print share the same spirit as the Ferlinghetti poem?

# Constantly Risking absurdity

*Aerial Act,* 1940.
Louis Schanker.
National Museum of American Art, Washington, DC.

## LAWRENCE FERLINGHETTI

Constantly risking absurdity
            and death
    whenever he performs
        above the heads
              of his audience
5    the poet like an acrobat
        climbs on rime[1]

---

1. **rime.** Alternate spelling of *rhyme*

to a high wire of his own making

and balancing on eyebeams[2]

10                  above a sea of faces

paces his way

to the other side of day

performing entrechats[3]

and sleight-of-foot tricks

15 and other high theatrics

and all without mistaking

any thing

for what it may not be

For he's the super realist

20                  who must <u>perforce</u> perceive

taut truth

before the taking of each stance or step

in his supposed advance

toward that still higher perch

25 where Beauty stands and waits

with gravity

to start her death-defying leap

And he

a little charleychaplin[4] man

30                  who may or may not catch

her fair eternal form

spreadeagled in the empty air

of existence            ■

*What types of tricks does the poet perform?*

*How does an acrobat risk absurdity? How does a poet risk absurdity?*

---

2. **eyebeams.** Glances of the eye
3. **entrechats.** In ballet, leaps straight upward during which the dancer beats his or her calves together
4. **charleychaplin.** Sir Charles Spencer (1889–1977), also known as Charlie Chaplin, English comic actor known for his portrayal of a duck-toed hobo in tattered evening dress

**WORDS FOR EVERYDAY USE**

**per • force** (pər fôrs′) *adv.*, necessarily. *The article must <u>perforce</u> be true.*

**Respond** *to the* **SELECTION**

Which is more difficult, being a tightrope acrobat or a poet? Why?

# INVESTIGATE, Inquire, Imagine

**Recall:** GATHERING FACTS

1a. What is the poet constantly risking? Where does the poet perform?

2a. On what does the poet balance? Where does he "pace"?

3a. What must the poet perceive? What is waiting for him on "that still higher perch"? What does Beauty do? What is the poet uncertain of catching?

➡ **Interpret:** FINDING MEANING

1b. Why do you think the speaker believes that the poet's job is risky? What kinds of risks does a poet face? How does the poet perform "above the heads / of his audience"?

2b. Why might it be difficult for the poet to perform these acts?

3b. What does the speaker believe the goal of the poet should be? Why may the poet be unable to catch Beauty? What will happen if the poet fails to catch her?

**Analyze:** TAKING THINGS APART

4a. Analyze the tone of the last six lines of the poem, in which the poet is compared to a "little charleychaplin man."

➡ **Synthesize:** BRINGING THINGS TOGETHER

4b. Why is the life of the poet sad and tragic?

**Perspective:** LOOKING AT OTHER VIEWS

5a. The speaker implies that the role of the poet is to capture Beauty in words for his or her audience. What subjects and themes might the speaker consider worth writing about?

➡ **Empathy:** SEEING FROM INSIDE

5b. If you were a poet and your audience did not understand your translation of Beauty, for what reasons might you continue writing poetry?

# Understanding Literature

**FREE VERSE.** Review the definition for **free verse** in the Handbook of Literary Terms. What does the line structure of the poem imitate? How is this achieved?

**SIMILE AND METAPHOR.** Review the definitions for **simile** and **metaphor** in the Handbook of Literary Terms, as well as the cluster chart you made for Literary Tools on page 869. In this poem, what is being compared? How does Ferlinghetti make it clear that he is comparing a poet to a tightrope acrobat? How are these two things similar? How are they dissimilar?

# WRITER'S JOURNAL

1. Imagine that you are the publisher of a poetry magazine. Write a **help wanted ad** for a poet, describing the qualities needed and the risks involved in the position.
2. Write a **paragraph** for your teacher defining Beauty as seen by the poet.
3. Imagine that you are employed in your chosen profession. Write a **poem** or **short essay** that uses a metaphor to describe the work that you do.

# Integrating
## *the* LANGUAGE ARTS

## Language, Grammar, and Style

**CORRECTING RUN-ONS.** Read the Language Arts Survey 3.34, "Correcting Sentence Run-ons." Then read each of the following sentences. If it is a run-on, rewrite it correctly.

1. Beat Generation authors were popular during the 1950s they rejected traditional social and artistic forms.
2. After moving to San Francisco, Ferlinghetti published many Beat writers' works.
3. Jack Kerouac wrote *On the Road* it was considered to be the testament of the Beat movement.
4. *Howl*, a long poem by Allen Ginsberg, attacks American values materialism is the most significant.
5. During the 1960s "beat" ideas and attitudes were absorbed by other cultural movements, and those who practiced the "beat" lifestyle were called "hippies."

## Speaking and Listening & Collaborative Learning

**INTERVIEW.** With a partner, play the roles of the poet and a member of his audience. The audience member asks the poet questions about the risks he takes, why he loves his work, what he hopes to accomplish with his poetry, and the definition of Beauty; the poet responds. Then switch roles. The poet asks the audience member why the audience member reads his poetry, what the role of the poet in society should be, what types of poems he or she likes, and so on.

## Study and Research & Speaking and Listening

**RESEARCHING THE BEAT GENERATION.** Research a beat poet or novelist. Poets include Gary Snyder, Jack Kerouac, Allen Ginsberg, Michael McClure, Gregory Corso, Kenneth Rexroth, and Lawrence Ferlinghetti. Novelists include Jack Kerouac, Chandler Brossard, and William Burroughs. Prepare a short biography for one of the writers, and describe the subjects and themes in his writing. Then select a cutting from a selection by your writer that you appreciate. Practice reading your cutting by using appropriate tone, gestures, facial expressions, and body movements. Finally, present your introduction and cutting to the class.

# Literary TOOLS

**CONFESSIONAL POETRY. Confessional poetry** is verse that describes, sometimes with painful explicitness, the private or personal affairs of the writer. Often confessional poetry has the quality of a diary entry or of an overheard interior monologue, but equally often it is highly artificial, employing much personal symbolism. As you read, think about what personal experience the poem relates.

**EPIGRAPH.** An **epigraph** is a quotation or motto used at the beginning of the whole or part of a literary work to help establish the work's theme. In the letter quoted in this poem's epigraph, van Gogh implies that painting the stars is for him a religious experience. Sexton sees mythic elements in the painting. As you read, make a chart. On the left, list elements from the poem that are related to religion or mythology. On the right, tell how these elements are used in the poem. One example has been done for you.

| Mythic Elements | Description |
|---|---|
| 1. god | The moon is described as a god. |

# Reader's Journal

What things in nature inspire you with awe?

## "The Starry Night"

BY ANNE SEXTON

## About the AUTHOR

**Anne Sexton** (1928–1974) made a significant contribution to American poetry, though she did not begin writing until she was twenty-eight years old. Born in Newton, Massachusetts, Sexton attended boarding school and Garland Junior College before marrying Alfred Sexton II in 1948. She began writing in 1956 after attending a class taught by Robert Lowell at Boston University.

In her work, Sexton presented painful memories and experiences in intensely personal poetry of a kind referred to by critics as confessional. Her first collection, *To Bedlam and Part Way Back* (1959), described her stay in a mental institution and her recovery from an emotional breakdown. In 1967, Sexton received the Pulitzer Prize for her collection *Live or Die*. Her shockingly personal poems brought her literary fame but received mixed reactions from critics. *Transformations* (1971) is a collection of her frightening, macabre retellings of fairy tales by the Brothers Grimm. Unfortunately, Sexton was plagued by depression and tragically ended her life on October 4, 1974. Two volumes of her poetry and a collection of her personal letters were published after her death by her daughter Linda.

## About the SELECTION

**"The Starry Night"** comes from Sexton's collection *All My Pretty Ones* (1962). The title of the collection comes from a statement made by MacDuff, in Shakespeare's tragedy *Macbeth,* upon hearing of the deaths of his wife and children. The title of the poem refers to a famous painting by Vincent van Gogh. Van Gogh, like Sexton, suffered from depression, which was intensified in van Gogh's case by a crisis of religious faith. The epigraph at the beginning of Sexton's poem comes from one of the remarkable letters that van Gogh wrote to his brother Theo.

# The Starry Night

*The Starry Night,* 1889. Vincent van Gogh. The Museum of Modern Art, New York.

## ANNE SEXTON

That does not keep me from having a terrible
need of—shall I say the word—religion.
Then I go out at night to paint the stars.
　　　　　—Vincent van Gogh[1]
　　　　　in a letter to his brother

1. **Vincent van Gogh.** (1853–1890) Dutch artist, first of the
great modern Expressionist painters. The letter from which this
passage is taken was written while Van Gogh was working on
another painting of the night sky, "Starry Night on the Rhône."

The town does not exist
except where one black-haired tree slips
up like a drowned woman into the hot sky.
The town is silent. The night boils with eleven stars.
5    Oh starry starry night! This is how
I want to die.

It moves. They are all alive.
Even the moon bulges in its orange irons
to push children, like a god, from its eye.
10   The old unseen serpent swallows up the stars.
Oh starry starry night! This is how
I want to die:

into that rushing beast of the night,
sucked up by that great dragon, to split
15   from my life with no flag,
no belly,
no cry.                                                    ■

To what is the tree
compared?

What is the "rushing
beast"?

# Respond to the SELECTION

Look at the reproduction of van Gogh's painting *The Starry Night* on page 875. Do you think
Sexton's poem captures the feeling of the painting? Do you think Van Gogh would appreciate
the poem? Why, or why not?

# INVESTIGATE, Inquire, Imagine

**Recall:** GATHERING FACTS

1a. What "does not exist"? What is the "one black-haired tree" like?

2a. What does the speaker see in the sky? What is the moon like? What is it doing? What is happening to the stars?

3a. What does the speaker address directly in the last two lines of stanza 2? What does she say to this thing?

➤ **Interpret:** FINDING MEANING

1b. What view overpowers and blots out the town? What is the town's response to the "drowned woman" who "Slips . . . into the hot sky"?

2b. What is the sky like? What emotions do you think the speaker feels looking at this sky?

3b. What is "The old unseen serpent"? What is being swallowed up? What is being born? In what sense are all things eventually swallowed up by night?

**Analyze:** TAKING THINGS APART

4a. Identify the main difference between the town and the sky.

➤ **Synthesize:** BRINGING THINGS TOGETHER

4b. What is the speaker's attitude toward life and death?

**Evaluate:** MAKING JUDGMENTS

5a. The speaker wants to split from her life with "no flag, / no belly, / no cry." To what degree has she abandoned life?

➤ **Extend:** CONNECTING IDEAS

5b. The poet Dylan Thomas wrote to his dying father, "Do not go gentle into that good night." Contrast the attitudes about death in the Thomas and Sexton poems.

# Understanding Literature

**CONFESSIONAL POETRY.** Review the definition for **confessional poetry** in Literary Tools on page 874. What personal experience does this poem relate? With what extremely personal subject does it deal?

**EPIGRAPH.** Review the definition for **epigraph** in Literary Tools on page 874 and the chart you made for that section. Which mythic elements are affiliated with the town? Which are affiliated with the night sky? To what extent does Sexton's experience with the night sky mirror van Gogh's? Explain.

# WRITER'S JOURNAL

1. Anne Sexton sees death in the night sky. Write a **paragraph** explaining what you see in the night sky.

2. Imagine that you are Anne Sexton. Write a **letter** to your editor explaining why you decided to use van Gogh's *The Starry Night* as the subject for your poem.

3. Write a **poem** or **paragraph** inspired by a painting that you like.

# Integrating *the* LANGUAGE ARTS

## Language, Grammar, and Style

**LINKING VERBS.** Read the Language Arts Survey 3.10, "Linking Verbs." On a separate sheet of paper, write the linking verb used in each sentence.

1. The town is silent.

2. The night sky looks hot; it boils with stars.

3. To the speaker, the night sky is a symbol for death.

4. Looking up at it, she becomes fascinated.

5. The speaker seems extremely depressed.

## Applied English

**BUSINESS LETTER.** Imagine you are Vincent van Gogh. Write a letter to your art dealer saying you have just completed a painting called *The Starry Night* that you would like him to sell. Explain what inspired you to paint it and describe it in detail. You might find it useful to describe the painting in terms of the foreground, center, and background. Be sure to mention how much money you hope to make from the sale of the painting. Before you begin writing, you might want to review the Language Arts Survey 6.5, "Writing a Business Letter."

## Speaking and Listening

**VISUAL LITERACY.** Visit the library with a partner and find an art book that contains paintings by van Gogh. Examine ten of these images carefully for details. Then write down their titles. Set the book aside and describe one of the paintings to your partner, beginning with the most minute details and building up to the more obvious characteristics of the painting. When your partner has identified the painting in question, switch roles. In your descriptions, mention the colors and textures, as well as the objects and figures in the scene.

## Study and Research & Media Literacy

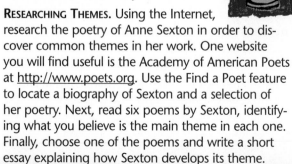

**RESEARCHING THEMES.** Using the Internet, research the poetry of Anne Sexton in order to discover common themes in her work. One website you will find useful is the Academy of American Poets at http://www.poets.org. Use the Find a Poet feature to locate a biography of Sexton and a selection of her poetry. Next, read six poems by Sexton, identifying what you believe is the main theme in each one. Finally, choose one of the poems and write a short essay explaining how Sexton develops its theme.

# "Those Winter Sundays"

BY ROBERT HAYDEN

## About the AUTHOR

**Robert Earl Hayden** (1913–1980) grew up in a poor neighborhood of Detroit, Michigan, a place to which he would return in poems collected in *Elegies for Paradise Valley* (1978). After attending Wayne State University, he received a master's degree from the University of Michigan, where he was professor of English from 1968 until his death in 1980. From 1946 to 1968, he taught at Fisk University in Tennessee.

Hayden built upon his experiences and on the heritage of African Americans to write poetry that spoke for different groups of people throughout history. He made connections to the universal from the experiences and voice of the individual, be it gypsy, slave, or slave trader. His poem "Middle Passage" uses the technique of collage, pioneered by writers such as John Dos Passos, T. S. Eliot, and William Carlos Williams, to evoke the many voices associated with the slave ships that brought African Americans to the New World.

Hayden was a versatile writer, trying various poetic forms and styles to express universally shared emotions. His collections include *Heart-Shape in the Dust* (1940), *The Lion and the Archer* (1948), and *A Ballad of Remembrance* (1962). At the First World Festival for Negro Arts in 1966, he received the Grand Prize for Poetry for *A Ballad of Remembrance*. From 1976–1978, Hayden served as poetry consultant to the Library of Congress in Washington, DC, a position later called Poet Laureate. He was the first black American to hold this position.

## About the SELECTION

**"Those Winter Sundays"** was published in Hayden's poetry collection *A Ballad of Remembrance* in 1962. It recalls a single, recurring event from the speaker's childhood and draws from it a moving generalization about the nature of love. The poem thus demonstrates how writers can arrive at and justify conclusions by presenting even minor events in concrete detail. The poem is remarkable for its simplicity, beauty, and precision of language.

## Literary TOOLS

**REPETITION. Repetition** is a writer's conscious reuse of a word, phrase, or other element. As you read, look for an example of repetition that ties into the poem's theme.

**ALLITERATION. Alliteration** is the repetition of initial consonant sounds, as in the words *babbling brook*. Make a cluster chart to illustrate the examples of alliteration you find in the poem. One example has been done for you.

> "clothes"/"cold" (line 2) — Alliteration

## Reader's Journal

What service did someone once do for you that demonstrated their love or concern?

## ArtNote

*Hometime,* 1970. Romare Bearden, page 880.

Ralph Ellison said that the collage technique of Romare Bearden (1914–1988) reveals "…the sharp breaks, leaps in consciousness, distortions, paradoxes, reversals, telescoping of time and surreal blending of styles, values, hopes and dreams which characterize much of Negro American history." How does the mood of *Hometime,* on page 880, compare to the poem "Those Winter Sundays"?

*Hometime*, 1970. Romare Bearden. The Butler Institute of American Art, Youngstown, Ohio.

# Those Winter Sundays

ROBERT HAYDEN

Sundays too my father got up early
and put his clothes on in the blueblack cold,
then with cracked hands that ached
from labor in the weekday weather made
5    <u>banked</u> fires blaze. No one ever thanked him.

I'd wake and hear the cold splintering, breaking.
When the rooms were warm, he'd call,
and slowly I would rise and dress,
fearing the <u>chronic</u> angers of that house,

10    Speaking indifferently to him,
who had driven out the cold
and polished my good shoes as well.
What did I know, what did I know
of love's <u>austere</u> and lonely offices?  ■

> What reaction did the father get for making the fire?

> What other task did the father do for the speaker? What didn't the speaker realize about the father's actions?

---

**WORDS FOR EVERYDAY USE**

**banked** (baŋkd) *adj.*, arranged to continue burning slowly. *If the small sticks, wadded newspaper, and dry logs are not <u>banked</u> properly, the fire will burn out quickly.*

**chron • ic** (krän´ ik) *adj.*, constant; perpetual. *Mrs. Dobbs experienced <u>chronic</u> arthritic pain.*

**aus • tere** (ô stir´) *adj.*, plain; without luxury or ornamentation. *The Murphys' <u>austere</u> apartment was softened with fresh flowers.*

If the speaker could relive a winter Sunday from his childhood, what would he do differently?

# INVESTIGATE *Inquire Imagine*

**Recall:** GATHERING FACTS

1a. What did the speaker's father do on Sunday mornings?

2a. When would the speaker's father call him to get up?

3a. What did the speaker fear, and how did he speak to his father?

➤ **Interpret:** FINDING MEANING

1b. Why does the speaker use the word *too* in line 1 of the poem?

2b. What did the speaker's father want to spare his child?

3b. What was the atmosphere in the speaker's home like? Was his relationship with his father always a warm one? Explain.

**Analyze:** TAKING THINGS APART

4a. Identify how the speaker's attitude toward his father has changed since he was a child.

➤ **Synthesize:** BRINGING THINGS TOGETHER

4b. Explain what the speaker means by "love's austere and lonely offices."

**Perspective:** LOOKING AT OTHER VIEWS

5a. Why did the father do special deeds for his son even though he did not receive thanks for them?

➤ **Empathy:** SEEING FROM INSIDE

5b. If you were the speaker, what would you do to let your father know that you appreciated his sacrifices?

# Understanding *Literature*

**REPETITION.** Review the definition for **repetition** in the Handbook of Literary Terms. What question is repeated in the poem? What does this repetition indicate about the emotion with which the line is spoken?

**ALLITERATION.** Review the definition for **alliteration** in the Handbook of Literary Terms and the cluster chart you made for Literary Tools on page 879. What example of alliteration relates to the poem's theme?

# WRITER'S JOURNAL

1. Imagine that you are the son. Write a **thank-you note** to your father for his acts of love.

2. Write a **journal entry** about the Sunday morning routine in your home.

3. Review the Reader's Journal question on page 879. Now, write a **lyric poem** addressed to the person who once did something nice for you out of love. Before you write, you may wish to brainstorm a list of sensory details connected with that person or with the nice thing he or she did.

# Integrating
## *the* LANGUAGE ARTS

## Language, Grammar, and Style

**ADDING MODIFIERS.** Read the Language Arts Survey 3.65, "Modifiers—Adverbs and Adjectives," 3.66, "Adjectives," and 3.67, "Adverbs." Then add appropriate adjectives and adverbs to the sentences below. Use your imagination to think of modifiers different from those Hayden used.

1. The speaker's father put his clothes on in the cold.
2. He started the fire.
3. His hands ached from labor.
4. The speaker feared the angers of that house.
5. He spoke to his father.

## Study and Research & Media Literacy

**RESEARCHING ON THE INTERNET.** Using the Internet, research Robert Hayden's legacy to twentieth-century American poetry. One site you will find useful is Modern American Poetry at http://www.english.uiuc.edu/maps. Then write a short essay, putting in your own words what you have learned. You might find it useful to review the Language Arts Survey 2.31, "Drafting."

## Speaking and Listening

**ORAL INTERPRETATION.** Have each person in your small group select a Robert Hayden poem in which the poet discusses his childhood in Detroit. Find an instrumental musical recording to accompany the poem you chose. Then take turns reading the poem to the students in your small group. Before you give your presentation, you might find it useful to review the Language Arts Survey 4.19, "Oral Interpretation of Poetry."

## Critical Thinking

**GENERALIZING.** Read the Language Arts Survey 5.5, "Generalizing." Then, as you reread the poem, think about what conclusions you can draw from it about the speaker's father and about the nature of love. What adjectives would you use to describe love as depicted in the poem? What characterizes the acts of love in the poem?

# "Morning Song"

BY SYLVIA PLATH

## About the AUTHOR

Despite her success as a writer, **Sylvia Plath** (1932–1963) lived a life full of depression and despair. Born in Boston, Plath published poems even as a child and won many academic and literary awards. Her interest in writing continued at Smith College. During her junior year she won a prize for fiction at *Mademoiselle* magazine and spent that summer as a guest editor in the magazine's New York office. After graduating *summa cum laude* from Smith, Plath accepted a Fulbright Scholarship to Cambridge University in England, where she met and married poet Ted Hughes. They had two children.

*The Colossus* (1960), the only volume of poetry published during Plath's short life, is intensely personal. *Ariel* (1968), her finest book of verse, was written in the last months of her life. Other volumes include *Crossing the Water* (1971) and *Winter Trees* (1972), which reveal an objective detachment from life and a growing fascination with death. Her novel, *The Bell Jar* (1963), chronicles the nervous breakdown she suffered while a college student. Plath committed suicide at the age of thirty, and most of her work has been published posthumously.

## About the SELECTION

Plath wrote **"Morning Song"** about the birth of her daughter, Frieda, in 1960. Like much of her work, this poem is highly personal and contains brilliant imagery. What might have been a joyful poem of celebration, however, is eerily dark: Plath's severe and crippling depression shows through in her description of her new baby as "a statue / In a drafty museum."

## Literary TOOLS

**RUN-ON LINE.** A **run-on line** is a line of verse in which the sense or the grammatical structure does not end with the end of the line, but rather is continued on one or more subsequent lines. As you read, identify a run-on line in "Morning Song."

**SIMILE.** A **simile** is a comparison using *like* or *as*. This figure of speech invites the reader to make a comparison between the two things being compared. The two "things" involved are the writer's actual subject, the *tenor* of the simile, and another thing to which the subject is likened, the *vehicle* of the simile. Make a chart for each of the three similes found in the poem. On the left, list the tenor. On the right, list the vehicle. One example has been done for you.

| Tenor | Vehicle |
|---|---|
| 1. you | fat gold watch |
| 2. | |
| 3. | |

## Reader's Journal

What sensory details such as sights, sounds, tastes, smells, and touch do you associate with morning?

# Morning Song

*Mother and Child*, 1967. Alice Neel.
Private Collection.

## SYLVIA PLATH

Love set you going like a fat gold watch.
The midwife slapped your footsoles, and your bald cry
Took its place among the
    elements.

> *What happens in stanza 1?*

Our voices echo, magnifying your arrival. New statue.
5  In a drafty museum, your nakedness
Shadows our safety. We stand round blankly as walls.

I'm no more your mother
Than the cloud that <u>distils</u> a mirror to reflect its own
    slow
<u>Effacement</u> at the wind's hand.

10  All night your moth breath
Flickers among the flat pink
    roses. I wake to listen:
A far sea moves in my ear.

> *What does the speaker hear in stanza 4?*

One cry, and I stumble from bed, cow-heavy and floral
In my Victorian nightgown.
15  Your mouth opens clean as a cat's. The window square

Whitens and swallows its dull stars. And now you try
Your handful of notes;
The clear vowels rise like balloons.

---

## ArtNote

**Mother and Child**, 1967.
Alice Neel.

By the 1960s, figurative art, which depicts the human form, was overshadowed by abstract art. But the portraits of Alice Neel (1900–1984) stood out for their stark honesty and the tension between the sitter and the viewer. What does Neel's portrait tell you about the mother's feelings for her child? How do these feelings compare to those of the mother in Plath's poem?

---

**WORDS FOR EVERYDAY USE**

**dis • till**, also **dis • til** (di stil′) *vt.*, let fall or precipitate in drops. *The moisture in the air, which had swelled up into black thunderclouds, was <u>distilled</u> by a sudden rainshower.*

**ef • face • ment** (i fās′ mənt) *n.*, disappearance or fading as if by wearing away. *The <u>effacement</u> of the date on the coin made Blake wonder how many people had handled it.*

# INVESTIGATE Inquire, Imagine

**Recall:** GATHERING FACTS

1a. Who "slapped your footsoles"?

2a. What does the cloud do?

3a. How does the baby's mouth open?

➤ **Interpret:** FINDING MEANING

1b. What event is described in stanza 1?

2b. What does the wind signify to the speaker?

3b. What does the baby want?

---

**Analyze:** TAKING THINGS APART

4a. Identify the sense with which the speaker is most aware of her child.

➤ **Synthesize:** BRINGING THINGS TOGETHER

4b. How does the speaker's attitude toward her child reflect her emotional state?

---

**Evaluate:** MAKING JUDGMENTS

5a. The speaker says that the new parents "stand round blankly as walls." In what ways is this reaction to the birth of a baby understandable? What types of things might the new parents be experiencing?

➤ **Extend:** CONNECTING IDEAS

5b. Read the poem "What Is Supposed to Happen" by Naomi Shihab Nye on page 1013. How does the speaker in this poem mirror the speaker's reaction to parenthood in "Morning Song"? What transition is the child experiencing in "What Is Supposed To Happen"? How does the mother react to this transition? What does she learn?

---

# Understanding Literature

**RUN-ON LINE.** Review the definition for **run-on line** in the Handbook of Literary Tools. Which line of the fifth stanza is a run-on line? What transition is marked by this run-on line?

**SIMILE.** Review the definition for **simile** in the Handbook of Literary Tools and the chart you made for Literary Tools on page 883. What does the vehicle for each simile reveal about the speaker's experience?

# Writer's Journal

1. Imagine that you are the speaker. Write a **letter** to your child to be opened on his or her eighteenth birthday. Describe your hopes and dreams for your child.

2. Imagine you are the speaker's child at age fourteen. Write a **journal entry** in which you describe your mother's parenting skills. Discuss the things she has done right and the things you would have liked her to do differently.

3. Write a **paragraph** explaining the meaning of the metaphor used in stanza 2.

# Integrating *the* LANGUAGE ARTS

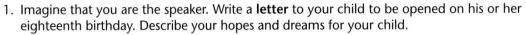

## Language, Grammar, and Style

**EDITING SENTENCES.** Read the Language Arts Survey 3.35, "Correcting Wordy Sentences." Then revise these sentences.

1. Sylvia Plath suffered from depression and she was often melancholy.
2. Plath won many academic awards and school prizes.
3. Plath graduated *summa cum laude* from Smith with the highest honors.
4. Plath wrote confessional poetry that was intensely personal.
5. Most of Plath's poetry has been published posthumously after her death.

## Media Literacy

**CREATING A POETRY BOOKLET.** Sylvia Plath wrote the poem "Morning Song" about the birth of her daughter. Research other poems about daughters, using the Internet or library resources. If you use the Internet, you may visit the **Academy of American Poets** website at http://www.poets.org. Conduct a search of the site using the "Find a Poem" feature and the keyword "daughter," or, visit the thematic exhibit "Daughters" by following the "Exhibits" link. After you have located at least four poems, put them together in a poetry booklet entitled "Daughters," including a short introduction for each poem that describes its treatment of the subject.

**INTERNET RESEARCH.** Explore a variety of Internet sites dedicated to Sylvia Plath and her work by visiting **PlathOnline.com** at http://www.plathonline.com. Prepare a brief description of five of the sites listed at this page.

## Collaborative Learning & Speaking and Listening

**DISCUSSION.** Read the Language Arts Survey 4.13, "Collaborative Learning and Communication." Then join a small group of classmates to discuss whether the speaker will be a good parent, based on evidence from the poem. Report your observations to the class.

# "The Secret"

### BY DENISE LEVERTOV

## About the AUTHOR

**Denise Levertov** (1923–1997) draws from many rich traditions to create her unique, visionary poetry, including the Welsh mysticism of her mother's ancestry and the Russian Hasidic Judaism of her father's. Born in Essex, England, Levertov was schooled at home. During the London blitz of World War II, she served as a nurse. She became a poet at a very early age, publishing her first collection, *The Double Image*, in 1946. In 1947, she moved to the United States. There she developed her distinctive voice, finding, in poem after poem, magic and mystery just behind the banal and ordinary.

Influences on Levertov's style include the poet H. D. (Hilda Doolittle) and, later, William Carlos Williams, whom she credits with helping her to find a voice as an American poet. During the 1960s, she translated, with Edward Dimock, Jr., *In Praise of Krishna: Songs from the Bengali* and became involved in the anti-Vietnam War movement. *Relearning the Alphabet* appeared in 1970 and contains some of her best verse, including the magnificent "A Tree Telling of Orpheus." Other collections of her poetry include *Here and Now* (1957), *Overland to the Islands* (1958), *Candles in Babylon* (1982), and *Breathing the Water* (1987). Levertov taught at Drew University, Vassar College, and Stanford University.

## About the SELECTION

**"The Secret"** is from Levertov's collection *O Taste and See,* published in 1964. The title poem of that collection encourages people to taste and see "all that lives / to the imagination's tongue." Levertov wants us not simply to exist from day to day but to live our lives fully, intensely, engaged with the wonders of the world around us. Such enthusiasm for life, active engagement in the world coupled with imagination, constitutes a secret worth remembering.

## Literary TOOLS

**SPEAKER.** The **speaker** is the character who speaks in, or narrates, a poem—the voice assumed by the writer. As you read, determine whether the speaker is the poet or a voice assumed by Levertov.

**FREE VERSE.** **Free verse** is poetry that avoids use of regular rhyme, meter, or division into stanzas. Notice that this poem is written in complete sentences. Notice also that the breaks between lines and stanzas often occur in the middles of sentences. A poet writing free verse can decide where to break a line or stanza based not on the number of beats, or stresses, in the line but rather on what he or she wants to emphasize. The materials before and after breaks receive the greatest emphasis.

As you read the poem, make a cluster chart to list what you learn about the secret. One example has been done for you.

the secret of life

The Secret

## Reader's Journal

What do you think is the secret of life?

# The Secret

## DENISE LEVERTOV

Two girls discover
the secret of life
in a sudden line of
poetry.

*What does the word sudden suggest here?*

5   I who don't know the
secret wrote
the line. They
told me

(through a third person)
10  they had found it
but not what it was,
not even

what line it was. No doubt
by now, more than a week
15  later, they have forgotten
the secret,

the line, the name of
the poem. I love them

for finding what
20  I can't find,

and for loving me
for the line I wrote,
and for forgetting it
so that

25  a thousand times, till death
finds them, they may
discover it again, in other
lines,

in other
30  happenings. And for
wanting to know it,
for

*What qualities do the two girls have?*

assuming there is
such a secret, yes,
35  for that
most of all.

■

What secret of life do you think the girls might have discovered?

# INVESTIGATE, *Inquire,* Imagine

**Recall:** GATHERING FACTS

1a. What do the two girls discover in a line of poetry? Who wrote the line?

2a. What does the speaker think most likely happened "more than a week / later"?

3a. Why does the speaker love these girls?

➤ **Interpret:** FINDING MEANING

1b. Does the speaker of this poem know the secret of life?

2b. Why is the speaker so sure that, a week later, the girls have forgotten the line?

3b. Why does the speaker love the fact that the girls have forgotten the line? What does the speaker's loving this fact reveal about her?

**Analyze:** TAKING THINGS APART

4a. Identify what you consider to be the theme of the poem.

➤ **Synthesize:** BRINGING THINGS TOGETHER

4b. Why doesn't the speaker think the girls are fickle to abandon the line of poetry in her poem?

**Evaluate:** MAKING JUDGMENTS

5a. To what degree have the girls, whom the speaker has never met, affected her life?

➤ **Extend:** CONNECTING IDEAS

5b. What secrets of life have you discovered? How did they become evident to you?

# Understanding *Literature*

**SPEAKER.** Review the definition for **speaker** in the Handbook of Literary Terms. In your opinion, is the speaker the poet or a voice assumed by Levertov? What can be inferred about the speaker?

**FREE VERSE.** Review the definition for **free verse** in Literary Tools on page 887 and the cluster chart you completed for that section. How many sentences make up the poem? Which sentence do you think reveals the poem's theme? Consider the breaks between stanzas 8 and 9. What two points are emphasized by breaking the sentence in this particular place?

# WRITER'S JOURNAL

1. Write a **paragraph** explaining what the speaker knows for sure and what she surmises about the girls.

2. Imagine that you are the speaker. Write a **journal entry** explaining why you were moved when you heard two girls found the secret of life in one of your poems.

3. Imagine that you are one of the girls who read the speaker's poem. Write a **letter** to the poet explaining what the poem you read means to you.

# Integrating *the* LANGUAGE ARTS

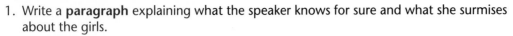

## Language, Grammar, and Style

**COMPARING ADJECTIVES AND ADVERBS.** Read the Language Arts Survey 3.47, "Recognizing Other Problems with Modifiers." Then use that information to correct the following sentences.

1. What could be more nicer than learning two girls liked your poem?

2. Of all her readers, the girls are the more reassuring because they found the secret of life in the speaker's poem.

3. The hopefullest thing about the girls is that they will keep looking for the secret of life in other places.

4. The speaker is the less angry of all poets because it doesn't bother her that the girls forgot the line a week later.

5. The speaker skillfulliest puts deep meaning in her poem without being aware of it.

## Media Literacy

**BOOKLET OF POEMS.** Using the Internet or resources at your local library, read other poems by Denise Levertov. Two websites you will find useful are the Academy of American Poets at http://www.poets.org and Modern American Poetry at http://www.english.uiuc.edu/maps. Make a booklet of six to eight poems that you like. Then write an index, listing the titles by subject or theme.

## Critical Thinking

**INTERJECTIONS.** Read the Language Arts Survey 3.74, "Interjections." Then, as you reread the poem, find one interjection and explain how it is used to emphasize the poem's main idea.

# "House *Guest*"

### BY ELIZABETH BISHOP

## About *the* AUTHOR

**Elizabeth Bishop** (1911–1979) was born in Worcester, Massachusetts, but, on the death of her father just eight months after her birth, Bishop was taken by her mother to live with her maternal grandparents in Nova Scotia, Canada. Her mother was permanently institutionalized when she was five years old, and Bishop became the pawn of warring family members, eventually being returned to Worcester by her paternal grandparents. Those early traumatic experiences left Bishop with a series of stress-related illnesses and an emotionally restrained personality that was later to characterize her poetry. While attending Vassar College in the early 1930s, Bishop became an ardent admirer of poet Marianne Moore and abandoned thoughts of medical school for the greater attraction of travel. She finally settled in Brazil and lived there for sixteen years. On her return to the United States, Bishop taught at Harvard from 1970 to 1977. Inspired by such events as the exile of her youth and her life as an expatriate in Brazil, Bishop's poetry is known for its meticulous detail and understated style. Her many honors include the 1956 Pulitzer Prize for the combined collection *Poems: North and South—A Cold Spring* and the 1969 National Book Award for *Complete Poems*.

## About *the* SELECTION

Some people's personalities challenge us, raising basic, uncomfortable questions. Elizabeth Bishop's **"House Guest"** presents a portrait of such a person. Bishop creates this portrait through precise description, vivid images, and bits of dialogue.

## Literary TOOLS

**ALLUSION.** An **allusion** is a rhetorical technique in which reference is made to a person, event, object, or work from history or literature. Look for allusions as you read "House Guest."

**TONE. Tone** is the emotional attitude toward the reader or toward the subject implied by a literary work. As you read, make a cluster chart to determine the tone of the speaker's comments toward the seamstress. In the first layer of circles, write a detail about the seamstress. In the next layer, write the speaker's comment about this detail. One example has been done for you.

> "No one can cheer her up"

> "is small and thin and bitter"

> SEAMSTRESS

## Reader's *Journal*

If one of your dreams became impossible to fulfill, would you retreat into disappointment, or would you seek another dream to take its place? Explain.

*Inside Looking Out,* 1953. Ben Shahn.
The Butler Institute of Ameriocan Art, Youngstown, Ohio.

# House guest

## Elizabeth Bishop

## Art Note

*Inside Looking Out,* 1953. Ben Shahn.

Ben Shahn's (1898–1969) painting seems
simplistic at first. Actually, it is a very complex composition. In
reality, where would the woman, the dresser, and the sewing
machine be located in relation to the viewer? How does this
painting correspond to Bishop's poem?

The sad seamstress
who stays with
us this month
is small and thin
and bitter.
No one can cheer her up.
5    Give her a dress, a drink,
roast chicken, or fried fish—
it's all the same to her.

She sits and watches TV.
No, she watches zigzags.
10    "Can you adjust the TV?"
"No," she says. No hope.
She watches on and on,
without hope, without air.[1]

Her own clothes give us pause,
15    but she's not a poor orphan.
She has a father, a mother,
and all that, and she's earning
quite well, and we're stuffing
her with fattening foods.

20    We invite her to use the binoculars.
We say, "Come see the jets!"
We say, "Come see the baby!"
Or the knife grinder who cleverly
plays the National Anthem[2]
25    on his wheel so shrilly.
Nothing helps.

She speaks: "I need a little
money to buy buttons."
She seems to think it's useless
30    to ask. Heavens, buy buttons,

*Who is visiting the speaker? What is the visitor like?*

---

1. **without air.** Without spirit
2. **National Anthem.** "The Star Spangled
Banner" by Francis Scott Key (1779–1843)

if they'll do any good,
the biggest in the world—
by the dozen, by the gross![3]
Buy yourself an ice cream,
35  a comic book, a car!

Her face is closed as a nut,
closed as a careful snail
or a thousand-year-old seed.
Does she dream of marriage?
40  Of getting rich? Her sewing
is decidedly <u>mediocre</u>.

Please! Take our money! Smile!
What on earth have we done?
What has everyone done
45  and when did it all begin?
Then one day she confides
that she wanted to be a nun[4]
and her family opposed her.

Perhaps we should let her go,
50  or deliver her straight off
to the nearest convent—and wasn't
her month up last week, anyway?
Can it be that we nourish
one of the Fates[5] in our bosoms?
55  Clotho,[6] sewing our lives
with a bony little foot
on a borrowed sewing machine,
and our fates will be like hers,
and our hems crooked forever?  ∎

What does the visitor ask for? What is her attitude toward her request? What is the speaker's response?

What personal secret does the visitor share? What light does this shed on her life?

What fear does the speaker raise at the end of the poem?

---

3. **gross.** Twelve dozen
4. **nun.** Religious woman who takes vows of obedience to the Roman Catholic Church
5. **Fates.** In Greek and Roman mythology, Clotho, Lachesis, and Atropos, the three goddesses who control human destiny and life
6. **Clotho.** Spinner of the thread of human life

**WORDS FOR EVERYDAY USE**

me • di • o • cre (mē´dē ō´ kər) adj., average; not very good. *Although only a <u>mediocre</u> artist, Brent put in the effort of a master.*

How would you respond to someone like the seamstress?

# INVESTIGATE Inquire, Imagine

**Recall:** GATHERING FACTS

1a. Who has come to stay at the speaker's house, and what adjectives are used in the first three lines to describe her?

2a. In what ways do the people in the house try to cheer up the seamstress?

3a. What questions does the seamstress raise in the mind of the speaker?

**Interpret:** FINDING MEANING

1b. How would you describe the seamstress's attitude toward life?

2b. What is unusual about the way in which the seamstress watches television? about her clothing? about the way in which she asks for money for buttons? What do these things reveal about her?

3b. How does the speaker feel about the seamstress staying longer than she was supposed to stay?

**Analyze:** TAKING THINGS APART

4a. A *pun* is a play on words, one that wittily exploits a double meaning. What pun exists in the name *Clotho*, applied to the seamstress?

**Synthesize:** BRINGING THINGS TOGETHER

4b. What fears about her own fate does the seamstress raise in the speaker?

**Perspective:** LOOKING AT OTHER VIEWS

5a. Explain why the seamstress is so unhappy with her life.

**Empathy:** SEEING FROM INSIDE

5b. If you were the speaker, what counsel would you give the seamstress?

# Understanding Literature

TONE. Review the definition for **tone** in the Handbook of Literary terms and the cluster chart you completed for Literary Tools on page 891. What is the tone of the speaker toward the seamstress? Why does the speaker take this tone?

**ALLUSION.** Review the definition for **allusion** in the Handbook of Literary Terms. In Greek mythology, the Fates were three goddesses, often pictured as extremely ancient sisters, who controlled the destinies of human beings. Clotho, the spinner, spun the thread of human fate; Lachesis, the allotter, spooled it out; and Atropos cut it, thus deciding when a person would die. To which of these sisters does the speaker allude in the final stanza of the poem? Why is this choice of allusion particularly appropriate?

# WRITER'S JOURNAL

1. Write a **want ad** that the speaker would have placed for a seamstress. Include mention of the living arrangement.

2. Write an **advice column** in which you respond to the speaker's complaints about her house guest.

3. Imagine that you are the seamstress. Write a **journal entry** in which you describe what it is like for you to work as a seamstress in the speaker's house.

# Integrating
## *the* LANGUAGE ARTS

## Language, Grammar, and Style

**Commas and Semicolons.** Read the Language Arts Survey 3.87, "Commas," and 3.88, "Semicolons." Then add the appropriate punctuation to the following sentences.

1. The seamstress referred by a friend came to live with us for a month.

2. We fed her entertained her and tried to make her happy.

3. The seamstress watched television she didn't mind the zigzags.

4. She had wanted to take her vows as a nun move into a convent and serve God.

5. I wasn't entirely happy with her work however I paid her what we had agreed upon.

## Applied English

**REFERENCE.** Write an honest reference for the seamstress, including personality traits so that prospective employers know what she's like. You may want to review the Language Arts Survey 6.5, "Writing a Business Letter."

## Speaking and Listening

**NONVERBAL COMMUNICATION.** Read the Language Arts Survey 4.1, "Verbal and Nonverbal Communication." Then, working with a partner, make a list of examples of nonverbal communication to go with each of the seamstress's activities mentioned in the poem. Finally, take turns interpreting the nonverbal communication on your list.

# "THE SLUMP"

BY JOHN UPDIKE

## Literary TOOLS

**METAPHOR.** A **metaphor** is a figure of speech in which one thing is spoken or written about as if it were another. This figure of speech invites the reader to make a comparison between the two things. As you read, decide what two things are being compared in the phrase "the sun seems a high fly I'm going to lose."

**DICTION. Diction**, when applied to writing, refers to word choice. Much of a writer's style is determined by his or her diction, the types of words that he or she chooses. Diction can be formal or informal, simple or complex, contemporary or archaic, ordinary or unusual, foreign or native, standard or dialectical, euphemistic or blunt. Updike's diction is characterized by the use of colloquial language. Make a chart of these expressions. On the left, list colloquial expressions. On the right, define them.

| Colloquial Expressions | Definitions |
|---|---|
| gag | prank |
| | |

## About the AUTHOR

**John Updike** (1932– ) is regarded by many critics and readers as one of America's great contemporary novelists. He grew up as an only child in Shillington, Pennsylvania. Hay fever, psoriasis, and a speech impediment isolated him from his classmates and compelled him to take up the solitary pursuits of drawing and writing. After graduating from Harvard, he spent a year in England at the Ruskin School of Drawing and Fine Art. Deciding on a career as a writer, he joined the staff of the *New Yorker* magazine.

Updike's novels and short stories usually deal with the tensions, frustrations, and tragedies of contemporary life. *Rabbit, Run* (1960) was the first installment in Updike's continuing saga of Harry "Rabbit" Angstrom, which would later include *Rabbit Redux* (1971), *Rabbit Is Rich* (1981), and *Rabbit at Rest* (1990). The series traces the life of Angstrom, a successful high school basketball player, from the early days of his precarious marriage to an alcoholic wife, through the turbulent 1960s, and into the compromises of middle and old age. Updike's other notable novels include *The Poorhouse Fair* (1959); *The Centaur* (1963), which earned the National Book Award; *Of the Farm* (1965); *Couples* (1968); *A Month of Sundays* (1975); the *Witches of Eastwick* (1984), later made into a major motion picture; *In the Beauty of the Lilies* (1996); and *Toward the End of Time* (1997). His volumes of short stories include *Pigeon Feathers* (1962), *The Music School* (1967), *Bech: A Book* (1970), *Museums and Women and Other Stories* (1972), and *Afterlife* (1994). Updike has also published volumes of poetry and essays.

## About the SELECTION

**"The Slump"** was first published in *Esquire* magazine in 1968. It was one of the few Updike short stories that did not first appear in the *New Yorker*. In 1972 it was published again in a collection of short stories called *Museums and Women and Other Stories*. In "The Slump" a nameless baseball player reflects on the extended slump that he is experiencing.

## Reader's Journal

Have you ever been in a slump? How did you get out of it?

# THE SLUMP

# They say reflexes,

the coach says reflexes, even the papers now are saying reflexes, but I don't think it's the reflexes so much—last night, as a gag to cheer me up, the wife walks into the bedroom wearing one of the kids' rubber gorilla masks and I was under the bed in six-tenths of a second, she had the stopwatch on me. It's that I can't see the ball the way I used to. It used to come floating up with all seven continents showing, and the pitcher's thumbprint, and a grass smooch or two, and the Spalding guarantee in ten-point san-serif,[1] and *whop!* I could feel the sweet wood with the bat still cocked. Now, I don't know, there's like a cloud around it, a sort of spiral vagueness, maybe the Van Allen belt,[2] or maybe I lift my eye in the last second, planning how I'll round second base, or worrying which I do first, tip my cap or slap the third-base coach's hand. You can't see a blind spot, Kierkegaard[3] says, but in there now, between when the ball leaves the bleacher background and I can hear it plop all fat and satisfied in the catcher's mitt, there's somehow just nothing, where there used to be a lot, everything in fact, because they're not keeping me around for my fielding, and already I see the afternoon tabloid has me down as trade bait.

> Who blames the baseball player's slump on his reflexes?

> How well did the ballplayer used to see the ball?

> What reason does the ballplayer give for his sudden inability to hit the ball?

# The flutters don't

come when they used to. It used to be, I'd back the convertible out of the garage and watch the electric eye put the door down again and drive in to the stadium, and at about the bridge turnoff I'd ease off grooving with the radio rock, and then on the lot there'd be the kids waiting to get a look and that would start the big butterflies, and when the attendant would take my car I'd want to shout *Stop*, *thief*, and walking down that long cement corridor I'd fantasize like I was going to the electric chair and the locker room was some dream after death, and I'd wonder why the suit fit, and how these really <u>immortal</u> guys, that I recognized from the bubble-gum cards I used to collect, knew my name. *They* knew *me*. And I'd go out and the stadium mumble would scoop at me and the grass seemed too precious to walk on, like emeralds, and by the time I got into the cage I couldn't remember if I batted left or right.

> Formerly, what did the ballplayer fantasize as he walked to the locker room?

# Now, heck, I move

over the bridge singing along with the radio, and brush through the kids at just the right speed, not so fast I knock any of them down, and the attendant knows his Labor Day tip is coming, and we wink, and in the batting cage I own the place, and take my cuts, and pop five or six into the bullpen as easy as dropping dimes down a sewer. But when the scoreboard lights up, and I take those two steps up from the dugout, the biggest two steps in a ballplayer's life, and kneel in the circle, giving

---

1. **ten-point sans-serif.** Size and style of the lettering
2. **Van Allen belt.** Belt of radiation that encircles the earth
3. **Kierkegaard.** Søren Kierkegaard, Danish philosopher and theologian

**WORDS FOR EVERYDAY USE** im • mor • tal (i môr′ təl) *adj.*, able to live forever; never to be forgotten. *Babe Ruth is an <u>immortal</u> baseball player.*

the crowd the old hawk profile, where once the flutters would ease off, now they dig down and begin.

What are the "biggest two steps" for a ballplayer? What does this ballplayer feel then?

# They say I'm not

hungry, but I still feel hungry, only now it's a kind of panic hungry, and that's not the right kind. Ever watch one of your little kids try to catch a ball? He gets so excited with the idea he's going to catch it he shuts his eyes. That's me now. I walk up to the plate, having come all this way—a lot of hotels, a lot of shagging—and my eyes feel shut. And I stand up there trying to push my eyeballs through my eyelids, and my retinas register maybe a little green, and the black patch of some nuns in far left field. That's <u>panic</u> hungry.

# Kierkegaard called

it dread. It queers the works. My wife comes at me without the gorilla

What does Kierkegaard call "panic hungry"?

mask and when in the old days, *whop!*, now she slides by with a hurt expression and a flicker of gray above her temple, I go out and ride the power mower and I've already done it so often the lawn is brown. The kids get me out of bed for a little fungo and it scares me to see them trying, busting their lungs, all that shagging ahead of them. In Florida—we used to love it in Florida, the smell of citrus and marlin, the flat pink sections where the old people drift around smiling with transistor plugs in their ears—we lie on the beach after a workout and the sun seems a high fly I'm going to lose and the waves keep coming like they've been doing for a billion years, up to the plate, up to the plate.

Kierkegaard probably has the clue, somewhere in there, but I picked up *Concluding Unscientific Postscript* the other day and I couldn't see the print, that is, I could see the lines, but there wasn't anything on them, like the

Where does the ballplayer seek the answer to his problem? Why doesn't it help?

rows of deep seats in the shade of the second deck on a Thursday afternoon, just a single ice-cream vendor sitting there, nobody around to sell to, a speck of white in all that shade, and Søren Sock himself, keeping his goods cool.

# I think maybe if I

got beaned. That's probably what the wife is hinting at with the gorilla mask. A change of pace, like the time DiMaggio[4] broke his slump by Topping's[5] telling him to go to a

What solution does the ballplayer think of?

night club and get plastered. I've stopped ducking, but the trouble is, if you're not hitting, they don't brush you back. On me, they've stopped trying for even the corners; they put it right down the pike. I can see it in his evil eye as he takes the sign and rears back, I can hear the catcher snicker, and for a second of reflex there I can see it like it used to be, continents and cities and every green tree distinct as a stitch, and the hickory sweetens in my hands, and I feel the good old sure hunger. Then something happens. It blurs, skips, fades, I don't know. It's not caring enough, is what it probably is, it's knowing that none of it—the stadium, the averages—is really there, just *you* are there, and it's not enough. ∎

---

4. **DiMaggio.** New York Yankee center fielder from 1936 to 1951

5. **Topping.** Yankee owner from 1945 to 1964

---

**WORDS FOR EVERYDAY USE**

**pan • ic** (pa' nik) *n.*, sudden, overpowering fright. *The child felt <u>panic</u> because he missed the school bus.*

INVESTIGATE **Inquire** *Imagine*

**Recall:** GATHERING FACTS

1a. What does Kierkegaard say?

2a. What surprised the narrator about his teammates when he was playing well? How does he convey that his attitude toward playing baseball has changed?

3a. What happens to the narrator's hunger at the end of the selection?

→ **Interpret:** FINDING MEANING

1b. How is the ballplayer's slump like a blind spot?

2b. How has the narrator's attitude toward baseball changed during the course of his career?

3b. What does the ballplayer experience at the end of the selection?

**Analyze:** TAKING THINGS APART

4a. Identify the two types of hunger described in this short story.

→ **Synthesize:** BRINGING THINGS TOGETHER

4b. How do you think the narrator will get out of his slump and overcome his panic hunger? Cite evidence from the story to support your answer.

**Evaluate:** MAKING JUDGMENTS

5a. "The Slump" captures the sense of uncertainty and insecurity that all people experience at some point during their lives. How effectively is this developed by the author?

→ **Extend:** CONNECTING IDEAS

5b. Explain why professional athletes are revered in our culture. Which professional athletes do you admire? Why?

# Understanding *Literature*

**METAPHOR.** Review the definition for **metaphor** in the Handbook of Literary Terms. In the phrase "the sun seems a high fly I'm going to lose," what two things are being compared? Why is this metaphor particularly appropriate for this story?

**DICTION.** Review the definition for **diction** in the Handbook of Literary Terms and the chart you made for Literary Tools on page 896. How would you characterize Updike's diction? From the colloquial expressions you listed in your chart, which appear dated? Which apply to baseball?

# Writer's Journal

1. Imagine that you are a sports writer for a newspaper. Write a **column** for sports fans contrasting the baseball player's past and current performance.
2. Imagine that you are a fan of the baseball player. Write a supportive **letter** giving him advice on how he should get out of his slump.
3. Write a **song or poem** that celebrates baseball. Be sure to include baseball diction.

# Integrating *the* LANGUAGE ARTS

## Language, Grammar, and Style

COMMON AND PROPER NOUNS. Read the Language Arts Survey 3.51, "Common Nouns and Proper Nouns." Then make two lists of the nouns in the sentences below, one headed *Common Nouns* and the other *Proper Nouns*.

1. The baseball player does not believe his reflexes are to blame for his slump.
2. The ballplayer used to see all seven continents on the ball made by Spalding.
3. Labor Day is coming, and the narrator plans to give a tip to the attendant.
4. Kierkegaard says you can't see a blind spot.
5. On the advice of Topping, Joe DiMaggio broke his slump by going to a night club.

## Critical Thinking

PRO AND CON CHART. Read the Language Arts Survey 2.21, "Pro and Con Charts." Then create a pro and con chart. Label the left column *Pro* and the right column *Con*. At the top, write the following statement, or proposition: "If given the chance, I should become a professional athlete." Then list arguments for and against becoming a professional athlete. For example, in the *Pro* column you might list, "might lead to fame," and in the *Con* column you might list "would be very stressful." When you are finished with the chart, write an essay explaining why, if given the opportunity, you would or would not want to become a professional athlete.

## Speaking and Listening

INTERVIEW. Choose a profession that interests you and interview someone in that field. Find out what training, education, and skills are required and what salary range is typical. You might also ask what tasks the person performs on a typical day. Then report on your findings to the class.

## Literary T O O L S

**POINT OF VIEW. Point of view** is the vantage point from which a story is told. Stories are typically written from a *first-person point of view*, in which the narrator uses words such as *I* and *we*; from a *second-person point of view*, in which the narrator uses the word *you*; or from a *third-person point of view*, in which the narrator uses words such as *he*, *she*, *it*, and *they*. As you read "Journey," decide which point of view the narrator uses.

**ALLEGORY.** An **allegory** is a work in which each element *symbolizes*, or represents, something else. As you read, make a chart. On the left, list elements of the selection that represent something else. On the right, explain what these elements represent. One example has been done for you.

| Elements | Represents |
|----------|------------|
| the city | the outcome of your life, or your goal |

### Reader's Journal

If you made a map of your life, what would it look like?

## "Journey"

BY JOYCE CAROL OATES

### About *the* A U T H O R

**Joyce Carol Oates** (1938– ) was born in Lockport, New York, a town so small that it had only a one-room schoolhouse. As a child she wrote her own stories. In her fiction, Erie County became Eden County, which she peopled with characters that reappeared in different books. At age twenty-six, Oates published her first novel, *With Shuddering Fall* (1964). She was awarded the National Book Award in 1970 for her novel *Them*. A prolific writer, she has published over forty novels, twenty-five collections of short stories, eight volumes of poetry, and numerous plays and books of essays, all while maintaining a full-time career as a university professor at Princeton.

Fellow novelist John Barth says that Oates "writes all over the aesthetical map." She reads widely and has been influenced by the entire Western literary tradition, making it difficult to categorize her writing style. The hallmark of her fiction, however, may be its exploration of the modern psyche. She says, "the main thing about me is that I am enormously interested in other people, other lives, and that with the least provocation . . . I could 'go into' your personality and try to imagine it, try to find a way of dramatizing it. I am fascinated by people I meet, or don't meet, people I only correspond with, or read about; and I hope my interest in them isn't vampiristic, because I don't want to take life from them but only to honor the life in them, to give some permanent form to their personalities. It seems to me that there are so many people who are inarticulate but who suffer and doubt and love, nobly, who need to be immortalized or at least explained."

### About *the* S E L E C T I O N

In **"Journey,"** Oates talks directly to the reader about the paths we take in life and the choices we make on our way to individuality. It was published in *The Poisoned Kiss and Other Stories* (1975).

# Journey

## JOYCE CAROL OATES

You begin your journey on so high an elevation that your destination is already in sight—a city that you have visited many times and that, moreover, is indicated on a traveler's map you have carefully folded up to take along with you. You are a lover of maps, and you have already committed this map to memory, but you bring it with you just the same.

*What can you see from the starting point of your journey?*

The highway down from the mountains is broad and handsome, constructed after many years of <u>ingenious</u> blasting and leveling and paving. Engineers from all over the country aided in the construction of this famous highway. Its cost is so <u>excessive</u> that many rumors have circulated about it—you take no interest in such things, sensing that you will never learn the true cost anyway, and that this will make no difference to your journey.

After several hours on this excellent highway, where the sun shines ceaselessly and where there is a moderate amount of traffic, cars like your own at a safe distance from you, as if to assure you that there are other people in the world, you become sleepy from the monotony and wonder if perhaps there is another, less perfect road parallel to this. You discover on the map a smaller road, not exactly parallel to the highway and not as direct, but one that leads to the same city.

*Why do you turn off the main highway?*

You turn onto this road, which winds among foothills and forests and goes through several small villages. You sense by the attitude of the villagers that traffic on this road is infrequent but nothing to

*What do you drive through on the second road?*

draw special attention. At some curves the road shrinks, but you are fortunate enough to meet no oncoming traffic.

The road leads deep into a forest, always descending in small cramped turns. Your turning from left to right and from right to left, in a slow <u>hypnotic</u> passage, makes it impossible for you to look out at the forest and discover that for some time you have not been able to see the city you are headed for, though you know it is still somewhere ahead of you.

By mid-afternoon you are tired of this road, though it has served you well, and you come upon a smaller, unpaved road that evidently leads to your city, though in a <u>convoluted</u> way. After only a moment's pause you turn onto this road, and immediately your automobile registers the change, the chassis[1] bounces, something begins to vibrate, something begins to rattle. This noise is disturbing, but after a while you forget about it in your interest in the beautiful countryside. Here the trees are enormous. There are no villages or houses. For a while the dirt road runs alongside a small river, dangerously close to the river's steep bank, and you begin to feel <u>apprehension</u>. It is necessary for you to drive very slowly. At times your speedometer registers less than five miles an hour. You will not get to the city before dark.

*What do you feel along the river's steep bank?*

The road narrows until it is hardly more than a lane. Grass has begun to grow in its center. As the river twists and turns, so does the road twist and turn, curving around hills that consist of enormous boulders, bare of all trees and plants,

---

1. **chassis.** Frame and working parts of a car, exclusive of the body

**WORDS FOR EVERYDAY USE**

**in • ge • nious** (in jēn′ yəs) *adj.,* marked by originality, resourcefulness, and cleverness in conception or execution. *The ingenious inventor patented a new invention every month.*

**ex • ces • sive** (ik se′ siv) *adj.,* exceeding what is usual, proper, necessary, or normal. *The excessive speed of the taxi driver made Gloria clutch the door handle.*

**hyp • not • ic** (hip nä′ tik) *adj.,* tending to produce sleep. *The hypnotic ticking of the clock lulled Eric to sleep.*

**con • vo • lut • ed** (kän və lü′ təd) *adj.,* twisting or coiling. *The convoluted garden paths made Sherry think of a labyrinth.*

**ap • pre • hen • sion** (a pri hen[t]′ shən) *n.,* fear. *Evan's apprehension mounted as the roller coaster went through a dark tunnel.*

covered only in patches by a dull, brown lichen[2] that is unfamiliar to you. Along one stretch rocks of varying sizes have fallen down onto the road, so that you are forced to drive around them with great caution.

Navigating these blind turns, you tap your horn to give warning in case someone should be approaching. But it is all unnecessary, since you come upon no other travelers. Late in the afternoon, your foot numb from its constant pressure on the accelerator, your body jolted by the constant bumps and vibrations of the car, you decide to make the rest of your journey on foot, since you must be close to your destination by now.

A faint path leads through a tumble of rocks and bushes and trees, and you follow it enthusiastically. You descend a hill, slipping a little, so that a small rock slide is released; but you are able to keep your balance. At the back of your head is the precise location of your parked car, and behind that the curving dirt road, and behind that the other road, and the magnificent highway itself; you understand that it would be no difficult feat to make your way back to any of these roads, should you decide that going by foot is unwise. But the path, though overgrown, is through a lovely forest, and then through a meadow in which yellow flowers are blooming, and you feel no _inclination_ to turn back.

*Why don't you turn back once on the footpath?*

By evening you are still in the wilderness and you wonder if perhaps you have made a mistake. You are exhausted, your body aches, your eyes are seared[3] by the need to stare so intently at everything around you. Now that the sun has nearly set, it is getting cold; evenings here in the mountains are always chilly.

You find yourself standing at the edge of a forest, staring ahead into the dark. Is that a field ahead, or a forest of small trees? Your path has long since given way to wild grass. Clouds _obscure_ the moon, which should give you some light by which to make your way and you wonder if you dare continue without this light.

Suddenly you remember the map you left back in the car, but you remember it as a blank sheet of paper.

## You resist telling yourself you are lost.

You resist telling yourself you are lost. In fact, though you are exhausted and it is almost night, you are not lost. You have begun to shiver, but it is only with cold, not with fear. You are really satisfied with yourself. You are not lost. Though you can remember your map only as a blank sheet of paper, which can tell you nothing, you are not really lost.

If you had the day to begin again, on that highway which was so wide and clear, you would not have varied your journey in any way: in this is your triumph. ∎

*What is your triumph?*

---

2. **lichen.** Fungus and algae that form a scaly or spongelike growth on rocks or trees
3. **seared.** Burned

WORDS FOR EVERYDAY USE

in • cli • na • tion (in′ klə nā shən) n., a tendency toward a particular goal; a particular disposition of mind or character. *Judith's inclination was to pursue a career in engineering.*

ob • scure (äb skyūr′) vt., conceal or hide by or as if by covering. *The people in front of us obscured our view of the concert.*

Do you think that you are lost or found at the end of the story?

INVESTIGATE

# Inquire *Imagine*

**Recall:** GATHERING FACTS

1a. What is your destination on this journey?

2a. What is the condition of the road on which you begin your journey?

3a. How do you assess your journey as a whole?

→ **Interpret:** FINDING MEANING

1b. What is the significance of the fact that you can no longer see the city from the second road?

2b. Why does the highway become monotonous? Why do you decide to find another road?

3b. What have you gained by following your own path?

**Analyze:** TAKING THINGS APART

4a. Into what four stages can your journey be divided?

→ **Synthesize:** BRINGING THINGS TOGETHER

4b. In the beginning of the story, "you are a lover of maps." What does it mean when you are well into your journey and you see the map "as a blank sheet of paper"?

**Evaluate:** MAKING JUDGMENTS

5a. Do you agree with the narrator that it is better to go through life without a map? What are some of the benefits of not planning your life in advance?

→ **Extend:** CONNECTING IDEAS

5b. Another selection that focuses on the idea of a personal quest is the excerpt from *Walden* on page 287. Review that selection. What map did Henry David Thoreau follow? Which roads did he take? Explain how "Journey" relates to the following Thoreau quote: "If a man does not keep pace with his companions, perhaps it is because he hears a different drummer. Let him step to the music which he hears, however measured or far away."

# Understanding *Literature*

POINT OF VIEW. Review the definition for **point of view** in the Handbook of Literary Terms. Which point of view is used in "Journey"? What impact does the use of this point of view have on the reader? How would the story's impact change if it were written from a different point of view?

**ALLEGORY.** Review the definition for **allegory** in the Handbook of Literary Terms and the graphic organizer you made for Literary Tools on page 902. What is the significance of the changing roads you take on your journey? What have you established by the time you reach the footpath? Besides a journey, how else could Joyce have written allegorically about life?

# Writer's Journal

1. Write a **tour guide** pointing out the key points of your journey.
2. Imagine that you write an advice column and a teenager has written you about what choices he or she should make. Write an **advice column** telling the teenager how to travel through life.
3. The narrator says, "You discover that for some time you have not been able to see the city you are headed for, though you know it is still somewhere ahead of you." Write a **paragraph** explaining the allegorical meaning of this sentence.

# Integrating the LANGUAGE ARTS

## Language, Grammar, and Style

Rewrite the first paragraph of "Journey" using a third-person point of view and the past tense to see how these changes alter the meaning of the story.

## Study and Research & Media Literacy

**TALK-SHOW INTERVIEW.** Research the life and career of Joyce Carol Oates. Then, with a partner, conduct a talk-show interview. One student plays the role of the interviewer, who asks Oates questions in an effort to connect "Journey" to personal choices she has made in her life. The other student plays the role of Oates, answering questions about her life and how her answers relate to "Journey."

## Applied English

**JOURNEY BROCHURE.** Imagine you work for a travel company. Design a brochure so that your clients will want to take the trip described in "Journey." Write a description of the trip. Then design a map that shows the transition from civilization to wilderness that the story describes.

# INAUGURAL ADDRESS

BY JOHN F. KENNEDY

## Literary TOOLS

**ANAPHORA.** An **anaphora**, as that term is used by linguists, is any word or phrase that repeats or refers to something that precedes or follows it. For example, the phrase "Let both sides" is repeated at the beginning of several paragraphs in Kennedy's speech. As you read, think about how this anaphora emphasizes Kennedy's ideas.

**PARALLELISM.** **Parallelism** is a rhetorical technique in which a writer emphasizes the equal weight of two or more ideas by presenting them in the same grammatical form. As you read, make a cluster chart to list examples of parallelism in the Inaugural Address. One example has been done for you.

"a victory of party"
"a celebration of freedom"

Parallelism

## Reader's *Journal*

If you were president, what goals would you set for your administration?

## About *the* AUTHOR

**John F. Kennedy** (1917–1963), thirty-fifth president of the United States, was born in Brookline, Massachusetts, to a family already very familiar with politics. Kennedy earned his undergraduate degree at Harvard University in 1940. That same year, his senior thesis, *Why England Slept,* was published. It examined Britain's reaction to the rise of the Nazi Party in Germany. From 1941 to 1945, Kennedy served in World War II as a torpedo boat commander and was honored for his bravery. His political career began when he returned home to Massachusetts. In 1946, he was elected to the United States House of Representatives and, in 1952, to the United States Senate. During his eight years as a senator, Kennedy married Jacqueline Bouvier and wrote the 1956 Pulitzer Prize winner *Profiles in Courage,* a book that examines the brave and moral actions of eight politicians. In 1960, he was elected president of the United States, the youngest person and the first Catholic to achieve that office. In 1962, President Kennedy faced a serious nuclear confrontation with what was then the Soviet Union in an episode known as the Cuban Missile Crisis. He also created the Peace Corps and was a supporter of civil rights legislation. Kennedy was assassinated on November 22, 1963, in Dallas, Texas.

## About *the* SELECTION

When John F. Kennedy was elected president of the United States, he took over the office from Dwight Eisenhower, who had been a much-decorated general in World War II. At the time of Kennedy's election, the nation was essentially peaceful and prosperous. Tensions existed, however, between the United States and the Communist-run Soviet Union—allies during World War II but later competitors for global influence.

In his **Inaugural Address**, presented January 20, 1961, Kennedy spoke of these tensions and rivalries on the world stage and set the goals of his presidency. He also sought to establish himself as a forceful leader, a special challenge for him as the youngest man ever elected president. This speech is considered one of Kennedy's most inspiring. Especially effective are his use of repetition and his references to "liberty," "freedom," and other words that reminded listeners of their shared American heritage.

# INAUGURAL ADDRESS

## JOHN F. KENNEDY

We observe today not a victory of party but a celebration of freedom—symbolizing an end as well as a beginning—signifying renewal as well as change. For I have sworn before you and Almighty God the same solemn oath our forebears[1] prescribed nearly a century and three-quarters ago.

The world is very different now. For man holds in his mortal hands the power to abolish all forms of human poverty and all forms of human life. And yet the same revolutionary beliefs for which our forebears fought are still at issue around the globe—the belief that the rights of man come not from the generosity of the state but from the hands of God.

We dare not forget today that we are the heirs of that first revolution. Let the word go forth from this time and place, to friend and foe alike, that the torch has been passed to a new generation of Americans—born in this century, <u>tempered</u> by war, disciplined by a hard and bitter peace, proud of our ancient heritage—and unwilling to witness or permit the slow undoing of those human rights to which this nation has always been committed, and to which we are committed today at home and around the world.

> *What are the characteristics of the new American generation?*

Let every nation know, whether it wishes us well or ill, that we shall pay any price, bear any burden, meet any hardship, support any friend, oppose any foe to assure the survival and the success of liberty.

This much we pledge—and more.

To those old allies whose cultural and spiritual origins we share, we pledge the loyalty of faithful friends. United, there is little we cannot do in a host of cooperative <u>ventures</u>. Divided, there is little we can do—for we dare not meet a powerful challenge at odds and split <u>asunder</u>.

To those new states whom we welcome to the ranks of the free, we pledge our word that one form of colonial control shall not have passed away merely to be replaced by a far more iron tyranny. We shall not always expect to find them supporting our view. But we shall always hope to find them strongly supporting their own freedom—and to remember that, in the past, those who foolishly sought power by riding the back of the tiger ended up inside.

To those people in the huts and villages of half the globe struggling to break the bonds of mass misery, we pledge our best efforts to help them help themselves, for whatever period is required—not because the Communists may be doing it, not because we seek their votes, but because it is right. If a free society cannot help the many who are poor, it cannot save the few who are rich.

To our sister republics south of our border, we offer a special pledge—to convert our good words into good deeds—in a new alliance for progress—to assist free men and free governments in casting off the chains of poverty. But this peaceful revolution of hope cannot become the prey of hostile powers. Let all our neighbors know that we shall join with them to oppose aggression or <u>subversion</u> anywhere in the Americas. And let every other power know that this hemisphere intends to remain the master of its own house.

> *Who is invited to join an "alliance for progress"?*

To that world assembly of <u>sovereign</u> states, the United Nations, our last best hope in an

---

1. **forebears.** Ancestors

**WORDS FOR EVERYDAY USE**

**tem • per** (tem´pər) *vt.*, toughen, as by rigors or trying experiences. *Joan was <u>tempered</u> by two years of service in the Marines.*

**ven • ture** (ven´chər) *n.*, risky or dangerous undertaking. *The cross-country bike trip was a courageous <u>venture</u> for the two disabled Vietnam veterans.*

**a • sun • der** (ə sun´dér) *adv.*, apart or separate in direction or position. *The party was split <u>asunder</u> by dissension.*

**sub • ver • sion** (səb ver´zhən) *n.*, systematic attempt to overthrow a government. *The dictator put the senators accused of <u>subversion</u> under house arrest.*

**sov • er • eign** (säv´ərn) *adj.*, independent. *<u>Sovereign</u> powers are dependent upon diplomacy.*

age where the instruments of war have far outpaced the instruments of peace, we renew our pledge of support—to prevent it from becoming merely a forum for <u>invective</u>—to strengthen its shield of the new and the weak—and to enlarge the area in which its writ may run.

Finally, to those nations who would make themselves our adversary, we offer not a pledge but a request—that both sides begin anew the quest for peace before the dark powers of destruction unleashed by science engulf all humanity in planned or accidental self-destruction. We dare not tempt them with weakness. For only when our arms are sufficient beyond doubt can we be certain beyond doubt that they will never be employed.

But neither can two great and powerful groups of nations take comfort from our present course—both sides overburdened by the cost of modern weapons, both rightly alarmed by the steady spread of the deadly atom, yet both racing to alter that uncertain balance of terror that stays the hand of mankind's final war.

So let us begin anew—remembering on both sides that <u>civility</u> is not a sign of weakness, and sincerity is always subject to proof. Let us never negotiate out of fear. But let us never fear to negotiate.

Let both sides explore what problems unite us instead of <u>belaboring</u> those problems which divide us.

Let both sides, for the first time, formulate serious and precise proposals for the inspection and control of arms—and bring the absolute power to destroy other nations under the absolute control of all nations.

> **LET US NEVER NEGOTIATE OUT OF FEAR. BUT LET US NEVER FEAR TO NEGOTIATE.**

What must be controlled?

Let both sides seek to <u>invoke</u> the wonders of science instead of its terrors. Together let us explore the stars, conquer the deserts, <u>eradicate</u> disease, tap the ocean depths, and encourage the arts and commerce.

Let both sides unite to heed in all corners of the earth the command of Isaiah—to "undo the heavy burdens . . . [and] let the oppressed go free."[2]

And if a beachhead[3] of cooperation may push back the jungle of suspicion, let both sides join in creating a new endeavor, not a new balance of power but a new world of law, where the strong are just and the weak secure and the peace preserved.

All this will not be finished in the first 100 days. Nor will it be finished in the first 1,000 days, nor in the life of this administration, nor even perhaps in our lifetime on this planet. But let us begin.

In your hands, my fellow citizens, more than mine, will rest the final success or failure of our course. Since this country was founded, each generation of Americans has been summoned to give testimony to its national loyalty. The graves of young Americans who answered the call to service surround the globe.

---

2. **"undo . . . free."** Isaiah 58:6
3. **beachhead.** Position gained as a secure starting point for an action

---

**WORDS FOR EVERYDAY USE**

**in • vec • tive** (in vek´tiv) *n.,* insulting or abusive language. *When Jed asked for the return of his baseball mitt, his request was met with <u>invective</u> from the angry boy he had lent it to.*

**ci • vil • i • ty** (sə vil´ə tē) *n.,* politeness. *With unexpected <u>civility</u> the wrestler shook hands with his opponent.*

**be • la • bor** (bē lā´bər) *vt.,* spend too much time or effort on. *"Do not <u>belabor</u> the point," the teacher instructed, "but go on to the next item."*

**in • voke** (in vōk´) *vt.,* call on for blessing, help, or inspiration. *At the beginning of the powwow, the chief spoke briefly to <u>invoke</u> the memory of the ancestors.*

**e • rad • i • cate** (ē rad´i kāt´) *vt.,* get rid of; wipe out; destroy. *The president proposed legislation intended to <u>eradicate</u> illiteracy.*

Now the trumpet summons us again—not as a call to bear arms, though arms we need—not as a call to battle, though embattled we are—but a call to bear the burden of a long twilight struggle, year in and year out, "rejoicing in hope, patient in tribulation"[4]—a struggle against the common enemies of man: tyranny, poverty, disease, and war itself.

*What challenge does this generation face?*

Can we forge against these enemies a grand and global alliance, North and South, East and West, that can assure a more fruitful life for all mankind? Will you join in that historic effort?

In the long history of the world, only a few generations have been granted the role of defending freedom in its hour of maximum danger. I do not shrink from this responsibility—I welcome it. I do not believe that any of us would exchange places with any other people or any other generation. The energy, the faith,

**ASK NOT WHAT YOUR COUNTY CAN DO FOR YOU— ASK WHAT YOU CAN DO FOR YOUR COUNTRY.**

the devotion which we bring to this endeavor will light our country and all who serve it—and the glow from that fire can truly light the world.

And so, my fellow Americans: ask not what your country can do for you—ask what you can do for your country.

My fellow citizens of the world: ask not what America will do for you, but what together we can do for the freedom of man.

Finally, whether you are citizens of America or citizens of the world, ask of us here the same high standards of strength and sacrifice which we ask of you. With a good conscience our only sure reward, with history the final judge of our deeds, let us go forth to lead the land we love, asking His blessing and His help, but knowing that here on earth God's work must truly be our own. ∎

---

4. **"rejoicing . . . tribulation."** Romans 12:12

# Respond *to the* SELECTION

Based on his Inaugural Address, did Kennedy seem prepared for the challenges ahead of him as president?

# INVESTIGATE, Inquire, Imagine

**Recall:** GATHERING FACTS

1a. What does Kennedy pledge to the nations of South and Central America? To whom is he also speaking?

2a. To what emotion does Kennedy link negotiation? What issue is at highest stake in the negotiations he discusses?

3a. In what way does Kennedy feel his generation is uniquely situated?

**Interpret:** FINDING MEANING

1b. Why might Kennedy's pledge be particularly important at this time in history?

2b. How does Kennedy suggest the two sides approach negotiation? What benefits for humanity might arise from his plans?

3b. What challenge and privilege does the unique situation of Kennedy's generation create?

**Analyze:** TAKING THINGS APART

4a. Identify the groups that Kennedy addresses in his speech.

**Synthesize:** BRINGING THINGS TOGETHER

4b. With what unifying concept does Kennedy address these groups?

**Evaluate:** MAKING JUDGMENTS

5a. How realistic is Kennedy's vision for the United States at home and abroad?

**Extend:** CONNECTING IDEAS

5b. In his speech, Kennedy refers to the United States at the time of its founding. What similarities do you see in Kennedy's Inaugural Address and Thomas Paine's *Crisis, No. 1* in Unit 3?

# Understanding Literature

ANAPHORA. Review the definition for **anaphora** in Literary Tools on page 908. How does the anaphora "Let both sides" emphasize Kennedy's ideas? What other examples of anaphora can you find in the speech?

PARALLELISM. Review the definition for **parallelism** in the Handbook of Literary Terms and the cluster chart you made for Literary Tools on page 908. What does Kennedy suggest about the ideas "victory of party" and "celebration of freedom" at the beginning of the speech? How does he link them?

# WRITER'S JOURNAL

1. Imagine you are Kennedy. Write an **outline** of the main points you plan to make in your Inaugural Address.

2. In his speech Kennedy states, "For only when our arms are sufficient beyond doubt can we be certain beyond doubt that they will never be employed." Write a **paragraph** for your history teacher supporting or refuting this statement.

3. Imagine that you are part of the "new generation of Americans" described by Kennedy. Write a **letter** to the president stating which ideas expressed in his Inaugural Address you agree and disagree with.

# Integrating *the* LANGUAGE ARTS

## Language, Grammar, and Style

**ACHIEVING PARALLELISM.** Read the Language Arts Survey 3.38, "Achieving Parallelism." Then rewrite each of the following sentences below to achieve the parallelism found in the selection.

1. We observe today not a victory of party but freedom's celebration—symbolizing an end as well as a beginning—signified renewal as well as change.
2. The torch has been passed to a new generation of Americans—born in this century, tempered by war, disciplined by a hard and bitter peace, showing pride in our ancient heritage.
3. We shall pay any price, be willing to bear any burden, meet any hardship, support any friend, opposing any foe to assure the survival and the success of liberty.
4. United, there is little we cannot do in a host of cooperative ventures. Being divided, there is little we can do—for we dare not meet a powerful challenge at odds and be split asunder.
5. To our sister republics south of our border, we offer a special pledge—to convert our good words into good deeds—in a new alliance for progress—assisting free men and free governments in casting off the chains of poverty.

## Study and Research & Collaborative Learning

**MURAL.** With a partner, research in the library the legacy of the Kennedy administration. Then draw a picture to represent each important contribution of his administration, such as the establishment of the Alliance for Progress and the Peace Corps. For your drawings, use a roll of blank shelf paper. Then present your mural to the class.

## Media Literacy & Applied English

**PRESS RELEASE.** Use the Internet or library resources to locate another historic speech by John F. Kennedy. If you use the Internet, one site you will find useful is John Fitzgerald Kennedy: 35th President of the United States at http://www.geocities.com/~newgeneration/. Then write a press release, giving the date of the speech and summarizing its main points. You may want to review how to write a press release by reading the Language Arts Survey 6.9, "Delivering a Press Release."

## Speaking and Listening & Media Literacy

**ANALYZING PUBLIC SPEAKING.** Begin by finding a recording of Kennedy's Inaugural Address. Check your school or community library for a recording on a record, CD, audiocassette, videotape, or other media and listen to it with other students in your class. Then analyze Kennedy's oratorical skills. You might find it useful to review the Language Arts Survey 4.18, "Guidelines for Giving a Speech."

# "ON THE MALL"

BY JOAN DIDION

## About the AUTHOR

**Joan Didion** (1934– ) is an acclaimed novelist, playwright, and journalist. Born in Sacramento, Didion studied at the University of California at Berkeley, and later worked as an editor at *Vogue* magazine after winning a contest for young writers. Her first novel, *Run River,* was published in 1963.

Didion is known for her spare and precise language, and for her exploration of the desolate cultural landscape of the contemporary United States. She has been called "the finest woman prose stylist writing in English today." In her nonfiction works, including magazine articles and essays, Didion writes in the first person, blending her own experiences with factual information to evoke a personal vision of her subject. Her essay collections *Slouching Towards Bethlehem* (1968) and *The White Album* (1979), which takes its name from a 1968 Beatles album with a white jacket, contain essays about life in California in the 1960s. Her other novels include *A Book of Common Prayer* (1977) and *The Last Thing He Wanted* (1996), both of which comment on American cultural and political attitudes.

## About the SELECTION

In her essay "**On the Mall**," Didion examines the obsessive consumerism of American society. Calling the years after World War II "a peculiar and visionary time," she sees shopping malls as emblematic of those postwar years, a time during which Americans believed that social and moral progress was infinite and that things could only get better. On this subject, Didion has said, "When we start deceiving ourselves into thinking not that we want something or need something, not that it is a pragmatic necessity for us to have it, but that it is a moral imperative that we have it, then is when we join the fashionable madmen, and then is when the thin whine of hysteria is heard in the land, and then is when we are in bad trouble." "On the Mall" was published in 1979 in Didion's collection of essays *The White Album.*

## Literary TOOLS

**IRONY. Irony** is the difference between appearance and reality. What is ironic about the names of the malls listed in the first paragraph of this essay?

**EXPOSITORY WRITING AND EXPOSITION. Expository writing,** also called informative writing, has the primary aim of informing the reader. Some examples of expository writing include news articles and research reports. **Exposition** is a type of writing that presents facts or opinions in an organized manner. There are many ways to organize exposition. The following are some of the most common: *Analysis* breaks something into its parts and shows how the parts are related. *Classification order* places subjects into categories, or classes, according to their properties or characteristics. *Comparison-and-contrast-order* presents similarities as it compares two things and presents differences as it contrasts them. *Process/How-to writing* presents the steps in a process or gives the reader directions on how to do something.

As you read "On the Mall," decide whether it can be considered an example of expository writing.

## Reader's Journal

Do you like shopping malls? Why, or why not?

# ON THE MALL

## JOAN DIDION

The Mall of America,
Bloomington, Minnesota.

They float on the landscape like pyramids to the boom years, all those Plazas and Malls and Esplanades. All those Squares and Fairs. All those Towns and Dales, all those Villages, all those Forests and Parks and Lands. Stonestown. Hillsdale. Valley Fair, Mayfair, Northgate, Southgate, Eastgate, Westgate. Gulfgate. They are toy garden cities in which no one lives but everyone consumes, profound equalizers, the perfect <u>fusion</u> of the profit motive and the <u>egalitarian</u> ideal, and to hear their names is to recall words and phrases no longer quite current. Baby Boom. Consumer Explosion. Leisure Revolution. Do-It-Yourself Revolution. Backyard Revolution. Suburbia. "The Shopping Center," the Urban Land Institute could pronounce in 1957, "is today's extraordinary retail business evolvement…. The automobile accounts for suburbia, and suburbia accounts for the shopping center."

It was a peculiar and visionary time, those years after World War II to which all the Malls and Towns and Dales stand as climate-controlled monuments. Even the word "automobile," as in "the automobile accounts for suburbia and suburbia accounts for the shopping center," no longer carries the particular freight it once did: as a child in the late Forties in California I recall reading and believing that the "freedom of movement" afforded by the automobile was "America's fifth freedom." The trend was up. The solution was in sight. The

To what time period are malls "pyramids" or "climate-controlled monuments"?

frontier had been reinvented, and its shape was the subdivision,[1] that new free land on which all settlers could recast their lives *tabula rasa*.[2] For one perishable moment there the American idea seemed about to achieve itself, via F.H.A.[3] housing and the acquisition of major appliances, and a certain <u>enigmatic</u> glamour attached to the architects of this newfound land. They made something of nothing. They gambled and sometimes lost. They staked the past to seize the future. I have difficulty now imagining a childhood in which a man named Jere Strizek, the developer of Town and Country Village outside Sacramento (143,000 square feet gross floor area, 68 stores, 1000 parking spaces, the Urban Land Institute's "<u>prototype</u> for centers using heavy timber and tile construction for informality"), could materialize as a role model, but I had such a childhood, just after World War II, in Sacramento. I never met or even saw Jere Strizek, but at the age of 12 I imagined him a kind of frontiersman, a romantic and revolutionary spirit, and in the indigenous grain[4] he was.

What was called "America's fifth freedom" during the postwar years? What was the shape of the new frontier?

Who was Jere Strizek, and how did Didion imagine him when she was young?

THEY MADE SOMETHING OF NOTHING. THEY GAMBLED AND SOMETIMES LOST. THEY STAKED THE PAST TO SEIZE THE FUTURE.

---

1. **subdivision.** Previously rural, unowned land surveyed and divided into lots for sale
2. *tabula rasa.* Clean slate; anything in its original and pure state (Latin)
3. **F.H.A.** Federal Housing Administration
4. **in the indigenous grain.** In the American way

---

WORDS FOR EVERYDAY USE

fu • sion (fyü′ zhən) n., merging of distinct elements into a unified whole. *The <u>fusion</u> of my love for music and my love for crafts led me to become a guitar maker.*

egal • i • tar • i • an (i ga′lə ter′ē ən) adj., asserting a belief in human equality, especially equality in terms of social, political, and economic rights. *When Thomas Jefferson wrote "All men are created equal," he expressed an <u>egalitarian</u> philosophy.*

en • ig • ma tic (e′ nig ma′ tik) adj., mysterious. *The actress's refusal to grant interviews made her seem very <u>enigmatic</u>.*

pro • to • type (prō′tō tīp) n., standard on which other things are modeled; the first working model of a new type. *In 1896, Henry Ford built his "Quadricycle," a <u>prototype</u> of the automobile.*

I suppose James B. Douglas and David D. Bohannon were too.

I first heard of James B. Douglas and David D. Bohannon not when I was 12 but a dozen years later, when I was living in New York, working for *Vogue*, and taking, by correspondence, a University of California Extension course in shopping-center theory. This did not seem to me eccentric at the time. I remember sitting on the cool floor in Irving Penn's[5] studio and reading, in *The Community Builders Handbook*, advice from James B. Douglas on shopping-center financing. I recall staying late in my pale-blue office on the twentieth floor of the Graybar Building to memorize David D. Bohannon's parking ratios. My "real" life was to sit in this office and describe life as it was lived in Djakarta and Caneel Bay and in the great châteaux of the Loire Valley, but my dream life was to put together a Class-A regional shopping center with three full-line department stores as major tenants.

What was Didion's dream?

That I was perhaps the only person I knew in New York, let alone on the Condé Nast[6] floors of the Graybar Building, to have memorized the distinctions among "A," "B," and "C" shopping centers did not occur to me (the defining distinction, as long as I have your attention, is that an "A," or "regional," center has as its major tenant a full-line department store which carries major appliances; a "B," or "community," center has as its major tenant a junior department store which does not carry major appliances; and a "C," or "neighborhood," center has as its major tenant only a supermarket): my interest in shopping centers was in no way casual. I did want to build them. I wanted to build them because I had fallen into the habit of writing fiction, and I had it in my head that a couple of good centers might support this habit less taxingly[7] than a pale-blue office at *Vogue*. I had even devised an original scheme by which I planned to gain enough capital and credibility to enter the shopping-center game: I would lease warehouses in, say, Queens, and offer Manhattan delicatessens the opportunity to sell competitively by buying cooperatively, from my trucks. I see a few wrinkles in this scheme now (the words "concrete overcoat" come to mind), but I did not then. In fact I planned to run it right out of the pale-blue office.

What words come to Didion's mind when she recalls her dream of creating a mall?

James B. Douglas and David D. Bohannon. In 1950 James B. Douglas had opened Northgate, in Seattle, the first regional center to combine a pedestrian mall with an underground truck tunnel. In 1954 David D. Bohannon had opened Hillsdale, a forty-acre regional center on the peninsula south of San Francisco. That is the only solid bio I have on James B. Douglas and David D. Bohannon to this day, but many of their opinions are engraved on my memory. David D. Bohannon believed in preserving the integrity of the shopping center by not cutting up the site with any dedicated roads. David D. Bohannon believed that architectural setbacks in a center looked "pretty on paper" but caused "customer resistance." James B. Douglas advised that a small-loan office could prosper in a center only if it were placed away from foot traffic, since people who want small loans do not want to be observed getting them. I do not now recall whether it was James B. Douglas or David D. Bohannon or someone else altogether who passed along this hint on how to paint the lines around the parking spaces (actually this is called "striping the lot," and the spaces are "stalls"): make each space a foot wider than it need be— ten feet, say, instead of nine—when the center first opens and business is slow. By this single stroke the developer achieves a couple of

---

5. **Irving Penn.** A photographer for *Vogue*
6. **Condé Nast.** Company that publishes magazines, including *Vogue*
7. **taxingly.** In a way that taxes a person, or in other words, demands a lot of work and energy

important objectives, the appearance of a popular center and the illusion of easy parking, and no one will really notice when business picks up and the spaces shrink.

Nor do I recall who first solved what was once a crucial center dilemma: the placement of the major tenant vis à vis[8] the parking lot. The dilemma was that the major tenant—the draw, the raison d'être[9] for the financing, the Sears, the Macy's, the May Company—wanted its customer to walk directly from car to store. The smaller tenants, on the other hand, wanted that same customer to *pass their stores* on the way from the car to, say, Macy's. The solution to this conflict of interests was actually very simple: *two major tenants*, one at each end of a mall. This is called "anchoring the mall," and represents seminal work in shopping center theory. One thing you will note about shopping-center theory is that you could have thought of it yourself, and a course in it will go a long way toward dispelling the notion that business proceeds from mysteries too recondite for you and me.

> *What did the major tenants of malls want? What did the smaller tenants want? How was their conflict solved?*

A few aspects of shopping-center theory do in fact remain impenetrable to me. I have no idea why the Community Builders' Council ranks "Restaurant" as deserving a Number One (or "Hot Spot") location but exiles "Chinese

Restaurant" to a Number Three, out there with "Power and Light Office" and "Christian Science Reading Room." Nor do I know why the Council approves of enlivening a mall with "small animals" but specifically, vehemently, and with no further explanation, excludes "monkeys." If I had a center I would have monkeys, and Chinese restaurants, and Mylar[10] kites and bands of small girls playing tambourine.

A few years ago at a party I met a woman from Detroit who told me that the Joyce Carol Oates novel with which she identified most closely was *Wonderland*.

> *Why did the woman from Detroit especially like the novel* Wonderland?

I asked her why.

"Because," she said, "my husband has a branch there."

I did not understand.

"In Wonderland the center," the woman said patiently. "My husband has a branch in Wonderland."

I have never visited Wonderland but imagine it to have bands of small girls playing tambourine.

## I HAVE NEVER VISITED WONDERLAND BUT IMAGINE IT TO HAVE BANDS OF SMALL GIRLS PLAYING TAMBOURINE.

A few facts about shopping centers. The "biggest" center in the United States is generally agreed to be Woodfield, outside

---

8. *vis à vis.* In relation to (French)
9. *raison d'être.* Reason for being (French)
10. **Mylar.** Polyester made in thin but durable sheets; used in some helium balloons

---

**WORDS FOR EVERYDAY USE**

**sem • i • nal** (se' mə nəl) *adj.,* planting the seeds for further development; creative; original. *One of the seminal writers of free verse poetry was E. E. Cummings.*

**re • con • dite** (ri kän´ dīt') *adj.,* difficult or impossible for the average person to understand; deep. *The laws of astrophysics are recondite for the person who has not studied gravitational theory.*

**im • pen • e • tra • ble** (im' pe′nə trə bəl) *adj.,* unable to be comprehended or penetrated. *Gillian's mind was impenetrable to me since she never spoke of her thoughts or motivations.*

**ve • hem • ent • ly** (vē´ə mənt lē') *adv.,* with force or intensity. *The defendant vehemently denied that he was guilty of the crime, insisting passionately that he had been falsely charged.*

Chicago, a "super" regional or "leviathan" two-million-square-foot center with four major tenants.

The "first" shopping center in the United States is generally agreed to be Country Club Plaza in Kansas City, built in the twenties. There were some other earlier centers, notably Edward H. Bouton's 1907 Roland Park in Baltimore, Hugh Prather's 1931 Highland Park Shopping Village in Dallas, and Hugh Potter's 1937 River Oaks in Houston, but the developer of Country Club Plaza, J. C. Nichols, is referred to with ritual frequency in the literature of shopping centers, usually as "pioneering J. C. Nichols" or "J. C. Nichols, father of the center as we know it."

Those are some facts I know about shopping centers because I still want to be Jere Strizek or James B. Douglas or David D. Bohannon. Here are some facts I know about shopping centers because I never will be Jere Strizek or James B. Douglas or David D. Bohannon: a good center in which to spend the day if you wake feeling low in Oxnard, California, is The Esplanade, major tenants the May Company and Sears. A good center in which to spend the day if you wake feeling low in Biloxi, Mississippi, is Edgewater Plaza, major tenant Godchaux's. Ala Moana in Honolulu is larger than The Esplanade in Oxnard, and The Esplanade in Oxnard is larger than Edgewater Plaza in Biloxi. Ala Moana has carp pools. The Esplanade and Edgewater Plaza do not.

These marginal distinctions to one side, Ala Moana, The Esplanade, and Edgewater Plaza are the same place, which is precisely their role not only as equalizers but in the sedation of anxiety. In each of them one moves for a while in an aqueous suspension not only of light but of judgment, not only of judgment but "personality." One meets no acquaintances at The Esplanade. One gets no telephone calls at Edgewater Plaza. "It's a hard place to run in to for a pair of stockings," a friend complained to me recently of Ala Moana, and I knew that she was not yet ready to surrender her ego[11] to the idea of the center. The last time I went to Ala Moana it was to buy *The New York Times*. Because *The New York Times* was not in, I sat on the mall for a while and ate caramel corn. In the end I bought not *The New York Times* but two straw hats at Liberty House, four bottles of nail enamel at Woolworth's, and a toaster, on sale at Sears. In the literature of shopping centers these would be described as impulse purchases, but the impulse here was obscure. I do not wear hats, nor do I like caramel corn. I do not use nail enamel. Yet flying back across the Pacific I regretted only the toaster. ∎

> What qualities distinguish the three malls from one another? What makes them "the same place"?

> What did Didion buy at the mall?

---

11. **ego.** In psychoanalysis, the part of one's mind that makes conscious decisions when dealing with the external world. One of its roles is to suppress urges and impulses.

---

**WORDS FOR EVERYDAY USE**

**le • vi • a • than** (li vī′ ə thən) *adj.*, gigantic and formidable. *The leviathan dinosaur towered over the treetops.*

**se • da • tion** (sə dā′shun) *n.*, the inducing of a relaxed state, especially by the use of sedatives. *The patient's sedation was ordered by her doctor to induce sleep.*

**a • que • ous** (ā′ kwē əs) *adj.*, of, relating to, or resembling water. *The darkness outside was so thick it seemed aqueous, and we felt as though we were swimming through the night.*

# Respond *to the* SELECTION

Do you ever feel that you lose your personality or judgment while shopping in malls? Explain.

# INVESTIGATE, Inquire, Imagine

**Recall:** GATHERING FACTS

1a. To what era are shopping malls "monuments"? What attitude did many Americans in the postwar period have toward the automobile and the development of rural areas?

2a. What does shopping center theory dictate about parking lots? What is "anchoring the mall"? What aspects of shopping center theory remain "impenetrable" to Didion?

3a. How does Didion describe the items she purchases at Ala Moana in Hawaii? Does she need these items?

**Interpret:** FINDING MEANING

1b. How does the automobile account for suburbia? How does suburbia account for the shopping center?

2b. In what sense can the mall developers be called "frontiersmen" or "pioneers"? What was their "frontier"? What is the ultimate purpose of the shopping mall techniques mentioned in this selection?

3b. What does the Detroit woman's remark about the novel *Wonderland* reveal about her priorities or about the priorities of many Americans? What is the purpose of making all malls alike? Why does Didion make these purchases?

**Analyze:** TAKING THINGS APART

4a. What two things does Didion say are fused, or combined, in shopping malls? Outline how shopping malls can be said to exemplify these things. How do malls represent the consumerist attitudes of postwar America? How do malls fit in with the new frontier of suburbia?

**Synthesize:** BRINGING THINGS TOGETHER

4b. How did Didion feel about malls when she was younger? What does she not understand about malls, and what does she criticize now that she is older? How does she show that she, too, is sometimes enchanted by malls?

**Evaluate:** MAKING JUDGMENTS

5a. How do you feel about the fact that mall developers design their buildings in order to influence you to buy more? Do you find this to be manipulative or just good business sense?

**Extend:** CONNECTING IDEAS

5b. Didion says that if she were to build a mall, she would have "monkeys, and Chinese restaurants, and Mylar kites and bands of small girls playing tambourine." What does this tell you about Didion's character? If you were planning your own mall, what would you include?

# Understanding Literature

**IRONY.** Review the definition for **irony** in the Handbook of Literary Terms. What is ironic about the names of some of the malls Didion mentions? What is ironic about the purchases Didion makes at Ala Moana?

**EXPOSITORY WRITING AND EXPOSITION.** Review the definitions for **expository writing** (listed under "aim") and **exposition** in the Handbook of Literary Terms. Is "On the Mall" an example of expository writing? Create a chart like the one on page 922 to show what method or methods of exposition Didion uses in her essay "On the Mall." On the left, list the methods used. On the right, refer to the part of the essay in which each method was used.

| Method of Exposition | Example |
|---|---|
| classification | A, B, and C types of malls |

# Writer's Journal

1. Write a **short story** about a person who enters a mall and surrenders his or her "ego" to the mall. What does he or she end up doing or buying?
2. Invent your own **classification system** for the malls or stores in your community. You can use any criteria you wish. For example, you could classify some stores under the heading "Teen Girl Trend Spot."
3. Imagine you own a mall. Write a **radio spot** advertising your mall. Appeal to human psychology in an effort to persuade people to come to the mall and buy as much as possible.

# Integrating the LANGUAGE ARTS

## Collaborative Learning

**DESIGNING A SHOPPING MALL.** Working in groups of four, plan a shopping mall for your area. First, decide what stores and other attractions you will have at your mall. Be creative! Then decide how they will be arranged. For example, do you want all clothing stores to be close together, or would it make more sense to scatter them so that people will be more likely to walk all the way around the mall? Using one large sheet of paper for each level, map out your mall plan. Include a directory of stores and color-code or number them on the map.

## Speaking and Listening

**HOLDING A CLASS DEBATE.** Suburban planning as it was first practiced in the United States in the 1940s has been widely criticized today as "urban sprawl." Critics blame sprawl for draining the economic vitality of inner city regions, for creating a greater dependence on the automobile and use of highways, and for eliminating the feeling of "community" that existed in older neighborhoods with smaller, localized businesses and parks. In groups of three or four students, research the controversy surrounding the development of suburbs. You may find relevant articles on the Internet or in the periodical section of the library. On the Internet, you might visit the **Sierra Club** at http://www.sierraclub.org or the website of journalist Alex Marshall at http://www.alexmarshall.org, and conduct a site search with the keyword "sprawl." Find at least two articles and discuss these in your small group. Try to find one article that refutes the problem of sprawl. Then come together as a class to discuss the issue of urban sprawl. Is it a problem? What are the pros and cons of suburban development?

## Study and Research

**RESEARCHING THE 1960s.** The 1960s was a decade of change in the United States. Research one of the following events or movements of the 1960s: the assassination of John F. Kennedy, the Equal Rights Amendment, the Black Panthers, the environmental movement, antiwar protests, and the experiments in communal living. You may also choose a particular figure from the 1960s to research, explaining how this person was involved in changing attitudes in American culture. Some examples might be Martin Luther King, Jr., Gloria Steinem, Betty Friedan, John, Jackie, and Robert Kennedy, Tom Wolfe, Angela Davis, Janis Joplin, and Jimi Hendrix.

## "Frederick Douglass"[1]
## by Robert Hayden

When it is finally ours, this freedom, this liberty, this beautiful
and terrible thing, needful to man as air,
usable as earth; when it belongs at last to all,
when it is truly instinct, brain matter, diastole, systole,
reflex action; when it is finally won; when it is more
than the gaudy mumbo jumbo of politicians:
this man, this Douglass, this former slave, this Negro
beaten to his knees, exiled, visioning a world
where none is lonely, none hunted, alien,
this man, superb in love and logic, this man
shall be remembered. Oh, not with statues' rhetoric,
not with legends and poems and wreaths of bronze alone,
but with the lives grown out of his life, the lives
fleshing his dream of the beautiful, needful thing.

## "For the Last Wolverine"[2]
## by James Dickey

They will soon be down

To one, but he still will be
For a little while      still will be stopping

The flakes in the air with a look,
5   Surrounding himself with the silence
Of whitening snarls. Let him eat
The last red meal of the condemned

To extinction, tearing the guts

From an elk. Yet that is not enough
10     For me. I would have him eat

The heart, and, from it, have an idea
Stream into his gnawing head
That he no longer has a thing
To lose, and so can walk

15     Out into the open, in the full

Pale of the sub-Arctic sun
Where a single spruce tree is dying

Higher and higher. Let him climb it
With all his meanness and strength.
20     Lord, we have come to the end
Of this kind of vision of heaven,

As the sky breaks open

Its fans around him and shimmers
And into its northern gates he rises

25     Snarling      complete      in the joy of a weasel
With an elk's horned heart in his stomach
Looking straight into the eternal

Blue, where he hauls his kind. I would have it all

My way: at the top of that tree I place

30     The New World's last eagle
Hunched in mangy feathers      giving

Up on the theory of flight.
Dear God of the wildness of poetry, let them mate
To the death in the rotten branches,
35     Let the tree sway and burst into flame

And mingle them, crackling with feathers,

In crownfire. Let something come
Of it      something gigantic      legendary

Rise beyond reason over hills
40     Of ice   SCREAMING      that it cannot die,
That it has come back, this time
On wings, and will spare no earthly thing:

That it will hover, made purely of northern

Lights, at dusk      and fall
45     On men building roads: will perch

On the moose's horn like a falcon
Riding into battle      into holy war against
Screaming railroad crews: will pull
Whole traplines like fibres from the snow

50     In the long-jawed night of fur trappers.

But, small, filthy, unwinged,
You will soon be crouching

Alone, with maybe some dim racial notion
Of being the last, but none of how much
55     Your unnoticed going will mean:

---

1. **Frederick Douglass.** Escaped slave who lived from 1817 to 1895. Douglass was involved in the Underground Railroad and became the publisher of the famous abolitionist newspaper the *North Star*, in Rochester, New York.
2. **Wolverine.** Fur-bearing animal related to the weasel and mink

How much the timid poem needs

The mindless explosion of your rage,

The glutton's internal fire        the elk's
Heart in the belly, sprouting wings,

60      The pact of the "blind swallowing
Thing," with himself, to eat
The world, and not to be driven off it
Until it is gone, even if it takes

Forever. I take you as you are

65      And make of you what I will,
Skunk-bear, carcajou,[1] bloodthirsty

Non-survivor.
                    *Lord, let me die        but not die*
*Out.*

## from *Tell Me How Long the Train's Been Gone* by James Baldwin

My brother, Caleb, was seventeen when I was ten. We were very good friends. In fact, he was my best friend and, for a very long time, my only friend.

I do not mean to say that he was always nice to me. I got on his nerves a lot, and he resented having to take me around with him and be responsible for me when there were so many other things he wanted to be doing. Therefore, his hand was often up against the side of my head, and my tears caused him to be punished many times. But I knew, somehow, anyway, that when he was being punished for my tears, he was not being punished for anything he had done to me; he was being punished because that was the way we lived; and his punishment, oddly, helped unite us. More oddly still, even as his great hand caused my head to stammer and dropped a flame-colored curtain before my eyes, I understood that he was not striking *me*. His hand leapt out because he could not help it, and I received the blow because I was there. And it happened, sometimes, before I could even catch my breath to howl, that the hand that had struck me grabbed me and held me, and it was difficult indeed to know which of us was weeping. He was striking, striking out, striking out, striking out; the hand asked me to forgive him. I felt his bewilderment through the membrane of my own. I also felt that he was trying to teach me something. And I had, God knows, no other teachers.

For our father—how shall I describe our father?—was a ruined Barbados[2] peasant, exiled in a Harlem[3] which he loathed, where he never saw the sun or sky he remembered, where life took place neither indoors nor without, and where there was no joy. By which I mean no joy that he remembered. Had he been able to bring with him any of the joy he had felt on that far-off island, then the air of the sea and the impulse to dancing would sometimes have transfigured our dreadful rooms. Our lives might have been very different.

But no, he brought with him from Barbados only black rum and blacker pride and magic incantations, which neither healed nor saved.

He did not understand the people among whom he found himself; they had no coherence, no stature and no pride. He came from a race which had been flourishing at the very dawn of the world—a race greater and nobler than Rome or Judea, mightier than Egypt—he came from a race of kings, kings who had never been taken in battle, kings who had never been slaves. He spoke to us of tribes and empires, battles, victories, and monarchs of whom we had never heard—they were not mentioned in our textbooks—and invested us with glories in which we felt more awkward than in the secondhand shoes we wore. In the stifling room of his pretensions and expectations, we stumbled wretchedly about, stubbing our toes, as it were, on rubies, scraping our shins on golden caskets, bringing down, with a childish cry, the splendid purple tapestry on which, in pounding gold and scarlet, our destinies and our inheritance were figured. It could scarcely have been otherwise, since a child's major attention has to be concentrated on how to fit into a world which, with every passing hour, reveals itself as merciless.

If our father was of royal blood and we were royal children, our father was certainly the only person in the world who knew it. The landlord did not know it; our father never mentioned royal blood to *him*. When we were late with our rent, which was often, the landlord threatened, in terms no commoner had ever used before a king, to put us in the streets. He complained that our shiftlessness, which he did not hesitate to consider an attribute of the race, had forced him, an old man with a weak heart, to climb all these stairs to plead with us to give him the money we owed him. And this was the last time; he wanted to make sure we understood that this was the last time.

Our father was younger than the landlord, leaner, stronger, and bigger. With one blow, he could have brought the landlord to his knees. And we knew how much he hated the man. For days on end, in the wintertime, we huddled around the gas stove in the kitchen, because the landlord gave us no heat. When windows were broken, the landlord took his time about fixing them; the wind made the cardboard we stuffed in the windows rattle all night long; and when snow came, the weight of the snow forced the cardboard inward and onto the floor. Whenever the apartment received a fresh coat of paint, we bought the paint and did the painting ourselves; we killed the rats. A great chunk of the kitchen ceiling fell one winter, narrowly missing our mother.

We all hated the landlord with a perfectly exquisite hatred, and we would have been happy to see our proud father

---

1. **Skunk-bear, carcajou.** Other names for the wolverine
2. **Barbados.** Island in the British West Indies
3. **Harlem.** Section of New York City

kill him. We would have been glad to help. But our father did nothing of the sort. He stood before the landlord, looking unutterably weary. He made excuses. He apologized. He swore that it would never happen again. (We knew that it *would* happen again.) He begged for time. The landlord would finally go down the stairs, letting us and all the neighbors know how good-hearted he was, and our father would walk into the kitchen and pour himself a glass of rum.

But we knew that our father would never have allowed any black man to speak to him as the landlord did, as policemen did, as storekeepers and welfare workers and pawnbrokers did. No, not for a moment. He would have thrown him out of the house. He would certainly have made a black man know that he was not the descendant of slaves! He had made them know it so often that he had almost no friends among them, and if we had followed his impossible lead, we would have had no friends, either. It was scarcely worthwhile being the descendant of kings if the kings were black and no one had ever heard of them.

And it was because of our father, perhaps, that Caleb and I clung to each other, in spite of the great difference in our ages; or, in another way, it may have been precisely the difference in our ages that made the clinging possible. I don't know. It is really not the kind of thing anyone can ever know. I think it may be easier to love the really helpless younger brother, because he cannot enter into competition with one on one's own ground, or on any ground at all, and can never question one's role or jeopardize one's authority. In my own case, certainly, it did not occur to me to compete with Caleb, and I could not have questioned his role or his authority, because I needed both. He was my touchstone,[1] my model and my only guide.

Anyway, our father, dreaming bitterly of Barbados, despised and mocked by his neighbors and all but ignored by his sons, held down his unspeakable factory job, spread his black gospel in bars on the weekends, and drank his rum. I do not know if he loved our mother. I think he did.

They had had five children—only Caleb and I, the first and the last, were left. We were both dark, like our father; but two of the three dead girls had been fair, like our mother.

She came from New Orleans. Her hair was not like ours. It was black, but softer and finer. The color of her skin reminded me of the color of bananas. Her skin was as bright as that, and contained that kind of promise, and she had tiny freckles around her nose and a small black mole just above her upper lip. It was the mole, I don't know why, which made her beautiful. Without it, her face might have been merely sweet, merely pretty. But the mole was funny. It had the effect of making one realize that our mother liked funny things, liked to laugh. The mole made one look at her eyes—large, extraordinary dark eyes, eyes which seemed always to be amused by something, eyes which looked straight out, seeming to see everything, seeming to be afraid of nothing. She was a soft, round, plump woman. She liked nice clothes and dangling jewelry, which she mostly didn't have, and she liked to cook for large numbers of people, and she loved our father.

She knew him—knew him through and through. I am not being coy or colloquial but bluntly and sadly matter-of-fact when I say that I will now never know what she saw in him. What she saw was certainly not for many eyes; what she saw got him through his working week and his Sunday rest; what she saw saved him. She saw that he was a man. For her, perhaps, he was a great man. I think, though, that for our mother any man was great who aspired to become a man: this meant that our father was very rare and precious. I used to wonder how she took it, how she bore it—his rages, his tears, his cowardice.

On Saturday nights he was almost always evil, drunk, and maudlin. He came home from work in the early afternoon and gave our mother some money. It was never enough, of course, but she never protested, at least not as far as I know. Then she would go out shopping. I would usually go with her, for Caleb would almost always be out somewhere, and our mother didn't like the idea of leaving me alone in the house. And this was probably, after all, the best possible arrangement. People who disliked our father were sure (for that very reason) to like our mother; and people who felt that Caleb was growing to be too much like his father could feel that I, after all, might turn out like my mother. Besides, it is not, as a general rule, easy to hate a small child. One runs the risk of looking ridiculous, especially if the child is with his mother.

And especially if that mother is Mrs. Proudhammer. Mrs. Proudhammer knew very well what people thought of Mr. Proudhammer. She knew, too, exactly how much she owed in each store she entered, how much she was going to be able to pay, and what she had to buy. She entered with a smile, ready.

"Evening. Let me have some of them red beans there."

"Evening. You know you folks been running up quite a little bill here."

"I'm going to give you something on it right now. I need some cornmeal and flour and some rice."

"You know, I got my bills to meet, too, Mrs. Proudhammer."

"Didn't I just tell you I was going to pay? I want some cornflakes, too, and some milk." Such merchandise as she could reach, she had already placed on the counter.

"When do you think you're going to be able to pay this bill? All of it, I mean."

"You know I'm going to pay it just as soon as I can. How much does it all come to? Give me that end you got there of that chocolate cake." The chocolate cake was for Caleb and me. "Well, now you put this against the bill." Imperiously, as though it were the most natural thing in the world, she put two or three dollars on the counter.

"You lucky I'm softhearted, Mrs. Proudhammer."

"Things sure don't cost this much downtown—you think I don't know it? Here." And she paid him for what she had bought. "Thank you. You been mighty kind."

And we left the store. I often felt that in order to help her, I should have filled my pockets with merchandise while she

---

1. **touchstone.** Test of genuineness or value

was talking. But I never did, not only because the store was often crowded or because I was afraid of being caught by the storekeeper, but because I was afraid of humiliating her.

When we had to do "heavy" shopping, we went marketing under the bridge at Park Avenue—Caleb, our mother, and I; and sometimes, but rarely, our father came with us. The most usual reason for heavy shopping was that some relatives of our mother's, or old friends of both our mother's and our father's, were coming to visit. We were certainly not going to let them go away hungry—not even if it meant, as it often did mean, spending more than we had. In spite of what I have been suggesting about our father's temperament, and no matter how difficult he may sometimes have been with us, he was much too proud to offend any guest of his; on the contrary, his impulse was to make them feel that his home was theirs; and besides, he was lonely, lonely for his past, lonely for those faces which had borne witness to that past. Therefore, he would sometimes pretend that our mother did not know how to shop, and our father would come with us under the bridge, in order to teach her.

There he would be then, uncharacteristically, in shirt sleeves, which made him look rather boyish; and as our mother showed no desire to take shopping lessons from him, he turned his attention to Caleb and me. He would pick up a fish, opening the gills and holding it close to his nose. "You see that? That fish looks fresh, don't it? Well, that fish ain't as fresh as I am, and I *been* out of the water. They done doctored that fish. Come on." And we would walk away, a little embarrassed but, on the whole, rather pleased that our father was so smart.

Meantime, our mother was getting the marketing done. She was very happy on days like this, because our father was happy. He was happy, odd as his expression of it may sound, to be out with his wife and his two sons. If we had been on the island that had been witness to his birth, instead of the unspeakable island of Manhattan, he felt that it would not have been so hard for us all to trust and love each other. He sensed, and I think he was right, that on that other, never to be recovered island, his sons would have looked on him very differently, and he would have looked very differently on his sons. Life would have been hard there, too; we would have fought there, too, and more or less blindly suffered and more or less blindly died. But we would not have been (or so it was to seem to all of us forever) so wickedly menaced by the mere fact of our relationship, would not have been so frightened of entering into the central, most beautiful and valuable facts of our lives. We would have been laughing and cursing and tussling in the water, instead of stammering under the bridge; we would have known less about vanished African kingdoms and more about each other. Or, not at all impossibly, more about both.

If it was summer, we bought a watermelon, which either Caleb or our father carried home, fighting with each other for this privilege. They looked very like each other on those days—both big, both black, both laughing.

Caleb always looked absolutely helpless when he laughed. He laughed with all his body, perhaps touching his shoulder against yours, or putting his head on your chest for a moment, and then careening off you, halfway across the room or down the block. I will always hear his laughter. He was always happy on such days, too. Caleb certainly needed his father. Such days, however, were rare—one of the reasons, probably, that I remember them now.

Eventually, we all climbed the stairs into that hovel which, at such moments, was our castle. One very nearly felt the drawbridge rising behind us as our father locked the door.

The bathtub could not yet be filled with cold water and the melon placed in the tub, because this was Saturday, and, come evening, we all had to bathe. The melon was covered with a blanket and placed on the fire escape. Then we unloaded what we had bought, rather impressed by our opulence, though our father was always, by this time, appalled by the money we had spent. I was always sadly aware that there would be nothing left of all this once tomorrow had come and gone and that most of it, after all, was not for us, but for others.

Our mother was calculating the pennies she would need all week—carfare for our father and for Caleb, who went to a high school out of our neighborhood; money for the life insurance; money for milk for me at school; money for light and gas; money put away, if possible, toward the rent. She knew just about what our father had left in *his* pockets and was counting on him to give me the money I would shortly be demanding to go to the movies. Caleb had a part-time job after school and already had his movie money. Anyway, unless he was in a very good mood or needed me for something, he would not be anxious to go to the movies with me.

Our mother never insisted that Caleb tell her where he was going, nor did she question him as to how he spent the money he made. She was afraid of hearing him lie, and she did not want to risk forcing him to lie. She was operating on the assumption that he was sensible and had been raised to be honorable and that he, now more than ever, needed his privacy.

But she was very firm with him, nevertheless. "I do not want to see you rolling in here at three in the morning, Caleb. I want you here in time to eat, and you know you got to take your bath."

"Yes, indeed, ma'am. Why can't I take my bath in the morning?"

"Don't you start being funny. You know you ain't going to get up in time to take no bath in the morning."

"Don't nobody want you messing around in that bathroom all morning long, man," said our father. "You just git back in the house like your ma's telling you."

"Besides," I said, "you never wash out the tub."

Caleb looked at me in mock surprise and from a great height, allowing his chin and his lids simultaneously to drop and swiveling his head away from me.

"I see," he said, "that everyone in this family is ganging up on me. All right, Leo. I was planning to take you to the show with me, but now I've changed my mind."

"I'm sorry," I said quickly. "I take it back."

"You take *what* back?"

"What I said—about you not washing out the tub."

"Ain't no need to take it back," our father said stubbornly. "It's true. A man don't take back nothing that's true."

"So *you* say," Caleb said, with a hint of a sneer. But before anyone could possibly react to this, he picked me up, scowling into my face, which he held just above his own. "You take it back?"

"Leo ain't going to take it back," our father said.

Now I was in trouble. Caleb watched me, a small grin on his face. "You take it back?"

"Stop teasing that child, and put him down," our mother said. "The trouble ain't that Caleb don't wash out the tub—he just don't wash it out very clean."

"I never knew him to wash it out," our father said,

"unless I was standing behind him."

"Well, ain't neither one of you much good around the house," our mother said.

Caleb laughed and set me down. "You didn't take it back," he said.

I said nothing.

"I guess I'm just going to have to go on without you."

Still, I said nothing.

"You going to have that child to crying in a minute," our mother said. "If you going to take him, go on and take him. Don't do him like that."

Caleb laughed again. "I'm going to take him. The way he got them eyes all ready to water, I'd better take him somewhere." We walked toward the door. "But you got to make up *your* mind," he said to me, "to say what *you* think is right. . . ."

# Guided Writing

## WRITING A RESEARCH PAPER

Kellie is on her high school basketball team. She is tall and incredibly agile. Her shot is silk. Although she's only a junior, college coaches are already sending her letters. The students who come to watch her play think she has it made—and she does. However, what most of them don't realize is that Kellie, since the eighth grade, has averaged two hours a day of playing basketball. Every summer she attends at least two basketball camps. Thousands of hours have gone into molding her natural ability. Kellie started playing basketball because she was a tall girl who was constantly tripping over her feet. Her dad got her dribbling and running to help her coordination. He knew that improving her coordination would make Kellie feel better about herself. What he didn't know was that she would develop a passion for the game and a future as a college star.

Writing a research paper follows a similar path. For whatever reason, you start with an issue, look into the background behind that issue, put in many hours finding history and expert opinion about this issue, and ultimately become more knowledgeable and passionate about it. The paper you write is the result of this research. Hours will be spent digging into sources. Some of the digging will be productive, some won't. But to write a good research paper, you have to be willing to put in the time. Putting in the time helped Kellie with basketball; time will also help you.

**WRITING ASSIGNMENT.** Early contemporary literature of the 1960s and 1970s raises many social and cultural issues. For this assignment, you will identify one of these issues, research it, and then write a research paper about it.

## Student Model—Draft
by Jerome Williams

> "The Greening of America?"
>
> This past winter, officials in Colorado reintroduced the lynx to its mountainous areas. Wearing radio-

> "You don't write because you want to say something; you write because you have something to say."
> —F. Scott Fitzgerald

tracking collars, these half-dozen cats were carefully monitored as they attempted to reacclimate themselves to the wilds of Colorado. In the first few months, several starved, one was shot, and one was hit by a truck. Some critics thought the whole endeavor was pointless. They argued that it was immoral to trap healthy lynx in Canada, ship them to Colorado, and let them die. Immoral or not, however, no one complained about the money being spent.

This past summer our small city spent over $1 million on new recycle bins. These huge, wheeled carts cost $200 each (Juras). Every two weeks, state-of-the-art recycle trucks come by, picking up the entire bin with a hydraulic arm that deposits the recyclables into the truck. There is no community outcry against these recycling expenditures. Recycling is now an accepted part of American life. So is the preservation of an endangered species.

I thought about this as I read James Dickey's "For the Last Wolverine." In the poem, Dickey mourns the slow disappearance of the wolverine and the eagle—"...let them mate / To the death in the rotten branches, / Let the tree sway and burst into flame / and mingle them, crackling with feathers." A member of the weasel family, the wolverine has become one of the rarest of all mammals. It has also come to represent the wilderness (Yukon Mammal Series). Elliott Coues, a renowned nineteenth century naturalist called the wolverine "...a ravenous monster of insatiate voracity, matchless strength, and supernatural cunning, a terror to all other beasts, the blood thirsty monster of the forest" (Yukon Mammal Series). There are tales of wolverines backing grizzly bears and packs of wolves down in confrontations over food. However, the myth of the wolverine seems to be greater than the reality (Yukon Mammal Series). Wolverines tend to survive as

**EXAMINING THE MODEL.** Jerome's interest was piqued in James Dickey's poem "For the Last Wolverine." A hiker, climber, and skier, Jerome had never seen a wolverine. He wondered whether they were extinct or not. The powerful, angry imagery, though, of the last wolverine mating with the last eagle in a spruce tree—"... let them mate / To the death in the rotten branches, / Let the tree sway and burst into flame / And mingle them, crackling with feathers"— moved Jerome. The poem made him want to know more about both wolverines and the environmental movement. He had taken it for granted that Americans had always been environmentally aware, but the passion in Dickey's poem suggested to him that perhaps that was not true.

Jerome begins his research paper with a look at some of the effects of environmental awareness. Through Dickey's poem, he questions the gulf between current environmental awareness and Dickey's fear that the environment is being destroyed. This launches Jerome's essay into the environmental conditions in Dickey's day and the history of the environmental movement.

> "Writing comes more easily if you have something to say."
>
> — Shalom Asch

scavengers, cleaning up the kills of wolves. Its hunting is limited to small mammals and the roots, berries, insects, and bird eggs that come with summer.

At one time the wolverine population extended south from the Arctic into Colorado, Indiana, Pennsylvania, and Michigan. Now, however, they are seldom found south of the Canadian Yukon (U of Michigan-Animal Diversity Web). Large wilderness areas—essential for the wolverine's survival—disappeared as roads, agricultural practices, and human inhabitation made inroads into the wolverine's habitat (Yukon Mammal Series). Would Dickey's lament come true?

Americans may have ignored environmental issues in the past, but in the last thirty years Americans have become environmentally aware. The eagle has come back from near extinction. How did this wondrous transformation come about? One of the first steps in the awakening of environmental awareness was the establishment of Earth Day.

## Writing Plan Checklist

- Find a topic that interests you
- Discuss pertinent issues
- Narrow your topic
- Identify reliable sources, three to five in print and at least one online
- Take research notes and document sources
- Write a thesis statement
- Establish main supporting points
- Organize your information

## Prewriting

**FINDING YOUR VOICE.** The research paper is one of the most formal pieces of writing you will do. Consequently, there are certain things to avoid, such as slang, contractions, and colloquialisms. Still, you can develop your own voice toward this topic. Kellie, who remains a fairly quiet and reserved young woman in the classroom, changes when she talks basketball; you can see it in her eyes. When you see her on the court, an even stronger voice emerges. She is aggressive and confident. Your topic and your relationship to it will help you determine what voice you will write in. Through your word choice, sentence structure, and tone, you can write in a way that makes your enthusiasm for your topic evident.

**IDENTIFYING YOUR AUDIENCE.** Your teacher is your main audience for your research paper, but you are also writing for your peers who may have a keen interest in the important contemporary issue that you have discovered. Keep in mind the varying backgrounds of these two audiences. Your teacher likely lived through the time period you are writing about and may have a good background knowledge of the issues and events of that time. Your peers will not have this background, so enough information needs to be included for them to understand the issue clearly.

WRITING WITH A PLAN. The literature in this unit covers a wide range of issues. Finding the issue that matters to you will take some time and thought. It will also take some creative thinking on your part. Reread some of the literature selections in this unit that you liked. Discuss them with your classmates. Reread the unit introduction on pages 862–867. What is a problem that intrigues you? What other issues might be related? What do you want to know more about?

For example, Jerome wanted to learn about wolverines. Where do they live? What are their characteristics? Are wolverines an endangered species? What relationship, if any, does humankind have with the wolverine? How are issues surrounding wolverines related to the environmental movement?

After you select a general topic, you will need to find out what information is available. Gather information from the library and electronic sources and start reading. When you have some background information, you should be ready to narrow your topic by developing a focus for presenting information about the issue.

As you read about your narrowed topic, take notes and document the sources. You will need this information later. For more information on documenting sources, see the Language Arts Survey 5.40, "Making Bibliographies and Bibliography Cards" and 5.36, "Documenting Sources."

Next, write a thesis statement that states your topic and your focus on that topic. Your thesis statement will serve as a guide to identify and develop the main points of support needed for your research paper.

After you have gathered information, organize it around the main points that support your thesis. Writers frequently organize their research in an outline because an outline gives a paper structure and order. Many students don't like to create an outline because they think an outline is limiting. Consider, though, that while an outline isn't the only way to organize a research paper, it does have benefits. For example, if it is difficult to put an outline together, there are probably some serious problems with the thesis, main points of support, research information, and structure of the paper. If you have trouble conceptualizing these elements, you might need to rethink your approach to the topic.

Details for some parts of the outline, such as the introduction and conclusion, may best be filled in as you develop your draft for the paper.

> "Words—so innocent and powerless as they are, standing in a dictionary, how potent for good and evil they become, in the hands of one who knows how to combine them!"
>
> —Nathaniel Hawthorne

**Techniques for Introducing Your Topic**

- Surprise your readers.
*On April 22, 1970, twenty million United States citizens participated in mass demonstrations all across the country.*

- Ask a series of questions.
*Are you environmentally aware? Do you recycle? Do you use the backside of notebook paper? Would anyone have asked you these questions thirty years ago?*

- Relate an **anecdote**.
*Every two weeks, I participate in an American recycling ritual. Before I leave for school in the morning, I drag a recycle bin to the curb. I watch new, state-of-the-art recycle trucks come by and pick up the entire bin with a hydraulic arm that deposits the contents into the truck. The truck moves on, collecting my neighbors' and their neighbors' recycling until the neighborhood is scoured of items that can be put to another good use.*

For more information on developing an outline, see the Language Arts Survey 2.28, "Rough Outlines," 2.29, "Outlining," and 2.30, "Formal Outlines."

## Language, Grammar, and Style

### Effective Documentation

IDENTIFYING EFFECTIVE DOCUMENTATION. You need to credit authors for the information from them that you use in your research. Citing your sources allows your readers to verify your research and protects you against plagiarism. Documentation that is effective for both these purposes is accurate and presented according to accepted style.

To quote an author's exact words, put the exact words in quotation marks and reference the last name and the page where you found those words.

**Direct quotation**
". . . let them mate / To the death in the rotten branches, / Let the tree sway and burst into flame / And mingle them, crackling with feathers." (Dickey 25)

At times, instead of using a direct quotation, you may paraphrase an author's idea in your essay. Even though you are paraphrasing—putting the author's idea into your own words—you must still credit

Jerome worked with the following graphic organizer as he took notes from his research materials and began to formulate his narrowed topic and thesis.

## Student Model—Graphic Organizer

**Topic:** concerns about the environment as shown in Dickey's poem

**Narrowed topic:** the history of the environmental movement

**Thesis:** Americans may have ignored environmental issues in the past, but in the last 30 years Americans have become environmentally aware.

**Outline:**
  I. Introduction
      **technique to develop interest**
          reintroduction of the lynx
          recycling bins
          question—Is Dickey right?
      **identify topic**
          caring about the environment—recycling and preservation of endangered species—is an accepted part of American life
      **thesis**
          not aware before, but aware now

 II. Body
      A. **1st main point**
          environmental problems not addressed
      B. **2nd main point**
          beginning concerns about the environment
      C. **3rd main point**
          birth of environmental movement
      D. **4th main point**
          growth of the environmental movement

III. Conclusion
      **summary statement**
          ways that Americans are environmentally aware today
      **motivation for thought or action**
          is it enough?

## Drafting

A good introduction is essential, but you don't need to write it first just because it comes first in the paper. Many times it is easier to write a great introduction after you have written the paper. This method helps you avoid sitting and staring at a blank piece of paper or computer monitor for hours while you try to compose the perfect introduction. Therefore, begin with your thesis statement. This gives you a concrete place to start.

The next logical step is to write about and support the main points. Focus on and write about only one point at a time. Insert the necessary parenthetical documentation as you quote or paraphrase specific information from your resources. After you have finished a section, you may find it beneficial to take a break before you go on to the next. It is important to keep a fresh mind while writing. See the Language Arts Survey 5.36, "Documenting Sources," for information about documenting sources.

After you have finished developing each of the main points and their supporting information, read your draft to gain a fuller understanding of how you have presented the issue. Then draft an introduction that uses an appropriate technique to develop interest in your topic. Include your thesis in the introduction. Finally, draft a conclusion that provides a summary of your point about the issue and that motivates your reader either to think further or take some action about it.

## Self- and Peer Evaluation

After you finish your first draft, complete a self-evaluation of your research paper. Read your draft as if you were unaware of the issue. This may help you identify background information or support that may be lacking. If time allows, you may want to get one or two peer evaluations. See the Language Arts Survey 2.37–2.40, "Self- and Peer Evaluation," for more information.

As you evaluate your draft or that of a classmate, answer the following questions:

- What would make the introduction more interesting or more focused?
- How clearly does the thesis statement present the issue?
- What main point is developed in each of the body paragraphs? How well is the main point supported?
- What questions does each body paragraph answer? What questions does each body paragraph leave unanswered?
- What do direct quotations add? What additional quotations would add meaningful support? Which quotations seem unnecessary?
- How logically do the main points support the thesis? What points might be missing? Which points might be extraneous to the issue?

the author by referencing the last name and page where you found the idea. See Language Arts Survey 5.43, "Paraphrasing, Summarizing, and Quoting" for additional information.

**Paraphrased statement**

However, the myth of the wolverine seems to be greater than the reality. (Yukon Mammal Series)

If you use two or more articles or books with the same author, include the author, title of article or book, and page number in the parenthetical reference. You also need to include this source in your bibliography at the end of your paper in the works cited page.

FIXING EFFECTIVE DOCUMENTATION. You need to document sources correctly. Explain how you would fix the documentation in each example below.

(Dickey, 25)

(p.235 Brown)

(Rachel Carson 19)

Read the quotation. Then determine which one of the following statements should be referenced because it paraphrases the author's idea.

"Earth Day achieved what I had hoped for. The objective was to get a nationwide demonstration of concern for the environment so large that

*continued on page 934*

it would shake the political arena. It was a gamble, but it worked. An estimated 20 million people participated in peaceful demonstrations all across the country. That was the remarkable thing that became Earth Day. April 22, 1970."

Earth Day was a success because it achieved its objective of demonstrating a large-scale concern for the environment that impacted political thinking.

On April 22, 1970, the first Earth Day was held. On that day, nearly twenty million people demonstrated their concerns for the environment.

**USING EFFECTIVE DOCUMENTATION.** Read through your paper again. Did you handle quotations correctly? Check carefully for paraphrased ideas. Are there any places where you paraphrased material that you need to reference? Is your works cited page done correctly?

- What transitions are used to hold the paper together? Where could the use of transitions be improved? Where could the types of transitions be varied?
- How well does the conclusion convince the reader?
- Is there adequate parenthetical documentation?

## Revising and Proofreading

Review your self- and peer evaluations. Revise your writing after considering these comments. Check that each paragraph has a topic sentence that relates to your thesis statement. Proofread your revised draft for spelling, mechanical, and usage errors. Don't merely rely on the spell check; be especially wary of such homonyms as *its* and *it's; to, two,* and *too;* and *their, there,* and *they're.*

Be sure that each source is referenced correctly in the paper. Be sure your works cited page is also done correctly. Finally, include a title page and a works cited page. Follow the Modern Language Association format for both. For more information, see the Language Arts Survey 5.36, "Documenting Sources."

## Publishing and Presenting

Your final product should be a paper that you are proud to present. What you say and how you say it should be done in the best possible fashion. When you have done your best, share your work with other members of your class. Your class may want to publish the papers as an anthology or post them on the Internet.

## Reflecting

Writing a strong research paper is a complicated process. What was the most difficult part of the project for you? What did you learn about your research skills, organizational skills, and the subject matter? How did your thoughts grow and evolve during the research and writing process? What goal can you set for yourself to accomplish the next time you are assigned to do research?

See Jerome's completed research paper on the following page.

The Greening of America?
by Jerome Williams

This past winter, officials in Colorado reintroduced the lynx to its mountainous areas. Wearing radio-tracking collars, these half-dozen cats were carefully monitored as they attempted to re-acclimate themselves to the wilds of Colorado. In the first few months, several starved, one was shot, and one was hit by a truck. Some critics thought the whole endeavor was pointless. They argued that it was immoral to trap healthy lynx in Canada, ship them to Colorado, and let them die. Immoral or not, however, no one complained about the money being spent.

This past summer, our small city spent over $1 million on new recycle bins. These huge, wheeled carts cost $200 each (Juras). Every two weeks, state-of-the-art recycle trucks come by, picking up the entire bin with a hydraulic arm that deposits the recyclables into the truck. There is no community outcry against these recycling expenditures. Recycling is now an accepted part of American life. So is the preservation of an endangered species.

I thought about this as I read James Dickey's "For the Last Wolverine." In the poem, Dickey mourns the slow disappearance of the wolverine and the eagle—". . . let them mate / To the death in the rotten branches, / Let the tree sway and burst into flame / and mingle them, crackling with feathers." A member of the weasel family, the wolverine has become one of the rarest of all mammals. According to the Yukon Mammal Series, an Internet site published by the Yukon Department of Renewable Resources, the wolverine has also come to represent the wilderness. Elliott Coues, a renowned nineteenth century naturalist called the wolverine ". . . a ravenous monster of insatiate voracity, matchless strength, and supernatural cunning, a terror to all other beasts, the blood thirsty monster of the forest." There are tales of wolverines backing grizzly bears and packs of wolves down in confrontations over food. However, the myth of the wolverine seems to be greater than the reality (Yukon Mammal Series). Wolverines tend to survive as scavengers, cleaning up the kills of wolves. Its hunting is limited to small mammals and the roots, berries, insects, and bird eggs that come with summer.

At one time the wolverine population extended south from the Arctic into Colorado, Indiana, Pennsylvania, and Michigan. Now, however, they are seldom found south of the Canadian Yukon (U of Michigan-Animal Diversity Web). Large wilderness areas—essential for the wolverine's survival—disappeared as roads, agricultural practices, and human inhabitation made inroads into the wolverine's habitat (Yukon Mammal Series). Would Dickey's lament come true?

Americans may have ignored environmental issues in the past, but in the last thirty years Americans have become environmentally aware. The eagle has come back from near extinction. How did this wondrous transformation come about? One of the first steps in the awakening of environmental awareness was the establishment of Earth Day.

In the nineteenth century when the population was relatively low and the amount of land and resources seemed unlimited, farmers frequently exhausted the fertility of the soil and then moved on. Rivers were used as sewers and receptacles of industrial waste. In the 1930s and again in the 1950s, the Cuyahoga River in Cleveland, Ohio caught on fire from burning chemical waste. Emissions from smoke stacks darkened American skies. There was no public outcry then (Brown USIA).

The sixties ushered in an outcry. In 1962, Rachel Carson, a marine biologist, published the book *Silent Spring,* describing the disastrous effects of agricultural pesticides that "have the power to kill every insect, the 'good' and the 'bad,' to still the song of the birds, and the leaping fish in the streams." (Carson 7). Apollo astronauts relayed photos from space, imprinting the picture of a beautiful and fragile planet Earth on millions of American psyches and influencing American public opinion. America's environmental awareness was awakening. When the Cuyahoga River caught fire again in 1969, Cleveland became a national laughingstock. Partially because of these events, Congress passed the first National Environmental Policy Act, declaring "a national policy which will encourage productive and enjoyable harmony between man and his environment" (Brown).

The time was ripe for the birth of America's environmental movement. Gaylord Nelson, senator from Wisconsin, had been a longtime conservationist. Borrowing from the antiwar movement, which had been having teach-ins to educate the populace about the Vietnam War, Nelson developed the idea to have an environmental teach-in. Earth Day was born (Brown). Nelson's plan was picked up by the wire services. The story went nationwide. He later said:

Earth Day achieved what I had hoped for. The objective was to get a nationwide demonstration of concern for the environment so large that it would shake the political arena. It was a gamble, but it worked. An estimated 20 million people participated in peaceful demonstrations all across the country. That was the remarkable thing that became Earth Day. April 22, 1970 (Brown).

After the initial event, the enthusiasm for Earth Day waned. Still, it was the start. In 1970, the National Environmental Protection Act became law (Levey and Greenhall 269). In 1971, the environmental organization Greenpeace formed in Canada. This group adopted principles of civil disobedience to raise public consciousness about the shrinking whale population and the danger of nuclear power. Another organization, The Nature Conservancy, began to buy undeveloped land for use as nature preserves. The Sierra Club and the National Audubon Society brought lawsuits against logging companies to slow the destruction of old-growth forests (Brown). In 1971, the chemical pesticide DDT was outlawed after scientists determined that it weakened the shells of birds and was a major factor in the reduction of numbers of eagles. In 1972, the Clean

Water Act was signed into law. In 1973, the Endangered Species Act became law.

Since that first Earth Day in 1970, Americans have become much more environmentally aware. Twenty million Americans took part in Earth Day events in 1970; in 1990, 200 million people all over the world took part in showing that they cared about the environment (Earth Day Network). In 1970, United Auto Workers led a parade through St. Louis featuring a smog-free car. In 1990, a 500 mile human chain was formed across France (Earth Day Network). In many ways, people have come a long way.

Still, these events must be kept in focus. Drivers are environmentally aware, yet gas-guzzling sport utility vehicles (SUVs) are the most popular vehicle in the U.S. market. Farmers are environmentally aware, but "pesticides . . . continue to raise public concern" (Ritter 1887). Families are environmentally aware, yet the average new American house is 3,500 square feet, compared to 1,700 square feet 25 years ago. Outdoor enthusiasts are environmentally aware, but their chance of seeing a wolverine in the United States is less than the chance of being struck by lightning. Yes, Americans are more environmentally aware today than they were thirty years ago. But after thirty years, an important question remains: Is the level of today's environmental awareness enough for the next thirty years?

## Works Cited

Brown, Tim. "What Is Earth Day?" United States Information Agency. 19 Oct. 1999 <http://www.usia.gov/topical/global/environ/earthday/brown.htm>

Carson, Rachel L., *Silent Spring*. Boston: Cambridge, Mass: Houghton Mifflin, Riverside Press, 1962.

"Earth Day 1970 & 1990: Historical Precedents." 14 Oct. 1999. Online posting. Earth Day Network. <http://www.cco.caltech.edu/~cetfers/unused/eday.history.html>

"Environmental Timeline: Earth Day." 19 Oct. 1999. Online posting. The Wilderness Society. <http://earthday.wilderness.org/history/timeline_list.htm>

Juras, Joshua. Manager, Public Works Department. Telephone interview. March 14, 2000.

Levey, Judith S. and Agnes Greenhall, eds. *The Concise Columbia Encyclopedia.* New York: Avon, 1983, 269.

Ritter, Len. "Report of a Panel on the Relationship between Public Exposure to Pesticides and Cancer." *Cancer* 80, 1997, 1887.

Weinstein, Bret and Liz Ballenger. "Gulo gulo: Wolverine." The University of Michigan, Museum of Zoology, Animal Diversity Web. 15 Oct. 1999 <http://animaldiversity.ummz.umich.edu/accounts/gulo/g._gulo>

Yukon Mammal Series. Yukon Department of Renewable Resources. Whitehorse, Yukon. 20 Oct. 1999 <http://206.12.26.168/wildlife/wolverine.html>

# UNIT REVIEW
## Early Contemporary Literature
## (1960–1980)

### Words for Everyday Use

Check your knowledge of the following vocabulary words from the selections in this unit. Write short sentences using these words in context to make the meaning clear. To review the definition or usage of a word, refer to the page number listed or the Glossary of Words for Everyday Use.

| | | |
|---|---|---|
| apprehension, 904 | eradicate, 911 | panic, 899 |
| aqueous, 920 | excessive, 904 | perforce, 871 |
| asunder, 910 | fusion, 917 | prototype, 917 |
| austere, 880 | hypnotic, 904 | recondite, 919 |
| banked, 880 | immortal, 898 | sedation, 920 |
| belabor, 911 | impenetrable, 919 | seminal, 919 |
| chronic, 880 | inclination, 905 | sovereign, 910 |
| civility, 911 | ingenious, 904 | subversion, 910 |
| convoluted, 904 | invective, 911 | temper, 910 |
| distill, 884 | invoke, 911 | vehemently, 919 |
| effacement, 884 | leviathan, 920 | venture, 910 |
| egalitarian, 917 | mediocre, 893 | |
| enigmatic, 917 | obscure, 905 | |

### Literary Tools

Define the following terms, giving concrete examples of how they are used in the selections in this unit. To review a term, refer to the page number indicated or to the Handbook of Literary Terms.

| | | |
|---|---|---|
| allegory, 902 | exposition, 915 | repetition, 879 |
| alliteration, 879 | expository writing, 915 | run-on line, 883 |
| allusion, 891 | free verse, 869, 887 | simile, 869, 883 |
| anaphora, 908 | irony, 915 | speaker, 887 |
| confessional poetry, 874 | metaphor, 869, 896 | tone, 891 |
| diction, 896 | parallelism, 908 | |
| epigraph, 874 | point of view, 902 | |

# Reflecting
## ............... *on* YOUR READING

### Genre Studies

1. **SHORT STORY.** "Journey" uses a second-person point of view. How is this point of view different from a first-person or a third-person point of view? How involved do you feel in the story? Who is included in the telling of this story? To whom does the lesson pertain? What other types of stories would use a second-person point of view effectively?

2. **CONFESSIONAL POETRY.** Confessional poetry is verse that describes, sometimes with painful explicitness, the private or personal experiences of the writer. Sexton's "The Starry Night" and Plath's "Morning Song" present different personal attitudes toward life. What are these attitudes? What figures of speech do the poets use to develop these attitudes?

# Thematic Studies

3. **REGRET.** What do the speaker of "Those Winter Sundays" by Hayden and the speaker of "The Slump" by Updike regret? Which speaker has the opportunity to change his regret? Which speaker does not? What lessons has each speaker learned from his regret?

4. **THE ROLE OF THE POET.** "Constantly risking absurdity" by Ferlinghetti and "The Secret" by Levertov discuss the role of the poet in contemporary society. Describe the images of the poet put forth in each of the two poems. What is the role of the poet in Ferlinghetti's poem? in Levertov's?

# Historical/Biographical Studies

5. **ANTI-CULTURAL POETRY.** Poet Karl Shapiro, in his 1960 work *In Defense of Ignorance*, advocated a move away from the complex, demanding style of T. S. Eliot and Ezra Pound toward the simple, straightforward style of Walt Whitman and Carl Sandburg. Which poems in the unit are most like the "poetry for the common person" of Whitman and Sandburg? in what ways?

6. **THE ROLE OF THE UNITED STATES.** In his Inaugural Address, President Kennedy set goals for his presidency. What role for the United States did he outline? How has the United States lived up to its role since this speech was given in 1961? What would Kennedy say should be the role of the United States in world events today?

7. **POSTMODERNISM.** What view of the automobile and the shopping mall does Joan Didion present in her essay "On the Mall"? How is her perspective in keeping with a postmodern viewpoint? Do you share Didion's viewpoint? Why, or why not?

*Gu, Choki, Pa*, 1985. Judy Pfaff.
Wacoal Art Center, Tokyo.

America is a vast conspiracy

to make you happy.

—John Updike

# ArtNote

*Gu, Choki, Pa,* 1985. Judy Pfaff,
pages 940–941.

Judy Pfaff (1946– ) is a pioneer of installation
art, large mixed-media sculptures that surround
the viewer. Her art is "site-specific," meaning
that she creates a unique work designed just for
that particular space, using local materials and
responding to the environment. What similarities can you find in this work to the Jackson
Pollock painting on page 756?

# CONTEMPORARY LITERATURE (1980–PRESENT)

## THE EIGHTIES

The decade opened in the heat of the negotiations over
the fifty-two remaining American hostages held by the
**Ayatollah Khomeini** in Iran. While President **Jimmy Carter**
had made progress, he was unable to obtain a release
before the 1980 presidential election. The voters turned
Carter and **Walter Mondale** out in favor of **Ronald Reagan**
and **George Bush**, who succeeded in bringing hostages
home after a few days in office. Six years later during the
**Iran-Contra hearings**, the American people learned that
officials in the Reagan administration had sent arms to Iran
in exchange for the hostages and had diverted the money from the sales to assist the
*contras* of Nicaragua against the Sandinistas. These proceedings, illegal because they
could be ordered lawfully only by Congress, ended in the conviction of four officials,
including Admiral **John Poindexter** and Lieutenant Colonel **Oliver North**.

Besides the hostage crisis, the Reagan Administration inherited an ailing economy,
one with inflation that reached 14 percent and interest rates as high as 21 percent.
Although Reagan campaigned on the platform of reducing the size of government and
cutting taxes to curb further federal growth, his Strategic Defense Initiative (SDI), also
known as "**Star Wars**," increased the national debt and budget deficit to an all-time
high. The budget deficit alone reached one trillion dollars, up from 321 billion dollars in
1980. By 1987, family farms were experiencing the worst depression in fifty years.
Clearly, the fiscal distance between the haves and have-nots grew considerably during
this period.

The economic collapse of the Soviet Union brought an end to the decades-long Cold
War between the United States and the USSR. The international stock market crash in
October 1987 delivered the final blow to the suffering economies of the Soviet Union's
Eastern bloc. The Soviet Union's new leader **Mikhail Gorbachev** promoted a more
democratic and capitalistic system that would allow for free elections and private

## LITERARY EVENTS

➤ = American Events

➤1981. Maxine Hong Kingston's *China Men* wins National Book Award for nonfiction

1980. Czeslaw Milosz wins Nobel Prize for literature

➤1980. Norman Mailer's *The Executioner's Song* wins Pulitzer Prize for fiction

➤1982. John Updike's *Rabbit Is Rich* wins Pulitzer Prize and National Book Award for fiction

➤1982. John Gardner, author of *On Moral Fiction,* killed in motorcycle accident

➤1983. Alice Walker's *The Color Purple* wins Pulitzer Prize

➤1986. Barry Lopez's *Arctic Dreams* wins National Book Award for nonfiction

1986. Elie Wiesel wins Nobel Peace Prize

➤1986. Robert Penn Warren named U.S. poet laureate

| 1980 | 1982 | 1984 | 1986 |
|---|---|---|---|

## HISTORICAL EVENTS

➤1980. Ronald Reagan wins presidency

➤1980. John Lennon assassinated

➤1981. Bill Gates introduces MS-DOS

➤1981. MTV goes on air for first time

➤1981. Sandra Day O'Connor first woman appointed to Supreme Court

1981. AIDS virus identified

➤1983. Sally Ride first woman in space

➤1983. Madonna tops pop charts

➤1984. Ronald Reagan re-elected president

➤1984. Nicaraguan contras receive private U.S. aid

➤1984. Apple Macintosh introduced as "insanely great" computer

➤1985. U.S. becomes debtor nation for first time since 1914

➤1987. October stock market crash

➤1987. Ivan Boesky sentenced to 3-year prison term for insider trading

➤1986. *Challenger* space shuttle explodes

1986. Chernobyl nuclear power plant disaster

responsibility for what had been government programs. From this new openness followed the collapse of Communist rule. The Soviet Union dissolved as the many ethnic groups that had been taken over by the empire demanded to reestablish their own nations. East and West Germany, divided for forty-five years, reunited, and the Berlin Wall came down. An international capitalism emerged, opening legitimate and black markets in the new economies, which created global economic interdependence in the nineties.

Throughout the 1980s within the Arab countries of Iran, led by Khomeini; Libya, led by **Moammar El-Kaddafy**; and Iraq, led by **Saddam Hussein,** religious and political extremists increasingly expressed their animosity toward the United States through acts of terrorism.

Revolutionary changes of a different kind were taking place in the United States economy. President Reagan fired striking federal air controllers, diminishing their union strength and employee benefits. Pensions were cut and replaced with 401k retirement plans that provided for individual tax-sheltered investment. Thus began the democratization of stock and mutual fund holdings, a movement that would lead to the booming stock market and consumerism in the 1990s. When **Tom Wolfe** wrote *The Bonfire of the Vanities* (1987), the novel was immediately recognized as a condemnation of the greed characterizing American society in the 1980s.

Interest in Earth Day and environmental causes had waned by the late 1970s. As economic expansion became an increasing priority, environmentalists criticized corporate greed and the disregard for environmentally sound practices. Such disregard led to huge human-made disasters, such as nuclear accidents in Bhopal, India; Chernobyl, Ukraine; and Three Mile Island in Pennsylvania; disastrous oil spills such as that of the *Exxon Valdez* in Alaska; and intensifying climate changes worldwide. The United States was documented as the

Dismantling the Berlin Wall, 1989.

➤1987. Joseph Brodsky wins Nobel Prize for literature

➤1987. Rita Dove's *Thomas and Beulah* wins Pulitzer Prize for poetry

➤1989. Anne Tyler's *Breathing Lessons* wins Pulitzer Prize for fiction

➤1990. August Wilson's *The Piano Lesson* wins Pulitzer Prize for drama

➤1990. Charles Johnson's *Middle Passage* wins National Book Award for fiction

➤1991. John Updike's *Rabbit at Rest* wins Pulitzer Prize

➤1992. Cormac McCarthy's *All the Pretty Horses* wins National Book Award for fiction

➤1993. Toni Morrison wins Nobel Prize for literature

➤1993. Rita Dove named U.S. poet laureate

➤1995. Doris Kearns Goodwin's *No Ordinary Time* wins Pulitzer Prize for nonfiction

➤1995. Robert Hass named U.S. poet laureate

➤1994. E. Annie Proulx's *The Shipping News* wins Pulitzer Prize for fiction

➤1994. Yusef Komunyakaa's *Neon Vernacular* wins Pulitzer Prize for poetry

**1988**     **1990**     **1992**     **1994**

➤1988. George Bush wins presidency

1988. Gorbachev implements perestroika

➤1988. U.S. deficit tops 3 trillion dollars

1988. Iran-Iraq war ends

1989. Hyper-text transfer protocol (http) invented

➤1989. Tiananmen Square massacre occurs in Beijing

➤1989. Eastern Communism collapses

➤1989. *Exxon Valdez* spills oil in Prince Edward Sound, Alaska

➤1991. U.S. launches Operation Desert Storm

➤1991. Clarence Thomas confirmed as Supreme Court judge

➤1992. Bill Clinton wins presidency

1993. World Wide Web goes public

➤1993. Terrorists bomb World Trade Center in New York City

➤1993. Shootout and burning occurs at Waco, Texas

➤1995. O. J. Simpson acquitted of murder

1994. Rwandan civil war; 100,000 people killed

1994. Nelson Mandela elected first black president of South Africa

➤1994. Republicans win control of House and Senate

A mural of Ayatollah Khomeini on a street in Iran, 1999.

largest emitter of greenhouse gases, a concern tied to the depletion of the ozone layer. The sudden detection in the mid-1980s of an ominous "hole" in the ozone layer of Antarctica prompted many governments to sign agreements to limit chemical compounds linked to such depletion. Acid rain, shrinking biodiversity (the extinction of many species of plants and animals), deforestation, and pollution of all kinds were some of the factors that led to a renewed sense of environmental commitment on **Earth Day 1990**, in which 200 million people around the globe participated.

## THE NINETIES

In 1991, Iraq, under the leadership of Saddam Hussein, invaded Kuwait to seize its oil fields. With the approval of most Americans, General Norman Schwartzkopf conducted "**Operation Desert Storm**," which forced Hussein's withdrawal. President George Bush, however, didn't use this success to his advantage and lost to the Clinton-Gore Democratic ticket in 1992.

In Eastern Europe, nations broke apart as formerly independent ethnic groups reclaimed their sovereignty. This was especially true in Yugoslavia. In 1992, NATO peacekeepers found mass graves of Bosnians killed by Serbian nationals who were attempting to crush the Bosnian independence effort. In 1994, NATO sent air attacks over Bosnia, forcing the Serbs to remove artillery surrounding the city of Sarajevo. NATO continued the conflict with air strikes against the Serbs, who were exterminating Albanians in Kosovo, to prevent what they considered to be their historic, sacred land from becoming an independent nation under the leadership of the Albanian majority. Even with the peace agreements in 1998 and the withdrawal of Serbian forces from Kosovo, peacekeeping forces had trouble controlling Albanians' retaliatory assaults against, and murders of Serbs.

**Bill Clinton** and **Al Gore** defeated incumbents George Bush and **Dan Quayle** for the presidency on a platform of fiscal responsibility, reduced government, welfare reform, support for education, a national health care program, and environmental protection. By 1994, however, under investigation for possible real-estate fraud in Whitewater,

## LITERARY EVENTS

➤ = American Events

➤1997. Robert Pinsky named U.S. poet laureate

➤1997. Frank McCourt's *Angela's Ashes* wins Pulitzer Prize for autobiography

➤1996. Richard Ford's *Independence Day* wins Pulitzer Prize for fiction

➤1999. Michael Cunningham's *The Hours* wins Pulitzer Prize for fiction

➤1998. Philip Roth's *American Pastoral* wins Pulitzer Prize for fiction

➤2001. Michael Chabon's *Amazing Adventures of Kavalier & Clay* wins Pulitzer Prize for fiction

➤2001. Billy Collins named U.S. poet laureate

➤2000. Stanley Kunitz named U.S. poet laureate

1996     1998     2000

➤1996. Bill Clinton re-elected president

➤1998. Clinton impeached by House but acquitted by Senate

➤1998. NATO air attacks against Serbs in Kosovo

1998. Wye river Accord for Mideast Peace signed by Israeli and Palestinian leaders

➤1999. Preparations made for Y2K computer failures

➤2000. Results of presidential election contested; Florida votes recounted; Al Gore concedes race to George W. Bush

➤2001. George W. Bush inaugurated as 43rd president of the United States

➤2001. Planes hijacked by terrorists destroy the World Trade Center in New York City and part of the Pentagon in Washington, D.C.; thousands are killed. In response, the United States sends troops to Afghanistan to destroy the terrorist network Al Qaeda, led by Islamic extremist Osama bin Laden.

## HISTORICAL EVENTS

Arkansas, Clinton lost both House and Senate to the Republicans' "Contract for America" championed by Congressman Newt Gingrich of Georgia. For Clinton and for the nation, the worst was yet to come. While investigating the Whitewater scandal, Independent Counsel **Kenneth Starr** and his committee received a tape recording from federal employee Linda Tripp of a conversation she had held with Monica Lewinsky, a White House intern. With permission to investigate, the Counsel plunged into an exhausting investigation of the President's sexual misconduct with this young intern and his attempts to cover it up. In 1998, Clinton was impeached by the U.S. House of Representatives and acquitted by the Senate, making him the first president to be impeached since Andrew Johnson. The public, though perturbed by Clinton's indiscretion and dishonesty, found themselves disgusted by the Independent Counsel's voyeuristic probing into Clinton's personal life. While seeming to have little regard for his character, the public maintained faith in the President's ability to govern.

One phenomenon that marked the 1990s was the transformation of private lives into public dramas. In what was to serve as a preview to the Clinton impeachment process, the public spent two years in front of their televisions watching the **O. J. Simpson** "trial of the century," in which the ex-football star was accused of murdering his wife, Nicole Simpson, and her friend, Ronald Goldman. The trial became a daily soap opera, to which many became addicted and later experienced withdrawal after Simpson's acquittal on inconclusive evidence. News analysts and commentators lived for their daily input and talk-show hosts found new, entertaining ways of probing the most sordid aspects of the lives of people more than willing to reveal personal secrets for fun, notoriety, and profit. In contrast, a few talk-show hosts, like **Oprah Winfrey**, provided award-winning, quality coverage and promoted such causes as health, wellness, and literacy.

## THE CULTURE FROM THE 1980s INTO THE FUTURE

The majority of the young **baby boomers**, the offspring of parents of the World War II and the Korean War eras, had evolved into the politically conservative "**yuppies**" of the Reagan era. Many, now in executive management positions, prided themselves on quick profits, corporate takeovers, and downsizing operations. They regarded business tycoons as heroes. Though many of their own children followed suit and succeeded professionally, many suffered. Statistically, children were among our nation's poor.

This generation of youth adopted the label "**Generation X**"—by their own definition they were nobodies, nameless and depressed by the burdens the adult world placed on them. Since both parents worked in many families, a phenomenon of the economy and the feminist movement, the Generation Xers often came home from school to empty houses. While some had large disposable incomes, many had no jobs, little money, and little hope of gaining more. They felt put upon by adults who lived well enough and left them with a huge national debt that they would have neither the means nor inclination to pay off. Characterized as being selfish, cynical, dependent, and demanding, this generation seemed to have no past and no future. They were materialists without the material. Madonna, Michael Jackson, Boy George, Cyndi Lauper, and many rock and rap groups contributed to the new culture aided by the exploding popularity of **MTV**. Advertising created an extraordinary consumerism and economic boom.

One of the most significant differences in our present world from our past is the pervasion of electronic media. The vast amount of information communicated via the **Internet** renders knowledge fragmentary and elusive. No central bank of knowledge

*Untitled (Your Fictions Become History),* 1983.
Barbara Kruger. Milwaukee Museum of Art.

exists. Each user compiles data according to a specific interest, only bits and bytes of what is available. Although the hyper-text-transfer protocol (http) was invented in 1989, the **World Wide Web** didn't open for public use until 1993. Since then the world has zoomed across space on the **"Information Superhighway,"** learning, gathering, buying, selling, chatting, joining, and investing. One can read the daily newspaper, subscribe to an e-zine, read an e-book, or check out reviews of movies, theater, music, and literature online. And this is only the beginning. Technology advances so rapidly that computer systems quickly become obsolete. TV, too, delivers virtual reality simulations based on digitized animations, cropped and reconstructed images, all of which break down the opposition of appearance and reality. Surface has become substance; the glitter is the gold. Today we record multiple copies of CDs, movies, e-books, and computer games that sell for a given price. We have immediate access to each other through e-mail, chat rooms, and cellular phones.

Communism's collapse has led to a new international consumer capitalism. Corporations are replacing nations as the dominant forces in people's lives. Trade agreements, the Internet, and standardizing currency such as the euro contribute to cross-cultural marketing and consumerism. Nations have split into political, ethnic, and/or religious entities with local and international economies, many of which struggle for identity and survival while others prosper. Borrowing from Marshall McCluhan's terms of the 1950s, the "global village" has become a reality.

The darkest side of the era was the discovery of the AIDS virus that spread rapidly throughout the world. Although the virus is still virulent, many who are HIV-positive are now able to control its effects through medication and to live quality lives. Despite progress having been made in treating the disease, the search for a cure continues.

During the latter part of the twentieth century we Americans reevaluated our own history. Now, as never before, writers examine events from perspectives of those who are not in power and who do not justify the status quo. In the last twenty years we have become more aware of the disregarded ethnic and racial minority contributors to our past and present. Women's voices have begun to be heard. We have had to re-examine the "discovery" of America, the frontier, the Civil War, the economy, and the sciences and arts of our nation to include those previously omitted. We have discovered a multicultural America that celebrates diversity while searching for unity.

## THE CONTEMPORARY LITERARY SCENE

Today it is difficult to speak of a contemporary literary canon, since the diversity of literature being published cannot be easily categorized. While critics and theorists may try to classify writers as minimalists, regionalists, feminists, multiculturalists, or neo-formalists, the contemporary literary collective is open for readers to enjoy and evaluate on the merits of each text.

Elements of painting, sculpture, text, video, sound, and theater have been brought together in new mixed-media forms, performance art and installation art. Well-known figures include **Laurie Anderson**, author of the international hit *United Stages* (1984), which used film, video, acoustics and music, choreography, and space-age technology. Performance poetry has entered the mainstream with **rap music**, while across the United States, **"poetry slams"**—open poetry reading contests held in literary bookstores and cafes—have become inexpensive, popular entertainment.

At the opposite end of the theoretical spectrum are the self-styled "**New Formalists**," who champion a return in poetry of form, rhyme, and meter. The New Formalists, although criticized for retreating to nineteenth-century themes, often draw on contemporary attitudes and images, along with musical language and traditional, closed forms.

Perhaps the most distinguishing characteristic of contemporary American literature has been the influence of **multiculturalism**. While the American population continues to grow increasingly diverse, American literature has been characterized by an unprecedented interest in and promotion of this diversity. The predominantly white male literary canon of the earlier part of this century has made room for works in all genres by women and people of color.

Minority literature has flowered with Hispanic-American writers such as poets **Gary Soto, Alberto Rios, Lorna Dee Cervantes, Pat Mora, and Jimmy Santiago Baca**. Much Chicano, or Mexican-American, poetry has a rich oral tradition in the *corrido*, or ballad, form. Recent works stress the traditions of the Mexican community and the discrimination it has sometimes experienced from whites.

Native Americans have written poetry and prose that excels in vivid, living evocations of the natural world, which become almost

Toni Morrison.

mystical at times. This work also voices a tragic sense of the irrevocable loss of a rich heritage. Native American writers include **Leslie Marmon Silko**, who wrote *Ceremony*, **Simon Ortiz, Louise Erdrich** (the *Beet Queen* trilogy), and **Sherman Alexie**, whose novel, *The Lone Ranger and Tonto Fistfight in Heaven,* was the basis for the critically praised movie *Smoke Signals* (1998).

African-American writers include poets **Amiri Baraka (LeRoi Jones), Lucille Clifton, Michael Harper, Nikki Giovanni,** and **Rita Dove**; novelists **Toni Morrison, Alice Walker,** and **Charles Johnson**, and short story writer **Toni Cade Bambara** (*Gorilla, My Love*). In 1993, **Maya Angelou** read "On the Wings of Morning," a poem that celebrates diversity, at the inauguration of President Clinton. That same year, **Rita Dove** was named poet laureate of the United States. Dove, a writer of fiction and drama as well, won the Pulitzer Prize in 1987 for *Thomas and Beulah,* a series of lyric poems honoring the lives of her grandparents. In 1993, **Toni Morrison**, author of such seminal works as *The Bluest Eye, Sula, Song of Solomon,* and *Beloved,* won the Nobel Prize for literature.

Asian-American literature is exceedingly varied as well. Poets include **Li-Young Lee, Cathy Song, Garrett Hongo, David Mura,** and **Janice Mirikitani**; prose writers include **Maxine Hong Kingston, Amy Tan, Frank Chin, Sylvia Watanabe, Gish Jen,** and **Gus Lee**. Americans of Japanese, Chinese, and Filipino descent may have lived in the United States for seven generations, while Americans of Korean, Thai, and Vietnamese heritage are likely to be fairly recent immigrants. Each group grows out of a distinctive linguistic, historical, and cultural tradition.

Other contemporary American voices making a strong contribution include prose writers **Allan Gurganus, Tim O'Brien, Anne Beattie, Anne Tyler,** Barbara Kingsolver, **Jane Smiley, Tom Wolfe, Frank McCourt, Garrison Keillor, E. Annie Proulx, Isaac Asimov, Kathleen Norris,** and **John Updike**; notable poets include **Diane Ackerman, Louise Glück, Phillip Levine, Sharon Olds, Charles Wright,** and **Donald Hall**.

# ECHOES

## CONTEMPORARY LITERATURE

Twenty years after the first Earth Day, those of us who set out to change the world are poised on the threshold of utter failure. Measured on virtually any scale, the world is in worse shape today than it was only two decades ago. People want to make the right choices in their lives, and now we have to. Talk is no longer sufficient. If we can adapt our lives to reflect our concerns for the environment and hold our elected leaders accountable for their promises, then perhaps we can truly make the 1990s the Decade of the Environment.

— Denis Hayes, Chairman, Earth Day 1990, and organizer, Earth Day 1970

Too bad that all the people who know how to run the country are busy driving taxicabs and cutting hair.

— George Burns, quoted in *Life*

Fear of success is one of the new fears I've heard about lately. And I think it's definitely a sign that we're running out of fears. A person suffering from fear of success is scraping the bottom of the fear barrel.

— Jerry Seinfeld

Our schools as much as our universities are given away to these absurdities: replacing *Julius Caesar* by *The Color Purple* is hardly a royal road to enlightenment. A country where television, movies, computers, and Stephen King have replaced reading is already in acute danger of cultural collapse.

— Harold Bloom, Introduction to *The Best of the Best American Poetry, 1988–1997*

It is ironical that, in this bad time, American poetry is of a higher quality than our criticism or teaching of poetry.

— Harold Bloom, Introduction to *The Best of the Best American Poetry, 1988–1997*

These three writers—Emerson, Whitman, and Dickinson—have been the primary and seminal influences on the American poets of the twentieth century: Emerson for his philosophical perspective; Whitman for his public celebration of the American themes of democracy, idealism, solidarity, equality, and love of nature; Dickinson for her finely discriminating probings of the soul in a spare poetic style, original in its elliptical syntax, its metaphorical daring, and its unconventional rhythm and rhyme.

— Robert DiYanni, Pace University

There are no secrets to success. It is the result of preparation, hard work, and learning from failure.

— Colin Powell

I like thinking big. If you're going to be thinking anything, you might as well think big.

— Donald Trump

We expect to eat and stay thin, to be constantly on the move and ever more neighbourly . . . to revere God and to be God.

— Daniel Boorstin

*Gu, Choki, Pa* [Detail], Judy Pfaff.

# "Hunger in NEW YORK CITY"

### BY SIMON ORTIZ

## About *the* AUTHOR

**Simon Ortiz** (1941– ) was born in New Mexico. After graduating from the University of New Mexico, he attended the University of Iowa Writers' Workshop. He is currently a professor at the University of New Mexico. Widely regarded as one of the country's most important Native-American poets, Ortiz places his focus on language. His poetry is rooted in the ancient oral traditions of the Acoma tribe. To Ortiz, Pueblo oral tradition "embodies the ceremonial, social life that has been kept within the continuum of the Acoma people. It includes advice and counsel, those things told to you by your elders to ensure that you're living responsibly, to ensure that the relationships among family members are correct and according to Acoma ways of life." Ortiz's collections of poetry include *Going for the Rain* (1976), *A Good Journey* (1977), and *Fight Back* (1980).

## About *The* SELECTION

**"Hunger in New York City"** first appeared in *Pembroke Magazine* in 1976 with the title "Hunger in New York." That same year it was published in Ortiz's collection of poetry called *Going for the Rain.* "Hunger in New York City" explores different types of hunger experienced by a Native American far from his native land.

## Literary TOOLS

**REPETITION. Repetition** is a writer's conscious reuse of a sound, word, phrase, sentence, or other element. As you read "Hunger in New York City," notice which words are repeated in the poem.

**PARALLELISM. Parallelism** is a rhetorical technique in which a writer emphasizes the equal value or weight of two or more ideas by expressing them in the same grammatical form. As you read, make a cluster chart to list examples of parallelism in the poem. One example has been done for you.

"or the concrete or the land / or the wind pushing you"

Parallelism

## Reader's *Journal*

For what things have you hungered?

# Hunger in NEW YORK CITY

### SIMON ORTIZ

Hunger crawls into you
from somewhere out of your muscles
or the concrete or the land
or the wind pushing you

*According to the speaker, from where does hunger come?*

5   It comes to you, asking
for food, words, wisdom, young memories
of places you ate at, drank cold spring water,
or held somebody's hand,
or home of the gentle, slow dances,
10  the songs, the strong gods, the world
you know.

That is, hunger searches you out.
It always asks you,
How are you, son? Where are you?

*What does hunger ask?*

15  Have you eaten well?
Have you done what you as a person
of our people is supposed to do?

And the concrete of this city,
the oily wind, the blazing windows,
20  the shrieks of <u>automation</u> cannot,
truly cannot, answer for that hunger
although I have hungered,
truthfully and honestly, for them
to feed myself with.

*What cannot answer for "that hunger"?*

25  So I sang to myself quietly:
I am feeding myself
with the <u>humble</u> presence
of all around me;
I am feeding myself
30  with your soul, my mother earth;
make me cool and humble.
Bless me. ∎

*With what does the speaker feed himself?*

**WORDS FOR EVERYDAY USE**

**au • to • ma • tion** (ô tə ma′ shən) *n.*, technique of making an apparatus, a process, or a system operate automatically. *When factory owners first began using <u>automation</u> to manufacture goods, many workers lost their jobs.*

**hum • ble** (hum′ bəl) *adj.*, reflecting, expressing, or offered in a spirit of deference or submission. *I rehearsed a <u>humble</u> apology to my brother for borrowing his car without permission.*

# INVESTIGATE, Inquire, *Imagine*

## Recall: GATHERING FACTS

1a. For what does the speaker hunger?

2a. Where is the speaker now? What does he say that this place is unable to do? What has he "honestly" tried to do?

3a. In the last stanza, what does the speaker say he is feeding himself with? What does he ask of "mother earth"?

## Interpret: FINDING MEANING

1b. What type of hunger does the speaker experience?

2b. How does the speaker feel about the city? How can you tell he feels this way?

3b. Explain why this food is able to help satisfy the speaker's hunger. How does he feel about nature and the earth?

## Analyze: TAKING THINGS APART

4a. What is revealed in this poem about the speaker's old home and way of life and his new home and way of life? How do these two places and ways of life differ? Which place is familiar? Which is unfamiliar?

## Synthesize: BRINGING THINGS TOGETHER

4b. What characteristically Native American values are revealed in this poem?

## Perspective: LOOKING AT OTHER VIEWS

5a. What might someone who loves urban life say to refute the speaker's negative depiction of the city?

## Empathy: SEEING FROM INSIDE

5b. If you were the speaker in the poem, would you move back home or try to adapt to life in the city? Explain what factors you would weigh in making your decision.

# Understanding *Literature*

REPETITION. Review the definition for **repetition** in the Handbook of Literary Terms. What words are repeated in this poem? Why does the poet repeat these words?

PARALLELISM. Review the definition for **parallelism** in the Handbook of Literary Terms and the graphic organizer you made for Literary Tools on page 949. What example of parallelism do you find in the final stanza? What idea is emphasized by the parallel structure?

# WRITER'S JOURNAL

1. Imagine you are the speaker. Write a **postcard** to a friend in your native land, expressing your feelings about living in New York.

2. Write a **dialogue** in which you interview the speaker about his spiritual beliefs.

3. Write a **poem** about something you have been deprived of that you have hungered for. You may choose to write either a free verse or a rhyming poem.

# Integrating the LANGUAGE ARTS

## Language, Grammar, and Style

**COMMON AND PROPER NOUNS.** Read the Language Arts Survey 3.51, "Common Nouns and Proper Nouns." Then make two lists of the nouns in the sentences below, one headed *Common Nouns* and the other *Proper Nouns.*

1. Simon Ortiz, an Acoma Pueblo of the Southwest, writes about New York City in the poem.

2. The Acomas live about seventy miles west of Albuquerque.

3. A small mesa rises three hundred feet in a vast landscape of low brown mountains and cliffs.

4. On top of this mesa sit the irregular adobe houses of Acoma Pueblo, or the Sky City.

5. According to legend, Masaweh, one of the Divine Twins, led the people up the cliffs to their new home.

## Speaking and Listening

**NONVERBAL COMMUNICATION.** Imagine how the speaker of this poem might look when he is walking down a street in New York. You can tell how he is feeling without his having to say a word because of his use of nonverbal communication. Review the Language Arts Survey 4.1, "Verbal and Nonverbal Communication." Then form groups of four or five students. Each member of your group attempts to convey one of the descriptions below using nonverbal communication.

1. A hungry person watching people dining through the window of a restaurant

2. A tourist enthusiastically exploring the sights of New York City

3. A lost child, alone and frightened in a shopping mall

4. Someone who feels proud of a hard-won accomplishment

5. Someone who fears that his or her misdeed is about to be discovered

## Study and Research & Collaborative Learning

**HUNGER AND HOMELESSNESS.** Working with a partner, do some online research to discover facts about organizations that fight against hunger and homelessness in America. The website of the National Coalition for the Homeless at http://www.nationalhomeless.org is one place to start. Finally, come up with a plan to help the hungry or the homeless where you live.

## "Wingfoot Lake"

BY RITA DOVE

## About the AUTHOR

**Rita Dove** (1952– ) was born in Akron, Ohio, to parents who greatly valued education. She began writing plays and stories at an early age. When a high-school teacher took her to a local writers' conference, she began to consider writing as a career. A high school Presidential Scholar in 1970, she went on to graduate from Miami University in Oxford, Ohio. She won a Fulbright scholarship to study in West Germany in 1974 and later did graduate work at the University of Iowa's Writers' Workshop. Dove has received a Guggenheim, a Lavan Younger Poets award, a Mellon Foundation grant, a Walt Whitman award, and fellowships from the National Endowment for the Arts and the National Endowment for the Humanities. In 1993 she became the first African American to be named poet laureate of the United States, an honor which she stated is "significant in terms of the message it sends about the diversity of our culture and our literature." In 1987, Dove won the Pulitzer Prize for poetry; she was the first AfricanAmerican to do so since Gwendolyn Brooks in 1950.

Dove's poetry collections include *The Yellow House on the Corner* (1980), *Museum* (1983), *Thomas and Beulah* (1986), *Grace Notes* (1989), and *Mother Love* (1995). In addition to her poetry, Dove has also published *Fifth Sunday* (1985), a collection of short stories, and *Through the Ivory Gate* (1992), a novel. Currently Dove teaches English at the University of Virginia in Charlottesville.

## About The SELECTION

"**Wingfoot Lake**" is taken from a collection of poems called *Thomas and Beulah*, which was awarded the Pulitzer Prize in 1987. Loosely based on the lives of Dove's maternal grandparents, the book is divided into two sequences: "Mandolin," devoted to Thomas, and "Canary in Bloom," devoted to Beulah.

"Wingfoot Lake" examines Beulah's life after the death of her husband, Thomas, and refers to the famous Civil Rights march of August 28, 1963, in which more than 250,000 protestors participated.

## Literary TOOLS

**ALLUSION.** An **allusion** is a rhetorical technique in which reference is made to a person, event, object, or work from history or literature. In this poem, Dove makes an oblique allusion to the Civil Rights march of August 28, 1963. As you read, find the lines in which Dove alludes to this historic event.

**CHARACTERIZATION. Characterization** is the use of literary techniques to create a character. Writers use three major techniques to create characters: direct description, portrayal of characters' behavior, and representations of characters' internal states.

## ArtNote

*Church Picnic,* 1988.
Faith Ringgold,
page 954.

The work of Faith Ringgold (1930– ) is indicative of a breakdown in the barrier between crafts and fine art in recent decades. Her paintings are combined with the tradition of the "story quilt" to celebrate African-American life. How does the picnic portrayed in Ringgold's picture on page 954 compare to the one depicted in the poem?

## Reader's Journal

What historic event has influenced you?

*Church Picnic,* 1998. Faith Ringgold. The High Museum, Atlanta, Georgia.

# Wingfoot Lake
## (Independence Day, 1964)

### RITA DOVE

On her 36th birthday, Thomas had shown her
her first swimming pool. It had been
his favorite color, exactly—just
so much of it, the swimmers' white arms <u>jutting</u>

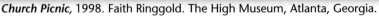

*What does Beulah see for the first time on her thirty-sixth birthday?*

WORDS
FOR
EVERYDAY
USE

**jut** (jut) *vi.,* extend out, up, or forward. *Michael's jaw <u>juts</u> forward.*

into the chevrons[1] of high society.
She had rolled up her window
and told him to drive on, fast.

Now this *act of mercy:* four daughters
dragging her to their husbands' company picnic,
white families on one side and them
on the other, unpacking the same
squeeze bottles of Heinz,[2] the same
waxy beef patties and Salem potato chip bags.
So he was dead for the first time
on Fourth of July—ten years ago

had been harder, waiting for something to happen,
and ten years before that, the girls
like young horses eyeing the track.
Last August she stood alone for hours
in front of the T.V. set
as a crow's wing moved slowly through
the white streets of government.
That brave swimming

scared her, like Joanna saying
*Mother, we're Afro-Americans now!*
What did she know about Africa?
Were there lakes like this one
with a rowboat pushed under the pier?
Or Thomas' Great Mississippi
with its <u>sullen</u> silks? (There was
the Nile[3] but the Nile belonged

to God.) Where she came from
was the past, 12 miles into town
where nobody had locked their back door,
and Goodyear[4] hadn't begun to dream of a park
under the company symbol, a white foot
sprouting two small wings.                    ∎

Where do Beulah's daughters bring her?

What did Beulah watch on TV last August?

What two things scare her?

According to Beulah, where does she come from?

---

1. **chevron.** A sleeve badge, often in the shape of a V, worn frequently in the military. *Chevrons of high society* indicates an elite and privileged group of people.
2. **Heinz.** Brand of catsup
3. **Nile.** Egyptian river
4. **Goodyear.** Tire company with the logo of a winged foot

**WORDS FOR EVERYDAY USE**

**sul • len** (sə′ lən) *adj.,* dull or somber in sound or color. *The <u>sullen</u> notes of the organ filled the congregation with grief.*

What advice would you give to Beulah to help her feel more a part of the present times?

# INVESTIGATE Inquire Imagine

**Recall:** GATHERING FACTS

1a. How old was Beulah when she saw her first swimming pool? What were the swimmers' arms like? What was her reaction to seeing the pool?

2a. Who sits on the other side of the white families at the picnic? What provisions does everyone bring to the picnic? Other than the picnic, what makes this Fourth of July different for Beulah?

3a. What did Beulah watch last August? What two things scare her? What does she wonder about Africa? Where does she believe she came from? What symbol does she notice?

→ **Interpret:** FINDING MEANING

1b. How did Beulah feel when she saw the white people swimming in the pool? How do you know she felt this way?

2b. Why do you think the fact that everyone brings the same food is pointed out in the poem? Does Beulah truly consider her daughters' bringing her to the picnic an "act of mercy"?

3b. What is Beulah scared of? What does her past represent? What does the Goodyear symbol represent?

**Analyze:** TAKING THINGS APART

4a. Identify how Beulah feels about her dead husband, her daughters, and her position in society.

→ **Synthesize:** BRINGING THINGS TOGETHER

4b. To what would you attribute Beulah's remembrance of her husband and her unwillingness to change?

**Perspective:** LOOKING AT OTHER VIEWS

5a. Imagine that you are the daughter who said "we're Afro-Americans now!" How do you see your mother? How do you see yourself?

→ **Empathy:** SEEING FROM INSIDE

5b. If you were Beulah, what would you object to in American society of the 1960s? How would you explain your lack of involvement in the Civil Rights movement?

# Understanding Literature

ALLUSION. Review the definition for **allusion** in the Handbook of Literary Terms. In which lines does Dove allude to the historic Civil Rights march of August 28, 1963? What is the significance of Dove setting this poem on the Fourth of July?

CHARACTERIZATION. Review the definition for **characterization** in the Handbook of Literary Terms. Does Dove use direct description, portrayal of the character's behavior, or representations of the character's internal states to depict Beulah?

# WRITER'S JOURNAL

1. Write a **greeting card** to commemorate the anniversary of the Civil Rights march on Washington.

2. Imagine you are one of Beulah's daughters. Write a personal **proclamation** stating the rights you want as an African American.

3. Write a **journal entry** about the first time you learned about an incident of discrimination because of race, sex, or religion. This might be a personal experience, an event you witnessed, something you read about, or something you heard on the news.

# Integrating *the* LANGUAGE ARTS

## Language, Grammar, and Style

**AGREEMENT OF PRONOUNS AND ANTECEDENTS.** Read the Language Arts Survey 3.45, "Getting Pronouns and Antecedents to Agree." Rewrite each sentence below to make every italicized pronoun agree with its antecedent. Circle the antecedent.

1. In the United States all people want *his* civil rights guaranteed in the Constitution.

2. After the Civil Rights Acts of 1866, 1870, 1871, and 1875, African Americans thought *her* freedoms were closer to the rights of whites.

3. Several states passed *its* own civil rights laws.

4. According to *her* wishes, President Lyndon Baines Johnson signed the most comprehensive civil rights legislation to date, the Civil Rights Act of 1964.

5. The Supreme Court was firm in *their* decision to desegregate public schools.

## Collaborative Learning

**TIME LINE.** With a partner, read the rest of *Thomas and Beulah*, the collection of poems from which "Wingfoot Lake" is taken. One person can read the section about Thomas; the other person can read the section about Beulah. Then make a time line, chronicling events in Thomas and Beulah's lives. Be sure to include the Civil Rights march on Washington and the Fourth of July picnic in your time line.

## Study and Research

**CIVIL RIGHTS MOVEMENT.** Research an aspect of the Civil Rights movement, such as the march on Washington, civil rights legislation, Rosa Parks, Martin Luther King, Jr., or Malcolm X. Then write a short composition summarizing what you have learned. Before you begin writing, read the Language Arts Survey 5.43, "Paraphrasing, Summarizing, and Quoting."

## Literary TOOLS

**IRONY.** **Irony** is a difference between appearance and reality. In *irony of situation,* an event occurs that violates the expectations of the characters, the readers, or the audience. As you read, find two examples of irony of situation.

**IMAGE.** An **image** is language that creates a concrete representation of an object or an experience. As you read, pay attention to the images Mura uses in the poem.

## Art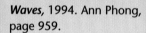Note

**Waves,** 1994. Ann Phong, page 959.

Ann Phong's art references her escape from Vietnam by boat, her life in refugee camps, and her immigration to America, but not in a literal way. As she explains, "Journalistic photos of fleeing, desperate people arouse pity and not pride in their bravery. I am not trying to illustrate my story but to communicate artistically to everybody about the feelings of a community whose voices often are heard in Vietnamese, not English." How does this compare to the way poetry communicates?

## Reader's Journal

When have you empathized with another person's suffering?

# "HUY NGUYEN: Brothers, Drowning Cries"

BY DAVID MURA

## About the AUTHOR

**David Mura** (1952– ) is a *sansei,* a third-generation Japanese American. He writes poetry about the Japanese-American experience, including the internment camps of World War II. After earning a B.A. at Grinnell College in Iowa, Mura went on to pursue graduate work in fine arts at Vermont College and in English at the University of Minnesota.

*After We Lost Our Way,* Mura's first volume of poetry, won the 1989 National Poetry Series Contest. His second volume, *The Colors of Desire* (1995), won the Carl Sandburg Literary Award. Mura has also been awarded an NEA Literature Fellowship and the Pushcart Prize. In the next millennium, Mura has stated that he would like to see the "diversity of America, many different populations and communities. An antidote to the mindlessness and shallowness of the mass media." To actualize this goal, the poet gives readings and speaks on the issues of race and multiculturalism throughout the United States. In addition to being a poet, Mura has written two memoirs, *Turning Japanese: Memoirs of a Sansei* (1991) and *Where the Body Meets Memory: An Odyssey of Race, Sexuality, and Identity* (1996).

## About The SELECTION

**"Huy Nguyen: Brothers, Drowning Cries"** was published in *After We Lost Our Way* (1989). It tells the story of a Vietnamese immigrant, contrasting his old life as a refugee with his new life as a student in the United States. Mura wrote the poem about a student he had in a writing class at the University of Minnesota.

# HUY NGUYEN:
# Brothers,
# Drowning Cries

### David Mura

*Waves,* 1994. Ann Phong. Private Collection.

**1**

Shaking the snow from your hair, bowl-cut
like an immigrant's, you hand me your assignment—
Compare and Contrast. Though your accent stumbles
like my grandfather's, you talk of Faulkner,[1]
*The Sound and the Fury.*[2] You mention Bergson,[3]
whom you've read in French. *Durée.* How the moment lasts.
Your paper opens swimming the Mekong Delta.[4]

*What does the student give the speaker? How does the paper begin?*

**2**

As you lift your face, the sun flashes
down wrinkles of water; blue dragonflies
dart overhead. You hear your brother call.
You go under again, down, down, till you
reach the bottom, a fistful of river clay,
mold a ball in the dark, feel your lungs struggle,
waiting to burst—

      Where is your brother?

*What does the student hear? What does he do?*

Against the current's thick drag, stumble
to shore, the huts of fishermen—
*My brother, my brother's drowned!*
Faces emerge from black doorways,
puzzled, trotting towards you, then
all of them running to the river,
diving and searching the bottom
not for clay but flesh,

*Where does the student seek help?*

and there the man
crawls up on the beach, your brother
slumped over his shoulder, bouncing up
and down as the man runs up and down,
water belching from your brother's mouth
but no air, no air: flings
your brother to the ground, bends,
puts mouth to your brother's lips,
blows in, blows out, until your brother's
chest expands once, once, and once,
and his eyes flutter open, not yet back
in this world, not yet recognizing the blue

*What is wrong with the student's brother? Who resuscitates him?*

---

1. **Faulkner.** William Faulkner (1897–1962), an American novelist who won the Nobel Prize for literature in 1950
2. *The Sound and the Fury.* Novel by Faulkner
3. **Bergson.** Henri-Louis Bergson, a French philosopher who won the Nobel Prize for literature in 1927. Bergson wrote that although we measure time in terms of minutes and hours, in reality we perceive it as duration (*durée* in French), a continuous flow, not divisible or measurable. In our minds, one moment—or one minute, hour, or day—can last forever.
4. **Mekong Delta.** Mouth of the Mekong River, which flows south from China into South Vietnam and empties into the South China Sea

of the sky, that your people see as happiness,
even happier than the sun.

3

Five years since you drifted on the South China Sea,[5]
and the night Thai[6] pirates sliced your wife's finger for
a ring, then beat you senseless. You woke to a merchant ship
passing in silence, as if a <u>mirage</u> were shouting for help.
Later, in that camp in Bataan,[7] loudspeakers told
of a boat broken on an island <u>reef,</u> and the survivors
<u>thrashing</u> through the waves, the tide pulling out,
and the girl who reached the shore and watched
the others, one by one, fall from starvation,
as she drank after each rain from shells on the beach.
At last only her brother remained, his eyes staring
upwards at the wind and the sun, calling her name . . .
The camp went silent, then a baby, a woman sobbing.
And you knew someone was saved to tell the story.

4

Now, through Saigon,[8] your mother carries kettles of soup to
    sell at dawn.
While <u>malaria</u> numbs your brother's limbs, he shivers on a
    cot in prison.
You write: "I wait for his death. Safe. Fat. World away." I
    red mark your English.
There was a jungle you fought in. There's a scar above your wrist.
A boy dives, splashes and, going down, clutches his stomach
    and twists.
You're at the bus stop by Target.[9] Snow still falling, a fine
    blown mist. ■

> Where does the student go next? What happens to his wife? to him?

> What disastrous story does the student hear at the camp in Bataan?

> What is happening to the student's mother and brother in Vietnam?

---

5. **South China Sea.** Body of water enclosed by Southeast China,
Taiwan, the Philippines, Indochina, Malaysia, and Borneo
6. **Thai.** From Thailand, a country in southeast Asia
7. **Bataan.** Peninsula in the Philippines
8. **Saigon.** Saigon was the capital of South Vietnam until the North
Vietnamese captured the city in 1975, at the end of the Vietnam War.
After Vietnam was reunified in 1976, Saigon was renamed Ho Chi
Minh City. That the author refers to the city by its old name indicates
that this section of the poem is probably set during the Vietnam War.
9. **Target.** Chain of discount department stores

**WORDS FOR EVERYDAY USE**

**mi • rage** (mə räzh′) n., optical effect sometimes seen at sea, in the desert, or over hot pavement; an illusion. *The soldier of the Foreign Legion thought he saw an oasis in the distance, but it was only a <u>mirage</u>.*

**reef** (rēf) n., chain of rocks or ridge of sand at or near the surface of the water. *Divers explore the coral <u>reef</u> off the Australian coast.*

**thrash** (thrash) vi., move or stir about violently. *The feverish patient <u>thrashed</u> about in his sleep.*

**ma • lar • ia** (mə ler′ ē a) n., disease transmitted by mosquitoes that is characterized by attacks of chills and fever. *During the construction of the Panama Canal, many workers died of <u>malaria</u>.*

If you were the student, what would you do to help your mother and brother back in Vietnam?

# INVESTIGATE Inquire, *Imagine*

**Recall:** GATHERING FACTS

1a. What is the relationship between the speaker and the immigrant? What details reveal that the immigrant is relatively new to the United States?

2a. What events does the student describe in his paper?

3a. What does the student reveal has become of his family in Saigon?

**Interpret:** FINDING MEANING

1b. How does the speaker feel about the immigrant student? What evidence do you find to support your opinion?

2b. In what way is the story heard in Bataan similar to the student's own story about his brother?

3b. How does the student feel about what is happening to his brother?

**Analyze:** TAKING THINGS APART

4a. How does the student perceive his homeland?

**Synthesize:** BRINGING THINGS TOGETHER

4b. Explain why the poem is called "Huy Nguyen: Brothers, Drowning Cries." In what way are the two brothers drowning?

**Evaluate:** MAKING JUDGMENTS

5a. This poem is about what the student wrote for a comparison and contrast essay. Based on what is revealed in the poem, evaluate whether the student's essay is effective.

**Extend:** CONNECTING IDEAS

5b. People who have lived through traumatic experiences in which others are hurt or die are sometimes afflicted with a condition known as "survivor's guilt." It is the feeling that one doesn't deserve to have escaped the fate that others suffered. Explain whether or not this term accurately describes what the student is experiencing.

# Understanding *Literature*

**IRONY.** Review the definition for **irony** in the Handbook of Literary Terms. What are two examples of *irony of situation* in the poem?

**IMAGE.** Review the definition for **image** in the Handbook of Literary Terms. Make a chart listing the images you find in the poem. Choose a vivid image of the student's new life in the United States and a vivid image of his old life in Vietnam. In what ways are they different?

| Sight | Sound | Touch | Taste | Smell |
|-------|-------|-------|-------|-------|
| Shaking the snow from your hair | | | | |

# WRITER'S JOURNAL

1. Imagine that you are the speaker who gave the comparison and contrast assignment. Write a **note** to the student, explaining how you reacted to his story and whether he completed the assignment well.

2. Imagine that you are the student in this poem. Write a **letter** to your brother in prison, telling about your new life in the United States and expressing how you feel about him.

3. Write a **short essay** comparing and contrasting two experiences in your life.

# Integrating *the* LANGUAGE ARTS

## Language, Grammar, and Style

USING COLORFUL NOUNS, VERBS, AND MODIFIERS. Read the Language Arts Survey 3.39, "Adding Colorful Language to Sentences." Then rewrite the sentences below, using colorful nouns, verbs, and modifiers.

1. Huy Nguyen turned in the paper.
2. He was from Vietnam.
3. There was a war in Vietnam and he had to get out.
4. He went through a lot of dangerous things before he could get away.
5. The teacher was sad when he learned about the student's life.

## Applied English & Media Literacy

LETTER-WRITING CAMPAIGN. In this poem, the student's brother is imprisoned in Vietnam. During the Vietnam War and in the postwar years, many Vietnamese were held as prisoners for their political beliefs. Groups such as Amnesty International ask people to write letters to free political prisoners. Information about their letter-writing campaigns can be found on their website at http://www.amnesty.org. Choose a campaign that you believe in and write a letter to support it. You might want to review the Language Arts Survey 6.5, "Writing a Business Letter," before you write your letter.

## Media Literacy & Speaking and Listening

REFUGEE STORIES. Research the stories of refugees in the news on the Internet or interview refugees in your community. The following are some basic research questions to investigate. What country did the refugees escape from? Why did they escape? Where did they go? How hard was their journey? What kind of life did they want in their adopted land? Then compare and contrast the experiences of these refugees with that of the student in the poem. Share your findings with the class.

# Literary
# T O O L S

**FREE VERSE. Free verse**, or *vers libre*, is poetry that avoids use of regular rhyme, meter, or division into stanzas. As you read, consider whether or not "Celestial Music" is an example of free verse.

**OBJECTIVE CORRELATIVE.** An **objective correlative** is a group of images that together create a particular emotion in the reader. As you read, make a cluster chart describing the images in the poem. One example has been done for you.

```
  ┌─────────────┐
  │ a caterpillar │
  │ dying in the  │
  │     dirt      │
  └─────────────┘
         \
          ┌──────────┐
          │  Images  │
          └──────────┘
```

# Reader's
## *Journal*

How have you overcome a moment of fear or timidity?

## *"Celestial Music"*

### BY LOUISE GLÜCK

# About *the*
# A U T H O R

**Louise Glück** (1943– ) was born in New York City and attended Sarah Lawrence College and Columbia University. Widely considered one of America's finest contemporary poets, Glück won the National Book Critics Circle Award for Poetry in 1985 and the Pulitzer Prize in 1993. She has received grants from the Rockefeller Foundation, the National Endowment for the Arts, and the Guggenheim Foundation.

Glück's poems, while appearing autobiographical, focus on larger human issues such as gender, nature, and family life. Her composed, reflective, often resounding disclosure of these issues gives much of her poetry a dark and unearthly tone. According to Glück, what keeps a poem alive "is not fixed discovery but the means to discovery." What attracts her to a poem is "a sense of speech issuing in the moment from a specific identifiable voice." Glück's collections of poetry include *Firstborn* (1968), *The House on Marshland* (1975), *Descending Figure* (1980), *The Triumph of Achilles* (1985), *Ararat* (1990), *The Wild Iris* (1992), and *Meadowlands* (1996). In addition to her volumes of verse, Glück has published a series of essays on poetry called *Proofs and Theories* (1994). Currently, she teaches English at Williams College in Massachusetts.

# About *the*
# S E L E C T I O N

**"Celestial Music,"** published in *Ararat* (1990), focuses on the speaker's attempt to understand the beauty and significance of ordinary things. The speaker's movement between dream and reality demonstrates Glück's ability to formulate the ordinary into something imaginative and unearthly.

# Celestial Music

## LOUISE GLÜCK

I have a friend who still believes in heaven.
Not a stupid person, yet with all she knows, she literally talks
     to god,
she thinks someone listens in heaven.
On earth, she's usually <u>competent</u>.
Brave, too, able to face unpleasantness.

> What do the speaker and
> her friend find in the dirt?

We found a caterpillar dying in the dirt, greedy ants crawling
     over it.
I'm always moved by weakness, by disaster, always eager to
     oppose <u>vitality.</u>
But timid, also, quick to shut my eyes.
Whereas my friend was able to watch, to let events play out
according to nature. For my sake, she intervened,
brushing a few ants off the torn thing, and set it down
     across the road.

My friend says I shut my eyes to god, that nothing else
     explains
my aversion to reality. She says I'm like the child who buries
     her head in the pillow
so as not to see, the child who tells herself
that light causes sadness—
My friend is like the mother. Patient, urging me
to wake up an adult like herself, a courageous person—

---

**WORDS FOR EVERYDAY USE**

**com • pe • tent** (käm′ pə tənt) *adj.*, properly qualified; capable. *Because he is a <u>competent</u> driver, Jeff passed his driver's test on his first try.*

**vi • tal • i • ty** (vī ta′ lə tē) *n.*, capacity to live and develop. *The vitamin ad promises the vitamins will add <u>vitality</u> to your life.*

In my dreams, my friend <u>reproaches</u> me. We're walking
on the same road, except it's winter now;
she's telling me that when you love the world you hear <u>celestial</u>
    music:
look up, she says. When I look up, nothing.
Only clouds, snow, a white business in the trees
like brides leaping to a great height—
Then I'm afraid for her; I see her
caught in a net deliberately cast over the earth—

In reality, we sit by the side of the road, watching the sun set;
from time to time, the silence pierced by a birdcall.
It's the moment we're both trying to explain, the fact
that we're at ease with death, with solitude.
My friend draws a circle in the dirt; inside, the caterpillar
    doesn't move.
She's always trying to make something whole, something
    beautiful, an image
capable of life apart from her.
We're very quiet. It's peaceful sitting here, not speaking, the
    composition
fixed, the road turning suddenly dark, the air
going cool, here and there the rocks shining and glittering—
it's this stillness that we both love.
The love of form is a love of endings. ∎

> *According to the friend, what do you hear when you love the world?*

**WORDS FOR EVERYDAY USE**

**re • proach** (ri prōch′) *vt.*, express disappointment in or displeasure with someone for conduct that is blameworthy or in need of amendment. *Dad <u>reproached</u> me for not doing the dishes after I made an omelette.*

**ce • les • tial** (sə les′ chəl) *adj.*, relating to heaven or divinity. *With a proper telescope, you can see many <u>celestial</u> bodies in the night sky.*

# Respond *to the* SELECTION

The speaker says, "The love of form is a love of endings." What endings does the speaker experience?

# Inquire Imagine

**Recall:** GATHERING FACTS

1a. How do the speaker and the friend react to the injured caterpillar?

2a. What does the friend do in the speaker's dream?

3a. What does the friend draw?

➤ **Interpret:** FINDING MEANING

1b. How do the speaker and her friend differ in their attitudes toward life?

2b. Why can't the speaker hear celestial music?

3b. Why does the friend draw the circle?

**Analyze:** TAKING THINGS APART

4a. Identify the change in the speaker at the end of the poem.

➤ **Synthesize:** BRINGING THINGS TOGETHER

4b. How is the speaker able to make this change?

**Perspective:** LOOKING AT OTHER VIEWS

5a. Why does the friend brush a few ants off the torn caterpillar and set it down across the road? Would you be able to watch the ants or prefer to look away?

➤ **Empathy:** SEEING FROM INSIDE

5b. If you were the speaker, would you want to "wake up an adult" like your friend or would you be content to stay the way you are? Explain your answer.

# Understanding Literature

**FREE VERSE.** Review the definition for **free verse** in the Handbook of Literary Terms. How is "Celestial Music" an example of free verse? How is the poem divided? Which stanza discusses the speaker's dream? Which stanzas oppose the dream with reality?

**OBJECTIVE CORRELATIVE.** Review the definition of **objective correlative** in the Handbook of Literary Terms and the graphic organizer you made for Literary Tools on page 964. What images does the poet create? What emotion, or mood, is created by the images in "Celestial Music"? What details in the poem contribute to the creation of this mood?

# WRITER'S JOURNAL

1. Imagine you are the speaker. Write a **journal entry** stating what you faced today and how your friend helped you face it.
2. Write a **character sketch** to describe the speaker and the friend.
3. Stanza 4 relates the speaker's dream. Write a **free verse poem** describing a dream you have had.

# Integrating *the* LANGUAGE ARTS

## Language, Grammar, and Style

**COMMAS.** Read the Language Arts Survey 3.87, "Commas." Then rewrite each sentence, adding commas where needed.

1. The speaker is timid fearful and unrealistic.
2. The friend talks to God faces life's unpleasantness and demonstrates competence.
3. The friend moves the caterpillar and she draws a circle around it.
4. The dream a sequence in which a dialogue takes place points out why the speaker is afraid for her friend.
5. While sitting with her friend during nightfall the speaker thinks how peaceful it is.

## Speaking and Listening & Collaborative Learning

**DIALOGUE.** With a partner, play the roles of the speaker and the friend in "Celestial Music." Discuss the caterpillar event and what it meant to you, your attitudes toward life, and the reason for your friendship.

## Applied English & Critical Thinking

**LETTER TO THE POET.** Write a letter to Louise Glück, explaining your interpretation of her poem. Tell her about the times you have heard celestial music. Before you begin writing, you might find it useful to review the Language Arts Survey 6.5, "Writing a Business Letter."

# "Reassurance"

BY ALLAN GURGANUS

## About the AUTHOR

**Allan Gurganus** (1947– ), novelist, short story writer, and essayist, was born and raised in North Carolina, where he lives today. He attended the University of Pennsylvania and Pennsylvania Academy of Fine Arts, Harvard, and Sarah Lawrence College, where he earned a B.A. During the Vietnam War, Gurganus served in the U.S. Navy.

In Gurganus's *Oldest Living Confederate Widow Tells All* (1989), his most acclaimed work, the character Lucy Marsden tells tales of her ninety-nine years, including her husband's experiences during the Civil War. In 1992, *Oldest Living Confederate Widow* was adapted into a television movie. Gurganus collected eleven of his short stories in *White People* (1991), which explores the place of Caucasians in a changing world. "My subjects embody the heroism still possible in middle-class life," says Gurganus. "If all my comedy and concerns were boiled down to a single word—let that word be 'Ethics.' Twentieth-century chaos makes our every try at kindness comic. From that rich tension, all my tales emerge." Gurganus has also written *Plays Well with Others* (1997) and *Angels Are Among Us* (1999).

## About the SELECTION

**"Reassurance"** takes place during the American Civil War (1861–1865). Section 1 is the complete text of an actual letter written by the American poet Walt Whitman to the mother of a dead Union soldier from Pennsylvania. Casualties were so high during the war that medical facilities were understaffed to treat all of the wounded. Volunteers filled in for nurses in many Union and Confederate hospitals, cleaning and bandaging wounds and assisting during surgery. Whitman was so moved by the suffering he saw that he moved to Washington, DC, to become a nurse in Union hospitals there. He offered conversation and comfort to the wounded and dying and frequently wrote letters to the families of the men he attended. In section 2 the Union soldier, Frank, fictionalized, writes a letter to his mother.

## Literary TOOLS

**STREAM-OF-CONSCIOUSNESS WRITING. Stream-of-consciousness writing** is literary work that attempts to render the flow of feelings, thoughts, and impressions within the minds of characters. As you read, look for examples of stream-of-consciousness writing in "Reassurance."

**REPETITION. Repetition** is a writer's conscious reuse of a sound, word, phrase, sentence, or other element. As you read, make a chart. On the left, write examples of elements that are repeated in the two sections of the story. On the right, explain the significance of the repetition. One example has been done for you.

| Repetition | Significance |
|---|---|
| "I myself liked him very much." | Whitman and Frank express admiration for each other. |

## Reader's Journal

When have you made a decision based on what others thought you should do, rather than following your heart?

Reassurance

*For David Holding Eil (1981–  )*
*and for Robert Langland Eil (1983–  )*

Death of A Pennsylvania Soldier. Frank H. Irwin, company E, 93rd Pennsylvania—died May 1, '65—My letter to his mother.

Dear madam: No doubt you and Frank's friends have heard the sad fact of his death in hospital here, through his uncle, or the lady from Baltimore, who took his things. (I have not seen them, only heard of them visiting Frank.) I will write you a few lines—as a casual friend that sat by his death-bed. Your son, corporal Frank H. Irwin, was wounded near fort Fisher, Virginia, March 25, 1865—the wound was in the left knee, pretty bad. He was sent up to Washington, was receiv'd in ward C, Armory-square hospital, March 28th—the wound became worse, and on the 4th of April the leg was amputated a little above the knee—the operation was perform'd by Dr. Bliss, one of the best surgeons in the army—he did the whole operation himself—there was a good deal of bad matter gather'd—the bullet was found in the knee. For a couple of weeks afterwards he was doing pretty well. I visited and sat by him frequently, as he was fond of having me. The last ten or twelve days of April, I saw that his case was critical. He previously had some fever, with cold spells. The last week in April he was much of the time flighty—but always mild and gentle. He died first of May. The actual cause of death was pyaemia,[1] (the absorption of the matter in the system instead of its discharge). Frank, as far as I saw, had everything requisite in surgical treat-

> *Why does Whitman write to Frank's mother? How does he describe his relationship with Frank?*

> **All the time he was out of his head not one single bad word or idea escaped him.**

ment, nursing &c. He had watches most of the time. He was so good and well-behaved and affectionate, I myself liked him very much. I was in the habit of coming in afternoons and sitting by him, and soothing him, and he liked to have me—liked to put his arm out and lay his hand on my knee—would keep it so a long while. Toward the last he was more restless and flighty at night—often fancied himself with his regiment—by this talk sometimes seem'd as if his feelings were hurt by being blamed by his officers for something he was entirely innocent of—said, "I never in my life was thought capable of such a thing, and never was." At other times he would fancy himself talking as it seem'd to children or such like, his relatives I suppose, and giving them good advice; would talk to them a long while. All the time he was out of his head not one single bad word or idea escaped him. It was remark'd that many a man's conversation in his senses was not half as good as Frank's delirium. He seem'd quite willing to die—he had become very weak and had suffer'd a good deal, and was perfectly resign'd, poor boy. I do not know his past life, but I feel as if it must have been good. At any rate what I saw of him here, under the most trying of circumstances, with a painful wound, and among strangers, I can say that he behaved so brave, so composed, and so sweet and

> *What things did Whitman do for Frank?*

> *What things did Frank speak about in his delirium?*

> *How does Whitman describe Frank's behavior?*

---

1. **pyaemia.** Form of blood poisoning by pus

---

**WORDS FOR EVERYDAY USE**

**req • ui • site** (reʹ kwə zət) *adj.*, essential; necessary. *Callie took the requisite number of classes and graduated on time.*

**de • lir • i • um** (di lirʹ ē əm) *n.*, a mental disturbance characterized by confusion, disordered speech, and hallucinations. *In his delirium Alonzo thought he was in Mexico instead of a California hospital.*

affectionate, it could not be surpass'd. And now like many other noble and good men, after serving his country as a soldier, he has <u>yielded</u> up his young life at the very outset in her service. Such things are gloomy—yet there is a text, "God doeth all things well"—the meaning of which, after due time, appears to the soul.

I thought perhaps a few words, though from a stranger, about your son, from one who was with him at the last, might be worth while—for I loved the young man, though I but saw him immediately to lose him. I am merely a friend visiting the hospitals occasionally to cheer the wounded and the sick.

> W.W.

2.

Dear Mother, It's Frank here, hoping a last time to reach you, and doubting I can but still I'm really going to try, ma'am. I want you to put your mind at rest about it all, Momma. That is why I am working hard to slip this through. You must really listen if this gets by the <u>censors</u> and everything, because I have limited time and fewer words than I'd like. I would dearly love to be there soon for breakfast and see that cussed little Wilkie come downstairs grumping like he always does till he's got a touch of coffee in him. I would even like to hear the Claxtons' roosters sounding off again. I remember Poppa, God rest him, saying as how other men kept hens for eggs but the Claxtons kept roosters for their noise and it was our ill luck to draw such fools as neighbors! The old man that wrote you of my end had the finest gray-white beard and finest-speaking voice I ever met with, finer even than parson Brookes we set such store by. The man who

> **Cold can be good. If you hurt enough, cold can be so good.**

Why does Frank write his mother?

wrote you was here most days after lunch, even ones I now recall but parts of. He brought ward C our first lilacs in late April, great purple ones he stuck into a bedpan near my pillow. Their smell worked better on me than the laudanum[2] that our Army chemists were so sadly out of.

He read to us from Scripture and once, my hand resting on his safe-feeling leg, I asked him for a ditty and he said one out that sounded fine like Ecclesiastes[3] but concerned our present war, my war. I told him it was good and asked him who had wrote it and he shrugged and smiled, he nodded along the double row of cots set in our tent here, like showing me that every wounded fellow'd had a hand in setting down the poem. He was so pleasing-looking and kind-spoken and affectionate, I myself liked him very much. Ice cream he brought us more than once—a bigger vat of it I've never seen, not even at the Bucks County Fair. Him and our lady nurses kept making funny jokes, bringing around the great melting buckets of it and the spoons and he himself shoveled a good bit of it into my <u>gullet</u>, grateful it felt all the way down. "Now for some brown." He gave me samples. "Now pink, but best for you is this, Frank. You've heard Mrs. Howe's line 'in the beauty of the lilies Christ was born across the sea'? This vanilla's that white, white as your arm here. Makes vanilla cool the deepest, my brave Pennsylvania youth." How I ate it. Cold can be good. If you hurt enough, cold can be so good. Momma? I do not love Lavinia like I forever said. I do not know how I got into being so mistruthful.

---

2. **laudanum.** Pain medication containing opium
3. **Ecclesiastes.** Book of the Old Testament, attributed to Solomon

---

**WORDS FOR EVERYDAY USE**

**yield** (yē[ə]ld) *vt.*, give or render as fitting, rightfully owed, or required. *Karen <u>yielded</u> her place in line to the elderly woman who walked with a cane.*

**cen • sor** (sen[t]′ sər) *n.*, official (as in wartime) who reads communications (as letters) and deletes material considered sensitive or harmful. *The <u>censor</u> deleted the platoon's location that the private had mentioned in his letter home.*

**gul • let** (gə′ lət) *n.*, throat. *"How many more tacos are you going to shove down your <u>gullet</u>?" Tom asked Brad.*

Maybe it was how her poppa was Mayor and I liked the idea of pleasing you with our family's possible new station or how everybody spoke of Miss Lavinia's attainments[4] and her skills at hostessing. It is my second cousin Emily I loved and love. She knew and knows, and it was just like Em to bide[5] that. Em met whatever gaze I sent her with a quiet wisdom that shamed and flattered me, the both. Once at the Fourth of July picnic where the Claxtons' rowboat exploded from carrying more firecrackers than the *Merrimac*[6] safely could, I noticed Emily near Doanes' Mill Creek gathering French lilacs for to decorate our picnic quilt later. You were bandaging Wilkie's foot where he stepped on a nail after you told him he must wear shoes among that level of fireworks but he didn't. I wandered down where Emily stood. She had a little silver pair of scissors in her skirt's pocket and I recall remarking how like our Em that was, how homely and prepared and how like you she was that way, Momma. She was clipping flowers when I drew up. I commenced shivering, that fearful of my feelings for her after everybody on earth seemed to think Lavinia had decided on me long-since. "Frank," Emily said. I spoke her name and when she heard how I said hers out, she stopped in trimming a heavy branch of white blooms (for, you know that place by the waterwheel where there are two bushes, one white, one purple, grown up side by side together and all mixed?). Emily's hands were still among the flowers when she looked back over her shoulder at me. Tears were in her eyes but not falling, just held in place and yet I saw the light on their water tremble with each pulse from her. It was then, Momma, I understood she knew my truest feelings, all.

"Why is it we're cousins and both poor?" I asked her. "Why could it not be just a little different so

What does Frank admit he has been untruthful about? Whom does he really love?

things'd fall into place for us more, why, Emily?" And she lifted one shoulder and turned her head aside. She half-fell into the sweet bushes then, white and green and purple, but caught herself and looked away from me. Em finally spoke but I half-heard with all the Roman candles going off and Wilkie bawling. She said quiet, looking out toward water through the beautiful branches, "We will always know, Frank, you and me will. Hearing as how you understand it, that already gives me so much, Frank. Oh, if you but guessed how it strengthens me just to say your name at night, Frank, Franklin Horatio Irwin, Jr., how I love to say it out, sir." Lavinia was calling that same name but different and I turned, fearful of being caught here by her, me unfaithful to the one that loved me if not strongest then loudest, public-like. "Excuse me, Cousin Emily," said I, and walked off and then soon after got mustered[7] in, then snagged the minie[8] that costs the leg then the rest of it, me, and no one knowing my real heart. Mother? I never even kissed her. Momma? Treat her right. Accord my cousin Emily such tender respects as befit the young widow of a man my age, for she is that to me, and not Lavinia that made such a show at the funeral and is ordering more styles of black crepe from a Boston catalogue even now, Momma. Have Emily to dinner often as you can afford it, and encourage her to look around at other boys, for there's not much sense in wasting two lives, mine and hers, for my own cowardly mistakes. That is one thing needs saying out.

I used to speak to my bearded visitor about brother Wilkie and all of you and I thought up things I'd tell my kid brother who has so bad a temper but is funny throughout. I'd want Wilkie to be brave and not do what the town

What stands in the way of Frank's and Emily's love for each other?

---

4. **attainments.** Acquired skills; accomplishments
5. **bide.** Accept the consequences of; tolerate
6. *Merrimac.* Iron-clad Confederate ship
7. **mustered.** Enrolled formally, as into the military
8. **minie** or **minié** (min' ē or mi nē ā'). Cone-shaped rifle bullet used in the nineteenth century

said he should, like pay court on a girl who's snooty and bossy just because of who her kin is and their grand home. I would tell Wilkie to hide in a cave and not sign up like I did, with the bands and drums and the setting off of all fireworks not burned up in the Claxtons' <u>calamity</u> rowboat—but, boy, it sure did look pretty going down, didn't it, Momma? My doctor took some time and pains with me and, near the end, got like Lavinia in telling me how fine a looking young man I was. That never pleased me much since I didn't see it all that clear myself and had not personally earned it and so felt a little guilty on account, not that any of it matters now. The Lady from Baltimore combed my hair and said nice things and I am sorry that she never got the watch and the daguerrotypes[9] to you. She is a confidence artist[10] who makes tours of hospitals, promising to take boys' valuables home but never does and sells them in the shops. Still, at the time, I trusted her, her voice was so refined and hands real soft and brisk and I felt good for days after she left, believing Wilkie'd soon have Poppa's gold watch in hand, knowing it had been with me at the end.

Just before they shot me, Momma, I felt scared to where I considered, for one second, running. No one ever knew of this but I must tell you now because just thinking on my failing cost me many inward <u>tribulations</u> at the last. "I could jump out of this hole and run into that woods and hide and then take off forever." So the dreadful plan rushed forth, and then how I stifled it, choked practically. I never in my life was thought capable of even thinking such a thing, and here I'd said it to myself! Then, like as

punishment, not six minutes after looking toward that peaceful-seeming woods, I moved to help another fellow from Bucks County (Ephraim's second cousin, the youngest Otis boy from out New Hope way) and felt what first seemed a earthquake that'd knocked the entire battle cockeyed but that narrowed to a nearby complaint known just as the remains of my left leg. It felt numb till twenty minutes later when I seriously noticed. It takes that kind of time sometimes to feel. It takes a delay between the ending and knowing what to say of that, which is why this reaches you six weeks after my kind male nurse's news, ma'am. I asked him once why he'd quit the newspaper business to come visit us, the gimps[11] and bullet-catchers, us lost causes.

> When did Frank's letter reach his mother?

He leaned nearer and admitted a secret amusement: said he was, from among the thousands of Northern boys and Reb prisoners he'd seen, recasting Heaven. Infantry angels, curly-headed all. "And Frank," said he, "I don't like to tease you with the suspense but it's between you and two other fellows, a three-way heat for the Archangel Gabriel." I laughed, saying as how the others had my blessings for that job just yet. He kept close by me during the amputation part especially. They said that if the leg was taken away, then so would all my troubles go. And I trusted them, Momma. And everybody

> ## They said that if the leg was taken away, then so would all my troubles go.

---

9. **daguerrotypes.** Early photographs made on light-sensitive silver-coated metallic plates and developed with mercury vapor
10. **confidence artist.** Swindler who gains the confidence of the victim in order to cheat him or her
11. **gimps.** Lame or crippled persons

---

**WORDS FOR EVERYDAY USE**

ca • lam • i • ty (kə laʹ mə tē) *n.*, extraordinarily grave event marked by great loss and lasting distress and affliction. *"Due to the <u>calamity</u>, we will have to completely rebuild the school," said the chair of the school board.*

trib • u • la • tion (tri byə laʹ shən) *n.*, distress or suffering resulting from oppression or persecution. *The Kosovars recounted their <u>tribulations</u> to the foreign press, who told the world about the systematic ethnic cleansing they had witnessed.*

explained and was real courteous and made the person feel manly like the loss of the leg could be his choice and would I agree? "Yes," I said.

My doctor's name was Dr. Bliss and during the cutting of my leg, others kept busting into the tent, asking him stuff and telling him things and all calling him by name, Bliss, Bliss, Bliss, they said. It helped me to have that name and word drifting over the table where they worked on me so serious, and I thanked God neither you nor Emily would be walking in to see me spread out like that, so bare and held down helpless, like some boy. Afterwards, my friend the nurse trained me to pull the covers back, he taught me I must learn to look at it now. But I couldn't bear to yet. They'd tried but I had wept when asked to stare below at the lonely left knee. It'd been "left" all right! Walt (my nurse's name was Walt) he said we would do it together. He held my hand and counted then— one, two, three . . . I did so with him and it was like looking at what was there and what was not at once, just as my lost voice is finding you during this real dawn, ma'am. He told me to cheer up, that it could've been my right leg and only later did I see he meant that as a little joke and I worried I had let him down by not catching on in time. I have had bad thoughts, lustful thoughts and evil. I fear I am yet a

**What does Frank confess to his mother?**

vain person and always have been secretly, Momma. You see, I fretted how it'd be to live at home and go downtown on crutches and I knew Lavinia's plan would change with me a cripple. Lavinia would not like that. And even after everything, I didn't know if I could choose Emily, a seamstress after all, over so grand a place on Summit Avenue as the Mayor'd already promised Lavinia and me (it was the old Congers mansion, Momma).

It seems to me from here that your Frank has cared way too much for how others saw him. It was Poppa's dying early that made me want to do so much and seem so grown and that made me join up when you had your doubts, I know.

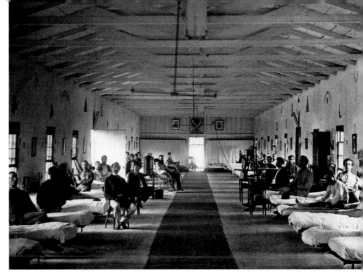

Civil War soldiers' hospital.

You were ever strict with me but I really would've turned out all right in the end . . . if it hadn't been for this.

Momma, by late April, I could feel the bad stuff moving up from the leg's remains, like some type of chemical, a kind of night or little army set loose in me and taking all the early lights out, one by one, lamp by lamp, farm by farm, house by house it seemed. The light in my head, don't laugh, was the good crystal lantern at your oilclothed kitchen table. That was the final light I worried for—and knew, when that went, it all went. But, through chills and talking foolish sometimes, I tried keeping that one going, tried keeping good parts separate, saved back whole. I felt like if I could but let you hear me one more time, it'd ease you some. Your sleeping so poorly since . . . that's just not like you, Ma, and grieves me here.

Dying at my age is an embarrassment, on top of everything else! It was just

**How does Frank view his death?**

one shot in the knee, but how could I have stopped it when it started coming up the body toward the last light in the kitchen in the head? You told me not to enlist—you said, as our household's one breadwinner, I could stay home. But the braided uniform

**What had Frank's mother urged him not to do?**

and the party that Lavinia promised tipped me over. Fevered, I imagined talking to Wilkie and all the younger cousins lined up on our front porch's seven steps, and me wagging my finger and striding to and fro in boots like our Lt.'s beautiful English leather boots, such as I never owned in life. I talked bold and I talked grand and imagined Emily was in the shady house with you, and beside you, listening, approving my sudden wisdom that'd come on me with the suffering, and on account of the intestine cramps, and after the worst <u>convulsion</u> Walt got me through, still that lead was coming up the thigh into my stomach then greeting and seizing the chest and then more in the throat and that was about all of it except for the great gray beard and those knowing eyes that seemed to say Yes Yes, Frank, even to my need to be done with it, the pain (the last white pain of it, I do not mind telling you, was truly something, Momma). I couldn't have held out much longer anyway, and the idea of choosing between my two loves, plus living on a crutch for life, it didn't set right with vain me.

This I am telling you should include that I hid the five-dollar gold piece I won for the History Prize at the Academy commencement up inside the hollowed left head-post of my bedstead. Get Wilkie to go upstairs with you and help lift the whole thing off the floor and out the coin will fall. Use it for you and Emily's clothes. Bonnets might be nice with it. Buy nothing but what's extra, that is how I want it spent. I should've put it in your hand before I left, but I planned to purchase my getting-home gifts out of that, and never thought I wouldn't. Selfish, keeping it squirreled back and without even guessing. But then maybe all people are vain. Maybe it's not just your Frank, right?

If you wonder at the color you are seeing now, Momma, the pink-red like our fine conch shell on the parlor's hearth, you are seeing the backs of your own eyelids, Momma. You will soon hear the Claxtons' many crowers set up their alarum[12] yet again and will catch a clinking that is McBride's milk wagon pulled by Bess, who knows each house on old McBride's route. Your eyes are soon to open on your room's whitewash and July's yellow light in the dear place. You will wonder at this letter of a dream, ma'am and, waking, will look toward your bedside table and its often-unfolded letter from the gentleman who told you of my passing. His letter makes this one possible. For this is a letter toward your loving Franklin Horatio Irwin, Jr., not only from him. It is your voice finding ways to smoothe your mind. This is for letting you get on with what you have to tend, Momma. You've always known I felt Lavinia to be well-meaning but right silly, and that our sensible and deep Emily was truly meant as mine from her and my's childhoods onward. You've guessed where the coin is stowed, as you did ever know such things, but have held back on account of honoring the privacy even of me dead. Go fetch it later today, and later today spend it on luxuries you could not know otherwise. This is the rich echo that my bearded nurse's voice allows. It is mostly you. And when the pink-and-red opens, and morning's here already, take your time in dressing, go easy down the stairs, let Wilkie doze a little longer than he should and build a fire and start a real big breakfast. Maybe even use the last of Poppa's maple syrup we tapped that last winter he was well. Use it up and then get going on things, new things, hear? That is the wish of your loving eldest son, Frank. That is the wish of the love of your son Frank who is

*Whose voice writes the letter?*

_____

12. **alarum.** Alarm

WORDS FOR EVERYDAY USE

**con • vul • sion** (kən vəl' shən) *n.*, abnormal, violent and involuntary contraction or series of contractions of the muscles. *The <u>convulsions</u> of the customer scared the server, who had never seen an epileptic seizure.*

no deader than anything else that ever lived so hard and wanted so so much, Mother.

Something holy will stand before you soon, ma'am. Cleave[13] to that. Forget me. Forget me by remembering me. Imagine what a boy like me would give now for but one more breakfast (ever my favorite meal—I love how it's most usually the same) and even Wilkie's crabbiness early, or the Claxtons' rooster house going off everywhichway like their rowboat did so loud. I know that you know, ma'am, and what you doubt, and so do you: but be at peace in this: Everything you suspect about your missing boy is true. So, honor your dear earned civilian life. Nights, sleep sounder. Be contained. In fifty seconds you will refind waking and the standing light. Right away you'll feel better, without knowing why or even caring much. You will seem to be filling, brimming with this secret rushing-in of comfort, ma'am. Maybe like some bucket accustomed to a mean purpose—say, a hospital slop pail—but one suddenly asked to offer wet life to lilacs unexpected here. Or maybe our dented well bucket out back, left daily under burning sun and daily polished by use and sandy winds, a bucket that's suddenly dropped far beneath even being beneath the ground and finally striking a stream below all usual streams and one so dark and sweet and ice-cream cold, our bucket sinks it is so full, Mother. Your eyes will open and what you'll bring to light, ma'am, is that fine clear over-sloshing vessel. Pulled back. Pulled back up to light. Be refreshed. Feel how my secrets and your own (I know a few of yours too, ma'am,

**Forget me. Forget me by remembering me.**

*What does Frank wish for his mother?*

oh yes I do) are pooling here, all mixed now, cool, and one.

I am not the ghost of your dead boy. I am mostly you. I am just your love for him, left stranded so unnaturally alive—a common enough miracle. And such fineness as now reaches you in your half-sleep is just the echo of your own best self. Which is very good.

Don't give all your credit to your dead. Fineness stays so steady in you, ma'am, and keeps him safe, keeps him lit continually. It's vain of Frank but he is now asking: could you, and Wilkie and Em, please hold his spot for him for just a little longer? Do . . . And Mother? Know I rest. Know that I am in my place here. I feel much easement, Ma, in having heard you say this to yourself.

There, worst worrying's done. Here accepting it begins.

All right. Something holy now stands directly before you. How it startles, waiting so bright at the foot of your iron bedstead. Not to shy away from it. I will count to three and we will open on it, please. Then we'll go directly in, like, hand-in-hand, we're plunging. What waits is what's still yours, ma'am, which is ours.

—Such brightness, see? It is something very holy.

Mother? Everything will be in it.

It is a whole day.

—One two three, and light.

—Now, we move toward it.

—Mother? Wake!

*What happens to Frank's mother at the end of the letter?*

■

---

13. **cleave.** Adhere firmly and closely or loyally and unwaveringly

**Respond** *to the* **SELECTION**

If you were Frank's mother, what would be your response to his letter?

# INVESTIGATE, Inquire, Imagine

**Recall:** GATHERING FACTS

1a. What reasons does Frank give for choosing to marry Lavinia instead of Emily?

2a. During battle, what did Frank briefly consider?

3a. Where is Frank's mother at the end of the story? What is "holy," according to Frank?

→ **Interpret:** FINDING MEANING

1b. How does Frank feel about this choice at the end of the story?

2b. Why does Frank admit his cowardice to his mother?

3b. What does it mean when Frank says, "Mother? Wake!"

---

**Analyze:** TAKING THINGS APART

4a. Identify the elements of section 1 that are elaborated on in section 2.

→ **Synthesize:** BRINGING THINGS TOGETHER

4b. Why is the story called "Reassurance"? Who is giving reassurance to whom? What reassurance is being given?

---

**Evaluate:** MAKING JUDGMENTS

5a. In section 2, Frank calls himself "cowardly." Using examples from the story, evaluate whether or not Frank is cowardly.

→ **Extend:** CONNECTING IDEAS

5b. Imagine that Frank does not die after his amputation but returns home. What actions does he take to secure a future for himself? What convictions does he act upon?

---

# Understanding Literature

**STREAM-OF-CONSCIOUSNESS WRITING.** Review the definition for **stream-of-consciousness writing** in the Handbook of Literary Terms. Then find an example of stream-of-consciousness writing in section 2 of the selection and explain what is going on in Frank's mind.

**REPETITION.** Review the definition for **repetition** in the Handbook of Literary Terms and the graphic organizer you made for Literary Tools on page 969. Since Frank's letter is really his mother's dream, how would you explain the use of repeated words and phrases in section 2?

# WRITER'S JOURNAL

1. Write an **obituary** for Frank. Be sure to include in it the following information: the names of the relatives he left behind, the name of the girl to whom he was engaged, and a brief summary of how he was wounded and died.

2. Imagine that you are Frank's mother and have just received Walt Whitman's letter. Write a **letter** to Walt Whitman, expressing your reactions to what he told you about your son.

3. Write a **dialogue** between Walt Whitman and Frank in the hospital that illustrates each character's personality and preoccupations.

# Integrating *the* LANGUAGE ARTS
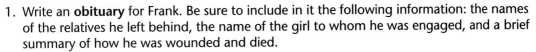

 ## Vocabulary

USING CONTEXT CLUES. Read the Language Arts Survey 1.16, "Using Context Clues to Estimate Word Meaning." Then read each of the following sentences. Write the definition of each underlined word, using context clues to deduce its meaning.

1. The surgeons <u>endeavored</u> to save all the wounded soldiers, but some died despite the doctors' best efforts.

2. Since Frank's behavior was beyond <u>reproach</u>, Walt Whitman could not find fault with either his words or behavior.

3. The censors <u>eradicated</u>, or erased, every mention of the battalion's location.

4. Although Parson Brookes was a great speaker, Frank thought Walt Whitman was even more <u>eloquent</u>.

5. When Frank <u>expired</u> on May 1, 1865, Whitman wrote a letter to Frank's mother informing her of his death.

 ## Speaking and Listening & Collaborative Learning

DIALOGUE. Imagine that Frank recovers from his amputation and returns home. With a partner, play the roles of Frank and Emily as they get reacquainted.

 ## Study and Research

CIVIL WAR MEDICINE. Research the state of medicine during the Civil War. What did soldiers routinely die of? Was anesthesia used during surgery? How frequently were amputations performed? What qualifications did the doctors and nurses possess?

## Media Literacy

HUMAN INTEREST STORY. Imagine you are a journalist during the Civil War and you have just learned that Walt Whitman is serving as a nurse in Union hospitals. Prepare a human interest story for a radio program. You might choose to do more research on Walt Whitman's experience as a hospital volunteer before you begin writing.

## Literary TOOLS

**CONFLICT.** A **conflict** is a struggle between two forces in a literary work. A struggle that takes place between a character and some outside force is called an *external conflict*. A struggle that takes place within a character is called an *internal conflict*. As you read, identify the external and internal conflicts that Laura, Yoyo, and Carlos experience.

**CLICHÉ.** A **cliché** is an overused or unoriginal expression such as *old as the hills* or *slow as molasses*. As you read, make a chart. On the left, list the clichés used mistakenly by Laura. On the right, correct them. One example has been done for you.

| Laura's Clichés | Corrected Version |
|---|---|
| "green behind the ears" | "wet behind the ears" |

## Reader's Journal

If you came from another culture, would you try to retain your traditions or assimilate completely into the new culture?

# "Daughter of Invention"

### BY JULIA ALVAREZ

## About *the* AUTHOR

**Julia Alvarez** (1950– ), poet, novelist, and nonfiction writer, was born in the Dominican Republic and emigrated to the United States with her family at the age of ten. Books provided a way for her to avoid feeling isolated, and by the time she was a teenager, Alvarez knew that she wanted to be a writer.

Alvarez uses her writing to discuss her experience as a person of two cultures, and she intends her audience to be both cultures. Although her novels have Latino characters, her treatment of them is not narrow; rather, Alvarez focuses on the intercultural idea of identity formation. A prolific writer, Alvarez has published essays, poems, and stories in *The New Yorker, Allure,* and *Hispanic Magazine.* She has also written several novels, including *How the García Girls Lost Their Accents* (1991), *In the Time of the Butterflies* (1994), and *¡Yo!* (1997). Her first book of nonfiction, *Something to Declare* (1998), contains twenty-four personal essays on her experiences as an immigrant and a writer. Currently, Alvarez teaches English at Middlebury College.

## About *the* SELECTION

**"Daughter of Invention"** is one of fifteen interconnected stories that form the novel *How the García Girls Lost Their Accents* (1991), which relates the experiences of four sisters who move to New York City from the Dominican Republic to escape the repressive regime of General Rafael Trujillo, who was dictator from 1930 until his assasination in 1961. "Daughter of Invention" focuses on how the mother, Laura, and her daughter, Yoyo, find their place in the new world of American culture, asserting their independence from the old world of Dominican tradition.

# Daughter of Invention

## JULIA ALVAREZ
### MAMI, PAPI, YOYO

For a period after they arrived in this country, Laura García tried to invent something. Her ideas always came after the sight-seeing visits she took with her daughters to department stores to see the wonders of this new country. On his free Sundays, Carlos carted the girls off to the Statue of Liberty or the Brooklyn Bridge or Rockefeller Center, but as far as Laura was concerned, these were men's wonders. Down in housewares were the true treasures women were after.

*What types of activities does Laura differentiate as men's and women's wonders?*

Laura and her daughters would take the escalator, marveling at the moving staircase, she teasing them that this might be the ladder Jacob saw with angels moving up and down to heaven. The moment they lingered by a display, a perky saleslady approached, no doubt thinking a young mother with four girls in tow fit the

**Woman with Medallion,** 1997. Matias Morales. Private Collection.

perfect profile for the new refrigerator with automatic defrost or the heavy duty washing machine with the prewash soak cycle. Laura paid close attention during the demonstrations, asking intelligent questions, but at the last minute saying she would talk it over with her husband. On the drive home, try as they might, her daughters could not engage their mother in conversation, for inspired by what she had just seen, Laura had begun inventing.

She never put anything actual on paper until she had settled her house down at night. On his side of the bed her husband would be conked out for an hour already, his Spanish newspaper draped over his chest, his glasses propped up on his bedside table, looking out eerily at the darkened room like a disembodied bodyguard. In her lighted corner, pillows propped behind her, Laura sat up inventing. On her lap lay one of those innumerable pads of paper her husband brought home from his office, compliments of some <u>pharmaceutical</u> company, advertising tranquilizers or antibiotics or skin cream. She would be working on a sketch of something familiar but drawn at such close range so she could attach a special nozzle or handier handle, the thing looked peculiar. Her daughters would giggle over the odd doodles they found in kitchen drawers or on the back shelf of the downstairs toilet. Once Yoyo was sure her mother had drawn a picture of a man's you-know-what; she showed her sisters her find, and with coy, posed faces they inquired of their mother what she was up to. *Ay*, that was one of her failures, she explained to them, a child's double-compartment drinking glass with an outsized, built-in straw.

Her daughters would seek her out at night when she seemed to have a moment to talk to them: they were having trouble at school or they wanted her to persuade their father to give them permission to go into the city or to a shopping mall or a movie—in broad daylight, Mami! Laura would wave them out of her room. "The problem with you girls . . ." The problem boiled down to the fact that they wanted to become Americans and their father—and their mother, too, at first— would have none of it.

What problem does Laura have with her daughters?

"You girls are going to drive me crazy!" she threatened, if they kept nagging. "When I end up in Bellevue,[1] you'll be safely sorry!"

She spoke in English when she argued with them. And her English was a mishmash of mixed-up idioms and sayings that showed she was "green behind the ears," as she called it.

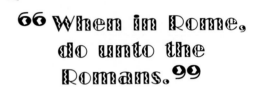

## 66 When in Rome, do unto the Romans. 99

If her husband insisted she speak in Spanish to the girls so they wouldn't forget their native tongue, she'd snap, "When in Rome, do unto the Romans."

Yoyo, the Big Mouth, had become the spokesman for her sisters, and she stood her ground in that bedroom. "We're not going to that school anymore, Mami!"

"You have to." Her eyes would widen with worry. "In this country, it is against the law not to go to school. You want us to get thrown out?"

---

1. **Bellevue.** Famous psychiatric hospital in New York

**WORDS FOR EVERYDAY USE**

phar • ma • ceu • ti • cal (fär mə sü′ ti kəl) *adj.*, of, relating to, or engaged in pharmacy or the manufacture and sale of drugs. *The <u>pharmaceutical</u> company was banned from producing the new drug it had developed.*

982    UNIT TWELVE / *CONTEMPORARY LITERATURE*

"You want us to get killed? Those kids were throwing stones today!"

"Sticks and stones don't break bones," she chanted. Yoyo could tell, though, by the look on her face, it was as if one of those stones the kids had aimed at her daughters had hit her. But she always pretended they were at fault. "What did you do to provoke them? It takes two to tangle, you know."

"Thanks, thanks a lot, Mom!" Yoyo stormed out of that room and into her own. Her daughters never called her *Mom* except when they wanted her to feel how much she had failed them in this country. She was a good enough Mami, fussing and scolding and giving advice, but a terrible girlfriend parent, a real failure of a Mom.

Back she went to her pencil and pad, scribbling and tsking and tearing off sheets, finally giving up, and taking up her *New York Times*. Some nights, though, if she got a good idea, she rushed into Yoyo's room, a flushed look on her face, her tablet of paper in her hand, a cursory knock on the door she'd just thrown open. "Do I have something to show you, Cuquita!"

This was Yoyo's time to herself, after she finished her homework, while her sisters were still downstairs watching TV in the basement. Hunched over her small desk, the overhead light turned off, her desk lamp poignantly lighting only her paper, the rest of the room in warm, soft, uncreated darkness, she wrote her secret poems in her new language.

"You're going to ruin your eyes!" Laura began, snapping on the overly bright overhead light, scaring off whatever shy passion Yoyo, with the blue thread of her writing, had just begun coaxing out of a labyrinth of feelings.

"Oh, Mami!" Yoyo cried out, her eyes blinking up at her mother. "I'm writing."

"*Ay*, Cuquita." That was her communal pet name for whoever was in her favor. "Cuquita, when I make a million, I'll buy you your very own typewriter." (Yoyo had been nagging her mother for one just like the one her father had bought to do his order forms at home.) "Gravy on the turkey" was what she called it when someone was buttering her up. She buttered and poured. "I'll hire you your very own typist."

Down she plopped on the bed and held out her pad. "Take a guess, Cuquita?" Yoyo studied the rough sketch a moment. Soap sprayed from the nozzle head of a shower when you turned the knob a certain way? Instant coffee with creamer already mixed in? Time-released water capsules for your potted plants when you were away? A keychain with a timer that would go off when your parking meter was about to expire? (The ticking would help you find your keys easily if you mislaid them.) The famous one, famous only in hindsight, was the stick person dragging a square by a rope—a suitcase with wheels? "Oh, of course," Yoyo said, humoring her. "What every household needs: a shower like a car wash, keys ticking like a bomb, luggage on a leash!" By now, it had become something of a family joke, their Thomas Edison Mami, their Benjamin Franklin Mom.

Her face fell. "Come on now! Use your head." One more wrong guess, and she'd show Yoyo, pointing with her pencil to the different highlights of this incredible new wonder. "Remember that time we took the car to Bear Mountain, and we re-ah-lized that we had forgotten to pack an opener with our pick-a-nick?" (Her daughters kept correcting her, but she insisted this was how it should be said.) "When we were ready to eat we didn't have any way to open the refreshments cans?" (This before flip-

Words For Everyday Use

cur • so • ry (kərs' rē) *adj.*, rapidly and often superficially performed or produced. *Brent's* cursory *rendition of the song made his band teacher frown.*

poi • gnant • ly (poi' nyənt lē) *adv.*, done in a manner that deeply affects the emotions. *Alicia waved* poignantly *at her new friends as she got on the train, knowing she would never see them again.*

lab • y • rinth (la' bə rin[t]th) *n.*, maze. *The twisting path of the* labyrinth *kept the children occupied for an hour.*

com • mu • nal (kə myü' nəl) *adj.*, participated in, shared, or used in common by members of a group or community. *Do you drink from a* communal *drinking fountain at school?*

top lids, which she claimed had crossed her mind.) "You know what this is now?" Yoyo shook her head. "Is a car bumper, but see this part is a removable can opener. So simple and yet so necessary, eh?"

"Yeah, Mami. You should patent it." Yoyo shrugged as her mother tore off the scratch paper and folded it, carefully, corner to corner, as if she were going to save it. But then, she tossed it in the wastebasket on her way out of the room and gave a little laugh like a disclaimer. "It's half of one or two dozen of another."

None of her daughters was very encouraging. They resented her spending time on those dumb inventions. Here they were trying to fit in America among Americans; they needed help figuring out who they were, why the Irish kids whose grandparents had been micks were calling them spics. Why had they come to this country in the first place? Important, crucial, final things, and here was their own mother, who didn't have a second to help them puzzle any of this out, inventing gadgets to make life easier for the American Moms.

Sometimes Yoyo challenged her. "Why, Mami? Why do it? You're never going to make money. The Americans have already thought of everything, you know that."

"Maybe not. Maybe, just maybe, there's something they've missed that's important. With patience and calm, even a burro can climb a palm." This last was one of her many Dominican sayings she had imported into her scrambled English.

"But what's the point?" Yoyo persisted.

"Point, point, does everything need a point? Why do you write poems?"

> What "important, crucial, final things" were the girls trying to figure out?

Yoyo had to admit it was her mother who had the point there. Still, in the hierarchy of things, a poem seemed much more important than a potty that played music when a toilet-training toddler went in its bowl.

They talked about it among themselves, the four girls, as they often did now about the many puzzling things in this new country.

"Better she reinvents the wheel than be on our cases all the time," the oldest, Carla, observed. In the close quarters of an American nuclear family, their mother's prodigious energy was becoming a real drain on their self-determination. Let her have a project. What harm could she do, and besides, she needed that acknowledgement. It had come to her automatically in the old country from being a de la Torre. "García de la Torre," Laura would enunciate carefully, giving her maiden as well as married name when they first arrived. But the blank smiles had never heard of her name. She would show them. She would prove to these Americans what a smart woman could do with a pencil and pad.

She had a near miss once. Every night, she liked to read *The New York Times* in bed before turning off her light, to see what the Americans were up to. One night, she let out a yelp to wake up her husband beside her. He sat bolt upright, reaching for his glasses which in his haste, he knocked across the room. "*¿Qué pasa? ¿Qué pasa?*" What is wrong? There was terror in his voice, the same fear she'd heard in the Dominican Republic before they left. They had been watched there; he was followed. They could not talk, of course, though they had whispered to each other in fear at night in the dark bed. Now in America, he was safe, a success even; his Centro de Medicina in the Bronx was thronged with the sick and the homesick yearn-

---

**WORDS FOR EVERYDAY USE**

**pat • ent** (pa' tənt) vt., obtain or grant authorization for an invention. *Mr. Swedarski patented a deicer tube designed to open frozen car doors.*

**hi • er • ar • chy** (hī'ə rär kē) n., graded or ranked series of things. *The English teacher asked the students to make a hierarchy of their personal values.*

**pro • di • gious** (prə di' jəs) adj., causing amazement or wonder. *Adam's prodigious drawing made his parents think that he might be an artist when he grew up.*

ing to go home again. But in dreams, he went back to those awful days and long nights, and his wife's screams confirmed

What does Carlos fear?

his secret fear: they had not gotten away after all; the SIM had come for them at last.

"*Ay*, Cuco! Remember how I showed you that suitcase with little wheels so we should not have to carry those heavy bags when we traveled? Someone stole my idea and made a million!" She shook the paper in his face. "See, see! This man was no *bobo!* He didn't put all his pokers on a back burner. I kept telling you, one of these days my ship would pass me by in the night!" She wagged her finger at her husband and daughters, laughing all the while, one of those <u>eerie</u> laughs crazy people in movies laugh. The four girls had congregated in her room. They eyed their mother and each other. Perhaps they were all thinking the same thing, wouldn't it be weird and sad if Mami did end up in Bellevue?

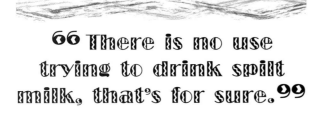

**66 There is no use trying to drink spilt milk, that's for sure. 99**

"*¡Ya, ya!*" She waved them out of her room at last. "There is no use trying to drink spilt milk, that's for sure."

It was the suitcase rollers that stopped Laura's hand; she had weathervaned a minor brainstorm. And yet, this <u>plagiarist</u> had gotten all the credit, and the money. What use was it trying to compete with the Americans: they would always have the head start. It was their country, after all. Best stick close to home. She cast her sights about—her daughters ducked—and found her husband's office in need. Several days a week, dressed professionally in a white smock with a little name tag pinned on the lapel, a shopping bag full of cleaning materials and rags, she rode with her husband in his car to the Bronx. On the way, she organized the glove compartment or took off

What work does Laura do for her husband?

the address stickers from the magazines for the waiting room because she had read somewhere how by means of these stickers drug addict patients found out where doctors lived and burglarized their homes looking for syringes. At night, she did the books, filling in columns with how much money they had made that day. Who had time to be inventing silly things!

She did take up her pencil and pad one last time. But it was to help one of her daughters out. In ninth grade, Yoyo was chosen by her English teacher, Sister Mary Joseph, to deliver the Teacher's Day address at the school assembly. Back in the Dominican Republic growing up, Yoyo had been a terrible student. No one could ever get her to sit down to a book. But in New York, she needed to settle some-

What does Sister Mary Joseph ask Yoyo to do? What change has Yoyo undergone since moving to New York?

where, and since the natives were unfriendly, and the country inhospitable, she took root in the language. By high school, the nuns were reading her stories and compositions out loud in English class.

But the spectre of delivering a speech brownnosing the teachers jammed her imagination. At first she didn't want to and then she couldn't seem to write that speech. She should have thought of it as "a great honor," as her father

---

**WORDS FOR EVERYDAY USE**

**ee • rie** (ir′ ē) *adj.,* so mysterious, strange, or unexpected as to send a chill up the spine. *The <u>eerie</u> sounds of the wild animals in the forest kept Donna awake in her tent.*

**pla • gia • rist** (plā′ jə rist) *n.,* someone who steals and passes off the ideas or words of another as one's own. *The <u>plagiarist</u> was expelled from the university for turning in papers he had gotten off the Internet.*

called it. But she was <u>mortified</u>. She still had a slight accent, and she did not like to speak in public, subjecting herself to her classmates' ridicule. It also took no great figuring to see that to deliver a <u>eulogy</u> for a convent full of crazy, old, overweight nuns was no way to endear herself to her peers.

But she didn't know how to get out of it. Night after night, she sat at her desk, hoping to polish off some quick, <u>noncommittal</u> little speech. But she couldn't get anything down.

The weekend before the assembly Monday morning Yoyo went into a panic. Her mother would just have to call in tomorrow and say Yoyo was in the hospital, in a coma.

Laura tried to calm her down. "Just remember how Mister Lincoln couldn't think of anything to say at the Gettysburg, but then, bang! *Four score and once upon a time ago,*" she began reciting. "Something is going to come if you just relax. You'll see, like the Americans say, *Necessity is the daughter of invention.* I'll help you."

That weekend, her mother turned all her energy towards helping Yoyo write her speech. "Please, Mami, just leave me alone, please," Yoyo pleaded with her. But Yoyo would get rid of the goose only to have to contend with the gander. Her father kept poking his head in the door just to see if Yoyo had "fulfilled your obligations," a phrase he had used when the girls were younger and he'd check to see whether they had gone to the bathroom before a car trip. Several times that weekend around the supper table, he recited his own high school valedictorian speech. He gave Yoyo pointers on delivery, notes on the great orators and their tricks. (Humbleness and praise and falling silent with great emotion were his favorites.)

Laura sat across the table, the only one who seemed to be listening to him. Yoyo and her sisters were forgetting a lot of their Spanish, and their father's formal, <u>florid</u> diction was hard to understand. But Laura smiled softly to herself, and turned the lazy Susan at the center of the table around and around as if it were the prime mover, the first gear of her attention.

That Sunday evening, Yoyo was reading some poetry to get herself inspired: Whitman's poems in an old book with an engraved cover her father had picked up in a thrift shop next to his office. *I celebrate myself and sing myself. . . . He most honors my style who learns under it to destroy the teacher.* The poet's words shocked and thrilled her. She had gotten used to the nuns, a literature of appropriate sentiments, poems with a message, <u>expurgated</u> texts. But here was a flesh and blood man, belching and laughing and sweating in poems. *Who touches this book touches a man.*

That night, at last, she started to write, recklessly, three, five pages, looking up once only to see her father passing by the hall on tiptoe. When Yoyo was done, she read over her words, and her eyes filled. She finally sounded like herself in English!

As soon as she had finished that first draft, she called her mother to her room. Laura listened attentively while Yoyo read the speech out loud, and in the end, her eyes were glistening too. Her face was soft and warm and proud. "*Ay,* Yoyo, you are going to be the one to bring our name to the headlights in this country! That is a beautiful, beautiful speech I want for your father to hear it before he goes to sleep. Then I will type it for you, all right?"

> Where does Yoyo find inspiration for her speech?

**WORDS FOR EVERYDAY USE**

**mor • ti • fied** (môr tə fīd) *adj.,* feeling severe and vexing embarrassment. *Shawn was <u>mortified</u> when his teacher read his composition to the class.*

**eu • lo • gy** (yü' lə jē) *n.,* speech of high praise. *The principal's <u>eulogy</u> praised the students for beautifying the campus.*

**non • com • mit • tal** (nän kə mi' təl) *adj.,* giving no clear indication of attitude or feeling. *Blake's <u>noncommittal</u> response made Kellie unsure if he would be at the dance.*

**flor • id** (flôr' əd) *adj.,* very flowery in style. *Ashley was impressed by Jacob's <u>florid</u> professions of admiration.*

**ex • pur • gat • ed** (eks' pər gat əd) *adj.,* having had appropriate parts removed before publication or presentation. *Julie had only read an <u>expurgated</u> section of* The Catcher in the Rye, *so she was eager to check the book out of the library.*

Down the hall they went, mother and daughter, faces flushed with accomplishment. Into the master bedroom where Carlos was propped up on his pillows, still awake, reading the Dominican papers, already days old. Now that the dictatorship had been <u>toppled</u>, he had become interested in his country's fate again. The interim government was going to hold the first free elections in thirty years. History was in the making, freedom and hope were in the air again! There was still some question in his mind whether or not he might move his family back. But Laura had gotten used to the life here. She did not want to go back to the old country where, de la Torre or not, she was only a wife and a mother (and a failed one at that, since she had never provided the required son). Better an independent nobody than a high-class houseslave. She did not come straight out and disagree with her husband's plans. Instead, she fussed with him about reading the papers in bed, soiling their sheets with those poorly printed, foreign tabloids. "*The Times* is not that bad!" she'd claim if her husband tried to humor her by saying they shared the same dirty habit.

*What is Carlos considering? Why?*

The minute Carlos saw his wife and daughter filing in, he put his paper down, and his face brightened as if at long last his wife had delivered the son, and that was the news she was bringing him. His teeth were already grinning from the glass of water next to his bedside lamp, so he lisped when he said, "Eh-speech, eh-speech!"

"It is so beautiful, Cuco," Laura coached him, turning the sound on his TV off. She sat down at the foot of the bed. Yoyo stood before both of them, blocking their view of the soldiers in helicopters landing amid silenced gun reports and explosions. A few weeks ago it had been the shores of the Dominican Republic. Now it was the jungles of Southeast Asia they were saving. Her mother gave her the nod to begin reading.

*What is the historical setting for this story?*

Yoyo didn't need much encouragement. She put her nose to the fire, as her mother would have said, and read from start to finish without looking up. When she concluded, she was a little embarrassed at the pride she took in her own words. She pretended to <u>quibble</u> with a phrase or two, then looked questioningly to her mother. Laura's face was radiant. Yoyo turned to share her pride with her father.

The expression on his face shocked both mother and daughter. Carlos's toothless mouth had collapsed into a dark zero. His eyes bored into Yoyo, then shifted to Laura. In barely audible Spanish, as if secret microphones or informers were all about, he whispered to his wife, "You will permit her to read *that?*"

Laura's eyebrows shot up, her mouth fell open. In the old country, any whisper of a challenge to authority could bring the secret police in their black V.W.'s. But this was America. People could say what they thought. "What is wrong with her speech?" Laura questioned him.

"What ees wrrrong with her eh-speech?" Carlos wagged his head at her. His anger was always more frightening in his broken English. As if he had mutilated the language in his fury—and now there was nothing to stand between them and his raw, dumb anger. "What is wrong? I will tell you what is wrong. It show no gratitude. It is boastful. *I celebrate myself? The best student learns to destroy the teacher?*" He mocked Yoyo's plagiarized words. "That is insubordinate. It is improper. It is disrespect-

*What does Carlos think of his daughter's speech?*

**WORDS FOR EVERYDAY USE**

top • ple (tä′ pəl) *vt.,* overthrow. *When the totalitarian regime was <u>toppled</u>, many citizens returned home from abroad.*

quib • ble (kwi′ bəl) *vi.,* find fault with. *Mrs. Modl <u>quibbled</u> with her daughter over how late she stayed out.*

ing of her teachers—" In his anger he had forgotten his fear of lurking spies: each wrong he voiced was a decibel higher than the last outrage. Finally, he shouted at Yoyo, "As your father, I forbid you to make that eh-speech!"

Laura leapt to her feet, a sign that *she* was about to deliver her own speech. She was a small woman, and she spoke all her pronouncements standing up, either for more projection or as a carry-over from her girlhood in convent schools where one asked for, and literally, took the floor in order to speak. She stood by Yoyo's side, shoulder to shoulder. They looked down at Carlos. "That is no tone of voice—" she began.

But now, Carlos was truly furious. It was bad enough that his daughter was rebelling, but here was his own wife joining forces with her. Soon he would be surrounded by a houseful of independent American women. He too leapt from the bed, throwing off his covers. The Spanish newspapers flew across the room. He snatched the speech out of Yoyo's hands, held it before the girl's wide eyes, a vengeful, mad look in his own, and then once, twice, three, four, countless times, he tore the speech into shreds.

> What does Carlos do to the speech?

"Are you crazy?" Laura lunged at him. "Have you gone mad? That is her speech for tomorrow you have torn up!"

"Have *you* gone mad?" He shook her away. "You were going to let her read that . . . that insult to her teachers?"

"Insult to her teachers!" Laura's face had crumpled up like a piece of paper. On it was written a love note to her husband, an unhappy, haunted man. "This is America, Papi, America! You are not in a savage country anymore!"

Meanwhile, Yoyo was on her knees, weeping wildly, collecting all the little pieces of her speech, hoping that she could put it back

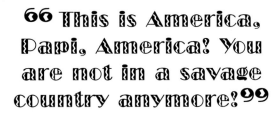

**This is America, Papi, America! You are not in a savage country anymore!**

together before the assembly tomorrow morning. But not even a <u>sibyl</u> could have made sense of those tiny scraps of paper. All hope was lost. "He broke it, he broke it," Yoyo moaned as she picked up a handful of pieces.

Probably, if she had thought a moment about it, she would not have done what she did next. She would have realized her father had lost brothers and friends to the dictator Trujillo.[2] For the rest of his life, he would be haunted by blood in the streets and late night disappearances. Even after all these years, he cringed if a black Volkswagen passed him on the street. He feared anyone in uniform: the meter maid giving out parking tickets, a museum guard approaching to tell him not to get too close to his favorite Goya.[3]

On her knees, Yoyo thought of the worst thing she could say to her father. She gathered a handful of scraps, stood up, and hurled them in his face. In a low, ugly whisper, she pronounced Trujillo's hated nickname: "Chapita! You're just another Chapita!"

It took Yoyo's father only a moment to register the loathsome nickname before he came after her. Down the halls they raced, but Yoyo was quicker than he and made it into her room

---

2. **Trujillo.** General Rafael Leónidas Trujillo Molina, dictator of the Dominican Republic who was assassinated in 1961
3. **Goya.** Francisco José de Goya y Lucientes (1746–1828), Spanish painter

---

**WORDS FOR EVERYDAY USE**

sib • yl (si′ bəl) *n.*, fortune-teller or female prophet. *In the* Aeneid, *the Cymaean* <u>sibyl</u> *offers Tarquin her prophetic writings.*

just in time to lock the door as her father threw his weight against it. He called down curses on her head, ordered her on his authority as her father to open that door! He throttled that doorknob, but all to no avail. Her mother's love of gadgets saved Yoyo's hide that night. Laura had hired a locksmith to install good locks on all the bedroom doors after the house had been broken into once while they were away. Now if burglars broke in again, and the family were at home, there would be a second round of locks for the thieves to contend with.

"Lolo," she said, trying to calm him down. "Don't you ruin my new locks."

Finally he did calm down, his anger spent. Yoyo heard their footsteps retreating down the hall. Their door clicked shut. Then, muffled voices, her mother's rising in anger, in persuasion, her father's deeper murmurs of explanation and self-defense. The house fell silent a moment, before Yoyo heard, far off, the gun blasts and explosions, the serious, self-important voices of newscasters reporting their TV war.

A little while later, there was a quiet knock at Yoyo's door, followed by a tentative attempt at the door knob. "Cuquita?" her mother whispered. "Open up, Cuquita."

"Go away," Yoyo wailed, but they both knew she was glad her mother was there, and needed only a moment's protest to save face.

Together they concocted a speech: two brief pages of stale compliments and the polite commonplaces on teachers, a speech wrought by necessity and without much invention by mother and daughter late into the night on one of the pads of paper Laura had once used for her own inventions. After it was drafted, Laura typed it up while Yoyo stood by, correcting her mother's misnomers and mis-sayings.

Yoyo came home the next day with the success story of the assembly. The nuns had been flattered, the audience had stood up and given "our devoted teachers a standing ovation," what Laura had suggested they do at the end of the speech.

She clapped her hands together as Yoyo recreated the moment. "I stole that from your father's speech, remember? Remember how he put that in at the end?" She quoted him in Spanish, then translated for Yoyo into English.

That night, Yoyo watched him from the upstairs hall window, where she'd retreated the minute she heard his car pull up in front of the house. Slowly, her father came up the driveway, a grim expression on his face as he grappled with a large, heavy cardboard box. At the front door, he set the package down carefully and patted all his pockets for his house keys. (If only he'd had Laura's ticking key chain!) Yoyo heard the snapping open of locks downstairs. She listened as he struggled to maneuver the box through the narrow doorway. He called her name several times, but she did not answer him.

"My daughter, your father, he love you very much," he explained from the bottom of the stairs. "He just want to protect you." Finally, her mother came up and pleaded with Yoyo to go down and reconcile with him. "Your father did not mean to harm. You must pardon him. Always it is better to let bygones be forgotten, no?"

Downstairs, Yoyo found her father setting up a brand new electric typewriter on the kitchen table. It was even better than her mother's. He had outdone himself with all the extra features: a plastic carrying case with Yoyo's initials decaled below the handle, a brace to lift the paper upright while she typed, an erase cartridge, an automatic margin tab, a plastic hood like a toaster cover to keep the dust away. Not even her mother could have invented such a machine!

But Laura's inventing days were over just as Yoyo's were starting up with her school-wide success. Rather than the rolling suitcase everyone else in the family remembers, Yoyo thinks of the speech her mother wrote as her last invention. It was as if, after that, her mother had passed on to Yoyo her pencil and pad and said, "Okay, Cuquita, here's the buck. You give it a shot."

■

*How does Carlos make amends with Yoyo after their fight?*

*What is Laura's last invention?*

How will Yoyo's talent for invention help her adjust to American culture?

# INVESTIGATE Inquire Imagine

**Recall:** GATHERING FACTS

1a. What do Laura and Yoyo like to do in their free time?

2a. What is Yoyo's initial reaction to having to write and deliver a speech at school?

3a. Why does Yoyo get angry at her father?

→ **Interpret:** FINDING MEANING

1b. How are Laura and Yoyo alike?

2b. How are the two speeches Yoyo writes different?

3b. Why does Yoyo call her father *Chapita?*

**Analyze:** TAKING THINGS APART

4a. Identify Yoyo's character traits and give evidence to support your assessment.

→ **Synthesize:** BRINGING THINGS TOGETHER

4b. Why do you think the selection is entitled "Daughter of Invention"?

**Perspective:** LOOKING AT OTHER VIEWS

5a. Carlos tears up Yoyo's speech so she cannot give it at school. Given his experiences in the Dominican Republic, is his behavior understandable?

→ **Empathy:** SEEING FROM INSIDE

5b. Describe a time when you acted to protect someone. Were your intentions mis-understood? Did the action bring you closer to that person?

# Understanding Literature

CONFLICT. Review the definition for **conflict** in the Handbook of Literary Terms. What *external* and *internal conflicts* do Laura, Yoyo, and Carlos experience? Which conflicts are resolved at the end of the story?

CLICHÉ. Review the definition of **cliché** in the Handbook of Literary Terms and the chart you completed for Literary Tools on page 980. Which cliché is the basis for the title of the story? What does Laura's use—or more often misuse—of clichés reveal about her?

# Writer's Journal

1. Imagine you are Yoyo and your cousin from the Dominican Republic is coming to visit you. Write an **e-mail message** to your cousin, explaining what she can expect on her visit to the United States.

2. Imagine you are Carlos. Write a **journal entry** describing the conflict you are having with Yoyo and Laura over Yoyo's speech. Why are you against the speech? What do you see as your role in the family? How has that role been thwarted?

3. Imagine you are Laura. Write a **note** to Yoyo explaining why you are giving up your inventions. What did your inventions mean to you? What is the "buck" you are passing on to your daughter?

# Integrating the LANGUAGE ARTS

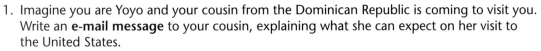

## Language, Grammar, and Style

**COMBINING SENTENCES.** Read the Language Arts Survey 3.36, Combining and Expanding Sentences. Then combine the following pairs of sentences using single words, phrases, or clauses.

1. Carlos was free on Sundays. He carted the girls off to the Statue of Liberty or the Brooklyn Bridge or Rockefeller Center.

2. Laura and her daughters would take the escalator. They marveled at the moving staircase.

3. A saleslady approached. She was perky.

4. Laura paid close attention during the demonstrations. She said she would talk it over with her husband.

5. Laura drew her inventions on notepads. They came from pharmaceutical companies.

## Study and Research

**EXPLORING CONTEXT.** When reading a story, one can find it helpful to have an understanding of historical events mentioned in the story to provide a contextual background. Research what conditions in the Dominican Republic were like under the dictator Trujillo. Then write a paragraph describing what you have learned.

## Applied English

**WRITING A SPEECH.** Yoyo is inspired by these lines from Walt Whitman's "Song of Myself": "I celebrate myself and sing myself. . . . He most honors my style who learns under it to destroy the teacher. . . . Who touches this book touches a man." Write Yoyo's Teacher's Day address based on these lines from the Whitman poem.

## Collaborative Learning

**CLICHÉS.** With a partner, make a list of clichés not mentioned in the story. Then describe a situation in which you could use each one.

# Literary TOOLS

**CRISIS.** In the plot of a story or a drama, the **crisis** is that point in the development of the conflict at which a decisive event occurs that causes the main character's situation to become better or worse. As you read "Ambush," identify its crisis.

**REALISM. Realism** is the attempt to render in art an accurate portrayal of reality. As you read, make a cluster chart that lists the realistic details of the story. One example has been done for you.

The platoon was spread out in the dense brush along the trail.

Realism

# Reader's Journal

When have you told a lie to protect someone?

# "AMBUSH"

BY TIM O'BRIEN

## About the AUTHOR

**Tim O'Brien** (1946– ), a veteran of the Vietnam War, is best known for his fiction about the wartime experiences of American soldiers in Vietnam. Born in Austin, Minnesota, O'Brien attended Macalester College in St. Paul. After graduating *summa cum laude* with a bachelor's degree in political science, he was drafted into the U.S. Army and sent to Vietnam, where he earned a Purple Heart. After a year of military service, O'Brien attended Harvard University. During the early 1970s, he worked as a national-affairs reporter at the *Washington Post* until he began writing fiction full-time. His novel *Going after Cacciato* (1978) won the National Book Award, and his short-story collection *The Things They Carried* (1990) was nominated for a Pulitzer Prize. O'Brien's other works include *If I Die in a Combat Zone, Box Me Up and Ship Me Home* (1973); *In the Lake of the Woods* (1994); and *Tomcat in Love* (1998).

## About the SELECTION

According to O'Brien, "The best literature is always explorative. It's searching for answers and never finding them." This approach sums up his short story collection *The Things They Carried* (1990), in which the interplay between memory and imagination makes it difficult for the reader to distinguish what really happened. In "**Ambush**," the narrator relives a moment of the Vietnam War when he killed another man with a grenade.

American
History Note:

When at Vietnam
WAR.
Read "Ambush"

in Literature
p. 992.

# AMBUSH

## TIM O'BRIEN

When she was nine, my daughter Kathleen asked if I had ever killed anyone. She knew about the war; she knew I'd been a soldier. "You keep writing these war stories," she said, "so I guess you must've killed somebody." It was a difficult moment, but I did what seemed right, which was to say, "Of course not," and then to take her onto my lap and hold her for a while. Someday, I hope, she'll ask again. But here I want to pretend she's a grown-up. I want to tell her exactly what happened, or what I remember happening, and then I want to

say to her that as a little girl she was absolutely right. This is why I keep writing war stories:

He was a short, slender young man of about twenty. I was afraid of him—afraid of something—and as he passed me on the trail I threw a <u>grenade</u> that exploded at his feet and killed him.

Or to go back:

Shortly after midnight we moved into the <u>ambush</u> site outside My Khe.[1] The whole <u>platoon</u> was there, spread out in the dense brush along the trail, and for five hours nothing at all happened. We

*How does the narrator of the story respond to his daughter's question?*

*What happened to the young man?*

---

1. **My Khe.** Village in Vietnam

**WORDS FOR EVERYDAY USE**

**gre • nade** (grə nād′) *n.*, small missile that contains an explosive or a chemical agent and that is thrown by hand or projected. *When the grenade exploded, tear gas was emitted, driving the student protesters outside.*

**am • bush** (am′ bŭsh) *n.*, trap in which a concealed person or persons lie in wait to attack by surprise. *The ambush surprised the stagecoach, and the robbers took all the passengers' money and jewelry.*

**pla • toon** (plə tün′) *n.*, subdivision of a company-size military unit normally consisting of two or more squads or sections. *The platoon ran two miles every day as part of its training.*

*U.S. Army Patrol in Vietnam,* 1968. Tim Page.

teen meters up the trail. The mosquitoes were fierce. I remember slapping at them, wondering if I should wake up Kiowa and ask for some repellent, then thinking it was a bad idea, then looking up and seeing the young man come out of the fog. He wore black clothing and rubber sandals and a gray ammunition belt. His shoulders were slightly stooped, his head cocked to the side as if listening for something. He seemed at ease. He carried his weapon in one hand, <u>muzzle</u> down, moving without any hurry up the center of the trail. There was no sound at all—none that I can remember. In a way, it seemed, he was part of the morning fog, or my own imagination, but there was also the reality of what was happening in my stomach. I had already pulled the pin on a grenade. I had come up to a crouch. It was entirely automatic. I did not hate the young man; I did not see him as the enemy; I did not ponder issues of <u>morality</u> or politics or military duty. I crouched and kept my head low. I tried to swallow whatever was rising from my stomach, which tasted like lemonade, something fruity and sour. I was terrified. There were no thoughts about killing. The grenade was to make him go away—just evaporate—and I leaned back and felt my mind go empty and then felt it fill up again. I had already thrown the grenade before telling myself to throw it. The brush was thick and I had to <u>lob</u> it high, not aiming, and I remember the grenade seeming to freeze above me for an instant, as if a camera had clicked, and I remember ducking down and holding my breath and seeing little wisps of fog rise from the earth. The grenade bounced once and rolled across the trail. I did not hear it, but

> What prompts the narrator to throw the grenade?

were working in two-man teams—one man on guard while the other slept, switching off every two hours—and I remember it was still dark when Kiowa shook me awake for the final <u>watch</u>. The night was foggy and hot. For the first few moments I felt lost, not sure about directions, groping for my helmet and weapon. I reached out and found three grenades and lined them up in front of me; the pins had already been straightened for quick throwing. And then for maybe half an hour I kneeled there and waited. Very gradually, in tiny slivers, dawn began to break through the fog, and from my position in the brush I could see ten or fif-

**WORDS FOR EVERYDAY USE**

**watch** (wäch) *n.,* act of keeping awake to guard or protect. *Private Johnson was reprimanded for falling asleep during his <u>watch</u>.*

**muz • zle** (mə′ zəl) *n.,* discharging end of a weapon. *The <u>muzzle</u> of the rifle was aimed at the deer.*

**mo • ral • i • ty** (mə ra′ lə tē) *n.,* doctrine or system of moral conduct. *The governor's speech about <u>morality</u> strengthened his support from the conservatives within his party.*

**lob** (läb) *vt.,* throw, hit, or propel easily or in a high arc. *Jamal <u>lobbed</u> the tennis ball over the net.*

# IT WAS NOT A MATTER OF LIVE OR DIE

there must've been a sound, because the young man dropped his weapon and began to run, just two or three quick steps, then he hesitated, <u>swiveling</u> to his right, and he glanced down at the grenade and tried to cover his head but never did. It occurred to me then that he was about to die. I wanted to warn him. The grenade made a popping noise—not soft but not loud either—not what I'd expected—and there was a puff of dust and smoke—a small white puff—and the young man seemed to jerk upward as if pulled by invisible wires. He fell on his back. His rubber sandals had been blown off. There was no wind. He lay at the center of the trail, his right leg bent beneath him, his one eye shut, his other eye a huge star-shaped hole.

It was not a matter of live or die. There was no real <u>peril</u>. Almost certainly the young man would have passed by. And it will always be that way.

Later, I remember, Kiowa tried to tell me that the man would've died anyway. He told me that it was a good kill, that I was a soldier and this was a war, that I should shape up and stop staring and ask myself what the dead man would've done if things were reversed.

> What did Kiowa tell the narrator about the kill?

None of it mattered. The words seemed far too complicated. All I could do was <u>gape</u> at the fact of the young man's body.

Even now I haven't finished sorting it out. Sometimes I forgive myself, other times I don't. In the ordinary hours of life I try not to dwell on it, but now and then, when I'm reading a newspaper or just sitting alone in a room, I'll look up and see the young man coming out of the morning fog. I'll watch him walk toward me, his shoulders slightly stooped, his head cocked to the side, and he'll pass within a few yards of me and suddenly smile at some secret thought and then continue up the trail to where it bends back into the fog. ∎

---

**WORDS FOR EVERYDAY USE**

**swiv • el** (swi′ vəl) *vi.*, swing or turn or pivot freely. *The child got dizzy when the chair <u>swiveled</u>.*

**per • il** (per′ əl) *n.*, exposure to the risk of being injured, destroyed, or lost. *The fire in the apartment building put the residents in <u>peril</u>.*

**gape** (gāp) *vi.*, gaze stupidly or in openmouthed surprise or wonder. *The students <u>gaped</u> at their teacher when he walked into the classroom wearing a Halloween costume.*

---

## Respond *to the* SELECTION

What kind of soldier did the speaker make?

# INVESTIGATE, Inquire, Imagine

**Recall:** GATHERING FACTS

1a. How did the young man carry his gun?

2a. What sound did the grenade make when it went off?

3a. What does the narrator see sometimes when he's reading a newspaper or just sitting alone in a room?

➤ **Interpret:** FINDING MEANING

1b. Why did the young man walk easily along the trail?

2b. What do the narrator's comments about the sound of the grenade going off tell you about the length of his combat experience?

3b. How does the narrator feel today about having killed the man?

---

**Analyze:** TAKING THINGS APART

4a. Analyze the thoughts and emotions the narrator experienced before, during, and after the moment he threw the grenade.

➤ **Synthesize:** BRINGING THINGS TOGETHER

4b. How did the narrator feel about throwing the grenade? Do you agree wth Kiowa's defense of the narrator's action? Explain.

---

**Evaluate:** MAKING JUDGMENTS

5a. Evaluate the effectiveness of the story as an antiwar message.

➤ **Extend:** CONNECTING IDEAS

5b. Compare and contrast the attitude toward war expressed in "Ambush" with the attitude toward war expressed in Stephen Crane's "Do not weep, maiden, for war is kind" (Unit 5).

---

# Understanding Literature

CRISIS. Review the definition for **crisis** in the Handbook of Literary Terms. What is the crisis of "Ambush"? Does the narrator's situation become better or worse after this event?

REALISM. Review the definition for **realism** in the Handbook of Literary Terms and the graphic organizer you made for Literary Tools on page 992. What realistic details does the story give about the man who was killed? Is he portrayed as the enemy?

# WRITER'S JOURNAL

1. Imagine that you are the narrator. Write a **journal entry** explaining how you feel about being drafted into the army. What are your hopes and fears?

2. Imagine that you are the sergeant in charge of the narrator's platoon. Write a **report** stating what happened in the ambush.

3. Imagine that you are the narrator's daughter, now eighteen. Write a **letter** to your father describing your reaction to reading "Ambush," especially in light of what your father told you when you were nine.

# Integrating
## *the* LANGUAGE ARTS

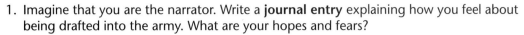

## Language, Grammar, and Style

**SUBORDINATE CLAUSES.** Read the Language Arts Survey 3.72, "Subordinating Conjunctions." Then write out any subordinate clauses that appear in each of these sentences.

1. Although Kathleen was only nine, she wanted to know if her father had killed anyone during the Vietnam War.

2. Since the man carried a gun, he wore an ammunition belt.

3. After killing the man, the narrator feels guilty.

4. The narrator has been haunted by the man he killed since he fought in the war.

5. The memories that the narrator has come to him when he is reading a newspaper or sitting alone in a room.

## Speaking and Listening

**DEBATE.** Research the United States' involvement in the Vietnam War. Then conduct a debate in a small group. Half of the group argues for involvement in the Vietnam War and half of the group argues against involvement in the war.

## Collaborative Learning

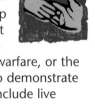

**MULTIMEDIA SHOW.** Work with a group to develop a multimedia show about war. Choose a topic, such as a patriotic look at war, the justification of warfare, or the tragedy of war. Then select media to demonstrate your point of view. Your show can include live demonstrations, such as skits, dance, or poetry; audiotapes; videotapes; and such visual media as sculpture, painting, and photography. Your show must include commentary and transitional material that holds the elements together.

# "Seeing" from Dakota

BY KATHLEEN NORRIS

## Literary
### TOOLS

ANECDOTE. An **anecdote** is a usually short narrative of an interesting, amusing, or biographical incident. As you read, notice the anecdotes in the selection.

DESCRIPTION. A **description**, one of the modes of writing, portrays a character, an object, or a scene. As you read, make a cluster chart of the selection's descriptions of the Great Plains landscape. One example has been done for you.

"Land, sky, and the everchanging light"

Great Plains

## Reader's
### Journal

What is your favorite landscape?

## About the
# AUTHOR

**Kathleen Norris** (1947–  ), poet and nonfiction writer, was born in Washington, DC, but grew up in different parts of the country. She spent most of her childhood summers in Lemmon, South Dakota. After high school in Hawaii and college in Vermont, she worked as arts administrator at the Academy of American Poets. In 1971, she published her first book of poems, *Falling Off*, which was followed by *How I Came to Drink My Grandmother's Piano*, *The Year of Common Things*, *The Middle of the World*, and *Little Girls in Church*. Norris's nonfiction books include *Dakota: A Spiritual Geography* (1993), *The Cloister Walk* (1996), and *Amazing Grace* (1998). She has received awards from the Guggenheim and Bush foundations.

In 1973 Norris moved from New York City to her late grandmother's home in Lemmon, South Dakota (population 1,614). She became a member of a Benedictine monastery in North Dakota, and her nonfiction exalts the rewards of monastic life, which gave her a greater appreciation of the concept of community, both social and spiritual. In Norris's words, "Any place has a spiritual geography. People can love Brooklyn or Chicago as passionately as a Dakota rancher loves the land, and there is much in American literature that attests to this. People tend to create small towns wherever they are. We don't live in big cities so much as in communities of friends, colleagues, relatives."

## About the
# SELECTION

**"Seeing"** is a chapter from Kathleen Norris's first nonfiction book, *Dakota: A Spiritual Geography* (1993), which was praised by critics, writers, and readers. The *New York Times Book Review* named it a Notable Book of the year, and *Library Journal* honored it among its Best Books of 1993. *Dakota* describes the harsh, desolate, yet sublime landscape of the Great Plains and its influence on the human spirit. "Seeing" is a visual account of that landscape.

# Seeing

## KATHLEEN NORRIS

> The midwestern landscape is abstract, and our response to
> the geology of the region might be similar to our response
> to the contemporary walls of paint in museums.
> We are forced to live in our eye.
> —Michael Martone

> Abba Bessarion, at the point of death, said, "The monk
> ought to be like the Cherubim and the Seraphim: all eye."
> —*The Desert Christian*

Once, when I was describing to a friend from Syracuse, New York, a place on the plains that I love, a ridge above a glacial moraine[1] with a view of almost fifty miles, she asked, "But what is there to see?"

> What place does Norris love?

The answer, of course, is nothing. Land, sky, and the everchanging light. Except for a few signs of human presence—power and telephone lines, an occasional farm building, the glint of a paved road in the distance—it's like looking at the ocean.

The landscape of western Dakota is not as abstract as the flats of Kansas, but it presents a similar challenge to the eye that appreciates the vertical definition of mountains or skyscrapers; that defines beauty in terms of the spectacular or the

---

1. **moraine.** Accumulation of earth and stones carried and finally deposited by a glacier

*Fort Pierre National Grassland, South Dakota.* Glen Allison.

busy: hills, trees, buildings, highways, people. We seem empty by comparison.

Here, the eye learns to appreciate slight variations, the possibilities inherent in emptiness. It sees that the emptiness is full of small things, like grasshoppers in their samurai[2] armor clicking and jumping as you pass. This empty land is full of grasses: sedges, switch grass, needlegrass, wheatgrass. Brome can grow waist-high by early summer. Fields of wheat, rye, oats, barley, flax, alfalfa. Acres of sunflowers brighten the land in summer, their heads alert, expectant. By fall they droop like sad children, waiting patiently for the first frost and harvest.

*Here, the eye learns to appreciate slight variations, the possibilities inherent in emptiness.*

What does the eye learn to appreciate in the Great Plains landscape? What small things fill the emptiness?

In spring it is a joy to discover, amid snow and mud and pale, withered grass, the delicate lavender of pasqueflower blooming on a ridge with a southern exposure. There is variety in the emptiness; the most prosaic pasture might contain hundreds of different wildflowers along with sage, yucca, and prairie cactus. Coulees harbor chokecherry, buffalo berry, and gooseberry bushes in their gentle folds, along with groves of silvery cottonwoods and Russian olive. Lone junipers often grow on exposed hillsides.

This seemingly empty land is busy with inhabitants. Low to the ground are bullsnakes, rattlers, mice, gophers, moles, grouse, prairie chickens, and pheasant.

What inhabitants reside in the Plains?

Prairie dogs are more noticeable, as they denude the landscape with their villages. Badgers and skunk lumber busily through the grass. Jackrabbits, weasels, and foxes are quicker, but the great runners of the Plains are the coyote, antelope, and deer. Meadowlarks, killdeer, blackbirds, lark buntings, crows, and seagulls dart above the fields, and a large variety of hawks, eagles, and vultures glide above it all, hunting for prey.

Along with the largeness of the visible—too much horizon, too much sky—this land's essential indifference to the human can be unnerving. We had a visitor, a friend from back East who flew into Bismarck and started a two-week visit by photographing the highway on the way to Lemmon; "Look how far you can see!" he kept exclaiming, trying to capture the whole of it in his camera lens. He seemed relieved to find a few trees in town and in our yard, and did not relish going back out into open country.

One night he called a woman friend from a phone booth on Main Street and asked her to marry him. After less than a week, he decided to cut his visit short and get off the Plains. He and his fiancée broke off the engagement, mutually and amicably, not long after he got home to Boston. The proposal had been a symptom of "Plains fever."

---

2. **samurai.** Relating to a Japanese warrior

**WORDS FOR EVERYDAY USE**

**in • her • ent** (in hir' ənt) *adj.,* belonging by nature or habit. *Raul's inherent good manners are the result of his parents' good example.*

**pro • sa • ic** (prō zā' ik) *adj.,* dull; unimaginative. *Jenny's essay was rather prosaic: she had added no original thoughts.*

**cou • lee** (kü' lē) *n.,* ravine, usually a small or shallow one. *The rabbit darted down into the hollow of the coulee.*

**lum • ber** (ləm' bər) *vi.,* move clumsily and in an unwieldy manner. *Ron lumbered across the living room, knocking a figurine to the floor.*

**am • i • ca • bly** (a' mi kə bəl ē) *adv.,* in a friendly or peaceable manner. *Leslie and Dianne settled their dispute amicably and remained friends.*

A person is forced inward by the spareness of what is outward and visible in all this land and sky. The beauty of the Plains is like that of an icon; it does not give an inch to sentiment or romance. The flow of the land, with its odd twists and buttes, is like the flow of Gregorian chant[3] that rises and falls beyond melody, beyond reason or human expectation, but perfectly.

*What is the effect of the "spareness" of the landscape?*

Maybe seeing the Plains is like seeing an icon: what seems stern and almost empty is merely open, a door into some simple and holy state.

Not long ago, at a difficult time in my life, when my husband was recovering from surgery, I attended a drum ceremony with a Native American friend. Men and boys gathered around the sacred drum and sang a song to bless it. Their singing was high-pitched, repetitive, solemn, and loud. As they approached the song's end, drumming louder and louder, I realized that the music was also restorative; my two-day headache was gone, my troubles no longer seemed so burdensome.

*What event did Norris attend? With whom did she go?*

I wondered how this loud, shrill, holy music, the indigenous song of those who have truly seen the Plains, could be so restful, while the Gregorian chant that I am just learning to sing can be so quiet, and yet as stirring as any drum. Put it down to ecstasy. ■

*What effect did the music have on Norris?*

---

3. **Gregorian chant.** A monotone and non-rhythmic liturgical chant of the Roman Catholic Church

---

**WORDS FOR EVERYDAY USE**

i • con (ī′ kän) *n.,* highly symbolic religious image. *The Russian icon portrayed Mary and the baby Jesus.*

in • dig • e • nous (in di′ jə nəs) *adj.,* having originated in and being produced, growing, living, or occurring naturally in a particular region or environment. *The indigenous Caribbean plants died when transplanted to South Dakota.*

---

## Respond to the SELECTION

If you were Norris, what would you hope readers would glean from "Seeing"?

# INVESTIGATE, Inquire, *Imagine*

**Recall:** GATHERING FACTS

1a. What did Norris's friend from Syracuse want to know about the landscape of the Great Plains?

2a. What aspects of the Dakotan landscape does Norris describe?

3a. Why did Norris's friend from Boston call a woman friend back East?

➤ **Interpret:** FINDING MEANING

1b. Based on Norris's response, is she a city person or a country person? How can you tell?

2b. How does Norris feel about the landscape?

3b. What do you think is meant by "Plains fever"?

**Analyze:** TAKING THINGS APART

4a. Explain what makes the Great Plains similar to a religious icon.

➤ **Synthesize:** BRINGING THINGS TOGETHER

4b. What do Norris's references to religious icons, Gregorian chant, and Native American drum ceremonies illustrate?

**Evaluate:** MAKING JUDGMENTS

5a. How effectively does Norris analyze the effect of the Dakotan landscape on the viewer?

➤ **Extend:** CONNECTING IDEAS

5b. The selection you have just read is called "Seeing." Select a different sense and explain how the essay would be different if it focused on that sense.

# Understanding *Literature*

**ANECDOTE.** Review the definition of **anecdote** in the Handbook of Literary Terms. What three anecdotes does Norris tell? What do they reveal about the Dakotas?

**DESCRIPTION.** Review the definition of **description** in the Handbook of Literary Terms and the graphic organizer you made for Literary Tools on page 998. What do Norris's descriptions reveal about the emptiness of the Dakotan landscape? What is your favorite description? Why?

# WRITER'S JOURNAL

1. Imagine you are visiting Norris. Write a **postcard** to a friend describing what you see on the plains.

2. Imagine you had a distant friend visit your part of the country. Write an **anecdote** describing an incident from his or her experience.

3. Imagine you are Norris's male friend from back East. Write a **letter** to your woman friend to whom you had proposed explaining that you want to break off the engagement, which was precipitated by "Plains fever."

# Integrating *the* LANGUAGE ARTS

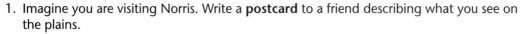

## Language, Grammar, and Style

**EXPANDING SENTENCES.** Expand each of the following sentences by adding modifiers, prepositional phrases, appositives, independent clauses, or subordinate clauses, as indicated. For more information, read the Language Arts Survey 3.36, "Combining and Expanding Sentences." Also refer to 3.65, "Modifiers—Adjectives and Adverbs," 3.68, "Linkers and Joiners," and 3.77, "Appositives."

1. There is nothing to see—only land, sky, and light. (modifier)

2. Norris's friend from Boston proposed to a woman he knew. (prepositional phrase)

3. A friend asked what there was to see. (appositive)

4. Norris attended a Native American drum ceremony. (independent clause)

5. Hills, trees, buildings, highways, and people are absent from the Great Plains landscape. (subordinate clause)

## Study and Research & Applied English

**TRAVEL BROCHURE.** Research a tourist site in North or South Dakota and discover what there is to do and see there. Then write a brochure that tourists would read. Describe and illustrate the locations in your brochure, providing historical background information and directions.

## Media Literacy

**INTERNET RESEARCH LOG.** On the Internet, research Native American drum ceremonies and powwows. Track your research path by keeping a log of the sites you visit. Try to find as many interactive sites as possible. You may want to begin your search by visiting **Minnesota Public Radio News** at http://news.mpr.org/ and searching for the documentary feature "Song Catcher, Frances Densmore of Red Wing." Densmore researched and recorded Native American music, and her audio recordings are included on MPR's Internet site.

# Literary TOOLS

THESIS. A **thesis** is a main idea that is supported in a work of nonfictional prose. As you read the essay, determine what you think is Boorstin's thesis.

COHERENCE. **Coherence** is the logical arrangement and progression of ideas in a speech or piece of writing. As you read, make a cluster chart to demonstrate Boorstin's coherence in discussing his optimism about America.

"One answer is very personal"— boosterism in Tulsa

Why Boorstin Is Optimistic about America

## Reader's Journal

For what reasons are you optimistic about the United States?

# "Why I Am *Optimistic* about AMERICA"

BY DANIEL J. BOORSTIN

## About the AUTHOR

**Daniel J. Boorstin** (1914–  ) was born in Atlanta, Georgia, but spent most of his youth in Tulsa, Oklahoma, as he describes in this selection. At Harvard he majored in English history and literature. After studying law at Oxford in England, he earned a law degree at Yale. He taught at Harvard, Radcliffe, and the University of Chicago, then moved to Washington, DC, in 1969 to accept the post of Director of the National Museum of American History at the Smithsonian. Seven years later, he was appointed Librarian of Congress, a position he held until his retirement in 1987. Boorstin has received three Pulitzer Prizes for his books, which include *The Mysterious Science of Law* (1941), *The Lost World of Thomas Jefferson* (1948), *The Americans* (1958–1973), *The Image* (1961), *The Discoverers* (1983), *The Creators* (1992), *Cleopatra's Nose: Essays on the Unexpected* (1994), and *The Seekers* (1998).

## About the SELECTION

**"Why I Am Optimistic about America"** was published in *Parade* magazine July 10, 1994. In this essay Boorstin explains the roots of his American brand of optimism and describes how the United States has made advances in the areas of religion, language, law, and wealth.

# Why I Am *Optimistic* about AMERICA

DANIEL J. BOORSTIN

*Americana*, 1999. Julie Delton. Private Collection.

You ask what is the basis for my optimism. With a Europe in <u>disarray</u> in a century plagued by two murderous World Wars, by <u>genocides</u> without <u>precedent</u>—the German-Nazi massacre of six million and the Stalin-Soviet massacre of 30 million—how can I speak so hopefully about the American future?

One answer is very personal. I was raised and went to public school in the 1920s in Tulsa, Okla., which then called itself "The Oil Capital of the World," but could perhaps have been called "The Optimism Capital of the World." Only 10 years before my family came to Oklahoma, the Indian Territory had been admitted to the Union as the 46th state.

*What personal reason does Boorstin give for his optimism about America?*

The city thrived on "booster" pride, and before I graduated from Central High School, it boasted two daily newspapers, three skyscrapers, houses designed by Frank Lloyd Wright and a public-school system superintended by the former U.S. Commissioner of Education. The Kiwanis, Rotary, and Chamber of Commerce competed furiously in projects of civic improvement. For our high school English classes, we memorized and <u>declaimed</u> patriotic orations—from Patrick Henry's "Give Me Liberty or Give Me Death" and Lincoln's "Gettysburg Address" to Henry Grady's "The New South" and Emile Zola's "Plea for Dreyfus." We wrote speeches on the virtues of the federal Constitution for a national contest, which held its finals before the Supreme Court in Washington.

Of course there were dark shadows—like the relentless racial segregation, the brutal race riots of the 1920s, and the Ku Klux Klan. But these were not visible or prominent in my life. The city <u>burgeoned</u>, proudly built a grand new railroad depot, a university, an elegant public library and a city hall—and soon it was <u>embellished</u> by art museums of national rank.

My father was one of the most enthusiastic "boosters," and the growing city seemed to justify his extravagant optimism. I came to sympathize with that American frontier newspaperman who was attacked for reporting as facts the mythic marvels of his upstart pioneer village—including its impressive hotel and prosperous Main Street. In America, he said, it was not fair to object to the rosy reports of community boosters simply because they had "not yet gone through the formality of taking place." I suppose I have never been cured of my distinctively American Oklahoma optimism, bred in the bone and confirmed by the real history of Tulsa.

Another reason for my optimism is in American history. The exhilarating features of our history and culture have in the past been captured in the idea of "American Exceptionalism." This is a long word for a simple idea: the traditional belief that the United States is a very special place, unique in crucial ways. American Exceptionalism is a name too for a cosmopolitan, optimistic and humanistic view of history—that the modern world, while profiting from the European inheritance, need not be imprisoned in Old World molds. And, therefore, that

*What is another reason for Boorstin's optimism?*

*What is "American Exceptionalism"?*

---

**WORDS FOR EVERYDAY USE**

**dis • ar • ray** (di sə rā´) *n.*, lack of order or sequence. *The outfits that Gina had tried on were in <u>disarray</u>—on the floor, on the bed, and on the chair.*

**geno • cide** (je´ nə sīd´) *n.*, deliberate and systematic destruction of a racial, political, or cultural group. *The <u>genocide</u> of Jews during the Third Reich was well documented by the Nazis.*

**prec • e • dent** (pre´ sə dənt) *n.*, something done or said that may serve as an example or rule to authorize or justify a subsequent act of the same or an analogous kind. *The judge ruled out Ms. Lawson's motion on behalf of her client because there was no legal <u>precedent</u>.*

**de • claim** (di klām´) *vi.*, recite a speech. *At the speech meet, Laurie <u>declaimed</u> a humorous selection by George Carlin.*

**bur • geon** (bur´ jən) *vi.*, grow and expand rapidly. *The suburb <u>burgeoned</u> with new housing once Snelling Avenue was paved.*

**em • bel • lish** (im be´ lish) *vt.*, make beautiful with ornamentation. *A Japanese screen <u>embellished</u> the set design for the play.*

the future of the United States and of its people need not be governed by the same expectations or plagued by the same problems that had afflicted people elsewhere.

How have we lost sight of this beacon?

We have been seduced by the rise of our country as a "superpower." For while power is quantitative, the uniqueness of the United States is not merely quantitative. We have suffered, too, from the consequences of our freedom. Totalitarian societies exaggerate their virtues. But free societies like ours somehow seize the temptation to exaggerate their vices. The negativism of our press and television reporting are, of course, the best evidence of our freedom to scrutinize ourselves. Far better this than the chauvinism of self-righteousness which has been the death of totalitarian empires in our time.

Yet we must never forget that, while to the Old World we were the Unexpected Land, we have ever since been the Land of the Unexpected. The main features of the culture of our United States are just what the wise men of Europe, looking at their own past, could not have conjured up. A short list of the American surprises includes what we have done here with four basic elements of culture— religion, language, law, and wealth.

*Which four areas of American culture represent historical "surprises"?*

*Who could have predicted that the United States, unlike the nations from which our people came, would never suffer a religious war?*

**Religion.** By the time of the European settlement of North America, the history of the rising nations of Western Europe had been punctuated by torture and massacre in the name of religion. There was the notorious Spanish Inquisition of the 15th century (1478), the bloody Massacre of St. Bartholomew (1572) in France and, in Germany during the very years of the Puritan settlements in New England, the Thirty Years War (1618–1648), which spread into a general conflict between Protestant and Catholic Europe. In that war alone, some 10 percent of the German population was slaughtered in the name of religious orthodoxy.

This seemed not to augur well for a nation like ours, whose Pilgrims were obsessed with religion and had fled England to fulfill their passionate dream. Their religious faith gave them courage to brave the ocean-crossing, the hardships of an unknown land and the risks of hostile natives, despite their lonely remoteness from ancestral homes.

Who could have predicted that the United States, unlike the nations from which our people came, would never suffer a religious war? That the Protestants and Catholics who had tortured and massacred each other in Europe would establish peaceful neighboring communities from New England to

*What is surprising about religion in America?*

**WORDS FOR EVERYDAY USE**

**bea • con** (bē′ kən) n., source of light or inspiration. *The beacon from the lighthouse guided the ship to safety.*

**quan • ti • ta • tive** (kwän′ tə tā tiv) adj., of, relating to, or expressible in terms of quantity. *Joseph favored qualitative rather than quantitative praise for his efforts.*

**to • tal • i • tar • i • an** (tō ta lə ter′ ē ən) adj., of or relating to a political regime based on subordination of the individual to the state and strict control of all aspects of the life and productive capacity of the nation, especially by coercive measures. *Millions of innocent Soviets lost their lives under Stalin's totalitarian regime.*

**scru • ti • nize** (skrüt′ ən īz) vi., examine closely and minutely. *Martin scrutinized the classifieds, searching every ad to find an apartment that allowed pets.*

**con • jure** (kän′ jər) vt., bring into being as if by magic. *Melissa conjured up twenty volunteers for the talent show.*

**punc • tu • ate** (pəŋk′ chə wāt) vt., break into or interrupt at intervals. *José punctuated his speech with exaggerated facial expressions and vivid gestures.*

**au • gur** (ô′ gər) vt., foretell, especially from omens. *Higher pay augurs a bright future.*

Maryland and Virginia? That Jews would here find asylum from ghettos and pogroms? That—though the U.S. would remain conspicuously a nation of churchgoers—the separation of Church and State would become a cornerstone of civic life? Or that public-school principals in the 20th century would be challenged by how to promote a holiday spirit without seeming to favor or neglect Christmas, Hanukkah or Kwanzaa?

**Language.** In Europe, languages had made nations. Spanish, Portuguese, English, French, German and Italian had produced their own literatures—even before there was a Spain, a Portugal, an England, a France, a Germany or an Italy. But the United States was the first great modern nation without its own language. Our country has been uniquely created by people willing and able to borrow a language.

Oddly enough, the English language has helped make us a congenitally multicultural nation, since most Americans have not come from the land of Shakespeare. So we have learned here that people do not lose their civic dignity by speaking the language of a new community. The English language has been invigorated and Americanized by countless importations of words from German, Italian, French, Spanish, Yiddish and American Indian tongues, among others.

The surprising result is that, without a unique national language, our community has developed a language wonderfully expressive of the vitality and variety of our people. Perhaps we should really call Broken English our distinctive American

*Why should our language be called "Broken English"?*

language, for it bears the mark of our immigrant history.

**Law.** Nowadays, we can be puzzled at the spectacle of peoples from Russia to South Africa contending over how, whether, and when to adopt a "constitution." They seem to have the odd notion that a "constitution" can be created instantly by vote of a legislature or by a popular election. All this offers a sharp contrast to our Anglo-American experience.

The tradition of a fundamental law—a "constitution"—that we inherited from England reached back

*Which country gave us the basis for our constitution?*

to at least the 13th century. The by-product of a nation's whole history, the unwritten English constitution was a pillar of government and of the people's rights. No one could have foreseen that such a tradition would find a transatlantic written reincarnation in the deliberations of 55 colonials meeting in Independence Hall in Philadelphia in 1787. So our United States was created by a constitution. With another surprising result—that our parvenu[1] nation at the end of the 20th century now lives by the most venerable (and probably most venerated) written constitution in the world. And that the constitution would survive by its very power to be amended (with difficulty).

Yet who could have predicted that a nation whose birth certificate bore the declaration that "all men are created equal" should have been one of the last to abolish slavery? Slavery was abolished in the British Empire in 1833. Still,

---

1. **parvenu.** Person who has recently or suddenly risen to an unaccustomed position of wealth or power and has not yet gained the prestige, dignity, or manner associated with it

---

WORDS FOR EVERYDAY USE

**asy • lum** (ə sī′ ləm) *n.*, place of retreat and security. *Mrs. Dobbs found asylum in a shelter for battered women.*

**con • spic • u • ous • ly** (kən spi′ kyə wəs lē) *adv.*, in a way that attracts attention. *The governor was conspicuously dressed at the press conference: he wore a pink feather boa and wraparound shades.*

**in • vig • o • rate** (in vi′ gə rāt) *vt.*, give life and energy to. *Mr. Broten's jokes invigorated the class.*

**con • tend** (kən tend′) *vi.*, strive in debate. *Students in the small group contended over the assignment of roles.*

**ven • er • a • ble** (ven′ ər ə bəl) *adj.*, calling forth respect through age, character, and attainments. *The venerable speaker has just founded his third company.*

**ven • er • at • ed** (ve′ nə rāt əd) *adj.*, regarded with reverential respect or with admiring deference. *The venerated writer was given an honorary degree by the university.*

three decades passed before Lincoln's Emancipation Proclamation of 1863 freed slaves in the Southern secessionist states, followed by the Thirteenth Amendment to the Constitution outlawing slavery in all the United States (1865). The slave trade survived only in certain Muslim states and in parts of Africa.

On the other side, we must note that our only Civil War was fought in a struggle to free a subject people. For this, too, it is hard to find a precedent. And a legacy of the history of slavery in the United States has been the equally unprecedented phenomenon of a conscience-wracked nation. This has led us to create a host of novel institutions—"equal opportunity" laws, "affirmative action," among others—in our <u>strenuous</u> effort to compensate for past injustices.

We should not be surprised that Russians are obsessively suspicious of foreigners coming to their country—after their long domination by the Mongols, their invasion by Napoleon and his forces of "liberation" who burned Moscow, and by the Germans in World War II who left 20 million casualties. No wonder the Russians see the foreigner as the invader or the agent of invaders.

In the United States, we have been luckily free of this stereotype. Instead, our vision of the newcomer has been <u>refracted</u> in the experience of our own recent immigrant ancestors. "Strangers are welcome," Benjamin Franklin explained in his *Information to those Who Would Remove to America* (1782), "because there is room enough for them all, and therefore the old inhabitants are not jealous of them." This has been the mainstream of our history: welcoming the newcomer as worker, customer, community-builder, fellow-citizen-in-the-making. The uniquely American notion of a Nation of Nations was never more vivid than today.

*The uniquely American notion of a Nation of Nations was never more vivid than today.*

**Wealth.** We are told that the United States is a *rich* nation. But what really distinguishes us is less our wealth than our radically novel way of measuring a society's material well-being.

Wealth—which was at the center of English mercantilist thinking before the American Revolution—was a static notion. The wealth of the world, measured primarily in gold and silver treasure, was supposed to be a fixed quantity, a pie that could be sliced one way or another. But the size of the pie could not be substantially increased. A bigger slice for Great Britain meant a smaller slice for France or Spain or somebody else, and one nation's gain was another's loss.

Our New World changed that way of thinking. People have come here not for wealth but for a better "way of life." America blurred the boundary between the material and the spiritual. All this was reinforced by the spectacular progress of our technology, exploiting the resources of a rich, little-known and sparsely populated continent.

The American Revolution then was, among other things, a struggle between the time-honored idea of "wealth" and a New World idea of "standard of living." This characteristically American idea appears to have entered our language only at the beginning of this century. It could hardly have been conceived in an Old World burdened with the legacy of feudal "rights," landed aristocracies, royal courts,

WORDS
FOR
EVERYDAY
USE

stren • u • ous (stren′ yə wəs) *adj.*, vigorously active. <u>*Strenuous*</u> *aerobic exercises kept Erica in shape.*

re • fract (ri frakt′) *vt.*, alter or distort. *The prism <u>refracted</u> the light, causing rainbows to form.*

<u>sacrosanct</u> guild monopolies and ancestral cemeteries. Wealth is what someone possesses, but a standard of living is what people *share*. Wealth can be secretly hoarded, but a standard of living can only be publicly enjoyed. For it is the level of goods, housing, services, health, comfort and education agreed to be appropriate.

**What distinction does Boorstin make between wealth and a standard of living?**

All these remarkable transformations of the culture of the Older World add up to American Exceptionalism.

Recently, we have heard apologies for expressions of belief in American uniqueness—as if it were somehow provincial or chauvinist. But our ex-Colonial nation in this post-Colonial age would do well to see what the <u>prescient</u> French man of letters André Malraux observed on his visit to President Kennedy in the White House in 1962: "The United States is today the country that assumes the destiny of man . . . For the first time, a country has become the world's leader without achieving this through conquest, and it is strange to think that for thousands of years one single country has found power while seeking only justice."

And, he might have added, while seeking community. We must see the unique power of the United States, then, not as the power of power, but as the power of example. Another name for history.

**What does Boorstin see as the unique power of the United States?**

The depressing spectacle today of a Europe at war with itself has offered us a melodrama of those same ghosts of ethnic, racial, and religious hate that generations of immigrants have come to America to escape. Now, more than ever, we must <u>inoculate</u> ourselves against these <u>latent</u> perils. Luckily, the states of our federal union are not ethnic, racial, or religious <u>enclaves</u>. Luckily, we have remained a wonderfully mobile people. There is no better <u>antidote</u> to these perils abroad than a frank and vivid recognition of the uniqueness of our history of the special opportunities offered us. Nor could there be greater folly than refusing to enjoy the happy accidents of our history.

The uniqueness that Jefferson and Lincoln claimed for us, we must remember, was for the sake of *all* mankind. Our Declaration of Independence takes its cue from "the course of human events." The Great Seal of the United States on our dollar bill still proclaims "Novus Ordo Seclorum"—a new order of the centuries. When before had people put so much faith in the unexpected? ∎

---

**WORDS FOR EVERYDAY USE**

**sac • ro • sanct** (saʹ krō saŋ[k]t) *adj.*, treated as if holy. *The child's hideaway in the closet under the stairs was <u>sacrosanct</u>, and he hid all his treasures there.*

**pre • scient** (preʹ sh[ē]ənt) *adj.*, possessing foreknowledge of events. *The journalist's <u>prescient</u> remarks about the country's readiness for war were remembered when it invaded a neighboring country.*

**in • oc • u • late** (i näʹ kyə lāt) *vt.*, protect as if by giving an inoculation. *Jeremy wanted to <u>inoculate</u> himself against the criticism he continually heard at home.*

**la • tent** (lāʹ tənt) *adj.*, present and capable of becoming obvious or active, though not now visible. *The doctor feared Darla suffered from a <u>latent</u> infection in her lungs.*

**en • clave** (enʹ klāv; änʹ klāv) *n.*, distinct territorial, cultural, or social unit enclosed within, or as if within, foreign territory. *Little Italy and Chinatown are famous ethnic <u>enclaves</u> in New York City.*

**an • ti • dote** (anʹ ti dōt) *n.*, something that relieves, prevents, or counteracts. *"What do you see as the <u>antidote</u> to the increased mechanization of society?" asked our social studies teacher.*

---

How would Boorstin explain the continued influx of immigrants into the United States?

# INVESTIGATE, Inquire, Imagine

**Recall:** GATHERING FACTS

1a. Why is Boorstin optimistic about America?

2a. What were the wise men of Europe incapable of imagining for the United States?

3a. What types of hate still exist in Europe?

**Interpret:** FINDING MEANING

1b. Why was Boorstin unconcerned about "the relentless racial segregation, the brutal race riots," and the Ku Klux Klan when he was growing up?

2b. What does "American Exceptionalism" allow?

3b. What attitude does Boorstin have toward the "special opportunities" of America?

---

**Analyze:** TAKING THINGS APART

4a. Identify major American accomplishments in the areas of religion, language, law, and wealth.

**Synthesize:** BRINGING THINGS TOGETHER

4b. Boorstin calls America a "Nation of Nations." What does he mean by this term, and what does it mean to incoming immigrants?

---

**Evaluate:** MAKING JUDGMENTS

5a. Evaluate how realistic a portrait of the United States Boorstin paints in his essay.

**Extend:** CONNECTING IDEAS

5b. Boorstin reminds us that the dollar bill proclaims "Novus Ordo Seclorum" (a new order of the centuries). Given his assessment of the United States today, what do you think Boorstin would foresee for our country in the twenty-first century?

---

# Understanding Literature

**THESIS.** Review the definition for thesis in the Handbook of Literary Terms. What do you think is the thesis of this essay? How does Boorstin support his thesis?

**COHERENCE.** Review the definition for **coherence** in the Handbook of Literary Terms and the graphic organizer you prepared in Literary Tools on page 1004. With what logical arrangement does Boorstin lay out his argument that there is reason for optimism about America? How do Boorstin's ideas progress?

# WRITER'S JOURNAL

1. Write an **editorial** for your local newspaper stating what reasons there are for optimism in your town or city.

2. Write Boorstin a **letter**, stating why you agree or disagree with his essay.

3. Boorstin states that American Exceptionalism is a name for a "cosmopolitan, optimistic and humanistic view of history." Write a **paragraph** explaining what Boorstin means.

# Integrating
## *the* LANGUAGE ARTS

## Language, Grammar, and Style

**CORRECTING RUN-ONS.** Read the Language Arts Survey 3.34, "Correcting Sentence Run-ons." Then rewrite the following run-ons. Correct each one, either by making it into two separate sentences or by adding a comma and a coordinating conjunction. If the sentence is not a run-on, copy it as it is.

1. Boorstin grew up in Tulsa, Oklahoma he declaimed patriotic speeches in school.

2. The city built a new railroad depot, a university, a public library, a city hall soon it was embellished by art museums.

3. American Exceptionalism means the United States is a very special place it is unique in crucial ways.

4. America celebrates religious diversity, there has never been a religious war in the United States.

5. American culture provides other reasons for optimism in the areas of religion, language, law, and wealth.

## Critical Thinking

**PRO AND CON CHART.** Read the Language Arts Survey 2.21, "Pro and Con Charts." Then make a pro and con chart using the following proposition: "Daniel Boorstin provides convincing evidence for being optimistic about America."

## Speaking and Listening & Study and Research

**STANDARD OF LIVING.** Boorstin differentiates between wealth and the standard of living when he states, "Wealth is what someone possesses, but a standard of living is what people *share*."

Research facts about the standard of living in the United States. Make charts and graphs to illustrate your findings and share them with the class in a presentation about America's standard of living.

## Study and Research

**REASONS FOR THE CIVIL WAR.** Boorstin states ". . . we must note that our only Civil War was fought in a struggle to free a subject people." Was the abolition of slavery one of the principal causes for starting the Civil War? Research the factors that led up to the Civil War and assess Boorstin's statement. Is his statement accurate, based on your research? Why, or why not?

## "What Is Supposed to Happen"
## by Naomi Shihab Nye

When you were small,
we watched you sleeping,
waves of breath
filling your chest.
Sometimes we hid behind
the wall of baby, soft cradle
of baby needs.
I loved carrying you between
my own body and the world.

Now you are sharpening pencils,
entering the forest of
lunch boxes, little desks.
People I never saw before
call out your name
and you wave.

This loss I feel,
this shrinking,
as your field of roses
grows and grows. . . .

Now I understand history.
Now I understand my mother's ancient eyes.

## from *Beloved*
## by Toni Morrison

I am beloved and she is mine. Sethe is the one that picked
flowers, yellow flowers in the place before the crouching.
Took them away from their green leaves. They are on the
quilt now where we sleep. She was about to smile at me when
the men without skin came and took us up into the sunlight
with the dead and shoved them into the sea. Sethe went into
the sea. She went there. They did not push her. She went
there. She was getting ready to smile at me and when she saw
the dead people pushed into the sea she went also and left me
there with no face or hers. Sethe is the face I found and lost in
the water under the bridge. When I went in, I saw her face
coming to me and it was my face too. I wanted to join. I tried
to join, but she went up into the pieces of light at the top of
the water. I lost her again, but I found the house she whispered to me and there she was, smiling at last. It's good, but I
cannot lose her again. All I want to know is why did she go in
the water in the place where we crouched? Why did she do
that when she was just about to smile at me? I wanted to join
her in the sea but I could not move; I wanted to help her
when she was picking the flowers, but the clouds of gunsmoke
blinded me and I lost her. Three times I lost her: once with
the flowers because of the noisy clouds of smoke; once when
she went into the sea instead of smiling at me; once under the
bridge when I went in to join her and she came toward me
but did not smile. She whispered to me, chewed me, and
swam away. Now I have found her in this house. She smiles at
me and it is my own face smiling. I will not lose her again.
She is mine.

• • •

Beloved
You are my sister
You are my daughter
You are my face; you are me
I have found you again; you have come back to me
You are my Beloved
You are mine
You are mine
You are mine

I have your milk
I have your smile
I will take care of you

You are my face; I am you. Why did you leave me who am you?
I will never leave you again
Don't ever leave me again
You will never leave me again
You went in the water
I drank your blood
I brought your milk

You forgot to smile
I loved you
You hurt me
You came back to me
You left me

I waited for you
You are mine
You are mine
You are mine

"There is no question that the transition from the culture of the book to the culture of electronic communication will radically alter the ways in which we use language on every societal level."

—Sven Birkerts

A **webzine,** an Internet magazine, is an exciting addition to the list of classroom publishing possibilities. Through a webzine, your class can reach a national, even global, audience. With nearly half of American households online, a webzine has the potential of reaching over 100 million people in America alone.

**WRITING ASSIGNMENT.** For this assignment, you will create a webzine or any other form of multimedia presentation about a contemporary author of your choice.

**EXAMINING THE MODEL.** Look at the faces in the class picture. Could that be your class, either online or in another type of multimedia project? One of Dr. Gary Wiener's AP English classes at Brighton High School in Rochester, New York, created this webzine to publish the essays about authors that they had written. Spend some time

# Guided Writing

## CREATING A MULTIMEDIA PRESENTATION

Writers write because they must; not because of an assignment, but because they have something to say—something that hasn't been said in quite that manner, something that others need to know. That something might be new information, or it might be an insight about life or human nature. Whatever the reason for writing, writers are voices that want to be heard. This is what publishing is: being heard.

In the classroom, publishing may mean that students read their papers out loud. Maybe the teacher prints and hands out copies of everybody's work. Perhaps there is there a bulletin board or a hallway where posters and artwork are displayed. However, classroom publishing is not limited to these forms. With the advent of easy access to technological publishing, new formats constantly appear as video, audio, and computer technologies combine to create multimedia presentations that dazzle audiences through their imaginative use of colors, patterns, music, text, and visuals.

### Professional Model
*The Bag Lunch* Webzine
by AP English Class, Brighton High School, Rochester, New York
http://www.bcsd.org/BHS/english/mag97/

# Prewriting

**FINDING YOUR VOICE.** A multimedia presentation gives you many new elements—colors, patterns, music, sounds, and graphics—to express your personality and attitude toward your topic author. However, the way you handle the text about the author is still crucial. Your text may be limited. It will be competing with other elements, so precise word choice and effective sentence structure are more important than ever.

If you write seriously about serious themes, your approach may be quite different from that of another writer who is pointing out the humorous flaws of humanity and society. How might your use of language reflect these different attitudes? How might your choices for colors, graphics, and music change? The essays in *The Bag Lunch* are quite serious, but the preface and afterword still maintain a friendly, light tone. While the graphics and photos seem to suggest that this is serious writing, the producers of *The Bag Lunch* don't take themselves too seriously.

**IDENTIFYING YOUR AUDIENCE.** *The Bag Lunch* is a scholarly effort written by high school students. Each student was responsible for writing a critical essay on an important American writer. The intended audience is other serious students, teachers, and lovers of literature. Consider potential audiences for your multimedia project about an author. Your teacher may show the efforts of your class to future students to give them an overview of American authors. Parents may view your multimedia presentation to learn about the skills you are learning. Your presentation might become part of your graduation portfolio. Your peers, too, will be interested in your message and the methods you chose to present it.

**WRITING WITH A PLAN.** Developing a multimedia presentation is a multifaceted undertaking. You will use several skills to accomplish many tasks. Start by breaking a multimedia presentation down into its major components. You will need:

- text about your author
- a presentation mode such as a video, computer presentation, or a webzine
- a design that incorporates your text and media elements and that works with your presentation mode
- media elements such as graphics, recordings, music, and movies

Next, consider the steps and needs for developing each of these components.

**TEXT.** You may already know which author you would like to use for your presentation. If not, review the literature selections and author information in your textbook, possibly discussing your ideas with other students. You might also consider the previous looking at the picture of *The Bag Lunch* home page, or if possible, open the webzine at http://www.bcsd.org/BHS/english/mag97/. As you explore the picture or the webzine, consider how artfully and deliberately the class combined text, graphics, and sound to contribute to the image and goal they wanted to achieve.

Consider the title. What might the title suggest about the webzine? How do the graphics and word choices complement the webzine's title and the theme? What information would you expect to find in this webzine? How does the layout contribute to accessing the information?

**VIEWING THE WEBZINE.** If you can view the webzine, consider these questions: What purpose does the preface serve? the afterword? What is the tone of the statement on plagiarism? What themes are developed in the students' essays?

Who is your favorite contemporary writer? Does one writer speak to you in a unique way? Which author do you most want to recommend to others? How might the author's life connect with the lives of your classmates? How does the author develop particular attitudes and philosophies? What themes does the author pursue in his or her work?

**PRESENTATION MODE.**
Depending on your resources, some presentation modes— video, electronic, or online— may come to mind immediately. In other cases, you may think that your resources are too limited to produce a multimedia presentation. Keep in mind that a multimedia presentation is not truly dependent on advanced technology. A reading, accompanied by music and graphics, can be one of the most effective multimedia presentations. Whichever method you use, remember that it is the content, not the format, that is most important. *The Bag Lunch* could have been done in another fashion and been as effective, as long as the quality of the writing remained high.

work you have done in Units 7 and 11. Then decide which author you will present.

Collect resources and begin your research about the author. As you are reviewing your resource materials, work on developing a purpose and focus for your presentation. Use your note-taking skills to record information that you will use. Use your documentation skills to credit your references.

Develop your thesis statement, the main point you want to present about the author. Decide on and organize the information you will use to support your thesis. Your presentation should demonstrate your ability to present scholarship in a fresh way, so don't recycle someone else's information. Make it your own. Then draft your text to prepare it for the next step— working it into a multimedia format. You will make decisions about the final draft as you prepare the presentation.

**DESIGN.** Multimedia presentations might dazzle the viewer; however, if they are designed poorly or lack interesting information, they will lose their appeal. Keep several basic principles of design in mind as you plan.

- **The text should be easy to read.** If all of the text is not presented in one place, as in an essay, divide the text into clear and logical topics and subtopics. Use short paragraphs, no longer than five to seven sentences. Use clear connections and transitions to help your reader follow the text. Keep in mind that on-screen text is more difficult to read than hard copy text.
- **The technology aspects should not get in the way of the presentation.** A presentation can easily be lost if the video doesn't play or a site does not operate efficiently. Avoid the temptation to overload your presentation. Clarity and sufficiency should serve as guidelines.
- **The presentation should be visually appealing.** Consider the shape and placement of text and graphics. Do they have a pattern and flow that is easy to follow? Do colors and shapes work with or against each other? Balance your creativity with your audience's need to visually understand your presentation.

The use of music, sounds, and voice-overs should also be balanced with your awareness of your audience's perspective. A dynamic song clip might actually detract from your purpose rather than enhance it if it is not used effectively.

**MEDIA ELEMENTS.** Start by considering the possibilities. Allow yourself to dream here. Picture what your multimedia presentation would be like if you had unlimited resources.

Next, consider availability. Your school library, art department, Internet sites, or your own personal materials may be rich depositories of video, sounds, and graphics. Explore to see what is available.

Finally, consider reality. Some media elements may be available, but you may not have the resources to work with them effectively. Experiment to see what works in your situation. A multimedia presentation that is somewhat limited in media elements but works flawlessly is of greater value than a presentation full of media that doesn't function.

## Student Model—Graphic Organizer

Marcus used the following flowchart to guide himself through the development of his multimedia presentation. Copy the flowchart onto your own paper. Use the flowchart as an organizational guide.

### Multimedia Presentation Flowchart
### 1. Gather Text and Media Elements

**Text Elements**
author _Amy Tan_
thesis statement _success came after many struggles_
main support points
    _parents' expectations_
    _becoming a writer_
    _accepting family &_
    _heritage_
title _Blessing from America_
draft completed _____
special word
choices      _blessing_
_____ _____ _____

**Media Elements**
      name  prepared  test
graphics  _tan.pct_  ✓  _____
    _U.S. map.pct_ ✓  _____
    _China.pct_  ✓  _____
video  _____  _____  _____
    _____  _____  _____
sounds  _____  _____  _____
    _____  _____  _____

### 2. Design Layout
ideas to reinforce theme    ideas for developing voice
_maps—China and US_    _make it look positive & balanced_
organization: topics,    considerations: audience
subtopics, transitions    and presentation mode
_link all of the topics_    _use links to information and interviews_

### 3. Test and Evaluate
self-evaluation  _____
peer evaluation  _____

### 4. Revise and Proof
revisions entered _____
proofed _____

### 5. Present
equipment    location    time

## Language, Grammar, and Style

### Effective Use of Visuals
**IDENTIFYING EFFECTIVE USE OF VISUALS.** Effective use of text, graphics, video, and layout strategies can greatly enhance the message you want to deliver. On the other hand, ineffective use can cause your audience to ignore your presentation. Several guidelines can help you to use visuals effectively. For more information, see the Language Arts Survey 6.11, "Displaying Effective Visual Information."

- Include a brief title to orient your viewer. Use lettering that fits the presentation style or theme.
- Select graphics that contribute to the overall theme you are trying to create. Consider how the use of colors may either add to or conflict with the theme.
- Use short paragraphs placed appropriately around graphics.
- Balance your text with your graphics. Too much text can be difficult to read. Too many graphics can overwhelm the viewer.

*continued on page 1018*

- Indicate the process that viewers should follow. Use standard formatting to indicate Internet links. Consider using arrows or numbers to indicate the flow of the process.

Review the screen capture of *The Bag Lunch* on page 1014. Locate places where the students followed the guidelines. How do the text and media elements contribute to the theme? How easy to read is the text? How are the media elements and text balanced? How is the process or navigation through the webzine indicated?

FIXING POOR USE OF VISUALS. Examine the following visual. What difficulties can you identify with the use of text, graphics, and process? How would you correct these problems? Create a thumbnail sketch on your own paper that shows your corrections.

In Chinese families, success means more than just being being personally successful. It involves successfully taking care of one's family too. For Amy Tan, an American novelist of Chinese descent, success—both personal and with her family—came after many struggles.

## Drafting

After you have made decisions about and compiled all the pieces of your multimedia presentation, you are ready to draft the presentation. Depending on the type of presentation you have chosen, your draft may take a variety of forms—page layouts and links for a webzine, screen layouts for a computer presentation, or stage directions for a video or live presentation. You goal at this stage is to incorporate your text with the media elements, working toward the development of your thesis, easy access of the information, and visual appeal.

Try several different layouts and designs for your elements. Practice using your designs to see how smoothly they function. Test each of the elements included in your presentation to make sure they all work in the intended way.

## Self- and Peer Evaluation

After completing your project, step away from it for a day or two and then come back and evaluate it. Complete a self-evaluation and then ask several of your classmates to examine your work using the following questions as an evaluation guide.

- What new, meaningful, and insightful information about the author does the presentation contain? What information seems to be missing or overstated?
- In what ways is the presentation visually appealing? Where might the visual appeal be lacking? Where might the presentation be visually confusing?
- How does the author's projected voice enhance the presentation's content and purpose? Which elements help to develop the voice? Which detract?
- Where are the rough spots—media elements that don't display properly or navigation that is hard to follow?

## Revising and Proofreading

Review your self- and peer evaluations. Revise your text, media elements, and layout after considering these comments. Complete a final proofreading of your text. After you have completed your revisions, test the entire presentation again to make sure all of the elements are functioning correctly.

## Student Model—Revised

USING VISUALS EFFECTIVELY.
Review your multimedia
presentation for effective use
of visuals. Where is the most
effective use? Where is the use
of visuals ineffective, perhaps
even confusing? Adjust the
text, graphics, or layout of
your presentation for the best
visual impact.

For more information, see
the Language Arts Survey
6.11, "Displaying Effective
Visual Information."

## Publishing and Presenting

After hours of hard work, it is time to publish and present.
Compile your presentation and then test each feature to make
sure it works smoothly. Before you present, make sure that all
the necessary equipment is in order. Then invite your
classmates, teachers, parents, and Internet community to share
your presentation.

As you participate in other presentations, study them to see
what information you gain. Ask questions both about the author
and about the process that was used to achieve certain effects.
As you explore the different Internet presentations, imagine
millions of people viewing the site. What will they take with
them when they exit? What will you?

## Reflecting

Think back to when you were first starting to read. You probably
experienced few words with many pictures. Gradually, as you
learned to read better, the number of words increased and the
number of pictures decreased. As your reading improved, your
mind filled in the pictures—better pictures, perhaps, than even
the best illustrator could produce.

Interestingly, the reverse of this process seems to be taking
place in some media. Watch an evening of TV advertising or
thumb through some glossy magazines. We live in an age of
increasingly dramatized media presentations. Some might argue
that these improve the quality of communication. Others would
argue just the opposite, that sizzle and glitz have replaced
substance. What are your views on this issue? How does your
presentation reflect your thinking on this? What might you
change the next time you develop a multimedia presentation?

# UNIT REVIEW
## *Contemporary Literature (1980–Present)*

## Words for Everyday Use

Check your knowledge of the following vocabulary words from the selections in this unit. Write short sentences using these words in context to make the meaning clear. To review the definition or usage of a word, refer to the page number listed or the Glossary of Words for Everyday Use.

ambush, 993
amicably, 1000
antidote, 1010
asylum, 1008
augur, 1007
automation, 950
beacon, 1007
burgeon, 1006
calamity, 974
celestial, 966
censor, 972
communal, 983
competent, 965
conjure, 1007
conspicuously, 1008
contend, 1008
convulsion, 976
coulee, 1000
cursory, 983
declaim, 1006
delirium, 971
disarray, 1006
eerie, 985
embellish, 1006
enclave, 1010
eulogy, 986
expurgated, 986
florid, 986

gape, 995
genocide, 1006
grenade, 993
gullet, 972
hierarchy, 984
humble, 950
icon, 1001
indigenous, 1001
inherent, 1000
inoculate, 1010
invigorate, 1008
jut, 954
labyrinth, 983
latent, 1010
lob, 994
lumber, 1000
malaria, 961
mirage, 961
morality, 994
mortified, 986
muzzle, 994
noncommittal, 986
patent, 984
peril, 995
pharmaceutical, 982
plagiarist, 985
platoon, 993
poignantly, 983

precedent, 1006
prescient, 1010
prodigious, 984
prosaic, 1000
punctuate, 1007
quantitative, 1007
quibble, 987
reef, 961
refracted, 1009
reproach, 966
requisite, 971
sacrosanct, 1010
scrutinize, 1007
sibyl, 988
strenuous, 1009
sullen, 955
swivel, 995
thrash, 961
topple, 987
totalitarian, 1007
tribulation, 974
venerable, 1008
venerated, 1008
vitality, 965
watch, 994
yield, 972

## Literary Tools

Define the following terms, giving concrete examples of how they are used in the selections in this unit. To review a term, refer to the page number indicated or to the Handbook of Literary Terms.

allusion, 953
anecdote, 998
characterization, 953
cliché, 980
coherence, 1004
conflict, 980

crisis, 992
description, 998
free verse, 964
image, 958
irony, 958
objective correlative, 964

parallelism, 949
realism, 992
repetition, 949, 969
stream-of-consciousness
   writing, 969
thesis, 1004

# Reflecting
......................... *on* YOUR READING

## Genre Studies

1. **NARRATIVE POETRY.** A narrative poem is a verse that tells a story. Which poem in this unit is a narrative poem? What story does it relate? What multicultural perspective does the poem represent?

2. **HISTORICAL FICTION.** Historical fiction is fiction that combines historical fact with imagined characters and events. In "Reassurance," what historical fact is used to make the Civil War period come alive? How does this fact impact the imaginary events that Gurganus describes? How well do the imaginary events reflect reality?

## Thematic Studies

3. **ETHNICITY.** "Daughter of Invention" describes the life of Puerto Rican immigrants in America. What effect does being Puerto Rican have on Laura and Yoyo? How would their experiences be different if they were not immigrants? How does ethnicity inform the theme of the story?

4. **SENSES.** Much of the writing in David Mura's "Huy Nguyen: Brothers, Drowning Cries" and Kathleen Norris's "Seeing" evokes the senses. To which senses do the authors refer the reader? How do they do this? In what ways do the senses help to relay the meaning of each selection?

## Historical/Biographical Studies

5. **MINORITIES.** Note the number of selections in this unit written by minorities. What does this tell you about the changing demography of the United States? How do minority authors enrich the texture of American literature? Be sure to use examples from the selections in this unit.

6. **SOCIOLOGICAL PROFILE.** Based on Daniel Boorstin's "Why I Am Optimistic about America," write a sociological profile of the American people today, covering the areas of religion, language, law, and wealth. Which characters and narrators in the selections in this unit reinforce Boorstin's sociological profile? Which oppose it? What is your own sociological profile of American society today?

# Part Three
## LANGUAGE ARTS SURVEY
### A HANDBOOK OF ESSENTIAL SKILLS

# READING Resource

## INTRODUCTION TO READING

### 1.1 Purposes of Reading

You as a reader read for different purposes. You might **read for experience**—for insights into ideas, other people, and the world around you. You can also **read to learn**. This is the kind of reading done most often in school. When you read to learn, you may read textbooks, newspapers and newsmagazines, and visual "texts" such as art and photographs. The purpose of this type of reading is to gain knowledge. Third, you can **read for information**. When you read in this way, you are looking for specific data in such things as reference materials, tables, databases, and diagrams.

### 1.2 Reading Independently

Learning to know and value your own response to what you read is one of the rewards of becoming an independent reader. Scanning, skimming, and reading slowly and carefully are three different ways of reading.

SCANNING. When you **scan**, you look through written material quickly to locate particular information. Scanning is useful when you want to find an entry in an index or a definition in a textbook chapter. To scan, simply run your eye down the page, looking for a key word. When you find the key word, slow down and read carefully.

SKIMMING. When you **skim**, you glance through material quickly to get a general idea of what it is about. Skimming is an excellent way to get a quick overview of material. It is useful for previewing a chapter in a textbook, for surveying material to see if it contains information that will be useful to you, and for reviewing material for a test or essay. When skimming, look at titles, headings, and words that appear in boldface or colored type. Also read topic sentences of paragraphs, first and last paragraphs of sections, and any summaries or conclusions. In addition, glance at illustrations, photographs, charts, maps, or other graphics.

SLOW AND CAREFUL READING. When you **read slowly and carefully**, you look at each sentence, taking the time to absorb its meaning before going on. Slow and careful reading is appropriate when reading for pleasure or when studying a textbook chapter for the first time. If you encounter words that you do not understand, try to figure them out from context or look them up in a dictionary. You may want to write such words in a notebook. The act of writing a word will help you to remember it later. When reading for school, take notes using a rough outline form. Writing the material will help you to remember it. For more information, see the Language Arts Survey 5.17, "Taking Notes, Outlining, and Summarizing Information."

## READING FOR EXPERIENCE

### 1.3 Reading Literature: Educating Your Imagination

The most important reason to read literature is to educate your imagination. Reading literature will train you to think and feel in new ways. In the process of reading literary works and thinking about your own and others' responses to them, you will exercise your imagination and grow in ways that might otherwise have been impossible.

### 1.4 Educating Your Imagination as an Active Reader

Reading literature actively means thinking about what you are reading as you are reading it. Here are some important strategies for reading actively.

ASK QUESTIONS AS YOU READ.

• How does what I am reading make me feel?
• What is the setting of this work? How do things look, sound, taste, feel, or smell?

- Do I identify with any of the characters? What would I do if I were in their place?
- Does what I am reading involve a conflict? If so, what is it? How might it be resolved?
- What main images, ideas, symbols, or themes appear in the work?
- What can be learned from the experiences of these characters?

**MAKE PREDICTIONS AS YOU READ.** While reading, think often about what will come next. Think about how situations might turn out and what characters might do.

**SUMMARIZE PARTS AS YOU READ THEM.** Especially when reading longer works, it is a good idea to stop, perhaps at the end of each chapter or section, to summarize on paper what you have read so far. Doing so will help you remember complicated literary works.

## 1.5 Keeping a Reader's Journal

Keeping a reader's journal will help you get the most out of your experience with literature. A reader's journal can first act as a log in which you record the title and author of the work you are reading. You may want to briefly summarize the work. You can write a journal response to questions such as those in the Reader's Journal and Respond to the Selection features of this textbook. Or you might write your own questions and respond to them.

> The way the narrator in "American History" shuts out the news of President Kennedy's death the day it happens is kind of strange, but I completely understand it. Here she's trying so hard to be accepted, especially by Eugene, and she has her one chance, and then the world comes to a complete stop with the death of the president. Maybe she's just selfish in her reaction, or maybe she's just in shock or denial . . .

## 1.6 Reading Silently versus Reading Out Loud

At times you will find it best to read silently and at other times to read out loud. When reading independently, you will probably make the most

progress by reading silently. However, you may find it most helpful to read difficult passages out loud, even if softly. Hearing the words spoken can help make sense of complex passages. Another good time to read out loud is with poetry. By speaking the lines, you will be able to hear the rhythm and rhyme. Plays are also intended to be performed, and as with poetry, they are best appreciated when they are read out loud. This can be particularly helpful when different people take on the roles of different characters.

## 1.7 Reading with a Book Club or Literature Circle

No two people are exactly alike. Because of this, the experience that you have when reading a particular story, poem, or play will be different from the experience of each of your classmates. That's what makes discussing literature with other students interesting.

In a classroom literature circle, students get together in a small group to exchange insights, interpretations, and questions about literature they have read independently. Students in a literature circle may gather to discuss a selection and work together to understand it. Or they might read different literary works and meet to compare themes, writing styles of different authors, or different selections by the same author. Personal insights recorded in a reading log or journal can be shared when the literature circle meets.

## 1.8 Guidelines for Discussing Literature in a Book Club

At first, your literature group might need help from your teacher to get started, but soon your group should be able to conduct its own sessions if you follow these guidelines.

**BEFORE THE SESSION**
- Finish reading the assignment on time.
- Write down ideas in your reader's journal to help yourself get ready for the discussion.
- Mark places in the reading that you don't understand or want to discuss with your group. Also mark passages that you like, disagree with, or find especially worth remembering.
- Make sure you bring the literature to school instead of leaving it home on discussion day.

- Share your ideas and offer suggestions.
- Speak clearly, loudly, and slowly enough.
- Make eye contact with others.
- Answer questions other people ask.
- Ask questions to help other members clarify or expand on their points.
- Help keep the group on track and focused.
- Encourage others to talk.
- Disagree when you find it necessary without hurting others' feelings.
- Summarize and repeat your ideas when necessary.
- Give reasons for your opinions.
- Listen politely and ask follow-up questions.
- Try to understand and carry out other members' suggestions.

AFTER THE SESSION
- Evaluate your contribution to the group.
- Evaluate the overall success of your group.
- List ways to improve the next time.

# READING TO LEARN

When you are reading to learn, you have two main goals: to expand your knowledge on a particular topic and to remember the information later. When you read to learn, you will often work with textbooks, nonfiction library books, newspapers, or journals, newsmagazines, and related art and photographs.

## 1.9 Reading Textbooks and Nonfiction Books

Textbooks provide a broad overview of a course of study. Textbooks should provide as much material as possible in an objective, factual way. Other nonfiction books provide information about actual people, places, things, events, and ideas. Types of nonfiction books include histories, biographies, autobiographies, and memoirs.

THE PARTS OF A BOOK. When previewing an entire book, you might want to glance at all of its parts. Every book will have some or all of the following parts:

### THE PARTS OF A BOOK

| | |
|---|---|
| Title page | Gives the title, author, and publisher |
| Copyright page | Gives information regarding the publication of the book and the copyrights protecting it from being copied or sold illegally |
| Table of contents | Lists the units, chapters, and/or subjects of the book and the page numbers where they are found |
| Preface, introduction, or foreword | Introduces the book |
| Text | Contains main part of the book |
| Afterword or epilogue | Gives conclusion or tells what happened later |
| Appendix | Gives additional information about subjects covered in the book, often in chart or table form |
| Glossary | Lists key words used in the book and their definitions |
| Bibliography | Lists sources used in writing the book or sources for further study |
| Index | Lists in alphabetical order the subjects mentioned in the book and pages where these subjects are treated |

## 1.10 Reading Newspapers, Journals, and Newsmagazines

Newspapers, journals, and newsmagazines contain an enormous amount of information. Few people have time to read everything that appears in a newspaper each day. Nonetheless, staying aware of the news is important.

To get an overview of a newspaper, journal, or newsmagazine, skim the headlines and leads (the first sentence in a news story that explains the who, what, where, why, and how of the story). Read any news summaries included in the publication. Then read in depth any stories that seem particularly important or interesting. Also take advantage of the features and entertainment sections, which often reflect contemporary culture or the particular flavor of a community.

When reading news stories and editorials, make sure to distinguish between facts and opinions. **Facts** are statements that can be proved by observation or by consulting a reliable and objective source. **Opinions** are predictions or statements of value or belief. When you encounter opinions in the news, try to determine whether they are sound. Sound opinions are supported by facts. For more information, see the Language Arts Survey 5.2, "Distinguishing Fact from Opinion."

## 1.11 "Reading" Art and Photographs

In today's visually stimulating world, books and news media rely on art, photographs, and other visuals as well as the printed word to convey ideas. Being able to understand and interpret graphic images is important in today's society. Visual arts offer insights into our world in a different way than print does.

Careful examination of a painting can lead you to discover meaning in it and to compare and contrast the painting's meaning with that of a literary work or other piece of writing. The same thing happens with photographs. Learning to interpret other graphics or images—drawings, diagrams, charts, and maps—will help you to more easily understand how things work, what things mean, and how things compare.

## 1.12 Seeking Knowledge as an Active Reader

Reading to learn requires you to develop and use key skills to acquire knowledge. Reading actively means thinking about what you are reading as you read it. Slow and careful reading—and sometimes rereading—is necessary when reading to understand new and complex material. There are five key skills required for active reading:

- asking questions
- using your prior knowledge to make inferences and predictions about what you are reading
- recognizing what you do not know
- being able to synthesize information or create summaries, and
- knowing when to adapt your reading approach.

**ASK QUESTIONS.** Questioning allows you to realize what you understand about what you are reading. Before you read, think about your prior knowledge about the subject. When confronted with new information, your brain is doing many things at once. It is trying to figure out what it already knows about the topic and how this information connects to the information in your brain. During reading, your brain is trying to answer these questions: What is the essential information presented here? How is this new information organized? After reading, you need to examine how your knowledge has grown, and identify the questions you still have about the material.

### BEFORE READING

What is this going to be about?
What do I already know about the topic?
What's my purpose for reading this?

### DURING READING

What does the author want me to know?
What is the significance of what I am reading?
What do I need to remember from this material?

### AFTER READING

What have I learned?
What else do I want to know about this topic?

**USE YOUR PRIOR KNOWLEDGE TO MAKE INFERENCES AND PREDICTIONS.** While you are reading, you need to use what you already know about the topic to make inferences about what the author is saying. As you read, think about what might come next and try to make predictions about the next section of material.

**KNOW WHAT YOU DO NOT KNOW.** Recognizing when you do not understand something is as important as knowing that you do understand it. Try to form questions about the material you do not understand. Reread the text. Explain the topic to another student. Teaching someone else forces you to work to understand the material in deeper ways.

**SUMMARIZE OR SYNTHESIZE TEXT.** Summarizing what you are reading not only helps you identify and understand the main and subordinate points in the text, it is essential for storing and retrieving the information from long-term memory. Write a summary for each major section of the text you read. Create meaningful labels for a list of things or actions.

**ADAPT YOUR READING APPROACH.** If you become aware that you are not comprehending the material, you need to try another approach. Expert readers alter their reading strategies to compensate for any problems they have. You may need to experiment with different tactics like whether to speed up, slow down, reread, stand up and read, read the same material from another book, read with a dictionary in your lap, or generalize or visualize what you are reading.

## 1.13 Strategies for Reading to Learn: SQ3R

A five-step reading strategy called SQ3R can help you reduce your study time and increase your ability to understand the essential information. The main steps of SQ3R are SURVEY, QUESTION, READ, RECALL, and REVIEW.

SURVEY
- Preview the organization of material.
- Glance at visuals and assess how they contribute to the meaning of the text.
- Skim headings and introductory paragraphs.

- Notice words in italics, boldface, and other terms that stand out.
- Ask yourself: What is the scope of the reading task? What should I learn from this material?

QUESTION
- Turn chapter titles and headings into questions.
- Ask yourself what the text is offering and what the author is saying.
- Ask yourself what you should know about the material and what you already know about it.
- Question graphics and visual materials. Try and translate the information they offer into your own words.
- Use words like *who, what, when, where, why*, and *how*.

READ
- Read and interact with the text.
- Underline or copy in your journal the main points.
- Make note of unusual or interesting ideas.
- Jot down words you need to define.
- Write your reactions to what you read.

RECALL
- Condense the major points of the text by writing recall cues.
- Summarize the material you have read. Reread any sections you don't clearly remember.
- Use graphic organizers to visualize or map out the material.
- Reread the text aloud if you need help recalling.

REVIEW
- After you have finished the chapter or book, go back and reread main headings and compare them to your notes.
- Review your notes, summaries, and definitions. Answer any questions you wrote.
- Ask yourself: What do I now understand? What is still confusing?

## READING FOR INFORMATION

## 1.14 Reading Internet Materials, Reference Works, Graphic Aids, and Other Visuals

When you are reading for information, you are looking for information that answers a specific, immediate question; that helps you learn how to do something; or that will help you make a decision or draw a conclusion about something. One of the most important tasks for you to learn in school is how to access, process, and think about the vast amount of information available to you on the Internet and in online and print reference works, graphic aids, and other visuals.

Skills critical to reading for information include:
- determining your specific purpose for reading
- determining the author's purpose
- knowing how to interpret symbols and numeric data, and
- using an appropriate approach for the reading task.

**DETERMINE YOUR SPECIFIC PURPOSE FOR READING.** Know why you are reading and what information you seek. State your purpose for reading as clearly as you can. Are you searching the Internet for a review of the movie you're unsure whether to see? Are you learning to operate a computer program? Are you researching data to determine if city regulations allow pet ferrets?

**DETERMINE THE AUTHOR'S PURPOSE.** It is important to interpret the author's viewpoint. Ask yourself what the writer wants the reader to think, believe, or do after reading this piece. Ask yourself if the author has bias on the topic that is affecting his or her views. If you are on the Internet, check for the following: Who is sponsoring the site? What hyperlinks are embedded in the site? Can you contact the web site? When was the content on the site written, and how might that affect the information it provides?

**DETERMINE HOW THE AUTHOR USES SYMBOLS AND NUMERIC DATA.** Work to understand how the author uses symbols, icons, and abbreviated headings on tables. Use any icons as shortcuts for navigating through the text and also for identifying the important from unimportant material.

**USE THE SEARCH APPROACH.** Although your reading strategies should vary and relate directly to your purpose for reading, you may find the SEARCH

method helpful when you are reading for information. SEARCH stands for Scan, Examine, Act, Review, Connect, and Hunt.

SCAN
- Look over the text and determine how the material is structured.
- Look for a table of contents, a glossary, an index, and other helpful sections.
- For an Internet site, look for a site map.

EXAMINE
- Do directions appear in a sequence of steps? Are there diagrams? Do directions reveal exactly what to do or do you need to experiment a little?
- Is there a pattern in headings or icons?
- Are there any references to other sources of information?
- If you are on the Internet, does the site provide any links?

ACT
- Explore the procedures you are reading and learn by doing.
- If you are seeking data, take notes about the information. Is it exactly what you were looking for, or do you need to keep looking?

REVIEW
- Revisit the steps of a procedure to make sure you have them clear in your head.
- Compare similar resources and read any additional references or links provided.

CONNECT
- Connect the information to what you previously knew about the topic. How did you build on what you knew?
- Connect text with visual aids. How do the visual aids supplement the text? What additional information do they provide?

HUNT
- Look up the meanings of any new words you found.
- Use the help feature on a computer program to find answers to your questions.
- Make a visual diagram of a procedure if it will help you remember it.

# 1.15 Using Graphic Aids

**Graphic aids** are pictures, maps, illustrations, charts, graphs, diagrams, spreadsheets, and other visual materials that present information. Many people, including scientists, sociologists, economists, business analysts, and school administrators, use graphic aids to present data in understandable ways. Information presented in tables, charts, and graphs can help you find information, see trends, discover facts, and uncover patterns. Here are some common types of structures for presenting data.

**PIE CHARTS.** A pie chart is a circle that stands for a whole group or set. The circle is divided into parts to show the divisions of the whole. When you look at a pie chart, you can see the relationships of the parts to one another and to the whole.

**BAR GRAPHS.** A bar graph compares amounts of something by representing the amounts as bars of different lengths. In the bar graph below, each bar represents the value in dollars of canned goods donated by several communities to a food drive. To read the graph, simply draw in your imagination a line from the edge of the bar to the bottom of the graph. Then read the number. For example, the bar graph below shows that the community of Russell Springs donated $600 worth of goods during the food drive.

**MAPS.** A map is a representation, usually on a surface such as paper or a sheet of plastic, of a geographic area, showing various significant features of that area.

## ARLINGTON HIGH SCHOOL POETRY SURVEY

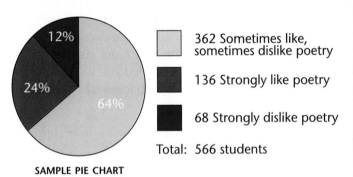

362 Sometimes like, sometimes dislike poetry

136 Strongly like poetry

68 Strongly dislike poetry

Total: 566 students

**SAMPLE PIE CHART**

**SAMPLE MAP**

## DOLLAR VALUE OF DONATED GOODS TO CANNED FOOD DRIVE

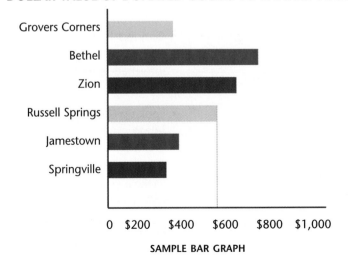

**SAMPLE BAR GRAPH**

Here are guidelines for working with graphics:

BEFORE READING
- Determine the subject of the graphic by reading the title, headings, and other textual clues.
- Determine how the data are organized, classified, or divided by reading the labels along rows or columns.
- Ask yourself: Why am I reading this document? What do I need to find? Where in this graphic is that information located?

DURING READING
- Survey the data and look for trends by comparing columns and rows, noting changes among information fields, looking for patterns, or navigating map sections.
- Use legends, keys, and other helpful sections in the graphic.
- Ask yourself: How do the data I need compare to other data on the graphic? What do those comparisons mean to me? What in this graphic can I skim or skip?

AFTER READING
- Check footnotes or references for additional information about the data and its sources.
- Ask yourself: Did this graphic answer my questions? If so, what are the answers? If not, where do I go to find the answers?

## DEVELOPING YOUR VOCABULARY

### 1.16 Using Context Clues to Estimate Word Meaning

If you come across an unfamiliar word in your reading and you can't access a dictionary, you can often figure out the meaning of a word by using context clues.

One type of context clue is **restatement**. The author may tell you the meaning of the word you do not know by using different words to express the same idea in another sentence.

EXAMPLE

The dog snarled at Donald malevolently.
The dog's vicious behavior warned Donald to stay away.

The restatement provides a context clue that *malevolently* means "maliciously, with intent to do harm."

Another type of context clue is **apposition**. An apposition is renaming something in different words. Look for a word or phrase that has been placed in the sentence to clarify the word you do not know.

EXAMPLE

Evan's conclusion was based on a fallacy, a false idea about how Maggie felt toward him.

Examples given in a sentence can also be used as context clues.

EXAMPLE

The words *dad, radar, noon,* and *tenet* are all palindromes; so is the phrase "A man, a plan, a canal, Panama!"

### 1.17 Using a Dictionary

Dictionary entries provide much more information about words than just their spelling and definitions.

The **pronunciation** is given immediately after the entry word. You can find a complete key to pronunciation symbols in the dictionary's table of contents. In some dictionaries, a simplified key is provided at the bottom of each page.

An abbreviation of the **part of speech** usually follows the pronunciation. This label tells the ways in which a word can be used (see the Language Arts Survey, 3.7, "Parts of Speech Overview"). If a word can be used in more than one way, definitions are grouped by part of speech.

An **etymology** is the history of a word. In the first entry, the word *pole* can be traced back through Middle English (ME) and Old English (OE) to the Latin (L) word *palus*, which means "stake." In the second entry, the word *pole* can be traced back through Middle English to the Latin word *polus*, which comes from the Greek word *polos*, meaning "axis of the sphere."

Each **definition** in the entry gives a different meaning of the word. When a word has more than one meaning, the different definitions are numbered. The first definition in an entry is the most common meaning of the word.

Sometimes the entry will include a list of **synonyms**. The entry may also include an **illustration of usage**, which is an example of how the word is used.

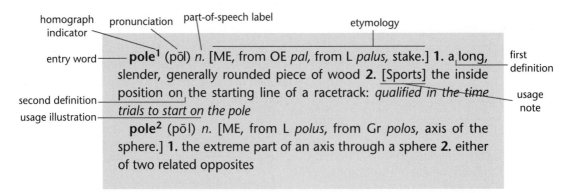

**homograph indicator** · **pronunciation** · **part-of-speech label** · **etymology**

**entry word** — **pole**¹ (pōl) *n.* [ME, from OE *pal,* from L *palus,* stake.] **1.** a long, — **first definition**
slender, generally rounded piece of wood **2.** [Sports] the inside — **usage note**
**second definition** — position on the starting line of a racetrack: *qualified in the time*
**usage illustration** — *trials to start on* the pole

**pole**² (pōl) *n.* [ME, from L *polus,* from Gr *polos,* axis of the
sphere.] **1.** the extreme part of an axis through a sphere **2.** either
of two related opposites

## 1.18 Using Glossaries and Footnotes

A **glossary** is an alphabetized list of words and their definitions. Glossaries usually appear at the end of an article, chapter, or book. **Footnotes** appear at the foot, or bottom, of a page. Sometimes they cite a source of information. Other times they define annotated words in order of appearance.

## 1.19 Learning Base Words, Prefixes, and Suffixes

Many words are formed by adding prefixes or suffixes to base words. (See the Language Arts Survey 3.101, "Using Spelling Rules I.") If you are unfamiliar with a word that is formed with a prefix or a suffix, check to see if you recognize the meaning of the base word and the meaning of its prefix or the suffix.

| PREFIX | MEANING | EXAMPLE | MEANING |
|--------|---------|---------|---------|
| anti– | "against" | antibacterial | against bacteria |
| dis– | "not, opposite" | disagreeable | not agreeable |
| hyper– | "over, excessively" | hyperactive | excessively active |
| im–, un– | "not" | unusual | not usual |
| post– | "after" | postseason | after the season |
| re– | "again" | reprint | print again |

| PREFIX | MEANING | EXAMPLE | MEANING |
|--------|---------|---------|---------|
| –er, –or | "one who" | narrator | one who narrates |
| –ful | "full of" | graceful | full of grace |
| –ish | "like" | childish | like a child |
| –ity, –ty | "state of, quality" | captivity | state of being captive |
| –less | "without" | fearless | without fear |
| –ment | "act of, state of" | achievement | act of achieving |

## 1.20 Learning Synonyms, Antonyms, and Homonyms

A **synonym** is a word that has the same or nearly the same meaning as another word.

EXAMPLES     discover, find, locate, pinpoint

An **antonym** is a word that means the opposite of another word.

EXAMPLES     discover, conceal     give, take     success, defeat

A **homonym** is a word that has the same pronunciation as another word but with a different meaning, origin, and usually, spelling.

EXAMPLES     bight, bite, byte

## 1.21 Exploring Word Origins and Word Families

The English language gains new words from many different sources. One source is the names of people and places. Another source of words in the English language is **acronyms**. Acronyms are words formed from the first letter or letters of the major parts of terms.

EXAMPLES

sonar, from sound navigation ranging; NATO, from North Atlantic Treaty Organization; NASA, from National Aeronautic and Space Administration

Some words in the English language are **borrowed** from other languages.

EXAMPLES    **deluxe** (French), **Gesundheit** (German), **kayak** (Inuit)

Many words are formed by **shortening** longer words.

EXAMPLES

ad, from advertisement; auto, from automobile; lab, from laboratory; phone, from telephone; stereo, from stereophonic

**Brand names** are often taken into the English language. People begin to use these words as common nouns, even though most of them are still brand names.

EXAMPLES    Scotch tape, Xerox, Rollerblade

HAMBURGER
Originally known as "Hamburg steak," the hamburger takes its name from the city of Hamburg, Germany.

SPOONERISM
A slip of the tongue whereby the beginning sounds of words are switched; named after the Rev. William A. Spooner, who was noted for such slips. For example, after officiating at a wedding, he told the groom, "It is kisstomary to cuss the bride."

## 1.22 Jargon and Gobbledygook

**Jargon** is the specialized vocabulary used by members of a profession. It tends to be difficult for people outside the profession to understand. A plumber may speak of a "hubless fitting" or a "street elbow" (kinds of pipe). A computer programmer may talk of "ram cache" (part of computer memory) or a "shell" (a type of operating software for computers).

Jargon is useful to writers who want to authentically describe situations in which jargon would naturally be used. A novel about fighter pilots would probably be full of aviation jargon. A science fiction film might include futuristic jargon about warps in space and energy shields.

**Gobbledygook** is unclear, wordy jargon used by bureaucrats, government officials, and others. For example, the failure of a program might be called an "incomplete success." A bureaucrat might say, "We are engaged in conducting a study with a view to ascertaining which employees might be assigned to the mobility pool and how we might create revenue enhancement" when he means, "We are planning to cut jobs and increase taxes." Gobbledygook should be avoided. Effective communication involves using precise language instead of muddy, vague vocabulary.

## 1.23 Clichés and Euphemisms

A **cliché** is an expression that has been used so often it has been colorless and uninteresting. The use of clichés instantly makes writing dull.

EXAMPLES    quick as a wink, pretty as a picture

A **euphemism** is an inoffensive term that substitutes for one considered offensive.

EXAMPLES    aerial mishap (for "plane crash")
building engineer (for "janitor")

## 1.24 Connotation and Denotation

A **connotation** of a word is all the associations it has in addition to its literal meaning. For example, the words *cheap* and *economical* both denote "inexpensive," but *cheap* connotes shoddy and inferior while *economical* connotes a good value for the money. A **denotation** of a word is its dictionary definition. Writers and speakers should be aware of the connotations as well as the denotations of the words they use.

EXAMPLES

curious: nosy, snoopy, prying, meddling

# WRITING Resource

## INTRODUCTION TO WRITING

### 2.1 The Writing Process

We live in an information age in which success in most fields requires well-developed writing skills. The most important action that you can take to shape a successful future for yourself is to learn how to write clearly and effectively. Almost anyone can learn to write well by learning the writing process. The writing process is simply the steps that a person takes to put together a piece of writing.

### SEVEN STAGES IN THE PROCESS OF WRITING

PREWRITING · DRAFTING · SELF- AND PEER EVALUATION · REVISING · PROOFREADING · PUBLISHING AND PRESENTING · REFLECTING

| STAGE | TASKS |
| --- | --- |
| 1. Prewriting | Plan your writing; choose a topic, audience, purpose, and form; gather ideas; and arrange them logically. |
| 2. Drafting | Get your ideas down on paper. |
| 3. Self- and Peer Evaluation | Evaluate, or judge, the writing piece and suggest ways to improve it. Judging your own writing is called **self-evaluation**. Judging a classmate's writing is called **peer evaluation**. |
| 4. Revising | Work to improve the content, organization, and expression of your ideas. |
| 5. Proofreading | Check your writing for errors in spelling, grammar, capitalization, and punctuation. Correct these errors, make a final copy of your paper, and proofread it again. |
| 6. Publishing and Presenting | Share your work with an audience. |
| 7. Reflecting | Think through the writing process to determine what you learned as a writer, what you accomplished, and what you would like to strengthen the next time you write. |

While writing moves through these seven stages, it is also is a continuing cycle. You might need to go back to a previous stage before going on to the next step. Returning to a previous stage will strengthen your final work. Note also that the Reflecting stage can be done between any of the other steps. The more you reflect on your writing, the better your writing will become.

# UNDERSTANDING THE WRITING PROCESS

## 2.2 Prewriting

In the **prewriting** stage of the writing process, you make a writing plan. You decide on a purpose, audience, form, and topic. You also begin to discover your voice and gather and organize ideas.

### THE PARTS OF A WRITING PLAN

| | |
|---|---|
| **Purpose** | A **purpose**, or **aim**, is the goal that you want your writing to accomplish. |
| **Audience** | An **audience** is the person or group of people intended to read what you write. |
| **Voice** | **Voice** is the quality of a work that tells you that one person wrote it. |
| **Form** | A **form** is a kind of writing. For example, you might write a paragraph, an essay, a short story, a poem, or a news article. |
| **Topic** | A **topic** is simply something to write about. For example, you might write about a sports hero or about a cultural event in your community. |

**2.3 IDENTIFYING YOUR PURPOSE.** A **purpose**, or **aim**, is the goal that you want your writing to accomplish. For example, you might write to inform, to entertain, to tell a story, to reflect, or to persuade. Your writing might have more than one purpose. For example, a piece of writing might inform about an important event while persuading the audience to respond in a specific way.

### MODES AND PURPOSES OF WRITING

| MODE | PURPOSE | EXAMPLE |
|---|---|---|
| **expository/informative writing** | to inform | news article, research report |
| **imaginative writing** | to entertain, enrich, and enlighten by using a form such as fiction or poetry to share a perspective | poem, short story |
| **narrative writing** | to make a point by sharing a story about an event | biography, family history |
| **personal/expressive writing** | to reflect | diary entry, personal letter |
| **persuasive/argumentative writing** | to persuade readers or listeners to respond in some way, such as to agree with a position, change a view on an issue, reach an agreement, or perform an action | editorial, petition |

**2.4 IDENTIFYING YOUR AUDIENCE.** An **audience** is the person or group of people intended to read what you write. For example, you might write for yourself, for a friend, for a relative, or for your classmates. The best writing usually is intended for a specific audience. Choosing a specific audience beforehand will help you make important decisions about your work. For example, for an audience of young children, you would use simple words and ideas. For an audience of fellow members of a technology club, you would use jargon and other specialized words that they already know. For more information, see the the Language Arts Survey 3.3, "Register, Tone, and Voice."

## THINKING ABOUT YOUR AUDIENCE

- What people would be most interested in my topic?
- How much does the audience that I am considering already know about the topic?
- How much background information do I need to provide?
- What words, phrases, or concepts in my writing will my audience not understand? For which ones will I have to provide clear explanations?
- What can I do at the beginning of my writing to capture my audience's interest?

**2.5 FINDING YOUR VOICE. Voice** is the quality of a work that tells you that one person in particular wrote it. Voice makes a person's writing unique. Beginning with the prewriting stage and continuing through the rest of the writing process, a writer discovers his or her own unique voice. For more information, see the section about voice in the Language Arts Survey 3.3, "Register, Tone, and Voice."

**2.6 CHOOSING A FORM.** Another important decision that a writer needs to make is what form his or her writing will take. A form is a kind of writing. For example, you might write a paragraph, an essay, a short story, a poem, or a newspaper article. The following chart lists some forms of writing that you might want to consider.

## FORMS OF WRITING

| | | | |
|---|---|---|---|
| Adventure | Directions | Letter | Rap |
| Advertisement | Dream report | Magazine article | Recipe |
| Advice column | Editorial | Memorandum | Recommendation |
| Agenda | Epitaph | Menu | Research report |
| Apology | Essay | Minutes | Résumé |
| Appeal | Eulogy | Movie review | Schedule |
| Autobiography | Experiment | Mystery | Science fiction |
| Biography | Fable | Myth | Short story |
| Book review | Family history | Narrative | Slide show |
| Brochure | Fantasy | Newspaper article | Slogan |
| Calendar | Greeting card | Obituary | Song lyric |
| Caption | Headline | Parable | Speech |
| Cartoon | History | Paraphrase | Sports story |
| Character sketch | Human interest story | Petition | Statement of belief |
| Children's story | Instructions | Play | Summary |
| Comedy | Interview questions | Police/Accident report | Tall tale |
| Consumer report | Invitation | Poem | Thank-you note |
| Debate | Itinerary | Poster | Tour guide |
| Detective story | Joke | Proposal | Want ad |
| Dialogue | Journal entry | Radio or TV spot | Wish list |

**2.7 Choosing a Topic.** A topic is simply something to write about. For example, you might write about a sports hero or about a cultural event in your community. Here are some ideas that may help you find interesting writing topics:

| WAYS TO FIND A WRITING TOPIC | |
| --- | --- |
| **Check your journal** | Search through your journal for ideas that you jotted down in the past. Many professional writers get their ideas from their journals. |
| **Think about your experiences** | Think about people, places, or events that affected you strongly. Recall experiences that taught you important lessons or that you felt strongly about. |
| **Look at reference works** | Reference works include printed or computerized dictionaries, atlases, almanacs, and encyclopedias. |
| **Browse in a library** | Libraries are treasure houses of information and ideas. Simply looking around in the stacks of a library can suggest good writing ideas. |
| **Use the mass media** | Newspapers, magazines, radio, television, and films can suggest good writing topics. For example, a glance at listings for public television programs might suggest topics related to the arts, to history, or to nature. |
| **Talk to people** | Friends, relatives, teachers, and other people you know make great sources for writing topics. |
| **Do some freewriting** | Simply put your pen or pencil down on a piece of paper and write about whatever pops into your mind. Write for two to five minutes without pausing to worry about whether your writing is perfect. Then look back over what you have written to see if you can find any good topics there. |
| **Ask "What if" questions** | Ask questions beginning with "What if" to come up with topics for creative writing. For example, you might ask, "What if a kid with a ham radio set received a message from space? Would people believe her?" |
| **Make a cluster chart** | Write some general subject such as music or sports in the middle of a piece of paper. Circle this subject. Then, around it, write other ideas that come into your mind as you think about the subject. Circle these and draw lines to connect the outer circles to the inner one. |

**2.8 Focusing a Topic.** Sometimes a topic is too broad to be treated in a short piece of writing. When you have a topic that is too broad, you must **focus**, or limit, the topic.

| WAYS TO FOCUS A WRITING TOPIC | |
| --- | --- |
| **Break the topic into parts** | For example, the topic "newspapers" could be broken down into reporting, copyediting, advertising, circulation, and so on. |
| **Ask questions about the topic** | Begin your questions with the words *who, what, where, when, why,* and *how.* Then ask what stands out about your topic or what interests you most. |
| **Make a cluster chart or do some freewriting** | For information on these techniques, see the Language Arts Survey 2.7, "Choosing a Topic." |

# Gathering Ideas

Once you have made your writing plan by identifying your purpose, form, audience, and topic, the next step in the prewriting stage is to **gather ideas**. There are many ways to gather ideas for writing. This section will introduce you to some of the most useful ones.

**2.9 BRAINSTORMING.** When you **brainstorm,** you think of as many ideas as you can, as quickly as you can, without stopping to evaluate or criticize the ideas. In brainstorming, anything goes. Sometimes even silly-sounding ideas can lead to productive ones. When you brainstorm in a group, often one person's idea will help another person to build on that concept. It is a good way to come up with creative, new ideas and innovative solutions to problems. Remember that no idea should be rejected in the brainstorming stage. Welcome all ideas with an encouraging response such as, "Great! Any other ideas?" Be sure to get contributions from everyone in your group and to record all ideas so they can be considered and judged later.

**2.10 LEARNING FROM PROFESSIONAL MODELS.** Professional models are works by published authors. They can be an excellent way to gather your own ideas. For example, Trevor was impressed by the way Sarah Orne Jewett wrote about endangered species in her short story "A White Heron" in Unit 6. He analyzed this short story and used it as a model when he wrote his own story about forest preservation. For more information, see the way Professional Models are used in the Guided Writing lessons at the end of each unit in this textbook.

**2.11 KEEPING A JOURNAL.** A **journal** is a record of your ideas, dreams, wishes, and experiences. Composition books, spiral notebooks, looseleaf binders, and bound books with blank pages all make excellent journal books. Some people even keep electronic journals on computers.

Journals can be classified according to purpose. The following chart shows different types of journals and their contents.

| TYPES OF JOURNALS | |
|---|---|
| **A Diary, or Day-to-day Record of Your Life** | August 3, 2003. Today I started keeping a journal. My brother Mickey saw me writing and asked me what I was doing. When I told him, he said, "Don't go writing about me in that thing!" I guess he thinks he has all kinds of fascinating secrets! In a family as large as ours, though, it is pretty difficult to have any privacy. . . . |
| **A Reader Response Journal** | The ideas that Robert Hayden expresses in "Those Winter Sundays" have really stayed with me, even though it's been a week since we read the poem in class. What I like about it is the way he describes such a harsh world—"blueblack cold"—and the way love expresses itself with its "austere and lovely offices." It's made me see a similar expression of love, though never spoken, in my own life . . . |
| **A Commonplace Book, or Book of Quotations** | "Many a thing is despised that is worth more than is supposed." <br>—Chrétien de Troyes, <u>Arthurian Romances</u> <br>"Who knows why people do what they do?" <br>—Barbara Kingsolver, <u>Animal Dreams</u> |
| **A Writer's Lab, or Collection of Ideas for Writing** | What if some new supercomputer fell in love with one of its programmers? That could be a very funny or a very sad story. How would it begin? Let's see. One day Randall Meeks, a programmer for the Department of Defense, goes in to work and sits down at a terminal connected to ERICA, a new top secret computer whose name means Efficient Risk-Instruction Computational Automaton. He logs onto the computer. A message appears, reading, "Good morning. You are looking quite handsome today." He thinks that one of the other programmers is playing a joke on him—but he's wrong. |

*continued*

| A Learning Log, or Record of What You Have Learned | Science: I read today in my science textbook that at the top of Mt. Everest, the highest point on the planet, there are rocks that were formed when sediment fell to the bottom of an ocean. How could the bottom of an ocean get pushed up to the top of the highest mountain? I'll have to ask in class tomorrow about that. Wow, Earth really is a turbulent thing, constantly changing. I wonder what it will look like millions of years into the future? |
|---|---|
| A Record of Questions | What causes the sky to glow at sunset? |
| | Chandra seems unhappy lately. How could I cheer her up? |
| | How does a person get a job as a zookeeper? Do you have to study animal behavior or biology or something like that in college? I think it would be fun to work with animals and to help save endangered species. |
| A Daily Organizer | Things to do tomorrow: |
| | • Go to library for book on Gandhi for social studies report |
| | • Go to football practice after school |
| | • Call Pete about concert tickets |
| | • Turn in overdue math homework |

**2.12 FREEWRITING. Freewriting** is simply taking a pencil and paper and writing whatever comes into your mind. Try to write for several minutes without stopping and without worrying about spelling, grammar, usage, or mechanics. If you get stuck, just repeat the last few words until something new pops into your mind.

I really don't get this freewriting stuff. Just write? About what? Hum. I don't think of myself as a writer. I mean, sure, I can write and all, but . . . OK, I'm stuck . . . OK, I'm stuck. Funny, I was just thinking, what if some character in a short story kept saying that this was just a story that he was stuck in and the other characters thought he was crazy, and maybe he manages to figure out a way to pop in and out of the story that he was in, or maybe he can get into different stories at different times. Weird idea, I know it's like that idea that "maybe this is all just a dream."

To gather ideas about a specific topic, you might want to try **focused freewriting**. In a focused freewrite, you still write nonstop for a few minutes, but you stick with one topic and write whatever comes to mind as you think about that topic.

**2.13 CLUSTERING.** Another good way to tap what you already know is to make a **cluster chart**. To make a cluster chart, draw a circle in the center of your paper. In it write a topic you want to explore. Draw more circles branching out from your center circle, and fill them with subtopics related to your main topic.

**SAMPLE CLUSTER CHART**

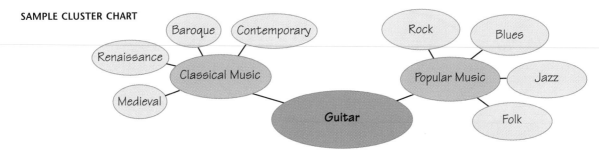

**2.14 QUESTIONING: USING THE 5 Ws AND AN H.** Using the 5 Ws and an H means asking the **reporting questions** who, what, where, when, why, and how about your topic. This questioning strategy is especially useful for gathering information about an event or for planning a story.

| USING QUESTIONING (TOPIC: COWBOY POETRY) | |
|---|---|
| **Who** | Cowboy poets from the United States and other parts of the world |
| **What** | The Cowboy Poetry Festival, where cowboy poets gather |
| **Where** | Elko, Nevada |
| **When** | Held annually the last week in January |
| **Why** | So cowboys who love performing their songs, poetry, and stories can share them with others |
| **How** | This happens because of the huge interest in cowboy poetry and because of the major help from volunteers; the Western Folklife Center in Elko is a major organizer. |

Sample paragraph using this information:

Cowboy poets from all over the United States and around the world will gather once again this January for the Cowboy Poetry Festival. Hosted annually in Elko, Nevada, by the Western Folklife Center and hundreds of volunteers, the largest cowboy poetry get-together draws huge crowds who love to listen to cowboys share their songs, poetry, and stories.

**2.15 IMAGINING: ASKING "WHAT IF" QUESTIONS.** If you are doing imaginative or creative writing, ask questions that begin with the words what if. "What if" questions can spark your imagination and lead you down unexpected and interesting paths. It can also help you see another side of things and to strengthen your own when writing a persuasive piece.

EXAMPLES  What if I could run school for a week? What changes would I make?
What if I could go back in time to speak with a historical figure?
What if the greenhouse effect melted the polar icecaps and raised the levels of the oceans around the world? How would people respond?
What if the city council rejects the proposal for a teen center? How will this affect me and the kids I know?

**2.16 COMPLETING VENN DIAGRAMS.** If you are writing a comparison and contrast essay, one of the best ways to gather ideas is by completing a Venn diagram. A Venn diagram shows two slightly overlapping circles. The outer part of each circle shows what aspects of two things are different from each other. The inner, or shared, part of each circle shows what aspects the two things share.

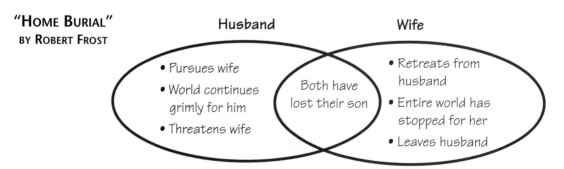

"HOME BURIAL"
BY ROBERT FROST

Husband
- Pursues wife
- World continues grimly for him
- Threatens wife

Both have lost their son

Wife
- Retreats from husband
- Entire world has stopped for her
- Leaves husband

**2.17 ANALYZING.** To **analyze** is to break something down into its parts and then think about how the parts are related. Analyzing is a way to sort out information about a topic. An **analysis chart** can help you to list the parts and to describe each one.

### ANALYSIS OF "THE VILLAGE BLACKSMITH" BY HENRY WADSWORTH LONGFELLOW

| PART | DESCRIPTION | RELATION OF PART TO WHOLE |
|---|---|---|
| Stanzas 1–2 | Gives physical description of blacksmith | Introduces blacksmith to reader |
| Stanza 3 | Describes blacksmith's workday | Underscores blacksmith's work ethic |
| Stanzas 4 | Shows children watching blacksmith | Shows them how blacksmith teaches them work ethic |
| Stanzas 5–6 | Describes blacksmith going to church | Shows blacksmith experiences both joy and grief |
| Stanza 7 | Tells how blacksmith spends his days/life | Summarizes admirable way blacksmith lives his life |
| Stanza 8 | Speaker of poem praises blacksmith | Reinforces importance of blacksmith, his work ethic, and his virtues |

**2.18 SENSORY DETAIL CHARTS.** Most people have the use of five major **senses**: sight, sound, touch, taste, and smell. The larger the number of these senses you use to observe something, the more you will notice about it. A **sensory detail chart** can help you to collect information about something so that you can describe it thoroughly. To make a sensory detail chart, begin by writing your subject at the top of the page. Make a box with a column for each of the five senses. In the column under each heading, list details about the subject that you learn from that sense.

### SENSORY DETAILS OF A MARATHON

| SIGHT | SOUND | TOUCH | TASTE | SMELL |
|---|---|---|---|---|
| hundreds of runners of all ages | starting gun | hot, sore feet from standing so long | hot dogs and lemonade from vendor carts | hot asphalt |
| news reporters and onlookers | crowds clapping | | | perspiration |
| running clothes | running shoes slapping on asphalt | stinging face from sun and wind | | |

**2.19 TIME LINES.** A **time line** can be useful when you are planning to write a story or a historical account. It gives you an overview of the sequence of events during a particular time period. To make a time line, draw a line on a piece of paper and divide it into equal parts. Label each part with a date or a time. Then add key events at the right places along the time line.

### Landmark Events in the History of the Civil Rights Movement (1950–1975)

| 1950 | 1955 | 1960 | 1965 | 1970 | 1975 |
|---|---|---|---|---|---|
| | 1954 *Brown v. Board of Education*: U.S. Supreme Court bans racial segregation in public schools | 1960 Sit-in at Greensboro, NC, lunch counter | 1965 March for voting rights from Selma to Montgomery, AL; Voting Rights Act passed; Malcolm X assassinated; race riots in Watts section of Los Angeles | 1971 Supreme Court rules that busing of students may be ordered to achieve desegregation | |

**2.20 STORY MAPS.** A **story map** is a chart that shows the various parts of a fable, myth, tall tale, legend, short story, or other fictional work. Most story maps include the following elements:

| ELEMENTS OF A STORY MAP | |
| --- | --- |
| **ELEMENT** | **DESCRIPTION** |
| **Setting** | The time and place in which the story occurs |
| **Mood** | The emotion created in the reader by the story |
| **Conflict** | A struggle between two forces in the story |
| **Plot** | The series of events taking place in the story |
| **Characters** | The people (or sometimes animals) who play roles in the story |
| **Theme** | The main idea of the story |

**2.21 PRO AND CON CHARTS.** A **pro and con chart** shows arguments for and against taking a particular position on some issue. To create a pro and con chart, begin by writing a statement, called a **proposition**, at the top of a piece of paper. Under the proposition, make two columns, one labeled *Pro* and the other, *Con*. In the pro column, list arguments in favor of the proposition. In the con column, list arguments against the proposition.

| PRO AND CON CHART | |
| --- | --- |
| **Proposition:** All students should take an hour of physical education each day. | |
| **Pro** | **Con** |
| —would keep students in good physical condition | —would take time away from academic studies |
| —improved health would also improve students' ability to think clearly and work hard | —the same ends might be achieved in less time per day |

**2.22 INTERVIEWING.** In an **interview**, you meet with someone and ask him or her questions. Interviewing experts is an excellent way to gain information about a particular topic. For example, if you are interested in writing about the making of pottery, you might interview an art teacher, a professional potter, or the owner of a ceramics shop. When planning an interview, list the questions you would like to ask, including some about the person's background as well as about your topic. Other questions might occur to you as the interview proceeds. See the Language Arts Survey 4.14, "Conducting an Interview."

**2.23 RESEARCHING FOR IDEAS.** No matter what your subject, you can probably find information about it by doing research in reference works. **Reference works** include encyclopedias, dictionaries, almanacs, atlases, indexes, Internet sites, and more. For additional information about reference materials and how to find them, see the Language Arts Survey 5.20, "Using Reference Works," and 5.37, "Keeping a Research Journal."

## 2.24 Organizing Ideas

After you have gathered ideas for a piece of writing, the next step is to organize these ideas in a useful way. One way is to write a thesis statement and several main ideas with supporting details. Another way to organize ideas is to arrange them in a particular order, as detailed in the Language Arts Survey 2.27, "Choosing a Method of Organization." Finally, an outline can help you organize your writing and prepare it for drafting, the next step in the writing process.

**2.25 WRITING A THESIS STATEMENT.** One way to start organizing your writing, especially if you are writing an informative or persuasive essay, is to identify the main idea of what you want to say. Present this idea in the form of a sentence or two called a thesis statement. A **thesis statement** is simply a sentence that presents the main idea or the position you will take in your essay.

THESIS FOR A PERSUASIVE ESSAY

> The development at Rice Creek Farm should be stopped because it will destroy one of the best natural areas near the city.

THESIS FOR AN INFORMATIVE ESSAY

> Wilma Rudolph was an athlete who succeeded in the elite sport of tennis before the world was willing to recognize her.

**2.26 WRITING MAIN IDEAS AND SUPPORTING DETAILS.** Once you have a thesis statement, the next step is to select several main ideas to support your thesis statement. Begin by writing your thesis at the top of a piece of paper. Then list the main points that you will use to support your thesis. For each main idea, list several supporting details—statements, facts, examples, quotes, and illustrations that explain or demonstrate your idea.

**THESIS:** The development at Rice Creek Farm should be stopped because people will be unable to enjoy the area, a considerable amount of wildlife will be harmed, and an important water resource will be lost.

- People will be unable to enjoy the area.
  - Hundreds of people of all ages now bike, run, and swim in the area in the summer and ski in the winter. Last year's recreation survey was completed by 653 people. Eighty-five percent said that they visited Rice Creek Farm at least twice a month.
  - The development of an industrial park would ban people from using the area. It will become a factory site instead of a wooded recreation area. "The industrial park site would be strictly off limits to the public for their own protection," developer Orrin Q. Smedley said in the *Rice Creek Times*.

- A considerable amount of wildlife will be harmed.
  - The wooded area will be completely eliminated, destroying habitat.
  - The species that will be lost will include deer, fox, racoons, skunks, and wild birds, according to the parks board supervisor.

- An important water resource will be lost.
  - The water resource has many uses, including recreational and agricultural.
  - The quality of our city water supply depends on the preservation of this habitat.

**2.27 Choosing a Method of Organization.** Writing can be organized in different ways.

| METHOD | DESCRIPTION |
|---|---|
| **Chronological Order** | Give events in the order in which they happen or should be done; connect events by using transition words such as *first, second, next, then,* and *finally.* Chronological organization would be a good method for relating a narrative, giving a recipe, writing a how-to article on building a bird-feeder, or to describe a process, such as what happens when a volcano erupts. |
| **Spatial Order** | Describe parts in order of their location in space, for example, from back to front, left to right, or top to bottom; connect your descriptions with transition words or phrases such as *next to, beside, above, below, beyond,* and *around.* Spatial order would be a useful form for an article describing a kitchen renovation, or a descriptive passage in a science fiction story set in a space station. |
| **Order of Importance** | List details from least important to most important or from most important to least important; connect your details with transition phrases such as *more important, less important, most important,* and *least important.* A speech telling voters why they should elect you class president could be organized from the least important reason and build to the most important reason. |
| **Comparison and Contrast Order** | Details of two subjects are presented in one of two ways. In the first method, the characteristics of one subject are presented, followed by the characteristics of the second subject. This method would be useful to organize an essay that compares and contrasts two fast-food chains. You could use this method to say why one is superior to another. "BurgerWorld has the most restaurants. They broil their hamburgers, and offer a line of low-fat meals. Ma's Burgers has far fewer restaurants, fries their hamburgers, and offers no low-fat choices." |
| | In the second method, both subjects are compared and contrasted with regard to one quality, then with regard to a second quality, and so on. An essay organized according to this method could compare the platforms of two political parties, issue by issue: the environment, the economy, and so on. |
| | Ideas are connected by transitional words and phrases that indicate similarities or differences, such as *likewise, similarly, in contrast, a different kind,* and *another difference.* |
| **Cause and Effect Order** | One or more causes are presented followed by one or more effects, or one or more effects are presented followed by one or more causes. A public health announcement warning about the dangers of playing with fire would be usefully organized by cause-and-effect. An essay discussing the outbreak of World War I and the events that led up to it could be organized by effect and causes. |
| | Transitional words and phrases that indicate cause and effect include *one cause, another effect, as a result, consequently,* and *therefore.* |
| **Part by Part Order** | Ideas are presented according to no *overall* organizational pattern. However, each idea is connected logically to the one that precedes it and/or to the one that follows it. A letter to a friend might be organized part by part. One paragraph might discuss a party the writer just attended and the next could focus on the writer's feelings about a person he or she met there. After chronological order, this is the most common method for organizing ideas in writing. |
| | Transitional words or phrases include anything that indicates the relationship or connection between the ideas. |

**2.28 OUTLINING.** An **outline** is an excellent framework for highlighting main ideas and supporting details. Rough and formal outlines are the two main types of outlines writers commonly use.

**2.29 ROUGH OUTLINES.** To create a **rough outline**, simply list your main ideas in some logical order. Under each main idea, list the supporting details set off by dashes.

### What Is Drama?

**Definition of Drama**
—Tells a story
—Uses actors to play characters
—Uses a stage, properties, lights, costumes, makeup, and special effects

**Types of Drama**
—Tragedy
  —Definition: A play in which the main character meets a negative fate
  —Examples: <u>Antigone</u>, <u>Romeo and Juliet</u>, <u>Death of a Salesman</u>
—Comedy
  —Definition: A play in which the main character meets a positive fate
  —Examples: <u>A Midsummer Night's Dream</u>, <u>Cyrano de Bergerac</u>, <u>The Odd Couple</u>

**2.30 FORMAL OUTLINES.** A **formal outline** has headings and subheadings identified by numbers and letters. One type of formal outline is the **topic outline**. Such an outline has entries that are words or phrases rather than complete sentences.

### What Is a Myth?

I. Definition of myth
  A. Ancient story involving gods
    1. Multiple gods in mythology
    2. Gods given human characteristics
  B. Often about origins
    1. Reflect prescientific worldview
    2. Gods and humans actively participate
  C. Often about heroes

II. Creation myths
  A. The Greek myth of the origins of the universe
  B. The Greek myth of the origins of human beings

III. Origin myths
  A. Arachne and the origins of spiders
  B. Phaëthon and the origins of deserts

IV. Hero myths
  A. Theseus and the Minotaur
  B. Herakles and the twelve labors

## 2.31 Drafting

After you have gathered your information and organized it, the next step in writing is to produce a draft. A **draft** is simply an early attempt at writing a paper. When working on a draft, keep in mind that you do not have to get everything just right the first time through. The beauty of a draft is that you can rework it many times until you are happy with the final product.

Different writers approach drafting in different ways. Some prefer to work slowly and carefully, perfecting each part as they go. Producing such a **careful draft** can be rewarding because you get to see a finished, polished piece emerging part by part. However, many writers find that perfecting each part as they come to it bogs down the process. These writers prefer to write a discovery draft, getting all their ideas down on paper in rough form and then going back over the paper to work it into shape. When writing a **discovery draft**, you do not focus on spelling, grammar, usage, and mechanics. You can take care of those matters during revision.

**2.32 DRAFTING AN INTRODUCTION.** The purpose of an introduction is to capture your reader's attention and establish what you want to say. An effective introduction can start with a quotation, a question, an anecdote, an intriguing fact, or a description that hooks the reader to keep reading.

An effective introduction can open with

| | |
|---|---|
| A QUOTE | "That's one small step for man, one giant leap for mankind." With these words, Neil Armstrong signaled his success as the first person to set foot on the moon . . . |
| A QUESTION | What would it be like if all the birds in the world suddenly stopped their singing? |
| AN ANECDOTE | When my brother was nineteen, he volunteered in a homeless shelter making sure people had a safe place to spend the night. He told me once that he would never forget the time he met . . . |
| A FACT | More than a million new web pages appear each day on the Internet . . . |
| A DESCRIPTION | Along the murky bottom of the ocean floor, at the deepest part of the ocean, lies the giant squid, a creature so elusive that few people have ever seen it. For hundreds of years, no one knew it really existed—although tales of sea monsters had long hinted of it. |

**2.33 DRAFTING BODY PARAGRAPHS.** When writing the body of an essay, refer to your outline. Each heading in your outline will become the main idea of one of your paragraphs. To move smoothly from one idea to another, use transitional words or phrases. As you draft, include evidence from documented sources to support the ideas that you present. This evidence can be paraphrased, summarized, or quoted directly. For information on documenting sources, see the Language Arts Survey 5.36, "Documenting Sources" and 5.43, "Paraphrasing, Summarizing, and Quoting."

**2.34 DRAFTING A CONCLUSION.** In the conclusion, bring together the main ideas you included in the body of your essay and create a sense of closure to the issue you raised in your thesis. There is no single right way to conclude a piece of writing. Possibilities include:

- making a generalization
- restating the thesis and major supporting ideas in different words
- summarizing the points made in the rest of the essay
- drawing a lesson or moral
- calling on the reader to adopt a view or take an action
- expanding on your thesis or main idea by connecting it to the reader's own interests
- linking your thesis to a larger issue or concern

**2.35 USING TRANSITIONS EFFECTIVELY.** Transitions are words and phrases that help you move smoothly from one idea to the next in your writing. The transition words themselves depend on the method of organization you are using in your paper. For lists of these words and when to use them, see the Language Arts Survey 2.27, "Choosing a Method of Organization."

**2.36 WRITING NARRATIVE, DIALOGUE, DESCRIPTION, AND EXPOSITION.** Some writing purposes do not require a thesis or a formal outline. They rely on other types of writing to present their ideas effectively. These types include narration, dialogue, description, and exposition.

| TYPE OF WRITING | DESCRIPTION AND ORGANIZATION |
|---|---|
| **Narrative** | Writing using this method tells a story or presents events using time, or **chronological order**, as a way of organization. |
| **Dialogue** | Writing using this method presents words as they were actually spoken by people. Quotation marks are usually used to set off direct speech. |
| **Description** | Writing with this method portrays a character, an object, or a scene. Descriptions make use of sensory details—words and phrases that describe how things look, sound, feel, taste, or smell. Descriptive writing frequently uses **spatial order** as a method of organization. |
| **Exposition** | Writing using this method presents facts or opinions in an organized manner. There are many ways to organize exposition. Among the most common are the following: |
| | **Analysis** breaks something into its parts and shows how the parts are related. |
| | **Cause and effect order** identifies and analyzes the causes and effects of something. |
| | **Classification order** involves placing subjects into categories, or classes, according to their properties or characteristics. These groups are then presented, one-by-one, in some reasonable order. |
| | **Comparison and contrast order** is a method of organization in which details about the similarities and differences between two subjects are presented in one of two ways. In the first method, characteristics of one subject are presented, followed by the characteristics of a second subject. In the second method, both subjects are compared and contrasted with regard to one characteristic, then with regard to a second characteristic, and so on. |
| | **Definition** explains a concept or idea and examines its qualities. |
| | **Problem/Solution** writing analyzes a problem and proposes possible solutions. It can be objective or persuasive. |
| | **Process/How-to** writing presents the steps in a process or gives the reader directions on how to do something. |

## 2.37 Self- and Peer Evaluation

When you evaluate something, you examine it carefully to find its strengths and weaknesses. Evaluating your own writing is called **self-evaluation**. A **peer evaluation** is an evaluation of a piece of writing done by a classmate, or peer.

**2.38 HOW TO EVALUATE A PIECE OF WRITING.** After producing a rough draft of a piece of writing, the next step is to evaluate that draft to find out what you or the writer you are evaluating should improve.

A good evaluation practice is to read through the piece of writing three times:

- **First, check for content.** If you are evaluating your own writing, make sure that you have said all that you want to say, that you have not left out important details, and that you have not included unimportant or unrelated details. If you are evaluating a peer's writing, make sure the content is clear, that nothing is missing to prevent the work from carrying the reader forward, and that the writer has not included any unrelated details.

- **Second, check for organization.** Make sure that the ideas in the writing are presented in a reasonable order.
- **Third, check the style and language** of the piece. Make sure that the language is appropriately formal or informal, that the tone is appropriate to the message and the audience the piece addresses, and that the writer has defined any key or unfamiliar terms.

As you check the writing piece, make notes about what the writer needs to revise, or change. See the Language Arts Survey 2.42, "A Revision Checklist," for further information on what to look for as you evaluate your or a peer's writing.

### 2.39 How to Deliver Helpful Criticism

- **Be focused.** Concentrate on content, organization, and style. Do not concentrate at this point on proofreading matters such as spelling and punctuation; they can be fixed later.
- **Be positive.** Let the writer know what he or she has done right. Show how the paper could be improved by making the changes that you are suggesting.
- **Be specific.** Give the writer concrete ideas for improving his or her work. For example, if you think that two ideas seem unconnected, suggest a way in which they might be connected clearly.
- **Be tactful.** Consider the other person's feelings, and use a pleasant tone of voice. Do not criticize the writer. Instead, focus on the writing.

### 2.40 How to Benefit from Helpful Criticism

- **Tell your evaluator specific concerns.** For example, if you are wondering whether something you have written is clear, ask the evaluator if he or she understands that part of what you have written.
- **Ask questions to clarify comments** that your evaluator makes.
- **Accept your evaluator's comments graciously.** Remember that criticisms can be helpful. They can help you to identify weaknesses and produce a better piece through revision. If, on the other hand, you think that a given suggestion will not truly improve your writing, you do not have to follow it. There are many ways to strengthen writing. By reflecting on reviewer comments and your own self-evaluation, you will be ready to go on to the next step: revision.

## 2.41 Revising

After identifying weaknesses in a draft through self-evaluation and peer evaluation, the next step is to **revise** the draft. Here are four basic ways to improve meaning and content:

**Adding or Expanding.** Sometimes writing can be improved by adding details, examples, or transitions to connect ideas. Often a single added adjective, for example, can make a piece of writing clearer or more vivid.

| | |
|---|---|
| UNREVISED | Wind whistled through the park. |
| REVISED | A **bone-chilling** wind whistled through the park. |

At other times, you will find you will need to add details to back up your main idea.

| | |
|---|---|
| UNREVISED | Everyone uses the park so its destruction would be a major loss to the community. |
| REVISED | Of the 653 people who responded to the survey, 85 percent said they would consider the destruction of the park a major loss to the community. |

**CUTTING OR CONDENSING.** Often writing can be improved by cutting unnecessary or unrelated material.

UNREVISED    Watson was firmly determined to find the structure of the DNA molecule.
REVISED      Watson was determined to find the structure of the DNA molecule.

**REPLACING.** Sometimes weak writing can be replaced with stronger writing that is more concrete, more vivid, or more precise.

UNREVISED    Several things had been bothering Bill.
REVISED      Several personal problems had been bothering Bill.
UNREVISED    Chandra lived in a house down the street.
REVISED      Chandra lived in a Garrison colonial down Mulberry Street.

**MOVING.** Often you can improve the organization of your writing by moving part of it so that related ideas appear near one another.

UNREVISED    Mince the garlic in very fine pieces. Then heat a tablespoon of olive oil in a small skillet. Stir it with a wooden spoon and saute just until it starts to brown. Then remove it. Oh—before you put it in the skillet, heat some oil. Use about a tablespoon. Olive oil is best. Use medium-low heat.
REVISED      Mince the garlic in very fine pieces. Heat a tablespoon of olive oil in a small skillet at a medium-low temperature. When the oil is hot, add the garlic. Stir it with a wooden spoon and saute it just until it starts to brown. Then remove the garlic.

When you mark a piece of writing for revision, use the standard proofreading symbols. The symbols for adding, cutting, replacing, and moving are the first four symbols in the Language Arts Survey 2.44, "Using Proofreader's Marks."

**2.42 A REVISION CHECKLIST.** The following chart lists some questions to ask yourself whenever you are revising your writing. If you cannot answer yes to any of these questions, then you need to revise your work. Continue revising until you can answer yes.

| REVISION CHECKLIST | |
|---|---|
| **Content** | • Does the writing achieve its purpose?<br>• Are the main ideas clearly stated and supported by details? |
| **Organization** | • Are the ideas arranged in a sensible order?<br>• Are the ideas connected to one another within paragraphs and between paragraphs? |
| **Style** | • Is the language appropriate to the audience and purpose?<br>• Is the mood appropriate to the purpose of the writing? |

## 2.43 Proofreading

When you proofread your writing, you read it through to look for errors and mark corrections. When you mark corrections to your writing, use the standard proofreading symbols. With just a little practice you'll find them very easy and convenient.

**2.44 USING PROOFREADER'S MARKS.** Consult the chart below for standard proofreading marks.

## PROOFREADER'S SYMBOLS

| Symbol and Example | Meaning of Symbol |
|---|---|
| The very first time | Delete (cut) this material. |
| cat cradle | Insert (add) something that is missing. |
| George | Replace this letter or word. |
| All the horses king's | Move this word to where the arrow points. |
| french toast | Capitalize this letter. |
| the vice-President | Lowercase this letter. |
| housse | Take out this letter and close up space. |
| book keeper | Close up space. |
| gebril | Change the order of these letters. |
| end. "Watch out," she yelled. | Begin a new paragraph. |
| Love conquers all | Put a period here. |
| Welcome friends. | Put a comma here. |
| Get the stopwatch | Put a space here. |
| Dear Madam | Put a colon here. |
| She walked he rode. | Put a semicolon here. |
| name brand products | Put a hyphen here. |
| cats meow | Put an apostrophe here. |
| cat's cradle (stet) | Let it stand. (Leave as it is.) |

**2.45 A PROOFREADING CHECKLIST.** After you have revised your draft, make a clean copy of it and proofread it for errors in spelling, grammar, and punctuation. Use the following proofreading checklist.

## PROOFREADING CHECKLIST

| | |
|---|---|
| **Spelling** | • Are all words, including names, spelled correctly? |
| **Grammar** | • Does each verb agree with its subject? |
| | • Are verb tenses consistent and correct? |
| | • Are irregular verbs formed correctly? |
| | • Are there any sentence fragments or run-ons? |
| | • Have double negatives been avoided? |
| | • Have frequently confused words, such as *affect* and *effect*, been used correctly? |
| **Punctuation** | • Does every sentence end with an end mark? |
| | • Are commas used correctly? |
| | • Do all proper nouns and proper adjectives begin with capital letters? |

**2.46 PROPER MANUSCRIPT FORM.** After proofreading your draft, you will want to prepare your final manuscript. Follow the guidelines given by your teacher or, if your teacher tells you to do so, the guidelines given here. After preparing a final manuscript according to these guidelines, proofread it one last time for errors.

---

### GUIDELINES FOR PREPARING A MANUSCRIPT

- Keyboard your manuscript using a typewriter or word processor, or write it out neatly using blue or black ink.
- Double-space your paper. Leave one blank line between every line of text.
- Use one side of the paper.
- Leave one-inch margins on all sides of the text.
- Indent the first line of each paragraph.
- In the upper right corner of the first page, put your name, class, and date. On every page after the first, include the page number in this heading, as follows:
  Keanna Pérez
  English 7
  May 3, 2002
  p. 2
- Make a cover sheet listing the title of the work, your name, the date, and the class.

---

## 2.47 Publishing and Presenting Your Work

In the **publishing and presenting stage**, you share your work with an audience.

**2.48 MAINTAINING A WRITING PORTFOLIO.** A **writing portfolio** is a collection of your writing. Usually, a portfolio is a file folder with your name on it and your writing in it. Your teacher may ask you to keep a complete portfolio, one that includes all the pieces that you write. Another possibility is that your teacher will ask you to keep a selected portfolio, one that contains only your very best pieces of writing.

When you put a piece of writing in your portfolio, make sure that your name and the date are on it. Attach any notes or earlier versions of the writing that you have.

From time to time, you and your teacher will evaluate, or examine, your portfolio. You will meet in a student-teacher conference and talk about your pieces of writing. Your teacher will help you to find strengths and weaknesses in your writing. He or she also will help you to make plans for improving your writing in the future.

Keeping a writing portfolio can be exciting. In very little time, you can build a collection of your work. Looking over this work, you can take pride in your accomplishments. You can also reflect on how you are growing as a writer.

**2.49 SHARING YOUR WORK WITH OTHERS.** Some writing is done just for one's self. Journal writing usually falls into that category. Most writing, however, is meant to be shared with others. There are many ways in which to share your work. Here are several ways in which you can publish your writing or present it to others:

- Find a local publication that will accept your work. (A school literary magazine, a school newspaper, or a community newspaper are possibilities.)

- Submit the work to a regional or national publication. Check a reference work such as *Writer's Market* to find information on types of manuscripts accepted, manuscript form, and methods and amounts of payment.

- Enter the work in a contest. Your teacher may be able to tell you about writing contests for students. You can also find out about such contests by looking for announcements in writers' magazines and literary magazines.

- Read your work aloud to classmates, friends, or family members.

- Obtain permission to read your work aloud over the school's public address system.

- Work with other students to prepare a publication—a brochure, online literary magazine, anthology, or newspaper.

- Prepare a poster or bulletin board, perhaps in collaboration with other students, to display your writing.

- Make your own book by typing or word processing the pages and binding them together. Or copy your work into a blank book.

- Hold a reading or performance of student writing as a class or schoolwide project.

- Share your writing with other students in a small writers' group that meets periodically to discuss one or two students' recent work. (Members of the group should receive the work to be discussed beforehand so they can read it and make notes on it.)

- If the work is dramatic in nature, work with other students to present a performance of it, either as straight drama or as reader's theater. If the work is poetry, fiction, or nonfiction, work with others to present it as an oral interpretation.

## 2.50 Reflecting on Your Writing

In the **reflecting** stage, you think through the writing process to determine what you learned as a writer, what you accomplished, and what skills you would like to strengthen the next time you write. Reflection can be done in a journal, on a self-evaluation form for writing, in small group discussion, or simply in your own thoughts. Here are some questions to ask as you reflect on the writing process and yourself as a writer.

### QUESTIONS FOR REFLECTION

- What have I learned in writing about this topic?
- What have I learned in writing for this purpose?
- What have I learned by using this form?
- How do I perceive my audience? What would I like my audience to gain from my writing?
- What kind of voice does my writing have?
- How have I developed as a writer while writing this piece?
- What strengths have I discovered in my work?
- What aspects of my writing do I want to strengthen? What can I do to strengthen them?

# LANGUAGE, GRAMMAR, AND STYLE Resource

## LANGUAGE

### 3.1 Appropriate Uses of English

Language is a powerful tool for conveying meaning. It is also a complex tool that must be used appropriately if genuine communication is to occur. In deciding how to communicate most effectively, a speaker must make choices concerning use of formal or informal English; what tone to use, the effects of irony, sarcasm, and rudeness; and how dialect affects the communicated message.

### 3.2 Formal and Informal English

Depending on the situation, you might use either formal English or informal English when you speak or write. Formal English is appropriate for school essays, newspaper and magazine articles, some literary works, oral or written reports, and test answers. Informal English is appropriate when speaking with a friend or writing personal letters or notes; it can also be used in some literary works.

How do you decide whether to use formal or informal English? You will naturally tend to use informal English, so all you need to remember are the situations just described in which formal English may be expected instead. Your audience and purpose help determine whether to use formal or informal English. For example, you would use formal English to discuss a grade with a teacher or to ask for a refund from a store manager. You would use informal English talking with your friends. You might use somewhat formal English in getting to know a new friend, and then relax and use more informal English as the friendship developed.

How do you tell the difference between formal and informal English? Informal English allows grammatical constructions that would not be acceptable in formal English. Many of these constructions are described in the Grammar Handbook on page 1055, where they are labeled "nonstandard." Informal English also uses *colloquialisms* and *slang*.

A **colloquialism** is a word or phrase used in everyday conversation.

COLLOQUIAL ENGLISH
> **You guys** must be **sick of** doing the same thing after day.
> He was **totally turned off** by the movie.

FORMAL ENGLISH
> **All of you** must be **weary** of doing the same thing day after day.
> He was completely **displeased** by the movie.

**Slang** is a form of speech made up of invented words or old words that are given a new meaning.

SLANG
> You better **chill out** for a while—you're too angry to talk to him now.

FORMAL ENGLISH
> You had better **relax** for a while—you're too angry to talk to him now.

### 3.3 Register, Tone, and Voice

To understand the concept of register, imagine that all the different kinds of usage in a language—both formal and informal—form one large set. A **register** is a subset of language usage specific to a particular relationship between people. In talking to a friend, for example, you speak in a register that is casual, warm, and open. In speaking to a young child, you speak in a register that is nonthreatening and simple to understand. In speaking to an official such as a police officer or a government clerk, you speak in a register that is polite but forthright—the same register that person should use with you. The words you choose, the grammar you employ to say those words, and your tone of voice will change depending on the register in which you are speaking.

Another way to understand register is to examine its meaning as a musical term. In music, register means the range of notes a singer or instrument is capable of producing. Your speaking and writing, however, are not limited to one range of usage. You can call on any part of a broad scale of usage, ranging from a grunt to a complex and formal declaration of your thought.

One hallmark of people who know how to use the power of language is their ability to choose and use the appropriate register for whatever situation they are in. They do not offend strangers by being too familiar or puzzle their friends by being too formal.

**Tone** is a writer's or speaker's attitude toward a subject. The tone of a message should reflect the speaker's attitude toward the subject and his or her audience. The speaker shapes the tone of a message by carefully choosing words and phrases. *Diction*, or choice of words, determines much of a speaker's tone. For instance, when writing a letter of complaint, do you want to say, "Your new product is so disgusting that I'll never buy anything you make ever again" or "I am concerned with the danger your new product poses to young children"? The tone you convey will depend greatly upon word choice.

The following examples give two different descriptions of the same scene. In one the scene is described in a tone of fear, and in the other it is described in a tone of awe. If you were telling a story about someone who was afraid of the ocean, you might use the more negative description. If you were writing about someone who enjoyed the ocean, you would probably use the more positive description.

**TONE OF FEAR**

Menacing black waves rolled in relentlessly, crashing down upon the rocks and threatening to sweep everything in their path out to sea. Mountainous and savage, the waves pounded the shore with a fury that sent a chill of dread through my soul.

**TONE OF AWE**

Powerful breakers rolled in majestically, splashing against the rocks and sending fountains of spray high into the air. I stood in awe of this force so mighty that nothing could stop it.

**Voice** is the quality of a work that tells you that one person in particular wrote it—not several, and not just anyone. Voice is one feature that makes a spoken or written work unique. The voice of a work can be difficult to define; it may have to do with the way a writer or speaker views people, events, objects, ideas, the passage of time, even life itself. If this treatment of the subject is consistent throughout, despite variations in tone, register, point of view, and topic, then the writer or speaker has established a voice, a sense of individuality, in the work.

In your own communication, whether in speaking or writing, you should strive to develop your own voice, not to imitate the voices of others. What that voice is, and how it compares to others, are matters no one can decide for you. "To thine own self be true," says Polonius in Shakespeare's *Hamlet*, "and thou canst not then be false to any man." Be true to your own voice, and your experience will speak directly to the experience of others.

## 3.4 Irony, Sarcasm, and Rudeness

It is easy to mistake the term *rude* to mean anything that is crude, distasteful, or not pleasing to someone. The word *rude* has been adapted and expanded into a general slang term. The standard definition of *rude* means bad-mannered, impolite, or inconsiderate. If someone says something a listener doesn't like, that person is not rude in the original meaning of the word. However, a person who interrupts someone else's conversation, curses, or forgets to say "please," "thank you," or "excuse me" is being selfish and inconsiderate—all characteristics of rude behavior within the original meaning of the word.

Frequently students confuse sarcasm or irony with rudeness. **Verbal irony** is present when someone says or writes the opposite of what he or she means in order to create humor or to make a point. It can be funny or serious. For example, if someone pushes to the front of a line, and someone else says, "What polite behavior," the speaker is expressing verbal irony. **Sarcasm** is a specialized kind of irony; the difference is the speaker's intentions. Sarcastic people say the opposite of what they mean in order to criticize, hurt, or humiliate someone. Sarcasm differs from other forms of irony because it is always unkind.

EXAMPLE OF SARCASM

> The other girls picked up the "pork chop" and made it into a refrain: "pork chop, pork chop, did you eat your pork chop?"
>
> —Judith Ortiz Cofer, "American History"

## 3.5 Dialects of English

A **dialect** is a version of a language spoken by people of a particular place, time, or group. Dialects are characterized by differences in pronunciation, word choice, grammar, and accent. They are usually based on social differences (upper class, middle class, and lower class) or on regional differences. In the United States, the major regional dialects are northern, southern, midland, and western.

All dialects are equally capable of expressing thought, which is what language is for. Therefore, no dialect is better than any other dialect. The dialect used by the most powerful social class is usually considered the **standard**, and other dialects are considered **nonstandard**. But standard does not mean "correct" or "better than others." Knowledge of the standard dialect is useful because it is widely understood, and because in many situations, speaking or writing in the standard dialect will ensure that people focus on what you say rather than how you say it. They will understand your meaning, without being distracted by your use of an unfamiliar dialect.

Knowing nonstandard dialect is also useful to writers. Consider the way Mark Twain uses dialect to make his writing more authentic.

> At the door I met the sociable Wheeler returning, and he button-holed me and recommenced;
> "Well, thish-yer Smiley had a yaller one-eyed cow that didn't have no tail, only jest a short stump like a bannanner, and—"
>
> —Mark Twain, "The Notorious Jumping Frog of Calaveras County"

Differences in dialect show up especially in the terms speakers use to refer to certain objects in various areas of the country. For example, the generic term for a carbonated beverage is "soda" in Florida and Washington, DC, "pop" in Ohio and Minnesota, "coke" in Georgia and Tennessee, and "tonic" in Boston. Similarly, the grassy strip separating the lanes of an interstate highway is called a "mall" in upstate New York, a "median" in Ohio, a "medial strip" in Pennsylvania, a "meridian" in the upper Midwest, and "neutral ground" in Louisiana.

# GRAMMAR

In English the basic unit of meaning is the sentence. In this integrated approach to grammar you will examine sentences to determine what they mean. This should help you to be a better reader and more skillful writer. This approach may be new to you, so here are a series of charts and references to help you as you begin. Do not memorize these charts. The more you use them, the less you will need them. With time, you will develop a feeling for the way language works so you will not need them at all.

## 3.6 Identifying the Parts of Speech

Each word in a sentence has one of four basic functions: it **names**, **modifies**, **expresses action or state of being**, or **links**.

A fifth "extra" function is to interrupt for effect; words that **interrupt** will be discussed at the end of this section.

English also has words that can work as more than one part of speech. Words that can take on different parts of speech are called **hybrids**. These words will be explained at the end of this section.

Below is an overview of the parts of speech. For a more detailed description of what each part of speech does, see the "Parts of Speech Summary" on page 1071.

## 3.7 Grammar Reference Chart—Parts of Speech Overview

| PARTS OF SPEECH | EXAMPLE(S) |
|---|---|
| **NAMERS** (nouns and pronouns) are subjects and objects. | |
| NOUN. A **noun** names a person, place, thing, or idea. | Adam, journalist, mountain, India, rose, motorcycle, honesty, feeling |
| PRONOUN. A **pronoun** is used in place of a noun to name a person, place, thing, or idea. | **I** bought the bricks and used **them** to build a wall.<br>Take Schuyler to the ice cream shop and buy **him** a cone. (**Him** is used in place of Schuyler.) |
| **EXPRESSERS** (verbs) name an action or state of being plus the conditions around it. | |
| VERB. A **verb** expresses action or state of being. | bake, glance, give, build, compose, think, look, feel, am |
| **MODIFIERS** (adjectives and adverbs) make other parts of speech more specific. | |
| ADJECTIVE. An **adjective** modifies, or changes the meaning of, a noun or pronoun. | **gray** skies, **deep** water, **eerie** laughter |
| ADVERB. An **adverb** modifies, or changes the meaning of, a verb, an adjective, or another adverb. | Leanne gripped the wheel **nervously**.<br>Elliot thought the exam was **extremely** easy.<br>Giovanni peered over the edge of the cliff **very** cautiously. |
| **LINKERS** (prepositions and conjunctions) join all the constructions of the English language. | |
| PREPOSITION. A **preposition** is used to show how a noun or a pronoun is related to other words in the sentence. Common prepositions are *in, after, among, at, behind, beside, off, through, until, upon,* and *with.* | Pablo enjoyed the concert **at** the Wang Center.<br>Theresa squeezed **through** the opening **of** the cave and crawled **into** the narrow passage. |
| CONJUNCTION. A **conjunction** joins words or groups of words. Common conjunctions are *and, but, for, nor, or, so,* and *yet.* | Wilhelm plays the guitar, **but** Leonard plays drums.<br>Wilhelm **and** Leonard play loudly. |
| **INTERRUPTERS** (interjections and other constructions) interrupt a sentence for emphasis. | |
| INTERJECTION. An **interjection** is a word used to express emotion. Common interjections are *oh, ah, well, say,* and *wow.* | **Hey!** What are you doing in there?<br>**Oh well**, I didn't expect to win the election anyway. |
| APPOSITIVE. An **appositive** is an interrupter that renames a noun. | My friend **Yang Yardley** did a beautiful project on birds.<br>Mrs. Cokely, **my favorite teacher**, will retire. |
| NOUN OF DIRECT ADDRESS. **A noun of direct address** says the name of the person or group spoken to and is never the subject of the sentence. | Wait until dark, **Audrey**.<br>**Class**, listen to the instructions. (*Class* is a noun of direct address; the subject of the sentence is *you*; the pronoun *you* is understood.) |

**CONTINUED**

| PARTS OF SPEECH | EXAMPLE(S) |
|---|---|

**HYBRIDS** (such as possessive nouns, pronouns, verbals) can act as more than one part of speech.

| | |
|---|---|
| **POSSESSIVE NOUNS AND PRONOUNS. Possessive nouns** and **pronouns** are nouns and pronouns that function as adjectives. | Angela read **Scott's** essay. (*Scott's* is a possessive noun modifying *essay.*)<br>Angela read **his** essay. (*His* is a possessive pronoun modifying *essay.*) |
| **VERBALS. Verbals** are verb forms such as participles, gerunds, and infinitives that can function as adjectives, nouns, and adverbs. | I love the **swimming** pool. (*Swimming* is a verbal called a participle and acts as an adjective.)<br>**Swimming** is my favorite sport. (*Swimming* is a verbal called a gerund and acts as a noun.)<br>I like **to swim**. (*To swim* is a verbal called an infinitive.) |

To understand how a sentence works, here are other groups of words that you should know about.

## 3.8 Grammar Reference Chart—Helping Verbs

A **helping verb** helps a main verb to express action or state of being.

| HELPING VERBS | | |
|---|---|---|
| be (am, are, is, was, were, being, and been) | have (has, had) | shall |
| | may | should |
| can | might | will |
| could | must | would |
| do (does, did) | | |

## 3.9 Grammar Reference Chart—The Verb *To Be*

Most languages use the verb *to be* more than any other verb because its forms have more uses than any other verb form. It can be the main verb of a sentence, used to express existence. It also can be a helping verb used with action verbs. Here are some forms of *to be:*

| THE VERB *TO BE* | |
|---|---|
| **Present:** am, is, are<br>**Past:** was, were, has been, had been<br>**Future:** will be, shall be, will have been | **Other expressions and forms that use *be*:**<br>being, can be, could be, could have been, may be, may have been, might be, might have been, must be, must have been, would be, would have been |

## 3.10 Grammar Reference Chart—Linking Verbs

A **linking verb** connects a noun with another noun, a pronoun, or pronoun adjective that describes or defines it. Note that some linking verbs can also be action verbs. For example, *I grow tired* uses *grow* as a linking verb. *I grow flowers* uses *grow* as an action verb. Notice how <u>I am a junior</u> and <u>A junior am I</u> mean exactly the same thing. This is because *am* is a linking, not an action verb. Sentences with action verbs cannot be reversed in the same way: *I made a bookshelf* and *A bookshelf* *made me* do not mean the same thing. Here is a list of common linking verbs. *Be* is the most common of all.

| LINKING VERBS | | |
|---|---|---|
| appear | grow | smell |
| be (am, is, are, was, were, been) | look | sound |
| become | remain | stay |
| feel | seem | taste |

## 3.11 Grammar Reference Chart—Prepositions

These are the most commonly used prepositions. Remember, though, that any word on this list may not always be used as a preposition. If it is a preposition, it will always have an object.

| PREPOSITIONS | | | | |
|---|---|---|---|---|
| aboard | at | concerning | off | until |
| about | before | down | on | up |
| above | behind | during | over | upon |
| across | below | except | past | with |
| after | beside | for | since | within |
| against | besides | from | through | without |
| along | between | in | throughout | |
| amid | beyond | into | to | |
| among | but | like | under | |
| around | by | of | underneath | |

## 3.12 What Is Grammar?

The **grammar** of a language refers to two different language areas. First, grammar is the collection of rules and standards that careful speakers use as they write and speak. Second, a **grammar** is any one of several possible descriptions of a language.

Classical grammar has troubled English students because it was originally designed to fit Latin, an inflected language. In Latin every word has an ending or inflection that defines its sentence function, so word order doesn't matter. About the middle of this century, different English grammars began to appear. The most successful of the new grammars were based upon rules of English word order, but frequently the terms used were too confusing to be widely used.

Consequently, the grammar presented here uses elements of both. It demands that students label words and language groups according to what language is doing (which we know by word order). Many terms are familiar because they come from classical grammar, but their meaning may change to fit the grammar of a syntactic language, English.

## 3.13 English Is a Syntactic Language

Scholars who study language have classified European languages into two major categories: **inflected languages** and **syntactic languages.** The words of **inflected** languages change their forms to tell speakers how the word is used. Word order isn't all that important to meaning. Some inflected languages are Latin and German. English is a **syntactic language**. Word order **(syntax)** determines meaning for **syntactic languages.**

## 3.14 The Importance of Syntax, or Word Order

EXAMPLE   The junior class plans the prom each spring.

In English sentences, words are arranged in specific patterns. In the most frequently used sentence, the sentence tells who *(The junior class),* and then it tells what that *who* does *(plans the prom each spring).* When word order changes, the  sentence changes meaning; if the pattern rules are ignored, the sentence may become awkward, or even meaningless.

EXAMPLES

Class the the prom plans each spring junior.
Plans the junior spring the prom class each.
Class the plans each the prom junior spring.

A change in syntax results in a change in meaning; different sentence positions of the same word results in different meanings.

EXAMPLES

Junior prom <u>plans</u> are finished by March.
<u>Plans</u> for our house were completed last fall.
Our family <u>plans</u> a vacation every summer.

In the first two sentences, *plans* names something. In the first sentence, it is used to mean arrangements; in the second it means blueprints. In the third sentence, *plans* is an action.
In all sentences the word form is the same, but different positions signal different meanings.

## 3.15 Inflections in English

Although word order is most important, English does have some **inflections**, or changes in form. English verbs, adjectives, and pronouns are inflected. Sometimes we add a suffix  (add *-ed* to *work*, *-er* or *-est* to *hard*); other times interior letters or the entire forms change: *drive* becomes *drove*, *my* becomes *mine*, *was* becomes *were*.

EXAMPLES

**INFLECTED VERBS**
Today I *carry* my lunch. Yesterday I *carried* it, too. (The *y* is replaced by *i*, and the suffix *-ed* is added.)

Today I *have* lots of homework; yesterday I *had* very little. (The entire verb form changes.)

**INFLECTED ADJECTIVES**
My sister is *wise*; my mother is *wiser*, but my grandmother is the *wisest* woman

in the family. (The suffixes *-er* and *-est* are added to indicate higher degrees of quality.)

Kevin's day was *good*; Tua's was *better*, but mine turned out *best*. (The form changes altogether.)

**INFLECTED PRONOUNS**
Most pronouns change forms: *me, mine; they, them.* A specialized group of pronouns, the reflexive and intensive pronouns, add the suffix *-self* to the singular possessive pronoun forms *my, him, her, it,* and *your,* and add *-selves* to the plural forms *them, your,* and *our.*

## 3.16 The Sentence: The Basic Building Block of the English Language

Since first grade you have been encouraged to write and speak in sentences because they are the basic units of meaning. English sentences are organized to tell us whom or what a speaker is talking about, and to give information about that person or thing. Classical grammar defines a sentence as "a group of words that expresses a complete thought."

## 3.17 Functions of Sentences

English speakers use four kinds of sentences to express four different kinds of complete thoughts:

- A **declarative sentence** informs us. First, it tells whom or what a speaker is writing or speaking about, and second, it gives information about that whom or what.

- An **interrogative sentence** asks a question.

- An **imperative sentence** gives orders or makes requests.

- An **exclamatory sentence** expresses strong feeling.

EXAMPLES

**DECLARATIVE:**   I am ready to eat dinner.
**INTERROGATIVE:** Is dinner ready?
**IMPERATIVE:**    Give me my food.
**EXCLAMATORY:**  I'm starving to death!

## 3.18 Subjects and Verbs: The Basic Building Blocks in a Sentence

Good readers and writers analyze meaning by examining the structure of sentences. Finding the parts of a sentence is a basic tool for people who use language well.

## 3.19 Finding the Complete Subject and Complete Predicate in a Sentence

All simple English sentences can be divided into two parts, the subject and the predicate. In the most common English sentence, the first part of the sentence tells us what it is talking about. This is the **complete subject**. Then it gives us information about the subject; this second part of the sentence is called the **complete predicate**. In the following examples, the complete subject is underlined once and the complete predicate is underlined twice.

> EXAMPLES
>
> One of my brothers fixed his own car.
> Sharyl and Ken will be presenting Friday's history lesson.
> Lala might have been given a wrong classroom number.

NOTE: Every word in every sentence is a part of the complete subject or the complete predicate.

## 3.20 Finding the Simple Subject and Simple Predicate in a Sentence

Most people need more specific information than that given by the complete subject and the complete predicate. The basic units of meaning are found in the **simple subject** and the **simple predicate** (more frequently called the **verb**). The **simple subject** is the **complete subject** without any of its modifiers. The **verb** is the **complete predicate** without any complements or modifiers.

The **simple subject** is the complete subject without any modifiers or linkers—the extra words.

> EXAMPLES
>
> Little **kids** like pet kittens and puppies.
> Telly's **mother** wants a new car.

The **simple predicate** or **verb** is the complete predicate without any complements, linkers, or modifiers.

> EXAMPLES
>
> Little kids **like** pet kittens and puppies.
> Telly's mother **wants** a new car.

NOTE: Verbs may be made up of more than one word—they may have as many as four! Each of the examples is one verb.

> EXAMPLES
>
> play (one word)
> is playing (two words)
> has been playing (3 words)
> may have been playing (4 words)

## 3.21 How to Find the Simple Subject and Verb

The following four-step method will help you to find the simple subject and verb.

> EXAMPLE
>
> My older sister might not get a motorcycle for high school graduation.

1. Ask, "What is the action of this sentence?" The action is *get*.

2. Using the Language Arts Survey 3.8, "Helping Verbs," check some of the words around the action word. For the sample sentence, you might want to check *might* and *not*. *Might* is on the list; *not* isn't. Only *might* is a helping verb. The verb of the sentence is *might get*.

3. After finding the verb, ask who (what) did the action? Who *might get . . . ? My older sister.*

4. Finally, what words aren't necessary for simplest meaning? *Older sister* makes sense, so omit *my; older* can be left out, too. *Sister* is the simple subject of the sentence.

## 3.22 Sentence Completers for Action Verbs: Direct and Indirect Objects

A sentence must have a subject and a verb, but sometimes sentences have other parts that complete the meaning. The completers for action verbs are **direct objects** and **indirect objects**.

**DIRECT OBJECTS.** If the action of the verb has a receiver, the receiver is a **direct object**. In each case, once the verb is found, the direct object answers the question "what?" about the verb.

> EXAMPLES
>
> Birds ate grain. (Birds ate what? *grain*)
> Work the problems fast. (Work what? *problems*)
> I walked the dog. (Walked what? *dog*)

Notice that the last step was to get rid of any modifiers. That tells you what the direct object itself is. Also note: the direct object is *never* found in a prepositional phrase.

**INDIRECT OBJECTS.** Sometimes the direct object is received by someone or something. This receiver is called the **indirect object**. A sentence without a direct object cannot have an indirect object.

EXAMPLE   Mike gave me a red pencil.

**What** is the *action* (the verb)? *gave*
*Who* gave? (the subject) *Mike*
*What* did he give? (the direct object) *pencil*

To find the indirect object, check to see if the direct object had a receiver. Who got the direct object? In this sentence we ask, "Who got the pencil?" The answer is *me*.

*Who* received the pencil? (the indirect object) *me*

## 3.23 Sentence Completers for Linking Verbs: Predicate Nouns, Pronouns, and Adjectives

Unlike action verbs, **linking verbs** do not describe an *action*. They simply join a subject to another word that describes or identifies it. Since no action is being performed, there are no objects or direct objects. Instead, the first noun, or naming word, is assumed to be the subject while the renaming or describing word is called its **complement.**

Because a linking verb has no object or direct object, the order of the sentence can sometimes be reversed without affecting the meaning. For example, *I am a student* and *A student am I* mean exactly the same thing. *Am* is merely linking the two nouns, no matter what the order. On the other hand, *I made dinner* and *Dinner made me* mean very different things. Because *made* is an action verb, the sentence cannot be reversed. There are three types of sentence completers for linking verbs: **predicate nouns**, **predicate pronouns**, and **predicate adjectives.**

EXAMPLES

**PREDICATE NOUN**         Tala is my best <u>friend</u>.
**PREDICATE PRONOUN**   We are the <u>ones</u>!
**PREDICATE ADJECTIVES** Tierre felt <u>ill</u>.

## 3.24 Predicate Nouns and Pronouns as Sentence Completers

Sentences with predicate nouns and pronouns do not use action verbs: they use forms of the verb *to be*. (Forms of *to be* are listed in 3.9, "Grammar Reference Chart—The Verb *To Be*.") To find a **predicate noun** or **predicate pronoun**, ask the same questions asked to find a **direct object**.

EXAMPLE   Mary will have been my friend for six years.

To find the predicate noun, ask, "Mary will have been what?" The answer is *friend*.

EXAMPLE   The most dangerous criminal was he.

To find the predicate pronoun, ask, "The most dangerous criminal was who?" The answer is *he*.

**NOTE:** Direct and indirect objects include *me, her, him, us,* and *them.* Predicate pronouns include *I, she, he, we,* and *they.*

## 3.25 Predicate Adjectives as Sentence Completers

A **predicate adjective** modifies, or describes, the subject of a sentence. Sentences with predicate adjectives may use a variety of linking verbs. Consult 3.10, the "Grammar Reference Chart— Linking Verbs," for a list of linking verbs. Most of these are used just with predicate adjectives, not with predicate nouns or pronouns.

EXAMPLE   Della feels blue today.

To find the predicate adjective, ask, "Della feels what?" The answer is *blue. Blue* describes Della.

# SUBJECTS AND VERBS: PROBLEM CONSTRUCTIONS

English speakers often rearrange or use different kinds of sentences. Some of these constructions can be very tricky!

## 3.26 Working with Inverted Sentences

A sentence is **inverted** when all or part of the complete predicate comes before the subject. When you ask a question, you automatically invert your sentence. Usually, part of the verb is in front of the subject.

EXAMPLES

**DECLARATIVE** Sitka did study the math problem.
**INTERROGATIVE** Did Sitka study the math problem?

In both sentences, the verb is *did study*. Part of the verb comes before the subject.

Other sentences may be inverted so that a modifier comes before the subject.

> EXAMPLE   Sitka studied the math problem <u>today</u>.
> <u>Today</u> Sitka studied the math problem.

Be sure to find all the words in the verb of an inverted sentence.

## 3.27 Working with *There* Sentences

The word *there* often appears as the first word or as one of the first few words in a sentence. *There* will never be a part of the sentence; it is a modifier. To make finding the subject and verb easier, cross out *there* before determining the basic parts of the sentence.

> EXAMPLE
>
> There will be two standardized tests given this week.
>
> Remove *there:*
> Will be two standardized tests given this week.
>
> Rearrange words:
> Two standardized tests will be given this week.

Now the subject and verb are easy to find. The subject is *tests;* the verb is *will be given*.

## 3.28 Working with Compound Subjects, Verbs, and Sentences

If a sentence has more than one subject, together they are called a **compound subject**.

> EXAMPLE
>
> <u>Frank and Jesus</u> work at a carwash.

If a sentence has more than one verb, the verbs together are called a **compound verb**.

> EXAMPLE
>
> Helen <u>cooked</u> dinner, <u>washed</u> dishes, and <u>swept</u> the floor.

Notice that each verb has its own direct object.

Sentences can have both a compound subject and a compound verb.

> EXAMPLE
>
> <u>Mikka</u> and <u>Juan</u> <u>cut</u> the grass and <u>washed</u> the car.

A **compound sentence** refers to two sentences that are either (1) connected by a semicolon *or* (2) connected with a coordinating conjunction and a comma. Each part of the compound sentence has its own subject and verb.

> EXAMPLES
>
> Sally wanted a car, but her family wouldn't buy one.
> Sally wanted a car; her family wouldn't buy one.

In both sentences, the subjects are *Sally* and *family;* the verbs are *wanted* and *would buy*. (*Not* is not part of the verb; it only modifies the verb.)

For more information, see the Language Arts Survey 3.36, "Combining and Expanding Sentences."

## 3.29 Working with Negatives and Contractions

**NEGATIVES.** Negatives such as *not* and *never* are considered adverbs because they change the meaning of the verb. The word *not* modifies the helping verbs *to be, to do* and *to be able to*, making them mean the exact opposite.

> EXAMPLES
>
> I play basketball.
> Negative: I do not play basketball.

Make sure to use only one negative in each sentence. Check your writing to be sure that you have not used a negative word such as *not, nobody, none, nothing, hardly, barely, can't, doesn't, won't, isn't,* or *aren't* with another negative word.

**DOUBLE NEGATIVE (NONSTANDARD)**
> I <u>hardly</u> <u>never</u> eat my lunch at school.
> <u>Didn't</u> Joyce <u>never</u> go to Chicago?
> It <u>doesn't</u> make <u>no</u> difference!
> Why <u>wasn't</u> Jerry hurt <u>no</u> worse when the car was destroyed?

**CORRECTED SENTENCES (STANDARD)**
> I hardly ever eat my lunch at school.
> Didn't Joyce ever go to Chicago?
> It doesn't make any difference!
> Why wasn't Jerry hurt any worse when the car was destroyed?

**CONTRACTIONS.** **Contractions** combine two words by shortening and joining them with an apostrophe.

isn't, aren't, don't, can't

When you are trying to determine subjects and verbs in a sentence, contractions need to be written out into the two words that they represent. After the contraction is written out, each word should be considered separately. Each of the contractions above contains a negative. Remember that a negative is never part of a verb but is an adverb.

| CONTRACTION | WORDS CONTRACTED | PARTS OF SPEECH |
| --- | --- | --- |
| isn't | is not | is (verb or helping verb), not (negative; adverb) |
| aren't | are not | are (verb), not (negative; adverb) |
| don't | do not | do (verb), not (negative; adverb) |
| can't | can not | can (helping verb), not (negative; adverb) |

## 3.30 Identifying Prepositional Phrases

The simple subject and verb is *never* in a **prepositional phrase.** If you think a word might be a preposition, check the chart of common prepositions in 3.11, "Grammar Reference Chart—Prepositions." If the word is there, find its object.

The prepositional phrases have been underlined in the example below:

EXAMPLE

One of my brothers is planning a medical career after college.

NOTE: The simple subject, verb, and complements are *never* in prepositional phrases, so before determining the subject and verb of a sentence, if you cross out the prepositional phrases, you will have fewer words to consider.

## 3.31 Using Indefinite Pronouns

You seldom have problems with personal pronouns in sentences because they are easy to recognize.

When you encounter an **indefinite pronoun** (used to replace a person or a group of people not specifically identified), you might make errors in subject and verb agreement. Subjects and objects are particularly tricky when they are followed by a prepositional phrase, as shown below.

EXAMPLES

Some of the students wrote excellent short stories.
Ten from the senior class were chosen for a legislative workshop.
Mr. James gave several of my friends top grades on their papers.

You might want to cross out prepositional phrases in a sentence before you determine subjects and verbs.

## 3.32 Avoiding Problems Caused by Understood Subjects and Nouns of Direct Address

**Understood subjects** are sometimes used in sentences that make requests or give commands. The subject is *you,* but it is not written out, because both the speaker/writer and listener/reader understand who is meant.

EXAMPLES

Open your books. Give me your attention.
Run outside; the school is burning down!

In each of these the speaker does not have to say the *you* because it is understood.

If you are not sure that the subject is understood, try using *you* in front of the verb.

**Nouns of direct address** are never a part of the sentence. They name the person talked to, and they are always set off from the rest of the sentence using commas. They can appear at any place in a sentence.

EXAMPLES

Hank, when did you plan to finish your project?
Have you seen the new science lab, Carrie?
I need to know, class, if you had any problems with today's homework.

By noticing the comma clues—the way the noun of direct address is set off from the rest of the sentence—you will see that these nouns are not actually an essential part of each sentence.

# WRITER'S WORKSHOP: BUILDING EFFECTIVE SENTENCES

## 3.33 Correcting Sentence Fragments

A sentence contains a subject and a verb and should express a complete thought. A **sentence fragment** is a phrase or clause that does not express a complete thought but has been punctuated as though it did.

**SENTENCE FRAGMENT**
So he could explore the clear waters of the lake.

**COMPLETE SENTENCE**
Teddy bought a new mask and snorkel so he could explore the clear waters of the lake.

**SENTENCE FRAGMENT**
Looking for the lost little girl.

**COMPLETE SENTENCE**
The searchers combed the woods looking for the lost little girl.

## 3.34 Correcting Sentence Run-ons

A **sentence run-on** is made up of two or more sentences that have been run together as if they were one complete thought. You can fix a run-on by dividing it into two separate sentences. Mark the end of each idea with a period, question mark, or exclamation point. Capitalize the first word of each new sentence.

**RUN-ON**
Jason tried to jump across the swollen stream he slipped in the mud on the other side.

**TWO SENTENCES**
Jason tried to jump across the swollen stream. He slipped in the mud on the other side.

**RUN-ON**
Mr. Strauss refused to reconsider his decision, he had made up his mind and didn't want to be bothered with the facts.

**TWO SENTENCES**
Mr. Strauss refused to reconsider his decision. He had made up his mind and didn't want to be bothered with the facts.

You can also correct a sentence run-on with a semicolon.

**RUN-ON**
I went to bed early I got up late.

**CORRECTED WITH SEMICOLONS**
I went to bed early; I got up late.

A **sentence string** is a run-on formed of several sentences strung together with conjunctions. Edit sentence strings by breaking them into separate sentences and subordinate clauses.

**STRINGY**
When I decided to audition for the part, I had no idea how to do it so I asked my friend Eileen who has some acting talent what to do and she said to practice in front of a mirror, but I tried that and it didn't help, so I had Eileen come over instead and when I read my lines to her that really helped.

**REVISED**
When I decided to audition for the part, I had no idea how to do it. I asked my friend Eileen, who has some acting talent, what to do. She said to practice in front of a mirror, but I tried that and it didn't help. I had Eileen come over instead. When I read my lines to her, that really helped.

## 3.35 Correcting Wordy Sentences

As you write, avoid **wordy sentences**. Use only the words necessary to make your meaning clear to a reader. Edit your sentences so that they are not wordy and complicated. Replace complicated or general words with simple and specific words.

**WORDY**
Make sure that you are very careful not to forget to lock the door to the house when you leave the house.

**CLEAR AND DIRECT**
Don't forget to lock the door as you leave.

## 3.36 Combining and Expanding Sentences

There are many ways to combine and expand sentences to achieve smooth writing and sentence variety.

**COMBINING SENTENCES.** If you use several short sentences in a paragraph, your writing might sound choppy, and your reader might have trouble understanding how ideas are connected.

**Combining sentences** is a good way to bring two sentences together that deal with the same main idea. If you combine short sentences, your writing will sound smooth and clear, and your reader will see how ideas are connected to one another.

One way of combining sentences is to take a word or phrase from one sentence and insert it into another sentence. You might need to change the form of the word.

**BORING, SHORT SENTENCES**

The cowboys walked into the saloon. Their walk was more like a swagger. They were boisterous.

**COMBINED SENTENCE**

The boisterous cowboys swaggered into the saloon.

Another way of combining sentences is to merge two related sentences into one sentence that states both ideas. Your two sentences can be combined with a comma and a **conjunction** such as *and, or, for, nor, but, so,* or *yet.*

**BORING, SHORT SENTENCES**

The storm was fierce. The captain brought the ship to safety.

**COMBINED SENTENCE**

The storm was fierce, but the captain brought the ship to safety.

**EXPANDING SENTENCES.** You can expand sentences and achieve sentence variety by combining clauses to form compound, complex, and compound-complex sentences.

An **independent clause** expresses a complete thought and can stand by itself as a simple sentence.

**INDEPENDENT CLAUSE**

The geese flew away.

To expand this simple sentence into a **compound sentence**, add one or more additional independent clauses beginning with a coordinating conjunction and a comma, or with a semicolon followed by a transition word such as *however* or *therefore* and a comma.

**COMPOUND SENTENCES**

The geese flew away at the sound of the plane, and all was quiet.
The geese flew away at the sound of the plane; however, the crows remained.

You can also expand a sentence that has only one independent clause by adding a dependent clause. You will then have a **complex sentence**—one formed of an independent clause and at least one dependent clause. A **dependent clause** contains a subject and a verb, but unlike an independent clause, it cannot stand on its own as a sentence because it begins with a **subordinating conjunction** such as *after, because, if,* or *when*, which automatically makes it depend on the rest of the sentence. NOTE: If the dependent clause comes before an independent clause, as in the example below, it must be followed by a comma.

**COMPLEX SENTENCES**

After the geese flew away, the crows remained.

If you combine a compound sentence and a complex sentence, you will have a **compound-complex sentence**. This kind of sentence must have two or more independent clauses and at least one dependent clause. In the following example, the dependent clause is underlined.

**COMPOUND-COMPLEX SENTENCES**

When the plane flew overhead, the geese flew away; however, the crows remained.

# 3.37 Making Passive Sentences Active

A verb is **active** when the subject of the verb performs the action. It is **passive** when the subject of the verb receives the action.

**ACTIVE**  Caroline delivered a powerful speech.
**PASSIVE**  A powerful speech was delivered by Caroline.

Poor writing uses too many passive verbs. Use active verbs unless you have a good reason for using the passive voice. In the examples that follow, note how the active verbs make the writing more natural and interesting.

**WITH PASSIVE VERBS**

The school was flooded with requests from students for a longer vacation. It was not decided by the school board until later to give them a hearing. The meeting was begun by the student council. The vote was unanimous to extend spring break an extra week. It was considered an unprecedented move favoring all students suffering spring fever.

**WITH ACTIVE VERBS**

Students flooded the school with requests for a longer vacation. The school board did not decide until later to give them a hearing. The student council began the meeting. Everyone voted to extend spring break an extra week. The unpredecented move favored all students suffering spring fever.

Note that the writer could still combine, expand, and add variety to these sentences. Making such sentences active instead of passive, however, is a good start toward livelier writing.

## 3.38 Achieving Parallelism

A sentence has **parallelism** when it uses the same grammatical forms to express ideas of equal, or parallel, importance. When you edit your sentences during revision, check to be sure that your parallelism is not faulty.

**FAULTY**

The teacher told me to think better and having more focus.

**PARALLEL**

The teacher told me to think better and to have more focus.

**FAULTY**

Being too late for the bus and to get something to eat, I decided to walk to the mall.

**PARALLEL**

Being too late for the bus and wanting to get something to eat, I decided to walk to the mall.

**FAULTY**

I really like playing chess, walking my dog, and vacations in Florida.

**PARALLEL**

I really like playing chess, walking my dog, and taking vacations in Florida.

## 3.39 Adding Colorful Language to Sentences

When you write, use words that tell your reader exactly what you mean. Precise and lively language makes your writing more interesting to your reader.

**DULL**

The people made noise.

**COLORFUL**

The mob made an uproar.

Specific verbs also help to create a clear picture in a reader's mind. Use verbs that tell the reader exactly what you mean.

**DULL**

He took the pitcher and drank the cool water.

**COLORFUL**

He grabbed the pitcher and gulped the cool water.

A **modifier** is a word that modifies—that is, changes or explains—the meaning of another word. Adjectives and adverbs are modifiers. Colorful modifiers can turn dull reading into dynamic reading.

**DULL**

The cold wind blew hard.

**COLORFUL**

The frigid wind blew furiously.

# EDITING FOR GRAMMAR AND USAGE ERRORS

## 3.40 Getting Subject and Verb to Agree

A word that describes or stands for *one* person, place, thing, or idea is **singular**. A word that describes or stands for *more than one* person, place, thing, or idea is **plural**.

| SINGULAR NOUNS | prize, child, instrument |
|---|---|
| PLURAL NOUNS | prizes, children, instruments |

In a sentence, a verb must be singular if its subject is singular and plural if its subject is plural. **A verb must agree in number with its subject.**

| SINGULAR AGREEMENT | Charles needs forty more dollars. |
|---|---|
| PLURAL AGREEMENT | They need forty more dollars. |
| SINGULAR AGREEMENT | She exercises every day. |
| PLURAL AGREEMENT | The girls exercise every day. |

The pronouns *I* and *you*, although singular, almost always take the same verb forms as for the plural pronouns *we* and *they*. The only exceptions are the forms *I am* and *I was*.

**EXAMPLES**

I believe the car industry will continue to rebound.
You sense my uneasiness.

**AGREEMENT WITH COMPOUND SUBJECTS.** A **compound subject** is formed of two or more nouns or pronouns that are joined by a conjunction and have the same verb. A compound subject joined by the conjunction *and* usually takes a plural verb.

EXAMPLE <u>Salt</u> and <u>acid rain</u> <u>are</u> hard on a car's body.

A compound subject in which the subjects are joined by the conjunction *and* takes a singular verb if the compound subject really names only one person or thing.

EXAMPLE His <u>work and love</u> <u>is</u> writing.

A compound subject formed of two singular subjects joined by the conjunctions *or* or *nor* takes a singular verb.

EXAMPLES

Neither <u>Streep</u> nor <u>Foster</u> <u>is</u> usually guilty of underpreparing.
Either <u>poetry</u> or <u>drama</u> <u>is</u> appropriate for public performance.

A compound subject formed of a singular subject and a plural subject joined by the conjunctions *or* or *nor* takes a verb that agrees in number with the subject nearer the verb.

EXAMPLES

Either <u>Kim</u> or the backup <u>vocalists</u> <u>are</u> responsible for the recording.
Either the backup <u>vocalists</u> or <u>Kim</u> <u>is</u> responsible for the recording.

**AGREEMENT WITH INDEFINITE PRONOUNS.** These indefinite pronouns are singular and take a singular verb: *anybody, anyone, anything, each, either, everybody, everyone, everything, neither, nobody, no one, nothing, one, somebody, someone,* and *something.*

EXAMPLES

<u>Nobody wants</u> to take the exam on Friday.
<u>Everybody enjoys</u> some kind of music.

These indefinite pronouns are plural and take a plural verb: *both, few, many,* and *several.*

EXAMPLES

<u>Both</u> of these choices <u>are</u> unacceptable.
<u>Several</u> new students <u>are</u> on the honor roll.

The following indefinite pronouns can be singular or plural: *all, any, most, none,* and *some.*

EXAMPLES

<u>All</u> of the cookies <u>were saved</u>. (*All* is plural.)
<u>All</u> of the pie <u>was eaten</u>. (*All* is singular.)

**AGREEMENT IN INVERTED SENTENCES.** When you invert sentences for emphasis, make sure you maintain agreement in number between subject and verb.

EXAMPLES

For those ghastly performances <u>he takes</u> full credit.
The last straw <u>she took</u>.

**AGREEMENT WITH *DOESN'T* AND *DON'T*.** The contraction *doesn't* (from *does not*) is third-person singular and should be used only with a third-person singular subject (*he, she,* or *it,* for example). The contraction *don't* (from *do not*) should be used with all other subjects.

EXAMPLES

<u>She doesn't</u> want material things.
<u>They don't</u> understand the procedure.
<u>I don't</u> find the subject boring.

**OTHER PROBLEMS IN SUBJECT-VERB AGREEMENT.** When a sentence begins with *here, there, when,* or *where,* often the subject follows the verb. In editing your writing, use extra care to check that the subject and verb of such sentences agree in number. Remember that the contractions *here's, there's, when's,* and *where's* contain a singular verb *(is)* and should only be used with a singular subject.

EXAMPLES

<u>Here's</u> the <u>team</u>.
<u>There is</u> one more <u>exam</u> being given.
<u>When's</u> the <u>test</u>?
<u>When are</u> the band <u>members</u> joining us?
<u>Where's</u> the <u>rub</u>?

Also check to be sure a verb in a sentence with a predicate nominative agrees in number with the subject and not with the predicate nominative.

EXAMPLES

<u>Essays</u> <u>are</u> the hardest part of school.
The hardest <u>part</u> of school <u>is</u> essays.

A collective noun takes a singular verb when the noun refers to the group as a unit, and it takes a plural verb when it refers to the members of the group as individuals.

| AS SINGULAR | The <u>team</u> <u>runs</u> laps every day. |
| AS PLURAL | The <u>team</u> <u>joke</u> among themselves behind the coach's back. |

While editing your work, check for nouns that are plural in form but singular in meaning. They should take singular verbs.

EXAMPLES   cryogenics, slacks, measles

The title of a creative work such as a book or song takes a singular verb, as does a group of words used as a unit.

EXAMPLES

The <u>book</u> *Aphorisms* <u>has</u> been on the bestseller list for two weeks.
<u>Sidney and Austen</u> <u>is</u> the smallest firm in Chicago.

An expression stating an amount is singular and takes a singular verb when the amount is considered as one unit. It is plural and takes a plural verb when the amount is considered as something with many parts.

AS SINGULAR

Three <u>eggs</u> <u>is</u> a high-cholesterol breakfast.

AS PLURAL

Three <u>eggs</u> <u>were</u> found splattered across the windshield.

A fraction or a percentage is singular when it refers to a singular word and plural when it refers to a plural word.

AS SINGULAR

One-fourth of the <u>text</u> <u>was</u> footnotes.

AS PLURAL

One-fourth of all the <u>pages</u> <u>were</u> footnotes.

AS SINGULAR

Over 60 percent of the <u>nation</u> <u>is</u> hopeful about the economy.

AS PLURAL

Over 60 percent of all <u>citizens</u> <u>are</u> hopeful about the economy.

Expressions of measurement, such as area, length, volume, and weight, are usually singular.

EXAMPLE

<u>Two quarts</u> <u>is</u> a lot of milk to drink in one sitting.

## 3.41 Using Irregular Verbs

To write about something that happened in the past, use past tense verbs (tense means time in grammar). For regular verbs, add *–ed* or *–d* to the present form of the verb. For more information, see the Language Arts Survey 3.62, "Properties of Verbs: Tense."

EXAMPLES

The bandit <u>guarded</u> the hideout.
*guard (base form) + ed*

Carmen <u>gazed</u> at the distant mountains.
*gaze (base form) + d*

**Irregular verbs** often have different past tense forms and are formed using a different spelling. The following chart lists some of the most common irregular verbs.

| IRREGULAR VERBS | | | |
|---|---|---|---|
| begin | / began | grow | / grew |
| bring | / brought | have | / had |
| burst | / burst | hurt | / hurt |
| choose | / chose | know | / knew |
| come | / came | lay | / laid |
| cut | / cut | make | / made |
| do | / did | ride | / rode |
| draw | / drew | run | / ran |
| drink | / drank | see | / saw |
| eat | / ate | sing | / sang |
| fall | / fell | take | / took |
| feel | / felt | teach | / taught |
| fly | / flew | wear | / wore |
| give | / gave | write | / wrote |
| go | / went | | |

When using irregular verbs in the perfect tense (with *has* or *have*), make sure you do not use the past form instead of the past participle.

NONSTANDARD

I <u>have knew</u> him since I was in middle school.

STANDARD

I <u>have known</u> him since I was in middle school.

Another error to avoid is using the past participle form without a helping verb, or mistaking the past participle for the past.

| NONSTANDARD | I flown this plane dozens of times. |
| STANDARD | I have flown this plane dozens of times. |

| NONSTANDARD | I done all I could do to convince him. |
| STANDARD | I did all I could do to convince him. |

Finally, do not add *–d* or *–ed* to the past form of an irregular verb.

| NONSTANDARD | I ated an apple. |
| STANDARD | I ate an apple. |

## 3.42 Avoiding Split Infinitives

In the English language, the infinitive is often in the form of two words, *to* and the base word.

EXAMPLES      to catch, to succeed, to entertain

Under traditional rules of grammar, the infinitive should not be "split." In other words, adverbs or other sentence components should not come between *to* and the base word.

| NONSTANDARD | Irving begged me to immediately show him the photos. |
| STANDARD | Irving begged me to show him the photos immediately. |

## 3.43 Using *I* and *Me*

Before you use the words *I* and *me* in a sentence, remember that *I* is always the subject of a verb and *me* is always the object of a verb or of a preposition.

EXAMPLES
I went sailing in Florida.
Amber and I went sailing in Florida.

*I* is the subject in both of these sentences.

Lester helped me set up for the party.
Lester helped Brianna and me set up for the party.

In both sentences, *me* is the object of the verb *helped*.

If you are not sure which pronoun to use with a compound subject, drop the other part of the subject and use your pronoun separately with the verb.

EXAMPLE
Sam and (I, me) went sledding at the golf course. (I went sledding at the golf course. OR Me went sledding at the golf course?)

*Correct:* Sam and I went sledding at the golf course.

Please apologize for Carol and (I, me). (Please apologize for me. OR Please apologize for I.)

*Correct:* Please apologize for Carol and me.

## 3.44 Using *Who* and *Whom*

The pronoun *who* has two different forms. *Who* is used as a subject of a sentence. *Whom* is used as the direct object of a verb or of a preposition.

**SUBJECT**
Who knows the answer?
Where is the boy who looks after the sheep?

**DIRECT OBJECT**
Whom did the police arrest?
The plumber whom we called charged a huge fee.

**OBJECT OF PREPOSITION**
By whom is this painting?
From whom is that gift?

## 3.45 Getting Pronouns and Antecedents to Agree

Make sure pronouns in your writing agree with their antecedents (the words they refer back to) in number and gender.

**Number** refers to singular and plural. If the antecedent is singular, the pronoun must also be singular; if the antecedent is plural, the pronoun must also be plural.

**INCORRECT NUMBER**
Each student must sit in their assigned seat.

**CORRECT NUMBER**
Each student must sit in his or her assigned seat.

**INCORRECT GENDER**
Humankind has his own flaws.

**CORRECT GENDER**
Humankind has its own flaws.

**Gender** is the form a word takes to show whether it is masculine, feminine, or neutral (neither masculine nor feminine). The pronoun must match its antecedent in terms of gender.

## 3.46 Avoiding Dangling and Misplaced Modifiers

A **dangling modifier** seems to modify a word it is not intended to modify. If this error occurs when the modifier is too far away from the word it is supposed to modify, it is called a **misplaced modifier**. Edit a dangling or misplaced modifier by rewording the sentence or moving the modifier closer to the phrase it modifies.

**DANGLING**
Valerie drove to the airport while <u>taking a nap</u>.

**WORDS ADDED**
Valerie drove to the airport while <u>I was taking a nap</u>.

**MISPLACED**
Alex walked his dog <u>wearing shorts</u>.

**REWORDED**
Alex, <u>wearing shorts</u>, walked his dog.

## 3.47 Recognizing Other Problems with Modifiers

*Them* is a personal pronoun. *Those* is a demonstrative pronoun, which means it points out a particular person, place, or thing.

**NONSTANDARD**    Them cars have four-wheel drive.
**STANDARD**    Those cars have four-wheel drive.

The words *bad* and *badly* often confuse writers. Use *bad* as an adjective, and *badly* as an adverb. The adjective *bad* should follow a linking verb such as *feel, see, smell, sound,* or *taste.*

**NONSTANDARD**
Reports of the forest fire sounded badly.

**STANDARD**
Reports of the forest fire sounded bad.

**NONSTANDARD**
Ricky behaved bad for the babysitter.

**STANDARD**
Ricky behaved badly for the babysitter.

The words *good* and *well* also tend to confuse writers. *Good* is an adjective used to modify a person, place, thing, or idea, not an action verb. *Well* is an adverb meaning "successfully" or "skillfully" and an adjective meaning "healthy" or "of a satisfactory condition."

**NONSTANDARD**
Allen swims good.

**STANDARD**
Allen swims well.
Allen is a good swimmer.
Allen is well now that he is over his cold.

Each modifier has a **positive, comparative,** and **superlative** form of comparison. Most one-syllable modifiers and some two-syllable modifiers form comparative and superlative degrees by adding *–er* and *–est.* Other two-syllable modifiers, and all modifiers of more than two syllables, use *more* and *most* to form these degrees.

|  | POSITIVE | COMPARATIVE | SUPERLATIVE |
|---|---|---|---|
| ADJECTIVES | hungry | hungrier | hungriest |
|  | daring | more daring | most daring |
| ADVERBS | late | later | latest |
|  | fully | more fully | most fully |

To show a decrease in the quality of any modifier, form the comparative and superlative degrees by using *less* and *least.*

EXAMPLES    dense, less dense, least dense
skeptically, less skeptically, least skeptically

Some modifiers form comparative and superlative degrees irregularly. Check the dictionary if you are unsure about the comparison of a modifier.

EXAMPLES    good, better, best
well, better, best
bad, worse, worst

Use the comparative degree when comparing two things. Use the superlative degree when comparing more than two things.

**COMPARATIVE**
Santha was the **more easily** intimidated of the two sisters.

**SUPERLATIVE**
The skin is the **largest** organ of the human body.

## 3.48 Correcting Common Usage Problems

Watch for these words and learn their correct usage as you edit your own writing.

**accept, except.** To *accept* is to "welcome something" or to "receive something willingly." To *except* is to "exclude or leave something out." *Except* is also used as a preposition meaning "but."

The Tigers accept our challenge to a rematch.
She excepted Roland from the guest list.
I will eat any vegetable except collard greens.

**advice, advise.** *Advice* is a noun meaning "guidance or recommendation regarding a decision." To *advise* is to "recommend or inform."

I took your advice about the movie.
I would advise you to avoid that movie.

**affect, effect.** *Affect* is a verb meaning "have an effect on." *Effect* is a noun meaning "the result of an action."

The short story <u>affected</u> me strangely.
The short story had a strange <u>effect</u> on me.

**altogether, all together.** *Altogether* is an adverb meaning "thoroughly." Something *done all together* is done as a group or mass.

She was altogether frustrated waiting all day.
We were all together awaiting news of the surgery.

**among, between.** Use the word *between* when talking about two people or things at a time. Use the word *among* when talking about a group of three or more.

Oscar and Lucas had five dollars between them.
There was disagreement among the team members.

**can, may.** Use the word *can* to mean "able to do something." Use the word *may* to ask or give permission.

Can you swim across Gull Pond?
May I go swimming? Yes, you may go.

**fewer, less.** *Fewer* refers to the number of units of something. *Less* refers to bulk quantity.

I have fewer than eight items.
I have less energy when it is very humid.

**in, into.** The preposition *in* indicates location. The preposition *into* indicates direction from the outside to the inside.

The meeting is being held in the gym.
The students are going into the gym now.

**its, it's** The word *its* is a possessive pronoun. The word *it's* is a contraction of *it is*.

The turtle dug its nest.
The sun will be up by the time it's over.

**lay, lie.** *Lay* means to "put" or to "place" and always takes a direct object. *Lie* means to "rest" or to "be in a lying position." *Lie* never takes a direct object. (Note that the past tense of *lie* is *lay*.)

Lay the map on the table.
Gretchen laid the map on the table.
Lie down and keep quiet.
Oliver lay down and kept quiet.

**like, as.** *Like* is a preposition meaning "similar to." *Like* usually introduces a phrase. *As* should be used as a conjunction. *As* usually introduces a clause that has a subject and a verb.

NONSTANDARD
The sun came out earlier, just like I had hoped.
STANDARD
The sun came out earlier, just as I had hoped.
NONSTANDARD
Rodney has been acting as a spoiled brat.
STANDARD
Rodney has been acting like a spoiled brat.

**their, they're, there.** These three *homonyms* (words that sound alike but that have different spellings and meanings) sometimes confuse writers. The word *their* is a possessive pronoun. The word *they're* is the contracted form of *they are*. The word *there* refers to a place.

Marsupials carry their young in a pouch.
They're complaining about the noise.
The lamp should go over there.

**to, too, two.** *To* is a preposition that can mean "in the direction of." *Too* is an adverb that means both "extremely, overly" and "also." *Two* is the spelling for the number 2.

Take the basket to Granny's house.
Ivan has too many fish in his tank.
Sharon is invited, too.
I have two wishes left.

**your, you're.** *Your* is a possessive pronoun. *You're* is the contracted form of *you are*.

Your mittens are in the dryer.
You're the winner!

# PARTS OF SPEECH SUMMARY

As you have seen, the meanings of words depend on their positions in a sentence. As their positions change, both meaning and function change. You have looked at function to determine parts of the sentence.

You can now go one step further. By looking at the relationship of a word to the rest of the words in a sentence, you can determine the parts of speech for individual words. Once again, you will be examining what a word does; then you will label its part of speech.

Remember two important facts: (1) words have four primary functions—they **name**, **express**, **modify**, and **link**. They can also **interrupt**. (2) Groups of words can function as one individual part of speech.

## 3.49 Namers—Nouns and Pronouns

**Namers** are **nouns** and **pronouns**, parts of speech that name people, places, ideas, and things or refer to them; you can tell what they are by what they do. Nouns and pronouns are subjects and objects: direct objects, indirect objects, objects of prepositions, and objects of infinitives. Namers:

| | |
|---|---|
| NAME PEOPLE | Dylan, principal, father, choreographer |
| NAME PLACES | home, Central Park, Joe's Tacos |
| NAME IDEAS | love, multiplication, tonality, smell |
| NAME THINGS | basketball, dance, orbit, trading card |

## 3.50 Specific Kinds of Nouns

There are many kinds of nouns. They include common and proper nouns, concrete and abstract nouns, and collective nouns.

**3.51 COMMON NOUNS AND PROPER NOUNS.** **Common nouns** are the names given to general objects. **Proper nouns** are names of specific people or things. They are always capitalized.

| COMMON NOUNS |
|---|
| girl, monument, government agency |

| PROPER NOUNS |
|---|
| Michelle, Washington Monument, United States Supreme Court |

Some proper nouns may have more than one word. These multiword names such as *Michelle Adams, Central High School,* and the *United States Department of the Interior* are still considered to be one noun because they name only one person or thing.

**3.52 CONCRETE NOUNS AND ABSTRACT NOUNS.** A **concrete noun** names anything you can physically taste, touch, smell, see, or hear. An **abstract noun** names something that cannot be physically sensed.

| CONCRETE NOUNS | automobile, textbook, lunchbox |
|---|---|
| ABSTRACT NOUNS | sadness, suffering, mood |

**3.53 COLLECTIVE NOUNS. Collective nouns** name groups—family, committee, class. Collectives are interesting nouns because, in their singular forms, they can be either singular or plural, depending upon how the group acts. When the group acts together as one unit to do something, the group is considered singular.

EXAMPLE    The <u>committee</u> <u>votes</u> on its agenda.

Because the committee acted as one unit (by everyone doing the same one thing at the same time), the noun is singular and takes a singular verb form. The possessive pronoun *its* also reflects that the noun is collective.

When the group acts as individuals instead of as one unit, the group is considered plural.

EXAMPLE    The <u>committee</u> <u>were</u> giving their reports.

Because individual members gave their reports at different times and functioned as individuals, the group is considered plural. Note how the verb *were giving* and the possessive pronoun *their* reflect this.

## 3.54 Types of Pronouns

**Pronouns** replace names (nouns) with reference words. Because we use these references in so many situations, there are four different kinds of pronouns and three hybrids. The four kinds of pronouns are **personal pronouns, indefinite pronouns, interrogative pronouns,** and **reflexive pronouns**.

The three kinds of hybrids are **possessive pronouns, relative pronouns,** and **intensifying pronouns. Possessive pronouns** are hybrids because they take pronoun forms but act as modifiers; **relative pronouns** are hybrids because they are pronoun forms that act as linkers; and **intensifying pronouns** use the same forms as reflexive pronouns, but they act as interrupters.

The three hybrids are discussed in the hybrids section (see Language Arts Survey 3.78, "Hybrids").

**3.55 PERSONAL PRONOUNS.** A **personal pronoun** is a substitute for the name of a person or thing. The personal pronouns are *I, me, we, us, he, she, it, him, her, you, they,* and *them.* Personal pronouns refer to three groups of speakers: first, second, and third person.

| | |
|---|---|
| **FIRST PERSON:** | the speaker or speakers talks about themselves: *I, me, we, us* |
| **SECOND PERSON:** | the speaker talks about the person talked to: *you* |
| **THIRD PERSON:** | the speaker talks about someone or something else: *he, she, it, they* |

All personal pronouns require clear **antecedents**, or nouns that come before the pronoun. That means that the person or thing that the pronoun refers to must be obvious. In the following example, *Mary* is the antecedent of *her.*

EXAMPLE  Have you seen <u>Mary</u>? Yes, I saw <u>her</u> yesterday.

**3.56 INDEFINITE PRONOUNS. Indefinite pronouns** are pronouns used when we may not be sure who we are talking about. They include *somebody, anybody, few,* and *many.* They also include numbers. Frequently they are used when the reference word is in a prepositional phrase. Below are some indefinite pronouns.

## INDEFINITE PRONOUNS

| | | |
|---|---|---|
| all | few | nothing |
| another | many | one |
| any | neither | other |
| anyone | no one | some |
| both | nobody | someone |
| each | none | something |
| either | | |

EXAMPLES

A <u>few</u> in our English class are reviewing a new textbook.
We asked for <u>some</u> of the details about the news story.
<u>Nobody</u> knows where the homecoming decorations were stored.
<u>Three</u> of the swimmers qualified for the state meet.

**3.57 INTERROGATIVE PRONOUNS. Interrogative pronouns** are the question-askers of the pronoun family. *Who, whom, whose, which,* and *what* are the interrogative pronouns.

EXAMPLES

<u>Which</u> of these buses do I take to reach my school?
<u>Whom</u> do I ask for directions?
<u>What</u> do I do now?

Be careful when identifying interrogative pronouns. The same words are used as relative pronouns (discussed in 3.79), but relative pronouns do not ask a question.

**3.58 REFLEXIVE PRONOUNS. Reflexive pronouns** refer back to a noun previously used and can be recognized because –*self* and –*selves* have been added to other pronoun forms. Some reflexive pronouns include *myself, herself, yourself, themselves,* and *ourselves.*

EXAMPLES

I talk to <u>myself</u>.
Mike and James helped <u>themselves</u> to more food.

**Reflexive pronouns** are often parts of the sentence or objects of prepositions. (Note that **intensifying pronouns**, discussed in 3.78, "Hybrids," use the same forms, but they are interrupters and are neither a part of a sentence nor an object of a preposition.)

## 3.59 Expressers—Verbs

**Verbs** are the **expressers** of the English language, and they carry more information than any other single part of speech because they have three major properties: *tense, mood,* and *voice.* They reveal the time something happened or will happen, whether the action is finished or continuing, whether the subject is the actor or receiver of the action, and the manner in which the action occurred. English verbs can be from one to four words long.

EXAMPLES      runs
has run
has been running
may have been running

**NOTE:** The same verb may fit into several of the classes that follow, depending on its uses in different sentences.

**3.60 ACTION VERBS AND STATE OF BEING VERBS.** The verb of any sentence is either an **action verb** or a **state of being verb**, depending on the message the verb expresses in the sentence. **Action verbs** refer to actions and to things you can do.

EXAMPLES    have, get, drive, run, sleep

**State of being verbs** indicate that something exists. These are all the forms of the verb *to be* that are listed in 3.9, "Grammar Reference Chart— The Verb *To Be*."

**3.61 TRANSITIVE AND INTRANSITIVE VERBS. Transitive verbs** are action verbs that have completers. If a verb has a direct object, it is a transitive verb.

EXAMPLE    Jamie writes short stories.

(*Short stories* is a direct object, so the verb *writes* is transitive.)

**Intransitive verbs** are action verbs that do not take objects.

EXAMPLE    The sun shines every day in Mexico.

The action *shines* is complete in itself; no extra material is necessary. This makes *shines* an intransitive verb.

## 3.62 Properties of Verbs: Tense

Verbs carry a concept of time, called **tense**. The **simple tenses** express simple past, present, and future. The **perfect tenses** give information about actions that take place over time. Each of the simple and perfect tenses has a **progressive form** that shows continuing action. The progressive form is made by using a tense of the helping verb *be* with the present participle.

SIMPLE TENSES. **Present tense** shows that something is happening now. **Past tense** verbs talk about something that happened before now, and **future tense** verbs talk about something that will happen in the future.

PRESENT TENSE
  Today I eat/do eat chocolate ice cream.
  Today I am eating chocolate ice cream. (progressive)

Notice that the past tense in English also uses the same three forms as present tense.

PAST TENSE
  Yesterday I ate/did eat strawberry ice cream.

PAST PROGRESSIVE
  Yesterday I was eating strawberry ice cream.

There are only two future tense forms.

FUTURE TENSE
  Tomorrow I will eat vanilla ice cream.

FUTURE PROGRESSIVE
  Tomorrow I will be eating vanilla ice cream.

PERFECT TENSES. The **perfect tenses** express past, present and future, but they add information about actions that continued over a period of time and were completed in the past or will be completed in the present or future. All perfect tenses use some form of the helping verb *to have.*

PRESENT PERFECT TENSE
  Mike has worn that sweater twice this week.
  We have been studying all day. [Progressive]

PAST PERFECT TENSE
  Maria had seen the movie before.
  Tyler had been planning to see it. [Progressive]

FUTURE PERFECT TENSE
  By the end of the year, I will have earned a prize.
  By the end of the year, I will have been earning my own money for five years.

## 3.63 Properties of Verbs: Voice

The **voice** of a verb refers to the relationship between the subject and the action. A verb is in the **active voice** if the subject did the acting. It is in the **passive voice** if someone or something else did the acting and the subject is the receiver of the action.

ACTIVE    Mary gave her sister Rhonda a new skirt.
PASSIVE    Rhonda was given a new skirt for her birthday.

For more information, see the Language Arts Survey 3.37, "Making Passive Sentences Active."

## 3.64 Properties of Verbs: Mood

The **mood** of a verb is the manner in which the verb relates the action. English uses three moods: the **indicative**, the **imperative**, and the **subjunctive**. Most declarative and interrogative sentences fall into the **indicative mood**.

LANGUAGE, GRAMMAR, AND STYLE RESOURCE

**INDICATIVE**
Gordon and Caley are my two brothers.
Don't you have two brothers, also?

Imperative sentences are in the **imperative mood**. These make requests or give commands.

**IMPERATIVE**
Please, hand me the salt.
Run before the flood gets you!

The **subjunctive mood** has few uses in English, and is used much less frequently than it is used in other languages. It is used to express a wish or a possible condition.

**SUBJUNCTIVE**
If I were you, I would dress more warmly.
If they were here, they would win the prize.

Notice the verb form in the first sentence. The only verb that has a unique form in the subjunctive is the verb *to be*. *Were* is used with all pronouns, not just the singular.

## 3.65 Modifiers—Adjectives and Adverbs

**Adjectives** and **adverbs**, two kinds of **modifiers**, add meaning to nouns, adjectives, verbs, and adverbs. To determine whether the word is an adjective or adverb, follow this procedure:

1. Look at the word that is modified.
2. Ask yourself, "Is this modified word a noun or a pronoun?"

If the answer is yes, the modifier is an adjective. **Adjectives** modify only nouns and pronouns. If the answer is no, the modifier is an **adverb**. **Adverbs** modify verbs, adjectives, and other adverbs.

**3.66 ADJECTIVES. Adjectives** modify namers by making nouns more specific.

| GENERAL REFERENCE | puppy |
|---|---|
| A LITTLE MORE SPECIFIC | the puppy |
| MORE SPECIFIC YET | the little puppy |
| EVEN MORE SPECIFIC | the little, black-spotted puppy |
| WITH A PREPOSITIONAL PHRASE | the little, black-spotted puppy with the shaggy coat |

As each step adds more modifiers (more information), it becomes more possible for the listener or reader to visualize the actual dog.

**3.67 ADVERBS. Adverbs** are the generalists of the modifier family. They modify anything that is not a namer (noun or pronoun)—verbs, adjectives, and other adverbs. Many times they will specify *where* or *when;* nouns and pronouns specify *who* or *what.*

**ADVERBS MODIFY VERBS**
Katie came home quickly.

*Quickly* tells how Katie came home.

**ADVERBS MODIFY ADJECTIVES**
She wore a really new dress.

*New* modifies *dress; really* modifies the modifier, *new*. Since *new* is an **adjective**, not a **noun** or **pronoun**, *really* has to be an **adverb**.

**ADVERBS MODIFY OTHER ADVERBS**
Katie scurried home really fast.

*Fast* modifies the verb *scurried; really* modifies *fast*. In this sentence, one adverb modifies another.

## 3.68 Linkers/Joiners

**Conjunctions** and **prepositions** are the joiners of the English language. These words join everything from individual words to complete thoughts to create compound sentences. Because there are many kinds of links that need to be made, there are many kinds of linkers: prepositions, coordinating conjunctions, correlative conjunctions, and subordinating conjunctions.

**3.69 PREPOSITIONS.** Prepositions are easy to identify because they have objects. If the word does not have an object, then it is another part of speech. See the Language Arts Survey 3.11 for a list of prepositions. If you find one of these words in a sentence, find its object. If it has an object, then the preposition and its object(s)—it may have more than one—form a prepositional phrase.

EXAMPLE   I went to the store for a loaf of sandwich bread.

In this sentence, three words are on the preposition list: *to, for,* and *of*. Does *to* have an object? Ask, *"to* what?" The answer is *the store. To* has an object, so it is a preposition. *To the store* is a prepositional phrase. After we apply the same test to *for* and *of,* we find that they are both prepositions and that the sample sentence has three prepositional phrases. These are *to the store, for a loaf,* and *of sandwich bread.*

**3.70 COORDINATING CONJUNCTIONS. Coordinating conjunctions** join words and groups of words of equal importance. The most common coordinating conjunctions are *and, or, nor, for, but* and *so*. The word is not important; what is important is that both words or word groups are equally important.

EXAMPLE

> Her morning schedule included math and history and music and home room.

Note that joining a series of words using coordinating conjunctions between them is perfectly acceptable grammar. Most writers use commas, however, and save multiple conjunctions for sentences with special emphasis. (Note: All but the last *and* could be replaced by commas.)

When coordinating conjunctions plus commas join two or more complete thoughts that could be separate sentences, the resulting structure is called a **compound sentence**.

COMPOUND SENTENCE

> I wanted to go to a movie, but nothing sounded very good.

Here a comma plus *but* join two short, complete, independent thoughts. Each of the two parts could be a sentence of its own. Since their ideas are closely related, we choose to join them using proper punctuation.

**3.71 CORRELATIVE CONJUNCTIONS. Correlative conjunctions** travel in pairs. Some of these pairs are *both...and, neither...nor, either...or, not only...but also*.

EXAMPLES

> <u>Both</u> art <u>and</u> graphic design are electives in our school.
> <u>Neither</u> Latin <u>nor</u> Greek languages are studied by most high school students.
> She wanted to study <u>either</u> architecture <u>or</u> industrial design.
> <u>Not only</u> did he speak German, <u>but</u> he was <u>also</u> fluent in French and Spanish.

**3.72 SUBORDINATING CONJUNCTIONS. Subordinating conjunctions** join two phrases or clauses that are not of equal importance. Subordinating conjunctions are used to establish that one idea in a sentence is more important than the other. Subordinating conjunctions include *after, before, if, than, since, unless, when,* and *while*; there are many more. All of the following examples contain subordinating conjunctions.

SUBORDINATING CONJUNCTIONS

> We will go on a picnic on Saturday <u>unless</u> it rains.
> <u>Whenever</u> the pollen count is high, I start to sneeze and get itchy eyes.
> I want to visit my grandmother in Detroit <u>if</u> I can save enough money.
> <u>When</u> the deadline arrives, students need to get their projects handed in.

Even though both clauses have subjects and verbs, the parts of the sentence of the most important clause (called the **main clause**) will be the subject and verb of the sentence. The parts of the sentence found in the less important clause (called the **subordinate clause**) are ignored. These are NOT the subject and verb of the sentence; they are only the subject and verb of a **dependent clause**.

## 3.73 Interrupters

Sometimes you will want to interrupt the flow of your sentences and thoughts by adding a word or phrase for emphasis. Most **interrupters** are set off from the rest of the sentences by commas because they are not basic building blocks of meaning. **Interrupters** include **interjections, parenthetical expressions, nouns of direct address,** and **appositives.** Another interrupter, **intensifying pronouns,** is discussed in the Language Arts Survey 3.78, "Hybrids."

Interrupters (with the exception of one-word appositives) are set off from other parts of the sentence using commas. It is important to note that no interrupter is ever any one of the basic parts of the sentence.

**3.74 INTERJECTIONS. Interjections** are parts of speech that express strong feeling or enhance meaning.

EXAMPLES

> <u>Yes</u>, I finished my homework.
> <u>Good grief</u>, you did what again?
> <u>Wow</u>, Sam got a new car for his birthday.

Note that omitting the interjection does not affect the meaning of the sentence. Each interjection is set off from the rest of the sentence by commas.

**3.75 PARENTHETICAL EXPRESSIONS. Parenthetical expressions** are those comments (set off by commas) that explain, comment, or qualify the ideas contained in the sentence. Common parenthetical expressions include *by the way, however, on the other hand, incidentally.*

EXAMPLES

I went right home after school; <u>however</u>, my sister went shopping for school supplies.
Mary misplaced her coat. <u>By the way</u>, have you seen a red raincoat in your closet?

**3.76 NOUNS OF DIRECT ADDRESS.** A **noun of direct address** says the name of the person or group spoken to. A noun of direct address is *never* the subject of the sentence. This becomes especially tricky when the subject is understood.

EXAMPLE    <u>Class</u>, listen to the instructions.

*Class* is a noun of direct address; the understood subject is *you.*

**3.77 APPOSITIVES. Appositives** rename a noun. Like all interrupters, appositives are enclosed or set off from the rest of the sentence by commas. There is one exception: word names do not require commas.

EXAMPLES

My friend <u>Yang</u> did a beautiful project on birds. (No punctuation is required.)

Mrs. Cokely, <u>my favorite teacher</u>, will retire this year. (Commas are needed.)

## 3.78 Hybrids

**Hybrids** are words usually thought of as one part of speech that occasionally function as another. Each word form should be labeled according to what it does in the sentence. Some common hybrids include **possessive nouns and pronouns, relative pronouns, intensifying pronouns,** and a group of verb forms called **verbals.**

**3.79 POSSESSIVE NOUNS AND PRONOUNS. Possessive nouns** and **possessive pronouns** are namer forms that work as modifiers. To form a possessive noun, an apostrophe plus an *s* is added to a singular; an apostrophe is added to a plural. Notice how the possessive noun uses a noun form, but with the suffix it becomes a modifier.

EXAMPLE    Linda proofread <u>Marty's</u> assignment.

*Marty's* modifies *assignment.* This construction is a hybrid: it looks like a noun, but it functions as an adjective. When listing parts of the sentence, label a possessive noun as an adjective.

**Possessive pronouns** act much the same way. Many possessive forms are the same as other pronouns, but a few pronoun forms are uniquely possessive. Some of the unique forms include *mine, your, yours, hers, its, our, their,* and *theirs.* Two other possessive forms, *her* and *him,* are not always possessive.

EXAMPLE    I ate <u>my</u> pizza.

*My* modifies *pizza. My* looks like a pronoun, but here it works as a modifier by telling who the pizza belongs to. Because we label parts of speech according to what they are doing in the sentence, this word should be considered a modifier—in this case, an adjective.

**Relative pronouns** are pronoun forms that function like **subordinating conjunctions.** The commonly used relative pronouns are *who, whom, whose, which,* and *that.* These words connect a subordinate clause to the main clause of the sentence. But they also will function as a subject, object, or predicate pronoun—these are exactly the same functions as naming parts of speech.

EXAMPLE

I want to meet the person <u>who painted that picture</u>.

*Who* is the **relative pronoun** that connects the subordinate clause (underlined) with the main clause. Also notice that *who* is the subject of the clause; the verb is *painted.*

EXAMPLE

I want to meet the cousin <u>whom you described</u>.

*Whom,* the **relative pronoun,** is the connection between the two clauses; it also is the direct object of the verb *described.*

Kate was the one <u>with whom I designed my art sculpture</u>.

In this sentence, *whom* is the object of the preposition *with;* it also connects the two clauses.

**3.80 VERBALS: PARTICIPLES, GERUNDS, AND INFINITIVES.**
**Verbals** are verb forms that act as namers or modifiers. There are three different forms of verbals. These include participles (that act as modifiers), gerunds (that act like nouns), and infinitives which can act like nouns, adjectives and adverbs.

To determine if a verb is used as a verbal, you must be aware of what the word is actually doing in the sentence. Like other verbs, verbals can take objects, modifiers, or both. When a verbal has modifiers and/or objects, the group of words is called a participial phrase, a gerund phrase, or an infinitive phrase. Like all phrases, verbal phrases function as one part of speech.

**Participles** are action adjectives. They have two forms: the present participle and the past participle. Both are used the same way.

The present participle uses the *–ing* form.

EXAMPLES   Jana jumped off the <u>diving</u> board.
My uncle has a <u>hearing</u> aid.
I love to listen to that <u>marching</u> band.

The past participle uses the *–ed* form.

EXAMPLES   A <u>raided</u> cookie jar is not a pretty sight.
The <u>forgotten</u> language will never be recovered.
A <u>watched</u> pot never boils.

Note that you can find the object of a **participle** by using the same questioning strategy you use to find the verb of a sentence. The participle and its object form a construction called a **participial phrase**. It acts as one part of speech, an adjective.

EXAMPLE   The student <u>taking notes</u> got an *A* last semester.

*Taking* is a participle. If you ask, "*taking* what?", the answer is *notes*. The object of *taking*, the **participle**, is *notes*. Since *taking notes* modifies *student*, the entire construction (called a participial phrase) is working as an adjective.

**Gerunds** are verb forms used as namers. When you use any action as a name (running, jumping, writing, singing, playing), you use a gerund.

EXAMPLES

<u>Running</u> was her favorite activity.
(The gerund is the subject of the sentence.)

He liked high <u>jumping</u>.
(The gerund is the direct object.)

She wanted a tutor for <u>writing</u>.
(The gerund is the object of a preposition.)

Like participles, gerunds can take objects. You can find the object of a gerund just as you find the object of a verb.

EXAMPLE   <u>Buying</u> a prom dress took all of Katy's money.

*Buying* is a **gerund**. If you ask, "Buying what?", the answer is *a prom dress*. After you eliminate the modifiers, you will see that the object of the gerund *buying* is *dress*.

Gerunds can also take modifiers; since the gerund acts as a noun, the modifiers are adjectives.

EXAMPLE   Dan began <u>ice skating</u>.

In this case, *ice* modifies *skating*.

EXAMPLE   Senna began <u>complaining</u> to her mother.

Note that the prepositional phrase *to her mother* modifies *complaining*. This makes the modifier a prepositional phrase.

In both of the sentences above, the entire **gerund phrase** (the gerund + objects and/or modifiers) acts as one noun. In both these sentences, the phrases are direct objects.

**Infinitives** are verbals that use the form *to* + the verb. Each of the examples below illustrates a different use of infinitives. Infinitives can be used as nouns or as modifiers (adjectives and adverbs).

EXAMPLES

Her desire <u>to win</u> dominated her entire life.
(Adjective)

The entire family gathered <u>to celebrate</u> my grandmother's birthday. (Adverb)

<u>To attend</u> college is my ultimate goal. (Noun)

Like other verbals, infinitives take modifiers and objects. In the second and third sample sentences, the infinitives have objects. *To celebrate* has an object, *my grandmother's birthday;* the object of *to attend* is *college.* The fourth, *to drive,* has an object, *my car,* and a modifier, *to school.*

Infinitives can get tricky because speakers and writers may leave out *to* when it follows some commonly used verbs. Sometimes the *to* is omitted in infinitives that follow *dare, do, feel, hear, help, let, make, need, see, watch.* These constructions, called **bare infinitives**, are usually direct objects that name an action. The *to* is understood.

EXAMPLES
I heard her (to) play the piano.
Help me (to) carry this table.

Be careful. The *to* is not always left out after these verbs, and no dependable rule seems to exist. Native speakers with good ears will have a sense of this, but others may find this difficult. Fortunately, it is never wrong to include the *to* with an infinitive, although it may sound a little awkward.

## 3.81 Groups of Words That Function as One Part of Speech

All through these grammar materials we have seen that groups of words sometimes function as one part of speech. These groups fall into two categories: **phrases** and **clauses**. Clauses have both subjects and verbs; **phrases** do not.

EXAMPLES
I need to get another spiral notebook. (Phrase)

She will be elected to the Student Council. (Phrase)

I will watch television when I finish my homework. (Clause)

Do you know who will be our next class president? (Clause)

Most clauses and phrases are named after the functions that they perform.

**3.82 PHRASES. Phrases** are groups of words that do not contain a subject and verb and that function as one part of speech. The following kinds of phrases are used in the English language:

**Adjective phrases** are prepositional phrases that modify nouns or pronouns.

EXAMPLE     Slim wanted a job with good hours.

**Adverb phrases** are prepositional phrases that modify anything except nouns and pronouns.

EXAMPLE     I spoke to the two-headed alien.

**Participial phrases** are verbal phrases that function as adjectives.

EXAMPLE     Their Victorian house, recently remodeled and repainted, is the jewel of the neighborhood.

**Gerund phrases** are verbal phrases that function as nouns.

EXAMPLE     Getting good grades is important to many students.

**Infinitive phrases** are verbal phrases that function as nouns, adjectives, or adverbs.

EXAMPLES     To see is to believe. (Noun)
The ride to go on is the Ferris wheel. (Adjective)
We are ready to go home. (Adverb)

**3.83 CLAUSES WITHIN A SENTENCE.** The **clauses** within a sentence are groups of words that (1) contain a subject and verb and that (2) function as one part of speech. The following kinds of clauses are used in English sentences:

**Adjective clauses** are subordinate clauses that function as adverbs; they modify nouns and pronouns.

EXAMPLE
I admired the girl who won the speech contest.

**Adverb clauses** are subordinate clauses that function as adverbs, modifiying anything except nouns and pronouns.

EXAMPLE
My mother got upset when she learned where I was going.

**Noun clauses** function as subjects and objects.

EXAMPLE
Whoever gets straight *A*'s in math gets a four-year scholarship from the school's foundation.

**3.84 The Clauses of a Sentence: Simple, Compound, and Complex Sentences.** The **independent clauses**, or **main clauses**, of a sentence are the parts that contain both a subject and verb. Without coordinating and/or subordinating words, they could stand alone. A sentence with only one independent clause is called a **simple sentence**.

> SIMPLE SENTENCE
> Mabel made a broccoli pizza.

A sentence with two or more independent clauses is called a **compound sentence**. The independent clauses are usually connected with a comma and **coordinating conjunction** such as *and, but, for, nor, or,* or *yet.*

> COMPOUND SENTENCE
> Mabel made a broccoli pizza, <u>but</u> I didn't eat it!

A sentence with one independent clause and one or more **dependent**, or **subordinate**, **clauses** is called a **complex sentence**. The dependent clauses are usually connected to the independent clause with a **subordinating conjunction** such as *after, because, if,* or *when,* or a **relative pronoun** such as *this* or *that.* The dependent clause may begin or end a complex sentence, but when it begins the sentence, a comma must follow it.

> COMPLEX SENTENCE
> I ate a big dinner after I returned home.
> After I returned home, I ate a big dinner.

If a sentence contains both kinds of clauses, it is called a **compound-complex sentence**.

> COMPOUND-COMPLEX SENTENCE
> When it started to rain, I put on my raincoat, but I still got wet.

For more information, see the Language Arts Survey 3.36, "Combining and Expanding Sentences."

## STYLE

## 3.85 Editing for Punctuation Errors

To avoid punctuation errors, you should know how to use end marks, commas, semicolons, colons, apostrophes, underlining, italics, quotation marks, dashes, and hyphens.

**3.86 End Marks. End marks** tell the reader where a sentence ends. An end mark also shows the purpose of the sentence. The three end marks are the period, the question mark, and the exclamation point.

A **declarative sentence** ends with a period.

> DECLARATIVE
> For many years the Empire State Building was the tallest skyscraper in the world.

An **interrogative sentence** ends with a question mark.

> QUESTION
> When did World War I begin?
> How do you spell your name?

An **exclamatory sentence** ends with an exclamation point.

> EXCLAMATION
> The view from the top is breathtaking!
> Help! Marvin is choking!

**3.87 Commas. A comma** separates words or groups of words within a sentence. Commas tell the reader to pause at certain spots in the sentence. These pauses help keep the reader from running together certain words and phrases when these phrases should be kept apart for clarity. Following is a list of the most common ways commas should be used.

| RULES | EXAMPLES |
| --- | --- |
| Use commas to separate **items in a series**. Three or more words make a series. | The primary particles in an atom are protons, neutrons, and electrons. Choices include carrots, green beans, and asparagus. |

**CONTINUED**

| RULES | EXAMPLES |
|---|---|
| Use commas when you **combine sentences using *and, but, or, nor, yet, so,* or *for*.** Place the comma before these words. | Casey was confident that he could hit a home run. He struck out.<br>Casey was confident that he could hit a home run, but he struck out.<br>Joanna will sing in the talent show. Margaret will accompany her.<br>Joanna will sing in the talent show, and Margaret will accompany her. |
| Use a comma to **set off words or phrases that interrupt sentences.** Use two commas if the word or phrase falls in the middle of the sentence. Use one comma if the word or phrase comes at the beginning or at the end of a sentence. | Emily's twin brothers, Eric and Derrick, look exactly alike.<br>Hercules, a hero of classical mythology, was said to be the strongest man on earth.<br>After the first quarter, the Knicks dominated the game.<br>How did you solve that problem, Jared? |
| Use commas to **separate the parts of a date.** Do not use a comma between the month and the day. | The Germans surrendered on May 8, 1945.<br>My appointment is on Wednesday, January 7. |
| Use commas to **separate items in addresses.** Do not put a comma between the state and the ZIP code. | Francisco was born in Caracas, Venezuela.<br>They live at 210 Newfield Road, DeWitt, New York 13214. |

**3.88 SEMICOLONS.** You have seen how two related sentences can be combined into one using a conjunction such as *and, but, so,* and *or.* Another way to join two related sentences into one is to use a semicolon. The **semicolon** can be used in place of the comma and the conjunction.

EXAMPLES

A fin was spotted moving through the water, so the bathers scrambled onto the beach.
A fin was spotted moving through the water; the bathers scrambled onto the beach.

Danielle is an exchange student from Paris, and everyone is enjoying getting to know her.
Danielle is an exchange student from Paris; everyone is enjoying getting to know her.

**3.89 COLONS.** Use a **colon** to introduce a list of items.

EXAMPLES

Don't forget the following items for the hike: water bottle, food, first-aid kit, extra sweater, and rain gear.
Make sure you have all your paperwork in order: passport, visa, and tickets.

You should also use a colon between numbers that tell hours and minutes.

1:07 P.M.      6:00 A.M.      9:54 P.M.

A colon is often used after the greeting in a business letter.

Dear Sirs:      Dear Ms. Flanagan:

**3.90 APOSTROPHES.** An **apostrophe** is used to form the possessive of nouns. To form the possessive of a singular noun, you should add an apostrophe and an *s* to the end of the word.

EXAMPLES

The sun's diameter is about 864,000 miles.
(sun + 's = sun's)

Isaac's room is plastered with posters of the Pacers.
(Isaac + 's = Isaac's)

The possessive of a plural noun is formed two different ways. If the plural noun does not end in *s*, you add an apostrophe and an *s* to the end of the word. If the plural noun ends with an *s*, add only an apostrophe.

EXAMPLES

The women's volleyball team is undefeated.
(women + 's = women's)

The Vikings' star quarterback is on the injured list.
(Vikings + ' = Vikings')

There are some words that end in *s* and are singular, such as *species* or *Jesus*, that have an irregular possessive form. Form the possessive of these words by adding only an apostrophe.

EXAMPLES

Moses' staff
Euripedes' tragedies

**3.91 UNDERLINING AND ITALICS. Italics** are a type of slanted printing used to make a word or phrase stand out. In handwritten documents, or in forms of printing in which italics are not available, underlining is used. You should underline or italicize the titles of books, magazines, works of art, movies, and plays.

| BOOKS | *How the Grinch Stole Christmas, Old Yeller* or <u>How the Grinch Stole Christmas</u>, <u>Old Yeller</u> |
| MAGAZINES | *Reader's Digest, Sports Illustrated* or <u>Reader's Digest</u>, <u>Sports Illustrated</u> |
| WORKS OF ART | *The Thinker, The Starry Night* or <u>The Thinker</u>, <u>The Starry Night</u> |
| MOVIES | *The Lion King, Dances with Wolves* or <u>The Lion King</u>, <u>Dances with Wolves</u> |
| PLAYS | *The Mousetrap, Hamlet* or <u>The Mousetrap</u>, <u>Hamlet</u> |

**3.92 QUOTATION MARKS.** When you use a person's exact words in your writing, you are using a **direct quotation**. Enclose the words of a direct quotation in quotation marks.

EXAMPLES

"It looks as if thunderclouds are gathering," Sylvia remarked.
Pietro said, "It's good to be back home."

A direct quotation should always begin with a capital letter. Separate a direct quotation from the rest of the sentence with a comma, question mark, or exclamation point. Do not separate the direct quotation from the rest of the sentence with a period. All punctuation marks that belong to the direct quotation itself should be placed inside the quotation marks.

EXAMPLES

"Your golf game has really improved," Avram remarked.
Victor lamented, "I wish Uncle Don were here."
"Did I turn off the iron?" wondered Mrs. Cameron.
Joy asked, "Have you seen my red blouse?"

Use quotation marks to enclose the titles of short works such as short stories, poems, songs, articles, and parts of books.

SHORT STORIES
"The Tell-Tale Heart," "The Magic Barrel"

POEMS
"Thirteen Ways of Looking at a Blackbird"

SONGS
"Swing Low Sweet Chariot," "The Battle Hymn of the Republic"

ARTICLES, ESSAYS
"Why I Am Optimistic About America," "How It Feels to Be Colored Me"

PARTS OF BOOKS
"Daughter of Invention"

**3.93 HYPHENS AND DASHES.** A **hyphen** is used to make a compound word.

EXAMPLES

four-year-old boy, great-grandmother, run-of-the-mill, seventh-grade student, three-time winner

A **dash** is used to show a sudden break or change in thought.

EXAMPLE

Juan surprised his teacher—and himself—by getting an *A* on the science test.

## 3.94 Editing for Capitalization Errors

To avoid capitalization errors, you should know how to capitalize proper nouns and adjectives; geographical names, directions, and historical names; and titles of art and history books.

**3.95 Proper Nouns and Adjectives.** Using capital letters is called **capitalization**. Always capitalize proper nouns and adjectives. A proper noun names a specific person, place, or thing. A **proper adjective** is an adjective formed from a proper noun.

**PROPER NOUNS**
Lebanon, Queen Elizabeth, Democrat

**PROPER ADJECTIVES**
Lebanese, Elizabethan, Democratic

Capitalize the names of people and pets.

**PEOPLE AND PETS**
Charles A. Lindbergh, Marie Curie, Smoky

There are many different kinds of proper nouns. The chart below should help you to recognize some of them.

### PROPER NOUNS

**TITLES USED WITH NAMES**
Dr. Stetson, Ms. Dixon, Mr. Meletiadis

**MONTHS, DAYS, HOLIDAYS**
January, Wednesday, Labor Day

**RELIGIONS**
Hinduism, Catholicism, Buddhism

**SACRED BEINGS AND WRITINGS**
the Great Spirit, the Bible, the Koran

**CITIES, STATES, COUNTRIES**
Seattle, Louisiana, Peru

**NATIONALITIES**
Danish, Brazilian, Greek

**STREETS, BRIDGES**
Highland Street, Tappan Zee Bridge

**BUILDINGS, MONUMENTS**
World Trade Center, Washington Monument

**CLUBS, ORGANIZATIONS, BUSINESSES**
Kiwanis Club, National Audubon Society, Sears Roebuck

**3.96 I and First Words.** Capitalize the first word of every sentence.

EXAMPLES
Did you see that meteor?
The river rose over its banks.

Capitalize the word *I* whenever it appears.

EXAMPLES
Janice and I will buy the present.
Whenever I see horses, I think of Uncle Sherman.

**3.97 Family Relationships and Titles of Persons.** A word for a family relation such as *Mom, Dad,* or *Grandpa* should be capitalized if it is used as the name or part of the name of a particular person. Do not capitalize a word for a family relation if a modifier such as *the, a, my,* or *your* comes before it.

**CAPITALIZED**
When they were children, Dad, Aunt Polly, and Uncle Richard went down the Grand Canyon on mules.

**NOT CAPITALIZED**
My grandma has a cousin who lives in Germany.

Capitalize the official title of a person when it is followed by the person's name or when it is used instead of a name in direct address.

President James Polk, Queen Mary, Sir Winston Churchill, Pope Paul
"I am honored to meet you, Ambassador."

Do not capitalize references to occupations.

the electrician, the doctor, the sergeant, the judge, the chef, the editor

**3.98 Geographical Names, Directions, and Historical Names.** Capitalize the names of specific places, including terms such as *lake, mountain, river,* or *valley* if they are used as part of a name.

| | |
|---|---|
| **BODIES OF WATER** | Colorado River, Black Sea |
| **CITIES AND TOWNS** | Kansas City, Fayetteville |
| **COUNTIES** | Cayuga County, Kosciusko County |
| **COUNTRIES** | Switzerland, Indonesia |
| **ISLANDS** | Ellis Island, Isle of Wight |
| **MOUNTAINS** | Pike's Peak, Mount Rainier |
| **STATES** | Montana, South Carolina |
| **STREETS, HIGHWAYS** | Erie Boulevard, Route 71 |

Do not capitalize general names for places.

**EXAMPLES**

The still lake beautifully reflected the white-capped mountain.

Follow this road for two more miles and you will reach a small town.

Capitalize geographical directions if they are part of a specific name or a commonly recognized region. Do not capitalize words such as east(ern), west(ern), north(ern), and south(ern) if they are used only to indicate direction.

**CAPITALIZED**

<u>Western</u> Samoa, <u>East</u> Africa, <u>South</u> Bend, <u>Northern</u> Ireland

**NOT CAPITALIZED**

<u>west</u> of Denver, <u>eastern</u> face of the mountain, <u>south</u> side of the city, <u>northern</u> regions

Capitalize historical events, special events, and recognized periods of time.

**HISTORICAL EVENTS**

Continental Congress, Boxer Rebellion

**HISTORICAL PERIODS**

Paleozoic Era, Industrial Age

**SPECIAL EVENTS**

Empire State Games, Rose Bowl

**3.99 TITLES OF ARTWORKS AND LITERARY WORKS.**
Apply title capitalization to titles of artworks and literary works. In title capitalization, capitalize the first word, the last word, and all other words except articles (*a, an,* and *the*) and prepositions.

**EXAMPLES**

Raphael's *The School of Athens*, Matisse's *Joy of Life*, Jackson Pollock's *Autumn Rhythm*, Shakespeare's *The Taming of the Shrew*, Faulkner's *The Sound and the Fury*, Ray Bradbury's "All Summer in a Day"

## 3.100 Editing for Spelling Errors

You can improve your spelling by following the rules given here, and by memorizing the list of commonly misspelled words.

**3.101 USING SPELLING RULES I.** Always check your writing for spelling errors, and try to recognize the words that give you more trouble than others. Adding prefixes and suffixes often causes spelling errors. A prefix is a letter or a group of letters added to the beginning of a word to change its meaning. When adding a prefix, do not change the spelling of the word itself.

dis + similar = dissimilar
un + necessary = unnecessary

A **suffix** is a letter or group of letters added to the end of a word to change its meaning. The spelling of most words is not changed when the suffix *–ness* or *–ly* is added.

even + ness = evenness
usual + ly = usually

If you are adding a suffix to a word that ends with y, and that y follows a vowel, you should usually leave the y in place. (**Vowels** are the letters *a, e, i, o,* and *u.*)

employ + ment = employment
stay + ing = staying
destroy + ed = destroyed

If you are adding a suffix to a word that ends with y, and that y follows a consonant, you should usually change the y to i. (**Consonants** are all letters that are not vowels.)

silly + est = silliest
sticky + ness = stickiness
cry + ed = cried
cheery + ly = cheerily

If you are adding a suffix that begins with a vowel to a word that ends with a silent e, you should usually drop the e.

shave + ing = shaving
value + able = valuable
rose + y = rosy
take + ing = taking

If you are adding a suffix that begins with a consonant to a word that ends with a silent e, you should usually leave the e in place.

tire + less = tireless
sincere + ly = sincerely
fate + ful = fateful
place + ment = placement

**3.102 USING SPELLING RULES II.** When a word is spelled with the letters *i* and *e* and has the long *e* sound, it is spelled *ie* except after the letter *c*.

> thief, relieve, yield, pierce
> ceiling, conceive, receipt, deceive

The only word in the English language that ends in *–sede* is supersede. Only the following three words end in *–ceed*: *exceed, proceed,* and *succeed.* Every other word that ends with the "seed" sound is spelled *–cede.*

> precede, recede, concede, accede

Most noun plurals are formed by simply adding *–s* to the end of the word.

> stairs, ducklings, kites, rockets

The plurals of nouns that end in *o, s, x, z, ch,* or *sh* should be formed by adding *–es.*

> tomatoes, classes, taxes, topazes, beaches, flashes

An exception to the rule above is that musical terms (and certain other words that end in *o*) are usually pluralized by adding *–s.*

> pianos, solos, concertos, sopranos, banjos, radios

Form the plurals of nouns that end in *y* following a vowel by adding *–s.*

| EXAMPLES | toy + s = toys |
| --- | --- |
| | donkey + s = donkeys |
| | Thursday + s = Thursdays |
| | ray + s = rays |

Form the plurals of nouns that end in *y* following a consonant by changing the *y* to an *i* and adding *–es.*

| EXAMPLES | pony + s = ponies |
| --- | --- |
| | spy + s = spies |
| | country + s = countries |
| | story + s = stories |

**3.103 COMMON SPELLING ERRORS.** Some English words are often misspelled. The following box contains a list of 150 commonly misspelled words. If you master this list, you will avoid many errors in your spelling.

## COMMONLY MISSPELLED ENGLISH WORDS

| | | | | | |
| --- | --- | --- | --- | --- | --- |
| absence | biscuit | enormous | liquefy | parallel | siege |
| abundant | breathe | enthusiastically | magnificent | pastime | significance |
| academically | business | environment | manageable | peasant | souvenir |
| accessible | calendar | exhaust | maneuver | permanent | sponsor |
| accidentally | camouflage | existence | meadow | persistent | succeed |
| accommodate | catastrophe | fascinating | mediocre | phenomenon | surprise |
| accurate | cellar | finally | miniature | physician | symbol |
| acknowledgment | cemetery | forfeit | mischievous | pneumonia | synonymous |
| acquaintance | changeable | fulfill | misspell | prestige | temperature |
| adequately | clothes | guidance | mortgage | privilege | tomorrow |
| adolescent | colossal | guerrilla | mysterious | procedure | transparent |
| advantageous | column | hindrance | naive | prophesy | twelfth |
| advisable | committee | hypocrite | necessity | prove | undoubtedly |
| ancient | conceivable | independent | nickel | receipt | unmistakable |
| annihilate | conscientious | influential | niece | referred | unnecessary |
| anonymous | conscious | ingenious | noticeable | rehearsal | vacuum |
| answer | consistency | institution | nucleus | relieve | vehicle |
| apparent | deceitful | interference | nuisance | resistance | vengeance |
| article | descendant | irrelevant | nutritious | resources | villain |
| attendance | desirable | irresistible | obedience | responsibility | vinegar |
| bankruptcy | disastrous | judgment | occasionally | rhythm | weird |
| beautiful | discipline | league | occurrence | schedule | whistle |
| beggar | efficiency | leisure | orchestra | seize | withhold |
| beginning | eighth | license | outrageous | separate | yacht |
| behavior | embarrass | lightning | pageant | sergeant | yield |

# SPEAKING AND LISTENING
## Resource

## THE POWER OF COMMUNICATION

Humans are by nature social creatures. **Communication** is a form of behavior that fulfills the basic human need to connect and interact with other individuals in society. Because democratic government requires the free exchange of ideas, communication is also fundamental to the political way of life in the United States.

## 4.1 Verbal and Nonverbal Communication

Human beings use both verbal and nonverbal communication to convey meaning and exchange ideas. When a person expresses meaning through words, he or she is using **verbal communication**. When a person expresses meaning without using words, for example by standing up straight or shaking his or her head, he or she is using **nonverbal communication**. When we speak to another person, we usually think that the meaning of what we say comes chiefly from the words we use. However, as much as 60 percent of the meaning of a message may be communicated nonverbally.

### ELEMENTS OF VERBAL COMMUNICATION

| ELEMENT | DESCRIPTION | GUIDELINES FOR SPEAKERS |
|---------|-------------|--------------------------|
| Volume | loudness or softness | Vary your volume, but make sure that you can be heard. |
| Melody, Pitch | highness or lowness | Vary your pitch. Avoid speaking in a monotone (at a single pitch). |
| Pace | speed | Vary the speed of your delivery to suit what you are saying. Excitement, for example, can be communicated by a fast pace, and seriousness can be communicated by slowing down and saying something forcefully. |
| Tone | emotional quality | Suit your tone to your message, and vary it appropriately as you speak. For example, you might use a light tone for a happy message and a heavier one for a sad message. |
| Enunciation | clearness with which words are spoken | When speaking before a group, pronounce your words more precisely than you would in ordinary conversation. |

## ELEMENTS OF NONVERBAL COMMUNICATION

| ELEMENT | DESCRIPTION | GUIDELINES FOR SPEAKERS |
| --- | --- | --- |
| Eye contact | Looking audience members in the eye | Make eye contact regularly with people in your audience. Try to include all audience members. |
| Facial expression | Using your face to show your emotions | Use expressions to emphasize your message—raised eyebrows for a question, pursed lips for concentration, eyebrows lowered for anger, and so on. |
| Gesture | Meaningful motions of the arms and hands | Use gestures to emphasize points. Be careful, however, not to overuse gestures. Too many can be distracting. |
| Posture | Position of the body | Keep your spine straight and head high, but avoid appearing stiff. Stand with your arms and legs slightly open, except when adopting other postures to express particular emotions. |
| Proximity | Distance from audience | Keep the right amount of distance between yourself and the audience. You should be a comfortable distance away, but not so far away that the audience cannot hear you. |

# LISTENING SKILLS

Learning to listen well is essential not only for success in personal life but also for success in school and, later, on the job. It is estimated that high school and college students spend over half their waking time listening to others, yet most people are rather poor listeners.

## 4.2 Active versus Passive Listening

Effective listening requires skill and concentration. The mind of a good listener is focused on what a speaker is trying to communicate. In other words, an effective listrener is an active listener. Ineffective listeners view listening as a passive activity, something that simply "happens" without any effort on their part. Passive listening is nothing more than hearing sounds. This type of listening can cause misunderstanding and miscommunication.

Different situations require different listening skills. The following suggestions can help you become a better listener in particular situations.

## 4.3 Listening to a Lecture or Demonstration

- Think of creative reasons to listen. It can be difficult to pay attention to a lecture or demonstration if you do not think the information being presented is important to you. Try to think of reasons why the information is important by asking yourself: How can I use this information?

- As you listen, show the speaker that you are involved. Remember that in a lecture or demonstration, as in a conversation, the speaker depends on you for positive feedback or response. Try to maintain an attentive posture by sitting up straight, making eye contact, and nodding when you understand.

- Listen for major ideas. Try to identify the speaker's main points and the facts or materials that are offered to support them. Check your understanding of what the speaker is saying by putting it into your own words, in your head, as you listen.

- Take notes as you listen. Note the major ideas and related details. Do not try to write down what the speaker says word for word. Use phrases, symbols, and abbreviations such as *w/* for *with, Amer.* for *American,* and *&* or *+* for *and.* (For more information, see the Language Arts Survey 5.17, "Taking Notes, Outlining, and Summarizing Information.")

- When you do not understand something that the speaker is saying, make a note. Save questions and comments for an appropriate time, usually when the speaker pauses or when he or she invites questions. Then raise your hand before asking your question or making your comment.

- Do not let yourself become distracted. Avoid such things as daydreaming, focusing on the speaker's delivery, or listening to background noise. Giving in to distractions can prevent you from understanding the speaker's message.

## 4.4 Listening in Conversations

- Do not monopolize the conversation. Give the other person plenty of opportunities to speak.

- When the other person is speaking, pay attention to what he or she is saying. Show through eye contact, body language, and facial expressions that you are interested and attentive.

- Avoid mentally debating the other person while he or she is speaking. This may distract you from truly hearing what the person has to say. Try to withhold judgment until the other person has finished.

- Ask the other person questions. Asking questions is a good way to start a conversation, to keep the conversation going, and to show the other person that you are really listening. The best questions are usually ones that directly relate to what the speaker has been saying.

- When you speak, respond to what the other person has been saying. Relate what you say to what he or she has said.

- Take time to think about what the other speaker has said before responding. Do not be afraid of a lull in the conversation while you think about what has been said and about your response.

- If you find yourself becoming overly emotional during a conversation, stop, take a deep breath, and bring your emotions under control before continuing. If controlling your emotions seems too difficult, consider continuing the conversation at a later time.

## 4.5 Listening to the Media

- Avoid being a "couch potato." Television, movies, and radio programs can be powerful manipulators. As you watch or listen, think critically about what you are seeing or hearing by evaluating these messages.

- When watching or listening to news programs or commercial advertisements, make sure to distinguish facts from opinions. *Facts* are statements that can be proved by checking a reference work or making observations. *Opinions* are statements of value or statements of policy that express personal beliefs. A statement of value expresses positive or negative attitudes toward a person, object, or idea. For example, "Albert Einstein was a great humanitarian" is a statement of value because it expresses a positive attitude toward Einstein. A statement of policy says what should or should not be done. "Congress should spend more money on education" is a statement of policy because it suggests what Congress should do. When you hear an opinion, ask yourself whether it is supported by the facts. For more information, see the Language Arts Survey 5.2, "Distinguishing Fact from Opinion."

- When watching or listening to an entertainment program, think about the quality of the program. Consider the quality of the acting, directing, and writing. Also consider the production qualities of the program—the lighting, sound effects, staging, camera work, costuming, properties, and music.

- Think about what message or messages are being delivered by the program and whether you agree or disagree with them. Do not assume that just because a program is entertaining, it does not communicate a message.

- Set standards about what you will watch or listen to. Learn to turn off a program or to switch to another program when something does not meet your standards.

- Limit the time that you spend watching or listening to the broadcast media. Remember that there is much more that you might be doing with your life such as reading, learning a new hobby or skill, writing in your journal, exercising, interacting with other people, creating works of art, or simply thinking.

## 4.6 Adapting Listening Skills to Specific Tasks

Just as different situations require different types of listening, different tasks or goals may also require different listening strategies and skills.

LISTENING FOR COMPREHENSION means listening for information or ideas communicated by other people. For example, you are listening for comprehension when you try to understand directions to a friend's house or your teacher's explanation of how to conduct a classroom debate. When listening for comprehension, your goal is to reach understanding, so it is important to recognize and remember the key information or ideas presented. Concentrate on getting the main points or major ideas of a message rather than all the supporting details. This can prevent you from becoming overwhelmed by the amount of information presented.

You might also use a technique called clarifying and confirming to help you better remember and understand information. The technique involves paraphrasing or repeating back to the speaker in your own words the key information presented to make sure that you have understood correctly. If the situation prevents you from using the technique—for instance, if there is no opportunity for you to respond directly to the speaker—it can still be helpful to rephrase the information in your own words in your head to help you remember and understand it.

LISTENING CRITICALLY means listening to a message in order to comprehend and evaluate it. When listening for comprehension, you usually assume that the information presented is true. Critical listening, on the other hand, includes comprehending and judging the arguments and appeals in a message in order to decide whether to accept or reject them. Critical listening is most useful when you encounter a persuasive message such as a sales pitch, advertisement, campaign speech, or news editorial. When evaluating a persuasive message, you might consider the following: Is the speaker trustworthy and qualified to speak about this subject? Does the speaker present logical arguments supported by solid facts? Does the speaker use unproven assumptions to make a case? Does the speaker use questionable motivational appeals, such as appeals to fear or to prejudice? These questions can help you decide whether or not to be convinced by a persuasive message.

LISTENING TO LEARN VOCABULARY involves a very different kind of listening because the focus is on learning new words and how to use them properly. For instance, if you were to hear a presentation on hip-hop music, the speaker might introduce some of the many slang terms used in this musical style and explain what they mean. Or you might have a conversation with someone who has a more advanced vocabulary and use this as an opportunity to learn new words. The key to listening in order to learn vocabulary is to pay attention to how words are used in context. Sometimes it is possible to figure out what an unfamiliar word means based simply on how the word is used in a sentence. Once you learn a new word, try to use it several times so it becomes more familiar and you become comfortable using it. Also be sure to look up the word in a dictionary to find out whether it has other meanings or connotations of which you are not aware.

LISTENING FOR APPRECIATION means listening purely for enjoyment or entertainment. You might listen appreciatively to a singer, a comedian, a storyteller, an acting company, or a humorous speaker. Appreciation is a very individual matter and there are no rules about how to appreciate something. However, as with all forms of listening, listening for appreciation requires attention and concentration.

## COMMUNICATING WITH OTHERS

### 4.7 Communicating with Another Person

The ordinary human interactions that take place in daily life involve a great deal of interpersonal communication, or communication between two individuals. The following guidelines will help you to communicate more effectively in such daily interactions.

- **Make eye contact** and maintain a relaxed posture.

- **Provide feedback as you listen**. Smile or nod to show understanding and/or agreement. Ask questions or make comments when the speaker pauses for feedback. Try not to interrupt or to finish the speaker's sentences for him or her.

- **Reflect back or rephrase what the speaker has said** to make sure that you understand him or her. For example, suppose that the speaker says, "Crazy Horse never allowed anyone to make a likeness of him or take his photograph." You could reflect back, "So, nobody ever made a likeness of Crazy Horse or took his photograph? That's interesting. Why do you think he felt that way?"

- **Control your emotions**. If you become angry while listening to the speaker, take a deep breath and count to ten. Make sure you haven't misunderstood by rephrasing the statement that angered you. If you can contain your anger, express your objections calmly. If you cannot contain your anger, end your conversation and say that you would like to continue it at another time.

- **Distinguish between facts and opinions**. Facts are statements that can be proven true, whereas opinions are expressions of personal belief that may or may not be true.  When presenting factual information in a conversation, it is helpful to explain what the basis for the fact is. When presenting opinions, try to indicate this by introducing these ideas with phrases like "I believe that . . ." or "In my opinion . . ."  If you are unsure whether another person is stating a fact or opinion, ask what his or her statement is based on.

### 4.8 Communicating in a Small Group

Much human activity takes place in small groups. A small group is defined as a group of three to fifteen people, interacting in a face-to-face situation, who have an awareness of a group identity. Everyone is involved in a small group at one point or another in their lives, whether it be a high school clique, an after-school organization, an athletic team, or a family. Although many of the principles of interpersonal communication hold true in small group situations, there are additional factors to consider because of the number of people involved. The following guidelines will help you become a better communicator and participant in small group situations.

- **Respect group norms and culture**. Most groups have norms or rules that govern appropriate behavior for group members. Groups also have their own culture or way of life that may include certain beliefs, rituals, or behaviors. When participating in a small group, be sure to pay attention to and respect the norms and culture of the group.

- **Understand group roles**. Individual members are likely to fulfill particular roles in a group based on what they do best. Constructive roles help the group to achieve its goals. These include the **leader** (directs the work of the group), **secretary** (keeps minutes of group meetings), **gatekeeper** (keeps communication open by encouraging and discouraging participation), and **harmonizer** (helps to resolve conflict or reduce tension between group members). Destructive roles may prevent the group from achieving its goals. These include the **joker** (distracts the group by engaging in horseplay), **dominator** (tries to control the group for his or her own interests), **blocker** (puts down the ideas of others or refuses to cooperate), and **deserter** (withdraws from the group and does not participate). Successful group participants attempt to fulfill positive and constructive roles within the group and encourage others to do so.

- **Take turns participating**. Good group members make contributions to the discussion, but also allow others to participate. If an overly talkative person seems to dominate the discussion, be willing to take on the role of gatekeeper and gently suggest that others be allowed to contribute. For instance, you might say, "I've been interested in what you have to say, Ed. What do other people think about this issue?"

- **Help to foster a positive group climate**. Group climate refers to the degree of warmth or coldness that group members feel toward each other. You have probably been in a group with a cold climate before, where members constantly bicker and argue and never seem to accomplish anything. Positive or warm group climates are characterized by trust, cooperation, and concern for others. Negative or cold group climates are characterized by suspicion, competition, and selfishness. As a good group member, you can help to create a positive and warm climate by being supportive of others ideas, empathizing with others, treating others as equals, and remaining flexible and open to new ideas and information.

- **Establish group goals**. Some groups have a difficult time accomplishing anything because it is not clear what the goals of the group are. Without goals, a group is like a ship that sets sail with no clear destination. Chances are the ship and the group will drift aimlessly until they run aground. You can help your group stay focused by encouraging its members to establish clear goals at the beginning, and referring to these goals whenever the group seems to run aground or lose its way.

## 4.9 Communicating in a Large Group

Large groups are those that contain more than fifteen people. Generally the larger the size of the group, the less opportunity there is for each individual to participate. However, there are still principles that can help you become a better communicator in large group situations.

- **Share group roles**. In larger groups, it may be difficult to decide who takes what role as many

members may have the skills needed for any one role. Sharing roles and responsibilities can allow everyone to contribute to the group.

- **Focus on key relationships**. It may not be possible to get to know everyone in a large group setting. Identify those key individuals in the group that you will most need to interact with in carrying out your assignments or duties, and focus on getting to know them.

- **Emphasize group identity, norms, and goals**. As groups become larger in size, they are likely to become less cohesive. Cohesiveness refers to the level of commitment and attraction members feel to each other and the group. Groups that experience low cohesion are usually not productive or successful. Try to increase cohesion by reinforcing the identity, norms, and goals of the group at every opportunity.

- **Stand up when speaking**. Make sure that everyone in the room can see and hear you. If there is a microphone available, use it. Speak in a normal tone four to six inches from the microphone.

- **Avoid the pressure to conform**. In larger groups, individuals are less comfortable speaking out if they disagree with an idea or decision. This can produce "groupthink," where members give in to the pressure to conform and do not critically evaluate information and/or decisions. If you disagree with an expressed idea or decision, do not hesitate to speak out and share your reservations.

- **Foster responsibility**. In large groups, it is relatively easy for individual members to shirk their duties and avoid responsibility. If something goes wrong, there are usually many people to blame so no one feels individually responsible for the outcomes of the group. Take responsibility yourself, and encourage others in the group to carry out their assigned duties.

## 4.10 Asking and Answering Questions

There are many situations in which you will find it useful to ask questions of a speaker, or in which you will be asked questions about a presentation. Often a formal speech or presentation will be followed by a question-and-answer period. Keep the following guidelines in mind when asking or answering questions.

ASKING QUESTIONS

- **Wait to be recognized**. In most cases, it is appropriate to raise your hand if you have a question and to wait for the speaker or moderator to call on you.

- **Make questions clear and direct**. The longer your question, the less chance a speaker will understand it. Make your questions short and to the point.

- **Do not debate or argue**. If you disagree with a speaker, the question-and-answer period is not the time to hash out an argument. Ask to speak with the speaker privately after the presentation is over, or agree on a later time and place to meet.

- **Do not take others' time**. Be courteous to other audience members and allow them time to ask questions. If you have a follow-up question, ask the speaker if you may proceed with your follow-up.

- **Do not give a speech**. Sometimes audience members are more interested in expressing their own opinion than in asking the speaker a question. Do not give in to the temptation to present a speech of your own.

ANSWERING QUESTIONS

- **Come prepared** for a question-and-answer period. Although you can never predict the exact questions that people will ask you, you can anticipate many questions that are likely to be asked. Rehearse aloud your answers to the most difficult questions.

- **Be patient**. It may take some time for audience members to formulate questions in response to your speech. Give the audience a moment to do so. Don't run back to your seat the minute your speech is over, or if there is an awkward pause after you invite questions.

- **Be direct and succinct**. Be sure to answer the question directly as it has been asked, and to provide a short but clear answer.

- **Rephrase difficult or ambiguous questions**. If you are not sure what an audience member's question is, repeat the question back to them to clarify. You may also want to repeat the question if not everyone in the audience could hear it.

- **Be courteous**. Sometimes audience members will ask a question you have already answered in your speech. Be tactful in such situations. Briefly repeat the information from your speech in case the audience member did not hear or understand you the first time.

- **Handle difficult audience members gracefully**. Sometimes audience members hog the stage or try to pick a verbal fight with a speaker. In such situations, keep your cool and gently suggest that the audience member talk to you privately after the presentation so you can discuss the issue with him or her more fully.

# COMMUNICATION STYLES AND CULTURAL BARRIERS

## 4.11 Being Considerate of Other Cultures and Communication Styles

Communication styles and behaviors vary greatly between people of different cultures—even those who live and were raised in the same country. There are many possible verbal and nonverbal sources of miscommunication between cultural groups. In some cultures, emotionally intense discussions and insults are expected forms of behavior. In other cultures, such behavior is considered rude. In traditional Asian cultures, a slap on the back is considered insulting and it is not customary to shake hands with people of the opposite sex. In other cultures, a slap on the back expresses friendliness and it is customary to shake hands with anyone you meet for the first time. When listening to someone speak, Native Americans consider a bowed head a sign of respect. In other cultures, lack of eye contact may be seen as a sign of shyness, weakness, or disrespect. In Latino cultures, two speakers in conversation may stand very close and even touch each other. In other cultures, standing close is considered an intrusion on personal space and thought to be rude, and touching is generally acceptable only with close friends or relatives.

These are only a few of the many communication differences that exist among people of different cultures. When interacting with a person from another culture, it is important to remember that such differences may exist and to respect the other individual's cultural practices and behaviors.

## 4.12 Overcoming Barriers to Effective Multicultural Communication

The following guidelines and suggestions will help you to overcome some common barriers and stumbling blocks to communicating with people of different cultural backgrounds.

- **Treat people as individuals**. Do not assume that everyone is "the same" as you are, or even that people with similar cultural backgrounds are the same. Avoid relying on preconceptions and stereotypes when interacting with someone from another culture. Regardless of what cultural practices, physical characteristics, or behaviors they might share, human beings are individuals and should always be treated as such.

- **Be sensitive to sources of miscommunication**. Remember that both verbal and nonverbal behaviors send messages to others, and that both can lead to miscommunication and misunderstanding. If you think you have done or said something that has offended someone from another culture, ask if this is the case. It may be uncomfortable to do so at first, but you are more likely to overcome your error and become friends if you show respect and sensitivity to the other person.

- **Seek common ground**. One reason people from different cultures may have difficulty communicating is because they focus on differences rather than similarities. A simple way to overcome this problem is to find some common interest, belief, or activity that you share with the other person and that can help to bridge differences.

- **Accept others as they are**. Avoid the temptation to evaluate or judge the behavior, beliefs, feelings, or experiences of others. Instead, learn to accept differences as valid, even if you personally disagree with what someone

else thinks or feels. It is also helpful to remember that the other person is probably doing the best he or she can with whatever resources are available at the time.

- **Avoid provoking language**. Racial, ethnic, or gender slurs have no place in an enlightened society and should never be used. Profanity or swearing is unacceptable, even among close friends, and should be avoided. You-statements ("You are not listening to me," "You should not do that," "You don't know what you're talking about") can feel like an attack, even when they are well intentioned. People often react to you-statements by becoming defensive or hostile. Try to use I-statements instead ("I feel like you aren't listening to me," "I don't think you should do that," "I'm not sure I agree with you").

## 4.13 Collaborative Learning and Communication

**Collaboration** is the act of working with one or more other people to achieve a goal. Many common learning situations involve collaboration:

- participating in a small-group discussion
- doing a small-group project
- tutoring another student or being tutored
- doing peer evaluation

### GUIDELINES FOR DISCUSSION

- **Listen actively during the discussion**. Maintain eye contact with the speakers. Make notes on what they say. Mentally translate what they say into your own words. Think critically about whether you agree or disagree with each speaker, and why.

- **Be polite**. Wait for your turn to speak. Do not interrupt others. If your discussion has a group leader, ask to be recognized before speaking by raising your hand.

- **Participate in the discussion**. At appropriate times, make your own comments or ask questions of other speakers.

- **Stick to the discussion topic**. Do not introduce unrelated or irrelevant ideas.

- **For a formal discussion, assign roles**. Choose a group leader to guide the discussion and a secretary to record the minutes (the main ideas and proposals made by group members). Also draw up an agenda before the discussion, listing items to be discussed.

GUIDELINES FOR PROJECTS

- **Choose a group leader** to conduct the meetings of your project group.

- **Set a goal** for the group, some specific outcome or set of outcomes that you want to bring about.

- **Make a list of tasks** that need to be performed.

- **Make a schedule** for completing the tasks, including dates and times for completion of each task.

- **Make an assignment sheet**. Assign certain tasks to particular group members. Be fair in distributing the work to be done.

- **Set times for future meetings.** You might want to schedule meetings to evaluate your progress toward your goal as well as meetings to actually carry out specific tasks.

- **Meet to evaluate your overall success** when the project is completed. Also look at the individual contributions of each group member.

GUIDELINES FOR TUTORING

- **Find out what the other student needs to learn**. Help him or her clarify assignments and areas of strength and weakness.

- **Break down your teaching into steps** that can be followed easily. Then help the other student to follow through on each step.

- **Review basic concepts, terms, and processes**. Encourage the other student to explain these to you in his or her own words.

- **Give the other student practice activities or exercises**, and help him or her to complete them.

- **Be patient**. Give the other student time to respond, to make mistakes, and to ask questions.

- **Be encouraging and supportive**. Remember that your job is to help someone else to learn, not to display your own knowledge.

GUIDELINES FOR BEING TUTORED

- **Bring with you all the materials that you need**, such as your textbook, study guides, notes, worksheets, pencils, and paper.

- **Explain as clearly as you can what you need help with**. Prepare questions beforehand.

- **Ask questions about anything that you do not understand.** Remember that no question is silly if it is sincere.

- **Be patient**. Learning takes time.

- **Do not give up if you do not understand immediately**. Practice makes perfect.

- **Be polite** and thank your tutor for his or her help.

GUIDELINES FOR PEER EVALUATION. For more information on peer evaluation, see the Language Arts Survey 2.37, "Self- and Peer Evaluation, " 2.39, "How to Deliver Helpful Criticism," and 2.40, "How to Benefit from Helpful Criticism."

## 4.14 Conducting an Interview

In an interview, you meet with someone and ask him or her questions. Interviewing experts is an excellent way to gain information about a particular topic. For example, if you are interested in writing about the art of making pottery, you might interview an art teacher, a professional potter, or the owner of a ceramics shop.

When planning an interview, you should do some background research on your subject and think carefully about questions you would like to ask. Write out a list of questions, including some about the person's background as well as about your topic. Other questions might occur to you as the interview proceeds, but it is best to be prepared. For guidelines on being a good listener, read the Language Arts Survey 4.2, "Active versus Passive Listening," and 4.4, "Listening in Conversations." Here are some more tips for interviewing:

- **Set up a time for the interview in advance**. Don't just try to work questions into a regular conversation. Set aside time to meet in a quiet place where both you and the person you are interviewing can focus on the interview.

- **Explain the purpose of the interview**. Be sure the person you are interviewing knows what you want to find out and why you need to know it. This will help him or her to answer your questions in a way that is more useful and helpful to you.

- **Ask mostly open-ended questions**. These are questions that allow the person you are interviewing to express a personal point of view. They cannot be answered with a simple "yes" or "no" nor a brief statement of fact. The following are all examples of open-ended questions: "Why did you become a professional potter?" "What is the most challenging thing about owning your own ceramics shop?" "What advice would you give to a beginning potter?" One of the most valuable questions to ask at the end of the interview is, "What would you like to add that I haven't asked about?" This can provide some of the most interesting or vital information of all.

- **If possible, tape-record the interview**. Then you can review the interview at your leisure. Be sure to ask the person you are interviewing whether or not you can tape-record the session. If the person refuses, accept his or her decision.

- **Take notes during the interview**, whether or not you are also tape-recording it. Write down the main points and some key words to help you remember details. Record the person's most important statements word for word.

- **Clarify spelling and get permission for quotes**. Be sure to get the correct spelling of the person's name and to ask permission to quote his or her statements.

- **End the interview on time**. Do not extend the interview beyond the time limits of your appointment. The person you are interviewing has been courteous enough to give you his or her time. Return this courtesy by ending the interview on time, thanking the person for his or her help, and leaving.

- **Write up the results of the interview as soon as possible after you conduct it**. Over time, what seemed like a very clear note may become unclear or confusing. If you are unclear of something important that the person said, contact him or her and ask for clarification.

## PUBLIC SPEAKING

## 4.15 Giving a Speech

The fear of speaking in public, although quite common and quite strong in some people, can be overcome by preparing a speech thoroughly and practicing positive thinking and relaxation. Learning how to give a speech is a valuable skill, one that you most likely will find much opportunity to use in the future.

The nature of a speech, whether formal or informal, is usually determined by the situation or context in which it is presented. **Formal speeches** usually call for a greater degree of preparation, might require special attire such as a suit or dress, and are often presented to larger groups who attend specifically to hear the presentation. A formal speech situation might exist when presenting an assigned speech to classmates, giving a presentation to a community group or organization, or presenting a speech at an awards ceremony. **Informal speech** situations are more casual and might include telling a story among friends, giving a pep talk to your team at halftime, or presenting a toast at the dinner table.

## 4.16 Types of Speeches

The following are the three main types of speeches:

- **Impromptu speech**. This is a speech given without any advance preparation. For example, if you were surprised by a gift or an award, you might be called upon to give a brief speech that was not written or rehearsed.

- **Memorized speech**. This is a speech that has been written out and memorized word for word. Your teacher may ask you to prepare a memorized speech on a topic you are studying at school.

- **Extemporaneous speech**. This is a speech in which the speaker refers to notes occasionally. Most professional speakers prefer to deliver extemporaneous speeches because they combine the liveliness of an impromptu speech with the careful preparation of a memorized or manuscript speech. While the speaker does not plan what he or she will say word for word, the speaker does create an overall plan for the speech, records important points on cards, and rehearses until she or he is comfortable with the material. You might give an extemporaneous speech at a city council meeting about funding for your school.

## 4.17 Steps in Preparing an Extemporaneous Speech

1. **Choose a topic for your speech**. Consider the audience, occasion, and your own strengths and weaknesses as a speaker when choosing a topic.

2. **Do prewriting to identify what you know or think about the topic**. As you write, think about different ways to approach the topic.

3. **Do research on the topic**. Use a variety of source materials, including newspapers, magazines, books, interviews, Internet sources, and personal experience.

4. **Determine your specific purpose in speaking about your topic**. What are you trying to accomplish in speaking to your audience? Are you trying to demonstrate something to them? Compare and contrast two things or ideas? Strengthen their commitment to something? Spur them to take action?

5. **Organize your material into three to five main points**. Use a clear, logical, and interesting organizational strategy that is suited to your specific purpose, the audience, and the occasion. Be sure each point flows logically and smoothly from the one that comes before it. Include transitions between main points, and between the introduction, body, and conclusion of the speech.

6. **Create visual aids**. Some material is too difficult to present orally and is best presented visually. Visual aids should be neat, attractive, visible from a distance, and relevant to your speech. For more information, see the Language Arts Survey 6.11, "Displaying Effective Visual Information."

7. **Prepare note cards**. Notecards should be no larger than 4 x 6 inches and should contain as much information as you need to present your speech, but not so much that you are tempted to read from the cards. Write clearly and legibly so you can read your notes at a distance.

8. **Rehearse with your note cards**. Never attempt to speak at length on a subject without practicing what you will say. If possible, practice a few times in front of a live audience. Otherwise, use a mirror or recording device. Rehearse until you feel comfortable with the material and can present the speech with minimal use of notecards. Be sure to rehearse with visual aids if you are using them.

9. **Deliver your speech**.

## 4.18 Guidelines for Giving a Speech

A speech should always include a beginning, a middle, and an end. The beginning, or introduction, of your speech should spark the audience's interest, present your central idea, and briefly preview your main points. The middle, or body, of your speech should expand upon each of your main points in order to support the central idea. The end, or conclusion, of your speech should be memorable and should give your audience a sense of completion.

### TIPS FOR SUCCESSFUL PUBLIC SPEAKING

- **Be sincere and enthusiastic**. Feel what you are speaking about. Apathy is infectious and will quickly spread to your audience.

- **Maintain good but relaxed posture**. Don't slouch or lean. It's fine to move around a bit; it releases normal nervous tension. Keep your hands free to gesture naturally instead of holding on to note cards, props, or the podium so much that you will "tie up" your hands.

- **Speak slowly**. Oral communication is more difficult than written language and visual images for audiences to process and understand. Practice pausing. Don't be afraid of silence. Focus on communicating with the audience. By looking for feedback from the audience, you will be able to pace yourself appropriately.

- **Maintain genuine eye contact**. Treat the audience as individuals, not as a mass of people. Look at individual faces.

- **Speak in a genuine, relaxed, conversational tone**. Don't act or stiffen up. Just be yourself.

- **Communicate**. Focus on conveying your message, not "getting through" the speech. Focus on communicating with the audience, not speaking at or to it.

- **Use strategic pauses**. Pause briefly before proceeding to the next major point, before direct quotations, and to allow important or more complex bits of information to sink in.

- **Remain confident and composed.** Remember that listeners are generally "for you" while you are speaking, and signs of nervousness are usually undetectable. To overcome initial nervousness, take two or three deep breaths as you are stepping up to speak.

## 4.19 Oral Interpretation of Poetry

**Oral interpretation** is the art of presenting a literary work aloud to an audience. It differs from theater in that the performers, known as interpreters, do not move around the stage. One type of oral interpretation is the dramatic interpretation of poetry. In the past, people often entertained one another by reading poems aloud. Here are a few basic guidelines to ensure the quality of an oral interpretation.

TYPES OF POEMS. The way you prepare your interpretation will depend on whether the type of poem you will interpret is a lyric poem, a narrative poem, or a dramatic poem.

- A **lyric poem** has a single speaker who reports his or her own emotions.

- A **narrative poem** tells a story. Usually a narrative poem has lines belonging to narrator, or person who is telling the story. The narrator may or may not take part in the action.

- A **dramatic poem** contains characters who speak. A dramatic poem may be a lyric, in which characters simply report emotions, or a narrative, which tells a story. A dramatic monologue presents a single speaker at a moment of crisis or self-revelation and may be either lyric or narrative.

Before attempting to dramatize any poem, read through the poem carefully several times. Make sure that you understand it well. To check your understanding, try to paraphrase the poem, or restate its ideas, line by line, in your own words.

ANALYZING THE SPEAKER OF A LYRIC POEM. When dramatizing a lyric or dramatic poem, think about the speaker of the poem. Ask yourself:

- Who is the speaker?
- How old is the speaker?

- Is the speaker male or female?
- What is the situation in which the speaker finds himself or herself?
- What does the speaker think about his or her situation?
- What values, opinions, beliefs, wishes, or needs does the speaker have?
- Is the speaker fully aware of the implications of what he or she is saying, or does the reader know more than the speaker?

Try to form a clear image of the speaker in your mind. Think about how such a person might sound, feeling and thinking as he or she does.

ANALYZING THE NARRATOR AND CHARACTERS OF A NARRATIVE OR DRAMATIC POEM. When analyzing a narrative or dramatic poem, ask about the narrator and the characters the same questions that you would ask about the speaker of a lyric poem. How are the narrator and the characters related to one another? In what ways are they different? Is there anything that the narrator understands that one or more of the characters do not?

List the narrator and each of the characters in the poem. After each, list his or her characteristics. Then try to form a clear image of each in your mind. Again, think about how each might sound, feeling and thinking as he or she does. If the poem is narrative, think of how each character reacts to the events in the story that the poem tells.

USING VERBAL AND NONVERBAL COMMUNICATION TO INTERPRET THE POEM. After analyzing the speaker (in a lyric poem) or the narrator and characters (in a narrative or dramatic poem), make a copy of the poem and mark it to show

- the different voices you will use when reading
- the emotions that you will express
- places to increase or decrease your pace
- places to raise or lower your volume
- gestures and facial expressions to use to communicate emotions

Strive to make voices of different characters sound different from the others by changing your tone (the emotion expressed) and pitch (the highness or lowness of your voice) and looking in a different direction each time you change voices.

**MEMORIZING A POEM.** To memorize a poem, work line by line. Look at one line. Look away and repeat it. Then check to see that you got it right. Once you get that line right, add a second line. Look away and repeat both lines. Then check them. Continue in this manner until the entire poem is memorized. You may wish to have someone else look at a copy of the poem while you recite it out loud. This second person can prompt you when you forget a line. Memorize the poem thoroughly before you begin working on the qualities of your reading. If you have not thoroughly memorized the lines, you will not be able to concentrate on how you sound.

**REHEARSING AND PRESENTING YOUR INTERPRETATION.** Rehearse your interpretation using a tape or video recorder or rehearse in front of a mirror so that you can view your facial expressions and gestures. Before actually presenting your interpretation, relax and adopt a confident attitude. If you begin to feel stage fright, try to concentrate on the poem and the audience, not on yourself.

## 4.20 Telling a Story

A **story** or **narrative** is a series of events linked together in some meaningful fashion. We use narratives constantly in our daily lives: to make a journal entry, to tell a joke, to report a news story, to recount a historical event, to record a laboratory experiment, and so on. When creating a narrative, consider all of the following elements:

- **Decide on your purpose.** Every story has a point or purpose. It may be simply to entertain or to share a personal experience, but it may have a moral or lesson. Your purpose in telling a story will shape many other parts of the narrative, so it is important to know your purpose before you construct your narrative.

- **Select a focus.** The focus for your narrative will depend largely on your purpose in telling it. For example, if you were telling the story of Abraham Lincoln's life, and your purpose was to show how someone could rise from humble roots to a position of greatness, you would probably choose a broad focus for the story. You might begin with Lincoln's birth in a Kentucky log cabin and end with his eventual rise to the position of president of the United States and his many accomplishments in office. If your purpose was to show that perseverance is an important virtue, you might choose a narrower focus. Your story could ignore Lincoln's early life and instead focus on his long political career and his many defeats on the way to the presidency.

- **Choose your point of view.** The storyteller or narrator determines the point of view from which the story will be told. You can choose to speak in the first person, either as a direct participant in the events or as an observer (real or imagined) who witnessed the events first hand. You can also use the third-person voice to achieve greater objectivity. Once again, your purpose in telling the story may affect your decision about what point of view you choose.

- **Determine sequence of events.** The sequence of events refers to the order in which they are presented. Although it might seem obvious that stories should "begin at the beginning," this is not always the best approach. Some narratives begin with the turning point of the story to create a sense of drama and capture the listener's interest. Others begin at the end of the story and present the events leading up to this point in hindsight. Wherever you choose to begin the story, your narrative should present events in a logical fashion and establish a clear sense of direction for your listeners.

- **Determine duration of events.** Duration refers to how long something lasts. Everyone has experienced an event that seemed to last for hours, when in reality it only took minutes to occur. A good storyteller can likewise manipulate the duration of events in order to affect the way listeners experience them.

- **Select details carefully.** Make them consistent with your focus and make sure they are necessary to your purpose. A well-constructed story should flow smoothly, and should not get bogged down by irrelevant or unnecessary detail. Details can also establish the tone and style of the story and affect how listeners react to the events being described.

- **Choose characters.** All stories include characters, who need to be developed so that they become real for listeners. Try to provide your listeners with vivid, concrete descriptions of the mental and physical qualities of important characters in the story. Remember that listeners need to understand and relate to the characters in order to appreciate their behavior.

- **Create dialogue**. Although it is possible to tell a story in which the characters do not speak directly, conversation and dialogue help to add life to a story. As with detail, dialogue should be used carefully. It is important that dialogue sound authentic, relate to the main action of the story, and advance the narrative. When telling a story, you might choose to enact the characters by creating an individual voice for each one.

## 4.21 Participating in a Debate

A **debate** is a contest in which two people or groups of people defend opposite sides of a proposition in an attempt to convince a judge or audience to agree with their views. **Propositions** are statements of fact, value, or policy that usually begin with the word *resolved.* The following are examples of typical propositions for debate:

| | |
|---|---|
| RESOLVED | That lie detector tests are inaccurate. (proposition of fact) |
| RESOLVED | That imagination is more important than knowledge. (proposition of value |
| RESOLVED | That Congress should prohibit the sale of handguns to private citizens. (proposition of policy) |

The two sides in a debate are usually called the affirmative and the negative. The **affirmative** takes the "pro" side of the debate and argues in favor of the proposition, while the **negative** takes the "con" side and argues against the proposition. Using a single proposition to focus the debate ensures that the two sides argue or clash over a common topic. This allows the participants in the debate to develop their logic and ability to argue their positions persuasively.

Sometimes you may find that you are defending a side of a proposition that you do not personally agree with. For example, you may be asked to defend gun control in class even though you believe that the Second Amendment to the Constitution prohibits regulations on the sale of guns. Although some people may find this distasteful, there is good reason to play the "devil's advocate." First, defending a position you do not believe in will allow you to better understand the position of those who disagree with you. Although you may not change your stance, you may come to appreciate why others see the issue differently. Second, in a society based on the free and open exchange of ideas, debate is a fundamental method for arriving at just and reasonable decisions. Every idea deserves consideration, even if it is ultimately rejected.

Typically, both sides in a debate are allowed an equal amount of time to prepare for the debate and to state their case for or against the proposition. To ensure fairness, the affirmative and negative teams take turns presenting speeches. There are two basic types of speeches: **constructive speeches** in which each side states its case for or against the proposition, and **rebuttal speeches** in which each side refutes or attacks its opponent's arguments, while defending its own case. Sometimes debaters are allowed to cross-examine or ask questions of their opponents during the debate. A typical debate might be organized as follows:

| | |
|---|---|
| AFFIRMATIVE CONSTRUCTIVE | 7 minutes |
| Cross-Examination by Negative | 2 minutes |
| Negative Constructive | 7 minutes |
| Cross-Examination by Affirmative | 2 minutes |
| Affirmative Rebuttal | 3 minutes |
| Negative Rebuttal | 5 minutes |
| Affirmative Rebuttal | 2 minutes |

In addition, each side might be granted 4 or 5 minutes of preparation time during the debate to prepare its upcoming speeches. Preparation time may only be used between speeches.

Once the debate is finished, the audience or judge is asked to consider the arguments that have been made and to vote for which side made the more persuasive case. Ideally, judges or audience members will try to be objective and make their decision based not on their personal views of the issue, but rather based on the arguments made by the debaters in the contest.

- **Be prepared.** In a debate, it will never be possible to anticipate all the arguments your opponent might make. However, by conducting careful and through research on both sides of the issue, you should be able to prepare for the most likely arguments you will encounter. You can prepare briefs or notes on particular issues in advance of the debate to save yourself preparation time during the debate.

- **Be organized.** Because a debate involves several speeches that concern the same basic arguments or issues, it is important that you remain organized during the debate. When attacking or refuting an opponent's argument, or when advancing or defending your own argument, be sure to follow a logical organizational pattern to avoid confusing the audience or the other team.

- **Take notes** by turning a long sheet of paper sideways. Draw one column for each speaker, taking notes on each speech going down one column, and recording notes about a particular argument or issue across the page as it is discussed in each successive speech.

- **Be audience-centered.** In the argument with your opponent it is easy to forget the goal of the debate: to persuade your audience that your case is correct.

- **Prepare in advance** for the most likely arguments your opponents will raise. Use time sparingly to organize your materials and think of responses to unanticipated arguments. Save time for the end of the debate, during rebuttal speeches, when it will be more valuable.

## 4.22 Preparing a Multimedia Presentation

Whether you use a simple overhead projector and transparencies or a PowerPoint presentation that involves graphics, video, and sound, multimedia technology can add an important visual element to a presentation. Consider the following guidelines to create a multimedia presentation:

- **Ensure that audio-visual elements enhance understanding.** The multimedia elements should add to the verbal elements, not distract from them. Be sure the content of the presentation is understandable, and that the amount of information—both verbal and visual—will not overwhelm audience members.

- **Make sure the presentation is clearly audible and visible.** Video clips or graphics may appear blurry on a projection screen, or may not be visible to audience members in the back or on the sides of the room. Audio clips may sound muffled or may echo in a larger room or a room with different acoustics. When creating a multimedia presentation, be sure the presentation can be easily heard from all parts of the room.

- **Become familiar with the equipment.** Well before the presentation, be sure you know how to operate the equipment you will need, that you know how to troubleshoot if the equipment malfunctions, and that the equipment you will use during the presentation is the same as that which you practiced with.

- **Be sure the room can accommodate your needs.** Once you know where you will make your presentation, be sure the necessary electrical outlets and extension cords are available, that lights can be dimmed or turned off as needed, that the room can accommodate the equipment you will use, and so forth.

- **Rehearse with the equipment.** Make sure that you can operate the equipment while speaking at the same time. Be sure that the multimedia elements are coordinated with other parts of your presentation. If you will need to turn the lights off in the room, make sure you can operate the equipment in the dark and can still see your note cards.

# STUDY AND RESEARCH *Resource*

## THINKING SKILLS

Everyone thinks, but not everyone realizes that thinking—like hitting a baseball or playing the piano—is a skill that you can improve by learning and practicing. This section gives you some tips that can greatly improve your ability to make decisions, to solve problems, and to learn and think critically.

### 5.1 Making Decisions and Solving Problems

**MAKING DECISIONS.** When you have a decision to make, the best approach is to weigh the alternatives available to you. You can do this by making a **criteria analysis chart**. To make such a chart, list the results that you want to achieve down the left side of the chart. List your choices across the top of the chart. Then assign points from 1 to 5 to each choice, with 1 being the lowest and 5 being the highest. Add up the points for each choice to see which one is best.

### CRITERIA ANALYSIS CHART

| Purchase of Portable Radio | Brand A | Brand B |
|---|---|---|
| 1. Low cost | 2 | 3 |
| 2. Good warranty | 2 | 1 |
| 3. Attractive design | 3 | 1 |
| 4. Many features | 2 | 3 |
| Total | 9 | 8 |

When making a decision, you often must weigh several factors. You can compare your options by making a **pros and cons** chart on paper. First make a list of all your options. For each option list the reasons for choosing it (the pros) and the reasons for not choosing it (the cons). Then compare the lists.

### PROS AND CONS

**Painting Yearbook Illustration or Drawing It in Pencil**

| | Painting | Drawing in Pencil |
|---|---|---|
| **Pros** | colorful | easier<br>less expensive |
| **Cons** | more expensive<br>more difficult | not colorful |

**SOLVING PROBLEMS.** There are many ways to solve problems. To solve a complex problem, you will probably need to use more than one strategy. Here are two approaches you can try:

- **Trial and error**. Sometimes when you have to solve a problem, you just make a guess and see if it works. In a **trial-and-error approach**, you try one possible solution and if it doesn't work you try another. If you don't know how to solve a particular math problem, you could guess the answer, plug it back into the problem, and then revise your answer as necessary.

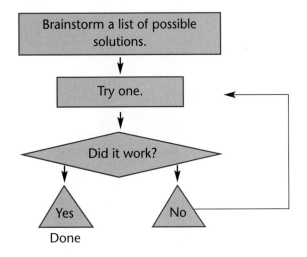

- **Divide and conquer**. Another strategy for problem solving is to divide the problem into parts and then solve each part one at a time in a logical sequence. Here is an example:

**PROBLEM**
A friend is coming to stay at your house for a few days and you need to prepare a room for him.

**SOLUTION**
Break down the job into small, manageable goals:

**STRATEGY**
(1) Move desk and computer from small downstairs room.
(2) Remove storage boxes from closet and put in basement.
(3) Clean the room.
(4) Put cot in room and make bed.

## 5.2 Distinguishing Fact from Opinion

What is the difference between the following statements?

The language with the greatest number of speakers, over nine hundred million, is Mandarin Chinese.

Mandarin Chinese is the greatest language in the world.

The first statement expresses a **fact**. You can prove this fact by looking in a reference book. The second statement expresses an **opinion**. This statement can be supported but not proved.

A fact is a statement that, at least in principle, could be proved by direct observation. Every statement of fact is either true or false. The following statement is an example of a fact:

Edgar Allan Poe wrote "The Pit and the Pendulum." (This statement can be proved by getting a published copy of the story to see who the author is.)

An opinion is a statement that expresses not a fact about the world, but rather an attitude or desire. Three common types of opinions are value statements, policy statements, and certain types of predictions.

A **value statement** expresses an attitude toward something. Such statements often include judgment words such as the following:

| | | |
|---|---|---|
| attractive | honest | ugly |
| awesome | junk | unattractive |
| beautiful | kind | valuable |
| cheap | mean | wonderful |
| dishonest | nice | worthless |
| excellent | petty | worthwhile |
| good | treasure | |

Ancient Greece produced some <u>beautiful</u> and <u>inspiring</u> myths.
Those violent "action films" are just <u>awful</u>.

A **policy statement** tells not what is, but what someone believes should be. Such statements usually include words such as *should, should not, ought to, ought not to, must,* or *must not.* Examples of policy statements include the following:

The president <u>should be</u> reelected.
You <u>must not</u> play your radio during study hall.

Closely related to policy statements are **requests** and **commands**:

Reelect the president.
Do not play your radio during study hall.

A **prediction** makes a statement about the future. Because the future is unpredictable, most predictions can be considered opinions:

People will live longer in the future.
Tomorrow will be partly cloudy.

**EVALUATING FACTS AND OPINIONS.** When evaluating a fact, ask yourself whether it can be proved through direct observation or by checking a reliable source such as a reference work or an unbiased expert. An opinion is as good as the facts that support it. The opinion that Mandarin Chinese is the greatest language in the world is supported by such facts as the number of speakers that it has. However, others might argue that English is the greater language because it is spoken more widely around the globe. Of course, no list of facts would conclusively prove or disprove the opinion.

When you write and speak, express opinions sparingly. Usually, you can make a stronger case by substituting related facts for opinions. For example, instead of saying, "This was a wonderful day," you could say something like, "Today the sun was shining, it was 74 degrees outside, and I got an *A* on my math test. That's what made it a great day." When you express an opinion, especially in writing, include facts to back up or support that opinion.

When reading or listening, be critical about the statements that you encounter. Ask yourself, "Is this a fact or an opinion?" If it is a statement of fact, consider whether it can be proved or seems likely. If it is an opinion, consider whether it is supported by facts.

## 5.3 Avoiding False Arguments and Propaganda

Another very important thinking skill is learning to use good logic. Life is a process of trying to learn what is true and then to live according to what you believe to be true. Not only do you need good facts, but you also need to know how to put those facts together to come up with the right conclusions. Learning how to think clearly will enable you to avoid errors in logic and to arrive at true conclusions. It will also help you to recognize the faulty thinking of others (especially advertisers) who might be trying to persuade you of something. The intentional use of false arguments to persuade others is called **propaganda**. Here are some of the many faulty arguments of which you should be aware.

**GLITTERING GENERALITIES AND "SPIN."** **Glittering generalities** are statements given to make something sound more appealing. Such statements can be hard to prove, as they appeal to the emotions.

EXAMPLE

These trading cards are the best ever in this limited-time collection!

**ANALYSIS**

Nothing in this statement tells the listener why the trading cards are the best ever. Adding "limited-time collection" to the statement vaguely implies that the trading cards will be available for only a short while, and that the listener should buy them quickly before they are unavailable.

**Spin** is a technique used to slant public perception of the news. Public relations firms and advertisers use this technique to create a favorable perception of a product or organization. Unlike more obvious forms of advertising, spin is hard to recognize because it can be invisible. It is important to know how to recognize such manipulative and misleading statements.

EXAMPLE

The accident was a minor incident because only twenty-five people were injured.

**ANALYSIS**

The fact is that twenty-five people were injured. This does not make it a minor incident; someone is merely interpreting the accident as minor.

**STEREOTYPES.** An overgeneralization about a group of people is known as a **stereotype**. Stereotypes are one of the most dangerous of all overgeneralizations. Remember that the differences among people within a single race or ethnic background are greater than the average differences between races or ethnic groups as a whole. Stereotyping is always based on lack of knowledge or experience. It is the basis of prejudice and is unacceptable in a civilized society.

**UNSOUND OPINIONS.** A fact is a statement that can be proved. An opinion is a statement that cannot be proved. An opinion is someone's personal idea of what is right and may or may not be true. A sound opinion is one that can be supported by facts. An **unsound opinion** is one that cannot be supported by facts. Always be sure that you make a clear distinction between facts and opinions and that you can back up your opinions with facts.

**FACT**

Miss Rivers won this year's award for excellence in teaching.

**OPINION**

Miss Rivers is the best teacher at Jordan High School.

**ANALYSIS**

The statement that "Miss Rivers is the best teacher at Jordan High School" is someone's personal feeling about her. However, it is probably a sound opinion because it is backed up by the fact that she received the award for excellence in teaching.

**CIRCULAR REASONING. Circular reasoning** is the error of trying to support an opinion by restating it in different words. You can avoid circular reasoning by always backing up your opinions with facts.

EXAMPLE

That adventure book was exciting because it was full of action.

**ANALYSIS**

The "reason" the speaker gives for saying that the book was exciting is really just another way of saying it was exciting. He or she should mention some specific examples to show what makes the story exciting.

**LOADED WORDS.** In trying to argue for or against something, people will often use **loaded words**, or words that stir up strong feelings, whether positive or negative. Be careful not to let your feelings interfere with your understanding of the facts.

EXAMPLE

Congressman Philbert is a lazy, good-for-nothing imbecile.

**ANALYSIS**

This statement, an emotional attack on the congressman, uses loaded words that will stir up feelings against him. It is not a reasonable evaluation of his policies or actions in office.

**BANDWAGON APPEAL. Bandwagon appeal** plays to your desire to be part of the crowd—to be like everyone else and to do what everyone else is doing. Beware of advertisements or arguments that try to get you to think or act like everyone else. Just because "everybody" believes or does something does not make it good or right for you.

EXAMPLE

Those who want to be cool wear Star jeans.

**ANALYSIS**

This statement suggests that you aren't really part of the "in" crowd unless you wear this brand of jeans. It does not prove, or even say, anything about the quality of the clothing.

## 5.4 Classifying

One of the many higher-level thinking skills you can develop is the ability to classify. To **classify** is to put into classes or categories. Items in the same category should share one or more characteristics. For example, whales are classified by their method of eating as baleen or toothed whales. The key step in classifying is choosing categories that fit your purpose. Make sure you clearly define your categories.

## 5.5 Generalizing

To **generalize** is to make a broad statement based on one or more particular observations. For example, suppose that you observe that several cats like to stare through windows. You might generalize, based on this discovery, that "cats like to stare through windows." Such generalizations are also called **inferences**. People have learned most of what they know about the world by making generalizations based on their experiences.

Generalizing is therefore an extremely important thinking tool. Unfortunately, it is not a perfect one. Generalizations can be proved false by only one exception. Since generalizations can be proved false by a new experience, avoid making generalizations based on too little evidence. Keep an open mind and be willing to revise your ideas about the world.

## 5.6 Making Inferences, Predictions, and Hypotheses

From careful observation, it is possible to make generalizations, or **inferences**, about the world around us. From there it is possible to **predict** what will happen and to form hypotheses. A **hypothesis** is an educated guess about a cause or an effect. A prediction based on a theory is a hypothesis. A possible explanation for an observed event is also a hypothesis. A hypothesis always needs to be tested against experience. You can test hypotheses the following ways:

- Conduct actual experiments to see if your prediction will occur.
- Examine many relevant examples.
- Conduct a "thought experiment" by asking "What if" questions. (See the Language Arts Survey 2.15, "Imagining: Asking 'What If?' Questions.")

Notice that a hypothesis can be disproved by only one exception. However, a hypothesis cannot be proved merely by gathering examples. Theories and hypotheses can change if a discovery shows that something is otherwise.

## 5.7 Deductive versus Inductive Reasoning

Deduction and induction are two types of logical reasoning. **Deductive reasoning** starts with a generalization to make a statement or statements about something specific. **Inductive reasoning** examines specific facts or instances to make a generalization.

**DEDUCTIVE**
All whales live in the sea. (general)
The beluga whale must live in the sea. (specific)

All students have signed the school policy statement. (general)
Tom is a student at the school. Therefore, he has signed the policy statement. (specific)

**INDUCTIVE**
The blue whale, beluga, and orca live in the sea. (specific)
Therefore, all whales live in the sea. (general)

More than 100 students have signed the school policy statement. (specific)

Therefore, all students have signed the policy statement. (general)

Note that with inductive reasoning, only one specific example is needed to prove the generalization false. See the Language Arts Survey 5.5, "Generalizing."

## 5.8 Estimating and Quantifying

To support an argument, you need to provide facts, and often facts are strengthened by numbers or quantities. If you claim, for instance, that too many people are without health insurance, you should **quantify** your claim by stating how many. The numbers you need may be available in reference works. If not, you might be able to **estimate**, or find the approximate quantity. Sometimes you will have only enough knowledge to estimate a range within which the actual number actually falls. If you need to estimate, always make clear that you are doing so.

**QUANTIFYING**
The science fair had 314 registered participants.

**ESTIMATING**
The science fair was attended by about 300 students and their parents.

## 5.9 Analyzing and Synthesizing

When you **analyze** something, you break it down into parts and then think about how the parts are related to each other and to the whole. For example, you might analyze a painting by describing its composition, shapes, lines, colors, and subject. You might analyze a short story by describing its conflict, plot, characters, setting, and theme. You might analyze a movie by describing its acting, directing, writing, settings, and costumes.

When you **synthesize** something, you bring everything that you were considering together into a whole.

## 5.10 Comparing and Contrasting

Comparing and contrasting are closely related processes. When you **compare** one thing to another, you describe similarities between the two things. When you **contrast** two things, you describe their differences.

To compare and contrast, begin by listing the features of each subject. Then go down both lists and check whether each feature is shared or not. You can also show similarities and differences in a Venn diagram. For more information, see the Language Arts Survey 2.16, "Completing Venn Diagrams," and 2.27, "Choosing a Method of Organization: Comparison-and-Contrast Order."

## 5.11 Evaluating

When you **evaluate,** you make a judgment about something. You may be asked to compare two things to determine which is more valuable or effective. Evaluate questions use such words as *evaluate, judge, justify, critique, determine whether, decide the effectiveness of,* and *appraise.*

> Determine how believably Hawthorne portrays Beatrice in "Rappaccini's Daughter," using evidence from the text to support your response.

## 5.12 Extending

When you **extend** your knowledge, you connect one experience to another. In the study of literature, you extend your knowledge by making connections between two pieces of literature, between the literary work and your own experience, or between a literary work and a cultural or current event. Extend questions use such words as *extend your knowledge, connect, relate,* and *apply.*

> In popular culture and throughout history, people have been accused of being poisonous, like Dr. Rappaccini. Name examples of such people and the ways they have influenced the world around them. Then name people who have countered them.

## 5.13 Perspective, Empathy, and Self-Understanding

When you are asked to use **perspective, empathy,** and **self-understanding** to answer a question, you are exercising an important ability to connect the experience of one person or group to your own. Such thinking allows you to see multiple perspectives, generated alternative viewpoints, and understand another person's feelings and worldview. These questions also allow you to understand your own perspective.

> Why do you think Susan B. Anthony was willing to be arrested for her convictions? How would you react if you lost your rights as a citizen? Would you be willing to risk arrest to fight for your rights, as Susan B. Anthony did? Why, or why not?

## STUDY SKILLS

## 5.14 Developing Good Study Habits

Success in a future career depends largely on success in school. No matter what your experience in school so far, you can improve your performance enormously by developing good study habits. Doing so will make learning easier and more enjoyable.

Find a place to work. Homework is best done in a special study area. Follow these guidelines for picking an appropriate place to study:

- Choose a quiet location, away from distractions such as conversation, television, or loud music.
- Choose a place that is well lit and comfortable. Adequate lighting will help you to avoid eyestrain and headaches.
- Choose a study area that is available at regular times. Set aside a specific time each day for study.
- Have all the tools that you will need, such as paper, pencils, textbooks, handouts, and reference works, at hand.

Make a study plan. Many of your assignments will be due on the following day. Others will be long-term projects. At the end of each school day, make a habit of looking over your assignment notebook. Decide what tasks you need to complete for the following day. Break down longer assignments into specific steps that need to be completed by specific times. Record all of these assignments on a calendar or study plan.

## 5.15 Keeping an Assignment Notebook

Keeping track of assignments in your head can be dangerous because of the possibility of forgetting important details. Instead, write down all your assignments in an assignment notebook. For each assignment, record:

- the name of the subject
- details of the assignment, including what, precisely, you need to do
- the date of the assignment
- the date when the assignment is due

## 5.16 Understanding the Assignment

Understanding an assignment depends on your ability to follow directions.

**FOLLOWING SPOKEN DIRECTIONS.** Often teachers give assignments orally. When listening to spoken assignments,

- Listen carefully. Write down the directions as you hear them.
- Notice what steps are involved in the assignment. Also notice the order of these steps.
- Listen for the key word in each step. A key word is one that tells you what to do. Examples are *read, write, organize,* and *memorize.*
- If you do not understand the directions, ask your teacher to explain them.

**FOLLOWING WRITTEN DIRECTIONS.** Directions for tests usually are written down. Assignment directions also sometimes appear in written form on the board, overhead transparencies, or handouts. When reading written directions,

- Read all the directions completely before you begin the assignment.
- Ask questions to clarify any points not covered in the directions.
- Divide the assignment into steps. Put these steps in a logical order.
- Decide what materials you will need, and assemble them before you begin.
- Reread each step before you actually do it.

## 5.17 Taking Notes, Outlining, and Summarizing Information

When **taking notes** in class or while conducting your own research, you may find it helpful to use a

**rough outline**, or modified outline, form. Write main ideas, capitalizing the first letter of the first word and all proper nouns and proper adjectives. Beneath the main ideas, write related subordinate ideas, preceded by dashes.

Major Cultures in N. Amer., 1492
- —Eastern woodland (incl. Iroquois & Algonquians)
- —Southeastern (incl. Cherokee & Chicasaw)
- —Plains (incl. Dakota, Pawnee, & Kiowa)
- —Southwestern (incl. Navajo, Hopi, & Apache)
- —Great Basin (incl. Ute & Paiute)
- —Plateau (incl. Nez Perce & Yakima)
- —Northwestern (incl. Chinook & Yurok)
- —California (incl. Shasta, Pomo, & Chumash)

Origins
- —Came to Amer. by land bridge across Bering Strait
- — ~ 35,000 bc
- —May have followed herds, mammoths, musk oxen, etc.

To review the material, you might find it helpful to read over your notes and outline, and then to **summarize** what you have learned. Writing a summary of the material is more powerful than thinking through your summary or even saying it out loud. The act of writing reinforces your memory of what you have learned.

## RESEARCH SKILLS

Learning is a lifelong process, one that extends far beyond school. Both in school and on your own, it is important to remember that your learning and growth are up to you. One good way to become an independent lifelong learner is to master research skills. Research is the process of gathering ideas and information. One of the best resources for research is the library.

## 5.18 How Library Materials Are Organized

Each book in a library is assigned a unique number, called a **call number**. The call number is printed on the **spine** (edge) of each book. The numbers serve to classify books as well as to help the library keep track of them.

Libraries commonly use one of two systems for classifying books. Most school and public libraries use the **Dewey Decimal System.** Most college libraries use the **Library of Congress Classification System** (known as the LC system).

## 5.19 How to Locate Library Materials

If you know the call number of a book or the subject classification number you want, you can usually go to the bookshelves, or stacks, to obtain the book. Use the signs at the ends of the rows to locate the section you need. Then find the

### THE LIBRARY OF CONGRESS SYSTEM

| Call Letters | Subjects |
|---|---|
| A | Reference and General Works |
| B–BJ | Philosophy, Psychology |
| BK–BX | Religion |
| C–DF | History |
| G | Geography, Autobiography, Recreation |
| H | Social Sciences |
| J | Political Science |
| K | Law |
| L | Education |
| M | Music |
| N | Fine Arts |
| P | Language, Literature |
| Q | Science, Mathematics |
| R | Medicine |
| S | Agriculture |
| T | Technology |
| U | Military Science |
| V | Naval Science |
| Z | Bibliography, Library Science |

### THE DEWEY DECIMAL SYSTEM

| Call Numbers | Subjects |
|---|---|
| 000–099 | Reference and General Works |
| 100–199 | Philosophy, Psychology |
| 200–299 | Religion |
| 300–399 | Social Studies |
| 400–499 | Language |
| 500–599 | Science, Mathematics |
| 600–699 | Technology |
| 700–799 | Arts |
| 800–899 | Literature |
| 900–999 | History, Geography, Biography[1] |

1. Biographies (920s) are arranged alphabetically by the name of the person whose life is treated in each biography.

particular shelf that contains call numbers close to yours.

Library collections include many other types of publications besides books, including magazines, newspapers, audio and video recordings, and government documents. Ask a librarian to tell you where to find the materials you need.

To find the call numbers of books that will help you with your research, use the library's catalog. The catalog lists all the books in the library (or a group of libraries if it is part of a larger system).

**COMPUTERIZED CATALOGS.** Many libraries today use computerized catalogs. Systems differ from library to library, but most involve using a computer terminal to search through the library's collection. You can usually search by author, title, subject, or key word. If your library has a computerized catalog, you will need to learn how to use your library's particular system. A librarian can help you to master the system. Here is a sample book entry screen from a computerized catalog.

| | |
|---|---|
| Author | **Wallace, David Rains, 1945–** |
| Title | **The Quetzal and the Macaw: The story of Costa Rica's National Parks** |
| Publication info. | **Sierra Club Books, 1992** |
| No. of pages/size | **xvi, 222p. : maps : 24 cm.** |
| ISBN | **ISBN 0–87156–585–4** |
| Subjects | **National Parks and reserves—Costa Rica—History** |
| | **Costa Rica. Servicio de Parques Nacionales—History** |
| | **Nature conservation—Costa Rica—History** |
| Dewey call number | **333.78** |

## COMPUTERIZED CATALOG SEARCHES

| Search By | Example | Hints |
|---|---|---|
| Author | gould, stephen j | Type last name first. Type as much of the name as you know. |
| Title | mismeasure of man | Omit articles such as *a, an,* or *the* at the beginning of titles. |
| Subject | intelligence tests; ability-testing | Use the list of subjects provided by the library. |
| Key words | darwin; intelligence; craniology | Use related topics if you can't find anything in your subject. |

**CARD CATALOGS.** Like a computerized catalog, a card catalog contains basic information about each book in the library. In a card catalog the information is typed on paper cards, and the cards are arranged alphabetically in drawers. For each book there is a title card, one author card for each author, and at least one subject card. All of these cards show the book's title, author, and call number, so you can search for a book by title, author, or subject. The following illustration shows a typical title card.

---

**A TITLE CARD**

333.78   The Quetzal and the Macaw : the story of
    Costa Rica's national parks.
    Wallace, David Rains, 1945–
    The Quetzal and the Macaw : the story of
    Costa Rica's national parks.—San
    Francisco: Sierra Club Books, 1992
    xvi, 222 p. : maps : 24 cm.
    1. National parks and reserves—Costa Rica—
    History. 2. Costa Rica. Servicio de
    Parques nacionales—History. 3. Nature
    conservation—Costa Rica—History. I. Title.
    ISBN 0-394-57456-7

---

When you find the entries for the books you want, write down the call number of each book and then go to the shelves. If you cannot find a particular book you need in the catalog, ask the librarian if your library can request books from another library through an interlibrary loan.

**INTERLIBRARY LOANS.** Many libraries are part of larger library networks. In these libraries, the computerized catalog covers the collections of several libraries. If you want a book from a different library, you will need to request the book at the library's request desk or by using its computer. Ask your librarian to help you if you have questions. He or she will be able to tell you when the book will be shipped to your library.

## 5.20 Using Reference Works

Most libraries have an assortment of reference works in which knowledge is collected and organized so that you can find it easily. Usually, reference works cannot be checked out of the library.

**5.21 TYPES OF DICTIONARIES.** You will find many types of dictionaries in the library reference section. The most common is a dictionary of the English language. Examples include *Merriam Webster Collegiate Dictionary, Webster's New World Dictionary,* and the multi-volume *Oxford English Dictionary.* Other word dictionaries focus on slang, abbreviations and acronyms, English/foreign language translation, and spelling. Biographical, historical, scientific, and world language dictionaries are also some of the works you will find in the reference section.

For more information on using a dictionary to look up specific words in English, see the Language Arts Survey 1.17, "Using a Dictionary."

**5.22 USING A THESAURUS.** A thesaurus is a reference book that groups synonyms, or words with similar meanings. Suppose that you are writing an essay and have a word that means almost but not quite what you want, or perhaps you find yourself using the same word over and over. A thesaurus can give you fresh and precise words to use. For example, if you look up the word *sing* in a thesaurus, you might find the following synonyms listed:

> **sing** (v.) carol, chant, croon, hum,
> vocalize, warble, yodel

**5.23 USING ALMANACS, YEARBOOKS, AND ATLASES.** **Almanacs** and **yearbooks** are published each year. An almanac provides statistics and lists, often related to recent events. In an almanac you can find facts about current events, countries of the world, famous people, sports, entertainment, and many other subjects. An overview of the events of the year can be found in a yearbook.

Some of the more widely used almanacs and yearbooks are *The Guinness Book of World Records;* the *Information Please, Almanac, Atlas, and Yearbook;* the *World Almanac and Book of Facts;* and the *World Book Yearbook of Events.*

An **atlas** is a collection of maps and other geographical information. Some atlases show natural features such as mountains and rivers; others show political features such as countries and cities. If you need to locate a particular feature on a map in an atlas, refer to the gazetteer, an index that lists every item shown on the map.

**5.24 USING BIOGRAPHICAL REFERENCES, ENCYCLOPEDIAS, AND PERIODICALS.** A **biographical reference** contains information on the lives of famous people. Examples include *Who's Who*, the *Dictionary of American Biography*, and *Contemporary Authors*.

**Encyclopedias** provide a survey of knowledge. General encyclopedias, such as *World Book*, contain information on many different subjects. Specialized encyclopedias, such as the *LaRousse Encyclopedia of Mythology*, contain information on one particular area of knowledge.

The topics in an encyclopedia are treated in articles, which are usually arranged in alphabetical order. If you look up a topic and do not find it, check the index (usually in the last volume). The index will tell you where in the encyclopedia your topic is covered.

A **periodical** is a publication that comes out regularly, usually once a week, once a month, or four times a year. Magazines and newspapers are periodicals. Because they are published frequently and quickly, periodicals are an excellent source for the latest news and information, but they may not be as accurate as some other sources.

**5.25 USING INDEXES, APPENDICES, AND GLOSSARIES.** An **index** lists in alphabetical order the subjects mentioned in a book or collection of periodicals and pages where these subjects are treated. Indexes help you locate possible sources of information about your topic. An index can be at the back of a book of nonfiction, or it can be a published book itself.

Examples of published indexes include *The Reader's Guide to Periodic Literature*, a comprehensive index to popular magazine and journal articles. Some periodicals, such as the *New York Times* and *National Geographic*, publish their own indexes, listing articles in past issues. Most indexes are published in sequential volumes that are issued yearly or monthly. Indexes are available as bound books, on microfilm, and online on the Internet.

An **appendix** provides additional material, often in chart or table form, at the end of a book or other writing.

A **glossary** lists key words in a book and their definitions.

## 5.26 Using the Internet

The **Internet** is a vast collection of computer networks that can provide you with a great wealth of information from libraries, government agencies, high schools and universities, nonprofit and educational organizations, museums, user groups, and individuals around the world. The Internet provides a valuable way to do research—if you know how to use it. Here are some guidelines.

**5.27 BROWSING VERSUS SEARCHING ON THE INTERNET. Browsing** means sifting through Internet sites through an Internet browser, or software that connects you to the Internet. **Searching** means conducting focused research by using an Internet search engine. By both browsing and searching, you can gain access to the information you want. Browsing allows you to navigate through different sites, either before or after you have conducted a search. Searching allows you to narrow and expand your research in a focused way to find the particular information you need.

### Internet Search Engines

**www.alltheweb.com**
This enormous engine tracks more than 200 million URLs (Uniform Resource Locators, or Internet addresses).

**www.altavista.digital.com**
This engine claims to index 30 million web pages.

**www.infoseek.com**
This search engine also contains a large database and an associated directory, Infoseek Guide.

**www.yahoo.com**
This popular search service is maintained by online editors who sift through Internet sites and keep only the valuable ones.

**5.28 CONDUCTING AN INTERNET SEARCH**

- Access a reliable search engine.
- Browse the search engine's links or do a keyword search.
- Use Boolean search strategies or other specialized search tools to narrow and expand your search as needed.
- Browse the results of your search.

- Repeat this process using different search engines until you find what you want.

To keep track of your Internet research, see the Language Arts Survey 5.41, "Documenting and Mapping Internet Research."

**5.29 USING BOOLEAN SEARCH STRATEGIES.** Boolean logic refers to the logical relationship among search terms. It is named for the mathematician George Boole. To conduct a focused search on the Internet, you should know Boolean operators such as AND, OR, NOT, and NEAR. These operators allow you to limit or expand your research. There are several guides to using Boolean search strategies on the Internet. They can be found by searching with the keyword "Boolean."

### Boolean Operators

| | |
|---|---|
| " " | Quote marks help limit your search to just the phrase in quotes. "Hitchhiker's Guide to the Galaxy" will find references to that specific book title. Without the quotes, a search engine might list numerous other sites, including those related to hitchhikers, guide, and galaxy. |
| AND | This operator lets you join two ideas. "Greece" AND "travel" would provide you with travel information to Greece. The two words by themselves would give you listings too general to be helpful. |
| OR | This operator gives you sites that carry information about one or the other of two groups. "Rottweilers OR Huskies" will give you sites that include either one of these dog breeds. "Rottweilers AND Huskies" will list only sites that include both dog breeds. |
| NOT | This command lets you eliminate certain sites. "American food NOT pizza" will find sites on American food but exclude sites related to pizza. |

## 5.30 Evaluating Information and Media Sources

To conduct your research efficiently, you need to evaluate your sources and set priorities among them. Ideally, a source will be:

- **Unbiased.** When an author has a personal stake in what people think about a subject, he or she may withhold or distort information. Investigate the author's background to see if she or he is liable to be biased. Using loaded language and overlooking obvious counter-arguments are signs of author bias.

- **Authoritative.** An authoritative source is reliable and trustworthy. An author's reputation, especially among others who conduct research in the same field, is a sign of authority. Likewise, periodicals and publishers acquire reputations for responsible or poor editing and research.

- **Timely.** Information about many subjects changes rapidly. An astronomy text published last year may already be out of date. In other fields—for instance, algebra—older texts may be perfectly adequate. Consult with your teacher and your librarian to decide how current your sources must be.

- **Available.** Borrowing through interlibrary loan, tracing a book that is missing, or recalling a book that has been checked out to another person takes time. Make sure to allow enough time for these materials.

- **At the appropriate level.** Find sources that present useful information that you can understand. Materials written for "young people" may be too simple to be helpful. Books written for experts may presume knowledge that you do not have. Struggling with a difficult text is often worth the effort, but if you do so, monitor your time and stay on schedule.

**5.31 HOW TO READ A NEWSPAPER OR NEWSMAGAZINE.** Newspapers and news magazines contain an enormous amount of information. Few people who are not professional politicians or news personnel have the time to read all or most of what appears in a newspaper each day. Nonetheless, reading the news is important. Only by doing that can you take advantage of democratic freedoms and make informed voting decisions.

An excellent way to approach reading a newspaper is as follows: Skim the headlines and leads for world, national, state, and local news stories. Read any news summaries included in your paper. Then read in depth any stories that seem particularly important or interesting. You may also wish to read the feature or entertainment sections of the newspaper, according to your own interests.

When reading news stories and editorials, make sure to distinguish between facts and opinions. Facts are statements that can be proved by observation or by consulting a reliable and objective source. Opinions are predictions or statements of value or policy. When you encounter opinions in a newspaper, try to determine whether these opinions are sound. Sound opinions are ones supported by facts. For more information on distinguishing between facts and opinions, see the Language Arts Survey 5.2, "Distinguishing Fact from Opinion."

**5.32 HOW TO EVALUATE A FILM.** We watch movies for a multitude of reasons, but perhaps the most common is that a movie allows us to escape our own realities for a couple of hours. It lets us visit new places, see and try exciting new things, and experience life in someone else's shoes. A great film gives us insight into the lives of others and so expands our understanding and our sympathies. Some films, however, are created solely for the purpose of making money through exploitation of sensational elements or gimmicks. Although you cannot control the types of movies Hollywood decides to make, you can control the types of movies you choose to watch. The following guidelines will enable you to become a more discriminating consumer of films.

- **Plan ahead**. Decide in advance which films you would like to see. Don't settle for just any movie that happens to be playing at your local theater or on television.

- **Listen, watch, and read what the critics have to say.** Take what the critics have to say into consideration to help you decide which movies to see. Once you have seen the movie, decide for yourself whether you agree or disagree with a particular critic. Consider what elements of the movie you liked or disliked, and what could have been altered to make it better. If, after a while, you find one particular critic with whom

you tend to agree on a regular basis, use his or her opinion to help you choose which movies to see.

- **Be a critic yourself**. Be critical of dialogue and story lines. Many films recycle conventional story lines and dialogue. Many contain sensational scenes that provoke audiences but forfeit quality in story line, dialogue, and content. When you see a film, ask yourself questions such as the following:

  – Does each scene move the story forward?

  – Do the characters' actions fit their motives? Is their dialogue believable?

  – Are the themes raised in the film fully developed?

- **Be aware of previews and coming attractions**. These are designed with the help of the production company's marketing and sales departments to motivate you to see their film. Previews can make a film seem more humorous, exciting, and powerful than it really is by showing only the best dialogue and action.

- **Try something new!** Try viewing a film that is much different from the type and genre that you usually see. Keep an open mind; you might just surprise yourself and enjoy it.

- **Never substitute.** Never see a film adaptation of a literary work as a substitute for reading the work itself. While seeing such an adaptation can be a good introduction to a literary work, do not rely on it to capture all the richness of the original.

**5.33 HOW TO EVALUATE RADIO AND TELEVISION.** Television and radio are other communication media. You may not be able to respond directly to the broadcaster, but you can still control the broadcast message. Follow the guidelines below to effectively control television output:

- **Plan your television and radio time.** Rather than accepting whatever program happens to be on, look at broadcast listings and choose programs that are of interest to you.

- **Be a critic.** Question what you see and hear. What criticisms do you have about a program:

its quality, its message, its originality, the depth and reliability of its coverage?

- **Remember that advertisers pay for most broadcast programs.** They also control the content of the programs they sponsor and pay for your attention because they want to sell you something. Listen to and watch these advertisements and programs critically. Read the Language Arts Survey 5.2, "Distinguishing Fact from Opinion," for tips on evaluating information critically.

**5.34 How to Evaluate Advertisements.** Advertising messages in the media are everywhere. To sharpen your skills in evaluating them, see the Language Arts Survey 5.2, "Distinguishing Fact from Opinion," and 5.3, "Avoiding False Arguments and Propaganda."

**5.35 How to Evaluate Internet Sites.** Most published print materials have been checked carefully before publication. But anyone can publish something on the Internet—without having to verify facts or guarantee quality. When you use the Internet for research, be careful to evaluate your sources. Here are some guidelines.

**Consider the resource's domain name.**
Documents that end with .edu and .gov are generally reliable, since they come from educational and governmental organizations. Commercial sites end in .com. They can be reliable, too, but watch for biases that favor the company's product. Sites ending in .org or .net can be trusted if they are from a reliable organization, but watch for special interest group sites that slant or "spin" information to their advantage.

| Key to Internet Domains | |
| --- | --- |
| .com | commercial entitity |
| .edu | educational institution |
| .firm | business entity |
| .gov | government agency or department |
| .info | organizations that provide information |
| .mil | military organization |
| .net | network resource |
| .org | other type of organization, usually nonprofit |
| .store | online stores |

**Consider the author.**
- Is the author's name listed?
- What are this person's credentials?
- What makes him or her qualified to provide this information?
- Does the author provide a way for you to contact him or her?

**Evaluate the quality of information.**
- How accurate is the information? Does it appear to be reliable and without errors?
- Are there links to other reliable sources? Do the links really work?
- How current is the information? Is the date provided for when the site was authored or revised? Is this the latest information on this topic?
- How clearly does the author provide information?
- How well does the author cover the topic, based on what you know from other sources?
- How does the author support the information—with charts, graphs, a bibliography?

**Look for objectivity.**
- Is the information given without bias?
- Is the author objective, or does he or she try to influence the way you think?

## 5.36 Documenting Sources

As you use your research in your writing, you must document your sources of information. Remember to:

- Credit the sources of all ideas and facts that you use.
- Credit original ideas or facts that are expressed in text, tables, charts, and other graphic information.
- Credit all artistic property, including works of literature, song lyrics, and ideas.

**5.37 Keeping a Research Journal.** Just as a writing journal can help you track your thoughts, experiences, and responses to literature, a research journal can help you track your research. A research journal is a notebook, electronic file, or other means to track the information you find as you conduct research. A research journal can include a list of questions you want to research. (Such questions can be an excellent source of writing topics.)

EXAMPLES

How did the Vietnam Veterans Memorial come to be? Why is it one of the most visited memorials in America?

Where can I find more artwork by Faith Ringgold?

Why was Transcendentalism such an important literary movement in America but not in Europe?

**5.38 USING YOUR RESEARCH JOURNAL FOR DOCUMENTATION.** As you conduct your research, rely on your research journal as a place to take notes on the sources you find and your evaluation of them. Keeping a research journal can be an invaluable way to track your research and to take notes.

**5.39 INFORMAL AND FORMAL NOTE-TAKING.** Use **informal note-taking** when you want information for your own use only, and when you will not need to quote or document your sources. You would take informal notes when preparing materials to use in studying, for instance, as you watch a film or listen to a lecture.

Informal note-taking is much like outlining (see the Language Arts Survey 2.29, "Rough Outlines"). Use important ideas as headings, and write relevant details below. You will not be able to copy every word, nor is there any need to. Write phrases instead of sentences.

QUOTATION   "Jerzy Kosinski came to the United States in 1957, and in 1958 he was awarded a Ford Foundation fellowship."

NOTES   Jerzy Kosinski
—came to US 1957
—Ford Foundation fellowship 1958

You will also want to record information about the event or performance, including the date, time, place, speaker, and title, as applicable. After you are done taking notes, read them over to ensure that they are legible and meaningful. If you have used idiosyncratic shorthand or abbreviations that you may not later recall, write out your notes more fully.

Use **formal note-taking** when you may need to quote or document your sources. When you are keeping formal notes for a project—for instance, for a debate or a research paper—you should use 4" x 6" index cards.

---

### PREPARING NOTE CARDS

1. Identify the source at the top right corner of the card. (Use the source numbers from your bibliography cards.)
2. Identify the subject or topic of the note on the top line of the card.
3. Use a separate card for each fact or quotation.
4. Write the pertinent source page number or numbers after the note.

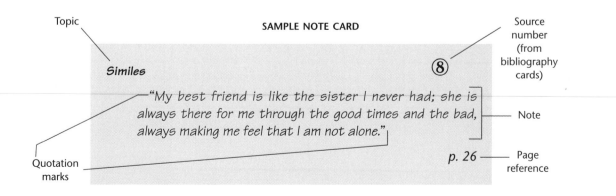

**SAMPLE NOTE CARD**

Topic

Similes ⑧

Source number (from bibliography cards)

"My best friend is like the sister I never had; she is always there for me through the good times and the bad, always making me feel that I am not alone." — Note

Quotation marks

p. 26 — Page reference

## FORMAL NOTE-TAKING

| Type of Note | When to Use | What to Watch For |
|---|---|---|
| Quotation | When the exact wording of a primary source is important to your topic | Copy spelling, capitalization, punctuation, and numbers exactly as in the source. |
| | When you are providing a definition | Place quotation marks around all direct quotations. |
| Paraphrase | When the wording of a secondary source is particularly memorable or insightful | Record, when appropriate, explanatory background information about the speaker or the context of a quotation. |
| | Most of the time | Focus on your main purpose, and note only points related to your topic. |
| | | Place quotation marks around any quoted words or phrases. |
| Summary | When the point you are making does not require the detail of a paraphrase | Reread the source after writing your summary to be sure that you have not altered the meaning. |

**5.40 Making Bibliographies and Bibliography Cards.** If you are writing a research paper, your teacher will ask you to include a bibliography to tell where you got your information. A **bibliography** is a list of sources that you used for your writing. A **source** is a book, a magazine, a film, or any other written or audio-visual material that you use to get information. As you work on your paper, you should be writing down on note cards the information for each source that you use. The chart below shows the correct form for different types of bibliography entries.

## FORMS FOR BIBLIOGRAPHY ENTRIES

**A. A book**
Douglass, Frederick. <u>Escape from Slavery: The Boyhood of Frederick Douglass in His Own Words</u>. New York: Alfred A. Knopf, 1994.

**B. A magazine article**
Reston, James, Jr. "Orion: Where Stars Are Born." <u>National Geographic</u>. December 1995: 90–101.

**C. An encyclopedia entry**
"Lewis and Clark Expedition." <u>Encyclopedia Americana</u>. Jackson, Donald. 1995 ed.

**D. An interview**
Campbell, Silas. Personal interview. 6 February 1997.

**E. A film**
<u>The Big Heat</u>. Dir. Fritz Lang. With Glenn Ford and Gloria Grahame. Writ. Sidney Boehm. Based on the novel of the same title by William P. McGiven. 90 min. Columbia, 1953.

**F. The Internet**
Durham, Dacia. The Charles A. and Anne Morrow Lindbergh Foundation. 24 Oct. 1995, updated 18 June 1999. <<u>http://www.mtn.org/lindfdtn/</u>>.

For each source used, prepare a bibliography card using an index card. Include all of the information in the following chart when preparing your cards.

## INFORMATION TO INCLUDE ON A BIBLIOGRAPHY CARD

| | |
|---|---|
| **Author(s)** | Write the complete name(s) of all author(s), editor(s), and translator(s). |
| **Title** | Write the complete title. If the piece is contained in a larger work, include the title of the larger work. (For example, write the name of the encyclopedia as well as the name of the article you used.) |
| **Publisher** | Write exactly as it appears on the title page. |
| **Place and date of publication** | Copy this information from the title page or copyright page of a book. For a magazine, write the date of the issue that you used. |
| **Location and call number** | Note where you found the book. If it is in a library collection, write the call number. |
| **Card number** | Assign a number to each bibliography card that you prepare. Write that number in the top right corner of the card and circle it. When you take notes from the source, include this number on each note card so that you will be able to identify the source of the note later on. |

**SAMPLE BIBLIOGRAPHY CARD**

②

Van Lawick-Goodall, Jane.
    <u>In the Shadow of Man</u>

      Boston: Houghton, 1971.

    Peabody Institute Library

599.8

**5.41 DOCUMENTING AND MAPPING INTERNET RESEARCH.** Your research journal is an excellent tool for tracking how you find information. It can be especially invaluable for documenting and mapping Internet research. As you browse and search on the Internet, it can be easy to jump from one Internet site to the next and to lose track of how you got from place to place. Especially as you conduct research, it is important to map your path. Here is one way to do so.

- Write a brief statement of the topic of your research.

- Write key words or phrases that will help you search for this information.

- Note the search engines that you will use.

- As you conduct a search, note how many "hits" or Internet sites the search engine has accessed.

Determine whether you need to narrow or expand your search. Write down new key words accordingly, and the results of each new search.

- When you find promising sites, write them down.

- Access each promising site. Evaluate its information using the guidelines in the Language Arts Survey 5.35, "How to Understand Internet Sites."

- Once you find information to include in your work, document it carefully. For more information on how to document Internet sites, see the Language Arts Survey 5.40, "Making Bibliographies and Bibliography Cards."

**5.42 AVOIDING PLAGIARISM. Plagiarism** is taking someone else's words or thoughts and pretending that they are your own. Plagiarism is a very serious problem and has been the downfall of many students and even famous people. Whenever you use someone else's writing to help you with a paper or a speech, you must be careful either to put the ideas in your own words or to use quotation marks. In either case, you must give credit to the person whose ideas you are using. Giving such credit to others is called documenting your sources.

**5.43 PARAPHRASING, SUMMARIZING, AND QUOTING.** As you do research, you notes will include paraphrases, and summaries, and quotations.

STUDY AND RESEARCH RESOURCE

**5.44 PARENTHETICAL DOCUMENTATION.** Parenthetical documentation is currently the most widely used form of documentation. To use this method to document the source of a quotation or an idea, you place a brief note identifying the source in parentheses immediately after the borrowed material. This type of note is called a **parenthetical citation**, and the act of placing such a note is called **citing a source**.

The first part of a parenthetical citation refers the reader to a source in your List of Works Cited or Works Consulted. For the reader's ease in finding the source in your bibliography, you must cite the work according to how it is listed in the bibliography. The reference to the source should also be as brief as possible. If the source is clearly identified in the text, omit it from the citation and give only the page number.

The second part of the citation refers the reader to a specific page or place within the source. If you are referring to a whole work, do not cite the page numbers since they are already given in the bibliography.

---

### SAMPLE PARENTHETICAL CITATIONS

**A. For works listed by title, use an abbreviated title.**

*Sample bibliographic entry*
"History." *Encyclopedia Britannica: Macropædia*. 1992 ed.

*Sample citation*
Historians go through three stages in textual criticism ("History" 615).

**B. For works listed by author or editor, use the author's or editor's last name.**

*Sample bibliographic entry*
Brown, Dee. *Bury My Heart at Wounded Knee: An Indian History of the American West*. New York: Holt, 1970.

*Sample citation*
"Big Eyes Schurz agreed to the arrest" (Brown 364).

**C. When the listed name or title is stated in the text, cite only the page number.**
Brown avers that Big Eyes Schurz agreed to it (364).

**D. For works of multiple volumes, use a colon after the volume number.**

*Sample bibliographic entry*
Pepys, Samuel. *The Diary of Samuel Pepys*. Ed. Robert Latham and William Matthews. 10 vols. Berkeley: University of California Press, 1972.

*Sample citation*
On the last day of 1665, Pepys took the occasion of the new year to reflect, but not to celebrate (6: 341–2).

**E. For works quoted in secondary sources, use the abbreviation "qtd. in."**

*Sample citation*
According to R. Bentley, "reason and the facts outweigh a hundred manuscripts" (qtd. in "History" 615).

**F. For classic works that are available in various editions,** give the page number from the edition you are using, followed by a semicolon; then identify the section of the work to help people with other editions find the reference.

**5.45 FOOTNOTES AND ENDNOTES.** Parenthetical documentation, described in 5.44, is the most common of many accepted systems. Footnoting and endnoting are two other accepted methods.

**FOOTNOTES.** Instead of putting citations in parentheses within the text, you can place them at the bottom or foot of the page; hence the term **footnote**. In this system, a number or symbol is placed in the text where the parenthetical citation would otherwise be, and a matching number or symbol, at the bottom of the page, identifies the citation. For example, *Literature and the Language Arts* uses numbered footnotes in the literature selections to define obscure words and to provide background information.

**ENDNOTES.** Many books use endnotes instead of footnotes. Endnotes are like footnotes in that a number or symbol is placed within the text, but the matching citations are compiled at the end of the book, chapter, or article rather than at the foot of the page.

Footnote and endnote entries begin with the author's (or editor's) name in its usual order (first, then last) and include publication information and a page reference.

---

### SAMPLE FOOTNOTE OR ENDNOTE CITATIONS

| | |
|---|---|
| **A BOOK WITH ONE AUTHOR** | [1]Jean Paul-Sartre, *Being and Nothingness* (New York: The Citadel Press, 1966) 149–151. |
| **A BOOK WITH ONE EDITOR AND NO SINGLE AUTHOR** | [2]Shannon Ravenel, ed., *New Stories from the South: The Year's Best, 1992* (Chapel Hill, NC: Algonquin Books, 1992) 305. |
| **A MAGAZINE ARTICLE** | [3]Andrew Gore, "Road Test: The Apple Powerbook," *MacUser,* December 1996: 72. |

---

## TEST-TAKING SKILLS

### 5.46 Preparing for Tests

Tests are a common part of school life. These guidelines will help you to prepare for and take a test.

**PREPARING FOR A TEST**

- **Know exactly what you will be tested on**. If you have questions, ask your teacher.

- **Make a study plan** to allow yourself time to go over the material. Avoid last-minute cramming.

- **Review the subject matter**. Use your notes, your SQ3R strategy, and any study questions given by your teacher.

- **Make lists** of important names, dates, definitions, or events. Ask a friend or family member to quiz you on them.

- **Try to predict questions** that may be on the test. Make sure you can answer them.

- **Get plenty of sleep** the night before the test.

Eat a nutritious breakfast on the morning of the test.

**TAKING A TEST**

- **Survey the test** to see how long it is and what types of questions are included.

- **Read all directions and questions** carefully. Make sure that you know exactly what to do.

- **Plan your time**. Answer easy questions first. Allow extra time for complicated questions. If a question seems too difficult, skip it and go back to it later. Work quickly, but do not rush.

- **Save time for review**. Once you have finished, look back over the test. Double-check your answers, but do not change answers too often. Your first ideas are often the correct ones.

### 5.47 Taking Objective Tests

**Objective tests** require simple right-or-wrong answers. This chart describes the kinds of questions you may see on objective tests.

| DESCRIPTION | GUIDELINES |
|---|---|
| **True/False.** You are given a statement and asked to tell whether the statement is true or false. | • If any part of a statement is false, then the statement is false.<br>• Words like *all, always, never,* and *everyone* often appear in false statements.<br>• Words like *some, usually, often,* and *most* often appear in true statements.<br>• If you do not know the answer, guess. You have a 50/50 chance of being right. |
| **Matching.** You are asked to match items in one column with items in another column. | • Check the directions. See if each item is used only once. Also check to see if some are not used at all.<br>• Read all items before starting.<br>• Match those you know first.<br>• Cross out items as you match them. |
| **Multiple Choice.** You are asked to choose the best answer from a group of answers given. | • Read *all* choices first.<br>• Rule out incorrect answers.<br>• Choose the answer that is most complete or accurate.<br>• Pay particular attention to choices such as *none of the above* or *all of the above.* |
| **Short Answer.** You are asked to answer the question with a word, a phrase, or a sentence. | • Read the directions to find out if you are required to answer in complete sentences.<br>• Use correct spelling, grammar, punctuation, and capitalization.<br>• If you cannot think of the answer, move on. Something in another question might remind you of the answer. |

## 5.48 Strategies for Taking Standardized Tests

**Standardized tests** are given to many students in a school district, a state, or a country. You may already have taken a standardized test, such as the Iowa Test of Basic Skills, and you certainly will take more during your school career. Some standardized tests, such as the Scholastic Aptitude Test, or SAT, are used to determine entrance to colleges and universities. Others must be passed to enter certain vocations or professions. A standardized test measures overall ability, or achievement over a period of time. Learning how to take standardized tests well can help you to achieve your academic and career goals.

When selecting an answer on a standardized test, remember these points:

• If you do not know the answer, try to rule out some choices and then guess from those remaining.

• If a question seems too difficult, skip it and go back to it later. Be aware, however, that most tests allow you to go back to questions only within a section.

- Always follow the instructions of the test monitor.

**5.49 ANALOGY QUESTIONS. Analogy questions** ask you to find the relationship between a given pair of words and then to recognize a similar relationship between another pair of words. In an analogy question, the symbols : and :: mean "is to" and "as," respectively. The example below would be "Mare is to horse as . . ." when read aloud. To answer an analogy question, examine all of the answers. If more than one answer seems correct, choose the best one.

To answer an analogy question, think of a sentence that relates the two words. For example, you might think of the sentence "A *mare* is a female *horse*." Then look for another pair of words that would make sense in that sentence: "A *doe* is a female *deer*."

EXAMPLE

MARE : HORSE ::
(A) lamb : sheep
(B) man : woman
(C) boy : girl
(D) bee : wasp
(E) doe : deer

The answer is E.

**5.50 SYNONYM AND ANTONYM QUESTIONS. Synonym** and **antonym questions** give you a word and ask you to select the word that has the same meaning (for a synonym) or the opposite meaning (for an antonym). You must select the best answer, even if none is exactly correct. For this type of question, you should try all the choices to see which one works best. Always know whether you are looking for a synonym or an antonym, because you will usually find both among the answers.

EXAMPLE

Write the letter of the word that is most nearly the opposite in meaning to the word in capital letters.
1. AMIABLE
 (A) capable
 (B) friendly
 (C) hostile
 (D) lovely

The answer is C.

**5.51 SENTENCE COMPLETION QUESTIONS. Sentence completion questions** present you with a sentence that has two words missing. You must select the pair of words that best completes the sentence.

EXAMPLE

The expansion of Cedar Hospital was largely_____by the citizens of Minor county, even though it was a major_____for the taxpayers.
 (A)   needed...contribution
 (B)   cheered...burden
 (C)   criticized...expense
 (D)   welcomed...dilemma

The answer is B.

**5.52 READING COMPREHENSION QUESTIONS. Reading comprehension questions** give you a short piece of writing and then ask you several questions about it. The questions may ask you to figure out something based on information in the passage. Use the following strategies when answering reading comprehension questions:

**STEPS IN ANSWERING READING COMPREHENSION QUESTIONS**

1. Read all the questions quickly.
2. Read the passage with the questions in mind.
3. Reread the first question carefully.
4. Scan the passage, looking for key words related to the question. When you find a key word, slow down and read carefully.
5. Answer the first question.
6. Repeat this process to answer the rest of the questions.

## 5.53 Taking Essay Tests

An **essay** is a short piece of writing that expresses the writer's thoughts about a particular subject. To answer an essay question, follow these guidelines.

- **Analyze each question**. Once you understand clearly what you have to do, you will be able to organize and write more effective essays in the time available.

  First, read the *entire* question carefully. Look for key words in the question that tell you what is expected. Underline these words or write them on your own note paper. Then make sure to answer *all* parts of the question.

- **Organize your answer.** Determining how you will spend the time available is an important part of planning an essay. Allow time for planning, writing, and reviewing. Before you begin writing, make a rough outline of the main points you will make. Include main points and key details. Later, if you find yourself running out of time, try at least to state your remaining main points and to add a conclusion.

- **Write a clear introduction.** This will help to keep you on track as you write each paragraph. Your introduction should state the thesis, or main idea, of your essay and should briefly answer the question. In the rest of the essay, you can elaborate on your answer, providing evidence to support it.

- **Review your answer**. Before you turn in your completed essay, take time to review and polish it.

### UNDERSTANDING AN ESSAY QUESTION

| TYPE OF ESSAY QUESTION | TASKS OF ESSAY |
|---|---|
| **analyze** | break into parts and describe the parts and their relationships |
| **compare; compare and contrast** | identify and describe similarities and differences |
| **describe; explain** | tell the steps in a process; identify causes and effects |
| **define; describe; identify** | classify and tell the features of |
| **interpret** | tell the meaning and significance of |
| **summarize** | retell very briefly, stating only the main points |
| **argue; prove; show** | tell and evaluate reasons for believing a statement |

### QUESTIONS FOR REVIEWING AN ANSWER TO AN ESSAY QUESTION

- Does the essay answer all parts of the question?
- Does the introduction state clearly the main idea of the essay?
- Does the body of the essay provide evidence to support the main idea?
- Does the essay cover all the points in my rough outline?
- Are there any points that could be made more strongly or clearly?
- Is every word in the essay easily readable?
- Is the essay free of errors in grammar, usage, and mechanics?

# APPLIED ENGLISH
## Resource

## THE IMPORTANCE OF APPLIED ENGLISH

**Applied English** is English in the world of work, or practical English. When you apply English skills to real-world situations, you are using your reading, writing, speaking, and listening abilities for practical reasons.

## 6.1 Filling Out Forms

Entering a new school, going to a new doctor, registering computer software, applying for a job—these are but a few of the thousands of activities that involve filling out forms. The following guidelines will help you to complete a form in a way that will make a good impression.

GUIDELINES FOR COMPLETING FORMS

- Get an extra copy or make a photocopy of the form so that you can complete a practice form.

- Read through the directions and the form itself before completing it.

- Gather the information you will need to complete the form. This information may include former addresses, dates of events, or a social security number.

- Complete the form neatly. Avoid smudges or cross-outs. Use the writing method requested on the form. Most forms request that you either type or use black or blue ink.

- Do not leave any lines blank. Use N.A. for "not applicable" if a request for information does not apply to you. For example, if you have always lived at the same address, you would write N.A. in the blank following "Previous Addresses."

- Proofread your information for errors in punctuation, spelling, or grammar. Make sure all information is correct.

- Submit the form to the appropriate person or address. Use an envelope or folder to keep the form neat and clean.

- Keep a copy of the form for your own records.

## 6.2 Following Directions

Every day people all over the world face the challenge of doing something they have never done before. Despite their inexperience, many people are able to succeed because they are able to follow directions. At the same time, someone must be able to give them clear, precise directions. Consider these guidelines before you begin following or giving directions.

GUIDELINES FOR FOLLOWING DIRECTIONS

- If the directions are being given in written form, read them carefully before beginning the procedure. If they are being given in spoken form, take notes as you listen. Ask for clarification if something is confusing.

- If written directions include any vocabulary or technical words you do not understand, look them up in a dictionary, or see if the materials include footnotes, a glossary, or an appendix. If an instructor uses words you do not understand, ask him or her to rephrase.

- Take your time and make sure you have performed each step carefully and accurately before proceeding to the next step.

- If you get stuck while following directions, retrace your steps or reread the step you are on. If they are available, consult diagrams, maps, or illustrations. You might find it helpful to ask someone else to read the directions and see if they arrive at the same conclusion as you do. If the directions include a "help hotline" or other contact information, you may want to use it.

## 6.3 Giving Directions

- Think through the directions completely, from start to finish, before you begin.

- Give each step in the order in which it should be taken.

- Include all necessary steps. Do not assume that your reader or listener already knows any part of the directions unless you are absolutely sure that this is the case.

- Do not include any unnecessary steps.

- Use simple language that can be understood easily.

- Use transition words such as *first, second, third, next, then,* and *finally* to connect your ideas.

- When possible, use a parallel or similar sentence structure for each part of the directions.

- When giving directions orally, ask the listener to repeat the directions to you when you have finished. This way you can check to make sure that your directions have been understood.

- If the directions that you are giving are complicated, put them into writing. Number each direction to help you and your reader to keep the steps separate and clear. You may also wish to include a map, diagram, or other illustration to accompany the written directions. For more information, see the Language Arts Survey 6.11, "Displaying Effective Visual Information."

## 6.4 Writing a Step-by-Step Procedure

A **step-by-step procedure** is a how-to or process piece that uses directions to teach someone something new. Written procedures include textual information and sometimes graphics. Spoken procedures can be given as oral demonstrations. They can include textual and graphic information and other props.

Examples of step-by-step procedures include an oral demonstration of how to saddle a horse; instructions on how to treat a sprained ankle; a video showing how to do the perfect lay-up in basketball; and an interactive Internet site allowing the user to design and send a bouquet of flowers.

To write a step-by-step procedure, review the Language Arts Survey 6.3, "Giving Directions," and 6.11, "Displaying Effective Visual Information."

- If you are showing how to make something, create several different samples to show each step of the procedure. For example, if you are showing how to make a wooden basket, you might want to display the raw materials, the started basket, the basket halfway finished, and then the finished product. You might also want to have a sample showing a variation—a different type of weaving, for example, that the finished product may not have.

- Be prepared. The best way to prevent problems is to anticipate and plan for them. Rehearse an oral demonstration several times. If you are preparing the procedure in written form, go through your directions as if you knew nothing about the process. Anticipate what it would be like to learn this procedure for the first time. See if you can follow your own directions or have a friend work through the procedure and offer suggestions for improvement.

- Acknowledge mistakes. If you are sharing a procedure "live" as an oral demonstration and you can't talk around or correct a mistake, tell your audience what has gone wrong, and why. If you handle the situation in a calm, direct way, the audience may also learn from your mistake.

- Know your topic well. The better you know it, the better you will be able to teach others.

## 6.5 Writing a Business Letter

A **business letter** is usually addressed to someone you do not know personally. Therefore, a formal tone is appropriate for such a letter.

Following appropriate form is especially important when writing business letters. If you follow the correct form, and avoid errors in spelling, grammar, usage, and mechanics, your letter will sound professional and make a good impression.

A business letter should contain an inside address above the salutation including the name and title of the person to whom you are writing and the name and address of that person's company or organization (see the model on the following page).

One common form for a business letter is the block form. In the block form, each part of the letter begins at the left margin. The parts are separated by line spaces.

Begin the salutation with the word *Dear*, followed by the courtesy or professional title used in the inside address, such as *Ms., Mr.,* or *Dr.,* and a colon. If you are not writing to a specific person, you may use a general salutation such as *Dear Sir or Madam*.

In the body of your letter, use a polite, formal tone and standard English. Make your points clearly, in as few words as possible.

End with a standard closing such as *Sincerely, Yours truly,* or *Respectfully yours*. Capitalize only the first word of the closing. Type your full name below the closing, leaving three or four blank lines for your signature. Sign your name below the closing in blue or black ink (never in red or green). Proofread your letter before you send it. Poor spelling, grammar, or punctuation can ruin an otherwise well-written business letter.

### GUIDELINES FOR WRITING A BUSINESS LETTER

- Outline your main points before you begin.
- Word process your letter, if at all possible. Type or print it on clean 8 1/2" x 11" white or off-white paper. Use only one side of the paper.
- Use the block form or another standard business letter form.
- Single space, leaving a blank line between each part, including paragraphs.
- Use a standard salutation and a standard closing.
- Stick to the subject. State your main idea clearly at the beginning of the letter. Keep the letter brief and informative.
- Check your spelling, grammar, usage, and punctuation carefully.

### STUDENT MODEL

Jorge loves snorkeling and wants to get a summer job working part time in a dive shop. This is a copy of the letter that he sent to the owner of the shop.

498 Blue Key Rd.
Charleston, SC 02716

May 3, 2002

Mr. Davy Jones, Owner
Deep Sea Divers, Inc.
73 Ocean St.
Charleston, SC 02716

Dear Mr. Jones:

Please consider me for a position as a part-time clerk in your store for the coming summer. I understand that in the summer your business increases considerably and that you might need a conscientious, hard-working clerk. I can offer you considerable knowledge of snorkeling and diving equipment and experience working in a retail shop.

I will be available for work three days per week between June 1 and August 12. I am enclosing a résumé and references. Please contact me if you wish to set up an interview.

Sincerely,

*Jorge Alvarez*

Jorge Alvarez

## 6.6 Writing a Memo

In businesses, schools, and other organizations, employees, students, and others often communicate by means of memoranda, or **memos.** For example, the director of a school drama club might write a memo to the editor of the student newspaper announcing tryouts for a new play.

Some memos will be more informal than others. If you know the person to whom you are writing well or if the memo has only a social function such as announcing a party, the tone can fairly informal. Most memos, however, have a fairly formal tone.

A memo begins with a header. Often this header contains the word *memorandum* (the singular form of memoranda) and the following words and abbreviations:

TO:
FR: (from)
DT: (date)
RE: (regarding)
cc: (copy)

### Student Model

Jack Hart, the president of the drama club at Wheaton High School, wishes to have the upcoming tryouts for his club's production of *Oklahoma!* announced in the school newspaper. He decides to write a memo to the editor of the paper, Lisa Lowry.

MEMORANDUM

TO: Lisa Lowry
FR: Jack Hart          CC: Ms. Wise
RE: Tryouts for the spring production of *Oklahoma!*
DT: February 12, 2002

Please include the following announcement in the upcoming issue of the *Wheaton Crier:* Tryouts for the Wheaton Drama Club's spring production of *Oklahoma!* will be held on Friday, February 26, at 6:00 P.M. in the Wheaton High School Auditorium. Students interested in performing in this musical should come to the auditorium at that time prepared to deliver a monologue less than two minutes long and to sing one song from the musical. Copies of the music and lyrics can be obtained from the sponsor of the Wheaton Drama Club, Ms. Wise. For additional information, please contact Ms. Wise or any member of the Drama Club.

Thank you.

## 6.7 Writing a Proposal

A **proposal** outlines a project that a person wants to complete. It presents a summary of an idea, the reasons why the idea is important, and an outline of how the project would be carried out. Because the proposal audience is people who can help carry out the proposal, a proposal is both informative and persuasive.

EXAMPLES

- You want funding for an art project that would benefit your community

- Your student council proposes a clothing drive for disaster relief

- You and a group of your friends want to help organize a summer program for teens your age

**Proposal:** To host a community arts day at the park behind Jordan High School that would allow high school artists to try new art forms and to exhibit their work.

**Rationale:** The art students at Jordan High School have shown there is a lot of talent here worth sharing. An Arts Day would let everyone interested get involved and build school and community pride. Art students could lead others through simple art projects and people could learn new things. At the end, the art could be displayed in an art fair at the community park. Artwork and refreshments could be sold, with all proceeds going to the Jordan High School Art Scholarship Fund.

### Schedule/Preparation Outline

| | |
|---|---|
| Present proposal to School Pride Committee | April 1 |
| Meet with art students to organize event | April 6–15 |
| Contact area businesses for donations | April 6–15 |
| Advertise event and sell tickets | April 16–25 |
| Practice day to make sure art activities work | April 20 |
| Community Arts Day | April 26 |

### BUDGET

**Expenses**

| | |
|---|---|
| Posters, mailings, tickets | $30 |
| Art supplies | $200 |
| Refreshments | $75 |

Note: Expenses will be fewer if we ask area businesses to help sponsor event

| | |
|---|---|
| Total estimated expenses | $305 |

**Income**

| | |
|---|---|
| Ticket sales  (estimated 150 tickets sold @ $3 each) | $450 |
| Refreshment sales | $100 |
| Earnings from art sold at exhibit | $200 |
| Total estimated income | $750 |
| Net proceeds | $445 |

Note: All proceeds will be donated to the Jordan High School Art Scholarship Fund

---

**GUIDELINES FOR WRITING A PROPOSAL**

- Keep the tone positive, courteous, and respectful.
- State your purpose and rationale briefly and clearly.
- Give your audience all necessary information. A proposal with specific details makes it clear what you want approved, and why your audience—often a committee or someone in authority—should approve it.
- Use standard, formal English.
- Format your proposal with headings, lists, and schedules to make your proposed project easy to understand and approve.

## 6.8 Writing a Résumé

A **résumé** is a summary of a job applicant's career objectives, previous employment experience, and education. Its purpose is to help the applicant obtain the job he or she seeks. A résumé should be accompanied by a cover letter to the employer (see an example in the Language Arts Survey 6.5, "Writing a Business Letter"). Many helpful books and articles are available in libraries and bookstores on writing a résumé. Here are some guidelines.

### GUIDELINES FOR WRITING A RÉSUMÉ

- Keep your information brief—to one page if possible. The goal of the resume is to give a potential employer a quick snapshot of your skills and abilities.

- Include all vital contact information—name, address, phone number, and e-mail address, if applicable—at the top of the page.

- Use heads to summarize information regarding job or career objective, education, work experience, skills, extracurricular activities, awards (if applicable), and references. Note that work experience should be listed starting with your most recent job and working backward.

- Key or type your résumé on white or cream-colored paper. Proofread it carefully for any errors; all facts must be accurate as well. Make it as neat as possible.

- You may list references, or simply state that they are available on request.

---

### Pat Mizos
5555 Elm Street
Anytown, NY 20111
(212) 555-5555

**Objective:**
To gain employment working in a summer camp program for children

**Education:**
Orchard High School, 2001 graduate

Major area of study: College preparatory, with concentration in science and physical education classes

Grade point average: 3.5 (B+)

**Work experience:**
Summer 1999    Summer youth counselor, Anytown Parks and Recreation Department

Summer 1998    Dishwasher, the Lobster Shack Anytown, NY

**Skills:**
Intermediate-level Spanish (Three years in high school)
Beginning-level American Sign Language (One semester at Anytown Vocational School)
Certified in CPR

**Extracurricular activities:**
Swim team, tennis team, youth hotline crisis volunteer

**References:**
Available on request

## 6.9 Delivering a Press Release

A **press release** is an informative piece intended for publication in local news media. A press release is usually written to promote an upcoming event or to inform the community of a recent event that promotes, or strengthens, an individual or organization.

EXAMPLES

- a brief notice from the choir director telling the community of the upcoming spring concert
- an informative piece by the district public information officer announcing that your school's art instructor has been named the state Teacher of the Year

GUIDELINES FOR WRITING A PRESS RELEASE

- Know your purpose. What do you want your audience to know from reading your piece?
- Use the 5 *Ws* and an *H*—*who, what, where, when, why,* and *how*—questioning strategy to convey the important information at the beginning of your story. (For more information, see the Language Arts Survey 2.14, "Questioning: Using the 5 *Ws* and an *H.*")
- Keep the press release brief. Local media are more likely to publish or broadcast your piece if it is short and to the point.
- Include contact information such as your name, phone number, and times you can be reached. Make this information available to the media representative or, if applicable, to the reading public.
- Type your press release using conventional manuscript form. Make sure the text is double-spaced and that you leave margins of at least an inch on all sides of the page.
- At the beginning of the press release, key the day's date and the date the information is to be released. (You can type "For immediate release" or designate the date you would like the press release to be printed in the newspaper.)
- At the end of the press release, key the word "END."
- Check a previous newspaper for deadline information or call the newspaper office to make sure you get your material there on time. Address the press release to the editor.

## 6.10 Writing a Public Service Announcement

A **public service announcement**, or PSA, is a brief, informative article intended to be helpful to the community. PSAs are written by nonprofit organizations and concerned citizens for print in local newspapers, for broadcast by television and radio stations, and for publication on the Internet.

EXAMPLES

- an article by the American Cancer Society outlining early warning signs of cancer
- an announcement promoting Safety Week
- an informative piece telling coastal residents what to do during a hurricane

GUIDELINES FOR WRITING A PUBLIC SERVICE ANNOUNCEMENT

- Know your purpose. What do you want your audience to know from reading or hearing your piece?
- State your information as objectively as possible.
- As with most informative writing, use the 5 *Ws* and an *H*—*who, what, where, when, why,* and *how*—questioning strategy to get your important information at the beginning of your story.
- Keep your announcement brief. Local media are more likely to publish or broadcast your piece if it is short and to the point.
- Include contact information in case the media representative has any questions. You might also include contact information in the PSA itself.
- Key or type your PSA in conventional manuscript form. Make sure the text is double-spaced and that you leave margins of at least an inch on all sides of the page.
- At the end of the PSA, key "END" to designate the end of the announcement.
- Be aware of print and broadcast deadlines and make sure your material is sent on time.

## 6.11 Displaying Effective Visual Information

People frequently learn things best and remember more when information is presented visually. Whenever possible, use charts, tables, pictures, slides, photographs, models, and art to express key points.

### Purposes of Visuals

- focus and hold audience attention
- help the audience grasp facts quickly
- clarify something complicated
- show comparisons
- emphasize key points
- summarize main thoughts
- serve as an outline or guide in a presentation

The quality of your visuals will affect your presentation. Depending on their use, visuals can detract from a presentation or enhance it. Before you use a visual, ask yourself:

- Is it attention-grabbing?
- Is it simple and neat?
- Does it serve a real purpose?
- Can I use it easily?
- Does it fit smoothly into the presentation?

The success of your presentation will depend on how you display visual information. Here are some guidelines.

### Guidelines for Displaying Visual Information

- Keep visual information simple. Do not clutter visual display with multiple lettering or font styles, too many small images, or too much textual or graphic information.
- Design your visual display in a way that the viewer's eye will naturally follow.
- Clearly label your visual display. Make it easy for the viewer to know what you are showing. Include a title or caption, labels for different parts, and simple, main points when needed.
- Make the visual visible. Type or graphics that are too small can make the best visual presentation useless. If the display is on a computer screen, make sure you can read it. If the display is for a speech or exhibit, stand back and see if you can see it from the back of the room or wherever your audience members will be. (A general rule is that one-inch letters can be read at 32 feet, two-inch letters at 64 feet, and three-inch letters at 128 feet.)
- Use bullets or numbering to organize your text. For simple presentations, use either one or the other; don't use both.
- Use color carefully. Color can add visual interest, but it can also be distracting or make a graphic or text area illegible.
- Document all sources of graphic information. The ideas in visual information are someone's intellectual property, just like the ideas in text material. Make sure you give proper credit for all work not your own.

For more information on types of visual presentations see the Language Arts Survey 1.15, "Using Graphic Aids."

## 6.12 Working on a Team

Working on a team, or doing collaborative learning, is an essential Applied English skill that depends on a strong ability to communicate. This ability can be strengthened with practice. For more information, see the Language Arts Survey 4.7–4.9, "Communicating with Others," and 4.13, "Collaborative Learning and Communication."

**ABRIDGMENT.** An **abridgment** is a shortened version of a work. When doing an abridgment, an editor attempts to preserve the most significant elements of the original. See also *abstract*, *bowdlerize*, and *paraphrase*.

**ABSTRACT.** 1. *n.* An **abstract**, *précis,* or **summary** is a brief account of the main ideas or arguments presented in a work. A well-made abstract presents those ideas or arguments in the same order as in the original. Writing an abstract is an excellent way to commit to memory the major ideas of a nonfiction work such as an essay or a chapter in a textbook. See *paraphrase*. 2. *adj.* An **abstract** word or phrase is one that refers to something that cannot be directly perceived by the senses. *Freedom, love, integrity, honesty,* and *loyalty* are examples of abstract terms. The opposite of *abstract* in this sense is *concrete*. See *concrete*.

**ABSURD.** See *literature of the absurd*.

**ACCENT.** See *stress*.

**ACRONYM.** An **acronym** is a word created from the first, or initial, letters of a series of words. Examples of acronyms include *scuba*, from the words *self-contained underwater breathing apparatus*, and *radar*, from *radio detecting and ranging*.

**ACROSTIC.** An **acrostic** is a poem organized so that the first or last letters of each line form a word, a phrase, or a regular sequence of letters of the alphabet.

**ACT.** An **act** is a major division of a drama. The first dramas were not divided into acts, but rather into scenes in which the actors performed and scenes in which the chorus spoke. The dramas of ancient Rome were generally divided into five acts, as were the plays of the Renaissance and the Enlightenment. In modern times, plays are most often divided into three acts, and short plays called "one-acts" are common. There are two acts in Tennessee Williams's play *The Glass Menagerie* in Unit 9.

**ACTION.** The **action** is the sequence of events that actually occur in a literary work, as opposed to those that occur off-scene or that precede or follow the events in the work itself. A common literary technique, inherited from

the classical *epic*, is to begin a work *in medias res*, in the middle of the action, and to fill in the background details later through flashbacks. This technique is often used in modern fiction, as in Ambrose Bierce's "An Occurrence at Owl Creek Bridge," in Unit 5. See *flashback*.

**ACTOR.** An **actor** is one who performs the role of a character in a play. The term is now used both for male and female performers.

**ADAGE.** See *proverb*.

**ADAPTATION.** An **adaptation** is a rewriting of a literary work in another form. In modern times, adaptations for film are often made of successful novels, musicals, and plays. Several film adaptations have been made of Tennessee Williams's play *The Glass Menagerie* (in Unit 9).

**AESTHETICS.** **Aesthetics** is the philosophical study of beauty. *Aesthetic principles* are guidelines established for the making and judging of works of art. From age to age, accepted aesthetic principles have differed, and these differences have dramatically influenced the nature of works of art produced in those ages. For example, the ancient Greek philosopher Aristotle propounded an aesthetic of *mimesis*, or *imitation*, believing that the proper function of art was to provide an accurate portrayal of life, an idea perhaps best expressed in Shakespeare's description of dramatic art as "a mirror held up to nature." In sharp contrast to such an aesthetic is the idea, derived from the Greek philosopher Plato, that the function of art is to rise above ordinary nature and to embody ideal, or *sublime*, forms of a kind not found in this material world of the ordinary and transient.

In Europe and the United States, the dominant aesthetics have been the Neoclassical, dating from the eighteenth century; the Romantic, dating from the nineteenth century; and the Realistic and Naturalistic, dating from the late nineteenth and early twentieth centuries. The Neoclassical aesthetic, typified by the works of Phillis Wheatley and Benjamin Franklin, values order, rationality, and artifice. The Romantic aesthetic, typified by the works of Edgar Allan Poe, values wildness, emotion, imagination, and nature. The Realistic aesthetic, typified by the works of Edith Wharton, Ernest Hemingway, and John Steinbeck, hearkens back to Aristotle and values imitation, but imitation of a modern kind—of the depths as well as the heights of human experience. The Naturalistic aesthetic, like the Realistic, views the purpose of art as the accurate imitation of life, but it also attempts to show how all things, including human actions, thoughts, and feelings, are caused, or determined, by circumstances. Superb Naturalist writers include Stephen Crane and Theodore Dreiser.

The critic I. A. Richards claimed that a radical shift away from an aesthetic based on beauty to one based on interest occurred in the twentieth century. While beauty, however defined, remains the guiding principle of artistic judgment in lowbrow circles—as for example, in popular judgments made about sentimental novels and verses—interest, both intellectual and emotional, has emerged as the primary standard by which professional critics today judge works of art. See *Naturalism, Neoclassicism, Realism,* and *Romanticism.*

**AFFECTIVE FALLACY.** The **affective fallacy** is the evaluation of works of art based not on their artistic merit but rather on their emotional effects on the reader, viewer, or listener. A person who holds a didactic or utilitarian view of the function of art would not consider this approach a fallacy. See *didacticism.*

**AFTERWORD.** An **afterword** is a statement made at the end of a work, often an analysis, a summary, or a celebration of the preceding work. See *epilogue.*

**AGE OF REASON.** See *Enlightenment* and *Neoclassicism.*

**AIM.** A writer's **aim** is his or her purpose, or goal. People may write with the following aims:

- to inform (expository/informational writing)
- to entertain, enrich, enlighten, and/or use an artistic medium, such as fiction or poetry, to share a perspective (imaginative writing)
- to share a story about an event, often to make a point (narrative writing)
- to reflect (personal/expressive writing)
- to persuade readers or listeners to respond in some way, such as to agree with a position, change a view on an issue, reach an agree-

ment, or perform an action (persuasive/argumentative writing)

Here are examples of writing that reflect these five aims:

*expository/informational*
    news article, research report
*imaginative*
    poem, short story
*narrative*
    biography, family history
*personal/expressive*
    diary entry, personal letter
*persuasive/argumentative*
    editorial, petition

**ALEXANDRINE.** An **Alexandrine**, or **iambic hexameter**, is a verse with six iambic feet.

**ALLEGORY.** An **allegory** is a work in which each element symbolizes, or represents, something else. Spirituals such as "Swing Low, Sweet Chariot," in Unit 5, are often allegorical. "Swing Low, Sweet Chariot" is on one level about the chariot of God that brings people to heaven, but on another level can be read as being about the Underground Railroad that carries slaves to freedom. The fiction of Nathaniel Hawthorne, in which characters, objects, and events often represent moral qualities or circumstances, is highly allegorical. In one sense, all literature can be viewed as allegorical in that individual characters, objects, places, and actions are types representing others of their kind. See *concrete universal* and *extended metaphor.*

**ALLITERATION.** **Alliteration** is the repetition of initial consonant sounds. Some writers also use the term to describe repeated initial vowel sounds. The following line from Henry Wadsworth Longfellow's "The Village Blacksmith," in Unit 4, contains the following example of alliteration:

They love to see the flaming forge

**ALLUSION.** An **allusion** is a rhetorical technique in which reference is made to a person, event, object, or work from history or literature. In *Walden,* excerpted in Unit 4, Henry David Thoreau makes allusions to many sources, including *The New England Primer,* the Bible, and Virgil's *Aeneid.* The alphabet rhymes in *The New England Primer,* excerpted in Unit 2, contain allusions to the Bible.

**AMBIGUITY.** An **ambiguity** is a statement that has a double meaning or a meaning that cannot be clearly resolved. In English, the word *cleave* is oddly ambiguous, for it can mean either "to cling together" or "to cut apart." Many literary *figures of speech*, including *metaphors*, *similes*, *personifications*, and *symbols*, are examples of intentional ambiguity, speaking of one thing when another is intended. In Poe's "The Pit and the Pendulum," in Unit 4, the prisoner exclaims "Free!—and in the grasp of the Inquisition!" after having won a small victory over his shackles. He has staved off immediate doom but is still held prisoner. Poe thus examines the ambiguity or shades of meaning of a state like freedom.

**AMPLIFICATION.** See *elaboration*.

**ANACHRONISM.** An **anachronism** is a reference to something that did not exist at the time being described. Thus, a reference to a computer in a story taking place during the Civil War would be an anachronism because computers had not been invented during the nineteenth century.

**ANAGRAM.** An **anagram** is a word or a phrase created by rearranging the letters of another word or phrase. The title of Samuel Butler's novel *Erewhon* is an anagram for *nowhere*. See *palindrome*.

**ANALOGY.** An **analogy** is a comparison of two things that are alike in some respects. Often an analogy explains or describes something unfamiliar by comparing it to something more familiar. A *simile* is an expressed analogy; a *metaphor* is an implied analogy. See *simile* and *metaphor*.

**ANALYSIS.** 1. **Analysis** is a thinking strategy in which one divides a subject into parts and then examines the relationships among the parts and between individual parts and the whole. An analysis of a short story, for example, might consist of a division of the work into such parts as the exposition, the rising action, the climax, the resolution, and the dénouement, along with an examination of the role played by each of these parts in advancing the plot. An analysis of a line of poetry might consist of a careful examination of its rhythm, its figures of speech, its images, and its meaning or meanings. 2. **Analysis** is also a way to organize exposition, a type of nonfiction writing.

**ANAPEST.** An **anapest** is a poetic foot containing two weakly stressed syllables followed by one strongly stressed syllable, as in the words *unimpressed* and *correlate*. A line of poetry made up of anapests is said to be *anapestic*.

**ANAPHORA.** An **anaphora**, as that term is used by linguists, is any word or phrase that repeats or refers to something that precedes or follows it. John F. Kennedy uses anaphora in his Inaugural Address, in Unit 11, when he repeats "Let both sides" in three successive paragraphs.

**ANECDOTE.** An **anecdote** is a usually short narrative of an interesting, amusing, or biographical incident. Although anecdotes are often the basis for short stories, an anecdote differs from a short story in that it lacks a complicated plot and relates a single episode. Anecdotes are sometimes used in nonfiction writing as examples to help support an idea or opinion.

**ANTAGONIST.** See *character*.

**ANTIHERO.** An **antihero** is a central character who lacks many of the qualities traditionally associated with heroes. An antihero may be lacking in beauty, courage, grace, intelligence, or moral scruples. Antiheroes are common figures in modern fiction and drama. In Bernard Malamud's short story "The Magic Barrel," in Unit 5, the rabbinical student Leo Finkle is an antihero. See *hero*.

**ANTITHESIS.** **Antithesis** is a rhetorical technique in which words, phrases, or ideas are strongly contrasted, often by means of a repetition of grammatical structures.

**APHORISM.** An **aphorism** is a short saying or pointed statement. Examples of aphorisms by Benjamin Franklin include "The early bird catches the worm" and "Time is money." An aphorism that gains currency and is passed from generation to generation is called a *proverb* or *adage*. See *proverb*.

**APOCRYPHA.** **Apocrypha** are works that are doubtful in their origin or authorship. The term was first used to describe works from biblical times not considered to be divinely inspired. It is now sometimes used to describe works of doubtful authorship.

**APOLOGY.** An **apology** is a literary defense. Emily Dickinson's "This is my letter to the World," in Unit 4, can be read as an apology.

**APOSTROPHE.** An **apostrophe** is a rhetorical device by which a speaker turns from the audience as a whole to address a single person or thing. Two examples of apostrophe can be found in "The Chambered Nautilus" by Oliver Wendell Holmes, in Unit 4, when the speaker addresses the sea creature and his own soul.

**APPOSITION.** An **apposition** is a grammatical form in which a thing is renamed in a different word, phrase, or clause. The title of Frederick Douglass's autobiography, excerpted in Unit 5, contains an example: *Frederick Douglass, an American Slave.*

**ARCHAIC LANGUAGE.** **Archaic language** consists of old or obsolete words or phrases such as *smote* for *hit.* Julia Ward Howe uses archaic language in "The Battle Hymn of the Republic," in Unit 5. For example, she says "Mine eyes" instead of "my eyes."

**ARCHETYPE.** An **archetype** is an inherited, often unconscious, ancestral memory or motif that recurs throughout history and literature. The notion of the archetype derives from the psychology of Carl Jung, who described archetypes as symbols from humanity's "collective unconscious." The term is often used, more generally, to refer to any element that recurs throughout the literature of the world. Thus the story of the journey, in which someone sets out on a path, experiences adventures, and emerges wiser, may be considered archetypal, for it is found in all cultures and in all times. In Eudora Welty's short story "A Worn Path" (Unit 10), the protagonist, Phoenix Jackson, makes an archetypal journey. See *motif.*

**ARGUMENT.** 1. An **argument** is a summary, in prose, of the plot or meaning of a poem or drama. 2. In nonfiction writing, an **argument** is the case for accepting or rejecting a proposition or course of action.

**ARGUMENTATION.** **Argumentation** is a type of writing that presents reasons or arguments for accepting a position or for adopting a course of action. In his essay "Why I Am Optimistic about America," in Unit 12, Daniel J. Boorstin uses argumentation to convince his readers why they should accept his position.

**ARGUMENTATIVE WRITING.** See *aim.*

**ARTICLE.** An **article** is a brief work of nonfiction on a specific topic. The term *article* is typically used of encyclopedia entries and short nonfiction works that appear in newspapers and popular magazines. The term is sometimes used as a synonym of *essay*, though the latter term often connotes a more serious, important, or lasting work. See *essay.*

**ASIDE.** An **aside** is a statement made by a character in a play, intended to be heard by the audience but not by other characters on the stage.

**ASSONANCE.** **Assonance** is the repetition of vowel sounds in stressed syllables that end with different consonant sounds. An example is the repetition in Emily Dickinson's "Because I could not stop for Death—" (Unit 4) of the long *a* sound:

We passed the fields of Gazing Grain—

**ATMOSPHERE.** See *mood.*

**AUTOBIOGRAPHY.** An **autobiography** is the story of a person's life, written by that person. Some editors and critics distinguish between autobiographies, which focus on personal experiences, and *memoirs*, which focus on public events, though the terms are often used interchangeably. *Black Boy*, excerpted in Unit 10, is the autobiography of Richard Wright.

**BACKGROUND INFORMATION.** See *flashback*, *plot*, and *setting.*

**BALLAD.** A **ballad** is a simple narrative poem in four-line stanzas, usually meant to be sung and usually rhyming *abcb. Folk ballads*, composed orally and passed by word of mouth from generation to generation, have enjoyed enormous popularity from the Middle Ages to the present. Examples of popular American ballads include "The Ballad of Casey Jones" and "Bonny Barbara Allan." *Literary ballads*, written in imitation of folk ballads, have also been very popular. The folk ballad stanza usually alternates between lines of four and three feet. Common techniques used in ballads include repeated lines, or *refrains*, and *incremental repetition*, the repetition of lines with slight, often cumulative, changes throughout the poem. See *refrain.*

**BIBLIOGRAPHY.** A **bibliography** is a list of works on a given subject or of works consulted by an author. See *List of Works Cited.*

**BIOGRAPHICAL CRITICISM.** See *criticism.*

**BIOGRAPHY.** A **biography** is the story of a person's life, told by someone other than that person.

**BLANK VERSE.** **Blank verse** is unrhymed poetry written in iambic pentameter. An *iambic pentameter* line consists of five *feet*, each containing two syllables, the first weakly stressed and the second strongly stressed. William Cullen Bryant's poem "Thanatopsis" (Unit 4) is written in blank verse.

**BLEND.** A **blend**, or **portmanteau**, is a word created by joining together two previously existing words, such as *smoke* and *fog* for *smog* or *whale* and *horse* for *walrus*.

**BOWDLERIZE.** To **bowdlerize** a piece of writing is to censor it by deleting material considered offensive. The term comes from the name of Thomas Bowdler, who published a "bowdlerized" edition of Shakespeare's works in the early nineteenth century.

**CACOPHONY.** **Cacophony** is harsh or unpleasant sound. Writers sometimes intentionally use cacophony for effect.

**CÆSURA.** A **cæsura** is a major pause in a line of poetry, as in the following line from T. S. Eliot's "The Love Song of J. Alfred Prufrock" (Unit 7):

Let us go then, | | you and I,

**CALVINISM.** **Calvinism** is a Protestant theology, or religious philosophy, based on the teachings of John Calvin. It stresses original sin, the inability of people to exercise free will, the preordination of events by God, and the choice (or election) by God of those who will be saved (the elect) and those who will be condemned. Puritanism was a Calvinist movement. See *Puritanism*.

**CANON.** A **canon** is a group of literary works considered to be authentic or worthy. The term was originally used for biblical books believed to be divinely inspired. It was later adapted to describe works that can be definitely assigned to a given author (as in *the canonical works of Mark Twain*). The term is also used to describe those works in a given literary tradition considered to be classics and thus worthy of inclusion in textbooks, in anthologies, and on the reading lists of courses in schools and universities. In the eighteenth century, there was much debate in France and England concerning whether the canon should include primarily modern or ancient works. In the twentieth century, debates over the canon centered on the inattention given works by non-male, non-European writers. Feminist critics, in particular, noted the tendency of male editors and anthologists to include in their collections works by male writers and to exclude works by female writers. See *feminist criticism* under the entry for *criticism*.

**CANTO.** A **canto** is a section or part of a long poem. The word comes from the Latin *cantus*, meaning "song." Ezra Pound's masterwork was a collection of poems called *The Cantos*.

**CARICATURE.** In literature, a **caricature** is a piece of writing that exaggerates certain qualities of a character in order to satirize or ridicule that character or type. See *satire*.

**CATALOG.** A **catalog** is a list of people or things. In his poem "Song of Myself" (excerpted in Unit 5), Walt Whitman catalogs plants, animals, people, and general elements of nature.

**CATASTROPHE.** The **catastrophe** is a conclusion of a work, particularly of a tragedy, marked by the fall of the central character. In the catastrophe, the central conflict of the play is ended, or resolved. See *plot*.

**CATHARSIS.** The ancient Greek philosopher Aristotle described tragedy as bringing about a **catharsis**, or purging, of the emotions of fear and pity. Some critics take Aristotle's words to mean that viewing a tragedy causes the audience to feel emotions of fear and pity, which are then released at the end of the play, leaving the viewer calm, wiser, and perhaps more thoughtful. The idea that catharsis calms an audience has been contradicted by recent psychological studies that suggest that people tend to imitate enacted feelings and behaviors that they witness. Much of the current debate over violence on television and in movies centers on this question of whether viewing such violence has a cathartic (calming) or an arousing effect on the viewer.

**CENSORSHIP.** **Censorship** is the act of examining works to see if they meet predetermined standards of political, social, or moral acceptability. Official censorship is aimed at works that will undermine authority or morals and has often in the past resulted in the suppression of works considered dangerous or licentious. Famous American novels that have been targets of censorship include *Adventures of Huckleberry Finn*, by Mark Twain, and *The Catcher in the Rye*, by J. D. Salinger. See *bowdlerize.*

**CENTRAL CONFLICT.** A **central conflict** is the primary struggle dealt with in the plot of a story or drama. See *conflict* and *plot.*

**CHARACTER.** A **character** is a person (or sometimes an animal) who figures in the action of a literary work. A *protagonist*, or *main character*, is the central figure in a literary work. An *antagonist* is a character who is pitted against a protagonist. *Major characters* are those who play significant roles in a work. *Minor characters* are those who play lesser roles. A *one-dimensional character*, *flat character*, or *caricature* is one who exhibits a single dominant quality, or *character trait*. A *three-dimensional*, *full*, or *rounded character* is one who exhibits the complexity of traits associated with actual human beings. A *static character* is one who does not change during the course of the action. A *dynamic character* is one who does change. A *stock character* is one found again and again in different literary works. An example of a stock character is the mad scientist of nineteenth- and twentieth-century science fiction.

**CHARACTERIZATION.** **Characterization** is the use of literary techniques to create a character. Writers use three major techniques to create characters: direct description, portrayal of characters' behavior, and representations of characters' internal states. When using direct description, the writer, through a speaker, a narrator, or another character, simply comments on the character, telling the reader about such matters as the character's appearance, habits, dress, background, personality, motivations, and so on. In portrayal of a character's behavior, the writer presents the actions and speech of the character, allowing the reader to draw his or her own conclusions from what the character says or does. When using representations of internal states, the writer reveals directly the character's private thoughts and emotions, often by means of what is known as the *internal monologue*. See *character* and *internal monologue.*

**CHIASMUS.** A **chiasmus** is a rhetorical technique in which the order of occurrence of words or phrases is reversed, as in the line "We can weather changes, but we can't change the weather."

**CHRONOLOGICAL ORDER.** **Chronological order** is the arrangement of details in order of their occurrence. It is the primary method of organization used in narrative writing. It is also common in nonfiction writing that describes processes, events, and cause and effect relationships.

**CLASSIC.** A **classic** is a work of literature that is widely held to be one of the greatest creations within a given literary tradition. The question of what works are to be considered classic, and thus the question of what constitutes the *canon*, is a much-debated one. See *canon.*

**CLASSICAL ERA.** The **Classical Era** is the period in European history that saw the flowering of the ancient Greek and Roman cultures. *Classical literature* is the literature of ancient Greece and Rome from the time of Homer and Hesiod to the fall of the Roman Empire in AD 410.

**CLASSICISM.** **Classicism** is a collection of ideas about literature and art derived from the study of works by Greeks and Romans of the *Classical Era*. Definitions of what constitutes the Classical style differ, but most would agree that the Classical aesthetic emphasizes authority, austerity, clarity, conservatism, decorum, imitation, moderation, order, reason, restraint, self-control, simplicity, tradition, and unity. Classicism is most often contrasted with *Romanticism*. See *Classical Era* and *Neoclassicism.*

**CLASSIFICATION ORDER.** **Classification order** is a method of organization in which subjects are divided into groups, or classes. These groups are then presented, one-by-one, in some reasonable order. Classification order is commonly used in exposition, or expository writing. See *exposition*, #1.

**CLICHÉ.** A **cliché** is an overused or unoriginal expression such as *quiet as a mouse* or *couch potato*. Most clichés originate as vivid, colorful expressions but soon lose their interest because of overuse. Careful writers and speakers avoid clichés, which are dull and signify lack of originality.

**CLIMAX.** The **climax** is the point of highest interest and suspense in a literary work. The term also is sometimes used to describe the *turning point* of the action in a story or play, the point at which the rising action ends and the falling action begins. See *crisis* and *plot.*

**CLOSED COUPLET.** See *couplet.*

**COHERENCE. Coherence** is the logical arrangement and progression of ideas in a speech or piece of writing. Writers achieve coherence by presenting their ideas in a logical sequence and by using transitions to show how their ideas are connected to one another. See *transition*.

**COINED WORDS. Coined words** are those that are intentionally created, often from the raw materials provided by already existing words and word parts. Examples of recently coined words include *spacewalk* and *e-mail*.

**COLLOQUIALISM. Colloquialism** is the use of informal language. Much modern poetry is characterized by its use of colloquialism.

**COMEDY.** Originally a literary work with a happy ending, a **comedy** is any lighthearted or humorous work, especially one prepared for the stage or the screen. Comedy is often contrasted with tragedy, in which the hero meets an unhappy fate. (It is perhaps only a slight exaggeration to say that comedies end with wedding bells and tragedies with funeral bells.) Comedies typically present less-than-exalted characters who display human limitations, faults, and misunderstandings. The typical progression of the action in a comedy is from initial order to a humorous misunderstanding or confusion and back to order again. Stock elements of comedy include mistaken identities, word play, satire, and exaggerated characters and events. See *tragedy*.

**COMIC RELIEF.** Writers sometimes insert into a serious work of fiction or drama a humorous scene that is said to provide **comic relief**, because it relieves the seriousness or emotional intensity felt by the audience. Paradoxically, a scene introduced for comic relief can sometimes, because of the contrast it provides, increase the perceived intensity or seriousness of the action around it.

**COMMONPLACE BOOK.** A **commonplace book** is a collection of quotations gleaned from various sources.

**COMPARATIVE LITERATURE. Comparative literature** is the study of relationships among works of literature written at different times, in different places, or in different languages. A study exploring the motif of the foundling left in a basket floating upon the waters in literature from different cultures would be an example. The latter motif is found in such widely separated stories

as Moses in the Bible and Romulus and Remus from Roman mythology.

**COMPARISON AND CONTRAST ORDER.** See *exposition*, #1.

**COMPLICATION.** The **complication** is the part of a plot in which the conflict is developed or built to its high point of intensity. See *plot*.

**CONCRETE.** A **concrete** word or phrase is one that names or describes something that can be directly perceived by one or more of the five senses. *Buffalo, geranium, storm,* and *heron* are examples of concrete terms. See *abstract*.

**CONCRETE POEM.** A **concrete poem**, or **shape poem**, is one printed or written in a shape that suggests its subject matter.

**CONFESSIONAL POETRY. Confessional poetry** is verse that describes, sometimes with painful explicitness, the private or personal affairs of the writer. Contemporary confessional poets include Sylvia Plath, Anne Sexton, and Robert Lowell.

**CONFLICT.** A **conflict** is a struggle between two forces in a literary work. A *plot* involves the introduction, development, and eventual resolution of a conflict. One side of the *central conflict* in a story or drama is usually taken by the *main character*. That character may struggle against another character, against the forces of nature, against society or social norms, against fate, or against some element within himself or herself. A struggle that takes place between a character and some outside force is called an *external conflict*. A struggle that takes place within a character is called an *internal conflict*. See *central conflict* and *plot*.

**CONNOTATION.** A **connotation** is an emotional association or implication attached to an expression. For example, the word *inexpensive* has positive emotional associations, whereas the word *cheap* has negative ones, even though the two words both *denote*, or refer to, low cost. Good writers choose their words carefully in order to express appropriate connotations. See *denotation*.

**CONSONANCE. Consonance** is a kind of slant rhyme in which the ending consonant sounds of two words match, but the preceding vowel sounds do not, as in the words *wind* and *sound*. The following line from Robert Hayden's poem "Those Winter Sundays" (Unit 11) provides an example:

then with cr**acked** hands that **ached**

**CONVENTION.** A **convention** is an unrealistic element in a literary work that is accepted by readers or viewers because the element is traditional. One of the conventions of fiction, for example, is that it uses the past tense to describe current or present action. Rhyme schemes and organization into stanzas are among the many commonly employed conventions of poetry. Violation of accepted conventions is one of the hallmarks of *avant garde* or *Modernist* literature. See *dramatic convention*.

**CONVENTIONAL SYMBOL.** See *symbol*.

**COUPLET.** A **couplet** is two lines of verse that usually rhyme. These lines from Anne Bradstreet's poem "To My Dear and Loving Husband" (Unit 2) provide an example:

If ever two were one, then surely we.
If ever man were loved by wife, then thee;

A closed couplet is a pair of rhyming lines that present a complete statement. These lines from Phillis Wheatley's "To S. M., a Young African Painter, on Seeing His Works" (Unit 3) are an example:

Cease, gentle muse! the solemn gloom of
    night
Now seals the fair creation from my sight.

A pair of rhyming iambic pentameter lines, like these, is also known as a *heroic couplet*.

**CRISIS.** In the plot of a story or a drama, the **crisis** is that point in the development of the conflict at which a decisive event occurs that causes the main character's situation to become better or worse. See *plot*.

**CRITIC.** A literary **critic** is a person who evaluates or interprets a work of literature. See *criticism*.

**CRITICAL ESSAY.** A **critical essay** is a type of informative or persuasive writing that presents an argument in support of a particular interpretation or evaluation of a work of literature. A well-constructed critical essay presents a clear *thesis*, or main idea, supported by ample evidence from the work or works being considered.

**CRITICISM.** **Criticism** is the act of evaluating or interpreting a work of art or the act of developing general guidelines or principles for such evaluation or interpretation. Over the centuries, many schools, or philosophies, of criticism have been developed. However, most readers and teachers are eclectic critics, drawing consciously or unconsciously upon various schools of critical thought. Common schools of criticism include the following:

**Biographical criticism** attempts to account for elements of literary works by relating them to events in the lives of their authors. Anne Bradstreet's "To My Dear and Loving Husband" read as a reflection of her life with her husband, Simon Bradstreet, would be an example of biographical criticism.

**Deconstructionist criticism** calls into question the idea that there is one "meaning" behind a literary work. Many works of literature contain binary, or two-part, relations that structure their meaning. For example, conventional critics believe that in *The Glass Menagerie* (Unit 9), Tennessee Williams criticizes the materialistic values of Jim as opposed to the artistic values of Tom. A deconstructionist might invite the reader to reverse the conventional assumptions about these two extremes. As such, a deconstructionist reading might argue that Williams actually meant to criticize Tom, the artist who produces illusions and believes them to be truths, a process leading inevitably to subjectivism and isolation, and that he approved of Jim because as a materialist, Jim successfully operates in the world, finding or creating purpose and connection. Such a reading deconstructs the conventional reading of the play. See *structuralist criticism*.

**Didactic criticism** evaluates works of art in terms of the moral, ethical, or political messages that they convey. Dismissal of a book as dangerous or obscene would be an example of didactic criticism.

**Feminist criticism** evaluates and interprets works of art with regard to their portrayal of or influence upon gender roles. Many feminist critics and scholars have been working to give women writers—often ignored in the past by male critics, editors, scholars, and teachers—the recognition they deserve. Other feminist critics point out gender bias in literary works by analyzing variations in literary depictions of males and females, and by analyzing the effects of literary works, activities, and movements on cultural norms related to gender. An example of feminist criticism would be an analysis of Kate Chopin's "The Story of an Hour" (Unit 6) as a representation of the effect the restricted role had on women in nineteenth-century American society.

**Formal criticism** analyzes a work of literature in terms of its genre or type. An explanation of those characteristics of Rita Dove's "Wingfoot Lake" (Unit 12) that make it a lyric poem would be an example of formal criticism.

**Freudian criticism** draws upon the works of the founder of psychoanalysis, Sigmund Freud, and generally views literary works or the parts thereof as expressions of unconscious desires, as wish fulfillment, or as neurotic sublimations of unresolved conflicts from childhood. An example of Freudian criticism would be the interpretation of the ancient Greek Oedipus myth, in which Oedipus unwittingly marries his mother, as an expression of the young male child's competition with his father for his mother's affection.

**Historical criticism** views the work of art as a product of the period in which it was produced. An example of historical criticism would be an analysis of the Puritan influence on Nathaniel Hawthorne's "Rappaccini's Daughter," in Unit 4.

**Jungian criticism** explores the presence in works of art of archetypes—unconscious images, symbols, associations, or concepts presumed to be a common inheritance of all human beings. An analysis of symbols of rebirth in a number of myths or folk tales would be an example of Jungian criticism.

**Marxist criticism**, based upon the work of the German-born political philosopher Karl Marx, evaluates and interprets works of art with regard to the material, economic forces that shape them or with regard to their origins in or depictions of struggle between the social classes. An example of Marxist criticism would be to explain the emergence of Realism in the novels of early twentieth-century American writers such as Theodore Dreiser and Sinclair Lewis as a result of increased awareness of the disparity between the classes, poor labor conditions, and urban discontent.

**Mimetic criticism**, which derives from the teachings of Aristotle, views works of art as imitations of nature or of the real world and evaluates them according to the accuracy of those portrayals. Insisting that a character is poorly drawn because he or she is unrealistic is an example of mimetic criticism.

The **New Criticism**, championed in the early-to mid-twentieth century by such critics as I. A. Richards and Cleanth Brooks, insists upon the interpretation and evaluation of literary works based on details found in the works themselves rather than on information gathered from outside the works. It disregards such matters as the life of the author, the period in which the work was written, the literary movement that led to its production, and the emotional effect of the work upon the reader. The New Critics insisted on the importance of close analysis of literary texts and the irreducibility of those texts to generalizations or paraphrases.

**Pragmatic** or **rhetorical criticism** interprets or evaluates a work of art in terms of its effects on an audience. An example of rhetorical criticism would be a reading of Poe's "The Raven" (Unit 4) that describes the various techniques used in the poem to evoke feelings of mystery, sorrow, and horror.

**Reader-response criticism** views the meaning of a text as resulting from a relationship between the text itself and the subjective experiences or consciousness of a reader. According to reader-response theory, a literary text has no meaning *per se*. It is, instead, an occasion for a participatory experience that the reader has. That experience may be meaningful or significant to the reader, but its meaning and significance will depend, in part, on what the reader brings to the text.

**Romantic** or **expressivist criticism** views a work of art as primarily an expression of the spirit, ideas, beliefs, values, or emotions of its creator. A reading of *Invisible Man* as expressive of the beliefs and emotions of Ralph Ellison would be an example of expressivist criticism.

**Structuralist criticism** analyzes works of literature and art in terms of binary, or two-part, relationships or structures. A structuralist analysis of Williams's *The Glass Menagerie*, for example, might view the characters as caught between dreams and realities, a rural Southern past and an urban Northern present, and so on.

**Textual criticism** analyzes the various existing manuscript and printed versions of a work in order to construct an original or definitive text for use by readers.

DACTYL. A **dactyl** is a poetic foot made up of a strongly stressed syllable followed by two weakly stressed syllables, as in the word *feverish*. A line of poetry made up of dactyls is said to be *dactylic*.

**DEAD METAPHOR.** A **dead metaphor** is one that is so familiar that its original metaphorical meaning is rarely thought of when the expression is used. An example is the word *nightfall*, which describes the coming of darkness as a falling object.

**DECONSTRUCTIONIST CRITICISM.** See *criticism*.

**DEFINITION.** A **definition** is an explanation of the meaning of a word or phrase. A dictionary definition typically consists of two parts: the genus, or class to which the thing belongs, and the differentia, or differences between the thing and other things of its class. Consider, for example, Ambrose Bierce's tongue-in-cheek definition of love: "A temporary insanity, cured by marriage." In this definition, insanity is the genus. The rest of the definition presents the differentia.

**DENOTATION.** The **denotation** is the basic meaning or reference of an expression, excluding its emotional associations, or *connotations*. For example, the words *dirt* and *soil* share a single common denotation. However, *dirt* has negative connotations of uncleanliness, whereas *soil* does not. See *connotation*.

**DÉNOUEMENT.** See *plot*.

**DESCRIPTION.** **Description** is a type of writing that portrays a character, an object, or a scene. Descriptions make use of *sensory details*—words and phrases that describe how things look, sound, smell, taste, or feel. Effective descriptions contain precise nouns, verbs, adverbs, and adjectives. Descriptions often use *imagery* and *figurative language*.

**DIALECT.** A **dialect** is a version of a language spoken by the people of a particular place, time, or social group. Writers often use dialect, as in Mark Twain's "The Notorious Jumping Frog of Calaveras County" (Unit 6), to give their works a realistic flavor. A *regional dialect* is one spoken in a particular place. A *social dialect* is one spoken by members of a particular social group or class.

**DIALOGUE.** 1. **Dialogue** is conversation involving two or more people or characters. Plays are made up of dialogue and stage directions. Fictional works are made up of dialogue, narration, and description. 2. **Dialogue** is also used to describe a type of literary composition in which characters debate or discuss an idea.

**DIARY.** A **diary** is a day-to-day record of a person's activities, experiences, thoughts, and feelings. Both Ralph Waldo Emerson and Henry David Thoreau kept diaries in which they recorded thoughts and feelings they later reworked into speeches and essays. See *journal*.

**DICTION.** **Diction**, when applied to writing, refers to word choice. Much of a writer's style is determined by his or her diction, the types of words that he or she chooses. Diction can be formal or informal, simple or complex, contemporary or archaic, ordinary or unusual, foreign or native, standard or dialectical, euphemistic or blunt. See *style*.

**DIDACTIC CRITICISM.** See *criticism*.

**DIMETER.** See *meter*.

**DOMINANT IMPRESSION.** See *effect*.

**DRAMA.** A **drama** is a story told through characters played by actors. The script of a drama typically consists of characters' names, *dialogue* spoken by the characters, and *stage directions*. Because it is meant to be performed before an audience, drama can be distinguished from other literary works by the central role played in it by the *spectacle*—the sensory presentation to the audience, which includes such elements as lighting, costumes, makeup, properties, set pieces, music, sound effects, and the movements and expressions of actors. Another important distinguishing feature of drama is that it is collaborative. The interpretation of the work depends not only upon the author and his or her audience, but also upon the director, the actors, and others involved in mounting a production. Two major types of drama are *comedy* and *tragedy*. See *comedy*, *dialogue*, *spectacle*, *stage directions*, and *tragedy*.

**DRAMATIC CONVENTION.** A **dramatic convention** is an unreal element in a drama that is accepted as realistic by the audience because it is traditional. Such conventions include the impersonation of characters by actors, the use of a curtain to open or close an act or a scene, the revelation of a character's thoughts through *asides* and *soliloquies*, and the removal of the so-called *fourth wall* at the front of the stage that allows the audience to see action taking place in an imagined interior. See *convention* and *suspension of disbelief*.

**DRAMATIC IRONY.** See *irony*.

**DRAMATIC MONOLOGUE.** A **dramatic monologue** is a poem that presents the speech of a single character in a dramatic situation. The speech is one side of an imagined conversation. A modern example of a dramatic monologue is "Lucinda Matlock" by Edgar Lee Masters, in Unit 7. See *soliloquy*.

**DRAMATIC POEM.** A **dramatic poem** is a verse that relies heavily on dramatic elements such as monologue (speech by a single character) or dialogue (conversation involving two or more characters). Often dramatic poems are narratives as well. In other words, they often tell stories. Types of dramatic poetry include the *dramatic monologue* and the *soliloquy*. See *poetry, lyric poem,* and *narrative poem*.

**DRAMATIS PERSONAE.** *Dramatis personae* are the characters in a literary work. The term is most often used for the characters in a drama.

**DREAM RECORD.** A **dream record** is a diary or journal in which a writer records his or her dreams. See *diary* and *journal*.

**DYNAMIC CHARACTER.** See *character*.

**DYSTOPIA.** A **dystopia** is an imaginary, horrible world, the opposite of a utopia. Dystopias are common in science fiction. A famous example of a dystopia is the society described in Ray Bradbury's *Fahrenheit 451*. See *utopia*.

**EDITORIAL.** An **editorial** is a short, persuasive piece that appears in a newspaper, magazine, or other periodical.

**EFFECT.** The **effect** of a literary work is the general impression or emotional impact that it achieves. Some writers and critics, notably Edgar Allan Poe, have insisted that a successful short story or poem is one in which each detail contributes to the overall effect, or *dominant impression,* produced by the piece.

**ELABORATION.** **Elaboration**, or **amplification**, is a writing technique in which a subject is introduced and then expanded upon by means of repetition with slight changes, the addition of details, or similar devices. In "Thanatopsis," William Cullen Bryant uses elaboration to depict the earth as a tomb.

**ELEGIAC LYRIC.** An **elegiac lyric** is a poem that expresses a speaker's feelings of loss, often because of the death of a loved one or friend. "Elegy for Jane," in Unit 10, is an elegiac lyric by Theodore Roethke.

**ELEGY.** An **elegy** is a poem that laments the dead. It is frequently long and formal in tone, but other poems can mourn death or loss as well. See *elegiac lyric*.

**ELIZABETHAN SONNET.** See *sonnet*.

**EMPHASIS.** **Emphasis** is importance placed on an element in a literary work. Writers achieve emphasis by various means, including repetition, elaboration, stress, restatement in other words, and placement in a strategic position at the beginning or end of a line or a sentence.

**END RHYME.** **End rhyme** is rhyme that occurs at the ends of lines of verse. See *rhyme*.

**END-STOPPED LINE.** An **end-stopped line** is a line of verse in which both the sense and the grammar are complete at the end of the line. The opposite of an end-stopped line is a run-on line. The following lines are end-stopped:

> Oh, oh, you will be sorry for that word!
> Give back my book and take my kiss instead.
> —Edna St. Vincent Millay

Excessive use of end-stopped lines gives verse an unnatural, halting quality. See *run-on line*.

**ENGLISH SONNET.** See *sonnet*.

**ENJAMBMENT.** See *run-on line*.

**ENLIGHTENMENT.** The **Enlightenment** was an eighteenth-century philosophical movement characterized by belief in reason, the scientific method, and the perfectibility of people and society. Thinkers of the Enlightenment Era, or Age of Reason, believed that the universe was governed by discoverable, rational principles like the laws of physics discovered by Sir Isaac Newton. By extension, they believed that people could, through application of reason, discover truths relating to the conduct of life or of society. Leading American thinkers of the Enlightenment included Benjamin Franklin and Thomas Jefferson. See *Neoclassicism*.

**EPIC.** An **epic** is a long story, often told in verse, involving heroes and gods. Grand in length and scope, an epic provides a portrait of an entire culture, of the legends, beliefs, values, laws, arts, and ways of life of a people. Famous epic poems include Homer's *Iliad* and *Odyssey*, Virgil's *Aeneid*, Dante's *The Divine Comedy*, the anonymous Old English *Beowulf*, and Milton's *Paradise Lost*.

**EPIC HERO.** See *hero*.

**EPIGRAM.** An **epigram** is a short, often witty, saying. An example of an epigram is Benjamin Franklin's "Three may keep a secret, if two of them are dead."

**EPIGRAPH.** An **epigraph** is a quotation or motto used at the beginning of the whole or part of a literary work to help establish the work's theme. T. S. Eliot uses an epigraph from Dante's *Inferno* at the beginning of "The Love Song of J. Alfred Prufrock," in Unit 7.

**EPILOGUE.** An **epilogue** is a concluding section or statement, often one that comments on or draws conclusions from the work as a whole.

**EPIPHANY.** When applied to literature, the term **epiphany** refers to a moment of sudden insight in which the essence, or nature, of a person, thing, or situation is revealed. The use of the term in this sense was introduced by James Joyce.

**EPISODE.** An **episode** is a complete action within a literary work.

**EPISTLE.** An **epistle** is a letter, especially one that is highly formal. Letters in verse are sometimes called epistles.

**EPISTOLARY FICTION. Epistolary fiction** is imaginative prose that tells a story through letters, or *epistles*. Allan Gurganus's "Reassurance," in Unit 12, is an example of epistolary fiction.

**EPITAPH.** An **epitaph** is an inscription or verse written to be used on a tomb or written in commemoration of someone who has died. The epitaph on the grave of Benjamin Franklin, written by Franklin himself, reads as follows:

> The body of
> Benjamin Franklin, printer,
> (Like the cover of an old book,
> Its contents worn out,
> And stript of its lettering and gilding)
> Lies here, food for worms!
> Yet the work itself shall not be lost,
> For it will, as he believed, appear once more
> In a new
> And more beautiful edition,
> Corrected and amended
> By its Author!

**EPITHET.** An **epithet** is a characteristic word or phrase used alongside the name of a person, place, or thing. Spring, "the season of new beginnings," is an example. Sometimes an epithet is so familiar that it can be used in place of a name. For example, you could use the epithet "Freer of Slaves" in place of "Abraham Lincoln."

**EPONYM.** An **eponym** is a person or character from whose name a word or title is derived, or a name that has become synonymous with some general characteristic or idea. Julius Cæsar is the eponym of the medical term *Cæsarean section*. The Greek actor Thespis is the eponym of the word *thespian*, another term for actor. A reference to Helen of Troy, used in place of the more general term *beauty*, or a reference to an Einstein, in place of a more general term such as *a smart person*, would be an eponym.

**ESSAY.** An **essay** is a brief work of prose nonfiction. The original meaning of essay was "a trial or attempt," and the word retains some of this original force. An essay need not be a complete or exhaustive treatment of a subject but rather a tentative exploration of it. A good essay develops a single idea and is characterized by *unity* and *coherence*. "On the Mall" by Joan Didion, in Unit 11, is an example of an essay. See *coherence* and *unity*.

**EUPHEMISM.** A **euphemism** is an indirect word or phrase used in place of a direct statement that might be considered too harsh or offensive. The phrase *passed away*, used instead of *died*, is a euphemism.

**EUPHONY. Euphony** is pleasing sound. Writers achieve euphony by various means, including repetitions of vowel and consonant sounds, rhyme, and parallelism. See *cacophony*.

**EXISTENTIALISM. Existentialism** is a twentieth-century philosophical school that assumes the essential absurdity and meaninglessness of life. Existentialist philosophers such as Albert Camus and Jean-Paul Sartre argued that existence, or being, emerges out of nothingness without any essential, or defining, nature. A human being simply finds himself or herself alive and aware without having any essential, defining direction. Any choices that a person makes in order to define himself or herself are made freely and therefore absurdly—one may as well make one choice as another. Freedom of the will is therefore seen by the Existentialist as a terrific burden, one causing anguish to people, who long for meaningfulness, not absurd choices. Another significant aspect of Existentialism is its insistence on the essential isolation of each individual consciousness and the consequent anguish of people looking for meaningful connection to others. Though many of the essential tenets of Existentialism have been discredited by contemporary philosophers, the school nonetheless exerted tremendous influence on mid-twentieth-century literature in Europe, Great Britain, and the United States. See *literature of the absurd* and *theater of the absurd*.

**EXPOSITION.** 1. **Exposition** is a type of writing that presents facts or opinions in an organized manner. Among the most common ways to organize exposition are the following: *analysis; classification; comparison-and-contrast*; and *process* or *how-to* writing. See Purpose and Organization in Nonfiction, pages 54–55, for more information. 2. In a plot, the **exposition** is that part of a narrative that provides background information, often about the characters, setting, or conflict. See *plot*.

**EXPRESSIONISM. Expressionism** is the name given to a twentieth-century movement in literature and art that reacted against *Realism* in favor of an exaggeration of the elements of the artistic medium itself, in an attempt to express ideas or feelings. The use in a play of characters named, simply, Person, Mother, and Character 1 is an example of Expressionism. Tennessee Williams's *The Glass Menagerie* (Unit 9), with its unrealistic setting and its generous use of symbolism, is an example of Expressionism.

**EXPOSITORY WRITING.** See *aim*.

**EXPRESSIVE WRITING.** See *aim*.

**EXTENDED METAPHOR.** An **extended metaphor** is a point-by-point presentation of one thing as though it were another. The description is meant as an implied comparison, inviting the reader to associate the thing being described with something that is quite different from it. Emily Dickinson's "Because I could not stop for Death—" (Unit 4) is an extended metaphor, in which Death is characterized as a carriage driver and the speaker of the poem as his passenger.

**EXTERNAL CONFLICT.** See *conflict*.

**EYE RHYME.** See *sight rhyme*.

**FABLE.** A **fable** is a brief story, often with animal characters, told to express a moral. Famous fables include those of Æsop and Jean de La Fontaine.

**FAIRY TALE.** A **fairy tale** is a story that deals with mischievous spirits and other supernatural occurrences, often in medieval settings. The name is generally applied to stories of the kinds collected by Charles Perrault in France and the Brothers Grimm in Germany or told by Hans Christian Andersen of Denmark. "Cinderella" and "The Little Mermaid" are famous examples.

**FALLING ACTION.** See *plot*.

**FANTASY.** A **fantasy** is a literary work that contains highly unrealistic elements. Fantasy is often contrasted with *science fiction*, in which the unreal elements are given a scientific or pseudo-scientific basis. See *magical realism* and *science fiction*.

**FARCE.** A **farce** is a type of comedy that depends heavily on so-called low humor and on improbable, exaggerated, extreme situations or characters.

**FEMINIST CRITICISM.** See *criticism*.

**FICTION. Fiction** is prose writing about imagined events or characters. The primary forms of fiction are the *novel* and the *short story*.

**FIGURATIVE LANGUAGE. Figurative language** is writing or speech meant to be understood imaginatively instead of literally. Many writers, especially poets, use figurative language to help readers to see things in new ways. Figurative language includes such literary techniques as *apostrophe, hyperbole, irony, metaphor, metonymy, oxymoron, paradox, personification, simile, synecdoche*, and *understatement*.

**FIRST-PERSON POINT OF VIEW.** See *point of view*.

**FLASHBACK.** A **flashback** is a section of a literary work that presents an event or series of events that occurred earlier than the current time in the work. Writers use flashbacks for many purposes, but most notably to provide *background information,* or exposition. In popular melodramatic works, including modern romance fiction and detective stories, flashbacks are often used to end suspense by revealing key elements of the plot such as a character's true identity or the actual perpetrator of a crime. One common technique is to begin a work with a final event and then to tell the rest of the story as a flashback that explains how that event came about. Another common technique is to begin a story *in medias res* (in the middle of the action) and then to use a flashback to fill in the events that occurred before the opening of the story.

**FLASH FICTION.** See *short short*.

**FLAT CHARACTER.** See *character*.

**FOIL.** A **foil** is a character whose attributes, or characteristics, contrast with, and therefore throw into relief, the attributes of another character.

**FOLK BALLAD.** See *ballad*.

**FOLK SONG.** A **folk song** is a traditional or composed song typically made up of stanzas, a refrain, and a simple melody. A form of folk literature, folk songs are expressions of commonly shared ideas or feelings and may be narrative or lyric in style. Traditional folk songs are anonymous songs that have been transmitted orally. Examples include the ballad "Bonny Barbara Allan," the sea chantey "Blow the Man Down," the children's song "Row, Row, Row Your Boat," the spiritual, "Go Down, Moses," the railroad song "Casey Jones," and the cowboy song "The Streets of Laredo." Contemporary composers of songs in the folk tradition include Bob Dylan, Joan Baez, Pete Seeger, and Joni Mitchell. See *ballad*.

**FOLK TALE.** A **folk tale** is a brief story passed by word-of-mouth from generation to generation. Writers often make use of materials from folk tales. Famous collections of folk tales include the German *Märchen*, or fairy tales, collected by the Brothers Grimm; Yeats's collection of Irish stories, *Mythologies;* and Zora Neale Hurston's collection of African-American folk tales and other folklore materials, *Of Mules and Men*. See *fairy tale, folklore,* and *oral tradition*.

**FOLKLORE.** **Folklore** is a body of orally transmitted beliefs, customs, rituals, traditions, songs, verses, or stories. *Folk tales, fables, fairy tales, tall tales, nursery rhymes, proverbs, legends, myths, parables, riddles, charms, spells,* and *ballads* are all common kinds of folklore, though each of these can be found, as well, in literary forms made in imitation of works from the oral tradition. See *folk tale, fable, fairy tale, tall tale, nursery rhyme, proverb, legend, myth, parable, riddle,* and *ballad*.

**FOOT.** In a poem, a **foot** is a unit of rhythm consisting of strongly and weakly stressed syllables. See *meter* and *scansion*. Also see the specific types of feet: *anapest, dactyl, iamb, spondee,* and *trochee*.

**FORESHADOWING.** **Foreshadowing** is the act of presenting materials that hint at events to occur later in a story. In "Rappaccini's Daughter" (Unit 4), when Guasconti first sees the figure of Rappaccini, the latter man's "demeanor was that of one walking among malignant influences, . . . which . . . would wreak upon him some terrible fatality." The events of the tale lead inexorably to the grim conclusion foreshadowed in that line.

**FOREWORD.** See *preface*.

**FORMAL CRITICISM.** See *criticism*.

**FOURTEENER.** See *meter*.

**FOURTH WALL.** See *dramatic convention*.

**FRAME TALE.** A **frame tale** is a story that itself provides a vehicle for the telling of other stories. Mark Twain's "The Notorious Jumping Frog of Calaveras County" (Unit 6) is written as a frame tale.

**FREE VERSE.** **Free verse** is poetry that avoids use of regular rhyme, meter, or division into stanzas. Much of the poetry written in the twentieth century is in free verse. Free verse is also referred to as *open verse*.

**FREUDIAN CRITICISM.** See *criticism*.

**FULL CHARACTER.** See *character*.

**GENRE.** A **genre** (zhän' rə) is one of the types or categories into which literary works are divided. Some terms used to name literary genres include *autobiography, biography, comedy, drama, epic, essay, lyric, narrative, novel, pastoral, poetry, short story,* and *tragedy*. Literary works are sometimes classified into genres based on subject matter. Such a classification might describe *detective stories, mysteries, adventure stories, romances, westerns,* and *science fiction* as different genres of fiction.

**GOTHIC FICTION.** **Gothic fiction** is a style of fiction characterized by the use of medieval settings, a murky atmosphere of horror and gloom, and grotesque, mysterious, or violent incidents. Essential to Gothic fiction is a setting that evokes strong feelings of foreboding or anticipation. Many of Edgar Allan Poe's stories, including "The Pit and the Pendulum" (Unit 4), are good examples of Gothic fiction. Toni Morrison is a contemporary writer who occasionally includes Gothic elements in her writing, most notably in her Pulitzer Prize-winning novel *Beloved*.

**HAIKU.** A **haiku** is a traditional Japanese three-line poem containing five syllables in the first line, seven in the second, and five again in the third. A haiku presents a picture, or image, in order to arouse in the reader a specific emotional and/or spiritual state.

**HALF RHYME.** See *slant rhyme*.

**HARLEM RENAISSANCE.** The Harlem Renaissance was a period of intense creative activity among African-American writers and other artists living in Harlem in New York City during the 1920s. Major writers of the Harlem Renaissance included Arna Bontemps, Countee Cullen, Langston Hughes, Claude McKay, and Jean Toomer.

**HEPTAMETER.** See *meter*.

**HERO.** A **hero** is a character whose actions are inspiring and courageous. An **epic hero** represents the ideals of the culture that creates it. In early literature, a hero is often part divine and has remarkable abilities, such as magical power, superhuman strength, or great courage. A **tragic hero** is a character of high status who possesses noble qualities but who also has a tragic flaw, or personal weakness. In much contemporary literature, the term *hero* often refers to any main character. See *antihero* and *tragic flaw*.

**HEROIC COUPLET.** See *couplet*.

**HEROIC EPIC.** A **heroic epic** is an epic that has a main purpose of telling the life story of a great hero. See *epic*.

**HEXAMETER.** See *meter*.

**HIGH STYLE.** See *style*.

**HISTORICAL CRITICISM.** See *criticism*.

**HOW-TO WRITING.** See *exposition*, #1.

**HYMN.** A **hymn** is a song or verse of praise, often religious. "The Battle Hymn of the Republic" by Julia Ward Howe (Unit 5) is an example.

**HYPERBOLE.** A **hyperbole** (hī pʉr′ bə lē) is an exaggeration made for rhetorical effect. Anne Bradstreet uses hyperbole when she writes,

My love is such that rivers cannot quench,
Nor ought but love from thee, give
recompense.

**IAMB.** An **iamb** is a poetic foot containing one weakly stressed syllable followed by one strongly stressed syllable, as in the words *afraid* and *release*. A line of poetry made up of iambs is said to be *iambic*.

**IAMBIC.** See *iamb*.

**IDIOSYNCRATIC SYMBOL.** See *symbol*.

**IMAGE.** An **image** is language that creates a concrete representation of an object or an experience. An image is also the vivid mental picture created in the reader's mind by that language. The images in a literary work are referred to, collectively, as the work's *imagery*.

**IMAGERY.** See *image*.

**IMAGINATIVE WRITING.** See *aim*.

**IMAGIST POEM.** An **imagist poem** is a lyric poem that presents a single vivid picture in words. "The Red Wheelbarrow" (Unit 7) by William Carlos Williams is an imagist poem. See *poetry* and *lyric poem*.

**IN MEDIAS RES.** See *action* and *flashback*.

**INCITING INCIDENT.** See *plot*.

**INCREMENTAL REPETITION.** See *ballad*.

**INFORMATIONAL WRITING.** See *aim*.

**INTERNAL CONFLICT.** See *conflict*.

**INTERNAL MONOLOGUE.** An **internal monologue** presents the private sensations, thoughts, and emotions of a character. The reader is allowed to step inside the character's mind and overhear what is going on in there. Which characters' internal states can be revealed in a work of fiction depends on the *point of view* from which the work is told. See *point of view*.

**INTRODUCTION.** See *preface*.

**INVERSION.** An **inversion** is a poetic technique in which the normal order of words in an utterance is altered. Robert Frost's famous line "Whose woods these are, I think I know" is an inversion of the usual order of expression: "I think I know whose woods these are."

**IRONY.** **Irony** is a difference between appearance and reality. Types of irony include the following:

*dramatic irony*, in which something is known by the reader or audience but unknown to the characters; *verbal irony*, in which a statement is made that implies its opposite; and *irony of situation*, in which an event occurs that violates the expectations of the characters, the reader, or the audience.

IRONY OF SITUATION. See *irony*.

JOURNAL. A **journal**, like a *diary*, is a day-to-day record of a person's activities, experiences, thoughts, and feelings. In contrast to *diary,* the word *journal* connotes an outward rather than an inward focus. However, the two terms are often used interchangeably. See *diary*.

JUNGIAN CRITICISM. See *criticism*.

LEGEND. A **legend** is a story coming down from the past, often based on real events or characters from older times. Unlike myths, legends are popularly regarded as historical; however, they may contain elements that are fantastic or unverifiable.

LIMITED POINT OF VIEW. See *narrator* and *point of view*.

LIST OF WORKS CITED. A **List of Works Cited** is a type of bibliography that lists works used or referred to by an author. A standard feature of a research paper, the List of Works Cited appears at the end of the paper and is arranged in alphabetical order.

LITERARY BALLAD. See *ballad*.

LITERATURE OF THE ABSURD. **Literature of the absurd** is literature influenced by Existentialist philosophy, which represents human life as meaningless or absurd because of the supposed lack of essential connection between human beings and the world around them. In brief, the Existentialist philosophers, such as Albert Camus and Jean-Paul Sartre, believed that a person's conscious existence precedes any essential self-definition and that self-definition can occur only as a result of making an absurd, completely free choice to act, think, or believe in certain ways. The literature of the absurd emphasizes the meaninglessness of life and the isolation, or alienation, of individuals. Much of the literature of the absurd is filled with horrors, anguish, random events, and illogical or improbable occurrences. Modern practitioners of the literature of the absurd include the novelists Franz Kafka,

Thomas Pynchon, and Kurt Vonnegut, Jr., and the playwrights Eugene Ionesco, Samuel Beckett, Edward Albee, and Harold Pinter. See *Existentialism* and *theater of the absurd*.

LOCAL COLOR. See *regional fiction*.

LOW STYLE. See *style*.

LYRIC POEM. A **lyric poem** is a highly musical verse that expresses the emotions of a speaker. Edna St. Vincent Millay's "Sonnet XXX" (Unit 1) and Amy Lowell's "Patterns" (Unit 7) are examples. Lyric poems are often contrasted with narrative poems, which have storytelling as their main purpose. See *poetry*.

MAIN CHARACTER. See *character*.

MAJOR CHARACTER. See *character*.

MARXIST CRITICISM. See *criticism*.

MEMOIR. A **memoir** is a nonfiction narration that tells a story. A memoir can be autobiographical (about one's life) or biographical (about someone else's life). Memoirs are based on a person's experiences and reactions to historical events. N. Scott Momaday's "The Way to Rainy Mountain" (Unit 1) is an example of memoir. See *autobiography* and *biography*.

METAPHOR. A **metaphor** is a figure of speech in which one thing is spoken or written about as if it were another. This figure of speech invites the reader to make a comparison between the two things. The two "things" involved are the writer's actual subject, the *tenor* of the metaphor, and another thing to which the subject is likened, the *vehicle* of the metaphor. In his essay *Self-Reliance* (Unit 4), Ralph Waldo Emerson uses this metaphor: "Society is a joint-stock company." The tenor of the metaphor is "society" and the vehicle of the metaphor is "joint-stock company."

*Personification* and *similes* are types of metaphor. See *dead metaphor, mixed metaphor, personification,* and *simile*.

METER. The **meter** of a poem is its rhythmical pattern. English verse is generally described as being made up of rhythmical units called feet, as follows:

| TYPE OF FOOT | STRESS PATTERN | EXAMPLE |
| --- | --- | --- |
| *iamb*, or iambic foot | ⌣ / | insist |

| | | |
|---|---|---|
| *trochee,* or trochaic foot | / ‿ | freedom |
| *anapest,* or anapestic foot | ‿ ‿ / | unimpressed |
| *dactyl,* or dactylic foot | / ‿ ‿ | feverish |
| *spondee,* or spondaic foot | / / | baseball |

Some scholars also use the term *pyrrhee,* or *pyrrhic foot,* to describe a foot with two weak stresses. Using this term, the word *unbelievable* might be described as consisting of two feet, an anapest followed by a pyrrhic:

‿ ‿ / | ‿ ‿
un be liev | a ble

Terms used to describe the number of feet in a line include the following:
*monometer* for a one-foot line
*dimeter* for a two-foot line
*trimeter* for a three-foot line
*tetrameter* for a four-foot line
*pentameter* for a five-foot line
*hexameter,* or *Alexandrine,* for a six-foot line
*heptameter* for a seven-foot line
*octameter* for an eight-foot line

A seven-foot line of iambic feet is called a *fourteener.*

A complete description of the meter of a line includes both the term for the type of foot that predominates in the line and the term for the number of feet in the line. The most common English meters are iambic tetrameter and iambic pentameter. The following are examples of each:

IAMBIC TETRAMETER
‿ / ‿ / ‿ / ‿ /
O slow | ly, slow | ly rose | she up

IAMBIC PENTAMETER
‿ / ‿ / ‿ / ‿ /
The cur | few tolls | the knell | of part |
‿ /
ing day,

**METONYMY. Metonymy** is the naming of an object associated with a thing in place of the name of the thing itself. Speaking of the *White House* when one means *the administrative or executive branch of the United States government* is an example of metonymy.

**MIDDLE STYLE.** See *style.*

**MIMETIC CRITICISM.** See *criticism.*

**MINOR CHARACTER.** See *character.*

**MIXED METAPHOR.** A **mixed metaphor** is an expression or passage that garbles together two or more metaphors. An example of mixed metaphor would be the sentence "The chariot of the sun screamed across the sky," in which the sun is described, inconsistently, as both a chariot and as something that screams. See *metaphor.*

**MODE.** A **mode** is a form of writing. One common classification system, based on purpose or aim, divides types of writing into five modes: expository/informative, imaginative, narrative, personal/expressive, and persuasive/argumentative. See *aim.*

**MODERNISM. Modernism** was an artistic and literary movement of the early twentieth century that championed experimentation, technicality, primitivism, impersonalism, aestheticism, and intellectualism. Important Modernists included the poets Ezra Pound and T. S. Eliot, the painters Pablo Picasso and Paul Klee, and the musicians Arnold Schönberg and Anton Webern.

**MONOMETER.** See *meter.*

**MOOD. Mood,** or **atmosphere,** is the emotion created in the reader by part or all of a literary work. The writer can evoke in the reader an emotional response—such as fear, discomfort, longing, or anticipation—by working carefully with descriptive language and sensory details.

**MORAL.** A **moral** is a practical or moral lesson, usually relating to the principles of right and wrong, to be drawn from a story or other work of literature.

**MOTIF.** A **motif** is any element that recurs in one or more works of literature or art. Examples of common folk tale motifs found in oral traditions throughout the world include grateful animals or the grateful dead, three wishes, the trial or quest, and the magical metamorphosis, or transformation of one thing into another. "Cinderella," "The Ugly Duckling," and the Arthurian "Sword in the Stone" are examples of the transformation motif, in which persons or creatures of humble station are revealed to be exceptional. Much can be revealed about a literary work by studying the motifs within it. In Sarah Orne Jewett's "A White Heron" (Unit 6), birds are a frequent motif.

**MOTIVATION.** A **motivation** is a force that moves a character to think, feel, or behave in a certain way. In Ambrose Bierce's "An Occurrence at Owl Creek Bridge" (Unit 5), the main character is motivated by a desire to save his own life by escaping from his captors.

**MUSE.** In ancient Greek and Roman myth, the **Muses**—the nine daughters of Zeus and Mnemosyne, or Memory—were believed to provide the inspiration for the arts and sciences. Calliope was the Muse of epic poetry; Clio, the Muse of history; Erato, the Muse of lyrical poetry; Euterpe, the Muse of music; Melpomene, the Muse of tragedy; Polyhymnia, the Muse of sacred choral poetry; Terpischore, the Muse of choral dance and song; Thalia, the Muse of comedy; and Urania, the Muse of astronomy. The idea of the Muse has often been used by later writers to explain the vagaries and mysteries of literary inspiration. For example, in Phillis Wheatley's poem, "To S. M., a Young African Painter, on Seeing His Works" (Unit 3), Wheatley writes: "And may the muse inspire each future song!" The connection of the Muses with entertainments and the arts survives in our English words *amusing* and *amusement*.

**MYTH.** A **myth** is a story that explains objects or events in the natural world as resulting from the action of some supernatural force or entity, most often a god. Every early culture around the globe has produced its own myths. An example of a myth is the explanation of the sky as a piece of weaving in "Song of the Sky Loom" (Unit 2).

**NARRATION.** **Narration** is a type of writing that tells a story, or describes events, most often using time, or *chronological order*, as a way of organization. See *chronological order*.

**NARRATIVE POEM.** A **narrative poem** is a verse that tells a story. See *poetry*.

**NARRATIVE WRITING.** See *aim*.

**NARRATOR.** A **narrator** is one who tells a story. In a drama, the narrator may be a character who introduces, concludes, or comments upon the action of the play. However, dramas typically do not have narrators. Works of fiction, on the other hand, always do, unless they consist entirely of dialogue without tag lines, in which case they cease to be fictions and become closet dramas, drama meant to be read but not performed. The narrator in a work of fiction may be a central or minor character or simply someone who witnessed or heard about the events being related. Writers achieve a wide variety of ends by varying the characteristics of the narrator chosen for a particular work. Of primary importance is the choice of the narrator's *point of view*. Will the narrator be *omniscient*, knowing all things, including the internal workings of the minds of the characters in the story, or will the narrator be *limited* in his or her knowledge? Will the narrator participate in the action of the story or stand outside that action and comment on it? Will the narrator be reliable or unreliable? That is, will the reader be able to trust the narrator's statements? These are all questions that a writer must answer when developing a narrator. See *point of view* and *speaker*.

**NATURALISM.** **Naturalism** was a literary movement of the late nineteenth and early twentieth centuries that saw actions and events as resulting inevitably from biological or natural forces or from forces in the environment. Often these forces were beyond the comprehension or control of the characters subjected to them. Taken to its extreme, Naturalism views all events as mechanically determined by external forces, including the decisions made by people. Much of modern fiction, with its emphasis on social conditions leading to particular consequences for characters, is naturalistic in this sense. Stephen Crane's "A Man Said to the Universe" (Unit 5) demonstrates a naturalistic attitude. Besides Crane, Jack London and Theodore Dreiser were writers informed by the philosophy of Naturalism.

**NEAR RHYME.** See *slant rhyme*.

**NEOCLASSICISM.** **Neoclassicism** is the term used to describe the revival during the European Enlightenment of ideals of art and literature derived from the Greek and Roman classics. These ideals included respect for authority and tradition, austerity, clarity, conservatism, decorum, economy, grace, imitation of the natural order, harmony, moderation, proportion, reason, restraint, self-control, simplicity, tradition, wit, and unity. Neoclassical literature was witty and socially astute but tended toward excessive *didacticism* and an excessive distrust of invention and imagination. Popular forms of

Neoclassical writing included the essay, the epistle, the satire, the parody, poems in rhymed couplets, and the earliest novels. Neoclassical writers wrote primarily about social life and social interactions. Of all American writers, Benjamin Franklin perhaps best reflects the Neoclassical spirit of urbane rationality. *Romanticism* can be seen as a reaction against Neoclassical restraint. See *Classicism, didacticism,* and *Romanticism.*

**NEW CRITICISM.** See *criticism.*

**NONFICTION. Nonfiction** is writing about real events. *Essays, autobiographies, biographies,* and *news stories* are all types of nonfiction. See *prose.*

**NONSENSE VERSE.** A **nonsense verse** is a kind of light verse that contains elements that are silly, absurd, or meaningless. Sometimes, as is the case with Lewis Carroll's "Jabberwocky," the apparent nonsense of the verse gives way to sense upon closer analysis. Carroll's poem turns out not to be nonsense at all, but rather an ingenious retelling, in a mock heroic ballad, of a stock folk tale story—that of a young person who sets off on a quest, slays a terrible beast, and returns home victorious.

**NOVEL.** A **novel** is a long work of prose fiction. Often novels have involved plots; many characters, both major and minor; and numerous settings. In Europe, the novel arose as a literary form soon after the publication of Miguel de Cervantes's *Don Quixote* in 1605. Novels soon gained lasting popularity throughout Europe. Nineteenth-century American novelists include Herman Melville, Mark Twain, and Stephen Crane. Some outstanding twentieth-century American novelists include Edith Wharton, Henry James, Ernest Hemingway, William Faulkner, Ralph Ellison, Alice Walker, and Anne Tyler.

**NOVELLA.** A **novella** is a short novel.

**NURSERY RHYME.** A **nursery rhyme** is a children's verse.

**OBJECTIVE CORRELATIVE.** An **objective correlative** is a group of images that together create a particular emotion in the reader. The term was coined by T. S. Eliot. See *image.*

**OCCASIONAL VERSE.** An **occasional verse** is one written to celebrate or commemorate some particular event. Phillis Wheatley wrote "To S. M., a Young African Painter, on Seeing His Works"

(Unit 3), for example, to celebrate the artistic gift of Scipio Moorehead.

**OCTAMETER.** See *meter.*

**OCTAVE.** An **octave** is an eight-line stanza. A Petrarchan sonnet begins with an octave. See *meter* and *sonnet.*

**ODE.** An **ode** is a lofty lyric poem on a serious theme. It may employ alternating stanza patterns, developed from the choral ode of Greek dramatic poetry. These stanza patterns are called the *strophe,* the *antistrophe,* and the *epode.* However, not all odes follow this pattern. William Cullen Bryant's "Thanatopsis" (Unit 4) is an example of an ode.

**OFF RHYME.** See *slant rhyme.*

**OMNISCIENT POINT OF VIEW.** See *narrator* and *point of view.*

**ONE-ACT.** See *act.*

**ONE-DIMENSIONAL CHARACTER.** See *character.*

**ONOMATOPOEIA. Onomatopoeia** is the use of words or phrases that sound like the things to which they refer. Examples of onomatopoeia include words such as *buzz, click,* and *pop.* Poets and other writers often make use of onomatopoeia.

**OCTAMETER.** See *free verse.*

**ORAL TRADITION.** An **oral tradition** is a work, an idea, or a custom that is passed by word-of-mouth from generation to generation. Materials transmitted orally may be simplified in the retelling. They also may be sensationalized because of the tendency of retellers to add to or elaborate upon the materials that come down to them. Often, works in an oral tradition contain miraculous or magical elements. Common works found in the oral traditions of peoples around the world include *folk tales, fables, fairy tales, tall tales, nursery rhymes, proverbs, legends, myths, parables, riddles,* charms, spells, and *ballads.* The spiritual "Follow the Drinking Gourd" (Unit 1) belongs to the African-American oral tradition. See *folklore.*

**OTTAVA RIMA.** *Ottava rima* is a stanza form made up of eight iambic pentameter lines rhyming *abababcc.* See *rhyme scheme.*

**OXYMORON.** An **oxymoron** is a statement that contradicts itself. Words like *bittersweet, tragicomedy,* and *pianoforte* (literally, "soft-loud") are oxymorons that develop a complex meaning from two seemingly contradictory elements.

**PALINDROME.** A **palindrome** is a word, a phrase, or a sentence that reads the same backward as forward. Examples include the word *radar* and the phrase *A man, a plan, a canal—Panama*.

**PARABLE.** A **parable** is a very brief story told to teach a moral lesson. The most famous parables are those, such as the parable of the prodigal son, told by Jesus in the Bible.

**PARADOX.** A **paradox** is a seemingly contradictory statement, idea, or event. All forms of *irony* involve paradox. An *oxymoron* is a paradoxical statement. Anne Bradstreet's line "That when we live no more, we may live ever" is paradoxical. Some paradoxes present unresolvable contradictory ideas. An example of such a paradox is the statement, "This sentence is a lie." If the sentence is true, then it is false; if it is false, then it is true. See *irony* and *oxymoron*.

**PARALLELISM.** **Parallelism** is a rhetorical technique in which a writer emphasizes the equal value or weight of two or more ideas by expressing them in the same grammatical form. Thomas Jefferson used parallelism in the Declaration of Independence (Unit 3) in his list of grievances against King George, starting each grievance with "He has. . . ."

**PARAPHRASE.** A **paraphrase** is a rewriting of a passage in different words. A paraphrase is often distinguished from an *abstract* or *summary* as follows: a summary is shorter than the original, whereas a paraphrase may be as long as or longer than the original. One of the central ideas of the so-called New Criticism was that it is impossible to paraphrase a literary work precisely. Much of the content or meaning of a literary work lies in how it is expressed. Changing the expression therefore inevitably changes the meaning. See *abstract*.

**PARODY.** A **parody** is a literary work that imitates another work for humorous, often satirical, purposes. In the idented stanzas of "Do not weep, maiden, for war is kind" (Unit 5), Stephen Crane subtly parodies hortatory patriotic speech.

**PATHETIC FALLACY.** The **pathetic fallacy** is the tendency to attribute human emotions to nonhuman things, particularly to things in the natural world. The term was coined by the Victorian critic John Ruskin and has often been used to describe the excesses of sentimental verse. The pathetic fallacy is used by Wallace Stevens when he ascribes human emotions to the season of winter in his poem "The Snow Man" (Unit 7).

**PENTAMETER.** See *meter*.

**PERIODICAL.** A **periodical** is a newspaper, magazine, journal, newsletter, or other publication that is produced on a regular basis. *The Dial*, a periodical, was the chief organ of American Transcendentalism. *Poetry* magazine has been a leading force in shaping the course of modern American poetry.

**PERSONA.** A **persona** consists of the qualities of a person or character that are shown through speech or actions.

**PERSONAL ESSAY.** A **personal essay** is a short work of nonfictional prose on a single topic related to the life or interests of the writer. Personal essays are characterized by an intimate and informal style and tone. They are often, but not always, written in the first person. See *essay*.

**PERSONAL SYMBOL.** See *symbol*.

**PERSONAL WRITING.** See *aim*.

**PERSONIFICATION.** **Personification** is a figure of speech in which an idea, animal, or thing is described as if it were a person. Edgar Allan Poe uses personification in his poem "The Raven" (Unit 4) when he addresses and questions the raven and has the raven answer, "Nevermore."

**PERSUASIVE WRITING.** See *aim*.

**PETRARCHAN SONNET.** See *sonnet*.

**PLAGIARISM.** **Plagiarism** is the act of using material gathered from another person or work without crediting the source of the material.

**PLOT.** A **plot** is a series of events related to a central *conflict*, or struggle. A typical plot involves the introduction of a conflict, its development, and its eventual resolution. Terms used to describe elements of plot include the following:

- The **exposition**, or **introduction**, sets the tone or mood, introduces the characters and the setting, and provides necessary background information.
- The **inciting incident** is the event that introduces the central conflict.

- The **rising action**, or **complication**, develops the conflict to a high point of intensity.
- The **climax** is the high point of interest or suspense in the plot.
- The **crisis**, or **turning point**, often the same event as the climax, is the point in the plot where something decisive happens to determine the future course of events and the eventual working out of the conflict.
- The **falling action** is all the events that follow the climax.
- The **resolution** is the point at which the central conflict is ended, or resolved.
- The **dénouement** is any material that follows the resolution and that ties up loose ends.
- The **catastrophe**, in tragedy, is the event that marks the ultimate tragic fall of the central character. Often this event is the character's death.

Plots rarely contain all these elements in precisely this order. Elements of exposition may be introduced at any time in the course of a work. A work may begin with a catastrophe and then use flashback to explain it. The exposition or dénouement or even the resolution may be missing. The inciting incident may occur before the beginning of the action actually described in the work. These are but a few of the many possible variations that plots can exhibit. See *conflict*.

**POETIC LICENSE.** **Poetic license** is the right, claimed by writers, to change elements of reality to suit the purposes of particular works that they create. Edgar Lee Masters's use in his *Spoon River Anthology* (excerpted in Unit 7) of characters who rise from their graves and talk is an example of poetic license. Such things do not happen in reality, but they are accepted by readers willing to suspend disbelief in order to have imaginary experiences. See *suspension of disbelief*.

**POETRY.** **Poetry** is imaginative language carefully chosen and arranged to communicate experiences, thoughts, or emotions. It differs from prose in that it compresses meaning into fewer words, and often uses *meter, rhyme*, and techniques such as *metaphor* and *simile*. Poetry is usually arranged in lines and stanzas as opposed to sentences and paragraphs, and it can be more free in the ordering of words and the use of punctuation. Types of poetry include *narrative, dramatic,* and *lyric*. See *meter* and *rhyme*.

**POINT OF VIEW.** **Point of view** is the vantage point from which a story is told. Stories are typically written from a *first-person point of view,* in which the narrator uses words such as *I* and *we*; from a *second-person point of view*, in which the narrator uses *you;* or from a third-person point of view, in which the narrator uses words such as *he, she, it,* and *they*. In stories written from a *first-person point of view*, the narrator may be a participant or witness of the action. In stories told from a *third-person point of view*, the narrator generally stands outside the action. In some stories, the narrator's point of view is *limited*. In such stories, the narrator can reveal the private, internal thoughts of himself or herself or of a single character. In other stories, the narrator's point of view is *omniscient*. In such stories the narrator can reveal the private, internal thoughts of any character.

**PORTMANTEAU.** See *blend*.

**PRAGMATIC CRITICISM.** See *criticism*.

**PRÉCIS.** See *abstract*.

**PREFACE.** A **preface** is a statement made at the beginning of a literary work, often by way of introduction. The terms *foreword, preface,* and *introduction* are often used interchangeably.

**PROCESS WRITING.** See *exposition, #1.*

**PROLOGUE.** A **prologue** is an introduction to a literary work, often one that sets the scene and introduces the conflict or the main characters.

**PROSCENIUM STAGE.** See *stage*.

**PROSE.** **Prose** is the broad term used to describe all writing that is not drama or poetry, including fiction and nonfiction. Types of prose writing include novels, short stories, essays, and news stories. Most biographies, autobiographies, and letters are written in prose. See *fiction*.

**PROSE POEM.** A **prose poem** is a work of prose, usually a short work, that makes such extensive use of poetic language, such as figures of speech and words that echo their sense, that the line between prose and poetry becomes blurred. Many passages from the work of William Faulkner have the quality of prose poetry.

**PROSODY.** **Prosody**, or **versification**, is the study of the structure of poetry. In particular, prosodists study *meter, rhyme, rhythm,* and *stanza* form. See *meter, rhyme, rhythm,* and *stanza*.

**PROTAGONIST.** See *character.*

**PROVERB.** A **proverb**, or **adage**, is a traditional saying, such as "You can lead a horse to water, but you can't make it drink" or the title of Shakespeare's play *All's Well That Ends Well.*

**PSALM.** A **psalm** is a lyrical hymn of praise, supplication, or thanksgiving. The biblical hymn, attributed to David, that begins with the line "The Lord is my shepherd," is an example.

**PSEUDONYM.** A **pseudonym** is a name assumed by a writer. For example, *Mark Twain* was the pseudonym of Samuel Clemens.

**PSYCHOLOGICAL FICTION.** **Psychological fiction** is fiction that emphasizes the interior, subjective experiences of its characters, and especially such fiction when it deals with emotional or mental disturbance or anguish. Kate Chopin's "The Story of an Hour" (Unit 6) is an example.

**PUN.** A **pun** is a play on words, one that wittily exploits a double meaning.

**PURITANISM.** **Puritanism** was a Protestant religious movement that emerged in England in the 1500s and later spread to the colonies of New England. The Puritans objected to the wealth, power, authority, and elaborate ritual of the Catholic Church. They professed a desire to "purify" the Church of England by ridding it of Catholic practices. The Puritans are known for their austerity and acceptance of the basic principles of Calvinism, including the ideas of preordination and original sin. The Plymouth Colony in Massachusetts was founded by Separatist Puritans who came from England via Holland. Important British Puritan writers include John Bunyan and John Milton. Important American Puritan writers include Cotton Mather and Jonathan Edwards. See *Calvinism.*

**PURPOSE.** See *aim.*

**PYRRHIC.** See *meter.*

**QUATRAIN.** A **quatrain** is a stanza containing four lines.

**QUINTAIN.** A **quintain**, or **quintet**, is a stanza containing five lines.

**QUINTET.** See *quintain.*

**RAP.** **Rap** is improvised, rhymed verse that is chanted or sung, often to a musical accompaniment.

**READER-RESPONSE CRITICISM.** See *criticism.*

**REALISM.** **Realism** is the attempt to render in art an accurate portrayal of reality. The theory that the purpose of art is to imitate life is at least as old as Aristotle. The eighteenth-century development of the novel, with its attention to details of character, setting, and social life, can be thought of as a step toward increased Realism in writing. However, the term *Realism* is generally applied to literature of the late nineteenth century, written in reaction to *Romanticism* and emphasizing details of ordinary life.

**REDUNDANCY.** **Redundancy** is needless repetition. The phrase *firmly determined* is redundant because the word *determined* already implies firmness.

**REFRAIN.** A **refrain** is a line or group of lines repeated in a poem or song. Many *ballads* contain refrains.

**REGIONAL DIALECT.** See *dialect.*

**REGIONAL FICTION.** **Regional fiction** is writing in which particular settings play an important role. The details used to create a particular regional setting are called *local color.* Many American novels and short stories deal with particular regions of the country (New York City, the western frontier, small towns in the South or Midwest, and so on). One example of regional fiction is Eudora Welty's novel *The Golden Apples,* which is set in the rural South and contains local idioms and color.

**RENAISSANCE.** The **Renaissance** was the period from the fourteenth to the early seventeenth century when Europe was making the transition from the medieval to the modern world. The word *renaissance* means "rebirth." The term refers to the rebirth of interest in ancient Greek and Latin writing that occurred during the period, a rebirth that is known as Humanism. The Renaissance was characterized by a lessening of reliance on authority, by a decline in feudalism and in the universal authority of the church, by increased nationalism, by increasingly active university and city life, by increased opportunities for individual economic attainment and freedom, and by increased belief in the value of this life (as opposed to the afterlife), in and of itself.

**REPETITION.** **Repetition** is the writer's conscious reuse of a sound, word, phrase, sentence, or other element.

RESOLUTION. See *plot.*

REVERSAL. A **reversal** is a dramatic change in the direction of events in a drama or narrative, especially a change in the fortunes of the protagonist. See *plot.*

REVIEW. A **review** is a written evaluation of a work of art, a performance, or a literary work, especially one that appears in a periodical or on a broadcast news program. Common subjects of reviews include books, films, art exhibitions, restaurants, and performances of all kinds, from rock concerts to ballets.

RHETORIC. **Rhetoric** is the art of speaking or writing effectively. It involves the study of ways in which speech and writing affect or influence audiences. Rhetoric has also been defined as the art of persuasion.

RHETORICAL CRITICISM. See *criticism.*

RHETORICAL QUESTION. A **rhetorical question** is one asked for effect but not meant to be answered because the answer is clear from context. Patrick Henry, in his Speech in the Virginia Convention (Unit 3), poses a series of rhetorical questions.

RHETORICAL TECHNIQUE. A **rhetorical technique** is an extraordinary but literal use of language to achieve a particular effect on an audience. Common rhetorical techniques include *antithesis, apostrophe, catalog, chiasmus, parallelism, repetition,* and the *rhetorical question.*

RHYME. **Rhyme** is the repetition of sounds at the ends of words. Types of rhyme include *end rhyme* (the use of rhyming words at the ends of lines), *internal rhyme* (the use of rhyming words within lines), *exact rhyme* (in which the rhyming words end with the same sound or sounds), and *slant rhyme* (in which the rhyming sounds are similar but not identical). An example of exact rhyme is the word pair *moon/June.* Examples of slant rhyme are the word pairs *rave/rove* and *rot/rock.* See *poetry, slant rhyme,* and *rhyme scheme.*

RHYME SCHEME. A **rhyme scheme** is a pattern of end rhymes, or rhymes at the ends of lines of verse. The rhyme scheme of a poem is designated by letters, with matching letters signifying matching sounds.

RHYTHM. **Rhythm** is the pattern of beats or stresses in a line of verse or prose. See *meter.*

RISING ACTION. See *plot.*

ROMANCE. **Romance** is a term used to refer to four types of literature: 1. medieval stories about the adventures and loves of knights; 2. novels and other fictions involving exotic locales and extraordinary or mysterious events and characters; 3. nonrealistic fictions in general; and 4. in popular, modern usage, love stories of all kinds. It was used by Nathaniel Hawthorne to describe such stories as his *Blithedale Romance* and *House of the Seven Gables* because of their deviations from *Realism.* Today, the term is quite widely used to refer to love stories, especially popular, sentimental stories.

ROMANTIC CRITICISM. See *criticism.*

ROMANTICISM. **Romanticism** was a literary and artistic movement of the eighteenth and nineteenth centuries that placed value on emotion or imagination over reason, the individual over society, nature and wildness over human works, the country over the town, common people over aristocrats, and freedom over control or authority. Much of Edgar Allan Poe's poetry is Romantic in its intensity of emotion. Transcendentalism was a particularly American form of Romanticism.

ROUNDED CHARACTER. See *character.*

RUN-ON LINE. A **run-on line** is a line of verse in which the sense or the grammatical structure does not end with the end of the line but rather is continued on one or more subsequent lines. The following lines from Dickinson's "This is my letter to the World" form a single sentence:

> This is my letter to the World
> That never wrote to Me—
> The simple News that Nature told—
> With tender Majesty.

The act of continuing a statement beyond the end of a line is called *enjambment.* See *end-stopped line.*

SATIRE. **Satire** is humorous writing or speech intended to point out errors, falsehoods, foibles, or failings. It is written for the purpose of reforming human behavior or human institutions.

SCANSION. **Scansion** is the art of analyzing poetry to determine its meter. See *meter.*

SCENE. A **scene** is a short section of a literary work that presents action that occurs in a single place or at a single time. Long divisions of dramas are often divided into scenes.

**SCIENCE FICTION. Science fiction** is highly imaginative fiction containing fantastic elements based on scientific principles, discoveries, or laws. It is similar to fantasy in that it deals with imaginary worlds but differs from fantasy in having a scientific basis. Mary Shelley's *Frankenstein* was an early precursor of modern science fiction. She based her idea of the creation of artificial life on nineteenth-century experiments with so-called animal magnetism, the electrical charge believed by some people in those days to be the force motivating living things and distinguishing them from nonliving things. Often science fiction deals with the future, the distant past, or with worlds other than our own, such as other planets, parallel universes, and worlds under the ground or the sea. The genre allows writers to suspend or alter certain elements of reality in order to create fascinating and sometimes instructive alternatives. Important writers of science fiction include H. G. Wells, Jules Verne, Ray Bradbury, Arthur C. Clarke, Isaac Asimov, Ursula K. Le Guin, Robert Heinlein, and Kurt Vonnegut, Jr. See *fantasy.*

**SENSORY DETAIL.** See *description.*

**SENTIMENTALITY. Sentimentality** is an excessive expression of emotion. Much popular literature of the nineteenth and twentieth centuries is characterized by sentimentality.

**SEPTET.** A septet is a stanza with seven lines.

**SESTET.** A **sestet** is a stanza with six lines, such as the second part of a Petrarchan sonnet. See *meter* and *sonnet.*

**SET.** A **set** is a collection of objects on a stage arranged in such a way as to create a scene.

**SETTING.** The **setting** of a literary work is the time and place in which it occurs, together with all the details used to create a sense of a particular time and place. Writers create setting by various means. In drama, the setting is often revealed by the stage set and the costumes, though it may be revealed through what the characters say about their environs. In fiction, setting is most often revealed by means of description of such elements as landscape, scenery, buildings, furniture, clothing, the weather, and the season. It can also be revealed by how characters talk and behave. In its widest sense, setting includes the general social, political, moral, and psychological conditions in which characters find themselves. See *set.*

**SHAKESPEAREAN SONNET.** See *sonnet.*

**SHAPE POEM.** See *concrete poem.*

**SHORT SHORT.** A **short short**, or **flash fiction**, is an extremely brief short story. This recently recognized genre of the short story is currently enjoying considerable popularity among readers of literary magazines and short story collections published in the United States. Short shorts sometimes take the form of anecdotes, or retellings of single incidents. Alternatively, they may attempt to develop an entire plot within the compass of a few paragraphs. Many short shorts are highly poetic and may be considered prose poems. See *anecdote* and *prose poem.*

**SHORT STORY.** A **short story** is a form of short prose fiction that relates a narrative. Short stories are typically crafted carefully to develop a plot, a conflict, characters, a setting, a mood, and a theme, all within relatively few pages. This form of literature gained popularity in the nineteenth century. See *conflict, character, mood, plot, setting,* and *theme.*

**SIGHT RHYME.** A **sight rhyme**, or **eye rhyme**, is a pair of words, generally at the ends of lines of verse, that are spelled similarly but pronounced differently. The words *lost* and *ghost* and *give* and *thrive* are examples. These lines from Claude McKay's poem "The Tropics in New York" (Unit 8) provide an example.

> Set in the window, bringing memor*ies*
> . . . And dewy dawns, and mystical blue sk*ies*

**SIMILE.** A **simile** is a comparison using *like* or *as.* Henry Wadsworth Longfellow uses a simile when he describes a blacksmith in "The Village Blacksmith" (Unit 4), saying, "And the muscles of his brawny arms / Are strong as iron bands." A simile is a type of *metaphor*, and like any other metaphor, can be divided into two parts, the *tenor* (or subject being described), and the *vehicle* (or object being used in the description). In the simile "your locks are like the snow," the tenor is locks of hair and the vehicle is snow. They can be compared because they share some quality, in this case, whiteness. See *metaphor.*

**SLANG. Slang** is extremely colloquial speech not suitable for formal occasions and usually associated with a particular group of people. An example of slang current among young people in the United States in the 1920s is "the bee's knees," for something uniquely attractive or wonderful. Among young people in the northeastern United States, the word *wicked* is now sometimes used as a slang term meaning "extremely," as in "That song is *wicked* good." Writers sometimes use slang in an attempt to render characters and setting vividly.

**SLANT RHYME.** A **slant rhyme, half rhyme, near rhyme,** or **off rhyme** is the substitution of assonance or consonance for true rhyme. The pairs *world/boiled* and *bear/bore* are examples. See *assonance, consonance,* and *rhyme.*

**SOCIAL DIALECT.** See *dialect.*

**SOLILOQUY.** A **soliloquy** is a speech delivered by a lone character that reveals the speaker's thoughts and feelings.

**SONNET.** A **sonnet** is a fourteen-line poem, usually in iambic pentameter, that follows one of a number of different rhyme schemes. The *English, Elizabethan,* or *Shakespearean sonnet* is divided into four parts: three *quatrains* and a final *couplet.* The rhyme scheme of such a sonnet is *abab cdcd efef gg.* The sonnets by Shakespeare in this book are examples. The *Italian* or *Petrarchan sonnet* is divided into two parts: an octave and a sestet. The rhyme scheme of the octave is *abbaabba.* The rhyme scheme of the sestet can be *cdecde, cdcdcd,* or *cdedce.* "Sonnet XXX" by Edna St. Vincent Millay (Unit 1) is an example of an English sonnet. Her sonnet "Euclid Alone Has Looked on Beauty Bare" (Unit 7) is an Italian sonnet.

**SONNET CYCLE.** See *sonnet sequence.*

**SONNET SEQUENCE.** A **sonnet sequence** is a group of related sonnets. Famous sonnet sequences include those of William Shakespeare. See *sonnet.*

**SOURCE.** A **source** is a work from which an author takes his or her materials.

**SOUTHERN GOTHIC. Southern Gothic** is writing containing elements of horror, suspense, mystery, or magic, produced or set in the southern United States. The writing of Flannery O'Connor, whose short story "The Life You Save May Be Your Own" appears in Unit 10, is typical of the Southern Gothic style. See *Gothic fiction.*

**SPEAKER.** The **speaker** is the character who speaks in, or narrates, a poem—the voice assumed by the writer. The speaker and the writer of a poem are not necessarily the same person. T. S. Eliot takes on the voice of J. Alfred Prufrock in "The Love Song of J. Alfred Prufrock" (Unit 7). In Carl Sandburg's "Grass" (Unit 7), the grass is the speaker.

**SPECTACLE.** In drama, the **spectacle** is all the elements that are presented to the senses of the audience, including the lights, setting, costumes, makeup, music, sound effects, and movements of the actors.

**SPIRITUAL.** A **spiritual** is a folk song of deep religious and emotional character. Spirituals were developed among African Americans in the southern United States during slavery. The words are most often related to biblical passages and frequently reflect patient, profound melancholy, even though the songs seldom refer to slavery itself. Spirituals influenced blues, jazz, and gospel songs. "Follow the Drinking Gourd" (Unit 1) and "Swing Low, Sweet Chariot" (Unit 5) are examples of spirituals.

**SPONDEE.** A **spondee** is a poetic foot containing two strongly stressed syllables, as in the words *compound* and *roughhouse.* Such a foot is said to be *spondaic.*

**STAGE.** A **stage** is any arena on which the action of a drama is performed. In the Middle Ages, stages often consisted of the beds of wagons, which were wheeled from place to place for performances. From the use of such wagons in inn yards, the *thrust stage* developed. This was a platform that extended out into the audience and that was closed at the back. In front of the platform in the first English theaters, such as Shakespeare's Globe Theatre, was an open area, the pit, where common people stood. Around the pit were balconies in imitation of the balconies of inns. The modern *proscenium stage* typically is closed on three sides and open at the front, as though the fourth wall had been removed. Sometimes contemporary plays are performed as *theater in the round*, with the audience seated on all sides of the playing area.

**STAGE DIRECTIONS. Stage directions** are notes included in a play, in addition to the dialogue, for the purpose of describing how something should be performed on stage. Stage directions describe setting, lighting, music, sound effects, entrances and exits, properties, and the movements of characters. They are usually printed in italics and enclosed in brackets or parentheses.

**STANZA.** A **stanza** is a group of lines in a poem. The following are some types of stanza:

| | |
|---|---|
| two-line stanza | *couplet* |
| three-line stanza | *triplet* or *tercet* |
| four-line stanza | *quatrain* |
| five-line stanza | *quintain* |
| six-line stanza | *sestet* |
| seven-line stanza | *heptastich* |
| eight-line stanza | *octave* |

**STATIC CHARACTER.** See *character.*

**STEREOTYPE.** A **stereotype** is an uncritically accepted, fixed or conventional idea, particularly such an idea held about whole groups of people. A stereotypical, or stock, character is one who does not deviate from conventional expectations of such a character. Examples of stereotypical characters include the merciless villain, the mad scientist, and the hard-boiled private eye. In his autobiography (Unit 5), Frederick Douglass disputes the stereotype of the contented singing slave because, in his experience, slave songs were a release of sorrow. See *character.*

**STOCK CHARACTER.** See *character* and *stereotype.*

**STORY.** A **story**, or **narrative**, is writing or speech that relates a series of events. When these events are causally connected and related to a conflict, they make up a *plot.* See *plot.*

**STREAM-OF-CONSCIOUSNESS WRITING. Stream-of-consciousness writing** is writing that attempts to render the flow of feelings, thoughts, and impressions within the minds of characters. Modern masters of stream-of-consciousness writing include Virginia Woolf, James Joyce, and William Faulkner. An example of stream-of-consciousness writing is the work of Katherine Anne Porter in "The Jilting of Granny Weatherall" (Unit 7).

**STRESS. Stress**, or **accent**, is the level of emphasis given to a syllable. In English *metrics,* the art of rhythm in written and spoken expression, syllables are generally described as being *strongly* or *weakly* stressed, in other words, *accented* or *unaccented.* A strongly stressed or accented syllable receives a strong emphasis. A weakly stressed or unaccented syllable receives a weak

one. In the following line from Walt Whitman's "When Lilacs Last in the Dooryard Bloom'd" (Unit 5), the strongly stressed or accented syllables are marked with a slash mark (/).

$$\text{/ \quad / \quad\quad / \quad\quad /}$$
When lilacs last in the dooryard bloom'd

**STRUCTURALIST CRITICISM.** See *criticism.*

**STYLE. Style** is the manner in which something is said or written. Traditionally, critics and scholars have referred to three levels of style: high style, for formal occasions or lofty subjects; middle style, for ordinary occasions or subjects; and low style, for extremely informal occasions or subjects. A writer's style depends upon many things, including his or her *diction* (the words that the writer chooses), selection of grammatical structures (simple versus complex sentences, for example), and preference for *abstract* or *concrete* words. Any recurring feature that distinguishes one writer's work from another can be said to be part of that writer's style. See *abstract* and *fiction.*

**SUBPLOT.** A **subplot** is a subordinate story told in addition to the major story in a work of fiction. Often a subplot mirrors or provides a *foil* for the primary plot. See *plot* and *story.*

**SUMMARY.** See *abstract.*

**SUSPENSE. Suspense** is a feeling of expectation, anxiousness, or curiosity created by questions raised in the mind of a reader or viewer.

**SUSPENSION OF DISBELIEF. Suspension of disbelief** is the phrase used by Coleridge in his *Biographia Literaria* to describe the act by which the reader willingly sets aside his or her skepticism in order to participate imaginatively in the work being read. In Nathaniel Hawthorne's "Rappaccini's Daughter," a certain flower is deadly. To enjoy the story, readers must suspend their disbelief in such flowers. The willingness to suspend disbelief, to participate imaginatively in a story being read, is the most important attribute, beyond literacy, that a person can bring to the act of reading literature.

**SYMBOL.** A **symbol** is a thing that stands for or represents both itself and something else. Writers use two types of symbols—conventional, and personal or idiosyncratic. A *conventional symbol* is one with traditional, widely recognized associations. Such symbols include doves for peace;

laurel wreaths for heroism or poetic excellence; the color green for jealousy; the color purple for royalty; the color red for anger; morning or spring for youth; winter, evening, or night for old age; wind for change or inspiration; rainbows for hope; roses for beauty; the moon for fickleness or inconstancy; roads or paths for the journey through life; woods or darkness for moral or spiritual confusion; thorns for troubles or pain; stars for unchangeableness or constancy; mirrors for vanity or introspection; snakes for evil or duplicity; and owls for wisdom. A *personal* or *idiosyncratic symbol* is one that assumes its secondary meaning because of the special use to which it is put by a writer. In "Song of Myself" (excerpted in Unit 5), Walt Whitman uses grass as a personal symbol for the beauty and value of simple, lowly things.

SYNAESTHESIA. **Synaesthesia** is a figure of speech that combines in a single expression images related to two or more different senses. In Emily Dickinson's "I heard a Fly buzz—when I died—" (Unit 4), the line "With Blue—uncertain stumbling Buzz—" contains an example of synaesthesia because "stumbling Buzz" is an image that appeals to both the senses of sight and of sound.

SYNECDOCHE. A **synecdoche** (sin ek´ də kē´) is a figure of speech in which the name of part of something is used in place of the name of the whole or vice versa. In the command "All hands on deck!" *hands* is a synecdoche in which a part (hands) is used to refer to a whole (people, sailors). Addressing a representative of the country of France as *France* would be a synecdoche in which a whole (France) is used to refer to a part (one French person).

SYNTAX. **Syntax** is the pattern of arrangement of words in a statement. Poets often vary the syntax of ordinary speech or experiment with unusual syntactic arrangements. Abraham Lincoln's Gettysburg Address is often noted for its unusual syntax. E. E. Cummings varies syntax in his line "anyone lived in a pretty how town / (with up so floating many bells down)" in "anyone lived in a pretty how town" (Unit 7). See *inversion*.

TAG LINE. A **tag line** is an expression in a work of fiction that indicates who is speaking and sometimes indicates the manner of speaking. Examples include the familiar *she said* as well as

more elaborate expressions such as *Raoul retorted angrily*.

TALL TALE. A **tall tale** is a story, often lighthearted or humorous, that contains highly exaggerated, unrealistic elements. Mark Twain's "The Notorious Jumping Frog of Calaveras County" (Unit 6) is an example.

TENOR. See *metaphor*.

TERCET. See *triplet*.

*TERZA RIMA*. **Terza rima** is a three-line stanza of the kind used in Dante's *Divine Comedy*, rhyming *aba, bcb, cdc, ded,* and so on.

TETRAMETER. See *meter*.

TEXTUAL CRITICISM. See *criticism*.

THEATER **(playing area)**. See *stage*.

THEATER IN THE ROUND. See *stage*.

THEATER OF THE ABSURD. The **theater of the absurd** is a kind of twentieth-century drama that presents illogical, absurd, or unrealistic scenes, characters, events, or juxtapositions in an attempt to convey the essential meaninglessness of human life, although playwrights have often used the form to convey significant moral messages. Practitioners of the theater of the absurd, which grew out of the philosophy of *Existentialism*, include Eugene Ionesco, Samuel Beckett, Edward Albee, and Harold Pinter. See *Existentialism* and *literature of the absurd*.

THEME. A **theme** is a central idea in a literary work. The value of each individual is the theme of Ralph Waldo Emerson's "The Rhodora" (Unit 4).

THESIS. A **thesis** is a main idea that is supported in a work of nonfictional prose. The thesis of Daniel J. Boorstin's "Why I Am Optimistic about America" (Unit 12) is that there are many reasons to be optimistic about the future of the United States.

THIRD-PERSON POINT OF VIEW. See *point of view*.

THREE-DIMENSIONAL CHARACTER. See *character*.

THRUST STAGE. See *stage*.

TONE. **Tone** is the emotional attitude toward the reader or toward the subject implied by a literary work. Examples of the different tones that a work may have include familiar, ironic, playful, sarcastic, serious, and sincere.

**TRAGEDY.** A **tragedy** is a drama (or by extension any work of literature) that tells the story of the fall of a person of high status. It celebrates the courage and dignity of a tragic hero in the face of inevitable doom. Sometimes that doom is made inevitable by a tragic flaw in the hero. In the twentieth century, writers have extended the definition of tragedy to cover works that deal with the fall of any sympathetic character, despite his or her status. Willie Loman in Arthur Miller's play *Death of a Salesman* is such a character. His downfall is precipitated by his adherence to the mistaken belief that success in life is gained by being "well liked" by people of importance.

**TRAGIC FLAW.** A **tragic flaw** is a personal weakness that brings about the fall of a character in a tragedy. See *tragedy*.

**TRAGIC HERO.** See *hero* and *tragedy*.

**TRANSCENDENTALISM.** As a variation of European Romanticism, **Transcendentalism** advocated a belief in spiritual, or transcendent, truths beyond sense perception and material existence. Placing oneself in natural environs would increase one's ability to attain transcendent thought. In contrast to the materialism valued by the Puritans and Benjamin Franklin, Transcendentalists exalted the spiritual and the individual. The group of Transcendental thinkers and writers gathered in Boston and Concord, Massachusetts, in the middle of the nineteenth century included Henry David Thoreau, Ralph Waldo Emerson, Bronson Alcott, Margaret Fuller, and W. H. Channing.

**TRANSITION.** A **transition** is a word, phrase, sentence, or paragraph used to connect ideas and to show relationships between them. *However, therefore, in addition,* and *in contrast* are common transitions. Repeated nouns, synonyms, and pronouns can also serve as transitions.

**TRANSLATION. Translation** is the art of rendering speech or writing into another language.

**TRIMETER.** See *meter*.

**TRIPLET.** A **triplet**, or **tercet**, is a stanza of three lines.

**TROCHEE.** A **trochee** is a poetic foot consisting of a strongly stressed syllable followed by a weakly stressed syllable, as in the word *winter*. A line of poetry made up of trochees is said to be *trochaic*.

**TURNING POINT.** See *plot*.

**UNDERSTATEMENT.** An **understatement** is an ironic expression in which something of importance is emphasized by being spoken of as though it were not important, as in "He's sort of dead, I think."

**UNITY.** A work has **unity** when its various parts all contribute to creating an integrated whole. An essay with unity, for example, is one in which all the parts help to support the thesis statement, or main idea. See *essay*.

**UNRELIABLE NARRATOR.** An **unreliable narrator** is one whom the reader cannot trust. See *narrator*.

**UTOPIA.** A **utopia** is an imaginary, idealized world. The term comes from the title of Sir Thomas More's *Utopia*, which described what More believed to be an ideal society. More took the word from the Greek roots meaning "no-place." See *dystopia*.

**VEHICLE.** See *metaphor*.

**VERBAL IRONY.** See *irony*.

**VERNACULAR.** The **vernacular** is the speech of the common people. The term *vernacular* is often used loosely today to refer to dialogue or to writing in general that uses colloquial, dialectical, or slang expressions.

**VERSIFICATION.** See *prosody*.

**VERS LIBRE.** See *free verse*.

**VOICE. Voice** is the way a writer uses language to reflect his or her unique personality and attitude toward topic, form, and audience. A writer expresses voice through tone, word choice, and sentence structure.

# GLOSSARY
## Of Words For Everyday Use

**PRONUNCIATION KEY**

**VOWEL SOUNDS**

| a | hat | i | sit | $\overline{oo}$ (or ü) | blue, stew | ə | extra |
|---|-----|---|-----|------|------------|---|-------|
| ā | play | ī | my | oi (or ȯi) | boy | | under |
| ä | star | ō | go | ou (or aů) | wow | | civil |
| e | then | ô (or ȯ) | paw, born | u | up | | honor |
| ē | me | oo (or ů) | book, put | ʉ | burn | | bogus |

**CONSONANT SOUNDS**

| b | but | j | jump | p | pop | th | the |
|---|-----|---|------|---|-----|----|----|
| ch | watch | k | brick | r | rod | v | valley |
| d | do | l | lip | s | see | w | work |
| f | fudge | m | money | sh | she | y | yell |
| g | go | n | on | t | sit | z | pleasure |
| h | hot | ŋ | song, sink | th | with | | |

**ab • di • cate** (abʹdi kātʹ) *vt.,* give up a right or a responsibility.

**a • bey • ance** (ə bāʹəns) *n.,* temporary suspension, as of an activity or function.

**ab • hor** (ab hôrʹ) *vt.,* shrink from in disgust.

**ab • ject • ly** (abʹ jektʹ lē) *adv.,* miserably; in a manner that shows utter hopelessness or resignation.

**a • bridge** (ə brijʹ) *vt.,* reduce in scope; make shorter.

**ab • sti • nence** (abʹ stə nən[t]s) *n.,* habitual abstaining or refraining from an action or practice.

**ab • strac • tion** (ab strakʹshən) *n.,* mental withdrawal; absent-mindedness.

**a • byss** (ə bisʹ) *n.,* bottomless hole.

**ac • cen • tu • a • tion** (ak sen chü āʹ shən) *n.,* emphasis; clear pronunciation.

**ac • cliv • i • ty** (ə klivʹə tē) *n.,* upward slope.

**ac • qui • esce** (akʹwē esʹ) *vi.,* agree without protest.

**a • cute • ly** (ə kyütʹlē) *adv.,* sharply, painfully, or severely.

**ad • jure** (ə jerʹ) *vt.,* urge; beg.

**ad • mon • ish** (ad mänʹish) *vt.,* caution against specific faults.

**af • fin • i • ty** (ə finʹi tē) *n.,* close relationship; connection.

**af • flic • ted** (ə fliktʹ əd) *adj.,* suffering from an illness or other painful physical condition.

**a • ghast** (ə gastʹ) *adj.,* feeling great horror or dismay.

**al • leged** (ə lejdʹ, ə leʹjəd) *adj.,* accused but not proven or convicted.

**am • bush** (am' bůsh) *n.,* trap in which a concealed person or persons lie in wait to attack by surprise.

**am • i • ca • bly** (a' mi kə blē) *adv.,* in a friendly or peaceable manner.

**a • nal • o • gy** (ə nalʹə jē) *n.,* similarity in some respects between things otherwise unalike.

**a • nath • e • ma** (ə nathʹə mə) *n.,* curse.

**a • noint** (ə nointʹ) *vt.,* rub with oil; apply oil to.

**an • ti • dote** (anʹ ti dōt) *n.,* something that relieves, prevents, or counteracts.

**ap • er • ture** (apʹər cher) *n.,* opening; hole.

**ap • pa • ra • tus** (apʹ ə ratʹ əs) *n.,* materials and tools needed for a specific purpose.

**ap • pend** (ə pendʹ) *vt.,* attach or affix.

**ap • pre • hen • sion** (a pri hen[t]ʹ shən) *n.,* suspicion or fear.

**ap • ti • tude** (apʹtə tüdʹ) *n.,* natural tendency or inclination.

**a • que • ous** (āʹ kwē əs) *adj.,* of, relating to, or resembling water.

**ar • bi • trary** (ärʹ bə trer ē) *adj.,* ruling by absolute authority.

**ar • dent** (ardʹ ʹnt) *adj.,* intensely enthusiastic or devoted.

**ar • du • ous** (är´jü əs) *adj.*, difficult.

**ar • is • toc • ra • cy** (ar ə stä´ krə sē) *n.*, government ruled by a small privileged class.

**ar • tic • u • lat • ed** (ar tik´ yü lāt´əd) *adj.*, made up of distinct syllables or words, as human speech.

**as • cet • ic** (ə set´ik) *adj.*, self-denying; austere.

**as • cribe** (ə skrīb´) *vt.*, assign; attribute.

**as • pi • ra • tion** (as pə rā´shən) *n.*, strong ambition.

**as • pi • rat • ed** (as´pə rāt´əd) *adj.*, articulated with a puff of breath before or after.

**as • sent** (ə sent´) *n.*, agreement.

**as • sert** (ə sʉrt´) *vt.*, declare; affirm.

**as • suage** (ə swāj´) *vt.*, lessen; calm; pacify.

**a • sun • der** (ə sun´der´) *adv.*, apart or separate in direction or position.

**asy • lum** (ə sī´ ləm) *n.*, place of retreat and security.

**au • gur** (ô´ gər) *vt.*, foretell, especially from omens.

**au • to • ma • tion** (ô tə ma´ shən) *n.*, technique of making an apparatus, a process, or a system operate automatically.

**aus • tere** (ô stir´) *adj.*, plain; without luxury or ornamentation.

**a • vail** (ə vāl´) *vi.*, be of use or advantage.

**a • ver • sion** (ə vʉr´zhən) *n.*, definite dislike.

**a • vert** (ə vʉrt´) *vt.*, prevent; turn away.

**a • vid • i • ty** (ə vid´ə tē) *n.*, eagerness; enthusiasm.

**a • vow** (ə vou´) *vt.*, admit frankly.

**bale • ful** (bā[ə]l´ fəl) *adj.*, sinister.

**balm** (bäm) *n.*, anything healing or soothing.

**balm • y** (bäm´ ē) *adj.*, soothing, mild, or pleasant.

**bane • ful** (bān´ fəl) *adj.*, causing distress, ruin, or death.

**banked** (baŋkd) *adj.*, arranged to continue burning slowly.

**bar • bar • ic** (bär ber´ik) *adj.*, wild, crude, and unrestrained.

**bea • con** (bē´ kən) *n.*, source of light or inspiration.

**beau** (bō) *n.*, boyfriend.

**be • guile** (bē gīl´) *vt.*, charm; lead by deception.

**be • la • bor** (bē lā´ bər) *vt.*, spend too much time or effort on.

**be • lea • guer** (bē lē´gər) *vt.*, besiege by encircling.

**bel • li • cose** (bel´i kōs) *adj.*, hostile; eager to fight.

**blight** (blīt) *n.*, anything that destroys or prevents growth.

**bom • bard • ment** (bäm bard´mənt) *n.*, attack by bombing.

**buf • fet** (buf´it) *n.*, blow with the hand or fist; *vt.*, batter or drive by force.

**bur • geon** (bʉr´ jən) *vi.*, grow and expand rapidly.

**bur • nish** (bʉr´nish) *vt.*, make shiny by rubbing.

**bur • nished** (bʉr´ nished) *adj.*, polished; made shiny by rubbing.

**ca • dence** (kā´dən[t]s) *n.*, rhythmic flow of sound or tone.

**ca • lam • i • ty** (kə la´ mə tē) *n.*, extraordinarily grave event marked by great loss and lasting distress and affliction.

**cal • low** (ka´lō) *adj.*, lacking adult sophistication.

**can • on • ize** (kan´ ən īz´) *vt.*, declare a deceased person a saint in formal church procedure.

**ca • price** (kə prēs´) *n.*, whim; change in way of thinking.

**car • riage** (kar´ ij) *n.*, manner of bearing the body; posture.

**ca • ter** (kāt´ər) *vi.*, take special pains in seeking to gratify another's needs or desires.

**cav • al • cade** (kav´əl kād´) *n.*, procession (of horses).

**ca • vort** (kə vôrt´) *vi.*, leap about, prance.

**ce • ler • i • ty** (sə ler´ ə tē) *n.*, rapidity of motion or action.

**ce • les • tial** (sə les´ chəl) *adj.*, relating to heaven or divinity.

**cen • ser** (sen´sər) *n.*, container for burning incense.

**cen • sor** (sen[t]´ sər) *n.*, official (as in wartime) who reads communications (as letters) and deletes material considered sensitive or harmful.

**ces • sa • tion** (se sā´shən) *n.*, ceasing or stopping.

**chron • ic** (krän´ ik) *adj.*, constant; perpetual.

**cir • cum • lo • cu • tion** (sʉr kəm lō kyü´ shən) *n.*, use of an unnecessarily large number of words to express an idea.

**ci • vil • i • ty** (sə vil´ə tē) *n.*, gentleness; a civilized manner; politeness.

**clod** (kläd) *n.*, lump, such as a lump of earth or clay.

**cog • ni • zance** (käg´nə zəns) *n.*, knowledge.

**com • men • su • rate** (kə men´ shür it) *adj.*, equal in measure or size; proportionate.

**com • mu • nal** (kə myü´ nəl) *adj.*, participated in, shared, or used in common by members of a group or community.

**com • mun • ion** (kə myün´yən) *n.*, act of sharing thoughts and actions.

**com • pe • tent** (käm´ pə tənt) *adj.*, properly qualified; capable.

**com • pli • ance** (kəm plī´ən[t]s) *n.*, act of giving in to wishes or demands.

**com • port** (kəm pôrt´) *vi.*, agree; go along.

**con • ceit** (kən sēt´) *n.*, idea, thought; personal opinion.

**con • fed • er • a • cy** (kən fed´ər ə sē) *n.*, people or groups united for a common purpose.

**con • found** (kən found´) *vt.*, confuse; bewilder.

**con • glom • er • a • tion** (kən gläm´ər ā´shən) *n.*, collection or mixture.

**con • jec • ture** (kən jek´chər) *n.*, prediction based on guesswork; speculation; *vi.*, guess.

**con • jur • a • tion** (kän jü rā´shən) *n.*, solemn appeal; magical spell.

**con • jure** (kän´ jər) *vt.*, bring into being as if by magic; call up.

**con • nois • seur** (kän´ə sʉr´) *n.*, person who has expert knowledge in some field.

**con • se • crate** (kän´si krāt´) *vt.*, make or declare sacred.

**con • sole** (kən sōl´) *vt.*, comfort.

**con • spic • u • ous • ly** (kən spi´ kyə wəs lē) *adv.*, in a way that attracts attention.

**con • sti • tu • tion** (kän´stə tü´shən) *n.*, physical makeup of a person.

**con • sul • ta • tion** (kän´səl tā´shən) *n.*, meeting to discuss, decide, or plan something.

**con • sum • mate** (kän´sə māt) *vt.*, complete.

**con • tem • pla • tion** (kän´ təm plā´ shən) *n.*, thoughtful inspection, study, or meditation.

**con • tend** (kən tend') *vi.*, strive in debate.

**con • tend • er** (kən ten´dər) *n.*, one who strives or fights in competition.

**con • tor • tion** (kən tôr´shən) *n.*, twisting out of shape.

**con • triv • ance** (kən trī´vəns) *n.*, invention; ingenious plan.

**con • viv • i • al** (kən viv´ yəl) *adj.*, relating to feasting, drinking, and good company.

**con • vo • lu • tion** (kän´və lü´shən) *n.*, twist; coil; fold.

**con • vo • lut • ed** (kän və lü´ təd) *adj.*, twisting or coiling.

**con • vul • sion** (kən vul´ shən) *n.*, abnormal, violent, and involuntary contraction or series of contractions of the muscles; sudden, violent disturbance.

**co • quet • ry** (kō´kə trē) *n.*, flirting.

**cor • di • al • i • ty** (kôr´jē al´ə tē) *n.*, warm, friendly act or remark.

**cou • lee** (kü' lē) *n.*, ravine, usually a small or shallow one.

**course** (kôrs) *vi.*, move swiftly; flow through.

**cowed** (koud) *adj.*, intimidated.

**cow • er** (kou´ər) *vi.*, crouch or shrink back in fear.

**cra • ven** (krā´vən) *n.*, coward.

**creed** (krēd) *n.*, statement of belief, principles, or opinions on any subject.

**crypt** (kript) *n.*, underground chamber.

**cul • ti • vate** (kul´tə vāt) *vt.*, acquire and develop.

**cur • so • ry** (kərs´ rē) *adj.*, rapidly and often superficially performed or produced.

**cur • tail • ment** (kər tā[ə]l´mənt) *n.*, abrupt ending.

**czar** (zar) *n.*, emperor.

**dal • ly** (dal´ē) *vi.*, waste time.

**de • cep • tion** (di sep' shən) *n.*, act of deceiving.

**de • ci • pher** (dē sī' fər) *vt.*, make out the meaning of.

**de • claim** (di klām') *vi.*, recite a speech.

**def • er • en • tial** (def´ə ren´shəl) *adj.*, respectful.

**de • lir • i • um** (di lir' ē əm) *n.*, mental disturbance charac-terized by confusion, disordered speech, and hallucinations.

**del • e • te • ri • ous** (del´ə tir´ē əs) *adj.*, harmful to health or well-being.

**de • lu • so • ry** (di lü´sə rē) *adj.*, quality of seeming unreal.

**de • mean • or** (di mēn´ər) *n.*, way of behaving; manner.

**de • mure** (di myür´) *adj.*, modest; shy.

**de • plore** (di plôr') *vt.*, regret strongly; consider unfortunate or deserving of criticism.

**de • pop • u • late** (dē päp´yə lāt´) *vt.*, reduce the population of, especially by violence or disease.

**de • port • ment** (dē pôrt´mənt) *n.*, manner of conducting or bearing oneself.

**de • praved** (dē prāvd´) *adj.*, morally bad; corrupt.

**de • rive** (di rīv´) *vt.*, take, receive, or make, usually from a specified source.

**de • vout** (di vout´) *adj.*, showing reverence.

**dif • fuse** (di fyüz´) *vt.*, spread out; pour out.

**di • gress** (dī gres´) *vi.*, deviate from the main topic in speaking or writing.

**di • lap • i • dat • ed** (də lap´ ə dāt´ id) *adj.*, falling to pieces or into disrepair; decayed; fallen into partial ruin through neglect.

**dil • a • to • ry** (dil´ə tôr´ē) *adj.*, causing delay.

**dil • i • gent • ly** (dil´ə jənt lē) *adv.*, painstakingly; industriously.

**dis • ar • ray** (di sə rā´) *n.*, lack of order or sequence.

**dis • bar** (dis bär´) *vt.*, deprive (a lawyer) of the right to practice law.

**dis • cord • ant** (dis kôr´dənt) *adj.*, disagreeing; conflicting.

**dis • creet** (dis krēt´) *adj.*, showing careful reserve in speech or action.

**dis • em • bark** (di səm bärk´) *vi.*, leave a ship to go ashore.

**dis • fran • chise • ment** (dis fran´ chīz mənt) *n.*, depriving of a legal right or privilege.

**dis • mal** (diz´ məl) *adj.*, causing gloom or misery.

**dis • po • si • tion** (dis´pə zish´ən) *n.*, state of mind; one's customary frame of mind or general nature.

**dis • si • pate** (di´sə pāt) *vi.*, break up; scatter; vanish.

**dis • suade** (di swād´) *vt.*, talk out of.

**dis • till** also **dis • til** (di stil´) *vt.*, let fall or precipitate in drops.

**dis • traught** (dis trôt´) *adj.*, upset by doubt or mental conflict.

**di • ver • si • ty** (də vʉr´sə tē) *n.*, variety.

**dole • ful** (dōl´fəl) *adj.*, full of or causing sorrow or sadness.

**dow • dy** (dou´ dē) *adj.*, unbecoming in appearance.

**dupe** (düp) *vt.*, deceive by underhanded means.

**dwin • dle** (dwin´dəl) *vt.*, languish; fade.

**ear • nest** (ʉr´nist) *adj.*, serious; intense; sincere.

**ebb** (eb) *n.*, flowing back of the tide toward the sea.

**eb • ul • li • tion** (eb´ə lish´ən) *n.*, boiling or bubbling up.

**ee • rie** (ir´ rē) *adj.*, frightening because of strangeness or mysteriousness.

**ef • face** (ə fās´) *vt.*, erase, wipe out.

**ef • face • ment** (i fās' mənt) *n.*, disappearance or fading as if by wearing away.

**ef • fec • tu • al** (e fek´chü əl) *adj.*, effective.

**ef • fi • ca • cious** (ef´i kā´shəs) *adj.*, producing or capable of producing the desired effect.

**egal • i • tar • i • an** (i ga´lə ter´ē ən) *adj.*, asserting a belief in human equality, especially equality in terms of social, political, and economic rights.

**e • late** (ē lāt´) *vt.,* raise the spirits of.

**ela • tion** (i lā´shən) *n.,* state of great joy and pride.

**elic • it** (i li' sət) *vt.,* draw forth or bring out.

**e • ma • ci • at • ed** (ē mā´shē āt əd) *adj.,* abnormally thin.

**em • bel • lish** (im be' lish) *vt.,* make beautiful with ornamentation.

**em • bra • sure** (em brā´zhər) *n.,* slanted opening in a wall (as of a fort) that increases the firing angle of a gun.

**em • is • sar • y** (em´i ser´ē) *n.,* person or agent sent on a mission.

**en • clave** (en' klāv; än' klāv) *n.,* a distinct territorial, cultural, or social unit enclosed within, or as if within, foreign territory.

**en • com • pass** (en kum´pəs) *vt.,* surround.

**en • cum • brance** (en kum´brəns) *n.,* hindrance.

**en • deav • or** (en dev´ər) *n.,* effort; attempt.

**en • dow** (in dou') *vt.,* provide with something freely or naturally.

**en • dow • ment** (en dou´mənt) *n.,* gift of nature; inherent talent.

**en • dure** (en dür´) *vi.,* continue in existence; last, remain.

**en • gen • der** (en gen' dər) *vt.,* cause to develop; produce.

**en • ig • ma • tic** (e' nig ma' tik) *adj.,* mysterious.

**en • mi • ty** (en´mi tē´) *n.,* active and typically mutual hatred or ill will.

**en • sue** (en sü´) *vi.,* come afterward; follow immediately.

**en • thralled** (in´thrôld´) *adj.,* held spellbound.

**en • treat** (en trēt´) *vt.,* beg; implore; ask earnestly.

**en • treat • y** (en trēt´ē) *n.,* earnest request.

**e • phem • er • al** (e fem´ər əl) *adj.,* short-lived; transitory.

**e • qua • nim • i • ty** (ek´wə nim´ə tē) *n.,* evenness of mind or temper; quality of remaining calm.

**e • rad • i • cate** (e rad´i kāt´) *vt.,* get rid of; wipe out; destroy.

**er • ro • ne • ous** (ər rō´nē əs) *adj.,* mistaken; wrong.

**e • the • re • al** (ē thir´ē əl) *adj.,* not earthly; heavenly, celestial.

**e • ther • ize** *or Brit.* **e • ther • ise** (ē´thə rīz´) *vt.,* render groggy or numb.

**es • ti • ma • tion** (es´tə mā´shen) *n.,* respect; value.

**eu • lo • gy** (yü' lə jē) *n.,* speech of high praise.

**eu • pho • ny** (yü´fə nē) *n.,* pleasing or sweet sound.

**e • vade** (ē vād´) *vt.,* avoid or escape from by deceit or cleverness.

**ev • a • nes • cent** (ev´ə ne´sənt) *adj.,* tending to fade; vanishing.

**eva • sive • ly** (i vā' siv lē) *adv.,* in a manner intended to evade.

**e • vince** (ē vin[t]s´) *vt.,* show plainly; indicate.

**ex • as • per • a • ting** (eg zas´pər āt iŋ) *adj.,* irritating; annoying.

**ex • ces • sive** (ik se' siv) *adj.,* exceeding what is usual, proper, necessary, or normal.

**ex • cru • ci • at • ing • ly** (eks krü´shē āt´iŋ lē) *adv.,* in a painful or agonizing manner.

**ex • hor • ter** (eg zôrt´ər) *n.,* one who urges earnestly, by advice or warning.

**ex • pa • tri • at • ed** (eks pā´trē āt´id) *adj.,* driven from one's land.

**ex • po • si • tion** (eks´pə zish´ən) *n.,* large, public exhibition or show, often international in scope.

**ex • pur • gat • ed** (eks' pər gāt əd) *adj.,* having had objectionable parts removed before publication or presentation.

**ex • tem • po • rize** (eks tem´pə rīz´) *vt.,* contrive in a makeshift way to meet a pressing need.

**ex • ten • u • at • ing** (ik sten' yə wāt iŋ) *adj.,* lessening seriousness of [a crime] by making, or serving as, an excuse.

**ex • trem • i • ty** (ek strem´ə tē) *n.,* state of extreme necessity or danger.

**ex • ult** (ig' zəlt) *vi.,* be extremely joyful.

**ex • ul • tant** (ig zəl´tənt) *adj.,* filled with great joy.

**ex • ult • ing • ly** (ig zəlt' iŋ lē) *adv.,* in a joyful manner.

**fate • ful** (fāt´ fəl) *adj.,* deadly.

**feign** (fān) *vt.,* pretend or imagine.

**fe • lo • ni • ous** (fə lō´nē əs) *adj.,* of a criminal nature.

**fer • vor** (fur´vər) *n.,* great warmth or emotion.

**fi • as • co** (fē as´kō) *n.,* complete failure.

**fin • ick • y** (fi' ni kē) *adj.,* excessively nice or exacting in taste or standards.

**fis • sure** (fish´ər) *n.,* long, narrow, deep cleft or crack.

**fix** (fiks) *n.,* position of difficulty or embarrassment.

**flar • ing** (flar´ iŋ) *adj.,* flaming brightly or unsteadily.

**flor • id** (flôr´ əd) *adj.,* very flowery in style.

**flour • ish** (flur´ish) *vi.,* grow vigorously; thrive; prosper.

**fluc • tu • ate** (fluk´chü āt´) *vi.,* change or vary continuously.

**for • lorn** (fər lôrn´) *adj.,* forsaken or miserable.

**for • mi • da • ble** (fôr´mə de bəl) *adj.,* overwhelming.

**for • mu • lat • ed** (fôr´myə lāt´əd) *adj.,* systematical; precise.

**fren • zied** (fren´zēd) *adj.,* marked by emotional agitation.

**fur • nish** (fur´ nish) *vt.,* supply or provide.

**fu • sion** (fyü' zhən) *n.,* merging of distinct elements into a unified whole.

**gal • lant • ly** (gal´ənt lē) *adv.,* politely, nobly.

**gape** (gāp) *vi.,* gaze stupidly or in openmouthed surprise or wonder.

**gar • ru • lous** (gar´ə ləs) *adj.,* talking too much.

**geno • cide** (je' nə sīd´) *n.,* deliberate and systematic destruction of a racial, political, or cultural group.

**ges • tic • u • late** (jes tik´yü lat´) *vi.,* make gestures with hands or arms.

**gid • dy** (gi´ dē) *adj.,* lightheartedly silly.

**glut • tony** (glut´nē) *n.,* habit or act of eating too much.

**grav • i • ty** (grav´i tē) *n.,* seriousness.

**gre • nade** (grə nād') *n.,* small missile that contains an explosive or a chemical agent and that is thrown by hand or projected.

**grov • el** (grä´vəl) *vi.,* give oneself over to what is base or unworthy.

**guf • faw • ing** (gə fô´ iŋ) *adj.,* laughing loudly and coarsely.

**guile • less** (gīl´lis) *adj.,* without deceit.

**gulf** (gulf) *n.,* wide, deep gap or separation.

**gul • let** (gə´ lət) *n.,* throat.

**gyp • sy** (jip´ sē) *n.,* wanderer; member of an itinerant people who live chiefly in Asia, Europe, and North America.

**hag • gard** (ha´gərd) *adj.,* having a worn, exhausted, or emaciated appearance.

**har • bor** (här´bər) *vt.,* serve as, or provide, a place of protection.

**he • do • nis • tic** (hē dən is´ tik) *adj.,* relating to or characterized by pleasure.

**hel • ter-skel • ter** (hel´ tər skel´ tər) *adj.,* marked by a lack of order or plan; haphazard.

**hem** (həm) *adj.,* encircle; surround.

**her • mi • tage** (hʉr´mi tij) *n.,* place where a person can live away from others.

**hi • er • ar • chy** (hī´ər är´ kē) *n.,* graded or ranked series of things.

**hoar • y** (hôr´ē) *adj.,* having white or gray hair.

**hul • la • ba • loo** (hə´lə bə lü´) *n.,* confused noise.

**hum • ble** (hum´ bəl) *adj.,* reflecting, expressing, or offered in a spirit of deference or submission.

**hyp • not • ic** (hip nä´ tik) *adj.,* tending to produce sleep.

**hys • ter • i • cal** (his ter´i kəl) *adj.,* displaying excessive emotion often through uncontrollable laughter or tears.

**i • con** (ī´ kän) *n.,* highly symbolic religious image.

**i • de • ol • o • gy** (ī´dē äl´ə gē) *n.,* doctrine, opinion, or way of thinking.

**im • bue** (im byü´) *vt.,* fill; saturate.

**im • mi • nent** (im´ə nənt) *adj.,* likely to happen without delay.

**im • mo • bil • i • ty** (im´mō bil´i tē) *n.,* state of being fixed or unmovable.

**im • mor • tal** (i môr´ təl) *adj.,* able to live forever; never to be forgotten.

**im • mu • ni • ties** (i myü´ nə tēs) , *n., pl.,* rights that are protected.

**im • pal • pa • ble** (im pal´pə bəl) *adj.,* that which cannot be felt by touching.

**im • pede** (im pēd´) *vt.,* obstruct; hinder.

**im • pend** (im pend´) *vi.,* be about to happen.

**im • pen • e • tra • ble** (im´ pe´nə trə bəl) *adj.,* unable to be comprehended.

**im • per • cep • ti • ble** (im´ pər sep´ tə bəl) *adj.,* not able to be detected by the senses or the mind.

**im • per • turb • a • ble** (im pər tʉr´bə bəl) *adj.,* that cannot be disconnected or disturbed.

**im • pla • ca • ble** (im plā´kə bəl) *adj.,* that cannot be appeased or pacified.

**im • plor • ing • ly** (im plôr´iŋ lē) *adv.,* in a beseeching manner.

**im • por • tu • nate • ly** (im pôr´chü nit lē) *adv.,* in an annoyingly urgent or persistent manner.

**im • por • tu • ni • ty** (im´pər tü´ nə tē) *n.,* persistent demand.

**in • a • ni • tion** (in´ə nish´ən) *n.,* lack of strength due to lack of food.

**in • au • di • bly** (in ô´də blē) *adv.,* not loudly enough to be heard.

**in • cen • di • ar • y** (in sen´ dē er ē) *adj.,* relating to or involving deliberate burning of property.

**in • ces • sant** (in se´ sənt) *adj.,* continuing following without interruption.

**in • cense** (in sens´) *vt.,* make very angry.

**in • ces • sant** (in se´ sənt) *adj.,* continuing or following without interruption.

**in • cli • na • tion** (in´ klə nā´shən) *n.,* a particular disposition of mind or character.

**in • co • her • ent** (in´ kō hir´ənt) *adj.,* unclear, not understandable.

**in • cred • u • lous • ly** (in kre´ jə ləs lē) *adv.,* in a doubting or skeptical manner.

**in • de • ci • pher • a • ble** (in´dē sī´fər ə bəl) *adj.,* incapable of being interpreted.

**in • def • i • nite** (in def´ə nit) *adj.,* having no exact limits.

**in • de • ter • mi • nate** (in di tʉr´mi nət) *adj.,* unspecific; unsettled.

**in • dict • ment** (in dīt´ mənt) *n.,* state of being charged with a crime or offense.

**in • dig • e • nous** (in di´ jə nəs) *adj.,* having originated in and being produced, growing, living, or occurring naturally in a particular region or environment.

**in • do • lent • ly** (in´də lənt lē) *adv.,* lazily.

**in • duce** (in düs´) *vt.,* persuade; prevail on.

**in • duct** (in dukt´) *vt.,* place in official position.

**in • dul • gence** (in dul´jəns) *n.,* favor or privilege.

**in • e • luc • ta • bly** (in´ē luk´tə blē) *adv.,* in an inescapable or unavoidable manner.

**in • es • ti • ma • ble** (in es´ tə mə bəl) *adj.,* too great to be measured.

**in • fat • u • a • tion** (in fa´ chü ā´shən) *n.,* foolish or shallow love or affection.

**in • fe • lic • i • tous** (in fə lis´ə təs) *adj.,* unfortunate; unsuitable.

**in • fest** (in fest´) *vt.,* overrun or inhabit in large numbers.

**in • fi • del** (in´fə del´) *n.,* person who does not believe in a particular religion.

**in • firm** (in fərm´) *adj.,* of weakened vitality; especially feeble from age.

**in • flec • tion** (in flek´shən) *n.,* change in pitch or tone of voice.

**in • fringe** (in frinj´) *vt.,* violate [a rule]; trespass [used with *on* or *upon*].

**in • ge • nious** (in jēn´ yəs) *adj.,* having great mental ability; marked by originality, resourcefulness, and cleverness in conception or execution.

**in • ge • nu • i • ty** (in´jə nü´ə tē) *n.,* cleverness.

**in • her • ent** (in hir´ ənt) *adj.,* belonging by nature or habit.

**in • her • ent • ly** (in hir´ ənt lē) *adv.,* characteristically; naturally.

**in • hu • man** (in hyü´ mən) adj., unfeeling; cruel; barbarous.

**in • oc • u • late** (i nä´ kyə lāt) *vt.,* protect as if by giving an inoculation.

**in • qui • si • tion** (in´kwə zish´ən) *n.,* severe or intensive questioning.

**in • quis • i • to • ri • al** (in kwiz´ə tôr´ē əl) *adj.,* prying.

**in • sen • si • ble** (in sen´sə bəl) *adj.,* lacking sensation; unaware.

**in • sid • i • ous** (in sid´ē əs) *adj.,* deceitful; sly; crafty.

**in • sin • u • ate** (in sin´yü āt) *vt.,* introduce or work into gradually.

**in • su • per • a • ble** (in sü´pər ə bəl) *adj.,* insurmountable.

**in • sur • rec • tion** (in´sə rek´shən) *n.,* uprising.

**in • ter • fer • ence** (in´ter fir´ens) *n.,* something that comes into collision or opposition.

**in • ter • fused** (in tər fyüzd´) *adj.,* combined, blended.

**in • ter • mi • na • ble** (in tʉr´mi nə bəl; in tərm´ nə bəl) *adj.,* without, or seemingly without, end.

**in • ter • mi • na • bly** (in tʉr´mi nə blē) *adv.,* endlessly.

**in • ter • mit • tent** (in tər mi´ tənt) *adj.,* coming and going at intervals; not continuous.

**in • tol • er • a • ble** (in täl´ər ə bəl) *adj.,* too severe, painful, or cruel to be endured.

**in • trigue** (in trēg´) *n.,* secret scheme.

**in • vec • tive** (in vek´ tiv) *n.,* insulting or abusive language.

**in • vi • o • late** (in vī´ə lit) *adj.,* sacred.

**in • vig • o • rate** (in vi´ gə rāt) *vt.,* give life and energy to.

**in • voke** (in vōk´) *vt.,* call on for blessing, help, or inspiration.

**jag** (jag) *n.,* sharp, toothlike projection.

**jaun • ti • ly** (jônt´ə lē) *adv.,* in a confident, carefree manner.

**jilt** (jilt) *vt.,* reject; cast off.

**joc • u • lar** (jäk´yə lər) *adj.,* humorous.

**joc • u • lar • i • ty** (jäk´ yü lar´ ə tē) *n.,* humor; joking

**ju • bi • lant** (jü´bə lənt) *adj.,* joyful, triumphant.

**jut** (jut) *vi.,* extend out, up, or forward.

**lab • y • rinth** (la´ bə rin[t]th) *n.,* maze.

**la • con • ic** (lə kä´nik) *adj.,* concise.

**lapse** (laps) *n.,* gliding or passing away.

**la • tent** (lā´ tənt) *adj.,* present and capable of becoming obvious or active, though not now visible.

**lat • tice** (lat´is) *n.,* shutter; openwork structure used as a screen.

**lav • ish** (la´ vish) *adj.,* abundant; excessive.

**lax • ly** (laks´lē) *adv.,* loosely; not strictly.

**lean** (lēn) *adj.,* lacking capital.

**leth • ar • gy** (leth´ər jē) *n.,* quality or state of being lazy.

**le • vi • a • than** (li vī´ə thən) *adj.,* gigantic and formidable.

**lilt • ing** (lil´ ting) *adj.,* characterized by a cheerful, rhythmical swing.

**lim • ber** (lim´ bər) *adj.,* having a supple and resilient quality.

**lime • light** (līm´ līt´) *n.,* prominent or conspicuous position, as if under a spotlight.

**lin • ger** (liŋ´gər) *vi.,* remain or stay longer than usual.

**lin • guist** (liŋ´gwist) *n.,* specialist in the science of language.

**list** (list) *vi.,* tilt to one side.

**list • less • ly** (list´lis lē) *adv.,* in a disinterested manner.

**loath • some** (lōth´səm) *adj.,* disgusting.

**lob** (läb) *vt.,* throw, hit, or propel easily or in a high arc.

**log • i • cal** (lä´ji kəl) *adj.,* governed by the scientific principles of reasoning.

**lo • cu • tion** (lō kyü´shən) *n.,* word; phrase.

**loi • ter** (loi´tər) *vi.,* remain in an area for no obvious reason.

**loi • ter • ing** (loi´tər iŋ) *n.,* act of lingering in an aimless way.

**lu • cid** (lü´sid) *adj.,* easily understood.

**lu • di • crous** (lо̄о̄´di krəs) *adj.,* absurd, ridiculous.

**lum • ber** (ləm´ bər) *vi.,* move clumsily and in an unwieldy manner.

**lu • rid** (lür´id) *adj.,* vivid in a harsh or shocking way.

**lus • trous** (lus´ trəs) *adj.,* reflecting light.

**mach • i • na • tion** (mak ə nā´ shən) *n.,* clever plot or scheme.

**mag • na • nim • i • ty** (mag´nə nim´ə tē) *n.,* state of being above pettiness.

**mag • nan • i • mous • ly** (mag na´ nə məs lē) *adv.,* showing nobility of feeling or generosity of mind.

**ma • lar • ia** (mə ler´ē ə) *n.,* disease transmitted by mosquitoes that is characterized by attacks of chills and fever.

**ma • lign** (mə līn´) *adj.,* malicious, evil.

**ma • lig • nant** (mə lig´nənt) *adj.,* harmful; evil.

**ma • lin • ger** (mə liŋ´gər) *vi.,* pretend illness.

**ma • neu • ver • ing** (mə nü´və riŋ) *n.,* strategic movement.

**man • i • fold** (man´ ə fōld´) *adv.,* in many forms or ways.

**mar • tial** (mär´shəl) *adj.,* warlike; of the military.

**mar • tyr** (märt´ər) *n.,* person who sacrifices his or her own life for the sake of a principle or cause.

**mas • ti • ca • tion** (mas´ti kā´shən) *n.,* chewing.

**ma • tric • u • late** (mə trik´yü lāt´) *vt.,* enroll.

**mea • ger** (mē´ gər) *adj.,* not rich or bountiful; inadequate.

**med • dling** (med´liŋ) *adj.,* interfering; concerning oneself with other people's affairs without being asked.

**me • di • o • cre** (mē´dē ō´ kər) *adj.,* average; not very good.

**me • nag • er • ie** (mə naj´ər ē) *n.,* collection of wild or strange animals kept in enclosures for exhibition.

**mien** (mēn) *n.,* manner; appearance.

**mi • rage** (mə räzh′) *n.*, optical effect sometimes seen at sea, in the desert, or over hot pavement; an illusion.

**mi • ser • ly** (mī′ zər lē) *adj.*, characterized by stinginess.

**mis • cel • la • ny** (mi′ sə lā′ nē) *n.*, mixture of various things.

**mock • er • y** (mä′ kə rē) *n.*, insulting or ridiculing action or speech.

**moi • e • ty** (moi′ə tē) *n.*, half.

**mol • li • fy** (mäl′ə fī′) *vt.*, soothe the temper of.

**mo • ral • i • ty** (mə ra′ lə tē) *n.*, doctrine or system of moral conduct.

**mor • ti • fied** (môr′ tə fīd) *adj.*, feeling severe and vexing embarrassment.

**mo • rose** (mə rōs′) *adj.*, having a sullen and gloomy disposition.

**mot • ley** (mät′lē) *adj.*, composed of many different elements.

**mute** (myüt) *adj.*, silent; unable to speak.

**muz • zle** (mə′ zəl) *n.*, discharging end of a weapon.

**nat • u • ral • i • za • tion** (nach′ər əl iz′ā shən) *n.*, bestowal of the rights of citizenship.

**noc • tur • nal** (näk tər′nəl) *adj.*, of, relating to, or occurring in the night.

**non • com • mit • al** (nän kə mi′ təl) *adj.*, giving no clear indication of attitude or feeling.

**nup • tial** (nup′ shəl) *adj.*, concerning marriage or a wedding.

**ob • dur • ate** (äb′dür it) *adj.*, unsympathetic; hardened.

**o • bei • sance** (ō bā′səns) *n.*, gesture of respect.

**ob • scure** (äb skyür′) *vt.*, conceal or hide by or as if by covering.

**ob • sessed** (əb sest′) *adj.*, greatly preoccupied or troubled.

**ob • tuse** (əb tüs′) *adj.*, slow to understand or perceive; insensitive.

**o • di • ous** (ō′dē əs) *adj.*, exciting or deserving hatred.

**ol • i • gar • chy** (ä′ lə gär kē) *n.*, government in which a small group exercises control, especially for corrupt and selfish purposes.

**om • i • nous** (äm′ə nəs) *adj.*, forewarning evil; threatening.

**o • paque** (ō pāk′) *adj.*, not admitting of light.

**op • pres • sion** (ə presh′ən) *n.*, keeping down by cruel or unjust use of authority.

**op • u • lent** (äp′yü lənt) *adj.*, very wealthy or rich.

**or • dain** (ôr dān′) *vt.*, officially give someone the authority and duties of a minister, priest, or rabbi.

**or • na • men • ta • tion** (ôr′na men tā′ shən) *n.*, decoration.

**or • ner • y** (ôr′nər ē) *adj.*, having an ugly or mean disposition.

**or • ni • thol • o • gist** (ôr′nə thäl′ə jist) *n.*, one who studies birds.

**os • cil • la • tion** (äs′ə lā′shən) *n.*, act of swinging back and forth.

**os • ten • ta • tious • ly** (äs ten tā′shəs lē) *adv.*, so as to attract attention.

**o • ver • ture** (ō′vər chər) *n.*, musical introduction to an opera or other long musical work.

**pal • try** (pôl′trē) *adj.*, insignificant.

**pan • ic** (pa′ nik) *n.*, sudden, overpowering fright.

**pan • to • mime** (pan′ tə mīm) *n.*, dramatic presentation without words.

**par • a • gon** (par′ə gän) *n.*, model or pattern of perfection or excellence.

**pat • ent** (pa′ tənt) *vt.*, obtain or grant authorization for an invention.

**pa • tri • arch** (pā′trē ärk′) *n.*, father; ruler; founder.

**pen • du • lum** (pen′ jə ləm) *n.*, body suspended from a fixed point so as to swing freely to and fro under the action of gravity and commonly used to regulate movements (as of clockwork).

**pen • sive** (pen′siv) *adj.*, expressing deep thoughtfulness, often with some sadness.

**per • en • ni • al** (pər en′ē əl) *adj.*, throughout the year; perpetual.

**per • force** (pər fôrs′) *adv.*, necessarily.

**per • il** (per′ əl) *n.*, exposure to the risk of being injured, destroyed, or lost.

**per • se • vere** (pʉr′sə vir′) *vi.*, continue in spite of difficulty; persist.

**per • ti • nac • i • ty** (pʉr′tə na′ sə tē) *n.*, stubbornness.

**phar • ma • ceu • ti • cal** (fär mə sü′ ti kəl) *adj.*, of, relating to, or engaged in pharmacy or the manufacture and sale of drugs.

**phe • nom • e • non** (fə näm′ə nän′) *n.*, extremely unusual or extraordinary thing or occurrence.

**phi • lan • thro • py** (fə lan[t]′ thrə pē) *n.*, act or gift of dispensing aid or funds set aside for humanitarian purposes.

**pic • tur • esque** (pik chə resk′) *adj.*, charming or quaint in appearance.

**pil • fer** (pil′fər) *vt.*, steal.

**pil • lage** (pi′ləj) *n.*, act of looting or plundering, especially in war.

**pin • ion** (pin′yən) *n.*, part of a bird's wing; *vt.*, disable or impede.

**plac • ard** (pla′ kärd; pla′ kərd) *n.*, notice for display in a public place; sign.

**plac • id** (pla′ səd) *adj.*, calm or free of disturbance.

**pla • gia • rist** (plā′ jə rist) *n.*, someone who steals and passes off the ideas or words of another as his or her own.

**pla • toon** (plə tün′) *n.*, subdivision of a company-size military unit normally consisting of two or more squads or sections.

**plume** (plüm) *n.*, feather.

**poi • gnant** (poi′ nyənt) *adj.*, deeply affecting the feelings.

**poi • gnant • ly** (poi′ nyənt lē) *adv.*, done in a manner that deeply affects the emotions.

**poise** (poiz) *n.*, ease and dignity of manner.

**pom • mel** (pə′ məl) *vt.*, pound or beat.

**pon • der • ous** (pän′dər əs) *adj.*, very heavy.

**pon • toon** (pän tün′) *n.*, flat-bottomed boat; floating object used for support.

**por • tal** (pôr´təl) *n.,* doorway, gate, or entrance.

**pos • ter • i • ty** (pä ster´ə tē) *n.,* all future generations.

**pre • am • ble** (prē´am bəl) *n.,* introductory statement.

**prec • e • dent** (pre´ sə dənt) *n.,* something done or said that may serve as an example or rule to authorize or justify a subsequent act of the same or an analogous kind.

**pre • cept** (prē´ sept) *n.,* command or principle.

**pre • cip • i • tous** (prē sip´ə təs) *adj.,* steep.

**pre • dis • pose** (prē dis pōz) *vt.,* give a tendency.

**pre • dom • i • nate** (prē däm´ə nāt´) *vi.,* have authority or influence over others.

**pre • em • i • nent • ly** (prē em´ i nent lē) *adv.,* first and foremost; most importantly.

**pre • lude** (prel´yüd; prä´ lüd) *n.,* first movement of an opera; introduction.

**pre • ma • ture** (prē´mə tür´) *adj.,* too early.

**pre • mo • ni • tion** (prē´mə ni´ shən) *n.,* feeling that something will happen.

**pre • scient** (pre´ sh[ē]ənt) *adj.,* possessing foreknowledge of events.

**pre • sume** (pri züm´) *vi.,* dare; venture; take upon oneself.

**pre • sump • tion** (prē zump´shən) *n.,* overstepping of proper bounds or the taking of something for granted.

**pre • vail** (prē vāl´) *vi.,* gain advantage or mastery; be victorious; triumph.

**pro • di • gious** (prə di´ jəs) *adj.,* causing amazement or wonder.

**prof • fer** (präf´ər) *vt.,* offer.

**pro • fu • sion** (prō fyü´zhən) *n.,* large number; abundance.

**prom • i • nent** (präm´ə nənt) *adj.,* widely and favorably known.

**prop • a • gan • dist** (präp´ə gan´ dist) *n.,* one who spreads ideas for a particular cause.

**pro • sa • ic** (prō zā´ ik) *adj.,* dull; unimaginative.

**pros • trate** (präs´ trāt´) *vt.,* bow down.

**pro • to • type** (prō´tō tīp) *n.,* standard on which other things are modeled; the first working model of a new type.

**pro • voke** (prō vōk´) *vt.,* anger, irritate, annoy.

**pul • let** (pu´ lət) *n.,* young hen.

**punc • tu • ate** (pəŋk´ chə wāt) *vt.,* break into or interrupt at intervals.

**pun • gent • ly** (pun´jənt lē) *adv.,* sharply; strongly.

**quad • ru • ped** (kwä´drü ped´) *n.,* animal, especially a mammal, with four feet.

**quaff** (kwäf) *vi.,* drink deeply.

**quan • ti • ta • tive** (kwän´ tə tā tiv) *adj.,* of, relating to, or expressible in terms of quantity.

**quer • u • lous** (kwer´yü ləs) *adj.,* full of complaint; peevish.

**quib • ble** (kwi´ bəl) *vi.,* find fault with.

**quiv • er • ing** (kwiv´ riŋ) *n.,* shaking or moving characterized by a slight trembling motion.

**rack • et** (ra´ kət) *n.,* confused, clattering noise; clamor.

**rai • ment** (rā´ mənt) *n.,* clothing.

**ram • bunc • tious** (ram bəŋk´ shəs) *adj.,* marked by uncontrollable enthusiasm; unruly.

**rap • tur • ous** (rap´ chər əs) *adj.,* full of joy or pleasure.

**rav • en • ous** (ra´ və nəs) *adj.,* eager or greedy for food, satisfaction, or gratification.

**rav • e • nous • ly** (rav´ ə nəs lē) *adv.,* in a greedy or wildly hungry manner.

**ra • vine** (rə vēn´) *n.,* small, narrow, steep-sided valley larger than a gully and smaller than a canyon.

**re • buke** (ri byük´) *vt.,* blame or scold in a sharp way.

**rec • om • pense** (rek´ əm pens´) *n.,* reward; compensation, payment; *vt.,* repay; reward.

**re • con • dite** (ri kän´ dīt´) *adj.,* difficult or impossible for the average person to understand; deep.

**rec • ti • tude** (rek´tə tüd´) *n.,* correctness.

**re • dress** (rē´dres´) *n.,* compensation.

**reef** (rēf) *n.,* chain of rocks or ridge of sand at or near the surface of the water.

**re • fract** (ri frakt´) *vt.,* alter or distort.

**re • frain** (ri frān´) *vi.,* hold back; keep oneself from doing something.

**re • lent • less** (ri lent´ ləs) *adj.,* harsh; pitiless.

**rel • ish** (rel´ish) *n.,* pleasure; enjoyment.

**rem • i • nis • cence** (rem ə nis´əns) *n.,* memory or something remembered.

**re • mon • strance** (ri män[t]´ stren[t]s) *n.,* protest, objection.

**re • mon • strate** (ri män´ strāt´) *vt.,* demonstrate.

**ren • dez • vous** (rän´ di vü) *adj.,* planned meeting.

**re • proach** (ri prōch´) *n.,* blaming or reproving; rebuke; *vt.,* express disappointment in or displeasure with someone for conduct that is blameworthy or in need of amendment.

**re • pug • nant** (ri pug´ nənt) *adj.,* exciting distaste or aversion.

**re • qui • site** (re´ kwə zət) *adj.,* essential; necessary.

**res • ig • na • tion** (rez ig nā´shən) *n.,* submission; patient acceptance.

**re • signed** (ri zind´) *adj.,* showing acceptance of the inevitable.

**res • o • lu • tion** (rez´ə lü´shən) *n.,* determined state of mind; faithfulness to some person or idea.

**re • spec • tive** (ri spek´tiv) *adj.,* as relates individually to each of two or more persons or things.

**re • splen • dent** (ri splen´dənt) *adj.,* shining brightly.

**re • sume** (ri züm´) *vt.,* take, get, or occupy again.

**ret • i • cent** (re´tə sənt) *adj.,* reserved or uncommunicative in speech.

**rev • er • ence** (re´ ver ənts) *n.,* honor or respect felt or shown.

**rev • er • en • tial** (rev´ə ren´ shəl) *adj.,* showing a feeling of deep respect, love, and awe.

**rev • er • ie** (rev´ər ē) *n.,* dreamy thinking.

**re • vert** (ri vʉrt´) *vi.,* return to a former practice or state.

**rick • e • ty** (rik´it ē) *adj.,* shaky.

**rouse** (rouz) *vt.,* awaken or stir up.

**ruf • fi • an** (ruf´ē an) *adj.,* brutal; violent; lawless.

**ru • mi • nate** (rü´mə nāt´) *vt.,* go over in the mind repeatedly; contemplate.

**rum • mage** (rum´ij) *vt.,* search through thoroughly; ransack.

**ruth • less** (rüth´ləs) *adj.,* merciless.

**sac • ro • sanct** (sa' krō saŋ[k]t) *adj.,* treated as if holy.

**sar • tor • ial** (sär tōr´ē əl) *adj.,* of or relating to clothes.

**sa • shay** (sa shā´) *vi.,* move or walk in such a way as to attract attention.

**sat • u • rat • ed** (sach´ə rāt´ əd) *adj.,* thoroughly soaked.

**saun • ter** (sôn' tər; sän' tər) *vi.,* walk about in an idle or leisurely manner.

**score** (skôr) *n.,* set of twenty.

**scorn** (skôrn) *vt.,* reject or dismiss as contemptible or unworthy.

**scru • ti • nize** (skrüt' ən īz) *vi.,* examine closely and minutely.

**se • da • tion** (sə dā' shun) *n.,* inducing of a relaxed state.

**sem • i • nal** (se' mə nəl) *adj.,* planting the seeds for further development; creative, original.

**sen • ti • nel** (sen´ti nəl) *n.,* person acting as a guard.

**sep • ul • cher** (sep´əl kər) *n.,* vault for burial of the dead.

**ser • vi • tude** (ser´vi tüd) *n.,* condition in which one lacks liberty, especially to determine one's course of life.

**sheep • ish • ly** (shēp' ish lē) *adv.,* in an embarrassed manner.

**shoal** (shōl) *adj.,* shallow.

**sib • yl** (si' bəl) *n.,* fortune-teller or female prophet.

**skir • mish** (skər' mish) *n.,* minor fight in war; minor dispute or contest between opposing parties.

**skulk** (skəlk) *vi.,* hide or conceal oneself, often out of cowardice or fear.

**so • lace** (säl´əs) *n.,* relief or consolation; *vt.,* comfort, relieve.

**sol • i • dar • i • ty** (säl´ə dar´ə tē) *n.,* combination or agreement of all elements or individuals.

**sov • er • eign** (sä´vərn; sä´və rən) *adj.,* independent; above or superior to all others.

**Spar • tan** (spärt´ən) *adj.,* like the Spartans; in other words, warlike, stoical, or disciplined.

**spas • mod • i • cal • ly** (spaz mä´dik lē) *adv.,* intermittently.

**spec • u • la • tive** (spe´ kyə lə tiv) *adj.,* theoretical.

**squal • id** (skwäl´id) *adj.,* wretched; miserable.

**squal • or** (skwäl´ər) *n.,* filth and misery.

**stren • u • ous** (stren' yə wəs) *adj.,* vigorously active.

**sub • jec • tion** (sub jek´shən) *n.,* bringing under control or dominion.

**sub • ju • ga • tion** (sub´jə gā´shen) *n.,* takeover; enslavement.

**sub • li • ma • tion** (sub´lə mā´shən) *n.,* expression of socially or personally unacceptable impulses in constructive, acceptable forms.

**sub • mis • sion** (sub mish´ən) *n.,* act of yielding; surrendering.

**sub • serve** (səb sʉrv´) *vt.,* be useful or helpful; serve.

**sub • ver • sion** (səb ver´zhən) *n.,* systematic attempt to overthrow a government.

**suf • fer • ance** (suf´ ər əns) *n.,* power to tolerate pain.

**suf • fice** (sə fīs´) *vt.,* be enough; be sufficient or adequate.

**sul • len** (sə' lən) *adj.,* dull or somber in sound or color; gloomily or resentfully silent.

**sul • try** (səl' trē) *adj.,* very hot and humid.

**sum • mon** (sə' mən) *vt.,* call forth.

**su • per • cil • i • ous** (sü´pər sil´ē əs) *adj.,* disdainful, contemptuous.

**su • per • flu • ous** (sə pʉr´flü əs) *adj.,* excessive.

**su • per • vene** (sü´pər vēñ) *vi.,* happen unexpectedly.

**su • pine • ly** (sü´pīn´lə) *adv.,* passively.

**sup • pli • ca • tion** (sə pli kā´shən) *n.,* humble request or plea.

**sur • cease** (sʉr sēs´) *n.,* respite; end.

**sur • mise** (sər mīz´) *n.,* conjecture; guess; *vi.,* guess.

**swiv • el** (swi' vəl) *vi.,* swing or turn or pivot freely.

**symp • to • mat • ic** (simp´tə mat´ ik) *adj.,* indicative; that constitutes a condition.

**tal • low • y** (tal´ō ē) *adj.,* fatty and pale.

**te • di • ous** (te´dē əs) *adj.,* long and tiresome.

**tem • per** (tem´pər) *vt.,* toughen, as by rigors or trying experiences.

**tem • pest** (tem´pəst) *n.,* violent storm.

**tem • po • ral** (tem´pə rəl) *adj.,* lasting only for a time; temporary.

**ten • ant** (te' nənt) *n.,* one who rents or owns; occupant.

**ten • dril** (ten'drəl) *n.,* something that curls in a spiral.

**ten • u • ous** (ten´yü əs) *adj.,* flimsy; weak.

**ten • ure** (ten´yər) *n.,* right to hold a position permanently.

**ter • mi • nate** (tʉr´mə nāt´) *vi.,* end; stop; cease.

**tes • ti • ly** (tes´tə lē) *adv.,* in an irritable manner.

**theo • log • i • cal** (thē ə lä´ ji kəl) *adj.,* of or relating to theology, or the study of religious faith, practice, and experience.

**thrash** (thrash) *vi.,* move or stir about violently.

**tin • ker** (tiŋ' kər) *vi.,* repair, adjust, or work with something in an unskilled or experimental manner.

**top • ple** (tä' pəl) *vt.,* overthrow.

**tor • pid** (tôr´pəd) *adj.,* dormant; sluggish.

**to • tal • i • tar • i • an** (tō ta lə ter´ ē ən) *adj.,* of or relating to a political regime based on subordination of the individual to the state and strict control of all aspects of the life and productive capacity of the nation especially by coercive measures.

**tran • si • ent** (tran´ sē ənt) *adj.*, not permanent; temporary.

**trans • fig • ure** (tran[t]s fi´ gyər) *vt.*, give a new and exalted or spiritual appearance to.

**trans • mute** (trans myüt´) *vt.*, change from one form, species, or condition into another.

**trans • port** (trans´ pôrt) *n.*, strong emotion; rapture.

**tra • vail** (trə vāl´) *n.*, very hard work; toil.

**tread** (tred) *n.*, manner of stepping.

**trem • u • lous • ly** (trem´yü ləs lē) *adv.*, in a trembling or quivering manner.

**trep • i • da • tion** (trep´ ə dā´ shən) *n.*, anxiety; nervousness.

**trib • u • la • tion** (trib´yü lā´shən) *n.*, distress or suffering resulting from oppression or persecution.

**trill** (tril) *vi.*, play or sing with a quaver.

**tu • mul • tu • ous • ly** (tü mul´ chü əs lē) *adv.*, wildly.

**ul • te • ri • or** (ul tir´ē ər) *adj.*, further; more remote; undisclosed; concealed.

**un • al • ien • a • ble** (un āl´ yən ə bəl) *adj.*, that which may not be taken away.

**un • daunt • ed** (ən dônt´ed) *adj.*, resolute in the face of danger.

**un • du • la • tion** (un dyü lā´shən) *n.*, act of moving in waves.

**un • furl** (un fʉrl´) *vt.*, unfold.

**un • in • tel • li • gi • ble** (un in tel´i jə bəl) *adj.*, that which cannot be understood.

**un • ob • tru • sive** (un əb trü´siv) *adj.*, not calling attention to itself.

**un • re • lent • ing** (un rē len´tiŋ) *adj.*, not softening or yielding in determination.

**un • to • ward** (un tō´ərd) *adj.*, improper; unseemly; not favorable.

**un • wield • y** (un wēl´dē) *adj.*, hard to manage.

**u • sur • pa • tion** (yü zər pā´ shən) *n.*, unlawful or violent taking of power.

**va • cu • i • ty** (va kyü ´ə tē) *n.*, empty space, void, or vacuum.

**vag • a • bond** (vag´ ə bänd´) *n.*, wandering, idle, disreputable, or shiftless person.

**va • ga • ry** (vā´ge rē) *n.*, odd, whimsical, or freakish idea or notion.

**ve • hem • ent • ly** (vē´ ə mənt lē´) *adv.*, with force or intensity.

**ve • loc • i • ty** (və läs´ə tē) *n.*, quickness or rapidity of motion or action.

**ve • neer** (və nir´) *n.*, superficial or deceptively attractive appearance, display, or effect.

**ven • er • a • ble** (ven´ər ə bəl) *adj.*, calling forth respect through age, character, and attainments.

**ven • er • at • ed** (ve´ nə rāt əd) *adj.*, regarded with reverential respect or with admiring deference.

**venge • ance** (ven´jən[t]s) *n.*, revenge.

**ven • ture** (ven´chər) *n.*, risky or dangerous undertaking; *vt.*, undertake the risk of.

**ven • ture • some** (ven[t]´ shər səm) *adj.*, daring; inclined to incur risk or danger.

**ver • i • ty** (ver´ə tē) *n.*, principle or belief taken to be fundamentally and permanently true.

**ver • min** (vʉr´mən) *n.*, small animals regarded as pests.

**ves • ti • bule** (ves´tə byül´) *n.*, hallway or small room at the entrance of a building.

**ves • tige** (ves´tij) *n.*, trace, mark, or sign of something that once existed but has passed away.

**vex** (veks) *vt.*, annoy.

**vi • and** (vī´ənd) *n.*, article of food, especially a tasty dish.

**vi • tal • i • ty** (vī ta´ lə tē) *n.*, capacity to live and develop.

**vi • tu • per • a • tive** (vī tü´ pə rā´tiv) *adj.*, abusive; viciously fault-finding.

**vi • vac • i • ty** (vī vas´ə tē) *n.*, liveliness of spirit; animation.

**vo • cif • er • a • tion** (vō sif´ər ā´shən) *n.*, shouting.

**vol • a • tile** (väl´ə təl) *adj.*, unstable; explosive.

**vo • li • tion** (vō li´ shən) *n.*, choice or decision made.

**vo • rac • i • ty** (vô ras´ə tē) *n.*, greediness.

**wa • ri • ness** (wār´ē nes) *n.*, prudence; careful cautiousness.

**watch** (wäch) *n.*, act of keeping awake to guard or protect.

**wean** (wēn) *vt.*, free from dependence or custom.

**whim** (hwim) *n.*, fancy, an eccentric and often sudden idea.

**wince** (win[t]s) *vi.*, shrink or draw back slightly, usually with a grimace, as in pain, embarrassment, or alarm.

**wist • ful • ly** (wist´ fə lē) *adv.*, expressing yearning or desire mixed with melancholy.

**wrath** (rath) *n.*, strong, vengeful anger.

**wretch • ed** (rech´id) *adj.*, miserable.

**writhe** (rīth) *vi.*, twist as if in pain or struggling.

**wrought** (rôt) *adj.*, worked; made; *alt. pp. of* work.

**xe • no • pho • bic** (zē nə fō´bik) *adj.*, fearful of or showing hatred toward foreigners.

**yield** (ye[ə]ld) *vt.*, give or render as fitting, rightfully owed, or required.

# INDEX
## Of Titles and Authors

# INDEX
### Of Skills

Romantic Movement, 143
Romantic poetry, 315
Romanticism, 284, 366, 401, 1153
rounded character, 29, 796
run-on lines, 249, 883, 885, 1153
scanning, 1024
scene, 1153
Schoolroom poets, 197
script, 42
second-person point of view, 641, 902
sensory details, 242
sentimentality, 419, 430, 1154
sestet, 16, 1154
set, 43, 50, 1154
setting, 29, 32, 39, 708, 713, 1154
Shakespearean sonnet, 21, 624
short short, 1154
short story, 27, 315, 859, 938, 1154
short story structure, 75
sight rhyme, 221, 1154
Silent Generation, 763
simile, 18, 118, 539, 546, 625, 630, 636, 638,
    640, 644, 869, 872, 883, 885, 1154
skimming, 1024
slang, 1154–1155
slant rhyme, 17, 221, 765, 769, 1155
soliloquy, 43, 1155
sonnet, 14, 19, 21, 624, 627, 1155
sound effects, 43
Southern Gothic, 686, 784, 794, 1155
speaker, 530, 531, 532, 533, 619, 622, 648,
    650, 887, 889, 1155
spectacle, 42, 43, 1155
speeches, 400, 435
spirituals, 4, 6, 10, 74, 322, 330, 401, 1155
spondaic foot, 632
spondee, 15, 1155
SQ3R, 1028
stage directions, 42, 46, 49, 687, 694, 1155
stages, 41, 43, 1155
stanza, 206, 209, 334, 1156
static character, 29, 721, 729
stereotype, 324, 328, 1156
stereotypical character, 419, 430
stock character, 29, 419, 430
stream-of-consciousness writing, 562, 570, 585,
    969, 978, 1156
stress, 1156
strongly stressed syllables, 14
style, 147, 151, 377, 1156
summarize, 1025
survey, 1028
symbol, 87, 90–91, 226, 251, 274, 365, 374,

508, 512, 658, 664, 700, 704, 705, 707,
    714, 720, 730, 743, 784, 794, 1156–1157
synaesthesia, 18, 226, 1157
synecdoche, 18, 1157
synonyms, 1031
syntax, 535, 537, 1157
tall tale, 4, 1157
tenor of metaphor, 92
tenor of simile, 640, 644, 883
tercet, 16, 1157
tetrameter, 15
textbooks, 1026
theme, 6, 10, 30, 50, 137, 277, 281, 330, 332,
    489, 494, 625, 630, 652, 656, 658, 664,
    730, 743, 1157
thesis, 1004, 1011, 1157
third-person point of view, 641, 902
three-dimensional character, 29, 796
thrust stage, 41
tone, 61, 64, 286, 297, 324, 328, 350, 352,
    484, 487, 530, 531, 632, 634, 641, 646,
    771, 773, 891, 894, 1157
tragedy, 41, 1158
Transcendentalism, 194–196
trimeter, 15
triplet, 16, 1158
trochaic foot, 632
trochee, 15, 1158
trope, 1158
turning point, 30
understatement, 18, 1158
vehicle, 18
vehicle of metaphor, 92
vehicle of simile, 640, 644, 883
verbal irony, 381
vers libre, 964
visuals, 1028–1029
voice, 1158
weakly stressed, 14

**Writing**
abstract, 50, 210
ad slogan, 11
address to the jury, 50
advice column, 152, 227, 275, 353, 561, 895,
    907
aim, 1035
analysis, 55, 915
analyzing, 1041
anecdote, 66, 665, 1003
annotated bibliography, 601–607
answer, 282
aphorism, 151

INDEX OF SKILLS

INDEX OF SKILLS

**Applied English**

# INDEX
## Of Internet Sites

At the time of publication, the following were valid, working Internet sites. Due to the changing nature of the Internet, some of these sites may no longer be accessible via the listed address. If an address does not work, try conducting a keyword search by the name of the site, author, or topic. If you find a non-working site, please notify us at educate@emcp.com so that we can update this index.

United States Mint
http://www.usmint.gov, 451
**Willa Cather Pioneer Memorial**
http://www.willacather.org, 547
**William Carlos Williams Links and Resources**
http://web.edcc.edu/gvb/wcw.html, 534

## RESOURCES BY AUTHOR NAME

**Anthony, Susan B.**
Susan B. Anthony House, http://www.susanb anthonyhouse.org, 453
**Brooks, Gwendolyn**
Academy of American Poets, http://www.poets.org, 779
**Cather, Willa**
Willa Cather Pioneer Memorial, http://willacather.org, 547
**Dos Passos, John**
PAL: Perspectives in American Literature, http://www.csustan.edu/english/reuben/home.html, 584
**Dunbar, Paul Laurence**
Paul Laurence Dunbar Digital Text Collection, http://www.libraries.wright.edu/dunbar, 623
**Faulkner, William**
*Faulkner News,* http://www.mcsr.olemiss.edu/~egjbp/faulkner/news/index.html, 592
Mississippi Writers Page, http://www.olemiss.edu/depts/english/ms-writers, 807
**Frost, Robert**
Academy of American Poets, http://www.poets.org, 519
**Hayden, Robert**
Modern American Poetry, http://www.english/uiuc.edu/maps, 882

**Hemingway, Ernest**
Ernest Hemingway Foundation of Oak Park, http://www.hemingway.org, 577
Hemingway Days Festival Site, http://www.hemingwaydays.com, 577
**Kennedy, John Fitzgerald**
"John Fitzgerald Kennedy, 35th President of the United States," http://www.geocities.com/~newgeneration, 914
**Levertov, Denise**
Academy of American Poets, http://www.poets.org, 890
Modern American Poetry, http://www.english.uiuc.edu/maps, 890
**Plath, Sylvia**
Academy of American Poets, http://www.poets.org, 886
PlathOnline.com, http://www.plathonline.com, 886
**Sexton, Anne**
Academy of American Poets, http://www.poets.org, 878
**Thoreau, Henry David**
Thoreau Institute http://www.walden.com, 298
**Welty, Eudora**
Mississippi Writers Page, http://www.olemiss.edu/depts/english/ms-writers, 807
**Williams, William Carlos**
William Carlos Williams Links and Resources, http://web.edcc.edu/gvb/wcw.html, 534
**Wright, Richard**
"Richard Wright: Black Boy" at PBS Online, http://www.pbs/org/rwbb, 829

# INDEX
## Of Fine Art

# ACKNOWLEDGMENTS

## Art Acknowledgments

**Cover** Something on the Eight Ball [Detail], 1953. Stuart Davis. CORBIS/Philadelphia Museum of Art/© Estate of Stuart Davis/Licensed by VAGA, New York; **Cover** Aspects of Negro Life: From Slavery through Reconstruction [Detail], 1934. Aaron Douglas. © Aaron Douglas/Schomberg Center, The New York Public Library/Art Resource, NY; **Cover** Watson and the Shark [Detail], 1778. John Singleton Copley. Museum of Fine Arts, Boston. Gift of
Mr. George von Lengerke Meyer; **Cover** In the Morning, Winslow Homer. Corel; **ix** Joslyn Museum, Omaha, Nebraska/SuperStock/© Estate of Grant Wood/Licensed by VAGA, New York; **viii** © Estate of T. H. Benton and R. P. Benton Testamentary Trusts/Licensed by VAGA, New York; **x** CORBIS/Francis G. Mayer/© 2000 Pollock-Krasner Foundation / Artists Rights Society (ARS), New York; **vi** New York State Historical Association, Cooperstown, NY; **vii** Glasgow Art Gallery and Museum, Scotland/ Bridgeman Art Library; **xii** National Museum of American Art, Washington, DC./Art Resource, NY; **2** Corel; **5** Rochester Museum and Science Center, Rochester, NY.; **7** Christie's Images; **13** CORBIS/ Philadelphia Museum of Art/ © Estate of Stuart Davis/Licensed by VAGA, New York; **19** Library of Congress; **22** William Abranowitz/A+C Anthology; **28** Christie's Images; **32** CORBIS/The Brett Weston Archive; **35** © Michelle Bridwell/PhotoEdit/PNI; **36** CORBIS; **42** © David Hockney/CORBIS/Sergio Dorantes; **44** CORBIS/ Hulton-Deutsh Collection; **45** CORBIS/Hulton-Deutsh Collection; **53** Oil on canvas 29" x 36" Sheldon Memorial Art Gallery. UNL-F.M. Hall Collection; **56** Photo by Robert Becker.; **57** Kiowa Funeral, opaque watercolor on paper, 1930, by James Auchiah. California Academy of Sciences.Courtesy of the California Academy of Sciences, Elkus Collection (catalog #370-1248); **78** Gift of Edgar William and Bernice Chrysler Garbisch, © 1999 Board of Trustees, National Gallery of Art, Washington; **81** Corel; **82** Corel; **84** Brooklyn Museum of Art, New York, USA/ Bridgeman Art Library; **86** Gift of Edgar William
and Bernice Chrysler Garbisch, © 1999 Board of Trustees, National Gallery of Art, Washington; **88** Bridge-man Art Library; **92** Planet Art; **93** © David Ryan/ Photo 20-20/PNI; **96** CORBIS; **97** Tozzer Library, Harvard University; **102** Portrait of John Smith, c.1617. After Simon van de Passe. National Portrait Gallery, Smithsonian Institution/ Art Resource, NY; **103** Sloane Manuscript, British Library, London, UK/Bridgeman Art Library; **106** National Portrait Gallery, Smithsonian Institution/ Art Resource, NY; **115** Worcester Art Museum, Worcester, Massachusetts; **118** Jonathan Edwards, 1793. Amos Doolittle, after Joseph Badger. National Portrait Gallery, Smithsonian Institution/ Art Resource, NY; **119** National Museum of American Art, Washington, DC/Art Resource, NY; **138** The Metropolitan Museum of Art, New York. Arthur Hoppock Hearn Fund, 1950 (50.117)/© Estate of Grant Wood/Licensed by VAGA, New York; **140** Museum of Fine Arts, Boston. Bequest of Maxim Karolik; **142** National Archives, Washington, DC; **143** Corel; **144** Corel; **145** The Metropolitan Museum of Art, New York. Arthur Hoppock Hearn Fund, 1950 (50.117)/© Estate of Grant Wood/Licensed by VAGA, New York; **146** Harvard University Portrait Collection. Bequest of Dr. John Collins Warren, 1856; **148** CORBIS/ Bettmann; **153** CORBIS; **154** The Granger Collection.; **159** Library of Congress; **163** Thomas Jefferson, 1800. Rembrandt Peale. CORBIS/ Bettmann; **164** SuperStock; **171** Gift of Robert Homans, Photograph © 1999 Board of Trustees, National Gallery of Art, Washington; **172** National Museum of American Art, Washington, DC./Art Resource, NY; **190** Museum of Fine Arts, Boston. Gift of Mr. George von Lengerke Meyer; **192** Museum of Fine Arts, Boston. Gift of Mr. George von Lengerke Meyer; **194** The Warner Collection of Gulf States Paper Corporation, Tuscaloosa, Alabama; **197** New York Public Library/Art Resource, NY; **198** Museum of Fine Arts, Boston. Gift of Mr. George von Lengerke Meyer; **199** William Cullen Bryant, c.1870. Jose Maria Mora. National Portrait Gallery, Smithsonian Institution/

Art Resource, NY; **200** New York Public Library/Art Resource, NY; **206** Oliver Wendell Holmes, c.1880. James Notman. National Portrait Gallery, Smithsonian Institution/Art Resource, NY; **207** PhotoDisc; **211** Library of Congress; **212** Museum of Fine Arts, Boston.Herman and Zoe Oliver Sherman Fund; **216** Amherst College Library; **217** Trustees of Amherst College; **223** New York State Historical Association, Cooperstown, NY; **228** Library of Congress; **230** Christie's Images; **236** Christie's Images; **244** Rosenwald Collection. Photograph © 1999 Board of Trustees, National Gallery of Art, Washington, DC./© Antonio Frasconi/Licensed by VAGA, New York; **247** Museum of Fine Arts, Boston.; **251** Peabody Essex Museum; **252** PhotoDisc; **261** PhotoDisc; **273** University of Minnesota Libraries Special Collections; **276** Distant View of Niagara Falls, oil on panel, 1830, 18 7/8 x 23 7/8".Thomas Cole, American, 1801-1848. Friends of American Art Collection, 1946.396. Photograph © 1998, The Art Institute of Chicago. All rights reserved.; **276** Library of Congress; **283** Christie's Images; **286** Library of Congress; **287** David Benoit; **291** David Benoit; **293** David Benoit; **296** University of Minnesota Libraries Special Collections; **317** The Metropolitan Museum of Art, New York. Gift of Mrs. William F. Milton, 1923 (23.77.1); **318** CORBIS/Bettmann; **319** Library of Congress; **320** Library of Congress; **320** Library of Congress; **321** Library of Congress; **322** Library of Congress; **323** The Metropolitan Museum of Art, New York. Gift of Mrs. William F. Milton, 1923 (23.77.1); **324** Library of Congress; **325** The Warner Collection of Gulf States Paper Corporation, Tuscaloosa, Alabama; **334** CORBIS/Bettmann; **335** CORBIS; **339** CORBIS/Bettmann; **340** CORBIS/Minnesota Historical Society; **344** National Archives; **347** Library of Congress; **350** Library of Congress; **354** Library of Congress; **355** Library of Congress; **360** Smithsonian Institution/Art Resource, NY. Photograph by Ken Pelka; **365** Walt Whitman. Daguerrotype, c.1854. Special Collections, Rare Books. New York Public Library/Art Resource, NY; **367** Glasgow Art Gallery and Museum, Scotland/ Bridgeman Art Library; **375** Brooklyn Museum of Art, New York, USA/Bridgeman Art Library; **379** UPI/Corbis-Bettmann; **380** PhotoDisc; **382** National Museum of American Art, Washington, DC/Art Resource, NY; **402** Brooklyn Museum of Art, Bequest of Edith and Milton Lowenthal/© 2000 The Georgia O'Keeffe Foundation/Artists Rights Society (ARS), New York; **405** CORBIS/

Bettmann; **406** CORBIS; **407** Library of Congress; **408** CORBIS/Bettmann; **409** Huckleberry Finn and Jim. Thomas Hart Benton. © T. H. Benton and R. P. Benton Testamentary Trusts/Licensed by VAGA, New York; **409** Jack London. Library of Congress; **410** Library of Congress; **411** CORBIS/Bettmann; **412** CORBIS/ Bettmann; **419** CORBIS; **420** Thomas Gilcrease Institute of American History and Art, Tulsa; **429** University of Califronia, Berkeley Art Museum, gift of Henry D. Bacon.; **432** CORBIS/ Bettmann; **434** Courtesy of the Southwest Museum, Los Angeles. Photo # CT.1.; **437** Library of Congress; **438** Rodney Busch; **448** CORBIS/ Bettmann; **455** CORBIS/Francis G. Mayer; **474** CORBIS/Philadelphia Museum of Art/© 2000 Artists Rights Society (ARS), New York / ADAGP, Paris; **477** National Archive; **478** Library of Congress; **479** Library of Congress; **480** Library of Congress; **481** Library of Congress; **482** National Archive; **483** CORBIS/ Philadelphia Museum of Art/© 2000 Artists Rights Society (ARS), New York/ ADAGP, Paris; **484** Library of Congress; **485** Joslyn Museum, Omaha, Nebraska/SuperStock/© Estate of Grant Wood /Licensed by VAGA, New York; **489** CORBIS/ Bettmann; **490** CORBIS/Burstein Collection; **496** Library of Congress; **497** Corel; **500** CORBIS/ Bettmann; **508** Library of Congress; **509** AP/ World Wide Photos; **513** CORBIS/ Philadelphia Museum of Art; **520** CORBIS/ Bettmann; **521** CORBIS/Philadelphia Museum of Art; **523** CORBIS/ North Carolina Museum of Art; **529** Library of Congress; **530** Jena Busch; **535** Library of Congress; **536** PhotoDisc; **539** Library of Congress; **540** Hirshhorn Museum, Washington, DC, Gift of Joseph H. Hirshhorn Foundation; **548** Minnesota Historical Society; **549** PhotoDisc; **552** PhotoDisc; **562** Library of Congress; **563** Courtesy of the Pennsylvania Academy of the Fine Arts, Philadelphia. Joseph E. Temple Fund.; **572** Library of Congress; **573** Planet Art; **578** Library of Congress; **579** Albright-Knox Art Gallery, Buffalo, New York/© 2000 Artists Rights Society (ARS), New York/VG Bild-Kunst, Bonn; **585** Library of Congress; **586** AP/Wide World Photos; **589** Library of Congress; **610** © Aaron Douglas/Schomberg Center, The New York Public Library/Art Resource, NY; **613** Library of Congress.; **614** Sheldon Memorial Art Gallery, NAA-Purchased with the aid of funds from the National Endowment for the Arts; **615** Library of Congress; **616** © Aaron Douglas/Schomberg Center for Research in Black Culture, New York/Art Resource, NY; **617** Archibald J. Motley, Jr. Saturday Night Street

Scene, 1936, oil on canvas, 36"x42" . © Estate of the Artist, Courtesy of Micheal Rosenfeld Gallery, NY; **618** Schomberg Center, The New York Public Library/Art Resource, NY; **619** Library of Congress; **620** © Lois Mailou Jones/National Museum of American Art, Washington, DC/Art Resource, NY; **624** Library of Congress; **625** Photo courtesy of the artist; **626** © Aaron Douglas/Howard University Gallery of Art, Washington, DC; **628** National Museum of American Art, Washington, DC/Art Resource, NY; **632** Library of Congress; **633** CORBIS/Bettmann; **636** CORBIS/ Bettmann; **637** National Museum of American Art, Washington, DC/Art Resource, NY; **640** Library of Congress; **641** CORBIS/Underwood & Underwood; **642** From the Collection of the Indiana State Museum and Historic Sites; **645** National Portrait Gallery. Washington, DC/Art Resource, NY; **648** Library of Congress; **649** National Museum of American Art, Washington, DC/Art Resource, NY; **652** AP/Wide World Photos; **653** National Museum of American Art, Washington, DC/Art Resource, NY; **658** Library of Congress; **659** National Portrait Gallery. Washington, DC/Art Resource, NY; **663** Library of Congress; **682** The Museum of Modern Art, New York; **684** Library of Congress; **685** The Museum of Modern Art, New York; **686** Library of Congress; **687** CORBIS/Bettman; **692** © Archive Photos/PNI; **695** Library of Congress; **700** Library of Congress; **705** Library of Congress; **708** Library of Congress; **714** Library of Congress; **721** Library of Congress; **730** Library of Congress; **756** CORBIS/Francis G. Mayer/© 2000 Pollock-Krasner Foundation / Artists Rights Society (ARS), New York; **759** AP/Wide World Photos; **760** Library of Congress; **761** CORBIS/Bettmann; **762** CORBIS/R. Beebe; **763** CORBIS/Bettmann; **764** CORBIS/ Francis G. Mayer/© 2000 Pollock-Krasner Foundation/Artists Rights Society (ARS), New York; **765** AP/Wide World Photos; **766** Inspection, 1943. Edward Steichen. CORBIS; **771** AP/Wide World Photos; **772** CORBIS/George Lepp; **775** Library of Congress; **776** Evans-Tibbs Collection, Washington, DC; **780** AP/Wide World Photos; **781** CORBIS/Seattle Art Museum; **784** AP/Wide World Photos; **785** Estate of Jerry Bywaters. Photo by Dallas Museum of Art; **796** Library of Congress; **797** National Museum of American Art, Washington, DC/Art Resource, NY; **808** Library of Congress; **809** CORBIS/Archivo Iconografico, S.A./© 2000 Artists Rights Society (ARS), New York/ADAGP, Paris; **824** Library of Congress; **825** © David C. Driskell/Fisk University, Nashville. Photo by Arthur Evans, Williamstown Art Conservation Center; **830** Richard De Combray; **831** CORBIS; **836** CORBIS/ Bettmann; **840** CORBIS/Paul Seheult; Eye Ubiquitous; **860** Tate Gallery, London/Art Resource, NY/© 2000 Andy Warhol Foundation for the Visual Arts / Artists Rights Society (ARS), New York; **863** AP/Wide World Photos; **864** CORBIS/ Bettmann; **865** AP/Wide World Photos; **866** CORBIS/Ted Streshinsky; **868** Tate Gallery, London/Art Resource, NY/© 2000 Andy Warhol Foundation for the Visual Arts / Artists Rights Society (ARS), New York; **869** CORBIS/Roger Ressmeyer; **870** National Museum of American Art, Washington, DC/Art Resource, NY; **874** Library of Congress; **875** Planet Art; **879** Library of Congress; **880** Watercolor collage on board, 26.25" x 45.62". Courtesy of The Butler Institute of American Art, Youngstown, Ohio./© Romare Bearden Foundation/Licensed by VAGA, New York; **883** CORBIS/Bettmann; **884** © The Estate of Alice Neel. Courtesy Robert Miller Gallery, New York; **887** AP/Wide World Photos; **891** Library of Congress; **892** Casein on paper, 17" x 15". Courtesy of The Butler Institute of American Art, Youngstown, Ohio./© Estate of Ben Shahn/ Licensed by VAGA, New York; **896** AP/ Wyatt Counts/Wide World Photos; **897** CORBIS/ Steve Chenn; **902** CORBIS/Oscar White; **908** Library of Congress; **909** CORBIS/Bettmann; **915** CORBIS/ Ted Streshinsky; **916** CORBIS/Owen Franken; **940** Courtesy of the artist; **943** CORBIS/ AFP; **944** CORBIS/AFP; **946** Photo: Milwaukee Art Museum, gift of Contemporary Art Society. Copyright courtesy: Mary Boone Gallery, New York; **947** Library of Congress; **948** Courtesy of the artist; **949** Photo by Alison Freese; **950** PhotoDisc; **953** AP/Wide World Photos; **954** © 1988 Faith Ringgold; **958** M.C. O'Leary; **959** Photo courtesy of the artist; **964** Sigrid Estrada; **965** PhotoDisc; **969** AP/Wide World Photos; **975** CORBIS/ Bettmann; **980** © Daniel Cima; **981** Kactus Foto, Santiago, Chile/SuperStock; **992** Jerry Bauer; **993** PhotoDisc; **994** CORBIS/Tim Page; **998** David Dwyer; **999** PhotoDisc; **1004** Jerry Bauer; **1005** Julie Delton.

# Literary Acknowledgments

**James Baldwin Estate.** "Pride and the Proudhammer" from *Tell Me How Long the Train's Been Gone* by James Baldwin. Copyright © 1968 by James Baldwin. Used by permission of the James Baldwin Estate. **Elizabeth Barnett.** "Euclid Alone Has Looked on Beauty Bare" by Edna St. Vincent Millay. From *Collected Poems,* HarperCollins. Copyright 1923, 1951 by Edna St. Vincent Millay and Norma Millay Ellis. All rights reserved. Reprinted by permission of Elizabeth Barnett, literary executor. "Sonnet XXX" of *Fatal Interview* by Edna St. Vincent Millay. From *Collected Poems,* HarperCollins. Copyright © 1931, 1958 by Edna St. Vincent Millay and Norma Millay Ellis. All rights reserved. Reprinted by permission of Elizabeth Barnett, literary executor. **BOA Editions, Ltd.** Li-Young Lee: "A Story" copyright © 1990 by Li-Young Lee. Reprinted from *The City in Which I Love You*, with the permission of BOA Editions, Ltd., 260 East Ave., Rochester, NY 14604. **Brighton High School.** Screen captures from the AP English Brighton High School 1997 website. Reprinted by permission of Brighton High School, Rochester, NY. **Gwendolyn Brooks.** "To Black Women", © 1991 by Gwendolyn Brooks. From *Blacks,* 1991. Published by Third World Press, Chicago. **Continuum International Publishing Company.** From *The Devastation of the Indies* by De Las Casas. Copyright © 1992 by Continuum Publishing Company. Reprinted by permission of Continuum International Publishing Company. **Estate of Elizabeth H. Dos Passos.** "Newsreel LXVIII" from *The Big Money* by John Dos Passos. Copyright 1936 J. Dos Passos, renewed 1964 John Dos Passos. Permission granted by the Estate of Elizabeth H. Dos Passos. **Rita Dove.** "Wingfoot Lake", from *Thomas and Beulah,* Carnegie-Mellon University Press. Copyright 1986 by Rita Dove; reprinted by permission of the author. **Faber and Faber Limited.** "The Love Song of J. Alfred Prufrock" from *Collected Poems 1909–1962* by T. S. Eliot. Reprinted by permission of Faber and Faber Limited, London. **Farrar, Straus & Giroux, LLC.** "Commander Lowell" from *Life Studies* by Robert Lowell. Copyright © 1959 by Robert Lowell. Copyright renewed © 1987 by Harriet Lowell, Sheridan Lowell, and Caroline Lowell. Reprinted by permission of Farrar, Straus & Giroux, LLC. "The Death of the Ball Turret Gunner" from *The Complete Poems* by Randall Jarrell. Copyright © 1969, renewed 1997 by Mary von S. Jarrell. Reprinted by permission of Farrar, Straus & Giroux, LLC. "House Guest" from *The Complete Poems 1927–1979* by Elizabeth Bishop. Copyright © 1979, 1983 by Alice Helen Methfessel. Reprinted by permission of Farrar, Straus & Giroux, LLC. "The Magic Barrel" from *The Magic Barrel* by Bernard Malamud. Copyright © 1950, 1958, renewed 1977, 1986 by Bernard Malamud. Reprinted by permission of Farrar, Straus & Giroux, LLC. "On the Mall" from *The White Album* by Joan Didion. Copyright © 1979 by Joan Didion. **Harcourt Brace & Company.** "Grass" from *Cornhuskers* by Carl Sandburg, copyright 1918 by Holt, Rinehart and Winston, Inc. and renewed 1964 by Carl Sandburg, reprinted by permission of Harcourt Brace & Company. "The Jilting of Granny Weatherall" from *Flowering Judas and Other Stories,* copyright 1930 and renewed 1958 by Katherine Anne Porter, reprinted by permission of Harcourt Brace & Company. "The Life You Save May Be Your Own" from *A Good Man Is Hard to Find and Other Stories* by Flannery O'Connor, copyright 1953 by Flannery O'Connor and renewed 1981 by Regina O'Connor, reprinted by permission of Harcourt, Inc. "A Worn Path" from *A Curtain of Green and Other Stories,* copyright 1941 and renewed 1969 by Eudora Welty, reprinted by permission of Harcourt, Inc. **HarperCollins Publishers.** Excerpt from *Black Boy* by Richard Wright. Copyright 1937, 1942, 1944, 1945 by Richard Wright. Copyright renewed 1973 by Ellen Wright. Reprinted by permission of HarperCollins Publishers, Inc. "Celestial Music" from *Ararat* by Louise Glück. Copyright © 1990 by Louise Glück. Reprinted by permission of HarperCollins Publishers, Inc. Excerpt from *Their Eyes Were Watching God* by Zora Neale Hurston. Copyright 1937 by Harper & Row, Publishers, Inc. Renewed 1965 by John C. Hurston and Joel Hurston. Reprinted by permission of HarperCollins Publishers, Inc. All lines from "Morning Song" from *Ariel* by Sylvia Plath. Copyright © 1961 by Ted Hughes. Copyright renewed. Reprinted by permission of HarperCollins Publishers, Inc. **Harvard University Press.** "Because I could not stop for Death", "'Hope' is the thing with feathers—" , "I heard a Fly buzz—when I died—", "Much Madness is divinest Sense", "The Soul selects her own Society—", "There's a certain Slant of light—", reprinted by permission of the publishers and the Trustees of Amherst College from *The*

*Poems of Emily Dickinson*, Thomas H. Johnson, ed., Cambridge, Mass.: The Belknap Press of Harvard University Press, Copyright © 1951, 1955, 1979, 1983 by the President and Fellows of Harvard College. Letter to John Adams, May 7, 1776, reprinted by permission of the publisher from *The Adams Family Correspondence Volume I* edited by L.H. Butterfield, Cambridge, Mass.: Harvard University Press, Copyright © 1963 by the Massachusetts Historical Society. **John Hawkins & Associates, Inc.** "Journey" from *The Poisoned Kiss and Other Stories from the Portuguese.* Copyright © 1975 by Joyce Carol Oates. Reprinted by permission of John Hawkins & Associates, Inc. **Henry Holt and Company.** "The Death of the Hired Man", "Home Burial", "Mending Wall", "An Old Man's Winter Night", from *The Poetry of Robert Frost,* edited by Edward Connery Lathem. Copyright 1944, © 1958 by Robert Frost. Copyright © 1967 by Lesley Frost Ballantine. Copyright 1916, 1930, 1939, © 1969 by Henry Holt and Company, LLC. Reprinted by permission of Henry Holt and Company, LLC. Letter to *The Amherst Student* from *Selected Prose of Robert Frost,* edited by Hyde Cox and Edward Connery Lathem. Copyright 1949, 1954, © 1966 by Henry Holt and Company, LLC. Copyright 1946, © 1959 by Robert Frost. Copyright, © 1956 by The Estate of Robert Frost. First appeared in *The Amherst Student.* Reprinted by permission of Henry Holt and Company, LLC. **Houghton Mifflin Company.** "Ambush" from *The Things They Carried.* Copyright © 1990 by Tim O'Brien. Reprinted by permission of Houghton Mifflin Co./Seymour Lawrence. All rights reserved. "Seeing", excerpted from *Dakota.* Copyright © 1993 by Kathleen Norris. Reprinted by permission of Ticknor & Fields/Houghton Mifflin Co. All rights reserved. "The Starry Night" from *All My Pretty Ones* by Anne Sexton. Copyright © 1962 by Anne Sexton, © renewed 1990 by Linda G. Sexton. Reprinted by permission of Houghton Mifflin Co. All rights reserved. "Wind and Silver" from *The Complete Poetical Works of Amy Lowell.* Copyright © 1955 by Houghton Mifflin Company, © renewed 1983 by Houghton Mifflin Company, Brinton P. Roberts, and G. D'Andelot Belin, Esq. Reprinted by permission of Houghton Mifflin Co. All rights reserved. **International Creative Management, Inc.** Excerpt from *Beloved* by Toni Morrison. Reprinted by permission of International Creative Management, Inc. Copyright © 1987, Alfred A. Knopf, Inc. **Alfred A. Knopf, Inc.** "Disillusionment of Ten O'Clock", "The Snow Man", "Thirteen Ways of Looking at a Blackbird" from *Collected Poems* by Wallace Stevens. Copyright 1923 and renewed 1951 by Wallace Stevens. Reprinted by permission of Alfred A. Knopf, Inc. "I, too, sing America" from *The Collected Poems of Langston Hughes* by Langston Hughes, copyright ©1994 by The Estate of Langston Hughes. Used by permission of Alfred A. Knopf, a division of Random House, Inc. "The Negro Speaks of Rivers" from *Collected Poems* by Langston Hughes. Copyright © 1994 by the Estate of Langston Hughes. Reprinted by permission of Alfred A. Knopf, Inc. "A Noiseless Flash" from *Hiroshima* by John Hersey, copyright 1946 and renewed 1974 by John Hersey. Used by permission of Alfred A. Knopf, a division of Random House, Inc. From *Of Plymouth Plantation 1620–1647* by William Bradford, edited with Notes and Introduction by Samuel Eliot Morison. Copyright 1952 by Samuel Eliot Morison and renewed 1980 by Emily Beck. "Reassurance" from *White People* by Allan Gurganus. Copyright © 1990 by Allan Gurganus. Reprinted by permission of Alfred A. Knopf, Inc. "The Slump" from *Museums & Women and Other Stories* by John Updike. Copyright © 1968 by John Updike. Reprinted by permission of Alfred A. Knopf, a division of Random House, Inc. **Liveright Publishing Corporation.** "anyone lived in a pretty how town", copyright 1940, © 1968, 1991 by the Trustees for the E. E. Cummings Trust, from *Complete Poems: 1904–1962* by E. E. Cummings, edited by George J. Firmage. Reprinted by permission of Liveright Publishing Corporation. "somewhere i have never travelled,gladly beyond", copyright 1931, © 1959, 1991 by the Trustees for the E. E. Cummings Trust. Copyright © 1979 by George James Firmage, from *Complete Poems: 1904–1962* by E. E. Cummings, edited by George J. Firmage. Reprinted by permission of Liveright Publishing Corporation. "Storm Ending", from *Cane* by Jean Toomer. Copyright 1923 by Boni & Liveright, renewed 1951 by Jean Toomer. Reprinted by permission of Liveright Publishing Corporation. "Frederick Douglass", "Those Winter Sundays" copyright © 1966 by Robert Hayden, from *Angle of Ascent: New and Selected Poems* by Robert Hayden. Reprinted by permission of Liveright Publishing Corporation. **David Mura.** "Huy Nguyen: Brothers, Drowning Cries" reprinted from *After We Lost Our Way* (E.P. Dutton, 1989). Copyright 1989 by David Mura. Reprinted by permission of the poet (e-mail: DAVSUS@aol.com). **New Directions Publishing Corporation.** "Constantly Risking Absurdity" by Lawrence Ferlinghetti from *A Coney Island of the Mind.* Copyright © 1958 by Lawrence Ferlinghetti. Reprinted by permission of New Directions Publishing Corp. "In a Station of the Metro" by Ezra Pound, from *Personae.* Copyright 1926 by Ezra Pound. Reprinted by permission of New Directions Publishing Corp. "The Red Wheelbarrow", "This is Just to Say" by William Carlos Williams from *Collected Poems 1909–1939, Volume I.* Copyright © 1938 by New Directions Publishing Corp. Reprinted by permission of New Directions Publishing Corp. "The Secret" by Denise Levertov, from *Poems 1960–1967.* Copyright © 1964 by Denise Levertov. Reprinted by permission of New Directions Publishing Corp. **Naomi Shihab Nye.** "What Is Supposed to Happen" from *Red Suitcase: Poems* by Naomi Shihab Nye (BOA Editions, Ltd., 1994). Reprinted by permission of the author. **Harold Ober Associates.** "A Black Man Talks of Reaping" by Arna Bontemps. Reprinted by permission of Harold Ober Associates Incorporated. Copyright © 1963 by Arna Bontemps. **Simon J. Ortiz.** "Hunger in New York", "My Father's Song", permission to reprint granted by Simon J. Ortiz. Poems originally published in *Woven Stone,* University of Arizona Press, Tucson, Arizona, 1992. **Parade Publications.** "Why I Am Optimistic About America" by Daniel J. Boorstin. Previously published in *The Discoverers* (1974), *The Creators* (1992), *The Seekers* (1998), *Parade Magazine,* July 10, 1994. Reprinted with permission from Parade, copyright © 1994. **Penguin Putnam Inc.** From *The Crucible* by Arthur Miller. Copyright 1952, 1953, 1954, renewed © 1980, 1981, 1982 by Arthur Miller. Used by permission of Viking Penguin, a division of Penguin Putnam Inc. "The Flower-Fed Buffaloes", from *Going to the Stars* by Vachel Lindsay. Copyright 1926 by D. Appleton & Co., renewed 1954 by Elizabeth C. Lindsay. A Hawthorn Book. Used by permission of Dutton Children's Books, a division of Penguin Putnam Inc. Chapter 1 from *The Grapes of Wrath* by John Steinbeck. Copyright 1939, renewed © 1967 by John Steinbeck. Used by permission of Viking Penguin, a division of Penguin Putnam Inc. "Sophistication" by Sherwood Anderson, from *Winesburg, Ohio* by Sherwood Anderson, introduction by Malcolm Cowley, copyright 1919 by B. W. Huebsch; Copyright 1947 by Eleanor Copenhaver Anderson. Used by permission of Viking Penguin, a division of Penguin Putnam Inc. **Princeton University Press.** Taylor, Edward. "Huswifery" from *The Poetical Works of Edward Taylor.* Copyright © 1943 by Princeton University Press. Reprinted by permission of Princeton University Press. **Random House, Inc.** "Darl" from *As I Lay Dying* by William Faulkner. Copyright © 1930 and renewed 1958 by William Faulkner. Reprinted by permission of Random House, Inc. "Elegy for Jane", copyright 1950 by Theodore Roethke. From *The Collected Poems of Theodore Roethke* by Theodore Roethke. Used by permission of Doubleday, a division of Random House, Inc. *The Glass Menagerie* by Tennessee Williams. Copyright © 1945 by Tennessee Williams and Edwina D. Williams and renewed 1973 by Tennessee Williams. Reprinted by permission of Random House, Inc. CAUTION: Professionals and amateurs are hereby warned that *The Glass Menagerie,* being fully protected under the copyright laws of the United States, the United Kingdom, Canada, and all other countries of the Copyright Union, is subject to royalty. All rights, including professional, amateur, motion picture, recitation, lecturing, public reading, radio-broadcasting, and the rights of translation into foreign languages, are strictly reserved. Particular emphasis is laid on the question of readings, permission for which must be secured from the author's agent in writing. All inquiries should be addressed to the author's agent, The Lantz Office, 888 Seventh Avenue, New York 10106. From *The Invisible Man* by Ralph Ellison. Copyright © 1952 by Ralph Ellison. Reprinted by permission of Random House, Inc. "Is Phoenix Jackson's Grandson Really Dead?" from *The Eye of the Story* by Eudora Welty. Copyright © 1978 by Eudora Welty. Reprinted by permission of Random House, Inc. "An Occurrence at Owl Creek Bridge" from *The Complete Stories of Ambrose Bierce,* published by Doubleday, a division of Random House, Inc. "The Richer, the Poorer" from *The Richer, the Poorer* by Dorothy West. Copyright © 1995 by Dorothy West. Used by permission of Doubleday, a division of Random House, Inc. "Upon Receiving the Nobel Prize for Literature" from *Essays, Speeches and Public Letters* by William Faulkner, edited by James B. Meriwether. Copyright © 1950 by William Faulkner. Reprinted by permission of Random House, Inc. **Simon & Schuster.** "A Clean, Well-Lighted Place", reprinted with permission of Scribner, a division of Simon & Schuster, Inc., from *The Short Stories of Ernest Hemingway.* Copyright 1933 by Charles Scribner's Sons. Copyright renewed © 1961 by Mary

Hemingway. "Richard Cory" from *The Children of the Night* by Edwin Arlington Robinson (New York: Charles Scribner's Sons, 1987). "The Sensible Thing", reprinted with permission of Scribner, a division of Simon & Schuster, from *The Short Stories of F. Scott Fitzgerald,* edited by Matthew J. Bruccoli. Copyright 1924 by Coloroto Corporation. Copyright renewed 1952 by Frances Scott Fitzgerald Lanahan. **Sunstone Press.** "Song of the Sky Loom" from *Songs of the Tewa* by Herbert Spinden appears courtesy of Sunstone Press, Box 2321, Santa Fe, NM 87504-2321, USA. **Susan Bergholz Literary Services.** "Daughter of Invention" from *How the García Girls Lost Their Accents.* Copyright © 1991 by Julia Alvarez. Published by Plume, an imprint of Dutton Signet, a division of Penguin USA, Inc., and originally in hardcover by Algonquin Books of Chapel Hill. Reprinted by permission of Susan Bergholz Literary Services, New York. All rights reserved. **Syracuse University Press.** Excerpt from *The Iroquois Constitution* from Arthur C. Parker, "The Constitution of Five Nations" in *Parker on the Iroquois,* edited by William N. Fenton. **Thompson and Thompson.** "Any Human to Another" and "Yet Do I Marvel" by Countee Cullen. Copyrights held by Amistad Research Center and administered by Thompson and Thompson, NY, NY. **The University of Georgia Press.** "American History" from *The Latin Deli: Prose & Poetry* by Judith Ortiz Cofer, published by The University of Georgia Press. Copyright © 1993 Judith Ortiz Cofer. Reprinted by permission of the publisher. **University Press of New England.** James Dickey, "The Last Wolverine" from *Poems 1957–1967,* © 1978 by James Dickey, Wesleyan University Press by permission of University Press of New England. **University of New Mexico Press.** "The Way to Rainy Mountain" from *The Way to Rainy Mountain* by N. Scott Momaday (University of New Mexico Press), copyright 1969. Reprinted by permission of the University of New Mexico Press. **University of North Carolina Press.** "To S.M., a Young African Painter, on Seeing His Works" from *The Poems of Phillis Wheatley,* edited and with an introduction by Julian D. Mason Jr. Copyright © 1966 by the University of North Carolina Press, renewed 1989. Used by permission of the publisher. **The University Press of Virginia.** "Do not weep, maiden, for war is kind", "A Man Said to the Universe" by Stephen Crane from *The Works of Stephen Crane,* edited by Fredson Bowers (Charlottesville: Virginia, 1975). "We Wear the Mask" by Paul Lawrence Dunbar from *The Collected Poetry of Paul Lawrence Dunbar* edited by Joanne Braxton (Charlottesville: Virginia, 1993). Reprinted with permission of The University Press of Virginia. **The Women's Press.** "The Resurrection of Zora Neale Hurston and Her Work", excerpted from *Anything We Love Can Be Saved* by Alice Walker, published in Great Britain by The Women's Press Ltd., 1997, 34 Great Sutton Street, London EC1V 0LQ. **Yale University Press.** From "Sinners in the Hands of an Angry God" by Jonathan Edwards from *Images or Shadows of Divine Things* (The Works of Jonathan Edwards). Reprinted by permission of Yale University Press.

We have made every effort to trace the ownership of all copyrighted material and to secure permission from copyright holders. In the event of any question arising as to the use of any material, we will be pleased to make the necessary corrections in future printings. Thanks are due to the aforementioned authors, publishers, and agents for permission to use the materials indicated.